I M C
Using Advertising and Promotion to Build Brands

Tom Duncan
University of Colorado-Boulder

Boston   Burr Ridge, IL   Dubuque, IA   Madison, WI   New York   San Francisco   St. Louis
Bangkok   Bogotá   Caracas   Kuala Lumpur   Lisbon   London   Madrid   Mexico City
Milan   Montreal   New Delhi   Santiago   Seoul   Singapore   Sydney   Taipei   Toronto

McGraw-Hill Higher Education

A Division of The **McGraw-Hill** *Companies*

IMC: USING ADVERTISING & PROMOTION TO BUILD BRANDS

Published by McGraw-Hill, an imprint of The McGraw-Hill Companies, Inc. 1221 Avenue of the Americas, New York, NY, 10020. Copyright © 2002 by The McGraw-Hill Companies, Inc. All rights reserved. No part of this publication may be reproduced or distributed in any form or by any means, or stored in a database or retrieval system, without the prior written consent of The McGraw-Hill Companies, Inc., including, but not limited to, in any network or other electronic storage or transmission, or broadcast for distance learning.

Some ancillaries, including electronic and print components, may not be available to customers outside the United States.

This book is printed on acid-free paper.

1 2 3 4 5 6 7 8 9 0 WCK/WCK 0 9 8 7 6 5 4 3 2 1

ISBN 0-256-21476-X

Publisher: *John E. Biernat*
Executive editor: *Linda Schreiber*
Developmental editors: *Christine Parker/Tracy Jensen*
Marketing manager: *Kim Kanakes-Szum*
Project manager: *Christina Thornton-Villagomez*
Lead production supervisor: *Heather D. Burbridge*
Cover design: *Matthew Baldwin*
Cover image: *© Corbis Images*
Interior design: *Kiera Cunningham*
Senior supplement coordinator: *Rose M. Range*
Producer Media technology: *E. Burke Broholm*
Photo research coordinator: *David A. Tietz*
Photo researcher: *Susan Holtz*
Printer: *Quebecor World Versailles Inc*
Typeface: *10/12 Palatino*
Compositor: *GAC Indianapolis*

Library of Congress Cataloging-in-Publication Data

Duncan, Tom (Thomas R.)
    IMC: using advertising and promotion to build brands / Tom Duncan.—1st ed.
      p. cm.—(The McGraw-Hill/Irwin series in marketing)
    Includes index.
    ISBN 0-256-21476-X (alk. paper)
    1. Brand name products—Marketing—Management. I. Title. II. Series
    HF5415.13 .D846 2002
    658.8′27—dc21

                       2001030302

INTERNATIONAL EDITION ISBN 0-07-112331-8
Copyright © 2002. Exclusive rights by The McGraw-Hill Companies, Inc. for manufacture and export. This book cannot be re-exported from the country to which it is sold by McGraw-Hill. The International Edition is not available in North America.

www.mhhe.com

To Sandra Moriarty,
a loving wife, best friend, and respected professional colleague.

About the Author

Tom Duncan, Ph.D.

Tom Duncan is the founder of the Integrated Marketing Communication graduate program at the University of Colorado–Boulder, where he currently teaches. He is also a consultant to both companies and agencies on IMC and brand building.

Before becoming a professor, Duncan worked in the industry for 15 years. He started his career in marketing research and account management at the Leo Burnett advertising agency's worldwide headquarters in Chicago. He worked on such accounts as Kentucky Fried Chicken and Procter & Gamble. He then went to the client side, where he was director of marketing services for Eckrich Processed Meats, a division of Beatrice Foods, and later vice president of marketing at Jeno's Frozen Foods, where he was responsible for new products.

Professor Duncan has done IMC consulting and workshops for companies such as Sun Microsystems, BBDO, Dentsu, Nestlé, Del Webb Properties, the U.S. Government Services Administration, Porter Novelli, American Marketing Association, Primedia (South Africa), Saudi Telecom Company (Saudi Arabia), Kreab Public Relations (Stockholm), McCann-Erickson. He is currently a member of IBM's Mobile Computing Marketing Advisory Board. He has done extensive speaking and conducted IMC workshops in Europe, Asia, Africa, and South America, as well as throughout North America. He is also a frequent expert witness in cases dealing with branding and marketing communications.

Professor Duncan has taught marketing communications for over 17 years. During this period he has been an invited lecturer at University of Kansas, University of Utah, BI School of Business (Oslo), Hanken Business School (Helsinki), Rau University (Johannesburg, South Africa), King Saud University (Riyadh, Saudi Arabia), and INFOTEC Mexico's federal program for information technology training, (as a participant in University of California at Berkeley's Worldwide Education Program).

In addition to writing articles for such publications as the *Journal of Advertising Research, Marketing Tools, Journal of Advertising,* and *Advertising Age,* and giving numerous academic presentations on IMC, Professor Duncan is coauthor of *Driving Brand Value* and *Creating and Delivering Winning Advertising and Marketing Presentations.* He holds a bachelor's and master's degree in advertising from Northwestern University and a Ph.D. from the University of Iowa.

Preface

Some interesting things happened on the way to the 21st century. Marketing communication (MC) functions such as advertising, public relations, sales promotion, and direct marketing became much more sophisticated, resulting in more commercial message clutter which made it more difficult for brands to be seen and heard. Emerging communication technology, especially the Internet, greatly empowered customers. Media became more fragmented, interactive, and global via satellite delivery. Databases became more pervasive and easier and less costly to use. Digitization made possible the convergence of computers, TV, and telephone. Customers became more business-savvy with higher expectations than ever before. And top management demanded even greater accountability as competition intensified.

These changes have both forced and enabled companies to change the way they communicate with prospects and customers. Customers are now more in command of the marketplace than ever before. They have more choices and more information on which to make brand decisions. They can buy 24-hours a day, seven days a week from anywhere in the world. The old marketplace motto "caveat emptor" ("Let the buyer beware") has become obsolete. Today, the more accurate axiom is "Let the company beware." Recognizing this change, smart companies have made greater efforts to *integrate* their marketing communications and all other brand messages, because this is the most cost-effective way to build brand relationships and brand value.

Nearly every type of business and organization you can think of uses MC functions and media to some extent. MC includes everything from signs in a retail-store window to multi-million dollar campaigns for global companies such as Coca Cola, Unilever, and 3M. MC is the way organizations communicate with customers, potential customers, donors, voters—whoever they want establish a relationship with and persuaded to think or act in a certain way. To maximize the work of the MC functions, it is essential that they are strategically integrated. This is the fundamental difference: IMC looks at and influences all brand messages, not just marketing communication messages. This is key because non-MC messages often have more impact on buying decisions than do MC messages.

As you read through this book, keep in mind that every business is unique as is its need for IMC. The objective of the book is to provide you with a basic understanding of the various marketing communication functions, media alternatives, and the integrated marketing communication concept and process. It will show you how these are used to develop long-term, profitable brand relationships.

To the Instructor

This textbook is about how to use communication to build stronger brand relationships. The IMC concept and process presented are those used by companies that truly put the customer first. It is about integrating *marketing* and *communication*. Although the title is IMC, some might call it integrated brand communication, customer relationship management (CRM), or even integrated corporate communication. This is because each of these has a strong common denominator: a customer focus. There is no question that IMC is still evolving. Each person who writes about IMC has a slightly different definition of it. Nevertheless, all of us who have worked on its development agree that the customer focus differentiates this new way of managing brand communication from traditional, one-way advertising and promotion.

Some say IMC is a management fad. Any relatively new business practice is always questioned, as it should be, during its evolution. Its ideas and practices need to be critically examined and challenged. IMC has successfully met these challenges and answered the hard questions. (See Schultz's and Kitchen's Sept./Oct. 2000 *Journal of Advertising Research* article, "A Response to '[IMC:] Theoretical Concept or Management Fashion?'"). The most important endorsement of the IMC concept, however, is its widespread adoption by both companies and agencies. As one top executive put it: "Why would a company want its operations to be *dis*-integrated? It's common sense that brand building should be as *integrated* as it can possibly be."

Some critics say IMC is nothing new because smart marketers have been integrating their marketing and marketing communication efforts for years. Conceptually, these critics are correct. IMC is basically what Peter Drucker has long said that marketing should be—a tool for creating customers for long term (e.g., customer relationships). The problem has been that as each of the MC functions and media became more sophisticated, their use became more fragmented. This fragmentation was further exacerbated by the new communication and information technologies. IMC came about in response to the need for a way to sort through all the MC and media options and to link and coordinate those selected for use in the most cost-effective manner.

IMC and traditional advertising and promotion make use of the same marketing communication functions and media, so some of the topics in this book are similar to those found in other texts. However, IMC differs significantly when it comes to objectives and strategies. Most advertising and promotion textbooks, even those that say they include IMC, simply do not mention or discuss in sufficient detail, the topics that are so critical in practicing integration. Some of the differentiating integration topics and factors that this book explains are:

- Building brands, not just brand images.
- Adding two-way to one-way brand communication.
- The strengths and weaknesses of the Internet in brand building.
- Discussion of brand messages rather than just ads.
- Identification and explanation of ALL brand contact points, not just those created by media.
- Customer-created brand contacts and how to respond.
- Cross-functional and zero-based planning.
- How to do and use SWOT analyses to determine the best mix of marketing communication functions and media.
- Using databases to segment, target, and create personalized brand messages.
- Importance of balancing efforts to acquire and retain customers and increasing their share of category spending.
- How to use an IMC Audit to evaluate IMC programs.
- Why a company can't be integrated externally until it is integrated internally.
- Brands, branding, and brand building explained in the context of creating and growing brand relationships. (Because brands are ephemeral compared to relationships, which are more tangible, the way to manage a brand is to manage the relationships that create and sustain that brand.)

- Explanation of why communication is the foundation of brand relationships.
- Discussion of why marketing communication cannot effectively operate in a corporate silo but rather must be integrated into the total business.

Acknowledgments

A book of this nature is only possible with the help and input of many people. I am indebted most to my wife, friend, and academic colleague, Professor Sandra Moriarty, whose wisdom and advice over the years has been invaluable in my development of an IMC concept and process. Her patience and understanding during the writing of this book is impossible to repay.

I am also indebted to practitioner and author Bill Arens who, early on in this project, shared and challenged my IMC ideas, pushing me to think in new directions. A big thanks to Steve Patterson, the McGraw-Hill/Irwin sponsoring editor who signed this book. His confidence and foresight six years ago regarding the academic and professional importance of IMC gave birth to the book's production. It has also been a pleasure to work with Christine Parker and Tracy Jensen, developmental editors, and Linda Schreiber, executive editor, who very professionally managed the development of the book. And many thanks to Jennifer Freedman, whose generous use of red ink during the initial editing process made this book a much better read.

Others who made significant contributions, for which I am extremely grateful, are:

Liz Bennett, Personal Research Assistant

Peggy Bronn, Professor of Marketing, BI School of Business, Oslo, Norway

Steven Carr, Senior Vice President, Integrated Public Relations, Cramer-Krasselt

Clarke Caywood, Former Director, IMC Graduate Program, Northwestern University

Ed Chambliss, Team Manager, The Phelps Group

Dustin Cohn, Vice President Account Director, FCB

Bruce Coulter, Corporate Account Representative, Rational Software Corp.

Bob Davies, Vice President, Price/McNabb

Michelle Fitzgerald, Connection Planner, Fallon

Mark Goldstein, Fallon's Worldwide Director of Integated Marketing

Richard Goode-Allen, Assistant Professor, University of Colorado—Boulder

Amy Hume, Media VP, Leo Burnett

Sam Kuczun, Professor Emeritus, University of Colorado—Boulder

Suzanne Lainson, President of SportsTrust

Loren Lindeke, Marketing Consultant

David Miln, marketing communication and brand consultant, London

Marieke de Mooij, International cultural marketing Consultant, the Netherlands

Brad Muller, Account Supervisor, Price/McNabb

Nancy Shonka Padberg, Vice President Promotion Marketing, The Phelps Group

Joe Plummer, Executive Vice President, Director of Brand Strategy and Research, McCann-Erickson World Group

Don Schultz, Founder of Northwestern University's IMC program

Karl Weiss, President, Marketing Perceptions, Inc.

Thanks to the following people who reviewed manuscript drafts in various stages and provided great insights, commentary, and suggestions that enhanced the quality and usefulness of this text:

Craig Andrews, Marquette University

Terry Bristol, Oklahoma State University

Wendy Bryce, Western Washington University

Melissa Burnett, Southwest Missouri State University

Todd Donavan, Kansas State University

Robert Ducoffe, The City University of New York

Alan D. Fletcher, Louisiana State University

Kate Gillespie, The University of Texas at Austin

Lisa M. Sciulli, Indiana University of Pennsylvania

Eric Haley, University of Tennessee

Patricia Kennedy, University of Nebraska

Tim Larson, University of Utah

Linda Miller, The University of Kansas

James Munch, University of Texas at Arlington

Terence Nevett, Central Michigan University

Joel Reedy, University of South Florida

Patricia B. Rose, Florida International University

Kris Swanson, Northern Arizona University

Brian Tietje, California Polytechnic University

Michael Weibad, Florida State University

Kurt Wildermuth, Northern Arizona University

Supplements

To assist the instructor in the classroom, the following supplements are available:

Instructor's Manual [0256215413]: The instructor's manual includes learning objectives, lecture outlines, additional mini-lectures, and further insights and teaching suggestions.

Test Bank [0256215421]: A test bank of over 1,300 questions has been developed to accompany the text. This test bank is comprised of multiple choice, true/false, and short-answer essay questions.

Video Library [0256215456]: A variety of perspectives on aspects of IMC along from real companies building and managing IMC campaigns, and with samples of relevant TV advertisements.

Instructor's Resource CD [0072481986]: This CD-ROM contains an electronic version of the Instructor's Manual, a computerized version of the test bank, a complete PowerPoint presentation, and a selection of video clips. This

CD-ROM allows instructors to customize classroom tests and presentations using images, PowerPoint text, and video clips.

Four-color Acetate package [0072481994]: These acetates contain ads and images for use in classroom lecture presentation.

Online Learning Center (OLC) [www.mhhe.com/duncan]: The OLC contains all instructor support materials, as well as student tutorials and self-assessment quizzing and additional materials, and a link to the Advertising PowerWeb.

Advertising PowerWeb [www.dushkin.com/powerweb]: This feature completes the online offering with access to current full-text articles, quizzing and assessment, validated links to relevant material, interactive glossaries, weekly updates, and interactive Web exercises. PowerWeb is organized by course area, ensuring that you and your students receive only the most pertinent and topical information.

Marketing Image Library CD-ROM [0072428511]: Containing 174 advertising images, the Marketing Image Library is a welcome fit with any advertising or marketing class. No matter which book you're using, or which concept you're explaining, you'll find plenty of up-to-date advertising images to perk up your lectures and make student comprehension easier. None of these images has appeared in a McGraw-Hill textbook before, so there will be no redundancy with your current book. Best of all, the images are organized by the concepts they illustrate, so that integrating them into your lecture is a breeze.

Oh, and did we mention it's free?

For a *complimentary* copy of the *Marketing Image Library CD-ROM*, contact your local McGraw-Hill/Irwin representative, call 1-800-338-3987, e-mail *listens@mcgraw-hill.com* or visit www.mhhe.com.

IMC is a process for managing communications that create the customer relationships that, in turn, drive brand value.

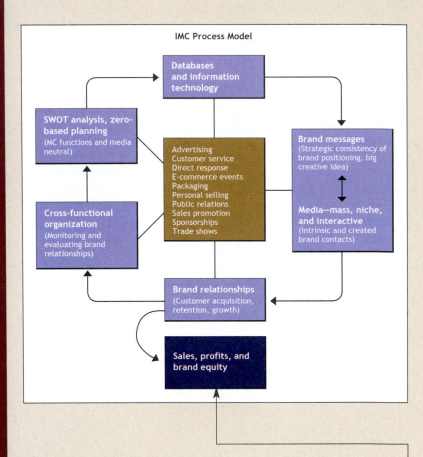

IMC Process Model

Databases and information technology

SWOT analysis, zero-based planning
(MC functions and media neutral)

Brand messages
(Strategic consistency of brand positioning, big creative idea)

Advertising
Customer service
Direct response
E-commerce events
Packaging
Personal selling
Public relations
Sales promotion
Sponsorships
Trade shows

Cross-functional organization
(Monitoring and evaluating brand relationships)

Media—mass, niche, and interactive
(Intrinsic and created brand contacts)

Brand relationships
(Customer acquisition, retention, growth)

Sales, profits, and brand equity

IMC Process Model

The integration process is illustrated here by the boxes surrounding the list of central marketing communication functions. Without this encompassing set of support functions, integration cannot take place.

NESCAFÉ SERVES CONTINUOUS HAPPINESS
McCann-Erickson, Osaka, Japan

When the Japanese economy went into a deep recession in the 1990s, and coffee category sales leveled off, the Swiss-based food-and-beverage giant Nestlé found it necessary to increase the prices of its instant-coffee brand Nescafé. Under such circumstances, how would you intensify the relationship Nescafé has with its Japanese customers, reach new customers, involve more retailers, and increase sales of instant coffee in Japan?

The Osaka office of international advertising agency McCann-Erickson decided that sales promotion was the marketing communication tool that could best lead this campaign for Nescafé. A strategic promotional idea under the theme "Continuous Happiness Present" was created by the McCann team and executed over a period of several years. This award-winning promotional campaign was designed to promote Nestlé's "friendly and caring" brand values while simultaneously increasing sales of Nescafé instant coffees at higher prices (see Exhibit 16-1).

To Western students of marketing communications, the "Continuous Happiness Present" campaign may seem overly polite, too much of a soft sell. It must be kept in mind, however, that the Japanese, like other Asian people, often find American and European advertising and sales promotion offers to be too pushy and intrusive.

The Marketing Challenge

The marketplace environment was the source of most of the problems faced by McCann's management team. Nescafé was the best-selling brand in the Japanese instant-coffee market, with a 72 percent share. However, its sales had been falling in recent years due to severe competition with growing liquid-coffee sales, a harder environment in which to get in-store display opportunities, and heavy-discount sale pricing of other competitive brands.

Campaign Strategy

EXHIBIT 16-1
A scene from one of the Nescafé TV commercials showing one of the winners of the flower promotion.

In 1998, the Nestlé Japan Coffee Beverage Group launched the "Continuous Happiness Present" campaign, which was designed to promote Nescafé's friendly nature to consumers rather than winning them with a discount price strategy. The promotion was a closed lottery in the sense that entrants had to provide a proof of purchase (a legal requirement in Japan), in this case the Nescafé proof-of-purchase mark, which appears on all Nescafé products. Winners whose entries were drawn received a present—a beautiful pot of flowers every month for a whole year (thus "continuous happiness"). It was a large-scale continuity campaign that ran for two years with a total of 10,000 winners.

(vertical sidebar) EFFECTIVENESS CASE

Chapter-opening cases show IMC at work in the real world, around the world. Cases are for goods, services, B2B, and for non-profit organizations.

Over half of the cases have an international emphasis.

14 of the opening cases are AME award winners.

USING A MEDIA CONTEXT TO HELP REVIVE AN OLD BRAND
Lee Jeans campaign by Fallon, Minneapolis, MN

Background: Why Buddy Lee Was Revived

Lee Jeans faced a critical brand problem. According to the heart of the jeans market, males and females ages 17–22, Lee Jeans were "not for me." They said Lee was "outdated," "boring," and "my mother's jeans." Fallon and Lee decided to reverse perceptions of the 105-year-old brand among these consumers by introducing a new sub-brand, Lee Dungarees, and reviving a diamond-in-the-rough icon uncovered in Lee's archives, Buddy Lee. (Buddy is Lee's vintage "spokes doll" from the 1920s (see Exhibit 13–1).

Lee's goal was to snap younger consumers' heads back and affect significant increases in key attribute measures including "brand for me" and "brand becoming more popular." In addition, Lee wanted to increase sales among young men and juniors.

The strategies: (1) guide fickle consumers down a path of discovery, allowing them to participate in discerning the meaning of the icon and the brand values; (2) fully integrate the positioning "jeans that won't hold you back" in all communications; (3) don't try too hard or risk rejection; and (4) use Buddy Lee to create a new definition of cool.

Stage I: Who is that cool guy?

Fallon designed a Discovery Phase to create intrigue in Buddy Lee and imbue him with coolness. The agency started by creating buzz locally and somewhat "underground." Using guerrilla tactics, brand communication was slightly ahead of the primary target, reaching leaders and influencers first. In these messages jeans were never mentioned . . . or the brand.

Consumers saw a phantom campaign of otherwise unidentified images of Buddy Lee wild posted, such as on walls bordering construction sites and other unusual places on the streets of trend areas in 15 major cities. Influential hipsters found random, small-space tune-in invitations to watch The Buddy Lee Story in music zines, alternative weeklies, and a CD-ROM (where Buddy became a fixture in the new music area). An underground network of web zines linked to the unbranded Buddy Lee website which told his story, but did not link to leejeans.com. The Buddy Lee site was interactive in that consumers could submit questions about Buddy and these were answered directly.

After bar-hopping and clubbing, the target came home and watched The Buddy Lee Story in between "South Park" episodes. The story ran as a two-part series of three-minute short films on late-late night

EXHIBIT 13-1
Reproduction of the original Buddy Lee "Spokes doll."

(vertical sidebar) EFFECTIVENESS CASE

IMC Mini-Audit

One of the key measurement and evaluation tools presented, is an IMC Audit.

FIGURE 21-1

This 20-question mini-audit is a good and easy way for an organization to quickly test its level of integration.

IMC Mini-Audit

Circle the number that best describes how your organization operates regarding each of the following statements. If you don't know how well your organization is doing for a given item, circle DK (Don't Know). If a question does not apply to your organization, leave it blank.

	Never				Always	

Organizational Infrastructure

1. In our company, the process of managing brand/company reputation and building stakeholder relationships is a cross-functional responsibility that includes departments such as production, operations, sales finance, and human resources, as well as marketing.   1 2 3 4 5 DK

2. The people managing our communication programs demonstrate a good understanding of the strengths and weaknesses of ALL major marketing communication tools such as direct response, public relations sales promotion, advertising, and packaging when putting marketing communication plans together.   1 2 3 4 5 DK

3. We do a good job of internal marketing, informing all areas of the organization about our objectives and marketing programs.   1 2 3 4 5 DK

4. Our major communication agencies have at least monthly contact with each other regarding our communication programs and activities.   1 2 3 4 5 DK

Interactivity

5. Our media plan is a strategic balance between mass media and one-to-one media.   1 2 3 4 5 DK

6. Special programs are in place to facilitate customer inquiries and complaints.   1 2 3 4 5 DK

7. We use customer databases that capture customer inquiries, complaints, compliments, as well as sales behavior (e.g., trial, repeat, frequency of purchase, type of purchases).   1 2 3 4 5 DK

8. Our customer databases are easily accessible (internally) and user-friendly.   1 2 3 4 5 DK

Mission Marketing

9. Our organization's mission is a key consideration and is evident in our marketing communication plans.   1 2 3 4 5 DK

10. Our mission provides an additional reason for customers and other key stakeholders to believe our messages and support our company.   1 2 3 4 5 DK

11. Our corporate philanthropic efforts are concentrated in one specific area or program.   1 2 3 4 5 DK

Strategic Consistency

12. All of our planned brand messages (e.g., advertising, sales promotion, PR, packaging) are strategically consistent.   1 2 3 4 5 DK

13. We periodically review all our brand messages to determine to what extent they are strategically consistent.   1 2 3 4 5 DK

14. We consciously think about what brand messages are being sent by our pricing, distribution, product performance, customer-service operations, and by persons and organizations outside the control of the company.   1 2 3 4 5 DK

Chapter Perspective:
A Special Relationship

Because IMC is a process, it is a means to an end. That end is brands and stakeholder relationships. The purpose of this chapter is to explain these two IMC end products. Companies make goods and provide services, but they sell brands. And as competing products proliferate and become more similar, the role of customer relationships becomes more critical. A company that has no customer relationships doesn't have a brand. Understanding how brands are built and managed requires an understanding of how relationships are built and managed. This chapter will first explain brands, then brand relationships (including stakeholder support, overlap, and capital), and finally the anatomy of profitable brand relationships.

Conceptually, neither IMC nor brand relationship building is new. What is new are the IMC *principles and practices* used to build these relationships. Recall from Chapter 1 that in the days of the old general store, owners knew their customers personally. But as companies and chains took over, these relationships gave way to mass marketing. With new information and communication technology, however, it is possible for companies to once again know their customers and operate on a more personal and responsive level.

A brand relationship strategy brings customers and branding together. According to Regis McKenna, a leading high-tech public relations consultant and author of *Relationship Marketing*, a successful brand is nothing more than a special relationship. A good brand relationship is one in which the relationship is of value to both the customer and company. A customer relationship building program, however, is a long-term strategy, unlike a more traditional marketing strategy that focuses on short-term transactions.

Chapter Perspectives

Each chapter's "Perspective" provides an overview of the chapter and explains how it fits into the overall IMC concept and process.

Video Series

A series prepared by the author provides illustration for the text concepts and video support to many of the cases.

The chapter objectives, summaries, and assessment exercises are all linked through each chapter's "Key Points." This inter-linked "safety net" gives students the assurance that they have mastered the basic content in the chapters.

Key Points in This Chapter

1. How does the creative process work to develop big ideas?

2. What are the message design needs of different MC functional areas?

3. What are the written parts of a brand message?

4. How do art and design contribute to MC executions?

Key Point Summary

Key Point 1: The Creative Process

The creative process is a step-by-step procedure that people use to discover original ideas. The first step is exploration, which means understanding all the background information and research from the creative brief. Second is insight, which means taking the facts and ideas from the research and backgrounding and using them to create a big idea. Third is execution, which means taking the big idea into all the various brand messages and producing the actual pieces. Fourth is evaluation, in which the creative team steps back, both during and after the process, and considers whether the big idea is on strategy.

Key Point 2: Designing for Different MC Functional Areas

1. What is the purpose of a headline?
2. What is the difference between display copy and body copy?
3. Find a print ad, make a copy of it, and on the copy in red ink identify the headline and the body copy. If any of the following are used in the ad, then identify them as well: captions, subheads, overlines, underlines, taglines, or call-out quotes. Finally circle the brand identification elements and label them as a logo or signature.

Key Point 3: Writing Copy

The key format elements which

Lessons Learned

Key Point 1: The Creative Process

a. Define creativity. What are its key characteristics?
b. What are the four steps in the creative process?
c. Set up a brainstorming session with some of your friends. Ask them to help you come up with an idea for a new Sonic Skating Gear ad. Experiment with all the brainstorming techniques. Which one led you to the most promising idea?
d. Find a marketing communication execution that you believe is highly creative and a similar one that isn't creative. Critique both pieces and explain your evaluation of them.

Key Point 2: Designing for Different MC Functional Areas

1. What is the purpose of a headline?
2. What is the difference between display copy and body copy?
3. Find a print ad, make a copy of it, and on the copy in red ink identify the headline and the body copy.

Assignments within the end-of-chapter "Challenges" and "Additional Readings" provide students with ample opportunity to explore concepts further and apply what they have learned.

Chapter Challenge

Writing Assignment

The Parkinson's Coalition case at the beginning of this chapter provides an example in which customers used both the head and the heart to make a decision. Explain how these different styles of reasoning work and how marketing communication can influence them. From what you have learned about customer decision-making processes, what would you recommend to the Parkinson's Coalition for next year's campaign?

Presentation Assignment

You have been hired by a local coffeehouse to analyze its customers' behavior. But first the manager wants you to give the organization's employees a crash course in brand decision-making basics. Go back through the entire chapter and list all the tips you can find about how to use marketing communication to effectively relate to customers. Prepare a presentation to the store owner and manager on those factors that you think are most relevant to their marketing situation. In particular, what are the various strategies you might recommend for their marketing communication that would influence behavior? Develop an outline of the key points you want to present. Give the presentation to your class or record it on a videotape (audiotape is also an option) to turn in to your instructor, along with the outline.

Internet Assignment:

Browse the Motley Fool website (www.fool.com) and find a discussion that relates to consumer behavior. Write a report on this topic, explaining it in terms of brand decision making as described in this chapter.

Additional Readings

Jones, John Philip. "Is Advertising Still Salesmanship?" *Journal of Advertising Research*, May-June 1997, pp. 9-15.

Fortini-Campbell, Lisa. *The Consumer Insight Workbook*. Chicago: The Copy Workshop, 1992.

Macdonald, Emma, and Bryon Sharp. "Brand Awareness Effects on Consumer Decision Making for a Common, Repeat Purchase Product." *Journal of Consumer Research*, April 2000.

Modahl, Mary. *Now or Never: How Companies Must Change Today to Win the Battle for Internet Customers*. New York: HarperBusiness, 2000.

Pine, B. Joseph, II, and James H. Gilmore. *The Experience Economy: Work Is Theatre & Every Business a Stage*. Boston: Harvard Business School Press, 1999.

Wicks, Robert. *Understanding Audiences*. Mahwah, NJ: Lawrence Erlbaum, 2001.

Research Assignment

Consult these articles and books and others that you find in the library that relate to consumer behavior and explain how advertising and other forms of marketing communication are successful (or not successful) in influencing the consumer decision process. Develop a marketing communications plan for the introduction of a new product of your own choice that makes the most effective use of marketing communication to influence the brand decision process of your target audience.

Brief Contents

Contents

Part Three
CREATING, SENDING, AND RECEIVING BRAND MESSAGES 307

9 IMC Message Strategy 308

10 Brand Message Execution 334

Photo Credits

p. 4 Ex. 1.1: © Copyright Atlanta Journal Constitution. p. 5 Ex. 1.2: Courtesy AirTran. p. 6 Ex. 1.3: Courtesy AirTran. p. 7 Ex. 1.4: Courtesy AirTran. p. 10 Ex. 1.5: Reprinted with permission of AT&T. p. 16 Ex. 1.6: Courtesy Cisco Systems and the United Nations Development Programme. p. 18 Ex. 1.7: Copyright © 1996 Sybase Inc. with Sybase logo as trademark of Sybase Inc. p. 25 Ex. 1.8: PR Newswire Disney Cruise Lines. p. 26 Ex. 1.9: © Anheuser-Busch, Inc. Budweiser® Beer is a trademark of Anheuser-Busch, Inc., St. Louis, MO. p. 27 Ex. 1.10: Courtesy *USA Weekend* magazine. p. 40 Ex. 2.1: Courtesy Boots the Chemist and J. Walter Thompson, London. p. 45 Ex. 2.2: Courtesy Gucci USA. p. 46 left Ex. 2.3a: Courtesy Hummer. p. 46 rt Ex. 2.3b: Courtesy Land Rover North America. p. 49 Ex. 2.4: Courtesy Cushman & Wakefield Worldwide. p. 51 Ex. 2.5: © 1996 Lucent Technologies. p. 52 Ex. 2.6: © 2000 Apple Computer Inc. All rights reserved. p. 54 Ex. 2.7: Copyright, Nissan (2000). Nissan and the Nissan logo are registered Trademarks of Nissan. p. 55 Ex. 2.8: Reproduced by permission of W. L. Gore & Associates, Inc. GORE-TEX is a registered Trademark of W. L. Gore & Associates. p. 61 Ex. 2.9: © 1997 IBM Corp. IBM, Solutions for a small planet and the e-business logo trademarks of International Business Machines Corporation in the United States and/or other countries. p. 63 Ex. 2.10: Edward**Jones**® is a registered trademark of Edward Jones, St. Louis, MO. p. 64 top Ex. 2.11: ® Good Housekeeping 2001. Hearst Communications, Inc. p. 64 bottom Ex. 2.12: Courtesy TRUSTe. p. 67 Ex. 2.13: Reprinted with permission of AchieveGlobal. p. 73 Ex. 2.14: ® St. Paul Fire and Marine Insurance Company, St. Paul, MN. p. 80 Ex. 3.1: Courtesy Salles and DMB&B. p. 81 Ex. 3.2: © Lawrence Migdale/Stock, Boston/Picturequest. p. 89 Ex. 3.3: Courtesy U.S. Air. p. 93 Ex. 3.4: © 2000 Apple Computer Inc. All rights reserved. p. 97 Ex. 3.5: Courtesy Poppe Tyson. p. 100 Ex. 3.6: Courtesy Cone. p. 101 Ex. 3.7: Reprinted with permission from the August 3, 1998 issue of *Advertising Age*. Copyright, Crain Communications, Inc. 1998. p. 103 left Ex. 3.8: Courtesy Rowland, Public Relations and Integrated Communications. p. 103 rt Ex. 3.9: Courtesy Golin/Harris. p. 105 Ex. 3.10: With permission of Landor. p. 113 Ex. 3.11: Magazine Publishers of America. p. 114 Ex. 3.12: © 2001 National Geographic Channel. p. 122 Ex. 4.1: Courtesy McCann-Erickson Dublin Ltd. and Unilever/HB Ice Cream. p. 123 Ex. 4.2: Courtesy McCann-Erickson Dublin Ltd. and Unilever/HB Ice Cream. p. 124 Ex. 4.3: Courtesy McCann-Erickson Dublin Ltd. and Unilever/HB Ice Cream. p. 128 Ex. 4.4: Courtesy Avaya Communications. p. 130 Ex. 4.5: © 1990 Southwest Airlines. p. 132 Ex. 4.6: Tupperware®. p. 134 Ex. 4.7: © 2001 Susan G. Holtz. p. 137 Ex. 4.8: Courtesy Ford Motor Company. p. 140 Ex. 4.9: Courtesy Motorola. p. 144 Ex. 4.10: Courtesy BMW America. p. 145 Ex. 4.11: © Gucci USA. All rights reserved. p. 147 Ex. 4.12: Courtesy FM Global. p. 158 Ex. 5.1: Courtesy McCann-Erickson Southwest and Parkinson Coalition of Houston. p. 159 Ex. 5.2: Courtesy McCann-Erickson Southwest and Parkinson Coalition of Houston. p. 162 Ex. 5.3: © 1998 BASF Corporation. p. 163 Ex. 5.4: Courtesy Liberty Mutual. p. 163 Ex. 5.4: Courtesy Liberty Mutual. p. 171 Ex. 5.5: Courtesy Oldsmobile. p. 172 Ex. 5.6: AP/Wide World. p. 174 Ex. 5.7: Courtesy Candies. p. 176 Ex. 5.8: mySimon is a division of CNET Networks, Inc. p. 177 Ex. 5.9: Courtesy WaterPik Technologies, Inc. p. 180 Ex. 5.10: Tobacco Education and Prevention Program, Arizona Department of Health Services. p. 181 Ex. 5.11: Courtesy Freshwater Software. p. 184 Ex. 5.12: Courtesy Swiss Army Brands, Inc. p. 194 Ex. 6.1:

Courtesy GMC Envoy and McCann Relationship Marketing. p. 196 Ex. 6.2a–b: Courtesy GMC Envoy and McCann Relationship Marketing. p. 197 Ex. 6.2c: Courtesy GMC Envoy and McCann Relationship Marketing. p. 199 Ex. 6.3: Lands' End® Direct Merchants. p. 205 Ex. 6.4: Courtesy Talisma. p. 206 Ex. 6.5: Courtesy Hewlett-Packard. p. 210 Ex. 6.6: Courtesy Motorola. p. 211 Ex. 6.7: Courtesy Nike. p. 212 Ex. 6.8: PR Newswire. p. 213 Ex. 6.9: Courtesy robertmondavi.com. p. 219 Ex. 6.10: Courtesy Amy Krammes. p. 234 Ex. 7.1: Courtesy Holden Ltd. and McCann-Erickson Melbourne. p. 236 Ex. 7.2: Courtesy Holden Ltd. and McCann-Erickson Melbourne. p. 237 Ex. 7.3: Courtesy Holden Ltd. and McCann-Erickson Melbourne. p. 241 Ex. 7.4: Coricidin® is a registered trademark of Schering-Plough HealthCare Products Inc. p. 243 Ex. 7.5: Courtesy SRDS. p. 244 Ex. 7.6: Courtesy Wendy's International Inc. p. 246 Ex. 7.7: © 2001 Susan G. Holtz. p. 249 top Ex. 7.8: Courtesy Helene Curtis Inc. p. 249 bottom Ex. 7.9: With permission Bristol-Myers Squibb Co. p. 251 Ex. 7.10: Courtesy Donnelley Marketing Information Services. p. 252 Ex. 7.11: © 1998, Pfizer Inc. p. 255 top Ex. 7.12: Courtesy worldcom. p. 255 bottom Ex. 7.13: Courtesy Clinique Laboratories, Inc. p. 262 Ex. 7.14: Courtesy Xerox, The Document Company. p. 272 Ex. 8.1: Materials courtesy British Airways and Carlson Marketing Group, London. p. 273 Ex. 8.2: Materials courtesy British Airways and Carlson Marketing Group, London. p. 274 Ex. 8.3: Materials courtesy British Airways and Carlson Marketing Group, London. p. 275 Ex. 8.4: Courtesy SAS Institute Inc. p. 282 Ex. 8.5: IBM, the e-business logo and Solutions for a small planet are trademarks of International Business Machines Corporation in the United States and/or other countries. © 1998 IBM Corp. All rights reserved. p. 285 Ex. 8.6: Courtesy Fenwick & West LLP. p. 286 Ex. 8.7: Courtesy jcpenney.com. © 2000 Levi Strauss & Co. p. 289 Ex. 8.8: Materials courtesy British Airways and Carlson Marketing Group, London. p. 292 Ex. 8.9: © 1999 The Coca-Cola Company. p. 293 Ex. 8.10: Courtesy PaineWebber Incorporated. p. 303 Ex. 8.11: Materials courtesy British Airways and Carlson Marketing Group, London. p. 310 Ex. 9.1: Courtesy Arnott's and Bates Advertising, Auckland. p. 312 Ex. 9.2: Courtesy Arnott's and Bates Advertising, Auckland. p. 317 Ex. 9.3: © 1999 Dayton-Hudson Corp. p. 318 Ex. 9.4: Jessica Wecker. p. 322 top Ex. 9.5: Courtesy Lancaster Group US LLC. p. 323 Ex. 9.6: Courtesy Acura. p. 322 bottom Ex. 9.7: © 3M 1996. p. 324 Ex. 9.8: Courtesy Hershey's. p. 326 Ex. 9.9: Courtesy Omaha Steaks. p. 328 Ex. 9.10: © 1990 Chemical Bank. p. 336 Ex. 10.1: Materials courtesy Andersen Consulting and Wunderman Cato Johnson, Franfurt. p. 338 Ex. 10.2: Materials courtesy Andersen Consulting and Wunderman Cato Johnson, Franfurt. p. 343 Ex. 10.3: © 1998 S. C. Johnson & Son, Inc. p. 345 Ex. 10.4: Courtesy Diesel. p. 346 Ex. 10.5: Courtesy Gillette. p. 348 Ex. 10.6a: Courtesy Washington Apple Commission. p. 348 Ex. 10.6b: Coopers & Lybrand. p. 350 Ex. 10.7: Courtesy American Greetings. p. 351 top Ex. 10.8: Courtesy Jeep. Jeep® is a registered trademark of Chrysler Corporation. p. 351 bottom Ex. 10.9: Courtesy Lufthansa. p. 352 Ex. 10.10: Courtesy Visio Corporation. p. 353 top Ex. 10.11: Courtesy Lufthansa. p. 353 bottom Ex. 10.12: Courtesy Lufthansa. p. 354 Ex. 10.13: © 3M 1989. p. 356 Ex. 10.14: Ford Motor Company. p. 357 Ex. 10.15: Courtesy Sprint. p. 358 Ex. 10.16: Materials courtesy Sprint. p. 359 Ex. 10.17: © 2001 Chris Hamilton Photography. p. 360 Ex. 10.18: © 2001 Susan G. Holtz. p. 361 top Ex. 10.19: © 2001 Susan G. Holtz. p. 361 bottom Ex. 10.20: Courtesy Dodge. p. 363 Ex. 10.21: AP/Wide World.

Part One

From Marketing Communication to IMC

Because of increasing brand competition, organizations need to design the most effective and efficient communication program possible to build relationships with customers and other key audiences. Integration is the key to superior brand communication.

The first three chapters explain the philosophy behind this book. Chapter 1 discusses the evolution of integrated marketing communication (IMC). Chapter 2 discusses branding and the key relationships that support a brand. Chapter 3 reviews the organizational dimensions of brand communication, including the critical relationship between agencies and clients.

1

From Marketing Communication to IMC

Key Points in This Chapter

1. How important is communication in building brand relationships?

2. How does relationship-focused marketing deliver on the marketing concept?

3. What is included in the marketing communication mix, and what more needs to be considered in an integrated program?

4. What industry trends are driving IMC?

Chapter Perspective

Moving from Transactions to Relationships

Advertising and promotion have been used by organizations for hundreds of years to sell goods, services, and ideas. But the marketplace has changed. Competition has increased in both the commercial and nonprofit worlds. Customers have become more distrustful of businesses. New communication and information technologies have been developed. Companies have discovered that its more profitable to sell to current customers than to new customers. The bottom line is that traditional advertising and promotional practices are no longer enough to do the job. Organizations now need more effective and efficient ways of communicating with customers than ever before. This is why so many companies today are using integrated marketing communications (IMC). They have learned that IMC practices and principles will help them build the customer relationships that create profitable brands.

Advertising and promotion are good ways to acquire customers and create a sales transaction. But a transaction is a single interaction that ends once the sale is made. A customer relationship, in contrast, consists of a number of interactions, including sales transactions, that are repeated over time. Just as one date does not constitute a personal relationship, one transaction does not create a customer relationship.

To develop a relationship with customers, a company must first know who its customers are. IMC uses customer databases to identify customers and thus to create the possibility of establishing a personal, two-way dialogue with them. IMC is neutral about marketing communication functions and the media, using a planning technique that lets each unique brand situation determine the best mix of marketing communication functions and media. IMC provides a system for integrating the planning and monitoring of brand-building activities. This system helps ensure that a brand has one voice, one look. IMC takes advantage of new media and new communication and information technologies. Finally, IMC can help build trust in a brand by creating an open, customer-focused culture.

Trust is something many brands have lost for one reason or another. Most often brands lose trust when they lose perspective on who their customers are. They lose trust when they overpromise or when they continually talk about price and discounts. Brands can also lose trust for other reasons, such as those highlighted in the opening case in this chapter. No matter what the situation, however, IMC can help build trust and relationships that create brands. This is because IMC is a process for listening as well as talking to customers. In essence, IMC is the big picture of brand communications.

AIRTRAN: HOW IMC HELPED REBUILD A BRAND
Cramer-Krasselt, Chicago

In May 1996, a low-fare regional airline called ValuJet received a lot of brand publicity. Unfortunately, it was all negative. One of the company's planes had crashed in the Florida Everglades, killing 110 people (see Exhibit 1–1). To make things worse, the Federal Aviation Administration (FAA) began a major investigation of the airline's safety practices, which resulted in the airline's being grounded. This generated further negative publicity. When ValuJet was finally allowed to resume flying, it could not regain enough customers to get its "load factor" (percentage of seats sold) above 50 percent, which meant it was unable to make a profit.

How this airline turned itself around to once again be profitable provides an excellent example of the benefits of using integrated marketing communications (IMC). You may not be familiar with this term or with some of the other terms in this opening case. Don't worry about it. The purpose of the book is to explain these to you. This case is intended to give you an overview of what this book is all about—the principles and practices of IMC.

The Turnaround Strategy

EXHIBIT 1-1

The negative media coverage of ValuJet's crash in the Florida Everglades led to the brand's demise.

To become profitable once more, ValuJet knew it had to accomplish two business goals: increase its load factor and increase its stock price. To do this required a major communication effort that would change attitudes and behaviors both inside and outside the company and rebuild its brand relationships. Customers needed "permission" to fly the airline again. Investors needed "permission" to buy or recommend the company's stock again. To make this happen the brand had to re-create trust, something that could not be done just with advertising—trust had to be earned.

To manage this critical communication challenge, ValuJet hired Cramer-Krasselt, an agency that specializes in integrated marketing communication. The agency was given three months to come up with a new positioning and an IMC reintroduction campaign.

In order to make sure all brand messages were integrated, Cramer-Krasselt set up a war room within the agency. In this converted conference room, daily meetings were held to keep track of what was being done for ValuJet—research, advertising, public relations, sales promotion, signage programs—and to discuss any other issues that needed to be addressed. Bringing all the marketing communications people together every day helped everyone

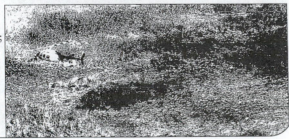

involved know what everyone else was doing. The result was that the IMC campaign had one voice, one look.

The agency's first step was to determine exactly what prospective passengers thought about ValuJet. Findings indicated that the 1996 crash had severely weakened relationships with customers, employees, communities, and the FAA. Research found that 22 percent of former customers said the airline was unsafe and that 49 percent said they were "very unlikely" to fly it again. Also, ValuJet, which had once been a highflier on Wall Street, had suddenly had its brand value greatly reduced by the financial community. The brand had been damaged beyond repair. Based on these findings, Cramer-Krasselt said the airline needed to achieve the following IMC objectives:

1. Relaunch the brand.
2. Redefine low-fare air travel.
3. Generate positive visibility of the airline in the media.
4. Recapture the business traveler.
5. Achieve an average fare of $65 and a load factor of 60 percent.

Recognizing that the brand name ValuJet had lost most of its brand value, the company merged with a Florida-based low-fare airline and took over its name—AirTran. The company made extensive changes in its operations and safety procedures. But the managers at the newly formed entity realized that changing the name and operations wasn't enough to completely rebuild confidence. To do this, they had to show that AirTran was more than just another low-fare airline. The marketing and communication challenge was for AirTran to redefine low-fare air travel—making it more than just a way to save money.

To that end, the IMC agency and its client came up with new strategies that would help further reposition the brand. One was to add a business-class service, which other low-fare airlines did not have. But to reinforce its low-fare image, AirTran priced its business-class tickets at only $25 more than a regular seat. The airline also implemented seat assignments and allowed travel agents to access its computer reservation system—additional things not done by other low-fare competitors. To make sure everyone knew exactly how the airline should be explained in brand messages, Cramer-Krasselt prepared the following positioning statement and printed it on a poster that was displayed in offices of those working on the account:

> AirTran Airways is the crusader for the under-appreciated, over-charged business flyer. We strive to exceed people's expectations about low-fare air travel through innovations that make flying as easy to enjoy as it is to afford.

To ensure that all brand messages were integrated, AirTran even had Cramer-Krasselt redesign the graphics on the exterior of its planes. The new design was anchored in a large signature "*a*." (See Exhibit 1–2. This is how the new logo was used on the airplanes.) Agency people also went to airports served by the airline and measured every interior billboard and terminal poster that needed to be replaced. Publicity releases were prepared for the financial as well as the mainstream media. Recognizing that employee morale, which had hit rock-bottom, was a critical element in determining the company's turnaround, company officials gave special attention to employees via newsletters and periodic update reports. On the day of the changeover, the company not only held a huge press conference at Atlanta International Airport but also issued new AirTran uniforms to employees.

In making the name change public, the company had a choice. One option was to simply begin using the AirTran name and hope customers and other stakeholders would not connect it to ValuJet. The other was to be open and straightforward,

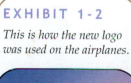

EXHIBIT 1-2

This is how the new logo was used on the airplanes.

saying that ValuJet had made major changes and was really a new airline with a new name, AirTran. Cramer-Krasselt recommended the straightforward approach, its client agreed, and the company took the first step in rebuilding brand credibility. Thus, the message in the introductory campaign was that ValuJet would now be AirTran, which was a whole new airline (see Exhibit 1–3). This head-on approach to acknowledging ValuJet's past prevented any possible media exposé stories claiming that the new company was trying to hide its connection to the old.

Three days before the grand reintroduction, Cramer-Krasselt pitched the story to *The Wall Street Journal*, the *Atlanta Journal-Constitution*, and the Reuters news service. All three agreed to do an interview with AirTran's chief executive officer (CEO) and hold the story until the introductory day. The publicity releases, newspaper and TV ads, new terminal signage, and new uniforms helped turn the changeover press conference into a party on the tarmac at the Atlanta Airport (home of AirTran). A redesigned airplane was ceremoniously rolled out from one of the hangars, and the new AirTran was on its way.

To continue to reinforce the idea that AirTran was a new and safe airline the company begin buying new planes. Brand messages were created to leverage the prestige of the new planes' manufacturer (Boeing) and engine makers (BMW and Rolls-Royce). According to Steve Carr, Cramer-Krasselt's director of integrated public relations, "This brand message, by associating AirTran with these three well-known and respected brands, reinforced the high safety standards of AirTran."

Wanting to stay as close to its customers as possible, AirTran set up a website (www.airtran.com) to allow customers to access flight information, purchase tickets, and find out just about anything else a potential passenger would want to know. Today, over 40 percent of AirTran customers purchase tickets online.

To help retain customers, AirTran set up a frequent-flyer promotional program called A-Plus Rewards. Like the airline's other programs, this one is extremely competitive. By buying just three business-class round-trips, for example, a passenger earns one free round-trip coach ticket to anywhere AirTran flies. Not only is the A-Plus Rewards program a good promotional tool for retaining customers, but it also provides the airline with a database of its customers so it can communicate with them on a one-to-one basis.

EXHIBIT 1-3

The company ran ads to explain openly, rather than trying to hide the fact, that ValuJet would henceforth be known as AirTran.

By the time we're through reinventing ValuJet you won't even recognize it.

It's much more than a new paint job. It's a brand new airline. ValuJet Airlines is now known as AirTran Airlines, an airline unlike anything you've flown before. And the changes are pretty dramatic. Because we're creating an entirely new way of looking at affordable air travel. Here's where we are so far.

Introducing AirTran Airlines. The product of new management, new thinking, and lots of new paint.

1. Starting in mid-October, we're assigning every seat. So you won't get stuck in one of those seat-grabbing, free-for-all boarding calls like on other low fare airlines. **2.** In late November, we're launching our Business Class. The first business class any business can afford. Two-by-two seats with extra legroom and—more importantly—decent seat room, for just a $25* upgrade. **3.** We also have new planes on the way—*one billion dollars* worth of state-of-the-art Boeing MD-95s to begin delivery in 1999. **4.** We'll be taking you to 45 cities so you'll have more help getting to where you're going without going broke. **5.** It's also easier to make reservations now that we're in your travel agent's computer reservation system. **6.** And you may have already noticed the new look. We think it shows how proud we are of the new airline we're building. The kind of airline our own CEO would like to fly. **7** No matter how much we examine, prod and re-think how we do things, you'll always be able to recognize our affordable fares everywhere we fly. Call your travel agent or **1-800-AIR-TRAN.**

Boston
$49
one-way

Some of our destinations

Atlanta	Macon*
Akron/Canton	Memphis
Boston	Mobile
*Chattanooga	New Orleans
Chicago (Midway)	Newport News/Norfolk
Dallas/Ft. Worth	Orlando
*Dalton	Philadelphia
Flint	Raleigh/Durham
Ft. Lauderdale	Savannah
Ft. Myers	Tampa
Houston (Hobby)	West Palm Beach
Jacksonville	

*FlightLink Service

All fares are one-way. All fares (except Business Class) are non-refundable, and a $35 fee applies to any change made after purchase plus any applicable increase in airfare. These fares require a 14-day advance purchase, are off-peak, and seats will be limited, subject to availability and may not be available on all flights. Off-peak for non-Florida markets is defined as every day except Friday and Sunday. Off-peak for Florida markets is defined as southbound Sunday, Monday, Tuesday, and Wednesday, and northbound Tuesday, Wednesday, Thursday, and Friday. Fares and schedules are subject to change without notice. Airport Passenger Facility Charges of up to $12 are not included. *Business Class upgrades are available for sale for $25 over the regular one-way coach fare for nonstop flights and for $40 over the regular one-way fare for connecting flights. Business Class will be available for sale in mid-October and will be available for travel in late November. AirTran FlightLink service is provided by buses operated by Greyhound Lines, Inc. AirTran Airlines operates using AirTran Airways' code. ©1997

It's something else.

EXHIBIT 1-4

AirTran began using new creative executions in 1999. Note the increased emphasis given to the signature "a" on this outdoor board.

Although AirTran has continued to use the integrated strategy that helped turn the airline around, its agency revised the creative execution in 1999 to place more emphasis on the brand name and signature "*a*," as shown in Exhibit 1–4.

The Results

The reintroduction and repositioning of ValuJet as AirTran has been extremely successful. As of September 2000, the airline's load factor was 70.4 percent (10.4 percentage points above its goal of 60 percent) and the average ticket price was over $80 ($15 above its goal of $65). The repositioning was so complete that when AirTran had a major press party to announce its new service to Minneapolis-St. Paul in mid-2000, not one reporter asked or wrote about AirTran's former existence as ValuJet. The success of this rebuilding was made possible by those at the company who valued the need for an integrated approach and chose to work with a communication agency that understood and practiced IMC.

Information for this case was provided by Steve Carr, VP, and other executives of Cramer-Krasselt, Chicago, agency for AirTran.

INTEGRATED MARKETING COMMUNICATION (IMC)

The number one marketing priority for a company should be to create customers. As management consultant Peter Drucker explained many decades ago, when this happens, the company is rewarded by making sales, which then produce profits. According to Drucker, building **customer relationships,** which involve a *series of interactions between individuals and a company over time,* will produce more sales and profits than will focusing on sales transactions alone. The objective of this book is to explain how companies can successfully integrate brand messages, media, and marketing communication functions to help create, retain, and grow brand relationships.

As the AirTran case that opens this chapter illustrates, marketing actions must take into consideration not only customers and potential customers but also other stakeholders, such as employees and investors. **Stakeholders** are *individuals or groups who can affect, or be affected by, an organization:* employees, customers, investors, suppliers, distribution channel members, the community, the media, special interest and activist groups, and government regulatory agencies. In other words, a stakeholder is anyone who has a stake in the success or failure of an organization.

A principle of integrated marketing communications (IMC) is that companies must continually be aware they operate within a public arena where their actions are scrutinized by all stakeholders. It used to be that business dealings were of interest to only a small percentage of the population—those directly involved with managing businesses. Today, however, with nearly half of the U.S. population owning shares of stock in one or more companies, business activity is front-page news. According to one study, "business" was the second most popular special interest topic in newspapers, scoring higher than sports, entertainment, and health.[1]

What IMC Means

With the increasing emphasis on customer and stakeholder relationships, both academics and professionals have come up with a variety of names for the processes designed to help organizations become customer-centric rather than company-centric. Besides integrated marketing communication (IMC), there is customer relationship management (CRM), one-to-one marketing, integrated marketing, strategic brand communication, and relationship marketing. Though each has its points of differences, all are designed to do one basic thing—increase the value of a company or brand by allowing the organization to cost-effectively acquire, retain, and grow customer relationships. "Growing" customers means motivating them to give your brand a greater share of their spending in a given product category.

IMC was one of the first processes to provide for managing customer relationships. It is also the most widely used. What differentiates IMC from the other customer-centric process is that its foundation is communication, which is the heart of all relationships, and that it is a circular process (as shown in Figure 1–1) rather than a linear one. There is no starting and stopping with regard to acquiring, retaining, and growing customers (unless a new brand is being introduced).

Figure 1–1 probably seems a little overwhelming since you are just beginning to study this book, whose purpose is to fully explain how to do IMC. The model is presented up front to provide you with an overview of what you will be reading about. At this point, the important thing to take away from the model is that IMC is a revolving process that creates brand value in the form of sales, profits, and brand equity.

Simply put, **IMC** is a *process for managing the customer relationships that drive brand value.* More specifically, it is a *cross-functional process for creating and nourishing profitable relationships with customers and other stakeholders by strategically controlling or influencing all messages sent to these groups and encouraging data-driven, purposeful dialogue with them.* To make sure the definition is clear, let's look at each of its major elements:

1. *Cross-functional process* means that all of the company's major departments (and outside communication agencies) that touch the customer must have a way of working together in the planning and monitoring of brand relationships. This is because, as you read in the AirTran case, customers are influenced by more than just marketing communication messages. A cross-functional process integrates managers from different departments and agencies who are working on the same brand in order to plan and manage all the messages a company sends to—and receives from—customers, prospects, and other stakeholders.

2. *Creating and nourishing stakeholder relationships* means attracting new customers and then interacting with them to find ways the company can further satisfy their wants and needs. The more satisfied customers or other stakeholders are, the more business or support they will generally give to a company.

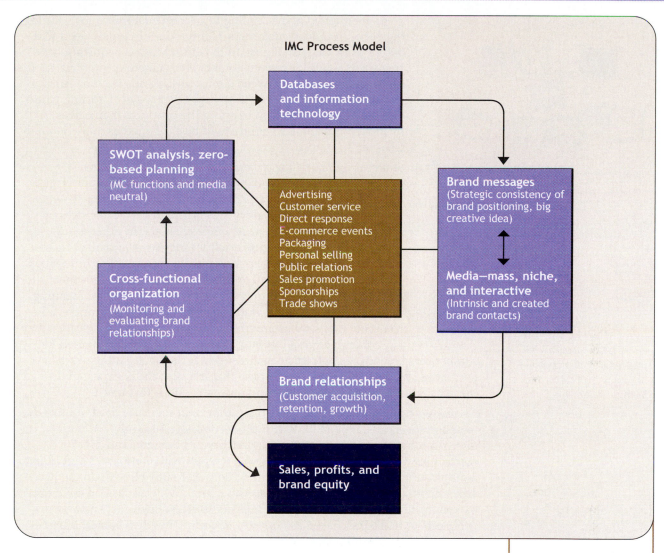

IMC Process Model

- Databases and information technology
- SWOT analysis, zero-based planning
  (MC functions and media neutral)
- Cross-functional organization
  (Monitoring and evaluating brand relationships)
- Advertising
  Customer service
  Direct response
  E-commerce events
  Packaging
  Personal selling
  Public relations
  Sales promotion
  Sponsorships
  Trade shows
- Brand messages
  (Strategic consistency of brand positioning, big creative idea)
- Media—mass, niche, and interactive
  (Intrinsic and created brand contacts)
- Brand relationships
  (Customer acquisition, retention, growth)
- Sales, profits, and brand equity

FIGURE 1-1

IMC is an ongoing process that "spins off" sales, profits, and brand equity.

Nourishing means not only retaining customers and stakeholders but also increasing the company's percentage of their category purchases and support. Each stakeholder group can affect a company in a different way: Employees can work harder and be more productive or go on strike; a local government agency can give a company a tax break or pass a law (such as a strict pollution regulation) that will make it more costly to operate; investors can hold or buy the company's stock or sell the shares they own. Customers, of course, can choose to buy or not buy from a company. Exhibit 1–5 explains AT&T's True Rewards membership program, which is designed to improve the brand's customer relationships.

3. *Profitable customer relationships* are specified because not all relationships are of equal value to a company. Some customers are more profitable to a company than others because of the quantity they buy, the types of products they buy, or the amount of servicing they require. For example, a person who has only a checking account with a bank doesn't generate nearly as much profit for that bank as the customer who has a checking account, a mortgage, and a savings account. IMC identifies the more profitable customers and directs a greater proportion of the marketing effort toward maintaining a relationship with those customers.

As mentioned above, selling to current customers costs far less than acquiring new customers. Companies obviously need to do both, but in the past almost all the effort was on acquiring new customers while current customers were taken for granted. As the physical differences between competing brands become smaller and smaller, companies need to find other ways of adding value to their products besides changing the products themselves. A relationship itself has value as will be explained in more detail in Chapter 2.

4. *Strategically controlling or influencing all messages* means recognizing that everything a company does sends a message— how it makes its products, how products perform, how it sets prices, through what kinds of stores it provides its services or sells its products, and how its employees act. In other words, all aspects of the marketing mix deliver messages and all of these messages need to be either strategically controlled or influenced.[2]

To strategically control or influence brand messages means to plan and monitor them to ensure they have consistent meaning. The messages must not contradict each other. For example, a company that says its laundry detergent gets clothes cleaner than any other detergent but then prices the detergent below all its competitors is sending contradictory messages. If the detergent really is best for getting out dirt, it doesn't make sense that it is also the cheapest in the category. Having the lowest price seldom says "best performance."

5. *Encouraging purposeful dialogue* recognizes that customers are tired of intrusive telemarketing calls, junk mail, interruptive commercials, and overcommercialization of events. They are tired of being talked at by companies. Customers want the ability to interact with companies and initiate a discussion when they have a need to do so, and to have this dialogue in a way and at a time convenient to them. The interactivity discussion in Chapter 8 explains how companies can make it easier for their customers and prospects to make purchases, ask questions, complain when something goes wrong, or give compliments when they are especially pleased. Communication, in other words, is at the heart of every relationship.

Communication Drives Relationships

The basic concepts of IMC are quite simple. As a matter of fact, you have been applying these concepts in your personal life for years. Think about the various relationships you have. One of the main things that helped you create these relationships and keep them going is communication. So a basic IMC principle is that **communication**—*the sending and receiving of messages*—is the foundation of all our relationships, including brand relationships.

As you communicate with friends, you consciously or subconsciously use certain words, actions, gestures, and facial expressions to send messages—even your appearance sends a message. With some people, such as teachers and other authority figures, your communication strategy is probably serious. With your friends, the messages are probably more freewheeling, sometimes even silly. Although you send a variety of messages to a variety of people, all of the content comes from you and has a consistency that lets the recipients know the messages are from you rather than anyone else.

Commercial brand relationships are created and terminated in a manner similar to personal relationships. In choosing brands, as in choosing friends, you have thousands from which to consider. Your choices are often based on what is communicated to you about these brands. In one study of customers who had switched brands, 70 percent said the switch had nothing to do with the specific good or service provided but rather with how they were treated. Reasons included being taken for granted, not getting answers to questions, not being able to get someone to listen and respond.[3]

IMC is about maximizing the positive messages and minimizing the negative messages that are communicated about a brand, with the objective of creating and sustaining brand relationships. But that's only one reason companies practice IMC. When used to build long-term relationships, IMC is also building and strengthening the brand. The stronger a brand is, the more value it has (as will be explained in Chapter 2). Positive brand relationships generate profits and increase the company's shareholder value.

The importance of brand relationships was illustrated when Coca-Cola was accused in 2000 of distributing contaminated products in Europe and taking too long to respond the problem. Six months later, after Coke's stock had lost nearly one-third of its value, a *Wall Street Journal* front-page headline read: "To Fix Coca-Cola, Daft Sets Out to Get Relationships Right." In the article, Coke's then-CEO Douglas Daft was quoted as saying, "Every problem we had can be traced to a singular cause: We neglected our relationships." Daft admitted the company had failed to adequately communicate with its European customers and other stakeholders—European Union bottlers, government regulators, and the media.[4] The result was that Coca-Cola's customers heard and read a lot of negative messages about Coke before the company finally explained the problem and what was being done to fix it.

IMC AND THE MARKETING UMBRELLA

To understand IMC, you must first have a basic understanding of marketing, because IMC functions under marketing's umbrella. For this reason, the next few pages will explain some of the basic elements of marketing. (If you have already taken a marketing course, you can probably skim this section as a review.) As Figure 1–2 illustrates, this discussion explains products, markets, brands, the exchange, the marketing process, the marketing concept, competitive advantage, and the marketing mix.

Marketing is more than selling; it is *the process of creating and providing what customers want in return for something they are willing to give (money, time, or membership).* The American Marketing Association (AMA) definition of the word *marketing* introduces a number of key concepts: "the process of planning and executing the conception, pricing, promotion, and distribution of ideas, goods and services to create exchanges that satisfy individual and organizational goals."[5]

Things that are bought and sold are often referred to as products but, as the AMA definition makes clear, the word *product* has come to mean more than just tangible goods. AirTran's product, for example, is taking customer from one city to another. Like the AMA, this book defines the word **product** as *any good, service, or idea produced and/or provided by an organization.* Banking, for example, is a service industry; however, banks refer to their various services such as checking accounts, mortgages, and personal loans as their "products." Sometimes what they are selling is an idea, such as saving money. Nonprofit organizations also use marketing to sell support for community service organizations (United Way), membership

FIGURE 1-2

These are some of the major elements that make up marketing.

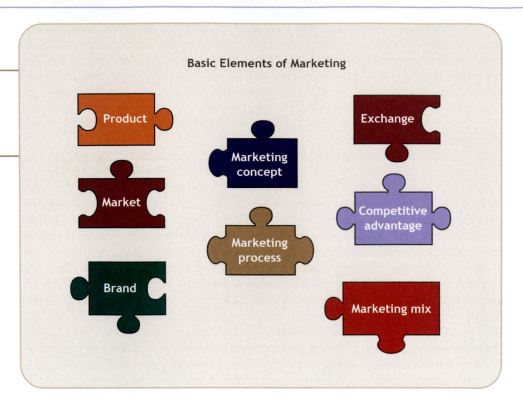

Basic Elements of Marketing

in an organization (symphonies, museums), higher education (universities and colleges), and volunteer groups (Habitat for Humanity). Although there are differences between goods, services, and ideas, a product is, basically, whatever an organization is selling.

A **market,** which is another key concept in marketing, is *the group of actual or potential buyers for a product.* The word can also refer to a geographical area, such as the "Chicago market." Every product category has one or more markets; some of these, which are referred to as **niche markets,** are *markets that are quite realtively or highly focused on one particular interest area.* A company should always estimate market size before launching a new product to determine if the potential revenue cannot only cover the costs of the product launch but also generate a profit.

Another basic element in the marketing definition is the notion of **exchange**, *the process by which money (or something else of value) is traded for goods or services, that is, the physical activity of a transaction.* Exchange is also an important communication concept and refers to information sharing.[6] This is discussed in more detail in Chapter 4, which connects marketing and communication. The **marketing process** is the *planning, executing, and evaluating of activities that produce exchanges between an organization and customers.*

Related to the concept of exchange is the concept of **demand**—*the amount of a good or service customers are willing and able to buy.* Some definitions of marketing talk about "creating demand" as one of marketing's responsibilities. Most psychologists would argue that demand cannot be created in people. Rather, if a company successfully relates brand benefits to customers' wants, needs, or desires, these customers will soon begin buying the brand. In this sense, a demand for the brand is "created." In the AirTran case, a large demand once existed, then became much smaller after the plane crash and the FAA grounding of the airline. Once the IMC campaign reassured passengers of AirTran's brand benefits, demand returned.

Another critical part of the marketing process is **competitive advantage,** which is *the market superiority created by offering customers something more or different than what is offered by other companies.* Achieving a competitive advantage is one of the ways a company can attract and keep customers. It used to be that companies thought of competitive advantage only in terms of how a good was made or a service was performed. Today, however, there are many different ways a company can have a competitive advantage. One of the most effective and efficient of these ways is to generate communication that results in a strong relationship between company and customer.

The Marketing Concept

Marketing is a concept as well as a process, and that concept is based on the notion of customer wants and needs. Historically, the **marketing concept** has been *a philosophy of business that focuses on meeting customer wants and needs*. Unfortunately, many companies have used marketing simply to create transactions. Such a transactional approach to business focuses on selling whatever a company produces. Companies that adhere to this approach have failed to understand the customer focus of the marketing concept.

The marketing concept suggests that marketing is a part of every employee's job since everyone in the organization is involved directly or indirectly in satisfying customers and other key stakeholders. Likewise, according to the marketing concept, brand communication should also be a part of every department and every employee's concern because all contacts with customers deliver brand messages that contribute to customers' perceptions of the brand. Marketing communication therefore helps create and maintain brand relationships that are a critical part of the marketing concept.

The Concept of a Brand

In marketing communication it is important to think not just of goods and services but also of the total brand offering. Customers typically see a brand as a total "product package." The product offering, as business author Frank Cespedes explains, involves not just the physical good or the primary service function but much more.[7]

How this total product package or offering is perceived is what makes up a brand. A **brand,** therefore, is *a perception of an integrated bundle of information and experiences that distinguishes a company and/or its product offerings from the competition*. When customers think about a specific store, company, good, or service, certain impressions come to mind, forming a sort of mental montage. What customers think of, for example, when they see or hear the words *Mercedes-Benz, Kmart, Wheaties,* or *Avis* is the *brand perception* of each of these companies and products.

A **brand identity** consists of *identification cues, such as brand symbols, colors, and distinctive typography, that together create recognition of the brand*. Creating and managing a brand identity is the responsibility of the total company, but the marketing department must be the champion of this effort and take the leadership in making sure it happens effectively and efficiently, with as little confusion and inconsistency as possible. Remember, however, that the brand itself is not a physical entity but rather a perception that lives in the mind of the customer,

> "The [total product] package includes the functional utility of the good or service; assistance in applications development provided before the sale; training or repair services provided after the sale; timely delivery; and any brand name or reputation benefits that help the buyer promote its own products or services."
>
> Frank Cespedes, *Concurrent Marketing*

based on the particular set of brand-related associations, experiences, and messages to which the customer has been exposed.

The Marketing Mix

The AMA definition of marketing given earlier contained a list of activities, or marketing strategy areas, that together are called the **marketing mix:** *product* (design, production), *price, place* (distribution), and *promotion* (marketing communication). These "four Ps" determine how a good or service is made or provided, how much it costs, where it is distributed, and how it is presented in all company communications.

In most organizations, changing from a focus on the traditional four Ps to more of a customer focus requires a major change in the corporate culture as well as in the marketing strategy. In other words, a company must move from using *inside-out thinking* (focusing internally on sales, shares, and quarterly reports) to using *outside-in thinking* (focusing externally on customers' needs and wants). Inside-out thinking starts with the organization's needs, whereas outside-in thinking starts with the customer's needs. A defining aspect of IMC is outside-in thinking. A good illustration of moving from an internal focus to an external focus is what one textbook describes as going from the four Ps (product, price, place, promotion) to the four Cs (customer, cost, convenience, communication).[8] Table 1–1 summarizes the difference between these two approaches.

In line with the marketing concept, this model shows that the focus should be on customer wants and needs versus products. That's the classic difference between inside-out and outside-in thinking. For example, say that a company can technically produce a videocassette recorder (VCR) that plays a happy-birthday song on a certain date. But if customers aren't interested in the song feature and find no value in having it on their VCRs, it is worthless, even if the manufacturer can add the feature at a low cost.

Pricing is another area where the focus can shift from inside-out to outside-in thinking. Instead of focusing on how to price a product, the company can focus on what it costs a customer to own it. For example, a certain car made by Renault may cost less than a similar model made by Ford. If the Renault breaks down more often, however, requiring more repairs, the Renault ends up costing the customer more than the Ford does.

Likewise, the shift from place to convenience indicates a focus on how easy it is for customers to acquire the product, rather than on how easy it is for the company to distribute it. This has been one of the primary reasons direct-response marketing has been so successful and why electronic commerce (e-commerce) has taken off so rapidly. Customers can now buy products easily without ever leaving their home or office—they merely get online or call a toll-free number, and the product is delivered within a few days. Similarly, one of the primary reasons for

TABLE 1-1	Moving from the Four Ps to the Four Cs	
Four Ps Inside-Out Focus		**Four Cs Outside-In Focus**
Product	→	Customer
Price	→	Cost
Place	→	Convenience
Promotion	→	Communication

- Promotion is what this class is all about
- it equals IMC

Coca-Cola's success is that the company has made a special effort over the years to have Coke vending machines in as many places as possible (a million more places than Pepsi in the United States). Coca-Cola has also been successful convincing restaurants to offer its products, as well as making them widely available in every type of store from supermarkets to drugstores.

The final and most important shift for marketing communicators is the one from promotion to communication. Traditionally, promotion has meant sending brand messages and offers to customers, using predominantly one-way communication. The new way of thinking focuses on opening up opportunities for dialogue. In other words, IMC moves a company from "telling and selling" to "listening and learning." This book will explain not only how companies can listen and learn but also why two-way, or interactive, communication is the lifeblood of strong brand relationships.

The four Cs model is a simplified way of demonstrating how the IMC focus is different from the traditional marketing focus. This does not mean the four Ps are unimportant, but rather that they have an external dimension that must be taken into consideration and managed when building a brand.

MARKETING COMMUNICATION

Marketing communication (MC) is *the collective term for all the communication functions used in marketing a product*—advertising, public relations, direct-response marketing, sales promotion and so on. (People in the industry sometimes use the shorthand term *marcom*; this book uses the simple abbreviation *MC*.) In traditional marketing, much of the communication is one-way. In other words, the messages are designed by a company (or its MC agencies) to be delivered to a target audience in a way that will have some desired impact, such as creating awareness or motivating a purchase. In more contemporary views, communication is used not only to impart information but also to create a dialogue, making it possible for the customer to initiate communication and the company to respond. The ad for the antipoverty group Netaid.org in Exhibit 1–6 clearly tells interested parties how to get involved.

The purpose of marketing communication is to add value to a product for both customers and the company. Customers gain value by learning about what features, benefits, improvements the product has; where the product can be purchased; and how to support a good cause like Netaid.org. They also gain value when they purchase a brand that is well known (high brand awareness) and has a good reputation (good brand image). As many sociologists have pointed out, people and companies use brands to help define themselves. Wearing a Rolex watch says something different about a person than does wearing a Swatch watch.

Companies gain value from marketing communication because, without brand awareness, there would be no demand for their products. In service businesses, employees would stand by idly twiddling their thumbs. In manufacturing plants, production lines and employees would have little to do.

The Marketing Communication Functions

Spending on traditional marketing communication in the year 2000 amounted to over $200 billion in the United States alone. It's a big business. And the reasons the

EXHIBIT 1-6

This Netaid advertisement not only introduces the nonprofit group, but it also explains how to make donations to good causes through the website.

MC industry keeps growing are that each MC function has its unique strengths and that companies and agencies are finding more and better ways to strategically use these functions.

The traditional MC functions include mass media advertising, marketing public relations, sales promotion, licensing, specialty advertising, merchandising and point-of-purchase (POP) materials, packaging, direct response, events and sponsorships, and trade shows (see Figure 1–3). Other communication functions that need to be coordinated with marketing communication include personal sales and customer service. (Part IV of this book discusses each major function in detail.) Most of these functions have been used for at least a hundred years, so individually they are not new. What is new is managing them in an integrated fashion as part of a strategic communication program.

Nearly every type of organization uses marketing communication to some extent. MC includes everything from signs in a retail store window, to multimillion-dollar campaigns for global companies such as Coca-Cola, 3M, and Unilever, to free computer disks sent through the mail by America Online. Marketing communication is the means by which organizations send brand messages to customers, potential customers, donors, voters—whoever it is that needs to be persuaded to think or act in a certain way—and the means by which the organizations receive messages back from these people.

Marketing communication is used to sell to all types of customers (children, retirees, companies, and institutions) and to sell all types of products and ideas (candy bars, locomotives, politicians, and forest fire prevention). Some companies make or provide products only for consumers (generically called *consumer products*), others only for other businesses (called business-to-business [BtB] products), and still others for both consumers and businesses. Some companies sell all their products under one brand name, while others use many different brand names. As you can imagine, with such a wide variety of companies, products, messages, and customer types, marketing communication takes on a vast number of forms. This means that there is no one formula that dictates how a company should use marketing communications—it all depends on the organization, its products, its customers and potential customers, its competition, and its financial resources.

A local shoe repair shop, whose use of marketing communication may be limited to a sign over the entrance and a Yellow Pages ad, does not need a director of marketing communication or an advertising, public relations, or sales promotion agency. At the other extreme is a company like Coca-Cola, which spends nearly $1 billion each year on marketing communication throughout the world. Unlike the local shoe repair shop, Coca-Cola has hundreds of employees working on its marketing communication plus dozens of MC agencies. Some industries spend less than 1 percent of their total budget on MC while others, such as the cosmetic industry, may spend up to 25 percent of their revenue in this area. There are no two organizations in the world that use marketing communication in exactly the same way.

As you read on, keep in mind that every business is unique, as are its needs for marketing communication. Two objectives of this book are to provide you with a basic understanding of the MC functions in an IMC context and to present guidelines on when and how to use them. The book will also explain how MC tools should be integrated into a total communication effort to develop long-term,

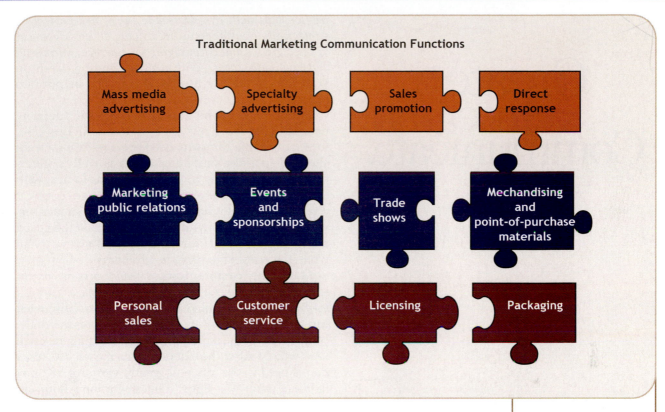

Traditional Marketing Communication Functions

- Mass media advertising
- Specialty advertising
- Sales promotion
- Direct response
- Marketing public relations
- Events and sponsorships
- Trade shows
- Mechandising and point-of-purchase materials
- Personal sales
- Customer service
- Licensing
- Packaging

FIGURE 1-3

These are the more popular MC functions used in IMC.

profitable brand relationships. Once you have this basic understanding of the IMC concept, you should be able to mix and match the various MC elements according to what an organization needs to do, regardless of the type or size of business.

Like marketing itself, integrated marketing communication is both a concept and a process. The IMC concept is creating customers and brand equity; the process in profitably managing long-term relationships with customers. The Sybase ad in Exhibit 1–7, though it wasn't designed for that purpose, refers to the basic dimensions of IMC.

Types of Brand Contact

Table 1–2 characterizes marketing communication functions in terms of the type of contact they create between a customer and a company. Traditionally, companies have used MC functions to talk to, rather than have a dialogue with, customers and potential customers. In other words, most marketing communication in the past was one-way contact. IMC still uses one-way communication but also makes much greater use of two-way communication tools. Two-way communication is facilitated through greater use of events, sponsorships, and trade shows as well as websites and 800 numbers. Also e-commerce and customer service each permit customers and other stakeholders to initiate or take charge of the communication.

The Marketing Communication Mix

Now that you have read about the marketing process and concept, marketing communications, and the meaning of integration, let's look once again at the definition of IMC: *a cross-functional process for creating and nourishing profitable*

Create.
Integrate.
Communicate.

At Sybase, we provide the extensible software platform enabling you to use information technology to [create] innovative, flexible applications. [Integrate] new and existing systems. And [communicate] throughout and beyond your organization. Create. Integrate. Communicate.

Solve problems. Gain advantage. Make money.

Watch for upcoming success stories about Sybase customers and partners. And see how we're changing business.

⑤SYBASE®

1-800-8-SYBASE   www.sybase.com/create/

©1996 Sybase, Inc. Sybase and the Sybase logo are trademarks of Sybase, Inc.

EXHIBIT 1-7

Sybase software uses this ad to promise companies it can help them meet the challenges of IMC.

relationships with customers and other stakeholders by strategically controlling or influencing all messages sent to these groups and encouraging data-driven, purposeful dialogue with them. With this definition fresh in your mind, consider now how IMC can be put into practice.

Seldom does a company use just one MC function; more often, it uses a mix of them. In the AirTran case, for example, the company used press releases, a website, and special promotional offers as well as advertising. It had to bring in public relations to deal with the negative publicity and the threat of government intervention, and it had to intensify its customer service function to deal with the complaints. It then used marketing public relations and advertising to explain what it was doing to solve its problems.

Marketing communication (MC) mix is *for the selection of MC functions used at a given time as part of a marketing program.* Unlike the marketing mix discussed earlier, where the four Ps are always represented, the components of the marketing communication mix will vary widely. Also, the extent to which each MC function is used in the mix will greatly vary. An MC mix is like a cake mix. Eggs, milk, sugar, and flour are each normally used to make a cake, but not always; numerous recipes exist for eggless or sugar-free cakes. Also, the amount of sugar and eggs used will vary from recipe to recipe, just as the amount of advertising or sales promotion will vary in an MC mix. The shape of the marketing communication mix is determined by analyzing the strengths of the various functions in terms of the communication objectives, a process that will be discussed in Chapter 6 as zerobased planning.

TABLE 1-2 Types of Brand Contact	
Nonpersonal Contact, One-Way	**Personal Contact, Two-Way**
Mass media advertising	Personal sales
Public relations	Direct response marketing
Sales promotion	
Specialties	**Involved Contact, One- and Two-Way**
Merchandising	Events and sponsorships
Packaging	Trade shows
Licensing	
	Customer-Initiated Two-Way Contact
	E-commerce
	Customer service

Recall that Figure 1–3 listed the traditional MC tools, from mass media advertising to packaging. In a totally integrated communication program, managers not only add a few items to the toolkit (such as e-commerce and internal sales) but also pay close attention to the characteristics and primary uses of each function. Table 1–3 presents this more expansive list of communication functions and groups them according to the type of contact they represent (mass media, situational, personal, and experiential). Each of the functions will be discussed in the context of these contact areas in Chapters 14 through 17.

Some people mistakenly believe that when a company uses a mix of MC functions, that company is practicing IMC. This is naive thinking. Companies have long used a mix of MC functions. What is different now is the strategy behind the use and the way the mix is coordinated. Because each MC function is different in how it creates and delivers brand messages, a company must develop a system for strategically determining which functions to use, and to what extent, in managing brand relationships. Also, because marketplace conditions as well as product categories and companies themselves are continually changing, those in charge of brand communications need to react and periodically adjust the marketing communication mix for maximum efficiency. IMC planning is specifically addressed in Chapter 6.

Once the company determines the MC mix, the next step is to make sure the various brand messages are strategically consistent and coordinated. The objective is to have all brand messages reinforce one another rather than working independently or, worse, at cross-purposes. Determining the proper MC mix to ensure "one voice, one look" is one of the things that integrated marketing communication does.

Integration Involves More Than Marketing Communication

Recall that integration involves unity and wholeness. Through this unity, synergy can be achieved. **Synergy** is *an interaction of individual parts that results in the whole being greater than the sum of those parts.* To achieve synergy, a company must integrate more than its marketing communication. As a matter of fact, unless integration occurs in a lot of other areas—such as customer service and product performance—the brand messages sent by the MC functions, no matter how well integrated, may ring hollow. Stewart Pearson, in his book on brand building, says the focus of integration should be on relationships rather than on creative executions.[9]

> " The basis for the integration of marketing is the *customer relationship*, not the creative execution."
>
> Stewart Pearson, *Building Brands Directly*

Although coordinating marketing communication functions is a key part of integrated marketing communications, it is just the tip of the integration iceberg. A larger definition of integration is well stated by Regis McKenna:

> The marketer must be the integrator. Both internally—synthesizing technological capability with market needs—and externally—bringing the customer into the company as a participant in the development and adaptation of goods and services. It is a fundamental shift in the role and purpose of marketing, from manipulation of the customer to genuine customer involvement: from telling and selling to communication and sharing of knowledge."[10]

Integrating the marketing communication functions alone is not enough to give a company a sustainable competitive advantage. Unless many other aspects of an

T A B L E   1 - 3   Characteristics and Uses of MC Functions

Function	Characteristics	Primary Uses
MASS MEDIA CONTACT		
Mass media advertising	Nonpersonal, paid announcements by identified sponsor	To reach large audiences, create brand awareness, help position brands, and build brand image
Public relations	Programs that focus on opinions of relevant publics, and manage corporate communication and reputation	To manage relationships with company's various publics to create and maintain goodwill, and to monitor public opinion and counsel top management
Marketing public relations	Product publicity; nonpaid stories or brand mentions in the mass media	To build brand credibility, make news announcements, and communicate with hard-to-reach audiences
SITUATIONAL CONTACT		
Sales promotion	Tangible incentives (such as coupons) to give sense of immediacy and stimulate behavior	To pull (i.e., to generate trial and repeat purchase) and to push (i.e., to encourage support of trade)
Merchandising	In-store promotional materials, activities, and messages	To promote in-store and create promotional ambiance
Point-of-purchase materials	Displays in the interior of stores where a product is sold	To serve as brand reminder and motivate trial and extra purchases
Packaging	Both a container and a communication medium	To give reminder message (the last message delivered at the point of sale)
Specialty advertising	Incentives given to customers to reward behaviors and keep the brand name visible	To serve as reminder advertising and a motivating incentive
Licensing	Selling the right to use some process, trademark, or patent	To increase a brand's visibility, and to enter new markets, particularly international ones
PERSONAL CONTACT		
Direct response marketing	A database-driven marketing approach that combines demand creation and fulfillment in one operation	To provide one-to-one marketing where customers are known and repeat sales can be cost-effectively motivated
E-commerce	Selling directly to customer through the Internet	To provide customer-initiated marketing
Personal sales	Real-time, two-way personal communication between a salesperson and a prospective buyer; most persuasive of all MC methods	To identify buyers' needs and match those needs to the firm's product offerings, and to allow seller to immediately respond to buyer's questions and objections

T A B L E   1 - 3   Characteristics and Uses of MC Functions *(continued)*

Function	Characteristics	Primary Uses
PERSONAL CONTACT *(continued)*		
Internal marketing	Selling marketing programs to the employees whose support is needed in order to make the program successful	To inform employees, motivate them, and create buy-in
EXPERIENTIAL CONTACT		
Events and sponsorships	Highly targeted brand associations that personally involve prospects	To help position a brand by associating it with certain causes or activities
Trade shows	Periodic gatherings where manufacturers, suppliers, and distributors in a particular industry display their products and provide information to potential buyers	To provide information, demonstrate and sample product, and engage in one-to-one dialogue with current and potential customers
Customer service	A customer-focused attitude toward business brought to life through all the nonproduct activities a company performs as a service to its customers	To reinforce positive feelings about a purchase and deal with any problems that might develop during use, and to maintain relationships after the sale

organization are integrated, the investment in marketing communication may have a minimal, or even negative, impact on customers. In other words, using IMC means integrating all the sources of brand messages.

What happened to a midwestern bank illustrates the basic truth that other business practices besides marketing communication send messages. Facing stiff competition from four other strong banks, this bank decided it needed a new marketing communication campaign. So the marketing department and its ad agency conducted some focus groups to ask bank customers what they liked and disliked most about banking. It was found that one of the things liked most was "friendly tellers."

Learning this, the ad agency developed a "most friendly bank in town" campaign. When pretested, the ads received high scores; nearly all respondents said "Yes, friendly service is very important when I do business with a bank." After the campaign ran, there was an initial increase in customers, but soon the bank began to lose more customers than it was attracting. To determine why this was happening, the bank conducted further research. What it quickly found was that customers did not find the bank's tellers to be the friendliest in town; in fact, some found the tellers to be rather cold and not friendly at all.

What happened? The bank's operations department, which was responsible for training and managing the tellers, was never told about the new ad campaign. Consequently, the tellers performed as they always had; they received no new training or additional incentives to be friendly. Before the campaign, the bank's customers didn't expect the tellers to be "the friendliest in town." But once promised this, the customers began to pay more attention to how they were greeted and treated. Customer expectations had been raised, but teller performance had not. The operations department was never *integrated* into the planning of the marketing communication campaign.

If the operations department had been integrated into the planning, it would have had time to retrain the tellers and set up a teller motivation program (such as a "smile contest") to help make sure the tellers delivered on the advertised promise. Or, if operations had no money for retraining, another department could have developed incentives for tellers (such as special rewards program) instead. Or the marketing people could have gone with another advertising strategy, one that did not set expectations that could not be met.

This example points to why integration must be applied to more than just marketing communication. Here's another basic principle of IMC: *When an organization is not integrated internally, it is difficult, if not impossible, for the brand to be integrated externally in the minds of customers, prospects, and other stakeholders.* When a brand isn't integrated, this becomes obvious to customers. They may say that the brand doesn't have its act together. As the bank example illustrates, there are many other brand messages that a company can send that can drown out its marketing communication messages. Therefore, it is in the marketing department's best interests to make sure its messages are not overpowered by other negative messages. Such messages may not be under the department's control, but it can influence them through integrated planning.

Some people may argue that integrating things other than marketing communication is outside the responsibility of marketing—and they are right. But, as stated at the beginning of this chapter, being customer focused is a companywide responsibility. Therefore, for a company to fully benefit from IMC, it must be willing to integrate, or coordinate, messages from all areas that affect brand relationships. Marketing managers are in a good position to evaluate the effectiveness of such integration and can set up cross-functional teams to manage the full range of brand messages. Even though a problem may arise in a different area, marketing can still send an alert.

What Needs to Be Integrated?

In order for marketing communication messages to have maximum impact, a company must integrate the following: employees, customers, business partners, databases, the corporate culture, corporate learning, and the corporate mission. Figure 1–4 refers to this larger set of integration components. Each of these is explained later in the book, but a brief explanation is given in the following sections to demonstrate the breadth of integrated marketing.

Employees

As strange as it might seem, many employees do not have a basic understanding of what their company makes, how their company operates, or what their role is in building customer relationships. They simply have not been integrated into the company, and many, especially, have not been educated about the need for being customer focused. One way to integrate employees into the spirit of serving customers is through **internal marketing**. This is *an ongoing program that promotes the customer-focus philosophy and keeps employees informed of important marketing activities that affect both them and the company's customers.* In a world of increasing interactivity, due to the Internet and other two-way communication opportunities, internal marketing is important because more and more employees have the opportunity to "touch" the customer. In the case of service brands, where there is

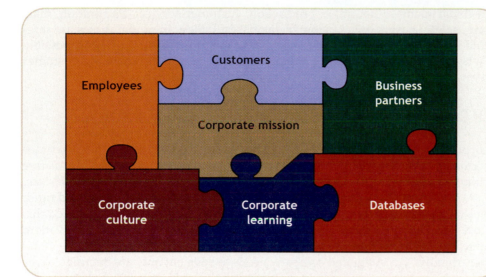

FIGURE 1-4

Integration Components

personal interaction with customers, employees *are* the brand. How they perform is how customers perceive the brand's performance. Finally, the more that employees feel like part of the company and the better informed they are about its business strategies, the higher their morale. Research has shown that companies with high employee morale have higher levels of customer satisfaction.

Customers and Business Partners

Saying that customers and other stakeholders (particularly suppliers, vendors, dealers, distributors) must be integrated into a company is another way of saying they need to have input regarding how the organization operates. Such input cannot help but make the company more customer focused. As Regis McKenna points out, customers must be integrated into such activities as product planning.[11]

> "Make customers partners in product development."
>
> Regis McKenna, "Real-Time Marketing"

Many companies have taken steps in this direction. Many business-to-business companies have customer advisory boards that meet periodically with company representatives to provide feedback on promotions, products, packaging, and other things that directly affect sales. The food company Kraft, for example, realigned sales and marketing into account teams to better manage its trade promotion, which is extremely important to Kraft's primary customers—the retail stores. This realignment was done from the point of view of a group of Kraft's retail customers.

Customers are also integrated into a company when they can easily contact the company with questions, complaints, and ideas. Toll-free numbers, interactive websites, and good customer-service departments facilitate contact. Integration in this area means bringing the company and its stakeholders closer together by increasing interaction with them. Databases are important for tracking these interactions. Interactive communication is fundamental to any relationship; that's why the definition of IMC includes interactivity as a critical component.

Databases

Employees who regularly interact with customers should have access to all the information the company has on each customer. Unfortunately, in many companies each department—accounting, production, customer service, distribution, marketing, sales—has its own customer databases. Unless these databases are integrated into a common database management system, it is difficult or impossible for whoever is contacted in the company to have a complete picture of a customer and give a knowledgeable response to requests or complaints.

Corporate Culture and Learning

A **corporate culture** reflects the personality of an organization; it is sometimes described as "the way we do things." *It is the pattern of shared values that structure the way an organization's employees work and interact with each other and with stakeholders.* For years, IBM's culture, for example, was professional, serious, and rigid. It was characterized by white shirts and dark blue suits. When IBM realized this culture had become outdated and was not conducive to encouraging innovation, interaction, and building relationships, it loosened up and became more "customer friendly." An integrated company needs to have not only an identifiable corporate culture but also a means of making sure this culture is integrated into the total organization.

An aspect of corporate culture is corporate learning. As companies expand their databases, buy more outside data services, and become more sophisticated in tracking interactions and transactions of customers, the information thus generated needs to be transformed into something meaningful—knowledge. And this knowledge then needs to be made available to everyone who can use it to increase customer service or add value to the brand in some other way. Shared information is the most important tool of corporate learning. Feedback programs make it possible for an organization to learn from its interactions with customers. By storing this feedback—and analyses of it—in databases that are available to those responsible for managing brand relationships, corporate learning can be integrated into the brand communication planning. This not only makes for better planning but also saves MC money by not repeating past programs that didn't work.

Corporate Mission

Most companies have a mission statement that was created after many hours of executive meetings, retreats, and consultation. The mission statement defines a company's raison d'être, or reason for existing, other than making a profit. Unfortunately, in many companies, once a mission statement is created, framed, and hung in the boardroom, it serves little purpose. Integrating the mission into the company's business operation, however, serves as a call to unity and provides a common, consistent focus for all employees.

An example comes from the growth of the Walt Disney Company, which in recent years has been guided by the relentless vision of its CEO, Michael Eisner, to focus on integration that produces synergy. *Brandweek* and *Adweek* magazines each named Michael Eisner "marketer of the year" in the mid-1990s. In explaining his selection, *Adweek* said:

> It is one thing to have an integrated strategy, to say that disparate divisions are going to work together, that growth will come from ideas that emerge across divisions, that there will be no turf wars. It is quite another to make it work. But under Eisner's direction, synergy works at Disney.[12]

In Disney's case, the company's mission is dedicated to producing high-quality, wholesome family entertainment. This mission is reflected not only in Disney's entertainment products but also in all of its marketing communication (see Exhibit 1–8). You might have noticed that in order to develop movies for a more mature audience, Disney established a second brand, Touchstone.

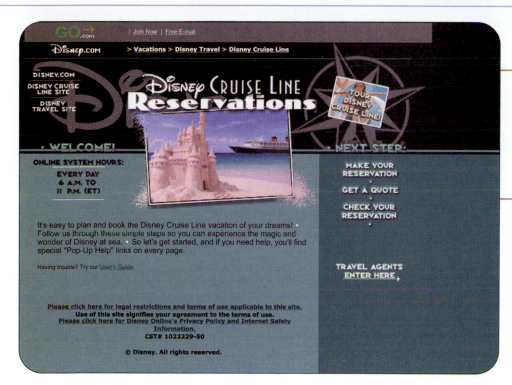

EXHIBIT 1-8

Although a new product category for the entertainment giant, the Disney Cruise Line can easily be integrated into the company's mission.

THE EVOLUTION OF IMC

Although the concept of IMC—managing customer relationships—is not new, the processes used in managing IMC are new. In the early 1990s, some academics as well as some professionals thought IMC was just a fad. But it has proved successful and is being increasingly used in a variety of forms. One of the best ways marketing can take advantage of the new communication and database technologies is by using IMC.[13] The Budweiser ad in Exhibit 1–9 gives an example of how technological change intersects with marketing. It has also been recognized as one of the best ways to do planning, coordinate executions, and create synergy for a brand.[14] Although most advertising agencies were slow in accepting IMC, nearly all have endorsed it by now and say they practice it.[15] Phil Kitchen and Don Schultz, in a 1999 study of U.S. advertising agencies, found that IMC was increasingly being used, although still a challenge for larger companies.[16]

The role of IMC and the need for greater integration and interaction between companies, customers, and other stakeholders are highlighted in the following sections, which look briefly at the socioeconomic and technological trends driving marketing communications.

Move to Mass Marketing

Up until the industrial revolution, which started in England in the mid-1800s and soon spread abroad, most manufacturing in the United States was done by local craftspeople such as blacksmiths, tanners, bootmakers, and grain millers. Those things that came from outside the villages and towns—such as spices, coffee and tea, and fine cloth—were sold by the local general store. Farmers sold their fruits, vegetables, meats, and dairy products in the town markets.

Telegraph   Electric Car   Movies   Color Television

Cordless Telephone   Laptop Computer   CD-ROM   Chat Rooms

http://www.budweiser.com   ©1997 Anheuser-Busch, Inc. Budweiser® Beer, St. Louis, MO.

The Classic American Lager Since 1876. *Budweiser*

EXHIBIT 1-9

This Budweiser ad is a time line that illustrates the evolution of the brand's label design in terms of broader technological advances in society.

What's interesting about this early period of marketing was that many producers had a direct personal relationship with their customers. The owners of general stores knew their customers' names, their children's names, their economic situation, their health status, and their product preferences. Another aspect of early marketing relationships was that products were often custom made. The primary marketing communication tool was personal selling based on a knowledge of each customer. This knowledge and interactivity resulted in strong relationships between merchants and their customers.

Then came the industrial revolution and mass production. Together these forces led to **mass marketing,** *selling the same product in the same way to "everyone."* Although mass marketing lowered prices and made a wide variety of consumer goods available to more people than ever before, it also limited choices in some ways. Henry Ford pioneered the mass production of automobiles but is also famous for having said that his customers could have any color of Model T they wanted so long as it was black. Mass marketing caused manufacturers and their customers to become separated because it required standardized production. It also required the help of intermediaries to handle the more widespread distribution. Finally, it brought about a new kind of good—**commodity products**, or undifferentiated products, which are *products made by different companies that have few or no distinguishing characteristics.*

Following World War II, increased production capacity in the United States placed increased pressure on sales and marketing departments to sell even more products. Sales quotas and market share became the primary business objectives, threatening product quality and customer service. Customers were told whatever it took to convince them to buy, and products were made to ensure that they could be sold at a competitive price and a profit, even if it meant reducing product quality. Customers didn't care about sales being the main business objective because they were getting products they had never before dreamed of—washing machines, cameras, cars, radios, TVs, and instant cake mixes, to name just a few. Quality seemed less of a concern than quantity.

Move to Mass Communication

As companies became more and more separated from their end-user customers, they turned to **mass media**, which consist of *all broad-based communication media that reach a large and diverse population.* Advertising and publicity arose to help catch the attention of the public and differentiate each company's brands from those of its competitors. First there were handbills and posters, print ads, and news releases in newspapers and magazines; then came broadcast ads on radio and television and now the Internet. The *USA Weekend* ad (Exhibit 1-10) symbolizes the magazine's mass audience.

One early marketer described advertising as "salesmanship in print." The idea was that an ad should communicate the same thing that a salesperson says when making a sales pitch. What this overly simplified definition overlooked was that in a personal sales call there was interactivity—dialogue and instant feedback. One of the things that has always made personal selling the most effective marketing communication tool is that a salesperson can immediately explain things that aren't clear and answer any objections a potential customer may have. Most mass media are unable to provide instant dialog and feedback.

During the 1950s and 1960s, mass media advertising accounted for more than two-thirds of the MC budget for most packaged-goods companies. As companies moved into the 1970s, however, management began demanding more accountability and more direct return on MC budgets. The result was a shift of the majority of MC dollars to sales promotion, whose results are more easily measured than advertising. At the Swiss-based food company Nestlé, for example, spending on mass media advertising decreased from 75 percent of the MC budget to 25 percent during this decade. As companies moved into the 1980s and 1990s, the bottom-line pressures continued. It was then that companies, both business-to-business (BtB) and consumer marketers, began making more use of sales promotion, product publicity, events, sponsorships, and direct marketing.

During the mass-marketing era, many companies became successful simply by producing a good or service, pricing it, placing it, and promoting it—hence the traditional four Ps of marketing. No more. The days of this type of linear thinking, whose primary objective is to make a transaction, are passing.

EXHIBIT 1-10

The mass appeal of USA Weekend *is illustrated by the various mass marketers that advertise in the publication.*

Trends Driving Integration

The history of marketing and marketing communication given above stresses the move away from personalized sales in the early years to mass marketing, with its emphasis on transactions, later on. Today's move toward relationship marketing brings us nearly full circle—back to more personalized selling. In addition to the gap between producers and customers created by mass marketing, there are other trends and situations, both inside and outside companies, that have made relationship building a critical element of any organization's success. As Figure 1–5 illustrates, these trends include internal, or organizational changes, and external, or marketplace changes. External changes are those things over which the organization has little or no control.

External Trends

There are eight external situations in the marketplace that affect brand relationships and call for the development of more integrated forms of marketing communication:

1. *Brand and product proliferation.* Forty years ago, the average grocery store carried about 8,000 items, counting all the brands and their different sizes and flavors. Today that number is closer to 30,000. Such proliferation is not limited to items in food, drug, and mass merchandising stores. The number of

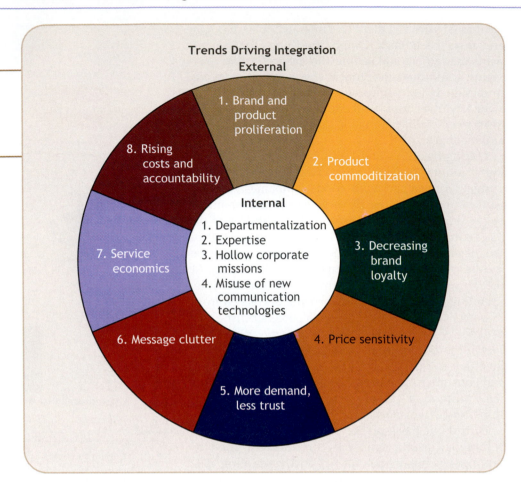

FIGURE 1-5

Both external and internal trends are driving integration.

services has also expanded. Look in the Yellow Pages and you'll find dozens of competing companies in most service categories. Customers can suffer from "brand-choice overload" when there are too many products, too many brands, and too many commercial messages.

2. *Product commoditization.* Although there are more brands competing against each other than ever before, there are often few differences between those brands. Because of technology, companies have the ability to quickly redesign their goods or services to match what their competitors are doing successfully. Even when a company makes a breakthrough in product performance, pricing, distribution, or even promotion, it may be only a matter of weeks or months—sometimes even days—before competitors copy. This does not mean that product differences are no longer important, but rather that few can be sustained. Product improvements are simply the ante that allows a company to stay in the game. Differentiation now must come from the "soft side" of business—such as providing superior customer service, useful information, and a commitment to shared values.

3. *Decreasing brand loyalty.* A result of brand proliferation plus product commoditization is that customers are less loyal now than in the past. They have discovered that one brand is often fairly similar to others in that price category, so they tend not to base their purchases on brand name alone.

4. *Price sensitivity.* As companies have fought to increase brand share, they have made more use of sales promotion techniques that reduce prices (e.g., get two for the price of one, take an additional 30 percent off, redeem coupons of all values). Consequently, customers have been conditioned to buy on price.

5. *More demand, less trust.* Customers in industrialized countries are sophisticated selectors of brands, and many in less developed markets are catching up fast. At the same time, they are smarter and more demanding, and they are also more distrusting. Findings from studies of U.S. consumers conducted by Yankelovich Partners (a marketing research and consulting firm) show that only 8 percent of consumers have a great deal of confidence in "advice and recommendations" from advertising, and only 6 percent have confidence in what major corporations have to say regarding their points of view on major issues.[17]

> "We all operate from the premise of being in the process of, or having just been, 'screwed.'"
>
> Watts Wacker, formerly with Yankelovich Partners

One reason these attitudes exist is that, although companies have made strides in lowering product defects, there are still too many instances of relationship defects—taking customers for granted, misleading them about what products will do, failing to listen and respond when customers complain or ask questions, and putting profits before everything else, including employees, customers, and the environment. In short, in many companies customer service has suffered as managers have failed to provide proper training, failed to reward employees for good customer service, and substituted technology for human contact.[18]

6. *Commercial message clutter.* In 1960, two-thirds of U.S. households could be reached by a company if it ran an ad in just three magazines: *Look, Life,* and the *Saturday Evening Post.* Today, only the latter two exist, and together they reach less than 2 percent of U.S. households. In 1970, by placing TV commercials during prime time on the three major networks—ABC, CBS, and NBC—a brand could reach nearly two-thirds of U.S. households; today a similar placement would reach half that many.

Today we live in a commercial message cocoon. The average person, for example, watches TV four hours a day, has a choice of over 50 channels, and is exposed to 42,000 TV commercials every year, even with zipping and zapping. Add in commercials on rented videotapes, radio commercials, ads in newspapers and magazines, ads on packages, billboards, junk mail, telemarketing calls, and commercial e-mail and you have an avalanche of brand messages.

7. *Service economics.* In the United States today, the service industry, not manufacturing, accounts for over three-fourths of the gross domestic product (the total dollar value of goods and services produced in a country in one year). The trend is the same in other developed nations. This is important because services, by their very nature, require buyers and sellers to interact. When the service is good, the brand message is positive; when the service is poor, the brand message is negative. And keep in mind that most products require supporting services—for example, delivery, product assistance, and repair. An airline that flies you safely between New York and Los Angeles is providing a primary transportation service. However, you also expect good supporting services such as a quick check-in, amenities while on board the plane, and quick and easy access to your luggage at the end of your trip. Because so many goods and services have become commodities, the supporting services often drive the buying decision. This is why many products—no matter whether goods or services—are really a "service" from the customer's perspective.

8. *Rising costs and accountability.* As media costs have escalated, more companies have begun to look for ways to measure the impact of their marketing communication efforts. It is easier to cost-justify communication programs in

some areas, such as direct mail, than it is in other areas, such as advertising and public relations, where the impact is subject to other activities inside and outside the company. Those who specialize in marketing communication are reacting to this increased accountability and are searching for ways to better prove their effectiveness.

Internal Trends

As noted earlier, integration must exist internally if a company is to communicate effectively with customers. Unfortunately, most companies suffer from a variety of internal situations that cause marketing efforts to *dis*integrate:

1. *Departmentalization.* As companies have grown bigger and bigger, they find themselves composed of highly separated departments and divisions that have been subdivided in order to maintain accountability and control. Take marketing, for example. The original concept of brand management was to integrate and coordinate all selling efforts, but the opposite—disintegration—has happened, as shown in Figure 1–6. It began when sales and marketing got separated. Then marketing subdivided into product/brand management and marketing services groups. To make things even more complex, marketing services, especially in the larger companies, further subdivided into specialty areas such as advertising, sales promotion, event sponsorship, direct response, and marketing public relations.

   With each new unit has come increased competition for budgets, staffs, and recognition. As Peter Senge, known for his theory of the "learning organization," explains: "Functional divisions grow into fiefdoms, and what was once a convenient division of labor mutates into the 'stovepipes' [departmental silos] that all but cut off contact between functions. The result: Analysis of the most important problems in a company, the complex issues that cross functional lines, becomes a perilous or nonexistent exercise."[19] Building brand relationships is a cross-functional issue. This means that unless companies integrate those operations that communicate with

FIGURE 1-6

The Disintegration of Marketing

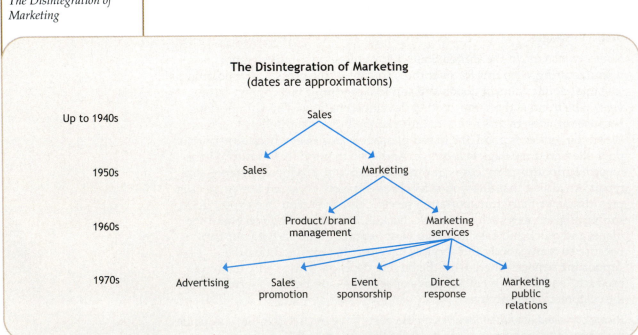

customers and other key stakeholders, they will have little success building profitable brand relationships.

2. *The two-edged sword of expertise.* Many marketing communication departments and agencies have become very good at what they do. This is both good news and bad news. The good news is that the organization benefits from the MC specialists' increased expertise. The bad news is that the more specialized these groups have become, the more likely they are to be isolated, seldom aware of what other MC departments are doing.

   As Mike White, former worldwide media director of the MC agency DDB, has observed: "Part of the problem is that as functional specialists develop expertise, they each have their own strategies on how to build the brand. Although many can contribute in the search for positioning and the big idea, in the end there can only be one strategy for the brand to remain cohesive."[20] Increased specialization without a system of integrating the planning and monitoring of brand relationships will only widen rather than narrow the company–customer gap. Although increased expertise certainly has its benefits, it can create such problems as turf battles.

3. *Hollow corporate missions.* The mission of most companies is either a corporate financial objective ("to be the most profitable," "to be the largest") or simply a lot of fancy words that, as noted earlier, hang on the boardroom wall or serve as window dressing in the annual report. When a company has a mission that goes beyond just making a profit (such as the pharmaceutical company Merck's, which is "preserving and improving human life") employees and other stakeholders have an additional reason to support the company. But this will happen only if they are made aware of the mission and are convinced that it is genuine.

4. *Misuse of new communication technology.* Computer-driven databases have made possible interactive, one-to-one marketing, moving the industry even further from its mass-marketing roots. The Internet, too, has opened up new lines of external communication. There are also automated voice response systems and automated e-mail responses. However, companies often use these technologies at the customer's expense. Automated voice response systems, for example, often make callers move through menu after tortuous menu and still not offer the desired option. Mass e-mailings (spam) and unsolicited faxes are considered by most people as intrusive and wasteful. Automated calling with a recorded message increases the number of unwanted telemarketing calls. All of these are done to save companies money and/or to increase sales efforts with little regard for those being contacted.

Integrity

One of the most important changes in our society in recent years is the increasing demand for integrity in business. The concept of integration is in tune with that trend. It is useful to note that the words *integrity* and *integration* come from the same Latin root, *integritas*, which means "honesty, completeness, soundness." In an era of customer and other shareholder distrust of just about everything, especially business and government, increasing the perception of a brand's integrity is a definite plus.[21] Integration produces integrity because an organization that is seen as a "whole" rather than as a collection of autonomous pieces and parts is perceived as being more sound and trustworthy, a prerequisite for sustaining relationships. Integrity also has a nuance that connects with values and moral principles, admirable characteristics for any brand that is concerned with social responsibility.

A FINAL NOTE: THE RELATIONSHIP REVOLUTION

If you're taking this course because you're planning to work in some area of marketing or marketing communication, congratulations—and fasten your career seatbelt. You have chosen what will be one of the most exciting, dynamic, and challenging careers in the 21st century. This is because both marketing and marketing communication are going through a major revolution.

The developments in computers and communication technology, the expansion of the global marketplace, the growing competition among the various internal departments and external agencies, the swing from a manufacturing-based economy to a service-based one, the increase in mergers and acquisitions, and the increase in customer demands requires that companies completely transform how they communicate with customers and sell their products.

If you are not planning to go into some area of marketing or marketing communication, you will still find this book valuable because it will show you what to expect and demand as a consumer. Over your lifetime you will spend hundreds of thousands of dollars buying things. How well you spend this money will depend on what you know about how marketing operates and how to best communicate with retailers and other people with whom you will do business. So welcome to the world of the educated consumer. After reading this book, you'll never again be able to look at an ad or other type of brand message in the same way.

Key Terms

customer relationships 7
stakeholders 7
IMC 8
communication 10
marketing 11
product 11
market 12
niche markets 12
exchange 12
marketing process 12
demand 12
competitive advantage 12

marketing concept 13
brand 13
brand identity 13
marketing mix 14
marketing communication (MC) 15
marketing communication (MC) mix 18
synergy 19
internal marketing 22
corporate culture 24
mass marketing 26
commodity products 26
mass media 26

Key Point Summary

This chapter introduces and defines integrated marketing communications (IMC). It discusses the IMC functions of planning and monitoring the activities that drive brand relationships.

Key Point 1: Marketing Communication and Brand Relationships

Relationship marketing uses a broad mix of communication tools, including two-way communication, to develop long-term relationships with customers and other stakeholders. Integrating and coordinating efforts to build long-lasting, profitable relationships is difficult when managers and their departments are totally focused on sales and transactions. A company with a relationship marketing orientation is more focused on maintaining and growing its customer base for long-term profits; such companies understand that it is less expensive and more profitable to encourage sales from existing customers than it is to continuously try to acquire new customers.

Key Point 2: Relationship Marketing and the Marketing Concept

Relationship marketing programs are designed to meet customers' wants and needs, thus delivering the ideal promised by the marketing concept. A transaction-focused marketing program uses the four Ps (product, price, place, promotion) to deliver sales; an integrated program uses the four Cs (customer, cost, convenience, communication) to deliver long-term brand relationships.

Key Point 3: The Marketing Communication Mix and Beyond

The marketing communication mix includes a wide array of functions and tools, such as mass media contact (advertising, marketing public relations); situational contact (sales promotion, merchandising, point-of-purchase materials, packaging, specialties, licensing); personal contact (direct response, e-commerce, personal sales, internal marketing); experiential contact (events and sponsorships, trade shows, customer service). Integration involves more than just marketing communication; other components of an integrated program include employees, customers, business partners, databases, corporate culture, corporate learning, and the corporate mission.

Key Point 4: Industry Trends

The trends driving the development of integrated marketing communication include both external and internal factors. External factors include brand and product proliferation; product commoditization; decreasing brand loyalty; price sensitivity; more demand, less trust; message clutter; service economics; and rising costs and accountability. Internal factors include departmentalization, expertise, hollow corporate missions, and misuse of new technologies.

Lessons Learned

Key Point 1: Marketing Communication and Brand Relationships

a. How is IMC defined, and what are the key elements in that definition?
b. Why is traditional marketing communication considered nonpersonal? Give two examples.
c. Define relationship marketing.
d. Explain why marketers care about building relationships with their customers.
e. Have you ever been exceptionally disappointed (or, if not, exceptionally pleased) by a personal experience you have had as a customer? Explain your feelings about that experience.

Key Point 2: Relationship Marketing and the Marketing Concept

a. Explain the marketing concept and how it relates to IMC.
b. What is the difference between a transaction focus and a relationship focus?
c. Explain the difference between the four Ps and the four Cs. What does the shift from the former to the latter mean for companies?

Key Point 3: The Marketing Communication Mix and Beyond

a.   Define marketing communication (MC).
b.   What types of marketing communication deliver personal communication?
c.   How does IMC differ from MC?
d.   Explain what a marketing communication mix is and how it is used.
e.   What other things in a company need to be integrated into a marketing communication program besides marketing?
f.   Choose a major brand and develop a list of the marketing communication efforts it uses. Also consult trade and professional magazine articles for discussion of these efforts. Is the brand using a "one voice, one look" strategy?

Key Point 4: Industry Trends

a.   What was sacrificed when marketing moved away from personal selling to mass marketing?
b.   Describe the key technological advances in the history of communication and explain how each has affected marketing communication.
c.   What has been the impact of (1) brand and product proliferation and (2) commoditization on marketing communication?
d.   Decreasing brand loyalty, price sensitivity, and more demand, less trust—how do each of these affect marketing communication?
e.   Internally, focusing on departmentalization and expertise has created what problems for marketing communication?
f.   How do the trends in the areas of corporate missions and new corporate technologies affect marketing communication?

Chapter Challenge

Writing Assignment

Identify a company or brand that you think needs to work on its relationship marketing. Analyze the company's problems and look at the way the company's marketing communication could be improved. Develop a white paper—a paper that analyzes a problem situation and states and explains your recommendations—for your instructor, whom you should address as the company's marketing director.

Presentation Assignment

Using what you have learned in this chapter, prepare a presentation on IMC for an organization to which you belong (or a company where you work). As part of the report, tell why IMC does or doesn't make sense as a philosophy of marketing communication for that organization. Develop an outline of the key points you want to present. Give the presentation to your class or record it on a videotape (audiotape is also an option); turn it in to your instructor, along with the outline.

Internet Assignment

Go to the websites for Barnes & Noble (www.barnesandnoble.com) and Amazon (www.amazon.com) and compare their operations. Pretend you are going to buy a book and analyze the differences in the way the two companies handle your transaction and attempt to create a relationship with you.

Additional Readings

Duncan, Tom, and Sandra Moriarty. *Driving Brand Value: Using Integrated Marketing to Manage Profitable Stakeholder Relationships*. New York: McGraw-Hill, 1997.

Schultz, Don; Stanley Tannenbaum; and Robert Lauterborn. *Integrated Marketing Communications*. Lincolnwood, IL: NTC Publishing Group, 1993.

Webster, Frederick E. *Market-Driven Management: Using the New Marketing Concept to Create a Customer-Oriented Company*. New York: John Wiley & Sons, 1994.

Whiteley, Richard C. *The Customer Driven Company: Moving from Talk to Action*. Reading, MA: Addison-Wesley, 1991.

Zyman, Sergio. *The End of Marketing As We Know It*. New York: HarperBusiness, 1999.

Research Assignment

Consult these books and other books and articles in your library on marketing communication and customer-focused marketing. Develop a questionnaire that you could use in interviewing managers at a company with which you are familiar that would determine the extent to which this company is market focused. Also determine the role that marketing communication plays in delivering this focus.

Endnotes

[1] Stewart Hoover, "Religion in Public Discourse: The Role of Media," report published by the Center for Mass Media Research, University of Colorado School of Journalism and Mass Communication, 1995.

[2] Tom Duncan and Sandra E. Moriarty, "A Communication-Based Model of Relationship Marketing," *Journal of Marketing* 62, no. 2 (April 1998), p. 1–13.

[3] Edward Forest and Richard Mizerski, *Interactive Marketing: The Future Present* (Chicago: NTC Business Books, 1996), p. 8.

[4] "To Fix Coca-Cola, Daft Sets Out to Get Relationships Right," *The Wall Street Journal*, June 23, 2000, p. A1.

[5] Peter D. Bennett, *Dictionary of Marketing Terms* (Chicago: American Marketing Association, 1988), p. 115.

[6] Duncan and Moriarty, p. 4. "A Communication-Based Model."

[7] Frank Cespedes, *Concurrent Marketing: Integrating Product, Sales, and Service* (Boston: Harvard Business School Press, 1995), p. 244.

[8] Don Schultz, Stanley Tannenbaum, and Robert Lauterborn, *Integrated Marketing Communications* (Lincolnwood, IL: NTC Publishing Group, 1993), p. 12.

[9] Stewart Pearson, *Building Brands Directly: Creating Business Value from Customer Relationships* (London: MacMillian Business, 1996), p. 55.

[10] Regis McKenna, "Marketing Is Everything," *Harvard Business Review*, January–February 1992, p. 65.

[11] Regis McKenna, "Real-Time Marketing," *Harvard Business Review*, July–August 1995, p. 92.

[12] Betsy Sharkey and T. L. Stanley, "Marketer of the Year, Michael Eisner," *Superbrands '96*, published by *Adweek*, October 9, 1995, p. 46.

[13] George Zinkam and R. T. Watson, "Advertising Trends: Innovation and the Process of Creative Destruction," *Journal of Business Research* 37, no. 3 (1996), p. 165.

[14]Bill Cook, "Integrated Marketing Communications: Performing Together," *Journal of Advertising Research* 37, no. 5 (1997), p. 5; and Joe Phelps, T. E. Harris, and E. Johnson, "Exploring Decision-Making Approaches and Responsibility for Developing Marketing Communications Strategies," *Journal of Business Research* 37, no. 3 (1996), p. 217.

[15]Laura Schneider, "Agencies Show that IMC can be Good for Bottom Line," *Marketing News,* May 11, 1998, p. 7.

[16]Phil Kitchen and Don Schultz, "A Multi-Country Comparison of the Drive for IMC," *Journal of Advertising Research* 39, no. 1 (1999), p. 21.

[17]Watts Wacker, partner at Yankelovich, personal correspondence, 1994.

[18]Watts Wacker, "The Information Highway: The Road to a New Paradigm for Consumer Decision-Making," Presentation to Creative Research International Group, May 17, 1994.

[19]Peter M. Senge, *The Fifth Discipline: The Art and Practice of the Learning Organization* (New York: Doubleday Currency, 1990), p. 24.

[20]Mike White, interview by author, Chicago, March 1996.

[21]Lynn Sharp Paine, "Managing for Organizational Integrity," *Harvard Business Review* 12 (March–April 1994), pp. 106–17.

2

Brands and Stakeholder Relationships

Key Points in This Chapter

1. What does it mean to say that a brand is more than a product?

2. Explain the five steps in building a brand.

3. What are the five strategic brand decisions that affect how marketing communication is used?

4. How does IMC build relationships that create brand value?

5. What is the anatomy of profitable brand relationships?

Chapter Perspective:
A Special Relationship

Because IMC is a process, it is a means to an end. That end is brands and stakeholder relationships. The purpose of this chapter is to explain these two IMC end products. Companies make goods and provide services, but they sell brands. And as competing products proliferate and become more similar, the role of customer relationships becomes more critical. A company that has no customer relationships doesn't have a brand. Understanding how brands are built and managed requires an understanding of how relationships are built and managed. This chapter will first explain brands, then brand relationships (including stakeholder support, overlap, and capital), and finally the anatomy of profitable brand relationships.

Conceptually, neither IMC nor brand relationship building is new. What is new are the IMC *principles and practices* used to build these relationships. Recall from Chapter 1 that in the days of the old general store, owners knew their customers personally. But as companies and chains took over, these relationships gave way to mass marketing. With new information and communication technology, however, it is possible for companies to once again know their customers and operate on a more personal and responsive level.

A brand relationship strategy brings customers and branding together. According to Regis McKenna, a leading high-tech public relations consultant and author of *Relationship Marketing*, a successful brand is nothing more than a special relationship. A good brand relationship is one in which the relationship is of value to both the customer and company. A customer relationship building program, however, is a long-term strategy, unlike a more traditional marketing strategy that focuses on short-term transactions.

BUILDING A RELATIONSHIP WITH BOOTS THE CHEMISTS
J. Walter Thompson, London, England

Retailers are particularly concerned about building lasting relationships with their customers. One way to create a bond with customers is to develop an IMC program whose strategic anchor is a customer loyalty card, like the airline frequent-flier card, that gives points or discounts on future purchases.

Boots The Chemists (BTC) is the largest pharmacy chain and the most visited retail chain in Britain. BTC began planning a loyalty card program in 1993 but decided to take the time to get the proposition right. The company spent many months conducting regional testing to ensure the card delivered the right benefits for customers. Meanwhile, the mid-1990s saw the explosion of this new retail marketing tool in the United Kingdom and, as its retail competitors handed out loyalty cards, Boots was left in the dust.

The national launch of the IMC campaign introducing the Boots Advantage Card was handled by the London office of international advertising agency J. Walter Thompson (see Exhibit 2–1). The campaign won a number of awards for its effectiveness and, in the process, proved that loyalty strategies were not just discounts in disguise, but rather a strategic relationship management tool.

The Relationship Challenge

The airlines and petrol (i.e., gasoline) retailers started it, but the supermarket chain Tesco triggered the landslide to customer loyalty cards in the United Kingdom. Retailers justified this headlong rush into expensive loyalty programs in a variety of ways:

- It maximizes the existing customer franchise because it is cheaper to keep an existing customer than it is to acquire a new one.

EXHIBIT 2-1

This frame from one of the Boots commercials shows a woman who represents the target audience enjoying the benefits of having used a Boots frequent-buyer card.

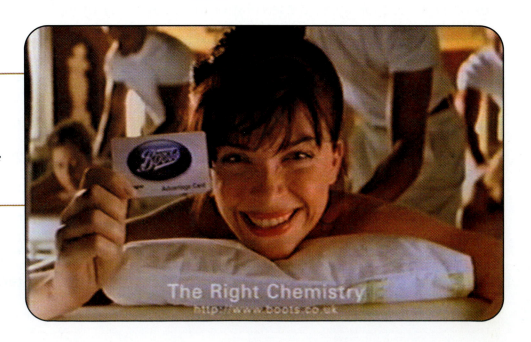

- It opens up the possibility to more accurately target individual customers using a database.
- It allows retailers to thank shoppers for their patronage and for allowing their customer information data to be captured.
- It affects shoppers' habits by discouraging them from straying to competitors, and it encourages the "weak loyalists" to shop more frequently at the store.

Such benefits, however, did not always materialize. Retailers were failing to bridge the gulf between the desirability of individual relationship-building programs and the difficulties of manipulating and interpreting databases of huge size and complexity.

Strategy for Building Brand Relationships

Boots' research found there were deep-rooted, widely held consumer perceptions about the Boots brand, personified as a trustworthy but potentially boring "man in a white coat." In contrast to its perceived position as a chemist (i.e., pharmacy), BTC's core areas of health and beauty offerings define it, in the company's view, as the store for products and services that make the customer "look good and feel good." However, its clinical image and store environment seemed to run counter to the brand attributes BTC needed in order to develop stronger customer relationships. According to survey respondents, missing from the "look good, feel good" image were the words *understanding, stimulating, personalized, fulfilling,* and *enjoyable*. Building a bridge from trust/authority to understanding/stimulating required the development of an emotionally differentiated image and more involved customers. In keeping with usual loyalty strategies, the Boots Advantage Card offered customers a way to earn points that could be traded in for free products from a list of 10,000 specially selected items.

Campaign Objectives

The Boots Advantage Card loyalty program was intended to accomplish the following:

- Increase profitability per customer by increasing frequency of visits and amount spent per visit.
- Provide a manifestation of the "look good, feel good" strategy with an aspirational, female focus.
- Enroll 8 million cardholders in the first 12 months.
- Achieve an incremental sales increase of 3.2 percent.

Targeting the Audience

Store exit research had determined that 83 percent of BTC's customers were women, so this was a key characteristic of the target audience. But BTC did not want to appeal to just any woman. Since the cost of maintaining the database was estimated at $2.25 per person, the campaign planners recognized that it was more important to get the right customers rather than simply lots of customers. More specifically, the campaign was designed to reach young women who could be motivated to treat themselves with something self-indulgent, rather than to reach the deal-seeking, discount-store shoppers. The campaign team knew it had to appeal to this target audience emotionally rather than purely rationally or on the basis of price.

Creative Strategy

BTC and J. Walter Thompson recognized that the frequent-buyer card needed to become a "must-have" item in an already crowded wallet. It had to strike a chord among the right kind of shoppers and become the flagship for the "look good, feel good" strategy. The objective of the resulting creative idea, called "the levels of pleasure" concept, was to tap into an attitude that allowed women to be self-indulgent. This "pleasure platform" was intended to set the card up to exploit the full potential of relationship marketing by making the transaction a win–win situation for both store and shopper. The first television commercial to use the self-indulgent pleasure theme showed a woman describing how she can treat herself by using the Boots Advantage Card to get her favorite indulgences for free.

Message Delivery

The Boots Advantage Card launch campaign used advertising and in-store merchandising along with publicity and staff training to deliver the new brand message. The campaign was launched first with in-store materials—posters and the application brochure. After two weeks, television was used to help demonstrate the card's benefits.

   The enrollment messages were carried on posters and point-of-purchase displays; the staff handed out the applications. The brochure, which incorporated the card application form, carried the pleasure theme and catalogued the indulgence items available for points. The publicity press launch was timed with the initial launch. A staff training manual continued with the theme. Three application forms were sent to each member of the staff to encourage early sign-up among their friends and family; 60,000 initial sign-ups were obtained from this effort, a successful example of using stakeholders (in this case, employees) as brand advocates.

Evaluation of the Boots Campaign

The Boots Advantage Card got off to a flying start, with the total number of applications running ahead of predictions by 20 percent. The customer database resulting from the launch campaign produced records on 8 million BTC customers. In its first year, the campaign delivered more than a 3 percent increase in sales; in the second year, an 8 percent increase. The company also found that the cardholders' average purchase amount was 8 percent more than that of noncardholder customers. The campaign reached the "right kind of person," as evidenced by its success in attracting upscale, young, and affluent women.

   As the Boots case demonstrates, relationships and brands are closely linked. This chapter focuses on how to understand and build the relationships that create brand value. Although relationships drive brands, the meaning of *brand* itself is discussed first, followed by a discussion of brand relationships—how they are constructed and evaluated. Finally, this chapter will look at brand value and brand equity.

This case was adapted with permission from the Advertising and Marketing Effectiveness (AME) award-winning brief for the launch of the Boots Advantage Card prepared by J. Walter Thompson, London.

WHAT "BRAND" MEANS

A brand is more than a product. Cars, checking accounts, candy bars, shoe repair, computers, and medical care are all products. What differentiates one car or one checking account from another is the brand. Take universities, for example. In their most basic form they all offer the same product—education. They all have instructors, courses, students, and in most cases classrooms and buildings. Despite this list of commonalities, however, there are major differences among them. These differences are determined by the quality of instructors, variety of course offerings, number of students, location, success of athletic teams, quality of facilities, and size of endowments, among other things.

When only commonalities are considered, universities, like all basic goods and services, are generic members of a product category. But when their differences are taken into consideration, they become brands. Brands are what separate similar products in a product category. What comes to mind when you think of each of the following—Notre Dame, MIT, Bryn Mawr, Tuskegee, and St. Olaf's College? Most people don't think about classrooms, students, and faculty. Rather they think about things such as football and Catholic (for Notre Dame); high tech (MIT); women's education (Bryn Mawr); African American student body (Tuskegee); small but highly respected liberal arts school (St. Olaf's College).

In this book, both products and companies are considered to be brands. This is because they both have significant intangibles manifested in their respective images and reputations. Also, sometimes a corporate name, such as Kraft, is used as a brand name or part of a brand name for a line of products, such as Kraft Singles (individually wrapped slices of American cheese). From an IMC perspective, customers have relationships with both products and companies.

Customers of both consumer and business-to-business (BtB) products carry in their minds a bundle of information about, and experiences with, a particular company's products. They integrate these bits of information and experiences into a perception. Customers of the automaker Lexus, for example, have visited a dealer and formed an impression of the showroom and sales staff; they hear other people say good things about the Lexus models; they have driven one, which gives them a sense of its quality; and they know the price. All of these messages and experiences are integrated into a basic perception of a Lexus. Some may be positive, some may be negative. Assuming the majority of the inputs are positive, then the resulting perception of Lexus will probably be positive. This is why a brand was defined in Chapter One as a perception, based on an integrated bundle of information and experiences.

Some stores sell **generic products**, which are *goods that are not labeled with a traditional brand name.* Typically, such products come in plain white packages with black lettering that gives basic product description (e.g., elbow macaroni, paper towels). The perception is that because they are not promoted, these generic product lines are less expensive than similar products. Many people also perceive them as low-quality products. Yet generic product lines are, in fact, very distinct brands. Their unique package design allows customers to recognize them easily. But more important, they have a certain association and bundle of perceptions that differentiates them from competing and traditional brand-name products.

A critical understanding for marketers and especially for marketing communication managers is that a brand is a perception. Cues, signals, and all other types of communication messages, as well as experiences, lead customers to form such perceptions. Marketing communicators either control or are able to influence most brand messages. To that end, they should also influence the type of interactions and experiences that customers have with a company and its products.

Needs, wants, and desires create demand for products (e.g., medicine for a headache, a car for convenient transportation, a fancy pen to impress others). People buy products whose benefits satisfy these needs, wants, and desires. For years, good marketers emphasized the *benefits* of their products rather than the *features*. As a manufacturer of electric drills once stated, he didn't sell drills but rather holes—the benefits of the drill. One benefit is the prestige associated with a brand; that is why people don't say they just bought a car or watch but rather a Pathfinder or a Rolex.

> " A brand signals to the customer the source of the product, and protects both the customer and the producer from competitors who would attempt to provide products that appear to be identical."
>
> David A. Aaker, *Managing Brand Equity*

There are some products, however, for which brands play an indirect role. Most people who need a broom, a rake, or some other utilitarian product, for example, do not search out a brand name. More likely, they look for a particular brand of store or catalogue from which such products can be purchased. Thus, for a high-quality broom, a person might go to Superior Hardware, for a low-cost broom to Kmart, or for an exotic broom to the Smith & Hawken catalog.

A brand, then, differentiates one product or company from another. It identifies the product and its source or maker, and often has a certain association and image. As David Aaker explains, a brand serves as a signal.[1]

How Brands Work: Transformation

Most customers are not willing to spend the time and energy needed to treat every purchase as a first-time buy. They use brand names and symbols as a form of mental shorthand, to immediately identify the specific product they have tried before and liked (or that they have been convinced they will like), reducing the need to shop around. Therefore, the more specific and less ambiguous the overall brand identity is, the more it helps customers recognize a product or company, and thus the more it adds value to the brand itself.

A basic principle of branding is that *brands transform products—goods as well as services—into something larger than the product itself*. A pair of Wrangler jeans is different from a pair of Levi's, even if they are both denim pants. They have different personalities because of the power of their brand image. If you give your mother a watch inside a Kmart box, she will react very differently than she would if you gave her the very same watch in a Gucci's box (see Exhibit 2–2).

In blind taste tests, where respondents were asked which of two (identical) samples of cornflakes tasted better, the number of those who chose sample A over sample B increased from 47 to 59 percent when respondents were told that sample A was Kellogg's cornflakes and sample B was not given a recognizable brand name. A brand, and what it represents, can also affect what people are willing to pay for a product. One study found that when identical TV sets were sold, those branded Hitachi sold for $75 more than those branded GE.[2]

No matter how much a company emphasizes being consistent in its marketing communication and other activities, a brand is seldom perceived in the same way by all customers. An example is when two people see the word Coke. To one of them what comes to mind is a cold, refreshing drink, while to the other one comes negative thoughts such as "too sweet" and "too fattening." The perceptions of these two people may differ because, over time, each had received different

TABLE 2-1   Brand Differentiation

TANGIBLE ATTRIBUTES	INTANGIBLE ATTRIBUTES
Design	Value
Performance	Brand image
Ingredients/components	Image of stores where sold
Size/shape	Perceptions of users of the brand
Price	
Marketing communication	

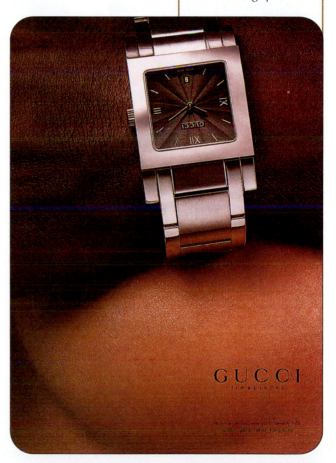

EXHIBIT 2-2

A respected brand name can transform the product into something special.

messages and different experiences regarding soft drinks, nutrition, and Coke itself. While a company may own a brand name and logo, and greatly influence what people think about its brands, the real brand meaning resides in the mind of each customer and is influenced by a wide variety of messages.

Studies have shown that consumers are more likely to use tangible attributes (size, shape, price) to decide *whether* competing products are different, and intangible attributes (quality, value) to decide *how* they are different (see Table 2–1). What this means is that intangible attributes, such as brand positioning and image, play a more significant role in making brand selections in those categories where there are few, if any, physical differences. This is another reason why it is important for marketers to develop strong brands. Intangibles are important in brand building for two reasons: because they are hard for competitors to copy and because they are more likely to involve consumers emotionally. Differentiation is an important factor in creating a link between a brand and its stakeholders.

The ads for the Hummer and Range Rover in Exhibit 2–3 illustrate just how different two brand personalities can be even when both brands are in the same narrow product category—in this case sport utility vehicles (SUVs). Study the two ads and determine what the intangible and the tangible attributes are that differentiate these SUVs.

The Brand Promise

The essence of a brand is a promise. Marketing communication has been used for years to make these promises in order to generate sales. But as Jean-Noël Kapferer explains, a brand is also a contract, albeit a virtual one, between a company and a customer.[3]

" By creating satisfaction and loyalty, the brand enters into a virtual contract binding it to the market."

Jean-Noël Kapferer, *Strategic Brand Management*

EXHIBIT 2-3A

The Hummer positions itself as a battlefield-tough vehicle that gives its owner a feeling of being invincible, at least in traffic.

EXHIBIT 2-3B

The Range Rover, in contrast to the Hummer, is positioned as a luxury off-road vehicle fit for royalty when they want to "rough it."

To increase sales, many companies increase the number and scope of their promises without making equivalent product improvements. This situation creates unrealistic expectations; when the products fail to deliver on the promise customers become dissatisfied, and the result is a weakening of their relationships with the brand. A basic principle of IMC, then, is that *a company must manage customer expectations.* This is the foundation of managing the brand promise and creating trust on which brands are built.

Brand Equity

There are two basic components that determine a company or brand's value. One is its physical net assets such as plants, equipment, and land. The other is **brand**

equity, which is *the intangible value of a company beyond its physical net assets*. In other words, a company's total value—what it would sell for—minus its net physical assets, equals brand equity. (The accounting term for brand equity is goodwill.) Although this definition suggests that brand equity is something "left over" after everything else is accounted for, it can actually be more valuable than physical assets. Currently, the average value of all American-based, publicly owned companies is 70 percent greater than the replacement cost of their physical assets.[4]

Two other methods of determining brand equity are the premium-pricing approach and the royalty approach.[5] The *premium-pricing method* determines how much more a branded product can charge for a product versus the same product that is unbranded. This difference is then multiplied by the estimated annual sales and by the number of years it is estimated the branded product will be able to maintain its premium price. The *royalty method* simply looks at the price that other companies are willing to pay (i.e., the royalty) to use the brand to sell a product that they make. Again, estimated sales and the number of years the licensed brand could be used in this way determine the brand equity.

When the tobacco giant Philip Morris acquired Kraft several years ago, for example, it paid six times the value of Kraft's physical net assets. The Philip Morris CEO said his company needed a portfolio of brands that had strong customer relationships that could be leveraged to enable the tobacco company to diversify itself (investor and financial relationships), especially in the retail food industry (trade relationships).[6] In other words, Philip Morris was willing to pay billions of dollars for a set of relationships and the anticipated support such relationships would provide. Likewise, the former CEO of automaker Chrysler once explained that the future success of his company was not determined by its past sales and profits, but rather by the relationships that it had with its dealers and customers.

Because brands are so relationship-dependent, defining brand equity in terms of brand relationships is a way to measure and justify marketing communication spending. David Aaker, a recognized brand authority, says brand equity is made up of five elements: brand-name awareness, brand associations, perceived quality, proprietary brand assets (patents, trademarks, and so on), and brand loyalty. Close analysis of this list shows that the first four elements are what determine the fifth element, brand loyalty. According to Aaker, **brand loyalty** is "a measure of the attachment that a customer has to a brand."[7]

Although brand equity is intangible, the elements that determine brand equity can be tracked and measured. Companies frequently conduct studies to determine the level of brand awareness, the level of perceived brand quality, and brand associations. They can also measure the level of brand loyalty, as determined by the percentage of customers' category purchases that a brand receives, especially where frequent-buyer cards are used and when names and addresses are captured as a part of making a transaction, as in most BtB and service transactions. Brand loyalty accumulates or dissipates as customers' buying experiences are tested against the expectations that have been created by brand messages.

IMC further describes brand equity as the value attached to a brand based on the quantity and quality of relationships with customers and other stakeholders. Brand equity represents the net-sum support that is determined by relationships a company has with its stakeholders—those who work for it, supply it, buy its products, buy its stock, recommend its stock, write about it in the media, and monitor how it conforms to government laws and regulations. Brand support, in other words, comes in many different forms and from many different stakeholders. When a relationship is negative or is lost altogether, the net-sum of support is reduced and the brand loses value.

HOW BRANDS ARE BUILT

Building a successful major brand, whether for a company or a new product, requires strategic planning and a major investment. When electronics manufacturer Hewlett-Packard spun off one of its divisions, it took many months to come up with a new brand name—Agilent. The new company then spent millions of dollars to create awareness and position this new brand. The basic steps in building a brand are shown in the following list and then explained below. Although these brand-building steps are numbered progressively, they often overlap, especially the second, third, and fourth—creating awareness, positioning the brand, and creating a brand image.

Steps in Building a Brand

1. Select a name and symbol to represent the company or product.
2. Create awareness/brand identity of name and symbol (if used) and what the product is or does (i.e., the product category).
3. Position the brand to begin differentiating it from competing brands.
4. Create a brand image to help further differentiate the brand and to make it easier to recognize and recall.
5. Create trust in the minds of customers, prospects, and other stakeholders about the brand by maintaining consistency and delivering on expectations.

1. *Select a name and symbol.* The name and symbol that are chosen to represent a brand can contribute to its success or failure. Names and symbols are what customers look for when shopping, whether in stores, in catalogs, on the Internet, or at trade shows and exhibits. The more memorable and relevant a chosen name and symbol are, the faster and less costly it will be to create awareness of a brand, position it, and develop an image for it. This chapter discusses name and symbol selection further in the section that follows this one.

2. *Create awareness and brand identity.* Once a company selects a name and symbol for its brand, the next step is to create awareness of these identity elements and what the product is or does. When Amazon.com started, it was important that people knew the site wasn't a place to learn more about the great river that runs through Brazil, but rather a company that sold books online. Brand identity needs to be created among many different audiences, not just prospective customers. As the dot-com companies have so well demonstrated, creating an identity within the financial community can help a company sell its stock, and in so doing can create additional awareness for the brand once the financial community has invested millions in it. A new company also needs to create awareness among the labor force if it wants to attract good employees. Another target audience should be suppliers and vendors, who supply not only necessary ingredients and equipment but also ideas for doing certain tasks cost-effectively.

3. *Position the brand.* Hand in hand with creating awareness of the brand name and symbol is positioning the brand. A **brand position** is *how a brand compares to its competitors in the minds of customers, prospects, and other stakeholders.* The positioning concept was articulated by Al Reis and Jack Trout 30 years ago and

is still a primary consideration in branding. What the positioning concept points out is that customers, who are generally aware of several brands in a product category, automatically compare and rank those brands according to how they perceive the differences among them. For example, when people think of cars, they might think of Volvo as being the safest, Corvette as being the sportiest, and Ford as being the most practical. These are the "positions" that each of these brands might hold in a person's mind. Although brand positions, like brands themselves, exist in people's heads and hearts and not on the sides of packages, a company can work to strengthen its brand's position. The challenge is to select a position that can be realistically supported by the product, the company, and the marketing communication and differentiate that brand favorably from competing brands.

4. *Create a brand image.* Giving a brand an identity and a position is not enough, however, to make it come alive and be easily remembered. Think of people you have met. Simply knowing their names, physical traits, and occupation doesn't tell you much about their personality. For brands, an image is its personality. A **brand image** is *an impression created by brand messages and experiences and assimilated into a perception through information processing.* A Harley-Davidson, with its spread-winged eagle symbol, is more than a motorcycle because it has an image as a brand for black-leather-clad, devil-may-care iconoclasts. Another classic example of a brand with a powerful image is Marlboro. Its identity includes its name and its red-and-white packaging. Its category is cigarettes. It is positioned as a masculine cigarette, while the image it calls to mind is that of a rough, romantic, macho cowboy who symbolizes the individualism of the West.

The reason an image adds value to a brand is because the image can communicate something about the buyer to other people. As Dutch authors Giep Franzen and Freek Holzhauer explain, the products you wear, drive, or subscribe to can tell others what you think is important.[8]

5. *Create trust.* The first four brand-building steps are most important in acquiring customers. In order to retain customers, however, brands must create trust (see Exhibit 2–4). This is done by making sure goods and services perform as promised. Facilitating interactivity with customers—making it easy for them to ask questions, complain, and interact with the brand when there is a need to do so—also does a lot to create trust. Trust in a brand develops over time and can be affected by many things, such as how well the product performs, how accessible and responsive a company is, and how consistent it is in what it says and does. As noted earlier, when brand messages promise more than products deliver, trust is weakened. This is why managing customer expectations is so critical.

TRUST. THE UNIVERSAL LANGUAGE FOR SUCCESSFUL PARTNERSHIPS.

The partnerships you formed in childhood have contributed to your success today. When you're exploring real estate opportunities 12 time zones away, global partnerships based on trust are crucial.

At Cushman & Wakefield, we're relationship-oriented, not just transaction-driven. That's why we've established a worldwide real estate services organization that offers the same standard of excellence on a global basis that distinguishes us in the U.S.

Today we provide real estate solutions tailored to our clients' specific needs in more than 30 countries, in the major business centers of the world.

Now that you're bigger, the world is even smaller. To put us to work for you call 1-800-346-6789.

Improving your place in the world.™

www.cushwake.com   Cushman & Wakefield Worldwide

EXHIBIT 2-4

The Cushman & Wakefield ad explains why trust is important in business relationships.

> "Not infrequently people use products—things they buy in a shop—as symbols. They use them in the communication process with other people: friends, partners, colleagues, strangers."
>
> Giep Franzen and Freek Holzhauer, *Brands*

Choosing a Brand Name

The number one priority for a brand name is that it be memorable. But choosing a memorable name is more art than science. Nevertheless, successful brand names share several common characteristics that help make them memorable: benefit description, association, distinction, and pronounceability. Generally speaking, the more of these characteristics a brand name has, the better.

Benefit Description

Brands like DieHard (batteries), Slim-Fast (diet foods), and Head & Shoulders (shampoo) position themselves by saying succinctly describing their benefits to customers. In this way, once awareness has been created of the name, the brand is automatically positioned, which, as explained above, is necessary in distinguishing it from competing brands. The name DieHard stresses the benefit of product longevity and suggests that users won't find themselves in a situation where they have to say those dreaded words "My car's battery is dead!" Slim-Fast not only promises weight loss (Slim) but promises it immediately (Fast). As for Head & Shoulders, an antidandruff shampoo, the brand name says this product is for people who worry about ugly dandruff falling from their heads onto their shoulders.

Association

A brand name achieves association by sounding like another word or concept, or by suggesting a connection to something desirable. Hewlett-Packard chose the name Agilent for a high-tech spin-off becasue it conferred a positive, relevant meaning to the new company—as agile. Because things change so fast in information technology and other high-tech areas, Agilent felt this name helped position the company. Nissan chose the name Pathfinder for a line of SUVs. Unlike DieHard, which speaks specifically to a car battery's performance, the name Pathfinder serves to associate this brand of SUV with off-road driving.

Distinction

Distinction can be achieved in any of several ways. One is to invent a name such as Exxon. There are brand-naming agencies that use computer programs to churn out combinations of letters forming nonsense words. The idea is to help companies find a unique brand name. Another approach is to take a simple word that is completely unrelated to the product such as Apple (computers) or Charlie (perfume). To an extent, this is the opposite of having a name that implies a benefit or an association. It is like wearing black accessories with a white outfit to create a contrast that is striking and distinctive. A distinctive name suggests a distinctive product and ensures that there are no similar brand names with which it will be confused. The Internet employment service Monster.com stands out from such sites as Jobs.com and JobFinder.com because of its name.

When a company chooses a name that either has no meaning or has a very common but unrelated meaning, then the company must invest heavily in marketing communication to create meaning and connect the name to the product.

Pronounceability

Names that are difficult to say or spell are less likely to be remembered. That is why many brands are short and phonetically easy such as Tide, Bic, Allstate, and Saturn. Pronounceability is thus a key consideration in choosing a brand name.

With the increase in multinational marketing, it is also important that names properly translate into other languages. This extends the importance of pronounceability for any company that expects to begin selling its brands outside its home country. When the phenomenally successful Harry Potter series of children's books was introduced to China, the lead publisher, Scholastic, translated the character's name phonetically as "Ha-li Bo-te" so that Chinese readers would find it easy to say. There are examples, however, where companies have been embarrassed by brand-name translations. The classic example is when Chevrolet began selling its Nova in Spanish-speaking countries and quickly found out that *no va* means "It doesn't go." When Clairol introduced its curling iron Mist Stick into Germany, it didn't realize that the German word *mist* means manure.[9]

Choosing a Brand Symbol

We live in a visual world. Newspapers, magazines, television, and the Internet constantly bombard us with visual images. We learn to see before we learn to speak, and throughout our lives 80 percent of what we perceive is visual. That is why having a symbol for a brand can greatly increase the brand's recognition. Cows and other livestock, for example, are "branded" with a symbol in order to tell which ones belong to which ranchers. A **logo** is *a brand symbol, or a distinctive graphic design used to indicate a product's source or ownership.* Corporate logos range from graphic treatments of a brand name to the most abstract design, such as Lucent's logo, the red brush-stroke circle (shown in Exhibit 2–5). As with brand names, good logos should communicate the image and positioning, be distinctive, be simple, and be relevant.

The General Food's International Coffee line logo uses a soft script typeface that says "feminine" and "relaxed" as compared to the bold, square-cornered typeface used in the logo for Sears's line of Craftsman tools, which says masculine and strong. Each of these logos helps reinforce their respective brand positions. McDonald's golden arches is an example of a logo that is both distinctive and simple. Apple computer's original logo—an apple with rainbow color—was long considered a classic logo because it was not only brightly colored and youthful (the early image of Apple computers) but also distinctive, simple, and relevant to the brand name. Recently Apple revised its logo, making it a solid color to appear more modern (see Exhibit 2–6).

Honey, I shrunk the supercomputer.

Power Mac™ G4 Cube. Think different:

Some companies that use electronic media to send out brand messages add another logo dimension: sound. An example is NBC's three-note chimes. As audio becomes more prominent in Internet communications, companies will be wise to add an audio element to their brand identity. The more perceptual clues a logo carries, the easier it will be for customers and prospects to recognize and find the brand when the need arises.

Because companies invest much effort, money, and time in creating brand names and logos, brand identity elements are extremely valuable. To ensure that companies have exclusive use of their brand names and logos, the government gives them legal protection. This protection guarantees companies that their brand identity elements are not being used in a similar way by another company but also requires that the names and logos be used in a consistent manner. A danger with popular brand names is that they become generic. For many years the Xerox Corporation ran a campaign aimed at both the consumer and business community telling people to ask for a photocopy rather than a "Xerox." When people said "Get me a Xerox," the brand name was being used in place of the word *photocopy*, turning it into a generic term. Xerox rightly feared that if the name *Xerox* was used generically, the company would lose its exclusive rights to using the brand. This is what happened to *linoleum* and *escalator*. At one time these were both brand names, but because they were allowed to be used generically—"Let's take the escalator" and "We'll linoleum the floor," the companies that owned these brands lost their exclusive right to use them.

Another word for a logo or brand name is **trademark** (*a sign of someone's trade designed to differentiate that person's work from others*). Some of the first uses of trademarks were initials and other symbols that silversmiths punched into the bottom of their products. Trademarks can be registered with state and federal governments. Before attempting to do so, a company would be wise to search current trademark registrations to make sure its intended brand identity elements have not already been registered and therefore protected from further use.

BRANDING STRATEGIES

A major responsibility of IMC is to manage brand identities and leverage brands once they have been established. Because of the increasing value of brands, the term *brand management* has taken on a new meaning. It originally meant managing a product line. Today it also means ensuring that the image and perception of a brand are maximized. This type of brand management is an increasingly important area of marketing. There are a growing number of brand consulting firms—such as Interbrand, the Brand Trust, the Brand Consultancy, and Landor—all of which help companies develop brand strategies. In addition, traditional marketing communication agencies are placing more emphasis not only on building brands for their clients but also on managing them for the long term as a way to provide more IMC services. The Leo Burnett advertising agency, for example, recently introduced a new research program called Brand Stock, DDB Worldwide has a research tracking study called Brand Capital, and the WPP Group has Brandz. For some years, Young & Rubicam has provided branding advice based on its Brand Asset Valuator model.[10]

How companies develop and use their brand identities is an important aspect of IMC. This is because brands themselves send strong messages that cue associations, feelings, and attitudes. Brand strategies are ways of maximizing the communication impact of brands. Because brands are so important and valuable, it is important that companies give thought to the most critical elements of a branding strategy, such as brand extension, multi-tier branding, co-branding, ingredient branding, and brand licensing.

Brand Extensions

Once a company has created awareness and trust in a brand name, it can then practice **brand extension**, which is *the application of an established brand name to new product offerings*. There are advantages and disadvantages of taking a successful brand and extending it to other products. The advantages are that it saves a company time and money when introducing new products because the brand is already known and instantly communicates a certain level of trust (assuming the brand already has that perception). If the new product is a success, this success can reinforce the brand and thus provide it with even more brand equity. From an IMC perspective, brand extension helps integrate a brand across a wider product line and creates more visibility.

The disadvantages of brand extensions include, first, the danger of diluting the power and meaning of the brand. If customers have come to associate the brand with a certain product, such as laundry detergent, and suddenly the association is extended to apparel or writing instruments, sales of the laundry detergent could suffer. In other words, a brand extension should have a compatible fit with the established brand and product. Second, if the new product fails, for whatever reason, that failure could reflect negatively on the brand's original products if a strong association was built with this failed product.

Brand extensions are generally most successful when they involve similar products. For example, after years of selling bars of soap under the Ivory brand name, the parent company, Proctor & Gamble, introduced a laundry detergent called Ivory Flakes. The new detergent was positioned as gentle detergent, which was consistent with the positioning of Ivory bar soap ("so pure it floats").

Multi-tier Branding

A variation of brand extension is multi-tier branding (also called brand hierarchies). **Multi-tier branding** is *when two or more brands (all owned by the same company) are used in the identification of a product.* Examples include IBM ThinkPad, General Mills Total, and Glad Cling Wrap. In the first two examples corporate names—IBM and

General Mills—have been combined with product-line brand names—ThinkPad and Total. In the third example, Glad is one of the divisions in the First Brands Corporation (a company you probably haven't heard of) and Cling Wrap is its product-line brand name. Exhibit 2–7 shows how both a corporate name (Nissan) and a product name (Maxima) are used in the same brand message.

Multi-tier branding is used for several reasons. The first is to leverage the value in the corporate name. The second is to strengthen the corporate brand by connecting it with another successful product line. The third is that the product brand helps differentiate the offering from other products sold by the company as well as from competing products. Multi-tier branding basically combines two or more sets of brand perceptions with the idea that two (or more) brands are stronger and more attractive than a single brand.

Corporate names generally communicate trust and quality because the company itself usually has been in existence longer than the product line and has already established perceptions of trust and quality. The product brand name is used to relate more directly to the product's performance. Take General Mills Total, for example. The name General Mills says the cereal is well made, well packaged, and fresh—things customers have come to associate with General Mills products. The name Total is designed to identify the product as a healthy cereal that contains 100 percent (i.e., the "total" amount) of the daily requirements for 12 key vitamins and minerals.

You can see how multi-tier branding creates strategic challenges for brand messages. When doing multi-tier branding, MC managers must decide how much emphasis to give each brand. In a print ad for Total, for example, how much space should be devoted to talking about General Mills and how much to Total's specific product features and benefits? To answer this requires input from customers and prospects. If customers express more concerns about product quality than about

EXHIBIT 2-7

This brand message is an example of multi-tier branding. The corporate brand is Nissan and the product-line brand is Maxima.

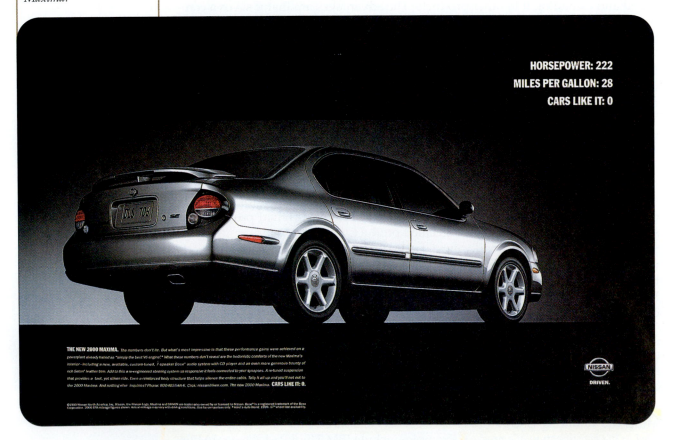

the healthy aspect of the product, then General Mills should be given more emphasis and vice versa. In the case of Total, the product name dominates.

A popular corporate strategy is to create a brand and eventually sell it off. Though Glad is now a division of First Brands Corporation, it was originally created by Union Carbide. Once the brand has established itself, it becomes a valuable asset that can stand (and be sold) on its own because it has created substantial brand equity. This is the idea that is driving the development of many new dot-com brands, which are often designed to be spun off.[11]

Co-branding

Like multi-tier branding, co-branding uses two brand names, but in most cases the names are owned by separate companies. Credit-card companies like to co-brand with other major organizations. The United Airlines Mileage Plus First Card, for example, is also a Visa card, carrying the blue-and-gold Visa logo. (Mileage Plus is the brand name of United Airlines' frequent-flyer program.) The idea behind co-branding is that it provides the customer value from both brands. The Mileage Plus card gives members of United's frequent-flyer program their own special card that automatically tracks purchases and generates free air travel, thus combining two services for the customer.

Co-branding also helps companies selling commodity products, such as credit cards, differentiate themselves. Co-branding is a contractual relationship between two marketing partners, such as Visa and United Airlines' Mileage Plus programs. It is also a challenge for IMC managers, who must decide how the various brand identity markers are to be used in the brand messages related to the products.

Ingredient Branding

One way to add value to a brand (and a brand message) is by **ingredient branding**, which means *using a brand name of a product component or ingredient, in the promotion of a product*. The Intel Inside campaign used by various computer hardware manufacturers is a good example; the manufacturers hope to reinforce the quality of the finished product by featuring its most important part: the processing chip. Another example is Gore-Tex. Despite what some people may think, Gore-Tex doesn't make gloves, shoes, coats, and jackets, but rather just the fabric from which these items are made by other manufacturers. But because Gore-Tex fabric, which is lightweight, warm, and water resistant, has become so well known and respected, and promoted so prominently (often even more than the apparel brand itself), many customers ask for a "Gore-Tex jacket" even though no such brand of jacket exists. Manufacturers who use Gore-Tex fabric have found they can sell their products at premium prices through ingredient branding (see Exhibit 2–8). Ingredient branding is also used by food-products manufacturers. Some dessert mixes, for example, promote the fact they contain Hershey's chocolate chips.

For ingredient branding to be successful, the ingredient brand must develop brand awareness just as a regular brand does. When it can accomplish this, the brand then becomes attractive to manufacturers who elect to promote the ingredient brand as a product feature.

EXHIBIT 2-8

Because Gore-Tex has developed so much brand equity, its name adds value to any product in which it is a part.

Brand Licensing

Another benefit of developing a strong brand is that it can be, in essence, rented to another company. The beauty of brand licensing is that the company owning the brand can continue to use it while also collecting a fee for the brand's use by another company. An example most students are familiar with is the licensing of a university's name, logo, and mascot to apparel makers. Licensing is of particular concern to an IMC manager because it means that critical aspects of the brand's identity are being used by unrelated companies that may not have the brand's best interests in mind. Consequently, monitoring brand licensing is an important role for IMC managers who want to maintain a consistent image. Licensing will be discussed in more detail in Chapter 15.

BRAND RELATIONSHIPS

A fundamental principle of IMC is that *a variety of groups can affect a company's bottom line and therefore should be taken into consideration when creating and sending brand messages.* As discussed in Chapter 1, these various groups are known as stakeholders. What the company does affects them, and what they do can likewise affect the company.

> "The focus shifts from products and firms as units of analysis to people, organizations, and the social processes that bind actors together in ongoing relationships."
>
> Frederick Webster, "The Changing Role of Marketing in the Corporation"

Although marketing's first concern is dealing with customers, it cannot ignore other stakeholders. The biggest reason comes from the increase in interactivity made possible by new communication technologies. As the practice of IMC provides customers with greater access to a company through toll-free telephone numbers, websites, and e-mail addresses, other stakeholders will also take advantage of this access, contacting customer-service and other departments with questions and complaints. Companies must be prepared to properly handle this increased interactivity with all stakeholder groups. As Frederick Webster points out, today's business focus has shifted to people, organizations, and processes that bind (i.e., integrate) stakeholders into ongoing relationships.[12]

Stakeholder Support

Figure 2–1 shows the different categories of stakeholders affected by marketing. The most important group of stakeholders is customers. The next most important group is employees. Then come all the other groups whose relative importance will vary by industry and over time: suppliers, and distribution channel members (distributors and retailers), the media, and MC agencies (for those companies that use agencies), government regulators, the communities in which businesses are located, the financial community and investors, and special interest groups. Although marketing interacts with some of these stakeholders more than others, each of these groups can have a major impact on a company, whether good or bad.

Customers

The most important stakeholder group is that of customers (or, in nonprofit companies, members) because customer support determines sales and profit. Frequent, in-depth interactions with customers can quickly reveal their changing wants, needs, and concerns. Interactivity, in other words, is a critical tool in creating customer integration into the company. The more customer feedback a company generates, the more integrated customers will be into the company's planning and operations.

Many companies, particularly BtB firms, have created partnerships with customers as a way to identify and then meet their needs. An example is Baxter International, a $9 billion health care products and services company that negotiates risk-sharing partnerships with its hospital and managed health care clients to set cost targets for supplies.[13] Participants in Baxter's ValueLink inventory management program entrust ownership and management of inventory to Baxter, which will deliver supplies directly to hospital floors and departments. Baxter has even taken over the task of cleaning and sterilizing equipment, freeing hospital staff to care for patients. At some hospitals, Baxter employees are on-site 24 hours a day. Chapter 5 goes into more depth regarding customer behavior and attitudes.

Employees

Customers often perceive the employees with whom they come in contact as "being the company." Some executives, especially in the service industry, believe that employees, rather than customers, should be a company's number one priority. The rationale for this approach is that unless employees know their job, feel they are being treated fairly by the company, feel like part of a team, and find meaning in their work, they are not going to provide excellent service to customers. How employees treat customers delivers a highly influential message. According to

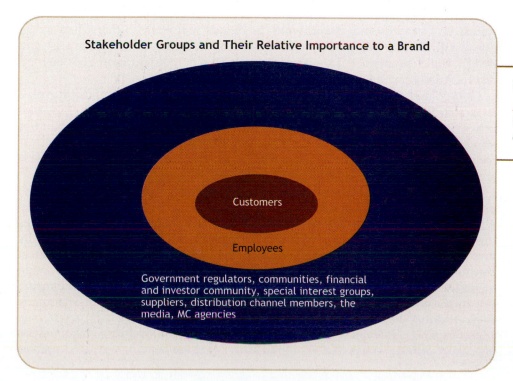

Stakeholder Groups and Their Relative Importance to a Brand

Customers

Employees

Government regulators, communities, financial and investor community, special interest groups, suppliers, distribution channel members, the media, MC agencies

FIGURE 2-1

An essential principle of IMC is that customers are at the center of a brand.

Frederick Reichheld, head of the customer-loyalty practice at the consulting firm Bain & Company, "It's impossible to build a loyal book of customers without a loyal employee base."[14]

As IMC encourages and facilitates customer interactivity, this means more customers will be talking with more people in a company. This is particularly true in BtB marketing, where customers take their questions, suggestions, and complaints directly to the different departments—accounting (questions about invoices), research and development (questions about new product ideas or complaints on product performance), and distribution (questions and suggestions about shipping), as well as customer service, sales, and marketing.

Companies that ignore employees pay the cost. A study conducted by the Food Marketing Institute found that 46 percent of employees in the companies surveyed argued with customers, 22 percent did slow or sloppy work on purpose, 20 percent came to work hung over, and 11 percent damaged property while horsing around.[15] IMC uses internal marketing (defined in Chapter 1) to help keep employees informed of marketing programs and to boost employee moral and involvement in MC programs. The IMC in Action box explains how a good employee relations program can increase employee loyalty.

Other Stakeholders

Besides customers and employees, various other stakeholder groups can also greatly affect the success of a company. Although marketing does not have the primary responsibility for maintaining relationships with these other stakeholders, marketers must constantly be sensitive to how these groups will react to what marketing does and what kinds of brand messages are being sent out.

Two stakeholder groups that have grown in importance over the last decade are *suppliers* and *distributors*. Auto companies, for example, are working with suppliers before cars are designed to head off design problems that, in turn, reduces the number of customer complaints. John Spoelhof, president of Prince Corporation, a company that makes armrests, sun visors, cup holders, and vanity mirrors, states: "We need to understand what car buyers will want so that when we sit down with the auto companies, we can figure out together what will surprise and delight the customers."[16] This is an example of where integration goes beyond just traditional media messages.

Competitors can impact a company's bottom line not only through competitive moves and countermoves but by how well they cooperate in supporting the product category. Major banks, for example, compete strongly against each other but also cooperate on getting legislation passed that is favorable to the banking industry as a whole. In Japan competitors often work together in industry conglomerates to compete in international markets.

Relationships with *media* stakeholders are important for several reasons. Reporters are always looking for expert opinions and explanations to help them write stories, and companies that have good media relationships will be the ones they call first. Another advantage of having good media relationships is that the media are more likely to be open-minded when a problem occurs. Finally, most medium and large-sized companies send out news and publicity releases. Having a good relationship can increase the chances that these will be used by the media (the media are very much aware that when they run a positive story for a company they are doing the company a favor).

Government regulators on the national, state, and local levels are stakeholders, especially for companies that are in industries that are heavily regulated such as

IMC IN ACTION

Pumping Up Employee Loyalty

PepsiCo has been paying attention to employee needs by providing many in-house services at its Purchase, New York, headquarters. A dry cleaner and tailor operates on-premises, a shoe shiner comes into the office twice a week, the cafeteria prepares take-home meals every day at 4:30 P.M., and a mobile oil-change service sets up shop in the parking lot twice a month. PepsiCo also provides a full-time concierge to help employees handle errands, line up day care, arrange home repairs, and reserve theater tickets and restaurant tables.

Rhône-Poulenc-Rorer (now merged into Aventis), a European pharmaceutical company, provides free shuttle and van service for employees who commute; an on-site credit union; a bank machine; a fitness center; a dry cleaner; shoe repair services; a florist; a pharmacy; a cafeteria with take-out dinners; a jeweler; a bed-and-breakfast for visiting executives; and three softball fields, two tennis courts, and three miles of jogging trails.

Why would PepsiCo and RPR do these things? So that employees can focus on their work and not be distracted by outside chores. Such services are often cheaper than many companies think because they can be handed over to outside contractors happy to set up shop on corporate campuses.

Southwest Airlines, headquartered in Dallas, Texas, goes so far as to put employees ahead of customers. CEO Herb Kelleher says customers are not always right: "The customer is frequently wrong. We don't carry those sorts of customers. We write them and say, 'Fly somebody else. Don't abuse our people.'"[1]

Why do all these companies care so much about their employees? In most cases, employees are a primary point of contact for customers. The theory is that creating happy employees in turn creates not only better work and a higher level of product or service quality but also more positive customer relationships.

Think About It

Why is employee relations an important part of a brand relationship program? If you were a company manager, what different techniques mentioned in this box might you use to motivate employees? How many of these techniques could you also use in a trade (supplier/vendor) relations program?

[1]Tom Peters, "Southwest Flying on a Wink and a Fare," Rocky Mountain News, September 27, 1994, p. 42A.

---

drugs, alcoholic beverages, and firearms. For example, the distinction between prescription drugs and over-the-counter drugs is one monitored carefully by the FDA (Federal Drug Administration) and one that has important implications for a brand's marketing and MC activities. Local and state governments are involved in such decisions as where a plant, office, or store is located and what kind of supporting services the respective governmental body will provide.

Special interest groups are groups of people who organize around a specific political or social issue, such as those that focus on pollution or environmental safety. They can be a company's friend and help it make responsible decisions that affect the community, or they can be enemies and actively work to block company proposals and organize brand boycotts. These stakeholder groups are important because they are often the source of negative word-of-mouth brand messages. The more a company can be aware of and work with these groups, the more these negative messages can be minimized.

The *communities* in which companies have offices, stores, and plants are stakeholders because they not only supply employees but also vote on city and county laws and regulations that can affect business operations. At the same time, municipalities depend to a great extent on local businesses as a source of tax revenue.

The *financial community* are investors, stockbrokers, financial analysts, who invest or strongly influence those who do have money to invest. Those who buy a company's stock become partial owners of the company and its brands. Stockbrokers and financial analysts influence the purchase of a company's stock by making positive or negative recommendations. One way McDonald's has kept the attention of the financial community is by inviting them to work in a store for a day, which the analysts think is really fun!

Stakeholder Overlap

Although brand messages are aimed at customers, companies must assume that all stakeholder groups will be exposed to those messages as well. Furthermore, a basic principle of IMC is that *stakeholders overlap*, a point illustrated in Figure 2–2. In an IMC brand audit done by the University of Colorado for a major bank, it was found that 95 percent of the bank's employees were also bank customers and that 75 percent owned shares of the bank's stock. Marketers must make sure that brand messages are acceptable to all stakeholders and that the presentation of the brand image and position is consistent. Fast-food franchise companies, for example, are always faced with the challenge of coming up with advertising that appeals not only to their targeted customers (who are often teenagers and young adults) but also to their franchisees (who are often older and more conservative than the brand's target audience). Finally, all stakeholders can also be customers.

FIGURE 2-2

As this figure shows stakeholders overlap.

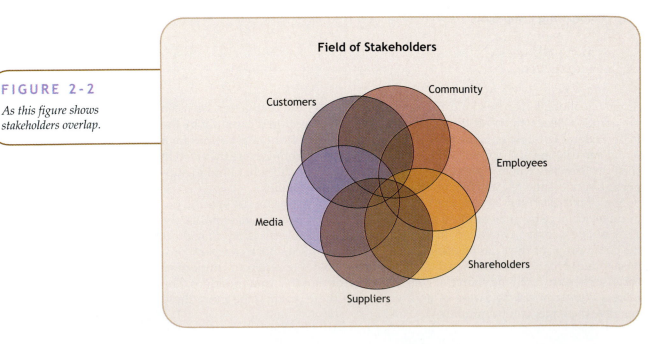

Field of Stakeholders

Customers
Community
Employees
Media
Shareholders
Suppliers

Stakeholder Capital Creates Brand Value

The broader and deeper the support of various stakeholders, the stronger a brand will be. Just as brand share is the result of the brand's customer franchise, i.e., its loyal customer base, brand value is the result of the company's stakeholder franchise, i.e., the loyalty of its various stakeholders. In this sense, stakeholder relationships are another form of capital (money in the bank). In terms of bottom-line impact, sales revenue and stock prices (in the case of public companies) can either increase or decrease depending on the behavior of customers, shareholders, the media, the financial community, and other stakeholders.

Depending on the situation, some of the noncustomer stakeholder groups (e.g., as investors, the financial community, and government officials) can have a greater impact on the bottom line than customers do. This is why most CEOs and presidents of major companies increasingly spend more time addressing the needs and concerns of stakeholder groups other than customers. It is estimated the average Fortune 500 CEO spends 85 percent of his or her time communicating with these various stakeholder groups.[17]

Importance of individual stakeholder groups will vary over time, depending on the situation. In a crisis, such as a product recall, the most important stakeholder group may be the media. During a stock offering by a public company, the most important group may be the financial community. During a restructuring or merger, the most important group may be employees, who should be kept up-to-date to minimize negative rumors that can lower morale and productivity. When these unusual situations occur, marketing communication managers should be willing to cooperate and do whatever is best for the company. Sometimes this can mean shifting money from the MC budget to another department whose brand messages are critical at that time.

Research has documented the benefits of having a multiple stakeholder focus. One study found that companies that emphasized three groups—employees, investors, and customers—significantly outperformed those that focused on only one or two of these groups.[18] Over an 11-year period, the companies that focused on all three groups had revenue increases four times greater than those with a more limited stakeholder focus. Furthermore, the multistakeholder-focused companies saw their stock appreciate 901 percent versus only 91 percent for the other companies during the same period.

The implication is that all businesses exist within a field of stakeholder interactions and these relationship interactions increase (or decrease) value for the brand. In other words, stakeholders interact with other stakeholders in a network of communication, and those messages may carry more weight than any ad or sales promotion. The issue of interwoven stakeholders is a theme in the IBM "e-business" ad in Exhibit 2–9.

EXHIBIT 2-9

The IBM e-business ad addresses the security concerns of information managers, employees, customers, and the financial community that provides online services.

THE ANATOMY OF A BRAND RELATIONSHIP

Traditionally, marketing communications has been a process of developing and sending out brand messages to create sales (i.e., transactions). Companies have learned, however, that they can be more profitable by focusing on building customer relationships rather than on just transactions. This does not mean, however, that transactions should be ignored. Without sales transactions, a company will soon go out of business. Transactions should be seen as a series of events that, besides increasing sales, provide an opportunity to begin and strengthen a brand relationship. This is because every time a company makes a sale, it is interacting, either directly or indirectly, with a customer. And each interaction is really a test—did the product and/or company perform well or not?

As part of its goals of creating and managing brand relationships, IMC first seeks to explain relationships by deconstructing them. Constructs are the components with which something, such as a brand relationship, is built. One way to learn how something is built is to take it apart—*de*construct it—and look at its constructs. That's what this section will do with brand relationships.

Acquisition versus Retention

When a company builds a strong relationship with customers, sales and profits are the result. As explained in the final section of this chapter, on profitable brand relationships, making a sale to a current customer is far less expensive than making a sale to a new customer. Also, the new customer is less likely than the old customer to be a heavy brand user, especially the first year. A basic principle of IMC, then, is that a *company should focus more on retention of current customers than on acquisition of new customers.*

Customer retention is the topic of numerous articles in the marketing press today. However, it is still not being well managed by most companies. One survey of 200 companies found that the vast majority still were doing little to create and manage customer relationships. Despite pledges of being customer driven, most were still cost driven and were losing, on average, 20 percent of their customers each year.[19] The percentage of such loss, however, differs by product category, brand, and company. In the automotive field, for example, over 55 percent of new car buyers don't buy the same nameplate they are replacing. Saturn, however, only loses 45 percent, and Infiniti loses 30 percent. Both of these companies are known for being more focused on relationships than on sales. The Tale of Two Companies box illustrates the difference between a transaction-focused and a relationship-focused way of doing business.

Trust

The reason customers most often give for making a particular brand choice is that they trust the chosen brand more than competing brands. Their trust is based on whether the company does what it says it will do—that is, whether its products and employees have integrity.

Trust anchors a company's reputation. As discussed in Chapter 1, image can be created, but a good reputation is a perception earned from repeated good experiences with a brand. Salmond says, "Trust between partners at a given time is a

A TALE OF TWO COMPANIES

Edward Jones and Prudential

An example of the positive results of focusing on relationships rather than transactions is the success of the Edward Jones brokerage company (see Exhibit 2-10). Concentrating on smaller towns outside the reach of major cities, Jones is the Wal-Mart of brokerage houses. Jones closely monitors its salespeople to make sure they are sending messages that create trust among customers and potential customers. To this end, salespeople are continually reminded that they are selling mostly to people who are not familiar with the stock market and therefore should steer customers away from risky investments. To make sure customers aren't being motivated to buy and sell unwisely just to generate commissions for the broker, the company also has a system to identify accounts that show excessive trading.

Most important, Jones has designed its compensation system to encourage its brokers to put the interests of their customers first and sales second. The company's success has resulted from a strategy of acquiring customers for the long term and providing them with the services they need in order to retain them. The result is that Jones's customers hold their funds for nearly three times the industry average. The company has over 3,350 offices and has watched its revenue nearly triple in the last five years, despite having a meager MC budget. Although Jones's rate of growth has leveled off as the big brokerage houses have begun moving into the smaller markets, the company is beginning to expand into larger markets with its successful customer-relationship strategy.

Compare this to the types of messages Prudential Securities (formerly Prudential-Bache Securities) used in building (or destroying) many of its relationships. In 1994, Prudential was forced to pay $1.4 billion to settle state and federal securities fraud charges that it supplied its brokers with misleading promotional literature. According to a *New York Times* investigation, one of the primary reasons for the misleading promotional material was Prudential's corporate culture, which emphasized transactions—short-term sales—over long-term relationships with customers. Unlike Edward Jones, Prudential Securities had, according to one observer of the situation, "utter disregard for the ultimate harm it might do to the customer."

Think About It

How can an emphasis on relationships versus transactions help a company's business? What exactly did the Jones brokerage do to create long-term positive relationships with its customers?

Sources: Greg Burns, "Can It Play Out of Peoria?" *Business Week*, August 7, 1995, p. 58; excerpt from Kurt Eichenwalk, *Serpent on the Rock*, published in *Sales and Marketing Management*, September 1995, p. 83.

EXHIBIT 2-10

Edward Jones

Serving Individual Investors Since 1871

---

bridge between past experiences and the anticipated future."[20] In order to facilitate trust, companies must be aware of the fact that trust is a factor of both reality and perception.

Like a person's reputation, trust in a company is built up over time and through a series of interactions between the company and its customers (and other stakeholders). Hot lines, customer-service departments, warranties, guarantees, and the like are designed to create higher levels of customer trust. Emblems like the Good Housekeeping Seal are also designed to make the customer's decision easier (see Exhibit 2–11). Since 1909, *Good Housekeeping* has guaranteed that if a product bearing the seal is defective (within two years of purchase), the magazine will replace it or refund the price. An organization dedicated to helping build trust in brands of websites is TRUSTe (see Exhibit 2–12).

Unfortunately, trust can be quickly lost. In most product categories, there are several brand choices, and a bad experience with one can cause customers to lose trust and switch to another brand. Although there are many factors that influence to what extent a customer trusts a company, research has shown the following constructs are most important in creating trust in a commercial relationship (see Figure 2–3).

- *Satisfaction.* Satisfaction is determined by a variety of inputs, such as positive product performance; beneficial brand attributes not offered by competitors; knowledge that others are using and happy with the brand; and the company's response to complaints or inquiries.

- *Consistency.* Consistency is communicated by product and service uniformity as well as the uniformity in the way a company positions itself and responds to situations. Consistency is important because it sets expectations and thus provides a way to reduce risk. When you go into a McDonald's restaurant, no matter where it is, you expect certain menu items, reasonable prices, and a clean eating area because these are the things you have experienced in the past when going to a McDonald's.

- *Accessibility.* When there is a problem, customers want to feel they have recourse, such as the ability to quickly contact someone and have the problem fixed.

- *Responsiveness.* When questions, inquiries, and complaints are quickly and thoroughly handled, customers are not only more satisfied, they feel a company really cares and appreciates their business.

- *Commitment.* Customers want to feel that a company has their best interest at heart rather than doing and saying anything they can just to make a sale. When a salesclerk tells you the store doesn't have your size but you might find it at one of the store's competitors, you feel that the store is committed to helping you and not just itself.

- *Affinity.* Affinity comes when customers identify with a brand or company, and relate to other people who use it.

- *Liking.* Liking something is often a reason for testimony—most people talk about their positive experiences and things they like. If a brand or company's commercials are irritating, its receptionist is snotty, its manufacturing plant is polluting the air and water, and its products break easily, then a person may decide that this is not a real likable company or brand. That's a strong reason for disassociation.

In IMC planning, these constructs are used to diagnose and measure the strength of brand relationships. By asking customers to what extent they feel

EXHIBIT 2-11

The Good Housekeeping seal works to build trust in any product on which it appears.

EXHIBIT 2-12

The TRUSTe website speaks to the importance of consumer trust.

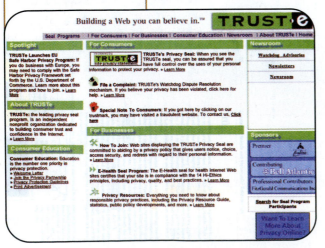

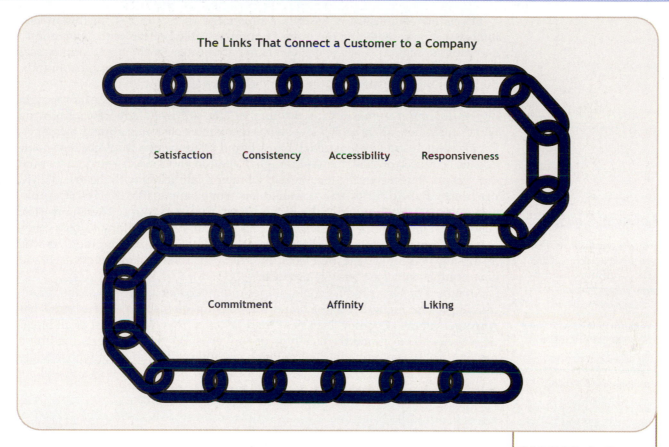

The Links That Connect a Customer to a Company

Satisfaction   Consistency   Accessibility   Responsiveness

Commitment   Affinity   Liking

FIGURE 2-3

The collective strength of these links determines the level of brand trust.

the company is responsive, consistent in performance and service, and accessible, for example, a company can begin to track whether its relationships are growing stronger or weaker. To give these measures meaning, the company should ask customers the same questions about its competitors.

Intensity

Another way to analyze brand relationships is to determine the intensity, or strength, of the relationship. Just as we have different levels of intensity in our personal relationships—from acquaintances to lovers—we have different levels of intensity in commercial relationships. The intensity of a brand relationship will vary for each customer and product category. An example of the benefits of brand intensity is the success of the Grateful Dead, whose popularity has lasted 30 years even though the group has never had a number one hit (only one top 10 hit). The reason for the band's longevity is that its followers have always been intensely loyal. Unlike most bands, which perform just one show in each city they tour, the Grateful Dead often does several shows in each city because the same fans attend night after night.

Customers have strong emotional feelings with some brands while seeing others as strictly utilitarian. A dedicated Pepsi loyalist, for example, would not be caught dead drinking Coke. Someone who religiously uses a particular shampoo is not going to feel comfortable using just any other brand. The same Pepsi or shampoo fan may not have a commitment to a particular brand of milk or laundry detergent. To successfully communicate with customers, a company needs to know the level of intensity that customers have for its brand and the product category.

Levels of relationship intensity are illustrated in Figure 2–4. In this model, intensity is represented by the levels beginning at the bottom with "awareness" and moving higher to where customers are advocates for the brand. Businesses usually will have a segment of customers at each of the levels. For most brands, the higher the intensity level, the fewer customers at that level.

The goal, of course, is to move as many customers as possible to the far top right on this continuum—maximizing the number who are brand advocates. Knowing which customers are at which level helps companies customize brand messages. For example, a strategy for strengthening brand relationships would be to encourage the "connected" customers—through invitation and rewards—to join a brand user group, thus increasing the intensity of their relationship with the brand. IMC programs can help create brand commitment. For example, IBM, Microsoft, Apple, and many other computer companies have set up user groups. These consist of customers who own the same brand of computer and enjoy talking to each other, learning from each other, and sharing new ways of using their computers, as well as getting help in solving problems. Internet chat rooms likewise create brand communities for a vast array of products.

Members of such product communities often become advocates of the brand, moving to the highest level of brand relationship intensity. When a brand has customers at the advocacy level, the brand benefits from the greatest of all brand messages—word of mouth. This type of "advertising" not only costs the brand nothing, but it also normally has very high credibility because those who listen to other customers know those people are sharing their own experiences and will not benefit personally if the listener decides to buy the brand.

FIGURE 2-4

As the graph shows, those customers who are brand advocates are a small percentage of total customers.

Adapted from Richard Cross and Janet Smith, *Customer Bonding: Pathway to Lasting Customer Loyalty* (Lincolnwood, IL: NTC, 1994), pp. 54–55.

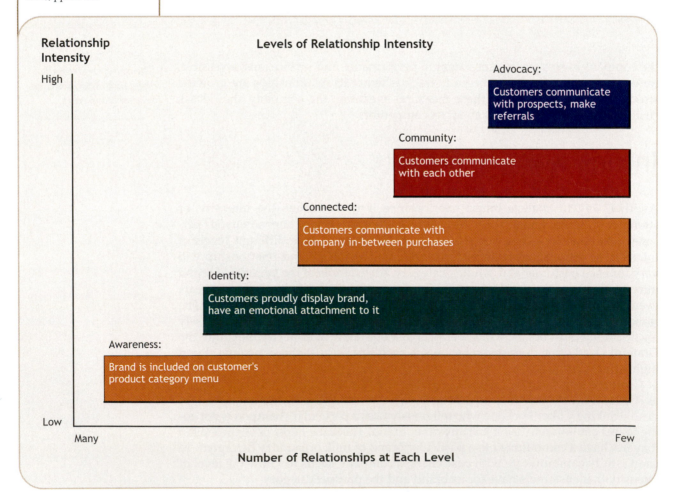

It's important to keep in mind that brand relationships are seldom built on transactions alone. Interactions of all kinds (e.g., requests for information, conversations with salespeople, product warranty registration, complaints) collectively determine the intensity of a relationship. One of the ways to evaluate an IMC program is to track the percentage of a company's customers that are in each of the intensity levels. In an effective IMC program, the percentage of people in the higher levels will increase over time.

Managing Expectations

"Relationship marketing is powerful in theory but troubled in practice . . . Consumers view companies as enemies, not allies."[21] This quote from a *Harvard Business Review* article points to a major industry problem—businesses are doing much more promising than delivering when it comes to managing their brand relationships (see Exhibit 2–13). Despite all their rhetoric about being customer focused and putting the customer first, the level of overall customer service has not been good. Too often, companies use "relationships" as a way to exploit customers rather than to provide a win-win situation: "There's a balance between giving and getting in a good relationship. But when companies ask their customers for friendship, loyalty, and respect, too often they don't give those customers friendship, loyalty, and respect in return."[22]

An important IMC practice is to create brand messages that make realistic promises that set expectations that the brand can meet. Brands fail to meet expectations generally for one of two reasons. The first is that expectations have been set too high, which is generally the fault of overzealous MC messages. (Recall from Chapter 1 the bank that wanted to be the friendliest in town, and created customer expectations beyond what it could deliver.) The other reason expectation gaps exist is that products or supporting services are defective. As Chapter 21 explains in more detail, companies must constantly monitor customer expectations and make the responsible departments aware when they are underperforming.

Loyalty

As discussed earlier, brands are built by focusing on customer retention rather than just acquisition. Repeat customers build brand loyalty. Note,

however, that brand-loyal customers do not always buy only one brand in a category. Most often the customers who buy one brand only are light users, meaning that their total purchases are relatively small. Medium and heavy users are much more likely to regularly buy two or three brands in a category.

Because most "loyal" customers are not 100 percent loyal, companies, regardless of product category, think in terms of **share of wallet**, *the percentage of a customer's spending in a product category for one particular brand*. This is because a firm's income depends not only on the number of customers it has but also on what percentage of each customer's category purchases it receives. Because few companies can capture 100 percent of a customer's share of wallet, heavy users are particularly important. A study of 83 grocery chains determined that the top 10 percent of customers, who were members of the chains' frequent-buyer programs, spent twice as much per week as the next 10 percent spent. It also found that the "top 30 percent of shopping-card holders account for approximately 75 percent of a store's total sales, versus only 2 percent for the bottom 30 percent."[23]

In other words, in most product categories a small number of heavy users account for a large percentage of the sales and profits, even though these customers may not be 100 percent loyal to the brand. **Heavy users** are *those customers who buy an above-average amount of a given product*. The exact definition of a heavy user differs by category. Heavy users are sometimes identified as the top quintile (the top 20 percent) of customers based on volume. A marketing rule of thumb known as the **Pareto rule** (named after Italian economist Vilfredo Pareto) states that *80 percent of a brand's sales come from 20 percent of its customers*. Although the precise ratio varies for every company, the reality is that the majority of sales and profits come from a minority of a company's customers.

To illustrate the 80/20 concept, let's say that a book publisher buys $10 million dollars worth of paper a year. If you represent the International Paper Company, you want to track what percentage of this $10 million your company receives. The book publisher likes to have more than one paper supplier, for a variety of reasons (it gains multiple sources of new ideas, makes sure product is still available if one company goes on strike, keeps each supplier from taking orders for granted). As a supplier, however, what you want is the largest percentage of the publisher's paper-buying business that you can get. Your goal may therefore be to have 80 percent ($8 million) of this business. An example from the service industry is discussed in the Technology in Action box.

PROFITABLE BRAND RELATIONSHIPS

The most important thing to remember about brand relationships is that they have bottom-line results. They cost money to create and maintain, but they can also generate sales or reduce the cost of doing business. Either way, they contribute to an organization's profit. Even nonprofit associations have to be sensitive to costs and how they handle their relationships with supporters regarding fund-raising, membership dues, and volunteers who contribute services. Unless an organization's brand relationships are profitable, it will soon be out of business.

When customers are manipulated into buying something they don't need or want, a company risks several things in addition to its good name. First, customers who have been manipulated will ultimately be less satisfied than those who haven't and consequently will be more likely to make a return or demand special handling, both of which increase operating costs. Second, disappointed customers are likely to become negative spokespersons for the brand. Third, they are less likely to buy again; therefore, the sale becomes a one-time transaction rather than

TECHNOLOGY IN ACTION

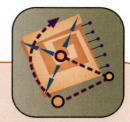

Cleaning Up on License Plates

Jimmy Branch, the owner of the Speedy Car Wash in Panama City, Florida, uses his customers' license plates to track the frequency of their purchases. With such information, he was able to determine that two-thirds of his customers came in only once or twice a year. What's more, he found that the remaining customers—those who washed their cars at Speedy three or more times a year—were responsible for two-thirds of his revenues.

He used this information to completely revamp how he markets his car wash business. He created discounts to encourage the lower-frequency customers to come in more often. For example, someone who has a car washed receives a coupon for $3 off another car wash if it's within two weeks. Frequent customers receive special recognition and efforts to persuade them to buy extra services, such as a wax or undercarriage wash, when they visit. If they respond to some short questions about their car-service needs—and thereby help Branch keep his computer information updated—

they qualify for a few dollars off the cost of the extra services.

Tracking customers by license plate number has also helped Speedy's salespeople individualize customer contact. When a customer pulls in, a salesperson at the front counter enters the customer's plate number into the computer. Repeat customers' names come up on the screen, so the salesperson can greet each of them personally. It's this kind of recognition and response that creates effective brand relationships.

Think About It

What did Jimmy Branch learn about the frequency with which his customers visited his car wash, and how did he learn that information? How has this information helped his staff build customer relationships?

Source: Laura M. Litvan, "Increasing Revenue with Repeat Sales," *Nation's Business*, January 1996, p. 36.

---

the beginning of a relationship, and the investment in getting that first (and only) sale is lost.

Profitability is a particularly important consideration with a loyalty program like the one designed for Boots The Chemists. Loyalty cards may attract people to the store, but they also have to have a financial payoff. In fact, clothing retailer Eddie Bauer stopped its loyalty program because it was losing money for the firm. In business terms, if you are going to give people money back or reward them in some other way, then you need to make enough additional money to cover the reward cost plus increase profits. The success of the Boots Advantage Card was evaluated according to the company's return on the investment in the loyalty program. By this measure, it turned out to be a very successful marketing effort.

Benefits of Brand Relationship Programs

There are several reasons why companies focus on building brand relationships in order to retain profitable customers (see Table 2–2). As the following list shows, some of these benefits come from increasing sales, but others come from reducing costs.

1. *It costs less to sell to a current customer.* There have been many estimates regarding the cost differential of acquiring versus retaining a customer. Most

TABLE 2 - 2   Profitable Relationships

Impact on Costs	Impact on Sales/Profits
• Costs less to sell to current customers	• Loyal customers buy more
• Relationships amortize costs of acquisition	• Loyalty increases long-term customer value
• Loyal customers are brand advocates reducing MC costs	• Decreasing defections increases sales
• Satisfied customers take less handholding	• Disappointed customers spread negative word of mouth, reducing sales revenue

of these have been based on the cost of selling to a customer for the first time versus the cost of making a repeat sale. The businesses with the best handle on this are those in direct marketing, where it is easiest to measure cost per sale. In most direct-marketing programs, a customer isn't profitable until the third time he or she buys. In BtB selling, research has shown that 80 percent of new customer sales require five or more brand contacts and that nearly two-thirds of all sales leads that turn into sales take three or more months to do so.[24] This is why selling to current customers lowers overall selling costs.

Sears has found a large differential between the cost of sales to new customers and the cost of sales to loyal customers—the former cost some 20 times more.[25] With this type of cost difference, you can see the wisdom of putting at least as much emphasis on selling to current customers as on acquiring new ones. This balance will differ in each product category and by brand. A company needs to continuously evaluate its relationship managing process to see if it is maximizing the sales potential of its current customers. In an effort to do this, some department stores send their credit-card holders as many as 16 catalogs and special sale announcements each year plus invitations to "private" sales and other special events. By maximizing the interactivity with customers, the stores are able to remain top of mind with customers and increase their buying. In maximizing this interactivity, however, a company must make sure it is not being intrusive. It can find out by simply asking customers whether it should scale back its mailings.

2. *Relationships amortize acquisition cost.* When customers no longer buy a brand, the company has a lower return on the investment it made to acquire those customers. In the telephone companies' recent battles for customers, for example, AT&T was offering some residential customers of other phone companies $100 to switch to AT&T. When this was added to the company's other MC expenditures, along with the processing costs of putting a new customer into its system, getting each new customer was really costing AT&T over $125. Now, say that a customer switches to another phone company five months later. The amortized $125 acquisition cost (i.e., the cost divided among those five months) is $25 a month. But if that customer had stayed with AT&T for five years, then that $125 could have been amortized over 60 months, amounting to only about $2 a month.

3. *A small decrease in defections means a large increase in sales.* Frederick Reichheld, of consulting firm Bain & Company, has found that decreasing customer defections by just 5 percent can boost profits per customer by 35 to 95 percent over the average lifetime of a customer.[26] One reason for this is that there is

always a fixed cost of doing business, called *overhead*, which includes salaries, cost of buildings and equipment, and utilities. These all have to be paid regardless of the number of sales made during a particular period. Therefore, the money from the first sales go to covering these costs. It's only after there have been enough sales made (minus variable costs) to cover these fixed costs that a portion of sales can be considered profit. And once the overhead is accounted for, then profit increases at a faster rate.

4. *Lost customers can cause other customers to also leave.* Just as positive word of mouth is a major benefit, negative word of mouth can be very damaging. It is not unusual for unhappy customers who quit buying because they are angry with the company to tell at least 10 others of their dissatisfaction. Such negative messages far outweigh the impact of a self-promotion such as advertising.

5. *Relationships increase value of the customer.* **Lifetime customer value (LTCV)** is *an estimate of how much a given customer contributes to a company's profit over the average number of years the average customer buys from a company.* LTCV is made up of product sales and aftermarket service revenue (direct revenue), and referrals and endorsements (indirect revenue). A worldwide luxury hotel chain has estimated that its average LTCV is $175,000. A men's retail store that has done this analysis came up with an average LTCV of $100,000. (LTCV will be explained in more detail in Chapter 7.)

6. *Loyal customers are more profitable.* **Profits per customer increase with customer longevity because the longer customers stay with a brand, the more willing they are to pay premium prices. An analysis of consumer buying data found that loyal packaged-goods customers generally are willing to pay 7 to 10 percent more than nonloyal customers.[27] Also, loyal customers are less costly to service, especially in business product categories. This is because they know the company they are dealing with, what it can and can't do, and whom to approach when they have a question or problem. This makes interactions smoother and more efficient.

7. *Capitalizing on advocates.* Finally, customers who have a good relationship with a company are more likely to be brand advocates, giving referrals and saying good things about the brand and company to potential customers. The value of a referral is illustrated by what an English company, Direct Line Insurance, did when it discovered that 50 percent of its new business was coming from referrals: It used its marketing communication to motivate current customers even more to recommend others. It was so successful doing this that it was able to bypass insurance brokers who sold on commissions. The company now has a 30 percent share of the insurance market in the United Kingdom.

How Customers Benefit from Brand Relationships

As part of customer retention, some MC messages should be designed to remind customers of the benefits of maintaining relationships with companies. These reminders also provide customers with counterarguments to use against other companies wanting them to switch. The following are some of the major ways customers benefit by having a relationship with a brand or company. They are summarized in Table 2–3.

1. *Less risk.* Knowing a company often reduces the inherent risk of making a purchase. For example, a business customer of a machine manufacturer

TABLE 2-3   Benefits of Brand Relationships to Customers

1. Less risk
2. Fewer decisions
3. Fewer switching costs
4. Greater buying efficiency
5. Increased association

knows the delivery time for replacement parts. A different company may not be able to match that delivery time, which could result in a production line being out of service during the unexpected wait.

2. *Fewer decisions.* Shopping around requires time and effort. Having a relationship with one or two brands simplifies choice since the customer is familiar with the companies' offerings and doesn't have to waste time collecting and analyzing brand information for each purchase.

3. *Fewer switching costs.* Staying with a brand eliminates switching costs. Although switching brands of candy bars or hair spray is not a major undertaking, finding and beginning to do business with a new hairdresser, a bank, or stockbroker can require a lot of time. In business product categories, changing raw material suppliers or buying production equipment from a different manufacturer often requires weeks and months of evaluating proposals. In some cases, such as computer hardware and software, changing brands may involve significant ramifications, forcing a customer to make a number of changes.

4. *Greater buying efficiency.* In companies practicing IMC, customers become known to the company. The results are personal recognition and working efficiency, something that must be re-created and earned in a new company. When a customer is recognized by a company, transactions happen quickly and smoothly—no credit checks necessary, no verification of name, address, phone numbers, and so on.

5. *Increased association.* The longer customers have been using a brand, the easier it is for them to "claim" it for their own. If the brand is a well-respected one, the customer can share in its aura. As will be explained more in Chapter 5, consumers (and sometimes businesses) buy certain brands because they feel those brands help explain who they are—they *associate* with something the brand represents. Wearing a Calvin Klein blouse or Abercrombie T-shirt may say to others that you are a "with-it" person who is both casual and classy.

A FINAL NOTE: IMC BUILDS THE RELATIONSHIPS THAT BUILD BRANDS

One of the most important reasons for using IMC is to build trust in a brand. The St. Paul Insurance company tries to convey its trustworthiness in its brand messages (see Exhibit 2–14). Trust is the best way to create the brand relationships that make successful brands. These relationships, however, must provide added value for customers, as well as the brand, or else expectations will be set but not met.

Is there someone who understands how

frightening a situation can be? Someone who

believes fear can be dismantled when we are

armed with confidence? Is there an insurance

company that is consistently rated superior by

independent rating services — a company with

a 146 year history of providing strength in the

face of uncertainty? Without Question.

Trust *is not being afraid even if you're vulnerable.*

Without Question. **The St Paul**
Property and Liability Insurance

EXHIBIT 2-14

Trust is at the heart of any brand relationship. This brand message about insurance does a good job of illustrating trust.

Remember, a brand is nothing more than a special relationship. And communication is what drives relationships.

How a company makes its goods or performs its primary services is no longer the number one factor in establishing a brand's value. The new priority is communication—how a company controls or influences the communication dimensions of everything it does, and how it manages the exchange of information between it and its customers and other stakeholders. The net result of this brand communication is what greatly affects the quantity and quality of brand relationships, not only with customers but with all stakeholders.

Key Terms

generic products 43
brand equity 46
brand loyalty 47
brand position 48
brand image 49
logo 51
trademark 52

brand extension 53
multi-tier branding 53
ingredient branding 55
share of wallet 68
heavy users 68
Pareto rule 68
lifetime customer value (LTCV) 71

Key Point Summary

This chapter is focused on the notion that a brand is a special relationship and that brand value is determined by a brand's stakeholder relationships.

Key Point 1: More Than a Product

The value of a brand is a product of the support of its stakeholders. This support is measured by the financial community in terms of brand equity, which represents the goodwill accrued to a brand by its brand relationships. Brand equity reflects the cognitive and emotional aspect of business, that is, the "human" side, and it is driven by communication.

Key Point 2: Brand-Building Steps

(1) Select a name and symbol to represent the company or product; (2) create awareness/brand identity of name and symbol; (3) position the brand to differentiate it from competing brands; (4) create a brand image to help further differentiate the brand and to make it easier to recognize and recall; and (5) create trust in the minds of customers, prospects, and other stakeholders about the brand through maintaining consistency and delivering on expectations.

Key Point 3: Brand Strategies

In addition to the identification elements (brand names and symbols), branding strategies include brand extensions, multi-tier branding, co-branding, ingredient branding, and brand licensing.

Key Point 4: Brand Relationships and Brand Value

Brand relationships are created from all the interactions and transactions a customer and other stakeholders have with the brand. Brand relationships are the net sum of stakeholder support that creates value for the brand.

Key Point 5: Anatomy of Profitable Brand Relationships

Brand relationships can be analyzed in terms of trust, intensity, expectation gaps, and loyalty. Maintaining and growing the business of current customers is more cost-efficient than acquiring new ones. Profitable relationships have benefits for both the brand and the customer or stakeholder.

Lessons Learned

Key Point 1: More Than a Product

a. What is a brand, and why is it more than just a product?
b. Explain how brands work to transform products.
c. Explain how brands work to create expectations.
d. Define brand equity and explain how it relates to brand relationships.
e. What is the difference between the tangible and the intangible components of brand equity? Why is the intangible side becoming a more important factor in estimating brand equity?
f. Analyze your brand relationships: Are there any brands that you buy consistently? Are there any product categories where you choose from a set of brands, any one of which is acceptable? Are there any product categories where you have no preference whatsoever about the brand? What's the difference among these three types of categories?

Key Point 2: Brand-Building Steps

a. List and explain the brand-building steps. How do they separate between acquiring and maintaining customers?
b. What is a brand position?
c. What is a brand image?
d. In choosing a brand name, what's the difference between using a benefit description strategy and an association strategy?
e. What is a trademark, and what is its role in a brand identity program?

Key Point 3: Brand Strategies

a. Why are brand extensions used, and what do they contribute to a brand from an IMC perspective?
b. How are multi-tier, co-branding, and ingredient branding different from one another?
c. What is the key problem brand licensing creates for IMC programs?

Key Point 4: Brand Relationships and Brand Value

a. List and describe the various stakeholder groups.
b. Why are employees considered to be a key stakeholder group?
c. Tell how the support of each stakeholder group affects brand equity.
d. If you were responsible for a chain of fast-food restaurants, what relationship policies would you establish for your employees? What suggestions would you make to better motivate the employees and increase the positive aspect of this contact point with customers?

Key Point 5: Anatomy of Profitable Brand Relationships

b. Why is trust the primary construct in a brand relationship?
c. What's the problem with manipulating a customer into buying something?
d. Explain the five levels of relationship intensity.
e. What needs to happen to turn stakeholders into brand advocates?
f. Explain why a totally brand-loyal customer is a rarity.
g. Explain the concept of share of wallet.
h. Is it more expensive to make a first sale or a repeat sale? Why?
i. Explain lifetime customer value (LTCV).

Chapter Challenge

Writing Assignment

You have invented a new type of lightweight folding bicycle that is easy to carry and store. Review this chapter and summarize all the important branding strategies that you will need to consider as you market this bike. What relationships will you need to develop? What tips about relationship management will you want to remember as you launch your new product? Prepare a memo to your instructor summarizing your ideas.

Presentation Assignment

Develop a presentation for a local bicycle store owner explaining this new product and how you intend to support its marketing with a relationship-building program. Develop an outline of the key points you want to present. Give the presentation to your class or record it on a videotape (audiotape is also an option) to turn in to your instructor, along with the outline.

Internet Assignment

Visit the Amazon.com and Barnesandnoble.com websites. Analyze how the two brands are presented on their sites. Is there a strong sense of brand identity? What relationship-building techniques do they use with their customers? Write a report on dot-com branding based on what you have learned from these two companies.

Case Assignment

What stores do you frequent that use loyalty cards similar to the Boots Advantage Card? Pick one and interview the store manager to determine the strategy behind the design and use of the card. How could the store make this card a more effective relationship-building tool?

Additional Readings

Aaker, David. *Building Strong Brands*. New York: The Free Press, 1996.
Arnold, David. *The Handbook of Brand Management*. Reading, MA: Addison-Wesley, 1992.
Jones, John Philip. *What's in a Name? Advertising and the Concept of Brands*. Lexington, MA: Lexington Books, 1986.
Keller, Kevin Lane. *Strategic Brand Management*. Upper Saddle River, NJ: Prentice-Hall, 1998.
McKenna, Regis. *Relationship Marketing*. Reading, MA: Addison-Wesley, 1991.
Upshaw, Lynn B. *Building Brand Identity*. New York: John Wiley & Sons, 1995.

Research Assignment

From your reading of these books and other books and articles on branding and relationship marketing, develop a set of interview questions that you would use to diagnose the state of your favorite brand's customer relationships.

Endnotes

[1] David A. Aaker, *Managing Brand Equity: Capitalizing on the Value of a Brand Name* (New York: Free Press, 1991), pp. 164–66

[2] Peter H. Farquhar, "Managing Brand Equity," *Journal of Advertising Research*, August–September 1990, p. RC-7.

[3] Jean-Noël Kapferer, *Strategic Brand Management: New Approaches to Creating and Evaluating Brand Equity* (New York: Free Press, 1994), p. 16.

[4] Floyd Norris, "According to the Q Ratio, The End Is Near," *International Herald Tribune*, May 29, 1996, p. 19.

[5] Raymond Perrier, ed., *Brand Valuation*, (London: Premier Books, 1989), p. 20.

[6] Tom Duncan and Sandra Moriarty, *Driving Brand Value: Using Integrated Marketing to Manage Profitable Stakeholder Relationships* (New York: McGraw-Hill, 1997), p. 16.

[7] Aaker, *Managing Brand Equity*, p. 39.

[8] Giep Franzen and Freek Holzhauer, *Brands: Signs, Names and Brands* (Amsterdam: BBDO Europe, 1989), p. 39.

[9] Kevin Keller, *Strategic Brand Management* (Upper Saddle River, NJ: Prentice-Hall, 1998), p. 138.

[10] Kathryn Kranhold, "Agencies Beefing Up on Brand Research," *The Wall Street Journal*, March 9, 2000, p. B14.

[11] Jim Collins, "Built to Flip," *Fast Company*, March 2000, pp. 131–43.

[12] Frederick Webster, "The Changing Role of Marketing in the Corporation," *Journal of Marketing*, October 1992, pp. 1–17.

[13] Rahul Jacob, "Why Some Customers Are More Equal Than Others," *Fortune*, September 19, 1994, pp. 215–24.

[14]Ronald Henkoff, "Service Is Everybody's Business," *Fortune*, June 27, 1994, p. 52.

[15]Kathy Boccella, "Study: Grocery Employees Steal More Than Customers Do," *Denver Post*, March 27, 1994, p. 71.

[16]Alex Taylor III, "Auto Supplier with an Attitude," *Fortune*, September 5, 1994, p. 60.

[17]Paul Argenti, *Corporate Communications* (Burr Ridge, IL: Richard D. Irwin, 1994), p. 58.

[18]John Kotter and James Haskett, *Corporate Culture and Performance* (New York: Free Press, 1992).

[19]Quoted in Peter Jordan, "Zero Defections," *Enterprise*, 1995, p. 29.

[20]Deborah Salmond, "Refining the Concept of Trust in Business-to-Business Relationship Theory, Research & Management," in *Relationship Marketing: Theory, Methods and Applications*, ed. Jagdish Sheth and Atul Parvatiyar, (Atlanta, GA: Emory Univerity, 1994), p. 2.

[21]Susan Fournier, Susan Dobscha, and David Mick, "Preventing the Premature Death of Relationship Marketing," *Harvard Business Review*, January–Feburary 1998, p. 44.

[22]Ibid.

[23]Arthur Middleton Hughes, "The Real Truth About Supermarkets—and Customers," *DM News*, October 3, 1994, p. 40.

[24]"The Last Frontier for Consistent, Predictable, and Profitable Growth," a presentation made by the Cargill Consulting Group at DCI's Field & Sales Force Automation Conference, Boston, Massachusetts, September 10, 1996.

[25]Jock Bickert, "A Look As We Leap into the Mid-1990's: Databases, Brand, and Common Realities," a presentation at the National Direct Marketing Institute for Professors, sponsored by the DMED, San Francisco, California, March 20, 1996.

[26]Fredrick Reichheld, *The Loyalty Effect*, (Boston: Harvard Business School Press, 1996), p. 36.

[27]Garth Hallberg, *All Customers Are Not Created Equal: The Differential Marketing Strategy for Brand Loyalty and Profits* (New York: John Wiley & Sons, 1995), p. 50.

3

IMC Partners and Cross-Functional Organization

Key Points in This Chapter

1. Who are the key players in the marketing communication world?

2. How is marketing communication managed on the corporate side?

3. How do the different types of agencies perform their services?

4. Why are media important partners in marketing communication?

Chapter Perspective

Organization Is the Foundation of IMC

Integration is an organizational challenge. This is because there are so many partners involved in managing brand relationships. The basic partners that work with companies to market their brands are media companies, distribution channels, and marketing communication agencies. A rigid structure of departmental silos—each working in its own world—is one of the major barriers most companies face when trying to do IMC.

A company can't build relationships externally until it builds them internally. The coordination of brand messages being created and delivered by all the departments in a company, its agencies, and the media is extremely difficult. That's why doing IMC often involves organizational restructuring. It is also why IMC is more widely and successfully practiced in smaller companies. Nevertheless, larger companies recognize the value of IMC and are working to be more focused through better internal integration.

During the time when the IMC concept and process were evolving, companies were busy reengineering and applying the principles of total quality management (TQM) to production, inventory control, distribution and accounting procedures. A fundamental principle of TQM is "unity of effort." One of the basic steps in TQM is breaking down barriers between departments. Along the same lines, reengineering creates integrated systems and processes to reduce red tape and redundant procedures. Although TQM and reengineering experts seldom talk about marketing or integrated marketing communications, they do say that the only way a cross-functional program can work efficiently is to look beyond functional departments to processes.

This chapter will discuss the major players who need to be integrated as partners in brand relationship building. Most often when people talk about marketing communication agencies and the media, it is in terms of how they help companies promote their brands. What is often overlooked is that agencies are companies, too, in business to make a profit just like their clients.

THE AGENCY OF THE CONSUMER
Salles/DMB&B, Sao Paulo, Brazil

A few years ago Salles/DMB&B, a Brazilian marketing communication agency, was hard hit by the loss of a prestigious, top-billing client. The impact of this loss caused the agency to restructure itself and take advantage of its international partner, DMB&B. This case will discuss how an agency positions itself relative to its clients' business needs. Salles undertook a review of its thinking, positioning, and operations, which led to a new business philosophy and organization. After becoming totally customer-relationship-oriented, the agency was labeled as Brazil's Agency of the Consumer (see Exhibit 3–1). The agency's house campaign (its promotional campaign for itself) won a gold medallion in the international Advertising and Marketing Effectiveness award program.

The Marketing Challenge

The Salles/DMB&B campaign was a response to radical changes taking place in the Brazilian communications market, which also reflected the sweeping changes taking place worldwide. With marketers rethinking their strategies in global terms, agencies had to rethink their strategies and operations to meet the challenge of global clients. Also, the Brazilian consumer was becoming increasingly knowledgeable and demanding—a sharp contrast with the consumer who had for years bought products in a protected market without questioning quality, price, or service. This new consumer, as never before, was becoming the deciding factor in every company's success. And the marketing communication agency that understood

EXHIBIT 3-1

A scene from the agency's promotional video in which its president explains the agency's new organization.

this—and fully focused its activities on the makeup and behavior of the emerging Brazilian consumer—would be a powerful force for its clients' marketing effectiveness (see Exhibit 3–2).

Salles/DMB&B had Brazilian market know-how born of 32 years successful operation. The agency wanted to focus its new communication philosophy on techniques that would effectively contribute to client success and adapt the proven research and strategic planning techniques developed by its international partner, DMB&B.

Campaign Objectives

The marketing objectives were to attract prospective clients and assure existing clients that Salles/DMB&B's domestic and worldwide market understanding would contribute to clients' success. The agency's message objective was to demonstrate the critical importance of understanding how consumers bond with a brand—that is, create a brand relationship—and establish Salles/DMB&B's expertise in reaching this new Brazilian consumer.

Targeting/Segmenting the Audience

The primary target audience for the Salles/DMB&B house campaign was top and middle management of domestic and multinational companies and other organizations involved in marketing communications in Brazil. This included CEOs, marketing directors and managers, product managers, financial officers, advertising directors and managers, research institutes, and the media.

Word of mouth is an important influence in decision making at this level and can come from myriad sources, many of which are unexpected. This campaign was aimed at reaching any person who could influence or make a decision about the choice of a marketing communication partner.

Communication Strategies

The marketing communication strategies used by Salles/DMB&B were designed to demonstrate the agency's new understanding of the consumer, which it maintained through extensive consumer research. To that end, its brand messages were designed to reposition itself by communicating the following:

- The importance of brand equity.
- How a consumer's relationship with the brand is created.
- Why it is important to understand and view the world through consumer eyes and to use tools and resources that enable this effort.

For the key target audience of executives, Salles used a direct, light tone to make it clear that the information presented was unvarnished fact, an approach that is more meaningful than fanciful language. The agency invested heavily in staff training and technology to galvanize its staff in this new direction.

EXHIBIT 3-2

Constant interaction with consumers, such as in this focus group, helps an agency understand how customers think and behave in the marketplace.

Message Delivery

A variety of nontraditional media were used to deliver the agency's messages to its tightly targeted business audience:

- *Direct mail:* A booklet containing the full message—from the meaning of consumption to Salles/DMB&B's role in creating consumer bonding with a product or service—was sent to key personnel at existing client and prospective client offices.
- *Print ads:* Business newspaper sections and magazines were chosen based on media research showing readership by the target audience.
- *Posters:* Specially designed posters were used in the agency, at associated agencies, at seminars, and other appropriate events.
- *Stickers:* Agency personnel, associated agencies, students, and suppliers made use of stickers where opportunities arose.
- *Nonbroadcast video:* A video describing the business philosophy was shown in new business presentations. The video used testimonials to show that consumers now have a much better understanding of their role in a free market economy and how they create relationships with products.

Campaign Effectiveness

The results so impressed potential clients that the agency won 23 new accounts over the next two years. Not only did billings and profits increase, but just as important, Salles was soon recognized as an agency that had the ability to react swiftly and transform crisis into opportunity. Since the reorganization, it has won awards from international shows such as the Cannes Advertising Festival, the Clio Advertising Festival, the Ibero-Americana Festival, the Marketing Awards for Excellence (MAX awards), and a number of Brazilian award shows.

An intangible result was a new spirited staff morale, which emerged forcefully during the transformation. Personal and professional benefits and the satisfaction received from investment in personnel upgrading, together with investments in technology and other staff support resources, fostered this response. The agency staff spirit and performance made the Agency of the Consumer a thriving reality and contributed significantly to establishing and strengthening Salles/DMB&B's new image and concept.

This case was adapted with permission from the Advertising and Marketing Effectiveness (AME) award-winning brief for the agency self-promotion prepared by the Salles/DMB&B agency in Sao Paulo, Brazil.

OVERVIEW OF THE MARKETING COMMUNICATION BUSINESS

The basic players in today's marketplace are the organization (whether profit or nonprofit), the media, and agencies. They are dependent on one another for their survival in a modern world. This basic "golden triangle" is depicted in Figure 3–1. In customer-centric marketing communication programs, customers are at the center of the planning. That was why Salles/DMB&B adopted the customer-focused philosophy as its business philosophy. Such an orientation helps agencies serve their clients better by supporting the relationship between the agency's clients and their customers.

The organization in the golden triangle can exist only if there are media to deliver its brand messages and customers to buy its goods or services. Both manufacturers and retailers rely on agencies to provide specialized marketing communication skills (unless they have those specialized skills in-house). The media can exist only if they sell enough advertising. And they can sell advertising only if they have a significant number of readers, listeners, or viewers. Customers, who are also the media's listeners and viewers, must have knowledge of the products they need and want.

But as companies get bigger, distribute their goods or services in more geographical areas, and work harder to compete with other companies, this basic golden triangle becomes more complex because the number of marketing partners significantly increases (see Figure 3–2).

The more companies spend on marketing communications, the more they are likely to use MC agencies. Backing up the work of MC agencies are production specialists such as film producers, freelance artists and photographers, typesetters, and

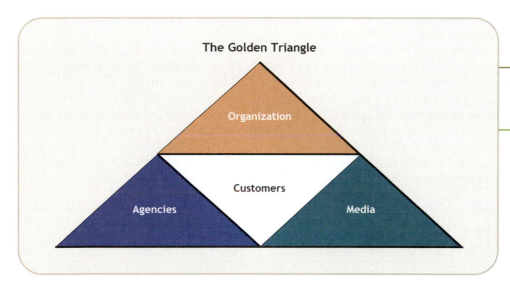

FIGURE 3-1

The Golden Triangle

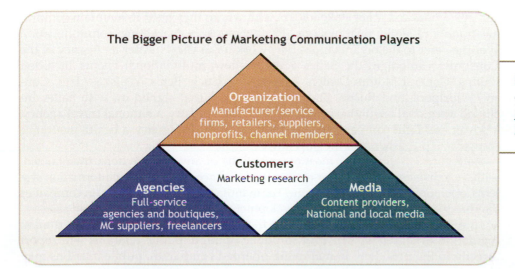

FIGURE 3-2

The Bigger Picture of Marketing Communication Players

printers. Media companies are greatly dependent on outside sources of content. For example, a newspaper's reporting staff produces only about 15 percent of a newspaper's total content; the remainder comes from advertisers, business (in the form of press releases), the community (schedules of events and letters-to-the-editor), news syndicates, and features syndicates (which provide such items as comics and crossword puzzles). The need for content is why NBC is willing to pay the National Collegiate Athletic Association billions of dollars for a multiyear contract to carry its basketball and football games. The TV networks know if they televise NCAA games, they will have millions of viewers. These millions of viewers then become a valuable asset they can "sell" to advertising agencies in order to carry their clients' messages. In this complex business situation, where there are many participants in creating, sending, and receiving brand messages, the need for integration should be obvious.

The Industry/Product Category

Every business operates within an industry or product category such as air travel, pharmaceuticals, high technology, fast food, or agribusiness. This means that marketing communication managers, whether they work for the company or an outside agency, must become experts in the industry or product category in which their company or client competes.

At the same time, those in marketing communication also have their own category or industry group. There are a variety of professional functions represented in marketing communication such as personal sales, advertising, direct marketing, sales promotion, and public relations. Each one of these MC areas is represented by an association that provides educational services and information to its members. The Public Relations Society of America (PRSA), for example, is made up of people who work in public relations. Part IV of this book goes into detail about each of the major marketing communication functions. This chapter examines how companies, agencies, and media are organized and relate to each other.

THE CORPORATE SIDE

All organizations, whether for profit or not for profit, have something to promote, and customers and other stakeholders with whom they need to maintain communications and build relationships. Professionals in marketing communication agencies refer to the organizations they work for as *clients*. After its Agency of the Consumer campaign, the Salles agency's new multinational clients included Philips, General Motors Dealers Association, Uncle Ben's, Whiskas/Trill, Consul/Whirlpool, and Roche. Brazilian companies that signed on with Salles included a regional telephone company, the labor ministry, a national travel agency, a power and light company, the São Paulo city tourist agency, a health insurance company, a publisher, and the post office.

As Figure 3–3 illustrates, most organizations of any size are departmentalized, with such divisions as human resources, legal, finance, management information systems, operations (in service companies) or manufacturing/production (in companies that produce goods), research and development (R&D), and marketing and sales.

In some companies, especially those that are highly controlled by government regulation or extremely sensitive to public opinion, public relations will report directly to the president. In marketing-oriented companies, public relations may

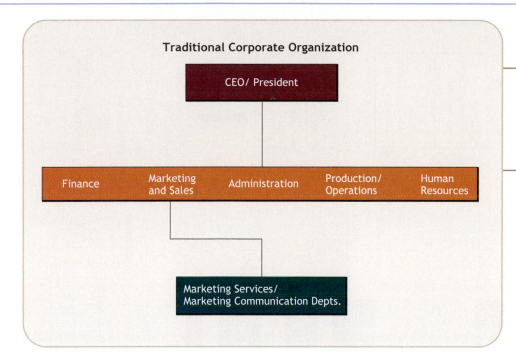

Traditional Corporate Organization

CEO/ President

| Finance | Marketing and Sales | Administration | Production/ Operations | Human Resources |

Marketing Services/ Marketing Communication Depts.

FIGURE 3-3

Generally speaking, the larger the company, the more complex the organization becomes.

be part of the marketing division or department. In some organizations one aspect of public relations—brand publicity—will be under marketing and the remaining public relations functions will be a stand-alone department.

The organizational chart in Figure 3–4 represents the way just one area—corporate communication—is organized at Nissan North America. Orchestrating the activities of all these corporate functions with brand relationship activities can be a major problem if the company is complex and the departments work in isolation.

Departments are usually organized according to functions or jobs. For example, the work of accountants is usually organized into an accounting department. Divisions are generally organized by product, market, or geography. Larger than departments, divisions sometimes resemble separate business units. Oldsmobile and Saturn are divisions within General Motors.

A typical corporate organization uses a top-down chain of command (such as that shown in Figure 3–4). Less hierarchical organizations use project-based teams that include representatives from the relevant areas, as depicted in Figure 3–5.

The more departments and divisions there are within a company, the harder it is to coordinate not only marketing objectives and strategies but all the brand messages that are being produced. Jack Welch, longtime CEO of General Electric, believes strongly in a "boundaryless" organization.[1] He says there's nothing worse in business than having departments. Why? Because the people in different departments don't talk to each other.

A product line, such as the various products that Procter & Gamble markets under the brand-name Ivory, may be considered a business unit. A **strategic business unit (SBU)** is *a product-, brand-, or market-based division that operates as a profit center within the company.* General Electric, for example, has 13 SBUs, including Aircraft Engines, Appliances, Lighting, and Medical Systems. Each of these units has its

" You have to make open behavior something that is rewarded. Finding an idea, sharing it, spreading it becomes rewarded behavior. Boundarylessness says that every time you meet somebody, you're looking for a better and newer and bigger idea. You are open to ideas from anywhere."

Jack Welch, longtime CEO of General Electric

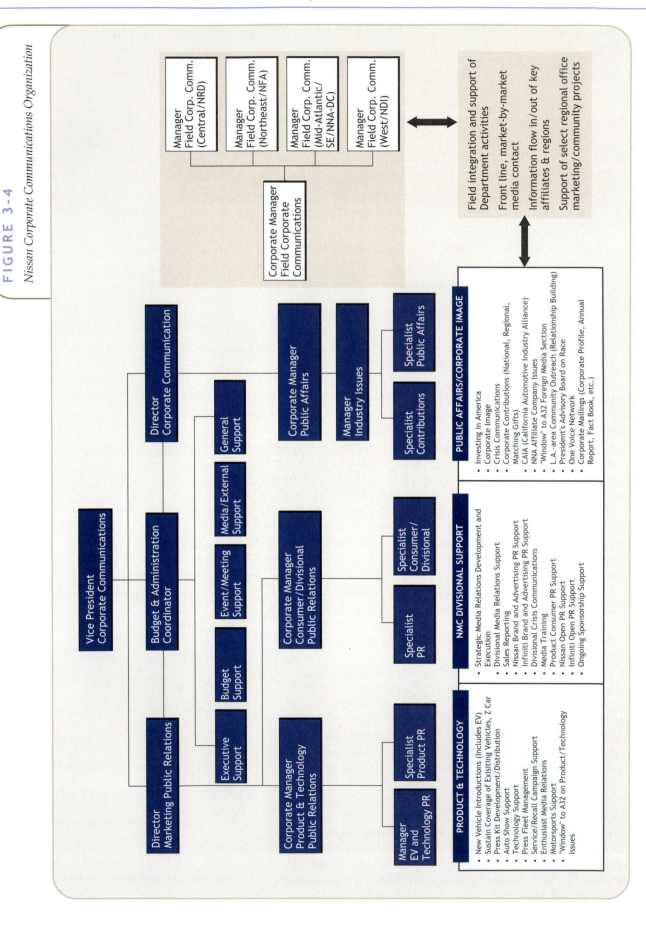

FIGURE 3-4
Nissan Corporate Communications Organization

own budget, objectives, and marketing strategies. A small business or start-up company, in contrast, operates as a whole—one unit.

Roles and Positions

Divisions and SBUs may be large enough to be managed by a president and have their own marketing departments. Whether for a division, an SBU, or a total company, when there is a marketing budget there is generally a director of marketing who often operates at the level of a vice president. In larger companies, where there are multiple brands or a brand with many product offerings, individuals are assigned to manage each brand or a certain group of products. *Those who manage a brand or product line* are called **brand managers** or **product managers** and report to the director of marketing. The scope of brand/product managers varies by company. In some companies they have responsibility for all business efforts relating to their particular product line or brand including the brand's profit and loss, as well as its budget and marketing efforts. In other companies, they advise on the development of a product, its pricing, and its distribution, but they don't have final say. In nearly all cases, however, brand/product managers are responsible for their brand's marketing communications.

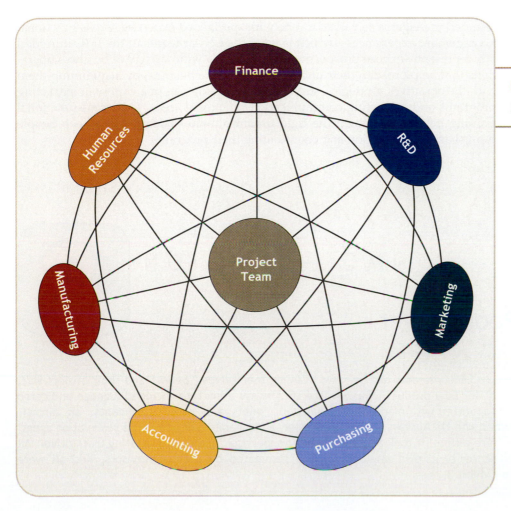

FIGURE 3-5

Project-Based Organization

In most cases, a company's sales force does not report to a brand manager but rather to a vice president of sales (or sales and marketing). In many companies, especially business-to-business companies, marketing is seen as support for the sales force. Frequently there is tension between sales and marketing. Marketing generally has a longer perspective, desiring to do things to build the brand. Sales, on the other hand, is more interested in generating transactions in the short term. Companies using IMC recognize the benefit of both short- and long-term needs of companies. This has resulted in changing how sales forces are compensated. Rather than paying sales representatives on commission only (that is, basing their pay only on a percentage of what they sell), increasingly companies pay sales representatives for extending the life of customer relationships and expanding the share of business for current customers. At the same time, marketing and marketing communication managers have been pushed into proving that they can increase sales (as well as build long-term brand relationships).

Larger companies often have a separate department to handle the marketing communication responsibilities. *The department that specializes in managing the marketing communication functional areas* is known as **marketing services** and is a support function for the brand managers. Such a department coordinates the work of internal communication specialists and external communication agencies. An exception is found in the case of brands with large advertising budgets, where the advertising agency generally reports to the brand manager and director of marketing rather than to the marketing services department. In these cases marketing services is responsible for all the other marketing communication functions.

As marketing executives move into top management, companies require that they have experience in many facets of the brand and company—that is, a well-rounded manager is as valued as one with specialized expertise. Cross-functional management experiences—which is what the US Air teams in the IMC in Action box represent—expose prospective managers to a wide variety of business operations that help broaden their understanding of the business by acquainting them with the objectives, strategies, strengths, and weaknesses of a variety of marketing programs and marketing communication functional areas. This cross-functional training helps break down the rigid organizational structures that keep people from sharing information and coordinating their programs.

IMC IN ACTION

Harnessing Peon Power

Companies generally depend on their research and development (R&D) department for new product ideas. Ideally this development is supported with marketing and consumer research. When the US Airways Group decided to start a new low-fare airline, it took an unusual approach: it enlisted scores of its own employees to do the planning (see Exhibit 3-3).

Calling themselves "peons" and their project US2, the US Airways think tank included luggage and cargo handlers, pilots and cabin attendants, an aircraft cleaner, a mechanic, a dispatcher, a reservation agent, a ramp supervisor, and even a catering truck driver. All were nominated by their supervisors, and all were proud of their role. One said, "We may be peons, but we're proud peons."

The unusual experiment in worker involvement in new product development made sense because US Airways' top management realized that each front-line employee knew his or her own little corner of the company and that if you could get a group of them talking together, you could find out all the ideas needed to make a great airline. Even though none of the self-proclaimed peons had any experience in starting a new business, they all had expertise in their own functional areas. Furthermore, the airline realized that because front-line employees were also the company's most important communication contact points, their involvement and buy-in would strengthen the delivery of positive brand messages.

Trying to protect US Airways from Southwest Airlines and AirTran, which were making inroads into the eastern markets, the US2 teams spent four months determining the best way to launch the new service. They priced peanuts, conducted focus groups, and argued over everything from the speed of the plane to luggage compartments, pillows, and ads.

US Airways' president, Rakesh Gangwal, and chairman Stephen Wolf used cross-functional management teams in undertakings such as this because they believe employee involvement brings fresh thinking and helps workers cope with change. Not only that, they get a lot of new ideas, including promotional ideas, from the people who know the business the best.

Organizational charts in most companies identify departments as well as chains of command and lines of communication. Hard boundaries create departments called *silos* (after the narrow, airtight storage structures built for animal feed or nuclear missiles) and, chances are, there won't be much communication between departments. There may even be "turf wars" as departments fight for budget and resources.

However, to undertake innovative programs that need shared information and communication, companies such as US Airways found ways to break through departmental walls. The important insight here is that a wide variety of people from all kinds of departments and outside firms have found information that needs to be captured and shared in making critical strategic decisions that will keep a company competitive.

Think About It

What is a corporate silo, and what organizational problems does it create? How did US Airways overcome the silo problem in its US2 product development?

Source: Adapted from Susan Carey, "US Air 'Peon' Team Pilots Start-Up of Low-Fare Airline," *The Wall Street Journal*, March 24, 1998, p. B1.

EXHIBIT 3-3

Involving employees at all levels was a critical part of creating this subsidiary of US Airways.

With more than 4,500 daily flights, the complex operations of US Airways are supported by countless examples of teamwork. From the everyday routine of loading baggage, greeting passengers and performing safety checks to large-scale projects such as integrating the new A330 widebody aircraft into our fleet—we work with the knowledge that we can accomplish extraordinary things through teamwork.

Captain John A. Williams Charlotte, NC and Michael L. Medina, II Mechanic, Charlotte, NC

As mentioned above, the brand publicity function may or may not be part of marketing or marketing services. When it is, those performing that function may still report to the director of public relations. Because public relations has by definition developed skills for building relationships, it is becoming a critical function in companies that are committed to building stronger and longer brand relationships.

Cross-Functional Planning and Management

As explained in the beginning of this chapter, integration is an organizational challenge. Turf wars in many companies make it difficult to plan and monitor comprehensive communication programs. Such wars break out when MC managers want to run their own show and start to fight for a greater portion of the MC budget. On the surface this may sound very self-serving (and sometimes it is), but it is often the result of managers' genuine beliefs in the power of their respective functional areas. Also, in most companies, the larger a manager's staff and budget, the larger the salary.

Cross-functional planning is *planning that involves multiple departments and functions.* A principle of IMC is that critical processes that affect customer relationships involve more than one department. Departmental silos should not be allowed to get in the way of creating and retaining customers. The benefit of the cross-functional IMC team is to ensure consistency in all brand messages, to see that the big creative idea is integrated in all messages, and to coordinate the timing and scheduling of the various MC programs. It is also a place where budgets are reallocated when necessary to address problems or take advantage of opportunities. Figure 3–6 illustrates the difference between a traditional silo organization and an IMC organization with cross-functional linking.

Cross-functional planning does not and should not mean "management by committee" or "management by consensus." The cross-functional team should have an executive head who is responsible for making sure plans are made and executed, and timetables are met. The primary purposes of cross-functional planning are to improve internal communication and to make sure programs are not redundant or

FIGURE 3-6

Silos

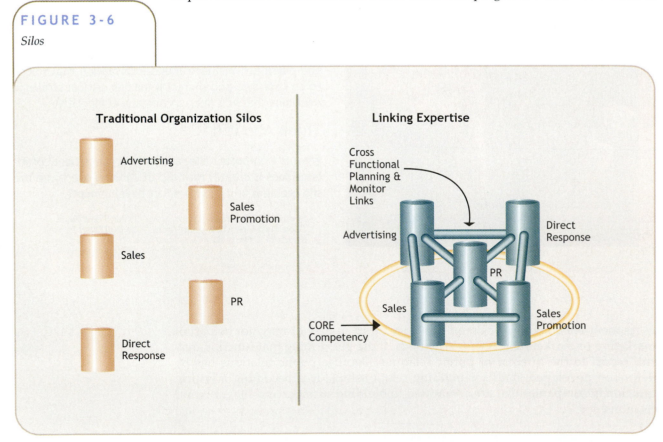

| Traditional Organization Silos | Linking Expertise |

in some other way at cross-purposes with each other. If people in different departments disagree about strategies, the cross-functional team, under the director of a marketing or other executive, should resolve the differences.

An example of the benefits of being internally integrated and using a cross-functional approach to planning comes from Hallmark Cards, Inc. The company significantly decreased its time-to-market by integrating its organizational structure for developing and introducing a new line of cards. According to a Hallmark executive, after setting up a cross-functional team, the company was able to develop a new line of cards in nearly half the time it took before:

> We grouped people together who had been separated by disciplines, departments, floors, and even buildings to cut down on the queue time, spur creativity, and end the throw-it-over-the-wall-it's-their-problem attitude. This [integrated team approach] worked so well that half of the line hit the stores . . . eight months ahead of schedule . . . We think the team worked because by bringing a group of people together like that, they got focused and [had] direct communication linkages.[2]

Reckitt Benekiser, a maker of cleaning products, uses cross-functional teams that include representatives from marketing, sales, trade marketing, and financial management. The company extends the cross-functional team concept by creating partnership "teams" of representatives of retailers. The result of these internal and external partner teams has been double-digit sales increases in each of the company's product categories.[3]

Cross-functional planning also helps employees become less myopic, which is one of the first steps in improving the relationship-building process. When people in an organization know and care about only their own positions and departments, they have little concern or sense of responsibility for the organization's collective results, as the Met Life experience demonstrates (see the Tale of Two Companies box). Such isolation is epitomized in the often-heard employee comment "It's not my problem!"

Cross-functional planning is not a new idea. In Peter Drucker's 1954 classic text, *The Practice of Management*, General Electric was cited as an example of a company that recognized the need for integrated thinking and a process for delivering synergy. According to an excerpt from GE's 1952 annual report, the firm's new (at that time) approach to operations was to introduce (i.e., integrate) marketing at the beginning rather than the end of the production cycle: "Thus marketing, through its studies and research, would establish for the engineer, the designer and the manufacturing person what customers want in a given product, what price they are willing to pay, and where and when it will be wanted."[4]

Unfortunately, however, many companies have been slow to develop the systems and organizational structures needed to effectively plan across functions. As Prensky, McCarty, and Lucas have concluded about integrated marketing, "at present marketing organizations are behind in developing the content of communication programs and the process of coordinating such programs."[5] Consulting companies and software manufacturers, however, are moving into this gap (see Exhibit 3–4).

Another reason for having a breadth of communication expertise represented on a cross-functional MC team is that it's a good way to generate new ideas. In consumer packaged goods, for example, it has been assumed that advertising was responsible for campaign ideas and that all the other MC functions were to merely follow advertising's lead. Now, however, many professionals in these "supporting" functions have developed their expertise to the point where they can go head-to-head with advertising when it comes to producing creative ideas. Every marketing communication agency—whether marketing public relations, sales promotion, direct response, or packaging—has case histories of successful programs they initiated, which is why they should all be represented on the cross-functional IMC team.

A TALE OF TWO COMPANIES

Cross-Functional Planning at Met Life and General Electric

Although cross-functional planning alone does not guarantee integration, the lack of it almost always guarantees *dis*integration. Metropolitan Life Insurance Company (MetLife), the second largest insurance company in the United States, offers a good example of what can happen when a cross-functional team is not in place and one department is allowed to operate unilaterally. Because MetLife agents were allowed to use questionable sales practices, promising more than they could, over 40 states levied fines, totaling $20 million, against the company. MetLife also faced the issue of making refunds of up to $75 million. Following public disclosure of all these problems, MetLife sales decreased by 25 percent. Finally, because of all the lawsuits and legal problems, the company's credit rating was reduced. (Its relationship with the financial community had also been damaged.)

According to a MetLife spokesperson, the company failed to enforce stated policies for sales messages. The MetLife auditors "would give a warning, lawyers would go down there [to Florida, where much of the trouble was centered] and say 'This has to stop,' but there wasn't follow-through." The internal pressure for sales performance drowned out the wiser voices. If a cross-functional management team had been in place, perhaps the voices of those concerned with the long-term impact on brand relationships and reputation would have been heard. Regardless of who was to blame, it was a marketing communication nightmare both internally and externally for MetLife.

In contrast, General Electric's Jack Welch created a forum dubbed "Pit" where, every two weeks or so, visiting GE employees gather to spot problems and argue for solutions. Pit sessions are held in the main auditorium of GE's Management Development Institute in Crotonville, New York. The pugnacious CEO challenges his staff to look for a fight when problems are spotted. He says, "The group has to get together and fix the problem. . . . You've got to take the responsibility to take the ball and run with it." He empowers them to intervene in the system in order to fix the problem. From his experience with the Pit, Welch has created a new organizational structure for GE called "Work-Out." The approach is to organize the GE workforce into flexible, natural teams that meet frequently to discuss how to improve processes. The objective is more efficiency, less waste and Welch's challenge is to "take work out of work," hence the phrase Work-*Out*.

The secret to GE's innovative management approach is communication. Welch's creations are not do-nothing corporate meetings but open, candid discussions—even arguments. Cross-functional teams with the authority to investigate various work processes come up with recommendations that managers must address on the spot and then fix. Such an approach not only opens up innovation but also protects a company against the kinds of problems that befell MetLife.

Think About It

What was the reason for MetLife's problems? What can you learn from GE's approach to management that applies to a marketing communication program?

Source: Adapted from Mark Suchecki, "Integrated Marketing: Making It Pay," *Direct*, October 1993, pp. 43–49; Weld Royal, "Scapegoat," *Sales & Marketing Management*, January 1995, p. 62; Judy Quinn, "What a Work-Out," *Performance*, November 1994, pp. 60–63; Marshall Loeb, "Jack Welch Lets Fly on Budgets, Bonuses, and Buddy Boards," *Fortune*, May 29, 1995, pp. 145–46.

Cross-Functional IMC Teams

Successful team management is an art, and an art that's very important in the IMC environment. For example, the IMC agency The Phelps Group has pioneered the use of self-managed, cross-functional teams in marketing communication agencies.

START REPLACING WALLS WITH WORDS.

It's time to remodel. And the Apple® Internet Server Solution is one of the fastest, easiest ways to transform your company. By dramatically improving communications. By unlocking hidden information. By knocking down a few walls.

With it, you can easily turn your network into an Intranet — an information warehouse where people can find answers to just about any question, and share results with just about anybody.

Now, virtually any document — from internal phone books to requisition forms to invoices — can be converted to electronic form and quickly updated. So people can more accurately and easily manage their work flow.

The Apple Internet Server Solution makes it easy for people to find new ways to communicate. Easy to support Windows and UNIX® Easy to grow. And, since security is built in, easy to prevent break-ins.

All the software that people need to set up, author and maintain their web page is included as well. Software available only for Macintosh® Like Adobe™ PageMill,™ which makes creating a web page as simple as creating a word processing page. No complex languages to learn. No editors or browsers to juggle.

To find out more, visit us at the web address below. And discover a whole new way to reengineer your business.

Apple Premium Server Reseller

Apple Premium Server Resellers are available to help you determine which solutions are best for your business.

EXHIBIT 3-4

Recognizing the growing demand for ways to eliminate organizational silos and facilitate cross-functional planning, this Apple BtB ad offers software that promises to dramatically improve organizational communications.

The unusual thing about these teams is that they are directly responsible to the client rather than to the agency's top management. The agency's culture is nonhierarchical. Instead of having managers who oversee the work of the group, the team itself provides its own leadership. The approach works because of the agency's effort at creating a corporate culture that values freedom, responsibility, and trust.[6]

Some basic IMC principles to managing cross-functional teams are as follows:

- *Long-term focus:* Keep team members in place for an extended period rather than assembling them for ad hoc projects. It takes time to develop team expertise and learn how to resolve group conflicts. By re-forming cross-functional teams on a task basis, the group is always in the learning curve of group dynamics, taking unnecessary amounts of time to test and learn to trust each other rather than focusing on customer relationships.

- *Constant contact:* Frequent meetings are important; however, if intranets or internal e-mail systems are available, members can keep in constant contact and minimize the number of face-to-face meetings.

- *Work space:* Assigning a cross-functional team its own work space helps keep team members informed. When General Motors integrated its corporate communication program, it established a "war room" where team members could meet, post project schedules, and track progress.

- *Support from the top:* Top management must support the idea of cross-functional planning by providing the necessary support systems, such as flexible budgeting, information sharing, compensation, rewards for teamwork and relationship building, and continuous monitoring of customer and other stakeholder perceptions.

- *Compensation:* In an integrated, cross-functional program, people should be rewarded not just for sales but for relationship-building activities and for activities that eliminate turf battles. Most compensation systems are based on performance—people are rewarded according to what they do for, or bring in to, the company. Increases in sales, brand share, or brand awareness are all important, but so are efforts that help build long-term profitable relationships.

AGENCY PARTNERS

Generally speaking, the larger the marketing communication budget, the more marketing communication agencies a company will hire. In most cases, these agencies provide specialized MC services the company can't or doesn't want to provide itself. There are dozens of different types of MC specialist agencies. Table 3–1 lists some of the agencies that make up Diversified Advertising Services, a division of Omnicom (a global marketing communication conglomerate discussed later in the chapter). Note that the list does not include BBDO, DDB, and Chiat-Day, three major advertising agencies also owned by Omnicom.

> "We are no longer simply purveyors and providers of advertising. That's only part of what's required. Stick with that exclusively and we will deserve to be dismissed as 'suppliers.'"
>
> Philip Geier, Jr., CEO of Interpublic

Although there are many different types of MC specialist agencies, the most common are those that specialize in advertising, public relations, direct marketing, sales promotion, and packaging/corporate identity. Because most agencies specialize in just one MC function, it is up to the client, in most cases, to ensure that the brand communication is integrated. According to Philip Geier, Jr., CEO of The Interpublic Group of Companies, more and more ad agencies and other specialized agencies are recognizing the power of IMC and are taking steps to being more IMC focused.[7]

Most MC agencies have between 20 and 40 clients (also called accounts). In most cases, an agency will handle only one company in a particular product category—no two competitors. This policy is intended to eliminate a conflict of interest in how the agency handles an account.

T A B L E   3 - 1   Some of the MC Agencies in Omnicom's Organization

MC Function	Agency*	Services Provided
Analytics and decision sciences	InforWorks	Customer profiling and segmentation, customer evaluation enhancement, predictive modeling
Branding and identity consulting	Interbrand	Brand strategy, naming, corporate identity programs, brand valuation
Consumer/corporate advertising	Merkley, Newman Harty	Advertising, strategic planning
Contract publishing	Premier Magazines	Creation and publication of customer magazines for promotional and loyalty-building purposes
Financial BtB advertising	Doremus	Financial advertising, financial printing
Design and image consultancy	The Designory	Graphics, collateral, package design, environmental design
Direct marketing	Rapp Collins	Creative and strategic planning for direct-response marketing, database creation and management, fulfillment, website design
Direct-response TV	SCP Directory Advertising	Strategic planning, response tracking, media management
Directory/Yellow Page advertising	Ketchum Directory Advertising	Market research, creative services
Event marketing	Kaleidoscope	Product launch events, trade shows, lecture bureau, field sampling, sports marketing
Field marketing	CPM International	Merchandising, personal selling
Graphic arts	RC Communications	Desktop publishing, color separations, photo labs, retouching, slide presentations
Health care	Targis Healthcare	Medical/pharmaceutical advertising and public relations
Information technology	Quantum Plus	Marketing process redesign, database development, decision support tools
Integrated communications	Focus Agency	Advertising, direct marketing, database modeling, forecasted sales results
Media planning/buying	Creative Media	Media planning and buying, direct response, new media, interactive media
Merchandising, POP displays	Schutz International	Design and manufacture of permanent POP display systems
Multiethnic	The Rodd Group	IMC agency for reaching ethnic audiences
Organizational communication	Smythe Dorward Lambert	Internal communications, reputation management, management education and training
Public affairs	GPC Communications	Government relations, communications PR
Public relations	Porter Novelli	Marketing support, media relations, crisis and employee communication
Recruitment communications	Bernard Hodes	Recruitment advertising, employee communications, diversity programs

TABLE 3-1 Some of the MC Agencies in Omnicon's Organization *(continued)*

MC Function	Agency[*]	Services Provided
Sales promotion	Alcone Marketing	Kids' marketing, interactive marketing, premium fulfillment, entertainment marketing, trade marketing
Research	M/A/R/C	Market segmentation, sales forecasting, customer satisfaction tracking, customer value analysis
Retail marketing	Integer Group	Retail merchandising, field marketing, consumer and trade promotions
Sports and event marketing	Millsport	Sponsorships, event administration, travel/hospitality
Telemarketing	Optima Direct	Outbound and inbound telemarketing, database-driven direct marketing
Trademark law	Marforce Associates	Trademark clearance, registration, enforcement, licensing, graphic design
Trademark licensing	The Beanstalk Group	Licensing representation, licensed property acquisition, strategic licensing planning

[*]All of these companies are members of Omnicom's Diversified Advertising Services.

Many large corporations not only work with a variety of MC agencies but also, when the budget is extremely large, use two or more agencies within a discipline such as advertising. In these cases, these competing agencies handle different brands, product lines, or geographical regions. In integration-driven companies, however, the trend is to pare down the number of agencies in order to get more consistency in the work. For example, 3M, which formerly had a network of 34 agencies in 23 countries, consolidated its work at the agency Grey Worldwide. IBM consolidated its $500 million global account at Ogilvy & Mather Worldwide, dropping about 50 other agencies.

Types of Agency Services

Although every agency is organized differently, there are some commonalities among them, such as whether they provide a full range of services to clients or specialize in certain types of work. The single largest number and type of MC agencies, especially when it comes to MC dollars handled, are advertising agencies. For this reason, much of the following discussion is about advertising agencies.

Full-Service Agencies

The phrase **full-service agency** is used to refer to *an agency that provides all or most of the services needed in its area of specialization.* In advertising, the full-service agency provides research services, creative development of brand messages, media planning and buying, and account management (which involves strategic planning). The Salles/DMB&B agency is considered a full-service agency in the Brazilian market. Full-service agencies do not actually make final print and broadcast ads, but rather they design them and then oversee their production by other specialists outside the agency. Increasingly, full-service agencies, especially midsized ones, have specialists in other marketing communication areas such as public relations, direct response, and sales promotion. Likewise, a direct-response or sales promotion agency, may on occasion create and place ads.

Interestingly, the very large full-service ad agencies such as J. Walter Thompson, Bates, Grey, and Young & Rubicam may not be as capable of providing a variety of marketing communication functions as the small and midsized full-service agencies, which for years have handled a variety of functions—sales promotion, direct response, and public relations—for clients. The ad in Exhibit 3–5 is for the Poppe Tyson full-service ad agency, which is trying to differentiate itself by telling prospective clients that it has extensive experience in the new and interactive media.

SO NOW EVERY AD AGENCY IN THE WORLD IS TRYING TO LOOK ELECTRONIC.

Online. Interactive. Multimedia. Whatever you call it, ad agencies are falling all over themselves to get into it. Setting up special departments. Changing their business cards. And treating the whole category as a new and unusual medium. Because it is new and unusual for them.

But for Poppe Tyson, it's already a proven part of our clients' communications portfolios. Clients like Hewlett Packard, Intel, Netscape, Penton Publishing, and Silicon Graphics. They're enjoying the benefits of technological sophistication in the hands of real marketing people.

Poppe Tyson has been a leading technology advertising agency for more than a decade. And we've constantly embraced the products we promote. So, long ago—when electronic media emerged as a viable communications tool—we integrated it into our services. This expertise is a component of Bozell Worldwide—Poppe Tyson's global parent. So you can get effective and appropriate electronic work serving larger business goals. Without having to deal with novices or geeks.

If your plans call for electronics— or if you just want to find out how they can work for you—please contact us. We'll be pleased to show you what we're doing for others right now. It's a wealth of information you could find positively illuminating.

Please visit our website at www.poppe.com or contact Nicholas Buck the traditional way at 415.969.6800.

Welcome to the White House

Yes, it's America's House. And our volunteer work helped completely refurbish its electronic entryway.

ABOUT INTEL
intel.
We fill the electronic needs for some of the world's technology and marketing leaders.

POPPE TYSON

www.poppe.com

In advertising agencies (and other MC agencies) an **account manager** is *a supervisor who serves as a liaison between the client and the agency.* The account management function varies somewhat by type of MC agency but generally oversees the development of the message strategy and coordinates the work of all the other agency people working for a particular client.

Often this account structure is designed to match the client's organization. For example, in staffing up its Oldsmobile account, the promotion agency Frankel assigned account directors to work one-on-one with Olds's sales promotion managers. Under General Motors' brand management structure, six Frankel sales promotion managers are each assigned as point persons to work with one or two brand managers at Olds.[8]

The people working in creative services are responsible for creating ideas, writing and designing marketing communication materials, and supervising production. The creative side of advertising is made up of **copywriters,** *the people who have the task of developing the verbal brand message (the copy),* and **art directors,** *the people responsible for the nonverbal aspect of the brand message—the design—which determines the look and feel of the ad.* They frequently work as a team under the guidance of a **creative director,** *an agent who supervises the development of the creative idea and its execution.* **Producers** are *agents either on staff or hired to handle such major tasks as the filming of television commercials and special events films.* In public relations firms, however, creative writing may be done by the account staff.

A position that links the creative staff with the account manager in large ad agencies is the **traffic manager,** *an agency person who controls the flow of work through the approval and production process.* Traffic managers track progress of the various MC materials as they are being produced, keep the job on deadline, and engage suppliers when needed.

Larger agencies may also have a research department that uses a variety of quantitative and qualitative research tools to better understand consumers and identify the most appropriate audiences for the marketing communication messages. Research departments in ad agencies are also involved in testing the strength of various message ideas and evaluating finished work in terms of how well it meets its objectives.

An increasingly popular position in ad agencies, and some public relations agencies, is the **account planner,** *who specializes in gathering consumer insights and using them to develop message strategies and who can speak on the consumer's behalf in the development of message strategies.* An account planner is responsible for understanding the target audience (using a variety of quantitative and especially qualitative research) and being the customer advocate within the agency. It's this person's job to make sure creative ideas and brand-positioning strategies are responsive to customer wants and needs. The account planner is a relatively new position in many U.S. agencies but one that has been used in England for some time.

Because agencies are businesses, just the same as clients are, they have departments such as finance and accounting, human resources, and legal. Most mass media advertising agencies strive to have a 20 percent profit margin. This means that for every $5 an agency earns, after paying salaries and all other expenses, $1 is gross profit (before taxes).

Agency Networks

Because the MC industry has been steadily growing and is quite profitable, there have been many mergers and acquisitions, which have created large networks or conglomerates of MC agencies. The Salles agency in Brazil, for example, is a member of the DMB&B international family of agencies.

The largest of these networks are Interpublic, WPP, and Omnicom. Having multiple "sister" agencies within a conglomerate is one way to get around a conflict-of-interest problem. On the surface, it looks as if these large networks are in the best position to offer IMC. In most of these networks, however, each agency remains a separate profit center, which means they compete with each other. Efforts are being made by these conglomerates, however, to motivate their separate agencies to work closer together for common clients. Executives in Omnicom agencies, for example, can receive special stock options as a reward for bringing two or more "family" agencies together to work for one client in an integrated way.

Another type of agency network is a group of independent agencies that affiliate in order to share resources and offer services on an international level. Among the 30 or so such groups is the International Communications Agency Network (ICOM), which is 50 years old and comprised of 77 independent agencies in 50 countries. ICOM promises it can serve clients in multiple countries with the same services that are provided by the large international agencies.

Media Buying Services

As the name implies, **media buying services** are *agencies that specialize in buying time and space, that is, placing brand messages in the media.* In advertising, these firms first started to serve small and medium-sized companies and other ad agencies that realized they were paying a high price for media because they were buying in relatively small quantities.

Media buying services are popular in advertising because they buy large quantities of time and space across a variety of client accounts, thereby earning sizable discounts for clients. By buying for many different clients, media buying services can have at least the same buying clout with the media as the large full-service agencies. Media buying agencies generally work on a commission of 2 to 4 percent of the media dollars they manage. The idea of media placement is also important in public relations, where there are companies that specialize in distributing publicity materials to the media.

In recent years large full-service agencies have spun off their media departments into freestanding media buying services. An example is Zenith Media Worldwide, which grew out of the merger of Bates and Saatchi & Saatchi (and still exists even though Bates and Saatchi & Saatchi have since split up). The result is that one agency does the creative work and another agency handles the media placement of that work.

How Agencies Specialize

Many companies hire MC agencies that specialize in an industry or product category. The ad in Exhibit 3–6 for the public relations firm Cone is a good example of how some MC agencies offer certain areas of expertise.

When producers of consumer goods and services hire an advertising agency they generally choose one that specializes in advertising to consumers such as J. Walter Thompson, Bates, BBDO, or Young & Rubicam. Likewise, pharmaceutical companies will often hire a public relations firm that has a special expertise in health care and government relations since the health care industry is so specialized and subject to so many governmental regulations.

Other agencies specialize in such areas as sports, technology, health care, agribusiness, and financial products. CKS, for example, is a California-based IMC agency that focuses on the high-tech industry and uses a wide variety of marketing communication tools in the delivery of its services for its high-tech clients. The Porter Novelli public relations agency, however, is divided by broad industrial categories such as health care (working for health maintenance organizations, hospitals, medical, and pharmaceutical companies); food practices (working for manufacturers of food products); and consumer products (nonfood goods and services).

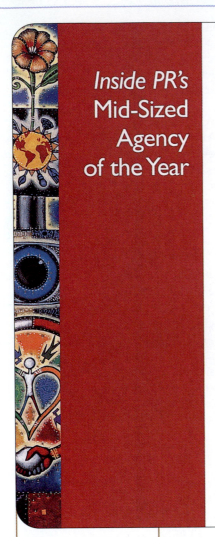

EXHIBIT 3-6

This BtB ad for Cone shows how the public relations agency has specialized in three communication areas, including interactive marketing.

Most large advertising agencies specialize in handling only consumer accounts. However, medium and small agencies often handle both consumer and BtB accounts.

Business-to-Business Specialists

Business-to-Business specialists represent clients that market products and services to other companies, such as parts sold to automotive manufacturers and chips sold to computer manufacturers. Often the primary MC function used by BtB companies is personal selling and the budget for other marketing communication functions is small compared to many consumer brand programs. BtB specialist agencies produce and place messages directed to business decision makers within a certain industry rather than to a broad audience.

Most BtB marketing communication is done through publicity and advertising in trade magazines, trade shows and exhibits, sales brochures and catalogs, direct-mail pieces, and telemarketing. Internet usage is increasing, although it still accounts for a relatively small percentage of total BtB MC spending. Because most BtB target audiences are relatively small, television commercials are seldom part of the MC mix. The exceptions are very large companies such General Electric, Kraft, and Sony that sell to both consumers and businesses and can cost-justify doing corporate advertising and public relations that run in both trade and consumer broadcast and print media.

Ethnic Agencies

As the size of ethnic populations has increased in the United States, so has the number of MC agencies that focus on certain ethnic groups. The Los Angeles–based Muse Cordero Chen, for example, specializes in reaching Hispanic, African-American, and Asian consumers. Many of the large consumer product companies with multimillion-dollar budgets will allocate a certain portion to reach minority audiences. For example, McDonald's has used Burrell Advertising, which specializes in creating and placing advertising for African-American consumers.

High-Tech Agencies

A number of agencies have recently appeared in the newly emerging area of Web-based marketing and advertising. One of the first was US Web, which merged with

AUGUST 3, 1998

AdvertisingAge®

CRAIN'S INTERNATIONAL NEWSPAPER OF MARKETING $3.00, IN CANADA $3.50   IN 2 SECTIONS, SECTION 1   http://adage.com

Latenews

JWT wins $26 mil in Unilever ad work

[LONDON] Unilever has dropped Ogilvy & Mather Worldwide from its laundry cleaning products advertising roster outside North America. J. Walter Thompson Co. picked up the $26 million assignment. Unilever said the move was made to "derive increased benefits of focus and scale, and to maximize the value derived from current centers of expertise." O&M's international work in other Lever categories is unaffected. The international move, involving creative only, does not affect the U.S., where O&M continues to handle Surf.

SRI gains support for Smart TV viewer audit

[WESTFIELD, N.J.] Statistical Research Inc. has received letters of intent from the major broadcast networks and six major media shops saying they will support a national rollout of Smart, SRI's TV audience measurement system that is a potential competitor to

Beyond Advertising

Strategic shift: Large ad agencies adopting the total communications solution; at long last, some execs say

By Kate Fitzgerald

A philosophical shift is sinking in deep at some major ad agencies, now embracing a way of doing business that doesn't always involve advertising.

sult in better outcomes for our clients and more profits."

In many cases, the long-promoted concept results in low-cost, highly effective campaigns and strategies using event marketing, sponsorships, sales

CBS Corp. signs first multi-unit ad package

Pennzoil cross-media pact valued up to $25 million

By Chuck Ross

CBS Corp. has signed Pennzoil Products Co. to a sweeping pact worth as much as $25 million, the media company's first-ever deal across all its divisions: the CBS-TV network, its TNN cable network, the CBS-owned radio stations, the CBS-owned TV stations and the company's Transit Displays Inc. outdoor ad unit.   **Pennzoil is**

EXHIBIT 3-7

The late 1990s found a lot of interest in IMC among the larger advertising agencies as this front page story in Advertising Age *suggests.*

another high-tech agency to create USWeb/CKS and then combined with Whittman-Hart to form marchFIRST. Others include iXL and Zentropy Partners. All of these offer their clients website design as well as the development and placement of online advertising.

IMC Agencies

Many agencies are now trying to position themselves as experts in IMC. Major advertising agencies that have handled integrated campaigns for various clients include BBDO, DDB, Leo Burnett, Ogilvy & Mather, and Young & Rubicam. The large agencies, however, still emphasize their creative advertising work despite the front-page *Advertising Age* story shown in Exhibit 3–7. Truly integrated agencies are more commonly found among midsized agencies such as Cramer-Krasselt and Fallon. Several agencies, such as The Phelps Group and Price/McNabb, have reinvented themselves as IMC agencies. Others that promise their clients IMC capabilities are Trinity Creative Communications, Tucker-Knapp, InterOne Marketing Group, and the Gage Marketing Group.

In-House Agencies

Some companies feel they can save money and have more control over their marketing communication by doing much of the work themselves. To do this, they may either create a department, which is very common in public relations, or set up what is called an **in-house ad agency**, *a department within a company that is responsible for producing some or all of that company's marketing communications.* Depending on the type of business, an in-house agency may also do brand publicity, sales promotion, and direct marketing as well as advertising.

In-house agencies are used by only a small percentage of large marketers, who hope to better control costs, eliminate the expensive overhead of external agencies, and take advantage of commissions offered by local media. Companies that do not have a large enough budget to attract the interest of outside marketing communication agencies often do their own marketing communications, working with freelance copywriters, artists, and publicists.

In-house agencies are commonly found in the headquarters of grocery and drugstore chains that must create new ads every week under the pressure of media deadlines. Because price is such a motivator of retail business, these chains use in-house agencies so that they can keep price features confidential until the very last minute that ads must be delivered to the media. The retail in-house agency must work closely with the chain's buyers and store managers to provide promotions against tight deadlines and in line with quantities that have been purchased (so customers will not be disappointed when they come to the stores).

Marketers such as designer-clothing manufacturer Calvin Klein handle their own marketing communication in-house because they believe they can better control the creative effort and bind it more closely to the brand image. Also, some companies believe they can save money by doing the work in-house and not paying typical agency salaries.

Although there can be economies in having an in-house agency, there are also several shortcomings. First, in-house control is often won at the expense of creativity. Because the in-house agency people work on only one account—the company that owns them—they don't have the benefit of interacting with and learning from people working on other types of business. Second, working for an in-house agency, versus an independent agency, is often less attractive to creative professionals, particularly in advertising, which means the talent pool is diminished. Third, because it is buying only its own media space and time, an in-house agency doesn't have as much media bargaining power as an advertising agency that is buying media for dozens of companies; therefore media costs can often be high.

In-house employees can become so conditioned to the way the company has always communicated that it is difficult for them to be creative. When in-house agency people do have a creative idea that is really different, they may not fight for it because they only have one account. If they lose that account, they are out of a job. External agencies offer an outside view that, for any company willing to listen, can be very helpful in identifying opportunities and problems.

Public Relations Firms

Like advertising agencies, there are many different sizes and types of public relations firms. (Because public relations organizations were never "agents" for the media, as were advertising organizations, they are called *firms* rather than *agencies*.) For an up-to-date overview of the public relations industry, visit www.prcentral.com, which provides current stores regarding the public relations industry. This site also will give you access to articles in *Reputation Management*, a public relations industry magazine.

Some of the largest public relations firms that have offices worldwide are Shandwick International, Burson-Marsteller, and Hill and Knowlton. Publicity, as will be explained in more detail in Chapter 14, is just one of the many services that public relations firms provide. The overriding function of public relations firms is to counsel companies on how to better manage their relationships with all stakeholder groups. Often a public relations firm will specialize in a certain industry or divide up its firm into industry-specific groups (see Exhibit 3–8).

Unlike advertising agencies, most public relations firms do not have a creative or media department. (The closest service to a media department is media relations, which helps companies respond to media inquiries as well as place stories favorable to the firm's clients.) Accounts are handled by assistant account executives, account executives, and account supervisors. For accounts in which the primary objective is to generate positive brand publicity, the account group not only does strategic planning but also writes press releases, organizes media tours and special events, and so on. In other words, it plans and executes.

Because many public relations firms generate most of their revenue for doing brand publicity, they have begun to use more "marketing" language in promoting themselves, as demonstrated in the ad for the public relations firm Golin/Harris in Exhibit 3–9. When it comes to helping their clients build brands, one of the most valuable attributes a public relations firm can have is a good relationship with the media. Account executives and supervisors must know what types of stories the media are interested in and must be able to get the attention of the media whose audiences most closely resemble clients' target audiences.

EXHIBIT 3-8

The Rowland ad demonstrates how the agency helps its clients in the health care industry communicate with distributors, consumers, and "influentials" (thought leaders, regulators, and the media).

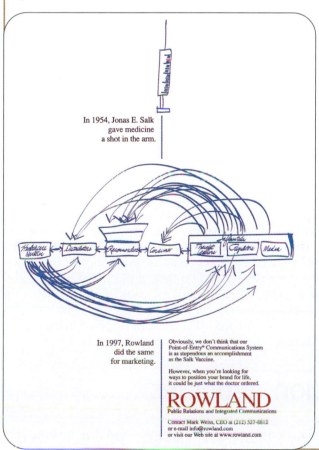

EXHIBIT 3-9

Although Golin/Harris is a public relations agency, its focus is on building brands. Note the firm's slogan used in this ad—"building trust worldwide."

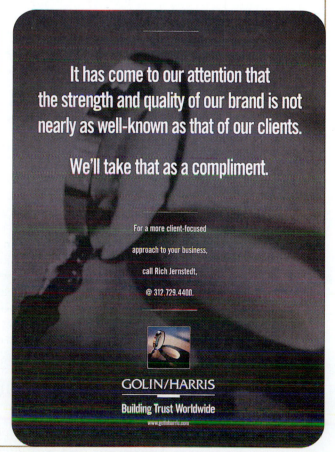

Direct-Response Agencies

Direct-response agencies are probably the closest in organization to advertising agencies. They have account executives and supervisors, creative departments, and media departments. The media departments are responsible for planning and buying media to carry direct-response offers. Unlike most advertising agencies' media departments, however, these deal not only with mass media but also with mail, e-mail, and telemarketing services. Direct-response agencies also have specialists who analyze and rent the databases used for doing mailings, telemarketing, and e-mailing. Primary outside support services for direct-response agencies include the following:

- *Data shops.* These agencies warehouse (i.e., store) databases, can combine several different databases and "de-dup" them (i.e., take out names that are on more than one list), code the various lists to indicate which lists produce the highest response rates, and compare lists to the national change of address (NCOA) lists in order to make address corrections.

- *List brokers.* These companies acquire customer lists that agencies then use for their clients; most lists handled by brokers are "response" lists, meaning they contain names of customers who have responded to other direct-response offers. The expertise of list brokers is determined by how well they are able to find lists that match the customer profile prepared by the direct-response agency.

- *Printers.* As the name suggests, printers actually produce the materials that will be sent out. Modern printers can customize brochures and letters using high-speed laser printers.

- *Letter shops.* After direct-mail materials have been printed, letter shops assemble the elements making up a mailing, stuff them into envelopes, and address the envelopes.

- *Creative services.* These agencies perform all the services of a creative department. They are used by small and medium-sized agencies that do not have enough work to have a creative department, and also by large agencies when the workload peaks.

Some of the major advertising agencies, such as Ogilvy & Mather and Grey, have set up direct-response services that operate as separate profit centers. As separate entities, they work not only for clients of their "mother" agencies but also for other clients. Examples of other direct-response agencies are Epsilon (which specializes in nonprofit work) and Carlson Marketing Group.

Companies that depend heavily on direct-response marketing, such as book and CD clubs, usually have an ongoing relationship with a direct-response agency. Companies that only occasionally include a direct-response promotion in their marketing programs may ask several agencies to bid on their project. The more strategic direct-response agencies recognize the benefit of coordinating marketing communication and will work closely with a client's other MC agencies to make sure the brand's positioning and major creative idea are both reflected in the direct-response offers. Chapter 16 discusses direct response in much greater detail.

Sales Promotion Agencies

Companies that do a lot of promotions—premium offers, sweepstakes, in-store special displays—use sales promotion and merchandising agencies. These are agencies made up of three groups: account service managers, creatives, and production people. The account managers do what all account managers do—serve as liaisons between the agency and clients. They also help come up with strategic ways of using promotions and merchandising programs (explained in more detail in Chapter 15).

As with direct-response agencies, sales promotion and merchandising agencies often work on a project basis. They are paid a flat fee determined by how much work is required to handle a project. Companies such as Burger King and PepsiCo that do a large number of promotions, or do them on a national scale, will have long-term relationships with several agencies. Some promotional agencies will also bring promotional and merchandising ideas to companies on a speculative basis, hoping that if a company likes the ideas they will get the assignment.

Other MC Agencies

Many different agencies offer specialized MC services. Each has its own type of organization and set of departments depending on the different skills needed. Corporate identity agencies such as Landor specialize in package design and identity programs for companies (see Exhibit 3–10). Landor built its reputation doing package designs. The more it dealt with package design, the more attention it found itself giving to brand names, the relationship of brands within a company, and overall branding strategies. Consequently, like many of its competitors, Landor has moved beyond being an agency composed of package and logo designers into one with strategic planners and brand strategists.

One of the fastest-growing types of specialist agencies is the online advertising agency. Although most advertising agencies say they can do online advertising, companies are finding that it takes a special expertise. As will be explained in Chapter 12, preparing and placing online advertising and leveraging the brand-building capabilities of the Internet requires more than knowing how to do banner ads. The top 12 online advertising agencies, based on billings, are listed in Table 3–2.

EXHIBIT 3-10

Landor is a leading package-design firm that has expanded its business services into brand consulting.

TABLE 3 - 2   Top 12 Online Advertising Agencies (as of June 2000)

Agency and City	Major Clients
1. MarchFIRST, Chicago	Williams-Sonoma, Boise Cascade, Apple, 3Com
2. Digitas, Boston	Amazon.com, American Express, AT&T, Dell
3. iXL Inc., Atlanta	Delta, Chase Manhattan, General Electric, WebMD
4. Grey Interactive, New York	Procter & Gamble, Liz Claiborne, Dell, AT&T, Autobytel
5. Sapient, Cambridge, Massachusetts	Adobe, Bank of America, 3Com, United, E*Trade
6. Modem Media, Norwalk, Connecticut	AT&T, Delta, IBM, J. C. Penney, Sony Entertainment
7. Aspen Interactive, St. Petersburg, Florida	Skyauction.com, New York State Lottery, Hewlett-Packard, Compaq
8. Ogilvy Interactive, New York	IBM, American Express, Ford, Jaguar, Kraft, Nestlé
9. Luminant, Dallas	AT&T, Harrods, IBM, M&M/Mars, MasterCard, Microsoft
10. AppNet, Bethesda, Maryland	Kellogg, Toshiba, U.S. Department of Health and Human Services
11. Euro RSCG Interaction, New York	Intel, Dior, Peugeot, Dell, Air France, Volvo, MCI
12. Organic, San Francisco	Avis, Barnes & Noble, Starbucks, British Telecom, Tommy Hilfiger

Source: *Forbes Critical Mass*, Fall 2000, p. 64.

MC Suppliers

MC suppliers are *the specialists who help MC agencies actually produce their work*. For example, ad agencies don't actually film commercials, take pictures, or do other final art treatments used in print ads, nor do they write music or record voices used in radio commercials. They hire suppliers who are professionals with specific types of expertise. These suppliers include people and companies involved in research, photography, illustrating, video production, printing, to name a few.

There are also companies that specialize in supplying premiums such as engraved ballpoint pens, caps, and mugs. There are mailing and fulfillment services for direct-marketing agencies, telemarketing call centers that are hired by direct-response agencies, and electronic commerce or interactive media consultants such as Web designers. In other words, there is a whole industry of support services that back up the agencies and firms that specialize in the primary MC functions. The following sections give brief descriptions of two such suppliers.

Creative Boutiques

A **creative boutique** is *an agency of creative specialists, usually writers and designers, who work for clients and other agencies in the development of the brand messages*. In essence, a boutique is the same as a creative department in a full-service ad agency. Likewise, there are agencies that focus only on brand, corporate, trade show, or package design, or print specialists who only work on designing brochures and other types of collateral materials such as sales literature.

Creative boutiques usually work on a project basis, turning over finished work to another agency for media placement. These boutiques are often started by creative people (e.g., a copywriter/art director team) who have worked for a full-service agency, done very well, and decided they want to be their own bosses.

Freelancers

Freelancers in marketing communications are *independent creative people who are self-employed and take on assignments for an agency or a marketer on a project-by-project* *basis.* Freelancers can be considered one-person "boutiques"; they specialize in copywriting, art direction, photography, or artwork. They normally work for small clients who can't afford an agency. They also do certain MC jobs that large agencies don't want to bother with, such as writing speeches.

Agency Approaches to IMC

The discussion of IMC and cross-functional management earlier in this chapter focused on the corporate side; however, organizational problems exist on the agency side as well. Typically, ad agencies assign creative, media, research, and client service people to work on a certain account. In many cases, however, these people also work on other accounts, which are seldom the same for all of them. In these cases, all of the media people may be in one area, all the creative in another, and all the account people in yet another. Although they have planning meetings, their primary allegiance is to their respective departments. Progressive agencies that recognize the value of IMC often have all members of a client team located together. Having greater physical proximity makes things run smoother and allows the work to be more integrated.

Integration problems occur, however, even with progressive agencies, when other MC functions are involved. Studies have determined that ad agencies, in particular, are reluctant to integrate other marketing communication agencies into any kind of cross-functional planning. According to one study, ad agencies "prefer to ignore the other communication channels or to operate independent firms under a corporate umbrella that offers full service but little integration."[9] But the integration problem is not restricted to advertising. Many nonadvertising agencies realize that they are always competing with ad agencies for budget allocations yet are often considered second-class MC players by both ad agencies and clients. There are even a few public relations academics who speak disparagingly of IMC as "marketing imperialism" and see it as a ploy for marketing and advertising to take over PR. Such an attitude is nonproductive and just the opposite of what IMC is all about.

Three typical ways agencies can organize themselves in order to offer integrated services are by adding on other MC functions, by reinventing themselves, and by operating as a lead agency with a team of supporting agencies.

Add-on Functions

With the add-on functions approach, an agency that specializes in one area (advertising, public relations, etc.) will add departments so that clients will not have to go elsewhere for specialized services. For example, FCB Worldwide several years ago added a sales promotion and a direct-response department to its full-service advertising agency.

Sometimes an agency will buy or partner with a specialist agency, although that can be problematic if there is no mandate to integrate the two at the strategic-planning level. Specialist departments can also be internally "grown." When Leo Burnett, for example, wanted to add direct-response services for its clients, it simply went out and hired people with direct-response experience.

Reinvention

Another approach requires an agency to start from scratch or to completely reorganize and reinvent itself. A good example of this approach is Price/McNabb, which was formerly a full-service advertising agency but reorganized to emphasize IMC and relationship marketing (see Table 3–3). Before the reorganization, each of the agency's MC functional groups was set up as a mini-agency within the overall agency. Each group was accountable for its own profit or loss. Consequently, groups competed with one another and often made recommendations that were more beneficial to a particular agency group than to the client. (The agencies that still use this type of organization, however, defend it by saying that the competition forces groups to perform better and that clients are smart enough to decide to what extent each MC function should be used.)

Figure 3–7 illustrates the Price/McNabb's organization after its reorganization. A key benefit of the new organization is the elimination of separate profit and loss centers. As Tom Eppes, president of Price/McNabb, explained, "The problem that affected us as separate profit centers was the same one that continues to affect major agencies: we focused on our individual areas and cared very little about the other areas."[10]

Because there are still companies that don't understand or are not ready to fully practice IMC, Price/McNabb has adjusted its organization to attract these clients. It allows new clients to "enter the agency door" by using the expertise of just one of its specialist teams (e.g., advertising, public relations, strategic planning, direct response). Once these clients are being served, they are encouraged to make use of a cross-functional retail or business-to-business team (depending on their type of business). This team then introduces the client to relationship-building philosophies and the benefits of practicing IMC. This practice also results in the agency getting more MC work from the client.

TABLE 3-3   Steps in Reinventing the Agency at Price/McNabb

The following are some of the specific changes the Price/McNabb agency made as it restructured itself to better deliver relationship-building programs for its clients:

- Wrote a focusing mission/vision statement that the agency lives by: "Our team mission is to set the standard for understanding and building relationships with the individual customer and prospects of our clients, and to use that knowledge to create communications that are recognized for extraordinary business results."

- Developed strategic alliances with other agencies specializing in product design, packaging, and sales promotion.

- Consolidated the profit and loss statements of its three regional offices so they wouldn't compete with each other.

- Eliminated incentive bonuses that were disincentive to IMC; they are no longer based on functional area performances.

- Eliminated media commissions and the standard 17.65 percent markup on nonmedia placement tasks.

- Designed office interiors to make employees more accessible to each other and dispersed specialists, such as PR people, around the agency.

- Developed its own proprietary step-by-step planning based on IMC theory.

Source: Tom Eppes, "Rebirth of an Agency: Challenges and Implications of Operating in an IMC Framework," *Journal of Integrated Communications* 9 (1998–99), pp. 28–38.

Lead Agency

Another IMC agency approach is to use an agency that coordinates the work of other MC agencies. Such an agency would operate in the same way primary care physicians handle their patients. When patients have medical problems that are beyond the expertise of the primary care doctor, he or she recommends the necessary specialists. The primary care physician stays in the loop, and, in terms of MC, continues to monitor the strategy as well as the consistency of the various treatments. This is the approach that BBDO has used in managing the Gillette account, which has involved sister companies Porter Novelli (public relations) and Rapp Collins Worldwide (direct marketing), along with several other specialist agencies.

Agency Compensation

There are several ways in which agencies are compensated: commissions, fees, retainers, and markups. The method of payment varies by type of MC agency and often by individual client, and is increasingly a mix of these various ways.

FIGURE 3-7

Price/McNabb organization after 1996

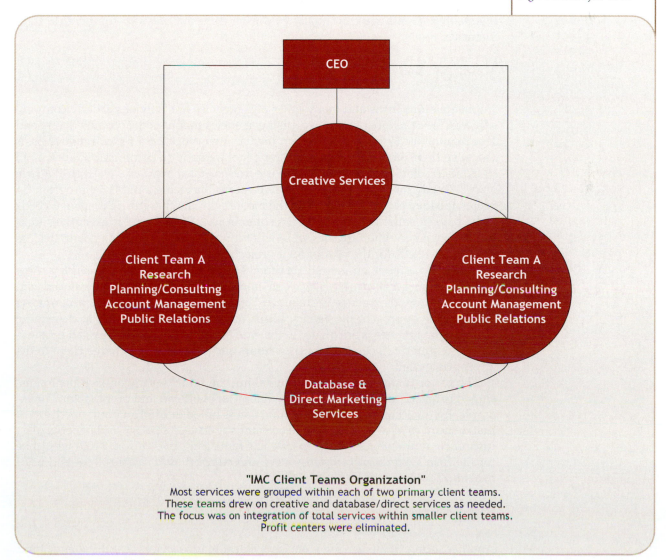

"IMC Client Teams Organization"
Most services were grouped within each of two primary client teams.
These teams drew on creative and database/direct services as needed.
The focus was on integration of total services within smaller client teams.
Profit centers were eliminated.

Commission

For years, most full-service ad agencies did all their work in return for a 15 percent **commission,** *a payment that represents a percentage of a client's total media spending.* For example, say a client spends $5 million a year on media. Over the course of the year, the agency would bill the client $5 million but pay only 85 percent of that amount ($4.25 million) to the media, keeping 15 percent, or $750,000 ($5,000,000 × 15% = $750,000). The commission system originated when agencies first began because their primary purpose was to act as sales representatives for the media. What the agencies soon found was that many companies didn't know how to create ads and thus were reluctant to buy advertising space. Seeing an opportunity to sell more space, the ad agencies began offering to do the ads for free for those companies that agreed to buy advertising space. The more space they sold, the more creative work they were willing to do for a client.

This system continued up until the 1980s, when media costs began increasing at a faster rate than inflation. This meant that clients were paying agencies more for the same amount of work. Under pressure for more profits, clients began to renegotiate contracts, forcing agency commissions down to between 8 and 12 percent, depending on the size of their media budgets. The larger the budget, the lower the percentage rate.

Not only has the traditional 15 percent commission been lowered for many clients, but clients are continually exploring different ways to compensate their agencies.

Fee or Retainer

Public relations firms and many other MC agencies are fully or partially compensated by fee or retainer. Also, advertising agencies that handle accounts that spend less than about $2 million a year on media often work on a fee or retainer basis (because their media spending doesn't generate enough commission, even at 15 percent, to cover agency costs). A **fee** is *a fixed payment based on standardized hourly charge.* To pay for all the time it takes to create and execute a publicity program (in which the idea is to place stories in the media without charge), a PR agency needs to be paid in some way other than a commission. Therefore, PR executives (and MC managers in other areas as well) will typically sit down with a client, discuss the client's needs for the year or for a project, and then set a monthly fee.

Similar to a fee is an annual **retainer.** This is *an arrangement in which a client contracts to work with an agency for a year or more and pay that agency a certain amount.* In other words, the agency is "retained" by the client to work on its account. As with the fee approach, the agency keeps track of employee hours to determine whether the retainer is adequate. In the case of public relations firms, all employees are required to keep track of their hours and expenses and charge them to the appropriate client.

The fee or retainer is estimated by taking the hourly wage of each person assigned to an account and multiplying that by an overhead and profit factor. For example, for an account supervisor's time that is billed at $150 an hour, one-third of that amount ($50) would go for the account supervisor's salary and benefits (e.g., insurance, retirement fund, bonuses). The remaining two-thirds ($100) would be for the firm's overhead (administrative and support staff salaries, rent and utilities) and profit.

Markups

Another source of income for agencies is marking up services that the agency buys for clients from another company. For example, when a direct-response agency designs a direct-mail piece, it has the printing, envelope addressing, and envelope stuffing done by outside companies that specialize in each of these areas. The printer and the letter shop (along with any other suppliers) will bill the direct-response agency for their services, and the agency will then mark up each bill by a certain percentage to cover the cost of administering the project. For example, if a printer charges $50,000, the agency may add a 20 percent markup (20% × $50,000 = $10,000) and send a bill to the client for $60,000. When the client pays the direct-response agency, the agency keeps $10,000 and sends the remaining $50,000 to the printer. Markups cover the cost of the agency dealing with these outside companies.

Performance-Based Compensation

As clients have focused more on accountability, advertising agencies in particular have seen an erosion of client budgets.[11] In response, some agencies and their clients have worked out a performance-based compensation plan. In most cases performance compensation is only a portion of the total amount a client pays (the remainder is commission and/or fee). Performance compensation is determined by the extent to which marketing communication objectives are achieved. For example, if campaign objectives are to (1) increase brand awareness by 10 percentage points, (2) increase trial by 25 percent among new users, and (3) generate 25,000 requests for additional information, the agency would be paid according to how many of these objectives were achieved within a set period of time. Bonus payments may be built in for results that exceed objectives.

The ideal arrangement, from a client's perspective, is to tie agency compensation directly to the company's sales and profits. This approach sounds better in theory than in practice, however, because there are so many variables, in addition to MC, that affect sales and profits, such as product performance, distribution, competitive activity, customer service, and effectiveness of the sales force. This is why most MC performance measures are based on awareness and other communication measures. In public relations, it is considered unethical to base compensation on factors that public relations firms cannot control, such as number of stories placed or sales.

In general, compensation is an area that is going through a great deal of change, and agency/client contracts are as individualized as the products they promote. A study by the Association of National Advertisers found that, as a percentage of the overall compensation to MC agencies, commission-based compensation declined from 61 percent in 1994 to 35 percent in 1997. At the same time, fee-based compensation approaches increased from 35 percent in 1994 to 53 percent in 1997.[12]

There is no longer only one set way to compensate agencies. As a president of a major ad agency said to this author, "The way we are compensated today varies by the number of clients we have. We have a different contract with each one because no two clients have the same needs or the same level of media spending." And one of the more innovative new approaches has come from e-commerce: agencies are being offered stock in dot-com companies in exchange for their professional MC services.[13]

Agency Evaluation

Companies should conduct periodic reviews of all agencies with which they have an ongoing relationship. This is done for the same reason companies evaluate employees, departments, and other suppliers. There are two basic types of agency evaluations. For agencies that are paid a fee (hourly or otherwise), a client can do a quantitative audit of an agency's records to determine that the hours and expenses for which the company has been billed are correct. The other type of evaluation is the qualitative survey, in which those employees who have frequent contact with an agency are asked to rate the agency on a variety of areas. Some of these areas are responsiveness, thoroughness, record of meeting deadlines, cooperativeness, level of initiative, source of new ideas, and creative abilities. Where budgets are quite large, a company sometimes conducts separate evaluations of the agency's creative department, media department, and account service area. The more money an agency handles for a company, regardless of the type of agency, the more critical periodic evaluations are.

Evaluations are beneficial for several reasons. Foremost, they help a company determine whether it is getting its money's worth. Unless the evaluation is based on performance measures, this is a subjective call and should reflect the thinking of not just one or two people. Second, most people like feedback. Real professionals even appreciate negative feedback, as long as it is constructive and objective, because they realize this will help them improve. Most agencies would rather be criticized and given a chance to improve their performance than to be simply fired. The primary purpose of agency evaluations should not be to determine whether the company should continue working with an agency (just as every employee evaluation is not about whether or not to fire that employee), but rather to determine how the agency and company can work better together.

Some companies, the more progressive ones, also ask their agencies to evaluate them. How are the company's people performing? Do they give clear directions? Are their critiques of the agency's work insightful, objective, and helpful? Are they competent? One of the most helpful questions a company can ask is how its MC people compare to those working for the agency's other clients.

MEDIA PARTNERS

Media partners provide *the vehicles through which marketing communication messages are carried to (and from) the target audiences.* Chapters 11, 12, and 13 discuss in more depth media characteristics and the planning and buying of media. This section introduces media companies, however, because they are an essential set of partners in doing IMC. Also, for many consumer and major BtB companies, the majority of MC dollars are spent on media.

There have been at least five recent changes in media, and in how media companies work with agencies and their clients. One is the new communication technologies such as wireless communications and high-speed Internet services. Another is an increase in media alternatives. With the exception of newspapers, most types of media such as magazines, cable TV, and radio have had a significant increase in the number of outlets (titles or stations). A new term is **place-based media,** which means *customer destinations where brand messages can be displayed.* There has been brand signage in public places such as sports arenas and transportation terminals for years, but these messages have gotten much more sophisticated and prolific. In addition, brand messages are now appearing in schools, in senior centers, on in-flight videos, and on gas pumps.

Third, media companies have recognized that they can add value to their delivery systems by providing potential advertisers not only more in-depth information about their respective audiences but also consumer research findings in general, such as spotting trends in certain product categories, showing what other media their audiences receive, and providing case histories of how their media have had certain effects on sales. Even local media are doing more consumer research to help attract more local advertising.

The fourth change came about as a result of the 1996 Telecommunications Act, which allows single ownership of competing media. This has resulted in larger media conglomerates. Disney's merger with the ABC TV network, for example, has resulted in a company that can provide marketers a wide range of media alternatives: radio stations, TV networks, cable channels, websites, sponsorships (Mighty Ducks hockey team), magazines, and movies (for product placements). In Europe, Bertelsmann is an example of a major media conglomerate. All of these media conglomerates say that the benefits for marketers include price and convenience in media buying. Unfortunately, these media bundles don't always match up to most companies' target audiences. Also, marketers and agencies have yet to see significant cost savings from buying these media packages.

Finally, because of media fragmentation (i.e., more media choices) and media ownership consolidation, media types and suppliers are trying harder than ever to establish their own identities.

As Jack Myers, the author of *Reconnecting with Customers* states in an article in *The Advertiser*: "The extent to which media companies can tie together program or editorial content, media buys and value-based promotions will dictate their value in the new media age."[14]

Most media (newspapers, magazines, radio, television, and outdoor, etc.) have their own national associations that promote their respective capabilities. The Magazine Publishers Association runs ads such as the one in Exhibit 3–11. The media promote themselves not only collectively but also individually such as *National Geographic* magazine is doing in Exhibit 3–12.

Nontraditional media include such innovative forms as painted buses, hot-air balloons, and signage in novel places such as on sidewalks and the sides of a building. New media are those that involve computers and telecommunication, such as the Internet (World Wide Web), intranets (networked communication systems within companies), extranets (networked communication systems that include external suppliers and agencies), pagers, and wireless devices.

An IMC program takes into consideration many ways of delivering messages besides advertising and media (whether traditional or nontraditional). These include employee communication, sales literature, package design, in-store merchandising materials, and customer service. These are all ways of not only delivering messages but, more important, responding to customers. Because IMC considers all points of contact to be opportunities for the exchange of brand messages, it redefines the word *media* as "message delivery systems." In other words, any company that delivers brand messages to (and from) customers and other stakeholders is in the media business.

Some companies represent the ultimate in integration because their product consists of both brand messages and media. The merger of Disney and ABC was mentioned above with regard to the merged company's role as a media provider. But Disney is also a marketer itself, and its merger has resulted in visual merchandising and mixture of special events together have made the Disney brand highly memorable (and profitable). Disney offers an example of what some call "closed-loop marketing"—it is a seamless company where the medium is the product as well as the

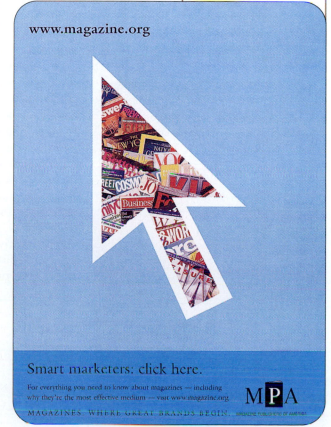

message. Disney characters are integrated into Disney movies, television programs, merchandise, and theme parks; any area in which children (and adults) come into contact with these characters may lead them to the other business areas. The Disney entertainment media empire now includes sports channels (including ESPN and ESPN2) and Internet services (with ABC Online, which is tied into America Online). Disney has also purchased the Web search engine Excite!, giving it a huge Web presence. Each entity reinforces the others but still offers something slightly different in the area of entertainment; such reinforcement creates synergy.

Another reason that IMC considers media part of the golden triangle (see again Figure 3–1) is because many media companies perform creative work for clients similar to that provided by agencies, especially at the local level. They help advertisers plan and create ads and other promotional materials. The most sophisticated media companies also sell other competing media because it generally takes a mix of media to maintain brand relationships. Meredith, a large magazine publisher, for example, can package a promotional effort for a client that includes advertising in its publications combined with supporting store promotions and direct-mail pieces.

A FINAL NOTE:
THE AGENCY/CLIENT RELATIONSHIP

EXHIBIT 3-12

National Geographic *promotes itself by demonstrating one of its primary benefits to an advertiser—engaging photographs.*

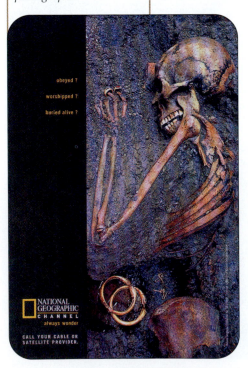

The extent to which a client trusts and respects the expertise of its MC agencies can significantly affect the quality of the agencies' work, not to mention the smoothness of the working relationship and the effectiveness of an IMC program. In good relationships (as in good relationship marketing), neither party is taken for granted.

What often determines the level of trust and respect is the client's attitude toward its agencies—does the client see the agency as a supplier or a partner? The answer is a major concern to agencies.

The agency/client relationship is critical to the successful functioning of an IMC program. IBM consolidated much of its global marketing communication activities with one agency, Ogilvy & Mather, believing that a centralized organization is the easiest path to achieving integration. At the same time, all of IBM's U.S. marketing communication disciplines were consolidated under a single management group, Marketing Services & Communications, which includes advertising, media relations, executive communications, direct marketing, trade shows, publications, employee communications, and more.

In an IMC program, the greater the distance between agency and client, and the more agencies involved, the harder it is to integrate programs. IBM's action is an important recognition of the need for a close and positive agency/client relationship.

Key Terms

strategic business unit (SBU) 85
brand managers (or product managers) 87
marketing services 88
cross-functional planning 90
full-service agency 96
account manager 98
copywriters 98
art directors 98
creative director 98
producer 98
traffic manager 98

account planner 98
media buying services 99
in-house ad agency 102
MC suppliers 106
creative boutique 106
freelancers 106
commission 110
fee 110
retainer 110
media partners 112
place-based media 112

Key Point Summary

Key Point 1: The Key Players

First are the marketers and the agencies who work for them; second are customers and other stakeholders; and third are the various media companies that sell time (broadcasting) and space (print media).

Key Point 2: Corporate Side

The corporate side, which represents marketers of all types, gives direction to the management of marketing communication. The cross-functional IMC team on the corporate side ensures consistency in all brand messages and coordinates the timing and scheduling of the various MC programs. It does this by linking specialized departments, making each one involved with brand relationships aware of what the others are doing, and making sure programs are not redundant, counterproductive, or in some other way at cross-purposes with each other.

Key Point 3: Agencies

Full-service agencies in the various areas of marketing communication provide a basic set of services, which can be supplemented by suppliers such as boutiques, freelancers, and media buying services. Agencies sometimes specialize by industry, and sometimes they are partners in networks of agencies. Compensation is usually through commission, fee or retainer, or markups. Performance-based compensation is becoming more prevalent. Agencies serve their clients in many different ways, which affects how they are staffed and compensated. The type of agency-client relationship also determines the degree to which agencies are able to support their clients with cross-functional planning. Agencies use several different organizational approaches—added functions, reinvention, and lead agency—to manage cross-functional planning.

Key Point 4: Media

Media partners are the channels through which marketing communication messages are delivered to (and from) target audiences. Recent media changes that have affected how media companies work with agencies and their clients include the development of new communication technologies, an increase in media alternatives, the provision of audience information, the legalization of single ownership of competing media, and attempts by media companies to establish their own identities.

Lessons Learned

Key Point 1: The Key Players

a. Diagram the marketing communication world and identify the key players. Explain the context within which they interact.
b. What is the relationship between customers and the other three key players?
c. Why did Salles/DMB&B adopt a customer-focused philosophy? How does it help cement the relationship between this agency and its clients?

Key Point 2: The Corporate Side

a. What are the common divisions within a company?
b. How can silos become a problem in traditional organizations?
c. Define cross-functional management.
d. Why is cross-functional management needed in integrated marketing communication programs?
e. Find an organizational chart for a company with which you are familiar. Analyze the structure of the company and explain how it organizes marketing and marketing communication functions.

Key Point 3: Agencies

a. What is a full-service agency, and how does it differ from a boutique?
b. What is an agency network, and what kind of services are included?
c. In what ways do agencies specialize?
d. What is an in-house agency, and in what situations is it used?
e. What kind of suppliers do agencies use? What services do they provide?
f. Explain the difference between commissions and fees.
g. Why are companies increasingly implementing performance-based compensation plans for MC agencies?
h. Of all the agency jobs described in the staffing discussion, which one most appeals to you? What skills and abilities do you have that might make this job a career for you?
i. Describe three ways agencies approach cross-functional management.

Key Point 4: Media

a. What are the five recent changes in the media world that affect the operation of MC programs?
b. What are place-based media, and how do they work?
c. Why should media consider themselves to be brands?

Chapter Challenge

Writing Assignment

Identify an MC agency about which you would like to know more. Look up the agency in the trade press (conduct an electronic search in your business school library), contact the agency's PR department for any brochures it might have produced, and look up the agency on the Web. Analyze the following:

1. What is the agency's area of business (i.e., its marketing communication specialty)?
2. How is it organized? What departments does it include? Is it part of a network?
3. What is its philosophy of business?

Presentation Assignment:

Partner with someone else in your class. Take turns conducting mock interviews for a job in an MC agency. Present your interviews to the class.

Internet Assignment:

Choose one of the agencies mentioned in this chapter and go to its website. From what you find on that site, develop a profile of the agency addressing the following points:

1. What is the agency's focus, specialty, or area of business? What services does it provide its clients?
2. What is the agency's philosophy of business?
3. How is the agency organized?

Additional Readings

Roddick, Anita. *Body and Soul: Profits with Principles—the Amazing Success Story of Anita Roddick and the Body Shop.* New York: Crown, 1991.

Scully, John. *Odyssey: Pepsi to Apple . . . A Journey of Adventure, Ideas, and the Future.* New York: Harper & Row, 1987.

Ziegler, Mel, Bill Rosenzweig, and Patricia Ziegler. *The Republic of Tea,* New York: Currency Doubleday, 1992.

Zyman, Sergio. *The End of Marketing As We Know It.* New York: HarperBusiness, 1999.

Research Assignment:

Consult these books and other books and articles in your library on the inner workings of business and marketing communication. What major marketing changes have affected the way these companies approach marketing communication?

Endnotes

[1] Marshall Loeb, "Jack Welch Lets Fly on Budgets, Bonuses, and Buddy Boards," *Fortune,* May 29, 1995, p. 145.

[2] Michael Hammer and James Champy, *Reengineering the Corporation* (New York: HarperCollins, 1993), p. 167.

[3] Wendy Marx, "The Co-Marketing Revolution," *Industry Week,* October 2, 1995, p. 77.

[4] As cited in Frederick E. Webster, *Market-Driven Management* (New York: John Wiley & Sons, 1994), p. 8, and quote from the 1992 GE annual report, p. 21.

[5] David Prensky, John A. McCarty, and James Lucas, "Integrated Marketing Communication: An Organizational Perspective," in *Integrated Communication: Synergy of Persuasive Voices,* ed. Esther Thorson and Jeri Moore (Mahwah, NJ: Lawrence Erlbaum, 1996) pp. 167-84.

[6] Joe Phelps, *Pyramids Are Tombs,* unpublished manuscript; Ed Chambliss, interview by author, February 2000.

[7] Philip Geier, Jr., "Beyond the New Horizon," *IAA Perspectives,* August 1999, p. 2.

[8] Betsy Spethmann, "Not Your Father's Oldsmobile," *Promo,* July 1997, p. 21.

[9] David Prensky, John A. McCarty, and James Lucas, "Vertical Integration and Advertising Agency Participation in Integrated Marketing Communications Programs," AMA Summer Marketing Educator's Conference, Washington, D.C., 1993.

[10] Tom Eppes, letter to author, February 24, 2000.

[11]Deborah Spake, Giles D'Souza, Tammy Crutchfield, and Robert Morgan, "Advertising Agency Compensation: An Agency Theory Explanation," *Journal of Advertising* 28, no. 3 (Fall 1999), pp. 53–72.

[12]Start Elliott, "Advertisers Shift Compensation Method," *New York Times,* June 11, 1998, p. D3.

[13]Suein L. Hwang, "Agencies Get Dot-Com Stock for Hot Spots," *The Wall Street Journal,* February 8, 2000, p. B1.

[14]Jack Myers, "Defining Media Brand Equity and Its Value for Measuring Advertising Effectiveness," *The Advertiser,* October–November 1999, p. 60.

Part Two

Strategic Foundations of IMC

Strategic planning in an IMC program demands an understanding of the communication process, as well as an understanding of how consumer attitudes and behaviors can be affected by persuasive messages. These topics are discussed in Chapters 4 and 5.

Once marketing communicators understand these basic concepts, they can design strategic IMC plans. IMC planning is the focus of Chapter 6. Chapter 7 looks at targeting and segmenting the audience, and Chapter 8 deals with designing data-driven strategies that address these audiences most effectively.

4

The Brand Communication Process

Key Points in This Chapter

1. How do the elements in a basic communication model relate to marketing communication?

2. What are the four types of brand messages?

3. How are media and brand contact points related?

4. How does noise affect marketing communication?

5. How can perception be more important than reality?

6. What is the difference between feedback and interactivity?

Chapter Perspective
A Gooey Interface

When we speak about a computer "interface," we mean the place where interaction occurs between a person and a computer. This interface—that is, the design of the way the computer interacts with users—is called a graphical user interface, or GUI (pronounced "gooey"). Nicholas Negroponte, director of the Massachusetts Institute of Technology's famed Media Lab, complains that most GUI designers focus on buttons, not users. He says that "interface is not just about the look and feel of a computer. It is about the creation of personality, the design of intelligence, and building machines that can recognize human expression."[1]

The same idea could be applied to companies. How easy is it for customers and other stakeholders to interact with a company? Is there a friendly interface? Negroponte recognizes that GUI is really about communication and that the best interface design is the one that comes closest to replicating the interaction between two people. Using this metaphor, marketing communication could be seen as the interface between customers and companies. The question is, How close does marketing communication come to replicating communication between two people?

The notion of GUI is also important because *gooey* means sticky and sweet. Since communication is the bond that holds relationships together, having a gooey interface means that the brand relationship is sticky; that is, there is loyalty between the brand and its customers. In order to analyze the role of sticky interfaces in marketing communication, this chapter first looks at how communication works and proceeds to analyze five steps in the brand communication process: creating the message, choosing the contact points (or media), minimizing noise, monitoring perceptions, and facilitating feedback.

LOVE AND ICE CREAM: THE HB CASE
McCann-Erickson, Dublin, Ireland

Marketing communication is about the messages companies send and receive and the media they use to send them. It's also about perceptions: every message you encounter about a brand contributes to your impression of that brand. In the late 1990s, HB Ice Cream, Ireland's number one ice-cream brand, decided it needed to change its stodgy brand perception. This is the story about how that message was communicated through every possible point of contact with the brand (see Exhibit 4–1).

With increasing competition facing its ice cream, HB's parent company, Unilever, decided to introduce a new brand identity for HB across Europe. McCann-Erickson Dublin was asked to develop a communication program capable of launching the new HB brand identity in Ireland. McCann's communication effort was so successful that not only did it achieve high awareness scores in a highly competitive product category, but it also was a winner in the Advertising and Marketing Effectiveness (AME) international award program.

The Marketing Challenge

Traditionally a poor relation on the fringe of Europe, the Republic of Ireland earned the tag "Celtic Tiger" through a sustained level of high economic growth during the 1990s. Unemployment rates, having remained stubbornly high for a long time, eased down toward the European average. Therefore, larger numbers of Irish young people (18–34 years old) are now opting to stay home rather than emigrate, creating the youngest population profile in Western Europe.

EXHIBIT 4-1

A Valentine's Day street fair was used to announce the new heart-shaped HB Ice Cream logo.

HB (whose initials come from the original founders, the Hughes Brothers) is *the* ice-cream brand in Ireland. Due to its long heritage in the Irish market (since 1926), HB is regarded with great affection by Irish consumers as "our ice cream." It still dominates the market despite being bought in 1973 by global marketer Unilever and forming a key element of the subsidiary Van den Bergh Foods' portfolio of products. The HB brand name acts as an umbrella for a wide range of products, with three take-home brands and five impulse brands (bars and cones you buy out of a cooler in a store).

Campaign Strategy

Because HB maintained a leading share of the Irish ice-cream market, the overriding business objective was to grow the category by increasing ice-cream consumption. That meant fighting for a share of the market in the bigger category of refreshment, using HB's impulse brands. This was to be essentially a battle for share of mind, pocket, and throat. Another objective was to communicate a new "togetherness" message along with the new brand identity by creating a more contemporary brand perception (and erasing the old perceptions), especially for the younger people in the HB market.

HB's consumer research had determined that the key target audience for the HB take-home brands consisted of housewives with children, and that for the impulse brands the target consisted of young adults aged 15 to 34. However, McCann decided that for a brand identity campaign, the strategy needed to move beyond these two audiences. Given HB's ubiquity and its broad acceptance, the identity effort was aimed at everyone in the Irish market.

The Brand Message

For 30 years the HB logo, with its initials in script mounted in an oval and printed over four bars, had been a familiar symbol in the Irish media, on signs in the streets, and in shops. The logo had appeared consistently on television and in other media as part of HB brand advertising, and the brand had a high pan-European advertising presence on TV and on billboards. Irish consumers came in contact with HB brands everywhere. It was impossible to walk down an Irish street without seeing HB signage, point-of-purchase displays, branded litter bins, or window stickers on the local corner shop. HB branded freezer cabinets were usually a prominent feature in these shops.

The original logo was appropriate to a relatively undeveloped market in both ice-cream consumption and other refreshments. However, the time had come to recognize consumers' greater familiarity with ice cream as well as the much fiercer competition in related refreshment areas where the lines were starting to blur between ice cream, carbonated soft drinks, confectionery, and yogurt categories.

The new design replaced the oval with a heart shape but continued to use the familiar HB initials (see Exhibit 4–2). The design was part of a pan-European brand identity change and sought to communicate the values of natural togetherness and warmth. "Natural togetherness" provided a key emotional benefit by focusing on people enjoying ice cream in a social, interactive environment.

The communication effort needed to touch the emotions of the audience. The message strategy was to use a major public

EXHIBIT 4-2

event to spearhead the campaign. The event would be supported by advertising so that when consumers saw on-pack and in-store changes, they would understand what was happening to the familiar HB brand. The event strategy was designed to create rapid and widespread awareness, excitement, and recognition of the new HB identity. The big idea was to capitalize on the heart-shaped logo by using the weekend around St. Valentine's Day (February 14) as a launch platform for the new logo (see Exhibit 4–3).

Delivering the Message

Fitting a brand of HB's stature and ubiquity with a new identity was clearly a task that needed to go far beyond advertising to engage all possible contact points. Changing over all HB's packaging, shopfront signage, point-of-purchase, and freezer cabinet branding messages in every supermarket and grocery store in the country was an unprecedented logistical challenge.

Rather than relying on the pan-European TV commercial to announce the logo, the McCann team felt strongly that the communication should include new media and contact points where appropriate. The core media idea was to create Ireland's first-ever themed weekend on Irish TV. St. Valentine's weekend was dubbed "The Love Weekend," and themed television programming sponsored by HB included movies such as *Sleepless in Seattle, Truly Madly Deeply,* and *Brief Encounter,* romantic episodes of *The Simpsons, Friends,* and *Golden Girls;* and a special called *An Intimate Evening with Michael Bolton.* In addition, a local television network created a phone-in music video request show called *Cupid's Corner.*

McCann's event-based plan allowed the agency to put in place a communication strategy that was completely integrated. That meant combining the three elements of the pan-European TV spot, a local media launch event, and on-the-street promotional activity so that consumers were involved with a 360-degree communication program for the new brand identity. In addition to traditional media time and space placements, the campaign used sponsorship "stings," short TV spots that announced HB's sponsorship of the Love Weekend. The networks also ran tie-in promotional teasers for the programs. In newspapers, the TV listings were printed over color watermarks of the heart logo.

A key element of HB's strategy to compete against the major refreshment brands was to establish a strong street presence in the main urban centers. To get the new HB logo on the street, McCann teamed up with a Dublin film-production company to project video images on large outdoor screens or walls. The Love Weekend TV reminder ads were also projected on large walls at city center locations on St. Valentine's night in Dublin, Cork, and Belfast. If the event didn't

It's Valentine's Weekend!
And to celebrate we're launching
our adorable new look with
an eye-catching new ad.

If you're in the mood for love,
don't miss the gigantic sneak preview
today from 2pm 'til late at the billboard
site on Dublin Road, Belfast.

So come along and start a new romance
with an old favourite.

quite cause national gridlock, it did manage to slow Saturday-night traffic near the light projections. McCann also had "hit squads" at each location distributing HB "Passion Test" cards, short questionnaires that tested the passion in one's life.

In an effort to further bring the event alive, McCann placed a color ad leading into the TV listings that offered people the chance to win a family holiday. This strengthened HB's ownership of the weekend's TV listings while at the same time the contest generated excitement and enthusiasm.

Evaluation of the HB Campaign

Market research two weeks after the Love Weekend, but prior to any signage or point-of-purchase changes, found that nearly half of all Irish recognized the new symbol without the HB signature cue. Furthermore, 70 percent of the 15–24 age group were aware of the logo, with 75 percent of these immediately associating the logo with HB Ice Cream.

Ice-cream sales in Ireland are seasonally biased to the summer months, so another objective was to stretch the impulse ice-cream season so that it starts earlier each year. Given the success of the Love Weekend with increasing sales in February, it is now part of HB's strategy to launch the new impulse season each year with a St. Valentine's weekend themed TV event.

Unilever managers were so impressed with the Irish campaign and the results it achieved that they decided to replicate the strategy in all their ice-cream markets. McCann's video of the whole campaign has become the template for similar launch activity in other markets.

This case was adapted with permission from the Advertising and Marketing Effectiveness (AME) brief for the HB brand identity campaign prepared by McCann-Erickson Dublin.

HOW COMMUNICATION WORKS

In order to understand why the HB brand identity campaign (discussed in the chapter opening case) was so successful, let's first consider how communication works in general. Conceptually, communication is a fairly simple process, as shown in Figure 4–1. It involves someone (the source, which can be a person or an organization) creating and sending a message and someone receiving that message. The message is transmitted through a communication channel; both the message and channel are subject to interference called noise. In interactive communication, the receiver responds, providing feedback to the sender or source. This chapter will transform this basic communication model into a model of brand communication and then into an integrated marketing communication model.

But first you need to understand the main acts of the sender and receiver: encoding and decoding. **Encoding** is *the process of putting a message into words, pictures, and/or sounds that convey the sender's intended meaning.* Encoding, in other words, is done by senders to translate their ideas into some message format. When you want others to know how you feel about them, for example, you can encode your feelings by doing such things as smiling at them, giving them verbal compliments, or buying them gifts. An important dimension of the source is its credibility, which affects how well the message is received.

What is often overlooked, however, is that everything you do, and sometimes what you don't do, sends a message. For example, what type of clothes you wear,

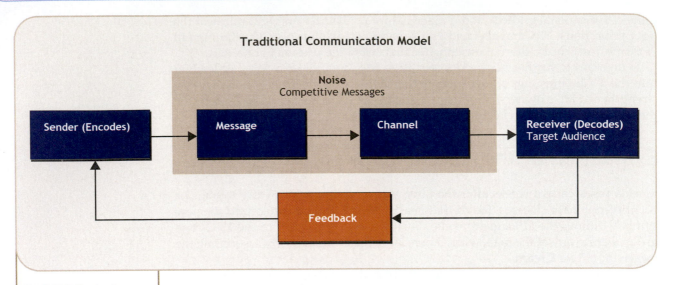

FIGURE 4-1

Note that the communication process is "circular."

where you work, how you spend your leisure time, who you choose for friends, where you live, and how you live (neatnik or slob), all are choices you make and are, either consciously or subconsciously, ways of encoding messages that tell others who you are. In other words, people are always sending messages about themselves and often don't even realize it. The same thing is true for brands and companies.

Decoding is *the process the receiver goes through to understand a message by interpreting what the words, pictures, and/or sounds in the message mean.* It's the reverse of encoding. When people see you smile at them, hear you give them compliments, or see that you have brought a gift, they can interpret these as signs of friendship or as a manipulative move to get them (the receivers) to do something for you.

How Marketing Communication Works

Figure 4–2 shows how the communication model described above can be translated into an interactive marketing communication model. In marketing communication, encoding is the creative task, which is done either by the company or its communication agency, as the McCann-Erickson's Dublin office did for its client HB. The encoding challenge is not only to describe a product's benefit in a way that is understandable and persuasive, but to do so in a way that will attract attention and make the decoding process as easy and enjoyable as possible for the receivers who are the targeted audience.

The **message** is *the information being transmitted from source to receiver.* In the case of HB, the message was that HB Ice Cream was not a stodgy relic but a modern brand that the Irish love as symbolized by the new heart-shaped logo and the associations it has with love. As explained above, the message itself can be encoded in many forms—words, pictures, actions, symbols, events, or even objects.

A communication channel, or **medium** (singular form of **media**), is *a means by which a message can be transmitted:* letter, e-mail, radio, television, newspaper, telephone, or an event. Recall from Chapter 1 that if they reach broad audiences in a variety of geographic areas, they are referred to as mass media. Mediated communication takes place when there is some physical entity between the sender and receiver of a message.

The communication process occurs in a context or environment where there are other things going on—other mass media messages, people walking by outside the

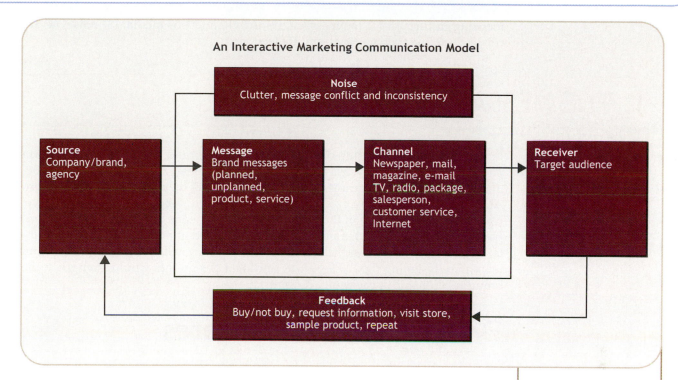

An Interactive Marketing Communication Model

Noise
Clutter, message conflict and inconsistency

Source
Company/brand, agency

Message
Brand messages (planned, unplanned, product, service)

Channel
Newspaper, mail, magazine, e-mail, TV, radio, package, salesperson, customer service, Internet

Receiver
Target audience

Feedback
Buy/not buy, request information, visit store, sample product, repeat

FIGURE 4-2

The basic communication model is basis for marketing communication.

window, a telephone ringing, conversations around you, as well as thoughts inside your head. **Noise** consists of *all the interferences and distractions that can negatively affect a message and its transmission.* One type of noise is message competition, or clutter, which results when there are a large number of sources trying to send a large number of messages to the same receivers. Clutter makes it difficult for a marketing communication message to get attention. Another type of noise comes from inconsistencies in the message presentation, which can cause confusion as the receiver tries to make sense of conflicting messages. In order to break through and create an impression, HB's campaign effort had to consider the many other competitive messages that were being sent at the same time.

After the receiver decodes a message, he or she responds in some way. This reaction is called **feedback,** or *a response to a message that is conveyed back to the source.* As will be explained later, "no response" is itself a response. In company-initiated communication, the response to the message may include trying or buying the product or visiting a store. For customer-initiated communication, the response may include a callback by a salesperson or customer-service representative.

The important thing about the version of the communication process illustrated in Figure 4–2 is that it depicts two-way communication. As you can see, the basic communication model is a loop, starting with the sender and then returning a response to the sender. In interactive brand communication, the source and receiver change places as people initiate contact as well as receive messages from a company. In IMC the important dimension is interactivity. The ad for the Lucent Technologies spin-off company Avaya in Exhibit 4–4 is focused on this interactive element.

Understanding this interactive approach to marketing communication is useful because it describes all the brand communication that determines the quantity and quality of brand relationships. It also identifies all the different points in the process where messages can go awry.

Chapter 2 discussed the sources of brand messages, companies and agencies, and briefly introduced the media. This chapter will fill in the rest of the model, focusing in turn on (1) the message, (2) the channels or media, (3) noise, (4) receiver decoding (perceptions), and (5) feedback.

1. THE MESSAGE

Building brand relationships requires managing a brand's total "communication package"—everything it says and does— and then analyzing all the messages being delivered at all the various contact points to see if they are working in concert. At each brand contact (e.g., seeing an ad, talking to a company representative, reading about the brand in the press, talking to someone who works for the company, using the product), a brand message is sent that either strengthens, maintains, or weakens the brand relationship. The biggest challenge facing the McCann team in redesigning the HB logo was finding a design that would strengthen the brand relationship at each contact point.

Everything Communicates

Brand messages are *all the messages customers and other stakeholders receive from and about a brand.* Recognizing that there are many different kinds of brand messages besides the ones put forth by marketing communication departments is a critical element of IMC. You will recall that marketing communication includes such things as advertising, product publicity, sales promotion, event sponsorships, and personal sales. Brand communication, however, is much broader, including not only marketing communication but all the other types of messages and signals that customers and other stakeholders receive from and about a company or brand.

Most marketing communication messages are a combination of *content* elements —words, sounds, actions, illustrations, symbols, or objects—and the meanings they represent. How they are applied and arranged is the *structure* of the message. The creative challenge for marketing communicators is to select the appropriate words, choose the right sounds, determine the volume and tone, select the graphic elements, and then combine them so they work together to present a coherent message that motivates the audience to respond in the desired way.

Whenever customers and other stakeholders have direct or indirect contact with a company, their eyes and ears pick up signals, all of which are brand messages. For example, distributing a product in Kmart as opposed to Bloomingdale's sends a signal about the quality, price, and value of the product. Such signals go to customers' heads and hearts, where they are decoded and integrated into impressions, thoughts, and feelings about the brand and/or company. It is this bundle of integrated brand messages that becomes the essence of a brand in someone's

EXHIBIT 4-4

Avaya is a spin-off of the telecommunications giant Lucent Technologies, which itself is a spin-off of AT&T. True to its mission, Avaya specializes in systems for interactive communication.

mind. A product's design, materials, performance, price, and distribution—along with the company's customer service, plant or store locations and hours, hiring practices, philanthropies, and marketing communications—all send messages about the brand or a company.

What all this means is that every department's activities have a communication dimension. For example, hiring new people or firing current employees sends a message about the company and how it is doing. New product introductions send a message that the company is innovative or expanding. Increasing or decreasing the supply of a product sends a message. Even silence or inaction can send a message. In other words, a company cannot *not* communicate. The Tale of Two Companies box illustrates a number of ways in which positive and negative messages can be sent in the daily operation of an airline.

Because marketing has the primary responsibility for the quality of brand relationships, and because these relationships are determined by how customers perceive an organization, marketing communication managers have a responsibility to track everything the organization does that sends messages about the brand and company.

The Four Sources of Brand Messages

Because everything a company does sends a message, the coordination problem is extremely challenging. Generally, the larger an organization and the more people involved, the larger the challenge and the more opportunity for message inconsistency. The first step in managing all brand messages is to identify their type and source.

Since controlling or influencing brand messages is the basis for managing brand relationships, it is critical to know where the messages originate. In other words, who or what is sending these messages? Once brand managers know the sources, they can design strategies and tactics to control or influence the messages so that they are strategically consistent. The four basic types of brand messages are determined by their sources and are identified as planned, product, service, and unplanned. Figure 4–3 illustrates this IMC message typology.

Planned Messages

Planned messages are the marketing communication messages delivered by advertising, sales promotion, personal sales, merchandising materials, press releases, events, sponsorships, packaging, and annual reports, to name a few. Traditional planned messages usually promote the brand or company, and their objectives include such effects as brand awareness, brand positioning, and brand knowledge. They also encourage action: buying, sampling, requesting additional information, or increasing purchase frequency or quantity.

Customers are not the only recipients of planned messages; companies also use such messages to address the concerns of employees, investors, and other key stakeholders using a variety of media such as press conferences, speeches, annual reports, recruitment advertising, annual meetings, sales meetings, notices in pay slips, bulletin boards (online as well as on a wall), and newsletters. In other words, messages come from a variety of company sources besides the

FIGURE 4-3

There are four basic types of brand messages.

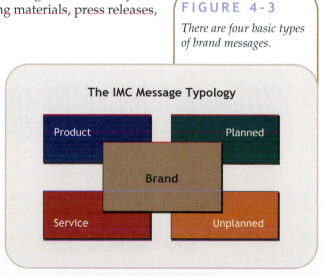

A TALE OF TWO COMPANIES

Southwest and American Airlines Deliver Messages

Southwest Airlines understands that everything sends a message. Its primary message source is its employees, whose loyalty and high morale were demonstrated in

EXHIBIT 4-5

This ad for Southwest Airlines emphasizes the company's low-cost business philosophy.

Southwest Airlines Tops $1 Billion, Becomes Major Carrier.

BY DAVID SMITH

(DALLAS) Southwest Airlines Chairman Herb Kelleher announced today that the Texas-based carrier has officially topped one billion dollars in annual revenues, thereby making it a "major carrier." Kelleher praised his employees and called them attentive...

IF WE CHARGED AS MUCH AS MOST AIRLINES, WE COULD HAVE RUN THIS AD YEARS AGO.

Our business philosophy is very simple. And it's been the same since 1971: Charge the traveler the lowest possible fare. And provide the highest quality Customer service. The idea being that Customers would naturally develop a loyalty toward our airline.

In 1990, the results speak for themselves. We just passed one billion dollars in annual revenues. And we're one of only two airlines that have been profitable for each of the last seventeen years.

Needless to say, we're proud of this milestone, and we have just one word for all of the people who helped us reach it. Thanks!

SOUTHWEST AIRLINES™

© 1990 Southwest Airlines

the 1970s when fuel prices skyrocketed. The airline's employees voluntarily took pay cuts so the company could continue operating in the black. Southwest Airlines has convinced its passengers that its rates are low, but more important, it has convinced them that flying is fun through the zany antics of its employees (see Exhibit 4-5). Relative to its competition, Southwest Airlines has spent far less per passenger mile on advertising and promotion and yet has been profitable every year since it started in the 1970s, something no other major airline has been able to accomplish. Also it has become the number one carrier on the majority of routes it serves.

Another airline company that tried to improve its message management was American Airlines. In most cases, providing useful brand information to customers adds brand value. That was why American Airlines spent $4 million erecting eight flight signs on the highway leading into the Dallas/Fort Worth airport with detailed arrival and departure information by flight number. The objective was to tell departing passengers and people picking up incoming passengers which terminal they needed to go to.

But for people in cars traveling at 55 miles per hour, the signs were difficult to read because they carried so much information. You can stand in front of a sign in a terminal until you find the flight you're looking for, but you can't stop in front of a sign on the highway. When several cars were involved in accidents on the airport highway, American was sued. Complainants claimed that the signs distracted drivers. American lost the $24 million suit. (It has, however, appealed the settlement.)

One of the arguments that helped persuade the jury to find in favor of the plaintiffs was that during the planning stages for the signs, some airport officials, as well as the police, had expressed concern about people looking away from the road to read the detailed information. Accident victim Anwar Soliman, who initiated the suit, said he had not planned to sue American until he read that airport officials had advised the airline that the signs could create a dangerous situation, and the airline ignored that advice.

Although this is a rare example of well-intended brand communications resulting in a costly problem, it reveals something that marketing communication and customer-service people need to keep in mind: Brand messages need to be examined from more than one perspective because the impact of what they say or how they are delivered can sometimes be different than intended.

Think About It

In what ways has Southwest Airlines created and sent positive brand messages? Why did American Airlines' attempt to provide customer information backfire? What should the airline have done to eliminate this traffic hazard?

Sources: Adapted from Jagdish Seth and Rajendra Sisodia, "Feeling the Heat," *Marketing Management* 4, no. 2 (Fall 1995), p. 12; Andrea Gerlin and Robert Tomsho, "Sign of Trouble: Why a CEO Sued American Airlines," *The Wall Street Journal*, December 3, 1996, p. A1.

marketing and MC departments, including the finance department (e.g., announcements of new stock issues or profit reports); human resources (e.g., job announcements); and research and development (e.g., engineers who write articles for, or are interviewed by, trade journals).

Product Messages

The second type of message is the produce message; these include all messages sent by a product's design, performance, pricing, and distribution.

Product Design

The design of a product can send powerful messages. Operating on the principle that if it looks good, it must be good, companies in the auto industry have always maintained a staff of industrial designers to style cars. The same principle operates in other industries as well, such as computers and appliances, where industrial designers are an important part of the product development team. In retail stores, the design of the store is an important signal of the quality of the merchandise or service. United Parcel Service (UPS) makes a point of washing its delivery trucks every evening on the assumption that clean trucks send a message of a professional level of service.

After years of sales increases, the plastic-container manufacturer Tupperware watched revenues stagnate for a decade. In order to regenerate sales growth, the company, which does little advertising, added bright colors and new styles to its functional products. Its products now quickly say "We're modern and contemporary, not your mother's old plastic storage bowls" (see Exhibit 4–6).[2]

Product Performance

Although product design is important, product performance is even more important when it comes to sending brand messages. As most marketers know, how well a product performs or how well a service is delivered, relative to expectations, is a major determinant of whether or not customers become repeat buyers. This is the rationale for spending large amounts on sales promotion to generate trial for a new product. As long as there are perceivable differences in brand performance, such investments are wise.

EXHIBIT 4-6

Tupperware redesigned and added bright colors to its products to send a message that its products were modern.

There are many variables involved in the product experience that can affect the product's use and therefore send a message. Take, for example, a VCR. Although it may do an excellent job of recording and playing tapes, if it cannot be easily programmed, a customer may infer that it's not a good product. Even if the technology is there to facilitate programming but the instruction manual is unclear, the result can be the same. Such communication problems are of concern to the whole company, but marketing communication managers must look for ways to prevent or correct them as part of their overall effort to send positive brand messages. Another reason for providing easy-to-follow instructions for complex products such as electronics, computers, and automobiles is to make sure the buyer can use and benefit from as many features as possible. By maximizing the customer's use of the product, the company can increase its brand's perceived value.

Pricing and Distribution

The brand messages sent by price and distribution are often not recognized for their importance in a brand's overall communication. There's a big perceived difference, for example, between cosmetics sold at Wal-Mart and those sold at Nordstrom.

Since there are a variety of brand choices for most product categories, the price of a particular brand is a message stating how it compares with competing brands. In marketing terms, brands are often positioned on price. In addition, the frequency and the extent of brand promotions also say something about a brand. The more a brand is on sale and the greater the discounts are, generally the more ordinary it is considered to be. Brands that compete consistently on price often have little else to say. And discount pricing can send negative messages, which McDonald's found out after it unveiled a plan to sell Big Macs and Egg McMuffins for 55 cents (to help commemorate its 55 years of being in business). The price cut probably made sense as an attempt to stem declining sales, but the negative fallout (which came from customers' perceiving the products as cheap) led investors to slice a big chunk off the company's share price. One financial analyst commented, "They have transformed one of the great brands in American business into a commodity." [3]

Seldom, however, can pricing messages stand alone. If a watch, say, is priced at $300, is the message "quality" or "overpriced"? Or, if it's priced at $15, is the message "bargain" or "cheap"? Without knowing more about the watch, it is impossible to say. Pricing messages, like all others, must be put into context and strategically integrated with all other brand messages in order to send customers and potential customers a coherent, meaningful message. The Technology in Action box discusses the issue of demand pricing.

Service Messages

Service messages come from contact with service representatives, receptionists, secretaries, delivery people, and all other representatives of a company. Service messages are usually personal, real-time interfaces between a company and a customer—and this is what makes them especially strong. Talking to a salesperson or customer-service representative will have much greater impact on a customer than will seeing an ad for that company because interactive communication is more personal and thus more persuasive.

The word *service* here refers to those activities that support a product, whether that product itself is a good or a service. For example, when you rent a car, getting transportation is the primary service provided. But there are supporting services that make your car rental experience good or bad. The courtesy you experience during check-in, the way you are treated by the counter staff, and the time it takes to get your car are supporting services that send brand messages.

In an effort to better manage service quality, researchers have combined five service measures in a method nicknamed SERVQUAL.[4] The five measures (sources of service messages) are tangibles, reliability, responsiveness, assurance, and empathy. The *tangibles* include the physical facilities that customers see and experience as well as the appearance of those providing the service. *Reliability* means consistency of performance. Does the company perform what it promises, and is this performance the same time after time? *Responsiveness* refers not only to how quickly a company responds but also to the quality of that response. *Assurance* is the ability of those performing the service to create within the customer a feeling of confidence and trust. *Empathy* means employees are perceived as feeling the customer's "pain."

An example of a negative service message occurs when bank customers are forced to wait in line for a teller while several bank employees are either working or talking together behind closed counters. These employees may not be tellers, but customers don't know this; they will assume the employees are tellers and are simply ignoring the customers. The message is that customers are less important than paperwork.

A positive service message when handling customer requests and complaints is created by a speedy response, which shows that the company is concerned and has made the customer's problem a top priority. A quick response can add a positive element even when the message content is not what a customer wants to hear. For example, a customer that needs parts for a discontinued product doesn't want to hear these parts aren't available, but letting the customer know this sooner rather than later minimizes the overall disappointment. (Offering alternatives can help, too.)

TECHNOLOGY IN ACTION

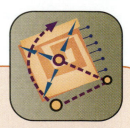

The Customer Side of Demand Pricing

What brand message is being sent when prices suddenly change? Computers and databases have enabled companies to use variations in price to help manage capacity and inventories. This is called demand pricing. When capacities decrease, prices are raised to maximize revenue return on products being sold. Oil and gas prices are good examples of demand pricing.

Airlines have been using demand pricing for years. As the date of a scheduled flight comes closer, the airlines' computers automatically raise or lower prices depending on how many seats for that flight remain unsold. Using a database of historical sales, the airlines have a good estimate of how many seats should be sold one week out, two weeks out, and so on. When seats for a particular flight are being sold faster than normal, the airlines raise the price for the remaining seats (and vice versa when sales are slower than expected). This is one reason why, for any given flight, the ticket prices paid by those on board will greatly vary.

Using the same supply and demand strategy, Coca-Cola is testing vending machines that raise and lower prices based on changes in the outside temperature (see Exhibit 4-7). Knowing that more people buy soft drinks on hot days than on cold days, machines are programmed to charge more for a can of Coke when temperatures go up. It is also possible to program vending machines to increase prices when sales significantly increase in a short period of time (due, for example, to a special event), in part to prevent the machine from running out before its regularly scheduled restocking.

Yet while demand pricing may help Coke maximize its profits on vending machines, it may also send a negative brand message to those who regularly use the vending machine. One day a Coke may cost 75 cents and the next day, when the temperature goes up, a can may cost $1.00. Will this make customers feel they are getting ripped off? Will it make them think of going to a Pepsi machine, where they know the price doesn't change? Will this make them switch from Coke to another brand the next time they go to the store and stock up on soft drinks for the home?

EXHIBIT 4-7

Coke is testing the effect of using demand pricing.

Think About It

What is demand pricing, and how might it send negative messages to customers? Why is demand pricing less of a problem for airlines than for soft-drink companies?

In most service companies, what service people do is not the responsibility of marketing, but rather of operations or some other department—such as human resources, customer satisfaction, accounting, credit, or sales, to name a few.

Nevertheless, one negative service message can more than counter the effects of dozens of positive, planned messages produced by marketing. In an integrated program, marketing works with operations and other departments to minimize negative service messages and create synergy between the planned and service messages for greater impact. Therefore, as explained in Chapter 3, effectively managing all the various supporting service messages requires a cross-functional organization.

Unplanned Messages

Unplanned messages include brand- or company-related news stories, gossip, rumors, actions of special interest groups, comments by the trade and by competitors, findings by government agencies or research institutions, and word of mouth. Companies can hope that unplanned messages are positive and consistent with all the other brand messages, but such messages are hard to control because they come from sources outside the company. These sources may be seen either as experts on the company (such as employees); protectors of the public interest (special interest groups, media, government agencies); or third parties who have no vested interest in the company (friends, associates, media).

Although it may seem like all unplanned messages are bad, such messages can also be positive. Shortly after Pfizer's new impotence drug, Viagra, was approved by the U.S. Food and Drug Administration, an estimated 35,000 prescriptions were being written a day—and that was before Pfizer had begun its marketing program for the new product. The demand was generated by positive word of mouth.[5]

An unplanned message may also arise (intentionally or not) from another company's planned message. In early 1998, ads warning travelers of the dangers of hepatitis A began appearing in national magazines in the United States. The ads pointed out that hepatitis A can be picked up in many parts of the world, especially in underdeveloped and developing countries, where sanitation standards are not always high. The sponsor of the ads was the Hepatitis Foundation International, which had recently received an unrestricted educational grant from the pharmaceutical giant SmithKline Beecham. Not coincidentally, SmithKline Beecham makes Havrix, which is a hepatitis A vaccine. (Merck, a competitor, also has a similar vaccine.) The ads did not mention specifically either SmithKline Beecham or Havrix. In other words, this was a generic promotion (a planned message) regarding the dangers of hepatitis A and the need to be vaccinated—yet it was a clever public relations move on SmithKline's part. The response to the campaign, according to several travel-medicine clinics, was a significant increase in demand for these vaccinations. While this was good news for SmithKline and Merck, the hepatitis A campaign upset many travel agencies. For them, it was an unplanned message; they complained that the campaign was creating undue fear of travel to many areas and thus hurting their business.[6]

Employee Messages

Employees are an important communication source, and their views are highly credible to people they know, as well as to reporters who interview them, particularly in a crisis situation. It is almost impossible to prevent employees from talking about their work experiences and, sometimes inadvertently, delivering negative messages. Employee grapevines and rumor mills can play havoc with carefully crafted planned messages.

A far-reaching marketing communication program, however, can dovetail with an open communication environment to influence the way employees express themselves at the conversational level. Companies that operate with this type of corporate culture find that their employees are generally more positive, as well as more informed, not only about the procedures that affect their jobs but about the bigger picture of the corporate mission and related issues such as profitability. The more informed employees are, and the better they feel about the company they work for and its mission, the more likely they are to send positive brand messages.

News Media

For most companies, the most critical unplanned messages come from the news media. Such messages often reach a relatively large audience and are seen as having especially high credibility. There will be more discussion of this in Chapter 15, on public relations; but the discussion here will give you a quick introduction to media relations.

Media stories can come from whistle-blowing employees, special interest groups, financial analysts, and many other sources over which MC managers have no control. Such stories can greatly affect business operations and, more important, the company's stakeholder relationships. According to one CEO:

> You have multiple publics. If you have a certain code of conduct on how you will handle your employees, how you're going to handle the [general] public, how you're going to handle your stockholders, how to handle your customers, you will go a long way toward preventing the kind of negative stories you see in business. You can improve [the situation caused by a negative unplanned message] by recognizing it is something you have to deal with like any other business problem and planning in advance a means of managing it. It's really about how you manage your own business and then how you communicate that to your various publics and how that gets translated in the electronic and print media.[7]

Influencing media behavior is difficult because many reporters are more distrustful of business executives than the general public is. A study of both journalists and business executives found that over two-thirds (69 percent) of the business executives admitted they had lied to the media at some time. Significant gaps were found between the perceptions of business executives and journalists. More than 75 percent of the journalists said business coverage has improved over the years, but only 30 percent of the executives believed this to be true. Nearly 75 percent of the business executives said the news media provide a negative view of business, but only 31 percent of the journalists believed this to be true.[8] Public relations media specialists develop relationships with reporters covering their business and the business of their clients in an attempt to make this relationship less confrontational.

Disasters and Crises

Another type of unplanned message handled by public relations is generated by company-related disasters. The crisis, disaster, or emergency is the most unwanted of unplanned messages, but crises are also a fact of life. Airline executives, for example, don't wonder *if* one of their planes will have a problem but rather *when.* Owners of fast-food restaurants closely follow stories about the shootings that occur periodically in public. The fact that millions of people each day walk into their stores means that their employees and customers are exposed to people with all sorts of problems. To minimize negative unplanned messages caused by news stories about shootings, fast-food chains have guidelines for district supervisors, store managers, and employees to follow when a crisis occurs.

One of the biggest corporate crises in recent years involved two companies: the automaker Ford and the tire manufacturer Firestone. Faulty Firestone tires were implicated in numerous crashes involving Ford's Explorer line of sport utility vehicles. Exhibit 4–8 is an ad created by Ford to announce its policy of replacing the tires on all its Explorers.

YOUR SAFETY IS OUR TOP PRIORITY.

"You have my personal guarantee that no one at Ford will rest until every recalled tire is replaced."

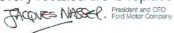 Jacques Nasser, President and CEO Ford Motor Company

You've been exposed to a whirlwind of information about the Firestone Tire recall. If you're still confused, that's understandable. Ford Motor Company would like to lay out, in four simple steps, the easiest way to ensure your safety and the safety of your family. All the following information is presented in even greater detail on our website at **www.ford.com**.

Which tires are affected?
• All Firestone ATX and ATX IIs of P235/75R15 size
• P235/75R15 Firestone Wilderness AT tires produced in Firestone's Decatur, Illinois plant
NO OTHER FIRESTONE TIRES ARE PART OF THIS RECALL.

Examine your tires.
To determine if your **15"** Wilderness ATs are affected, find the U.S. DOT Safety Standard Code. (Simply look under your vehicle with a flashlight. There is no need to raise the vehicle.) If the code reads DOT VDHL, your tires should be replaced.

Which vehicles are involved?
• '91-'00 Ford Explorers
• '96-'00 Mercury Mountaineers
• 91-'00 Ford Rangers
• '91-'94 Ford F-Series
• '91-'94 Ford Broncos
• '01 Ford Explorer Sport Tracs
• '94-'00 Mazda B-Series
• '91-'94 Mazda Navajos

DOT Code

The DOT code is located on the inboard sidewall of Wilderness AT tires. Inspect tire DOT code with vehicle on ground.

Make an appointment.
If your tires are part of the Firestone recall, contact one of the following authorized replacement outlets. As of this moment, there are over 13,000 outlets nationwide. Any one of them will be happy to assist you.

• Ford Motor Company at **www.ford.com** or **(800) 660-4719**
• Firestone at **www.firestone.com**
• Midas at **www.midas.com**
• Sunoco Ultra Service Centers at **(800) 786-6261**
• Monro Muffler/Brake at **www.monro.com**
• Costco Wholesale Member Services at **(800) 774-2678**

To find the outlet nearest you, go to **www.ford.com**, click on the Firestone Information box and select your preferred outlet under "Locate An Authorized Replacement Center."

Choose from over 30 replacement tires.
To date, over a million tires have been replaced. That's good progress, but not good enough. That's why we've now gained commitments from other tire manufacturers, including Goodyear, Michelin and Continental to double their production and help make replacement tires available sooner.

Select tires from nine manufacturers have been approved as certified replacement tires. The complete list appears at **www.ford.com**. Click on the Firestone Information box and select "Recommended Replacement Tires" under Owner Information. Also, the tire professionals listed above will be familiar with these tires and can help make the selection that's best for your vehicle.

Let us know if we can still help.
For the latest news and information, click on **www.ford.com**. If you have any further questions or concerns, call us 24 hours a day, 7 days a week at **(800) 660-4719**, or e-mail us at **tireinquiry@ford.com**.

Ford Motor Company

As discussed in Chapter 14, although not all companies face the same possibilities for having a crisis, every company should have a **crisis management plan,** *a plan for handling the types of disasters that can be anticipated.* Planning ahead of time for the worst that can happen is one of the most important things a company can do to influence unplanned messages.

Managing the Message Typology

What the message typology described in the preceding sections should help you realize is that, although coordinating a one-voice approach in planned messages (advertising, public relations, etc.) is desirable, it is a waste of a company's money and effort if the other types of brand messages are contradicting the planned messages. Advertising, in other words, can be canceled out by a bad experience with customer service or with a product that fails the first time it's used. Marketing communication managers can create synergy among all the brand messages only when they consider all the various types of brand messages and the way they reinforce or contradict one another.

2. MEDIA CHANNELS AND BRAND CONTACT POINTS

Think of media as bridges that carry messages from senders to receivers. They allow a brand and all its stakeholders to come in contact with each other. Any person, event, or thing that provides exposure to a brand message is considered a medium. Marketing communication messages are normally carried by mass media such as TV, radio, newspapers, magazines, mail, and outdoor boards. Other types of media that carry planned messages are signage, buildings, sports stadiums (e.g., brand logos and signs on the walls), e-mail, faxes, kiosks, and packaging.

Some media, such as newspapers and TV, are primarily one-way bridges in that messages travel only from a company to customers. In contrast, **interactive media**—*media that offer two-way communication, making it possible to both send and receive messages*—such as the telephone and the Internet, can be used by customers as well as by companies for sending and receiving messages. The phone is one of the most important interactive media. Exhibit 4–9 illustrates its use in a business-to-business situation.

But there are other types of media, and here is where it can get a little confusing. Products themselves—both goods and services—also perform as media because they carry brand messages. The box of Tide you pick up at the store carries messages that help you form a judgment about the laundry powder inside. Another example is a videotape of the movie *101 Dalmatians* that was made by Disney and sold in retail stores. The videotape is an entertainment product, but it is also a medium that carries the Disney brand name and says something about Disney. Products-as-media are important because they enable a brand and customer to interact.

Every brand-related, information-bearing interaction that a customer or potential customer has with a brand is called a **brand contact point.** Brand contact points include such things as using the branded product, hearing or reading about the brand in the mass media or from another person, talking with someone from the company making or selling the branded product, driving behind the company's truck on the highway, or receiving a direct mail offer. Every point of contact delivers a brand message of some sort. The Global Focus box illustrates how an automotive dealership makes terrific use of its showroom to creatively make brand contacts.

Three Types of Brand Contact Points

The concept of brand contact points was first popularized by Jan Carlson, former chairman of Scandinavian Airlines System (SAS). During the time he managed this

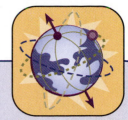

Coffee with Car to Go

The Volvo Conservatory in Manila, the capital city of the Philippines, is an airy, sparkling-white showroom for Volvo cars that bears no resemblance to any other car showroom you have ever seen. It offers a coffee shop, a bank, music concerts, and art exhibits, as well as lectures on values and on the environment. The Volvo Conservatory has taken the concept of an entertaining location to the extreme. Except for a display of three Volvo models and one auto accessory shop, there is no obvious connection to a car dealer's showroom. The Coffee Beanery, a chic local café, serves customers all day at one end of the showroom; at the opposite end sits a branch of the Urban Bank. People come to the Conservatory to use these facilities, so Volvo becomes part of their daily lives. This unusual marketing approach has connected with many Filipino coffee drinkers, who became Volvo buyers because of this subtle marketing approach.

The owner of the dealership, Selene Yu, says he has created a unique culture that appeals to Philippine sensitivities. He explains that the name Conservatory, which suggests an English greenhouse, is relevant because it is a place to nurture the four values that the Scandinavian automaker wants to impart: safety, protection of the environment, social values, and support for the arts. All of these have broad appeal in the Philippines.

In addition to selling cars, the Volvo Conservatory holds concerts by local bands to convey the message that the car is not only for middle-aged executives but for young people as well. It sponsors environmental films to emphasize that Volvo is committed to preserving nature. It sends car experts to colleges to educate students on car safety and responsible driving. Volvo brochures are passed around during all these events. The Conservatory works—and sells cars—because it appeals to the values of its Filipino customers.

Think About It

What is a contact point, and why should MC managers be concerned with contact points other than marketing communication? In what ways did the Volvo Conservatory create unusual and effective customer contact points?

---

world-class company, Carlson realized that there were certain company/customer interactions that had a significant impact on whether customers chose SAS the next time they flew. He called these contact points "moments of truth." They included on-time departures and arrivals, careful handling of luggage, and courteous interactions with airline personnel.[9]

To manage brand contacts, therefore, a company must first identify all of them. Next, it must prioritize them based on the following criteria: (1) impact on brand loyalty, (2) ability of the company to influence the contact-point experience, (3) cost of making each contact a positive experience, (4) the extent to which contacts can be used to gather customer data, and (5) the extent to which contacts are appropriate for carrying additional brand messages.

There are three types of brand contact points: **brand created,** which are the result of specific communication efforts by the company; **intrinsic,** which are the contacts that automatically take place during the buying and using of a product; and **customer created,** which are *customer-initiated contacts*.

Company-Created Contact

Company-created contact points are planned marketing communication efforts that were explained above. When Lexus, for example, creates and places an ad in *Time,* the automaker has created a brand contact with the magazine's readers. The

Volvo Conservatory (highlighted earlier in the Global Focus box) is an interesting example of creating contact points for the automobile brand among a variety of daily activities. A highly controversial created contact point comes from the Channel One Network. This service (begun by Whittle Communications and sold in 1994 to media giant Primedia) has given participating schools thousands of dollars' worth of TV equipment in exchange for the opportunity to show a daily 10-minute program containing news and a few TV commercials aimed at teenagers. Some companies advertising on Channel One have found that this created contact point has generated a great deal of hostility, aimed at both Channel One and themselves as sponsors. The critics are not necessarily against advertising, but they question the appropriateness of creating a brand contact point in a school setting.

Intrinsic Contact Points

Before investing in new message opportunities, a brand should identify and examine those that already exist and make sure the messages being delivered are consistent and on strategy. The following list illustrates some of the intrinsic contact points encountered when you rent a car:

- Company representative answering toll-free reservation number.
- Clerk at rental counter.
- Driver of van to car holding area.
- Attendant at car holding area.
- The rental car itself.
- Attendant at car return area.

From a communication standpoint, the interactions at each of these car rental contact points either strengthen, weaken, or reconfirm your impression of the company. Besides the behavior and attitude of the car rental representatives, there are other things sending brand messages: signage and directions, appearance of the car lot, cleanliness of the van and rental office lobby, and the overall convenience and ease of completing the paperwork and getting on your way.

Because intrinsic contact points occur when buying and using a brand, these contacts primarily affect current customers' perceptions, whose retention and growth in business dealings are extremely important.

In the cable television industry, which has never been known for its high level of customer service (perhaps because most cable services have a monopoly in

EXHIBIT 4-9

This ad demonstrates "the power to communicate" in the context of the World Wildlife Fund's use of a Motorola cellular phone to circulate alerts about situations that endanger wildlife.

The power to communicate in an instant can provide the hope for survival to some of the earth's most endangered creatures. That's why Motorola's Land Mobile Products Sector has partnered with the World Wildlife Fund to bring state-of-the-art wireless communications technology to environmental teams working in some of the most primitive places on the planet. Working to deter poaching and encourage conservation in places as remote as the tropical rain forests of South America, the mountainous forest terrain and Savannah grasslands of Bhutan, the dense forests of West Africa, and the marine habitats of the Turtle Islands in Southeast Asia. For with the power to communicate, comes the power to survive. And their survival empowers us all.

WWF

"THE POWER TO COMMUNICATE CAN MEAN THE DIFFERENCE BETWEEN LIFE AND DEATH FOR SOME OF THE EARTH'S MOST ENDANGERED CREATURES."

Kathryn S. Fuller, President WWF–US

Ⓜ **MOTOROLA**

What you never thought possible.™

For information on Motorola products visit our website at http://www.mot.com/LMPS

their respective geographical areas), some cable companies are finally realizing that installation is an intrinsic brand contact point, and therefore installers should be seen as more than just technicians. Some companies are conducting special training for installation workers—teaching them not only how to politely deal with customers but also how to do low-key suggestive selling of different cable offerings.

One industrial company strengthening its relationships with customers by identifying and responding to intrinsic contact points is 3M. The company put together a cross-functional team of representatives from the three operational areas that were responsible for managing intrinsic contact points—sales, management information systems, and logistics. Working together, this 3M team was able to come up with ways for one of its BtB customers, Boise Cascade, a distributor of office products and building materials, to reduce its warehouse operating costs by $500,000 per year. One of the team's suggestions, for example, was "logistics labels" showing appropriate slot locations for its products in the warehouses, making it easier and faster for Boise Cascade employees to place 3M products into inventory. According to a 3M vice president, "Each of these people [on the team] have contact points with the customer. Each point of contact is a point of ownership to satisfy the customer."[10] By collectively discussing each of their contact points, the 3M team was able to strategically focus on the warehousing process and come up with cost reductions, which in turn reinforced its brand relationship with Boise Cascade.

Customer-Created Contacts

One of the communication areas most overlooked by marketing departments is the customer-created brand contact. As the communication model in Figure 4–4 shows, customers (and prospects) can be the source of brand messages in the same way as can a company and its MC agencies. The feedback that customers receive when they initiate communication can either strengthen or weaken the brand relationship.

Managing customer-created contacts is a critical part of IMC because it deals primarily with current customers and thus, significantly impacts customer

FIGURE 4-4

Basic communication model applied to customer-created brand communication.

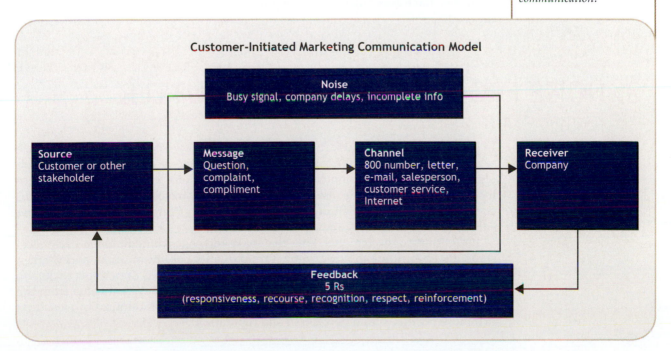

retention. Two of the main reasons customers contact a company is because they are unhappy with a product or have a question about its use or care. In other words, these customers are at a critical point regarding brand satisfaction. How a company responds, therefore, significantly impacts the repurchase decisions of these customers.

Companies are increasingly inviting customers and prospects to contact them by providing 800 numbers, e-mail and websites addresses displayed on packages and in most other planned messages. The problem is, most companies have not yet learned how to respond properly to customer-initiated messages. The annual company-response studies done by the University of Colorado's IMC program, for example, have found that the majority of company responses to e-mail and phone contacts rate only fair or poor.[11]

A dramatic example of how a company can go wrong in handling customer-created brand contacts is what happened to the telephone company US West (now named Qwest) in the mid-1990s when it consolidated its customer service centers from 530 to 26 offices.[12] The result was, when customers called their phone company they got busy signals or were put on hold for lengthy periods. Out of frustration, these customers began calling and complaining to their public utility commissions. The result was, US West ended up not only getting fined millions of dollars for failure to respond promptly and properly to customer contacts, the media picked up the poor customer service story providing even more negative publicity for the company. Not only did some top executives lose their jobs as a result of these problems, the company's CEO eventually made a public statement admitting the company had to change its ways if it was going to successfully compete in the new deregulated telecommunications marketplace.

At the same time US West was not properly managing the customer-created contacts, it was spending approximately $50 million a year on brand-created messages (heavy TV and newspaper advertising). One of the products being advertising, ironically, was a special phone service for small businesses to help them improve their customer service.[13]

US West could very well have received a much better return on its MC investment if it had moved some of its advertising dollars over to its customer service departments. Not only could this have provided customers with better service, it could also have avoided a lot of unplanned, negative brand messages appearing in the media.

3. NOISE FROM CONFLICT AND CLUTTER

In the marketing communication model, noise is shown as surrounding the message and channels and ultimately interfering with the receiver's message decoding. Defects in brand communication that create noise and obliterate messages include such things as inconsistency and broken promises. Environmental conditions that create noise include conflicting messages from competitors and other stakeholders, and message clutter in general.

Poor timing or executional flaws that make messages difficult to read or understand also contribute to noise, detract from quality communication, and weaken brand relationships. Although zero-defect communication is impossible to obtain, understanding the sources of the noise and eliminating any that came from the marketing program itself can raise the quality of brand communication, resulting in a more positive brand perception and reputation.

Mixed Messages and Message Conflict

One of the most troublesome sources of noise is inconsistent marketing communication produced by the company itself. Creating a variety of messages from a variety of different sources can introduce points of confusion. The result may be a fuzzy brand image. If investors are being told the company is in great shape and employees are being told that the company has to reduce costs and lay off staff, then mixed messages are being sent by and within the organization. (And don't forget that many employees are sometimes also investors, so these messages overlap.)

An IMC audit of a regional retail chain, for example, revealed inconsistent service messages. Most of the clerks were knowledgeable, patient, and personable when helping customers make purchase decisions—positive service messages. However, although the chain had a liberal return policy, some of these same clerks became sullen and mechanical, and made limited eye contact when handling returns—sending negative service messages that overpowered the positive ones.

Conflicting messages can also come from external stakeholders, such as the media, as well as competitors. Not only do MC managers need to know what competitors are saying, but how, when, and where they are saying it. In other words, marketers not only compete *with* brands but they also compete *for* the attention and support of customers and potential customers as well as other stakeholders such as investors and suppliers. What other people say, particularly important people such as employees or financial analysts, can create conflict by causing customers to change their perceptions and rethink their purchasing strategies.

Message Clutter and Overload

The problem of noise requires integrated marketing communicators to recognize that messages come from many different sources. A large number of commercial messages directed at customers can overwhelm them with message clutter. If you are a marketing manager responsible for reaching customers with planned messages, you often lay awake at night wondering whether your ad or direct-mail piece will be one of the few brand messages that will actually have an impact on your target audience.

Clutter includes other planned messages but it also includes a variety of environmental factors. You are reading this chapter, for example, in an environment that is sending you messages—a classroom littered with today's college newspaper and old messages on the blackboard; the interior of an airplane with seats too close together and a talkative seatmate; your apartment with a radio playing, a dog barking, and a siren blaring from an ambulance outside.

In addition to these physical noises are psychological noises such as all those things on your mind—the fight with your boss, the ski gloves you lost this afternoon, the $50 your favorite aunt just sent you, and your plans for the weekend to get away from all this stress. All of these things—your surroundings, your thoughts, and your internal states—are noise because they have the potential to interfere with new messages.

Clutter creates communication overload. People are inundated with more information than they know how to handle. And the problem has only gotten worse with the spread of the Web. Businesspeople, especially those in positions to make purchasing decisions, live in a double cocoon of brand messages. They drown in both consumer and business-to-business messages. A good example is what happens inside business magazines such as *Forbes, Fortune,* and *Business Week.* Look at how many ads are for consumer products even though these magazines are aimed at people who are supposed to be thinking "business" when they read the magazines. The problem of clutter is the reason advertising and other marketing communication areas emphasize using a creative idea in their messages to increase attention and interest. The BMW motorcycle ad (Exhibit 4–10) uses a twist to spark interest in the brand message and break through the commercial message clutter.

4. RECEIVER DECODING AND PERCEPTIONS

EXHIBIT 4-10

To make the point about the excitement of riding the motorcycle, the BMW ad entices your interest by twisting the notion that you may hate to get up at 6 A.M. on a Saturday.

6 am, Saturday morning.
I hate it when I oversleep.

BMW
Motorcycles

The *receiver* is the targeted audience—the customer, potential customer, or other stakeholder. (If the message is customer-initiated, then the receiver may be a salesperson, a customer-service representative, or a webmaster.) The audience members targeted by planned communication will decode brand messages based on past experience with that brand; what they know about the product category in general from friends, news stories, and personal experience; and their immediate needs, wants, and concerns. Everything the receiver brings to the decoding process will shape and shade the meaning of a brand message. Note that both the encoding and decoding steps require people to use their knowledge and experiences to create or interpret a message. Of course, no two people are alike, so there are always going to be some differences between encoders and decoders no matter what experiences they have had.

The extent of decoding—how much time and effort people will put into reading, watching, or listening to a brand message—also determines how successful the message is. One problem is that so many MC messages have overpromised, intruded upon privacy, and otherwise irritated consumers that many people, as soon as they recognize something as a commercial message, try to block it out; they turn the page, throw it in the waste basket, or change to another station.

To help prevent *misinterpretation*—which happens when the perceived message does not match the intended message—there are several things marketers can do. One is to keep messages simple in order to reduce the complexity of what needs to be encoded and decoded. There is an old rule of thumb in advertising that says "Be single-minded." This means that there should be only one main idea in a brand message. Another rule is to build in redundancies. This means you should say the same thing in several different ways so that receivers will have several chances rather than just one to get the message. In fact, that's one of the big advantages of an IMC program—it is designed to build in strategic redundancy by coordinating all the messages so they reinforce one another.

The Importance of Perceptions

Why does one brand have twice the share of another when there is no difference in the product attributes or performance and they both sell for the same price? The answer is a difference in perceptions. As noted in Chapter 2, a brand is a perception, not a strategy statement or a logo or the design on the side of a package. It exists only in people's minds. In the marketplace, perceptions are the collective result of everything a stakeholder sees, hears, reads, or experiences about a company and its brands. In other words, perceptions are the products of communication. In the head and heart of each person who is aware of a brand exists a perception that *is* the brand. That perception can be influenced through positive (and negative) communication experiences, but not controlled. The intangible nature of a brand led to the creative idea used in the Gucci ad in Exhibit 4–11.

A perception is real, at least for the person who holds it. Messages can influence these perceptions, but the perception is in the consumer's mind, not the company's messages. People's opinions are governed by their own perceptions, as are their responses to communication. Perceptions are reality because they determine behavior.

An example comes from the automotive industry. A creative director for Chrysler's in-house MC agency observed that the auto industry has a lot of parity products (i.e., products with few distinguishing features). In such a situation, perceptions become very important. He explained, "Practically the only difference that's left is the perception of what the car feels like and how it's gonna make you feel when you drive it."[14] The IMC process helps guard against a *perception virus* that can infect and weaken communication strategies or kill relationships.

Because communication is the lifeblood of any relationship, whether personal or commercial, managing brand relationships means managing all the communication that influences what people think about a brand—the impressions that lead to a brand perception. First encounters with a company always make an impact. Receptionists, telephone operators, and sales clerks are particularly important

GUCCI

EXHIBIT 4-11

The Gucci ad presents ties as art, a perception that is easy to understand because it connects with the upscale image that the Gucci brand has in people's minds.

in the management of this first impression. Midwesterners who occasionally call into New York or New Jersey offices, for example, often report that the people answering the phone are abrupt or rude. The fact is that people from different parts of the country often have different communication styles. It may be just a cultural thing, but a receptionist perceived to be unfriendly can send the wrong message. If the company cares about its business relationships with people from other parts of the United States or foreign countries, it needs to be sensitive to these differences and train its people accordingly.

The Role of Communication in Perception

Marketing communication can close the gap between intended and perceived messages. This is because MC messages can set brand expectations. When expectations are too high, a company must work to bring its product performance up to the proper level or send different messages to create a new set of perceptions. When a product has a higher level of quality than is perceived, marketing communication needs to raise the level of expected quality (i.e., promise more) to make the brand more competitive.

A company can add value to its brands by enabling customers to ask questions. Feeding a baby, for example, may sound like a simple thing, but many new parents find that it isn't always so. The baby-food company Gerber has a toll-free telephone number that parents can call with questions about feeding and raising a baby. Although the company does not give medical advice, its representatives do answer thousands of questions each month from new parents. Merely knowing that there is a place they can call and get answers is a tremendous added value to the parents buying Gerber baby food.

Since a perception is the result of communication, it provides a window on the success of the message strategy. In other words, tracking customer perceptions is an important source of feedback in evaluating brand messages.

5. FEEDBACK AND INTERACTIVITY

Companies are recognizing that two-way communication gives them immediate access to the receiver's response (i.e., feedback), as Anders Gronstedt explains in his book on world-class IMC companies.[15]

In addition to comments and dialogue, feedback also includes such responses to a marketing communication message as buying (or not buying) the product, asking for a demonstration or sample, requesting more information, visiting the store or showroom, or responding to a survey. New interactive media allow companies to evaluate responses in real-time research. Some companies listen in on Internet chat boards as a way to monitor real-time feedback.

When the feedback is no response or a negative response, a company needs to find out why. If the message was never received, it could mean that the wrong message delivery system (i.e., channel) was used, that it was sent to the wrong place or sent at the wrong time, that there was

> "The promotional monologue of advertising at the seller's convenience is being replaced by dialogue at the customer's convenience."
>
> Anders Gronstedt, *The Customer Century*

too much commercial message clutter or other noise, or that it was just the wrong message. If the message was received but misinterpreted, it could mean that the message was poorly encoded. If the message was received and properly decoded, but still there was no response, it could mean that either the message was not persuasive enough or the receiver was not a potential customer. When the latter is determined, the company should not waste money designing and sending further messages to this target audience or should significantly change the message to appeal to the recipient's other needs or interests.

Purposeful Dialogue

Integrated programs use two-way communication to send messages efficiently and to receive and capture messages from customers (and other stakeholders) in order to create a long-term, purposeful dialogue. **Purposeful dialogue** is *communication that is mutually beneficial for the customer and the company.* IMC does *not* mean just collecting customer and potential customer names and addresses in order to send them more and more brand messages. It *does* mean learning about customers in order to have a purposeful dialogue with them.

Although corporate executives and marketing managers talk a great deal about creating a dialogue with customers, in too many cases their brand communication is intrusive and irritating, and thus perceived as self-serving with no added value for the customer. Marketers obviously want to tell customers about products and persuade them to buy. For the communication to be mutually useful, however, the customer must want to hear about the products and choose to be exposed to this information, as the FM Global ad in Exhibit 4–12 demonstrates.

Companies should not, however, stimulate and facilitate interactivity indiscriminately. Because brand relationships are not all equal, and because having a dialogue with stakeholders costs the company money, gathering feedback should be done selectively. One of the early mistakes made by companies using the Internet was to invite everyone to talk to them. As a result, many of those who responded were not customers or potential customers, but merely disinterested people surfing the Internet. Few companies can afford the luxury of unproductive interactivity.

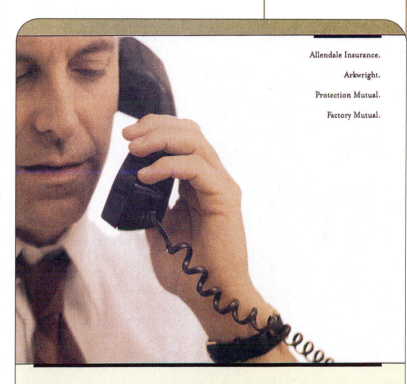

One of the easiest and most useful things a marketer can do to ensure that customers perceive the dialogue to be purposeful is to ask them what information they want about the brand, when and where they want it, and in what form they want it. This is especially true for business-to-business marketers selling complex goods and services in which there are many different product variations and divisions, often selling to the same customers. Some customers prefer receiving brand information by mail, others electronically; some wish to meet with sales representatives only on certain days. However, unless a marketer asks for this information and makes it available to everyone in the company who has contact with these customers, customers will not perceive brand messages as being respectful of their time.

The Five Rs of Purposeful Dialogue

Purposeful dialogue must embody the "five Rs" of interactivity: Customers are looking for *recourse*, *recognition*, and *responsiveness*—and companies must conduct their dialogue with *respect* in order to *reinforce* customer support.

Recourse

A major concern of most customers is how to avoid risk when buying a product. What are their options—that is, what recourse do they have—if they don't like the product, if it doesn't work properly, or if it breaks? How companies handle complaints will affect repeat purchases. This aspect of customer relations is second only to product quality in building customer loyalty.

The recourse problem begins with *ease of contact*. The easier it is for a customer to get questions answered and problems dealt with, the easier it will be for that customer to develop a supporting relationship with that company. The approachability of an organization, particularly when there is a problem, is an added value to customers. In a focus group for IBM customers a couple of years ago, one of the participants asked: "How do you call IBM?" Trying to call a company, particularly a large, multinational company, is a discouraging thought for most people.

Another critical aspect of recourse is *ease of solution*. A company's willingness to replace a product is negated if customers must fill out numerous forms, find receipts, send in the product at their own expense, and then wait weeks for a decision on the replacement. A manufacturer of telephones handles problems by having the customer mail the phone back to the company (at the customer's expense) and agree up front to a $35 service/handling charge. And customers learn of this policy only after they develop a problem. Think of the implied negative messages this policy sends: First of all, the product broke, so it did not meet performance expectations; second, there is no information on the product itself concerning what to do or where to send it, so customers must take the initiative to call the company; and finally, customers must go to a lot of trouble and expense to have the problem fixed.

In contrast, The Bombay Company, a furniture manufacturer and retailer, has a no-questions-asked policy. Said President and CEO Robert Nourse, "We'll take the thing back with no hassle, no questions, no guff about 'Where's the receipt?' The cost of that is peanuts compared with what you gain in customer loyalty."[16] Retailers have benefited by handling defective products for consumers. In other words, retailers are reducing risk for consumers, and consumers, in return, are transferring their loyalty to the retailer's brand rather than the manufacturer's brand.

Recognition

Customers and other stakeholders like to be personally *recognized*; that's one of the first steps in a relationship. When customers have given a company their business (or buy stock in the company), they feel a relationship has been established, even if the company sees it as an "acquisition." If the company fails to recognize this connection, then the customer or investor sees a disconnect in the relationship.

Even better is when a company knows a customer's transaction history and incorporates this into future transactions. Customers who are frequent buyers will receive special recognition. And customers who have had problems with the company in the past can receive empathetic attention. However, consumers are sophisticated enough to see through insincere recognition. In direct-mail solicitations, for instance, companies often address a potential customer by name. If the company has had no prior relationship with the customer, the person being contacted will recognize this as a ploy.

Responsiveness

Merely providing customers a toll-free number or an e-mail address so they can easily reach the company is not being *responsive*. Responsiveness consists of a company representative listening to the customer, putting the conversation into a context in light of the customer's profile and history, and staying with the customer until the problem is solved or next steps are agreed to. The amount of time that elapses between a customer's order, complaint, or request and the company's response sends a strong service message. Texas Instruments receives approximately 200,000 inquiries a year. Over 95 percent are answered within 2 hours and virtually all within 24 hours.[17]

Respect

Howard Gossage was a partner of a San Francisco advertising agency in the 1950s and 1960s. He has gone down in advertising history as one of the most insightful and intelligent people to ever work in this industry. Among many of his insights was that a marketer's audience was more important than the product or brand. He preached that, without *respect* for the audience, a company's advertising was sure to be a waste of money.

Focusing on customers doesn't mean smothering them with brand contacts. Customers aren't interested in interrupting their lives to receive corporate messages, idly chatting with marketers, or continually being offered another product or line extension that they don't need. Typical BtB customers, for example, receive between 20 and 60 pieces of mail each business day—the last thing they want is more junk mail. They resent intrusive messages and are creating more and more defense mechanisms against them. They will be more willing to be part of a commercial relationship if it is clear that the company respects them and their time.

In a focus group of business customers for a major computer company that had recently discovered database marketing, those in the group were quick to tell how intrusive this company's brand messages had become. The company had been bombarding these customers with surveys, customer satisfaction checks, new product information, and "courtesy calls." When this company was mentioned, one of the respondents said he had both their software and hardware, but if he received one more disruptive call from the company, he would move to a different brand, no matter how much the cost. He was just plain tired and disgusted, he said, of being bothered by this company.

Fifteen minutes later in this same discussion, respondents were asked if they would attend one of several half-day seminars sponsored by this particular computer company. One of the first people to say "yes" was the person who had threatened to drop the company. When asked why the change in attitude, he explained that he could schedule the seminar at his convenience. In other words, he was willing to give the company a half-day of his time on *his* schedule, but not two minutes on *its* schedule.

Reinforcement

One of the important benefits of mass-media advertising is reinforcement for people who have already purchased the product. In fact, studies have shown that in many cases the majority of ad readers are current customers. Reinforcement of a purchase decision, especially on high-ticket items, should be part of a company's communication strategy. The more expensive the item, the more likely it is that "buyer's remorse" (cognitive dissonance) may set in. Car dealers, for example, often call new buyers to make sure everything is working properly and to answer any questions customers might have about their new car's operation. This is another opportunity for dialogue that begins a long-term relationship.

FINAL NOTE: TWO-WAY COMMUNICATION

Because stakeholder and customer relationships are influenced heavily by messages from and to a company, marketing approaches that focus on relationship building operate with a marketing model that includes more than the traditional four Ps of product, price, place, and promotion (as discussed in Chapter 1). Figure 4–5 provides a model that depicts the relationship-creating elements of communication. It identifies (in the boxes on the left) all the various message sources at the corporate, marketing, and marketing communication levels, and (on the right), all the various stakeholder and customer audiences. Interactivity (in the middle) is what connects the company and its stakeholders and makes the brand relationships possible that lead to the creation of brand value.

In the past, feedback was limited to periodic customer tracking studies and ad hoc market research surveys. When IMC is used, however, the concept and processes of acquiring feedback are greatly expanded. For one thing, as you will learn in Chapter 5, in most buying situations there are numerous steps in the buying process, and it is possible to involve customers and get feedback at each step in order to know what the customers are thinking and planning to do. Also, brand relationships encourage interactions and dialogue, each of which can be considered feedback to brand messages.

New telecommunication and computer technologies have made it more cost-effective to listen to customers, record their comments, and facilitate their questions, complaints, and concerns. They have also made it possible for customers and other stakeholders to initiate conversations with companies about their brands. Because of this new world of two-way communication, the interface between companies and their customers and stakeholders is becoming more important than ever before.

FIGURE 4-5

This model shows how interactivity links a company and its stakeholders.

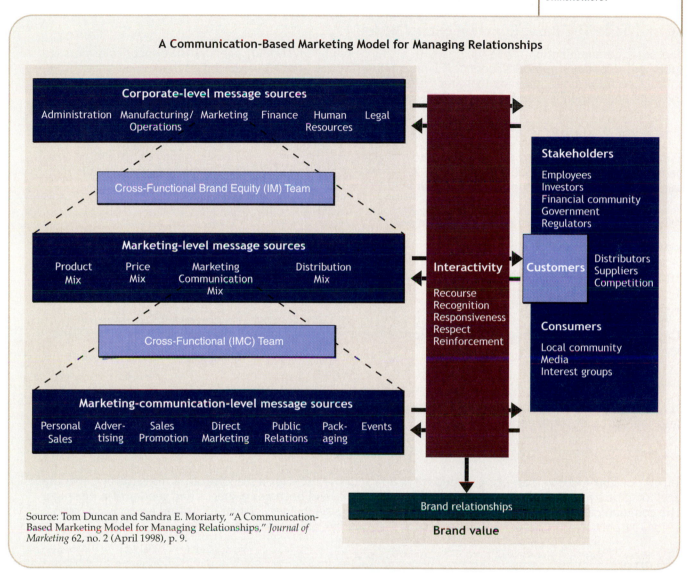

A Communication-Based Marketing Model for Managing Relationships

Corporate-level message sources

Administration   Manufacturing/   Marketing   Finance   Human   Legal
                 Operations   Resources

Cross-Functional Brand Equity (IM) Team

Marketing-level message sources

Product   Price   Marketing   Distribution
Mix   Mix   Communication   Mix
                  Mix

Cross-Functional (IMC) Team

Marketing-communication-level message sources

Personal   Adver-   Sales   Direct   Public   Pack-   Events
Sales   tising   Promotion   Marketing   Relations   aging

Interactivity

Recourse
Recognition
Responsiveness
Respect
Reinforcement

Stakeholders

Employees
Investors
Financial community
Government
Regulators

Customers   Distributors
Suppliers
Competition

Consumers

Local community
Media
Interest groups

Brand relationships

Brand value

Source: Tom Duncan and Sandra E. Moriarty, "A Communication-Based Marketing Model for Managing Relationships," *Journal of Marketing* 62, no. 2 (April 1998), p. 9.

Key Terms

encoding 125
decoding 126
message 126
medium (plural: media) 126
noise 127
feedback 127

brand messages 128
crisis management plan 137
interactive media 138
brand contact point 138
purposeful dialogue 147

Key Points Summary

This chapter covers the communication theories that help us understand IMC and, particularly, the interactive dimension of brand communication.

Key Point 1: The Basic Communication Model

The basic communication model begins with a source (company/brand, agency) that encodes a message (planned, unplanned, product, service), which is transmitted through media (mass media and other brand contact points). Amid noise (clutter and conflict), a receiver then decodes (perceives and interprets) the message and responds with feedback (response, behavior).

Key Point 2: Everything Sends a Message

Everything a company does (and sometimes what it doesn't do) sends a message about the brand or company; a company cannot *not* communicate. The message typology identifies four basic types of brand messages: planned, product, service, and unplanned.

Key Point 3: Media and Contact Points

Media include any person, event, or thing that carries a brand message. Every interaction that a customer or other stakeholder has with one of these message delivery points is called a brand contract point, and every point of contact delivers brand messages that are either intrinsic or created.

Key Point 4: Noise

The noise that affects marketing communication messages consists of mixed messages, conflicting messages, and clutter.

Key Point 5: Receiver Perceptions

Perceptions, which are the products of communication, are the collective result of everything a customer sees, hears, reads, or experiences about a company and its brands.

Key Point 6: Feedback and Interactivity

In relationship-focused marketing, feedback is not only the receiver's response to a message but also the beginning of a new message as the receiver switches roles and becomes a source and sender of a message. The communication expectations of customers and other stakeholders can be identified as recourse, recognition, responsiveness, respect, and reinforcement—the 5Rs of interactivity.

Lessons Learned

Key Point 1: *The Basic Communication Model*

a. List the key elements in a basic communication model and the order in which they occur in the communication process.
b. What's the difference between encoding and decoding?
c. Using the communication-based model of marketing, analyze the HB Ice Cream case and explain how the various elements in the case fit into the model.

Key Point 2: *Everything Sends a Message*

a. Define a message in an IMC program.

b. Explain the four types of IMC messages and give examples of each from the HB Ice Cream case. If an area isn't discussed explicitly in the case, then recommend a way to introduce that element into the next year's campaign plan.

c. Have you ever had a bad experience with a service company? Analyze how the messages were delivered and what messages were being sent. What would you recommend that the company do to improve the problems you uncovered?

Key Point 3: Media and Contact Points

a. How are messages delivered in an IMC program?

b. Define the term *brand contact point* and explain the difference between the two types of brand contact points. Analyze the HB Ice Cream case for examples of contact points. If an area isn't discussed explicitly in the case, then recommend a way to introduce that element into the next year's campaign.

c. Develop a list of contact points for your college or university that a potential student might encounter. Analyze the messages delivered at those points, and prioritize them in terms of their importance.

Key Point 4: Noise

a. Explain mixed messages, message conflict, and message clutter.

b. What problems does noise create in the marketing communication process?

c. You are working on the Pepsi account. What types of noise might interfere with this brand's communication?

Key Point 5: Receiver Perceptions

a. What does it mean to say that perceptions are the product of communication?

b. What does it mean to say that perception is reality?

c. Develop a list of products for which your perception of *value* is the most important decision factor in whether or not you buy them. Now create a list of products you buy based on *price* and another based on *perceived quality*. What are the differences among the three lists? What do these lists say about your personality and values?

Key Point 6: Interactivity and Feedback

a. What is feedback, and how is it generated in IMC programs?

b. What is involved in real-time market research?

c. By reading professional or trade magazines, find a company that you think does a good job of managing feedback from its stakeholders. Outline how feedback operates for this company.

Chapter Challenge

Writing Assignment

You have been asked to advise a club to which you belong on how to manage its communication program. Develop for the club its own communication model and explain how the model can help the club identify its communication problems and develop better communication programs and activities.

Presentation Assignment

For a club or other organization to which you belong, develop a presentation to give to the club's executive committee that focuses on how understanding the communication model can help the club develop better communication strategies. Develop an outline of the key points you want to present. Give the presentation to your class or record it on a videotape (audiotape is also an option) to turn in to your instructor, along with the outline.

Internet Assignment

Have you ever had a bad experience traveling by air? Or a good experience? Did you make an effort to complain to or compliment the company? There are a number of websites that handle complaints on behalf of travelers for a fee, particularly the complaints that can result in ticket refunds. The Department of Transportation has set up an electronic in-basket for complaints about two particular topics, airline pricing and overbooking (go to www.oig.dot.gov). The Better Business Bureau of New York also compiles complaints from its site (www.newyork.bbb.org) and relays them to the Department of Transportation. Travel agency OneTravel.com has set up a website (www.1travel.com) with complaint channels and consumer-affairs materials. Consult two of these websites and compile their advice and your own ideas on how to write both a complaint letter and a compliment letter.

Additional Readings

Duncan, Thomas R., and Sandra E. Moriarty. "A Communication-Based Marketing Model of Managing Relationships." *Journal of Marketing* 62, no. 2 (April 1998), pp. 1–13.

Christopher, Martin; Adrian Payne; and David Ballantyne. *Relationship Marketing: Bringing Quality, Customer Service, and Marketing Together*. Oxford, UK: Butterworth-Heinemann, 1991.

Dawar, Niraj, and Philip Parker. "Marketing Universals: Consumers' Use of Brand Name, Price, Physical Appearance, and Retailer Reputation as Signals of Product Quality." *Journal of Marketing* 58 (April 1994), pp. 81–95.

McCracken, Grant, and Victor J. Roth. "Does Clothing Have a Code? Empirical Findings and Theoretical Implications in the Study of Clothing as a Means of Communication." *International Journal of Research in Marketing* 6 (1989), pp. 13–33.

Research Assignment

This chapter notes that a lot of marketing communication messages, as well as other marketing mix decisions, are really designed to be signals to customers. Consult the articles and books listed above, and others you find on the concept of marketing signals and how they work. Find a brand for which you can compare advertising as a signal of the product's quality to other signals such as the price of the product and the place where it is distributed. What are their relative effects as quality signals? Do the signals send conflicting messages? Which signals seem to have the most impact? Write up the results of your analysis in a short paper for your instructor.

Endnotes

[1]Nicholas Negroponte, *Being Digital* (New York: Alfred A. Knopf, 1995), p. 92.

[2]Pam Weisz, "Times Sure Have Changed When Tupperware Is Cool," *Brandweek,* November 21, 1994, p. 18.

[3]Greg Burns, "McDonald's: Now, It's Just Another Burger Joint," *Business Week,* March 17, 1997, p. 38.

[4]A. Parasuraman, V. A. Zeithaml, and Lenoard Berry, "SERVQUAL: A Multiple-Item Scale for Measuring Consumer Perceptions of Service Quality," *Journal of Retailing* 64, no. 1 (1988), pp. 12–40.

[5]Robert Langreth and Andrea Petersen, "A Stampede Is on for Impotence Pill," *The Wall Street Journal,* April 20, 1998, p. B1.

[6]Thomas Goetz, "Viruses on Vacation? Vaccine Ad Bugs Travel Industry," *The Wall Street Journal,* April 20, 1998, p. B1.

[7]Mike Haggerty and Wallace Rasmussen, *The Headlines vs. The Bottom Line* (Nashville, TN: Vanderbilt University First Amendment Center, 1994), p. 23.

[8]Ibid.

[9]Roger Hallowell, Leonard A. Schlesinger, and Jeffrey Zornitsky, "Internal Service Quality, Customer and
    Job Satisfaction: Linkages and Implications for Management," *Human Resource Planning* 19, no. 2,
    1996, pp. 20-32.

[10]Rahul Jacob, "Why Some Customers Are More Equal Than Others," *Fortune,* September 19, 1994, p. 218.

[11]Jason Riley, "How Companies Handle Customer-Created Brand Contacts," *IMC Research Journal,* 2001,
    p. 6.

[12]Tom Williams, "US West Revamps Customer Service," *Telephony* (February 12, 1995), p. 7: Julia King,
    "US West's Failed Restructuring Spells IS Overhaul," *Computerworld* (February 17, 1995), p. 6.

[13]Tom Duncan and Sandra Moriarty, *Driving Brand Value,* (New York: McGraw-Hill, 1997), p. 6.

[14]Stan Gelsi, "Detroit's Model Year," *Brandweek,* January 1, 1996, pp. 19-23.

[15]Anders Gronstedt, *The Customer Century: Lessons from World-Class Companies in Integrated Marketing
    and Communications* (New York: Routledge, 2000), p. 7.

[16]Jay Finegan, "Survival of the Smartest," *Inc. Magazine,* December 1993, p. 88.

[17]Earl Naumann, *Creating Customer Value,* (Cincinnati: Thompson Executive Press, 1995), p. 82.

5

The Brand Decision Process

Key Points in This Chapter

1. What are the three factors that influence brand decision making?

2. What distinguishes the three buying-behavior situations and their models?

3. What are the five basic brand decision-making steps?

4. How do hierarchy-of-effects persuasion models work?

Chapter Perspective

Speaking to the Head and the Heart

In order to acquire, retain, and grow customers, companies need to know how customers and prospects make brand decisions—how they decide to buy and repurchase one brand versus others. The brand decision process can be primarily cognitive (rational) or primarily experiential (emotional) depending on the product category and situation. Is the customer solving a problem or taking advantage of an opportunity? The process is also different for current customers versus prospective customers, and for consumers versus business customers.

Buying behavior is complex. People do not make decisions in a vacuum, nor does everyone act in the same way. Every brand contact point contributes to attitudes about a brand and affects behavior. Because brand decision making is partly rational and partly emotional, brands must speak to both the head and the heart. The overriding objectives of marketing communications are to ignite and/or intervene in the brand decision process. Reaching these objectives requires a keen understanding of the process in all its major variations.

There are several pathways through the brand decision process. Some customers spend time searching for information, while others buy without much thought. Two customers who appear to be similar may have entirely different needs that must be addressed in different ways by marketing communications. In most brand situations, there are a variety of brand messages aimed at different customer types, which can result in a jumble of messages. The marketing communication challenge is to create brand messages that are consistent but at the same time relevant to each target audience.

This chapter first looks at factors that influence brand decision making and discusses three buying-behavior situations (cognitive, experiential, and repeat/habit). It then outlines the five basic brand decision steps (recognition, search, evaluation, action, and review). Finally, it discusses persuasion in terms of a model called think/feel/do.

USING HEADS AND HEARTS TO MAKE HEALTH DECISIONS
McCann-Erickson Southwest, Houston, Texas

In the late 1990s, the Parkinson Coalition of Houston obtained funding to expand its reach to minorities afflicted with Parkinson's disease, a progressive disorder of the nervous system marked by shaking limbs, muscle weakness, and difficulty in walking (see Exhibit 5–1). The assignment given to MC agency McCann-Erickson Southwest was to create a campaign that would inform minorities of the symptoms and motivate them to contact Parkinson care facilities to seek treatment or offer support.

The Marketing Challenge

The Parkinson Coalition of Houston was formed by an alliance between the Houston Area Parkinson Society and the Parkinson Foundation of Harris County. The Houston Area and the Harris County groups had been around for 24 and 18 years, respectively. Most people with Parkinson's disease in greater Houston were moderately aware of the two groups. However, awareness and interest among racial and ethnic minority groups were low. So this campaign was designed to create a change in the attitudes and behaviors of minorities and to touch their minds as well as their feelings.

This "Real Victims" campaign was the first campaign in the local area designed to reach minority populations with information about Parkinson's. Previous marketing efforts of the Houston Area and Harris County groups had been limited to brochures primarily distributed to medical practitioners, hospitals, and care centers.

EXHIBIT 5-1

The blurred image of a man with Parkinson's disease helps to emotionally illustrate the confused world in which these patients live.

Knowledge and Attitudes

Three key audience factors made the development of this campaign a strategic and creative challenge: (1) skepticism regarding the helpfulness of the Parkinson's organizations (an emotional barrier), (2) embarrassment among those with the disease (an emotional barrier), and (3) an overall lack of knowledge of the disease (a rational barrier). For example, Parkinson Coalition staff members noted that some people believed the disease was caused only by repeated trauma to the head. Others confused the symptoms with signs of old age. This overall lack of knowledge of the disease often kept those who suffered it from seeking help, leaving many people untreated. Members of the target audience were also believed to be more skeptical about whether the Parkinson organizations could actually help them. Thus, it was important for the Parkinson Coalition to establish trust and credibility with them.

Campaign Strategy

The McCann team identified its primary target audience in Houston as African Americans and Hispanics 50 years or older who were afflicted with Parkinson's disease. The broader secondary target audience included all adults 50 or older with Parkinson's disease. The campaign objective was to expand the target market for the services of the Parkinson Coalition in order to reach these segments of the population, who were largely underserved by the organization's programs. Specifically, the campaign was designed to increase the amount of minority contact with the coalition.

The communication strategy was designed to inspire and connect with the primary and secondary target audiences on an emotional level by focusing on people who had the disease but were hiding it; these people were identified sympathetically as the "real victims." The ads used a general theme of "how I once was versus how I am now" that was designed to connect with the target audiences as well as provide empathy. Demonstration of the disease's most common symptom (trembling) was used to clarify what the symptom looked like to distinguish it from other, similar disease symptoms.

The Parkinson Coalition's "Real Victims" campaign used television exclusively because it was really the only medium through which the McCann team could visually show the key symptom, and it also provided the best opportunity to create an emotional response among viewers (see Exhibit 5–2). The campaign planners felt that an emotional response was necessary to maximize contact with the coalition.

Another important strategy was to provide different commercial executions for the two different minority groups that made up the primary audience. This allowed McCann to construct each spot with the different cultural and racial differences in mind. The characters in the different ads could speak in a language or accent that the target audience could relate to and appreciate.

EXHIBIT 5-2

Closing shot of Parkinson Coalition TV commercial providing phone number so those interested can call and request more information.

Creative Tactics

The commercial targeted to the African-American audience used a blues guitar player who was having trouble getting his fingers to cooperate the way they used to. The key line in this spot was, "living life in slow motion."

The spot targeted to Hispanics featured an older Hispanic gentleman trying to tie his shoes with trembling hands. He explained that he felt like he was getting old before his time and that his body had a mind of its own. A key visual effect used in this spot showed the lead character moving in and out of focus, the blurring creating a visual metaphor for the loss of control that haunts those with Parkinson's disease.

Touching Hearts and Minds

The "Real Victims" campaign created by McCann-Erickson for the Houston Parkinson's Coalition was a highly successful public service campaign that motivated a significant percentage of the target audiences to respond. The commercial touched the hearts and minds of minority populations with empathetic and believable messages, as measured by the sizable portion of minorities with Parkinson's disease who had been reluctant in the past to contact Parkinson centers for help but who began to take advantage of the services available to them following the campaign.

This case was adapted with permission from the Advertising and Marketing Effectiveness (AME) award-winning brief for the Parkinson Coalition of Houston, Texas, prepared by McCann-Erickson Southwest.

FACTORS THAT INFLUENCE BRAND DECISIONS

To understand how IMC works, you must first understand the decision-making process from the customer's or prospect's perspective. How do prospects decide to buy for the first time (and thus become customers)? How do customers decide to make repeat purchases? How do customers decide to increase their business with a company? Answers to these questions lie in this chapter.

Although individuals approach buying decisions in unique ways because of past experiences and cultural surroundings, there are three basic factors that help predict what type of decision model a given customer will use. The first factor is the extent of the customer's involvement (high to low) with the product category. The more involved they are, the more complex the decision-making process. Second is whether the decision is being made by a current customer or a prospect. Third is whether the buyer is a consumer (who chooses the product for personal use) or a business buyer (who chooses the product for use in making or selling other products, or for resale).

Involvement

The more involved customers and prospects are with the product category and brand, and the more relevant they are to their lives, the more likely a prospective customer will spend time searching for the "right" brand. Involvement is in the heads and hearts of customers. Although we talk about high- and low-involvement *products*, involvement is a *perception* attributed to products by customers. Nevertheless, there are many product categories that most customers approach with a fairly common level of involvement. Most customers are highly involved with their choice of doctors and dentists, for example, while most are not highly involved in deciding between several brands of frozen vegetables or brands of gasoline.

High-involvement products are considered to be *products for which customers perceive differences among brands and are willing to invest prepurchase decision-making energy*. Such products represent above-average risk and expense. Obvious examples are computers, cars, brokerage services, and real estate. Other possibilities are jewelry, wine, and (for some people) even such items as ice cream or golf course memberships. High-involvement products are those that customers especially care about. Other types of products, such as candy bars, detergent, and toilet paper, are considered to be **low-involvement products**, or *products bought on impulse or without much consideration*. These purchases have low risk and few, if any, important consequences.

Customers base most high-involvement decisions on lots of information. There are, however, high-involvement products (such as fine jewelry, expensive cars, and works of art) that appeal first to feelings. Messages about these products appeal to customers' desires, wants, emotions, and self-image. This is also the type of strategy McCann-Erickson used in its "Real Victims" campaign for the Parkinson's Coalition (see the chapter opening case).

Customers and Prospects

In most courses and textbooks on buying behavior, customers are considered to be anyone who has bought or might buy a product. IMC speaks in terms of **prospects** (*those who have not bought the brand but who might be interested in it*) and **customers** (*those who have purchased the brand at least once within a designated period*). From a company perspective, motivating a prospect to buy for the first time is the process of acquiring a customer and thus requires an *acquisition strategy*. Motivating a customer to make repeat purchases is a *retention strategy*. Getting customers to buy more frequently or in greater quantity than they have in the past is a *growth strategy*. Acquisition, retention, and growth call for different types of message strategies because the groups involved in each use different pathways in making a brand decision, and those pathways affect their response to marketing communication.

One of the biggest mistakes a company can make is to take it for granted that current customers will continue to make repeat purchases. Persuading current customers to stay loyal to a brand may be easier and less costly than motivating a prospect to buy, but it still requires some effort in maintaining the customer relationship.

With new brands, everyone is a prospect rather than a customer. To acquire customers for a new brand, companies need to know how customers find out about brands and decide to adopt them. (This will be explained in more detail in Chapter 7, on segmentation and targeting.) Keep in mind that there are two types of "new." From a company's perspective, a brand is new when it is first introduced into the marketplace. For prospects, a brand is new when they first learn about it. A brand can be on the market for years before some people see it or hear of it. The BASF ad in Exhibit 5–3 celebrates the spirit of innovation that leads to a parade of new products.

Consumers and Businesses

Create a new world where lightweight plastics can outfly metals.

Aerospace designers are limited by their materials, not their dreams.

At BASF, we looked at the design limitations of metals and saw the need for a radically new generation of materials. The result: strong, lightweight, carbon fiber reinforced plastics. These Advanced Composite Materials will enable future designs to carry more, faster, farther.

In one industry after another, from aerospace to automotive, our broad-based technologies help us create new worlds by seeing in new ways.

The Spirit of Innovation

BASF

EXHIBIT 5-3

Knowing that manufacturers often have the choice between using metals or plastics for certain products, this brand message created by chemical products company BASF urges adoption of its "radically new generation of materials."

A business, like a consumer, can be either a prospect or a current customer and can also approach different buying decisions with different levels of involvement. Other than that, however, consumer decision making and business decision making differ in several ways. The major differences are that businesses are more likely to use a cognitive decision-making process than an experiential one (discussed later in this chapter) and are likely to go into more depth at each step in this process than consumers are. The Liberty Mutual ads in Exhibit 5–4 illustrates a business-to-business (BtB) marketing communication campaign that uses a problem-solution message.

There are other factors that also differentiate between consumer and business buying. Recognizing the following differences enables marketers to create relevant messages and target them accurately:

- Most businesses buy goods in larger quantities than consumers do, which means the average business transaction is generally worth considerably more than the average consumer transaction. A consumer, for example, may buy one pair of shoes on a given shopping trip, but a shoe manufacturer buys tons of leather at one time.

- Business-buying decisions generally involve inputs from more than one person. The larger the decision, the more people involved. While some businesspeople have buying authority, others who do not have such authority can still greatly influence the buying decision. Identifying who has the buying authority is usually not as difficult as determining who can influence the buying decision.

- Large business transactions often affect other activities within a company. Therefore, business buying carries higher risk than consumer buying. Minimizing risk is always an objective of business buyers.

- Businesses, unlike consumers, make few impulse decisions.

- Many business-buying decisions are made according to how those wanting to sell to them respond to requests for proposals (RFPs). When a business wants to make a major purchase, it will often announce its want or need and invite companies to propose how they would satisfy the needs and wants as specified in the announcement. The Internet has enabled companies to send out their RFPs to more bidders and made the response process faster than ever before. RFPs form a common business platform on the Internet and have even moved into business-to-consumer marketing with the success of such companies as Priceline.com.

Some companies sell to both consumer and BtB markets, which means they must be aware of, and respond to, different buying-decision processes. For example, Kleenex doesn't sell its tissues to consumers the same way it sells them to retailers or to hospitals and retirement homes.

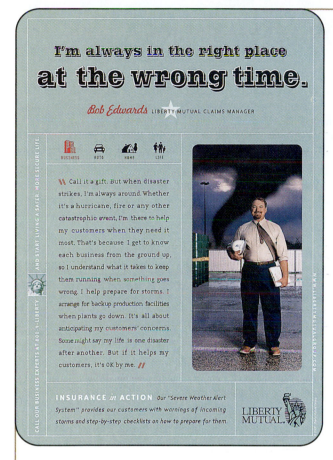

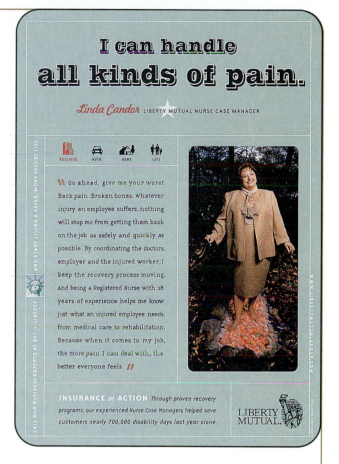

EXHIBIT 5-4

Using a problem-solution strategy and headlines that seem to say the opposite of what one would expect, this Liberty Mutual campaign is aimed at businesses.

Companies buy goods and services from other companies for one of three purposes: (1) to resell to individuals or other companies such as distributors and retailers, (2) to use in the production of other goods and services, and (3) to use in the process of running a business or office. Their buying decisions are (or should be) based on what the end user wants and is willing to pay for. This is called *derived demand* because a company derives its need for a particular product from another company or a group of consumers.

For example, when General Motors (GM) makes cars, it buys from other companies many of the things that go into its cars, such as radios, tires, and batteries. Car buyers demand that such components be of a certain quality and design. Therefore, a manufacturer of car radios will market not only to General Motors, but also to General Motors' dealers and customers, because both dealers and customers influence how GM makes and equips its cars. Consequently, the radio manufacturer should get to know the needs and wants of its customer's customers (i.e., GM's customers) and address these in its sales materials. In this way the radio maker can anticipate what its business customers will be buying. Also, it can influence the customers of the targeted businesses to request the company's products.

The Intel Inside campaign is an example of a marketing communication effort that encourages customers to demand Intel processors in the computers they buy. This, in turn, puts pressure on computer manufacturers to buy computer chips from Intel. This is called a "pull" strategy.

THREE BUYING-BEHAVIOR SITUATIONS

Some people approach the purchase of a product like a car from a cognitive, rational viewpoint, searching for information in order to better understand the product and its features, and how the product compares to those of competitors. Other people purchase a car because of its styling or its association with a certain lifestyle or status level; this is an experiential, emotional approach (see Figure 5–1). The two approaches to decision making are not mutually exclusive, as illustrated in the chapter opening case, where the target audience for the Parkinson Coalition of Houston used both their heads and hearts in deciding how to respond. However, in most buying situations, one approach is generally more dominant than the other.

Although marketers have known for years that buying decisions are influenced by both the head and the heart, they assumed the head played a much more important role. This resulted in a series of models that were designed to explain decision making rationally. In recent years, however, marketers have been giving more attention to the role that emotion plays in decision making, as Mike Solomon points out: "Consumer behavior has been strongly influenced by the information-processing paradigm, which views consumers as rational decision makers; but many in the field are now beginning to embrace the experiential paradigm, which stresses the subjective, nonrational aspects of consumption as well as cultural influences on consumer behavior."[1]

One of the biggest problems marketers face, say Kevin Clancy and Robert Shulman in their book *Marketing Revolution,* is the dependency on a cognitive model for consumer behavior.[2] In an article in *American Demographics,* David Wolfe cites research to show that different mental processes lead to different kinds of decision making.[3] In sum, it is dangerous to oversimplify the decision-making process and think it can be explained in just one way with just one model. This chapter will explain three different models, the cognitive model, which is the traditional and most popular; the experiential model, which is growing in acceptance; and the habit/repeat model, which, although relatively simple, actually explains the majority of purchases that are made.

Cognitive Decision Making

The cognitive model of buying behavior is based on a type of information processing. It says that once customers recognize a problem or opportunity, they (1) think about it; (2) search for the information, comparing product features that will help solve the problem or take advantage of the opportunity; (3) rationally evaluate the alternatives; and (4) make a decision that is as objective as possible. Emotion can exist within this model, but it plays a minor role. Customers are said to use the cognitive model in situations where there is a significant element of risk and they are aware of the consequences of their actions. They are thus inclined to take more time (than in the other models) to become informed and think carefully about the alternatives before taking some kind of action. That is why such purchases are sometimes called *considered purchases.*

Prospects and customers are, according to this model, likely to use rational criteria when considering an expensive product (car, insurance policy, computer, furniture); an unfamiliar product category (medicine, legal counsel, or financial services); an infrequently purchased product (kitchen appliances, exotic foods,

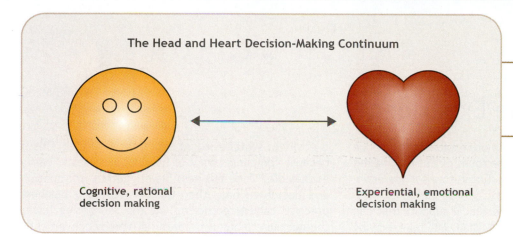

The Head and Heart Decision-Making Continuum

Cognitive, rational
decision making

Experiential, emotional
decision making

FIGURE 5-1

Head and Heart Decision-Making Continuum

rodent extermination services, transmission fluid for cars); or a high-involvement product category (pets, education, clothing). Once consumers take an action, they evaluate it rationally as well. If this evaluation is positive, customers give themselves permission to repeat the action or purchase.

Experiential Decision Making

In the experiential model of decision making, customers recognize problems and opportunities from an emotional perspective. When a person no longer feels good about wearing a particular suit, for example, this experience can motivate a search for information on suits and where they are sold. When the person sees an ad for a new suit, his or her response will include such thoughts as "I wonder how I would look in that?" How well the suit is made, the price, and the credit terms are not likely to be factors in this decision process, since information is less important to this customer than are his or her feelings about the alternatives. The customer's evaluation of the decision is likewise emotionally based, with either good or bad feelings about the action taken. A good feeling says it is OK to make the same decision again.

There is an increasing interest in the experiential aspect of brands. Joseph Pine and James Gilmore's book, *The Experience Economy,* shows how "experiencing" is becoming a major consideration in marketing.[4] One of the main reasons for this is the significant increase in service businesses. Because services are "experiences," and both consumers and businesses are using more services than ever before, it should be no surprise that brand decisions are increasingly being made with an experiential decision-making approach.

Whereas the cognitive model focuses heavily on information processing, the experiential approach aims to intensify the customer's level of involvement with a brand and can therefore stimulate a deeper emotional response. The concept of experiences provides another way to increase the involvement a prospect or customer has with a product category, even with traditionally low-involvement products. Pine and Gilmore explain that the experience realm is characterized by absorption and immersion, what they describe as the kind of connection that unites customers with the buying experience (see the IMC in Action Box).[5]

> "The newly identified offering of experiences occurs whenever a company intentionally uses services as the stage and goods as props to engage an individual."
>
> Joseph Pine and James Gilmore, *The Experience Economy*

IMC IN ACTION

Marketing the Experience

As Joseph Pine and James Gilmore explain in their book *The Experience Economy*, the focus of business in the last half of the 20th century shifted to a service economy, and even goods now have service elements, such as financing programs and technical support that can sometimes drive the buying decision. And now, moving into the 21st century, where competitive advantage is increasingly difficult to find, the focus of business is on experiences and how they transform commodity goods and services into products that engage customers in personal ways and create brand relationships.

The buying experience, as Pine and Gilmore explain it, is based on the concept of marketing as theater. That's why theme restaurants and department stores such as Bloomingdale's and Nordstrom have focused on creating an exciting retail environment. The retail store becomes an environment in which customers are participants in the "staging of the shopping play." In such a setting, peripheral processing (discussed later in this chapter) becomes increasingly important because the environmental cues are what set the stage.

Although companies can use an experience-based approach to motivate prospects to buy, it is naturally a way to reach customers who have already bought the product and hence have experience with the brand. The goal of experiential marketing is to make the brand experience so positive and so engaging that customers keep coming back.

The business-to-business buying situation begins with the cognitive model and then, if the experience is positive, switches to an experiential model. This is because companies want to handle purchases as easily as possible. Once business buyers gather information and decide to buy, they then switch to a business practice called reordering. At the reordering level, the decision to buy is primarily driven by convenience and trust; these become peripheral factors that can be evaluated only through experience. Even business buyers can be delighted and surprised, however, when the reordering process is effortless.

The experiential approach to marketing is also in line with IMC's emphasis on customer retention. Pine and Gilmore emphasize that staging experiences in business is not about entertaining customers but rather about engaging them. They more they are engaged in brand-related experiences, the more likely they are to begin and maintain a relationship with that brand.

Think About It

What does an experience-based approach to marketing contribute to the customer's brand decision process? How does it intersect with IMC? What brand-related experiences have you participated in and how did they affect you?

Source: B. Joseph Pine and James H. Gilmore, *The Experience Economy: Work is Theatre & Every Business a Stage* (Boston: Harvard Business School Press, 1999).

Another dimension of this intensified involvement is lifestyle relevance. Marketing programs, such as promotions and public relations, that link a brand with a good cause can drive up the emotional involvement between a customer and a brand. That's why Avon has adopted breast cancer research as a cause to support, one that has a deep meaning for its women customers.

Habit/Repeat Decision Making

Habit or repeat decision making comes into use after one of the other two models have been used and a brand is evaluated as being OK to repurchase. This means that when a customer recognizes a problem or opportunity similar to the one that prompted the original purchase, the same response is triggered. There is little or no information search or evaluation of choices. An example in BtB buying would be a utility company that needs gasoline to operate its service trucks. The company uses a cognitive model to find which brand of gasoline will provide not only the best performance but also the best price. Once the utility company makes a decision and the brand's performance meets or exceeds expectations, utility truck drivers are told to buy that brand of gasoline whenever they need it. The information search is eliminated on these repeat purchases, although there is ongoing evaluation of the brand's performance.

This is an extremely important model in IMC because it is the one that most customers use when they repurchase a brand, especially those brands that are purchased frequently and are not extremely expensive. This is the decision-making model that drives customer retention. Although this model can replace either a cognitive or experiential model, neither cognition nor emotion plays a major role in this type of decision making because it is so automatic. It is the automatic part, especially for consumers, that turns brand selection into a habit. Ask your parents or friends why they always buy a certain brand, and they likely will tell you, "I have just always bought that brand." Sometimes they can't even remember why they first started buying it.

The main things that will make a current customer quit using habit/repeat decision making is when the brand is not available or when the ongoing review of the brand shows it to be unsatisfactory. An unsatisfactory evaluation could result from a price increase, a change in performance or quality, or the recognition of a better way to solve the problem.

An example of a decision process that requires little or no thinking or emotional involvement is just-in-time (JIT) ordering, where the customer's supply level is monitored by the supplier and the order is automatically placed when the level falls to a certain point. JIT is all done electronically, with the customer and supplier tied together through linked databases.

Figure 5–2 shows the three decision models and the steps used in each. Note that the steps are fewer in the habit/repeat model than in the first two models. But all begin with problem/opportunity recognition and end with decision review.

FIGURE 5-2

Most customers use a variety of ways to make brand decisions.

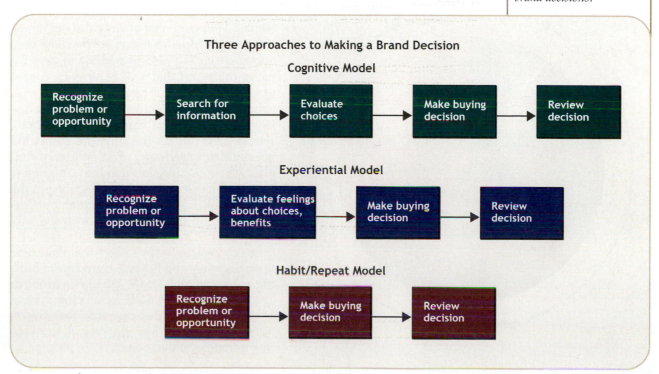

Three Approaches to Making a Brand Decision

Cognitive Model

Recognize problem or opportunity → Search for information → Evaluate choices → Make buying decision → Review decision

Experiential Model

Recognize problem or opportunity → Evaluate feelings about choices, benefits → Make buying decision → Review decision

Habit/Repeat Model

Recognize problem or opportunity → Make buying decision → Review decision

Figure 5–3 illustrates how the three decision models interrelate with high- and low-involvement products. Note that the habit/repeat model is at the bottom and straddles the differentiation between the cognitive and experiential models. This is because this model can begin with either a cognitive or a nonrational motivation. Because the habit/repeat model requires little involvement, it is at the bottom of the involvement circle. This figure also illustrates that there are various degrees of involvement in both of the other models.

BASIC BRAND DECISION-MAKING STEPS

Each step of the cognitive decision-making model (and thus also of the other two models) contains several psychological dimensions, as shown in Table 5–1. The explanations of these dimensions in the following sections will give you a deeper understanding of the role and importance of each step in the brand decision process.

Step 1: Problem and Opportunity Recognition

FIGURE 5-3

Generally speaking, the more important the brand decision, the higher the involvement.

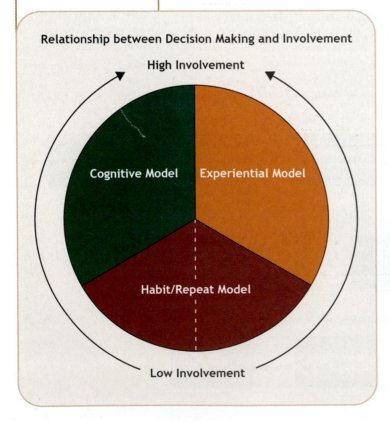

Relationship between Decision Making and Involvement

Purchase decisions begin in one of two ways: either by recognizing a problem that creates a need (or want) or by recognizing an opportunity that will provide a benefit not previously thought of or considered possible. The opportunity is presented by a brand message.

Think how you take class notes and then use these notes to study. If you are like most students, you don't see this as a problem but rather a usual, necessary procedure. You know how to do it and are satisfied with the results. Then you read an article about a new software product that not only makes note taking easier but also provides a system for using the notes that will raise your course grade by one letter. The product comes with a money-back guarantee. The brand message in the article (which came from a publicity release sent out by the software company) presents an *opportunity*. You suddenly find yourself in a decision-making situation— should you buy the product described in the article, look for something similar but less expensive, or just be satisfied with the way things are?

In contrast, if you are aware that your note taking is lousy and that your grades are hurting as a result, you know you have a problem and thus a need—a need for a better system of note taking. In this case it is the *problem recognition* rather than the brand message that initiates the decision-making process.

TABLE   5 - 1   The Cognitive Decision Process

Steps	Psychological Dimensions
1. Problem/opportunity recognition	Needs and wants Attention Selective perception
2. Information search	Awareness Brand knowledge Central/peripheral processing Active and passing processing
3. Evaluation of choices	Cognitive/affective response Evoked sets Preference and conviction Likability Source credibility
4. Behavior, action	Sample, visit, try/buy
5. Review of buying decision, repeat buy	Cognitive and conditioned learning Learning from satisfaction and dissatisfaction Cognitive dissonance

Recognizing either a problem or an opportunity creates wants. Say you have finished your grocery shopping and are standing in line to check out. Although you have just eaten lunch and are not hungry, you notice the display of candy bars and remember how good your favorite one tastes. Suddenly, you *want* a candy bar. Because wants and needs—regardless of what triggers them— are what drive the decision-making process, let us take a close look at how marketers use needs and wants to influence the buying behavior.

Needs and Wants

Needs are *the biological and psychological motivations that drive impulses and actions.* Biological motivations satisfy survival needs associated with hunger, thirst, cold, heat, pain. Psychological motivations satisfy social and emotional wants and needs such as status, affiliation, excitement, love, respect. Biological needs are easily felt, such as a need for food when you are hungry; psychological needs are more considered, such as the need for a new book to read on a trip. A psychological need such as belonging, esteem, and self-actualization can lead you to want friends, status, or luxury products.

Psychologist Abraham Maslow's *hierarchy of needs* (see Figure 5–4) helps explain what motivates people to respond to messages. From lowest to highest, the five need levels are physiological (food and water), safety and security (protection from physical dangers), belongingness (social acceptance), esteem (self-confidence and satisfaction), and self-actualization (self-development, maximizing personal talents and abilities). According to Maslow, people are motivated to satisfy their most basic needs first, and having done so, move on to higher needs and wants, those that are more social and psychological rather than physical. The hierarchy is referred to as a theory of motivation because it identifies the factors that drive a person to act in a certain way.

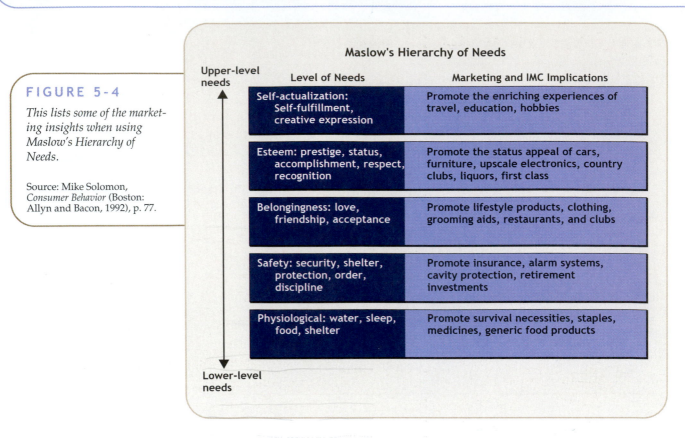

Maslow's Hierarchy of Needs

The ad in Exhibit 5–5 for General Motors' Aurora model, for example, addresses a need for self-expression, a form of self-actualization.

In industrialized societies, because most people have the basic physical needs, selling strategies focus mainly on the higher needs, such as belonging and self-actualization. However, there are ways to ignite basic needs such as safety. A good example comes from competition for market share among two products: roller skates versus in-line skates. U.S. sales of roller skates had plunged from $100 million in 1990 to $30 million in the mid-1990s, while sales of in-line skates took over during that period. However, from 1992 to 1996 there were some three dozen deaths in the United States related to in-line skates. Roller-skate manufacturers began to call attention to the hazards of in-line skating. As a result, in-line skate sales started falling in 1995 and the market for traditional roller skates was revitalized.[6]

Prospective customers can have different *aspirational levels* reflected in a similar motivation. Two people, for example, may each want to buy a computer. One has never purchased a computer before and has relatively little money to spend; this person may be satisfied with an entry-level model. The other, who is an experienced computer user, wants the fastest processor available and lots of memory. Thus, though their motivation is the same, their aspirations differ widely with regard to this product.

The more a marketing communication strategy considers customers' aspirational and self-actualization levels, the more it can direct them to the products that best satisfy their needs. Databases are used to store information about customers' and prospects' purchases, as well as the psychographic and demographic characteristics that make it possible to predict such things as aspirational levels.

The Attention Factor

In order for brand messages to present customers or prospects with an opportunity or to influence how they go about satisfying a need or want, the messages must first get the attention of these customers and prospects. **Attention** means *the conscious narrowing of mental and emotional focus.* In a perception course, you would learn that there are many things in your environment that are competing for your attention. **Selective perception** is *the process used to decide what is worthy of attention.* Imagine yourself walking down a street and seeing signs, stores, trees, the sky, other people, and so on. Your attention shifts from one thing to another as you select something from this vast panorama to focus on. The same process operates when you watch television or read a magazine. You consciously attend to some things but not to others. Every magazine carries ads, but that doesn't mean you pay attention to all the ads, or to any of them, unless you select an ad from the stream of things you see as you page through the magazine and stop and concentrate on it.

In a considered purchase situation, once a brand message has gotten customers' attention, customers focus their minds on some communication related to the brand, which is usually a claim or benefit about the brand. In marketing communication, attention is attracted by creative ideas that help a brand message stand out among the hundreds of other brand messages that bombard customers everyday. Effective marketing communication consists of those brand messages that attract people's attention.

Is What You Drive

A Reflection Of Who You Are?

Or Is Who You Are

A Reflection Of What You Drive?

THE ANSWER, OF COURSE, DEPENDS ON WHAT YOU DRIVE. Lucky you. Because for a limited time, we're offering a special lease on the new 1997 Aurora, by Oldsmobile. This is your opportunity to experience the Aurora's 32-valve dual-overhead-cam V8, wrapped in what is arguably the world's most beautiful package. Certainly, a proposition worthy of your reflection. **AURORA** by Oldsmobile.

$399/36	$2,700 +	$399 +	$450 =	$3,549
a month months	Total down payment	1st month's payment	Security deposit*	Total due at inception

*Security deposit is refundable. Aurora M.S.R.P. $36,400. Taxes, license, title fees, insurance extra. 36,000 miles allowed. GMAC must approve lease. Example of base model. Payments may be higher in AL, CT, HI, NY, RI, TX and VA. You must take delivery from dealer stock by 4/30/97. See your participating dealer for details.

© 1997 GM Corp.
All rights reserved. Buckle Up, America!   www.auroracar.com

EXHIBIT 5-5

Aurora is appealing to those who feel a car is an important part of expressing themselves.

Step 2: Information Search

During the information search, brand awareness becomes important. Customers or potential customers may first begin searching their memories for information to help satisfy their needs and wants. For a brand message to have an impact on this search, it must do more than simply gain attention.

The Awareness Factor

Attention is of little value unless brand awareness is also created or brought to mind. **Awareness** is *getting a message past the senses—the point of initial exposure—and into the consciousness.* Awareness creates brand knowledge or reminds customers of what they already know about the brand. Gaining **brand knowledge,** which means *acquiring an understanding of the brand and its benefits,* is an essential element in a customer's brand decision. Obviously, the greater the brand awareness and brand knowledge, the more impact a brand will have on a customer's decision-making process. This is why a common MC objective is to maintain or increase brand awareness.

Some marketers use research to determine the level of brand awareness. Typically, researchers will mention a product category to consumers and ask what brands they can think of in that category. A common type of research for magazine advertising takes readers through an issue and afterward asks if they remember seeing certain ads. For every ad to which they respond yes, they are presumed to be aware of the brand.

Some marketing communication, however, uses creative elements that are good at attracting attention but poor at communicating a brand message. The battery maker Energizer found out that brand knowledge does not always come easily or automatically. After it began its now-famous Energizer bunny ad campaign, a study showed that nearly half of the people who remembered a bunny selling batteries on television said they were Duracell batteries. Energizer therefore had to adjust its marketing communication to make the association between its bunny and brand name stronger (see Exhibit 5–6).

If simple brand awareness does not give customers enough information to make a purchase decision, they will look elsewhere—to past experiences, personal sources (e.g., referrals from friends or co-workers); marketing communication (e.g., advertising, packaging, displays, salespeople); public sources (e.g., mass media, organizations, *Consumer Reports*); or product examination and trial (e.g., test drives, free samples). Each of these sources of information requires a different amount of effort and carries a different amount of believability (see Table 5–2).

How much time and effort customers are willing to spend searching for information depends on how involved they are with the product category or brand and how relevant it is to their lives. One of automaker Saturn's selling strategies, for example, is to equip its sales associates with information about competitors' cars. The idea is not to argue against competing models, but rather to give prospects as much information as possible so they can make informed decisions.

During the information search, customers usually focus on the differences they perceive among competing brands. For example, if consumers are primarily concerned about price, they are likely to look at low-priced brands first, considering differences among these brands and picking the one that best meets their needs. This is why brand differentiation is important. A study of 1,000 television commercials found that the most persuasive ones included a brand-differentiating message. In other words, the commercials that helped customers distinguish one brand from another were the most effective.[7]

The Relevance Factor

As mentioned earlier, an appeal to self-interest is a good technique for attracting attention. Research has shown that when customers see marketing communication that is *relevant* to them, they are more likely to pay attention and think about it. If the communication

EXHIBIT 5-6

Energizer did a great job of creating awareness of its pink "demonstrator" bunny; however, the link between the bunny and the brand was initially not strong.

is not relevant, they are likely to pay attention only if it catches their attention in some other way. Attractive models, glitzy celebrities, bright colors, clever plays on words, and so on can create something called **borrowed interest** (*interest created in a brand message through associating it with something else, related or not, that customers find relevant*). What makes a message or message element relevant is a customer's wants and needs. Message planners find these points of relevance by trying to see the product through the customer's eyes and asking themselves, "What's in it for me?" According to the Elaboration Likelihood Model, the more involved consumers are, the more likely they will think about facts in a brand message.[8] Although involvement is a customer condition, products—and their brand messages—are described as low- or high-involvement depending on how much relevance they typically have to customers' lives.

Central and Peripheral Routes

There are two routes, or paths, used in information searching: the *central route*, which is followed when the customer is highly involved and the product is highly relevant, and the *peripheral route*, which is followed when the customer is less involved and the product has a lower level of personal relevance.[9] Peripheral-route decisions are based on such things as imagery, colors, celebrity spokespeople, or music—all of which can create borrowed interest.

Consumers traveling the central route are likely to actively engage in information searching and thinking that generates cognitive responses to brand messages. In contrast, those following a peripheral route are likely to respond to such visual cues as the attractiveness of the presenter talking about the brand or the setting in which the brand is presented. Central-route searches are active, peripheral-route searches more passive. Event marketing, like trade shows and retailing, uses the environment as a way to attract and focus people's attention, eliciting a similar type of peripheral processing that is characteristic of image and lifestyle advertising.

Some planned messages are designed to stimulate the senses without being very informative—that is, to address the consumer through the peripheral route. **Image messages** are *messages that either present an attractive personality for the product or indirectly suggest to customers that they can acquire a certain style by using a particular brand* (see Exhibit 5–7). This type of message operates through the process of association; that is, it associates a quality (sexiness, speed, strength) or a lifestyle with the product.[10]

TABLE 5 - 2   A Comparison of Information Sources

Source	Effort Required	Believability
Past experiences	Low	High
Personal sources (e.g., friends)	Low	High
Marketing communications	Medium	Low
Public sources (e.g., media)	Low	High
Product examination and trial	High	High

Source: Adapted from Paul Peter and Jerry Olson, *Consumer Behavior and Marketing Strategy* (Burr Ridge, IL: Irwin, 1996), p. 311.

Step 3: Evaluation of Choices

After customers have recognized a problem or opportunity and searched for relevant information, they must evaluate their findings. This is when prospects and customers think about the options that might satisfy their needs. Evaluation is both a cognitive and an experiential activity; in this context, the experience is described using the psychological term *affect;* as described below, affective responses include emotions and feelings as opposed to thoughts.

Cognitive Response

A **cognitive response** *involves reasoning, judgment, or knowledge.* This kind of response is typically limited to the consideration of a high-involvement product where the prospect or customer is engaged in central-route information processing. Brand messages for low-involvement products are less concerned with developing a cognitive response.

Types of cognitive responses include asking questions, elaborating on the message by reinterpreting it in terms of one's own life and needs, and making associations with other products and ideas. These are ways people respond to a brand message and, in the process, acquire brand knowledge. Another type of cognitive response is counterarguing against the points being made in the brand message. Arguing back to the television, for example, is a form of negative cognitive response.

Marketing communicators must understand their customers' cognitive responses in order to predict the effectiveness of brand messages. For example, companies will offer a high rebate on a product when they expect that not all of their customers will make the effort to apply for the rebate. Some companies have found that contests and sweepstakes aren't great motivators of response when customers realize they are not likely to win anything. Companies can gain such insights into customer response patterns by researching proposed promotional ideas or simply through the process of doing business. Companies that see themselves as "learning organizations" make an effort to collect information about such promotional efforts in a database so they are better able to predict the effectiveness of their brand messages.

Evoked sets

Evaluation of choices sometimes involves examining alternative product categories (SUVs versus vans) as well as a set of brands (a Ford van versus a Chrysler van). Evaluation helps narrow brand choices from all those customers are aware of (*awareness set*), to those they are considering (*consideration set*), to those they are most likely to purchase (*evoked set*).

In making a brand decision, most people evoke, or call to mind, a set of acceptable or liked brands within a product category. Thus, an **evoked set** is *all those brands that customers have judged to be acceptable*. Think of coffee—which brands would you be comfortable buying without knowing any more about them than you know now? Businesses function the same way as customers do, using the term *approved* or *authorized* brands rather than evoked sets. Often a business will have a list of approved suppliers for each product category it frequently purchases. For both consumers and businesses, using an evoked set of brands in frequently purchased product categories greatly simplifies choice evaluation. If only one brand ends up in the evoked set for a particular category, customers will most likely begin to use the repeat/habit decision-making model.

Because most customers use evoked sets it is no surprise that a study conducted by Grey Worldwide determined that pure brand loyalty is rare.[11] Grey found that consumers in the United States, the United Kingdom, and Australia routinely make their choices from a group of brands they consider acceptable. Consequently, the drive for complete brand loyalty is not realistic in many categories. More appropriate is an objective that calls for companies to increase their share of wallet or share of evoked set purchases.

Fear of making a mistake in the brand decision process, particularly for expensive products, can motivate consumers to carefully evaluate brand choices. There are six different risks that both consumers and businesses try to minimize:[12]

> "Brand loyalty—one of the most critical factors in long-term corporate profitability—barely exists. In fact, 'brand promiscuity' is a global phenomenon."
>
> Adam Shell, "Brand Loyalty? Fugged about it!"[11]

- *Financial risk.* Customers lose money when a brand doesn't work; they have to replace the product or spend extra to make it work.
- *Performance risk.* Product failures can cause other failures such as missed deadlines or inability to produce other goods or services.
- *Physical risk.* The brand may hurt or injure those who use it.
- *Psychological risk.* The brand may not fit in well with the consumer's or company's self-image or corporate culture.
- *Social risk.* The brand may negatively affect the way others think of the customer.
- *Time-loss risk.* If a product fails, the customer must spend time to get it adjusted, repaired, or replaced.

Affective Responses

As explained at the beginning of this chapter, most buying decisions involve both cognitive and experiential inputs. It is therefore important to give customers and prospects reasons to buy that are emotional as well as rational. This is especially true for low-involvement products. There is an important role in marketing communication for messages that stimulate feelings. Such feelings are called an **affective response,** or *a response that involves emotional processing and results in preferring (or not preferring) a brand and developing a conviction about it.* Affective responses are feelings, but they are generated in conjunction with cognitive responses. (The noun *affect* is used by psychologists to describe an overall emotional state; it is not simply the same thing as an *effect*.)

Some marketing communication may call for deliberate affective messages that directly engage customers' emotions such as fear or love. The "Real Victims" campaign described in the chapter opening case used a combination emotional/rational message strategy designed specifically to touch the feelings of Parkinson's disease victims in order to convince them to take action. The mySimon.com ad in Exhibit 5–8 is an example of an affective approach that tries to use feelings about love to sell an Internet search engine.

A consumer's purchase anxiety is another affective response that marketing has to confront. Researchers have determined, for example, that an increase in product choices can actually cause a reduction in sales for the whole product category. A study of student buying habits found that the more brand/size/flavor choices they were given for a particular product, the less likely they were to buy at all. Seemingly, the increased number of choices increased the purchase anxiety to the point that it actually reduced category sales.[13]

Companies use the affective approach in the marketing of luxury products such as Nikon cameras and Lexus cars. Yet a potential problem is that while affective messages may convince people that these brands are prestigious, the cognitive messages may not convince them that the brands are worth the high prices. See the Technology in Action box, though, for an example of effective use of affective messages.

EXHIBIT 5-8

In an effort to create a positive affective response—that is, to make a customer feel good—this ad for a Web search engine illustrates "feeling" by showing the act of giving flowers.

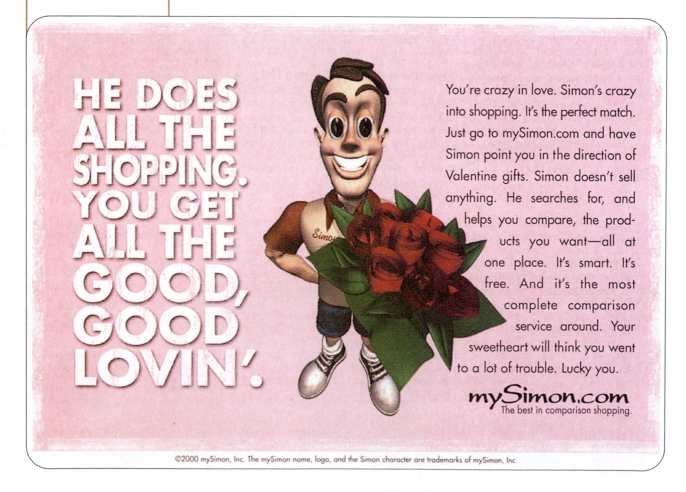

©2000 mySimon, Inc. The mySimon name, logo, and the Simon character are trademarks of mySimon, Inc.

TECHNOLOGY IN ACTION

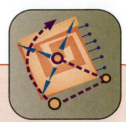

Shower Yourself with Pleasure

The decades of the 1980s and 1990s introduced a new consumer term: *the "me" generation.* Somewhat hedonistic, consumers of this generation have focused more on their own pleasures than their predecessors ever did. Direct marketers and retailers such as Williams-Sonoma have ridden on that consumer trend, delivering the commercial upscaling of everyday life from the kitchen to the garage. Others call it "the democratization of good taste."

One outgrowth of this trend has been the high-tech luxury bathroom with glass and brass or gleaming tiles and fancy jetted tubs. Sales of bathroom fixtures and related products have blossomed because consumers see the bath as their private place for pampering themselves. New bathroom gimmicks continue to be introduced to increase the pleasure of the bath or, more specifically, the shower. As one bathroom-products executive explained, "People see showering as 'my time.' It's very personal and self-indulgent." The shower and bath are places for escape, offering precious time alone for people leading hectic, demanding lives.

Responding to this consumer trend, Teledyne Water Pik (now Water Pik Technologies) introduced the Flexible Shower Massage, a showerhead with a 15-inch hose that can be adjusted to most any position—and stays put until adjusted again (see Exhibit 5-9). Why do customers need such a product? Company research found that:

- Those with bursitis want a pulsating stream to massage their throbbing shoulders.
- When two people of different heights share the same shower, they want a showerhead that can be easily moved up or down.
- Women who sit on a seat in the shower while shaving their legs want to aim the water on their back.

The company took 18 months to develop its flexible showerhead, and spent about $1 million in research and new manufacturing equipment leading to its domination of this new product category.

EXHIBIT 5-9

waterpik™

118 spray channels for full body coverage

CENTER SPRAY
a concentrated, full force spray

SPRAY-PULSE
a pulsating massage combined with a soothing body spray

PULSE
a steady, pulsating spray massage

OUTSIDE SPRAY
a soft and generous body spray

TURBO PULSE
a powerful hyper massage

5 YEAR LIMITED WARRANTY
Your Original Shower Massage® Showerhead is warranted for five years against defects in materials and workmanship. Warranty details enclosed.

EASY INSTALLATION
Installs in minutes onto any 1/2" standard shower arm. Complete parts and easy-to-follow instructions are included.

Think About It

What products do you buy for affective reasons? In other words, when are your feelings driving your purchases more than your reason? Think of a product that would appeal to the "me" generation and decide what type of communication you could use to introduce it to the market. Locate your communication objective on the hierarchy of needs in Figure 5-4, and give an example of a message that would achieve this objective.

Sources: Tara Weingarten and John Leland, "The Tastemaker," *Newsweek*, June 9, 1997, pp. 60–61; Coleman Cornelius, "Shaping a Trend in Showering," *Denver Post*, May 9, 1997, p. C1.

Attitude Formation

As a result of evaluating brand choices, customers form **attitudes**, or *dispositions regarding objects, people, and ideas associated with a brand.* These attitudes are an important underlying factor in creating brand loyalty. In contrast, a **belief** is a *conclusion based on information and/or experiences with a brand.* Both attitudes and beliefs are based on what customers and prospects see, hear, experience, and learn about brands.

Attitudes represent a frame of mind. Public opinion surveys and other types of consumer surveys attempt to identify changing consumer attitudes. For example, a study by *Glamour* magazine investigated how women aged 18 to 54 perceived "value." The study found that product performance was at the top of the list (92 percent said product performance was the most important indicator of value), followed by "getting my money's worth" (90 percent). After a big jump, the next most important factors in determining value were "durable/stays in style" (74 percent), "makes me feel good about using/owning it" (63 percent), on sale or had a coupon (50 percent), and impresses others (22 percent).[14] Compare these findings with your own attitudes toward product value: How would you rank each factor?

Consumer attitudes have important implications for marketing and brand message strategies. In building a strategy, therefore, it is useful to know something about attitude structure. As depicted in Figure 5-5, attitudes have two dimensions—direction and degree of conviction. *Attitude direction* is whether the feeling is positive or negative. *Degree of conviction* is how sure customers are about their attitude and how strong the feeling is (e.g., slightly positive, very positive, slightly

FIGURE 5-5

The strength and direction of an attitude toward a brand influences behavior.

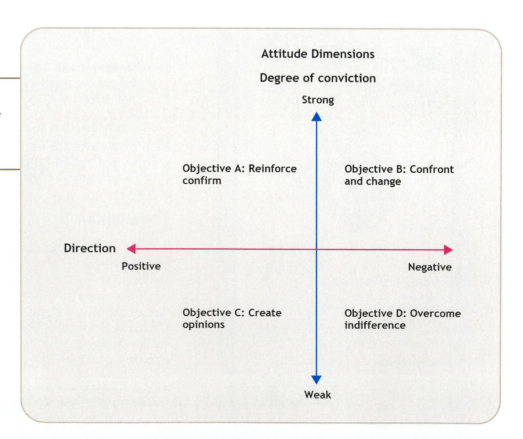

negative, very negative). Message strategies are designed to either reinforce strong, positive attitudes (Objective A); confront and change strong, negative attitudes (Objective B); create positive attitudes where convictions are weak (Objective C); and overcome negative, weak attitudes (Objective D). The IMC Strategy box describes an antismoking campaign that works to reinforce the opinion that smoking is unhealthy (Objective A) and change the attitudes of teens who think it is "cool" (Objective B). In order to accomplish Objective B, the campaign has attempted to demonstrate that smoking is gross.

Attitudes and opinions can be changed at a variety of levels. There are basically four types of attitude and belief change strategies:[15]

1. *Beliefs about consequences of behavior.* Customers might be persuaded that a new ice cream isn't as fattening as they think.

2. *Evaluations of consequences.* Customers might be persuaded that eating a new ice cream is OK, even if it is fattening.

3. *Beliefs about perceptions of others.* Customers might be persuaded it's OK to eat the new ice cream because everyone says it's special.

4. *Motivations to comply.* Customers might be persuaded to eat a new ice cream because everyone else is eating it.

In addition, companies can attempt to change a customer's attitudes about a competing brand either by decreasing the likelihood of a positive consequence being associated with a competitor's product or by increasing the likelihood of a negative consequence being associated with a competitor's product.

In the chapter opening case on the Parkinson's Coalition of Houston, the campaign planners admitted that before they could encourage people to contact the coalition—the behavioral objective of the campaign—they had to first change the attitudes of skepticism and embarrassment. The IMC in Action box on the Arizona Tobacco Education and Prevention Program also illustrates how important attitudes are in a behavior-change campaign.

Likability

The appeal to the heart is very much a part of most brand decisions, even those that appear to be driven by rational thinking. *Liking the brand* is an important attitude that affects decision making; another is *liking the message.*

Some MC managers argue that liking a brand message is not important as long as customers remember the brand; they say that irritating messages may even attract more attention and stay in memory longer than appealing messages. Research has found, however, that there is a link between liking the message and liking the brand.[16] Ultimately, liking how a brand presents itself is a critical factor in the development of a long-term brand relationship.

Credibility

As explained in Chapter 4, brand perceptions are the result of planned, product, service, and unplanned messages. In other words, there are many different types of messages, and all of them bring different types of credibility, impact, and likability to brand messages. When messages are effective at combining these factors, they also create conviction.

Customers never receive marketing communication messages in isolation. An important factor in attitude formation is the perceived **source credibility**—*the extent to which the message sender is believable.* This relates to the trust factor in relationships

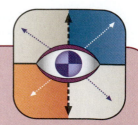

IMC STRATEGY

Changing Attitudes and Behaviors with a Gross-out Campaign

Since 1996, the Arizona Tobacco Education and Prevention Program (TEPP) has been seeking to change the attitudes and ultimately the behaviors of teenagers about smoking. The strategy is to speak to teens in their own language and use gross humor to get their attention.

In one television commercial, for example, a teenager sitting in a movie theater with his date spits gooey, chewed tobacco into a cup. His date absent-mindedly reaches over and takes a drink from the cup. Gross! In another, the mad doctor creating Frankenstein chastises an assistant for bringing him the lungs of a smoker. In yet another (which has stimulated some complaints from adults), a smoking teen tries to be cool by telling a story about how smart dogs are. "I mean, dogs got, like, giant brains. They know when things suck," the boy says as the dog lifts his hind leg and extinguishes the cigarette in his master's hand (see Exhibit 5-10).

Since making its debut in Arizona, the campaign, which uses the tagline "Tobacco: tumor-causing, teeth-staining, smelly, puking habit," has been distributed in other states by the U.S. Centers for Disease Control and Prevention. The ABC television network has run the ads as a public service during its Saturday-morning programming. Within weeks of the campaign's first appearance, Arizona teens were repeating the slogan and mimicking lines from the ads.

In addition to the television ads, the Arizona campaign has blitzed teens with merchandise such as T-shirts, hats, and pens with the campaign's slogan. More than 300,000 items have been sold through the Smelly, Puking Habit Merchandise Center, which has taken orders from as far away as Alaska. Its online marketing can be seen at www.tepp.org.

The Ash Kicker is a 43-foot-long trailer, pulled by a Hummer, that visits schools, state fairs, and other events. Inside the trailer are such gross items as a simulated cancerous lung, a chewing-tobacco-spewing mannequin, and a figure whose head spins from that of a young girl smoking a cigarette to that of a sickly, wrinkled woman. The Ash Kicker campaign has used a variety of communication tools to convey the message that smoking isn't cool.

Traditional marketing communication such as advertising has focused on building awareness and getting attention. Although those are important objectives, the bottom line now is changing behavior. The questions raised by the Arizona TEEP campaign center on its effectiveness in preventing teens from starting to smoke or getting them to quit if they are smokers.

Think About It

How has the TEPP campaign attempted to change attitudes? What would you say to the researcher who observed that teens' awareness of the slogan doesn't prove the ads are working? Can such a campaign lead to behavior change?

Sources: Adapted from Barbara Martinez, "Antismoking Ads Aim to Gross Out Teens," *The Wall Street Journal*, March 31, 1997, p. B1; Amy Silverman, "Mrs. Good Retch," *Phoenix New Times*, April 24, 1997; Millie Takaki, "Arizona Anti-Smoking Ads Gain National Momentum," *Shoot*, April 18, 1997, p. 7.

EXHIBIT 5-10

discussed in Chapter 2. How trustworthy is the medium in which the message appears? Who paid to produce the message? Is the person talking or writing about the brand paid by the company to do so? Is the spokesperson knowledgeable about the product or just an actor reading lines?

Product publicity is an important MC tool because the editorial part of media has a relatively high level of credibility compared to the commercial part. Exhibit 5–11 shows a magazine story that says positive things about Freshwater Software, a start-up that provides software and management services for e–commerce companies. Such stories will generally have more impact than if the same claims had been stated in a typical ad, whether or not readers know that the story was initiated by a publicity release from the company.

Yet many consumers today show widespread lack of faith in all sources of information. A recent survey of 1,100 consumers by the Porter Novelli public relations agency found that Americans in general are increasingly cynical about all sources of information—political ads and election coverage, media (one-third say the media have become less credible in the last five years), and corporations (44 percent said companies are less credible than five years ago). Only 20 percent believe companies are completely truthful during a corporate crisis; more than a third think corporations withhold negative information.[17] Whom did these respondents say they trust? Consumer advocacy groups ranked highest, with the media coming in at a distant second.

A similar study by the Cummings Center for Advertising Studies at the University of Illinois found that, although Americans report that they do not generally trust advertising, they tend to feel more confidence with ad claims that are focused on the consumer's actual purchase decisions than in ads that try to create an affective response. In general, though, more respondents said that they like rather than dislike advertising.[18]

A message source that has an important impact on attitudes is what sociologists call the **opinion leaders,** *people who are highly visible in the community, in the media, or in industry and who are consulted about their opinions.* Such people are generally outgoing and have higher-than-average social status. Knowing that opinion leaders can influence purchase decisions, companies sometimes seek them out for testimonials. When Johnson & Johnson launched its disposable contact lenses, under the brand name Acuvue, it first contacted eye care specialists with information about the product so they could have informed discussions with potential customers. Only after experts and opinion leaders had a chance to assimilate the brand information and talk about it in their columns, newsletters, and trade journals did the company then begin sending brand messages to customers.

Information that strengthens the credibility of a message is called a *support argument.* Information that challenges the credibility of a message is called a *counterargument.* Studies have shown that the opinions of highly credible sources may outweigh a message receiver's initial opposition or counterargument to the message. Johnson & Johnson involved eye care specialists as experts in order to overcome customers' fear of, or resistance to, leaving the contact lens in the eye overnight. Thus, the company turned to credible sources to provide support arguments and to defend itself against potential counterarguments from prospective customers.[19]

EXHIBIT 5-11

This newspaper article, which was the result of a publicity release, positively reflects on the company as it helps to build the Freshwater Software brand.

Step 4: Behavior and Action

Attitudes and behavior are linked, although the links are not always direct or clear. People act according to their attitudes and beliefs, as well as according to what they know. The behavioral stage is the one in which a customer takes some type of action in response to a message. At one time, marketers were concerned about generating only one type of behavior—a purchase. However, they have learned that there are other behaviors that are important for many product categories and for customers.

An example comes from the automotive industry. Ninety percent of new-car buyers visit a dealership multiple times before they buy, and they do so three times on average. A visit is an action in the decision-making process. Car shoppers must act to choose a dealer and then to determine which model to buy, what options to select, and what form of financing to use.

The objective of most automotive-related brand messages in the mass media is to get prospects to visit a showroom in order to learn more about a particular car. Once prospects come to a showroom, it is obvious they are in the information-seeking and evaluation stages. Auto dealers satisfy customer needs at this point with brochures, test drives, and, hopefully, informed sales representatives. After the initial visit, a smart dealership will send the prospect a "thank-you" mailing and offer a small premium (such as a pen flashlight, a can of compressed air for inflating flat tire, or an emergency flasher) for making a return visit and taking a test drive. This repeat visit is carefully designed to move prospects closer to making a buying decision.

Step 5: Review of Buying Decision

After making a purchase, customers consciously or subconsciously evaluate their decision and arrive at some level of satisfaction or dissatisfaction, which then leads to either a repeat purchase or a return to the evaluation step to search for a different brand.

Learning

The review process involves **learning,** which is *a change in the knowledge base that comes from exposure to new information or experiences.* Learning is ongoing for most consumers and companies in the brand decision process. It happens as customers and prospects acquire information, evaluate alternatives, and try the product. It all comes together, however, after a purchase has been made, at the point of reflection on the outcome.

Psychologists have two basic theories about how most of us learn; these correspond to the cognitive and experiential decision-making models we have been discussing. The first is the **cognitive learning theory,** which is *a view of learning as a mental process involving thinking, reasoning, and understanding.* According to this theory, we think by comparing new information to what we already know (i.e., thoughts and information filed away in our memory). The second is **conditioned learning theory** (also called stimulus-response theory), which is *a view of learning as a trial-and-error process.* We confront a new situation, respond in a certain way, and something happens. If what happens is good, then we are likely to develop a positive feeling about it and respond the same way every time we are in that situation. If the experience is bad, then we'll change our response and try something else. Such patterns of behavior represent the way we approach most simple purchases, from soap to soup. Reinforcement advertising is used to remind people of the good experience. Learning also intersects with involvement in that cognitive learning typically occurs with high-involvement products, and conditioned learning with low-involvement products.

Cognitive Dissonance

Cognitive dissonance is *the contradiction between two or more beliefs or behaviors.* When such dissonance (or clashing) occurs during the review of a buying decision, customers generally search for more information to help decide between two attractive choices. An example is making the decision to go skiing over spring break when you know you have two midterms and a major research paper due shortly after spring break. The tension this decision creates can lead to dissatisfaction with not only the purchase decision (i.e., your purchase of the plane ticket or hotel package) but also the ski destination as it becomes associated with guilt. When marketers know that cognitive dissonance can occur, they can often create messages designed to lessen the tension. For example, the company that sold you the spring-break ski trip could emphasize students' need to take a mental break in order to think smarter and more creatively afterward. The ski destination could promote the fact it provides study time every morning and afternoon in a specially equipped area for students.

PERSUASION: HIERARCHY-OF-EFFECTS MODELS

Because the role of marketing communications is to ignite and/or intervene in the decision process, brand messages are designed to be persuasive. **Persuasion** is *the act of creating changes in beliefs, attitudes, and behaviors.* Marketing communication messages are designed to affect how customers and prospects think about the brand, feel about a brand, and make a brand choice. In other words, brand messages are designed to have an *effect* on customers and prospects.

A classic persuasion model is AIDA, an acronym derived from four persuasive steps or desired effects that a brand message should have on customers and prospects: *attention, interest, desire, action.* The first effect is a brand message attracting the *attention* of a prospect (see Exhibit 5–12); the next effect is *interest* in the brand, followed by *desire* for the brand. The final desired effect is *action*, which may be one of several responses—seeking additional information, talking to others who have used the brand, or making a purchase.

Four decades ago , the Association of National Advertisers issued a report titled *Defining Advertising Goals for Measured Advertising Results,* which has become known by its acronym, DAGMAR.[20] It is similar to the AIDA model but specifies a slightly different set of steps: awareness, comprehension, conviction, and action. The AIDA and DAGMAR models, and others like them, are called *hierarchy-of-effects* models because they assume that customers and prospects are affected in certain ways as they move through a decision-making process that is organized in a hierarchy.

Think/Feel/Do Model

The AIDA model's hierarchy of effects corresponds to the five steps in the decision process (see Figure 5–6). Both include three kinds of activities—thinking, feeling, doing—as shown in the right-hand column of Figure 5–6. The think/feel/do model helps explain in simple terms how customers respond to brand messages.[21]

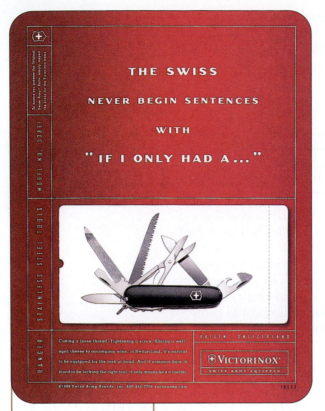

Although the think/feel/do model appears to be a linear process, it is not always so. More recent theories about buying behavior show that buyers don't always take the decision steps in this specific order. The think/feel/do order of responses varies by product category, level of involvement, and type of buyer (business or consumer, customer or prospect).

Most people approach high-involvement purchase decisions by "thinking" about them first. In contrast, the first response when considering a convenience or impulse is more likely to be "feeling" or "doing". You buy a package of gum, for example, because you feel like having some gum. Or you see a magazine next to the cash register as you're checking out at a food store, and you simply reach over on an impulse and grab it without really thinking or feeling strongly about the decision to act.

Rather than looking at the think/feel/do model as a linear hierarchy, it is more accurate to think of it as circular (see Figure 5–7). In this circle the spokes set out the three categories of think, feel, and do; a buyer can begin and end the process at any place on the circle. Note that the segments in the circle contain the psychological dimensions that were explained earlier in this chapter as elements in the decision-making steps.

The point is that not all brand decision-making situations inspire people to move through a hierarchy in the same way. To better understand the various ways brand decisions can be made, consider the scenarios below. See if you can determine which order of think/feel/do has been used in each one.

- *Scenario 1.* Bradley stopped at the drugstore on the way home from work to have a prescription filled. While checking out, he bought on impulse a copy of *Time* magazine. When he got home, he found himself reading the magazine rather than watching his favorite Thursday-night TV show. When

FIGURE 5-6

This shows how the Think/Feel/Do model relates to the other decision models.

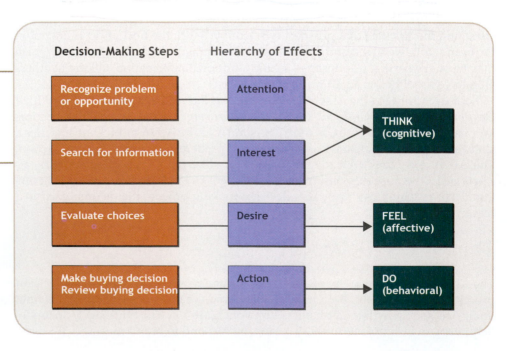

he realized he had missed his show, he was pretty surprised. The next day he picked up from the floor one of the subscription cards that had fallen out of the magazine. After looking at the price and recalling that his checking account was in pretty good shape, he realized that subscribing to the magazine would be cheaper in the long run than buying it from a store.

- *Scenario 2.* Liz and Mike needed an apartment in Atlanta, Georgia, where Mike was being transferred by his company. To make the decision on an apartment, the couple first determined how much they could spend each month on rent, then how much room they needed, and finally the part of town in which they wanted to live. Next they began looking at what was available that met their criteria. As they went through six different apartment units, they could tell that some were more comfortable and pleasing than others. Finally, after settling on the one that was second-closest to Mike's new office, they signed a contract and made a damage deposit.

- *Scenario 3.* Lindsay was very frugal with the money she earned. She had a credit card, for example, but made a point of paying off the balance every month to avoid finance charges. But for some time, she had been walking on her lunch hour past a store window close to her office. In the window was a beautiful leather jacket. One day, she was having lunch with a friend and pointed out the jacket. Her friend said she had one similar to it. That did it: Lindsay walked in, handed the clerk her credit card, and pointed to the jacket in the window. That evening, when she took the jacket out of its box, the first thing she saw was the price tag. She spent the rest of the evening trying to figure out how she was going to pay the credit-card bill that would come in two weeks and include the cost of the jacket.

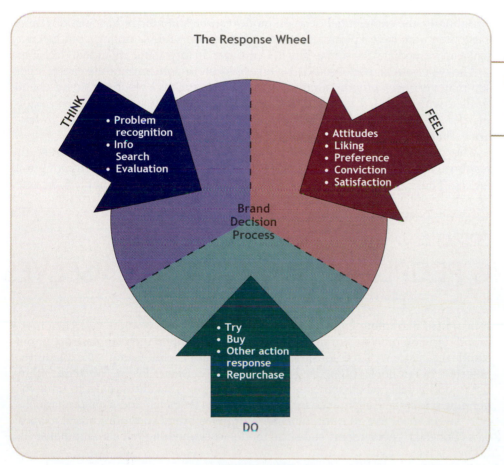

FIGURE 5-7

Components of Think/Feel/Do.

TABLE 5-3   Four Paths to a Brand Decision

Type of Decision Process	Route	Products
Cognitive processing	Think/feel/do	Cars, major appliances, high-involvement and new products
Experiential processing: impulse	Do/feel/think	Snacks, beverages, cigarettes, small household items featured at the checkout stand
Experiential processing: experiences	Feel/do/think	Restaurants, sporting events, trade shows, new products where sampling and demonstration are important
Repeat/habit processing	Do/think/feel	BtB supplies; routine purchases, repeat purchases leading to brand loyalty

To better understand the circular think/feel/do model, remember that the cognitive decision-making model was described as eliciting a decision path focused on rational thinking activities that ended with some type of behavior. In other words, think/feel/do is a shorthand version of the cognitive model. This is an appropriate model, as stated earlier, for high-involvement products, particularly new product purchases that call for searching and product comparison.

Similarly, the experiential decision model can be summarized as feel/do/think. Customers who have a pleasant, satisfying experience while sampling a product may make an immediate decision to buy it. Only later do they think about that decision.

The experiential model could also take a different path around the circle. A person may very well buy on impulse, then have an affective response such as being thrilled with the purchase. Only after the feeling good about the experience does the person begin thinking about whether it was really the smart thing to have done. This process could be summarized as do/feel/think.[22]

The repeat/habit model can be summarized as do/think/feel because the response is automatic, with an ongoing evaluation based on both thinking and feeling. These four paths to a buying decision are summarized in Table 5–3.

A FINAL NOTE:
PERSUADING PEOPLE TO PERSUADE THEMSELVES

In a sense, marketing communication is a type of intervention in a customer's brand decision process. But the intervention works only if the planner truly understands the customer's relationship to the brand. Lisa Fortini-Campbell explains that objective in her book *Hitting the Sweet Spot: The Consumer Insight Workbook:* "think how good it feels when someone really understands us and speaks to us with a genuine understanding of who we are."[23] She says that such understanding touches our "sweet spot." We all want someone (a friend, a brand communication) to speak to us honestly, "not as some statistical model, or something to be manipulated like a marionette in the marketplace, but from one living breathing human being to another—with caring, understanding, and shared values." She concludes, "You don't persuade people. They persuade themselves."[24]

From an IMC perspective, communication that aids customers and responds to them in a personal way is much more persuasive than communication that tries to manipulate them. That's also the lesson from the Parkinson's campaign described in the chapter opening case.

Think about all the points in the brand decision process where communication is welcome. Imagine that you need to buy a washing machine (not usually the type of product that you get excited about shopping for and spending a lot of money on). You see an ad or hear about a new type of Maytag washing machine from friends or a salesclerk. This message may offer an opportunity to solve a laundry problem in a way you had not thought about before. As uninterested as you may be in washing machines, that's still a useful piece of information. In addition, the message may also present comparative information that leads you to think a second time about the brand relative to the competition. So that helps you with the buying decision. And when someone you know says something good about the brand, then that helps even more with the decision. In other words, at every step in the decision-making process, there is an opportunity for a message to move you toward (or away from) a brand. The problem for IMC planners is knowing how these consumer insights connect with brand perceptions. The chapters that follow will discuss in more detail how this is done.

Key Terms

high-involvement products 161
low-involvement products 161
prospects 161
customers 161
needs 169
attention 171
selective perception 171
awareness 171
brand knowledge 171
borrowed interest 173
image messages 173
cognitive response 174

evoked set 175
affective response 176
attitude 178
belief 178
source credibility 179
opinion leaders 181
learning 182
cognitive learning theory 182
conditioned learning theory 182
cognitive dissonance 183
persuasion 183

Key Point Summary

Key Point 1: Three Factors

The brand decision process is governed by three key factors: high-involvement versus low-involvement products, customers versus prospects, and consumers versus business buyers.

Key Point 2: Three Buying-Behavior Situations

The cognitive decision-making model involves five steps: problem and opportunity recognition, information search, evaluation, action, and review of buying decision. The experiential model is shorter because feelings replace the information search and evaluation steps. The habit/repeat buying model, is even shorter because it is essentially just the replication of three steps in the cognitive model: problem recognition, evaluation leading to a buying decision, and then a review of the decision.

Key Point 3: The Five Decision Steps

The five basic decision steps are (1) problem and opportunity recognition, which also considers needs and wants, and the attention factor; (2) information search, which includes awareness, relevance, and the two routes of central and peripheral processing; (3) evaluation, which considers cognitive and affective responses and attitude formation; (4) behavior, which is the action step that follows a decision; and (5) the review step, where the decision maker learns from satisfaction and dissatisfaction.

Key Point 4: Hierarchy-of-Effects Persuasion Models

The most traditional hierarchy-of-effects model is AIDA (attention, interest, desire, action) which summarizes the types of impact a brand message has on a prospect or customer. The think/feel/do model moves away from the idea of a hierarchy and introduces different paths to a decision depending on the buying-behavior situation.

Lessons Learned

Key Point 1: Three Factors

a. What is the difference between prospects and customers?
b. What are the two basic types of customers?
c. Find ads that represent low- and high-involvement products. How do you recognize the involvement level of the product?

Key Point 2: Three Buying-Behavior Situations

a. Distinguish between cognitive and affective responses.
b. Explain how the experiential approach to brand decisions differs from the cognitive approach.
c. Why are there fewer steps in the habit/repeat model than in the cognitive or experiential models?

Key Point 3: The Five Decision Steps

a. Distinguish between needs and wants, as well as problems and opportunities. Give an example of each that might motivate the purchase of a product.
b. Find an article in the business press about consumer trends. Brainstorm with others in your class and come up with ideas for new products that would address these consumer needs and wants.
c. Distinguish between central and peripheral processing.
d. What are the two dimensions of attitudes? Identify a product category with which you are familiar and identify your own attitude structure about that category.
e. Collect cigarette ads that you feel are aimed at young people. Analyze how they affect attitudes in their attempt to sell cigarettes. Compare these ads with those in the Arizona antismoking campaign and other such campaigns. Which ones do you feel are most effective? Why?
f. What is an evoked set, and why is that concept important in marketing communication?
g. What's the difference between cognitive and conditioned learning?
h. What is the role of satisfaction in brand decision making?

Key Point 4: Hierarchy-of-Effects Persuasion Models

a. What does AIDA stand for, and why is it referred to as a model of persuasion?
b. How does the think/feel/do model differ from AIDA?

c. What does it mean when we say that the hierarchy-of-effects models are more important in understanding the decision making of new buyers than repeat buyers?

d. What are the variations on think/feel/do that represent four different paths to a brand decision? Explain each variation.

e. Find ads (or other examples of marketing communication) that illustrate the four variations on think/feel/do. Analyze how they work.

Chapter Challenge

Writing Assignment

The Parkinson's Coalition case at the beginning of this chapter provides an example in which customers used both the head and the heart to make a decision. Explain how these different styles of reasoning work and how marketing communication can influence them. From what you have learned about customer decision-making processes, what would you recommend to the Parkinson's Coalition for next year's campaign?

Presentation Assignment

You have been hired by a local coffeehouse to analyze its customers' behavior. But first the manager wants you to give the organization's employees a crash course in brand decision-making basics. Go back through the entire chapter and list all the tips you can find about how to use marketing communication to effectively relate to customers. Prepare a presentation to the store owner and manager on those factors that you think are most relevant to their marketing situation. In particular, what are the various strategies you might recommend for their marketing communication that would influence behavior? Develop an outline of the key points you want to present. Give the presentation to your class or record it on a videotape (audiotape is also an option) to turn in to your instructor, along with the outline.

Internet Assignment:

Browse the Motley Fool website (www.fool.com) and find a discussion that relates to consumer behavior. Write a report on this topic, explaining it in terms of brand decision making as described in this chapter.

Additional Readings

Jones, John Philip. "Is Advertising Still Salesmanship?" *Journal of Advertising Research,* May–June 1997, pp. 9-15.

Fortini-Campbell, Lisa. *The Consumer Insight Workbook.* Chicago: The Copy Workshop, 1992.

Macdonald, Emma, and Bryon Sharp. "Brand Awareness Effects on Consumer Decision Making for a Common, Repeat Purchase Product." *Journal of Consumer Research,* April 2000.

Modahl, Mary. *Now or Never: How Companies Must Change Today to Win the Battle for Internet Customers.* New York: HarperBusiness, 2000.

Pine, B. Joseph, II, and James H. Gilmore. *The Experience Economy: Work Is Theatre & Every Business a Stage.* Boston: Harvard Business School Press, 1999.

Wicks, Robert. *Understanding Audiences.* Mahwah, NJ: Lawrence Erlbaum, 2001.

Research Assignment

Consult these articles and books and others that you find in the library that relate to consumer behavior and explain how advertising and other forms of marketing communication are successful (or not successful) in influencing the consumer decision process. Develop a marketing communications plan for the introduction of a new product of your own choice that makes the most effective use of marketing communication to influence the brand decision process of your target audience.

Endnotes

[1]Mike Solomon, *Consumer Behavior* (Boston: Allyn and Bacon, 1992), p. 15.

[2]Kevin J. Clancy and Robert S. Shulman, *Marketing Revolution* (New York: HarperBusiness, 1993).

[3]David Wolfe, "What Your Customers Can't Say," *American Demographics,* February 1998, pp. 1–3.

[4]B. Joseph Pine II and James H. Gilmore, *The Experience Economy: Work Is Theatre & Every Business a Stage* (Boston: Harvard Business School Press, 1999), p. 11.

[5]Ibid. p. 31.

[6]Joseph Pereira, "Classic Roller Skates Return as Safety Fears Dull Blades," *The Wall Street Journal,* October 24, 1997, p. B1.

[7]David W. Stewart and David H. Furse, *Effective Television Advertising* (Lexington, MA: Lexington Books, 1986).

[8]Richard E. Petty, John T. Cacioppo, and David Schumann, "Central and Peripheral Routes to Advertising Effectiveness: The Moderating Role of Involvement," *Journal of Consumer Research,* September 1983, pp. 153–46.

[9]Ibid.

[10]Ivan L. Preston, "The Association Model of the Advertising Communication Process," *Journal of Advertising,* 1:2 (1982), 3–15; Ivan L. Preston and Esther Thorson, "Challenges to the Use of Hierarchy Models in Predicting Advertising Effectiveness," in *Proceedings of the 1983 Convention of the American Academy of Advertising,* ed. Donald W. Jugenheimer (Lawrence, KS: American Academy of Advertising, 1983).

[11]Adam Shell, "Brand Loyalty? Fuggedaboutit!" *Adweek,* May 12, 1997, p. 40.

[12]David L. Loudon and Albert J. Della Bitta, *Consumer Behavior: Concepts and Applications,* 3rd ed. (New York: McGraw-Hill, 1988), p. 532. Loudon and Della Bitta adapted this list from Martin Fishbein and Icek Ajzen, *Belief, Attitude and Behavior: An Introduction to Theory and Research* (Reading, MA: Addison-Wesley, 1975), p. 610.

[13]"Market Makers," *The Economist,* March 14, 1998, p. 67.

[14]Mark Dolliver, "Value Your Own Savvy As a Consumer," *Adweek,* May 19, 1997, p. 18.

[15]Loudon and Della Bitta, *Consumer Behavior.*

[16]Esther Thorson, "Likability: 10 Years of Academic Research," paper presented at the Eighth Annual ARF Copy Research Workshop, New York, September 11, 1991.

[17]"Who Do You Believe?" *Marketing Tools,* October 1996, p. 33.

[18]Sharon Shavitt, Pamela M. Lowrey, and James E. Haefner, *Public Attitudes Toward Advertising: More Favorable Than You Might Think* (Urbana, IL: The Cummings Center for Advertising Studies at the University of Illinois, 1997).

[19]John Deighton, "Features of Good Integration: Two Cases and Some Generalizations," in *Integrated Communication: Synergy of Persuasive Voices,* ed. Esther Thorson and Jeri Moore (Mahwah, NJ: Lawrence Erlbaum, 1996), pp. 243–58.

[20]Russell Colley, *Defining Advertising Goals for Measured Advertising Results* (New York: Association of National Advertisers, 1961).

[21]Robert C. Lavidge and Gary A. Steiner, "A Model for Predictive Measurements of Advertising Effectiveness," *Journal of Marketing,* October 1961, pp. 59–62.

[22]Ibid.

[23]Lisa Fortini-Campbell, *Hitting the Sweet Spot: The Consumer Insight Workbook* (Chicago: The Copy Workshop, 1992), p. 7.

[24]Ibid., p. 36.

IMC Planning

Key Points in This Chapter

1. How does IMC planning work, and where does it fit in an organization's strategic planning process?

2. What are the eight steps in the IMC planning process?

3. What is a SWOT analysis, and how does it relate to zero-based IMC planning?

4. Why is internal marketing important in IMC planning?

Chapter Perspective
Knowing the Score

Integrated marketing communication is often compared to an orchestra. As a matter of fact, at one time the marketing communication agency Ogilvy & Mather called its approach to IMC "Orchestration." Like IMC's various marketing communication functions and all the different media, an orchestra has many different instruments, each of which produces a different sound. If the sounds of these instruments are not coordinated according to a plan, the orchestra produces noise rather than music.

An orchestra performs according to a written musical score. In the same way, an IMC campaign must have a written score, or plan, that details which marketing communication functions and what media should be used at which times and to what extent. An IMC plan can be as minimal as a set of organized thoughts in the head of a person running a small retail business or as complex as a 100-page document for a multimillion-dollar brand campaign. But all good plans, regardless of size, have three basic elements: objectives, strategies, and tactics. All three are determined after doing research and considering the situation and environment in which the communication effort will take place.

This chapter explains how IMC planning is done. It explains the differences between objectives, strategies, and tactics and then describes each of the eight steps in the zero-based planning process. The chapter ends with a discussion of internal marketing since companies cannot plan IMC strategies without the full knowledge and cooperation of all their members.

TRAVELING WITH AN ENVOY
McCann Relationship Marketing, New York

Ask 10 different people what an envoy is and, odds are, you'll get 10 different answers. Formally, it means a diplomat who ranks slightly below an ambassador; informally, it means a messenger or representative. General Motors' truck division GMC asked McCann's Relationship Marketing office in New York to get people excited about the launch of its Envoy, a small, luxury sport utility vehicle (SUV) and to inspire them to test-drive one. The challenge was to build interest in the car even though it wouldn't be available for seven months. In essence, GMC was asking McCann to start from a base of zero and build an identity and consumer demand for a vehicle nobody could yet see, touch, or drive. It was a hill climb, but the McCann team was able to come up with a plan that made the GMC Envoy ready to hit the road (see Exhibit 6–1).

The Marketing Challenge

The GMC Envoy was scheduled for release in the late spring of 1998. Market research indicated that the SUV product category was extremely competitive. GMC was therefore concerned that potential customers would purchase competitors' models before the Envoy hit the showrooms. Obviously, the company wanted to prevent this from happening, but it wouldn't be easy, considering that

- There would be no Envoys available for consumers to test-drive or even look at for seven months.
- Consumers were not aware of the Envoy (because it was a new brand).
- There was no budget for a regular introductory campaign until early summer (four months after the beginning of the heavy SUV buying period).
- Many SUV brands were already well established.
- Several new SUV brands were scheduled to come into the market at the same time as the Envoy.
- There would be competition between the Envoy and GMC's already-existing compact SUV, the Jimmy.

Although the Envoy had these things working against it, research also showed the brand had several conditions working in its favor:

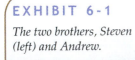

EXHIBIT 6-1

The two brothers, Steven (left) and Andrew.

- The manufacturer, GMC, had a good reputation.
- GMC had a good dealer network.
- SUV prospects were fairly easy to identify.
- The demand for SUVs was strong and growing.
- The economy was healthy and growing which meant that consumers had a reasonable amount of disposable income.

By combining traditional direct-marketing and sales-promotion tactics with some very creative advertising elements, the McCann team created an award-winning IMC campaign that excited prospects' interest and kept them waiting by their mailbox to learn more about the new Envoy.

Strategic Planning

A critical element of the IMC plan for the Envoy was to track interim responses to know who was interested, who visited showrooms, and who placed orders for the car. In addition, the McCann team set forth several specific communication and behavioral objectives:

1. Create awareness of the Envoy launch among 50 percent of the target audience.

2. Keep the target audience from buying another brand of SUV before the Envoy was available.

3. Motivate 10 percent of the target audience to visit a showroom and ask for the Envoy by name.

4. Create a brand identity and position for the Envoy as an SUV that combines both luxury and technology.

5. With a minimal MC budget, generate sales of 3,500 units within the first three months of the Envoy's launch.

Target

McCann determined the target audience to consist of three segments: current GMC Jimmy owners, current competitive SUV owners, and current luxury-car owners with a high likelihood of purchasing an SUV. McCann chose this upscale audience because these people were the most likely to be interested in purchasing the Envoy.

The Envoy campaign used direct-response media (specifically, a series of mailings to the target audience) because the company was able to obtain names and addresses of the people to whom it was targeting this exclusive offer. Like most MC clients, GMC didn't want to spend a lot of money—in fact, the budget was quite small for a new-car launch—but did want to make a big impact. In order to announce the car and prevent the target audience from purchasing other SUVs before the Envoy became available, the campaign had to create interest, intrigue, a position, and a brand identity virtually immediately.

Creative Strategy

The overall marketing strategy was to position the SUV to appeal to the upscale target audience's sophistication. The McCann team was confident it could get the attention of the target audience by playing up the fact they were being given the inside track on Envoy.

Since there were no Envoys available to test-drive, the big creative idea was to invite prospects on a vicarious test drive, described by a fictitious American diplomatic envoy and his brother who worked for GMC. A critical creative element of the big idea was to have the test-drive story take place in Europe, since the audience had a propensity for international travel (see Exhibit 6–2a).

McCann planned a set of direct-mail pieces featuring two brothers, whose pictures were included in one of the mailings and who each represented an aspect of the Envoy. In developing these characters, the McCann team went so far as to create their biographies, complete with education, marital status, and favorite foods, music, and drink. The first brother was Steven Bank, the director of GMC's Envoy development. The fictitious Steven was the brain behind the Envoy. He talked in "marketing speak." A left-brain character, he embodied the rational reason for buying this vehicle. His brother, Andrew, was a right-brain person. An American

diplomat stationed overseas, he provided the emotional reasons for owning the Envoy. He described the Envoy as if he were describing a friend. Together, Steven and Andrew presented two perspectives on why buying a GMC Envoy was a smart decision.

The mailings to the target audience took the form of a series of engaging letters between the two brothers. In one letter, for example, Andrew refers to the Envoy's high-intensity discharge headlamps, calling them "some new-generation thingamajig." In the next letter, Steven gives technical reasons to explain why this "thingamajig" is so revolutionary. The letters were not only written in a personal and often humorous manner but also contained things such as a paper cocktail napkin that contained a sketch of Andrew; the idea was to make the mailings look noncommercial (see Exhibit 6–2b).

Each letter also presented selected aspects of the Envoy, such as its luxurious features, rugged capabilities, innovative technologies, and the rich history of GMC truck making. To help keep the letters interesting and not just about the product, Andrew gave a glimpse into the mysterious world of the diplomatic envoy, talking about interactions with political personalities such as Jacques Chirac, Tony Blair, and Margaret Thatcher.

Media Strategies

With direct mail being the primary medium used in the GMC Envoy launch, the brand messages were targeted to a very select, upscale audience, as described above. To get the attention of these sophisticated people (who received many direct-mail offers), the Envoy campaign letters were actually mailed from Europe, using fictitious hotel return addresses, foreign stamps, real cancellation marks, and no GMC branding. McCann chose these elements to create impact and ensure the mailings were opened.

There were six mailings in all. The timing of the mailings was important. If they arrived too close together, prospects wouldn't have time to really begin thinking seriously about purchasing an Envoy. If they arrived too far apart, recipients would lose track of the travel story and the mailings would lose their synergy. McCann decided that intervals of 10 to 14 days would be optimum.

In two of the later mailings, targets were asked if they would like to visit a GMC showroom to see the new Envoy. This helped maintain an ongoing dialogue between the prospects and the two characters who embodied the Envoy brand. The direct-mail campaign also made it possible for the agency and GMC to instantly track results so that they would know who was interested and to what extent.

Promotional Strategy

A sweepstakes with the opportunity to win a free two-year Envoy lease was part of the third direct mailing (see Exhibit 6–2c). It was included to motivate a higher level of response and find out who the real prospects were. The sweepstakes entry form asked five questions regarding interest in buying a new SUV and interest in the Envoy. A postage-paid business reply envelope was included to make it easy for prospects to respond.

Those who responded were immediately sent more information about the Envoy, and their contact information was sent on to the GMC dealership nearest them. Dealers then made further follow-ups, letting prospects know when the Envoy would be available for a real test drive.

Evaluation of the Envoy Campaign

By closely analyzing its target audience, taking advantage of the strengths of direct mail, and using an engaging, creative message strategy, GMC and McCann were able to introduce the Envoy with a great impact but without a huge budget. The dueling letters from the dueling brothers were able to sustain the target audience's interest over a seven-month period. Because of the high level of interest, the campaign created an instant brand identity and image for the Envoy.

The direct-mail campaign had a response rate of 10.5 percent, which is considerably higher than the usual direct-mail response rate of 1 to 2 percent. Of those who responded, there was a conversion rate (i.e., a commitment to buy) of 19 percent. The cost per response was $19.21, and the cost per conversion (actual sale made) was $184. This $184 investment was only one-fifth of the automotive industry's normal MC allocation per car, which meant that this campaign was highly cost-effective. GMC tracked 4,162 unit sales to this campaign. This total included sales made to people who came to dealerships in response to the Envoy campaign and ended up buying other GMC models.

Another measure of the campaign's success was that the mailings were so compelling that GMC received more than 40 actual marriage proposals for the fictitious Andrew and Steven Bank.

GMC believes these results are noteworthy for the automotive and relationship marketing industries because they show that (1) consumers can be motivated to purchase a $33,000 vehicle through direct-mail brand messages without the benefit of costly broadcast and print mass media advertising or traditional "cash-back" offers, and (2) the Envoy's targeting approach was able to identify the very best prospects for the direct-response campaign.

This case was adapted with permission from the award-winning Advertising and Marketing Effectiveness (AME) brief for the launch of the GMC Envoy prepared by the McCann-Erickson Relationship Marketing office in New York.

EXHIBIT 6-2C

Mailing with sweepstakes entry form and postcards.

STRATEGIC PLANNING

The process described in the chapter opening case on the GMC Envoy launch is called **strategic planning,** "a process of developing and maintaining a fit between the organization's goals and capabilities and changing marketing opportunities."[1] It is based on researching the brand's internal operations, the marketplace, the target audience, competitive offerings, and the satisfaction of current customers, as well as the perceptions of prospects. An organization analyzes this information in terms of the brand's product offerings, marketing abilities, and the company's overall business and marketing objectives and strategies. IMC planners must do their work to help accomplish the larger marketing and corporate objectives.

A well-run organization has a **corporate** or **business plan,** *that states the company's financial objectives and strategies for achieving those objectives.* Once this plan has been determined, each of the major corporate divisions such as production, operations, finance, human resources, and marketing then develop their own plans to help achieve the corporate marketing plan.

New companies must also have a **business model**. Simply put, a business model explains the company's idea for making money. A critical part of the model is an explanation of how the new company will create interest in and sell its products—which is the company's marketing plan.

A **marketing plan** is *a set of objectives, strategies, and tactics orchestrating all of the organization's marketing activities designed to help the company achieve its financial objectives.* As Roman Heibing and Scott Cooper explain, a marketing plan must use a disciplined, step-by-step approach: "To truly integrate marketing tools, one needs a very set methodology to sort out and interface the many overlapping elements."[2] The plan must include, for example, the target audience and a time frame.

The launch of the Envoy, for example, was a business strategy used by GMC to achieve the objectives of moving GMC into the luxury SUV category and broadening its customer reach. The marketing objective was to establish and position the Envoy brand and sell 3,500 units. Its strategy was to create enough curiosity about the Envoy among the target audience to delay purchase of other SUVs until the Envoy was available. This strategy then became one of the critical MC objectives.

As part of IMC planning, each marketing communication function, such as advertising and direct marketing, may have its own annual plan if the brand budget is large enough to warrant doing so. Annual MC plans are generally composed of a **campaign**—*a set of various brand messages designed with a common theme to meet marketing communication objectives.*

Strategic planning recognizes that some activities are more long-term and have more impact than others. As Figure 6–1 illustrates, a promotion has a relatively short-term effect; a campaign is longer and has greater impact. Brand positioning is a long-term effort that is highly in important to a brand. Promotions and campaigns can be designed to launch a brand or establish a position, as the Envoy case demonstrates, but once a brand is no longer new, then promotions and campaigns are used to focus, reinforce, or change a position and/or brand identity.

FIGURE 6-1

The Relative Impact and Longevity of Planning Decisions

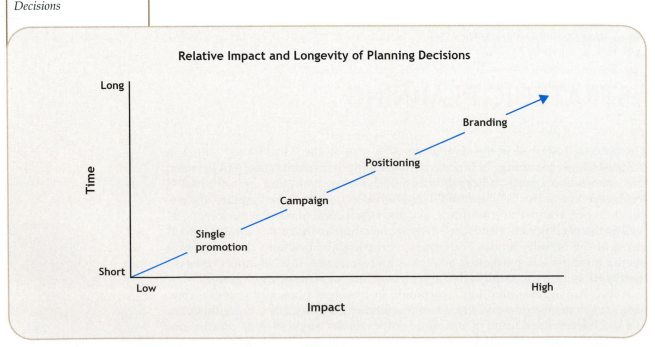

How Planning Works

There are three critical tasks in planning: setting objectives, deciding on strategies, and selecting tactics. **Objectives** are *what you want to accomplish*, **strategies** are *ideas for accomplishing objectives*, and **tactics** are *the specific actions that must be taken in order to execute a strategy*.

Objectives

The primary purpose of setting objectives is to state what is to be accomplished in order to direct an organization's efforts and allow it to evaluate effectiveness. When top management allocates money, it wants to know specifically what it's going to receive for the investment. Objectives describe the results that are expected. Objectives also serve as a communication and integration tool by keeping everyone working on the brand focused on what needs to be done.

Because the marketing plan defines the target audience at the outset, objectives do not have to mention the target. Only when the target audience is different from the stated one is it necessary to define it in an objective. Also, it is assumed that each objective must be achieved within the year for which the plan is designed. As with the target audience, the time period is stated only when it differs from the overall plan (e.g., "Within the first three months, obtain 75 percent awareness among the retail trade of the brand's new, improved formula").

Well-written objectives pass the SMAC test; they are Specific, Measurable, Achievable, and Challenging. The more *specific*, the better. Rather than setting an objective of "increasing brand knowledge by 15 percent," a company would do better to set an objective of "increasing knowledge of the brand's superior warranty by 15 percent."

Objectives should be stated in *measurable* terms. As the headline in the Lands' End ad in Exhibit 6–3, states, numbers don't lie. When objectives are measurable, it is easy to determine whether or not they have been achieved. Many companies make the mistake of having "directional objectives" such as "Increase brand awareness." The problem with directional objectives is that it is difficult to tell when the objective has been reached. For example, does a 1 percent increase in brand awareness achieve the objective "Increase brand awareness"? Technically speaking it does, but in most situations a 1 percent increase is not statistically significant and is not likely to satisfy management. When the objective is stated in measurable terms, such as "Increase awareness 10 percent," the organization can tell when the objective has been achieved (assuming, too, that the plan defines *awareness* and proposes a valid means of measuring it).

In order to set a realistic measurable objective, you first need a quantifiable measure of the current situation. This measure is called the *baseline* or *benchmark*. For example, if you want to set a share increase objective, you first need to know what the current share is.

If the current share is 10 percent and you want to increase it to 12 percent, then you are proposing a change of 2 share points. This is a 20 percent increase ($2 \div 10 = .20$). But herein lies a problem for most companies: They are not willing to spend the money required to determine the necessary benchmarks. Unless a company knows what percentage of its target audience is aware of its brand, has tried it, has made repeat purchases, and so on, there is little or no basis for setting measurable objectives.

Objectives should be *achievable;* otherwise, those responsible will not take them seriously. Some managers set objectives too high, hoping to maximize the effort of those involved. Since meeting objectives gives employees a sense of satisfaction, employees will likely come to resent managers who consistently set unreachable objectives. Yet, objectives should be *challenging* in order to push employees to be creative and do their best work. Admittedly, there may be a thin line between challenging and achievable, and it takes experience to know where that line is.

Another advantage of setting objectives is to help make sure those working on a brand are working strategically. Without objectives, employees and departments most likely will focus only on generating sales. This can lead to short-term thinking that may harm brand relationships in the long run. Having thought-out objectives that address all major aspects of managing brand relationships much improves the chances that the focus will be on building brand relationships rather than on just generating sales.

Strategies

Inexperienced marketers often mistakenly think that simply selecting a particular MC function constitutes a strategy. "Use brand publicity," for example, is not a good strategy statement because it doesn't contain an idea of how to use the publicity. A better strategy statement would be: "Use a team of doctors to conduct a media tour of the top 10 markets, explaining the breakthrough qualities of the brand in curing cancer." This is still a publicity strategy but, more important, it contains an idea of how the publicity function will be used.

Because strategies are so important, let's look at another example. Michelin is a manufacturer of premium-priced automobile tires whose objective is to convince car owners that its tires are the most durable and safest tires on the market. A weak strategy statement with regard to this objective would be "Use television advertising." A much stronger statement is: "Associate the Michelin brand name with protecting babies, by creating advertisements that visually link babies and tires in a way that emphasizes the ideas of protection and safety." Using this association to sell tires is the strategic idea.

Tactics

Specific short-term actions are called tactics; they are the executional details that bring a strategic idea to life. These are the details that are decided as the strategy is implemented, such as the typography, layout style, or images used in the design of a specific brand message. IMC planners must choose tactics for all the various MC messages used in the campaign by artists, writers, producers, and creative directors who make the strategic ideas come to life in the form of commercials, brochures, or merchandising kits.

In the case of Michelin, the tactics are to use a simple visual showing a cute baby sitting inside a tire. That visual executes the strategy by not only associating the brand with babies but also showing the baby surrounded and protected by the Michelin tire.

Cascading Objectives and Strategies

To understand what influences marketing and marketing communication objectives, we need to step back and look at an organization's total planning process. At the corporate level, underlying goals are to increase: a) profits, b) return on investment, and c) shareholder value (i.e., brand equity). For nonprofit organizations, underlying corporate goals are to increase or maintain financial support (through donations of money and time) and increase or maintain social impact. At the marketing level, the underlying goals are always, to some extent, to acquire, retain, and grow customers. The purpose of planning is to determine objectives and strategies for achieving these goals at the respective organizational levels.

Marketing and marketing communication objectives derive from two areas: a SWOT analysis (discussed later in this chapter) and high-level objectives and strategies. As shown in Figure 6–2, which uses the example of a U.S. food-products manufacturers whose overall goal is to successfully enter the Canadian market, high-level strategies from the business plan and marketing plans often become objectives for the next level of planning. Note how the 50 percent brand awareness strategy for marketing communication then becomes an objective for advertising. This process is called *cascade planning* because each stage spills over into the next. In very large companies, SWOT analyses are done at both the corporate and marketing levels. At all levels, objectives and strategies should be based on research and a thorough analysis of the corporation and brand market situation.

THE ZERO-BASED PLANNING PROCESS

Because the primary responsibility of IMC is to help organizations acquire, retain, and grow customers, all IMC objectives and strategies should directly or indirectly

FIGURE 6-2

Cascading Objectives and Strategies

Organizational level	Objectives	Strategies
Corporate	Increase profits 10%	Begin selling in Canada
Marketing	Have sales of $2 million in Canada by year end	Focus efforts in top 10 Canadian markets
Marketing communication	Acquire 100,000 new customers from top 10	Create 50% awareness, 35% brand knowledge, 20% trial
Advertising	Create 50% brand awareness in top 10 markets	Revise TV spots using Canadian cities as background
Sales promotion	Generate 20% trial among those aware	Distribute 500,000 free samples in top 10 markets
Publicity	Create 35% brand knowledge in top 10 cities	Do nutritional study and distribute findings in publicity

T A B L E   6 - 1   The Zero-Based Planning Process

Step	Description
1. Analyze SWOTs	Summarize internal (strengths, weaknesses) and external (opportunities, threats) brand-related conditions; determine the success of the MC functions and media used in preceding year.
2. Analyze targets and relationships	Analyze the various customer and prospect segments and determine which should be targeted and to what extent.
3. Determine MC objectives	Determine what marketing communication programs should accomplish.
4. Develop strategies and rationales	Determine which MC functions should be used and to what extent. Choose brand messages and means of delivery. Support each strategy with a rationale.
5. Determine the budget	Determine what the overall MC budget will be and then how money will be divided among the selected MC functions.
6. Determine the timing	Determine when each MC program will begin and end.
7. Test market MC mixes	Conduct ongoing MC tests in an effort to find more effective ways to do IMC.
8. Evaluate effectiveness	Monitor and evaluate all the IMC efforts to determine effectiveness and accountability.

be designed to support these three things. The challenge is to determine specifically how to get customers to be attracted to the brand, continue to buy the brand, and increase their share of category spending with the brand. At the same time, the brand must also maintain good relationships with all other stakeholders, who can impact the success of a brand.

Because market conditions are continually changing, IMC planners should use **zero-based planning,** which consists of *determining objectives and strategies based on current brand and marketplace conditions.* (The current conditions are considered the zero point.) This means not simply repeating last year's plan. As marketplace conditions change and a brand's needs change, the use of marketing communication functions and media should change accordingly. Sometimes it makes sense to use more advertising at the expense of sales promotion; at other times, under different marketplace conditions, it may be smarter to do just the opposite. Zero-based planning means starting at the beginning to make a plan based on what needs to be done rather than what has always been done. Merely repeating last year's plan with only slight tweaking seldom makes good sense.

Zero-based planning takes more work than other kinds of planning. Many organizations have gotten into the habit of using certain MC functions and downplaying or ignoring others. As will be explained in Part IV of this book, each MC function has its own unique strengths. The organization can determine the right mix of these functions only after it has analyzed the brand's Strengths, Weaknesses, Opportunities, and Threats (SWOT)—as they exist at the current time in a dynamic marketplace. To that end, the first step in the eight-step zero-based planning process outlined in Table 6–1 is a SWOT analysis. This eight-step planning process is equally applicable to consumer and BtB brands; to companies of every size, from

TABLE 6-2   SWOT Analysis Categories

Internal Factors	External Factors
Strengths: a brand's competitive advantages	Opportunities: marketplace conditions that are favorable for a brand
Weaknesses: a brand's competitive disadvantages	Threats: marketplace conditions that are unfavorable for a brand

the smallest retailer to the largest global brand; to service providers as well as manufacturers; and to nonprofit organizations.

Step 1: Analyzing SWOTs

Many marketing plans in the United States are based on an annual **situation analysis** which is basically *an analysis of marketplace conditions*. The problem with this type of analysis is that it doesn't categorize and prioritize findings from a strategic viewpoint, which is what a SWOT analysis does in an IMC plan. A **SWOT analysis** is *a structured evaluation of internal situations (strengths and weaknesses) and external situations (opportunities and threats) that can help and hurt a brand.* It is the first step in planning marketing communication, as Figure 6–3 illustrates.

Internal factors are all those that are under the company's control; external elements are those over which the company has little or no control (but on occasion can influence). Table 6–2 summarizes the four categories of information needed for a SWOT analysis.

Internal Factors

A company's internal factors—its strengths and weaknesses—include a wide range of variables, such as the company's expertise in R&D, the value of the patents it holds, its distribution system and product availability, its pricing, the depth and breadth of its sales force, its brand positioning, the extent and condition of its physical facilities, its brand share, and its overall financial strength. Brand image, corporate reputation, corporate culture, and core values can also be either strengths or weaknesses.

Most companies include communication and resulting customer and prospect perceptions as internal elements even though the formation of perceptions is not directly under the company's control. This is because customers develop attitudes and beliefs about a brand because of things the brand has or has not done, and such actions are in fact under the brand's control. The internal factors are defined as follows:

- *Strengths:* Competitive advantages; resources that allow the company to offer benefits competitors cannot offer or do not offer at the same level of quality or as economically. GMC had successfully marketed its Jimmy SUV model and could leverage this strength when launching the new upscale Envoy.
- *Weaknesses:* Competitive disadvantages; areas in which customers perceive competitors to have an advantage. GMC faced a huge weakness in the launch of Envoy because the car would not be available until seven months after the beginning of the traditional SUV buying period. Furthermore, since it was a new brand, it had no brand awareness—another major weakness.

External Factors

A company's external factors—its opportunities and threats—include competitive activity, laws and regulations, technological innovation, industry trends, socio-economic conditions, and changes in the marketplace. These can be defined as follows:

- *Opportunities:* Social and economic conditions and situations in the marketplace that can positively alter customers' attitudes about and behavior toward the company's products. GMC determined that there was an opportunity to extend its market appeal into the upscale SUV category because of the growth in the overall upscale car category.

- *Threats:* Marketplace conditions that reduce the perceived value or attractiveness of a product or that result in its being more costly to make or

FIGURE 6-3

SWOT-based Campaign Planning

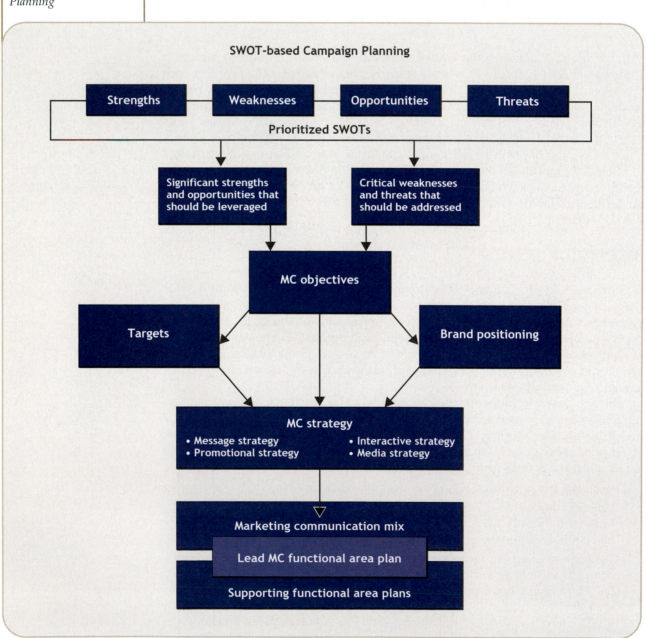

provide. For example, GMC could see the level of competition building in the upscale SUV category and was worried that prospects would purchase competitors' models before Envoy was in the showroom.

By definition, threats can't be controlled, but sometimes a company can lessen their impact. The idea is to anticipate them and make efforts to counteract them. Exhibit 6–4 is an ad that addresses a threat common to most companies doing e-commerce.

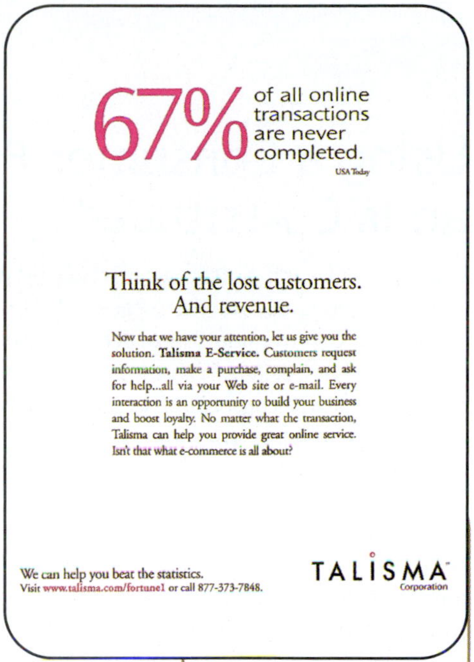

Customer-Focused Analysis

A SWOT analysis should take an outside-in perspective—from the customer's viewpoint—rather than relying on internal judgments to analyze the company, brand, and competitive situation. Perceptions determine to what extent customers and prospects will buy a brand, as the IMC in Action box illustrates. The gathering of SWOT data needs to be managed by a cross-functional team that has the responsibility to plan and monitor all corporate messages for strategic consistency.

Brand audits of companies conducted by the author have found that not only do managers' perceptions differ from customers' perceptions, but managers are not always in agreement on the brand's strengths, weaknesses, opportunities, and threats. An IMC audit of a financial services company, for example, found that top management believed that one of the company's key strengths was its employees; however, the company's marketing managers believed that the employees were a key weakness. Customers, meanwhile, perceived the employees to be no better and no worse than those in competing companies. This points to the need for a company to make sure its SWOT analysis is accurate. When different managers have different perceptions of the company's SWOTs, the company needs to conduct customer and market research to resolve these differences.

One way to ensure that the SWOT analysis has a customer focus is to think in terms of the four Cs, defined in Chapter 1 as customers, cost, convenience, and communication.[3] Rather than focusing on the product (where production and cost savings are most important), think from a customer's perspective—that is, ask *customers* how the brand compares to competing brands rather than doing just internal competitive-product lab tests. Rather than comparing prices to competitors, ask customers how they perceive the *cost* of buying and using the brand in relation to competing brands. Rather than doing store checks to determine the extent of brand distribution, ask customers how *convenient* it is for them to find and buy the brand. Finally, rather than just looking at promotional redemption figures, ask customers if they are receiving the kinds of *communication* from the company that they need to make their buying decisions. Ask, too, whether the company is accessible and responsive to their complaints and inquiries.

In addition to asking customers about the brand's strengths and weaknesses, the company should determine the basis for these perceptions. What brand contact points led customers to believe the brand is better or worse than competing brands? Flimsy packaging, for example, may cause customers to say that the brand is inferior to competing brands even if the actual product is superior. A company can address negative messages only if it knows their source.

A company can learn about customer perceptions through customer surveys, analyses of service calls, and interviews with the sales force. Additional sources of customer-focused SWOT information include observation studies of customers shopping and using both the company's brand and competing brands, comparing

EXHIBIT 6-4

Talisman has a way to help e-commerce companies address a common brand threat, which is that two-thirds of online shoppers don't complete their transactions.

IMC IN ACTION

Using a Consumer Focus to Create an IMC Attitude*

For its SoftBench Suite, a Unix application program sold to businesses, Hewlett-Packard (HP) developed a marketing communication program based on defining customers' needs (see Exhibit 6-5). The division began its planning with a product positioning workshop that defined *customers' dilemmas with Unix* and identified *HP's resources that could be used to address these dilemmas*.

One result of this customer-focused approach was that planners determined that *various HP departments—sales, product marketing, engineering, customer support—each understood a different aspect of customers' needs.* According to a HP marketing manager, "By integrating all perspectives, we were able to think constructively about how our product addressed those dilemmas. Out of all this, we developed a creative strategy focused on customer need."

The creative strategy used the theme "We understand" to emphasize HP's understanding of the issues, pressures, and constraints that software developers and software development managers faced, such as *unrealistic deadlines, hidden code errors, simultaneous development of multiple application versions, and transition problems in moving to object-oriented programming*.

This theme was launched in a print advertising campaign, reinforced in three direct-mail pieces and a trade-show handout, showcased on the company's website, and then later picked up in another division's direct-marketing campaign promoting a product bundled with SoftBench.

As HP managers discovered, true integration goes much further than coordinating graphic designs and key messages. Entire divisions or companies need to adopt an integrated attitude to implement an effective marketing communication program. HP used that approach so that customers would be greeted at all levels with the idea that HP understood their dilemmas. For example, in speaking to customers, all HP employees—from customer-service representatives to sales associates to product marketing engineers—focused on the same thing: understanding and solving the customer's problem.

Integration as a process makes everyone in the company a salesperson. Integration as an attitude allows employees to offer solutions, not just programmed responses, to customer needs.

Think About It

Why is it important to use a customer focus in planning an IMC program? How was this done in HP's SoftBench Suite campaign planning? In what way were cross-functional teams needed to plan, implement, and monitor the "We understand" campaign?

* SWOT findings are in italics.

Source: Adapted from Lindell, P. Griffith, "Lining Up Your Marketing Ducks: Integrated Marketing Communications," *Marketing Computers*, October 1996, p 27.

EXHIBIT 6-5

the brand's website to competitors' sites, review of what the trade press and the popular press are saying about the brand, and formal or informal surveys of the brand's suppliers and channel members.

Prioritizing SWOTs

Once the SWOTs have been identified, they need to be prioritized. Although many things can be taken into consideration when prioritizing SWOTs, the following criteria can be used for most product categories:

1. *Realistic damage* to brand relationships and brand equity if a weakness or threat is not addressed (i.e., anticipated and counteracted).
2. *Realistic benefit* if a strength or opportunity is leveraged (i.e., used to its full potential).
3. *Cost* of addressing or leveraging each SWOT.
4. *Time* company has to address or leverage each SWOT.

Each criterion should be weighted for importance depending on the product category and the company's long-term objectives. Table 6–3 shows how the GMC Envoy's SWOTs, as outlined in the chapter opening case, could be evaluated and given priority scores.

Once the SWOTs have been scored, the scores can be graphed as shown in Figure 6–4, which more clearly identifies key SWOTs than does Table 6–3. Notice that strengths and opportunities, which need to be leveraged, are charted above the middle line and that weaknesses and threats, which need to be addressed, are below the middle line. SWOTs that extend beyond the dotted "critical" lines are deemed to be most in need of being either leveraged or addressed. A company determines the critical lines based on past experience. As you can see, there were four key SWOTs on which the Envoy campaign needed to act.

After the company has prioritized the brand's SWOTs, it must use them to set objectives that will leverage the key strengths and opportunities and address the most serious weaknesses and threats. No company will have the time or resources to address and leverage all the SWOT findings, but the prioritization can help IMC planners determine where to focus their attention.

A prioritized SWOT analysis also leads to decisions about which marketing communication tools to use. As shown earlier, in Figure 6–3, the SWOTs lead to objectives and strategies for using the appropriate MC functions. The Envoy campaign, for example, used direct response because the brand's SWOTs dictated the use of an exclusive offer to a relatively small group of identifiable prospective customers whose interest had to be maintained over seven months. Although awareness was a key objective, it did not make sense to use mass media advertising because of the small target audience. In this case, the company understood that it could make good use of the awareness-building dimensions of direct response. Somewhat unusual in the Envoy example is the fact that the direct-response function was able to support strategies for accomplishing all the major objectives (see Table 6–4).

Account Planning

A particular type of planning that is useful in IMC is called **account planning**, which means *using research and brand insights to bring a strong consumer focus to the planning of marketing communication*. As explained in Chapter 3, an account planner is both a researcher and a strategic thinker whose mission is to see the brand's communication effort through the customer's eyes and represent the customer's viewpoint in planning meetings.

T A B L E   6 - 3   Prioritizing the GMC Envoy's SWOTs

Rank each SWOT item from 1 to 3 according to its importance to the company's objectives (with 3 being the most important).

	Damage If Not Addressed	Benefit If Leveraged	Cost of Addressing or Leveraging	Window of Time	Total*
Strengths					
• Strong GMC consumer franchise	—	2	3	1	6
• Good dealership network	—	2	3	1	6
• Identifiable target	—	3	3	3	9
Weaknesses					
• No Envoy brand awareness	3	—	2	3	8
• Not available until spring	3	—	3	3	9
• Small budget, no major MC support until spring	3	—	2	3	8
Opportunities					
• Increasing interest in SUVs	—	2	1	2	5
• Good economy	—	2	1	2	5
Threats					
• Established competitive brands	3	—	3	1	7
• New brands coming into market	2	—	2	1	5

*The higher the number, the higher the priority.

T A B L E   6 - 4   Zero-Based Plan for Envoy

Key SWOTs	MC Objectives	Best MC Function	Rationale
No brand awareness	Create 50% awareness among target audience	Advertising	Not appropriate because of small audience, product availability, and small budget
Identifiable target	Create 50% awareness among target audience	Direct marketing	Small audience; contact information available
Availability problem	Get 10% to visit Showroom when available	Direct marketing	Build curiosity and draw out interest over a longer period of time
Low budget and little MC support	Sell 3,500 units in advance of availability	Direct marketing	Use personal contact medium to presell target

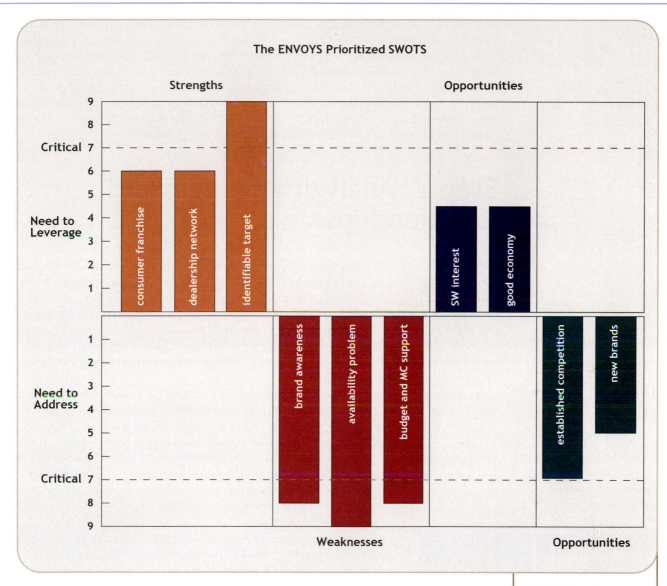

FIGURE 6-4

SWOTs that score beyond the critical limits (dotted lines) should be given top priority.

A researcher traditionally conducts market studies and interprets the data, but an account planner takes the interpretation a step further and analyzes how best to use the insights from the research in the development of the message and media strategies. Account planners write **briefs**, which are *statements that summarize the research and the insights for the creative team, and help the team identify the direction and focus for their creative and media ideas.* The insights uncovered by account planners can very easily be moved into a SWOT analysis to strengthen the plan's customer focus.

Account planning is used primarily in advertising agencies but also in some other marketing communication agencies. In advertising, Abbott Mead Vickers BBDO (AMV) in the United Kingdom and Goodby, Silverstein & Partners and TBWA Chiat/Day in the United States are agencies that have pioneered the use of account planning. Porter Novelli is a public relations agency that also has used account planning to develop strategies.

AMV, for example, used account planning to puzzle out a strategy for British Telecom as it moved through privatization and faced competition from US telecommunications giants such as AT&T and US West (now Qwest Communications International). The objective was to increase overall phone usage in the consumer marketplace and retain British Telecom's large customer base. A traditional approach to achieving this objective would have been to offer promotional incentives for increased usage. AMV account planners, however, used customer research to learn that men were concerned about the costs of telephone usage and women therefore felt guilty about how much time they spent on the phone. Based on these insights, the account planners recommended a strategy based on (1) convincing men of the value, not the cost, of the calls and (2) giving support to women about phone use because of the value of the calls. The strategy worked.

Step 2. Analyzing Targets and Relationships

Step 2 of the zero-based planning process is identifying the key customer and prospect segments, as well as the brand's relationship with each key segment. Because of its emphasis on consumer insights, account planning can help a company identify and understand its target audiences. This step must be completed before the organization can develop objectives. (Because segmenting and targeting are so important, this book devotes a whole chapter—Chapter 7—to explaining how segmenting and targeting are done. Therefore, only a brief mention of segmentation and targeting will be made here.)

Targeting is used to focus the MC effort on (1) current customers who are most likely to repurchase and/or influence purchases; (2) those who need special attention for whatever reason (e.g., have slowed their frequency of purchase, have had a bad customer service problem, have had a dialogue with the brand but have not yet purchased); and (3) those who have not bought the brand before but are likely prospects based on their profiles. Other stakeholders who affect or influence these three categories of customers and prospects may also be targeted. Exhibit 6–6 shows how Motorola targets different user groups of cellular phones.

Because it is expensive to send out brand messages, the more precise the targeting, the less the media waste. Only by knowing whom to target can a brand develop objectives and strategies that are relevant and therefore persuasive. For example, by knowing they needed to reach an upscale audience interested in SUVs, the IMC planners in the Envoy case were able to develop a big creative idea that would appeal to this type of sophisticated prospect.

Most IMC efforts are designed to reach a variety of targets: current customers, prospective customers, and channel members (e.g., distributors and retailers). Also, in large companies, it is wise to use internal marketing to reach those who play a critical role in managing brand relationships (this is explained in more detail at the end of this chapter). Unless these people know what marketing is trying to do, it is difficult for them to support that effort.

Companies should use continuous customer feedback and specific customer research to determine the strength of customer relationships. As you will recall from Chapter 2, the anatomy of brand relationships includes trust, intensity, expectations, and loyalty. These aspects can be divided into eight constructs, which can be used to measure to what extent customers:

EXHIBIT 6-6

A part of Motorola's MC plan is to target a variety of cellular phone users.

1. *Trust* the brand.
2. Are *satisfied* with the brand.
3. Perceive the company as *consistent* in its dealings and product performance.
4. Perceive the company as *accessible*.
5. Perceive the company as *responsive*.
6. Feel the company is *committed* to customers and puts them first.
7. Have an *affinity* for the company and its other customers.
8. *Like* the company and enjoy doing business with it.

Customers and other stakeholders can be asked to rate the brand and its competitors on each of these constructs, indicating where the brand is relatively weak and strong. Just as important as *how* a brand scores on these relationship constructs is *why* it scores high or low. For example, if a brand scores low on trust, the company can do little to correct that perception until it determines the source of the distrust (e.g., poor customer service, overpromising in planned messages, poor product performance) and takes whatever action is necessary to solve the problem. As explained earlier in the book, negative performance messages can make millions of dollars in marketing communication a wasted investment.

An example of the benefits provided by relationship analysis comes from athletic shoe manufacturer Nike's early experiences of selling to women. In the early 1990s, women made up only about 5 percent of Nike's customer base. Nike used customer-focused research and discovered that one reason for this was that women did not find advertising that featured Michael Jordan and other male athletes relevant; these messages didn't talk to women. As a result, the company created a separate women's campaign with advertising copy that addressed how women felt about their bodies and themselves. The ads included lines like "Did you ever wish you were a boy?" "You were born a daughter," and "A woman is often measured by the things she cannot control." Soon after this campaign, women accounted for 15 percent of Nike's sales.[4] Such success is what led Nike to move further into the women's market, reaching the market niches of girls and young women (see Exhibit 6–7).

Although it is important that marketers stay focused on marketing communication issues, they have a responsibility to recommend changes whenever other areas of the marketing mix or company operations are delivering inconsistent or negative brand messages. Negative product and service messages especially need to be brought to the attention of top management. In other words, if customers perceive a product as being low in quality yet blind tests show it is equal to competing brands, a cross-functional team needs to determine the source of the misperception. The Tale of Two Companies box illustrates how one area of the marketing mix can negatively affect an otherwise strong brand.

Most of the guidelines for analyzing brand relationships apply to both consumer and BtB customers, but there are some differences. As you will recall, business-to-business marketers must get to know their customers' businesses as intimately as possible in order to anticipate their needs and go beyond satisfying just their specific requests. Such customer knowledge enables a company to respond not only to customer needs and wants but also what causes these needs and wants. Only then can it determine if there is a

EXHIBIT 6-7

A larger-budget advertiser like Nike can afford to target individual customer segments, as in this brand message aimed at women.

A TALE OF TWO COMPANIES

Snapple before and after Quaker

This is really a tale of three companies, or rather one company at three different points in its marketing history. The Snapple brand of fruit and tea beverages became a huge marketing success based on its relationship with its customers, whose cult like devotion even involved customers sending in ideas for new flavors. Wendy, the "Snapple lady," was the star of marketing communication that featured her as epitomizing the brand's personality. Originally a receptionist for Snapple, Wendy was shown opening the mail and reading letters from enthusiastically satisfied customers. Because of her success in this role and the strength of this idea as a campaign theme, Wendy eventually became head of a six-person customer-service department that handled an average of 2,000 letters a week.

Despite its successful customer relationships, Snapple had problems expanding its distribution beyond the mom-and-pop stores that had been its loyal supporters in the beginning; larger retail chains simply would not carry the brand.

Enter (the giant packaged-foods company) Quaker, which had solved a similar problem when it took over Gatorade. Investors believed that Snapple had grown as much as it could as an independent and needed the marketplace power of a large company like Quaker to solve its distribution problems. Unfortunately, Quaker's pressure on retailers to stock the full line of Snapple beverages irritated these retailers and left many of the brand's loyal distributors out in the cold. Furthermore, Quaker seemed not to understand the magic of the marketing communication that had created the Snapple cult; instead, it moved toward more traditional image-oriented campaigns.

Quaker's major marketing effort became an ambitious sampling program in the summer of 1996 intended to expand Snapple's market and reach consumers at every possible point of contact from beaches to parks to Little League games to office buildings. Unfortunately the "Snapple Sample Guys" didn't connect with enough consumers to rebuild the Snapple franchise. In 1997, Quaker sold Snapple to Triarc Companies, taking an estimated $1.4 billion loss. Triarc focused on the youth market and increased Snapple's distribution before selling the brand, in turn, to Cadbury Schweppes in October 2000 (see Exhibit 6-8)

Think About It

What was the source of the success of Snapple in its early days? What caused Snapple sales to tumble? Could that problem be solved with a new or different marketing communication program?

Sources: "Phyllis Berman, "Juicing It Up," *Forbes*, May 18, 1998, pp. 134-136; Cliff Edwards, "Quaker Oats Co. Sells Snapple at $1.4 Billion Loss," *Daily Camera*, March 28, 1997, p. 6b: Greg Gattuso, "Drinking It in Communication Is Key to Snapple's Customer Loyalty," *Direct Marketing*, October 1995, pp. 26-29.

EXHIBIT 6-8

Part of Snapple's plan is to use distinctive packaging design.

better solution than what the customer is asking for, and become proactive rather than just reactive. According to authors Michael Treacy and Fred Wiersema, "Deep customer knowledge and breakthrough insights about the client's underlying processes are the backbone of every customer-intimate organization today."[5]

Regardless of whether the targeting is for consumers or BtB customers, an effective IMC program seeks to use communication opportunities to strengthen relationships. A smart company makes sure that customers see such opportunities as a benefit of having a relationship with the company.

Step 3. Determining MC Objectives

In setting objectives, marketers determine what needs to be accomplished in order to address and leverage the key SWOT findings. An example of setting an objective to address an external threat to a brand comes from the wine industry. Retailing in the wine and liquor industry has moved from small family stores to large self-service stores. Because of this, customers must make their own selections with little or no help from informed salesclerks. For years, winemaker Robert Mondavi had depended on the retail sales staff to explain and sell its brand. The loss of this support has become an increasing threat to the brand. It is an external threat because it is a situation over which Mondavi has no control.

To make this condition even worse for Mondavi, the number of wine choices has significantly increased (another external threat), making it even more difficult for a single brand to be noticed and selected. To address these two external threats, Mondavi and its agency, Ketchum, San Francisco, agreed that one of the company's primary MC objectives should be to increase direct contact with customers and prospects, regardless of where they buy their wine (see Exhibit 6–9). To make this objective measurable, Mondavi stated its objective as follows: "Generate 500,000 unique website visits and 150,000 customer-initiated calls to customer-service center by year-end."

Because IMC is about building and managing brand relationships, objectives are of two types, communication and behavioral. All marketing communication should have a positive impact on one or both of these areas. Increasing credibility of claims and reinforcing or changing brand positioning are examples of communication effects; increasing trial, sales, and requests for information are examples

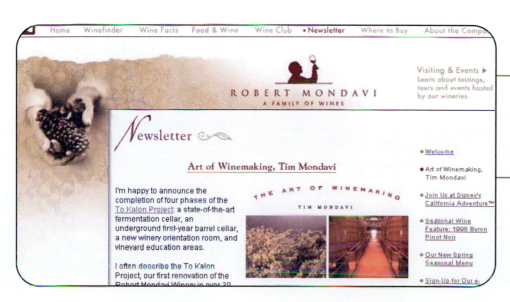

EXHIBIT 6-9

The Mondavi Newsletter was designed to increase the opportunity for direct contact with customers.

of behavioral effects. The important thing to remember is that both types of objectives are needed because customers and prospects can't be expected to "behave" in the desired way without being convinced that it is in their best interest to do so.

Communication Objectives

As explained in Chapter 5, there are various hierarchy-of-effects models that explain how brand messages affect the brand decision process. The steps in these models can be used to set communication objectives. The awareness, interest, desire, action (AIDA) model, for example, suggests that a brand have communication objectives for achieving certain levels of brand awareness, interest in the brand, and desire for the brand. The last step, action, is a behavioral objective. In the case of BtB products and high-priced consumer products, communication objectives can be set to address where customers are in their buying process. An insurance company may set a communication objective for its sales representatives as follows: "All customers who request a quote on their home and automobile insurance policies will be contacted personally within 72 hours of their quote requests."

Figure 6–5 shows that the percentage of the target audience affected at each of the hierarchical steps gets decreasingly smaller as customers move toward the last step, action. In other words, it is easier to accomplish communication objectives than it is to accomplish behavioral objectives. The figure gives hypothetical response rates (i.e., rough approximations) in order to demonstrate that, generally, the impact reduces by half as customers move through the hierarchy. This is

FIGURE 6-5

As figure shows, it's easier to achieve communication than behavioral objectives.

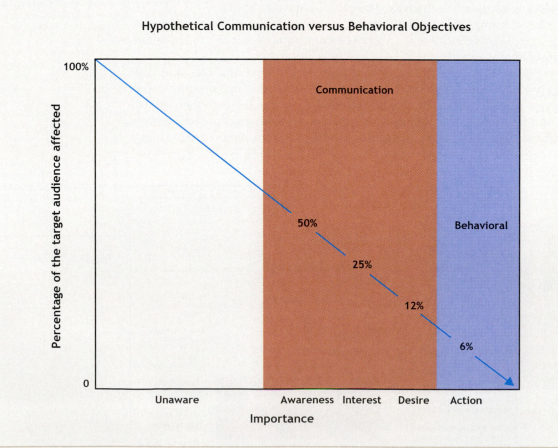

Hypothetical Communication versus Behavioral Objectives

because it is much easier to make people aware of a brand than it is to persuade them to buy it or take some other kind of action. The level of expected impact will obviously vary with the product category and the strength of the brand message.

Communication objectives can also be based on the think-feel-do model. Once a company decides what a target audience should think and feel about a brand, it can determine a desired percentage for each. The following are examples:

"Think" communication objectives

- Convince 50 percent of the target audience that Brand X is the most durable.
- Make 35 percent of the target audience aware that Brand X has the longest warranty.

"Feel" communication objectives

- Have 40 percent of the target audience rate Brand X as the one "easiest to do business with."
- Convince 55 percent of the target audience that Brand X is the most prestigious of all brands in its category.

The quantitative aspect of an objective—the percentage or raw number to be achieved—depends on the brand's past performance and how much MC support is available. The more research that has been done on past MC efforts, the more educated the current estimate can be. For example, if customers' measured interest in the brand is generally half of their measured awareness of the brand, and their action was half of their desire for the brand, it would be realistic to set an awareness objective of 80 percent, an interest objective of 40 percent, and a desire objective of 20 percent in order to justify increasing the action objective to 10 percent. To help determine how realistic these objectives are, one would need to look back at past response tracking for that brand to see how the numbers (in relation to each other) have changed over time.

Communication objectives should also be set for one or more of the eight relationship constructs listed earlier in this chapter. Knowing that trust, for example, is the most important relationship component, a brand would be smart to have a trust objective, such as "Determine that at least 85 percent of current customers *trust* our brand more than any other." Other such objectives could include the following: "75 percent say our brand is the most *responsive*," "80 percent say brand is the most *consistent* in its dealings with customers," and "90 percent say our company is more *accessible* than any other competing company."

Some marketers don't focus too much on communication objectives because, they argue, there is no absolute link between achieving them and achieving behavioral objectives. While it is true that increases in awareness, trust, or other communication measures do not necessarily guarantee increases in sales, common sense says that if no one is aware of a brand, or that those who are aware of it don't trust it, the chances of it selling well are small. The exact relationship between communication and behavior differs by brand and over time as marketplace conditions change, but there is always some level of relationship. This is why it is imperative that brands conduct ongoing evaluations of customer perceptions and behavior.

One of the concerns of using mass media advertising has always been the inability to precisely determine its impact on sales. A statement made many years ago by the owner of a major department store underlines this problem: "I know that half my advertising is wasted, I just don't know which half." The Association of National Advertisers' DAGMAR report (mentioned in Chapter 5) proposes that measurable objectives focused on awareness, comprehension, conviction, and action will help companies sort out the impact of advertising and other types of marketing communication.[6]

TABLE 6 - 5   Sample Behavior Objectives

Behavior Desired	Examples of Relevant Objectives
Request information	Receive 10,000 requests a month for new product brochure.
Sample product	Distribute samples to 35% of target households.
Visit showroom	Motivate 50 or more visits to showroom each week during promotion period.
Make brand referrals	Generate 20,000 applications in which applicants indicate they were referred by a current customer.
Make multiple purchases	Have 20% of all brand purchases be multiple purchases.
Buy more frequently	Increase average rate of purchase from 2 times a month to 2.5 times a month.

Behavioral Objectives

As noted earlier, the most desirable customer behavior is the product purchase (and, even more important, the repeat purchase). However, having prospects request more information, visit a showroom, sample the brand, or have customers refer the brand to others are also desired behaviors that can be objectives. Table 6–5 illustrates how objectives for each of these examples could be written.

Most marketing communication efforts by retailers have behavioral objectives, as do direct-response and promotional programs. Those doing online marketing also use behavioral objectives for website visits, inquiries, and transactions. Once the objectives have been determined, in terms of leveraging or addressing the key SWOTS, the next step in the zero-based planning process is determining how to achieve the objectives. The "hows" are strategies.

Step 4: Developing Strategies and Rationales

The essence of zero-based planning is to be neutral in choosing MC functions and media, which means letting the SWOT analysis and resulting objectives determine the best MC mix and media mix. Long-distance telephone service provider MCI (now WorldCom) created its successful "Friends and Family" promotion, for example, because its analysis indicated it was more cost-effective to have customers selling other customers on the service than it was using a telemarketing campaign. In the promotion, customers were financially rewarded when they recruited other households to become MCI customers. To make this possible, MCI moved dollars from its telemarketing program into sales promotion.[7]

In most cases developing strategies involves selecting the most relevant MC mix to help achieve the objectives, creating (or seeing) a "big idea," and selecting the best media mix. The development of a positioning and creative strategy can be a very in-depth process. For example, the Price/McNabb agency in Charlotte, North Carolina, uses a "Brand Studio," which is the name of the agency's planning process for brand positioning (see IMC Strategy box).

IMC STRATEGY

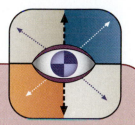

Price/McNabb's Brand Studio

The Brand Studio begins with a Context Analysis which analyzes the perspectives of stakeholders, the company, and the competition. Price/McNabb's planning approach includes four tools: Mosaic, Laddering, Portrait, and the I-Statement

1. *Mosaic.* Mosaic is a workshop technique the agency uses with clients to build consensus by analyzing 16 brand opportunity areas. The workshop groups create key positioning ideas in four areas: company, product, user, and symbolism. Then the workshop rates every idea based on the three evaluation factors of validity, motivation, and differentiation, described in the Context Analysis. The map of the opportunities will reflect the categories in Table 6-6. Typically a Mosaic session will produce from 50 to 150 ideas. The total list is ranked and the teams work with the top 20 or so ideas to build a positioning strategy.

2. *Laddering.* Using the output from a process like Mosaic, the teams have many ideas with which to work. The question becomes one of creating a logical connection between different types of information. The premise behind Laddering is that information can be labeled as relatively feature-oriented, benefit-oriented, or reward-oriented. Features are concrete, objective, rational, and, normally, "close to the company or product." At the other end of the continuum, rewards are abstract, subjective, emotional, and, normally, "close to the customer." Laddering provides a systematic way to connect different levels of information. Features support benefits; features and benefits support rewards. Figure 6-6 gives several illustrations of how these are linked.

3. *Portrait.* Using collage-building techniques, the teams create detailed visual profiles of competitors' brands and/or constituencies (stakeholders). Portrait is a projective technique that uses laminated images and adjectives to tell a story about a brand.

4. *The "I-Statement."* This last tool moves the planning into the realm of message strategy. It uses five components: a behavioral outcome, a replacement or competitive behavior, a motivation or benefit, support for the claim, and validation. The format, which is based on reflecting a customer viewpoint, is as follows:

When I _____ (outcome)
instead of _____ (replacement)
I _____ (benefit)
because _____ (support)
and _____ (validation)

An example is: "When I visit a Drexel Heritage Home Inspirations showroom instead of going to an Ethan Allen store, I get excited and inspired about my home because of the beauty of the product and the expert designers they have to help me, and I will feel like I fit in with my friends but still express my personal taste."

TABLE 6-6   Opportunity Analysis

Company	Product	User	Symbolism
History/legacy	Scope	Psychology	Graphic
Culture	Performance	Self-image	Abstract
Country of origin	Price/value	Emotion	
Persona	Feature/ingredient	Usage experience	
	Unique method		
	Quality		

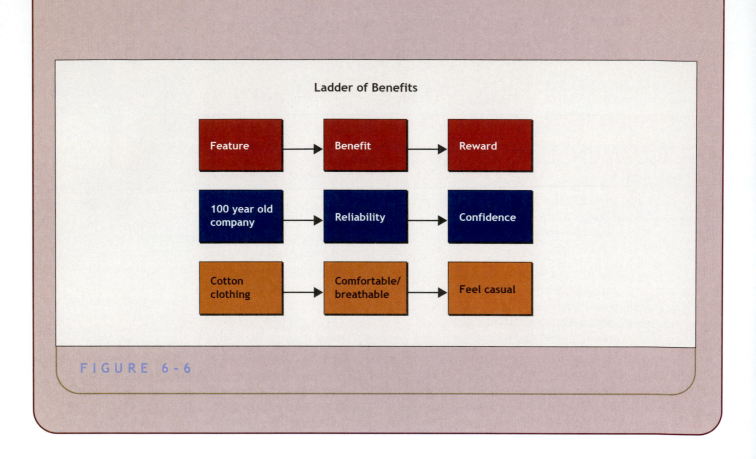

FIGURE 6-6

Selecting the MC Mix

Most marketing communication plans use a mix of MC tools because each tool has different communication and persuasive strengths (see Exhibit 6–10). Deciding which MC tool can most efficiently and effectively help achieve a particular objective is not too difficult if you stop and think about what each function does best. For example, to help achieve the objective of "Increase belief of brand claims by 15 percent," publicity would be used because it has relatively high credibility. If the objective is "Increase trial by 25 percent," then sales promotion may be the best MC tool to use because sales promotion adds tangible value to a brand offering. (The strengths of each MC tool are explained in Chapters 14–17.)

The hard part of planning an MC mix is deciding how best to mix the various functions for maximum efficiency and impact. One MC function may take the lead while others are used to support it. The big idea, for example, may call for an event. The event is the lead tool, but it must be announced by advertising and publicity. Sales promotion may also be used to create reminder pieces that event participants take home with them.

A problem can occur when one MC tool dominates simply out of tradition, regardless of the objectives. This domination happens most often with mass media advertising, especially on consumer brands. There are several reasons for this. First, mass media advertising has been extremely successful in creating brand awareness and in positioning brands. Consequently, many consumer brands start out by allocating the majority of their MC budgets to advertising and then find it hard to change the allocation because departments and agencies become involved and continue to perpetuate their own preeminence. Second, many brands still place too much emphasis on acquiring customers. Finally, advertising may seem to be the most "glamorous" of the various MC tools. Most marketers prefer to identify themselves with a TV or magazine advertising campaign rather than with

EXHIBIT 6-10

As shown here, examples of the variety of pieces in an IMC mix can include such things as ads, brochures, and direct mail pieces.

a direct-marketing campaign (involving telemarketing or "junk mail") or a sales promotion campaign (involving cents-off coupons or free coffee mugs).

Because advertising has been so successful, many of those working in advertising agencies have come to believe advertising can do it all. There is an old industry joke about the advertising agency executive who is making a new business pitch and says to the prospective client: "Advertising is the answer. What's the question?" Smart advertising agencies, of course, realize they don't have all the answers, which is why so many today are buying or merging with other MC agencies.

Creating the Big Idea

Once the company selects an MC mix, the creative people develop a "big idea" that will solve the key problem and anchor all the marketing communication. The big idea provides a single focus to all the communication efforts, gives direction to both message design and message delivery, and must be reflected in the executions. (Message strategy and execution will be discussed in Chapters 9 and 10.) Recall that in the GMC Envoy case, the big idea was to take the target audience on a virtual test drive of the Envoy via a series of direct mailings from two brothers touring Europe.

Idea development must be carefully managed; otherwise, a variety of unrelated ideas may be produced. Offering a six-pack of beer or a pair of panty hose to motivate people to try on a Rolex watch at a jewelry store would not be a good idea since these promotional offers are not consistent with the upscale image of a Rolex watch. Offering a chance to win a Montblanc pen or a Hermes scarf, however, would be consistent. For strategic consistency in brand messages, there needs to be a *fit* between brands and offers. Keep in mind that promotional offers will serve two purposes: to motivate behavior and to reinforce a brand's image.

Traditionally, for many consumer products and BtB products, advertising agencies have been given the responsibility for developing the main strategic creative idea, and then all the other MC functions have been told to use that idea in executing their respective functions. Today, more and more companies are asking all of their MC agencies for big ideas and then choosing the best one, with which all the others must work.

Selecting the Media Mix

Media and message strategies are interdependent. This is why the media strategy needs to be developed at the same time as the message strategy. The media analysis should be neutral and broad in scope. For each target audience, the company and its MC agency develop a strategic **media mix**, *a plan that identifies the most effective ways to create positive contacts that cost effectively deliver brand messages*. In any given campaign, the media can be used at different times and at different levels to deliver specific types of messages. (The media mix will be discussed in more detail in Chapters 11–13.)

The Robert Mondavi winery's relationship-building campaign discussed earlier included not only advertising in specialty magazines (a medium Mondavi had used rarely over the years) but also a newsletter and direct-mail pieces sent to people who visited the Mondavi winery or its Internet site (which receives about 5,000 visits a month).[8] By using addressable media aimed at customers who initiated contact with the brand, Mondavi hoped to at least partially replace the personal attention its buyers and potential buyers once received in the family-owned stores.

Providing the Rationale

The last component in developing strategy is to explain why the strategy ideas are sound—that is, to state the rationale. Executing ideas, particularly the production and media placements, is what costs money. Therefore, those responsible for approving expenditures want to be given reasons why the strategic ideas being presented will work. If the agency or department recommending strategies cannot articulate why their ideas should work, then the ideas are probably not very good. ("Trust me" is not a good rationale, even though more than one person in the marketing communication business has tried using it over the years.)

The rationale for the GMC Envoy's direct-mail, two-brothers-in-Europe campaign was given as follows: (1) The target audience was identified as sophisticated world travelers, so the foreign stamps and return addresses of upscale European hotels would be attention-getting and enticing; (2) the upscale direct mailing was strategically consistent with the image objective for the new Envoy; and (3) the budget was not enough to do mass media advertising.

Step 5: Budgeting

A universal curse of planning is that you never have a large enough budget to do everything that needs to be done. This is why SWOT analysis findings are prioritized. Marketing and MC planners need to put their resources against the most important situations that need to be addressed or leveraged.

Marketing and marketing communication departments (and their campaigns) are allocated *a fixed amount of money for a fixed period of time*—in other words, a **budget.** Marketing competes with all other corporate departments (finance, production, human resources, etc.) for its share of the total corporate budget. Then, marketing communication and its various functional areas have to compete among themselves for the money they need to run their programs.

The normal corporate budgeting process begins by asking each department how much money it needs to meet its objectives. What makes budgeting so difficult is the difficulty a marketing department has in predicting the return on what it spends. This is because results are affected by so many variables such as competitors constantly changing their offerings and promotions and customers needs and wants constantly changing.

Recognizing their inability to predict the future, most companies use a combination of methods—percentage-of-sales, objective and task, share-of-category spending, and return on investment (ROI)—to determine how much MC money they will need. These four major budgeting inputs are discussed below.

Percentage-of-sales This method uses two variables—the sales forecast for the coming year and an arbitrary percentage of that forecast. For example, if a manufacturer of maple syrup forecasts sales for next year to be $25 million, and marketing's MC budgeting allocation is 10 percent, then it will have $2.5 million to spend on MC. This percentage is found in a brand's financial **pro forma**, which *is a breakdown of forecasted sales on a per case basis* as shown below:

Pro Forma for Maple Syrup Manufacturer

Forecasted number of cases that will be sold next year	1,000,000	
Sales price per case	$25.00	
Forecasted sales revenue	$25,000,000	

(dollar allocation per case)

Cost-of goods	$10.00	40%
Labor	2.50	10
Warehousing and distribution	1.25	5
Sales commission	2.50	10
Marketing communication	2.50	10
Administration and overhead	3.75	15
Profit before taxes	2.50	10
TOTAL	$25.00	100%

As you can see, for every case sold at $25 a case, marketing communication receives $2.50 or 10 percent. A critical element of a pro forma is the forecast. If a company doesn't make its forecast and sells only 800,000 cases but still spends $2.5 million on marketing communication, it will in fact spend 12.5 percent rather than 10 percent of sales (800,000 × $25 = $20,000,000 − $2,500,000 = 12.5%) on marketing communications. This is why companies, when they see they are not going to make their forecast, very frequently cancel some of their marketing communication programs.

In most companies, the percent-of-sales spent on marketing communication is similar from year to year. Unfortunately, many companies also use the same allocation percents from year to year. For example, if 50 percent of the MC budget was spent on mass media advertising last year, that is what they do the next year. As you might imagine, merely repeating the previous year's spending mix, regardless of changes in the marketplace, is the easiest but often not always the smartest way to budget. What is smart is to analyze what last year's budget was able to produce and to determine, to the extent possible, which MC functions and media were responsible for producing results. These findings along with an analysis of what it will cost to accomplish specific objectives is the next important input on deciding how much to spend on MC.

Objective-and-task This input starts with zero-based planning which determines the marketing communication objectives and what "tasks" needs to be done to accomplish each objective. Then estimates are made for how much each task will cost to do. For example, if an objective is to increase customer retention 10 percent, and it's decided that the most cost-effective way to do this is to send each customer a New Year's "thank you" basket of fruit and candy, this cost can be easily estimated. If this, or a similar program, has been used before, and the company has kept a record of these programs and their results, the costs can be more accurately estimated.

Other sources of useful information on the cost to achieve certain objectives with certain programs are MC agencies. Frequently they have used similar programs with other companies and know the costs and results. (It must be kept in mind that agencies are anxious to sell their programs and therefore will sometimes select the more positive results to share with clients.)

As you will read later in this book, sales promotion and direct response functions have been receiving a greater proportion of MC budgets. One reason is because the return on spending in these functions is much easier to determine than, for example, the spending on image advertising and brand publicity.

Share-of-category spending The third major input into budgeting is determining what is the brand's current portion of total MC spending in the product category. Advertising agencies, for example, talk about share-of-voice which is a brand's portion of the total media spending in that brand's product category. For example, if the total media spending in the small battery category is $300 million a year, and Duracell is spending $100 million, Duracell's share-of-voice is 33 percent. The share-of-voice percent is compared to a brand's share of market. If Duracell's share of market is 45 percent, most advertising agencies would say that the brand was underspending. If such a difference existed, Duracell's marketing managers would have a strong argument for asking for a larger budget. It is assumed by many marketers that share-of-spending should be fairly close to a brand's share of market. If a brand wants to significantly increase its share, it must be prepared to increase its share of spending as that can drive the share of market.

Return-on-investment The last major input is the estimated return on the MC investment. One of top management's major responsibilities is to maximize the return of the monies it spends. The more a department can support a high level of return, the more likely it is to receive the budget it requests. Budgeting is also a highly political process; the more political power a department has, the more likely it is to receive the budget it requests. This is why internal marketing is important. The more others in a company know what the marketing department does and accomplishes, the more political support it is likely to have.

In the case of marketing and marketing communications, ROI is determined by doing a **marginal analysis**, which is *examining the ratio of spending to sales and profit*. For example, as long as the maple syrup manufacturer (see pro forma above) can increase sales by spending no more than $2.50 per case to do so, it is a smart thing to do. However, when a brand finds it is spending more than has been budgeted per case to generate additional sales, this extra expense will reduce profits and is normally not a good investment.

Large companies that use different agencies for each of the MC functions sometimes have the agencies compete for their share of the MC budget. The more creative and effective the ideas are that an agency crafts to achieve the stated objectives, the greater share of the budget pie it may be given to execute those ideas.

According to IMC studies done by both the University of Colorado and Northwestern University, the biggest barriers to practicing IMC are egos and turf battles.[9] Because most managers' and executives' pay is proportional to the size of their staff and budget, it is only natural for them to want the largest staff and budget that they can get. Consequently, the decision to reallocate MC monies to where they can do the most good is often hampered by executives who stand to lose out personally. To overcome this barrier, companies and agencies should design compensation and reward systems so that people are not penalized when their budgets are temporarily reduced.

Step 6: Timing and Scheduling

An important aspect of zero-based planning is timing and scheduling—determining which media placements, promotional programs, and other MC activities should happen first or last or in between. For example, most brands have seasonal buying patterns, meaning that sales are higher during some months and lower during others. Most swimsuits in the United States, for example, are sold in late spring and early summer. Strategic planners must decide how far in advance of the buying season to start sending out brand messages and how late into the buying season to maintain marketing communication support.

There is no magic formula for timing promotional programs. Normally each product category has its own seasonal pattern. Companies can apply some logic, however. Staying with the swimsuit example, most promotional support begins in late winter and early spring. This is when people begin to tire of cold weather and begin thinking about the pleasures of summer. During this time, people seem to be receptive to swimsuit brand messages. Another factor is when retail stores begin displaying the suits. When stores set out new merchandise, they expect manufacturers to have marketing communication programs running that will help generate sales.

Another timing concern is when other MC functions are used. For a direct-response campaign that uses mass media advertising, direct mail, and telemarketing, timing is extremely important. The mass media advertising should run two to three weeks before the direct mail is sent out. Two to three days after the direct mail hits, the telemarketing should be done. The mass media advertising urges the target audience to look for the direct-mail offer, which helps take it out of the "junk mail" category. But if the telemarketing starts too early, before the direct mail hits, the response will be significantly less because the telemarketing calls will not be expected. If the telemarketing starts a week or more after the direct mail has hit, the impact of the direct mail will have been lost and again the response rate will be less.

A challenge often faced by both consumer and BtB companies is coordinating the timing between marketing, production, and sales. Each of these areas need lead times of several months (sometimes even more). Once a new product has been given the go-ahead for production, three to six months may elapse before the first product is actually manufactured. At the same time, sales is making calls and presenting the new product so that when production starts, finished goods will not have to sit in a warehouse for long. To support the sales effort, marketing communication materials—ads, direct-mail pieces, special events, trade-show exhibits—need to be produced, which can take several months. In the case of some consumer products, media time and space need to be bought three to six months ahead to guarantee the best rates and placement.

If any of these departments—production, sales, marketing communication—fails to perform as planned, then the company begins to lose money, top management starts asking embarrassing questions, and customers become disillusioned because things didn't happen as they had been promised. When timing fails, relationships both internally and externally can be hurt.

In the case of new consumer products, most companies don't like to begin marketing communication support in a market area until the product has at least a 60 percent "all commodity volume" (ACV). In other words, until the product is on display and available for consumer purchase in stores that account for 60 percent of all retail sales in the product category, a company feels it is wasting its marketing communication dollars. And even with 60 percent ACV, this means only 6 out of 10 consumers who see the marketing communication and then look for the product will find it.

Timing is also important when publicity is part of an MC campaign. Where the publicity angle has news value (e.g., a new product or a significant improvement in an old product), it is better to do the brand publicity before advertising. This way, the information is still news and editors will be more likely to run the stories.

Timing and coordination go together. They are both critical elements of integration. The best way to ensure right timing is to discuss individual department plans in cross-functional meetings, letting everyone know what everyone else is planning to do and when they are planning to do it.

Step 7: Test Marketing MC Mixes

Because MC causes and effects are constantly changing and are different for each product category, about the only way to know whether something will work is to try it. This is why it is good to build into every annual plan some type of testing.

Procter & Gamble is always testing new advertising approaches. For most of its brands, it has three different creative campaigns in the works. One is the national campaign. The second is a campaign that has beaten the national campaign in a laboratory test and is now running in a few markets to determine whether it does, in fact, produce better results than the national campaign. The third campaign is the one being developed to beat the campaign that is in the test market.

Another important factor to constantly test is the level of media spending. How much media spending is too much? How much is too little? Many brands select two or three markets and increase media spending (and other marketing communication support) to see whether sales increase enough to pay for the extra spending and also earn the company a profit. At the same time, brands try to determine what the minimal level of spending is to maintain their market share.

Step 8: Evaluating Effectiveness

The effectiveness of a campaign is evaluated according to how well the effort meets its objectives. This is why a company should clearly define its objectives in measurable terms and specify a time frame within which each objective is to be achieved.

The company can gather the sales response impact from corporate and industry reports, and it can conduct research to determine whether there has been a change in awareness or perceptions. Evaluation of IMC must also include measures of relationship strengths in addition to the usual sales, share, and awareness measures. Sales and share are historical measures, but relationship strengths are predictors of future sales. Chapter 21 discusses evaluation in more detail and presents some methods for evaluating the effectiveness of marketing communication in brand relationship building.

One aspect of IMC that is different from traditional marketing communication is the emphasis on continuous feedback. Current, shared information is critical for decision making by the cross-functional team. That means companies must have new ways of listening to customers wherever contacts with the customer occur, particularly from front-line employees. The overnight delivery company Federal Express, for example, tracks performance measures that are distributed daily. In addition, it tracks monthly indicators for all areas, including public relations and conducts an online employee survey every three months. Managers use the results for discussions with employees and act on the survey information immediately wherever change is needed. Senior managers are required to spend a few days every year in a given sales district to get close to both customers and the front line of the sales and marketing efforts.[10] Continuous feedback programs help the company become a *learning organization*.

INTERNAL MARKETING

One of the primary responsibilities for marketing departments is to interpret the needs of the customer and the marketplace and bring that information to all departments. In addition, MC planners must involve other departments in the planning process, and then inform these other departments of the final plan and why it is worth supporting. Marketing needs buy-in and support from all departments whose work affects customers. That's everyone: Even employees who do not deal directly with customers support other employees who do.

As mentioned in Chapter 1, this communication to internal stakeholders is called internal marketing. Internal marketing consultant Sybil Stershic defines it as "the application of marketing inside the organization to instill customer-focused values."[11] Employees, especially those "touching the customer," should be thought of as customers also. The more they are satisfied, the more they will satisfy customers. Companies can increase morale and productivity keeping employees informed so they aren't embarrassed when asked about certain progams, letting them have a sneak preview of promotional materials before they begin running, and letting them know the results of their efforts to build strong brand relationships.

> " The more of your employees that touch the customer, the more critical it is to have internal marketing."
>
> Sybil Stershic, " Internal Marketing: Getting Employees to Be Customer-Focused"

It is important to note that in some industries (e.g., office machines, automobiles), service personnel rather than sales and marketing people are the ones most likely to have ongoing contact with customers. For suppliers to grocery and discount stores, the truck's driver may be an important contact point and may even have the responsibility of shelving the products or setting up merchandising materials. Thus, the truck drivers not only represent the company but also are the first to be aware of product and marketing communication problems and other customer concerns. Customer-contact employees can be a primary resource about the state of the marketplace, product performance, and provide opportunities for continuing sales and relationship marketing communication.

Internal marketing puts a process in place for employees to report back to marketing. Front-line employees, in particular, need to be linked to a company's information-gathering system in order to give feedback about what customers are thinking and how they are acting. Formal programs enable customers to participate in roundtables, where customers are brought together to discuss a brand's and company's operations and product performance.[12]

Communication Dimensions

Like external marketing, internal marketing is communication-dependent. This communication takes many forms including intranets, company newsletters, e-mail, voice mail, and bulletin boards. There are three basic aspects of internal communication: informing employees, empowering them, and listening to them.

Informing

Communicating a customer-first business policy, as well as other marketing programs to employees, is a responsibility of internal marketing. Such a philosophy is an outgrowth of the recent upsurge in emphasis on customer service and customer relationship management (CRM). Another objective is to continually impress on employees the importance of being responsive to customers.

Empowering

Internal marketing, because it provides employees with more information, is also a natural program to support **employee empowerment** programs, which means *giving front-line employees the power to make decisions about problems that affect customer relationships*. As companies downsize and place more responsibility at lower levels, more decisions that affect customer relations are being made by service employees who are on the front line of customer contact. The more information these employees have, generally the better decisions they will make. Empowerment programs must therefore be supported by training and information about company policies. Automaker Nissan requires all dealer employees (including clerks and receptionists) for its Infinity models to attend six-day training programs designed to teach employees how to recognize legitimate customer problems and how to address them. The necessary elements of a support program that creates empowered and responsive employees are presented in Table 6–7.

Listening

Just as external marketing should include two-way communication, so should internal marketing. If an internal marketing program only sends messages, employees will see the program as propaganda. In order for its messages to have integrity, internal marketing must encourage and facilitate employee feedback, which then enables managers to know if employees understand the internal marketing messages, agree with these messages, and are willing to support the various marketing programs. Even more important, because employees usually are closer to customers than are managers, internal marketing feedback can provide valuable real-time customer research to help in planning and budgeting.

TABLE 6-7   Empowering Employees

The more employees are empowered to make their own decisions when responding to customers, the more they need to be:

- Informed of their role in satisfying customers.
- Informed of their role in the company's success.
- Rewarded based on a balance of their individual performance and the company's overall performance.
- Listened to when they have ideas how to better serve customers even when those ideas involve other areas of operations.
- Given easy access to customer information files and other databases that enable them to make quick and knowledgeable responses.

A benefit of internal marketing programs is enhanced employee loyalty. Reducing employee turnover means reduced training costs and an overall increase in experience throughout the company. A study of employee loyalty in 1999 found that even though the old idea of brand loyalty is questionable, it is possible to generate commitment with good communication, opportunities for personal growth, and more workplace flexibility.[13] And don't forget, employees are often customers, too.

An example of internal communication gone awry comes from a chain of natural foods stores, named Wild Oats, headquartered in Boulder, Colorado. The company was known for its social responsibility and sensitivity to employees. Customers, employees, and the media were all amazed to learn that Wild Oats' CEO had ordered managers to search employees' bags twice a day as part of an antitheft policy. Several managers resigned in protest and negative stories appeared in the local media. In response, the CEO wrote a letter to the local newspaper admitting that the store's "infamous loss control memo was not well thought out, impossible to enforce, and, in retrospect, just plain Dilbertesque." (The latter was a reference to the well-known comic strip "Dilbert," which lampoons poor management practices.) He concluded that the ruckus had caused the company to conduct "a comprehensive internal review of how we communicate to our staff members and the need to think more completely about the consequences of our actions."[14] In this case, the company learned, to its chagrin, that everything it does and says, including in-house staff policies, sends a brand message.

Internal Communication Systems

In order to make internal marketing work, a company must establish systems of communication that make internal employee dialogue possible. In a survey of internal communication of U.S. companies, it was found that half of the managers and front-line supervisors surveyed cited inadequate interdepartmental communication as the number one problem behind poor customer service. According to the marketing manager of a major bank, which has hundreds of branches, making employees aware of current marketing programs is an ongoing challenge: "We're doing well if 80 percent of our tellers are aware of a new promotion when it runs." If communication were measured using the quality standards applied to production, an 80 percent rate would be considered a failure. Most quality programs on the manufacturing side strive for 98 to 99 percent efficiency.

New communication technologies include **intranets,** which are *computer networks that are accessible only to employees and contain proprietary information.* Intranets facilitate the following:

- Communication (e-mail, messaging).
- Collaboration (shared databases, conferencing).
- Coordination of work flow (work flow applications that integrate messaging and databases).

A limited-access computer network that links suppliers, distributors, and MC agencies to the company is called an **extranet.** (Both internets and extranets will be discussed in more detail in Chapter 12.)

Many companies are discovering that using intranets and extranets eliminates tons of paper flow and, at the same time, places accurate and timely information at everyone's fingertips (see the Technology in Action box). Some of the basic organizational communication and information resources that are now being distributed electronically are telephone directories that are never more than 24 hours out of date, requisition forms, employee announcements, changes in procedures, training materials, and organizational databases.

TECHNOLOGY IN ACTION

Creating a Brochure via an Intranet

How do you create a brochure in a company where the people writing the text are in one country, the artist who will be designing it is in another country, and members of the management team that has requested the brochure are in offices all over the globe? And furthermore, how do you create such a brochure when it is for a particularly sensitive new product and everyone has to sign off on it, including the corporate attorney, the accountants, and the engineers back in headquarters? Oh, and can you do it in less than three weeks?

As an example of how an intranet stimulates internal communication, consider the development of a typical company brochure. The public relations department drafts some text and sends it by e-mail to everyone involved in the development of the product asking for comments. An engineer checks out the product specifications that are described in the brochure, the financial people review the numbers, the legal staff checks for liability, the marketing people check for strategy, and a copyeditor checks for language and style problems as well as factual errors—and they all send it back within two working days. Because employees can access the system when away from the office, their absence does not slow down the process as it does when everything is done on hard copy, passing paper from one person to another. And in this case, there is no need to wait for international mail to deliver drafts to various offices around the world.

At the same time, the designer begins working on a preliminary layout and the staff photographer either locates photos or schedules a photography session. When the copy is finalized and the photos have been scanned, all the pieces are sent back to the designer, who assembles everything and then e-mails it back to everyone involved for a second check. This time they are looking at an electronically generated proof of the finished brochure. Meanwhile, a proofreader in headquarters is going over the text word by word to check for mistakes. Everyone who needs to be involved has two opportunities for review, and it can all be done in a week or two, rather than months.

Think About It

What problems drive the need for an internal electronic communication system within a company? What kind of intranet would enable a company to handle a project like this?

Source: Adapted from Vicki Gordon, "The Role of Groupware in IMC," *Integrated Marketing Communications Research Journal* 2 (Spring 1996), pp. 32–36.

A FINAL NOTE: PLAYING FROM THE SAME SCORE

An IMC plan defines the way a company does business by creating a customer and stakeholder focus rather than department-focused programs that can work at cross-purposes and send mixed messages. The more focused a company is on transactions rather than building long-term relationships, the weaker its relationships with customers will be. In particular, the less interaction there is between a company and its customers, the more likely the marketing communication plan will be off-target and not effective. The successful launch of the GMC Envoy demonstrates how effective a single-minded effort can be when it is designed to build relationships over time.

In order to create this customer focus throughout the company, it is necessary that everyone play from the same score: an integration-driven marketing communication plan. And this plan also demands internal marketing in order to deliver messages with consistency by everyone who touches a customer. The more inconsistent the messages are at these touchpoints, the less integrated the brand positioning will be in the minds of customers and other stakeholders.

IMC is not easy to accomplish. As more stakeholders are taken into consideration, as more functional areas are used in support of the big idea, as more message delivery systems are added to the media mix, both planning and monitoring for consistency become very complex. Such complexity demands more time from the cross-functional management team as it manages a company's internal communication processes. Although integrated planning isn't easy, it is essential for companies that want to compete in the 21st century.

Key Terms

strategic planning 197	zero-based planning 202	budget 220
corporate or business plan 197	situation analysis 203	marginal analysis 222
marketing plan 198	SWOT analysis 203	employee empowerment 226
campaign 198	account planning 207	intranets 227
objectives 199	briefs 209	extranet 227
tactics 199	media mix 220	

Key Point Summary

Key Point 1: How IMC Planning Works

A marketing plan is governed by the company's overall business plan and gives direction to the marketing communication plan. MC planning can be expressed in separate plans for all of the key MC areas, as well as in a campaign plan that unites the activities of various MC functional areas. An IMC plan contains objectives and strategies, which cascade from the marketing plan, and tactics, which guide the execution of the plan.

Key Point 2: The IMC Planning Process

The IMC planning process involves the following eight steps: (1) analyze SWOTs, (2) analyze targeting and brand relationships, (3) determine the MC objectives, (4) develop strategies and rationales, (5) set a budget, (6) determine timing, (7) test the MC mix, and (8) evaluate the effectiveness of the IMC program.

Key Point 3: SWOT Analysis and Zero-Based Planning

A SWOT analysis looks systematically at internal Strengths and Weaknesses and external Opportunities and Threats. Objectives are developed to address and leverage key SWOTs. Zero-based planning (which starts from current conditions rather than past or expected future conditions) is used to identify the appropriate MC area that can best deliver on the objectives.

Key Point 4: Internal Marketing

Internal marketing is the process of involving other employees in the planning process and then communicating the plan back to them to get their buy-in and support.

Lessons Learned

Key Point 1: How IMC Planning Works

a. What's the difference between a business plan and a marketing plan?
b. What's the difference between a strategy, an objective, and a tactic?
c. What is a benchmark, and how is it used in stating an objective?
d. How was strategic planning used by Hewlett-Packard in its SoftBench Suite campaign, and what does it mean to make integration an attitude?
e. Convert the six "tasks" McCann-Erickson faced in the GMC Envoy case into measurable objectives.

Key Point 2: The IMC Planning Process

a. What is zero-based planning? What assumption does it challenge?
b. Define account planning. Why is it used?
c. How do you know if an IMC campaign is effective?
d. Explain the steps in Price/McNabb's Brand Studio approach to planning. How can the information obtained from each be used in an IMC plan?
e. Using the eight-step planning process, reconstruct the key planning decisions behind the GMC Envoy campaign.

Key Point 3: SWOT Analysis and Zero-Based Planning

a. What is the difference between a situation analysis and a SWOT analysis?
b. What are the internal and external factors involved in a SWOT analysis?
c. Why is SWOT analysis the first step in zero-based planning?

Key Point 4: Internal Marketing

a. Define internal marketing.
b. What is the role played by communication in internal marketing?
c. Analyze the HP SoftBench Suite campaign in terms of its internal marketing dimensions. What was done? What other activities and programs would you recommend?

Chapter Challenge

Writing Assignment

Look up Snapple in current articles in your business school library. What was Triarc's strategy to turn around this troubled brand? Did it work? What objectives and strategies would you recommend to Snapple's current parent, Cadbury Schweppes; in particular, what needs to be done to build this brand and its brand relationships? Using the eight-step IMC planning process, develop a marketing communication plan for Snapple for next year. Develop a set of visuals that summarizes your key recommendations. Present your plan to the class.

Presentation Assignment

Using Price/McNabb's Brand Studio approach, develop a set of recommendations for the positioning strategy for GMC's Envoy as it moves away from being a new product. Concentrate on Opportunity Analysis, the Ladder of Benefits, and an "I-Statement." How should the marketing communication plan change now that the SUV has been launched?

Internet Assignment

Consult the website for the John W. Hartman Center for Sales, Advertising, and Marketing History at Duke University (http://scriptorium.lib.duke.edu/adaccess). The site contains more than 7,000 print advertisements that were produced between 1911 and 1955. To demonstrate that the basics remain the same, find an ad in the collection that demonstrates one of the following:

1.   Leveraging an opportunity.
2.   Addressing a threat.
3.   Leveraging a strength.
4.   Addressing a weakness.

Additional Readings

Cohen, William A. *The Marketing Plan*. New York: John Wiley & Sons, 1995.

Hiebing, Roman G. Jr., and Scott W. Cooper. *How to Write a Successful Marketing Plan*. Lincolnwood, IL: NTC Business Books, 1990.

Ind, Nicholas. *Great Advertising Campaigns*. Lincolnwood, IL: NTC Business Books, 1993.

McDonald, Malcolm H. B., and Warren J. Keegan. *Marketing Plans That Work*. Boston: Butterworth-Heinemann, 1997.

Steel, Jon. *Truth, Lies & Advertising—the Art of Account Planning*. New York: John Wiley & Sons, 1998.

Research Assignment

Find a write-up about a successful advertising campaign. (Nicholas Ind's book is a good place to start; also check the advertising trade press.) Using your understanding of the IMC planning process plus ideas you gather from the books listed above, develop a marketing communication plan for that product that moves its focus from advertising to IMC.

Endnotes

[1]Philip Kotler and Gary Armstrong, *Principles of Marketing* (Upper Saddle River, NJ: Prentice Hall, 1999), p. G9.

[2]Roman G. Hiebing Jr. and Scott W. Cooper, *How to Write a Successful Marketing Plan* (Lincolnwood, IL: NTC Business Books, 1997), p. xxvi.

[3]Don Schultz, Stanely Tannenbaum, and Robert Lauterborn, *Integrated Marketing Communications* (Lincolnwood, IL: NTC Publishing Group, 1993), p. 12.

[4]Allan J. Magrath, *How to Achieve Zero-Defect Marketing* (New York: American Management Association, 1993), p. 14.

[5]Michael Treacy and Fred Wiersema, *The Discipline of the Market Leaders* (Reading MA: Addison-Wesley, 1995), p. 125.

[6]Russell Colley, *Defining Advertising Goals for Measured Advertising Results* (New York: Association of National Advertisers, 1961).

[7]Louise O'Brian and Charles Jones, "Do Rewards Really Create Loyalty?" *Harvard Business Review*, May–June 1995, p. 79.

[8]Gerry Khermouch, "Mondavi Seeks ID above Wine Glut," *Brandweek*, September 11, 1995, p. 14.

[9]Tom Duncan and Steve Everett, "Client Perceptions of Integrated Marketing Communications," *Journal of Advertising Research* 33, 1993, pp. 30-39; Clarke Caywood, Done Schultz, and Paul Wang, *A Survey of Consumer Goods Manufacturers* (New York: American Association of Advertising Agencies, 1993).

[10]Anders Gronstedt, "Integrated Communications at America's Leading TQM Corporations," doctoral dissertation, University of Wisconsin-Madison, 1994.

[11]Sybil Stershic, "Internal Marketing: Getting Employees to Be Customer-Focused," AMA Marketing Workshop, Oak Brook, IL, fall 1999.

[12]Ibid.

[13]"Employers Can Create Loyalty," *Tampa Tribune,* May 7, 1999, p. 5.

[14]Mike Gilliland, "CEO Admits Mistake, Changes Store Policy," *Boulder Daily Camera*, March 14, 2000, p. 6A

7

Segmenting and Targeting

Key Points in This Chapter

1. How is marketing moving away from mass marketing to smaller yet more profitable market and customer segments?

2. Why is segmenting out your most profitable customers important?

3. What characteristics can companies use to identify customer segments?

4. How does targeting work?

Chapter Perspective
Carving Up the Market

Some marketers believe that it is important to reach as many potential customers as possible with a marketing communication message; they don't want to pass up a single one. Although this might seem to make sense, it ignores the factor of cost efficiency. Reaching "everyone" costs money and sends lots of unwanted messages to people who aren't customers or prospects. It makes more sense to narrow the audience to people who are most likely to buy the brand.

Segmenting and targeting are used to identify those groups of customers and prospects for whom a brand can get the best return from its marketing communication efforts. Segmenting and targeting start with a brand's current customers, because current customers are a brand's best customers. It costs significantly less to create a transaction with a current customer than with a prospect.

Progress in market research and database technology has allowed companies to learn more about current customers and the differences among them. Now companies are able to track which consumers purchase what products, how often, and what quantities. Companies can often track which messages customers heard or saw, what else their customers are buying, and who they are (e.g., how old they are, where they live, and other profile information). But most important, companies can determine which customers are profitable and which are not.

Because different customers and prospects have different needs, wants, and desires, brand communications must differ accordingly. In other words, segmenting and targeting are interrelated strategic decisions. This chapter is organized around four main topics: reasons for segmenting and targeting, segmentation strategies, types of market segmentation, and how targeting works.

INSIGHTS FROM EVERYWHERE
McCann-Erickson, Melbourne, Australia

Holden Ltd. is Australia's premier automaker. Its Barina is its smallest model and, at 14 years, one of the oldest models in the Australian market. It had been a success in the small-car market for many years; however, in the 1990s, it became clear that the model was on a decline and had lost its way. This situation raised a number of questions for Holden: how do you get a small car back on track and design a marketing communication program that will help it finish ahead of the competition? Who should be involved in planning the turnaround? Is it a pricing problem? a targeting or positioning problem? a promotional problem? Where do you start?

The McCann-Erickson office in Melbourne saw it as a research problem, but one that needed to be handled by a cross-functional team of planners. This broad-based agency team came together for a better understanding of the car's target market in order to create a creative strategy and communication mix that would make the Barina a winner in the automotive race.

The Marketing Challenge

The Barina was originally launched in the Australian market with an advertising campaign called "Beep, Beep," which used the Road Runner character from the old Warner Bros. cartoon series. This campaign transcended the memorable limits of most advertising and became part of the Australian vernacular. The car was soon affectionately referred to as the "Beep Beep Barina." Even when Holden abandoned the Road Runner visual, the "Beep, Beep" was maintained as an advertising sign-off and a powerful mnemonic device.

However, in the early 1990s, the Barina's sales declined by 16 percent and then an alarming 43 percent. There were a number of reasons for this, including an increase in small-car brand alternatives and greater price competition. The most critical change, however, was the decline in interest by the traditional small-car target market—young women.

Segmenting and Targeting

McCann-Erickson Melbourne formed a multidisciplinary task force to gather information about trends important to the Barina's key target market. This task force included personnel from advertising, market research, public relations, and promotions, as well as innovators from other consumer categories such as music producers, magazine publishers, and clothing marketers.

Using the research, the McCann task force determined that the primary target audience would be a subsegment of young women—those in their early 20s who were also characterized as "early adopters," that is, the first to try something and then influence the opinions of others. The broader target audience was identified as "single, female optimists" aged 18–34. The third most important segment was all remaining 18–34-year-olds, male and female.

The research was designed to determine why young women had abandoned the Barina. Knowing the *why* is what enables a company to create brand messages relevant to a targeted segment. The McCann task force found that safety was not particularly relevant to young women. Further, Barina's image, which was still associated with the dated "Beep, Beep" campaign, did not match the segment's aspirations—it was considered too young and "girlie." This research also revealed that young women have a great affinity with their cars—they see their car as an "accomplice" in their life. Therefore, a car's image and personality is important to this group. And the car must suit their lifestyle. McCann also found that this segment considered traditional car advertising dull, uninspiring, and unengaging. What scored high with this segment was unexpected advertising conveyed with wit.

To convince young-female-early-adopters that Barina was "cool," the McCann team first had to understand what this group considered cool in general and then anticipate the next trend. To do this, the team conducted innovative multidisciplinary research designed to monitor the lifestyle and attitude trends of this group. This research unearthed two key facts: (1) The target needs to identify with the brand, via identifying with a projected brand user who represents someone they would like to be, and (2) the target was interested in Japanese *manga* (a highly identifiable style of comics and animated cartoons), which if translated into advertising could potentially be a very original and unique communication device for Barina (see Exhibit 7–1).

Strategy

McCann determined that the Barina campaign's communication objectives were to project a far "cooler" image for the car than currently existed and associate it with the personality attributes of fun, smart, independent, outrageous, and stylish. The consumer research and resultant understanding of the key target audience indicated that if the McCann team was going to change perceptions of Barina and leave "Beep, Beep" behind, a radically different creative approach was critical. Barina needed to break the rules of traditional car advertising, in terms of both medium and message. The resulting communication strategy recommendation was to:

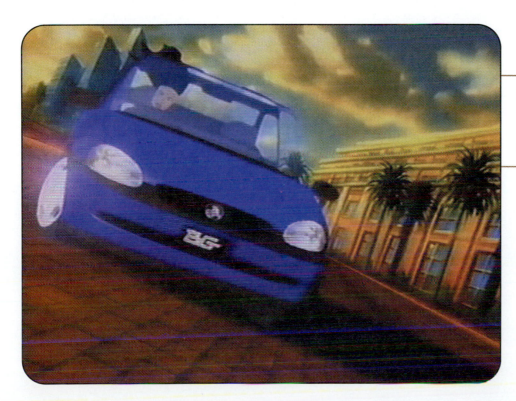

EXHIBIT 7-1

This is a frame from the new Barina TV advertising using the manga execution style.

EXHIBIT 7-2

Print ad examples using the BG character which was created to appeal to the segment of females in their 20s who were "early adopters."

- Develop a character who reflected the identified lifestyle aspirations of the target audience.
- Develop a sense of intrigue and consumer involvement. (The target audience needed to discover Barina for itself, not be told.)
- Build the brand in a consistent supporting manner across all communication expressions.

Creative Strategy

The Japanese cartoon style provided an approach that was fresh, original, and in tune with the early-adopters' aspirations. The result was an animated character called "BG"—Barina Girl—which represented the target audience's lifestyle, aspirations, and personality (see Exhibit 7–2).

Creatively, the storylines described BG as handling life's highs and lows with intelligence, wit, and spunk. For example, a "Bad Hair Day" commercial was inspired by discussions in a focus-group session. In this commercial, BG uses her Barina to deal with her bad-hair problem in an imaginative way.

Message Delivery and Media

The McCann team could not simply rely on conventional media to reach its target and achieve the campaign's objectives. Television alone, for example, would not bring about the changes in attitudes needed. The brand needed to capitalize on niche activities to capture the target's spirit and enthusiasm.

McCann repositioned Barina as a hip brand by building a strategic street presence prior to the launch of the multimedia campaign. This was accomplished by creating a BG Roller Blading Team that appeared at selected trendy festivals and gave away premiums that were branded "BG." Recipients had no way at that point of knowing what "BG" meant, and the simple "BG" logo was reminiscent of a secret underground nightclub symbol. The BG premiums included T-shirts, sun cream, backpacks, stickers, and key rings. Posters designed to look like those for underground bands were hung in selected inner-city areas.

The agency then launched a multimedia advertising campaign that capitalized on the broader target's unique relationship with each medium. The BG commercials appeared only in a select list of television programs considered to be leading-edge, must-see programs among the target. This selected programming included *Melrose Place*, which had become a cult program among young women in Australia. BG movie advertising also appeared along with a group of targeted films.

The character BG was given her own weekly radio program on a key radio network. McCann developed new adventures each week to keep the campaign fresh, maintain consumer involvement, and capitalize on topical issues.

A half-page comic strip appeared in another popular medium for the target, a weekly magazine (see Exhibit 7–3). The strip cartoons were supplemented with full-page color ads themed around the magazine's special issues such as most beautiful people, celebrity weddings, best and worst dressed, and best bodies.

McCann also capitalized on early-adopter's trends by using the Internet: BG was given her own highly successful and constantly changing interactive website (www.bg.com.au).

EXHIBIT 7-3

The cartoon style of this ad and the message about BG getting an exclusive interview with an American basketball team were both designed to get the attention of young single women—the Holden Barina's primary target audience.

Evaluation of the BG Campaign

Quantitative testing of the BG campaign was positive, with 97 percent of targeted respondents liking the manga-style animation approach. Findings from ongoing qualitative tracking studies found that the targeted segment was shifting its perceptions of the Barina and its manufacturer, Holden. In approximately 20 focus groups, the campaign was discussed spontaneously and enthusiastically. In terms of the behavioral objectives, the campaign had a positive impact on sales. Since the BG campaign launch in 1998, the Barina sales decline has been reversed and sales have grown by 30 percent. This case demonstrates the importance of segmenting a market, identifying a target, and then learning as much as possible about that target in order to create messages and select media that will have an impact.

This case was adapted with permission from the award-winning Advertising and Marketing Effectiveness (AME) brief submitted by McCann-Erickson, Melbourne.

REASONS FOR SEGMENTING AND TARGETING

Segmenting and targeting are processes for determining who companies want to reach in order to build brand relationships. **Segmenting** is *grouping customers or prospects according to common characteristics, needs, wants, and/or desires*. Segmenting can be done at different levels of specificity. For example, a manufacturer of bicycles could begin by dividing a market into bike owners and non-owners. Bike owners could be further segmented into bike racers, mountain bike riders, leisure riders, children, and parents. An important part of segmenting is specifying the characteristics that successfully predict who will be in the groups. In the chapter opening case on Holden Ltd.'s Barina car, the early adopters made up the segment the company's MC agency initially identified as being the most desirable group with which to build brand relationships.

Targeting is *analyzing, evaluating, and prioritizing those market segments deemed most profitable to pursue*. Figure 7–1 illustrates the Barina targeting decision. As you will recall, the brand identified "young-female-early-adopters" as being the most responsive and profitable segment and thus is the center of the target. McCann realized it also had to reach beyond this initial segment. Its next most important targets were "single, female optimists" aged 18–34, followed by all remaining 18–34-year-olds, male and female. Compared with those in the center, those farther from the middle of the target are less likely to respond and are therefore less profitable. Targeting thus allows companies to focus their MC efforts on segments that promise the greatest return on investment (ROI).

Moving Away from Mass Marketing

Segmentation is not a new concept. Soon after Henry Ford became successful selling his mass-produced Model T, which was introduced in 1908 and came in one color only (black), Alfred Sloan, then head of General Motors, realized his company would have to do something different to compete with Ford. The more Sloan learned about who bought cars, the more he realized that different segments of customers wanted different types of cars. He also figured out that once he got a customer, he could keep that customer if he could provide different cars to match customers' changing needs for cars as customers grew older and more financially secure and moved from one segment to another.

This is why General Motors (GM) was one of the first companies to offer a range of models for each customer segment, from the low-priced Chevrolet; through the Pontiac, Oldsmobile, and Buick; to the most expensive family car (at that time), the Cadillac. Sloan figured that as his Chevrolet customers advanced in life and could afford a better car, his company could still target them, but with a different car and message. In this way, GM could retain those customers. Sloan also realized that cars allowed the more successful people to show they were different from middle class or the less successful. GM's early segmentation efforts allowed the company to beat out Ford for first place in the automotive industry in the late 1920s.

Even so, as described in Chapter 1, with the rapid growth of mass media in the United States, mass marketing became the norm in the middle of the twentieth century. In the late twentieth century, media technologies changed marketing yet again. Segmentation took on more and more importance as marketing moved away from mass marketing. As this book notes throughout, marketing today is, in the name of

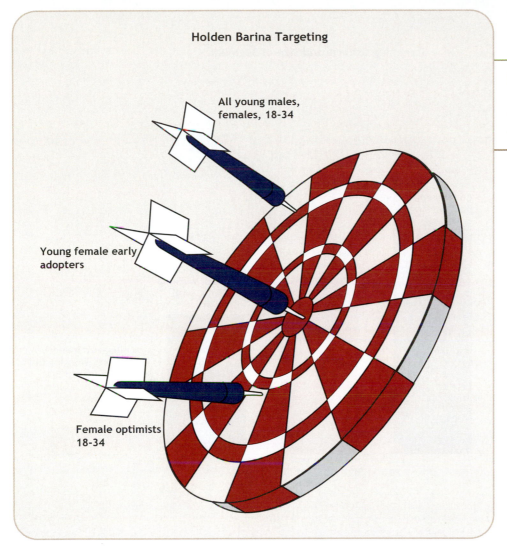

Holden Barina Targeting

All young males,
females, 18-34

Young female early
adopters

Female optimists
18-34

FIGURE 7-1

*"Young female early
adopters" were the primary
target segment for HB.*

efficiency and effectiveness, becoming more focused on smaller but more profitable segments of the market.

Mass marketing is an attempt to sell the same thing to everyone. No effort is made to target messages to certain groups. The obvious problem with mass marketing is that a lot of money is wasted reaching people who have no interest in the product. Yet, despite pronouncements by some in the MC industry who say that mass marketing is dead, the reality is, the marketplace is someplace in-between.

A good example is how large retailers such as Target, Kmart, Wal-Mart, Kroger, Safeway, and Walgreen operate. They advertise heavily in mass media, especially newspapers and supplements, but are still quite successful. This is because they have redefined mass marketing by offering a variety of products and brands in most product categories. In this way, they are able to satisfy many different customer segments. In their shampoo sections, for example, there are shampoos for regular versus dry versus oily hair, for dandruff control, and for babies, as well as shampoos with built-in conditioners. In essence, these mass marketers *are* practicing segmentation because they are offering products and brands that appeal to different customer segments. Furthermore, individual stores in national chains are increasingly being encouraged to customize their merchandise mix to best suit customers in their geographic area.

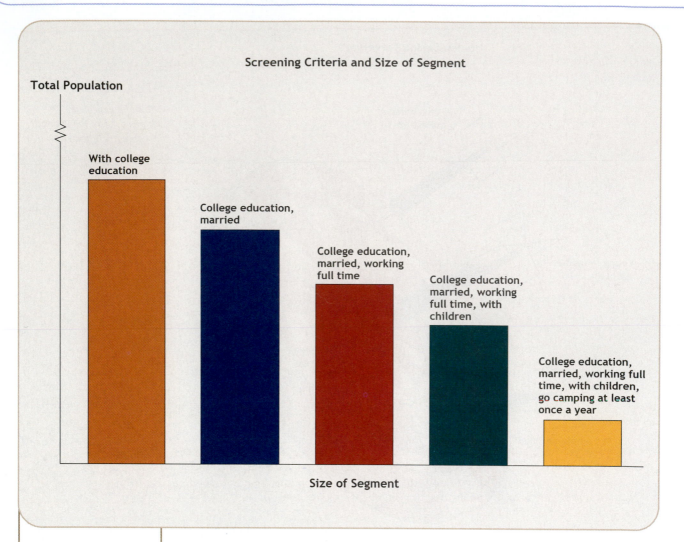

Screening Criteria and Size of Segment

Total Population

With college education

College education, married

College education, married, working full time

College education, married, working full time, with children

College education, married, working full time, with children, go camping at least once a year

Size of Segment

FIGURE 7-2

The more the screening criteria, the smaller the segment.

Segments and Niches

Smart marketers recognize that certain segments of customers like certain types of products. The question that marketers must always answer is, How narrowly do we want to segment? As shown in Figure 7–2, the more narrowly you target, the smaller the segment will be.

In the Barina case, females were segmented by age and type of "adopter" (early versus late). Some marketers would refer to this group of early adopters as a *niche*, or *subsegment*, within the young female segment. Niche markets are defined by very distinct commonalities among their members. Skateboarders and snowboarders, for example, are each niche markets with their own equipment magazines, sporting events, and even clothes. The Coricidin advertisement in Exhibit 7–4 shows a product (CoricidinHPB) that has been reformulated for a niche market: people with colds who also have high blood pressure.

Although niche markets, by definition, are smaller than mass markets, they can still include millions of customers. *Modern Maturity* magazine, for example, is considered a niche publication because it is sent only to those seniors who are members of the American Association of Retired Persons (AARP), yet it is one of the largest publications in the United States, with a circulation of over 20 million.

In business-to-business marketing, there are also niches in most product categories. Take printing presses, for example. The niche market for high-end, six-color presses includes companies like Hallmark Cards, Inc., that demand very sophisticated, high-quality performance. At the other end of the printing-press market is the niche of "job printers," who use small printing presses that are only a step above a photocopy machine in their level of quality.

What smart marketers have been doing in recent years is dividing their markets into smaller and smaller segments—to a degree. For example, all the people who buy cars can be divided into segments according to such factors as the size of car, its styling and handling, its price tag, and its engineering. On the one hand, it would be stupid to try to sell an inexpensive car to everyone in the car market because some customers are willing to pay a premium for engineering (BMW), styling (Corvette), or size and functionality (SUVs). On the other hand, it is not cost-effective for car manufacturers to create a unique car for each individual (although customization is being done more often now then ever before, and the costs are coming down). Manufacturers and service providers are still interested in taking advantage of economies of scale whenever they can, but they are doing so by targeting smaller segments and niche markets rather than providing just one product for all customers in the category.

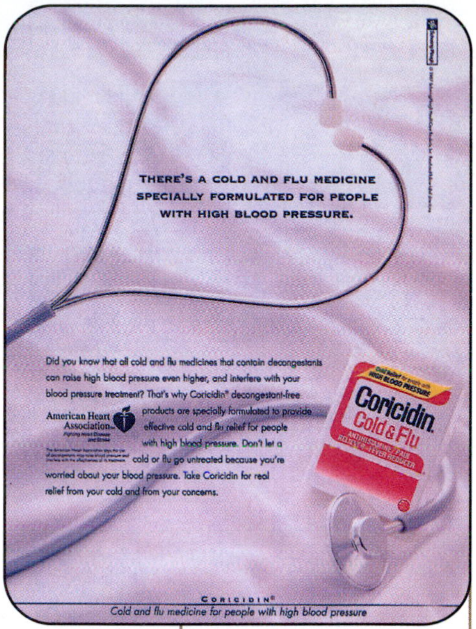

EXHIBIT 7-4

The headline in this ad is designed to attract the attention of that segment of consumers who have high blood pressure and a cold.

Segments of One

Along with the increase in niche marketing has come an emphasis on **one-to-one marketing**, which means *customizing products and marketing communication for an individual person or company according to individual needs.* The highly successful computer hardware manufacturer Dell has built a multibillion-dollar brand by customizing computers for individuals and companies.

Because marketing communication is a support function for marketing and selling, the more products become customized, the greater the need for customizing brand messages. With good customer databases in product categories where it can be cost-justified, marketing can produce individualized, personalized sales messages. New technologies allow new forms of interactivity, such as e-mail and individually printed coupons at checkout. All of this is bringing one-to-one targeting to consumer marketing as well as extending its use in BtB marketing.

A popular marketing book that came out in the mid-1990s, *The One to One Future*, is testimony to this trend.[1] Nevertheless, one-to-one marketing is still generally affordable only for higher-priced consumer and BtB products. Where one-to-one messages can and should be used, regardless of a brand's price point, however, is in responding to complaints and inquiries.

SEGMENTATION STRATEGIES

Segmentation and targeting are used in both consumer and business-to-business marketing. The more diverse a company's line of products, generally the more customer segments it will have. As shown in Figure 7–3, there are seven basic steps in segmenting and targeting. The first three steps concern current customers, and the last four concern prospects; the following discussion explains in more detail.

Current Customers

A key principle of IMC is "Know thy customers." Segmentation, therefore, should start by identifying and profiling current customers. There are three main principles behind this: (1) It costs less to sell additional products to customers than it does to sell first purchases to new customers (recall the discussion of retention versus acquisition in Chapter 2); (2) some customers are more profitable than others; and (3) common characteristics of a brand's most profitable customers can be used to find new customers. A brand cannot apply these three principles unless it tracks customers and maintains an up-to-date profile database. SRDS, for example, supplies companies and MC agencies with profiles of the audiences of most media vehicles (see Exhibit 7–5).

As discussed in Chapter 5, *current customers* are those who have a relationship with a company and have made one or more purchases within a given period. *Prospects* are consumers who have not yet purchased but who can benefit from using the brand, can afford it, and have access to it. In most cases prospects are buying one or more competitive brands.

The first segmentation principle, that current customers are generally more valuable to a company than potential customers, is true because current customers don't have to be "brand-educated" on each transaction to nearly the same extent as first-time buyers do. Because they have already purchased the brand, current customers should have a positive attitude toward it. The cost-per-sale for a current

FIGURE 7-3

Steps in Segmenting and Targeting

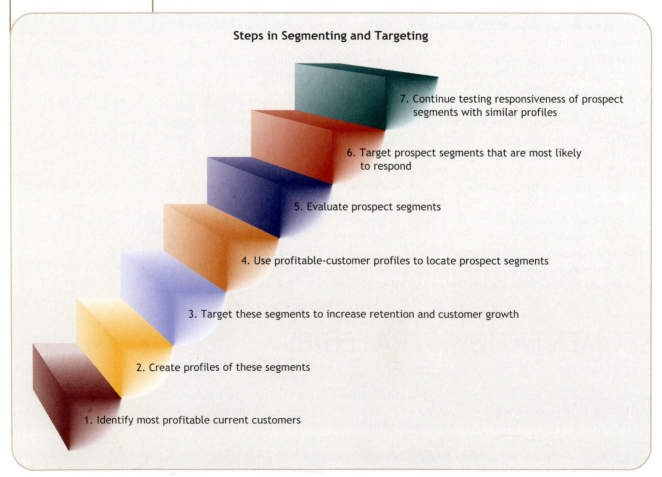

Steps in Segmenting and Targeting

7. Continue testing responsiveness of prospect segments with similar profiles

6. Target prospect segments that are most likely to respond

5. Evaluate prospect segments

4. Use profitable-customer profiles to locate prospect segments

3. Target these segments to increase retention and customer growth

2. Create profiles of these segments

1. Identify most profitable current customers

customer (assuming he or she has been satisfied with the prior purchases) is estimated to be 5 to 10 times less than for selling to a prospect.

Current customers, however, should not be taken for granted—though in many companies, unfortunately, they are. Past purchases do not guarantee future ones. The only way customers will continue to buy the brand is to receive superior satisfaction in product performance and customer service. Although ensuring satisfaction is costly, it is far less expensive than acquiring new customers to replace unsatisfied ones. That is why a brand should think first about how best to retain customers before investing in new customers. Also, since most current customers give a single brand less than 100 percent of their category purchases, encouraging additional brand purchases is also possible.

The second principle, that not all current customers (and prospects) are equally valuable, is valid because in nearly every company the Pareto rule (introduced in Chapter 2) holds true. A close examination of customer transactions and profitability will show that a minority of customers generate the majority of business. Although this ratio will vary by company, the high-profit segment of customers should be satisfied before all others. Segmentation is essential for identifying the company's most valuable customers.

The last principle, that common characteristics of the high-profit segment can be used to identify high-probability prospects, is true because similar people tend to like similar things. In essence, brands try to clone their most profitable customers among prospects.

Buyers versus Users

In some product categories, the person making the brand decision—the person doing the shopping—may not be the primary user of the brand. In such cases, a company must decide to what extent it should target the buyer versus the user. Before this decision can be made, a company needs to fully understand the role that the user plays in influencing the brand decision.

Consider the following example: Before beginning an MC campaign, a processed-meat company used market research to determine that most hot dogs are eaten by children but purchased by mothers. The company then conducted focus groups to better understand the dynamics of these two key segments—buyers and users. Moms said they made the brand decision, but their children had veto power over the brand choice. What they meant was that, when children refused to eat a certain brand, the mothers would no longer buy that brand. As one mother put it: "Buying something that I have to throw away because they won't eat it is a waste of money." At the same time, mothers also said they paid little attention to brands requested by their children. The meat company decided that the best strategy was to target moms with a message that showed children enjoying the brand. The strategy was quite successful.[2]

Profitability Segmentation

Effective targeting is based on overall business and marketing objectives. When a company wants to expand by targeting a new segment of customers, it must weigh the *benefits* of doing so (growth potential, market dominance) against the *costs* of doing so (expanding beyond its area of expertise, diluting its focus by serving too many diverse customer groups). Creating and sending brand messages, and listening and responding to customers, all represent expenses, so segmenting and targeting decisions ultimately have bottom-line implications.

EXHIBIT 7-5

Many businesses do not have a good idea of the types of people that buy their brands. SRDS has research data from thousands of households that provides this essential information.

If you had *BrandAdvantage*, you'd already know who this is.

When you want the whole picture of your consumer, focus on *BrandAdvantage*.

This annual directory profiles over 5,200 brands and breaks them down into 340 categories. Designed for SRDS by Simmons Market Research, *BrandAdvantage* features fresh data compiled from a sample of 28,000 households that represents the U.S. population.

It's time to get the complete picture of who's buying your products.

srds

Call Today
1-800-851-SRDS

BrandAdvantage. The complete picture of who's buying what.

EXHIBIT 7-6

Wendy's brand messages are aimed at fast-food users and not at the very health conscious, which it knows would be impossible to attract.

Although the focus of IMC is on building brand relationships, companies do not want to invest in building and maintaining relationships with customers who are unprofitable or who don't have the potential to become profitable. As the ad in Exhibit 7–6 illustrates, the fast-food chain Wendy's recognizes that the very health-conscious consumer will never be a profitable segment for its business; that's why the target for its brand communications is fast-food customers.

One approach to profitability begins with analyzing the size of customer segments. The primary question to answer is, Is each segment large enough to generate enough revenue to cost-justify a customized marketing effort? An example of a company that did this analysis was Midas, which offers repairs on auto brakes and exhaust pipes (among other services) with no appointment required (see the IMC in Action box).

Some marketers naively think that if a transaction is handled badly, the cost is simply the loss of a single sale. They do not consider that such a loss may represent the loss of a lifetime of transactions. Other costs may include the cascading impact that the dissatisfied customer can have through negative word-of-mouth testimonials. To determine which relationships are profitable, a company must analyze more than just how much a customer buys each year. Different customers provide different types of financial support. For example, a customer whose sales volume is only average might be a strong brand advocate who refers the brand to many new customers. Also, customers who buy the most are sometimes not the most profitable because they often use their buying power to bargain for the lowest prices.

Relationship Maintenance Costs

Customers can be classified in terms of both their spending patterns and their relationship maintenance costs.[3] This suggests four classifications of customers (unprofitable low-volume, unprofitable high-volume, profitable low-volume, and profitable high-volume) and corresponding strategies; these are outlined in Table 7–1.

One way to encourage low-volume customers to buy more is to offer them incentives for doing so. One of the best examples of doing this are the airlines' frequent-flyer programs. The more miles a customer travels a year, the more benefits and privileges that passenger is offered, such as first choice on seating and coupons for free upgrades.

Some low-volume customers, however, cost too much to retain. For example, GE Capital charges credit-card holders who pay off their balances every month an annual $25 fee. The company realizes this fee may motivate some customers to switch to another credit-card brand, but GE Capital would rather lose these customers than continue to lose money by providing them services for little in return. In contrast, some of GE Capital's credit-card customers who pay off their monthly balance have an extremely high level of charges; GE Capital makes money off them via the 2 to 4 percent the company charges retailers for handling transactions. GE Capital uses specially written software programs to identify this profitable, but small, customer segment—early-pay, high spenders.

Another consideration in segmenting on the basis of profitability, especially with BtB customers, is that today's marginally profitable customers can become tomorrow's profitable customers as their businesses grow. In the 1980s and early 1990s, some of the large computer companies screened and rejected prospective customers if they spent below a certain amount each year on computer software and hardware. IBM, for example, rejected prospects spending under $40,000 a year. What IBM came to realize, however, was when these companies grew and

T A B L E   7 - 1   Profitability Segments

Classification	Description	Strategy	Example
Unprofitable or Marginally Profitable			
Low-Volume	Customers who do little business with the company and who cost more to service than the company receives in profit from them; a drain on resources.	Charge them for services.	A credit-card company may install a service charge for customers who pay off their balance each month.
High-volume	Customers who buy in large quantities and therefore demand discounts and a high level of service.	Use a graduated level of discounts to ensure profitability.	An office supply company may stop offering volume discounts and instead charge a handling fee.
Profitable			
Low-volume	Customers who are generally happy but who do the bulk of their business elsewhere.	Design marketing programs to increase brand's share of wallet.	A retail store may set up a frequent-buyer program.
High-volume	Customers who buy in large quantities and generate the majority of profit; the company's best customers.	Reward and recognize them.	A department store may send its high-volume customers "exclusive invitations" to special sales.

began spending much more than $40,000, they remembered IBM's rebuff and consequently gave their business to IBM's competitors. (IBM has since changed this screening strategy.) The bottom line? When using profitability as a screen, it is important also to analyze prospects' potential for growth.

Recency, Frequency, Monetary (RFM)

Information about past purchase behavior is particularly useful in segmenting current customers and predicting which ones are most likely to respond to a new offer. From tracking the response to each offer and tracking the behavior of each customer, direct-response marketers have learned that a customer who has bought most recently, who buys frequently, and who has spent an above-average amount over a designated period is most likely to respond to a new offer. **Recency** is *a measure of how long ago a customer has purchased from the company.* Those who have purchased in the last 60 days, for example, are more likely to buy again than those who have purchased months or years before. **Frequency** is *a measure of how often, within a given period a customer has purchased the brand.* Frequency is somewhat less valuable as an indicator than recency because new customers will obviously not have had time to make repeated purchases. **Monetary** is *a measure of the amount a customer has spent with the company over a given period.* Direct marketers use these measures in combination—called RFM—to analyze lists of past and potential customers.

IMC IN ACTION

Midas Turns Segments into Gold

In the past, the main market segments for the auto service chain Midas have been derived from three criteria: age of the car (the older the car, the more likely it will need repairs); size of the car (repairs on big cars are expensive for customers but profitable for Midas); and driver (women offer more potential for cross-selling). There was, however, no way for Midas to know if these segments were real and, if so, profitable.

However, when Midas conducted research into customer service expectations and satisfaction, it became clear there were just two segments: the car lover and the utilitarian. Both segments were sizable enough to be profitable and both wanted fast, reliable, no-surprise, one-time repair. However, their interest in the way the service was delivered was different, and that meant the messages delivered by the service, as well as the marketing communication messages, had to change for the two different groups (see Exhibit 7-7).

Knowing these service segments exist, the question for Midas becomes: Is it economical to serve both the utilitarian and the car lover? A quantitative check of the economics in this particular case revealed that about 50 percent of Midas customers fell in each segment, making it viable to create different relationship programs to serve both.

In order to target the car lover, Midas designed brand messages to talk specifically about the car, offering to check on maintenance and service items (wash wheels when brakes have been changed) and call every six months or yearly to inform the customer it is time for a checkup. These messages also stressed that Midas allows customers to watch the repair process and to see old parts and the packaging from the new ones.

For the utilitarian segment, Midas used a different strategy. People in this group didn't want to feel they were wasting time, so the brand messages emphasized that Midas shops would give them a newspaper or a game to play while they wait (so the time didn't seem so long), offer to call a taxi, or, better still, provide a replacement car. Further, the messages explained that at the end of the repair, Midas employees would reassure them that the work was well done, that the bill would conform with the estimate (no surprises), and that they should be able to drive their car for a certain number of miles without any problems.

What this example demonstrates is that segmenting requires, above all, a customer orientation. Company managers must put themselves in the shoes of the different customer segments and not be limited by traditional company practices.

Think About It

How did Midas change its segmentation strategy? How did it know this was a profitable strategy?

EXHIBIT 7-7

Activity-Based Costing

The most precise way of determining customer profitability is done by **activity-based costing,** *a process for capturing and allocating the cost of handling each customer on a customer-by-customer basis.* For example, when a customer calls into a company for technical support, the amount of time company representatives take to discuss and provide responses is recorded, and a cost is calculated based on their hourly billing rate. If the customer wants a special report, the costs of locating the report, making copies, and sending it are also allocated to that customer. Customer-specific marketing and sales costs associated with entertaining, special merchandising materials, sales calls, and so on are allocated to each customer accordingly. Marketing expenses that can't be attributed to individual customers, along with the company's overhead costs (e.g., the company's electric bill, the receptionist's salary and benefits, the insurance and taxes on the building), are divided proportionally among all clients on the basis of each client's total billings. Each customer's total costs are then subtracted from his or her total purchases (revenue). The difference is the gross profit per customer.

Companies then identify the unprofitable customers and analyze why they are not profitable. If the analysis shows, for example, that they are demanding too many support services, the company can institute service fees accordingly. It is up to sales and marketing to explain any new charges in a way that maintains customer goodwill.

New Customers and Self-Selection

Segmentation strategies for prospects are similar to those for current customers. The idea is that similar people respond to similar messages. Thus, companies can use profitability profiles of current customers to find prospective customers.

Self-selection (or **aggregation segmentation**) *is a method of segmenting prospects that motivates potential customers to "raise their hands"—that is, identify themselves as being interested in what the brand has to offer.* In this strategy, mass and niche media are initially used to reach a broad range of prospects with a brand offering. Brand messages invite those interested in the brand to respond by sending back a form, calling a toll-free number, sending an e-mail, visiting a store, or responding in some other way. Frequently, companies use incentives to increase response. Companies must be careful, however, to make sure that the incentives are not the sole motivation for responding. In most cases, especially with BtB products, if prospects are not willing to invest some effort in order to learn more about a new brand, then they probably are not valuable prospects.

Self-selection is exemplified by what Procter & Gamble did when it introduced Cheer Free, a detergent without perfumes created especially for customers who are allergic to such additives. Not knowing who these allergy-sensitive customers were, Cheer ran mass media ads that offered a free sample to people allergic to detergent perfumes. In this way, Cheer was able to aggregate high-potential customers and build a segment based on self-identification. For the most part, those responding to this free offer identified themselves (or someone they knew) as being in need of the product. At that point, the company was able to switch to more highly targeted direct mail.

Another benefit of self-selection strategy is that it is respectful of customers' privacy and avoids the wastefulness that comes from overdependence on intrusive forms of brand message delivery. As noted earlier in this book, prospective customers are becoming increasingly resistant to what one British advertising executive has called "the stab 'em in the heart till they buy" selling strategy.

TYPES OF MARKET SEGMENTATION

On the surface, segmentation can seem like something easy to do. A company that sells fishing rods, for example, obviously should send brand messages to those who fish. But unfortunately, it's not that simple. There are many kinds of fishing, such as deep-sea fishing, fly fishing, trout fishing, and ice fishing. Each requires different kinds of fishing gear and attracts different types of people. Therefore, it is necessary to look at the distinguishing commonalities of each fishing segment.

Taken together, the commonalities will create a *profile* of each segment. The more detailed the profiles are, the more useful they are in helping a company find prospects likely to become customers. The most commonly used characteristics, or variables, for profiling are behavior (usage/benefits), demographics, psychographics, and level of brand relationship (see Figure 7–4). Most companies use more than one set of characteristics for each profile. With the exception of psychographics, these sets of characteristics can be used for profiling both consumer and BtB segments. The following sections discuss each set of variables in turn.

Behavior/Benefit Segments

Behavioral segmenting is a widely used practice; it involves *segmenting a market according to product usage*. The factors that influence brand decision making identified in Chapter 5—involvement level, customers versus prospects, and consumers versus businesses—can be used to identify segments. Segments can also be based

FIGURE 7-4

There are four basic segmentation variables.

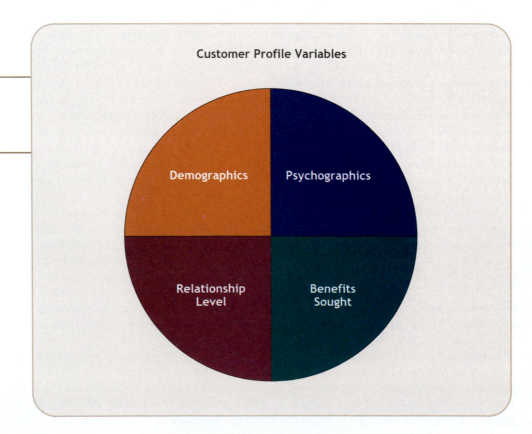

Customer Profile Variables

Demographics | Psychographics

Relationship Level | Benefits Sought

on different positions in the adoption process, such as Barina's initial targeting of the early-adopter category in the small-car market. The Thermasilk ad in Exhibit 7–8 is directed at the segment of shampoo users who also use a blow dryer.

Customers in every product category can be divided into four groups: heavy users, medium users, light users, and non-users. Non-users are not currently buying this product but might be prospects in the future. The criteria for placing customers in each group vary for each product category. For example, a person who buys a new car every year is a heavy user of cars, but if that same person buys laundry soap only once a year, he or she is a light user of laundry soap.

To identify the usage groups for a given product, the company must determine what amount the *average* customer purchases per year. Those who purchase above-average amounts of the product can be placed in the heavy user group, and so on down the line. For example, if the average buyer of shampoo buys four bottles a year, the shampoo industry may consider those who buy six or more bottles a year heavy users, those who buy three to five bottles a year medium users, and those who buy one to two bottles a year light users.

Current customers can be further segmented by what and where they buy. For example, some customers buy the majority of their clothes from discount stores, while others prefer more service and greater selection, and therefore buy the majority of their clothes from department or specialty stores. A similar type of segmentation can be done on the basis of what type, flavor, model, or style of a product customers buy. Take clothes, again. Students who buy mostly T-shirts and jeans may be labeled as the "casual segment," whereas executives who buy mostly suits may be labeled as a "business segment."

Patrons of fast-food restaurants can be segmented not only by how frequently they visit a fast-food restaurant but also by meal occasion: breakfast, lunch, dinner, or snack. Knowing who makes up these meal segments allows a fast-food chain to (1) design messages for each meal segment that reinforce usage of that meal occasion and (2) cross-sell other meal occasions. For example, if Burger King can identify heavy breakfast users, it can offer them a frequent-buyer incentive (to retain them) and also offer them an incentive to come in for lunch or dinner. This type of **cross-selling**, or *using the sale of one product to promote the sale of related products*, is one way to "grow" customers and get more of their fast-food dollar. A related concept, **up-selling**, means *encouraging customers to buy a more expensive product than they had in mind*. For example, car dealers frequently offer accessories or low financing rates in order to motivate customers to buy a more expensive model car than they would otherwise choose.

Benefit segmenting means *segmenting a market according to the benefits customers seek as the result of using a brand*. Consider how diverse and "segmented" the lodging industry has become. OAG's HotelDisk, for example, is an electronic directory of North American hotels available in CD-ROM format. In the section for business travelers, it separates hotels into 30 categories. Some have star chefs in the dining room or state-of-the-art fitness centers; others have in-room faxes and computer printers. There are even hotels with special rooms designed to fight the effects of jet lag to ensure long-distance travelers a better night's sleep. Customers can pick a hotel that offers the specific benefits they want to receive. Exhibit 7–9 illustrates a brand message offering a very specific benefit—relief from a migraine headache.

Another example of a strategy developed from a benefit perspective comes from the airport food service industry. Restaurant managers were

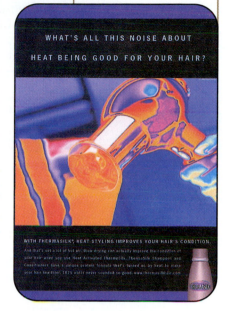
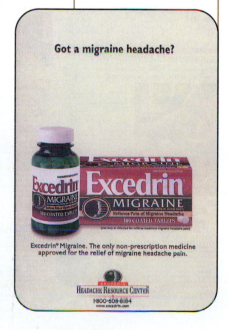

asked to identify customer segments for a customer satisfaction study. These managers identified business travelers, tourists, local airport employees, and travel groups. Although that may seem to make sense, the study found that these labels didn't correspond to actual customer segments. Instead, those who ate at airport restaurants could be grouped into one of two service segments—"in a hurry" and "not in a hurry." In other words, half of the group was looking for a quiet place and relaxation; the other half was hurrying through the airport and simply wanted a fast meal. The conclusion was that the staff should be trained to identify customers in terms of these two benefit segments and then serve them accordingly, with either a quiet corner or fast service. This type of service benefit segmentation is based on understanding whether or not all customers have the same service needs and, if not, how can they be grouped into manageable clusters that better identify their needs.

Demographic Segments

Once a segment is identified by its behavior, the next step is to further profile it according to its **demographics,** which are *definable statistical measures, such as age and life stage, gender, ethnicity, religion, income, education, occupation, marital status, household size, age of children, and home ownership*. Credit-card companies, for example, use age as part of their demographic segmenting. Those most likely to sign up for their first credit card are in the age category 16–19. Table 7–2 identifies the most commonly used demographic measures.

For many brands, demographics are often the best predictors of consumer behavior and therefore the primary means of segmentation. What customers buy often reflects how old they are, how much money they make, and how well educated they are. Said another way, certain demographic characteristics often correlate with certain product and brand choices. A highly paid executive is more likely to buy a Mercedes than is someone who just graduated from high school.

Age groups are indicators of purchasing power, as well as the type of products purchased. Senior citizens control a great deal of the wealth in the United States; in Asian countries they have a great deal of the population's respect, so they have a great deal of influence on family purchases. Young people in the United States are also a significant economic segment. Teenage Research Unlimited has estimated that the 31.6 million U.S. teens (ages 12 to 19) each week spend, on average, $66 of their own money (from jobs and allowances) and $27 of their parents' money.[4]

One of the challenges a company faces in maintaining brand relationships is that customers change in age, income, education, and in other ways. These changes cause changes in wants, needs, and desires. A company must decide whether to expand its product offerings to meet these changing needs, which may confuse brand identity, or implement an ongoing customer replacement strategy.

TABLE 7 - 2 Demographic Characteristics	
Age	Family size
Education	Family life stage
Income	Residence type
Gender	Ethnicity
Occupation	Religion
	Geography

A good source of basic demographic information is census data, which are available in most industrialized countries. The 2000 United States census, for example, collected 220 different pieces of demographic information on households and compiled them by residential block. The Donnelley Marketing ad in Exhibit 7–10 for its Hispanic segmentation program illustrates how demographics relating to ethnicity and location can be used. Note that even within an ethnic segment, there are differences in age, education, income, and other important product-usage predictor factors.

Ethnic Segments

Segments based on ethnicity are increasingly important in the United States, where ethnic markets include such segments as African Americans, Asians, and Latinos or Hispanics. But it's not just in the United States that ethnic marketing is an important strategy. In Malaysia, for example, the Malay population is large and politically powerful; however, the Chinese segment is nearly as large and very important in the business sector. There is also an Indian segment, which is smaller in number but still important in the business sector.

In the United States, disposable income of ethnic segments is increasing faster than that of the total U.S. market. The Hispanic share of U.S. spending, for example, rose from 5.2 to 6.2 percent between 1990 and 1997, an amount estimated at $348 billion. The African-American share of spending in the same period rose to 9 percent, an estimated $469 billion.[5] The 1990 U.S. census found over 22 million Hispanic persons, making this group 10 percent of the population. Based on the 2000 census, Hispanic people are projected to be 15 percent of the U.S. population by 2020 and 25 percent by 2050.

In some cases, brands are designed specifically for an ethnic group; in other cases mainstream brands have marketing communication campaigns tailored to specific ethnic cultures and values. Both of these approaches can have unexpected negative consequences if the targeting is not handled with sensitivity, but can work quite well if it is. The first example of this strategy dates to the 1940s when Pepsi-Cola developed a sales team to market its soft drinks to African Americans, a group that showed high loyalty to Pepsi.[6] The Pfizer ad in Exhibit 7–11 shows a niche product (Viagra) being advertised to an African-American audience.

An ongoing industry question is whether marketers are doing a good job targeting these ethnic groups, given their market growth. Critics have noted that companies spend a disproportionately small amount of money for advertising in ethnic media. A study of radio, for example, found that stations targeting minority listeners earn about 29 percent less than stations that offer more general programming.[7]

Geodemographic Segments

Another important way to describe a segment is to look at geographical information. Called **geodemographic segmenting**, this is *a process that combines geographic and demographic data to identify residents of a particular area with certain demographic traits.*

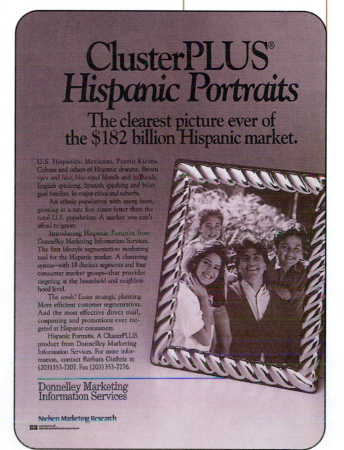

EXHIBIT 7-11

This Pfizer ad is aimed at a very specific segment— older African-American couples in which the male suffers from impotency.

Geographic descriptions of a segment consider such factors as international, national, region, state, city, climate, topography, and urban/suburban/rural. Pharmaceutical manufacturers, for example, know that different allergies appear in different geographic areas, and they market their over-the-counter remedies accordingly. In Indiana, it's ragweed; in California, it's grass; in the Northeast, it's trees. In the car category, four-wheel drive vehicles are marketed more to people living in the Rocky Mountain states than to people in Florida because of obvious geographic differences.

There are also some interesting marketing anomalies in product-related areas, such as health care and education, that are based on geography. For example, a Dartmouth study found that elderly patients in Miami, New York City, and parts of south Texas are especially likely to spend their final days in a hospital and often in an intensive care unit. Elderly patients in other parts of the country are much more likely to die at home with much less medical intervention. In other words, different approaches to end-of-life care were found to be reinforced by uneven distributions of hospital beds, specialists, and other medical resources.

A number of business information programs, such as Cluster-PLUS (Donnelley Marketing) and PRIZM (Claritas) model census data down to zip codes and blocks to describe segments and predict their size and behavior. The census residential block information, for example, can be inserted into mapping software that companies use to chart where their best customers are located in terms of their zip codes. Demographic information is also available from companies that compile lists of driver's licenses and auto registrations.

ClusterPLUS and PRIZM are offered by competing companies that have created 40 to 50 lifestyle profiles based on where consumers live and their purchase behaviors. The programs then assign each neighborhood, defined by zip codes, to one of the profiles. The underlying assumption is that customers who live close to each other have similar wants and needs. Once brands develop a profile of their customers, they use PRIZM or ClusterPLUS to create segments they want to target by grouping zip codes that best match their profiles.

Keeping up with the changing tastes of segments requires creative research techniques. To keep track of the urban youth market, one company used "Street Teams," a network of some 80 kids in 28 cities in the United States. These teams roam clubs, malls, sports fields, playing courts, and record stores looking for the urban buzz before it starts buzzing. Such an urban intelligence network is often able to predict trends for the global teen market and therefore is used by global marketers such as Nike and Tommy Hilfiger.

Psychographic Segments

The problem with using only demographics to segment markets is that, although they provide a great deal of factual information, they do not explain what people like, think, and believe. This is why many companies also use **psychographics**, which are *measures that classify customers in terms of their attitudes, interests, and opinions as well as their lifestyle activities* (see Table 7–3).

The reason for identifying this type of information is that certain consumer decisions are driven more by psychological needs and wants than by physical realities. Hallmark Cards, Inc., for example, places more emphasis on psychographics than on demographics when segmenting and targeting its customers. A writer for the card company explained: "To reach consumers, we consider the

T A B L E   7 - 3   Psychographic Characteristics

Interests	Lifestyle activities:
Opinions	Hobbies
Attitudes	Clubs
Personality	Entertainment
Social class	Shopping
Values	Vacations
	Other social activities

states of a relationship rather than an age. Whether you're 25 or 65, you have the same feelings—that giddy uncertainty in the beginning, the bottomless thrill of falling in love. Targeting a 40-year-old makes no sense because that 40-year-old may feel like a teenager.[8]

A research company that specializes in developing personality and lifestyle classification information is SRI Consulting Business Intelligence (SRIC-BI), which produces a research product called Values and Lifestyles (VALS). The company's original segmentation study divided U.S. consumers into nine groups based on Maslow's hierarchy of needs (see Chapter 5) and the inner-directed/outer-directed theories of sociologist David Reisman. It was criticized because it tended to place the majority of consumers into only a couple of the groups. The current version, VALS 2, combines demographics and lifestyle data gathered from two national surveys of 2,500 consumers who responded to 43 lifestyle questions. It places people into one of eight groups.

In Figure 7–5, the eight VALS 2 groups are arranged in a rectangle with the vertical dimension representing resources (income, education, self-confidence, health, intelligence, energy level, eagerness to buy) and the horizontal dimension representing self-orientation (principles, status, and action). Each group orients itself to its world and social environment differently and displays distinct decision-making patterns, product usage rates, and media behaviors. At the top of the figure is a group called "actualizers," people with abundant resources and a great deal of self-confidence. At the bottom is a group called "strugglers," people who have few resources and find it challenging just to get by. In between, the figure identifies six other groups that are broken into three categories: "fulfilleds" and "believers," who are principle-oriented; "achievers" and "strivers" who are status-oriented; and "experiencers" and "makers," who are action-oriented.

Lifestyle and Life Stage Segments

A form of psychographic segmentation is grouping customers in terms of how they live. The word **lifestyle** refers to *the way people live their lives as well as how they choose to spend their money, time, and energy.* Exhibit 7–12 is an example of a BtB ad that talks to a segment of business customers defined by its comfort with and use of new communication technology.

The term **life stages** refers to *the different periods in life of an individual or family.* Life stages may be labeled as single, young family, single-parent family, family with older children, and empty nesters (couples whose children have grown and left home). This is a helpful segmentation strategy because people have certain needs and wants during different stages in their lives. People in the young family segment, for example, are more interested in furnishing their homes and buying

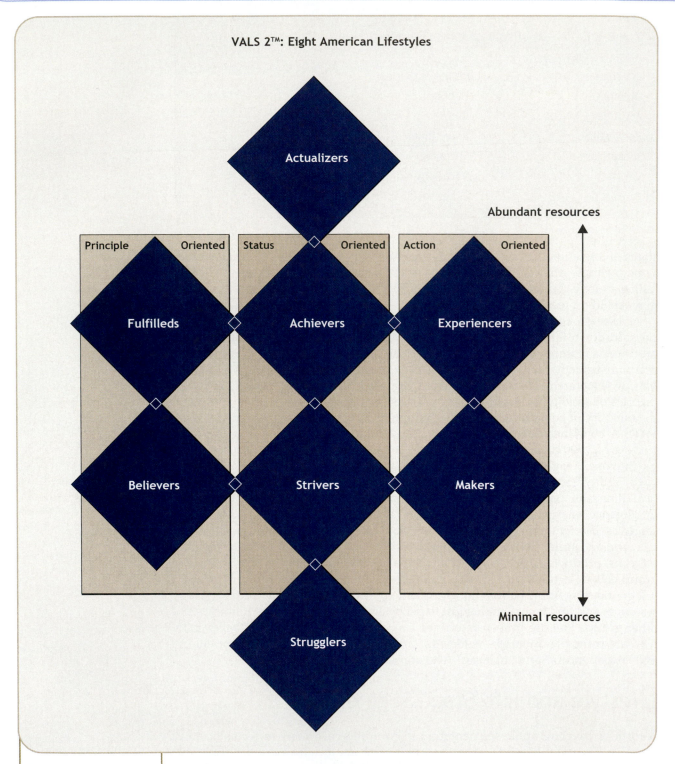

VALS 2™: Eight American Lifestyles

FIGURE 7-5

Lifestyles can be used to segment and prioritize customers and prospects.

children's products than are empty nesters, who are more interested in travel and luxury items that they can now afford.

Lifestyles often cut across demographic segments. For example, in the hunting and fishing lifestyle segment, there is a wide range of ages, incomes, and education. Marketers must determine for their own brands which commonalities are most relevant to their products. Sometimes lifestyle profiling is more important, and sometimes demographics takes precedence. The best approach to segmentation is to use

a combination of both. As the CEO of a European company remarked: "In the 1980s we looked for the customer in each individual. In the 1990s we [looked] for the individual in each customer."[9] The latter is likely to hold true in the twenty-first century as well.

The most famous lifestyle term—yuppies—was one used in the 1980s and 1990s to describe young, urban professionals who aspire to a good life. Yuppies were characterized as driven by their desire to be upwardly mobile and accumulate possessions. As status-conscious parents, yuppies tended to marry later than average, then had "yuppie puppies" or "gourmet babies," recognizable by their expensive status-brand clothing. Although you don't hear much about yuppies anymore, their babies are still a growing market for designer products. It's not just OshKosh B'Gosh in the closet. Trendy children's brands also include Versace, Moschino, Hermes, and Kenzo.[10] In addition, yuppie parents seriously plan their infants' intellectual development around educational toys, developmental experiences, and tests.

Other interesting labels, such as baby boomers (people born between 1946 and 1964), baby busters (the generations that followed boomers), and echo boomers, (the children of baby busters), have been coined to describe people in terms of their age and life stage. The unusually large number of births after World War II created a bulge in the U.S. population statistics. Baby boomers, most of whom are now middle-aged, comprise some 38.4 percent of U.S. households but control 49 percent of all dollars spent each year, which is why companies like Clinique, maker of upscale beauty and skin care products, design ads specifically for them (see Exhibit 7–13).

More recently, a slew of lifestyle terms has been created to identify particular segments of the population. They include:

Formulated for baby boomers.

It won't put up with the status quo. Refuses to accept skin that's looking a little dull, flat, lined.

No wonder Turnaround Cream is considered the perfect "formula" for us baby boomers.

A constant exfoliant, it helps get rid of the old, the uneven, the poorly textured.

So that the new, the radiant can shine through.

Takes a very pro-active approach, using salicylic acid to gently but quickly reveal a brighter, finer, more energized complexion.

Over time, even gets fine lines to get a move on.

Yes, it's true, we're not as young as we once were.

But we still want our bottle. Clinique.

Allergy Tested. 100% Fragrance Free.

www.clinique.com

Dinkies: Double income young couples with no kids.

Biddies: Baby boomers in debt.

Skippies: Schoolkids with income and purchasing power.

Guppies: Gay upwardly mobile professionals.

Maffies: Middle-aged affluent folks.

Mossies: Middle-aged, overstressed, semi-affluent suburbanites.

Dimps: Dual-income couples with money problems.

Woopies: Well-off older persons.

The term *Generation X* has been used to identify the group whose 45 million members were born between 1965 and 1979. "Gen Xers" grew up on television and computers, and are described as independent-minded and cynical due to the economic and social problems present when they were young (e.g., the AIDS epidemic, an economic recession, corporate downsizing, and a doubling of the U.S. divorce rate). They have also been found to be skeptical of advertising and other promotional activities. Though marketing strategists have found the label Gen X useful, the group's members have been found to dislike it, because of its negative connotations. An interesting campaign conducted by the wine industry targeted this segment by using the slogan "Forget the rules! Enjoy the wine," an iconoclastic appeal to people who were presumed not to be concerned about the traditions of matching the right kind of wine to meat.

Generation Y, which was born after 1980, is an elusive group with far greater diversity than any other lifestyle group and a spending power of $150 billion per year. Generation Y, in contrast to Generation X, is generally thought to be more optimistic and entrepreneurial because of being raised in a more nurturing style amid an economic boom. Gen Y has also been called the Digital Generation (Generation D) because it has grown up with the Internet and other computer technologies. It has been described as better informed, more empowered, and more cause-oriented than preceding generations. The 1999 Cone/Roper Cause-Related Teen Survey found that 55 percent of teens would switch brands based on social issues and that 90 percent want to know about a company's cause-related activities as part of their buying decision.[11] The newest generation, sometimes dubbed the Millennium Generation, has not been profiled very well yet by marketers, but demographers have predicted that it will be an even larger group than the boomer market.

And then, of course, there are the seniors. Mostly born before or during World War II, this "gray market" includes young seniors (60–74) and older seniors (75-plus). A huge market, there are over 68 million U.S. seniors alone, which is more than the population of France, Canada, Italy, or the United Kingdom. One of the wealthiest retired generations in history, seniors have over $1.6 trillion in buying power and hold approximately two-thirds of the wealth in the United States.[12] And with baby boomers heading into their 50s and early 60s, the market size of the senior group is going to get even bigger and more important relative to the rest of the population.

Relationship Segments

Companies that understand the importance of creating long-term relationships with customers will base their segmentation strategies on both customers' perceptions of their relationships with a company and their behavior within that relationship. Table 7–4 describes four loyalty segments that indicate the nature of the relationship a customer has with a brand.[13] These relationship levels

T A B L E   7 - 4   Relationship Loyalty Segments

No loyalty	Customers feel little attachment to the brand and are not likely to make repeat purchases: hence, there is little return to be expected from these switchers or non-users. Seldom a targeted segment.
Inertia loyalty	Customers feel little attachment to the brand, but continue to make repeat purchases out of habit. The best strategy to use for this group is to make the purchase as easy as possible. Frequent Purchase clubs, like those that send women's hosiery to members on a regular schedule, exemplify the strategy for this segment.
Latent loyalty	Customers feel strong attachment to the brand, but make few repeat purchases. This is particularly true for major purchases, such as cars or large appliances. A customer may only purchase a washing machine once every 20 years or so, but Maytag wants this person's loyalty when it comes time to replace that machine. Maytag also wants this person as an advocate who testifies on the brand's behalf to family and friends, to maximize the power of word-of-mouth advertising. Reminder marketing communication, reward programs, and programs to stimulate word-of-mouth testimonials are important strategies for this segment.
Premium loyalty	Customers feel strong attachment to the brand and also make frequent repeat purchases. Abercrombie & Fitch is determined to retain the loyalty of youthful customers who wear the label as a badge to impress friends. A strategy for this segment involves developing a sense of belonging to a special club, either in spirit (Abercrombie shoppers, Saturn owners) or in actuality, such as the self-organized Harley Owners Group (HOG).

emphasize the point that not all customer relationship segments are equal. Recognizing the differences between them can be helpful in targeting the most important groups as well as designing messages to address their interests.

AT&T has invested in a future customer segment (no loyalty yet) by giving over $150 million worth of telecommunications equipment and services to elementary and secondary schools. The company is hoping that its donations will make the AT&T brand a familiar one with young people. Building brand awareness among students may be the first step in creating a long-term relationship. In addition to someday getting the students' telecommunications business, the company also hopes to motivate students to think positively about working for AT&T.

Combining Profile Variables with Size Segments

As you will recall, the first section in this chapter described how segmentation dimensions range from mass to segments of one (Figure 7–3). By combining these size segments with the profile variables of behaviors, demographics, psychographics, and levels of relationship, a brand can increase the accuracy of its targeting (see Figure 7–6).

FIGURE 7-6

Targets can vary in size by the type of segmentation used.

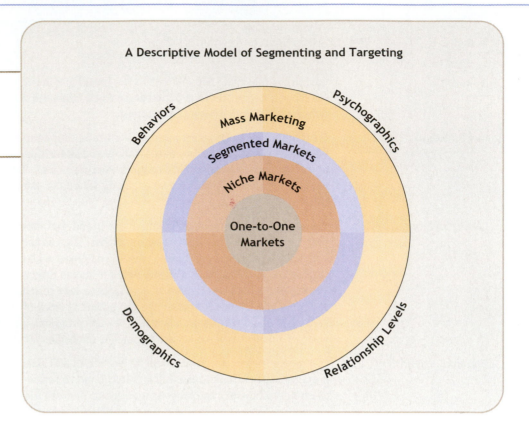

A Descriptive Model of Segmenting and Targeting

Adopter Segments

The term *new product* can refer to a product that is new in the market or one that is new to the prospect (i.e., it has been on the market for some time, but the prospect hasn't been aware of it and/or hasn't bought it before). People adopt new brands at different rates, and information about these adoption patterns can also be used to segment markets, as the chapter opening case on Holden Barina illustrated. In that case, the young women coming into the market were making their first new-car purchase; even though the Barina had been around, it was a new product purchase for them. Furthermore, the Barina repositioning campaign also was designed to create a new product feeling for the brand.

Adoption segments reflect the fact that some people are more willing to take a risk than others. Think about Internet users. Who was the first person you knew to get online and explore the Web? Would you identify that person as an innovator? Do you know any people who still have not learned to use the Internet? As Table 7–5 shows, customers can be divided into five categories: innovators, early adopters, early majority, late majority, and laggards. These categories are frequently used in marketing communication strategies, particularly to define the target audience for the introduction of new products.

Understanding the differences in people's attitudes toward innovation is important in identifying audiences to target with different kinds of messages about new products or product changes. For example, innovators and adopters are most likely to be attracted by messages stressing a product's newness; the late majority are most likely to be attracted by a message that stresses that the product has been well tested and well received. These different segments, like other segments, vary by product category.

TABLE 7-5   Categories of Adopters

Category	Percentage of Population	Characteristics	MC Strategy
Innovators	2.5%	Risk-takers, cosmopolitan; often affluent and well-educated	Use publicity releases and the Internet; retention is extremely important, because innovators influence early adopters.
Early adopters	13.5	Leaders in their communities and a source of information about new things; above average in income and education	Use the Internet, direct response, events, and advertising that lets them raise their hands to try; retention also very important, because early adopters influence early majority.
Early majority	34	Take their lead from the early adopters and wait for them to be satisfied first; slightly above average in age and education	Use advertising emphasizing "new" and "better," with case histories/demonstrations, comparisons with competition.
Late majority	34	Older than average and less well-educated; tend to be skeptics and more comfortable with old values	Use sales promotion and guarantees/warranties to reduce risk; advertising should focus on demonstrations.
Laggards	16	Suspicious of innovation and its source; have little education, low income, often social outsiders	Use advertising as brand reminder; use price-oriented sales promotion.

Source: Adapted from Everett Rogers, *Diffusion of Innovations* (New York: Free Press, 1983).

HOW TARGETING WORKS

As defined earlier, targeting involves analyzing market segments to determine which groups are most profitable. It also involves developing a marketing communication program to reach those groups. Targeting is done by using the profile characteristics of the segments to draw boundaries around a particular group of customers or prospects who are projected to respond well to a brand and its marketing communication.

The segmentation factors, such as demographics and psychographics, can be used to predict how customers with certain characteristics will behave. These become the key "predictor variables" used in identifying a target. As Figure 7–7 illustrates, a segment becomes smaller each time one of the critical predictor variables is added to the profile. Once the marketer delineates an identifiable, high-potential group, it estimates the group's size by consulting such information sources as census data, industry market analyses, and companies that specialize in collecting customer data.

The next step is to prioritize the segments based on a combination of business and marketing objectives and profit potential. For example, in the category of children's

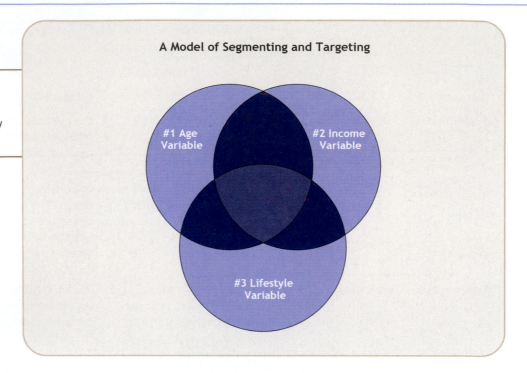

FIGURE 7-7

These three segmentation variables produce a relatively small target.

clothing, the primary target may be parents, because they make the purchase and the secondary target may be children, who influence the decision.

The company then develops message strategies and media plans for the segments that have been identified as most important. This makes it possible to explain various product features in terms of a particular segment's needs, wants, and interests. Not every product feature is equally important to every segment. The cereal maker Kellogg's may target parents by emphasizing that its products have some good nutritional features, while sending messages to kids that emphasize how good the cereals taste. At the same time, Kellogg's may be telling another target—retailers—about the product's market share and high potential for repeat sales. The IMC Strategy box explains how different companies have targeted certain youth segments.

Media and Message Dimensions of Targeting

The targeting decision is carried out in both the message and media strategy. A company, such as a pharmaceutical company, can have several different high-priority customer targets, all of which require different message strategies, as shown in Table 7–6.

As you can see, this pharmaceutical company has targeted four segments: primary care physicians, insurance companies, hospital administrators, and patients. Each group has its own special interest regarding drugs. Primary care physicians, for example, are most interested in the efficacy of the drugs, meaning how well they work and what side effects they cause. Insurance companies are most interested in how much the drugs cost. Hospital administrators are interested not only in how the drugs perform but also in how easily the hospital can reorder supplies as well as train nurses to administer the drugs. Patients want to know about reliability and trustworthiness of the drugs, as well as side effects. Because of the

IMC STRATEGY

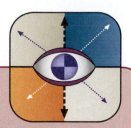

Hip-Hop and the 'Hood

Fila USA started as a sportswear marketer that made tennis togs for the country-club set. So why did it run edgy, dark ads against graffiti-filled inner-city playground walls with a chorus of clanging garbage cans in the background? Fashion designer Tommy Hilfiger has made a fortune selling preppie wardrobes to well-bred suburbanites. So why did he give away wardrobes to rap stars, send rappers down his fashion runway, and add athletic shoes to his brand's lineup?

The answer is that the funky street culture that embraces rap and hip-hop has become a fashion statement among teenagers, sort of a universal youth badge. Even white kids in Kansas wear the flamboyant fashions of the inner city—baggy jeans, green hair, camouflage T-shirts, vintage lambskin-lined flight jackets, metallic sweatshirts, and, of course, Nike shoes.

Mistic Beverages, the many-flavored soft-drink brand, used Dennis Rodman's chameleonlike hair in a "Show Your Colors" promotion. And Sprite, Coca-Cola's spirited lemon-lime drink, pitted rappers MC Shan and KRS One against each other in a verbal duel that became an ad. Sprite also inked a deal with Shabazz Brothers Urbanwear to give away $1 million worth of the clothing with a mean street attitude in a bottle-top promotion. Riding on the popularity of the black street culture, Sprite's volume jumped almost 18 percent, three times as big an increase as the next most successful soft drink.

Shabazz Fuller, owner of Urbanwear, explains why these major corporations are looking to "the 'hood" (the neighborhood) for inspiration: "They want to piggyback on our brand equity, which caused us concern at first, but it's cool. They're supporting the whole rap community."

Why does the kid from Kansas, or the Euroyuppie from Haarlem, the Netherlands, want to emulate black kids from New York's Harlem? A researcher who heads the BrainWaves Group (a division of MC agency D'Arcy Masium Benton & Bowles) speculates that "kids figure that to make out in life, you have to live by your wits, and black kids on the streets of the city are the epitome of that." It is this type of consumer insight that enables a company to be precise and cost-effective in targeting brand messages.

But most of all it's about brands. The African-American market, with its $325 billion in spending power, cares intensely about brand names. A rapper called Q-Tip sends that message in a song that starts with Tommy Hilfiger and then goes on to list a dozen other brand names such as Tanqueray, Lexus, Donna Karan, and BMW. As *Brandweek* observed, "street certification in a rap song is a marketer's dream come true."

Think About It

How does this box explain or relate to niche marketing, and how does that differ from mass marketing? Why would marketers want to mimic the styles of the urban streets in marketing their products to young people?

Sources: Adapted from Joshua Levine, "Badass Sells," *Forbes*, April 21, 1997, 142–148; Nicole Crawford, "The Worm Proves Mistical," *Promo*, July 1997, p. 8; and Sarah Van Boven, "Toeing the Designer Line," *Newsweek*, November 17, 1997, p. 77.

TABLE 7-6 A Pharmaceutical Company's Targeting Strategy

Targeted Segments	Message Emphasis
Primary care physicians	Efficacy of the drugs; side effects
Insurance companies	Cost
Hospital administrators	Performance of the drugs; training needs; inventory and ordering
Patients	Reliability and trustworthiness of drugs; side effects

EXHIBIT 7-14

Xerox BtB ad says its copy machines can be used to easily customize messages in order to "profit from today's highly targeted marketing."

respective needs of each segment, the pharmaceutical company, if it wants to maximize chances of success, must send each of these segments a different set of brand messages that interpret the brand's benefits in terms of each segment's interests; at the same time, it must maintain certain message consistencies that help position and reinforce the brand's overall image.

Usually the initial pieces of a marketing communication—such as the headline in an ad or the cover on a brochure—will speak to the interests of the target audience and separate those people from all others. An example of how messaging is used to target is the Xerox BtB ad shown in Exhibit 7–14.

Marketers select media on the basis of each medium's ability to reach the targeted audience. One of the benefits of the Web is that it enables companies to practice narrow targeting; the Internet also can be used to reach many different audiences. Heidi Kay of the former Internet ad agency Flycast Communications (now part of Engage, Inc.) suggests several targeting strategies for the Internet, which are listed in Table 7–7.

Profitability-Based Targeting

As stated earlier, the key to effective targeting is the estimation of the group's profitability. As stated before, one of the principles of IMC is to think first of current customers. To what extent current customers are

TABLE 7-7   Online Targeting Strategies

Targeting Method	Strategy
Content	Use specific websites whose content is of interest to target audience.
Timing	Run brand messages during times of day or days of week when audience is most likely to be surfing.
Organizational name	Expose campaign to surfers belonging to certain companies or organizations.
Geography/Internet service providers	Run brand messages in designated locations or have them carried by selected Internet service providers.
Profile data	Show banner ads only to those who have provided profile information that matches target profile.

Source: Heidi Kay, "Media Planning, A Targeting Tutorial," ClickZNetwork, www.searchz.com/Articles/0614993.shtml, September 21, 2000.

targeted will differ for every brand. The primary deciding factor is how much it costs to generate a sale from current customers versus the cost per sale for new customers. The greater the difference, the more one segment should be targeted over another.

Another consideration is how fast a company wants to grow and how much it has to invest in acquiring new customers. Just because new customers cost more to acquire doesn't mean that the investment won't pay off in the long term. In addition to profitability, there are other criteria that companies should use (see Table 7–8).

Segmenting and Targeting BtB Customers

If segmenting and targeting profitable customers is important in consumer marketing, it is even more so in BtB marketing. This is because the average BtB customer spends more and costs more to acquire than the average consumer. And as with consumers, most companies don't give one company 100 percent of their category spending, so there is always the opportunity to increase the spending of these customers. Although this chapter has discussed segmenting mostly in terms of consumer marketing, most of the segmenting concepts, such as customer profitability, are also applicable to BtB marketing. However, there are some different terms and special considerations in BtB segmenting and targeting that you should know.

In the United States, businesses have been segmented by the government according to the North American Industry Classification System (NAICS), formerly

T A B L E 7 - 8 Profitability Criteria for Targeting a Segment	
1. Measurable	Can those making up the segment be identified and counted? A company may know that redheads like its brands. However, unless there are ways of identifying where redheads live, work, or what media they consume, the segment is too nebulous to work with, other than through a self-selection strategy.
2. Accessible	Can those in the segment be reached with the product and brand messages? A segment of prospects that live outside a brand's area of distribution may not be attractive because expanding distribution may cost more than the new sales would justify.
3. Substantial	How many customers or businesses make up the segment? Unless the segment has enough critical mass it may not be worth singling out. Size of the segment differs by product category—convenience goods need large segments but manufacturers of airplane carriers may need only one customer.
4. Differential	Does the segment have commonalities that distinguish it from other segments? A segment needs to have certain needs, wants, or desires that will motivate those in the segment to respond to certain messages and offers.
5. Actionable	Can the segment be served? The company must have the capacity to make enough product to serve the segment, enough salespeople to reach the segment, and enough marketing communication budget to send messages to the segment.

Source: Phil Kotler and Gary Armstrong, *Principles of Marketing* (Upper Saddle River, NJ: Prentice Hall, 1999), p. 215.

TABLE 7-9   Sample NAICS Codes

Major Group Category Range	20-39	Manufacturing Industrial Division
Major Group (first two digits)	34	Fabricated metals
Industry Group (three digits)	342	Cutlery, hand tools
Specific Industry (four digits)	3423	Hand & edge tools
Product Class (five digits)	34231	Mechanics' hand service tools
Specific Product (six digits)	342311	Pliers

called the Standard Industrial Code (SIC) system. The NAICS system provides multilevel segmentation. The sample listing in Table 7–9 shows how this works. A manufacturer of pliers is assigned the code number 342311. The "34" indicates that the company falls within the range of manufacturing industrial companies and, specifically, is a fabricated metals company. Study the table to see how the rest of the code number is derived. The same system operates in all major business product categories.

NAICS codes are helpful for a company selling a product like computers, which have applications in many different kinds of industries. IBM, for example, frequently puts together marketing communication programs aimed at certain NAICS codes, such as companies involved in distribution, manufacturing, or service industries. By segmenting on the basis of these well-defined sets of criteria, everyone involved in marketing at IBM knows exactly which types of companies are being targeted based on the code numbers.

Other common BtB segments are based on company size, which is determined by total sales or number of employees. Companies can also be segmented based on characteristics similar to those used in consumer marketing:

Purchase behavior: large or small volume; brand loyal or price sensitive; usage rates, order size, order frequency

Benefits: special needs, level of service required

Demographics: company size or sales level, type of firm, organization, or industry

Geographics: areas in which company is located and/or does business

Psychographics: corporate culture, level of risk taking

Relationship level: how loyal the customer is

Ethics of Targeting

Some of the criticisms of marketing and marketing communication arise from controversial targeting decisions related to special groups: many people feel, for example, that children shouldn't be targeted for certain kinds of products, such as sweetened cereals or violent video games; and ethnic groups resent what they see as a bombardment of "sin product" ads, such as those for liquor and cigarettes. As the Ethics and Issues box discusses, companies need to consider ethics when targeting certain segments.

ETHICS AND ISSUES

Offensive Targeting

For some food manufacturers, particularly those who sell candy and sugared cereals, running ads for food products on Saturday-morning cartoon shows and before child-oriented feature films is targeting at its best; they can economically transmit their sales messages to a demographically perfect audience.

But to opponents of advertising to kids, such targeting is just another example of socially irresponsible marketing. Critics warn that advertising directed toward children may be contributing to alcohol abuse, violence, childhood obesity, an increased level of childhood diabetes, and compulsive buying by young adults.

There are other ways targeting can raise hackles. Credit-card companies have been criticized for targeting college students who have little income. Critics have charged that cartoons such as Joe Camel and the Budweiser frogs entice young people to buy cigarettes and beer. Although the tobacco company R. J. Reynolds claimed that the Joe Camel campaign was not directed at children, it was compelled to abandon the cartoon image in all of its marketing. In 1998, an agreement was reached between 46 states and several tobacco companies to settle lawsuits that had been filed by the states. Part of the agreement was that the companies would not advertise in media whose audiences had more than 15 percent in the 12-17 age range. However, two studies done in 2000, one by the Massachusetts Department of Health and the other by the American Legacy Foundation, determined that tobacco companies had actually increased their levels of advertising in magazines reaching the youth audience.

Other critics have focused on the targeting of alcohol and tobacco products to racial and ethnic minority groups. The billboard issue is a particularly sensitive one in urban areas where ethnic groups feel they are being massively targeted for these products. The products that generated the greatest criticism included Uptown, a low-menthol cigarette formulated for African Americans; Dakota cigarettes, which were targeted to young, poorly educated, blue-collar women; and PowerMaster malt liquor, a high-alcohol beer marketed to young black men that emphasized getting a fast buzz in its advertising.

PowerMaster's maker, G. Heilman, subsequently got in trouble with the U.S. Bureau of Alcohol, To-

bacco, and Firearms (BATF) when it introduced a line extension called Colt 45 Premium, which the BATF felt was really PowerMaster in a new package. The BATF doesn't permit brewers to advertise alcohol strength, regardless of the brand name.

Similarly, in Britain, Bass PLC has marketed low-alcohol drinks that critics say encourage underage drinking. With a sugary flavor, offbeat packaging, and quirky names such as Hooper's Hooch and Stunn Potent Passion, these "alco-pop" drinks have been denounced by the government and consumer groups who claim that their makers are inappropriately targeting young people.

Target marketing of such products raises the paradox of "good marketing but bad ethics." A study of such practices found that people believe that a targeting strategy is unethical if it involves targets perceived as vulnerable and products perceived as harmful. These concerns can cause an uproar leading to protests, bad publicity, and costly legal battles.

The Code of Ethics of the American Marketing Association states, among other things, that (1) products should be safe and fit for their intended use, (2) communication about products should not be deceptive, (3) companies should disclose risks associated with products, and (4) companies should not use false and misleading marketing communications.

Think About It

What are the issues associated with the targeting efforts described in this story? Why are people critical of such practices? Consult a general interest magazine and find an ad for a product that you think needs to be reconsidered, based on the American Marketing Association's Code of Ethics. Explain why you question the ethics of the marketing of this product.

Sources: Joan Lowy, "Kidblitz: Do Advertisers Rob Cradle?" *Daily Camera*, December 11, 1999, p. D1; Nancy Millman, "Tonning Up Kids," *Chicago Tribune*, January 9, 1997, p. 3-1; "Cigarette Billboards Draw Heat, Fire over Tasteless Message," *Daily Camera*, July 9, 1998, p. 7C; Ernest Beck, "Bass to Reformulate Low-Alcohol Drink to Address Criticism," *The Wall Street Journal*, September 11, 1997, p. B4; N. Craig Smith and Elizabeth Cooper-Martin, "Ethics and Target Marketing: The Role of Product Harm and Consumer Vulnerability," *Journal of Marketing* 61 (July 1997), pp. 1–20; and "Tobacco Ads Targeting Teens, Study Says," *Daytona Beach News Journal*, May 5, 2000, p. 2A.

A FINAL NOTE: BALANCING ACQUISITION AND RETENTION

Segmentation emphasizes the importance of knowing and targeting current customers. Most companies seldom have a proper balance of targeting current customers (for retention) and prospective customers (for acquisition). Because of the traditional emphasis on transactions rather than relationships, and acquiring new customers rather than retaining and growing the current ones, many marketing programs have not been as cost-effective as they could be.

A survey conducted by *Direct* magazine, for example, found that marketers are more likely to use their direct-marketing budgets to gain new customers rather than to retain current ones.[14] Obviously, a real strength of targeting with direct marketing messages and media is the ability to individualize and customize messages. Current customers should be the first target of this type of marketing communication. Strategic segmenting and targeting allow a company to use marketing communication tools efficiently. They are an essential part of zero-based planning, as discussed in Chapter 6.

In the chapter opening case, Holden made a major effort to retain its current customers—young women in the small-car market—by completely repositioning its Barina model. It was also essential that Holden reach young women as they came into the market. The BG campaign was designed both to retain the interest of young women in the market and to reach new prospects as they matured. In most cases, segmenting and targeting calls for a careful balancing of the two objectives of acquisition and retention.

Key Terms

segmenting 238
targeting 238
one-to-one marketing 241
recency 245
frequency 245
monetary 245
activity-based costing 247
self-selection (aggregation segmentation) 247
behavioral segmenting 248

cross-selling 249
up-selling 249
benefit segmenting 249
demographics 250
geodemographic segmenting 251
psychographics 252
lifestyle 253
life stages 253

Key Point Summary

Key Point 1: Moving Away from Mass Marketing

Because there are few real mass market products, marketers are targeting ever smaller and more profitable segments for the sake of message efficiency and effectiveness. The segmentation process involves identifying the types of customers in the market, analyzing them for their common characteristics and profitability, and then targeting those who are most likely to respond with messages and media designed specifically for the group. Segmentation leads to niche markets and "markets of one." A niche market is a tightly defined group of customers often served by some highly specialized product or interest; one-to-one marketing means custom-tailoring a product, and its marketing communication, to a particular customer's needs.

Key Point 2: Profitability

Segmentation identifies and prioritizes groups of customers with common characteristics in order to target the most profitable groups and develop retention programs for them. Segmentation starts with the identification of characteristics of current customers. After the segments have been identified, the next step is to target the ones that offer the most profit potential by analyzing their recency, frequency, and monetary characteristics.

Key Point 3: Identifying Segments

Segments are defined in terms of such characteristics as behavior and desired benefits, demographics (including ethnic segments and geodemographics), psychographics, relationship levels, and adopter status. These are the variables that can be used to match a segment with current high-profitability customers.

Key Point 4: Targeting

Targeting is the process of selecting high-priority segments that are most likely to respond to marketing communication programs. Self-selection, which lets customers aggregate themselves as a target market, locates the most interested and responsive target.

Lessons Learned

Key Point 1: Moving Away from Mass Marketing

a.   Distinguish between segmenting and targeting.
b.   List and describe the steps in the segmentation process.
c.   Explain why there has been a move away from mass marketing and toward segmented marketing.
d.   Define a market niche.
e.   What is one-to-one marketing? How is it different from mass marketing?
f.   Define self-selection and explain why it is considered to be the technique that locates the most interested and responsive target audience.
g.   Find an advertisement for a product that you think is marketed to a niche. (Hint: look in special interest magazines.) Explain the characteristics of those who make up the niche, and analyze how the message is designed to speak their interests.

Key Point 2: Profitability Segmentation

a.   Why should companies start with current customers in developing a segmentation and targeting strategy?
b.   What is the difference between buyers and users?
c.   What is profitability segmentation?
d.   What does RFM stand for? How are these factors used to ensure customer profitability?

Key Point 3: Types of Market Segmentation

a.   What are the five types of customer segmentation discussed in this chapter? Give an example of each.
b.   Distinguish between demographics and psychographics, and explain the role of each in segmentation.
c.   Explain how a company can develop segmentation strategies based on a knowledge of relationship factors.

Key Point 4: Targeting

a. Check out your three favorite websites. Using the list in Table 7-7, identify what type of online targeting strategy the site represents.
b. How does business-to-business segmenting and targeting differ from consumer segmenting and targeting? How are they similar?
c. Analyze the contents of your closet or medicine cabinet. Find one brand that you think was targeted to you. Explain why and how that brand's targeting works in general, and tell how it speaks to you personally with its brand messages.
d. Analyze the ethics of targeting to children on Saturday-morning cartoons. If you were working on the advertising for a sugar-laden cereal, is there any socially responsible way to advertise it on Saturday-morning cartoons to children? What would be your personal opinion about this assignment?

Chapter Challenge

Writing Assignment

As discussed in the beginning of this chapter, automaker Holden wants to market its Barina model to young women. Review this chapter on segmenting and targeting, and Chapter 5, on the brand decision process. How many ideas from these two chapters would you recommend that the Holden marketing manager consider in developing the next year's marketing plan? List all the principles and strategies that you think might be useful in developing this strategy.

Presentation Assignment

Develop a class presentation on the use of stars as campaign spokespersons. Choose from Dennis Rodman, Magic Johnson, Kristi Yamaguchi, Gabriela Sabatini, Amy Van Dyken, Michael Jackson or some other star with whom you are familiar. Analyze the effectiveness of this star in reaching either mass or niche audiences. How does the use of stars assist in the segmenting and targeting of a campaign. Develop an outline of the key points you want to present. Give the presentation to your class or record it on a videotape (audio tape is also an option) to turn in to your instructor, along with the outline.

Internet Assignment

Go to the SRI Consulting Business Intelligence's VALS website www.future.sri.com/vals and then click on "survey," and match your own lifestyle with the VALS typology. Where would you be located, and how well do you think that designation fits you?

Additional Readings

Hallberg, Garth. *All Customers Are Not Created Equal: The Differential Marketing Strategy for Brand Loyalty and Profits.* New York: John Wiley & Sons, 1995.

Lowenstein, Michael W. *Customer Retention: An Integrated Process for Keeping Your Best Customers.* Milwaukee: ASQC Quality Press, 1995.

Peppers, Don, and Martha Rogers, *The One to One Future: Building Relationships One Customer at a Time.* New York: Currency Doubleday, 1993.

Enterprise One to One: Tools for Competing in the Age of Interactivity. New York: Currency Doubleday, 1997.

Webster, Frederick E. *Market-Driven Management: Using the New Marketing Concept to Create a Customer-Oriented Company.* New York: John Wiley & Sons, 1994.

Whiteley, Richard C. *The Customer Driven Company: Moving from Talk to Action*. Reading, MA: Addison Wesley, 1991.

Research Assignment:

Consult the books above or any other books or articles that relate to targeting, segmenting, and positioning. What guidelines can you develop from your readings on the different procedures used in retaining customers and acquiring new ones. How is a manager to make the decision about which one of these to emphasize?

Endnotes

[1] Don Peppers and Martha Rogers, *The One to One Future: Building Relationships One Customer at a Time* (New York: Currency Doubleday, 1993).

[2] Author experience when he was Director of Marketing Communications for Eckrich Processed Meats.

[3] Kaj Storbacka, "Segmentation Based on Customer Profitability: Retrospective Analysis of Retail Bank Customer Bases," in *Contemporary Knowledge of Relationship Marketing*, Atul Parvatiyar and Jagdish Sheth (Atlanta: Emory University, 1996. p. 32)

[4] "The Hearts of New-Car Buyers," *American Demographics*. August 1991, p.14.

[5] Dave Carpenter, "Businesses Tune In to Teens," *Associated Press*, November 11, 2000, reporting on a study done by Teenage Research Unlimited, Northbrook, IL.

[6] Leon E. Wynter, "Blacks and Hispanics Gain Spending Clout," *The Wall Street Journal*, September 3, 1997, p. B1.

[7] Stephanie Capparell, "Ed Boyd Tore Down Race Barriers to Build a Market for Pepsi," *The Wall Street Journal*, August 29, 1997, p. B1.

[8] Keith L. Alexander, "Communications Study Finds Ad Bias," *USA Today*, January 14, 1999, p. 1B.

[9] Judith D. Schwartz, "What is a Family Today? For Hallmark, a Challenge," *Brandweek*, June 14, 1993, p. 24.

[10] Jacques Horovitz and Nirmalya Kumar, "Getting Close to the Customer," *Financial Times*, February 2, 1996, p. 13.

[11] Robert Berner, "Now Even Toddlers Are Dressing to the Nines," *The Wall Street Journal*, May 27, 1997, p. B1.

[12] Tina Furuki, "Why Ask Y?" *American Advertising*, Winter, 2000, pp. 11-14.

[13] "Senior Spending," *American Advertising*, Winter, 2000, p. 13.

[14] "What's in Store? *Direct* 4, no. 12 (December 1992), p. 26.

8

Data-Driven Communication

Key Points in This Chapter

1. What is data-driven communication?

2. What are the privacy and security issues associated with databases?

3. How are data collected, and how is a database mined for strategic use?

4. How do companies use databases to manage different types of customer relationships and to customize messages?

Chapter Perspective
Relationships of Steel

What will separate successful from unsuccessful companies in the coming years will not be the quantity of customer data they collect but rather how they turn those data into actionable marketing strategies and programs. Databases are like iron ore, and the data within them like iron—the raw material used to make steel. Making high-quality steel starts with taking high-quality iron ore, extracting the iron, and then refining it to increase its strength and durability.

Good brand communication follows a similar process. Properly collected and stored data must be refined before they can be used to form brand communication strategies and programs that result in steel-strength brand relationships. Data alone have minimal value. They become valuable only when turned into information that makes companies smarter about their customers, prospects, and the marketplace.

Companies collect data to learn about customers—who they are and what they need, want, and desire. Companies use data to segment and target customers—how they respond to offers, what they buy and don't buy, why they buy and why they don't buy, how much they buy, when they buy, and which customers are profitable and which are not. The sophistication of today's information technology (IT) systems makes it possible to cost-effectively collect and analyze data.

Databases and IT are thus the engines that drive integration and interactivity. IT enables a large number of employees to have access to current customer data, which is a must in IMC. Finally, IT enables faster and broader evaluation of IMC programs, making marketing people more accountable than ever before. The challenge is to know how best to use the technology to develop efficient and effective data-driven communication strategies that enrich relationships that produce sales and profits.

This chapter first introduces some components of data-driven communication, then discusses privacy and security issues related to data collection and use, explains how to design database programs, and, most important, explores the management and use of customer databases in IMC programs.

BRITISH AIRWAYS' LEISURE RELATION-SHIP MARKETING PROGRAM TAKES OFF
Carlson Marketing Group, London, England

Traditionally known as an airline for business travelers, British Airways (BA) recognized a huge growth opportunity in the leisure travel market—one of the world's fastest-growing travel sectors. The questions was how could BA best penetrate this market. After conducting extensive research into the leisure travel market, BA identified the type of offering that would be most suited to this segment of travelers. The answer was to create the Travel Service, a one-stop service for leisure travelers. BA's challenge to the London branch of the Carlson Marketing Group was to launch this new service. The resulting campaign was unique in that it matched product offerings to members' interests (see Exhibit 8–1). Furthermore, it used a database to profile BA's most profitable customers in order to identify high-profit prospects.

The Personalized Strategy

At the time British Airways was developing its program, a number of competitors were offering consumers a "travel service." These consisted of travel agents offering customers the convenience of an electronic or phone sales service, or banks and credit-card companies extending their product offerings. However, these services used blanket communications that were nonpersonalized and nonspecific. BA believed its Travel Service could better meet the needs of individual leisure travelers by using more personalized brand messages.

The British Airways Travel Service was unique in that it was the only travel service that proactively mailed members the "inside information" on the latest offers and holiday destinations from BA and its partners, relevant to members' interests and lifestyles. It also provided members with new ideas and suggestions on when and where to go, where to stay, and what to do at each destination.

EXHIBIT 8-1

An introductory ad for BA's new Travel Service.

More important, where possible, it matched the offering to specific details provided by members through their "preference forms." The product offering included flights, holidays, accommodation, car rental, and foreign currency exchange—the full travel experience (see Exhibit 8–2).

Campaign Strategy

The Carlson Marketing Group designed the launch campaign for the Travel Service to recruit high-value members who fit the profit profile and would generate new revenue opportunities for BA. The campaign's marketing communication strategies were to:

- Drive additional in-store traffic and encourage enrollment at point-of-purchase.
- Develop a distinct set of brand values that complemented British Airways' master brand while still permitting the Travel Service to stand alone.
- Create a cohesive approach to all aspects of marketing communication.
- The target audience was identified as two key groups:
  - ☐ "Dinkies": Dual-Income, no kids; young independents, 25–35 years of age, affluent; sophisticated and ambitious when making travel arrangements; plenty of spontaneity and spare income to match.
  - ☐ "Global Greys": 45-plus years of age, affluent, children have left home, plenty of time to enjoy newfound freedom; enough financial resources to travel.

The campaign consisted of three parts. First, a self-selection recruitment strategy that used direct mail, posters, and point-of-purchase materials to encourage prospects to raise their hands and sign up. Second, the agency chose an activation strategy using direct mail to maximize the relationship with members after recruitment; the objective was to encourage members to book and repeat-book. Third, Carlson established a training program (internal marketing) to educate BA staff about the program and their role in the recruitment process and ongoing service delivery.

Due to the highly targeted nature of the program, the success of the effort depended on building a solid database. BA generated the database from prospects identified as having an appropriate profile for a BA leisure offering. The airline selected data from existing databases consisting of customers who had previously purchased direct from BA. Prospects were sent a "recruitment pack" containing the preference form, which generated

How the Travel Service benefits you

Here at the Travel Service we're always striving to look after you and offer you the ultimate travel experience. That's why we offer you a number of benefits:

★ The Travel Service gives you the inside information on the latest flights and holidays from British Airways and partners including exclusive offers and advance notice of exciting travel promotions.

★ Our unique Matching Service enables us to bring you the latest offers relevant to your travel interests.

★ Our specially trained Travel Consultants can give you all the advice you need to plan and book your holiday.

★ We bring you new and inspirational holiday ideas and in depth destination information.

★ Together with our partners, we can fly you to over 240 destinations worldwide.

★ We work with over 20 travel partners, specifically chosen for the quality of products and service they offer.

★ We're there for you seven days a week, 8.30am - 8pm Monday to Friday and 9am - 5pm at weekends.

★ We're operated by British Airways, bringing you worldclass expertise and an unparalleled level of service - all your meals and drinks free on board our aircraft, a complimentary overnight bag on longhaul flights and free headphones for our award winning in-flight entertainment.

Surfing With British Airways Travel Service

We intend that the Travel Service should always make the most of today's technology for the benefit of our members, which is why we've enhanced and improved our web site. Simply log on and you can get full details about any of the holidays we've featured in this pack - plus much more information about our many inspirational travel opportunities. There's page after page of ideas - it's the innovative way to plan your next holiday!

You can find our web site at www.britishairways.com/travel-service. Once on line, you can explore at your leisure.

additional information for the database, such as frequency of travel, travel plans, types of offers of interest, travel partners, annual household spending on travel, and particular interests while on holiday. This database enabled the company to generate highly targeted, personalized direct-mail communications on an ongoing basis.

The strategy behind the Travel Service and its launch campaign was that by gathering data from customers and developing relationships with them, BA could better understand their needs, aspirations, and travel desires in order to proactively target them with the latest, most relevant offers and destinations on an ongoing basis. This would increase members' propensity to make leisure bookings with BA. Hence, BA created its Matching Service to enable the Travel Service to deliver to members details of offers that matched their preferences. The benefit to members was twofold: inside information on the latest offers from BA and their partners, along with a degree of proactivity that no other travel service provider could equal.

The creative proposition driving the campaign was based on the concept of "inside information": "Only the British Airways Travel Service proactively sends you the 'inside information' on the latest offers and destinations that are relevant to you . . . so you never miss out."

By targeting prospects from current BA databases and setting up its own database to record the additional information obtained from the campaign's responders, the Travel Service was able to effectively match member interests and behavior with BA offerings (see Exhibit 8–3). Through the Travel Service, BA was able to develop strong, personalized relationships with its leisure customers.

The British Airways Travel Service launch campaign, driven by a customer database and a multistage direct-mail program, met its key performance objectives and successfully recruited a critical mass of 170,000 members into the program by the end of year one. It also reached incremental and gross revenue targets. Finally, it won a Gold Medallion in the international Advertising and Marketing Effectiveness award competition.

This case was adapted with permission from the Advertising and Marketing Effectiveness (AME) award-winning brief for British Airways prepared by the Carlson Marketing Group agency in London.

EXHIBIT 8-3

The BA Travel Service's mailing focused on ideas for holiday vacations. Included in the package was a group of inserts that described various destinations and provided important travel information for travel planning.

WHAT IS DATA-DRIVEN COMMUNICATION?

As explained in Chapter 1, the integrated marketing communication process has been designed to do three things more effectively and efficiently than traditional marketing: acquire, retain, and grow profitable customers. IMC achieves all three in part by using prospect and customer information compiled in some form of a database. That's how British Airways was able to match a product offering—its new Travel Service—to its customers' interests.

There are also many other types of databases that companies can use to add value to brands. For example, by putting product offerings, price lists, and inventory reports into electronic databases, companies can provide information to customers and other stakeholders much quicker and much less expensively than they can by printing and distributing paper catalogs and brochures. Making timely and accurate information easy to access not only saves the company money but adds value to the brand. Often, increases in operating efficiency lead to price reductions. This chapter explains how to collect and manage data to that end.

Customer Relationship Management (CRM)

An increasingly popular phrase used to describe a data-driven approach to being customer focused is called **customer relationship management (CRM),** which was mentioned briefly in Chapter 7. As with IMC, different people have different definitions of CRM. A narrow one is that CRM is *a type of database software for tracking customers*. Ruth Stevens, a professor and consultant, says it is "a combination of retention marketing and customer service."[1] A much broader definition describes it as being very similar to IMC:

> Total Customer Relationship Management is the optimization of all customer contacts through the distribution and application of customer information. Simply stated, it is your promise, that no matter how your customers interact with you, you will always recognize who they are. Total CRM requires the cooperation of all departments and divisions within an organization around this concept.[2]

The CRM consulting firm Front Line Solutions has set up a website (www.CRMguru.com) that features the latest CRM practices and applications; the CRM Guru site is open to students for free. Other major CRM consulting services are Siebel; the SAS Institute (see Exhibit 8–4); and German-based SAP, which will custom-design a firm's CRM system. A major step forward in information technology allows companies to use the Internet to carry their data transfers on an as-needed basis rather than paying millions of dollars to customize their own

in-house CRM systems. SAP, for example, is using the Web to provide customer service by providing a free online database of CRM problems and solutions, which customers and prospects can search and apply to their own situations.

Databases

A **database** is *a collection of related information that is stored and organized in a way that allows access and analysis*.[3] A customer database can be as simple as a shoe box full of index cards containing the names and addresses of customers. Although some small retailers are quite successful with a shoe-box database, most companies use computerized databases. A company's customer database is a strong competitive tool because no competitor knows what a company knows about its own customers. In other words, this proprietary (i.e., privately owned, exclusive) information can provide a company with a strong competitive advantage when dealing with its own customers.

Occasionally you will hear people talk about *database marketing* as being the same thing as *direct marketing*. This is incorrect. Direct marketing is just one of the marketing communication functions. Database marketing goes further; it can and should be used with all marketing communication functions and in the selection of media. Database marketing helps companies manage brand relationships in a variety of ways:[4]

- Understanding customers and prospects.
- Managing customer service.
- Understanding the competition.
- Managing the sales operation.
- Managing the marketing and marketing communication campaigns.
- Communicating with customers.
- Providing information resources to customers and therefore added brand value.

A company's first objective in using a customer database is to identify who its customers are. Surprisingly, many retail businesses, especially, have only a vague notion of who it is that buys the products they offer. Even BtB companies often don't know who their end users are, because their products are sold through distributors and retailers. As explained in Chapter 4, it is difficult to have a meaningful dialogue with someone whom a company knows nothing about, and nearly impossible to design goods and services that will satisfy the needs of these "unknown" consumers and companies.

An important reason for capturing customer behavior information in databases is to determine just how effective the company's various marketing programs are. For years, marketing departments have been criticized for their inability to show how their spending has affected sales and long-term brand relationship building. By using databases to track how customers respond to campaigns and promotional offers, marketers are better able to show a cause and effect, and to more accurately calculate the return on a marketing program investment.

But customer identification and accountability are only two of the many uses of customer databases. The Database Application Checklist (Table 8–1), developed by the advertising agency Saatchi & Saatchi, provides examples of the many business and marketing questions that customer database systems can help answer and address.

T A B L E   8 - 1   Database Application Checklist

To help its clients increase the efficiency of their marketing communications, Saatchi & Saatchi asks them the following questions to see to what extent they are maximizing the use of their databases in strategic planning and managing their brand relationships:

- Do you know how much promotional money you can afford to spend to attract a new customer?
- When you undertake sales promotion or other direct-response activities, do you keep in contact with the respondents?
- What resources does your company have at present to capture data on your customers and prospects?
- Do you know what proportion of your sales comes from what proportion of your customers?
- Can you identify existing customers of one brand who might be receptive to promotion and cross-selling of another?
- Do you know if your number of accounts is the same as your number of customers?
- Can you determine the lifestyles of your customers?
- Can you quickly and inexpensively identify actual customers of your product for inclusion in focus group panels or for other research purposes?
- Do you know if your sales representatives visit all your potential customers?
- If you could differentiate between your high-, medium-, and low-value customers, would you spend your marketing money the way you do today?
- Have you monitored the relationship between various schedules of media activity with brand awareness and sales across countries?
- Do you regularly test different uses of media across brands and countries?

Source: Adapted from *The Total Communications Audit* (London: Saatchi & Saatchi), pp. 6–7.

Digitization

A database can hold anything that can be digitized, that is, converted into a numerical form (most often using a binary number system of 1s and 0s). Everything you see on a computer monitor, including everything on the Internet, has been digitized so a computer can store or find information and provide it when you want it. Words, pictures (both moving and still), and sounds can all be converted from their normal analog form into a digital form. Thus, databases can contain text, videos, graphics, music, and numbers. Computer programs retrieve digitized data and place them into recognizable forms for easy use. Digitization is the driver of *convergence*, the term now used to describe how different media are blending. Reducing words, pictures, and sounds to a common-denominator form allows the television, computer, and telephone to be combined into a single communication device. A good example is the mobile phone that contains a web browser.

Digitization allows us to collect, store, retrieve, analyze, and transmit data quickly and cost-effectively. In addition, digitization allows data to be compressed, something that cannot be done with printed books and reports (other than using thinner paper), thus minimizing the space needed for storage. Finally, one of the most important benefits of digitization is its accuracy in reproduction. In the case of digitized music recordings, for example, listeners talk about the fine quality and clean sound of the recording.

For years, digitization and databases have been used in the production of printed information—magazines, newspapers, reports, and catalogs. Magazines are now electronically produced (using dozens of databases and computers) until the very last step, when ink is applied to paper. This is why it is relatively easy to think about Internet delivery of magazines, newspapers, and so on possibly overtaking the printed versions.

Information Technology (IT)

A database by itself just sits there. It takes an information system to make the database useful. The department responsible for managing an organization's hardware (computers), software (programs), and databases (information) is called one of several names depending on the company—data processing, information systems (IS), information technology systems (ITS), or information technology (IT). The latter is the most common.

The company's IT department usually operates a **database management system (DBMS)**, which is *software that records customer information, tracks customer interactions, and links customer databases that are already in existence* (e.g., product orders, accounting records, service and repair records, customer service). A good DBMS allows users to look up the status of a customer's order (which is in one database) and compare it to that customer's order history or customer service history (which often are in separate databases). This makes it possible, say, for a customer-service representative to know what a particular customer has ordered in the past and what problems he or she is currently experiencing; such knowledge should help greatly in solving problems and improve the level of customer retention.

> " It can be argued that the database is the greatest single application of information technology within marketing. "
>
> John O'Connor and Eamonn Galvin, *Marketing and Information Technology*

A good database also often contains information about other stakeholders, such as supplier and distributor orders. Some experts, such as John O'Connor and Eamonn Galvin, feel that a database is the greatest single application of information technology available to companies.[5] Figure 8–1 explains its central role in marketing management.

DMBSs vary with the company, ranging from relatively simple systems that run on PCs to highly complex systems that require mainframe computers. The growing importance of computer technology in business today is exemplified by the fact that, since the mid-1990s, more than 50 percent of all capital equipment expenditures of U.S. companies has been for information technology.[6]

Databases and their attendant DBMSs are the tools that enable companies to do integrated marketing communication and allow them to give more than lip service to a customer-first philosophy. An information system for use in IMC should contain data that can be mixed and matched in a variety of applications. Recall from the chapter opening case how British Airways was able to match its travel offerings with its customer preferences.

Marketing communication managers do not need to be information technology experts, but it is essential that they have a basic understanding of how IT operates and what IT can do to improve MC planning. Unless marketing people know what information exists within the company's systems and in what forms it can be provided, they will find that working with IT people can be extremely frustrating. One of the most important things marketing managers can do is to build a strong working relationship with one or more people in the IT department. This is not just organizational politics but rather a move to make sure all employees can get support when they need it—for the good of all the company's stakeholders. Even

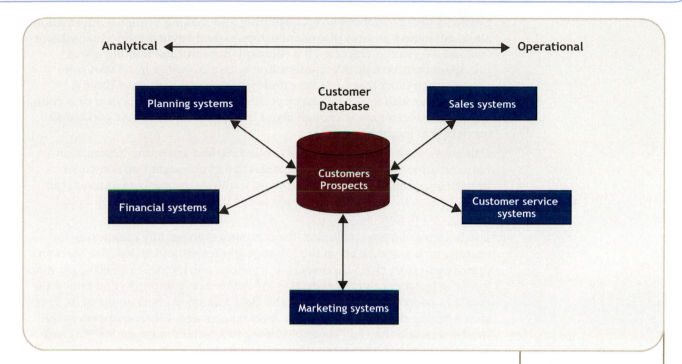

Analytical ⟷ Operational

Planning systems

Customer Database

Sales systems

Customers Prospects

Financial systems

Customer service systems

Marketing systems

FIGURE 8-1

This illustrates the central role of the customer database

Source: John O'Connor and Eamonn Galvin, *Marketing and Information Technology* (London: Pitman, 1997), p. 66.

more than other departments, most corporate IT departments have an ongoing backload of work. Marketing may be competing with many other departments for getting help and must remember that part of internal marketing involves getting buy-in and support from their fellow workers.

Learning Organizations

Databases are the institutional memory of an organization. Before the widespread use of DBMS systems—and still in companies that do not use them—customer responses to MC programs and other important pieces of customer relationship dealings often resided only in the heads of individual employees. When those employees leave a department or company, that information goes with them. Capturing responses to marketing programs and customer feedback make it possible for companies to record and learn from their past experiences, and thus create a "learning organization."

A learning organization has a feedback program that involves four dimensions: (1) ongoing data collection, (2) continuous aggregation of this data, (3) periodic trend analysis (looking for a "critical mass" of comments or behaviors suggesting problems or opportunities), and 4) making information available to those who need it to do their jobs better. Capturing, analyzing, and sharing customer feedback not only increases corporate learning, but also communicates to employees that such learning is a top priority.

Data-driven marketing and corporate learning are structural issues because they demand that information systems be set up so that information can be shared. As Ron Kahan, president of a Denver database company, explains, "The knowledge gleaned from a marketing database must fuel a corporate culture of service. It should act as a strategic hub with spokes permeating every business unit within the enterprise."[7]

The following list summarizes four important ways in which databases contribute to organizational learning:

1. *Databases record customer history.* Capturing and making available information about customers ensures that relationships extend beyond individual sales or customer-service interactions. If a company has recorded nothing about previous contacts, then every interaction with a customer must start from scratch, something that customers find irritating and a waste of time. A company can also miss business opportunities if a new salesperson or account supervisor doesn't know enough about the customer to suggest goods and services that might be useful.

2. *Databases are the source of insights.* By collecting and analyzing information on how consumers use products, companies can gain insight into consumer behavior. Complaints, compliments, and inquiries, properly quantified, can help companies design new products, solve problems, and develop brand message strategies.

3. *Databases uncover market changes.* If a company is constantly monitoring its customers, it will pick up on their changing interests and tastes. The Mervyn's department store chain captures conversations with 50,000 to 70,000 customers a year in its stores. Survey responses are entered on computers and tallied the next day. Mervyn's benefited from this data collection effort in one of its Texas stores during the Christmas season several years ago. When shoppers in the local stores said they had started listening to a certain radio station that had recently changed to country-and-western music, Mervyn's was able to instantly revise its radio buy to include this station and more effectively drive its Christmas business. In the past, an outside firm took six weeks to tabulate data, and Mervyn's would not have known until after Christmas that its customers' radio listening habits had changed.

4. *Helping the sales staff.* Databases allow companies to share timely information with sales representatives, giving them the opportunity to change their presentations to match rapidly developing markets. This is particularly important for sales to the trade. Since business customers are most likely gathering information on changing developments in their own markets, those who sell to them must know about these changes to meet their needs. Del Monte, known for its canned fruits and vegetables, maintains a database of nearly 55,000 food stores, drugstores, and mass merchandisers that carry its products. It can analyze the buying patterns at each store and provide a profile of the store's most frequent customers. This information is then passed along to its sales force to help them target stores with specific products and also to share information with the stores to build relationships with the trade.

Another important aspect of customer databases is that they are themselves valuable assets. Because the primary purpose of business is to create customers, the databases that contain profiles of these customers in some cases are more valuable than land, labor, and capital. When airline company Pan Am declared bankruptcy, United Airlines bought its South American routes—more for Pan-Am's frequent-flyer database than for the routes themselves. United was already servicing South America, which made the list of Pan Am's best customers for flights in that region all the more valuable. (The various privacy issues surrounding such sales of databases are discussed later in this chapter.)

Database Applications

Collecting data without becoming inundated by them is a challenge. The key to meeting this challenge is data management. Some companies overanalyze data and end up focusing on the minutia of business; other companies underanalyze data, which leads to an inability to track and analyze business patterns. The IBM ad in Exhibit 8–5 addresses the problem of managing data so it contributes to business intelligence.

There are two primary applications of customer databases—operational and analytical. **Operational database applications** are those *where the data are used to help the company to improve its interactions with customers.*[8] At customer-service contact points—such as when customers have questions about the status of an order, when a car rental representative checks in a returned car and needs to print out a receipt for the customer, or when a manufacturer calls a supplier to check on current pricing and availability of certain items—certain applications of databases help companies *operate* quickly and effectively. Improved operation is an added value to customers.

Analytical database applications are *those that allow companies to examine customer transactions and interactions.* Companies can *analyze* data for such things as trends (e.g., responses to direct-mail offers are falling); commonalities (e.g., customers that buy early in the season are more likely to buy on credit than those who buy late); and profitability (e.g., the longer customers have been buying, the more profitable they are). British Airways, for example, was able to build profit profiles by analyzing its customer database and using those profiles to identify which customers had potential to become high-profit customers.

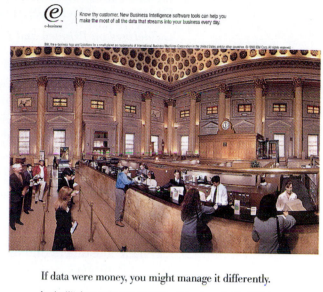

If data were money, you might manage it differently.

EXHIBIT 8-5

Business intelligence is based on the ability to track and analyze data in order to spot market trends and set up customer relationship programs.

PRIVACY AND SECURITY ISSUES

In the battle of profits versus privacy, companies have to decide how important their customer relationships are in the long term and whether they can afford potentially alienating customers by tracking their shopping behaviors (with or, especially, without their knowledge). Whenever consumers see examples where personal information about an individual or group has been misused, they become wary of all information gathering, even by reputable companies.

Data Collection

Companies that practice IMC gather customer profile data so that they can personalize their interactions with customers. Collection of personal data, however, has been attacked in recent years by consumer watchdog groups as an invasion of privacy.

A company that buys customer data from other companies, compiles the lists, and from them develops a customer profile to send out personalized brand messages can be seen as crossing the privacy line. Many customers do not understand list brokerage and thus cannot figure out how the company acquired such information. Another consumer concern is that companies will link individuals' names with incorrect data (e.g., false information on credit reports, Internet reading patterns based on an accidental visit to a porn site, and so forth).

The Direct Marketing Association, comprised of a group of companies particularly interested in database marketing, has developed data collection guidelines for its members. Another set of guidelines (which follows) is a list based on the Code of Fair Information Practices, developed by an advisory panel of the U.S. Department of Health, Education, and Welfare.[9]

Guidelines on Privacy and Personal Information

1. Personal data record-keeping practices should not be kept secret.
2. An individual should have the ability to find out what information about him or her is on record and how it is disclosed.
3. An individual should have the ability to correct or amend a record of identifiable information about him or her.
4. An individual should have the ability to limit the disclosure of information about her or him that was obtained for some other purpose.
5. An organization creating, maintaining, using, or disseminating records of identifiable personal data must guarantee the reliability of the data for their intended use and must take precautions to prevent misuse of the data.

When consumers find out that their purchases and lifestyles have been or are being monitored, particularly for commercial purposes, it is a concern to them. Consumers are more likely to be receptive to personal data collection if:

1. They know it is being collected.
2. They have given their permission for it to be collected.
3. The information being asked for is relevant to buying or using of the product.
4. Its use will benefit them and not just the company (e.g., speeds up the delivery time of the goods and services they want, alerts them to information they want, shields them from information they do not want).
5. They feel they have control over what is done with the information.

Some people have realized that credit-card companies have been collecting data on their purchase behavior for years and that grocery stores are now able to collect very specific information about their purchases. Customers who use a frequent-buyer card may protest when they realize what information is being collected and how that information is used. One woman, for example, canceled her food-store loyalty card when she received a personal letter reminding her it was probably time to buy more tampons.[10]

Privacy and Situational Ethics

When your doctor asks you questions about your personal health, you are not likely to consider this an invasion of privacy. However, should the doctor ask you what your annual income is and what shares of stock you own, you may rightly feel that he or she has crossed the privacy line. When you are talking to your stockbroker, however, just the opposite is true. The point is that *privacy is situational*. When a company asks questions that do not seem relevant to its products or business dealings, then customers can become suspicious (which weakens trust).

Since medical records are moving from paper files in doctors' offices to electronic files, the possibility of a national health-record network exists. That will be great if you are traveling and need medical attention. If will not be so good if your family's secret about alcoholism, abortion, or venereal disease comes to light, and you are sent unsolicited product offers relating to one or more of these conditions. The Ethics and Issues box asks you to analyze different situations in terms of ethical behavior when collecting customer data.

ETHICS AND ISSUES

How Much Is Too Much?

Where should the line be drawn regarding collecting customer data? Following are several examples of things companies have done that have caused customers and consumer watchdog groups to complain. Keep in mind that when a brand is accused of violating the privacy of its customers, not only are relationships weakened but resulting negative publicity may weaken all of a brand's stakeholder relationships. How would you react in each of the following situations?

- A researcher developed a watch that could be activated by a microchip embedded in a magazine page. The watch would monitor how long a person was looking at the page. The inventor proposed that the device be given to a sample of a brand's customers and prospective customers. However, in order to get a more objective measurement, the company would not tell the customers about the watch's dual function.

- Porsche stirred up a storm when it sent a direct-mail piece to its upscale users. The copy in the mailing identified the prospects in terms of sensitive demographic information such as job title and income level.

- When Blockbuster Video announced that it was planning to sell information about its customers' viewing habits, it received letters from thousands of angry customers.

- A little-noticed section of the Health Care Portability and Accountability Act, passed by Congress in 1996, could make it easier for all kinds of strangers to find out if you've ever had a heart attack, an abortion, a medically treated depression, or a positive HIV test. A number of companies are already compiling information from consumers' medical records, so health secrets are not as secret as they used to be.

- Parents and legislators are particularly concerned when companies collect data on children. Legislation has been proposed to prevent companies from selling or purchasing personal information about a child without the consent of his or her parents.

An entire industry has grown up to collect data on millions of people from public and private sources. Information brokers dig through public records—birth certificates, court records, driver's licenses, real estate deeds, and change-of-address forms—to compile lists that they sell to direct-mail firms, retailers, insurers, lawyers, and private investigators. One of these vendors offers a service that searches more than 100 million records and can return with a person's Social Security number and other information that can be used by scam artists to set up phony bank and credit-card accounts, a crime known as "identity theft."

Think About It

What privacy issues do sensitive marketers who use database information have to consider? What practices are particularly irritating to many consumers?

Sources: Tom McNichol, "The New Privacy Wars," *USA Weekend*, May 16, 1996, p. 16–17; Ellyn E. Spragins and Mary Hager, "Naked Before the World," *Newsweek*, June 30, 1997, p. 84.

Ethical Data Use

Companies are becoming more sensitive, as well they should do, to the ethics of customer privacy. For example, Experian Information Solutions (formerly a unit of TRW) which maintains credit records on some 180 million Americans, has spent over $30 million in the last few years updating its computer network and launching programs to soothe customer concerns. This was partially in response to laws passed in several states requiring credit-reporting agencies (which provide credit checks of individuals for companies) to provide consumers a free copy of their credit record and information about the companies that have asked for checks on them. TRW's efforts led to an 80 percent reduction in mix-ups on financial data from people with similar names. "Consumers have interests in economic choices and privacy," says Martin E. Abrams, director of the former TRW's privacy and consumer policy. "Our job is to find an equilibrium between the two."[11]

Nike used a direct approach to addressing customers' feelings about privacy when it gave each purchaser of its All Conditions Gear a survey card. The headline, in large, bold print, asks, "Would you like to receive Nike publications?" Then several descriptions with "yes" or "no" replies are listed, for instance, "If Nike makes its mailing list available to other companies, do you wish to be included?" The options are immediately visible and well explained, giving the consumer the feeling that it's his or her own choice.

Major information companies such as Equifax even bank on the fact that companies will pay to know which customers do not want to hear from them. They compile lists of customers according to whether or not they wish to receive mail offers for different categories of products and services. This information is then sold to direct marketers so they can be more effective in their targeting.

Companies who want to respect their customers' privacy, build trust, and thus strengthen brand relationships need to put in place a privacy program. The steps for developing such a program are listed below. The department responsible for monitoring customer dialogue should be responsible for also monitoring the company's privacy program.

Steps in Developing a Privacy Program

1. Create a privacy policy.

2. Educate employees, especially those who "touch" the customer and handle customer profile data, about the policy.

3. Make customers and other stakeholders aware of the policy.

4. Know what customer information is being collected.

5. Know how this information is being used.

6. Provide customers with options for controlling how their personal data are used (especially if the company is in the practice of selling customer data).

7. Periodically ask customers if they have any concerns regarding the company's privacy policy. This will indicate to what extent the company is following its policy.

DESIGNING DATABASE PROGRAMS

The more information a company captures and stores in a database, the more expensive the database is to construct and maintain. Also, as the database increases in complexity, it becomes increasingly difficult to use. One of the most important considerations is to design a database management system that all the various people who need access to customer information can easily use. This task should be carried out by a cross-functional team so that all departments have input into what data to capture, what role they will play in capturing and using the data, and how the data will be configured for easiest retrieval by each user group. The Sun Microsystems ad in Exhibit 8–6 dramatizes this point.

Setting Up a Customer Database

Because tracking and capturing customer information is costly, the database setup must be clearly thought out ahead of time. The more complex a company's sales transactions and aftermarket service (service provided after a product, like a car, has been purchased), the more demands will be made of the database and the more important it is to consider the following questions before investing in a database management system.

1. *What data are needed? How much does the company need to know about prospects and current customers? What specific pieces of information are actionable?* Deciding what data to collect is one of the biggest challenges. Companies can be just like people who go through a cafeteria line and select much more than they can consume; what they can't use goes to waste. The challenge is to be realistic about what data will be used to make strategic decisions and what data would simply satisfy curiosity.

2. *How will the data be collected? From whom will it be collected? What are the least costly ways to obtain the desired data? How much can the company spend to collect customer data?* Although the cost of collecting data depends on the amount collected, data collection is definitely an expense. The way to minimize the cost is to have the data provider (whether an information company or a customer group) do as much of the data entry as possible. United Airlines, for example, does an annual survey of its high-volume flyers. If these customers respond to the survey online, they are rewarded with 2,000 frequent-flyer miles; however, if they chose to respond to a paper-and-pencil survey, they only receive 1,000 miles. The difference in the rewards reflects the fact that it cost United money to input the answers from the paper survey into the database whereas online survey answers go directly into the database.

3. *How will the data be stored? How much data can your system process and at what speed?* Data storage is conceptually similar to inventory storage. Both require a warehouse whose architecture determines its efficiency for various functions such as storing, assimilating, and keeping track of contents. Database designs are heavily influenced by either financial needs, production needs, or sales needs. The more manipulation that must occur to satisfy each of these area's needs, the more costly and time-consuming database management is. Therefore, it is important that marketing be involved in database planning to make sure that its information needs can be met.

4. *How will the data be used? What kinds of analyses will the company conduct? What kinds of decisions will be based on the results? What reports will be prepared directly from the database?* Marketing uses database information to determine lifetime customer value, calculate customer profitability, measure the extent of cross-category buying,

profile heavy buyers, and track frequency of complaints, inquiries, and compliments. Since 1990, Levi Strauss & Co. has been building a database of its customers. Through various direct-response techniques, such as toll-free numbers and sweepstakes, the company has created customer profiles. According to P. J. Santoro, the company's database marketing specialist, "Everything we find out about customers is being put on the database. It helps us identify where our customers live, their spending habits throughout their life cycles, finances, value of their home, and kind of car they drive."[12] The information has generated 50 different psychographic profiles. Levi Strauss has used this segmented list to do cooperative promotions with retailers (see Exhibit 8–7).

5. *Who will manage the database? Will the marketing department or information systems management be in charge? How user-friendly must the system be? What individuals and departments will have access to what information? Who will be able to add and delete information?* "Power used to mean that you controlled information. Now, power comes from providing greater access to the information," says Robert M. Howe, head of IBM's consulting business.[13] A survey of business-to-business marketers found that the marketing department handles the databases in 44 percent of companies, the information technology department in 15 percent, and both departments work together in 26 percent of companies.[14] At Kao, Japan's largest packaged-goods company, all marketing and sales managers have access to a database that contains shipping, point-of-purchase, market share, product cost, and qualitative consumer feedback information.

A major question every company must deal with is who will be allowed to add, delete, and change data in the database? The more people within a company who interact with customers, the more who need authority to change data. At the same time, the more people who are making changes to the database, the more opportunities there are for errors.

6. *How accurate and secure does the database need to be? How frequently does the information need to be updated? How confidential is the data?* The integrity of data can be a problem. A survey found that 61 percent of the respondents in one customer database had changed either their name, title, company affiliation, address, or phone number within the past year.[15] Because databases are becoming so valuable as corporate assets, security is also a major issue. Companies set up "firewalls" to prevent people from outside the company from getting into company databases. Inside the company, people are given passwords that allow them to access certain databases on the basis of job need.

EXHIBIT 8-7

This is an example of how two companies, Levi's and JC Penney, use profile data to do an online promotion.

Database Architecture

As shown in Figure 8–2, which visually depicts the architecture of a database, the simplest information is a customer's name and contact information—street address, city, zip code, fax, e-mail address, telephone number, and fax number. The next level of information is the customer's purchase history and record of responses to various promotional offers. Next are what are called enhancement data, which include demographic and lifestyle data about each customer or household. Then come records of specific interactions, including any repairs, returns, complaints, or inquiries the customer has made. The final data set details customer preferences (such as the information collected by British Airways).

The most sophisticated databases capture all of these elements and, furthermore, include such things as credit rating, use of customer service, preferred delivery schedules and methods, and status of current order.

Until recent years, most executives felt that creating and using customer databases could be justified only for business-to-business and high-ticket consumer products. But as the cost of database use continues to fall, this is changing. Over half of the major packaged-goods companies in the United States have built or are building consumer databases.[16]

Collecting Customer Data

Building a good customer database is easier for some companies than for others. Most BtB companies automatically record customer names, addresses, and phone numbers and maintain a history of transactions as a regular part of doing business. There are also many consumer product categories, especially services, where customer data are automatically collected in the course of doing business. Inter-Continental Hotels and Resorts, for example, compiles a multitude of valuable data every time a customer reserves a room or checks in; however, it has discovered that its customer information database was cumbersome and difficult to access for marketing purposes. To correct this, the company designed a global marketing initiative designed to provide a standard procedure for creating and managing its customer database. Customer information is now captured from 80-plus hotels all over the world and is transferred electronically every week to its central customer database. For a recent five-year period, the database processed over 5.9 million stays, aggregated this data, and developed customer profiles and interaction history for 2.9 million guests.[17]

FIGURE 8-2

Generally speaking, the more data collected about a customer, the more personal it will be.

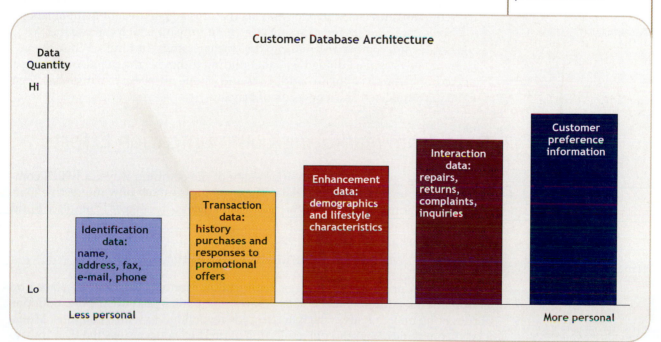

Customer Database Architecture

Scanner Data

Often the most important customer information is derived from the sale itself. For consumer goods and services, point-of-purchase (also called point-of-sale) information is gathered at the retail level by chains that have frequent-buyer programs and by research companies such as ACNielsen Corporation and Information Resources, Inc. Most chains encourage customers to have a frequent-buyer card scanned each time they shop at one of their stores. To get a card, consumers fill out an application that requires them to provide demographic and lifestyle information. This information is then cross-listed with each customer's purchases.

Companies motivate customers to use their cards by offering them frequent promotional deals (available only to cardholders) or rewards when they reach certain levels of spending within a specified time period.

Retailers not only use scanner-built databases for their own marketing efforts but also sell the data to manufacturers. Kraft Foods, for example, collects demographic and product-buying information for customers from over 30,000 food stores. For many years, Radio Shack has simply asked customers for basic information—address and phone number—as the sale is made. Other means of gathering information as part of a transaction include the following:

- *Proprietary credit cards.* Many retailers have long offered their own credit cards, primarily to capture reliable information about customer purchasing patterns.

- *Membership programs with ID cards.* Online computer equipment retailer and auctioneer Egghead.com tracks sales through the use of a scanner card. Each time a customer uses the Egghead card, he or she receives an automatic 5 percent discount on purchases. The company has issued over 1 million cards; to obtain one, a customer has to fill out an extensive questionnaire. This information, in turn, is used to develop customized quarterly newsletters. Exhibit 8–8 is an example of the questionnaire that British Airways uses to collect customer data from those who join its Travel Service.

- *Credit bureau appending services.* When a retailer does not have its own frequent-buyer card, it can build a customer database by taking names from credit-card and check purchases. This requires a great deal of manual labor. Credit-card charges must be sent to a credit bureau, which can use the charge-card number and name to find the customer's address. While there are no laws against doing this data building in-house, the practice of using a credit bureau to "append" addresses and phone numbers to names has been heavily criticized as an invasion of privacy.

Data from Marketing Communication Efforts

The following subsections summarize some of the common ways in which companies collect and use customer data. These examples show how interactive marketing communication programs not only deliver messages but also build customer relationships.

Coupons, Sweepstakes, and Promotional Offers

With modern printing technology, identification numbers can now be placed on coupons and address labels. This allows companies that distribute coupons through the mail to know which households responded to which coupons. Multibrand companies that send out a selection of product coupons use the ID numbers to determine which households are redeeming coupons for baby products, dog food, diet foods, snack foods, or other products. This information gives a company opportunities for cross-selling additional products where appropriate. For example, a household that is a heavy consumer of diet foods is likely to be a poor prospect for snack items; a company can thus save money by not sending coupons for snack foods to those households.

Promotional offers should be designed to identify potential customers, not just those interested in getting free merchandise. Responses that request informational pamphlets on product-related subjects, for example, identify serious prospects. Crayon and marker manufacturer Crayola generated names by running a sweepstakes in its first free-standing insert (FSI), a manufacturer-produced flyer inserted into a newspaper. Parents could enter by filling in a coupon with their children's names, birthdates, addresses, and phone numbers. In return, each child received two free Crayola markers. The company received approximately 400,000 coupons—that is, 400,000 names of current and prospective customers.[18]

Warranty Cards

Gates Energy Products offered $20 rebate coupons to encourage consumers to return product registration cards when it introduced its new rechargeable batteries. The company used this information to market its products directly to customers, thus bypassing the retailer.

EXHIBIT 8-8

The British Airways Travel Service used a questionnaire to gather new customer information. To motivate people to respond, the questionnaire was supported with a drawing for free travel for two from London to New York.

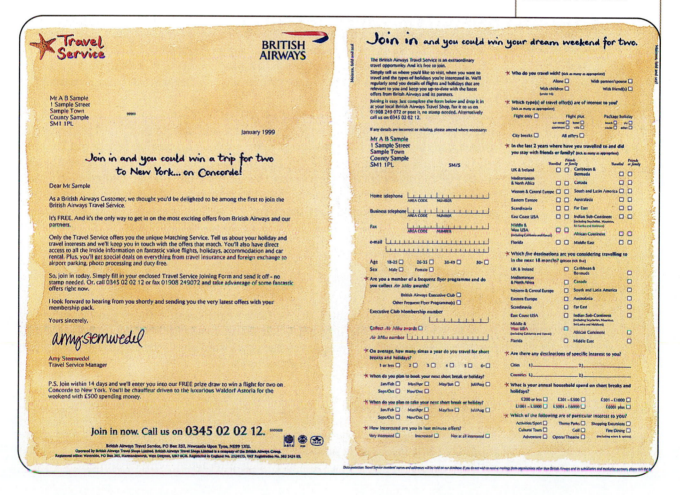

Membership Clubs

Toymaker Mattel has been gathering names through its Magic Nursery line. After purchasing or receiving a doll, the child sends in the name she's given it, and her address, age, and the store where it was purchased. In return, the child receives a Mother's Day card signed with the baby's name and a coupon. When the company introduced another doll into the product line, those children in areas where the doll was available received an announcement. Mattel has also used the list, containing approximately 100,000 names, to mail out coupons for its Barbie line.

The Swiss watchmaker Swatch started a collectors club in 1993, which is promoted in more than 500 designated "collector" stores in Europe. Collectors pay approximately $80 a year for membership. In return, they receive a laundry list of special privileges: a Swatch watch produced exclusively for club members; a catalog of every Swatch watch ever produced; special offers on collectible watches and accessories like T-shirts and artwork; invitations to attend at least six special events a year, which include special travel and hotel arrangements; VIP seating at Swatch-sponsored music concerts, some of them held exclusively for members; and the quarterly *Swatch World Journal* with information on all new product launches and styles. The club boasts more than 100,000 members in seven European countries and the United States. Ten thousand of them showed up for an exclusive rock concert in Italy.

Catalogs

Bloomingdale's, the New York–based department store, produces approximately 300 different catalogs and promotional mailings per year. Customer purchases are tracked to determine who receives which offers. Someone who bought a men's suit would receive notice about a sale on men's accessories. The data collected have revealed that 75 percent of the company's business comes from 25 percent of its customers.

Little Tikes, which makes a large variety of toys for young children, uses its mailing list to send a catalog twice a year, although customers cannot purchase directly from the catalog but must go to retail stores. The catalog is sent out to those who have called the company's toll-free number (featured in all advertising and on all packaging) and asked to be on the mailing list—a list that contains over 1 million names. When customers call, the company collects information on the ages of the children and whether the caller is a parent or grandparent. In addition, minicatalogs are placed in all toy packaging along with information on how to join the mailing list.

Toll-Free Numbers

Health Valley Foods was able to move from health food stores to grocery stores by tracking consumers. The company collected names from letters and calls to a toll-free number. Once a loyal customer base was established, the company was able to show supermarkets that its products would sell.

E-Mail and Websites

Many companies have created websites, chat rooms, user groups, and Web communities for users of their products or people wanting information. These are excellent vehicles for collecting data as well as interacting with customers.

Surveys

Our Own Hardware, a 1,200-store, 24-state chain, uses an electronic survey box in each of its stores. In return for sharing their names, addresses, preferences, and purchasing information, customers receive on-the-spot discounts and coupons.

Relationship Tracking

In some product categories, companies need to make special efforts in order to identify customers and learn more about them. In other words, tracking is easier to do in some categories than in others. This is an important consideration in the decision to invest in an expensive database management system. Table 8–2 lists product categories where tracking customer interactions are easy and those categories where it is more difficult.

When a company's primary customers are distributors or retailers, it must make special efforts to gather information about its products' end users. One way to do this is through establishing partnerships with retailers. Motorola, for example, rewards its dealers with points for acquiring new customers. To get these reward points, dealers must supply Motorola with information on these new customers. The company not only puts this information into its customer database but also sends these new customers $100 certificates that they can redeem at their local dealer when they refer a new customer to that dealer. In this partnership effort, Motorola owns the database and the retailers benefit from a customer-acquisition incentive program.

There are some manufacturers of packaged goods who say that they cannot justify the cost of building a database of end users. What they overlook is that it is not necessary to track every single customer but only the most profitable ones. As

---

T A B L E   8 - 2   Tracking Relationships

Easy-to-Track Product Categories
- Financial institutions: banks, brokers, insurance
- Monopolies: public utilities
- Contractual services: club memberships, trash removal, lawn care
- Personalized services: doctor, dentist, lawyer, hair care, car repair
- Big-ticket goods: real estate, cars
- Retail stores with their own charge cards: department and specialty stores
- Rental agencies: video, car, hotel, sporting equipment
- Direct-response companies: mail order, telemarketing, online services
- Business-to-business companies

Difficult-to-Track Product Categories
- Packaged goods and consumer durables
- Retail stores: food, drug, discount
- Retail services: restaurants, movie theaters, dry cleaners
- Products bought in bulk by a company that are then passed out to employees (e.g., cell phones, laptop computers, company cars, uniforms)

EXHIBIT 8-9

Marketed to college students, this Coke Card promotion contains a list of partner businesses— restaurants, clothing stores, movies and video rental stores, e-commerce companies, and many more—where the Coke Card delivers discounts.

explained before, a relatively small percentage of customers accounts for the majority of sales and profits. Therefore, rather than trying to track all customers, these manufacturers should begin by trying to identify their heavy users. The Coke Card in Exhibit 8–9 rewards customers with discounts from Coke's marketing partners. This is the first step in Coke's effort to build a database of its loyal customers.

Consider a mass marketer like Colgate-Palmolive. Although it cannot justify individually capturing and responding to every purchase of its many product varieties, the company can use retail store scanner data to identify and respond to heavy-user households of its bar soaps, toothpastes, shaving lotions, and so on. Collective sales can amount to as much as $400 a year per household. With this type of customer information, it now becomes cost-effective for Colgate-Palmolive to mass-customize and reward brand-loyal customers for their past business (with special high-value coupons, for example), and to motivate them to buy even more of the company's brands and products. Manufacturers of consumer products can also create affinity clubs, which are manufacturer-sponsored clubs like the one Procter & Gamble sponsors for mothers who buy Pampers.

Data Overlays

It is not always necessary for a company to invest in gathering *all* the desired customer profile information, especially for consumer packaged goods. Often this additional data can be rented from outside sources such as Equifax. The new data are then "overlaid" on a company's customer database. **Data overlay**, thus means *enriching one database by adding another to it.* For example, the Polk Company, which specializes in gathering information related to the automotive industry, captures new car purchase information. Equifax, which bought Polk's Consumer Information Solutions division in 2000, collects and processes "warranty card" profiles. The latter are the cards you get when you purchase appliances and other consumer goods such as cameras and suitcases. The cards ask where the product was purchased, the price, if it was on sale, if you bought it or received it as a gift, plus several demographic and psychographic questions. Most warranty cards also contain a few questions that relate directly to the brand and product bought.

Companies such as Samsonite and Canon hire companies such as Equifax to tabulate and analyze these cards. All of the data collected are given back to the respective companies, including responses to the specialized questions. The company then uses the demographic and psychographic data to expand and update its national household database (e.g., overlays the new data), which it sells to other companies who are willing to pay for such information. For example, Kodak could buy names of households that have expressed an interest in photography (a general category question) but could not buy responses to Canon's specialized questions.

Data Mining

As the Technology in Action box illustrates, companies too often do not make use of data they already have that could improve their customer communications. Completed warranty cards are often filed away and are never used as a source of

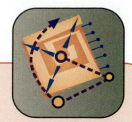

TECHNOLOGY IN ACTION

The Data Gold Mine

The full-service brokerage firm Paine Webber learned the value of customer databases when, with the help of its advertising agency, Saatchi & Saatchi, it did a communication audit of its customers. Although the company knew how many *accounts* it had, it did not know how many *actual customers* it had, because it didn't know which customers had more than one account. It also didn't know the characteristics of customers who had more than one account. Consequently, it was not able to efficiently focus its efforts on growing its current customers.

Paine Webber, like many other companies, was ignoring the fact that the data already in its possession could be extremely valuable in developing more profitable business strategies. It preferred to market each of its products to the "average customer," overlooking the fact that many of these people were already buying more than one of its products.

Saatchi's audit discovered that Paine Webbers's 1.8 million accounts were held by 717,000 individual customers. This revelation resulted in significant savings in the company's marketing communication, not to mention the reduction in customer aggravation from continually receiving multiple mailings and being offered products that they already had purchased. The audit identified the penetration of the 22 products by each customer, making it possible to begin a customized cross-selling program. It also enabled Paine Webber to identify its most profitable customers and their lifetime customer value. Finally, by combining databases, the company was able to identify which of its products were most effective as "beachheads" for selling related products.

As a result of Saatchi's audit, Paine Webber's marketing communication strategies became better focused and its targeting more precise. The analysis involved data that were already captured but not fully utilized by the company's marketing department. In other words, Paine Webber only needed to mine its own gold (see Exhibit 8-10).

Think About It

How did Paine Webber go about analyzing what data it collected and how the data were used? How was the Saatchi & Saatchi agency able to use the information from its audit to help Paine Webber turn data into communication strategies?

Source: Saatchi & Saatchi promotional piece (no date).

EXHIBIT 8-10

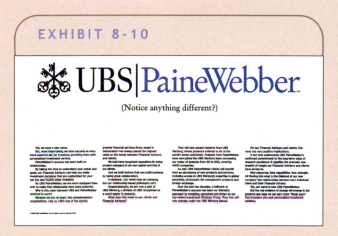

---

vital data for customer profiling. After rebate offers are fulfilled, the forms are often destroyed and thus vital customer information is lost.

Data mining is a useful metaphor for *the sifting and sorting of the information warehoused in a company's database.* The purpose of data mining is to spot trends, relationships (e.g., heavy users buy less frequently than the average customer but in larger quantities), and other nuggets of information and insights in order to make better marketing decisions. The following subsections contain examples of the types of information and insights that can be gained by digging into customer databases and analyzing the information for insights. Data mining can help marketers accomplish one of their most important responsibilities, which is customer segmentation.

Customer Gains and Losses

Companies should examine data related to both new customers and lost customers to see if there are obvious similarities or differences. For example, a provider of office cleaning services might use data on hand to find that most of its new customers are small firms and those that are being lost are large companies. Such a finding would suggest further research is needed to determine why this is happening.

Acquisition and Retention Costs

By analyzing how many new customers were brought in by a particular marketing communication program, the cost of the program, and the profitability of these first-time sales, a company can determine its customer acquisition costs. The same type of analysis can be done for sales made to current customers; the result is called retention cost.

Customer Profitability Analysis

Customer profitability analysis involves tracking customer interactions with the company, and finding out what marketing communication each customer has been exposed to (so that a prorated cost can be applied). This involves mining both sales data and customer-service data. Profitability analysis requires the help of the accounting department, which understands the procedures that capture customer-service costs. As discussed in Chapter 6, more and more companies are finding it useful to determine the lifetime customer value (LTCV) of their customers. Gerber, the baby-food manufacturer, knows that the average baby consumes about 600 jars of baby food before he or she progresses to solid food. If Gerber is able to keep a baby's mother loyal to Gerber during this period of the baby's growing up, that baby's LTCV to Gerber could be $350 to $400.

Evaluation of MC Offers and Campaigns

Major offers and campaign ideas should be tested whenever possible. By tracking these efforts, determining which customers responded and to what extent they responded, and knowing the cost of the offer or campaign, a company can determine each promotional program's success or failure.

Analysis of Purchasing Patterns

Customers often vary in their purchase behavior by season, occasion, frequency of purchases, and quantity purchased per transaction. The more a company can identify these, the more strategic planning it can do. For example, if a company finds that one-third of its customers buy only once a year, but the average customer buys once a month, it can design an MC program specifically geared to the infrequent buyer.

Geographical Sales Analysis

A **geographical information system (GIS)** is *a software program that combines geographical databases with customer databases and analyzes sales and other transactions based on geography.* This type of information helps marketers determine where to deliver different types of brand messages. When a discount store like Target learns that it is pulling heavily from areas to its north and west, but not pulling as well from neighborhoods to its south and east, it can either increase its marketing communication activities in these underdeveloped areas or focus on its current heavy users in the developed areas.

GIS information can also help a company choose the types of messages to use. A GIS report might show that the reason the Target store is attracting a lower percentage of customers from the south and east neighborhoods is that those areas are close to Kmart and Wal-Mart stores. Knowing this, Target can use competitive messages in these areas specifically designed to lure customers away from Wal-Mart and Kmart.

GIS also includes such things as traffic patterns and traffic density by day of the week and even times of the day. By combining such information with customer data, retailers can determine when and where to place MC messages. Fast-food stores, for example, use traffic flow analysis to determine where to place outdoor boards that help direct customers to the store (e.g., "Burger King 2 miles east on Interstate 65").

An ongoing challenge to companies using mass media advertising is to determine to what extent the media's geographic coverage is consistent with the brand's distribution. GIS can help answer this question by overlaying the reach of the various media used with a map of its distribution points. It can also show how far customers will travel in response to certain promotions and from which specific areas they come.

Channel Analysis

Most manufacturers distribute their products through a variety of channels. But which channels operate the most efficiently? Which are the most profitable? Channel analysis reminds manufacturers that customers are not always the end users of their products. Sometimes, it is more important to those that sell to intermediaries to have databases of their channel members than it is to have databases of end users. The findings from channel analysis enable companies to reward those channel members that are being exceptionally supportive and to design new communication programs to help improve the performance of those that are underperforming.

Data Maintenance

Companies should think of their customer databases as living, dynamic entities. In order for a database to be healthy and grow, it needs to be fed and cared for just like a living creature. A database containing only names and addresses is suffering from malnutrition and will not support sophisticated marketing communication activities. Customer databases need to be maintained and updated because customer needs and wants, buying patterns, and key personnel (particularly important in BtB marketing) are constantly changing.

Database maintenance includes such things as merging and purging and data integration. **Merge/purge** is *a process that eliminates duplications in a database*. It is necessary anytime two or more customer files are combined. For example, a company interested in renting customer databases of outdoor sports enthusiasts would need to do a merge/purge of all the lists rented because heavy users of outdoor equipment most likely buy from many different outdoor equipment companies. Performing a merge/purge operation prevents a company from sending duplicate offers to the same customer—which saves money and keeps the company from looking foolish and disorganized.

HOW TO MANAGE AND USE CUSTOMER DATABASES

FIGURE 8-3

Marketing/customer databases are the core of IMC.

Source: John O'Connor and Eamonn Galvin, *Marketing and Information Technology* (London: Pitman, 1997), p. 84.

Databases can be used in a number of critical points in the management of a marketing communication campaign as shown in Figure 8–3: analysis, planning, contact, response, follow-up, and monitoring. The figure also identifies the functions and media used at each stage.

Having good customer databases, unfortunately, doesn't guarantee that they are fully utilized. A survey of BtB marketers found that 85 percent use their marketing databases only for building and using a customer and prospect mailing list.[19] Another survey of 179 companies found that less than a third were using their databases to profile and segment customers according to their buying habits. Some of the reasons for underutilization of databases are that they have not been designed with marketing in mind; marketing people have not taken the time to learn how to use the databases; databases have not been properly managed,

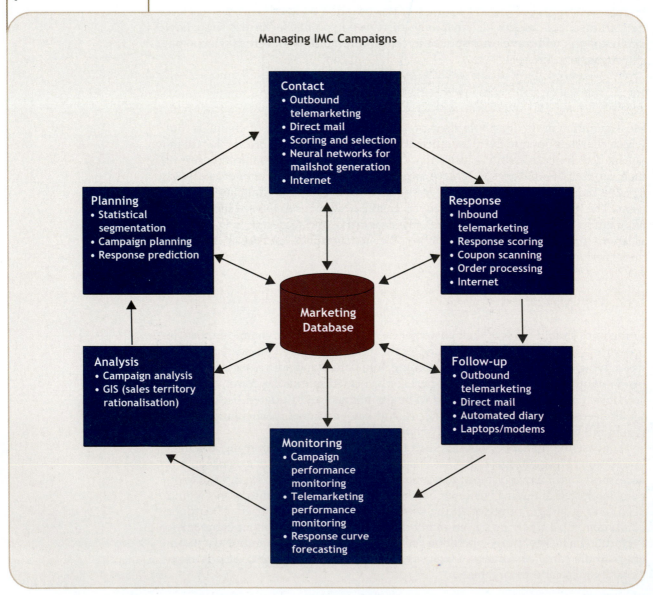

Managing IMC Campaigns

Contact
- Outbound telemarketing
- Direct mail
- Scoring and selection
- Neural networks for mailshot generation
- Internet

Planning
- Statistical segmentation
- Campaign planning
- Response prediction

Response
- Inbound telemarketing
- Response scoring
- Coupon scanning
- Order processing
- Internet

Marketing Database

Analysis
- Campaign analysis
- GIS (sales territory rationalisation)

Follow-up
- Outbound telemarketing
- Direct mail
- Automated diary
- Laptops/modems

Monitoring
- Campaign performance monitoring
- Telemarketing performance monitoring
- Response curve forecasting

resulting in inaccurate and out-of-date data; and marketing has not been allowed to access the databases in a meaningful way.

Using Databases to Manage Relationship Stages

Customer databases can be used at each stage of brand relationships: acquisition, retention, growth, and reacquisition (i.e., recovery of lost customers). Generally a single database can contain all the information that is needed for developing strategies and tactics at each relationship stage.

Acquisition Programs

When putting together a data-driven customer acquisition program, the first thing a company should do (as explained earlier) is to examine the profiles of its most profitable customers to identify their common demographic and lifestyle characteristics. It can then use these characteristics to find prospective customers. A practice called **prospecting** (*using data on hand to identify prospective customers types*), fits in with the data mining metaphor. Prospecting works for both consumer and BtB marketing.

Once a company has found commonalities of profitable customers, it can then go to a list broker for help in finding the lists that most closely match.

The *Courier*, a newspaper in Evansville, Indiana, used this data-driven technique to determine how to attract more subscriptions. It identified three distinct profiles of current subscribers. Since subscriptions do not vary in price, the criterion of "most profitable" was determined by the number of years households had been subscribers—the more years, the more profitable. The *Courier* then sent a promotional offer to 1,000 prospective households in each of the three profiles. All were offered a 30-day trial subscription. The lowest response rate was 24 percent, the highest 82 percent. As a result of that test, the newspaper decided to concentrate its marketing efforts on nonsubscribers who matched the highest response segment's profile. The IMC Strategy box illustrates how such acquisition programs can be designed.

Retention Programs

In retention programs, listening to customers is as important, if not more so, than talking to them. Some business-to-business companies are now making a special effort to ask customers when and how they would like to be contacted by the company. This information is placed in the customer database so it is readily accessible when doing one-to-one messaging. This shows respect for the loyal customer's time and schedule, and allows him or her to direct the brand communication in a positive way.

But just listening isn't enough. Companies must respond and in some cases make changes when what they hear indicates problems or opportunities. Figure 8–4 shows how a customer database can be used for doing "exception analyses." This type of analysis uses a special software program to periodically scan the database and indicate when an above-average number of complaints, inquiries, or compliments have been received within a certain period. The critical number will vary depending on the size of the customer base and product category. Note that the database captures all interactions, not just sales, with input from customer contacts handled by marketing, sales, and customer service.

IMC STRATEGY

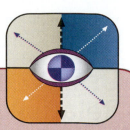

Skiing Goes Downhill

In the 1990s, the U.S. ski industry began to be concerned that the number of skiers nationwide had stayed level, at approximately 5 percent of the population, for the past 10 years. In a speech at a ski industry conference, the CEO of a major ski area said one of the reasons the industry was getting fewer new customers was that most of the marketing communication was in such publications as *Ski* and *Skiing*, aimed at current skiers, with each resort simply trying to steal customers from all the others. To get new skiers, he recommended reaching nonskiers by advertising in magazines such as *Time*, *Newsweek*, and *People*. Unfortunately, his recommendation was not a good one. These recommended magazines appeal to mass audiences that, if anything, lean toward older readers (especially *Time* and *Newsweek*) and have few key characteristics similar to skiers, other than income.

What the CEO should have recommended was that the ski industry analyze its customer databases to identify the key characteristics of its current heavy skiers, and then look for groups of nonskiers who had similar characteristics. Heavy skiers may be those who like outdoor sports, enjoy many short vacations throughout the year as opposed to one long one, are college graduates and are single or are young couples without kids. The heavy skier profile can be used to find similar groups that might include rock climbers, bicyclists, amateur pilots, hikers, tennis players, in-line skaters, and owners of cross-country motorcycles. Advertising in magazines that reach these groups could easily result in response rates several times higher than would result from advertising in the mass-market magazines that go to "everyone."

Think About It

What information led ski resort managers to advertise in ski publications and general interest publications? What information might be used to better target advertising to acquire new customers?

Excessive inquiries about a product or subject—such as "How do I eject a disk without turning off my computer?" or "Have my parts been shipped yet?"—indicate that either more information needs to be made available to customers or the product needs to be redesigned so that it stimulates fewer questions about its use. To illustrate, NEC, a manufacturer of computers and monitors, ran an "exception analysis" of its customer database and found that it was receiving 1,500 calls a month from customers saying they couldn't get their CD-ROM to read. As it turned out, in nearly every one of the cases, the caller had forgotten to insert the CD into the disk drive. Although this sounds like a small thing, each customer service call was costing NEC about $20 to handle. After discussions with its research and development team, NEC decided to add a small display panel to the front of the monitors that indicated whether or not a disk had been inserted. This change virtually eliminated calls for this problem, saving the company approximately $360,000 a year, far less than the cost of the minor modification to this product.[20]

When an above-average number of compliments are recorded in a given period, the company should examine them to see if they relate to some benefit of the product that could be further leveraged in the brand's marketing communication messages. Compliments should also be forwarded to the departments and people responsible for them as a way of recognizing good work and praising employees. Increased morale improves customer service and lowers the number of product defects.

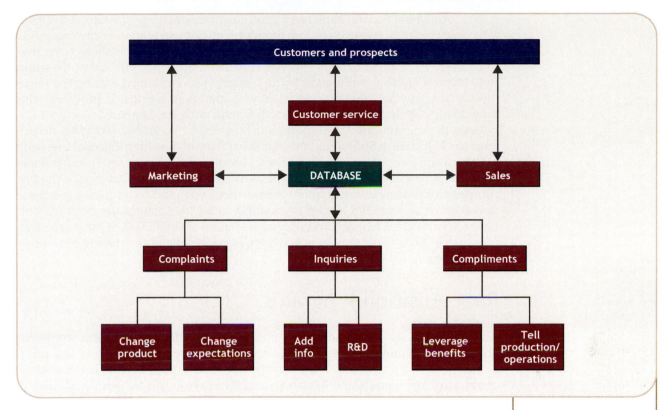

FIGURE 8-4

This illustrates sources of customer data and how data can affect operations.

Source: Tom Duncan and Sandra Moriarity, *Driving Brand Value: Using Integrated Marketing to Manage Profitable Stakeholder Relationships* (New York: McGraw-Hill, 1997), p. 216.

All companies, no matter how good they are, receive complaints. What is critical, therefore, is to note when too many are being received about a particular good or service. Negative exception reports act as an early warning system. Complaints indicate that either the company's products or customer handling methods are faulty or that customer expectations are not being properly managed. As explained in Chapter 2, managing expectations is one of the primary responsibilities of marketing communications.

Here's an example: A national car rental company, soon after putting a new fleet of cars into service, sees that customer complaints about the lack of certain features are increasing month to month. The company can decide whether the cars need to be upgraded or the MC messages need to be changed to lower customer expectations of the cars' features. One possibility would be an MC campaign stressing that economy cars mean economy rates.

Customer Growth Programs

Growth programs encourage current customers to give a brand a greater share of their category spending. Consumer panel data, collected by independent information companies, can show a company's share of customers' category spending. For BtB companies, average customer category spending is often available from industry associations as well as from independent research studies.

The Hertz Gold Club, designed for business travelers who need rental cars at airports, charges a $50 annual membership fee (though for very frequent flyers the fee is waived). Gold Club services include being picked up at airline terminals and taken directly to the rental car. Often the car's motor is running, the heat or air conditioning is on, and the trunk is up waiting for the luggage—value-added brand services that motivate customers to increase the frequency of using Hertz.

California First Federal bank has a good customer database and uses it to cross-sell other products. Banks often lose money on customers who use only one product such as a checking or savings account. By cross-selling, Cal Fed has been able to decrease its number of single-service customers by 11 percent and at the same time increase customer retention by 58 percent.[21] As explained earlier, the more links a company has with its customers (e.g., the more services it provides), the more likely it is that those customers will remain with the company.

Growth programs are also important in business-to-business marketing. An example is Meridian, a $100-million-a-year subsidiary of Northern Telecom that sells high-tech software systems to businesses. Meridian pulled from its customer database five potential customers for one of its software products. Each was invited to complete a needs-assessment questionnaire. Four companies completed the questionnaire, three attended a sales presentation, and two bought the product. The payback from these two contacts was sales of more than $75,000.[22] One reason this was such a successful program is that there was virtually no marketing communication waste.

Reacquisition Programs

Customers will leave a brand for any number of reasons. Reacquisition programs, however, can minimize the ultimate loss. Because these programs by nature must be customized, it means they are relatively expensive to administer. Therefore, they can be most appropriate in BtB dealings and for expensive or frequently purchased consumer goods and services. Recognizing how critical this area is, Ford-Mexico, for example, has a department called Customer Recovery. Its responsibility is to research and develop communication strategies for getting former Ford customers, who have bought another car brand, to once again buy a Ford-made car. At the other extreme are small businesses such as beauty shops. Hairdressers who keep a database of their customers can quickly determine when customers are overdue for their next appointment. Reminder phone calls to these people can determine whether they have simply forgotten to make an appointment or have in fact switched salons.

Some former customers are impossible to reacquire, such as those who have moved out of the shopping area or, in the case of a BtB, gone out of business. But most often, customers who quit buying have switched to another brand or to another company because they were dissatisfied.

The first step in customer recovery is to determine as quickly as possible when a customer is no longer a customer. Because customer databases capture purchases, computers can be programmed to periodically examine transaction frequencies and create a list of all customers who have not made a purchase within a set number of days, weeks, or months. Also, since each customer generally has a certain purchase frequency, software can be used to determine when each customer's purchase frequency has been broken. After a certain nonbuying period, these customers' files should be flagged.

Once lapsed customers are identified, the next step is to contact them to determine why they have stopped buying. In some cases, the mere act of contacting lost customers and showing an interest in them is enough to bring them back. Those who are no longer in the product category can be forgotten. But for that majority who have had a bad brand experience, the next step is to determine why this occurred. Competing long-distance phones companies, for example, have found that perceived or actual cost savings have caused some customers to switch carriers and have therefore offered lost customers up to $100 for switching back.

Reasons for leaving need to be captured into the database and periodically analyzed. As with other complaints, when a particular reason appears more frequently than expected, it is time the relevant operational, manufacturing, or customer service procedures are reexamined and revised or brought back into standards. Although, as mentioned above, recovery programs are relatively expensive, many companies have found that recovered customers are more loyal and profitable than are average customers who never left.

Personalizing the Message

Once a company has mined and analyzed its customer and prospect data, the next step, especially for BtB and certain consumer goods and service companies, is to design and execute marketing communication efforts that include personalized brand messages.

You have most likely received phone calls and mailings in which your name has been inserted into what is obviously a form message. Although you probably recognize right away that this is not really a personal message, the technique, which uses a database to match names to phone numbers and addresses, can significantly increase the level of response. Nevertheless, it remains the lowest level of message personalization (see Figure 8–5).

At the second level, personalized brand messages refer to some aspect of a customer's interaction with a company, such as a previous transaction, complaint, or inquiry. Clothing retailer Gap, for example, captures transaction information for all charge-card purchases. The chain can then program its computers to find, say, all customers who have purchased sportswear in early spring for the last three years. A computer-written but personalized letter can be sent to each of these, noting their habit of buying sportswear each spring and even referring to specific items purchased. The primary purpose of the letter may be to invite these customers to a special showing of this year's newly arrived spring sportswear or to make some other special offer.

The term **mass customization** has been used to describe *the process of personalizing customer interaction with a company on a large scale.* To the customer, these letters, e-mails, and telemarketing calls can be made to seem personal because there is

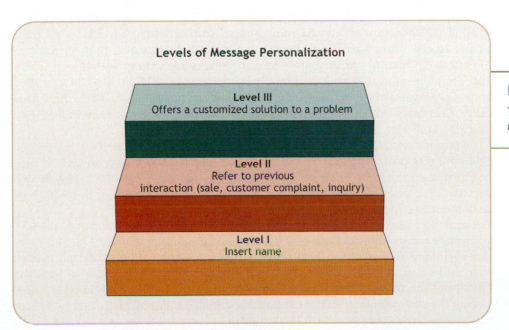

Levels of Message Personalization

Level III
Offers a customized solution to a problem

Level II
Refer to previous
interaction (sale, customer complaint, inquiry)

Level I
Insert name

FIGURE 8-5

There are various levels of message personalizations.

customer-specific information in them. However, they were created by simply grouping all those customers with like behavior (buying each spring), referring to specific items purchased from the customer's purchase history in the database, and making a common offer (come to special spring showing and have first choice of the new spring fashions).

The third and highest level of personalized messages are those that address an individual customer's specific problem. These are most common in BtB messaging where salespeople have learned enough about their customers and prospects to formulate a solution to a particular company's problem or overlooked opportunity. But they can also be used for some consumer products. Take an insurance company, for example, that keeps an up-to-date database of all its policyholders, including names and birthdates of children. When a policyholder's child turns 16, the insurance company automatically sends a computer-generated letter offering car insurance for the new driver in the family. The policyholder sees this as a personal letter (even though it was computer generated) and welcomes the reminder. Customized brand messages are also seen as less intrusive than run-of-the-mill junk mail.

Southern California Gas Company used its database to identify customers who had large differences between their summer and winter utility bills, creating problems in the months when the bills were high. These customers were targeted for a level payment plan that averaged payments over a 12-month period. By allowing customers to level out their monthly payments, the company was able to add value to its service. Personalization of the communication ensured a high response rate for the payment-plan program.

Customer Recognition and Reward

When a company is able to recognize customers by remembering who they are and how they have interacted with the company, it adds value to its brands. Both BtB customers and individuals appreciate being remembered and recognized. Harris Bank's emphasis on collecting customer information and using that information to provide personalized communication and services, for example, has resulted in an average customer relationship of 20 years versus the industry average of only 4 years.[23]

Another example is Domino's Pizza. Domino's has installed a caller ID system in all of its 700 company-owned and operated stores and close to half of its franchised stores. The system is tied in to a customer database so that repeat customers' order histories immediately come up on a screen along with their address and phone number. Those in a hurry have only to say "The usual" before they hang up because the screen has all the necessary information. For a first-time caller, Domino's can have his or her name and address on the screen in less than four rings (as long as the caller has a listed phone number).

Databases also allow companies to do more than just recognize their customers. Companies that surprise and delight their high-profit customers with reward programs are more likely to keep these customers for the long term. The British Airways Travel Service program, for example, provides discounts to its best customers (see Exhibit 8–11).

Department store chain Neiman Marcus discovered that even affluent customers appreciate recognition and rewards. The retailer annually rewards its most important customers with a free airline trip for two plus a lunch with the local store manager. In its ongoing customer-satisfaction research with these big spenders, the lunch, not the trip, is usually mentioned as being the more appreciated reward; having the store manager sit across the table and call them by name is much more valuable to these customers than the airline tickets are.

Traditional retailer Sears has used a simple, low-cost customer database method to strengthen brand relationships with top customers: It identified and sent top customers a small, pressure-sensitive "Best Customer" label to put on their Sears charge cards. Employees were instructed to give these customers special attention, such as personally introducing the customers to the department or store manager or making a special effort to point out items on sale.

A FINAL NOTE: RELATIONSHIP MEMORY

EXHIBIT 8-11

This mailing by the British Airways Travel Service offered select customers a 10 percent saving on travel costs.

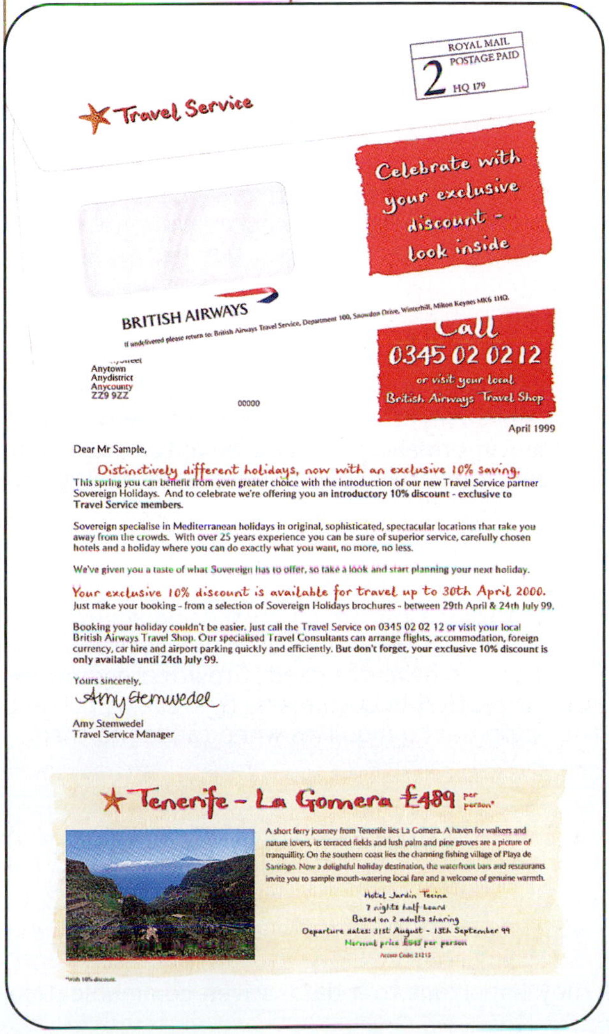

In data-driven communication, the proper focus is not on information technology and information systems but rather on how these systems are integrated into marketing communication activities. The British Airways campaign described in the chapter opening case was so successful because it created bonds with its customers.

In a similar vein, a company may have a large sales force, several of whom call on the same clients. Without a common database, one sales rep cannot know what another sales rep has promised and sold. All of them may find they are competing with each other or that they are wasting the customer's time by making duplicate presentations. Customer information files create "interaction memory" for the company and thus minimize duplication.

Consumers' brand perceptions and experiences are recorded in their memories; they learn something new with each new experience. Likewise, businesses can learn about their customers if transactions and interactions are recorded in their institutional memory. In order for there to be a successful relationship between a company and its customers, there needs to be a relationship memory on the company's side similar to the customer's memory.

Key Terms

customer relationship management (CRM) 275
database 276
database management system (DBMS) 278
operational database applications 281
analytical database applications 281
data overlay 292

data mining 293
geographical information system (GIS) 294
merge/purge 295
prospecting 297
mass customization 301

Key Point Summary

Identifying profitable customers and knowing how, when, and in what way they have interacted and want to interact with a company, depends on collecting information in an accessible database.

Key Point 1: Data-Driven Communication

A customer information system compiled as a database is the institutional memory system used by companies to become smarter in order to better meet the needs of its customers. Such an information system records, stores, aggregates, and shares customer and other stakeholder information throughout an organization. Using customer databases, a company can track and segment customers in order to make its marketing communication more efficient and effective. Capturing customer information makes it possible for companies to become learning organizations.

Key Point 2: Privacy and Security

Companies gather customer profile data in order to personalize their interactions with customers. Misuse of this personal data constitutes an invasion of privacy. Customers may worry that a company will either cross the privacy line or link their names with inaccurate data. The Direct Marketing Association has established guidelines for the ethical use of personal data (see pp. 281–282).

Key Point 3: Database Mining

Managing databases involves setting up systems, collecting data, and manipulating the databases. The hardware and software known as a database management system (DBMS) tracks customer interactions and links customer databases that are already in existence. Customer information is collected automatically at the point of purchase and through customer-initiated communication. Data overlay and data mining are techniques used to make the data more useful.

Key Point 4: Managing Customer Relationships

New customers are developed in acquisition programs through prospecting, which profiles heavy users to find potential new customers with matching characteristics. Retention programs identify ways to please current customers. Reacquisition programs seek to lure back those who have defected. Growth programs increase the purchase activity of regular customers and identify unprofitable customers. By tracking current customer behavior, companies can personalize messages and responses to inquiries when talking to them.

Lessons Learned

Key Point 1: Data-Driven Communication

a. What do the initials IS and IT stand for, and why are they important to a data-driven communication program?
b. Define and explain the word *database*.

c. Define the term *learning organization* and give an example.
d. Explain how databases are used by a learning organization.
e. Explain how large and small companies might use databases in an IMC program.
f. Explain the difference between operational and analytical database applications.

Key Point 2: Privacy and Security

a. What are two major consumer concerns about privacy?
b. What is situational ethics, and how does the concept apply to database programs?
c. What is "identity theft," and how does it tie in to database management?
d. What can a company do to make sure its database program is responsive to privacy issues?

Key Point 3: Database Mining

a. Why is a cross-functional team needed in designing a database systems?
b. What are the six decisions that need to be made in setting up a database program?
c. Explain two ways customer data can be collected, and give examples of each.
d. What is the purpose of data mining? Give an example of how it can be used to develop better market-
    ing communication strategies.
e. If you were designing a membership recognition program for an association to which you belong, how
    would you go about setting up a database system?
f. You have been asked to build a database of friends and supporters of your school or department. What
    types of databases might be available to you? How would you go about combining them, and what would
    you need to do to make the new list as efficient and effective as possible?

Key Point 4: Managing Customer Relationships

a. What are the four types of programs used in relationship management, and how do they work?
b. Explain how prospecting works.
c. What is cross-selling, and how is it used in growth programs?
d. How and why are profitable customers identified?
e. Have you (or someone you know) been targeted by an acquisition or retention program? How did the
    program operate, and how did you respond?
f. Define the term *mass customization* and explain how companies use it to create brand messages.
g. A local store has asked you to help design a customer recognition program. What are some techniques
    that you might recommend?

Chapter Challenge

Writing Assignment

Go back through this chapter and list all the ways you can find that database use improves marketing communication. Then discuss the problems and concerns that you need to keep in mind when using databases.

Presentation Assignment

Assume that you have a new job or an internship. You have been asked to prepare a presentation for a marketing staff training program on the strategic use of databases. Develop an outline of the key points you
want to present. Give the presentation to your class or record it on a videotape (audiotape is also an option) to turn in to your instructor, along with the outline.

Internet Assignment

Visit www.CRMguru.com for an in-depth understanding of the latest CRM practices and applications. This
website is open to students for free. Analyze the materials and discussion items on this site and identify a
problem or debate that is engaging the CRM community. Explain the problem and the differing viewpoints
in a written report to your instructor.

Additional Readings

Hughes, Arthur M. *Strategic Database Marketing: The Masterplan for Starting and Managing a Profitable, Customer-Based Marketing Program*. Chicago: Probus, 1994.

Jackson, Rob, and Paul Wang. *Strategic Database Marketing*. Lincolnwood IL: NTC Business Books, 1994.

Newberg, Jay, and Claudio Marcus. *TargetSmart! Database Marketing for the Small Business*. Grants Pass, OR: The Oasis Press, 1996.

Newell, Frederick. *The New Rules of Marketing: How to Use One-to-One Relationship Marketing to Be the Leader in Your Industry*. New York: McGraw-Hill, 1997.

O'Connor, John, and Eamonn Galvin. *Marketing and Information Technology*. London: Pitman, 1997.

Pine, Joseph. *Mass Customization: The New Frontier In Business Competition*. Harvard Business School Press, 1993.

Research Assignment

From your reading of these books or other books and articles on data-driven marketing and communication, develop an analysis of how different categories of customers should be targeted by marketing communication campaigns. What information is needed, and how is that information used in the development of the message strategy for various types of customer segments and stakeholder groups?

Endnotes

[1]Ruth Stevens, "It's Time to Return Meaning to CRM," *iMarketing News,* November 20, 2000, p. 16.

[2]Melinda Nykamp and Carla McEachern, as quoted in *The New Rules of Marketing* newsletter, published by Seklemian/Newell, October 2000, p. 1.

[3]John O'Connor and Eamonn Galvin, *Marketing and Information Technology* (London: Pitman, 1997), p. 273.

[4]I. Linton, *Database Marketing: Know What Your Customer Wants* (London: Pitman, 1995).

[5]O'Connor and Galvin, *Marketing and Information Technology,* p. 79.

[6]John F. Rockart, Michael Earl, and Jeanne Ross, "Eight Imperatives for the New IT Organization," *Sloan Management Review,* Fall 1996, p. 47.

[7]Ron Kahan, *DM News* 19, no. 2 (January 13, 1997), p. 1.

[8]O'Connor and Galvin, *Marketing and Information Technology,* p. 65.

[9]*A Direct Marketer's Guide to Fair Information Practices.*

[10]"Market Makers," *The Economist,* March 14, 1998, p. 68.

[11]Presentation by Martin Abrams to Direct Marketing Association Educators' Conference, San Francisco, 1996.

[12]Jim Emerson, "Levi Strauss in the Early Stages of Shift to Database Marketing," *DM News,* December 7, 1992, p. 1.

[13]Ira Sager, "The Great Equalizer," *Business Week Special Issue, The Information Revolution* (New York: Business Week, 1994), p. 104.

[14]"DMA: Over 90% of BtBers Use Databases," *DM News,* January 31, 1994, p. 10.

[15]John Coe, "The Decay Rate of Business Databases—a Surprise," *DM News,* February 14, 1994, p. 25.

[16]"Using Databases to Build Brands; Consumer Database Marketing Requires a Long-Term Focus and Retailer Input," *Potentials in Marketing* 26, no. 8 (September 1993), p. 20.

[17]Annette Kissinger, "You Say London, I Say Londres," *Marketing Tools,* May 1997, pp. 12–14.

[18]Risa Bauman, "Making Play Pay," *Direct* 5, no. 4 (April 1993), p. 29.

[19]Kim Cleland, "Few Wed Marketing, Communications," *Advertising Age,* February 27, 1995, p. 10.

[20]Jennifer Dejong, "Smart Marketing," *Computerworld,* February 7, 1994, p. 118.

[21]Brent Keltner and David Finegold, "Adding Value in Banking: Human Resource Innovations for Service Firms," *Sloan Management Review,* Fall 1996, p. 63.

[22]Diane Luckow, "Better Selling through Technology: Companies of All Sizes Are Using Database Marketing to Boost Sales through Old-Fashioned Personal Service," *Profit* 13, no. 4 (January 1995), Sec. 1, p. 43.

[23]Brent Keltner and David Finegold, "Adding Value in Banking: Human Resource Innovations for Service Firms," *Sloan Management Review,* Fall 1996, p. 63.

Part Three

Creating, Sending, and Receiving Brand Messages

With an understanding of how communication works in IMC, companies can develop messages that accomplish certain objectives. In this part of the book, the design of the message is discussed in terms of message strategy in Chapter 9 and message execution in Chapter 10.

In IMC, the role of media is not just to deliver brand messages, but to help create, sustain, and strengthen brand relationships by connecting companies and customers. Chapter 11 is about the characteristics of one-way media; Chapter 12 explains characteristics of two-way, interactive media, with specific attention given to the Internet; and Chapter 13 explains how to strategically develop an integrated media plan, using a combination of one- and two-way media.

9

IMC Message Strategy

Key Points in This Chapter

1. What are the elements in a creative brief?

2. What marketing decisions need to be considered in planning IMC messages?

3. What are the key elements in a creative strategy?

4. Why is strategic consistency an important consideration in message strategy?

Chapter Perspective:
Strategic Mandates for the Creative Side

Brand messages are not just designed to entertain: they have some very specific mandates. All planned brand messages should (1) create brand awareness; (2) change or reinforce customers' attitudes; (3) stimulate some kind of response or action; and/or (4) stimulate the interactivity that helps build brand relationships.

These mandates are related to the think/feel/do dimensions of the customers' brand decision process outlined in Chapter 5. For example, brand messages are designed to ignite the decision process by pointing out a problem or opportunity—or in the case of customers who already recognize they have a problem or opportunity, it helps them realize how the brand can solve their problem or take advantage of an opportunity. Likewise, brand messages ignite feelings and attitudes when customers are evaluating their choices. Finally, brand messages, particularly interactive ones, motivate action and reinforce brand choices leading to repeat action.

The IMC Creative Brief is based on these mandates and how they relate to the brand decision-making process. This chapter focuses on the first two parts of the brief: Marketing Strategy Decisions and Selling Strategy Decisions. These are the parts designed to affect consumer attitudes and their impact is governed by the consistency with which these messages are delivered, which is the last section of this chapter. The third part—Creative Execution Decisions—is the subject of Chapter 10.

CREATING BRAND VALUE FOR A BISCUIT
Bates Advertising, Auckland, New Zealand

Arnott's is an Australian biscuit and cracker manufacturer that has successfully expanded its market to many areas of the Pacific region. In Australia, biscuits are what Americans call cookies. In neighboring New Zealand, however, Arnott's was seen as an "Aussie interloper" and was having a tough time competing against locally entrenched New Zealand brands. If you were assigned to develop a meaningful relationship between Arnott's and current and potential customers in New Zealand, what would you recommend?

That was the challenge given to Auckland's Bates Advertising, which created a moving, award-winning campaign for Arnott's. The assignment was a major one—to revitalize the brand. Using an IMC campaign and a great creative idea, Bates was able to involve New Zealand consumers with the brand in an emotional way (see Exhibit 9-1).

The Marketing Challenge

Arnott's had been in the New Zealand marketplace since 1983 and by the early 1990s had nearly a 30 percent market share. However, by the mid-90s, growth had begun to stagnate and the trade had begun introducing imported brands, as well as private labels, in order to generate greater profitability. This additional competition for shelf space was threatening the profitability and market share of established brands.

The biscuit category is characterized by low consumer loyalty. Focus group research found that, because of the product proliferation, consumers in New Zealand had developed a large repertoire of favorite brands. From the consumers' perspective, there were few points of difference among the product offerings. Category research also found that recall of advertising for specific brands was low.

EXHIBIT 9-1

The Arnott's campaign focused on repositioning the "biscuit" with a strong brand identity and association.

Griffin's, the market leader, had the highest level of loyalty. As Bates Advertising was planning the Arnott's campaign, Griffin's market share was 55 percent and Arnott's was 28 percent, with the remaining 17 percent representing other imported brands and private labels.

Brand Analysis

Griffin's had come to own the biscuit category's primary values (warmth, approachability, trust, caring, everydayness, and friendliness). What's more, it was a brand that easily outspent its competitors. Arnott's was seen as expensive since its price was 7 percent above the market average. Also, the brand's relationship with the trade (retailers, distributors) was a distant one, a problem compounded by its Australian origins. Furthermore, Arnott's had a perception problem. The company's own research found that the brand was seen as cold and inaccessible, and thus at odds with the overall "warmth" of the biscuit category.

Arnott's had a seemingly insurmountable problem. It was a brand without positive core values in a category that was rapidly fragmenting. And Griffin's was outspending it by 2½ to 1.

Campaign Strategy

Bates decided that the solution for Arnott's was to create an emotional connection to the brand. Brand building in a category increasingly driven by price promotion is risky, but in this case it paid off. In fact, while the category "zigged" with price-focused promotional strategies, Arnott's "zagged" with a brand-building strategy.

In addition to the core consumer target market, which Arnott's identified as household shoppers aged 18–49 with children, the brand also needed to focus attention on the retail trade target.

Bates undertook benchmark research at the start of the campaign and, from this information, set the communication objectives. It then incorporated key positioning statements relevant to the objectives into tracking studies. The communication objectives were (1) to improve the brand positioning on key biscuit values (caring and friendly); (2) to increase perceptions of the brand's modernity, quality, and relevance to New Zealand; and (3) to increase trust with the trade (i.e., business-to-business) audience.

Creative Strategy

Arnott's was a brand looking for a relationship with the New Zealand consumer. This came together in a big idea based on "soap-opera" format commercials that featured Michael, an attractive young man, and his search for a meaningful relationship. For two years, the entwined stories of Michael and the Arnott's brand unfolded in the style of a long-running television series, an approach that was very different from traditional marketing communication in this category. Together Arnott's and Michael won the hearts of New Zealanders.

Bates introduced Michael to the target audience via a lonely-hearts advertisement. In the commercials, his words struck a chord with New Zealand women, thousands of whom responded to his plea for "old-fashioned love." As the campaign evolved, New Zealanders joined Michael in his search for happiness. Arnott's products were featured as integral components of each commercial, providing occasions for meeting and sharing (see Exhibit 9-2).

The series had three phases: The first phase focused on Michael's experiences as he dated the array of women who answered his advertisement, the second on the development of a significant relationship, and the third on its outcome. The final

EXHIBIT 9-2

Arnott's developed a romantic lead character, Michael, to appeal to its target audience and demonstrate the need for and power of a relationship.

phase used an interactive approach that involved customers in the campaign. Arnott's biscuits were at the heart of every commercial episode.

In the second phase of the series, Michael bumps into his perfect match in the supermarket parking lot. Not only does he get her name—Jessica—but he also manages to get her phone number. Their relationship begins. During the ensuing episodes, Michael falls hopelessly in love. But for Jessica, Michael's ardor is too much, too soon. Like most divorced women living in the modern world, she has a lot to juggle: her commitment to her son Billy, the challenges and opportunities of her career, and the possibilities that a more independent life can bring. There's also Billy's dad—how does he fit into all of this? Phase two concludes with a cliffhanger: Jessica's ex turns up at the local park and tension mounts as Jessica seems to be following Billy straight back to his daddy's arms.

The conclusion used an innovative interactive television commercial that allowed viewers to vote on Michael's fate. They were offered four possible conclusions to Michael's search for old-fashioned love:

1. Jessica returns to Billy's dad.

2. Jessica chooses neither man.

3. Michael wakes up to discover that the whole thing was a dream.

4. Jessica chooses Michael, and the two get married and live happily ever after.

These alternative scenarios were launched on television and the voting forms were available on point-of-sale posters and in magazines. A combination of public relations and an "advertorial" in a women's magazine then took over to build further interest in the outcome.

The winner: a wedding! More than 15,500 consumers participated in this campaign by voting for one of the options. The greatest number of votes was tallied for the wedding. And in a break from convention, Arnott's announced and staged the wedding in a joint venture with the women's weekly magazine. A front cover and an "editorialized" photo spread reported on the event. The wedding took on a life of its own, as New Zealand consumers identified with the fictional Michael and Jessica.

Evaluation of the Arnott's Campaign

This highly successful campaign stopped Arnott's share-of-market erosion and changed consumers' perceptions of the brand. Results show that in the space of two years, Arnott's moved from being a brand without meaning or relevance to the New Zealand consumer to being a favorite brand, closing the "preference gap" between itself and its juggernaut competitor, Griffin's. Even more important, Arnott's has protected its market share while at the same time increasing its average price to 10 percent above the category average. Finally, as a test of its emotional strength, the campaign was voted Most Romantic television commercial by the Romance Writers Guild.

The multidimensional, integrated campaign that told the story of a meaningful relationship also built a caring image for the Arnott's brand. This image in turn helped the company develop customer relationships that provided a sweet foundation for building brand equity in a competitive grocery market.

This case was adapted with permission from the Advertising and Marketing Effectiveness (AME) award-winning brief for Arnott's prepared by Bates Advertising agency in Auckland, New Zealand.

BRAND MESSAGE STRATEGY DEVELOPMENT

Chapter 6 presented the IMC planning process, which begins with a SWOT analysis, moves on through target and relationship analysis to objective setting, and then reaches the fourth step: developing message strategies. That's where this chapter, along with the one that follows on message execution, takes over.

Companies and their marketing communication agencies employ strategic thinking at a variety of levels in the marketing communication process. No one company follows all of the steps or uses all of the documents presented in this chapter, but the discussion that follows should help you see the typical chain of strategic decisions that occur at different stages in the design of a brand message.

The Creative Message Brief

When MC agencies create brand messages, whether ads, publicity releases, packaging, or sales promotion offers, the development of these messages is guided by a document called one of several names: creative brief, creative platform, creative plan or workplan, creative strategy, or copy strategy. This book uses the term **creative brief** to refer to this document which provides the guidelines for creating brand messages.

Over the years, many of the major advertising agencies have customized the elements that make up their set of guidelines for creating brand messages. As you can see in Table 9–1 (which lists the creative brief outlines used by six major advertising agencies), although each outline contains slightly different elements,

---

T A B L E   9 - 1   Outlines of Advertising Agency Creative Briefs

Ogilvy & Mather	DDB Worldwide	Young & Rubicam
Product	Marketing Objective	Key Fact
Key Issue/Problem	Competitive Advantage	Consumer Problem
The Promise	Advertising Objective	Advertising Objective
The Support	Action by Target	Creative Strategy
Competition	Key Insight	1. Prospect Definition
Target	Reward/Support	Product Use
Demographics	Brand Personality/Tone	Demographics
Psychographics	Position	Psychographics
Desired Behavior	Media	2. Competition
Target's Net Impression		3. Consumer Benefit
Tone & Manner		4. Reason Why

Tracy-Locke	Leo Burnett	Campbell Mithun
Target	*Convince*: Target	Business Goal
Brand	*That*: Desired Belief	Consumer Profile
Reason Why	*Support*: Reasons Why	Current Attitudes
Brand Character	*Because*: Proposition	Desired Attitudes
Focus of Sale	(Key Drama)	Desired Action
Tone		Selling Proposition

there are many similarities. Probably some of the terms used by these creative briefs are unfamiliar to you at this point; don't worry, they will start to make sense as you go through this chapter.

The MC account planners' first step in developing a message strategy is to review the marketing plan and the SWOT analysis. As part of that step, planners identify the brand's competitors, the brand's competitive advantage, and their message strategies. For the client's brand, this backgrounding step includes some or all of the following basic information:

- Marketing objectives (share of market, sales levels, share of wallet).
- Marketing strategies (timing, geographical focus, market segments).
- Brand identity, image, and/or personality.
- Brand attributes and distinctive features.
- Competition's attributes and distinctive features.
- Existing position and desired position (how customers see the brand relative to its competition; how the client wants it to be seen).
- Key SWOTs.

All of this information is compiled and analyzed, along with additional research into consumer and customer insights and behavior, and is used to give direction to the creative team's work.

Figure 9–1 illustrates how the public relations agency, Citigate Cunningham, has applied its creative platform to its work for client Freshwater Software. The firm calls its message strategy document a Positioning Platform. At the top is a "positioning statement," one sentence that sets forth the client's main brand message. Beneath this is a set of "value propositions," or statements of what benefits the brand offers to customers. The three key value propositions for Freshwater are: e-business growth; rapid, and global scalability (meaning it can help companies

FIGURE 9-1

Citigate Cunningham's "Positioning Platform" for its client, Freshwater Software

Positioning Statement	Freshwater Software is the leading provider of comprehensive Internet growth solutions for eBusiness		
Value Propositions	*eBusiness growth*	*Rapid, global scalability*	*Brand integrity*
Key Messages	*Our services, technologies and expertise are critical enablers of eBusiness growth*	*We help companies scale their Internet businesses quickly and globally*	*We create trust in our customers' Internet brands*
Sample Proof Point	**2,500 growing businesses outsource website monitoring to Freshwater**	**Freshwater measures website availability from 11 global networks**	**Freshwater helps meet unique eBusiness brand requirements, including 24-hour availability**
Sample Sound Bite	*"We have time and resources to build other areas of our business when Freshwater monitors our Web environment."*	*"As we add customers around the world, Freshwater makes sure they can reliably complete transactions on our website."*	*"Freshwater makes sure my website is available 24 hours a day, seven days a week, so it can support my overall business brand."*

determine the proper scale for their operations); and brand integrity. As you look down the columns, you will find a key message associated with each proposition; the proof or information supporting the proposition; and, at the bottom, a set of quotes ("sound bites") that bring the value propositions to life.

Compare the Citigate Cunningham platform to the six advertising agency platforms summarized in Table 9-1. How do they differ in structure? How are they alike?

Creative briefs typically include such things as a restatement of the marketing strategy, a restatement of the marketing objectives in terms of the intended message impact, the message format or approach, the psychological appeal, the selling premise, the big idea or creative concept, and the message execution details.

Targeting and Customer Insight

As discussed in Chapter 7, segmentation starts broad and narrows down to an identifiable group or set of groups that has a reason to be in a relationship with the brand. A target market is a segment most likely to buy the brand. Recall from the chapter opening case that Arnott's targeted household shoppers aged 18–49 with children and, secondarily, retailers.

Message strategies are intimately tied to segmentation and targeting strategies because a message strategy is about the impact of the brand message on the target audience. Current customers are largely aware of the brand (although maybe not all of its features or benefits) and probably have some attitudes about it. Users of competitive brands are aware of the product category, but may or may not be aware of your brand and may have either unfocused or negative attitudes about it.

Before a creative brief can be written, marketers and account planners need answers to questions such as: How is the brand positioned in the minds of current customers and users of competitive brands? Who are the best prospects for the brand? How strong are brand relationships? What can be done to strengthen brand relationships and increase the brand's share of customers' category spending? These answers, which should be found in the SWOT analysis findings, help brands to more accurately target their messages and media.

To further increase the impact of targeted messages, account planners also try to put into the creative brief as much customer insight as possible. **Customer insight** is *gained by looking below the surface of what customers say they want and need in regards to a brand and product category.* A good account planner will use, for example, observational research and in-depth probing to see how and why customers behave as they do. With this knowledge account planners can find ways in which a brand can be made more relevant to customers and prospects. Back in the 1950s Leo Burnett came up with the idea of associating Marlboro cigarettes with rugged, masculine cowboys working in the wide-open spaces of the West. This was not, however, because cowboys were the primary target. It was because Leo Burnett had the insight that young and middle-aged men fantasized about the freedom and independence of being a cowboy. By offering a cigarette that symbolized this romantic idea, men could briefly escape into this fantasy each time they lit up. This simple (but creative) insight is what has made Marlboro one of the top brands in the world.

In her book, *The Consumer Insight Handbook,* Lisa Fortini-Campbell gives another example. Having customer insight, she says, is what explains why the movie, *Pretty Woman,* was so successful with the female audience ". . . it touched a dream [that every woman has] always harbored . . . if we're in the right spot at the right time, someone rich, handsome, sophisticated and kind will see us for who we really are and carry us off on his white horse. Or in his white limousine. And we'll live happily ever after."[1]

Finding the consumer insight for a brand has become the responsibility of the account planner in many agencies. Some consider the account planner to be the "voice of the customer." Unfortunately, most definitions of account planning say little or nothing about creating and managing a dialogue or an ongoing relationship with customers. This will change, however, as more agencies and companies adopt IMC, as the two concepts and processes complement each other.

Selling Strategies

Selling strategy decisions begin with the question "For each major contact point, what is being said about the brand?" This analysis, plus the analysis of the SWOTs, leads planners to decide on the primary problem (or opportunity) that is solvable (or taken advantage of) with communication. From this comes the message objectives for the various functional areas.

Purpose or Key Problem

Philosopher John Dewey once said, "A problem well-stated is a problem half-solved." In strategic thinking, recognizing the problem to be solved is the hard part. A company's sales may be stagnating or even falling, but no improvement can come unless the company knows why this is happening. For example, Quaker State Motor oil for years had good distribution in gasoline stations but did not realize that its products were being poorly displayed. Once it realized that this was the case, the company designed a "pull strategy" that was aimed at end users: "Ask for Quaker State. Your local station has it even if you don't see it on the shelves."

An account planner can write a problem statement that helps creatives know what to look for and how to gauge the effectiveness of their ideas. In other words, creatives will evaluate alternative message strategies by asking themselves, "Will this idea solve the central problem?"

Identifying the company's main opportunity or key problem is the first step in developing a selling strategy. This key problem should summarize the most important finding from the SWOT analysis described in Chapter 6. A common problem, for example, is the need to sharpen or change how a brand is positioned. Exhibit 9–3 is an example of an ad for Target designed to address such a purpose.

One technique the creative team can use to keep its work focused on the key problem is to complete the following statement:

> The purpose of this marketing communication message is to convince
>
> _____ [target audience] _____ that _____
>
> [brand] _____ will _____ [benefit] _____
>
> because _____ [proof]. The result should be _____ [message
>
> objectives: impact on consumer].

For the Arnott's campaign, the statement might be worded as follows: "The purpose of this marketing communication message is to convince New Zealand mothers 18–49 that Arnott's biscuits will be emotionally satisfying because the brand has warmth. The result should be measurably stronger brand loyalty among Arnott's customers." Of course, the creative team may alter the wording of the statement as needed.

Functional-Area Message Objectives

Chapter 1 defined the term *marketing communication mix* as the combination of MC functions used in IMC campaigns. Choosing this mix is part of the second selling strategy decision. For example, perhaps the SWOT analysis determined that the brand's image is fuzzy, and the chosen purpose of the message is to clarify, sharpen, or refocus that image. That may give the creative team an insight about what MC function to use: advertising. Advertising is especially good at creating, changing, and reminding customers about a brand's position or image. If, instead, the brand has a credibility problem or needs to create an immediate sales response that will have bottom-line impact, the primary MC function would be brand publicity to increase credibility or sales promotion to create an immediate response.

MC efforts are measured against their objectives, so stating appropriate message objectives is an important part of determining the desired impact. For that reason, planners often base creative message objectives on some notion of a *hierarchy of effects*, as explained in Chapter 5. The AIDA model, the most common of these hierarchies, identifies a set of consumer decision points where a message might be able to have some impact—awareness, interest, desire, and action. What this and the other hierarchy models all provide is a logic for setting objectives and for evaluating the effectiveness of messages in terms of their communication effects.

The Tale of Two Companies box focuses on the objectives of two different beverage companies—Mott's and Nestlé—and reviews their effectiveness in terms of message impact on consumers.

A less hierarchical approach reflects the four message mandates discussed in the Chapter Perspective—awareness, attitude, action, and relationship building. Note that in the relationship-building step, action is repeated and attitudes are reinforced over and over. These four mandates can also be used to frame a set of message objectives. Not all of these are equally important in every situation, but they all are important to some degree in most marketing communication plans. Table 9–2 presents a list of typical objectives for each mandate category. These objectives can also be linked to a set of fairly standard message strategies.

Remember this principle: *The brand message objectives and strategies need to dovetail with the marketing plan.* Recall that the Arnott's campaign was designed to build brand values, which is an objective derived from the marketing plan, and create a strong brand relationship between the brand and its various stakeholders. The brand-building strategy was a novel approach in the biscuit category and involved a fair share of risk. And a relationship-focused strategy that involved the trade, as well as customers and media, was also new to the category. New creative ideas like these tend to be risky because the planners have no previous experience from which they can draw to to predict the impact.

Standard Message Strategies

There are a number of standard message strategies MC planners use to deliver on the message objectives. For example, the awareness and attitude objectives

EXHIBIT 9-3

This ad attempts to move Target's image from that of an average discount store to one that offers quality merchandise at a value price. The quality message is communicated through the high-fashion model and the value message is delivered through the accompanying prices.

A TALE OF TWO COMPANIES

Clamato and Quik

Nestlé Quik Banana Milk, which was launched in 1990, used a banner on its package in the late 1990s that bragged: "America's Favorite Banana Milk." Paul Lukas, a columnist for *Fortune*, asked: "So what?" and then proceeded to try to document the claim. He concluded that the "America's favorite" phrase doesn't refer to a state of cutthroat competition in the banana milk category but rather to the fact that Quik is the best-selling branded banana milk in the United States. There are other brands of banana milk, but they are all regional. In other words, Nestlé Quik Banana Milk positions itself as number one in a category of one, and it's a small category at that.

In terms of message objectives, the brand is trying to get attention for itself and build awareness by using a common promotional technique called puffery, which refers to an overly exaggerated claim that can't be proved or disproved. Lukas's "So what?" response demonstrates the type of impact puffery usually elicits.

In contrast, the beverage maker Mott's found out from research on its Clamato brand that the reason for the clam/tomato juice's low household penetration of 2 percent was that people feared the amount of clam juice in the beverage was too much. Furthermore the brand's lack of personality (i.e., poor brand image) suggested that it was time for a repositioning. After conducting an integrated campaign that included advertising, sales promotion, and public relations, Mott's saw a double-digit increase in Clamato buyers. How was it done?

The message strategy was to use a quirky, irreverent positioning, cued by a simple tagline that assuaged the fears of prospective Clamato tryers: "99.9% Clam Free." To build the quirky personality, the creative team borrowed French Stewart, the wacky brother from the sitcom *3rd Rock From the Sun*, to deliver the pitch. A "Just for Laffs" promotion used Stewart to announce a contest for best jokes. Public relations coverage included a piece on *Entertainment Tonight*, and outtakes from the ad shoot were used on *America's Funniest Home Videos*. These efforts both built awareness of the brand and delivered the repositioning message (see Exhibit 9-4).

Think About It

Why was the Nestlé Quik Banana Milk package promotion panned as being a "So what?" strategy? What is puffery, and what is the danger in using it? How was the Clamato repositioning strategy carried out, and why do you think it was successful?

Source: Paul Lukas: "The Persistence of 'So What?' Marketing," *Fortune*, November 10, 1997, pp. 48–49; Stephanie Thompson, "Juicing Clamato Sales," *Brandweek*, January 19, 1998, pp. 20–21.

EXHIBIT 9-4

[Nestlé Quik Banana Milk carton: "AMERICA'S FAVORITE BANANA MILK"]

are often achieved using two general types of message strategies known as *informational* and *transformational*.[2] The action and relationship objectives (action, repeat purchase, interactivity) can be met by using *behavioral* and *relational* strategies.

TABLE 9 - 2   Brand Message Mandates and Objectives

Typical Objectives

Awareness

Make an impression

Get attention

Create brand identity; aid recognition

Create differentiation

Create interest

Remind, aid recall

Announce news

Inform: aid understanding/comprehension of claims, benefits

Create associations

Increase importance (salience)

Attitude

Affect feelings and emotions

Create brand image, personality

Create liking

Create conviction/belief

Create positive attitudes and opinions, change indifferent or negative

Influence opinion leaders

Defend, neutralize opposition or counter competitive activities

Action

Stimulate behavioral response

Motivate trial

Motivate immediate action/response (provide incentives to add value)

Stimulate other behaviors: return card, visit dealer, visit website

Relationship Building

Connect the customer to the brand; extend the action over the long term

Create or increase preference leading to some level of loyalty

Stimulate repeat purchase

Increase share of wallet

Create or increase trust in brand

Create or increase brand liking

Aid self-identification with the brand

Support brand affiliation

Encourage dialogue: contact company (toll-free number, e-mail address)

Encourage positive word-of-mouth

Stimulate advocacy

Figure 9–2 identifies these categories of common strategic approaches used in developing brand messages for various kinds of marketing communication and links them to the four message mandates described in the Chapter Perspective; note also that the strategies relate to the think/feel/do model described in Chapter 5. The terms in this figure provide planners and creative people a way to talk about the logic of the message according to what it is trying to accomplish.

Informational strategies focus on concrete details, such as product attributes and performance, and showcase product differentiation. The result of an informational message is that customers know or understand certain objective facts about the brand. Such strategies rely heavily on the execution to gain the target audience's attention, unless the offer or benefit has high news value or is so dynamic that the announcement itself is attention-getting (e.g., "XYZ cures cancer").

Transformational strategies change the perception of a brand in emotional ways. The result is that people *feel* differently about the brand. The idea is to create a positive expectation and personalize the brand experience. Image building is a relatively long-term strategy, but association, lifestyle, emotion, relevance, and credibility strategies can deliver impact in the short term.

Common Message Objectives and Strategies

Think   Feel

1. Informational
Create awareness
or attention

2. Transformational
Create an attitude,
feeling, emotion,
belief, or opinion

3. Behavioral
Create action
4. Relational
Create interactivity
and repeated action

Do

FIGURE 9-2

This illustrates how the think-feel-do model relates to various message objectives and strategies.

Behavioral and relational strategies are used to create action. The choice of strategies is determined by the complexity of the brand decision process. The decision process associated with buying a car is generally several months long. In such a situation, incremental action or "do" strategies may be designed to lead prospects through a series of small steps (such as responding to a direct-mail invitation, visiting a showroom, and comparing one car make against another) that ultimately lead to a purchase. In the case of packaged goods, such as buying a can of soup, the desired action may not just be the purchase but the actual use. If the soup maker wants customers to take the can off the shelf at home and use it, it can provide menu ideas to remind people that they have soup on hand, and that it is a convenient and quick food for everyday use, not just for rainy days or when someone is sick. This action approach includes a value-added strategy (a recipe), and a reminder strategy.

The last types of objectives—interactivity and relationship building—are addressed through strategies that engage the customer and provide psychological links with a brand. These are the links that lead to brand loyalty. To intensify loyalty, MC planners can use other strategies, such as involvement in brand experiences and personalization, to support the interactivity dimension of a relationship. The following describes the basic message strategies.

Informational Message Strategies

Brand identity: Creates a competitive difference by establishing brand familiarity; used to create recognition of the brand identification marks (name, logo, colors, etc.) for new brands and to help focus a fragmented identity for an existing brand.

Generic: Makes no effort at brand differentiation and, instead, focuses on selling the category; primarily used in monopolistic or brand-dominant situations. Because Campbell Soup has over 70 percent share of the soup market, it can simply sell the goodness of soup.

Preemptive: Focuses on a common attribute or benefit that any product in the category could claim; however, gets there first and locks the brand into that association; forces competition into "me-too" positions; used in categories with little product differentiation and in new product categories.

Positioning: Although developing a brand position is a marketing strategy, sometimes the message strategy is focused on establishing, reinforcing, or changing a position; used by new products, small brands that want to challenge a market leader, or older products that need to be repositioned.

Transformational Message Strategies

Brand image: Creates superiority based on factors such as psychological appeals and brand personality cues; used with homogeneous, low-technology goods with little physical differentiation, also with any product that wants a distinctive identity in a competitive category.

Association: Makes a psychological connection between a brand (its attributes or image characteristics) and its customers and prospects; particularly used with lifestyle products.

Lifestyle: Uses situations, lifestyles, and emotions that the target audience can identify with—that is, the situation "strikes a chord" or resonates; used with highly competitive product categories with little differentiation.

Emotion: Uses an emotional message to break through indifference and charge the consumer's perception of the product with strong feelings; used with "sentiment" products like greeting cards and in situations where competitors are focused on product features.

Credibility: Uses demonstrations and endorsements (third-party confirmations) to make a point and establish believability; used with new products and those with some risk or reliability issues.

Relevance: Speaks to customers about brand-related features and benefits that are important to them, things they especially care about; used with brands that have competitive differentiation, or to intensify a sense of importance for features that may not be seen as relevant but could be with a focused message.

Behavioral Message Strategies

Added value: Used to create a sense of immediacy and give an incentive to respond quickly; used in product situations where a quick bump in the sales curve is desired, and as a defensive strategy to counter a competitor's strategy.

Reminder: Keeping the brand top-of-mind with the target; used with mature brands that have an established brand identity, and to jog the customer's memory at a point-of-purchase.

Relational Strategies

Loyalty programs: Used to encourage repeat purchases and to increase the customer's share of wallet by encouraging them to buy more often and to buy other brand offerings (i.e., cross-selling); used with brands where heavy users can be identified.

Involvement: Used either to move a product from low involvement to high involvement, or to more directly involve the customer in a brand through some kind of participation experience; used with low-involvement products, and with products that have a long lifetime and offer opportunities for participatory experiences.

Dialogue: Used to move from one-way to two-way communication programs in order to open up communication with customers and capture their feedback; used with any product where it makes sense for a customer to contact a company.

Account managers, planners, and creatives use terms such as these to talk about the logic behind message strategy—that is, the target audience's message needs and how these needs will ultimately direct the message strategy. Citigate Cunningham's Positioning Platform for Freshwater Software (see again Figure 9–1) is an informational strategy and the Arnott's campaign used a brand-image strategy built on emotion. The ad for Davidoff's line of Cool Water body care products in Exhibit 9–5 uses association to create an emotional, or affective, response in the viewer.

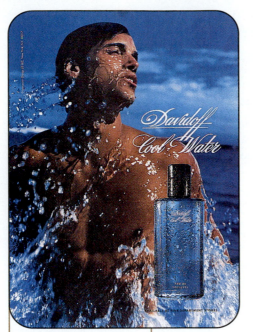

Appeals and Selling Premises

Marketing communication uses psychological **appeals**, which are *ideas that motivate the audience or excite their interest.* The appeals should correspond to wants and needs uncovered in the market research. Common appeals include motivators such as aspiration, comfort, convenience, economy, efficiency, reduction of fear, love, nostalgia, pride, health, luxury, patriotism, responsibility, safety, and sex. In the ad industry, these are referred to as "hot buttons."

Whereas appeals speak to the heart and are more appropriate for targets and product categories in which decision making is primarily experiential, **selling premises** *speak more to the head and cognitive decision making.* Selling premises focus on the logic behind an offer.

For the selling premises, it is important to state the proof on which the claim, benefit, or proposition rests. In some industries, such as pharmaceuticals and food, any health claims, as well as any other statements of superiority, have to be supported by research. If there is support for the selling premise, then the creative platform should identify this proof so the copywriter can use it in writing the brand message.

Whether the basis for a creative strategy is an appeal or a selling strategy, all creative strategies should include two basic things—the brand benefit and the reasons why the benefit will occur. A **benefit** is *a promise that is made in a message.* The **reasons why** are the *proof claims or features of a brand that explain why it will provide the promised benefit.* Sometimes the benefit and reasons why are very specific and direct in a brand message. For example, Crest ads promise fewer cavities (benefit) because Crest contains sodium floride which is an active ingredient that prevents decay (reason why). Generally, the reasons why describe product features.

The 3M ad in Exhibit 9–6 is an example of an implied benefit (e.g., safer roads) but it highlights a specific reason why—3M's microreplication technology. Fashion ads which contain only an illustration and brand name are good examples of using both implied benefits and reasons why. The strategy behind these ads is that viewers will look at the illustration and say to themselves: "I can look like that or have that type of experience if I wear that brand" (i.e., an implied promise). The reasons why in these ads lie in the association of the illustration with the brand name. After seeing so many Ralph Loren ads, a customer begins to associate Ralph Loren with sophisticated, interesting, successful-looking people. This is what is called "soft" reasons why.

The Acura ad in Exhibit 9–7 is one that combines both an appeal and a selling proposition—both a rational and an emotional—message strategy. The message promises that driving an Acura is a luxurious experience and gives many reasons why including the fact it has

NORTH TO RED ROCK COUNTRY

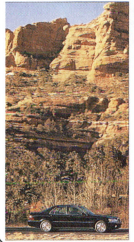

ACURA RL

Experiencing the crown jewels of Scottsdale and the curves of Tortilla Flats.

◆ The Phoenician is the ultimate Scottsdale resort, a marble-lined extravaganza of scenery, service, shopping and golf. It's the quintessential luxury experience.

It's also the perfect location to examine Acura's flagship 3.5RL, an elegant, roomy luxury sedan that looks right at home parked by the fountain at the main entrance.

As does The Phoenician, the big Acura 3.5RL 5-seater pampers you by supplying everything you could possibly need or want, usually before you even realize you need or want it. While both give you your money's worth, the $41,900 (MSRP) 3.5RL is actually a great value among luxury sedans.

The 3.5RL sports some restyling touches this year including new grille, hood and bumpers along with H.I.D. headlights. Inside the cabin are new front-passenger smart airbags.

Mechanical highlights include a fully independent double wishbone suspension system as specified on the finest racing cars. Four-wheel disc brakes with ABS, high-performance tires on alloy wheels and a 3.5-liter single-overhead-cam engine driving through a computer-controlled 4-speed automatic transmission complete the running gear.

To test out all this high technology, we head for the decidedly low-tech old cowboy trading post at Tortilla Flats. Scenic Route 88 to Tortilla Flats is a very, very twisty road with astonishing elevation changes. Having read the specs, we're ready for the big Acura's 140-mph performance and superb braking. What we

don't anticipate is the 3.5RL's world-class level of comfort.

Early the next morning, we're on the winding road to Sedona. We head out Route 87, a spectacularly curving divided highway that twists and climbs into the pine-covered Sierra Ancha Mountains. Here we find Payson, a little hill settlement whose main claims to

The RL cabin coddles you in world-class comfort. Glove-soft leather-trimmed upholstery and a 225-watt Acura/Bose sound system create a delicious environment. And with the RL's formidable trunk, you can take it all with you.

H.I.D. headlights, smart airbags, and a fully independent wishbone suspension system that is the same as used on racing cars. At the same time the ad implies the promise and provides the "proof" of this promise by visually associating the Acura with the beauty of the West and the luxury of the Phoenician resort in Scottsdale, Arizona.

STRATEGIC CONSISTENCY

A challenge in brand communication is to develop brand messages that are strategically consistent with the brand position and image, and, at the same time, with all the other brand messages. The objective is to eliminate inconsistent messages. When products perform consistently and companies behave and communicate in a consistent way, people can trust them.

Trust, however, can erode if a brand presents itself inconsistently. Examples of brand message confusion are not difficult to find, and they plague big, sophisticated marketers as well as small ones. Pepsi, for example, announced in 1996 that it was scrapping its familiar red-white-and-blue design and switching to a radically, new electric-blue design. The reason was that Pepsi's message, particularly in international markets, had been losing something in translation. As *The Wall Street Journal* observed in reporting on "Project Blue's" launch, Pepsi's image was "all over the map." A grocery store in Hamburg was using red stripes, a bodega in

UNCHANGED **HERSHEY'S** MILK CHOCOLATE SINCE 1899

CHANGE IS BAD

EXHIBIT 9-8

This Hershey's ad shows why the package and position of Hershey's has been relatively unchanged over a 100-year period, creating a very strong brand image.

Guatemala was using 1970s-era lettering, a Shanghai restaurant was displaying a mainly white Pepsi sign, and a hodgepodge of commercials featured a variety of spokespeople, ranging from cartoons and babies to doddering butlers. Not only were the marketing communication efforts inconsistent from country to country, but consumers were also complaining that the cola tasted different in different countries. To address this problem, Pepsi had to revamp its manufacturing and distribution systems, as well as its marketing communication, in order to achieve strategic brand consistency worldwide.[3]

"One-Voice, One-Look"

IMC planners focus their attention on two types of consistency: "one-voice, one-look" and strategic consistency. This one-voice, one-look strategy needs to be consistent over time if a strong brand is the objective, as Exhibit 9–8 illustrates.

One-voice, one-look is the most elementary level of consistency and delivers a campaign in which all advertising, sales promotion, sponsorships, publicity, direct response, and packaging have the same appearance and feel. All the media messages reinforce one another. For example, when Levi Strauss broke a new campaign for its Dockers khakis, it relied on a Dockers-dedicated team at agency Foote, Cone & Belding in San Francisco to create messages using the Dockers "Nice pants" theme for everything from posters to bus shelters to the Dockers.com website.

Many companies, especially larger ones, have a difficult time integrating brand messages. For example, an IMC brand audit of a major beverage brand (with a marketing communication budget of $150 million) found that the marketing services and brand managers were working against 10 different MC objectives. Not surprisingly, a content analysis of a year of planned brand messages found little consistency.

Strategic Consistency

In spite of the importance of maintaining one-voice, one-look consistency, using exactly the same message in all marketing communication is usually not done because most markets are divided into customer segments, and even subsegments, and because companies must communicate with a variety of other stakeholders besides customers. For example, in selling educational toys, the message to parents will be different from the one aimed at the kids. This does not mean, however, that there can't be certain consistencies in both sets of messages. The brand's personality, positioning, and identification cues, for example, should be consistent, but the individualized selling propositions may differ (for kids: "exciting fun"; for parents: "they learn while playing").

To achieve strategic consistency MC planners must walk a fine line between tailoring different messages to the various target audiences and maintaining a constant brand image. McDonald's, for example, serves beer in Germany and sushi in Japan, but it is still McDonald's. Why? Because it continues to offer a basic standard menu, in spite of the regional additions, and the cost-value of its offerings is predictably always very good. A McDonald's exterior is reasonably easy to recognize worldwide; however, the company uses its interiors to connect

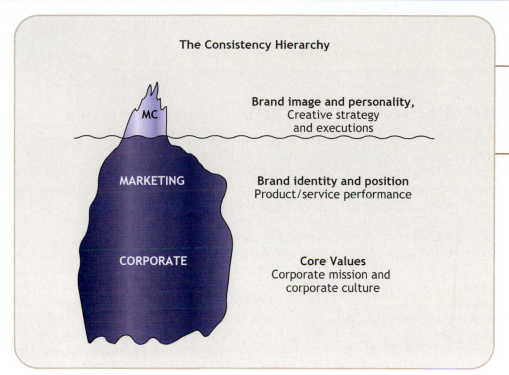

The Consistency Hierarchy

MC

Brand image and personality,
Creative strategy
and executions

MARKETING

Brand identity and position
Product/service performance

CORPORATE

Core Values
Corporate mission and
corporate culture

FIGURE 9-3

Consistency in marketing communication is only the tip of the iceberg.

with each local community. For example, in Peru, Indiana, which used to be the winter quarters for several circuses, the interior of the McDonald's has a circus motif and many pictures of the old circus days in the city.

As Figure 9–3 illustrates, having consistency in the marketing communication is only the tip of the iceberg. The deeper you go in analyzing the brand and corporate strategy, the more important consistency becomes throughout the organization's operations. At the bottom, the foundation on which all communication is built, is the corporate mission, culture, and core values. The company's business philosophy comes next, followed by the various elements of brand strategy: product and service performance, brand identity, and brand position. Omaha Steaks, in the IMC Strategy box, credits its success to a well-managed team approach that integrates all its marketing efforts behind its gourmet image and position.

Core Values

The bedrock of consistency is the corporate mission, business philosophy, and corporate culture. A **mission** is what the company stands for, represents, or does well. A corporate mission is the critical integrative element because coming up with a consistent message is impossible if no one in the company knows what the company stands for. Putting the customer first as a business philosophy is an easy promise to make in planned messages but often difficult to practice, especially when it comes to service messages, which involve sales, customer service, repairs, and handling returns. Sometimes expressed as "the way we do business around here," a corporate culture, as defined in Chapter 1, is the pattern of shared values and beliefs that determine how an organization's employees work and interact. This corporate "culture" should serve as a guideline in all business communication situations no matter whether it involves dealings with distribution, customer service, selling, or the media.

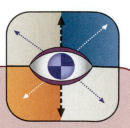

IMC STRATEGY

"Steaking Out" a Quality Position

Unless you're a vegetarian, there's nothing that symbolizes a celebratory dinner better than a good steak. And for Omaha Steaks, the Nebraska-based gourmet food provider, there is nothing that delivers quality as much as a carefully integrated marketing program (see Exhibit 9-9).

The quality control begins with the product. Todd Simon, vice president and general manager of the family-owned company, says, "We keep control of the process from beginning to end." The steaks, for example, start with only the finest USDA-approved corn-fed beef, aged for 21 to 28 days. "We're control freaks," Simon explained when talking about the rigorous standards his family applies to its own business as well as its suppliers.

The marketing communication program is driven by direct marketing, including direct-mail pieces and catalogs. Omaha Steaks won the coveted *Catalog Age* Catalog of the Year Award in 1997 based on "its manifest excellence," which is more evidence of its dedication to quality. The direct-marketing program is backed up by select television and print media advertising.

Other marketing channels include retail (with some 30 stores), a food-service operation, and business-to-business gifts and incentives. There's even a lone Omaha Steaks restaurant that operates independently under a licensing arrangement.

Co-branding is used with the recent issuance of an Omaha Steaks credit-card promotion in conjunction with MBNA and with other marketing promotions through the American Express Membership Rewards program.

An Internet operation (www.omahasteaks.com) brings it all together with an online catalog, a 100 percent satisfaction guarantee, current specials, an offer for a free *Good Life Guide & Cookbook*, customer-service information, a gift guide, and a consistent emphasis on the company's quality position.

The firm tracks results, not by demographics, but rather by responsiveness. "We run a sophisticated database, tracking the order history of each customer. This information is right in front of each sales representative when talking with our customers," Simon says. So even the customer relationship is a quality operation.

But the reason for the firm's success is its emphasis on quality and the way that is reflected in its business philosophy, corporate culture, and caring employees. In conferring its award on Omaha Steaks, *Catalog Age* cited the company's exceptional customer service and active participation in the catalog community.

Think About It

How has Omaha Steaks used its positioning strategy as a consistency platform? How many different instances of integrated planning can you find in this Omaha Steaks example?

EXHIBIT 9-9

Marketing Level

At the marketing level, consistency is signaled by the product and service performance messages, as well as the brand positioning and the brand identity, which are very much controlled by marketing managers. Maintaining consistency in product and service performance has been a primary thrust of marketing programs and is also critical in integrated marketing communication. As mentioned before, product and service performance have communication dimensions that send some of the most powerful brand messages. Most important, the product and service messages must be reflected in the marketing communication and be in sync with customers' own experiences. A few years ago automaker Oldsmobile tried to change its brand image by explaining how contemporary its cars were. The MC theme was "This isn't your father's Oldsmobile." Unfortunately, although the product had been improved, potential customers didn't see as much change in the cars as the ads led them to expect. Subsequent efforts have also failed to revitalize the brand causing GM to announce the line will be discontinued.

As the IMC Strategy box illustrates, there is more to integration than just having all the pieces in a campaign look alike. An IMC program has to be reflected in the company's total business operations, not just its marketing communication messages.

Marketing Communication Level

Consistency at the marketing communication level generally means maintaining one voice and one look in all planned messages, particularly in campaigns. However, as already pointed out, strategic consistency allows for different executions that are aimed at different segments. The creative concept behind the promotional activity, along with the design and tone of the brand message, should remain the same. These executional factors will be discussed in more detail in Chapter 10.

The Consistency Triangle

The consistency triangle shown in Figure 9-4 is a simple way to analyze how all of a company's brand messages relate to each other. Strategic brand consistency exists when a brand does what it says, from the customer's perspective. What the brand says and what it does are reinforced by what others say about it. In other words:

- *"Say" messages* are the planned communication delivered by the company through its marketing communication program. These set expectations.

- *"Do" messages* are those delivered by the company's product and service messages. They are conveyed by how products actually perform, what they

FIGURE 9-4

Gaps in the consistency triangle are red flags.

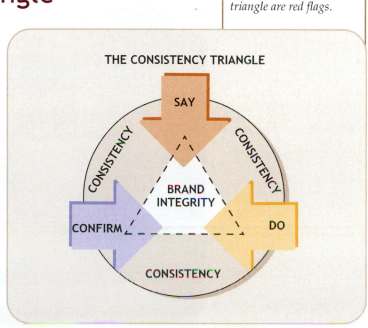

THE CONSISTENCY TRIANGLE

actually cost, how convenient they are to get and use, and the product's supporting services.

- *"Confirm" messages* are those from other people who either criticize (e.g., don't confirm) or praise the brand or company (see Exhibit 9–10). Personal and positive third-party communication is considerably more persuasive than most planned brand messages.

Consistency Gaps

The consistency triangle is used to identify gaps in brand communication and alert a company to potential relationship problems. In other words, the "say" messages delivered by marketing communication must be consistent with the "do" messages of how products and services perform, as well as with what others say or

EXHIBIT 9-10

Marketing communication significantly increases its impact when it leads to word of mouth, particularly the kinds of conversations where someone refers a friend to your brand.

Most of our clients are referred by a source far more compelling than any advertising.

When it comes to innovative, responsive financial services, people of influence are recommending Private Banking at Chemical Bank.
In fact, our clients themselves are our single most reliable source of new client relationships.

If you wish to discover how your financial needs can best be met, please call Gitelle Cardin or Richard Foley at (212) 621-2583.
If you prefer, write to Chemical Bank, Private Banking, 30 Rockefeller Plaza, New York, NY 10112.

© 1990 Chemical Bank
Member FDIC

CHEMICALBANK
PRIVATE BANKING

"confirm" about the brand. Gaps between any of these points of the triangle threaten brand relationships.

When an airline puts "special handling" tags on the bags of its frequent flyers it seems to be promising these customers that they will be the first ones to receive their bags upon landing. If the frequent flyers find that their tagged bags arrive no sooner than everyone else's on the flight, then there is a gap between the "say" and "do" messages. Consistency gaps, if they occur too often or become too large, will make the brand image seem unfocused, diffused, and fuzzy. From the customer's point of view, consistency means "no negative surprises" as well as easy recognition of the brand.

A FINAL NOTE: A MESS OF MESSAGES

When the full array of brand messages is considered, one can quickly see the communication complexity involved—and the reason why most companies are dealing with a mess of messages. As the chief strategist for General Motors once explained:

> Every point of customer contact—from printed material to products to after-sale service—must present the customer with a clear and harmonious impression of the company, its products, and its services. And this unified outward image is a reflection of the company's internal consistency.

Consistency, however, is a means to an end. That end is positive brand relationships. Success at creating this level of consistency is what made the Arnott's campaign an example of an effective message strategy that was able to turn around a troubled brand.

Key Terms

creative brief 313
customer insight 315
appeals 322
selling premises 322

benefit 322
reasons why 322
mission 325

Key Points Summary

Key Point 1: The Creative Message Brief

The IMC Message Strategy Brief has three main sections: the summary of the marketing strategy decisions, the selling strategy decisions, and the creative execution decisions.

Key Point 2: Marketing Strategy Decisions

The key marketing decisions that give direction to the message strategy include the marketing objectives and strategies, the competitive analysis leading to an analysis of the brand's competitive advantage, key SWOTs, the target audience, and brand positioning.

Key Point 3: Selling Strategy Decisions

The strategic elements in the Creative Brief include the purpose or key problem/opportunity, the communication needs to address, functional-area message objectives, appeals and selling premises, and the consistency factors.

Key Point 4: Strategic Consistency

Having one-voice, one-look consistency means communicating a consistent message across a variety of media and other functional areas; it stems from a unified creative strategy in the planned messages. Strategic consistency varies the messages with the needs of the audience; however, it maintains brand consistency by using a set of core consistency elements. Strategic consistency also means coordinating all types of messages (product, service, and unplanned, as well as the planned messages) in order to guarantee that there are no gaps between the say, do, and confirm messages.

Lessons Learned

Key Point 1: The Creative Message Brief

a. What are the three main sections in the Creative Brief?
b. Study the six agency creative briefs in Table 9-1. What elements appear most consistently in them? What elements appear infrequently? Do you believe the ones that appear infrequently are needed to develop a message strategy?
c. How does the Arnott's story in the chapter opening case exemplify a Creative Brief? In other words, what elements of the brief can you identify in the Arnott's campaign?.

Key Point 2: Marketing Directions

a. What are the various marketing decisions that need to be reviewed as part of the backgrounding step?
b. What is a key customer insight? Give an example of how customer insights contribute to the development of message strategy.
c. What are the three areas considered in the development and management of a brand? Find an ad that you believe demonstrates the three elements and explain how they work in that ad.

Key Point 3: Selling Strategy Decisions

a. What are the main categories of selling strategy decisions outlined in the Creative Brief?
b. What are the four general communication impact goals? Give an example of an objective for each category.
c. What is the difference between an appeal and a selling premise? Find a piece of marketing communication that illustrates each and explain how each one works.
d. Discuss the selling premise of Nestlé Quik Banana Milk. What might you recommend as a better approach? Why?
e. What selling strategies lay behind the Clamato "99.9% Clam Free" campaign?
f. Review the sample purpose statement on p. 353. Now try to write one of these statements for the Omaha Steaks campaign.

Key Point 4: Strategic Consistency

a. What is one-voice, one-look consistency, and how does it differ from strategic consistency?
b. Define and distinguish between mission, corporate culture, and core values and explain how these elements can anchor a consistency strategy.
c. What consistency problems are embedded in product and service performance?

Chapter Challenge

Writing Assignment

a. Find an article in the trade press that describes a new marketing communication campaign or program. Critique the marketing communication message strategy based on the information given in the report. What is missing? If you were working on this account as a planner, how would you develop the strategy? Prepare this in a memo format and address it to your instructor.

b. Collect all the communication materials you can find from a local bank. Analyze them and your experiences using the bank in terms of the Consistency Triangle. Can you identify any gaps between the say, do, and confirm messages?

c. Find a product or service that demonstrates inconsistency in the materials developed by the various marketing communication areas. Redesign the materials using a one-voice, one-look approach to create more consistency in these planned messages. Explain your changes.

Presentation Assignment

Adopt a local client, either a store, a manufacturer, or a nonprofit organization. Analyze the strategy behind this organization's marketing communication messages. In particular, look for IMC issues such as the four sources of messages, the messages the organization is communicating, and what messages the organization is sending to its stakeholders. Using the consistency triangle in Figure 9-6, identify any gaps in consistency among these various messages. Prepare your analysis for presentation to your client.

Internet Assignment

Look up the website for any of the brands mentioned in this chapter and find a site that presents the company's brand strategy. Summarize what you find there in terms of the marketing strategy decisions and how that strategy is made visible on the website.

Additional Readings

Bendinger, Bruce. *The Copy Workshop Workbook*. Chicago: The Copy Workshop, 1993.
Fill, Chris. *Marketing Communications: Frameworks, Theories, and Applications*. London: Prentice Hall International, 1995.
Harris, Thomas L. *Value-Added Public Relations: The Secret Weapon of Integrated Marketing*. Lincolnwood, Il: NTC Business Books, 1998.
Jewler, Jerome. *Creative Strategy in Advertising*, 3rd ed. Belmont, CA.: Wadsworth, 1989.
Jones, Susan K. *Creative Strategy in Direct Marketing*. Lincolnwood, IL: NTC Business Books, 1991.
Moriarty, Sandra E. *Creative Advertising: Theory and Practice*, 2nd ed. Englewood Cliffs, NJ: Prentice Hall, 1991.

Research Assignment

How do these different books and other books and articles you might find in your library approach message strategy? What are the differences? If you were to develop your own version of an IMC message strategy document, based on everything you have read in this chapter and in these other books and articles, what would it look like?

Endnotes

[1]Lisa Fortini-Campbell, *The Consumer Insight Handbook,* The Copy Workshop, 1992, p. 19.

[2]Chris Fill, *Marketing Communications* (London: Prentice Hall, 1995), pp. 259–60; and Bill Wells, "How Advertising Works," speech to American Marketing Association, St. Louis, MO, September 17, 1986.

[3]"Seeing Red Abroad, Pepsi Rolls Out a New Blue Can," *The Wall Street Journal*, April 2, 1996, p. B1.

10

Brand Message Execution

Key Points in This Chapter

1. How does the creative process work to develop big ideas?

2. What are the message design needs of different MC functional areas?

3. What are the written parts of a brand message?

4. How do art and design contribute to MC executions?

Chapter Perspective
The Big O

To paraphrase the words of Keith Reinhard, chairman and CEO of MC agency DDB Worldwide: Today, more than ever, if marketing communication is not *relevant,* it has no purpose. If it is not *original,* it will attract no attention. If it does not strike with *impact,* it will make no lasting impression. In the DDB approach to creative planning, the initials *ROI* (for relevant, original, impact) are equated with the investment made by clients in marketing communication. To be effective, the creative planning must also deliver bottom-line ROI (return on investment).

The brand messages that move consumers to respond contain the big O—the originality dimension in Reinhard's ROI formula. The originality factor first springs to life in the big idea. How this creative concept is executed determines to a great extent how effective the brand message will be in creating impact.

There are essentially two sets of decisions to make in brand message execution: what elements to use and how to structure those elements. The elements include all the bits and bytes of a brand message—the words, the sounds and music, the photos and illustrations, the costumes and settings, the lighting. The structure is the way these elements are combined—the layout, the flow, the form of the message. This chapter continues Chapter 9's discussion of message strategy and how to put the creative brief to work. The chapter first gives an overview of creative thinking, then discusses the functional areas of execution, looks briefly at tone and style, and then looks at two main divisions of creative executions: words and pictures.

HOW A SHARK SWIMS PAST THE SECRETARY
Wunderman Cato Johnson, Frankfurt, Germany

Andersen Consulting, now called Accenture, is the world's largest consulting company and, in Germany, one of the most important. Decisions on hiring a business consulting firm of this caliber are made at the CEO level. The problem Accenture faced in the 1990s was: How do you get a message about your consulting services on the CEO's desk? It's hard to reach chief executives via traditional media and their mail is filtered through one or more executive secretaries who function as gatekeepers.

That was the problem Accenture in Germany gave to the Frankfurt office of MC agency Wunderman Cato Johnson (WCJ), now called Impiric. The assignment was to develop a direct-mail message that would get past the secretary. Impiric rose to the challenge and developed a mailing that not only got past the secretaries and onto the desks of CEOs but also became a finalist for an AME Award (see Exhibit 10–1).

The Challenge

Accenture's core business is in the field of business process reengineering. Since reengineering a company's organization is very much a top management responsibility, the CEO is the one who must decide whether or not to hire a consulting firm and, if so, which one.

EXHIBIT 10-1

The cover of the direct mail piece that was designed to be interesting enough to get by the CEOs' gatekeeper (secretaries). This dramatic illustration did the trick!

A marketing problem for a company like Accenture is that CEOs are insulated from most commercial messages. Their mass media use is limited, and most of their reading consists of clippings preselected by their staff members. In terms of sales techniques, cold calls at this level are almost impossible. And traditional direct mail rarely passes the secretary who screens and filters the CEO's mail.

The Campaign Strategy

The objective of the campaign was to position Accenture as an expert of redesign of an organization, one that achieves its success by providing a holistic solution to its clients' problems. To achieve this objective, Impiric had to ensure that Accenture's message would get past the executive secretary and, as an Impiric team member explained, intrigue the CEO to the point that he or she would take the piece home: "If the CEO takes our mailing home and reads it to his [or her] children or grandchildren, then we've surpassed our objectives."

More specifically, the direct marketing objectives were stated as follows:

- Get the Accenture message on the CEO's desk.
- Build the Accenture brand at the "point of decision."
- Significantly increase brand awareness. (Because the mailing was image-oriented, no response was expected.)
- Reinforce the creative message presented in television commercials and in the print corporate campaign under the theme "Master of Design."
- Position Accenture as the expert for redesign of an organization.

In order to solidify this position, Accenture leveraged what would become its key differentiating position—the holistic approach to solving business problems, or business integration. Accenture's positioning statement then became: "To organizations and individuals who are committed to continuously strengthening performance, Accenture is the critical resource and partner to ensure that they achieve their goals." Accenture, then, was positioned as the master of organizational design.

The target audience for the mailing was taken from a list of 350 CEOs, chairpersons, general managers, and vice presidents in the leading industries and trade and service companies in Germany. These top managers represented Accenture's existing customers as well as prospective customers with the highest potential for hiring the company's services. Existing customers were included because the primary objective was to increase awareness of the position, rather than generating an immediate response. The campaign was designed not to sell a product but rather to make CEOs more aware of Accenture's services and place the company at "top of mind" when executives were considering their organizational problems and reengineering opportunities. Current Accenture customers were the ideal target for this redefined consulting opportunity.

Message Delivery

The "Master of Design" campaign used television commercials and a print corporate campaign that included airport posters. It also used a mailing designed to reinforce the umbrella campaign that had been presented in the more traditional media. The very sophisticated and obviously expensive mailing, however, was also designed to get past the secretaries by piquing their curiosity and motivating them to want to share the story with the CEO, who then would share it with his or

EXHIBIT 10-2

The Accenture "Shark" mailing was a large interactive book enclosed in a matching box cover. It featured a number of eye-catching print production techniques designed to appeal to a busy senior executive who might want to take it home and share it with his or her children or grandchildren.

her children or grandchildren at home (see Exhibit 10–2). The mailing, in turn, was supported by matching communication pieces such as invitations, stickers, shaped marzipan, and posters.

The Creative Strategy

A long-running advertising campaign using a "school of fish" theme had been evolving through the mid-1990s for Accenture. The evolution followed the company's shift from a solutions provider on a project basis to a consulting service that provides ongoing guidance to continuously strengthen the business performance of its clients.

The key element of the "Master of Design" campaign came to be known as the "Shark" mailing. It was built on a short fairy tale about a school of goldfish that live in an undisturbed and peaceful world where they happily perform their work. Suddenly things get tougher as enemies enter the marketplace—the goldfish are in danger. Another fish—the Master of Design—becomes their consultant and redesigns the loosely grouped school of fish into a new, more powerful organization using a familiar shape—the profile of a shark.

The Shark mailing, which was much more than a brochure, invited the reader to take an active part in the story development. The story could be read at several levels—as a simple fairy tale for children or as a sophisticated metaphor for business executives. It was presented in a hard-cover blue box with a laser graphic of a fish on its cover that appeared to be moving in water. When the lid was opened, water sounds and music could be heard. The first page showed a school of fish, swimming through the streets of a city, many wearing homburg hats. Some of the fish were mounted on magnets, which gave a three-dimensional effect and invited readers to move them around as they progressed through the story.

Evaluation of the Shark Mailing

Accenture initially sent 140 pieces to its target audience. Some 20 percent of the recipients responded with a personal letter that the marketing department captured for follow-up contact.

Not only did the innovative Shark mailing catch the attention of CEOs, it also won a number of awards at the New York Festivals, the Clio Festival, and the AME Award Show. But the real success of the Shark mailing lay with its integration into the ongoing "Master of Design" campaign that successfully repositioned Accenture as a leader in reengineering consulting services

This case was adapted with permission from the Advertising and Marketing Effectiveness (AME) award-winning brief for Accenture prepared by the Wunderman Cato Johnson agency in Frankfurt, Germany

BRAND MESSAGE EXECUTIONS

Chapter 9 introduced the process for creating a message strategy and a creative brief. This chapter will discuss the creative execution decisions (see Table 10-1).

An execution is the form of the completed advertisement, brochure, or sales piece—that is, how the planned message will appear when it is finished, which means managing all the details and decisions involved in the production of the brand message. The strategy statement describes what the piece is intended to accomplish; the execution statement describes how it will appear when it is completed.

CREATING THE BIG IDEA

Accenture's powerful use of imagery, copy, and even humor in the Shark mailing described in the chapter opening case demonstrates how creativity can enhance marketing communication. But what, exactly, is creativity? What is its role in marketing communications? Where does creativity come from, and how is it developed?

The Creative Concept

A creative concept transforms the message strategy into an exciting, attention-getting, and memorable idea. This move from the dry language of strategy to ideas that engage attention has been called the "creative leap" by advertising legend James Webb Young, founder of the Young and Rubicam agency.[1] In all forms of marketing communication, professionals are searching for the **big idea**, *a creative concept that translates the strategy into a catchy umbrella theme that unites all the various brand messages and contributes consistency to the brand image.*

T A B L E   1 0 - 1   Creative Execution Decisions

1. Creating the Big Idea
   - The creative concept that translates the strategic decisions into an attention-getting, interesting, and memorable message
2. Functional-Area Executions
   - Details about how the different functional areas will be used and what dimensions are important
3. Tone and Style
   - The "tone of voice" used by the brand to deliver its message
4. Words and Pictures
   - How the message is written and what it will look like

IMC IN ACTION

Black Gold: Turning a Brand Around with an Event

Black Gold had been one of Denmark's premium beers, but after many years on the market, the brand's user base was aging and sales were declining. The brand managers understood that they needed to reposition the beer as a more youthful brand. But, at the same time, they didn't want to lose their premium image. The problem, therefore, was credibility. How could they get young beer drinkers to believe that Black Gold, which had an "older drinker" image, was still cool—that it was the drink for them?

The traditional solution to such a problem would have been to launch an aggressive image campaign via mass media (specifically, television advertising) showing hip, youthful drinkers enjoying Black Gold. That would be traditional, but not very credible—and certainly not very creative.

Instead, the brand managers decided to take an IMC approach. The company's ad agency, DDB recommended a big idea in the PR/event arena—develop a marketing communication campaign around a film noire festival sponsored by Black Gold, thereby associating the brand with a stylish art form that was very much in vogue at that time with young adults. The campaign's objectives were to establish the association, make it credible, and make it relevant to the target audience.

The film festival, held in three major cities, anchored the campaign and, most important, created a lot of brand involvement. The company supported the festival with news releases; sales promotion in the form of posters and postcard premiums which showed dramatic scenes from the films; and mass media advertising to announce the time and place of the showings. Plus, it created a special film trailer that was shown in regular movie theaters.

Targeted customers were able to respond in numerous ways: they could attend the festival, read about it, collect the postcards and posters, and, of course, drink Black Gold. In short, the event provided a behavioral dimension to the brand's new positioning as well as a basis for an attitudinal change regarding the brand.

Think About It

What marketing problem did the Black Gold planners face? What consumer insights led to the development of the event-based IMC campaign?

Source: DDB in-house training video. Undated.

The big idea is usually associated with advertising, but big ideas can spring from, and are used in, other MC functional areas as well. The IMC in Action box describes a campaign that stood out because of its vivid presentation of a big idea for an event. This particular big idea—a film noire festival—demanded both artistic vision and insight into the target audience's interest in such an event.

A creative idea is "big" when it attracts the attention of the targeted audiences; is relevant to the brand's selling proposition; is memorable; is conceptually strong enough to be executed in a number of ways by a variety of marketing communication functions (i.e., is not just an idea that works in advertising or PR); and can last for years. Think of the Energizer bunny, the Budweiser frogs, and the milk mustache campaign—all were based on a big creative idea.

The big idea synthesizes the purposes of the strategy; joins the product benefit with consumer desire in a fresh, involving way; brings the subject to life; and makes the reader or the audience stop, look, and listen. As John O'Toole, former president of the American Association of Advertising Agencies, has noted, big ideas are not necessarily products of thought but rather of inspiration.[2]

David Ogilvy, a founder of the highly successful agency Ogilvy & Mather, pointed out that campaigns that have run five years or more are the superstars—they keep on producing results and memorability because of the strength of their big ideas. Superstar campaigns have run for Dove soap (33 percent cleansing cream), Ivory soap (99 44/100 percent pure), Perdue Chickens ("It takes a tough man to make a tender chicken"), and the U.S. Army ("Be all that you can be"). Many of these campaigns are all still running, and some have run for as long as 30 years. That's a big idea![3]

> **"While strategy requires deduction, a big idea requires inspiration."**
>
> John O'Toole, *The Trouble with Advertising*

Although big ideas are important for campaigns, the practice of continually searching for a creative concept that will break through the message clutter (described in Chapter 4) can create consistency problems. No matter how creative, messages that change frequently can cause confusion and undercut brand consistency. Relationships and brand equity are hard to build on an endless stream of unrelated big ideas. As many companies have learned, it's a challenge to come up with a big idea and then stick with it for an extended period (more than a year).

As the big idea is developed by the creative team, it is conceptualized in terms of its visual and verbal elements. Accenture's "Shark" mailing was essentially a visual idea used because of its attention-getting power. It was supported by a written story that helped to explain the point. Language affects imagery, and vice versa. However, because of the explanatory power of language, the verbal elements often come together first as an executional strategy statement for most promotional efforts, whether they be ads, brochures, or news releases.

Although the big campaign idea can come from any MC function, it is logical to search for it primarily within the MC function that is most appropriate to address or leverage the situation. Once the creative team has determined what the lead MC function will be, it must select other MC functions to round out the support.

For clients, evaluating a big idea is almost as difficult as coming up with one. When the agency (or the advertising department in an in-house situation) presents creative concepts, the client is suddenly in the role of a judge—without having gone through the other steps in the creative process first. David Ogilvy recommended that clients ask themselves five questions when evaluating new work:[4]

1. Did it make me gasp when I first saw it?
2. Do I wish I had thought of it myself?
3. Is it unique?
4. Does it fit the strategy to perfection?
5. Could it be used for 30 years?

Creative Thinking

Big ideas are the product of creative thinking. To *create* means to originate—to conceive a thing or idea that did not exist before. It can, though, and typically does, involve taking two or more previously unconnected objects or ideas and combining or arranging them to form something new. Most people believe that creativity springs directly from human intuition. But as we'll see in this chapter, creativity is very much a way of thinking, and the creative process is a step-by-step procedure that can be learned and used for generating original ideas and concepts.

Where does such creativity come from? Can it be developed? Or is it just a gift that only special people have? Obviously some people exhibit more than others, but creativity lives within all of us. If we weren't creative as a species, we wouldn't have discovered how to harness fire, domesticate animals, irrigate fields, or manufacture tools. And as individuals, we use our natural creativity every time we select clothes from out of the wardrobe in the morning, contrive an excuse, cook a meal, or choose a costume for a party.

In business, the **creative process** is recognized as *a formal procedure for increasing productivity and innovative output by an individual or a group.* It is used to get ideas and solve problems. Those responsible for creating ads, packages, sales promotions, websites, and news releases use various approaches in the development of new ideas. One approach is **brainstorming**, a technique developed many years ago by Alex Osborn, one of the founders of the agency BBDO.[5] It is *a formal process in which a group of 6 to 10 people gather together for the purpose of generating a multitude of new ideas.* The goal is to record any inspiration that comes into anyone's mind, allowing each new idea an opportunity to stimulate other people's thoughts.

Another approach is based on a combination of linear reasoning (moving logically through induction and deduction) and lateral thinking (bouncing around from one thought to another based on free association) that one creativity expert, Edward De Bono, has described as the Six Hats (see Table 10–2). In De Bono's workshops, people are assigned a hat to wear and asked to respond to a creative problem using the viewpoint represented by the hat.

Whatever specific approaches a company or agency develops, the creative process has a fairly predictable set of steps: exploration, insight, execution, and evaluation. Let's look at each step in turn.

Exploration

In the exploration stage, copywriters and art directors begin by assembling the raw materials from which ideas are made—facts, experiences, history, knowledge, and feelings, along with all the information gathered in the review of the marketing situation that is summarized in the creative brief. Brainstorming is useful at this stage.

TABLE 10-2   De Bono's Six Hats

White: Facts, data, and information. "What info do we have? What is missing? What information would we like to have? How can we get it?"

Red: Feelings, intuitions, hunches, emotions, and gut feelings. "Here's how I feel . . ."

Yellow: Optimism, the logical positive view of things; focus on benefits. "This might work if . . .; The benefit would come from . . ."

Green: New ideas, alternatives, possibilities. "We need some new ideas here—are there any other alternatives? Could we do this in a different way? Is there another explanation?"

Blue: Analysis of the process being used, priorities, agendas. "We have spent too much time looking for something/one to blame; Let's figure out the priorities; Let's try some green-hat thinking to get some more new ideas."

Black: Cautions and critical judgments. "The regulations say . . .; When we did it before . . .; It would be a mistake to . . ."

Source: Edward De Bono, *Six Thinking Hats* (New York: Little, Brown, 1986).

Insight

In the second step of the creative process, insights are extrapolated through the tedious task of reviewing all the pertinent information, analyzing the problem, identifying patterns, and searching for a key verbal or visual concept to communicate what needs to be said. This is the point where the search for the big idea—that flash of insight—takes place. It may come all at once, but sometimes it doesn't come until the creative team just lets the information stew simmer for a while.

Techniques used by creative people to stimulate this insight include changing patterns (unexpected juxtaposition) and looking at things in different ways (make the strange familiar and the familiar strange). Other techniques include adaptation (change the context), imagine (ask what if), reversal (look for the opposite), connection (join two unrelated ideas), comparison (build a metaphor), elimination (subtract something or break rules), and parody (fool around, look for the humor). An example of juxtaposition of unexpected images is found in the Skintimate ad in Exhibit 10–3.

An example of how a twist can be applied to an otherwise routine idea is a campaign for credit-card agency Visa that uses well-known people in predictable situations. The Bob Dole commercial, which was a Super Bowl favorite and a Cannes International Advertising Festival winner, showed the former (unsuccessful) presidential candidate returning home to Kansas, where he is simply known by everyone as "Bob." But the rousing welcome turns sour when a local store owner refuses to accept his check without an ID. With deadpan humor, Dole quips, "I just can't win." In another commercial, actor and New Age spiritual writer Shirley MacLaine, too, is asked to show ID, even though the cashier claims to have known her in past lives.

Execution

The third step in the creative process focuses on the way the idea is executed, which is sometimes as important as the idea itself. Since this chapter is about execution, the topic will receive more attention in the following pages. To give just one example, consider the Polo ad for Ralph Lauren underwear in which a good-looking guy is lying on a cot, wrapped in a half-open sleeping bag that reveals a lack of underwear. While the image is designed to get women's hearts pumping, the little executional detail that makes it an unexpected image is the tatoo, which you might not expect to find on a Ralph Lauren model.

An aspect of execution that isn't discussed much is presentation—the selling of the ideas. Ideas don't sell themselves; they have to be explained in terms of how they deliver on the strategy. In a workbook for copywriters, Bruce Bendinger says that "how well you sell ideas is as important as how good those ideas are."[6] To get the big idea approved, creative people may have to convince not only the client but others within the agency as well. Winning over the agency account team turns them into partners for the presentation to the client. It helps when the creative strategy clearly delivers on the creative brief and the overall marketing communication strategy.

Evaluation

Creatives use both judgment and research to evaluate their big ideas, which is the last step in the creative process. Evaluation for big-budget

EXHIBIT 10-3

Juxtaposing a pair of legs with a pair of scissors creates a provocative image for the moisturizing shaving gel Skintimate.

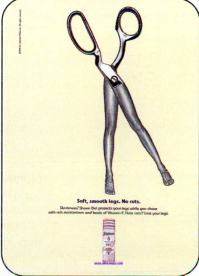

Soft, smooth legs. No cuts.

MC efforts may rely on a process called **copytesting,** which is *testing the effectiveness of brand message, a creative concept, or elements such as a headline, slogan, or visual for creative impact and understandability.* Testing is conducted at all points during the development of the creative strategy and executions, and even after the completed materials are in use.

A well-known example of the use of testing to determine the power of alternative creative elements comes from an early pioneer in the direct-response area, John Caples. For *Reader's Digest,* Caples determined which articles would be the most popular, both to feature in the magazine and in its promotional copy, by writing small ads offering many different articles for free and placing them in a daily newspaper. Readers selected the ones they wanted, and this "vote" gave Caples information about the popularity of the article titles.

The creative team carries out evaluation in the light of everyday practicality in order to decide what to do with an idea: implement it, modify it, or discard it and start over. Even though some agencies conduct research to test ideas, a lot of marketing communication go/no-go decisions are based on the judgment of the creative team and the client's marketing staff. They ask themselves questions such as: What's wrong/right with this idea? What if it fails? And, most important, does this idea achieve the message and MC objectives? Test yourself and your own judgment against the strategy calls described in the Ethics and Issues box. (See Chapter 21 for a more in-depth discussion of evaluating creative ideas and messages.)

FUNCTIONAL-AREA EXECUTIONS

As noted throughout this book, a typical IMC campaign will use a variety of MC functions. Each one chosen in any given marketing mix will need a different execution (or set of executions). Highly skilled professionals carry out the functional-area execution. This section is intended to give you only a brief overview of MC production processes and some familiarity with the terms. Expertise in this area comes from further, specific study and years of practice.

The Anatomy of a Brand Message

Before talking more about execution strategies and details, let's first take a tour through the anatomy of a brand message. This will introduce you to the language of the creative team and the elements of a creative message.

Printed Pieces

In a print piece like the Gillette ad in Exhibit 10–5 on page 346, for example, you will note that the selling premise—"Three Revolutionary Blades"— is introduced in the headline. The ad also contains other types of **display copy** (*copy in a type size that is larger than the body copy*): underlines and overlines ("Introducing Gillette"), picture captions, and subheads. Display copy is meant to entice the reader into continuing on to the **body copy,** *the text of the brand message.* The terminology is the same for brochures and direct-mail pieces as for advertisements.

Captions are used to explain the point of a visual. Call-outs are like minicaptions; they are positioned around the illustration and point to various parts of the visual, or they are pulled from the text and displayed for more prominence. Call-outs, for example, have been used throughout this textbook to call attention to important

ETHICS AND ISSUES

You Be the Judge

Reaching Generation Y is not easy for middle-class, middle-aged MC executives. Consequently, the brand messages targeted to this group sometimes fail to carry exactly the right nuance and are therefore seen as jokes. However, ads and other MC materials that do speak to this group in its own language may be panned by the rest of the marketing communication industry (as well as by parents and community leaders) for being too outrageous.

An example comes from the inline skate category. Sonic Skating Gear was chastised by *Adweek* for an ad designed to sell its tools and accessories to young people. The headline "The Homeless Have It Easy" was placed against a picture of a young skater sliding on his skates down a railing. The follow-up line—"They get to stay out on the streets all day"—explains the point but doesn't take the edge off the offensiveness.

The ad's creators obviously thought the hard-core Sonic skaters would enjoy the joke about the homeless. *Adweek's* columnist, however, found it to be offensive, not so much for what it says about the homeless, but for what it says about Sonic's customers: "Sonic blithely takes it for granted that these readers will lap up a witless joke about society's most hapless losers. How flattering is that?"

What's your call? Do you think irreverent hard-core skaters would identify with the ad or dismiss it as trying too hard to be hip? How would you evaluate this creative concept if you were on the creative team?

Another creative approach that works on the edge is the Diesel campaign by the Italian jean maker. Diesel's objective seems to be to position its clothing brand as outside or beyond the predictable, and its ads turn convention upside down (see Exhibit 10-4). For example, in one ad, which is a takeoff on an old western, the good-looking young hero, who is first seen putting on his jeans, kisses his beautiful wife and cute baby good-bye. In the next scene a grubby old nasty guy is seen waking up in bed next to an ugly woman. He sneers at her, kicks a dog on the steps outside the saloon, and generally behaves abominably. A gunfight between the two in the street takes place, and the nasty guy wins. The gunfight scene closes with him picking his nose.

What do you think? Does the bad-guy-wins idea appeal to a youthful audience? Is the ad bizarre and fun, or does it just go over the top? Where do you draw the line?

Think About It

How do you know if a narrowly targeted message works for its audience? How can you extend your judgment to a target audience you may not know much about? Is it okay to be offensive to broader social views if the message speaks to the interests of your target audience?

Source: "What's New Portfolio," *Adweek*, December 22, 1997, p. 24.

EXHIBIT 10-4

Diesel is known for its outrageous and provocative imagery.

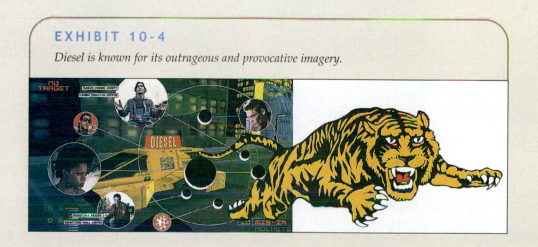

quotes. The illustration in Exhibit 10–5 uses call-outs to point to the various parts of the product—specially positioned blades, comfort edges, lubricating strip, springs, pivot design, contour grip, single-point docking, and flexible microfins.

At the end of the printed piece, a tagline may be found that provides either a call to action (e.g., instructions on how to respond) or a slogan that serves as a brand or campaign reminder cue. A tagline is often used to summarize in a catchy way a campaign's big idea. The Gillette tagline reads: "The Closest Shave in Fewer Strokes with Less Irritation." Also at the end of an ad are facilitators, which include the information that makes an inquiry or purchase easier, such as a map, a toll-free number, or an e-mail or website address. In this ad, a website address is featured: www.MACH3.com.

Typically at the bottom of the piece, the brand identification information is showcased, usually in the form of a distinctive **logo** (*a word, phrase or graphic element used to identify a brand*) or a **signature** (*a distinctive way of printing the brand name*). A signature can also be a logo, as in the case of Coca-Cola, whose familiar brand name is written in all planned messages in a distinctive Spencerian script. Sometimes a creative message can be delivered, or at least dramatized, by an unusual production technique.

The Accenture "Shark" mailing described in the chapter opening case was defined by its creative production. One spread featured buildings on a pull card that tilted when the tab was pulled, as well as a wheel in the background that showed the school of fish swimming around and around in its underwater environment. On the next spread, a giant menacing octopus popped up with several fish captive in its tentacles. Next came another popup—a box depicting five levels of circles with a silver fish (the Master of Design) in the middle. Printed alongside were rows of chairs with the fish in their homburg hats all lined up on the seats. On the next page a tab operated a moving iris that could either isolate the silver fish or show it in the middle of the school of fish. The last page of this fish story opened with a popup in the shape of a shark, whose body was made up of the school of fish swimming in unison.

Broadcast Pieces

A broadcast message, whether designed for television or radio, uses a script to outline the critical elements and the structure of the brand message. At the top of the script is information about the client and product, the title of the piece, the date, the writer's name, the length of the segment, and other identification information, such as a script number. An audio script, such as the one in Exhibit 10–6a for a radio commercial, contains the auditory descriptions that help identify the source and content of the message. Typically the source is identified on the left side in capital letters (the person speaking, music, or sound effects). The text on the right contains the dialogue.

A video script is more complex than an audio script because it contains both audio and video instructions. In order to illustrate the visual ideas, a storyboard is used to provide a pictorial diagram of the scenes. The storyboard coordinates the action with the dialogue by showing key frames with their associated audio track underneath the various scenes. Once a TV commercial is produced, photoboards are often made as shown in Exhibit 10–6b. Photoboards are very similar to storyboards, the only difference being the use of actual scenes rather than drawings of them.

Message Formats

The first step in the execution of a brand message is to identify the appropriate presentation for the message. Experienced creative people look for the technique and style with the greatest persuasive appeal for the idea being presented. The term *execution strategy* describes the message format or approach. Some message formats are referred to as "formulas" because they are used so frequently. The following list describes the 12 most common message formats:

1. *News announcement:* Uses a straightforward, factual presentation and emphasizes a news angle; used for press releases in publicity and as a straight-sell approach in advertising that emphasizes an appeal to reason; useful for new products or products with a new formulation or use.

Washington Apple Commission
Washington Apples
They're As Good As You've Heard.
C. Kram
Radio :30
WAC-3

(SFX):	a telephone rings; the cradle lifts
MAN:	(an avuncular voice) Hello.
CALLER:	Oh. I'm sorry. I was looking for another number.
MAN:	976-EDEN?
CALLER:	Well. . . yeah.
MAN:	You got it.
CALLER:	The flyer said to ask for Eve.
MAN:	Yeah, well, she's not here. I can help you.
CALLER:	Oh. . . no. That's okay. I'll just. . .
MAN:	Hold on, hold on. Let me get the apple.
CALLER:	The apple?
MAN:	You ready? Here goes. . .
(SFX):	crunch
CALLER:	That's. . . you're eating an apple. That's the "little bit of paradise" you advertised?
MAN:	Well, that's a little *bite* of paradise. The printer made a mistake.

CALLER:	I'm supposed to sit here and listen to you eat an apple?
MAN:	Well, it is a Washington Apple. . .
(SFX):	crunch
CALLER:	Look, I'm not going to pay three dollars a minute just to sit here while you. . .
MAN:	Nice, big, Red Delicious Washington Apple. . .
(SFX):	crunch
CALLER:	. . . eat an apple. . . it does sound good.
MAN:	It is nice and crisp, you know.
CALLER:	Sounds good. . .
MAN:	Kinda sweet.
CALLER:	Uh-huh. . .
MAN:	Fresh. . .
CALLER:	I shouldn't. . . this is silly. . .
(SFX):	crunch
CALLER:	What are you wearing?
MAN:	Well, a flannel shirt and paisley ascot.
CALLER:	Oh. Describe the apple again.
MAN:	Mmmm-hmmm
V.O.:	Washington Apples
(SFX):	crunch
V.O.:	They're As Good As You've Heard.

EXHIBIT 10-6A

An example of a radio script that is used to guide the production of the commercial.

2. *Inherent drama:* Focuses on finding the characteristic of a brand that lends itself to storytelling or mythmaking in a way that sets the brand apart from competitors; used in categories with little product differentiation.

3. *Testimonial/endorsement:* Uses celebrities, experts, or typical users to deliver a message endorsing a product; used in categories where there is product differentiation or where credibility is important.

4. *Talking head:* Lets the characters tell a story in their own words using dialogue, monologue, or interview techniques; used to explain things and to add believability.

5. *Lifestyle:* Focuses on the user rather than the product; for example, beer and soft-drink advertisers like Mountain Dew frequently target their messages to active, outdoorsy young people, focusing on who drinks the brand rather than on specific product advantages.

6. *Problem/solution:* Identifies a problem that the product can solve—often the premise behind "slice-of-life" episodes; used to dramatize product differentiation and entertain at the same time.

7. *Demonstration:* Invites audience members to believe the evidence of their own eyes; for highly persuasive communication, "don't just say it, show it;" used with products that have a demonstrable point of difference.

Coopers &Lybrand

NOT JUST KNOWLEDGE. KNOW HOW.

"Best of Times"   30 Seconds

(MUSIC THROUGHOUT)
ANNCR: (VO) It's a whole new world facing
today's chief executive.

The economy is global. Competition is fierce.

Financial pressures are unrelenting.

But, there is one firm that can help CEO's make
the difference between the worst of times

... and the best of times. (CROWD APPLAUDS)

Coopers & Lybrand.
Not just knowledge. Know how.

EXHIBIT 10-6B

This is an example of a TV :30 photoboard.

8. *Picture caption:* Tells a story with illustrations and captions; particularly useful for products that have a number of different uses or come in a variety of styles or designs; a comic-strip panel approach also can deliver this type of story.

9. *Jingle:* Uses music and catchy words to entertain and remind the audience of brand values; used for products with little product differentiation and for brand image messages; an old maxim in advertising is "If you can't say it, sing it."

10. *Humor:* Entertains, dispels negative images, and creates a fun, likable personality for undifferentiated products. Note: humor is subjective and can distract from the product; it should be used with caution—watch for issues of questionable taste. Exhibit 10–7 Is an example of an American Greetings ad that uses humor along with an unpredictable production technique to get attention.

11. *Animation/cartoons:* Uses drawings, puppets, and claymation characters (made out of clay but filmed like puppets movement by movement) for their entertainment value as well as for communicating difficult messages and reaching specialized markets.

12. *Special effects:* Uses visually interesting production techniques to catch attention and entertain. In broadcast, computer graphics can create almost unimaginable effects, like those in science-fiction movies; print forms such as posters, brochures, and ads may use special printing and binding effects to create unusual folds, 3-D forms, images that appear to move, scratch-and-sniff scents, and computer chips that sing.

Understanding how to structure promotional messages in terms of these common formats, and when to use them, helps creative people figure out what they need to say and how they need to say it. Because using one of these common formats produces a predictable message, some creative people will start with an idea for one format and then twist it into something that unexpectedly violates or parodies the format. That's another way to take a predictable idea and turn it into a creative one.

TONE AND STYLE

EXHIBIT 10-7

American Greetings used this ad to call attention to its Bubblegum line of funky cards. It consists of an actual card glued to the page. When you open the card, you find that "Sis" has handwritten: "At least there was one opening at that company."

In marketing communication, the tone is a cue about the nature of the message and the personality of the brand. The word **tone** describes *a general atmosphere or a manner of expression*, as in "He speaks in an angry tone of voice." Tone of voice—businesslike, solemn, angry, happy, cheering, fearful, sympathetic, frustrated—implies shades of coloring and nuances in the style of the message and signals the appropriate emotional response. The Jeep ad in Exhibit 10–8, for example, uses a threatening tone to make a point about its trademark.

Tone can also imply a conversation, and that's an important dimension of relationship-focused communication. The personality of the brand speaks through the planned messages, but the style of the language also signals the target audience. Ads with an "attitude," for example, are frequently targeted to young people, particularly the Generation X group, who are presumed to be anti-advertising. In other words, the tone surrounds the message and sets up audience expectations about the brand relationship.

The word **style** also describes *a manner of expression;* in contrast to tone, which has to do with how a message sounds, style has to do with how it looks or feels more generally.

There are some styles that don't work very well in marketing communication—such as pedantry, preachiness, and pomposity. Creative teams generally avoid messages using the corporate "we" or brag-and-boast approaches. Negative messages, particularly those that patronize or put down the audience, are especially ineffective. One thing to avoid when setting the tone or developing the style of a brand message is the typical marketing language of the strategy statements. Sandra Moriarty warns against "strategy hypnosis."[7] She admits that creative people have to understand the strategy, but they also have to move beyond it.

WORDS AND PICTURES

Words and pictures play different roles in the logic of a brand message. Pictures—or, more broadly, *visuals*—are usually designed to catch attention and to move the reader on into the copy. As the ad for the German airline Lufthansa in Exhibit 10–9 demonstrates, the rose dripping with water sets up an interesting visual and arouses curiosity. The headline—"Shower in Our Lounge"— is also provocative in that it picks up on the dripping water imagery but doesn't really explain the visual per se. In order to get the point of this ad, you have to read on into the body copy, where the idea of luxury is equated with business travel. The words and the picture work together to deliver the concept.

As Figure 10–1 shows, in print messages the visuals and headline create the attention step in the hierarchy of effects. The interest step typically corresponds to the subheads and the first or lead paragraph of body copy. Body copy, along with other elaboration devices such as boxes and supporting visuals, helps build credibility and stimulates desire. The action step takes place with the closing paragraph or other copy at the end of the piece. The closing may sometimes include a last line that functions as a call to action—in other words, it tells the target audience what to do or gives helpful information such as where the product might be found. Other action items at the end—the logo, slogan, tagline, signature—provide brand identity and reinforce the brand position.

Although it is important that the words and pictures work together in creative messages, it helps if the visual adds something to the words and the words extend the idea presented in the visual, as the Lufthansa ad demonstrates. If the visual is a literal translation of the words, you may have a rather predictable, perhaps even boring, concept. But, as is the case with true synergy (where the sum is greater than its parts), a unique conjunction or juxtaposition of words and pictures can create a richer meaning than either element carries by itself.

A good example of words-and-pictures synergy comes from the ad in Exhibit 10–10 for Microsoft's Visio, a software program for business diagrams. The headline on the left page says "Save a Thousand Words." The illustration on the right page shows a perceptual map that diagrams a product idea. The ad thus calls to mind the old adage "A picture is worth a thousand words" without stating it explicitly.

EXHIBIT 10-8

The tone of the headline, which is shown inscribed on a metal sign on a fence that comes in front of the brand name, Jeep, is tongue-in-cheek, but still threatening.

Writing

Whether copywriters apply their skills to a variety of MC functions or specialize in only one, they need to understand the similarities and differences in writing for print media and writing for electronic media. Writing publicity messages (whether print or electronic) presents special challenges to copywriters.

The Role of Display Copy

As mentioned earlier, the display copy, particularly the headline, is the major attention-getting device in print messages. The writer's goal is to express the big idea with verve. The headline also needs to work with the art in order to develop the creative idea, as Exhibit 10–11 illustrates.

To be effective, a headline must serve a set of purposes—attracting attention is the foremost, but it must also engage the audience, explain the visual, lead the audience into the body of the copy, and cue the selling message. The average MC

EXHIBIT 10-9

In this Lufthansa ad, the dripping rose is a symbol of a luxurious bathroom and represents the idea of taking a shower after a long flight, which is a strong benefit of the brand.

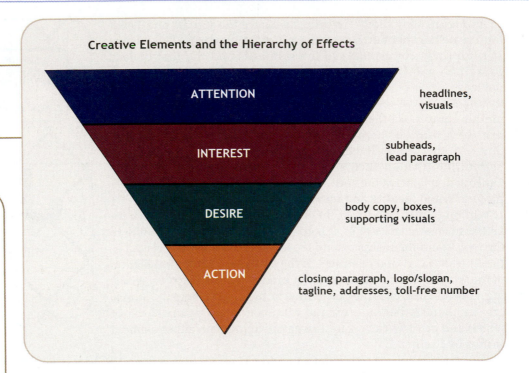

Creative Elements and the Hierarchy of Effects

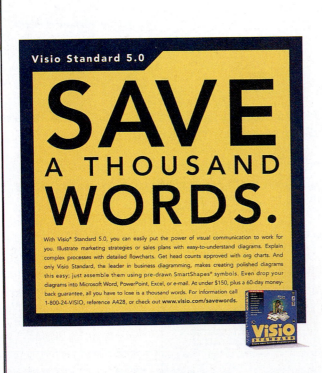

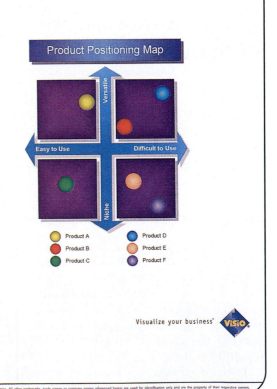

message has only a couple of seconds to capture the reader's attention. The Lufthansa ad in Exhibit 10–12 illustrates how a relevant claim, "More Space: Our New First and Business Class" can be used to attract the attention of business travelers.

Ideally, headlines present a complete selling idea. Research has found that, on average, three to five times as many people read the headline as read the body copy. So if the selling premise isn't clear in the headline, the message may be wasting the client's money. In outdoor posters or billboards, the headline may be the only copy, so it has to communicate the entire message. The difficulty is that the headline needs to be short and succinct. The traditional notion is that short headlines with one line are best but that a second line is acceptable. In one study of over 2,000 ads, most headlines averaged about eight words in length.[8]

Publicity writers also pay close attention to creating provocative, newsworthy headlines. The headline will determine how much attention an editor pays to the publicity release. If the editor doesn't find it interesting and engaging, the article will never make it into print.

Finally, headlines, particularly in publicity writing, are used to showcase news. Consumers look for new products, new uses for old products, or improvements on old products. "Power words" that imply newness (e.g., New, Improved, Redesigned) can increase readership and should be employed whenever honestly applicable.

The Role of Body Copy

The writer tells the complete story in the text, or body copy. Set in smaller type than headlines or subheads, the body copy is a logical continuation of the ideas introduced in the display copy. The body copy creates interest, credibility, and desire. Body copy appears in brochures, news releases, and advertisements. Exhibit 10–13 demonstrates how body copy works.

As noted above, fewer people read body copy than read headlines. Thus, to gain attention, the copywriter must speak to the target audience's interests. Imaginative ideas carefully phrased can increase the attention span of busy readers. Refer to the Lufthansa ad in Exhibit 10–12, whose body copy explores the value of personal space—"Having more to claim as your own is especially valuable when you travel." Body copy explains the features, benefits, and utility of the product or service, and handles the sales appeal and the call for action.

Copywriters often read their copy aloud to hear how it sounds—even if it's intended for print media. The ear is a powerful copywriting tool, so good writers pay close attention to the phonic characteristics of the words they use. For example, notice the rhythm of the parallel construction in the last two sentences in the Lufthansa ad: "With room to relax, business travel becomes infinitely less stressful. And less stressful travel is exactly what people have come to expect from Lufthansa."

Writing for Electronic Media

Some of the same rules that pertain to writing copy for print media also hold true for radio, television, and other types of video. Yet electronic media have special dictates.

EXHIBIT 10-11

Usually designed by the art director to appear in the largest and boldest type in the ad, the headline is often the strongest focal point, next to the art.

EXHIBIT 10-12

Not only does this headline work to catch attention of business travelers but the rose visual also links it with other pieces in this campaign and continues to serve as a symbol of the luxury positioning.

Writing Audio Copy

Copywriters for radio first need to understand the nature of the medium. Radio provides entertainment or news to listeners who are busy doing something else—driving, washing dishes, reading the paper, or even studying. To be heard, a message must be catchy and interesting. Radio listeners usually decide within seconds if they're going to pay attention. Therefore, to attract and hold listeners' attention, radio copy must be designed to be intrusive and break through the clutter of other environmental stimuli. Radio copy also uses music to connect with listeners; as noted earlier, jingles are highly memorable; they offer copywriters a way to repeat a line in a nonirritating way.

But keep in mind: intrusive, yes; offensive, no. An insensitive choice of words, an overzealous effort to attract listeners with irritating sounds (car horns, alarm clocks, screeching tires), or a character that sounds too exotic, odd, or dumb can cause listener resentment and ultimately inattention.

Radio and other audio copy has to be clearer than any other kind of copy. The listener can't refer back, as in print, to find, say, an antecedent for a pronoun, so it has to be very clear what the pronoun refers to. Likewise, the English language is so full of homonyms (words that sound like other words) that listeners can easily confuse the meaning of a word that does not have a clear or sufficient context. Think of the confusion that can result if a listener can't tell whether a radio commercial is using the word *cereal* or the word *serial*.

One of the most challenging aspects of writing for broadcast media is making the script fit the time slot. The copywriter may type the script on a normal page and then count the lines, allowing approximately five seconds for each 80-character line. However, the delivery changes for different types of messages, so writers must read the script aloud for timing. With electronic compression, recorded radio ads can now include 10 to 30 percent more copy than text read live. Still, the following list is a good rule of thumb:

10 seconds: 20–25 words.

20 seconds: 40–45 words.

30 seconds: 60–70 words.

60 seconds: 130–150 words.

Writing Video Copy

Video uses the standard techniques of audio; however, its visuals can attract attention and describe something better than words—by showing it. Video copywriters can use action, music, sound effects, and special effects, all of which can add an element of drama to the message. An example of a visually interesting video message is a series of commercials for clothing retailer Gap, which uses musical styles to sing the praises of its pants. The "Khakis swing" ad featured Louis Prima and energetic swing dancers in khaki pants; the "Khakis rock" spot has skaters dancing to an electronic beat. Clearly, in creating these ads, the copywriters also understood the power of music.

To illustrate some basic principles of writing video copy, let's describe a commercial in detail. Champagne producers have tried in the past to convince people that it is okay to drink champagne at times other than New Year's Eve. How would you break through this wall knowing that people may like the sense of festiveness associated with champagne more than they like the taste? A campaign for Moët & Chandon by the agency Kirshenbaum Bond & Partners uses the distinctive pop of the cork to announce times for small celebrations. Rather than focusing on holidays, the campaign shows two intriguing women lying on their backs in a field, an amorous couple in a dark café, a woman rising from a bathtub, and a woman and two men in a rowboat. All the characters become alert as they hear a sound— though the audience doesn't hear it (a technique designed to pique the viewers' interest—"What did those people all hear?"). The ad then uses a voice-over (the sound of an unseen narrator speaking) in which a woman asks in a sultry tone, "Is it possible for one sound to do more than break the silence?" The voice-over continues: "Can one sound be inherently French, yet transcend every language?" The spot ends with a visual of a Moët cork being shot toward the viewer, accompanied by an unmistakable popping sound.

The copywriter wrote only two sentences, but the challenge came in matching those sentences, in style and tone, to the visuals and sounds.

Writing Publicity Messages

As will be discussed further in Chapter 15, most public relations communications are not openly sponsored or paid for. People receive these communications in the form of news articles, editorial interviews, or feature stories after the messages have been reviewed and edited—filtered—by the media. Since the public thinks such messages are coming from the medium rather than a company trying to promote a product or service, it accepts and trusts them more readily than it does commercial brand messages.

Although PR may offer greater credibility, advertising can offer greater awareness and control. For this reason, many companies relay their public relations messages through corporate or institutional advertising. An example is the Ford Motor Company's recycling ad in Exhibit 10–14.

The most widely used PR tool is the **news release**, which is *a news story written by an organization to get publicity for its products or services.* It consists of one or more typewritten sheets of information issued to shed light on a particular subject. They may announce the development of a new product, the promotion of an executive, an unusual contest, the landing of a major contract, or establishment of a scholarship fund, to name just a few common topics. Exhibit 10–15 shows a standard news release format.

EXHIBIT 10-14

Ford Motor Company uses this ad to demonstrate how much of an effort it makes to recycle and reuse materials in its cars.

Many publications, particularly trade publications, run **feature articles,** which are *colorful stories with high human or business interest,* about companies, products, or services. Features are also called *soft news;* timeliness is less important in them than in hard news. Whether for print or electronic media, features may be written by a PR person working for a company or its agency, the medium's staff, or a third party (such as a freelance business writer). They may include case histories, how-to's (such as how to use the company's product in a new way), problem-solving scenarios (how one customer uses the company's product to increase production), and state-of-the-art technology updates. Other formats include roundups of what's happening in a specific industry and editorials, such as a speech or essay by a company executive on a current issue.

A **media kit** is *a package of publicity information that includes a variety of materials related to an event, including background information* (Exhibit 10–16). Such a kit may includes a basic fact sheet of information about the event, news releases and feature stories, a program or schedule of activities, and a list of the participants and their biographical data. In addition, the kit may contain photos, brochures, maps, and other artwork.

Art and Design

In any MC message, the visual elements carry an important responsibility in attracting attention and communicating something about the brand or company. The appearance of an annual report, for example, can create a positive or negative impression that stays with a potential investor. That mood, in turn, helps or hinders the acceptance of the verbal message. The creative team must also be sure that the various elements in a piece of marketing communication flow logically. To have a sense of how creatives do that, we need to understand how visual elements are selected and assembled. As noted in Chapter 9 the art director is responsible for photos, illustrations, filming, logos, and so on—anything that has to do with the look of the brand message.

News Release

  Sprint

Press Contacts: For Immediate Release
Russ Robinson
Sprint
Phone: (913) 624-3417
Email: russ.robinson@mail.sprint.com

Jenifer Sarver
Citigate Cunningham
Phone: (512) 652-2751
Email: jsarver@cunningham.com

Sprint Forms Broadband Wireless Group To
Deploy Fixed Wireless Broadband Services Across the U.S.

Tim Sutton Named President of New Organization

OVERLAND PARK, Kan. — Aug. 9, 1999 — Sprint announced today the creation of a new organization which will build the facilities and develop the wireless broadband services the company will deliver over the nationwide fixed wireless network that Sprint is creating. Timothy Sutton, formerly vice president, Technology and Corporate Development, has been named president of the Broadband Wireless Group (BWG).

Sprint has acquired five companies with licenses in the Multichannel Multipoint Distribution Service (MMDS) spectrum: Peoples Choice TV, American Telecasting, Inc., Transworld Telecommunications Inc., Videotron USA and WBS America. These licenses will give Sprint up to 200 MHz of spectrum in over 65 markets across the nation, covering about 30 million households. BWG will be responsible for building a broadband fixed-wireless network in these markets, and bringing to market high-speed Internet service for homes and small businesses that will compete with cable data offerings, the xDSL offerings of local Bell companies and with data CLECs.

— more —

EXHIBIT 10-15

This is an example of a news release. Notice how the headline summarizes the point of the story, however, you have to read on to truly understand what the story is about.

Visualizing Creative Strategies

Art directors and other graphic artists must decide on a theme and then must translate that concept into visual elements. This process, which is called **visualization,** refers to *the first step in turning the creative concept into a visual.* Both copywriters and art directors are imaginative, and they put their imagination to work through the four-step creative process outlined earlier in this chapter. An example of art director creativity comes from an advertisement for Amica, which specializes in automobile insurance. The ad shows a car on a dark road, beneath a headline that says to hold the ad up to the light. When you do, you can see a huge truck bearing down on the car. The truck and the Amica logo and copy block are all printed on the back side of the page and can only be seen and read when light shines through the page.

Another dimension of visualization involves how the message elements—the words, pictures, and sounds of the message—will be presented and ordered to best communicate the big idea. MC messages often use a specific word or phrase

EXHIBIT 10-16

In addition to a news release, this press kit for Sprint includes photos, answers to frequently asked questions, and an overview of the schedule for the new product roll-out.

to connect the text to the images—like "the Master of Design" in Accenture's Shark mailing. However, think what this message would look like without the silver fish representing the master and the school of fish surrounding the master. If the creative team had just placed the headline and body copy on an otherwise bare full page, it could have saved some production money, but how much would the brand message have lost because of low visual interest and thus low readership?

The Role of Visuals

As noted earlier, the word *visual* is interchangeable with the word *picture*, but *visual* also encompasses any kind of art. In print advertising, the art usually consists of a photograph, a computer-generated image, or a hand-drawn illustration. In video, the art element may be live-action film, still photos, or animation. The style of the art is also important. An intimate style uses soft focus and close views; a documentary style portrays the scene without pictorial enhancements such as fancy editing; and a dramatic style features unusual angles, distorted color, fast pacing cuts, or blurred action images.

But don't forget the earlier discussion of the synergy of words and pictures: In most brand messages, particularly advertising, the nonverbal message should be inseparable from the verbal. Either one can enhance the other, or destroy it. The remainder of this section, therefore, discusses the execution of the big idea from the standpoint of the visual elements and how they relate to and support the verbal details.

The Visual Focus

Selecting the focus for the visuals is a major step in the creative process. It often determines how well the big idea is executed. Refer back to the "Can't Rush Perfection" ad for Lufthansa in Exhibit 10–11; the dominant visual (the rosebud) illustrates an idea—a visual metaphor— rather than the product itself. The visual idea wouldn't make sense, however, without the headline, so the two elements work synergistically to create the proposition: "something good takes time to unfold." Just as important, the visual projects a style and creates a feeling—a context for the consumer's perception of the quality of the brand.

It may appear self-evident to say that the kind of visual used is often determined during the visualization process. But frequently, the visual is not determined until the art director or designer actually lays out the ad (designs its look and locates its elements). Advertising managers and art directors often keep checklists—as well as an extensive file, or morgue, of noteworthy ads, photos, and illustrations—to serve as idea ticklers. Brand messages use many standard subjects for visuals, both product-related and image-focused. Here are a dozen sources art directors commonly use to determine the focus of the visual:

1. The product alone or in use, or its package.
2. The context or setting.
3. Product features.
4. Comparison of products.
5. Users benefiting from or enjoying the product.
6. Established brand symbols (e.g., the Jolly Green giant).

7. Story elements (e.g., babies, puppies).

8. A humorous visual, whether or not previously related to the product.

9. People as spokespersons or giving a testimonial.

10. Demonstration of the problem (what happens if you don't use the product) and the solution (what happens if you do).

11. A visual association (i.e., a connection between the product and something it looks like).

12. A visual metaphor (i.e., something that stands for the product).

In advertising and sales promotion materials, the visual shapes the message into a complete communication package that appeals to the senses as well as the mind. The exotic undersea imagery, for example, in the Accenture's package was reinforced by the water sounds that started up when the cover was opened.

As an example of the sensory impact a promotional visual for a brand can deliver, consider the 42-foot-high Coke bottle on the rooftop of Atlanta's Turner Field in a public park called the Sky Field.[9] Made of 983 bats, 79 mitts, and 5,788 baseballs, the Coke bottle is visible from most anywhere in downtown Atlanta (Exhibit 10–17). Oversize Adirondack chairs with back slats in the distinctive hourglass shape of the Coke bottle are spread around the Sky Field as well. Such creative visuals signify a new age of architecture and furniture as marketing communication.

However, there is more than one kind of art in an MC message. There is also the typography, which has a design dimension and contributes to the style of the message. When artfully designed and crafted, a **typeface**—*a set of letters and numbers with a particular or distinguishing design*—evokes a mood. Thus, different typefaces convey different tones (formal, funny, regal, casual, etc.) and must be coordinated with other elements of the brand message.

EXHIBIT 10-17

The gigantic Coke bottle at Atlanta's Turner Field is constructed of bats, balls, and mitts.

Corporate and Brand Image Design

One area of design that is particularly important in IMC is corporate or brand image design. There are two levels of design strategy involved in such efforts: the design of an identity program and the design of the brand or corporate image.

The word *identity* refers to the design of the public face or distinctive visual appearance of an organization or brand. This "look" should be reflected in every aspect of the business from architecture to, of course, marketing communication. It provides the elements needed to recognize the brand. The pieces of a corporate identity program include logos, trademarks, distinctive colors, typography, brand characters, and graphic styles.

Companies successful at maintaining a consistent brand identity, such as Lucent and Intel, have established a set of graphic standards, a set of rules that establish consistency in the use of the brand or corporate identification elements. These standards explain how to use logos and other brand marks and colors on signage, truck side panels, letterheads, ads, and so on. Having and enforcing graphic standards also helps to legally protect trademarks and logos. The graphic standards (often printed in a book or manual) need to be in the hands of every department and agency that develops materials bearing the brand name, trademark, or logo. As the organization's "beauty regimen" the standards ensure consistency in corporate and brand identity.

One problem that bedevils corporate identity programs is the protection of brand names and trademarks. Corporate advertising is often managed by a public relations department to protect product names and trademarks. As noted in Chapter 2, a successful brand that dominates its product category must guard against becoming seen as generic. Kleenex, for example, uses advertising to remind consumers that its name is a brand name in the product category of tissues. Xerox, Formica, Frigidaire, and other companies have either lost the right to the exclusive use of their names or have been threatened by the Federal Trade Commission with such a loss because the brand name has moved into common usage for the product category.

A **corporate image** is broader than a brand image in that it is defined as "the perceived sum of the entire organization, its objectives, and its plans. It encompasses the company's products, services, management style, communication activities, and actions around the world."[10] It reflects the company's philosophy of business as well as its corporate culture— "the way we do things around here."

Even though they reside in the minds of customers and other stakeholders, both the brand image and the corporate image are managed strategically by the marketing communication program. When the product brand name and the company name are the same (Sony, for example), the company can, with relative ease, establish consistency of image. When the brand name is different from the company name, consistency may be harder to maintain. Different product brands may be managed by entirely different departments in an organization.

A corporate advertising campaign is often used to announce a new corporate image or a change in image. Corporate image for Ford, for example, is generally the responsibility of the public relations staff; the brand image of the various Ford makes and models are generally the responsibility of marketing and/or advertising divisions. A strategic management decision involves the extent to which the two should reinforce or support one another. Furthermore, where a brand has subbrands, then similar strategies are needed to plot the interrelationships between the umbrella brand and the subbrands.

Changing an image can be even more difficult than creating one. Clothing retailer Gap, for example, has had to work very hard to transform its image from a store that sells funky jeans for teens to a chain that sells simple, tasteful clothing for adults as well. Ads for the Gap reflect that new image; they are simple, striking, dramatic, and almost avant-garde. The stores, in their interior design and merchandising displays, project the same personality as the ads. Even more dramatic has been the image change for Abercrombie & Fitch, which used to be a store for older well-to-do customers, and is now a mecca for teenage fashion leaders (see Exhibit 10–18).

Design programs that seek to make cosmetic changes will probably not be very effective unless they also reflect the corporate culture. An identity program, like a personality, must come from within.

Package Design

A package, especially for consumer goods, is an important communication vehicle. Its front panel or label defines the product category, identifies the brand, delivers short copy points, and functions as the "last ad a customer sees" before making a purchase decision. It's more than just a physical container for a product.

A package reflects the brand image and delivers visual impact. Consumers pick a brand, in many cases, because the package delivers a welcome familiarity. In such a situation, consistency of design— between the package design and other brand design

EXHIBIT 10-18

Abercrombie & Fitch, which used to be a stuffy store for aging want-to-be explorers, has become a fashion statement for young people.

elements—delivers a key visual message. Coca-Cola's hourglass-shaped bottle continued as a brand icon even when the company switched from glass to plastic bottles. Realizing the need to stand out in a world of clutter, Coke plans to put a picture of its bottle shape on its cans as well. The objective is to generate near instantaneous and universal recognition. Other classic packaging examples include the Mrs. Butterworth's syrup bottle, the L'eggs egg-shaped hosiery containers, and the artful boxes that hold Celestial Seasonings herbal teas (see Exhibit 10–19).

Packages also link to other marketing communication efforts. If the brand is involved in other major promotional activities, for example, the creative team can design a tie-in message for the package to serve as a reminder. Most package front panels are designed with space for **promotional flags**, *banners that call attention to current sales-promotion programs and advertising theme*s, such as "official sponsor of the Olympics" with an Olympics rings logo.

Packaging also provides the link between MC messages and the product on the shelf. Notice in soft-drink commercials how much time is devoted to showing the can or bottle. Likewise, the package may extol a product's benefits by showing mouth-watering pictures of such food products as ice cream, cereals, cake (always baked, seldom in the mix stage), and pizza. Packages for appliances such as food processors, slow cookers, and hand drills often show dramatic shots of the product in use or the food created by the product. The package, in other words, uses a sophisticated form of visual persuasion to deliver a benefit strategy message.

Print Layout and Design

In print media, the word **layout** refers to *an orderly arrangement of the elements making up an MC message:* visuals, headlines, subheads, body copy, captions, trademarks, slogans, and signatures. It is during the layout process that the creative team creates coherence in the visual message and uses style to help create meaning.

By creatively arranging elements—for example, surrounding the text with lines, boxes, shades, and colors—and relating those to one another in size and proportion, the designer can further enhance the message. In layout, the design principles of balance, proportion, and movement are guides for uniting images, type, sounds, colors, and qualities of the medium into a single communication. The Dodge Dakota ad in Exhibit 10–20 demonstrates how a layout can contribute meaning to the ad's theme, which is the "new" Dodge has lots of new "stuff."

In advertising, there are a number of standard layouts. Traditionally, print ads scoring the highest recall have used a poster-style format with a single, dominant visual that occupies between 60 and 70 percent of the ad's total area. In fact, some research shows that ads scoring in the top third for "stopping power" (getting attention) devote an average of 82 percent of their space to the visual.

The layout also serves as a blueprint for production. It shows the size and placement of each element; it tells the copywriter how much copy to write; it suggests the size and style of the image to the illustrator or photographer; and it helps the art director specify

the type. Also, once the production manager knows the dimensions of the piece, the number of photos, the amount of typesetting, and the use of art elements such as color and illustrations, he or she can accurately determine the cost of producing it.

The Print Design Process

The design process serves as both a creative and an approval process. In the conceptual phase for print media, the designer uses a variety of "rough" art to establish the message's look and feel. The following list describes the evolution of a print message.

- The *thumbnail sketch*—or, simply, thumbnail—is a small, very rough, rapidly produced drawing used to try out ideas. The artist uses the thumbnail to visualize a number of layout approaches without wasting time on details; the best sketches are approved and then developed further.

- In a *rough layout,* the artist draws to the actual size of the ad. Headlines and subheads suggest the final type style; illustrations and photographs are sketched in; and body copy is simulated with lines.

- The *comprehensive layout,* or comp, a highly refined facsimile of the finished piece, allows the client to judge how the brand message will look. A comp is generally quite elaborate, with colored photos, text lettered or typeset, photostats of subvisuals, and a glossy spray-coat. When the process reaches the comp stage, all visuals should be final.

- A *dummy* is used to present the actual size, look, and feel of brochures, multipage materials, packages, or point-of-purchase displays. Dummies may be done as thumbnails, roughs, or comps. The artist assembles the dummy by hand, using colored markers and computer proofs, mounting them on sturdy paper, and then cutting and folding them to size. A dummy for a brochure, for example, is put together, page by page, to look exactly like the finished product and may be as polished as a comp.

- The *mechanical* is the final camera-ready artwork. In print production, the type and visuals must be placed into their exact position for reproduction by a printer. Today, most designers do this work on the computer, completely bypassing the need for old-fashioned paste-up. The art goes directly from disk to an output device that makes negatives for the printing process.

Anytime during the design process—until the printing press lays ink on paper—an artist or designer can make changes on the piece. Today, the expense of making changes and corrections in a layout done on the computer with digitized artwork is far less than it used to be.

Exhibit Design

Another execution of corporate or brand design is found in exhibits, displays, and booths, particularly those used for trade shows. In most cases, these are exciting, visually intensive, three-dimensional formats, requiring the creation of a much more complicated design concept than a two-dimensional print ad. All the brand identity information needs to be easily observable, but exhibit designers may also have to worry about traffic patterns as people move through the space and within and around the designed environment. The design is often complicated by the inclusion of other message sources such as video screens and computer systems, as well as people staffing and visiting the booth.

Most exhibits go beyond sending messages in words and pictures by allowing for actual product demonstration. Models, mockups, and actual product demonstrations

EXHIBIT 10-21

Because trade shows are a major BtB marketing communication function, booths are often extremely elaborately designed.

will be showcased to the extent space permits. It's very much a hands-on environment, and the messages are enhanced by the credibility that comes from face-to-face communication (see Exhibit 10–21).

Video Design

The strength of video is its real-life believability, which comes from moving pictures and sound. A humorous example that also demonstrates the shock potential of video comes from London, England, where the Borough of Islington ran a public service commercial about picking up after your dog. The commercial shows a man outside a Georgian home squatting in front of its wrought-iron fence with his pants down. The next shot shows a standard Islington street sign with the words "You wouldn't." Next is a shot of the man pulling up his pants as a neighbor in a business suit walks by, followed by another street sign that reads, "Don't Let Your Dog."

The creative process for a radio or TV commercial, a sales video, or a Web page is similar to the process for print materials, except the planning pieces are different. The first step in print is to develop a layout; in video, however, the art director works with a **storyboard,** *a sheet preprinted with a series of blank windows (frames) in the shape of television screens.* The completed storyboard presents all the design decisions in such areas as scene, setting, characters, action, lighting, props, camera movements, and film editing techniques.

In video, the art director is very much involved in artistic development and determining the look of the scene. Using the script, the art director draws a series of frames on a storyboard to present the look of the image and the flow of the action sequences, or shots. The art director sketches the video image scene by scene and establishes the nature of the action. He or she carefully designs how each scene should appear, arranging actors, scenery, props, lighting, and camera angles to maximize impact, beauty, and mood.

The storyboard is the guide for filming. Upon approval of the storyboard, the commercial is ready for production, a process that involves preproduction planning, the production shoot, and postproduction editing. In the production stage, art directors must be able to work with a variety of professionals—producers,

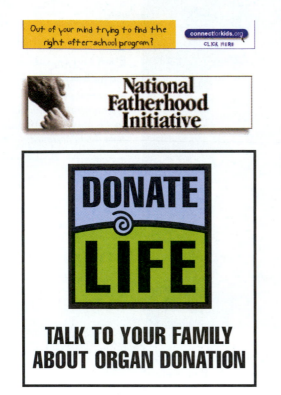

EXHIBIT 10-22

Examples of online banners that are also links to the respective websites.

directors, lighting technicians, and set designers to successfully develop and produce a commercial.

Online Design

Online design is similar to video design in that both work with a screen as a frame. The content, however, is entirely different. Video has all the benefits of cinematic techniques and realistic action. Online images are still dominated by words—although it is changing rapidly as the technology improves. Web-page design begins with an outline of the content and a flow chart that shows how the site will be navigated and how the links perform. The art director then creates the design of the pages as well as any photos or animation that might be used on each page.

What complicates online design is the need to understand how viewers will navigate through the site. In other words, a route has to be mapped that represents a typical viewer's pattern of information processing. What complicates this map is that most Web pages have various options that can be accessed through **hyperlinks** (also called links), which are *buttons or other sensitive areas on the page that, when clicked on, move the viewer to another page*. These links have to be plotted into the design. Part of mapping this route includes making it easy for viewers to go whatever way they want to go, whenever they want to go there.

Another element of Web design is the **banner**, which is *a small ad on some other company's Web page*. These function like outdoor boards in that they have to grab attention quickly with highly condensed information and interesting animation. Hyperlinks on banners move the Internet user to the sponsor's website. Their function is to tease the viewer into investigating the company behind the banner. Exhibit 10–22 shows some banners produced by the nonprofit Ad Council as a public service.

A FINAL NOTE: THE ROI OF THE CREATIVE SIDE

There are two dimensions to a brand message: what to say and how to say it. The previous strategy chapter focused on the first of those decisions and this chapter focused on the second. Within the general area of "how to say it," are the elements of a message—words, pictures, motion, sound, and so forth—and the structure, or how the elements are put together to create impact. In other words, "how to say it" means the elements and the structure must be relevant (determined by the strategy) and original (determined by the creativity of the message) in order to create impact.

Creativity, then, is the way to arrive at a Big Idea that stands out amidst the clutter of other brand messages. The structure, or anatomy, of various types of brand messages can vary with the functional area. However, certain basics, such as tone and style and how they are conveyed in writing and design are the tools by which creative people in marketing communication create messages with impact. And that's how the ROI of brand messages is executed.

Key Terms

big idea 339	signature 347	typeface 359
creative process 342	tone 350	corporate image 360
brainstorming 342	style 350	promotional flags 361
copytesting 344	news release 355	layout 361
display copy 344	feature articles 356	storyboard 363
body copy 344	media kit 356	hyperlinks 364
logo 347	visualization 357	banner 364

Key Point Summary

Key Point 1: The Creative Process

The creative process is a step-by-step procedure that people use to discover original ideas. The first step is exploration, which means understanding all the background information and research from the creative brief. Second is insight, which means taking the facts and ideas from the research and backgrounding and using them to create a big idea. Third is execution, which means taking the big idea into all the various brand messages and producing the actual pieces. Fourth is evaluation, in which the creative team steps back, both during and after the process, and considers whether the big idea is on strategy.

Key Point 2: Designing for Different MC Functional Areas

1. What is the purpose of a headline?
2. What is the difference between display copy and body copy?
3. Find a print ad, make a copy of it, and on the copy in red ink identify the headline and the body copy. If any of the following are used in the ad, then identify them as well: captions, subheads, overlines, underlines, taglines, or call-out quotes. Finally circle the brand identification elements and label them as a logo or signature.

Key Point 3: Writing Copy

The key format elements which writers focus on are the display copy, body copy, and closing elements. Headlines create attention, subheads and the opening paragraph create interest, body copy delivers desire, and action is delivered by the closing paragraph as well as the reminder information such as slogans and taglines.
- Audio messages must be catchy, interesting, unforgettable, and intrusive enough to attract and hold listeners' attention.
- Video uses moving visuals to add action to the drama of the message.
- Publicity writing delivers news announcements and feature stories that build human interest through the editorial side of the media.

Key Point 4: Art and Design

Visualization means envisioning the translation of the big idea into a tangible ad, commercial, or product brochure; art direction involves choosing the symbols—the words, pictures, and sounds of the message—and deciding how they'll be presented and ordered to best communicate the big idea. Specific areas of creative execution are as follows:
- In addition to a distinctive look, a corporate and brand design includes recognition elements and the personality cues for the brand image.
- In print, a layout is an overall, orderly composition or arrangement of all the format elements of a MC message—headline, subhead, visual, display and body copy, caption, trademark, slogan, and signature.

- Package design defines the product category, identifies the brand, reflects its brand image, delivers short copy points, and functions as the "last ad a customer sees" before making a purchase decision.
- Exhibit designs are three-dimensional formats with easily observed identity information and space for product demonstrations.
- In video, an art director creates a storyboard to communicate the design decisions relating to scene, setting, characters, action, lighting, props, camera movements, film editing and the flow of the shots and scenes.

Lessons Learned

Key Point 1: The Creative Process

a.   Define creativity. What are its key characteristics?
b.   What are the four steps in the creative process?
c.   Set up a brainstorming session with some of your friends. Ask them to help you come up with an idea for a new Sonic Skating Gear ad. Experiment with all the brainstorming techniques. Which one led you to the most promising idea?
d.   Find a marketing communication execution that you believe is highly creative and a similar one that isn't creative. Critique both pieces and explain your evaluation of them.

Key Point 2: Designing for Different MC Functional Areas

1.   What is the purpose of a headline?
2.   What is the difference between display copy and body copy?
3.   Find a print ad, make a copy of it, and on the copy in red ink identify the headline and the body copy. If any of the following are used in the ad, then identify them as well: captions, subheads, overlines, underlines, taglines, or call-out quotes. Finally circle the brand identification elements and label them as a logo or signature.

Key Point 3: Writing Copy

a.   What is the role of a headline?
b.   What is the role of body copy? How does body copy differ for various types of marketing communication tools?
c.   What is a script? How does it differ for audio and video media?
d.   Find a broadcast announcement that you think is particularly intrusive. Why is it irritating? What might be done to soften the irritation and still keep the message on strategy?
e.   Find an ad that you think is particularly well written and one that isn't. Compare the two and explain your evaluation.

Key Point 4: Art and Design

a.   Define art direction and explain the role of an art director.
b.   What does visualization mean?
c.   What is a layout and how does it work?
d.   What is a storyboard and how does it work?
e.   Twelve ways to determine the focus of a visual were given on pp. 358-359. Find ads that illustrate all twelve. Which one of the ads do you think is the most effective, and what does the visual contribute to your evaluation?

Writing Assignment

Find an organization that needs some help with its marketing communication. Write the copy for a brochure for that organization. Then write a cover memo to your instructor that explains your strategy, the logic behind your copy, and your big idea.

Presentation Assignment

Collect all the MC materials you can find for one of your favorite brands. Analyze them in terms of their creativity, big idea, writing, and design. How is the brand image being expressed in these pieces? What might be done to strengthen the presentation of the brand image and personality? Present your analysis to your classmates.

Additional Readings

Andersson, Axel, and Denison Hatch. "How to Create Headlines that Get Results," *Target Marketing*, March 1994, pp. 28–35.

Burton, Philip Ward. *Advertising Copywriting*, 6th ed. Lincolnwood, IL: NTC Business Books, 1991, pp. 65-66, 70.

Collins, Julia M. "Image and Advertising," *Harvard Business Review*, January-February 1989.

Goldman, Kevin. "The Message, Clever As It May Be, Is Lost in a Number of High-Profile Campaigns," *The Wall Street Journal*, July 27, 1993, pp. B1, B8.

Nelson, Roy Paul. *The Design of Advertising*, 5th ed. Dubuque, Iowa: Brown, 1985.

O'Toole, John. *The Trouble with Advertising*, 2nd ed. New York: Random House, 1985.

Ogilvy, David. *Ogilvy on Advertising*. New York: Random House, 1985.

Roman, Kenneth, and Jane Maas. *How to Advertise*. New York: St. Martin's Press, 1992.

Seiden, Hank. *Advertising Pure and Simple*, new ed. New York: AMACOM, 1990.

Research Assignment

All of the books and articles listed above are focused on advertising. Review them and any others you can find in your library, and compile a set of guidelines for the creative team working on IMC projects. In other words, what rules of thumb from the advertising area are universal in application and could help an IMC team develop creative ideas, write effective copy, and design impactful visuals?

Endnotes

[1] James Webb Young, *A Technique for Producing Ideas,* 3rd ed. (Chicago: Crain Books, 1975).

[2] John O'Toole, *The Trouble with Advertising,* 2nd ed. (New York: Random House, 1985), p. 132.

[3] David Ogilvy, *Ogilvy on Advertising* (New York: Random House, 1985), pp. 17-18.

[4] Ibid, pp. 88-89.

[5] Alex F. Osborn, *Applied Imagination,* 3rd ed. New York: Scribners, 1963.

[6] Bruce Bendinger, *The Copy Workshop Workbook,* Chicago: The Copy Workshop, 1993, pp. 170-74.

[7] Sandra Moriarty, *Creative Advertising: Theory and Practice,* 2nd ed. Englewood Cliffs, NJ: Prentice Hall, 1991, p. 172.

[8] Murray Raphel, "Ad Techniques: Off with the Head," *Bank Marketing*, February 1988, pp. 54-55.

[9] Joshua Levine, "Zap-proof Advertising," *Forbes*, September 22, 1997, pp. 146-50.

[10] G. A. "Andy" Marken, "Corporate Image—We All Have One, But Few Work to Protect and Project It," *Public Relations Quarterly*, Spring 1990, pp. 21-23.

11

Media Characteristics

Key Points in This Chapter:

1. What are media and how can they be classified?

2. What role does media play in IMC?

3. What are the characteristics of the major one-way media types?

4. What are the relative strengths and weaknesses of the major one-way media?

Chapter Perspective
Connecting with Customers

Over the years the word *media* has become tightly associated with the word *advertising*, leading many to think that media are used only for advertising. Nothing could be further from the truth! All marketing communication messages are carried by some form of media. Brand publicity, sales promotion offers, direct-response offers, and sponsorships all use various media to deliver messages to customers. These media include not only the obvious and traditional advertising media—radio, TV, outdoor billboards and posters, newspapers, and magazines—but also the Internet, telephone, mail services, coffee mugs, signs, company trucks and cars, package labels, Yellow Pages, company stationery and business cards, pens, T-shirts, and matchbook covers.

Another myth is that the media's only job is to provide opportunity for message exposure. The reality is that companies are not satisfied just to have their messages sent or shown to target audiences. They demand that media add value to messages by increasing their impact on attitudes and behaviors; and this can only happen when media create connections.

In IMC the role of media is not just to deliver brand messages, but to help create, sustain, and strengthen brand relationships by connecting companies and customers. The difference between delivery and connection is significant. To deliver means "to take something to a person or place"; to connect means "to join together." Delivery is only the first step in connecting.

This chapter begins with a look at the media business in general. It then focuses in turn on three main one-way media categories: print, broadcast, and out-of-home. These categories encompass the most traditional and still most widely used media for delivering brand messages (newspapers, magazines, directories, radio, television, and billboards), but the chapter also highlights new developments in each area that are in line with the IMC focus on connectivity.

DRIVING A RELAUNCH
Team One, El Segundo, California

Lexus markets a line of luxury cars. When it introduced its GS sports sedan several years ago, however, the GS proved a disappointment in the highly competitive luxury sports sedan category. How would you go about reintroducing this car and overcoming the negative impression of the previous model? That was the assignment the California-based MC agency Team One was given. The goal was to create awareness of the new GS and effectively position the vehicle as a viable contender in the category. Team One used the most integrated launch campaign in Lexus's history, one that generated a high level of traffic in dealer showrooms (see Exhibit 11–1).

The Marketing Challenge

Lexus first launched the GS in the fall of 1992. Initially, there was a great deal of interest in the first Lexus sport sedan. Unfortunately, the product did not live up to the performance standards of its primary competitors. Thus, the next-generation GS faced a difficult challenge. In addition to the negative heritage of the original product, it faced a market that had become even more competitive, with highly acclaimed new models from BMW and Audi. It was important to communicate that the new Lexus sports sedan outperformed every other car in the category.

Campaign Strategy

Team One's campaign for the GS was designed to create high consumer awareness and consideration of the new model, position it as the most credible sport sedan in its class, and associate it with the luxury and value associated with Lexus. The IMC strategy was to convert people who intended to buy competing midsize luxury cars. Reaching and convincing these prospects was important because Lexus needed credibility with them. The secondary goal was a relationship objective focused on customer retention by building interest among both move-up and move-down Lexus owners.

The target audience consisted primarily of married men, with half having children under 18 in their home. The majority were well-educated college graduates, with a household average income of at least $125,000 and a median age in their mid-40s. These people perceive themselves as youthful, energetic, self-confident, and independent. They are passionate about driving, and they view their car as an extension of themselves. Additionally, they don't think Lexus has ever offered the type of car they are looking for. Because Lexus is known for quiet, smooth cars (perceived as conservative), one of the challenges was convincing the target audience that Lexus could make a credible sport sedan.

Creative Strategy

Creatively, the most challenging aspect of the launch was communicating to consumers that the new GS was unlike any other Lexus ever made. The launch of the GS was the beginning of the repositioning of the total Lexus as a younger, exciting, more contemporary

EXHIBIT 11-1

Lexus campaign used "walls-of-fire" to attract attention.

brand. The marketing communication needed not only to stand out from competitive advertising but also to be completely different from anything Lexus had done in the past.

"Something wicked this way comes," a line from Shakespeare's *Macbeth*, announced the arrival of the new GS. The tag line "Faster. Sleeker. Meaner." was developed to provide additional support for the idea that the GS was unlike any other Lexus, and it was used in place of the brand's "Relentless Pursuit of Perfection" tag line.

To communicate the "wicked" nature of the new GS, the television spots featured the car approaching calm, tranquil settings. As the GS enters and passes through, it brings with it a powerful storm, which wreaks havoc as the voiceover says "Something wicked this way comes." The spots closed with each setting returning to "normal" as the car leaves the area.

The print ads used other dramatic elements to communicate emotional and factual aspects of the GS. A medieval-looking typeface was designed specifically for the print executions (see Exhibit 11–2). The photography used dark, dramatic visuals to communicate the "wicked" nature of the car (see Exhibit 11–3). The campaign was designed to deliver an integrated communication plan across a variety of media and message delivery points.

Message Delivery

The GS relaunch campaign used a wide range of MC functions and media (television, print, outdoor, direct marketing, and event marketing) to create awareness of the new Lexus model. What made the campaign different, however, was the use of an innovative interactive media approach that tied in to traditional mass media.

The message-delivery strategy had two parts: prelaunch, which was driven by the interactive strategy; and the launch, which used more traditional media. In the prelaunch, the Lexus website posted a preview page of the High Performance Sedan (HPS). A mass e-mailing invited people to view the page and enabled Lexus to capture 7,000 names and addresses of people who indicated they were interested in the vehicle. Additionally, during the prelaunch, outdoor "tease boards" and 10-second TV "teaser ads" ran in selected markets.

EXHIBIT 11-2

This brochure for the relaunch of the Lexus GS has a medieval-looking type on the cover and copy that sounds like Shakespeare. Inside, the car is featured against a dark dramatic background aflame with the orange of a setting sun. The campaign theme "Something wicked this way comes" is used as a headline, followed by the "Faster. Sleeker. Meaner." tag line at the bottom of the page.

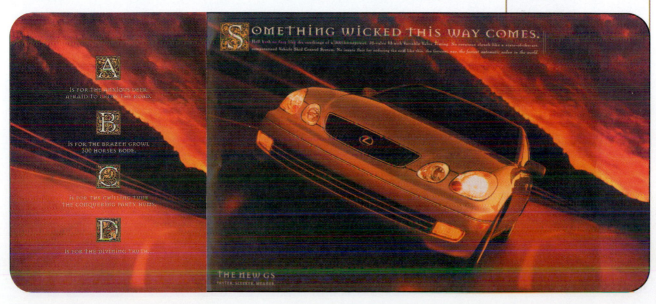

The Lexus GS website, which went "live" a month before the launch, included a 360-degree view of the car and invited viewers to "customize" the car with the color of their choice. Additionally, Team One developed special commercials to run on technology pioneer PointCast's online advertising network. (PointCast is now Infogate.) These commercials were rated in the top 10 in "click through" by PointCast—a first for an automotive manufacturer. The website also offered an opportunity for an interactive element in the "Wicked" campaign. Visitors to the page were encouraged to jump directly to their local Lexus dealer's website.

During the launch, automotive enthusiasts got the first look at the GS launch campaign via a dramatic four-page gatefold ad in October issues of automotive publications such as *Car & Driver* and *Road and Track*. Television was used to create high-impact coverage and build awareness quickly. The campaign launched with a "stunt night" on NBC's Thursday-night "must see" TV; multiple spots were featured in shows such as "Seinfeld" and "E.R." Programming was selected based on the Nielsen Affluent Study to reflect the target audience's mind-set and lifestyle. To reach the younger segment of the target audience, Team One chose to run ads on Fox Television Network shows such as "Millennium" and "X-Files."

Media Tie-In Strategies

Two of the "Wicked" campaign's unique message delivery strategies were a purchase incentive program developed and delivered in conjunction with United Airlines and a direct-mail program with television commercials aired during the United in-flight entertainment. Following each spot, an announcer directed viewers to the GS ad running in United's in-flight magazine, *Hemispheres*. These ads included a business-reply card that incorporated information on the purchase incentive program. Over 800 vehicles were sold as a result of the program.

Event marketing developed a first-ever partnership with artist Robert Risko, who designed special GS art. Team One also set up a four-city tour (New York, Los

EXHIBIT 11-3

This is the style of print ad that Team One used to relaunch the Lexus GS. It uses the Shakespearean style of copy, the "something wicked this way comes" theme line; and a dramatic visual with the darkness of the inside of the car contrasting against a spray of light outside the window.

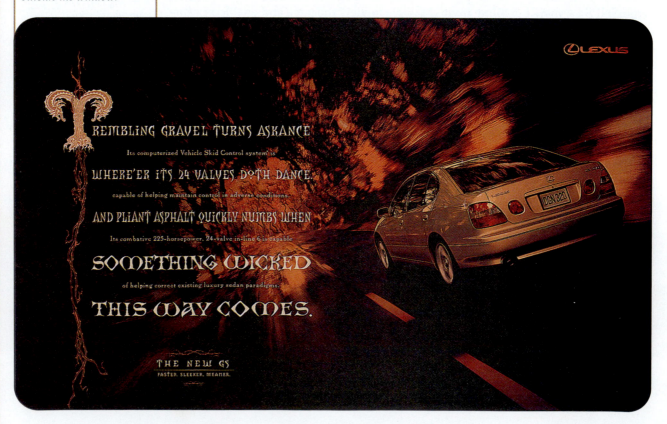

Angeles, Dallas, and Chicago) for which Lexus owners and prospects were invited to meet the artist and view his work.

Evaluation of the Lexus GS "Wicked" Campaign

The results tell the story of this successful relaunch campaign. Due to the strong interactive and direct-mail programs, Lexus had 2,000 advance orders for the new GS. Furthermore, the "Wicked" campaign for the Lexus GS relaunch generated tremendous dealer traffic, which resulted in the GS exceeding its sales goals every month in the period after the launch. Additionally, the GS outsold key competitors for the first time in the history of the brand. This inventive campaign made a truly wicked move on the luxury sport sedan market, winning a number of awards as it moved cars out of the dealers' showrooms.

This case was adapted with permission from the Advertising and Marketing Effectiveness (AME) award-winning brief for Lexus, which was prepared by its agency, Team One, El Segundo, California.

THE MEDIA BUSINESS

The word *media* comes from the Latin word "middle." Media carry messages to or from a targeted audience and can add meaning to these messages. This chapter is the first in a series of three that focus on media; as noted in the Chapter Perspective, this chapter is concerned with one-way media: print, broadcast, and out-of-home. Chapter 12 will look at the Internet and other forms of two-way, or interactive, media. Chapter 13 will focus on media planning. These three media chapters will explain media as media planners view them. But remember, although media are channels that can convey commercial messages to and from a company, they first of all are channels and stations and publications that people watch, listen to, and read.

Media Overview

Every person has a media menu, that is, a set of media that they use or consult most frequently. From the perspective of an MC planner, however, the media menu is the set of media used to reach a target audience and open up two-way, as well as one-way communication with them. In other words, the concept of **media menu** refers to *all the communication vehicles available to the consumer, as well as to the marketer.*

The selection and use of media can be just as creative as the writing of a publicity release or developing an ad. It used to be that media planners were subservient to the creative team. In IMC, however, media people work alongside the creative people in developing campaigns. The importance of media is demonstrated in the chapter opening case, which describes the relaunch of Lexus's GS sports sedan.

How brands choose to connect with prospects and customers can influence a brand's image. For example, status and luxury brands use magazines because the high production quality of magazine advertising sends an appropriate message. Intel has used TV not only to reach a broad audience but also because TV's audio dimension has enabled Intel to establish an audio brand identity—the four tones that play when the "Intel inside" logo is shown. Signage, which is a type of media, has become a brand signature and popular brand identifier for many companies such as McDonald's—"Let's go to the golden arches." The point is, media can add or subtract from a brand experience depending on which media are used and in what way.

Using media to deliver brand messages is big business. It is estimated that companies in the United States alone spent $235 billion on media (not including telemarketing) during 2000.[1] One of the primary ways brands are built is through media exposure. There is probably no better example of this than Martha Stewart, the subject of the IMC in Action box. Through magazine and television exposure, Martha Stewart has not only become a household name, but has also built her own media empire based on the cultivated brand image of her name.

Media exposure, however, does not guarantee *message* exposure. While media planners try to gain the most cost-effective media exposure they can for a brand, it is up to the individual brand messages to attract attention, change attitudes, and motivate behavior. As shown in Figure 11–1, most brand messages generate a response from only a small percentage of those who are exposed to the message. The challenge is to find media whose audiences are most likely to respond and thus narrow the difference between the number exposed (which is what media prices are based on) and the number who respond (the return on the media investment).

Broadcast media sell time; print and out-of-home media sell space. Interactive media (such as telephone and the Internet) sell access. As shown in Table 11–1, the media used most extensively to carry brand messages are television and newspapers, followed by direct mail. Notice that dollars spent for delivering brand messages through the Internet, despite all the talk about this new medium, is still a very small portion of total media spending (1 percent).

Media Classifications

FIGURE 11-1

This is the hypothetical relationship between levels of message involvement and response to that message.

One way to classify media is by level of inclusiveness. Figure 11–2 illustrates the different terminology used for talking about levels of media. The word *media* simply refers to all channels of public communication. Most *mass media* guarantee only the opportunity for a large, heterogeneous audience to be exposed to a brand

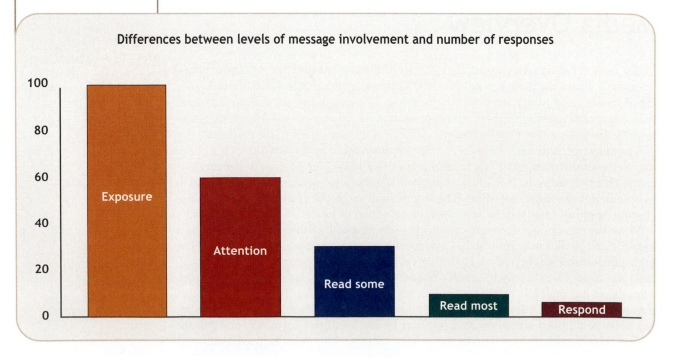

IMC IN ACTION

Martha Stewart's Omnimedia Empire

While she's known for her color-coordinated bedrooms and bathrooms, Martha Stewart's real design genius lies in her ability to create a big brand for her company, Martha Stewart Living Omnimedia, Inc.

The multimedia empire started in 1982 with Stewart's landmark book, *Entertaining,* which has since sold more than 500,000 copies and is in its 30th printing. The company's book line has continued to grow, with dozens of titles for cooking, weddings, decorating, and so on. In 1989, Stewart developed the prototype for an upscale how-to magazine, *Martha Stewart Living,* which was published by Time Warner. In 1997, she bought back control of her "crown jewel" from Time Warner, and it joins her other magazine titles: *Martha Stewart Weddings, Entertaining,* and *Clothes-*

EXHIBIT 11-4

Cover of Martha Stewart's' magazine which is just one of her media vehicles.

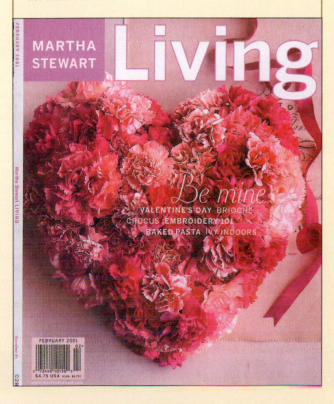

keeping. She visualizes her typical reader as a supremely confident 40-year-old woman with a family and a part-time job, living in a nice house in the suburbs. Rather than running articles about getting a man, dieting, or the latest hairstyles, Stewart aims her how-to content at this audience's sense of self-reliance (see Exhibit 11-4).

Martha Stewart produces and owns rights to her daily TV show and radio program, plus TV specials, such as her holiday special in 1999, which reached 7.8 million households. She also makes regular appearances on other TV programs. She writes a syndicated weekly newspaper column, "Ask Martha." Altogether, her media properties reach 88 million people a month and, because of the quality demographics of her audience, her media also command premium ad rates. The books and magazines generate 65 percent of the company's sales, with TV and radio accounting for another 12 percent.

Her Web entries include MarthaStewart.com, which, with its 1 million registered users, is a hit with advertisers as well as consumers, who actively participate in its chat rooms. A related site is MarthasFlowers.com, and Stewart owns a minority interest in BlueLight.com, Kmart's e-commerce venture with Yahoo! Inc. In 1999, her Internet and catalog sales accounted for roughly 13 percent of the company's revenues.

The secret to Stewart's media success is her ability to create original, high-quality content (stories and programs) for media networks that are strategically consistent and that can cascade through various media, retail outlets, and the Web. The shared costs and cross-promotions ultimately lead to higher revenues and earnings. Another secret is the powerful image that makes Martha Stewart the walking, talking personification of her brand. That's led to a tightly controlled brand image—but one that worries investors, who wonder whether the brand can outlast her.

Think About It

How many different media are involved in the Martha Stewart Omnimedia empire? What makes the Martha Stewart media brand so powerful?

Source: Diane Brady, "Inside the Growing Empire of America's Queen," *Business Week,* Jan. 17, 2000, p. 63.

message. *Specific publications, networks, channels, stations, and programs that make up a medium* are called **communication vehicles.** Examples of vehicles are the *New York Times*, MTV, *Newsweek,* and the America Online portal on the Internet. When a company "buys media," it is really buying access to the audiences of specific vehicles.

Another way to classify media is by audience orientation. Here, media planners use such terms as mass media versus niche media, addressable media, and interactive media.[2]

Mass versus Niche Media

Mass media are communication channels through which messages may be sent to the "masses"—large, diverse audiences. Niche media, of course, are communication channels through which messages are sent to niche markets (defined in Chapter 1). Channel One is a niche medium that reaches teenagers while in school.

TABLE 1 1 - 1   Estimated U.S. Media Spending in 2001 (in Billions of Dollars)

	National Spending	Local Spending	Total	%
Television	$ 39.1	$ 13.6	$ 52.7	22
Radio	4.6	14.8	19.4	8
Newspapers	7.1	42.3	49.4	21
Magazines	12.3	—	12.3	5
Yellow Pages	2.1	11.2	13.3	6
Internet	3.4	—	3.4	1
Direct mail	44.7	—	44.7	19
Other media	28.4	11.6	40.0	17
Total	$141.7	$ 93.5	$235.2	99%*

*Adds to less than 100 because of rounding.

Source: *Bob Coen's Insider Report*, McCann-Erickson Worldgroup website <www.mccann.com>, June 2000.

FIGURE 1 1 - 2

This shows the different media classification levels.

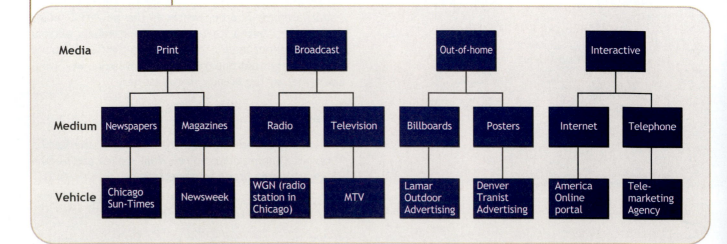

The distinction between mass and niche media is not always easy to make. Recall from Chapter 7 that *Modern Maturity* magazine is considered to be a niche medium, but it has a circulation of over 20 million people who are very diverse except for one factor—they are 55 or older. Similarly, millions of people worldwide watch soccer's World Cup playoffs. Like *Modern Maturity* subscribers, the World Cup's audience is extremely large and diverse, yet the soccer fans are younger than the world population in general. Even so, most would argue that the World Cup coverage, like the coverage of most major sporting events, has a mass rather than a niche audience.

Thus, a media planner's primary concern should not be how a medium is labeled but, rather, to what extent its audience composition suggests that the audience would be interested in what a brand has to offer. Subject content and distribution patterns are indicators of an audience's interests.

Addressable and Interactive Media

Media that carry messages to identifiable customers or prospects are referred to as **addressable media** because all can be used to send brand messages to specific geographic and electronic addresses. Addressable media include the Internet, postal mail, fax, and telephone. These media will be discussed in Chapter 12. Addressable media are used primarily to communicate with current customers or with carefully selected prospects. In the Lexus GS case, e-mail was sent to people who registered at the Lexus website and direct mail was sent to current customers (see Exhibit 11–5).

Two-way media, which allow both companies and customers to send and receive messages are called **interactive media.** The benefit of interactive media such as telephone, the Internet, and personal salespeople is that they allow an instant exchange of information to take place. More important, they make it possible for a customer to contact a company.

Media Intrusiveness

Because of the high level of commercial message clutter, companies need all the help they can get in attracting attention to their messages. Media planners know that media vary in their degree of intrusiveness, as shown in Figure 11–3. The most intrusive medium is personal selling because the sales representative's presence demands attention. The least intrusive media are print—newspapers, outdoor boards, magazines—because users choose when and to what extent to use these media. The more intrusive a medium is, generally speaking, the more it can be personalized but the more costly it is to use.

Admittedly, the word *intrusive* has negative connotations. If a message is disruptive, it is not exactly something that helps build brand relationships. This often puts companies in an awkward position. While they know it is to their advantage to get brand messages

EXHIBIT 11-5

As part of the Lexus GS launch, this reply card was sent to current customers.

25,000 FREE MILES

Purchase or lease a new 1998 Lexus GS between November 1, 1997, and

YOUR WAY COME.

April 30, 1998, and receive 25,000 United Airlines Mileage Plus miles, courtesy of Lexus.

Visit your nearest Lexus dealer to see the new 1998 Lexus GS models, including the GS 400, the fastest automatic sedan in the world. Fill out and return this reply card, and we'll send you program details on how to take advantage of this offer, and a GS brochure.

NAME

ADDRESS

CITY   STATE   ZIP CODE   TELEPHONE

If you are not currently a Mileage Plus member, call 1-605-399-2400** to enroll.

*Based on 0–60 mph acceleration times listed in major U.S. and international enthusiast magazines. **All United Airlines Mileage Plus rules and regulations apply. All information on the reply card must be filled in completely. LEXUS MILEAGE PLUS UNITED AIRLINES

©1997 Lexus, A Division of Toyota Motor Sales, U.S.A., Inc. Lexus reminds you to wear seatbelts, secure children in rear seat and obey all speed laws.

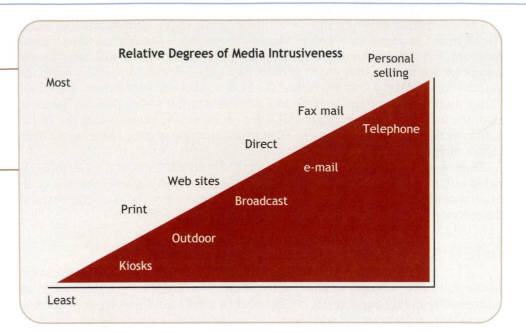

to customers and prospects, they also know that many of these message may not be welcome. There are several ways intrusiveness can be minimized. One is to choose media whose target audience is interested in the product category. Research has shown that one of the benefits of specialized magazines is that readers enjoy learning about new products from the advertising in these publications. Another way is to ask customers what type of information they would like to receive, in what ways (fax, website, phone call, personal sales call), and when. Good sales reps, for example, know how to make themselves seem less intrusive. One simple way to do this is to make an appointment to meet with a customer or prospect. When a person is expecting a sales call, it is no longer perceived as intrusive.

Media Strengths and Weaknesses

The strengths and weaknesses of each medium are relevant to any type of brand messages they carry, regardless of the type of marketing communication message. This includes everything from traditional advertising to publicity resulting from a news release. Table 11–2 is a summary of the major strengths and weaknesses of each medium as discussed in this chapter and the next. Some terms may be unfamiliar to you; these will be defined as needed in each discussion. The information summarized in Table 11–2 is the most important of all the information in the three media chapters.

PRINT MEDIA

The print media, of course, includes newspapers and magazines, but they also include directories, mail, brochures, packaging, and all other forms of message delivery that are produced by printing on paper or some other material. Print messages are relatively permanent compared to broadcast messages, which are fleeting.

TABLE 11-2   Strengths and Weaknesses of Major Media

Medium	Strengths	Weaknesses
Newspapers	• Reader education and income • Tangible • Reader habit, loyalty, involvement • Short lead time • Low production cost • High one-time reach • Good for detailed copy	• Poor reproduction, especially color • Decreasing readership • Clutter • Media waste
Magazines	• Audience selectivity • Expertise environment • High-quality reproduction • Long life • High credibility	• Long lead time • Low "mass" reach • Costly production • Low frequency (weekly, monthly, or quarterly)
Television	• Impact—Sight, sound, motion • Good builder of reach • Local and national • Targeted cable channels	• Broad audience • High production cost • Intrusive • Messages short lived
Radio	• Audience selectivity • "Theater of the mind" • Frequency builder • Relatively low product cost	• Background (low attention) • Low reach • Sound only • Messages short lived
Outdoor	• Localized • Frequency builder • Directional signage	• Low attention • Short exposure time • Poor reputation (visual pollution)
Direct mail*	• Highly selective • Measurable results • Can be personalized • Demands attention	• Clutter/junk mail perception • High cost per message • Long lead time
Telemarketing*	• Personalized • Real-time interaction • Attention getting • Measurable results	• Costly • Ugly image • Intrusive
Internet*	• Mass and addressable • Can be personalized • Extremely low cost • Can be interactive	• Clutter • Limited reach • Limited creative options

* Direct mail, telemarketing, and the Internet are discussed in Chapter 12.

In this case *permanence* means that the message can be kept (clipped and filed, for example) and revisited.

Sales brochures and product literature (sometimes called *collateral materials*) are designed to assist sales representatives in making calls and taking orders. Training materials may also be available in printed form. Annual reports are a good example of more elaborate publications that are meant to be kept, at least for a year.

Newspapers

Although readership of U.S. daily newspapers has been in a slow decline over the last 25 years relative to population increases, newspapers are still a major medium, especially for carrying local advertising. In fact, 45 percent of all local advertising is carried by daily newspapers. At the same time daily newspaper circulation has been declining, there has been growth in weekly, alternative, and ethnic newspapers. Active urban singles are particularly interested in the alternative papers, which are usually given away free at newsstands and in busy spots such as coffee shops and restaurants. The *Chicago Reader* and the *Denver Westword,* for example, offer exhaustive coverage of popular culture and local events. Mostly targeted at 20-somethings who find the local daily to be largely irrelevant to their lives, these Generation X newspapers are beginning to attract national advertising from companies who long to reach this group.

Hispanic newspapers in the United States have grown much faster than the Hispanic population itself. In 1970, there were 232 Hispanic newspapers with a combined circulation of 1 million and total advertising revenues of $14 million. By the end of 1998, there were 515 Hispanic newspapers with a combined circulation of 12.7 million and ad revenues of $445 million.[3]

To fight the readership decline and competition from other media, many daily newspapers have invested heavily in redesign and in the addition of special-topic sections. Also, all major U.S. papers now have websites that contain past stories as well as news updates throughout the day.

Formats and Features

Most medium- and large-circulation newspapers divide their content into topic sections such as sports, entertainment, lifestyle/fashion, finance/business, and food in addition to the local/national/international news section that usually fronts the paper. Many of the special-interest sections rely heavily on news releases provided by public relations departments and agencies. Companies can quasi-target their paid brand messages by asking the newspaper to place their advertisements in the most relevant section (e.g., leisure-oriented brands in the sports section, food items in the food section, personal care brands in the lifestyle/fashion section).

Classified, Display, and Inserts

Newspapers offer three basic types of advertising: classified, display, and supplement inserts. **Classified ads** are *small-space, words-only ads presented in a clearly labeled section with no editorial content.* They are priced according to word count and generally run multiple times. Classifieds are organized by category (items for sale, automobiles, apartments for rent, help wanted, etc.) which helps readers quickly find what they are looking for. In recent years, there has been an increase in **classified display ads,** which are *ads in the classified section that include graphics and larger* *sizes of type.* Approximately one-third of a newspaper's advertising revenue comes from its classified section.

The majority of a newspaper's advertising space is filled with **display ads,** which are *ads that generally contain more graphics and white space than copy and appear next to editorial content.* Unlike those who buy space in the classified ad section, where readers seek out certain goods and service providers, most users of display advertising assume that customers and prospects will not specifically search out their ads. Thus, they depend on the editorial content to pull readers through the paper, providing exposure to their ads.

Display ad space is sold either by the column inch or by the standard advertising unit (SAU). A **column inch** is *a space that is one column wide and one inch tall.* (Most columns are approximately two inches wide.) A space that is four columns wide and 10 inches tall is 40 column inches (4 columns × 10 inches). The **standard advertising unit (SAU)** is *a set of predetermined spaces that are constant in size in every newspaper that has adopted the SAU standards* (see Figure 11–4). These standards were set up in response to complaints from national advertisers that using local newspapers was too costly because every paper had its own dimensions, which meant that separate ads had to be produced for each paper used. Now, a national brand that wants to buy newspaper space can have its agency create an ad that conforms to one of the SAU sizes and know it will be acceptable at most papers. (This has still not encouraged many national advertisers to use newspaper advertising, however, as will be explained below in the discussion of newspaper rates.)

Supplement inserts, the third way to advertise in newspapers, are *inserts that are preprinted by an advertiser and enclosed with the newspaper.* These inserts are usually 100 percent advertising and often each one is for a separate company. Retailers such as Target, Walgreens, and Home Depot commonly use inserts. *Supplements that contain ads, most with coupons, for a variety of national brands* are called **free standing inserts (FSIs)** and are sold primarily by two national sales-promotion companies, ADVO and Valassis Communications. Companies using supplements and FSIs supply their own printed materials, but papers charge an insert fee based on the size of the insert and the paper's circulation.

Coverage and Audiences

Newspapers today, as in their beginning, are primarily a local medium in the United States. National advertisers generally use newspapers only on a market-by-market basis for adding extra media weight to markets where competition may be extremely strong or the brand is having trouble building its consumer franchise. Newspaper penetration in large metro

FIGURE 11-4

Standard Advertising Units (SAUs)

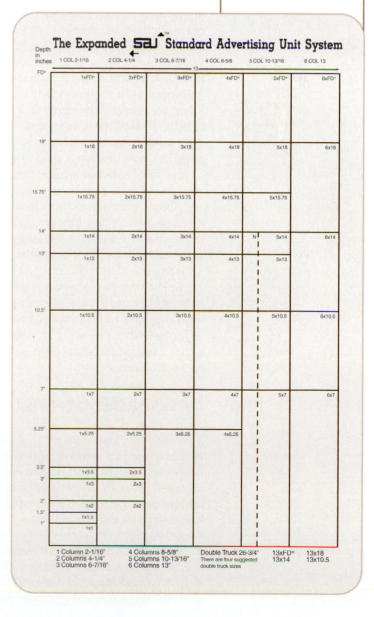

areas is 25 to 35 percent by the major daily (or dailies) in that market; in smaller cities the penetration may be as high as 75 percent. Newspaper readership is highest in middle- and upper-income neighborhoods, and lowest among teenagers (regardless of socioeconomic status).

Sales and Pricing

Newspaper representatives sell advertising space and promotions, such as event sponsorships or special editions. These people generally work totally or partially on commission. Besides local sales reps who work directly for a newspaper full-time, there are national "rep firms" that represent many different newspapers across the country. These firms sell to regional and national brands that want to buy newspaper space in more than one city. A major benefit to ad agencies for using rep firms is receiving only one invoice for all the space bought in different papers.

Most newspapers publish a **rate card,** which is *a list of advertising space costs and discounts.* For very large accounts (usually retailers that place one or more full pages of advertising each week), the advertisers may negotiate an annual rate that is lower than anything shown on the rate card. Newspaper rates are determined by circulation and the amount of space a brand uses. There are also extra charges for the use of color and sometimes for placement in special locations within the paper.

Newspapers charge national brands as much as 50 percent more than local retailers. They justify these higher rates by claiming that it costs more to do business with national advertisers than with local retailers because newspapers have to pay a commission (15 percent) to agencies that place ads for national and regional brands. This is one reason national marketers don't like to use newspapers. For local retailers, there is an "open rate," which decreases based on the amount of space a retailer buys during a year—the greater the volume, the lower the rate.

One way national brands can advertise at local rates is to have their local franchisees (such as Avis, Kentucky Fried Chicken, H&R Block) place and pay for the ads. Often franchisees form local co-op groups that pool their marketing communication dollars and hire an agency to handle their marketing communication. In automotive marketing, for example, dealer groups often organize to create and place advertising within a metropolitan area or region.

Many manufacturers offer a **cooperative advertising program,** *a system in which a manufacturer pays a portion (normally half) of the cost when a local retailer advertises the manufacturer's brand.* Many newspapers keep track of which manufacturers are offering these programs. Because some retailers, particularly the smaller ones, often forget about these funds, the newspaper provides a service to its retail customers and, at the same time, sells more ad space by making the retailer aware of co-op allowances.

Newspaper Strengths and Weaknesses

Newspapers boast a number of strengths. They reach a mass local audience, between 25 and 75 percent of households in their metro area. Generally speaking, however, the greater the metro population, the lower the percentage of households reached. As with magazines, newspaper readers are above average in education and income. The fact that newspapers are tangible allows customers and prospects to be exposed to brand messages when and where they prefer, and to read and reread messages at their own pace for better comprehension.

Because most newspaper circulation is daily (i.e., the number of times a person is exposed to a brand message), frequency can be quickly built among those who regularly read the newspaper. The average newspaper reader spends 29 minutes a day reading a weekday edition, and slightly more reading a Sunday edition.[4] For subscribers, the newspaper has a designated place in their daily routine. The fact that newspapers are a constant supply of information and entertainment, means that most subscribers have an emotional involvement with their daily newspaper, which is a benefit to advertisers. Finally, daily newspapers provide marketers with flexibility and short lead time—that is, it's a quick production process. Interestingly, research has shown that newspaper readers often consider advertising to be news, too.

Newspapers also have several weaknesses. Because their average life is one day, newspapers are printed on low-quality porous paper (called newsprint). Consequently, when ink is applied, it spreads, which is why newspapers have relatively poor reproduction qualities for any kind of graphics. Clutter is also a problem in newspapers. Not only does a brand message compete with other ads for attention, but it must also compete with all the editorial content, which also includes publicity stories. Further, newspapers have a relatively high cost for ads taking up a half page or more. Perhaps the most serious weakness, from an IMC perspective, is that newspapers are a mass medium. Even though an advertiser can quasi-target a message by requesting it appear in a special topic section (e.g., sports, food), cost of the space is based on the paper's total circulation. This means that there can be a high percentage of media waste.

Magazines

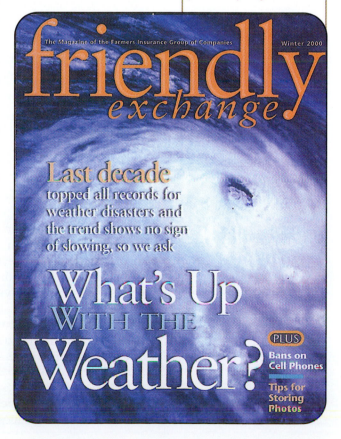

Magazines are classified by frequency of publication (weekly, monthly, bimonthly, quarterly) and by type of audience (consumer, business, trade, and professional). Magazines are also classified by how they are distributed. *Magazines that sell subscriptions* are classified as **paid-circulation publications.** Even these publications, though, receive approximately three-fourths of their income from space sales. In contrast, **controlled-circulation publications** are *trade, industrial, and organizational magazines that are distributed free to those working in a given subject area or affiliated with a given organization.* These magazines make up for the lack of subscription income by selling ads, selling their database of subscribers, and in some cases sponsoring annual trade shows in their subject area.

Although there are some very good controlled-circulation publications, most media planners prefer buying space in paid-circulation magazines. Logic tells us that people are more likely to spend more time reading a magazine they have paid for than one they have received for free.

Magazine Formats and Features

Unlike newspapers, which strive to provide news and information coverage of a geographical area, most magazines focus their content coverage on a particular subject. Professional and trade journals often take either a horizontal or a vertical approach to a subject. An example of a *horizontally focused* magazine is *Chain*

Store Age, which discusses the operation of chain retail stores (drug, food, mass merchandisers, sporting goods, hobby shops) regardless of the type of merchandise being sold. An example of a *vertically focused* magazine is *Supermarket News,* which discusses issues related to just one industry, selling products in food stores.

A major characteristic that differentiates magazines from newspapers is production quality. Because magazines are, usually, printed on coated paper, photographs reproduce particularly well, as do tiny details in typography. The Lexus GS relaunch campaign described in the chapter opening case took advantage of magazine production values to reproduce its dramatic visuals and medieval-looking typeface, which helped position the car as a luxury brand.

In an effort to strengthen relationships with current customers, some very large companies publish their own magazines (see Exhibit 11–6). On first glance, these look like most other magazines with full-color pictures and interesting layouts. However, the subjects discussed are all related in some way to the company's products. Some of these customer-focused magazines have ads only for company brands, while others sell space to noncompeting brands.

Although both are print media, magazines offer a wider range of ways to present brand messages than newspapers do. The following are types of advertising specific to magazines:

- *Gatefolds:* two or more pages that literally fold out from the magazine.
- *Preprinted ads:* bound into the magazine but of heavier-stock paper than that used in the magazine itself, attracting attention when people are thumbing through.
- *Business-reply cards (BRCs):* postcard-sized cards that are (*a*) slipped in-between the pages (so they easily fall out when the magazine is read), (*b*) tipped into the binding so they are easily seen but held in place, or (*c*) stuck onto an ad. BRCs provide a good way to begin a customer dialogue or to measure to what extent an ad has generated a response.
- *Pop-up ads:* three-dimensional ads that stand up when the magazine is opened to that page.
- *Scent strips:* patches that readers can scratch or pull off to elicit a smell (used for perfumes, air fresheners, foods, etc.).

All of these options help attract attention to a brand message. They also can greatly increase the price of advertising in a magazine. The media planner must determine that the increased cost will be justified by increases in message exposure and customer response.

Magazine Coverage and Audiences

Standard Rate and Data Service (SRDS) provides magazine profiles, production requirements, and advertising rates to marketers and agencies. SRDS has two main magazine directories—one for consumer magazines and one for business publications. In the business and industrial product categories, there are magazines for virtually every type of service and manufacturing area imaginable. The business directory has over 7,500 listings divided into 186 market classifications ranging from architecture to woodworking. Because magazines' rates, specifications, circulations, and printing options periodically change, SRDS publishes a new directory each month. It also has an online edition that is constantly being updated. The consumer directory has 86 category listings for over 3,000 magazines, including 380 international magazines and 300 farm magazines.

Although most magazines (both consumer and BtB) have national distribution, several consumer magazines are targeted regionally and locally. Major metro areas have their own magazines such as *Tampa Bay Life* and *San Francisco Focus;* examples of regional magazines are *Sunset* and *Yankee,* which serve the Southwest and Northeast, respectively. Large-circulation magazines such as *Sports Illustrated* and *Business Week* also have regional and even metro editions. Like zone editions of newspapers, these local and regional editions of magazines provide area companies the prestige of using national publications but advertising rates based on the circulation in their trading area plus a slight premium.

When buying space in regional or local editions, media planners must remember that even a large-circulation magazine like *Time,* which reaches about 4 percent of U.S. households, will reach only a proportional percentage of households in a local market. The good news for *Time* is that many of the households in its 4 percent local reach are desirable ones, those whose income, education, and professional levels are above average. Some magazines also have demographic editions. *Newsweek,* for example, prints a special edition that goes just to female executives; Exhibit 11–7 shows that the women reached by *Newsweek*'s special edition index is much higher than the average adult female.

Another way to think about magazine coverage is from a product category or subject area perspective. For *House and Garden,* a media planner would want to know what percentage of homeowners it reached, since homeowners make up the magazine's target audience. For a trade magazine serving the institutional food service industry, it is important to know what percentage of food service managers the magazine reaches.

Since circulation is a major factor that determines how much a magazine charges for its space, agencies and marketers do not just take the word of the magazine, but use third-party research services to verify circulation. The Audit Bureau of Circulation is the primary verification service for consumer magazines. Besides certifying circulation, this bureau also gives a geographical breakdown of the circulation and indicates the amount of paid versus controlled (e.g., free) circulation. The circulation of business and professional magazines is monitored by the Business Publication

EXHIBIT 11-7

Newsweek, like many other large-circulation magazines, has special editions that go to specific audiences. Marketers can buy in just this edition, thus minimizing media waste.

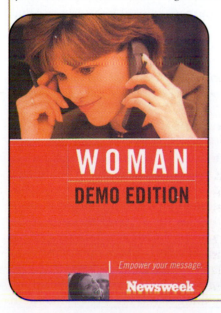

Audit service. Magazines pay for having their circulations audited and the findings published.

Circulation figures, however, do not tell the whole story. Compared to newspapers, magazines have a higher **pass-along rate,** that is, *the number of people who read the magazine in addition to subscribers or buyers.* Business and professional magazines, especially, have high pass-along rates because they are often routed to different people within an organization and kept in the company library. *Newsweek*'s edition sent to women executives, for example, has a circulation of 800,000 but an audience of 3 million. This means, on average, each copy is read by more than four women. Pass-along rates, of course, are estimates; media planners must keep in mind that actual readership may vary.

Magazine Sales and Pricing

Magazine space is sold in portions of a page—quarter-, half-, and full-page ads, as well as double-page spreads. There are also custom space buys, such as "islands," which are spaces in the middle of editorial content. As with newspapers, the more magazine space a brand buys, the lower the rate. Four-color ads cost more than black-and-white ads. *Ads with graphics that go to the very edge of the page,* called **bleed ads,** also cost more but are more attention-getting.

As with newspapers, magazine space is sold by salespeople working directly for the magazine and by media representatives who sell space in a variety of magazines. Magazines also have rate cards, as newspapers do, but are known to do more negotiating on rates. This is because most space sales are for bigger dollars, which allows more room for negotiation. When comparing magazine costs, cost-per-reader reached is more informative than cost based on circulation. As explained above, some magazines, especially trade and professional publications, are passed along to several others before being discarded or placed in the company's library.

Magazine Strengths and Weaknesses

Because most magazines are subject-specific, one of their greatest strengths is their audience selectivity. Although there are a few general-interest magazines such as *Time, Newsweek,* and *Reader's Digest,* the vast majority of magazines focus on one area. Not surprisingly, Cuisinart, which makes food processors, advertises in *Gourmet* and *Better Homes & Gardens* because these magazines often run stories that attract readers interested in learning about new and better ways of preparing food. Such readers are high-potential prospects for Cuisinart. Subject-specific magazines are seen as being authorities on their respective subject areas. Therefore, brands that advertise in them become part of this expertise environment, an added value for a brand message. As mentioned earlier, another advantage to magazines is their high-quality reproduction.

Like newspapers, magazines are tangible and thus allow readers to read them at their own pace. Magazines also have strong reader involvement because readers (of paid circulation magazines) have selected and paid for their magazines, a strong indication that they are interested in the magazine's subject and will spend time with the magazine. Magazines are even more permanent than newspapers because they are kept much longer and are frequently picked up and read more than once, which provides additional opportunities for a brand message to be seen, read, and have an effect.

A feature of magazines that many marketers particularly like is the ability to do a **split-run,** *a process in which a marketer places one ad in half of a magazine's circulation and a different ad in the other half.* This allows marketers to test one offer, headline, or creative approach against another. The only thing that is required is that both ads contain a response device such as a toll-free number, coupon, or order form that is coded so that the marketer can tell which ad produced a higher response.

Magazines, too, have weaknesses that concern advertisers. Although highly targeted, most magazines have relatively limited reach of a brand's target audience. This is more true of consumer than of BtB magazines. Magazines also have a long lead time; it can take two to three months for publication of some. Consequently, magazines do not offer the scheduling flexibility of newspapers and some other media. Another drawback is their lack of frequency. As noted earlier, many appear only once a month or even less frequently, especially industry magazine and trade journals. Magazine ads are more costly to produce than newspaper ads (but far less expensive than TV commercials).

Directories

The most widely used and known directory is the Yellow Pages, either a section within a phone book or (in large cities) a separate book that contains listings of businesses by product and service category. No one company owns the name "Yellow Pages," so many of the 2,000-plus publishers of telephone directories across the United States use the term.

All businesses that have a telephone are listed in the Yellow Pages; however, a business must pay extra for a display ad. Yellow Pages display ads not only repeat (from the one-line listing) the business's phone number and address but may also provide a locator map, business hours, a list of services or brands carried, number of years in business, and other claims to help differentiate the business from its competitors. Display space is contracted annually but paid for monthly via a fee added to the business's phone bill. As with magazines, space is sold by portions of a page—full, half, quarter, eighth.

A directory is both a reference source and an advertising medium. Not only do customers go to the Yellow Pages to look up telephone numbers but also to see which businesses offer a certain product, what their hours are, and where they are located. The amount of information, its arrangement, and its accuracy can send a brand message—positive or negative. What makes a Yellow Pages brand message valuable is that those who see it are seeking information about the product category. In other words, customers reached by Yellow Pages ads are generally in the second or third step of the AIDA model described in Chapter 5—*interested* in a product (see Exhibit 11–8).

The Yellow Pages may be the primary, and sometimes only, form of advertising used by a small, local business. National advertisers, especially franchised businesses such as car rental firms, fast food, and airlines, often have display ads listing all their locations and/or different telephone numbers for different types of product information.

A weakness of the Yellow Pages is that they are printed only once a year. This means that new businesses that begin midyear must wait to be listed (unless they plan far ahead). It also means that any changes in contact information, hours of operation, and so on cannot be made until the next directory is published. To help circumvent this weakness, most Yellow Pages are now available on-line as well as in print (see the Technology in Action box).

There are thousands of directories published by trade associations, industrial groups, and special

EXHIBIT 11-8

Because of its reach to an interested target audience, Yellow Pages are said to "close the loop" for product preferences that were developed through advertising and other forms of marketing communication.

interest groups—and most of them accept advertising. Whether aimed at BtB customers or consumers, directories facilitate customer dialogue, steering people to places where they are most likely to get their questions answered.

BROADCAST MEDIA

As broadcast media, radio and television have several common characteristics. On average, people spend 85 percent of their media time with broadcast media and only 15 percent with print media.[5] On the surface, this would seem to indicate that broadcast is the best place for brand messages. It should be kept in mind, however, that people do other things while listening to radio and watching TV, especially when commercials are on.

As noted in Chapter 10, both radio and television accept news releases; video news releases, especially, can be effective in generating brand publicity. Local stations will often cover special events—such as a grand opening of a store or a sports event—by doing on-site broadcasts; thus broadcast media can be helpful in supporting event marketing programs.

Compared to print messages, however, broadcast messages are fleeting. Once a message appears, it is gone until it runs again. (People rarely record commercials in order to watch them over and over.) The fleeting nature of broadcast media is one reason cable news stations like CNN, sports stations like ESPN, and

TECHNOLOGY IN ACTION

Directories Go Electronic

You can now use your personal computer to find all the restaurants within driving distance that serve Mexican food at moderate prices. You can probably also check out their menus online and, perhaps, study a photo of their dining room. And then, when you do choose one to go to, your computer can plot a route from your home to its door.

The electronic directories (e-directories) that are coming online can do all of this. Yellow Pages publishers, as well as independent directories, are developing these new e-directories as supplements to the familiar printed directory. They aggregate business listings, just like a regular printed directory, and accept paid advertising. There are more than 600 directories of this type. (A complete listing of Internet Yellow Pages is maintained by the Kelsey Group at www.kelseygroup.com.)

Electronic Yellow Pages have advantages for both companies and consumers. Companies can continu-

ously update their listings—your Mexican restaurant, for example, can add new menu specialties or change its prices. E-directories can also provide in-depth information to customers by setting up links to other sections or websites. This feature is particularly useful for companies (like banks) that offer complex product packages. E-directories thus give customers and prospects instantaneous access to searchable information that may not be available in any other format.

Think About It

When would you ever want to consult an electronic directory? Go to the Kelsey Group directory of electronic directories and see how close it comes to providing information you might use in your city or town.

Source: Adapted from Joel J. Davis, *Understanding Yellow Pages* (Troy, MI: Yellow Pages Publishers Association, 1998).

the Weather Channel have been so successful—they can provide programming 24 hours a day for people who want to tune in for a short while to catch the latest update (see Exhibit 11–9).

In terms of advertising, broadcast commercials are more intrusive than brand messages in print media. This is because programming and commercials are presented in a stream, one after another. With print media, readers can select stories and ads in whatever order they want and even completely ignore whole sections. With broadcast media, this is difficult to do. The remote control and VCR have made it possible to time-shift programs and zip past commercials, but the presentation form is still linear and viewers and listeners have to attend to information in the order it is presented.

Audience Measurement

Broadcast media are measured in terms of rating points. A **rating point** is *1 percent of a communication vehicle's coverage area that has been exposed to a broadcast program*. If the Super Bowl is said to have had a 43 rating, this means that during an average 15-minute segment of the program, 43 percent of U.S. households were tuned in. At the local level, a radio or TV program that has 3 percent of the households in its market tuned in is said to have a 3 rating.

Broadcast ratings are based on a communication vehicle's coverage area in terms of geography and target profile—for example, households in the Detroit area, adults nationwide, or women 25–49 in the Northwest. Although broadcast time is priced according to the ratings, media planners must remember that ratings are only a measure of households with a TV or radio on and tuned to a certain program. They are not a measure of the number of people paying attention to commercials. As noted earlier in this chapter, media exposure does not equal message exposure. For broadcast media, actual message exposure can be 25 to 50 percent less than program exposure.[6]

A broadcast term related to a rating is **share,** *the percentage of those using a radio/TV at a particular time which are tuned to a particular station*. For example, during the evening hours, about one-half of U.S. households have their TVs on. This number, called households using TV (HUT), is the base number on which share is figured. If one-fourth of all the sets on are tuned to "Who Wants to be a Millionaire?", then this program is said to have a 25 percent share. A program's share is always larger than its rating because there is never a time when *everyone* is listening to radio or watching TV. Stations that have relatively low ratings sometimes talk about their share rather than their rating, because share numbers are larger.

TV audiences are measured by companies such as Nielsen Media Research, Inc., which provides the ratings on which television networks and stations base the cost of their air time. Ratings for radio are determined by Arbitron. These audience measurements are taken four times a year in periods known as "sweeps." During the sweep periods, networks run special programming and stations heavy-up their self-promotions. The idea is to maximize viewing and thus create higher ratings, which then allow networks and stations to increase their prices for commercial time.

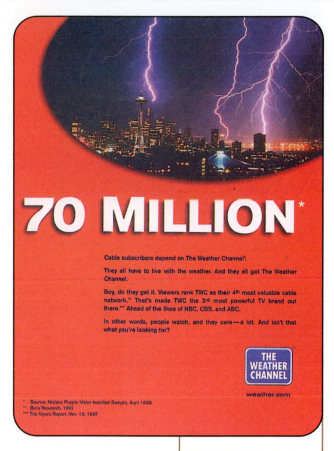

EXHIBIT 11-9

One of the advantages of cable broadcasting has been the introduction of full-time news, sports, and weather channels. This ad identifies the number of cable subscribers who turn to the Weather Channel.

In the case of TV, Nielsen does its research in 210 television markets, where it asks a sample of the population to record their viewing behaviors in diaries. Nielsen also uses "people meters," boxes wired to TV sets in a sample of homes in 47 markets. The meters track daily viewing data and automatically relays this data to a central location for analysis.[7] One of Nielsen's newer measurements is a share-of-viewing report that separates the TV audience into the following categories: network, syndication, cable, PBS, pay cable, and local/other. This makes it possible for companies to compare network, syndication, and cable viewing patterns for 32 time periods.

Another company that collects TV viewing data, along with demographic and lifestyle data, is MRI.

Because ratings are a major factor in determining what advertising rates broadcasters can charge for their various programs, the major TV networks have been complaining for years that the Nielsen ratings understate the size of their audiences. Consequently, these networks (CBS, ABC, NBC, and Fox) have formed a joint venture with Statistical Research, Inc., creating a rating service called Systems for Measuring and Reporting Television (SMART). One of the primary objectives of SMART is to include out-of-home viewing (at, for example, barber shops, transportation terminals, bars, and restaurants), which Nielsen does not include in its research.

Sales and Pricing

Broadcast time is sold in units. Stations often quote prices in terms of 30- and 60-second units (written as :30 and :60). Of course, costs vary not only by the amount of time but also by the estimated size of the audience. For example, Station A charges $1,000 for a :60 commercial while Station B charges only $800. If Station A's audience is twice as large as Station B's, then Station A's unit is a much better value even though its unit cost is $200 more. Pricing is on a per point (e.g., rating point) basis, which is discussed in more detail in Chapter 13.

Although size of audience is important, other audience characteristics, such as income and lifestyle also are important in putting a price on a program or channel's time. The ad in Exhibit 11–10 for the Food Network promises potential advertisers an upscale audience.

Ad rates for broadcast media are much more negotiable than for print because broadcast commercial time is both fixed and perishable. Subtract programming time from 24 hours in a day and the remaining time is what is available for commercials. The only way to get more commercial time is to cut back on programming, which most stations are reluctant to do because it is the programming (not the commercials) that attracts audiences. Unlike print media, which can increase or reduce the number of pages in each edition based on how many pages of advertising have been sold, broadcasters cannot increase or decrease the number of hours in a day. Therefore, when there is an above-average demand for commercial time, stations increase their prices; when the demand is below average, stations decrease their prices to attract more buyers. In other words, broadcast pricing is based on supply and demand.

Broadcast time is said to be perishable because, if a unit of commercial time goes unsold, then it is simply gone—the opportunity to sell it will not come again. It's the same for airlines: Once the November 22, 2002, New York City to London flight departs at 9 A.M. with empty seats, those seats can never be sold again for that particular flight. Another reason broadcast rates are negotiable is that a station's cost-of-operation remains the same whether some, all, or none of the commercial time has been sold. A station may choose to cut its rates rather than to get nothing at all for a given unit of time.

Another pricing characteristic that is common to both radio and TV is that rates vary according to how much guarantee an advertiser wants that a commercial scheduled to run will actually run. Because stations never know how much demand they will have for commercial time, they have what is called a **preemptable rate.** This is *a relatively low rate that doesn't guarantee a given commercial will run at a given time.* If another advertiser is willing to pay more for the time, it can preempt the advertiser that accepted the low rate. If a retailer is buying time to support a grand opening or special event, it is not a good idea to buy preemptable time because the promotional support may not be there. On the other hand, this is a money-saving choice for reminder and image messages that can run anytime.

Another overall difference between print and broadcast media is that broadcast audiences constantly fluctuate, whereas print audiences stay fairly constant issue to issue. The size of a station's audience varies significantly by time of day and program offering.

Radio

Today in the United States there are more than 10,000 commercial radio stations, split about evenly between AM and FM. Signals from AM stations can travel up to 600 miles (depending on atmospheric conditions), while the range of FM signals is only 40 to 50 miles. There are also noncommercial stations, many of which are affiliates of the nonprofit National Public Radio (NPR) network. Although NPR stations are referred to as noncommercial, they do carry brand messages, and these have in fact slowly expanded from simple "sponsored by" lines to soft-sell commercials. (Nonprofit stations are not allowed to make direct offers.) Finally, online radio stations—both commercial and noncommercial—are also beginning to build audiences.

In addition to radio, marketing communicators may also consider various types of audio formats for brand messages and brand reinforcement. For example, CDs are often used by brands or in support of brand events; McDonald's, for example, has used CDs by pop icons Britney Spears and 'N Sync as premiums (giveaways). Custom CDs, such as the Wrangler Jeans "Country Christmas," are assembled specifically for the brand's use. Sometimes these efforts represent several partners in addition to the product sponsor. One recent promotion by bootmaker Doc Martens also had the support of Warner Bros. Records, American Eagle Outfitters, and *Spin* magazine. Such a promotion can cost over a million dollars, depending on the amount of support in the form of advertising or publicity.[8]

Radio Formats and Features

Research has shown that radio is a background medium, meaning it is often on while people are doing other things (multitasking). This means that listeners tune in and out as something catches or loses their attention. Because people get used to having

radio in the background, brand messages must break through this background mode in order to get and retain attention. In spite of the background nature of radio, however, radio programs and stations generally have loyal audiences. Radio listening can be an intimate and personal experience, as the ad in Exhibit 11–11 demonstrates. The effectiveness of radio as an advertising medium comes from its ability to use its programming to target audience interests.

Although radio is a broadcast medium, it differs in several significant ways from television. First, and most obvious, it is just sound. Second, while TV viewers select programs, most radio listeners select stations, meaning radio stations have more brand loyalty than do TV stations and networks. Third, the majority of television advertising is national, while the majority of radio advertising is local. Most national advertising that radio stations do receive comes as spot buys from national brands who want to have extra weight in certain markets. Fourth, networks play a major role in TV but a minor one in radio.

Probably the most significant feature of radio is that each station has one specific kind of programming, called a *format*. While most stations provide news and weather to some degree, the majority of all their other programming comes in one of the formats listed in Table 11–3. The four most popular radio formats are country, adult contemporary, religion/gospel, and Top 40. Because each format attracts a different type of audience, planners can easily match station and brand audience profiles.

Most stations using a music format buy their programming from syndicators. These companies record and distribute the various music formats either by satellite or CD, so all a station has to do is plug in and play. These computer-driven format packages come complete with automated commercial breaks and station breaks, during which the correct time is announced along with the local station's call letters. If a station wants to have its own live news reports periodically throughout the day, that time is automatically scheduled in. The format packages also contain a few national commercials that the syndicate has presold. Most radio stations run between 15 and 20 minutes of commercials an hour, the majority of which are local. Syndicated programs, both music and talk, are sold to only one station in a market.

There are a couple of dozen national radio networks, but, only about 5 percent of the average local station's advertising revenue comes from them. Most of the national networks supply news segments throughout the day. There are also special networks such as the National Black Network, which is carried by about 100 stations. There are certain programs, such as those hosted by Paul Harvey and Rush Limbaugh, that are sold to stations on a market-by-market basis. Popular programs such as these can be heard in almost every radio market in the country. These programs also carry national commercials.

In radio, the on-air personalities (e.g., talk-show and music-format hosts) are often "brands" and listeners often relate more to them than to the station. To leverage these radio personalities, some advertisers do not run prerecorded commercials. Instead, they supply the on-air personalities with a list of their brand's attributes. The hosts then talk about the products for 30 or 60 seconds in their own words, making sure to include the majority of the brand's selling points.

EXHIBIT 11-11

Radio reaches its audience at the personal level with the potential to deliver a very powerful impact because of the relationship between listeners and the stations they love to listen to.

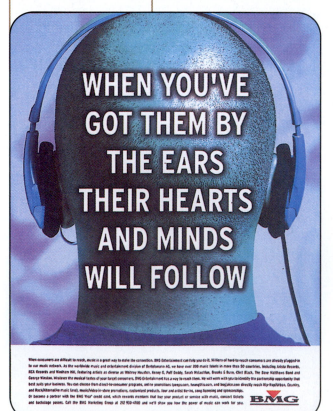

WHEN YOU'VE GOT THEM BY THE EARS THEIR HEARTS AND MINDS WILL FOLLOW

BMG

T A B L E   1 1 - 3   Radio Formats

Format	Description
Top 40	Contemporary hit rock songs
Album-oriented rock	Recent or current rock music, usually with a driving beat, and often with electric sound
Alternative or progressive rock	Various types of music, especially those not found on conventional music stations, such as avant-garde rock
Classic rock	Like album-oriented rock, but emphasizing music from the 1960s, 70s, and 80s
Adult contemporary	Soft, light vocals and instrumental music with a jazzy or soft rock sound
Urban contemporary	Upbeat, usually current dance or rap music
Blues	Music with its roots in rural black America used to communicate the trials and tribulations of life, especially in the delta area of the Deep South
Rhythm and blues	Soul music with a mellow beat and rich vocals—more traditional than urban
Country	Ballads, contemporary, and classic songs with a traditional, rural American influence
Jazz	Vocals or instrumentals, ranging from blues ballads of the 1930s and 40s to the electronic sounds of the 1990s
New Age	Soft instrumental music or soft jazz, also known as "fusion"
Easy listening	Light instrumental and vocal music largely from the 1940s through the 1970s
Oldies	Popular vocal or instrumental music from the 1950s through the 1980s
Classical	Symphonic, chamber, operatic, and show music
Spanish	Music, news, and information programming in the Spanish language
Talk	Topical programming on a wide range of subjects, from personal to political, often in the form of interview and/or call-in shows with a dynamic host
Religious	Music, information, or teaching; music may include Christian rock, gospel, choral, or instrumental

A manufacturer of breakfast sausage used radio advertising in several markets during morning drive time. The company chose stations with live DJs. Company sales representatives took electric skillets into each station and helped the DJs fry the sausage on-air, talking about the brand while periodically holding the mike near the skillets so listeners could hear the delicious sizzling sound of the sausage being prepared. Not only was the brand message delivered but, the selling points were given greater credibility because the DJs were known and respected by their listeners. The risk of using such a strategy, however, is that there is no guarantee the DJs will cover the important brand points. Also, not all on-air personalities have large, loyal audiences or are willing to do "live" commercials.

Another unique feature possible with radio is the remote broadcast from a retailer's place of business. Most stations will agree to do a remote broadcast when a retailer buys a certain amount of air time, and usually such buys are used for special promotional events like store openings. Remote broadcasts are especially effective when the host is well known and listeners are promised hot dogs and drinks or other premiums for visiting the business during a certain period.

Another way a brand can get extra air time for little cost is to provide stations with the brand's products, which can be given away. Radio stations are always doing things to encourage more listeners to tune in. Frequently used incentives are quizzes and drawings. Brands that donate merchandise to be used as prizes get their names and key brand claims mentioned every time listeners are told about the prizes that can be won in a drawing or contest.

Coverage and Audiences

Radio is primarily a local, consumer medium, seldom used for BtB brand messages. It is considered the most pervasive medium because it can be listened to anytime, anywhere. According to the Radio Advertising Bureau, the average person listens to radio about three and a half hours a day and in the course of a week 96 percent of Americans 12 and over have listened to radio at least once.

Although most radio stations can be received easily throughout a metro area and even farther with AM, an average station reaches (e.g., is listened to by) only between 1 and 3 percent of the local audience because of the proliferation of stations. For this reason, most marketers who use radio use it as a supplement to other media buys. It is difficult to get a high level of audience reach unless heavy schedules are bought on the majority of stations, which is generally cost-prohibitive. This is why media planners often use radio as a supplemental medium to build frequency. To this end, radio sales representatives often talk about **image transfer** from TV. This is *a process by which those exposed to the sights and sounds of a brand's TV message, recall the visual elements of the message when they are exposed to a similar sound track on radio.* Because radio is often less expensive than TV, radio can be a cost-effective way to extend the impact and length of a TV campaign.

Radio listening varies by time of day, as Figure 11–6 shows. The term **daypart** simply refers to *a block of time identified by a station for the purpose of setting ad rates.* The "morning drive time" daypart has the largest radio audience, reaching over 85 percent of the adults and teens who listen to radio. During these hours people are getting dressed, fixing and eating breakfast, or commuting—activities that can be done without too much concentration, which facilitates radio listening.

Radio Audience Measurement

Several companies measure radio audiences: Arbitron, RADAR, and Birch/Scarborough. RADAR and Birch do their research by phone, calling a sample of listeners each day for seven consecutive days and asking which stations they listened to and at what times, on the previous day. Arbitron, which is the most widely used service, recruits samples of households in each major U.S. metropolitan area. These areas are called designated marketing areas (DMAs). The larger DMAs are measured four times a year and the smaller ones once a year. Respondents are sent a diary in which they are asked to record, on a quarter-hour basis, the stations they listen to over seven days. Arbitron then collects the diaries and tabulates the data

FIGURE 11-6

Radio listening varies significantly by time of day.

Radio's Daily Reach by Daypart for Adults 18+				
6-10 am	10 am-3 pm	3-7 pm	7 pm - Midnight	Midnight - 6 am
50%	43%	43%	23%	16%

to show each station's ratings and share at each quarter hour for selected demographic groups. Other important figures from the diaries are daypart and station cumulative (called cume for short) ratings. The cume is the number of different people who are reached within each daypart, day, and week.

Radio Sales and Pricing

For radio time, which is sold in units of 10, 30, and 60 seconds, the most common length is the :60 commercial. Few 30-second commercials are used because they are the same price as 60-second commercials.[9] Thus, a brand can have twice the time exposure for the same price (or only slightly more, since the longer commercial will cost a little more to produce). Second, because radio is a background medium, more time allows the advertiser more of a chance to gain attention and exposure.

Some people think of radio as being an "inexpensive" medium to use. This is because the cost of one commercial unit is considerably less than the cost of a newspaper ad or a TV commercial unit (within the same market). The reality, however, is that radio's costs can be nearly the same as spots on TV and newspaper placements when you consider the size of the audiences reached by each medium. Also, the impact of a radio spot is, on average, less than that of a TV spot because radio is dealing with only one of the senses—hearing.

Radio rates are determined by a station's ratings and its audience's demographics. As shown above, ratings vary by time of day. If a media planner wants a schedule of commercials to run only in morning drive time, the cost will be higher than if the schedule is for "run-of-station," which means the spots would be spread throughout the various dayparts. Audience demographics affect rates because some audiences are more valuable to brands than others. A station with an audience that skews high on women aged 18–49, for example, will be able to charge more than one with an audience of teens or adults 55 and over.

When a company buys radio time, the "buy," as it is called, includes a number of commercial units. Buying radio is like eating potato chips—no one thinks of just one. Because the average radio exposure is so small, repetition is important.

Strengths and Weaknesses of Radio

Radio is called "theater of the mind" because listeners must provide their own mental visuals for the words, sound effects, and music they hear. This means listeners create mental pictures for not only programming content but also for commercials. Such a high level of mental involvement happens, however, only when the programming or commercial messages are attention-getting and the words and sounds are rich in imagery.

Station programming formats provide radio with its most important strength—selectivity. As with magazines, when an audience has a common interest, it is relatively easy for media planners to match the audience to a brand's audience profile. For example, the audience for a golden-oldies station is much older than the audience for a top-40 station, and has different wants and needs. All-news and classical formats have audiences that skew higher in education and income than most other formats.

As with newspapers, there is a short lead time for preparing and running a low-budget radio commercial. A radio spot can be written and produced in a couple of days and placed into a station's schedule in less than a week. Radio spots with custom-written music, special sound effects, and well-known talent, however, can take a couple of months to arrange and produce.

Like TV, radio is intrusive, which is both a strength and a weakness. On the one hand, it is a strength because it presents brand messages whether the audience wants to hear them or not. On the other hand, some people find offensive the fact that it does this and many have conditioned themselves to mentally ignore the messages.

Radio's other limitations are that it has no visuals and is fleeting. Another serious limitation is the fact that radio is used as background entertainment by people who are doing other things. Finally, even with sophisticated audience measurement techniques, it is difficult to determine what percent of brand messages are actually heard.

Television

Television has the most exposure of any medium. In the United States, almost 99 percent of homes have TV, the average home has 2.2 sets, and one or more sets is on an average of seven hours and 26 minutes a day, according to Nielsen Media Research. Television is used by both consumer and BtB companies to deliver brand messages. This is because it reaches a large audience and can deliver messages with highly dramatic effects, as the Lexus GS commercial in Exhibit 11–12 illustrates. Many large companies, both consumer and BtB, also recognize TV's potential for keeping their brand top-of-mind with stakeholders other than customers—investors, employees and prospective employees, suppliers, and the financial community.

An often-heard criticism of television is that it reaches such a wide and diverse audience that most brands that use it are paying to reach many who are neither customers nor prospects. (See Chapter 13 for a discussion of media waste.) This criticism was more true 20 years ago than it is today with dozens of specialized network and cable channels. Although the average TV program audience is

EXHIBIT 11-12

In this commercial, titled "Steeplechase," horses and riders are shown competing until a Lexus GS drives by and the beautiful day turns mysterious. The horses rear, the wind comes up, and then things return to normal as the car passes.

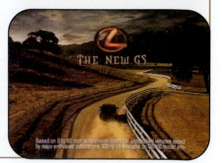

significantly smaller than in the past, many of these audiences have specific commonalities that can now easily be matched to a brand's target audience.

Most people have little interest in or knowledge of the organizational structure of television. To viewers, TV is simply a bunch of channels with programs and commercials. Media planners, however, need to understand this structure, especially since more media dollars are now spent on television than any other medium. The major growth area in TV spending is cable, where budgets have increased by over 400 percent in the last 10 years. As shown in Table 11–4, television spending has five classifications: national TV networks, national spots, local spots, syndicated programming, and cable stations.

Spot buys are *when regional or national companies buy TV time only in certain markets.* Spot buys are used to react to certain local market situations or to leverage an opportunity such as gaining new distribution or responding to seasonal changes. For example, in the northern part of the United States, when the weather turns cold, it's a good time to begin promoting antifreeze and snow tires. The point is that doing a "national" TV campaign doesn't necessarily mean using the same media plan in every market.

Network TV is made up of six national networks: ABC, CBS, NBC, Warner Bros. (WB), Fox, and UPN. Each of these has **affiliates,** which are *local market stations that agree to carry programming and commercials provided by the network.* In Denver, for example, KDVR is the Fox affiliate and KCNC is the NBC affiliate. Local affiliates often co-brand themselves by building awareness of their own call letters, as well as the name of their network. Networks originate programming and sell commercial time to national brands that appear on all affiliate stations. (Occasionally an affiliate will preempt network programming to broadcast a local event.) Networks supply program content throughout the day, but not continuously, allowing time for local news shows, syndicated programs, and locally produced programs. During the time periods when content is supplied by the networks, local stations have only a few minutes per hour for local advertising.

Syndicated programs such as "Oprah," "Wheel of Fortune," and "Jerry Springer," are created and sold to stations by independent producers. Initially, stations paid a fee for these shows and then recovered their costs by selling time within the shows. Today, however, stations seldom pay for syndicated programming because the syndicators have already sold most of the commercial time to national brands, leaving a few unsold time slots for stations to sell locally. The syndicators try to have their shows carried in as many markets as possible (though only one station in a market), because the more households a show reaches, the

TABLE 11-4 MC Spending for TV, 2000

Spending Classification	Amount ($ in Billions)
National network	$15.6
National spot	11.4
Local spot	13.6
Syndication	3.1
Cable	9.0
Total	$52.7

Source: *Bob Coen's Insider's Report*, McCann-Erickson Worldgroup website, June 2000, <www.mccann.com>.

more the syndicators can charge for spots within the show. Local stations like syndicated shows because they provide programming for free.

In many markets there are independent stations that don't belong to any network. The vast majority of their content is syndicated programs and network reruns (a form of syndication). Because the cost of producing original programming has become so high, especially when the shows have high-priced talent like Jerry Seinfeld, networks lose money if they cannot sell reruns.

TV Formats and Features

Television is frequently referred to as either broadcast or cable. This can be confusing because those who have cable receive *both* cable and broadcast channels via their cable service. But the distinction remains because the networks for many years were received only over the air (i.e., broadcast). At one time, three networks (ABC, CBS, NBC) dominated TV viewing in the United States; however, cable channels have been making steady inroads. In the last 10 years, according to Nielsen reports, sets tuned to cable channels have more than doubled, going from about 1.5 to 3.5 hours a day, leaving the major networks with only half of the total viewing audience. Exhibit 11–13 shows, for example, the various types of programming available on the Discovery Channel on cable.

In 2000, 68 percent of U.S. households had cable, 31.5 percent subscribed to pay TV, and about 7 percent subscribed to a direct broadcast satellite provider, according to the Television Bureau of Advertising. Because the majority of U.S. homes receive their TV signals via cable, a new channel that wants to gain distribution of its programming has to buy its way into the marketplace. When the Fox News channel began operating, for example, it had to pay cable companies a set amount per subscriber. If a cable operator had 100,000 subscribers and charged Fox News $8 a subscriber, this was $800,000. In return, cable companies agreed to pay back to Fox 20 cents a month per subscriber. Thus, it would take over three years for Fox to make back its investment ($8 ÷ $0.20 ÷ 12 months = 3.3 years).

Those households that do not have cable or a satellite dish can receive only local, over-the-air channels. Up until 1999, direct broadcast satellite companies such as DirecTV and EchoStar could not transmit local stations, which put them at a competitive disadvantage with local cable operators. The change allowing satellite companies to carry local stations has resulted in more rapid growth of satellite customers. In February 2000, Nielsen reported that penetration was at or above 15 percent in 85 TV markets (primarily the smaller markets where cable competition was not as great as in major metro areas).

Breaking down hours of viewing according to demographic categories shows that women are heaviest viewers of TV, followed by men (see

EXHIBIT 11-13

These four ads illustrate the diversity of programming available on cable television.

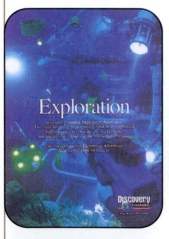

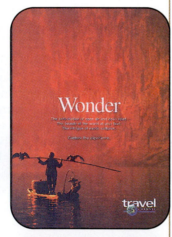

Table 11–5). These hours of viewing may be misleading, however, because viewers tend to do other things while the television is on, particularly during commercial breaks.

The networks claim that they can still reach every corner of the country, something that cable companies can't do. NBC, for instance, says it reaches 59 percent of all adults under the age of 50 in a single week, which is 21 percent more than the top 10 cable networks combined. It also boasts that it reaches 32 percent more upper-income viewers—those with more than $75,000 in household income—than the top 10 cable channels combined.[10] The fact that cable TV is made up of dozens of channels is both good and bad for marketers. The good aspect is that it allows marketers to select channels with audiences that have a common interest in such areas as cooking, gardening, and home repair. On the other hand, companies selling mass-marketed products are forced to buy many different cable channels in order to have broad reach.

TV Sales and Pricing

In the early days of TV, the most frequently used commercial lengths were one minute and two minutes. As TV time has become more expensive and marketers have looked for ways to get more for their media dollar, the average length of TV commercials has significantly shortened. In 1999, 60 percent of all network TV commercials were 30 seconds, 31 percent were 15 seconds, and only 6 percent were 60 seconds.

In television, as in radio, marketers buy time in dayparts (morning, prime time, late night) or in specific programs whose audiences are likely to match their target profile. Television's eight dayparts vary significantly in price (see Table 11–6). You will recall that 1 point is 1 percent of households (or any other defined population). Since there are approximately 100 million households in the United States, 1 point represents 1 million households. Cost varies significantly by daypart. The cost-per-point (CPP) or the cost of reaching 1 million households, for example, is nearly four times as much during prime time ($27,000) as during early morning ($7,300) and daytime ($7,400).

There are several reasons for this extreme difference in costs. First, viewers pay more attention to sets that are on during prime time than they do to sets that are on in other parts of the day. Second, prime-time audiences are generally the most desired daypart audience. A much higher percentage of those who watch TV during early morning, daytime, and early and late fringe dayparts are either retired, unemployed, low-wage earners, or chronically ill—not the ideal target audience for most brands. Finally, most marketers feel that prime time has a certain prestige environment, and being a part of that environment adds prestige to their brands.

TABLE 11-5   Average Hours Spent Viewing TV Per Day

Category	Hours:Minutes
Women	4:40
Men	4:02
Teens	3:02
Children	2:58

Source: TV Bureau of Advertising, 1999.

TABLE 1 1 - 6   Total U.S. Household Cost per Point (CPP)
by TV Daypart

Daypart	CPP
Early morning	$ 7,300
Daytime	7,400
Early fringe	10,100
Early news	12,900
Prime access	16,500
Prime time	27,000
Late news	18,600
Late fringe	12,500

Source: Estimated second quarter, 2001 prices for United States from Media Market Resources.

Although TV networks sell time direct to agencies (and companies), national spot buys are sold by national "rep" firms, which are companies that represent local stations. If a company wants to advertise in only the top 25 markets, it will generally negotiate with a TV rep firm. Syndicated programs are sold by the syndicators or their representatives. Each cable channel, such as ESPN or Discovery, has its own sales force, along with national sales firms that represent more than one channel. At the local level, each station has its own sales force that calls on retailers and other local organizations.

As explained earlier in this chapter, TV advertising rates are based not only on ratings but also on how much inventory (i.e., time) is available. If a station is 80 percent sold out two weeks from now, rates will be higher for the remaining time than they would be if the station were only 60 percent sold out. When buying commercial time on TV, media people seldom depend on a rate card; instead, they call stations or their representatives, explain how many points they are interested in buying, and then ask for a price.

TV Strengths and Weaknesses

Because TV is so dynamic (due to its ability to carry sound and moving visuals), it is often considered the prestige medium for marketing communication. When retailers consider taking on a new line of products, they often want to know to what extent this line will be promoted on TV.

One of the major limitations of using TV, especially for smaller brands, is the high production cost. The average cost of making a national 30-second spot is over $350,000. (Spots produced by a local TV station cost far less than this, but they also often look far less professional.)

Another limitation of TV is clutter. Almost one-third of prime time, for example, is now being used for nonprogram content (commercials, station and network identification and promos, and promos for upcoming programs). A **commercial pod** (*the commercial break in a TV program*) can carry 10 or more different brand messages. Nevertheless, according to the Television Advertising Bureau, 76 percent of viewers feel commercials are "a fair price to pay for being able to watch TV." Lead times for TV can also be a limitation, especially at the national level. The best programs and time slots are often sold four to six months in advance.

Infomercials

Besides traditional commercials, another way to deliver a brand message using TV is with an **infomercial.** This is generally *a 30-minute commercial program that demonstrates a product, presents testimonials from satisfied users, and offers viewers one or more ways to buy the product direct* (toll-free telephone number, website address, or mailing address). Infomercials typically feature complicated products that need demonstration—everything from sophisticated consumer electronics to exercise and body-shaping equipment.

For products sold only through an infomercial, companies need to generate $3 in sales for every $1 spent on TV time. If the product is also available in retail stores or on the brand's website, the ratio is only about $2 to $1.

Interactive TV

The convergence of computers, television, and the Internet is referred to as **interactive TV,** a technology that allows viewers to directly respond to TV commercials with a click of their remote control or a remote keyboard. Viewers can order movies instantly, for example, rather than having to make a phone call. By clicking on a website address in a commercial, a viewer can go directly to the site to get further brand information or place an order. Interactive TV also allows viewers to obtain information while watching a program. For example, while watching a baseball game, a viewer can bring a player's profile on screen as the player is coming to bat. The work to make television a two-way medium has been going on for several decades. Although the technology now exists for interactive TV, customers have been slow to embrace it; many are not yet convinced of its value.

OUT-OF-HOME MEDIA

In addition to print and broadcast, another large group of media are best described as **out-of-home media.** These include *communication vehicles that the target audience sees or uses away from home.* A more specific term, *place-based media,* was defined in Chapter 3 as message-delivery opportunities at places where the target audience goes. Billboards (sometimes called outdoor boards) and transit posters are two of the most common categories of out-of-home media. Others include theater and video ads; product placements in movies; aerial advertising (see Exhibit 11–14); electronic kiosks; ads in elevators or bathroom stalls; banner displays on automated teller machines (ATMs); chalk-and-stencil sidewalk messages; placards on shopping carts—the list could go on and on. Posters and small digital screens are making it possible to reach people almost anywhere they go, and particularly in situations where they have nothing else to do, as when they are riding on a bus.

Outdoor

Outdoor goes back in history at least to the Roman Empire, when commercial signs were painted on city walls. In modern times, as cars and highways took over the landscape, large signs along highways and streets became message-delivery points. A classic example is the "See Rock City" campaign that began appearing on barn roofs in 1936. Since then, the Lookout Mountain rock formations in Tennessee

EXHIBIT 11-14

This ad for the Aviad company, which creates and delivers aerial advertising, targets high-tech and dot-com companies.

have been promoted on some 900 barns in 19 states from Michigan to Florida. Although many of the barns have disappeared, the remaining ones are celebrated as pieces of pop culture.[11] Today the outdoor advertising industry remains strong and profitable; annual expenditures are estimated to be $4.8 billion.[12]

Modern outdoor advertising comes in three standard forms: bulletins, 30-sheet posters, and 8-sheet posters. A nonstandard form, called a spectacular, is used for extra attention-getting power (see Table 11–7). The most widely used is the 30-sheet poster. (The "30" once referred to the number of sheets of paper that were pasted together to form a message on a single board. Although individual sheets are larger today, requiring fewer per board, the industry continues to use the term). Whereas 30-sheet posters are purchased for only a month or two, the contracts for spectaculars often run for several years.

Spectaculars are generally permanent, lighted, and often animated in some way. They are also extremely expensive compared to other outdoor forms. Times Square in New York City has a number of spectacular boards, including ones that carry live TVs (see Exhibit 11–15). As the name suggests, these boards are visually stunning and often quite memorable. Design of spectaculars in recent years has included images that extend beyond the traditional rectangular borders and popouts that make the boards three-dimensional.

Signs and Posters

Exploiting the concept of creating effective brand contact points, out-of-home message delivery includes a wide range of locations where brand messages can be posted. Besides traditional outdoor boards, outside signage includes signs on trucks and shopping bags; even uniforms serve as vehicles for brand messages. These are the media we encounter as we go about our daily business (see Exhibit 11–16).

Advertisers commonly purchase space from public transit authorities. Posters appear on (and inside) buses, subway trains, and taxis, as well as in bus shelters and subway stations. Other place-based media include malls, stores, health clubs,

---

T A B L E   1 1 - 7   Outdoor Advertising Forms

- *Bulletins:* 14 by 48 feet; either painted or printed panels; usually created for a local marketer in the outdoor company's shop and then assembled on the billboard structure.

- *30-sheet posters:* 12 by 25 feet; the basic outdoor format for national marketers; printed on large sheets in multiple copies and then distributed to local outdoor companies, which mount the sheets on the outdoor board.

- *8-sheet panels* (also called *junior panels*): 5 by 11 feet; good with pedestrian traffic; used by food-product manufacturers as a reminder near a grocery store.

- *Spectaculars:* nonstandard; used in busy metro areas such as New York, Hong Kong, London, and Las Vegas; electronic signs with movement, color, and flashing lights designed to grab attention in high-traffic areas.

and libraries, as well as community, student, and senior centers. Posters inside a conveyance or waiting place generally have a captive audience that can spend some time with a message, so those posters are designed to deliver complex messages or to be highly involving.

Nontraditional posters have appeared in chalk on city streets, as well as on the sides of buildings. Some buildings have been wrapped with huge preprinted vinyl images. The old Burma-Shave signs that used to adorn highways with little limericks about the shaving cream have inspired modern advertisers to use this low-tech form. In order to reach dot-com companies, the owner of Bostonhire.com, a job-posting site, screwed all-weather posterboards with the company's name to trees along Route 128, New England's high-tech corridor. The owner reported lots of calls from his $500 investment. A similar scheme in California uses tall billboards mounted on barges to reach people traveling on 101 South from San Francisco. The signs are so tall they can be seen from the Bay Bridge, 10 miles north. The "barge boards" are attractive to marketers because the traditional billboards along 101 are sold out for years in advance.

Audience Measurement

Outdoor advertising reaches people as they travel by the sign's site. Thus, reach is determined by the percentage of people (based on car or pedestrian counts) within a 24-hour period who are exposed to one or more boards carrying the brand message. This number is a percentage of the population of the total market.

The basic units of sale for outdoor advertising are called **showings;** they are estimated in terms of 25, 50, or 100 gross rating points daily. This means the brand message will appear on as many panels as needed to provide the desired level of exposure—25, 50, or 100 percent, which is equal to the market's total population. For example, a 50 showing means that 50 percent of the market's population was exposed to one or more of the outdoor brand messages in one day. Outdoor space is sold in terms of sets of boards spaced throughout a market that will deliver the desired 25, 50, or 100 showing. Although this medium receives only about 2 percent of all media dollars spent in the United States, in some countries, especially developing countries, it is one of the most widely used to deliver brand messages.

Strengths and Weakness of Outdoor

Using outdoor boards in a local market is a good way to extend reach and, even more so, extend frequency of a brand message. Outdoor boards also provide geographical flexibility for targeting. Another advantage of outdoor media is that they can attract people with certain commonalties. People attending baseball games, for example, obviously have an interest in sports. People in airline terminals are more likely than the average population to be businesspeople or vacation travelers. When using transit media, the challenge is to select communication vehicles whose audience demographics most closely match those of the brand's target audience. Outdoor boards are used to keep established brands top-of-mind and their primary function is as a brand reminder. They are also widely used to provide directions— "Shell at next exit" and "KFC two blocks ahead." For the most part, outdoor boards are used for consumer brands.

Limitations of outdoor boards are several. Outdoor boards have "passing" exposure, meaning that most people who are exposed are passing by, often at fairly high speeds! This fact, plus the fact that outdoor boards must fight for attention with all the other visual stimuli that surround them, means they must carry simple yet highly attention-getting messages. The more visual the message is, the more impact an outdoor board is likely to have. Another limitation is that, when used extensively, the messages may suffer from "wear out," with customers subconsciously ignoring boards they have seen several times before.

Outdoor's biggest limitation is its negative perception. As mentioned earlier, many people consider billboards as nothing more than visual clutter. Environmentalists have referred to outdoor advertising as "visual pollution on a stick." Some states (Maine, Vermont, Hawaii, and Alaska), as well as some communities, have outlawed or greatly restricted the use of outdoor boards. Many metro areas now have restrictions on the heights and placements of billboards. The Highway Beautification Act of 1965 controls outdoor advertising on U.S. interstate highways.

In this day of marketing accountability, another big limitation is measuring outdoor board effectiveness. Since most outdoor campaigns are part of larger media plans, it is next to impossible to break out the incremental impact of outdoor messages. Many people passing by in cars never see or read the posted messages. Testing product use is the primary way companies determine billboards' effectiveness. Most companies that sell outdoor advertising keep detailed case histories showing impact on sales. Media planners must interpret these cases carefully, though, before assuming that the results for one brand will transfer to another brand and marketing situation.

Cinema and Video

Movie theaters have found that besides selling tickets and concessions, they can generate revenue by running commercials before movies. Videocassette producers, too, have found that commercials on rented movies can reach a mass audience. Yet these communication vehicles have some inherent problems. It is difficult to target other than by the type of movie—G or PG movies, comedies or dramas. Also, people have not readily accepted brand messages that accompany movies. Feeling that commercials take away from the main features, Disney has refused to distribute its movies to cinemas that run commercials for anything other than upcoming movies.

Advantages of using movie-theater commercials include the captive audience and the lack of clutter. Seeing fewer than a half-dozen commercials within a two-hour period while sitting in a movie theater represents far less clutter than seeing 60 or more messages within the same time period while watching television. The cost of cinema advertising is based on monthly attendance. The cost per person exposed goes down as more theaters are added. Generally, though, the cost of in-theater commercials is around a $22 per thousand people reached, which is the equivalent to the cost of a 30-second prime-time TV spot.

Video is playing an increasingly important role in message delivery for both consumer and BtB brands. Unlike movie theaters, which still tend to run brand messages for movies only (i.e., previews or trailers), rental videos are carrying more and more message for nonmovie products. According to findings from one study, two-thirds of those who rent videos resent the presence of commercials, yet even so, over half reported they watched the commercials.[13]

Another type of video advertising is the product video produced by a company as an individual infomercial. Nearly every major brand in the United States now has a product video, video catalog, or CD-ROM to augment the efforts of its sales staff or to use for prospecting. Many car manufacturers, for example, produce videos of their new models that let people take "virtual test drives" on their televisions at home. These test-drive videos are advertised in the conventional way and then sent to those who request them. The overall cost for these videos is extremely high when production and distribution are added together. Yet their impact is much greater than that of a typical television commercial and the high cost may be justified by the positive reactions of high-potential prospects. Payout, or impact on sales, can be easily determined since there is a record of those to whom the videos are sent.

Promotional video networks are *companies that use either videos or satellite transmission to distribute programs and commercial messages.* Such networks (e.g., the Airport Channel, the Medical News Network, and the Truck Stop Channel) supply various organizations (airports, hospitals, truck stops) with programming that carries brand messages. The Kmart in-store channel, for example, is sent by satellite to 2,300 stores, and Wal-Mart has set up an ad network that will play brand messages on those long rows of television sets lined up for sale in the chain's 1,950 stores nationwide.

Nontraditional Media

Nontraditional media—hot-air balloons, sidewalk painting, toilet doors, painted buses and cars (see Exhibit 11–17), disposable coffee-cup holders (java jackets), mouse pads, ATM screens, race cars, rolling billboards pulled through city streets, and much more—are increasingly attracting the attention of media people. There is even a company in Paris, France, that places ads on the small tables used by sidewalk cafés and bars. The company furnishes the tables for free, making its money from selling the advertising space. Consider the following:

- Actor Jim Carrey's face on one-inch-high peel-off stickers appeared on 12 million California apples to promote the home video release of *Liar Liar*.

- Virtual reality entertainment centers are being used in malls to promote merchandise from goods to hit science-fiction movies such as *Star Wars*.

- Buick used the packages of airplane peanuts and cookies to market its new Regal sedan. The

EXHIBIT 11-17

These are examples of using nontraditional media to deliver brand messages.

packages were wrapped in plastic covered with Buick and Regal emblems. Inside, along with the snacks, were photos of the Regal and a chart comparing the car to its competition.

- The Body Shop, an upscale seller of personal care items, has had good luck building awareness with its mobile truck program. The company has transformed the vehicle into a source of revenue by linking the traveling display to its growing catalog business.

- Advent Advertising Corporation has announced plans to begin selling space on airplane overhead storage bins.

- Otis Elevators and IBM have joined together to use flat-panel computer screens to display news and brand messages in elevators.

- When Seattle-based Millstone Coffee moved into the Denver market, it used a technology called the Mobile-Image Projector to beam images of 300-foot-tall cups of coffee and bags of beans on buildings.

- In Cairo, Egypt, the feluccas, the ancient sailboats that travel up and down the Nile, are carrying multinational brands embossed on their sails.

The past decade has seen an increase in everything from video shopping carts to in-store video networks.[14] One of these growing alternative media is **audiotext,** which is *a recorded message that provides information (e.g., the weather, sports scores) via a toll-free (800) or toll (900) number.* The 900 number can handle thousands of calls at a time, but it is expensive to install.

While nontraditional media may never achieve the status of major media forms, they should be considered for use in narrowly targeted programs. The challenge is to use nontraditional media when they strategically fit into a media mix and not merely because they are different. According to the director of out-of-home and nontraditional media at BBDO, these media have several limitations: lack of audience measurement, equipment failure (such as breakdowns of recorders supplying video messages in elevators), and high production and operating costs.[15]

Product Placement

In Steven Spielberg's 1993 movie *Jurassic Park,* there were more than 1,000 marketing and product tie-ins. **Product placement** is *when branded products or brand names are featured visibly in a movie or television program.* For years, movie producers took care not to show brand names on the screen. As times changed, both marketers and producers realized that product placement could be an effective means of sending brand messages. Many moviegoers remained unaware of the practice for some time—a situation that may have been changed by the prominent use of Reese's Pieces candy in Spielberg's 1982 hit *E.T.—the Extra-Terrestrial.* While product placement is often associated with movies, the biggest showcase for placements is actually on television, most specifically in popular sitcoms.

Product placements are of two types. One is the incidental inclusion of a brand such as a car driving past an Amoco filling station or a bottle of Bayer aspirin sitting on a bedside table. In some movies, producers agree to place their actors in cars made by only one manufacturer. The exposure of brand names in these situations is subtle. The other type of placement is when a brand receives prominent exposure. In the James Bond movie *The World Is Not Enough,* the BMW sport car model Z28 was launched with a starring role. Several scenes had close-ups of Bond driving the car, leaving no question as to the brand.

Product placement offers marketers a unique way to reach mass markets. It does, however, have its limits. Last-minute editing can play havoc with promotional plans. For example, when a Reebok ad was cut from the movie *Jerry Maguire*, the sneaker company sued Sony for violating the terms of the product placement agreement. The placement had been the centerpiece of a planned Reebok retail promotion that subsequently had to be dumped.[16]

Evaluating and comparing media alternatives is done on the basis of reaching those most likely to respond, and at this time, it is not very precise.

A FINAL NOTE: "CONNECTIVITY"

Media are used to create a connection between an audience and a brand—and doing so in the most cost-effective way. But it is also important to connect with the audience in a way that reinforces the brand's image.

In the past, media planners were concerned primarily with delivering messages to customers and prospects—primarily one-way communication telling customers what the company wanted them to know. A media mix that connects companies and customers not only informs and persuades but also can begin two-way communication and feedback.

Key Terms

media menu 373
communication vehicles 376
addressable media 377
classified ads 380
classified display ads 380
display ads 381
column inch 381
standard advertising unit (SAU) 381
supplement inserts 381
free standing inserts (FSIs) 381
rate card 382
cooperative advertising program 382
paid-circulation publications 383
controlled-circulation publication 383
pass-along rate 386
bleed ads 386

split-run 386
rating point 389
share 389
preemptable rate 391
image transfer 394
daypart 394
spot buys 397
affiliates 397
commercial pod 400
infomercial 401
interactive TV 401
out-of-home media 401
showings 403
promotional video networks 405
audiotext 406

Key Points Summary

Key Point 1: Media Classifications

How brands choose to connect with prospects and customers can influence a brand's image. Media carry messages to or from a targeted audience and can add meaning to these messages. There are four basic types of media: print, broadcast, out-of-home, and interactive. Within these are the mass media (newspapers, magazines, radio, television, etc.), which further contain specific communication vehicles (the *Chicago Sun-Times*, *Newsweek*, etc.). When a company "buys media," it is really buying access to the audiences of specific communication vehicles.

Key Point 2: Print Media

Print media includes newspapers, magazines, brochures, directories, packaging, and all other forms of message delivery that are produced by printing on paper or some other material and are relatively permanent (as opposed to broadcast messages, which are fleeting). Their permanence means they can be kept, filed, or revisited.

Key Point 3: Broadcast Media

Broadcast media include radio and television. Their messages are more fleeting and more intrusive than print messages yet they have great reach and high levels of involvement and impact.

Key Point 4: Out-of-Home Media

Out-of-home media are media that the target audience sees when they are away from home. The most common are outdoor boards, transit posters, commercials in movie theaters, various nontraditional media, and product placements in films and TV shows.

Lessons Learned

Key Point 1: Media Classifications

a. What are the four major types of media?
b. What does the following sentence mean: "Media exposure does not guarantee message exposure"?
c.   What do the different types of media each sell? On which media do advertisers spend the most money?
d. What's the difference between a mass medium and a communication vehicle? Give examples.
e. What is the difference between mass and niche media? Between mass media and addressable media? Between addressable and interactive media?
f.   Why is intrusiveness a problem for some of the one-way media? Give an example from your own personal experience of a highly intrusive message and describe your response to it.

Key Point 2: Print Media

a. List the various forms of print media.
b. Find examples of classified and display advertising, and explain how they differ.
c. How do newspapers and magazines set their advertising rates?
d. Compare the strengths and weaknesses of newspapers and magazines.
e. What are some of the advantages and disadvantages of advertising in the Yellow Pages?
f.   You are designing a marketing communication program for a restaurant near your campus. Would you want to use any of print media in your advertising plan? Why or why not?

Key Point 3: Broadcast Media

a. What is a rating point? What is the difference between *ratings* and *share?*
b. What are some of the most popular radio formats? What types of products might be advertised effectively on each?
c. Explain the concept of image transfer. Give an example of a brand message that you have heard that uses image transfer.
d. What is a daypart? Which dayparts in radio carry the most expensive advertising time slots? Which do in television? Explain the differences.
e. Compare the strengths and weaknesses of radio and television.
f.   What is a spot buy? Give an example.
g. You are designing a marketing communication program for a restaurant near your campus. Would you recommend using any broadcast media? Why or why not?

Key Point 4: Out-of-Home Media

a. Describe the different forms of outdoor boards.
b. What is a showing?
c. What are the biggest strengths and weaknesses of outdoor boards?
d. What are some of the problems associated with cinema- and video-related commercial messages?
e. List and describe some of the nontraditional media, and discuss their role in an overall MC campaign.
f. Explain product placement and what it brings to a brand.
g. You are designing a marketing communication program for a restaurant near your campus. Would you recommend any out-of-home media? Why or why not?

Chapter Challenge

Writing Assignment

Review the definition of *media menu* at the start of this chapter. Study your own media behavior. Buy a notepad or diary, pick a typical day in your life, and record every medium with which you come in contact. Group and classify the different types of media in your life. Analyze your involvement with media—do you consider yourself to be a media-intense person or a media-averse person? Write a report on your media diary for your instructor that describes a profile of you as a media consumer.

Presentation Assignment

Choose two college-age friends and develop a media menu for each one. Take them through a typical day and ask them what they see, read, view, watch, or listen to. Then consult with your parents, or two older adults, and develop their media menus. Compare and contrast the two sets. Develop a presentation for your classmates that explains how these two groups of people differ in their media menus.

Internet Assignment

Check out the MarthaStewart.com website. Compare this site with Stewart's section on the Kmart website BlueLight.com. Are the brand images identical or has there been any change to adapt to the Kmart audience? Do you feel this branding strategy is effective? Why or why not?

Additional Readings

Fine, Jon. "Cross-Media Catches Fire," Advertising Age, October 23, 2000, p. S2.
Zufryden, Fred S. "Predicting Trial, Repeat, and Sales Response from Alternative Media Plans," Journal of Advertising Research's Special Classics Issue, December 2000, p. 65
Radio Advertising Bureau Radio Marketing Guide and Fact Book for Advertisers (www.rab.com), 2000.

Research Assignment

Different media mixes create different results. What are the media variables that create these different results? Describe at least three ways that the results of two media mixes will most likely differ.

Endnotes

[1]*Brandweek* website, November 4, 2000, quoting Robert Coen, SVP Universal McCann.
[2]Tom Duncan and Sandra Moriarty, *Driving Brand Value* (New York: McGraw-Hill, 1997), pp. 102-3.

[3]National Hispanic Media Directory, 1998.

[4]Television Advertising Bureau, as cited on TVBasics website, July 2000.

[5]Radio Advertising Bureau's website <www.rab.com>, June 2000.

[6]*TV Dimensions '98* (Media Dynamics, Inc., 1998), p. 335.

[7]Richard Siklos, "Will the Nielsen Spin-Off Be a Hit?" *Business Week,* July 20, 1998, pp. 66–67.

[8]Richard Hendersen, "Over One Million Sold," *Brandweek,* November 6, 2000, special advertising section, p. 6.

[9]Author interview with Amy Hume, Leo Burnett media department, September 2000.

[10]Kyle Pope, "In Battle for TV Ads, Cable Is Now the Enemy," *The Wall Street Journal,* May 6, 1998, p. B1.

[11]Rachel Zoll, "Up on the Roof," *Boulder Sunday Camera,* June 14, 1998, p. 1B.

[12]Cara Beardi, "From Elevators to Gas Stations, Ads Multiplying," *Advertising Age,* November 13, 2000, p. 40.

[13]Scot Hume, "Consumers Pan Ads on Video Movies," *Advertising Age,* November 13, 2000, p. 40.

[14]Kevin B. Tynan, *Multi-Channel Marketing: Maximizing Market Share with an Integrated Marketing Strategy* (Chicago and Cambridge, UK: Probus, 1994), pp. 91–98.

[15]Rebecca Gardyn, "Moving Targets," *American Demographics,* October 2000 <www.americandemographics.com>.

[16]T. L. Stanley, "Place-Based Media," *Brandweek,* May 11, 1998, pp. 34–35.

12

The Internet and Interactive Media

Key Points in This Chapter

1. What are the technologies that have created the new electronic marketing frontier?

2. How do the older forms of addressable, interactive communication—phone and mail—compare with e-mail?

3. In what ways has the new technology affected marketing communication?

4. What are the important aspects of website design, operation, and management?

Chapter Perspective

Adding Two-Way to One-Way Media

The majority of most companies' sales and an even greater proportion of their profits come from current customers with whom the company has established a connection. To motivate repeat purchases, companies need to continually connect and reconnect with customers. The media most suited for doing this are addressable, interactive media. The importance of interactive media is reflected in the fact that 39 percent of U.S. media dollars in 2000 were spent on phone, mail, and the Internet. This does not include face-to-face personal selling, which some say is the most powerful interactive medium of all (and which is discussed later in this book as one of the MC functions—see Chapter 17).

You will recall from Chapter 11 that one-way media are used most often for creating brand awareness, helping position a brand, and keeping the brand at top-of-mind with customers and prospects. In contrast, interactive media are used not only for generating repeat purchases but also for communicating with prospects who have expressed interest in a brand. Interactive media are extremely valuable in building brand relationships because they enable companies and customers to get to know and trust each other.

This chapter gives an overview of the recent technological advances that have shaped interactive media. From a general discussion of communication and technology, it moves to an analysis of interactive media characteristics and then to discussions of e-commerce and online marketing communication. Another section focuses on website design and operation, and the final section touches on Internet privacy issues.

AN E-BUSINESS PIONEER
Cisco Systems, San Jose, California

Cisco Systems Inc., a business-to-business marketer, sells routers, switches, access devices, Internet appliances, website management tools, and network management software. The company's basic business mission is to be a marketer and assembler of high-tech products and systems. It has more than 17,000 employees and claims to have the world's largest Internet commerce site. Without a doubt, it is a pioneer in using the Internet to communicate with its key stakeholders—customers, employees, suppliers, and distributors. The secret to Cisco's success has been its ability to manage its communication, both internally and externally. The company is communication driven (see Exhibit 12–1).

Cisco began getting closer to its customers in the early 1990s when it set up a bulletin board system for customer questions and comments. In 1993, the company was one of the first to offer graphical interaction through the use of an early Internet browser, Mosaic. Online sales began in 1995, making it easier for customers to do business with the company (see Exhibit 12–2). Initially, the internal sales staff was wary. They were worried that they would lose commissions and had to be assured that they would get the same commission whether the order was placed over the phone or on the Internet.

Cisco's ordering system is complex because the company sells virtually all of its products made to order. In the past, a customer would create a purchase order and send it to the company by fax, phone, or e-mail. The order was then entered into Cisco's database. Approximately 25 percent of all orders had errors, were rejected by Cisco, and had to be resubmitted by the customer, weakening the relationship. Most of the errors occurred during the data entry phase at Cisco. In 1996, Cisco developed software programs that fed orders automatically into production

EXHIBIT 12-1

This double-page magazine ad shows how Cisco communicates on an emotional as well as a rational level with customers and prospects.

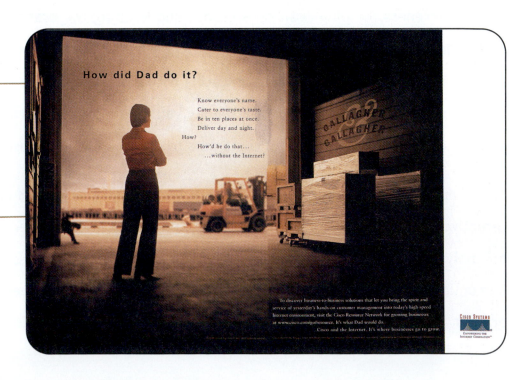

schedules, inventory control, and shipping databases. This eliminated the data-entry problem. In addition, customers were able to check the status of their orders online, which was a significant competitive advantage because it was an added value for customers.

Four months after it started taking online orders in 1995, Cisco handled 10 percent of its orders that way. By 2000, Cisco was receiving 97 percent of its orders over the Internet. Today, orders are routed within minutes after being received to an assembly vendor (there are 32 supplier plants worldwide), which then builds Cisco products to order. This system has cut product lead time in half, from a maximum of six weeks to a maximum of three weeks. Sales data are updated three times a day. The quarterly books can be closed in 24 hours. This improved communication has added value for customers while at the same time reducing the company's operating costs—an excellent example of e-business in action.

EXHIBIT 12-2

Cisco Systems was an e-commerce pioneer moving into online sales in 1995.

Cisco's electronic communication and ordering system also works for resellers. Orders are placed at the Cisco site and then routed through a distributor's system, where the distributor can add features such as pricing discounts. Various stakeholders, such as customers, suppliers, distributors, and other business partners, have access to Cisco's extranet.

Cisco uses the Internet to benefit other internal operations, such as human resources, which offers Internet-based training programs. Employees can also look up benefits and file expense reports online. Job seekers can apply online—and 85 percent do so, eliminating 25,000 paper résumés a month. Also, information goes into the database about the companies where Cisco job applicants are working, which can alert Cisco to competitors that might be having problems.

Customer service is another area where Cisco uses online communication. Roughly 85 percent of Cisco's 800,000 monthly customer queries are handled via the Web, eliminating the need to train thousands of customer-service reps to handle phone-call questions. As you can see, Cisco is a good example of a company that understands e-commerce and how to use the Internet to create and manage brand relationships.

Sources for this case included the following: "The 100 Hottest Companies," Business 2.0, *May 1, 1999 <www.business2.com/content/magazine/indepth/1999/05/01/19647>; U.S. Government Electronic Commerce Policy, Chapter 3 <www.ecommerce.gov/chapter3.htm>; Brian Riggs, "Cisco Simplifies Business,"* Information Week, *December 13, 1999 <www.informationweek.com/765/ciscoebiz.html>; Bill Roberts, "E-commerce Poster Child Grows Up,"* Datamation, *August 1998 <http://datamation.earthweb.com/ecomm/08ecom.html>; and Scott Thurm, "Eating Their Own Dog Food: Cisco Goes Online to Buy, Sell and Hire,"* The Wall Street Journal, *April 19, 2000, p. A1.*

COMMUNICATION AND TECHNOLOGY

As the price of computing power has dropped and more companies and individuals have joined the computer revolution, new business opportunities have been created, both in starting up information-based companies and in moving old businesses, such as car manufacturers, to using the new electronic media. Just as the industrial revolution shifted people from farms to factories, the information age is shifting people from manufacturing to service industries (see Exhibit 12–3).

Moore's law, named after Intel's Gordon Moore, who formulated the concept in 1965, says that microchip capacity, and consequently computing speed, doubles every 18 months. This accelerating speed has affected every aspect of marketing communication. Today, a major problem with a brand can be communicated around the world within days or even hours—the greater the problem, the faster the word is spread. Intel itself found this out several years ago when a user discovered a problem with one of Intel's chips. In a matter of days, the faulty chip became a discussion topic in dozens of high-tech chat rooms and the issue was picked up by the offline mass media and further publicized.

Television, cable, computer, and phone companies all are scrambling to take leadership positions in the new world of telecommunication convergence. Sprint, for example, describes itself as a global communication company that integrates long distance, local, wireless, and Internet communication. It claims to operate the only nationwide, all-digital, fiber-optic network in the United States, making it a leader in advanced data communication.

More complex communication requires more **bandwidth,** which is *what governs the amount of digital information or data that can be sent from one place to another in a given time.* Limited bandwidth is a particular problem for exchanging large data files that contain graphic and video elements. However, because of the speed of technological evolution identified in Moore's law, data-transmission capacities are increasing monthly. This means that, as more consumers buy faster computers and have access to more bandwidth, companies can deliver more complex brand messages than ever before.

EXHIBIT 12-3

This ad speaks to the need to use the Internet efficiently.

THE TROUBLE WITH EXPLORING THE INTERNET IS THE TIME IT TAKES EXPLORING THE INTERNET.

You have needs, you have wants. Sometimes they involve the act of shopping. But what you probably don't have is a lot of time. Introducing forbes.clique.com. A unique shopping destination designed specifically for Forbes readers. Filled with the kinds of products you want. Uncluttered with the kinds of products you don't. Visit forbes.clique.com and discover a smarter way to shop. It's about time, isn't it?

forbes.clique.com

clique.com
Shop Smarter

Forbes

The Internet has become the fastest-growing communication technology in history, according to Harris Interactive, and has made the concept of interactive communication much more feasible. As noted in the chapter opening case, Cisco Systems claims to be the biggest Internet business in the world because it understands the power of interactivity in building and maintaining customer relationships. Yet, although the Internet is the fastest-growing medium and is getting a lot of attention, it still accounts for only a very small portion of all business interactivity. The two media that carry the most interactive communication—mail and phone—have been around for years. These two "old" media, however, have been modernized so that much of their use today is data-driven. These media help companies collect data about customers and then use that data to generate further communication with both current customers and prospects.

Through the use of sophisticated profiling techniques and complex networks of databases, which hold information about customers' online (and offline) behavior and interests, companies can target brand messages to individuals and alter message content on the fly with customized images and appeals. Real-time, targeted, and personalized brand messages—that's the difference in marketing communication created by the new electronic technologies.

The Internet

While there have been important technological advances throughout history, computers, integrated circuits, and microprocessors opened a new electronic frontier of interactive communication in the twentieth century. One of the primary new media players, of course, is the **Internet,** which is, simply, *a worldwide system of linked computer networks.*

The Internet has actually been around since 1969, but for many years was used exclusively by government officials and academics to exchange research data. It wasn't until the early 1990s that the Internet moved out of the research world into the marketplace. This transition was made possible by the development of the World Wide Web, an information interface, and Mosaic, the first major Web browser, which *allowed people to view the Web through a user-friendly graphical format.* The Web made it possible to exchange audio and visual information as well as text messages, and thus allowed the Internet to become a powerful marketing communication medium as well as a research platform.

The Internet's greatest function is as a communication link. It helps companies build stronger brand relationships with customers, suppliers, distributors, and other stakeholders by increasing the power of interactivity. As a medium, it combines the characteristics of many other media—newspapers, magazines, catalogs, TV, and directories. Its communication versatility is why people have invested billions of dollars in online ventures, some of which have worked, and some of which have been financial disasters. It has by far the richest and most diverse content of any medium that has ever existed. For a current overview of the economic impact the Internet is having on the marketplace, go to the Internet Economy Indicators website (www.internetindicators.com), which not only carries current articles on the Internet but also has links to all the major publications and other sites related to e-commerce. Among its most important characteristics, the Internet:

1. *Shifts power from companies to customers.* Customers can do comparative shopping and learn more about brands from third parties more quickly and easily than ever before.

2. *Is accessible to the majority of the population.* Those who do not have access at home can go online at work or schools. Access is also available in public locations such as libraries and Internet cafés.

3. *Provides an extensive range of information.* Internet users have access to a wealth of information on companies, brands, and virtually every subject there is.

4. *Allows for unsurpassed speed and coverage.* Especially since the advent of high-speed connection services, information travels across the Internet almost instantaneously in most parts of the world.

5. *Reduces the cost of selling and acquisition.* The cost of taking a business online is far less than opening a traditional brick-and-mortar business.

Consumer and business use of the Internet is expanding rapidly because the Internet is both inexpensive and easy to use. Most computers today come with modems that can send and receive data over ordinary phone or cable lines or via satellite. By 2000, more than half of all U.S. households were online.[1] Interactivity has progressed due to advances in three different areas: hardware, software, and connectivity. The hardware has become less cumbersome as it has become more powerful; the software has become more sophisticated as it has become easier to use; and the networks that link computers and their users have spread like wildfire throughout the industrialized world. But the rapid growth has created a problem for many companies, namely, how to handle and manage the increase in interactivity. According to an article in *The Economist,* the marketing world was much simpler when all companies did was send out brand message.[2] With the increasing use of interactive technology, customers have come to expect high levels of service. They want to ask questions, place orders, and register complaints anytime—and companies are having to make major adjustments.

> " Most organizations find it . . . difficult to make the intellectual and cultural shifts necessary to succeed in a much more interactive business environment."
>
> " Business and the Internet," *The Economist*

Websites and e-mail are the two most obvious communication tools that have grown up with the World Wide Web. These will be discussed in more depth later in this chapter. The Internet offers users several other communication features. **Listservs,** which work like electronic bulletin boards, are *voluntary electronic mailing lists.* These are often used by organizations to keep members informed. **Forums** are *public websites where people can post notes on a given topic,* such as a current movie or news events like a product recall. **Chat rooms** are *websites in which people can engage in real-time interaction with other people.*

Communication and searching for information are currently the dominant uses of the Internet. According to a Gallup Poll conducted in 2000, among those who have used the Internet, 95 percent have done so to obtain information, 89 percent to send or receive e-mail, 45 percent to shop, and 21 percent to visit in chat rooms.[3] Approximately 10 percent of Internet users have visited online brokerages, banking services, or auction houses.

E-mail is so popular that, in 2000, 60 percent of U.S. adults surveyed said they preferred e-mail to reading traditional mail, and 34 percent said they preferred it to phone calls.[4] This is good news for marketers because e-mail is a less expensive form of one-to-one communication than either regular mail or long distance telephone calls. Users also report spending about one-fourth of their online time gathering information.[5] This is more good news for companies. It indicates that an increasing number of customers and prospects are getting used to gathering information online, suggesting that the Internet is an economical medium for distributing brand information.

Communication Networks

Networked communication is not a new concept. Broadcasting chains of linked stations have long been known as "networks." But it is Web-based technology that has had the most impact on how businesses interact with their customers, employees, business partners, and other stakeholders. According to Ed Zander, president of computer hardware giant Sun Microsystems, BtB interactivity has been revolutionized.[6]

Intranets and Extranets

As explained earlier in this book, a company cannot be integrated externally until it is integrated internally. The Internet has made it possible for companies to better manage their internal and external communication. Increasingly, companies are choosing Internet-based networks for corporate communication, as opposed to maintaining their own private networks. The two types of proprietary communication systems—intranets and extranets—were introduced in Chapter 6; this section looks at them in more detail.

Intranets are private online communication systems whose access is restricted to members of a company or organization. Before the Internet was widely available, companies had to pay for expensive private networks (called wide area networks) to link their various offices. In 1998, one out of every four dollars spent on U.S. companies' Web initiatives was spent on intranets.[7] Intranets are password-protected with specialized software programs known as firewalls to prevent external access. They can be set so that employees in a variety of locations can access information. Table 12–1 summarizes the most popular uses of Intranets.

> " The real revolution [in the marketplace] is how the Internet is enabling companies to interact more efficiently with suppliers and partners as well as customers—not to mention their own employees."
>
> Ed Zander, Sun Microsystems press release

To further facilitate intranet usage, a number of companies are providing employees with free or low-cost home computers and Internet access, thus allowing them to access corporate intranets from home. Ford Motor Company, for example, gave all its employees a computer and Internet access. According to a survey of approximately 5,000 Internet users, 26 percent said the Internet has increased the amount of time they spend working at home.[8]

The next level of Web-based interactive communication, the *extranet,* allows approved outside stakeholders such as suppliers, channel members, business partners, support agencies (e.g., legal firms, MC agencies, accounting firms), as well as customers, to have access to selected organizational information. An extranet, like an intranet, facilitates interactions and communication. Cisco's extranet connects the company with its customers, suppliers, distributors, and other business partners. The goal is to increase communication efficiency while not breaching critical security. Often different stakeholders have access to different parts of the extranet (e.g., suppliers can monitor inventory, MC agencies can monitor corporate communications). This is controlled by assigning each group an access code.

Benefits of Network Technology

Network technology has given more control to customers, reinforcing their relationship with a company or brand. Like Cisco Systems, the overnight delivery company Federal Express (FedEx) found that it provided an added valued when it

---

T a b l e   1 2 - 1   Popular Uses for Intranets

Corporate Use	Employee Use
Document management	Calendars
Meeting management support	Meeting announcements
Project management	Newsletter distribution
Knowledge management	Human resources information
Training programs	Corporate directory access
	Personal Web page creation
	Employee discount shopping
	Cafeteria menus
	Discussion groups

opened up its online tracking system to its customers. Both individuals and companies that use FedEx for package delivery can check the extranet for the status of a given shipment whenever they wish. By not having to hire extra phone representatives to handle these inquiries, FedEx has saved millions of dollars. UPS and other competitors have implemented similar extranets in order to stay competitive with FedEx (see Exhibit 12–4).

In sum, network technology has helped companies improve communication both internally and externally and thus to become more integrated. More specifically, an intranet or extranet:

- Decreases costs through increased efficiencies.
- Facilitates record keeping.
- Provides new channels of distribution.
- Makes companies more flexible and responsive to the marketplace.
- Eliminates distance barriers.
- Increases globalization (and global competition).
- Increases knowledge in all areas and enhances analysis; makes it possible for a company to be a learning organization.

Wireless Communication

EXHIBIT 12-4

UPS advertises that its tracking system helps companies manage their inventory and streamline their distribution.

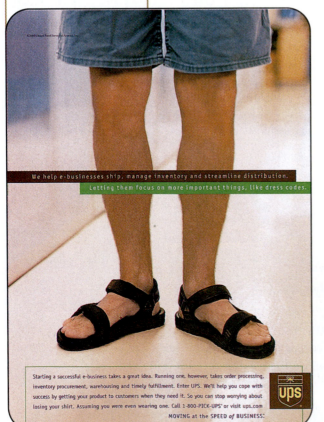

We help e-businesses ship, manage inventory and streamline distribution. Letting them focus on more important things, like dress codes.

Starting a successful e-business takes a great idea. Running one, however, takes order processing, inventory procurement, warehousing and timely fulfillment. Enter UPS. We'll help you cope with success by getting your product to customers when they need it. So you can stop worrying about losing your shirt. Assuming you were even wearing one. Call 1-800-PICK-UPS® or visit ups.com

MOVING at the SPEED of BUSINESS®

Wireless transmission of data and information will probably be the single most significant change in media technology during the first decade of the new millennium. Developing countries such as China and India, which don't have enough existing telephone and cable lines to support all the new media, are investing heavily in wireless communication, leapfrogging the in-ground stage of communication infrastructure. In the United States, one of the fastest-growing telecommunication areas is direct broadcasting satellites. The fact that customers are now able to access the Internet and send and receive e-mail via cellular phones is another indication of the growth in wireless. Although many companies are getting into the wireless business most marketers of consumer and BtB goods are still waiting to see how viable it is to send brand messages to cellular phones.

According to London-based Ovum, a research and consulting firm, $4 billion will be spent in 2002 on wireless advertising; that number is expected to quadruple to $16 billion by 2005. Marketers will be attracted to using wireless advertising for several reasons: (1) customers are increasingly mobile, (2) messages can be targeted not only by individual cellular phone number but also by time and location of targeted customers, and (3) wireless provides one more way to reinforce brand awareness and motivate customers to respond (see the Technology in Action box). It is expected that wireless messages will be most successful when used to redirect customers to certain websites, sponsor Web pages that are most likely to be accessed with cellular devices, and for

TECHNOLOGY IN ACTION

M-commerce Is the Future of Interactive Media

One of the most rapidly advancing types of interactive media is wireless digital communication. Its application to business is referred to as m-commerce (*m* for *mobile*). Devices for using this medium include cell phones, some personal digital assistants (PDAs), and global positioning systems (GPSs). The first generation of wireless devices consisted of analog cellular phones. The second generation consisted of digital cellular phones. The third generation will be those that can transmit voice, data, and video. Beginning in 2001, all wireless phones were being equipped with wireless application protocol (WAP), an industry standard that allows phones to receive content from the Internet. It has been estimated that by 2003 there will be more people interacting with the Internet by a handheld wireless device than by a PC.

In some countries, such as Finland and Japan, there are already more wireless phone subscribers than fixed line subscribers. In 1999, over 275 million cellular phones were sold worldwide, with most of the sales being in Europe and Asia. The owners use their phones not only to talk to each other but also to send e-mail messages back and forth, pay for small-ticket items such as soft drinks, and subscribe to text messages such as horoscopes and jokes. But the uses are fast expanding. According to one observer, " People will be accustomed to getting up-to-minute personal and customized news, from traffic and weather to sports; stock quotes; and even when movies are playing." Such use, if it becomes widespread, will make wireless communication a particularly attractive way to deliver brand messages.

Retail marketers are excited about the prospect of tying messages to location. A shopper in a mall will be able to request on-the-spot information concerning sales in the mall. A shopper in a grocery store will be able to obtain electronic coupons. A tourist walking past a restaurant can be alerted to a lunch special.

Think About It

What types of brand messages—from what types of businesses—seem the most logical to send brand messages over wireless devices? Will the proliferation brand messages sent via wireless media finally cause customers to revolt against commercial messaging?

Source: Brad Applegate, "From 'Appointment Viewing' to 'News on Demand,'" posted on MediaPost Monitor, July 18, 2000. <www.masha@mediapost.com>

"click-and-dial." An example of the latter would be a message that appears on your mobile phone's message screen asking if a birthday or special occasion is near for which flowers would be an appropriate gift. The message would then allow you to click though to an online florist to place an order.[9]

ADDRESSABLE AND INTERACTIVE MEDIA

While Chapter 11 defined addressable and interactive media, this chapter will discuss them in more depth. Recall that companies use *addressable media* primarily to communicate with current customers at their individual point of contact (home or work address or phone number, e-mail address). Besides serving as a communication vehicle for product offers to customers, addressable media (mail, e-mail, phone, fax) can deliver messages asking research questions about level of brand satisfaction, further purchase intentions, and so on. Rewards, discounts, and special offers can also be delivered to heavy users via addressable media. With the right messages, these media can help retain current customers and increase their share of business. For major-purchase goods and services, these media are also used to reach identified prospects.

Another benefit of using addressable media is that each message can be personalized. As explained in Chapter 8, however, this is generally cost-prohibitive unless the customization can be done by computer. Even with highly sophisticated database-driven printing processes, the cost of using addressable media is relatively high compared to mass media. This cost continues to come down, however, as the use of customized e-mailings grows.

Cable television operators that have digital systems have addressable capabilities, meaning they can send a tailored selection of programs and brand messages to a particular subscriber's TV set. A recent deal between TCI and Kraft, for example, experimented with sending different ads to different televisions within the same home. This means that in the near future, a TV in the kitchen would receive an ad for Kraft Singles cheese, while the TV in the basement workshop runs an ad for Black & Decker power tools.

Interactive media have four major characteristics that set them apart from mass media: (1) they can target individuals as well as customer segments, (2) they enable customers and prospects to talk back to a company, (3) they are more measurable and accountable than mass media, and (4) they demand more attention than mass media because of the personalized brand messages they carry. The ability to deliver tight targeting is a particularly important benefit.

Companies have traditionally asked, "How can *we* best send messages to our customer and prospects?" They are now beginning to recognize there is another question that is just as important: "How can our *customers* easily send messages to us?" Interactivity is one of the primary ways in which customers are "integrated" into a company. Customers can and should contribute to the product planning and development process, as well as to distribution and marketing decisions. Interactivity is increasingly seen as a customer's "right." If customers can easily ask one company a question or voice a complaint, they expect to be able to do so with all companies with whom they do business. Companies that do not keep up risk sending the message that they are antiquated and don't care about their customers.

In sum, from a customer's perspective, interactivity means *accessibility*, *recognition*, and *responsiveness*—all the things people require in a relationship, whether personal or commercial. From a brand perspective, it means the ability to listen as well as speak and then modify corporate behavior as a result of customer feedback.

Companies that sincerely want customers and prospects to talk to them need to provide options for communicating with the company—fax, phone, e-mail, a website, or mail. The more flexibility there is to talk to a company, the more consumers will respond. Microsoft's ad in Exhibit 12–5 invites customers to interact with the company.

Interactivity can be either active or passive. "Active interactivity" is when a company and a customer talk to each other in real time (e.g., via the telephone or live chat). "Passive interactivity" involves a time delay of some kind. A customer may get a fax on demand or use a company-sponsored kiosk or website to ask questions, retrieve information, and request information that arrives later by mail, fax, or e-mail. Interactive media include many of the addressable media described above. The difference between the two is simply in how they are used. As mentioned earlier, the Internet can be used as a mass medium (banner ads), an addressable medium (e-mail), or an interactive medium (live chat).

Mail Formats and Features

Mail may not be as sexy as newer media such as the Internet, but, it is the third largest medium behind TV and newspapers in terms of MC spending. It accounts for approximately 20 percent of all media spending.[10] Mail is a pervasive medium that reaches every U.S. business and household. In the late 1990s, more than half of all U.S. adults placed one or more product orders by mail. Although mail is primarily considered an addressable medium, it is a medium that customers use extensively to communicate with companies. Also, many direct-mail offers contain business reply cards and stamped, addressed envelopes to encourage response. For this reason, it is also considered an interactive medium.

The following are considerations that affect how mail should be most effectively used in marketing communication:

- Young adults 18–21 are more likely than any other demographic group to respond to a direct-mail offer.
- Offers sent in oversized envelopes have a higher response rates than those sent in standard letter-sized envelopes.
- The average adult receives 22 pieces of mail per week.
- The higher a person's socioeconomic level, the more pieces of mail he or she receives.
- By month, the highest mail volume comes in December, followed by May and June.

Costs

In the United States, marketers use any of several classes of mail: Express, Priority, first class, and third class. (Second class mail is reserved for authorized publishers and news agents.) The majority of mailings use either first or third class. The U.S.

Why is our company tagline a question?

In part, it is meant to be an invitation to you.

In part, it's a question because we really need to know. We don't have all the answers. We just make software and then we watch you use it. And we've noticed you tend to do some pretty amazing things, some things we never would've imagined. We do a lot of our best work trying to keep up with your imagination.

So, for us, this isn't just a slogan; it's an honest question, and how you answer makes all the difference. So we'll ask it again: Where do you want to go today?

Where do you want to go today?

Microsoft

EXHIBIT 12-5

This ad for Microsoft explains the company's tag line, "Where do you want to go today?" as an invitation for customers to interact with the company.

Postal Service does not have a volume discount on postage. There are certain things marketers can do, however, to reduce mailing costs. When there are 500 or more pieces to deliver, presorting by zip code will reduce the cost per piece. Third-class mail must be presorted and classified by destination and delivered to the post office in bags or trays.

BtB mailings aimed at top executives are often sent by UPS, FedEx, or some other private carrier—all of which charge more than the U.S. Postal Service. Two main reasons for using private mail services are, first, that packages delivered by private carriers demand more attention and are perceived as being more important than those received by regular mail and, second, private carriers are in general highly dependable and able to track mailings.

Strengths and Limitations

The number one strength of mail is its addressability. If a company is able to identify its customers and prospects, mail can be a cost-effective medium because it minimizes waste—response rates are consistently higher than those of other brand messages. Addressability also enables a company to personalize its messages. With newspaper and magazine ads, each reader receives exactly the same message. (A few magazines offer some minimal customized messaging, such as printing the recipient's name on the cover, but this significantly increases the cost.) Marketers that use mail should also tap the power of their databases to tailor their messages to customers and prospects as specifically as possible. Unfortunately, most companies use this addressable medium to send mass messages that are not personalized.

Addressability allows marketers to measure response rates to direct mailings. This makes mail a much more accountable medium than most other media. Companies can use mail's addressability to test many different offers, and use only those that generate the highest response rates to be sent to a large number of target customers and prospects.

Despite the perception of direct mail as junk mail, a piece of mail receives more attention than any *mass* media message. Few people take things from their mailbox and just throw them away without first sorting through them. This fact alone virtually guarantees that a direct-mail envelope will be noticed and given some consideration. Unlike ads in newspapers and magazines, direct mail has no editorial competition for attention (just other direct mail). According to household diary reports, 52 percent of unsolicited mail pieces are opened.[11] The percent of mass media messages that receive similar attention ranges only between 8 and 35.

Another advantage of direct mail is that the brand message can be of any size or configuration. In general, the more complex and expensive-looking it is, the more likely it will attract attention and be opened—although some marketers have found that small postcards inscribed with a "handwritten" message can cut through mailbox clutter.

As you might guess, any medium that has this many advantages must be costly to use, which is one of mail's major weaknesses. Not only is postage costly, but most mailings are considerably more costly to produce than other types of brand messages (see Chapter 17). Another weakness is long lead time. It can take weeks and even months to create, produce, and send out a mailing. The more complex the piece is, generally the longer the lead time.

Phone Formats and Features

Some people have a problem thinking of the telephone as a marketing communication medium. But it definitely must be included when you think back to the definition of *media* as a means of connecting companies and customers. Like mail, **telephony** *(the technical name for the transmission of sound between two points)* is big business. In 2000, U.S. companies spent $44.7 billion on telephone marketing—almost as much as was spent on TV.[12] And this figure includes neither handling incoming calls that are in response to offers made in other media (e.g., toll-free numbers) nor handling incoming calls to customer service.

Telemarketing, *the practice of using the telephone to deliver a brand message designed to create a sale or sales lead,* will be discussed in more detail in Chapter 17. Although the telephone is no longer the "most economical" way of connecting buyer and seller, as a Bell Telephone sales manual claimed in 1927,[13] it is still the most effective selling medium other than a face-to-face sales call.

> " The telephone provides the simplest, most effective and most economical means of increasing the number of contacts between salesman and buyer."
>
> Bell Telephone Co. of Pennsylvania's *Telephone Sales Manual*, 1927

Outbound Calls

The business use of telephony is divided into two types of calls, outbound and inbound. *Outbound calls* are those initiated by an organization. Since it's the human interaction that makes outbound calls so expensive, some companies use automated calls, especially for sending reminder messages. A chain of local oil-change service centers, for example, can turn its customer database over to a telemarketing service that will script and produce a brief recorded message reminding customers when it is time for their next oil change. The same can be done for dental, doctor, and veterinary appointments, and for office supplies and other products where there is need for periodic repurchase of products that most consumers and companies don't keep top-of-mind.

Some companies have made creative use of technology with regard to telemarketing. When people in large numbers began to screen incoming calls to avoid telemarketers, some companies began using automated dialing equipment that hangs up if a human answers. These companies are finding more success by leaving their sales message on answering machines than by trying to talk to a live person. They say the response rate compares favorably to that of direct mail.[14]

Inbound Calls

Inbound calls are those initiated by prospects and customers who are either responding to a brand offer delivered in some other medium or calling with an inquiry, complaint, or request for more information. As you are probably well aware, most businesses today use some form of automated answering system. To many people, such a system is a "voice-mail jail," a place that is not very customer-friendly. This being true, why do companies use them? The answer—to save money. Such systems can reduce customer-service operating costs by 20 to 50 percent.

But such systems don't have to be irritating for a company to save money. Capital One Finance Corporation, one of the 10 largest credit-card issuers in the United States, uses an automated answering system that handles customer calls efficiently and effectively. Capital One receives 1 million calls a week from customers who want to check their credit-card balances, question a charge on their monthly card invoice, ask why their interest rate has changed, and so on. As soon as a call comes in, Capital One's computers (which hold profile data on 17 million customers) go instantly to work. They identify the caller in the customer database (based on the telephone number of the incoming call), analyze that customer's profile data, predict why the person may be calling, sort through 50 possible internal call destinations, and even determine what company products may be of greatest interest to the caller. For frequent callers, computers have been programmed to learn all the numbers from which they usually call (e.g., work, home, cell phone). According to an article on Capital One's system, "All these steps—the incoming call, the data review, the analysis, the routing, and the recommending—happen in just 100 milliseconds."[15]

As the Capital One example illustrates, the "old" medium of telephone has gone high-tech. Because the phone is the primary medium customers use for initiating communication with a company, how companies choose to receive phone calls can affect customer relationships. There is a range of automated answering systems, as shown in Figure 12–1. An automated attendant (AA) offers a recorded menu from which the caller chooses an appropriate number. An interactive voice response (IVR) system does everything an AA does but, in addition, allows callers to interact with the company. For example, callers can punch in their account number to find out their bank balance or type in a flight number to find out a departure times. The IVR can handle multiple calls at the same time, so callers are rarely put on hold.

When computer technology integration (CTI) is combined with an IVR system, a call can go into the customer database and bring up the caller's profile, as is done at Capital One. This way customer-service representatives know who is calling even before the caller speaks (although most callers still are asked for some form of identification). A CTI system also allows the customer-service rep to transfer the caller's profile to another person or department so the customer does not have to repeat any information after a transfer. This is called "screen popping."

The most advanced systems are the automated voice recognition (AVR) systems. With these systems, customers don't have to punch any buttons but simply give a verbal response to questions being asked. At the current level of development, most AVR systems pose questions that can be answered with a yes or no. Because of accents and different voice levels and manners of speaking, there is still much work to be done in perfecting AVR systems.

Part of a company's media evaluation should be an ongoing monitoring of its automated answering system. After company personnel learn how to use the system and its shortcuts, its complexity may not seem like a problem for them. But for prospects and new customers, an automated system can be intimidating and irritating if not set up with customer needs in mind. The following list contains guidelines for creating user-friendly automated answering systems:[16]

1. Designate a cross-functional team to own the process.

2. Conduct a situation analysis to understand customer needs.

3. Design IVR appropriately to meet those needs.

4. Choose a system with reporting capabilities.

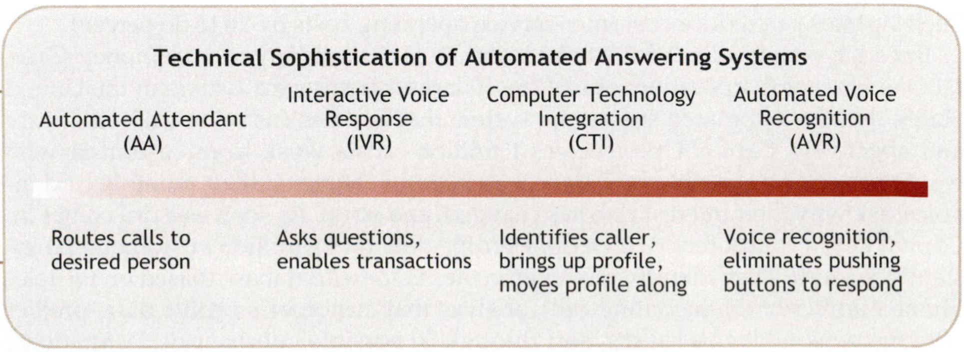

FIGURE 12-1

Companies can choose from a variety of automated phone systems.

Technical Sophistication of Automated Answering Systems

Automated Attendant (AA)	Interactive Voice Response (IVR)	Computer Technology Integration (CTI)	Automated Voice Recognition (AVR)
Routes calls to desired person	Asks questions, enables transactions	Identifies caller, brings up profile, moves profile along	Voice recognition, eliminates pushing buttons to respond

5. Design menu options to meet customer needs.

6. Incorporate procedure for capturing customer feedback.

7. Provide motivation for employees to submit customer and personal feedback.

8. Monitor system and analyze reports to determine impact on customer relationships.

9. Update system based on results of analysis.

10. Repeat steps 8 and 9 at designated intervals.

Phone rates, like most other media rates, can be negotiated—the more long-distance volume, for example, the lower the rate. According to one study, the average cost per hour of doing outbound BtB telemarketing is $53, which is twice the cost of making outbound consumer calls. This figure includes a telemarketer's salary, commissions, equipment, and facilities, as well as phone line charges. Since 1996, when the Telecommunications Act deregulated telephone service, no phone company can hold a monopoly, especially in long distance. With the growth of wireless service, telephony has gotten even more competitive.

Strengths and Limitations

Besides having all the strengths of other interactive media, telephony also has the advantages of being real-time and making a brand more personal. As with face-to-face personal selling, the telephone allows companies to personalize sales calls. The telephone also allows for an immediate response. Another advantage of telephony is that it demands attention. Although some consumers use answering machines to screen calls, most people will pick up a ringing phone.

The phone's major weakness is cost, especially when calls are being made by a human (rather than a computer). Also, when used for delivering commercial messages, the phone probably has one of the worst images of all the media because of its intrusiveness. An unwanted phone call from a telemarketer can upset even the gentlest, kindest, and most mature of people.

E-mail Formats and Features

Although phone and mail are huge media in terms of MC spending, the fastest-growing interactive medium is e-mail. E-mail and websites use different technologies and are used differently by both customers and businesses. For these reasons they will be discussed as different media, although both travel over the Internet.

E-mail has proven to be a popular and effective way to reach customers, because, as writer Jim Sterne has noted, it is so simple and inexpensive to use.[17] Yet unsolicited e-mail has become a source of customer irritation. Nevertheless, some Internet service providers, such as Hotmail, provide customers with free e-mail and Internet services in return for their agreeing to view advertising (see Exhibit 12–6).

Customer permission is an important consideration in the proper use of e-mail campaigns. *Unsolicited e-mail whose purpose is to sell a product or service* is called **spam.** Spam is not only bothersome to individuals but also a growing concern for government regulators and other consumer action groups. In IMC, spamming is not

> "Faster than a postal letter. More powerful than a banner ad. Able to leap tall organizational structures in a single bound. It's E-MAIL."
>
> Jim Sterne, "In Praise of E-Mail"

done. A step below spamming is **opt-out e-mail,** which is *a series of messages that a company sends automatically until notified not to.* For example, when you sign up for an online newsletter, the Web page will often have a box, already checked, that says something like "Please send me news about special offers." Unless you uncheck the box, the company will feel free to send you brand messages at regular intervals. This technique has been used for years by book and record clubs—unless you tell them not to send next month's selection, you will receive it.

The strategy that is most respectful of customers is **opt-in e-mail,** which means *e-mail that is sent only to those who have indicated they want to receive it.* Some refer to this as *permission marketing.* With this approach customers agree to be contacted and voluntarily provide the contact information. For opt-in to work, companies generally use offline media to invite those interested to "raise their hands" and sign up. Opt-in strategies have two benefits. First, they qualify the person (or company) as being interested in the product category. Second, when customers do sign up, smart companies ask profile questions so they have a better idea of their customers' demographics and lifestyles. An example of opt-in comes from companies that offer free event-planning or reminder services in exchange for personal data, which can be used to drive customized e-mail ads. One strategy is to use e-mail to announce a website launch to potential customers.

E-mail marketing can be done in a variety of formats. Examples include:

- *Ads.* Companies can send out e-mail advertising as plain text or as "rich media," *which features audio and/or video formats.* Rich media e-mails, like those designed by the RadicalMail company, use technology that permit streaming video, among other special effects, to be distributed within an e-mail message rather than in an attachment. They can be extremely effective in terms of attracting people to a company's website. For example, when Warner Bros. sent potential licensees an e-mail message featuring a trailer for an upcoming film, the response rates were exceptionally high.[18]

- *Discussion lists.* E-mail discussion lists (or listservs) can include hundreds or thousands of people. Advertisers can add marketing messages at the bottom of each message sent out to the list, which allows them to continually send messages to a targeted group of people.

- *Newsletters.* Marketers send mass e-mailings set up as newsletters on brand-related topics. Unlike members of discussion lists, newsletter recipients can't communicate directly back to the marketer or to other recipients.

- *Publicity.* News releases are being distributed online not only to editors but also to others who need to know about a company's announcements.

Since there is no cost to distributing e-mail per se, there are no space, time, or postage expenses to add up. What is sold, however, are e-mail services. The software and hardware required for handling large e-mail distributions can cost millions of dollars. This is why nearly all companies making use of e-mail as an MC medium hire services such as MessageMedia and Yesmail. These are companies that specialize in helping a brand put together an effective e-mail program. When the cost of the service is included, it is possible to estimate opt-in e-mail at about $2 per sale.

EXHIBIT 12-6

This ad for Internet service provider Hotmail is addressed to companies that might want to attach ads to the e-mail being delivered free by Hotmail. Advertising is the way Hotmail, and other providers of free online services, support themselves.

Put your message on something that people use everyday - their email. Email is the #1 application on the Web and Hotmail is the #1 Web email service. We profile each of our 8 million subscribers, so we can put your ad in front of the people who you want to see it. For a free trial, visit: www.hotmail.com/offer.html

hotmail.

YOUR AD HERE

In contrast, banner ads (discussed later in this chapter) have an average cost per sale of $100, and direct mail of approximately $71.[19]

Strengths and Limitations

Research has shown that e-mail is the most effective form of online marketing because it is personalized and inexpensive.[20] It is a particularly effective way to attract customers to a company's Website. Most e-mail ads are designed to encourage **click-through,** *the act of responding by clicking on a link to go directly to a particular website.* Users are 3 to 10 times more likely to click through to a company's website from an e-mail than from a banner ad. One study found that 63 percent of consumers surveyed about how they found their way to the website credited e-mail campaigns, compared to 29 percent for traditional advertising.[21]

Another advantage of e-mail is that, once a message has been produced, it has no distribution costs. Neither the size of the audience nor the size of the message affects the overall cost. As with direct mail, however, there is the cost of producing the message, obtaining and processing addresses, and managing the distribution and response.

Judging the effectiveness of e-mail is relatively straightforward: Costs are balanced against revenues. Marketers must remember, though, that it is the sale that is important, not the number of e-mails opened or the number of responses achieved. For example, in the table below consider three different e-mails—all of them sending 1,000 messages—and the responses they elicited. Note that e-mail C was the most frequently opened and that B attracted the most visitors to the website. E-mail A, however, produced the most sales.[22]

	E-Mail A	E-Mail B	E-Mail C
E-mail opened	300	400	500
Click-throughs	30	45	40
Sales	5	4	3

E-COMMERCE

To marketers, the Internet is not only a medium but also a business platform. Like direct marketing, electronic commerce (e-commerce) can either stand alone or be one aspect of a company's overall marketing communication effort. E-commerce is used by online-only (e.g., pure-play) companies such as eBay and Amazon.com and by offline companies such as Lands' End and Cisco Systems that make sales both online and offline. At first it seemed that online companies would dominate e-commerce; however, now that many "brick-and-mortar" companies have added e-commerce to their marketing operations (thus becoming "click-and-mortar" companies), a major portion of online sales are from offline-based companies. Recall from the chapter opening case that Cisco Systems began offline but that now 97 percent of its business is done on the Internet. Of the top three websites at the end of 2000, two— Toysrus.com and Walmart.com—were sponsored by click-and-mortar retailers; the other one, Amazon.com, is exclusively an online retailer.[23]

It is estimated that by 2002, e-commerce will generate more than $1.1 trillion in revenue.[24] Companies have found using the Internet to be a low-cost, convenient way to reach target audiences around the world; at the same time customers have found it to be a convenient way to shop. The Bluefly ad in Exhibit 12–7 shows how websites reach these new customers.

The product categories with the highest volume of online sales are books, CDs, computer software, and toys and games. Online ticketing is another growing category. People have found they can print out tickets for air travel, sports events, and so on from their home printers, along with other information that wouldn't fit on conventional printed tickets, such as schedules and maps. In order to make sure tickets are not counterfeited, a supporting BtB business has been developed that sells encryption and bar code technology to online ticketmasters.

According to the Small Business Association (SBA), in the year 2000, about 40 percent of small businesses had posted websites, which was up from 10 percent the year before.[25] SBA members who do business through e-commerce say that 50 percent of their online sales are coming from new customers, demonstrating the reach of e-commerce. The following are the primary marketing reasons why businesses use e-commerce. Note that e-commerce includes much more than just making a transaction.

- To reach broad worldwide audiences.
- To have a cost-effective dialogue with customers and prospects.
- To provide an extremely cost-effective way to distribute brand information.
- To aggregate niche audiences to reach a critical mass of customers.
- To provide alternative channels of distribution.
- To provide frequently updated prices and information.
- To improve customer service by providing company access 24 hours a day, seven days a week.
- To collect instant feedback and conduct market research, which can be interactive and immediately tallied.

For all these reasons, e-commerce is proving to be a viable way to generate sales. For example, after General Motors' Saturn website transformed itself from a passive site (featuring car information, data comparisons, and dealer referrals) to an active selling tool (featuring an online order form, a lease-price calculator, and an interactive design shop for choosing car options), site visits tripled. Eighty percent of Saturn's customer leads now originate on the Internet.[26]

Although most people agree that e-commerce has great potential, they also know that several barriers must first be overcome. The Internet has become an information jungle that is cluttered and difficult to navigate. It is estimated that 7 million pages are added to the Internet *each day*.[27] For companies using e-commerce, the marketing communication challenge is to make the company's website easy to find amid this clutter and, once found, easy to navigate.

Another weakness of e-commerce is the low level of computer and Web literacy among the general population. Although the growth has been fast, only slightly over half of U.S. homes have online access, and the majority of this access is via standard, narrowband telephone lines.

Concerns about the Internet include how it will be used, who will control it, and whether it will make businesses even more impersonal than they already are. One organization that has been created as a result

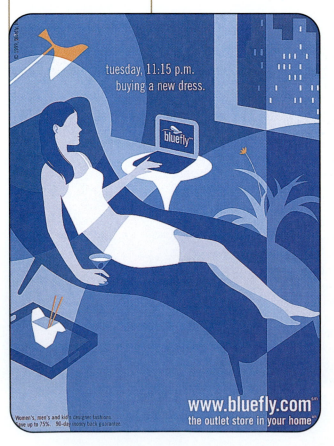

of these concerns is Cluetrain, which is devoted to warning businesses that the Internet enables people to network and build coalitions that can be more powerful than businesses themselves. Founders of the organization have published a book, *The Cluetrain Manifesto: The End of Business As Usual,* and set up a website (www.cluetrain.com), which lists the group's 95 "theses."

Offline Advertising

Originally, online companies tended to place their brand messages only on other websites, on the assumption that marketing offline was a waste of money. If you only want to reach people who have Internet access, why advertise elsewhere? Internet companies soon realized, however, that they needed to drive more traffic to their sites than could be done with just online messaging. For example, one way to reach busy commuters is not online, but by radio. This explains why two public radio stations, WNYC in New York and KQED-FM in San Francisco, receive around half of their advertising revenue from Internet companies.[28]

The ad in Exhibit 12–8 for the sugar substitute Equal is an example of advertising in a Sunday newspaper coupon supplement designed to heighten the visibility of Equal's website with its target audience. The ad adjoins a coupon, but its goal is to offer recipes as an incentive to entice Internet users to visit its website.

Another realization was that people often surf the Web and watch television simultaneously. This tendency to multitask was evident during the 2000 Super Bowl. Twenty-two percent of Internet users who watched the game were also on line during the broadcast. Twelve percent said they navigated to an advertiser's website during or after the game.[29]

Brand building is just as important for online companies as it is for other companies. More than 80 percent of commercials on American television feature a Web address and 30 percent promote a website. Currently, marketing costs account for 40 percent of Web development budgets.[30] On average, new dot-com companies have spent $25 million per year on marketing communication aimed at building their brands. In the 1999 holiday season alone, more than $1 billion was spent to advertise Internet companies in traditional media, and the average annual spending in the first years of the new century have been estimated at $3 billion.[31]

E-Commerce Navigation

A **home page** is *the opening page of a website.* The best home pages succinctly summarize the business the companies are in, reinforce their brand identities, and provide a site

> " Networked markets [people] are beginning to self-organize faster than the companies that have traditionally served them. Thanks to the web, [people] are becoming better informed, smarter, and more demanding of qualities missing from most business organizations."
>
> *Cluetrain Manifesto* website home page

You'll love this sweet little number ... (0 calories)

For recipe ideas, visit our website at www.equal.com

EXHIBIT 12-9

Crayola's home page is a good example of being visitor friendly.

map so visitors can easily navigate the site. Some good examples of corporate home pages can be found at the following URLs: www.altoids.com, www.apple.com, www.crayola.com, and www.saturncars.com. (see Exhibit 12–9).

As you probably know, many searches begin with a search engine or Web portal. That's because the Web is like a vast library with no card catalog. A **search engine** (Sherlock, Excite, Ask Jeeves), is a *service that finds websites based on keywords.* A **portal** is *a search engine for a select number of sites.* Lycos and Yahoo! also serve as portals, along with America Online. Yahoo! is trying to become an online shopping center as well (see Exhibit 12–10).

The term *search engine* usually refers to either of two different types of navigational aids, although only one type is technically a search engine. *Crawler- or spider-based* search engines scan sites across the Web and follow all the URLs found. The crawler feeds all the text from every URL it finds into an index that is then sorted and ranked by special software. When keywords are specified by a user, crawlers scan the text of all indexed sites looking for requested words. *Directories* serve as Yellow Pages and list websites by category. The lists are created by people who decide which categories should be created and what websites should be put into them. Keyword searches can be used here as well, although the only websites that will turn up are those that have been included in the directory and may only include keywords used in the description of the site.

As online businesses mature, marketing is becoming more important with new online companies now spending 25 to 50 percent of their total budgets on marketing communications to help build their brands. Unfortunately, many of the first companies to set up e-commerce sites did so with little or no marketing experience. They were heavily focused on the technology, building an organization, and grabbing market share. Thus, they paid little attention to maintaining customer relationships. In some cases they struggled to understand how brands are built and what kind of brand messages are appropriate for what kinds of brand images.

According to an analysis of 50 leading consumer sites:[32]

- Only 38 percent cross-marketed to customers within 90 days.
- E-mail follow-ups contained an average of 4.4 offers.
- Sixty-three percent of follow-up offers were simply sale announcements or monthly specials that had no customer focus.
- Only 5 percent of offers were related to the original purchase.
- Only 16 percent used personalization in follow-up marketing campaigns.
- Eighty-nine percent of offers were not targeted to individual customer needs or buying behavior.
- Ninety-five percent allowed customers to opt out of receiving promotions.

EXHIBIT 12-10

Yahoo! presents its travel service as an easy and dependable way to make travel arrangements.

Weak online marketing practices are changing because the venture capitalists who have invested (and lost billions of dollars) in dot-com companies are now more focused on brand building than they once were. "The Mantra . . . is build a brand," says a marketing communication agency executive. "If a brand is built there will be equity in selling the company, and that benefits the venture capitalist."[33]

Brand building has become crucial for companies seeking a beachhead in the rapidly moving e-commerce stream for two reasons. First, the Internet lowers barriers to competition. A company now has a smaller window of time than ever before to establish itself before competitors appear. Second, the Internet makes it possible to build brands incredibly fast. Amazon.com did it in less than five years.[34] One organization that help companies make better use of the Internet medium is the not-for-profit Internet Advertising Bureau (www.iab.net).

ONLINE MARKETING COMMUNICATION

Most of the major marketing communication functions use the Internet, along with the other major media, to connect with customers and prospects. Some forms of online communication though, are unique, such as online communities, chat rooms, and e-mail. The greatest MC challenges are attracting people to a website, keeping them on the site, and, when they do leave, giving them motivation to return again.

According to Forrester Research, search engines are the single best marketing vehicle to help users find websites (see Table 12–2). Therefore, the most important first step in reaching the Web audience is to register with as many search engines as possible in order to gain visibility and site visits. Exhibit 12–11 is an ad for a company that registers the keywords people might use in a Web search. Web marketers often structure their websites using common keywords in order to maximize how often they turn up in searches.

Online Advertising

There are two aspects to online advertising. First, as discussed earlier, many Web-based companies advertise offline (in other media) to bring customers to a site (see Exhibit 12–12). This is particularly true for e-commerce companies, which have found that they need to advertise in traditional media to drive viewers to their sites.

Second, of course, is online advertising itself. Although still a fraction of total media spending, online advertising is growing faster than any other type of advertising. DoubleClick, which refers to itself as a global Internet advertising solutions company, places more than 1.5 billion ads on the Internet each day. Advertising online offers a number of advantages: *interactivity*, which means companies and customers can engage in dialogue; *flexibility*, which allows companies to change their information rapidly; and *precise targeting*, because people who come to a website are already interested in the topic, product category, or brand.

Web companies that advertise on other websites are aggressively trying to become visible. Ad spending on the Web increased from just $300 million in 1996 to about $5.3 billion in 2000 and is estimated to be $16.5 billion by 2005.[35] However, as advertising has become more common on the Web, users have learned to ignore it; thus the search is on for new and better ways to attract attention, which can make online advertising increasingly intrusive. It's difficult to find the right balance between attraction and irritation.

TABLE 12-2   How Websites Are Found

Medium	Percentage of Respondents Reporting Use
Search engines	57%
E-mail messages	38
Links from other websites	35
Word of mouth	28
Magazine ads	25
TV commercials	14
Periodic articles	11
Vendor catalogs	11
Newspaper ads	9
Banner ads	7
Radio ads	2
Direct mail	2

Source: Heather McLatchie, "E-Business Essentials," *clipwebzine*, August 23, 1999 <www.clipwebzine.com/article.cfm?storyid=163>.

The creativity of the message design is an important factor in attracting attention to the Web ad. As an example of the power of a well-designed ad, Scott Kurnit, CEO of iVillage Inc., told this story: "Just the other day I was going through a food site and saw an unbelievable ad for Coca-Cola. I had to use my mouse to take a bottle of Coke and pour it into an empty glass. Then I added ice cubes and a straw. I was so fascinated by it I kept doing it over and over. I spent several minutes of my precious time with this one brand."[36]

Another way to attract attention is with frequency. Web advertisers are turning out ads at an unheard-of rate. According to a study conducted by AdRelevance in late 1999, approximately 850 new ads a day, or 6,000 per week, were hitting the Web. While the average number of online ads created for a company's use was 8 and almost half of all companies were using less than 2, the 10 largest Web advertisers averaged 290 different ads. Amazon.com has the most, with some 360 different ads in its portfolio. Production and placement costs in traditional media make such volume prohibitive, but on the Web creating a variety of messages is an important (and less costly) strategy.

Banners

Small ads placed on websites, generally running at the top, bottom, or side of a screen page, are called **banners.** Usually they are configured so that users can click on the ad and be taken to the brand's website. To grab attention,

EXHIBIT 12-11

No matter how beautiful the site, if people can't find it, then they won't become customers. The Internet Keywords service helps companies reach customers by merging the Web address and the product name.

BRAND MANAGER NIGHTMARES

☐ WAKING UP AT 4 AM FACE DOWN IN A PILE OF CHARTS AND SPREADSHEETS.

☐ YOUR CELEBRITY SPOKESPERSON ANNOUNCES THEIR ENGAGEMENT TO SOMEONE THEY MET IN RE-HAB.

☐ YOUR BRAND NAME TRANSLATES INTO "BARNYARD DUNG" IN YOUR NEWEST OVERSEAS MARKET.

☑ 50% OF YOUR CUSTOMERS CAN'T FIND YOUR PRODUCT ON THE WEB.

INTERNET KEYWORDS: A DREAM COME TRUE FOR ALL YOUR BRANDING EFFORTS.

INTERNET KEYWORDS by RealNames

banners increasingly employ animation and/or sound. Tracking technology can monitor website visitors and select from a variety of banners to display depending on the visitor's profile—two people may view the same page at exactly the same time; one may be shown an ad for financial services, and the other an ad for an online bookstore.

The cost of banner ads is generally determined by the number of ad views (impressions) and sold on the basis of cost per thousand people reached (abbreviated as CPM, where M is the Roman numeral for 1,000). Banner ads can also be sold based on an expected number of click-throughs (the number of times an ad is clicked within a given period of time). Some companies barter advertising space; that is, they trade space on each other's sites rather than exchanging money. Competition among sites, along with the fact that banner ads are not generating the click-through rates they once did, has caused the cost of online advertising to fall in recent years. Nevertheless, the average banner ad CPM on popular sites is still more than the average CPM for a 30-second spot on prime-time TV.

Response rates for banner ads are lower than those for direct mail. The average click-through rate is between three-tenths and five-tenths of 1 percent (i.e., 3 to 5 responses for every 1,000 people who see the ad).[37] Of those who do click through, only about 1 percent make a purchase. Assuming a click-through rate of five-tenths of 1 percent, this means that only 1 out of 20,000 people who see the average banner ad actually ends up responding (20,000 × .01 click-through × .005 who respond = 1). And this rate continues to decrease despite new audio and visual techniques designed to make ads more attention-getting. Not surprisingly, customers interested in high-involvement products are more likely to click through than are those interested in low-involvement products. What is a surprise is that larger banner ads and animation can lift the click-through rate for low-involvement products but not for high-involvement products, at least according to one study.[38]

One of the first Web advertising design considerations is deciding how intrusive a banner ad should be. Do you need to attract attention, even if that means "clicking off" a few surfers in the process? Or are you concerned about building a brand relationship with your users? According to a presentation co-sponsored by three major online advertising companies, there are five "Golden Rules of Online Branding" regarding banner ads:[39]

- Keep banner simple—the more creative elements (graphics and words) the less ability a banner has to raise brand awareness.

- Maximize size of logo—the bigger the logo, the more likely the banner will send a clear message to customers.

- Maximize size of banner—just as with print ads, the larger the size the greater impact it has.

- Use frequency—the optimal frequency number differs by product category and banner design, but overall, research findings indicate that a frequency of five impressions is the most efficient.

- Include a human face—the presence of a human face was found to increase attention more than other design elements.

Clearly, not all Web advertisers follow these rules. Some of the new techniques that use a "click or die" strategy can only be described as obnoxious. The idea is to design a site that is "sticky" enough to keep viewers "glued" to it. Web gremlins

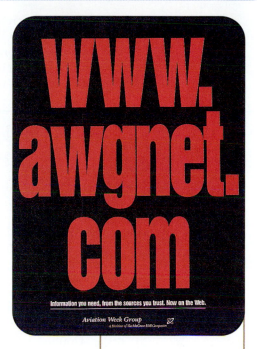

Information you need, from the sources you trust. Now on the Web.

Aviation Week Group
A Division of The McGraw-Hill Companies

EXHIBIT 12-12

This ad for the Aviation Week's website is designed to drive interested readers to the publication's online information

have been created that hijack your cursor and won't release it until you click on its mother site.

Another problem lies with **interstitials**, a type of ad that is similar to a banner ad, but more intrusive. These are *ads that pop up in a separate frame on a screen page.* The user has to stop reading and click on them to eliminate them. These have become highly controversial because they are so irritating. Media buyers say the intrusiveness is needed; viewers hate them. A class-action suit has been filed against America Online by members who feel that since they pay an hourly fee to use the service, they shouldn't have to deal with such annoyances. According to a study by Grey/ASI, interstitials had the highest online irritational factor of all Web advertising (15 percent). Some interstitials have been designed that treat you with several minutes of full-screen movies, whether you want to watch or not. Barb Palser, of Internet Broadcasting Systems, has described such ads in terms normally reserved for predators.[40]

> "Today's cutting-edge [online] ads are more than distracting flashes and fake dialogue boxes; they howl, prowl, and pounce."
>
> Barb Palser, "Attack of the Killer Ads"

Customization may be the answer to the intrusiveness problem. Marketing companies such as Be Free, LinkShare, Phase2Media, and SmartAge create advertising for a network of sites that attract users with similar interests. Similar to DoubleClick, Engage Technologies, with its click-through data on 42 million Web surfers and their visits to some 900 websites (see Exhibit 12–13), is another company that provides this service to advertisers. When an Engage-profiled shopper, many of whom aren't even aware that Engage is watching them, visits an electronic retailer (e-tailer), that site gets the shopper's profile instantly and can then use it to tailor its offerings and ads. Engage does hide shoppers' identification information, providing only the serial number of their profiles to the retailer. Engage claims that Web users are 50 percent more likely to click on Web ads picked by its profiling technique than on ads placed to fit a page's content.

EXHIBIT 12-13

Services like DoubleClick track the behavior of online customers and provide e-tailers with information about their online consumer behavior.

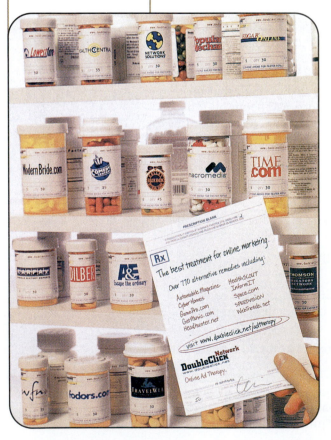

Because business is driven by customers' wants and needs, it is not surprising that ad-blocking software has been developed. AdKiller, Junkbuster Proxy, and AdSubtract are some of the software programs that do this. What is especially concerning companies such as DoubleClick and others that sell online advertising is that some of this ad-blocking software is being installed in modems. If ad-blocking becomes pervasive, it will mean many online service providers will be forced to begin charging for their services since they will no longer be supported by advertising revenue.[41]

Classified Advertising

The ease with which consumers can use keywords to search for only those ads pertinent to them makes online classified advertising a particularly attractive proposition. In addition, online classified advertising can deliver far more than print classified ads. For example, compared to a page in a newspaper, a website has far more space for photos and can offer multimedia enhancements, such as interactive video tours of homes. Further, since the Internet is global far beyond traditional classified advertising outlets, such as local newspapers.

Ad Targeting

Early systems and many of today's small-scale operations simply targeted the broad Web audience with brand messages either fixed on a Web page for a certain time period or rotated randomly. As technology has grown more sophisticated, businesses are increasingly able to place specifically targeted advertisements online. Online targeting strategies can be divided into three types:[42]

- *Editorial.* Banners are targeted by site or page topic. For example, advertisers on the Yahoo! search engine can place ads on any of the more than 100,000 categories featured in its Web directory.

- *Filtered.* In the most popular form of professional Web advertising today, advertisers can specify targeting parameters, such as the user's operating system or browser software, time period, country, or even the Internet service provider (ISP). The selection mechanism on the service provider's server analyzes the request and selects only those sites for placement that match the ad's specifications.

- *Personalized.* Next-generation systems will use neural networks and other proprietary learning methods to allow personalized content and advertisement selection based on the browsing and interaction history of a particular user, as well as other demographic information. *Ad servers* (computers that control the ad placements, which are often run by someone other than either the advertiser or the content website, such as DoubleClick) can be programmed so that they can continue to fine-tune ad placement depending on response rates.

Online Public Relations

Because websites can contain a vast array of information, they can be designed to be useful to all of a company's stakeholders. For media relations, a site can contain a description of a company's business operations, a listing of all its brands and products, a listing of all executives, and, most important, company contact information. Some sites, such as that of AirTran (see Chapter 1), also carry selected photos so that media representatives can retrieve and use them easily (www.airtrain.com). Most companies post their press releases on their website and maintain a file of these for a certain period of time.

Human resources department often use a company's website to publicize job openings and provide prospective employees easy access to the company. As explained in the chapter opening case, Cisco Systems' intranet company's policies, retirement procedures, and insurance offerings.

Public companies find that their websites can be an important source of information for the financial community. After the story broke regarding defective Firestone tires on Ford Explorers, which were blamed for dozens of rollover accidents, Ford's stock price declined. To help address concerns of the financial community, along with other Ford stakeholders, Ford began using a special button on the opening page of its corporate website that said: "For official Ford News on the Firestone recall, click here." This link took the online users to a listing of news releases and other information that Ford had made public regarding both the recall and the automaker's future use of Firestone tires.

Online Sponsorship and Events

Rather than simply placing ads on sites, some companies prefer to sponsor entire sites. The site's content may come from a nonprofit association, but is specifically created to attract target audiences for the corporate sponsor and to promote that sponsor's products. Online educational seminars (just like in-person seminars) represent one of the most common sponsorship opportunities. Other sponsors attempt to create a "halo effect" for their brand by associating it with something positive. An example is the Women's Auto Center sponsored by Ford Motor Company on iVillage, a network of women's sites. Sponsorships are more about building customer relationships long term than about driving sales short term.

The importance of sponsorships is increasing. In 1998, banner advertising accounted for 52 percent of online advertising dollars, with sponsorships getting 40 percent. For 2001, it was expected that banners would receive only 26 percent of online ad dollars and sponsorships 58 percent.[43]

Online events are also being used to attract audiences. Music sites such as CD-now and CD Universe sponsor online concerts. Among other things, these events reward regular customers and allow them to sample new music.

Promoting Brands through Online Communities

One of the earliest online marketing techniques involved bringing together customers and prospects who might share ideas on how to use a company's products. **Virtual communities** are *groups who focus on certain online activities and whose members establish relationships with one another*. The easiest way to understand this is to think about fan clubs. Major league athletic teams often have websites where their fans congregate and communicate with the team as well as with each other. It is a virtual community based on fan loyalty.

In business communication, Adobe offers user-to-user forums for each of its products that operate like bulletin boards where customers can post and read notes. At the Kraft Foods website, there is a bulletin board called the Wisdom of Moms Exchange where people can post such things as recipes and Mother's Day memories. Such sites not only allow loyal users to share tips with each other but also reinforce their commitment to the sponsoring brand. Chat rooms are also available on some corporate sites that allow people to talk to one another in real time.

Collecting Internet users into like-minded groups has three primary marketing benefits: It aggregates people into addressable target markets; it creates bonds, which may deliver goodwill to community sponsors; and it allows the company to listen to its customers, providing a type of real-time research.

WEBSITE DESIGN AND OPERATION

According to a study by the Yankee Group, 87 percent of business executives interviewed about their company's use of websites said "building brand awareness" and "providing marketing information" were the primary objectives.[44] These responses illustrate the lack of understanding of the true value of websites: inter-activity. A printed brochure can build brand awareness and supply marketing in-formation, but a website can engage customers and other stakeholders in valuable dialogues. Unless a website is interactive, the major portion of its value is wasted.

Every element of interactive marketing should be done with the customer in mind. Building a website that meets the needs of the target audience is difficult, but research is there to help, as Table 12–3 demonstrates. The figures, compiled by For-rester Research, indicate that users are most likely to return to sites that have high quality content, are easy to use, are quick to download, and are updated frequently.

There are two basic types of websites: The first, and simplest, is essentially an online brochure that gives information about a company; details about its prod-ucts, brands, and services; and contact information. More complex is a website that is interactive, allowing customers to contact the company with questions, shop on-line, and link to other products and services, such as chat rooms and product-related reference information (see Exhibit 12–14). Both will be reviewed here in terms of strategic planning and setup, design, and management.

Strategic Planning for a Website

The first step in creating a successful website is to set objectives: What is the pur-pose of the site? There are a multitude of possible answers, including education, conversation and dialogue, feedback and research, entertainment, and sales.

The next step is to identify the target audience: Who are they? How long have they been online? What kinds of browsers and computers will they be using? What languages do they speak? Why will they come to the site? How often will they come to the site? Will they want to download, print, or e-mail website infor-mation? What are their product needs?

TABLE 12-3   Factors Driving Repeat Site Visits

Factor	Percentage of Respondents Citing This Factor As Important
High-quality content	75%
Ease of use	66
Quick to download	58
Updated frequently	54
Coupons and incentives	14
Favorite brands	13
Cutting-edge technology	12
Games	12
Purchasing capabilities	11
Customizable content	10
Chat rooms	10
Other	6

Source: Heather McLatchie, "E-Business Essentials," *clipwebzine*, August 23, 1999 <www.clipwebzine.com/article.cfm?storyid=163>.

EXHIBIT 12-14

This travel website is provided by the Houston Chronicle. *It contains a number of links to other travel services such as* Travelocity.com, *as well as allowing its users to make reservations online.*

The operation side is a huge issue: Who will be responsible for the website? Will it be set up and maintained in-house? If so, by whom? How will the site be evaluated? And if there is contact information, such as an e-mail address or toll-free number, then how will this back-end operation be staffed? How many people are needed to handle the response?

Finally, since nothing is free, another critical question is: What is the budget? How much can you spend on website development, operations, and other expenses? These questions must be answered in order to build a site that is customer driven and sustainable.

Setting Up the Website

Setting up a site involves some important initial decisions, such as naming and hosting the site. The shorter and more distinctive the name is, the easier it will be to remember and use. The first step in setting up a website is to purchase a **domain name** *(the general term for the name of a node on the Internet).* This name includes a suffix that identifies the type of organization. The three suffixes most commonly used by businesses are *.com* (for *commercial* enterprises) *.net* (for organizations involved in *network* maintenance), and *.org* (usually used by nonprofit *organizations*). It's best to buy your domain name in all three forms or you may find yourself with a confusing competitor. For example, www.whitehouse.org will take you to the website of the White House; www.whitehouse.com, however, is a pornography site.

Companies can design and host their own websites, but most are managed by outside service providers who own the **server,** *a computer with huge memory capacities that links individual sites to the Web. Outside companies that handle transactions and distribute products* are called **fulfillment companies** (see Exhibit 12–15).

Designing the Website

In the early days of the Web, sites were overloaded with every new graphic trick designers could find. The new credo in website design, however, is to make the page user-friendly. As business columnist Paul Tulenko has observed, the goal is to "get the basics out there quickly with a bit of class."[45] A good example of a website that is simple yet involving is that for Purina's brand of cat-litter products, Tidy Cats (www.tidycats.com). The home page has five main elements: a brief description of the product line, a picture of a package of Tidy Cats Crystals, a listing of website categories (which are link buttons), and a bold linking banner: SEE THE PRODUCT DEMO. The last is a Website Feedback button that links to a page titled "Tell Us What You Think" (see Exhibit 12–16). The company uses data gathered from this page to continually refine the website. An even more important link on the home page is one of the website categories: CONTACT US. This further encourages customers to ask questions, complain, or make suggestions. The product demo link brings up a screen from which a cartoon demo can be downloaded. Viewers are told approximately how long the download will take. The animated demo is both informative and fun to watch. Check it out.

Sites should load quickly and be viewable on a variety of browsers. This ease of access is determined by the complexity of the design and the use of animation and multimedia formats. Some companies make the mistake of adding unnecessary audio and animation that consumers do not want. For example, outdoor-products retailer REI reported that when users have been given the option to choose either a multimedia format or a text-and-photos-only format, most chose the latter. However, those who chose to look at the video presentations bought significantly more than those who chose not to.[46] The following list contains some guidelines for creating websites that work:

- Make the home page work hard to establish your identity and tell what you do.
- Make the interface intuitive—people shouldn't need training in order to use the site; all operations should be obvious.
- Make content prominent—don't bury the content under a lot of graphics, ads, or complicated site design.
- Make navigation user-friendly.
- Don't create too many levels.
- Make sure menu options are complete.
- Give users a way to return to main menu.
- Use links rather than long periods of scrolling.
- Include navigation aids at both the top and bottom of the page.
- Provide a site map and perhaps a search engine.
- Create a website that can also be read in a text-only format.
- Flashing banner ads are irritating, especially those with little connection to your page. If you have to use them, put them on the bottom of the home page or elsewhere in the site.
- Give users a contact-and-response mechanism.
- Don't open new windows or redirect the viewer when he or she hits the back button. Leave the back-button route alone so viewers can retrace their path to get back to the home page.

Great! Your CEO just announced sky-high online orders.

Too bad your order fulfillment system can't deliver.

FullStream
Full-cycle e-commerce software

TECSYS

EXHIBIT 12-15

FullStream is an order fulfillment service that handles the back end of e-commerce, providing online order processing to distribution and replenishment.

One of the greatest challenges in website design is **navigation**—*the process by which people access the site, find the information they want, and move around within the site and to other related sites.* Stephen Wildstrom, a *Business Week* technology writer, took several big companies—United Airlines (www.ual.com), Hertz (www.hertz.com), and Microsoft (www.microsoft.com)—to task for their difficult designs. He observed that it is faster to make a reservation or get a question answered by phone than it is to use these sites.[47]

As noted above, contact information is particularly important in this day of interactivity—yet it is also highly problematic. For example, a study of Fortune 100 companies found that 50 percent did not have a simple e-mail link through their websites. Instead, visitors had to click four or more times and then fill out extensive forms with personal information. Ten companies had no e-mail links at all.[48]

Websites can be designed from the very simple to the very complex. Figure 12–2 illustrates the range of complexity a site can have. For examples of a listing of good BtB websites go to www.netb2b.com and click on "The NetMarketing 200" mini-banner; the site is owned by *Advertising Age* magazine. Another site that offers advice on Web marketing is www.ClickZ.com.

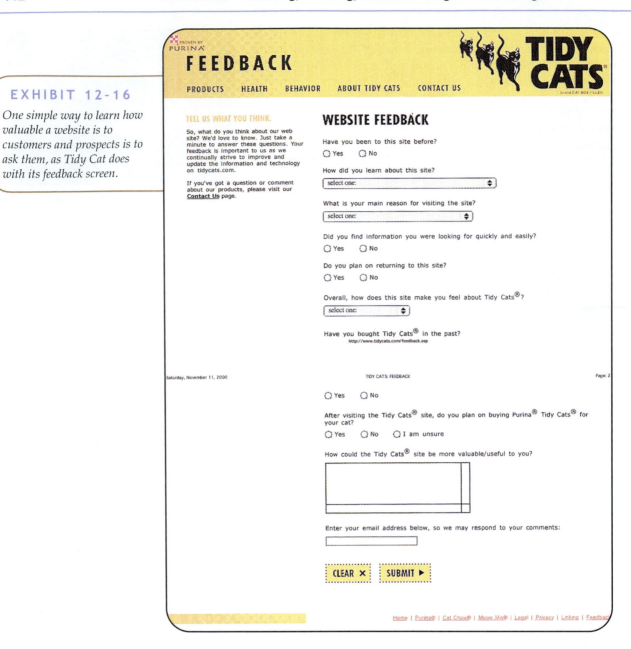

Managing the Website

Most companies hire a **webmaster,** *someone who understands the design of a site and how it works.* A webmaster's duties normally include the following:

- Monitor and analyze site activity.
- Use database logs to document hits and visitor usage.
- Continually check for problems.
- Capture consumer profiles and tracking information about site visits.
- Post new information so content is always fresh.
- Continually test content, navigation, offerings, and response mechanisms.
- Work with all departments to ensure that the information is current and correct.

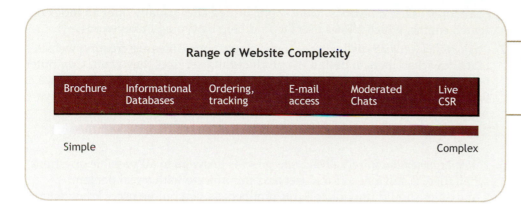

Range of Website Complexity

| Brochure | Informational Databases | Ordering, tracking | E-mail access | Moderated Chats | Live CSR |

Simple   Complex

FIGURE 12-2

Websites can be very simple to very complex.

Monitoring the site's activity is a particularly important activity. Most servers can track the number of **hits** (*individual site visits*). If a company counts the hits, it must make sure employees' computers do not open up on the website when they turn on their computers. That would inflate the data.

Keeping track of hits is good, but more important is the number of unique visits in a designated time period and user sessions. The definition of a "user session" may vary from site to site, but the idea is to find out how often people spend a significant amount of time at the site. Other tracking information includes how people get to the site (where they are coming from), what they do once they get to the site, how long they stay around, and what features of the site are getting the most use. Webmasters can also monitor what keywords people are typing in to find the site in order to make the links with those keyword clusters even stronger.

Customer Service

Responding to customers is a critical management responsibility. James Daly, editor of *Business 2.0,* predicted that customer service would separate the winners from the losers in the dot-com shakeout that began in 2000 with the devaluation of Web stocks. He points out that customer service is not the last rung on the ladder at the end of the sale, but rather the first—it begins the moment someone arrives on a website.[49]

Service, in other words, must begin with building good brand relationships at the first contact and continue through fulfillment and postpurchase customer service. A study of 621 large companies in 12 countries found that online customers receive 20 percent of their orders late. This logistics problem is compounded by the fact that customers expect to receive their orders within two days, rather than the current industry average of four days.[50]

In the new age of interactivity, customer service needs to be available 24 hours a day and seven days a week—a practice called 24/7 service. That's particularly true for multinational companies. In addition to making it possible to do business and communicate with customers anywhere in the world in real time, new technology has also made it possible to shift time. For example, a number of companies have found that call centers can be located anywhere; in some cases they even shift all calls to any one of their call centers around the globe so they are always operating during normal work hours on a 24-hour schedule.

There are three necessary elements for delivering good customer service online:

1. *Thorough and easy-to-use information at the website.* Simple sites may employ a frequently asked questions (FAQ) list, which supplies the answers to

commonly asked questions. More sophisticated sites usually offer an index or search engine, which allows users to find help by typing in keywords.

2. *Customizable products and services.* Increasingly companies are creating websites that allow customers to design the products and services they want. Computer manufacturer Gateway, for example, allows both individuals and businesses to design the computers to order. Customers are presented with an extensive menu of features, and their computers are built to those specifications. Similarly, Nike allows some of its website visitors to order custom-made shoes.

3. *Human interaction.* Rarely does a site provide answers to all possible questions. Often there is still a need for a user to communicate with a real person. Companies should provide toll-free numbers so that online users know where to call. They should also allow for easy use of e-mail, although this option should not be provided if the response rate is going to be slow. No online consumer should have to wait more than 24 hours for an answer by e-mail. A quicker solution is a direct online link to a customer-service representative. The user is able to type in questions and receive immediate responses. Another variation allows a user to type in a question and then receive an immediate telephone call back from a customer-service rep.

A number of companies have created new products to help meet online customer-service needs. For example, eGain is an online customer communication company that provides "integrated multichannel solutions" including e-mail management, interactive Web and voice collaboration, intelligent self-help agents, and proactive online marketing. Another company, eTetra.com, offers software that allows a site visitor to click an icon that brings him or her directly to a real person. The program collects information about the site visit and then finds the right person to assist with whatever the customer needs.

Infrastructure

It's an old principle, one that's easily forgotten: If you publish a phone number (or e-mail address), there has to be someone to respond. That is, there has to be an infrastructure in place to handle the details of the business—stocking merchandise, delivering it, and, yes, answering the phone. Research at the University of Colorado has been tracking this interactivity element since 1997 and found that most companies are not totally prepared to respond. On average, less than half of the mystery-shopper contacts made by phone and e-mail have been rated *good* (the contact was satisfied easily and thoroughly); the majority were rated *fair* (one or more shortcomings) or *poor* (no response, excessive delay, rude and unfriendly, off-target response).[51] In other words, the majority of companies do not have a good enough infrastructure to handle interactivity. There must be an infrastructure in place to deliver on customers' expectations.

INTERNET PRIVACY

As the Internet use has grown, privacy has become an increasing concern. Georgia Institute of Technology's Visualization and Usability Center did a study of 10,000 Web users and found that 71 percent thought there should be privacy laws governing use of online personal data. Over four-fifths of the respondents objected to companies selling customers' personal data to other companies.[52]

In a survey that asked online users if they want targeted advertising and content, the majority of respondents said yes. When people realize, however, how much information is being gathered about them and the fact that it might be shared with other companies, most express reservations, a fact discovered in a study done by the Pew Foundation. According to this study of 1,017 Internet users, 86 percent were in favor of companies asking permission to use personal data (i.e., having an *opt-in policy*). About half (52 percent) said that tracking online activities is an invasion of privacy. The study found that 54 percent of respondents had provided personal data to online companies, while 27 percent said they never would. The study also found that approximately one-fourth of online users use false identities. When asked about the placing of *an online tracking tool*—a **cookie**—on their computers, 56 percent said they didn't know how to tell if this had been done. (See the Ethics and Issues box.) Although computers can be set to reject cookies, only 1 in 10 online users has done so.

Despite the above findings, one of the conclusions of the study was: "The actual incidence of unpleasant events is modest, the incidence of criminal events online is miniscule, and the incidence of *trusting is high.*"[53]

According to research done by Pennsylvania's Wharton School of Business, people who have backed away from online shopping have often done so because of privacy concerns. The study indicated that concern about "monitoring by third parties" was the highest predictor for not purchasing online and an unwillingness to "trust the business with private data" was another question that scored high.[54] The "privacy" ad for Promotions.com in Exhibit 12–17 illustrates the seriousness with which marketing communication companies approach this problem.

Privacy Policies

Understanding the company's offline privacy policy and giving permission for certain kinds of data to be collected are the most important elements in an online privacy policy. In Internet marketing, that means posting a highly visible link to the company's privacy policy on the opening page. In addition, companies that are sensitive to their customers' privacy concerns may also register with a program like TRUSTe. The TRUSTe icon functions like the Good Housekeeping Seal to monitor companies' privacy performance (see Exhibit 12–18). Other such services include Pricewaterhousecoopers' BetterWeb, Good Housekeeping's Web Site Certification, the Better Business Bureau's privacy guarantees.

In the United States, the Federal Trade Commission (FTC) has been carefully watching the development of the Web privacy issue. It released a report in 2000 that found that only 20 percent of sites with 39,000 or more unique visitors per month adequately protect their consumers' privacy. To help companies address the privacy concern of citizens, the FTC recommends practices for industry self-regulation:[55]

Fair Information Practices

- *Notice.* Give clear and conspicuous notice of what information is collected and how it will be used.
- *Choice.* Let consumers choose whether their information can be used for any purpose besides fulfilling the transaction.
- *Reasonable access.* Consumers should be able to access the information collected on them and have a reasonable opportunity to correct any errors or delete the data.
- *Adequate security.* Companies should ensure proper handling of consumer information to prevent unauthorized access of identity theft.

EXHIBIT 12-17

Privacy is such a concern that this online promotional company uses it as its key selling proposition.

America Online (AOL) is in a tricky position regarding privacy issues. It keeps records on more than 21 million subscribers, including names, addresses, and credit-card numbers. AOL says it has never sold data about its members' movements within its systems, which are tracked by AOL's proprietary service. The company believes that its privacy policy is one of the best in the industry. It does, however, sell names and addresses of subscribers to direct mailers, a practice it admits in its privacy policy, and it also buys information about its members from outside suppliers and uses that information for targeting brand messages to its new subscribers.

In contrast, Amazon.com has come under attack by two privacy groups. The Electronic Privacy Information Center (EPIC), a Washington-based advocacy group that was part of Amazon's affiliates program, has decided to end its partnership with Amazon. Likewise, Jason Catlett, of the private

"We are witnessing the slow erosion of online privacy under the industry's self-regulatory approach."

Marc Rotenberg, EPIC

ETHICS AND ISSUES

The Cookie Monster

You may think that, when you are browsing the Web or participating in a chat room, you are hiding behind the anonymity of your clever user name; however, you may not realize the extent to which your private interests can be tracked on the Internet with Internet bugs called cookies. If a cookie is issued by a company that has a presence at hundreds of websites, it can capture customers' comings and goings all over the Web. Cookies may simplify things, like site registration, but they can also leave a trail of the sites you've checked.

In a Cathy cartoon strip, Cathy is confronting old boyfriend and computer guru, Irving, about what he has found out about her from his online snooping. He reports that she browsed four diet websites, downloaded flea remedies, clicked on "European Airlines," and cruised the personals. He observed that the next time she logged on, she would receive banner ads for "singles weight-loss spas in Italy that allow dogs."

Mirroring Cathy's expression of horror was the public outcry that arose in 2000 when it was revealed that DoubleClick, a company hired to handle other companies' advertising across a network of some 1,500 websites, was being investigated by FTC for possible deceptive data-collection and sharing practices. Complaints arose when DoubleClick revealed that it planned to amass personal information about Internet users' habits and identities to sell to advertisers, a practice that has long been done by traditional direct marketing companies.

The DoubleClick problem came to the surface after the company bought AbacusDirect, a direct-marketing company that holds information on some 88 million households that buy from catalogs. DoubleClick had planned to combine the contact information with online viewing information and catalog purchase history to create a deep profile of customers' behavior. One of DoubleClick's clients responded by announcing that it would no longer share customer information unless its visitors "opt in" or gave permission. (Many other sites make users specifically choose to opt out, otherwise they are included.) Eventually DoubleClick reversed itself, deciding to hold off on merging the data until government privacy guidelines were in place.

Consumer activists have been following this issue and can provide some of the best consumer information about cookies and the practice of online profiling. You may not know that when you buy a new computer and transfer your files over, the cookies transfer along with the other data. You also may not realize that most computers can be set up to not accept and store cookies. If you want to learn more, check out the privacy watchdog site Junkbusters (www.junkbusters.com) and the U.S. government's Electronic Privacy Information Center (www.epic.org). Webwasher.com or your Internet service provider can help you eliminate cookies.

Think About It

What are cookies? What are the good and bad sides of cookies? Do you care if a site you visit installs a cookie? How can cookies be used in a way that's sensitive to privacy issues?

Source: Jane Bryant Quinn, "Fighting the Cookie Monster," *Newsweek*, February 28, 2000, p. 63; "Bad Cookies," *Newsweek*, February 28, 2000, p. 12; Andrea Petersen, "A Privacy Firestorm at DoubleClick," *The Wall Street Journal*, February 23, 2000, p. B1; Andrea Petersen, "DoubleClick Reverses Course After Privacy Outcry," *The Wall Street Journal*, March 3, 2000, p. B1.

advocacy firm Junkbusters, pulled out of the program, saying that Amazon.com's new privacy policy is "unacceptably weak."[56] Amazon.com's problem arose when it stopped letting customers opt out of having their personal information shared with other marketing companies and Amazon.com retail partners. It also told customers that it considered customer information to be a company asset that can be sold if Amazon.com goes out of business.

EXHIBIT 12-18

TRUSTe is a company that certifies that online companies are complying with a set of privacy standards

A question that remains unanswered is to what extent the Internet industry will regulate itself on the privacy issue. When the Federal Trade Commission surveyed 1,400 websites in 1998, it found that a year after having warned businesses to adopt privacy guidelines or face government regulations, 92 percent collected personal information but only 14 percent disclosed how the information would be used.[57] A study done by the University of Massachusetts for the Direct Marketing Association (DMA) found that only 38 percent of DMA members informed site visitors that they were collecting information on them and only a third sought permission to use this information.[58]

Marketing to children on the Internet has warranted special attention. The FTC found that 89 percent of the children's sites surveyed collected personal information. Of those, only 23 percent told children to seek parental permission, less than 10 percent provided parents a way to control the collection and use of information, and only 7 percent said they would notify parents about information-gathering practices. Some sites even used promotions, games, and cartoons to encourage children to provide personal information.[59]

Security

Security of financial transactions is a major concern of online consumers. According to a Gallup Poll conducted in 2000, slightly over half (55 percent) of all Internet users did not feel confident or totally secure that their credit-card information would remain secure.[60]

When the Web-design firm InteractionArchitect was researching security issues for a major European airline, it discovered "that people's perception of security when doing online transactions depends on the simplicity of the site and on the availability of user support." The company suggested that to increase a sense of security, an online transaction site should be comprehensible, predictable, flexible, and adaptable.[61] In other words, perception of security may extend beyond actual security and reassurances of security. Privacy and ease of use are two issues, but payment is of the most concern.[62] And without security, a customer relationship is weakened.

A FINAL NOTE: HYPERCHARGED CYBERMARKETING

There are a number of communication technology challenges facing the 21st-century organization. An obvious one is the speed with which changes are introduced. Old businesses are transformed, new businesses are created, competitors come and go—all faster than the blink of an eye.

In the two years spanning the turn of the century (1999–2000), for example, the hot Internet business focus went from portals to business-to-consumer retailing to BtB e-commerce. Because technology allows businesses to quickly spot changes and react to them, the focus has shifted to results measured in days and hours rather than months or years. Airlines, for example, can adjust ticket prices from minute to minute based on seat availability. Cheap fares are offered via websites like Travelocity.com to those who can travel on short notice.

Another dimension of hypercharged marketing is the speed with which business is now being conducted. The chapter opening case on Cisco Systems tells a story about how one company reduced its order handling for its customers to a matter of minutes.

To meet these challenges, companies are doing more outsourcing of their customer management functions. This allows a company greater flexibility. Staffs can be expanded and contracted as necessary and specialized skills can be acquired as needed. The concept of the *virtual corporation,* where people around the world are pulled together to work on a project-to-project basis, has made the distinction between employee and contractor much less significant and increased the need for intranets, extranets, as well as increased dependency on the Internet for e-business and e-commerce. This practice also raises questions about communication consistency and gaps and makes the management of customer communication more difficult than ever before.

Key Terms

bandwidth 416	opt-out e-mail 428	virtual communities 438
Internet 417	opt-in e-mail 428	domain name 440
listservs 418	click-through 429	server 440
forums 418	home page 431	fulfillment companies 440
chat rooms 418	search engine 432	navigation 441
telephony 425	portal 432	webmaster 442
telemarketing 425	banners 434	hits 443
spam 427	interstititals 436	cookie 445

Key Points Summary

Key Point 1: New Technologies

Technological change is accelerating and getting more complex as the Internet, intranets, extranets, and wireless communication systems have developed.

Key Point 2: Interactive and Addressable Media

Three types of personal media—mail, phone, and e-mail—are used in marketing communication because they are interactive and addressable. Although mail and phone still dominate in terms of MC spending, the fastest-growing addressable and interactive medium is e-mail.

Key Point 3: Internet-Based Marketing Communication

Most of the MC functions (advertising, sponsorship, events, etc.) use the Internet. Some of the uses are particularly important for the Web, such as online communities and customized messages.

Key Point 4: Websites

Web-based marketing involves strategic planning for a website, setting up the website, designing the website, and managing the website, with a particular focus on customer service.

Lessons Learned

Key Point 1: New Technologies

a. In the last half of the twentieth century, a number of technological advances led to the new electronic frontier. What are they?
b. What is Moore's law, and what does it say about the future of the Internet?
c. What are the differences between intranets and extranets?

Key Point 2: Addressable and Interactive Media

a. Why is the use of addressable, interactive media increasing?
b. How are interactive media different from mass media?
c. How important is mail as a marketing communication medium?
d. How does the cost of mail compare to that of other mass media forms? With this in mind how could you justify using mail?
e. How important is the phone as a marketing communication medium?
f. Compare and contrast outbound and inbound calls in a marketing communication program.
g. What is the difference between opt-in and opt-out e-mail?
h. Would it be accurate to say that there is no cost to e-mail campaigns? Explain.

Key Point 3: Internet-Based Marketing Communication

a. How can a company make its website more visible in order to attract more visitors?
b. Explain the attraction-versus-irritation problem with online advertising.
c. How effective are banner ads? How is their effectiveness determined?
d. Why have Web-based companies turned to offline advertising? Find an example and analyze its effectiveness.
e. Explain online communities, forums, and chat rooms in terms of how they can be used in marketing programs. On the Web, find a product-related forum or chat room and explain what you learned at that site.
f. What are two methods of delivering customized messages on the Web?
g. Go to the Cisco Systems website (www.cisco.com) and list ways (other than those mentioned above) this site is of value to customers and prospects.

Key Point 4: Websites

a. What is the first step in creating a website?
b. What are three things to think about when you set up a website?
c. What is the most important consideration in website design and, on the other side of the coin, what is the biggest problem?
d. What is a webmaster, and what are his or her responsibilities?
e. What are two areas of customer service where online companies tend to fall short?
f. Why is infrastructure an issue in customer service?
g. Visit the following sites, which were listed in *Business Week's* "Favorite Clicks" column. Pick one and analyze it using the guidelines listed on p. 000:

www.ragingbull.com (a stock market site)

www.zagat.com (a restaurant site)

www.guild.com (a high-end, art-and-crafts site)

www.bizrate.com (a place to check out other people's experience with online stores)

Chapter Challenge

Writing Assignment

To analyze the advertising of dot-com companies, find three examples in magazines and three examples of broadcast ads. For the TV ads, you can videotape them off-air, or you can consult www.superbowl-ads.com, which compiles the ads from the Super Bowl. Analyze the six ads you chose in terms of the following: (*a*) the purpose, (*b*) effectiveness of product explanation, and (*c*) brand-building efforts. Write up your analysis in a report for your instructor.

Presentation Assignment

Pick a local company that does Web marketing. Interview its webmaster and analyze its website. Identify its other uses of the Internet. Does it sell products both online and offline? What is its privacy policy? How might this company's Internet use be improved? Prepare a presentation on what you have found out to give to your classmates.

Internet Assignment

Consult the Cluetrain website (www.cluetrain.com). Write a report for your instructor on the founders' viewpoint and concerns about the use of the Internet for business. Draft a set of guidelines for responsible online marketing communication that address the issues raised by Cluetrain.

Additional Readings

Garfinkel, Simson. *Database Nation: The Death of Privacy in the 21st Century.* New York: O'Reilly and Associates, 2000.

Kleindl, Brad Alan. *Strategic Electronic Marketing: Managing E-Business.* Cincinnati, OH: South-Western Publishing, 2001.

Locke, Christopher; Rick Levine; Doc Searles; and David Weinberger. *The Cluetrain Manifesto: The End of Business As Usual.* New York: Perseus Books, 2000.

Newell, Frederick. *Loyalty.com.* New York: McGraw-Hill, 2000.

Turban, Efraim; Jae Lee; David King; H. Michael Chung. *Electronic Commerce: A Managerial Perspective.* Upper Saddle River, NJ: Prentice Hall, 2000.

Research Assignment

Review these books or other articles on Internet marketing or Internet privacy issues. Assume you are working for a company that intends to set up a website for e-commerce. Write a report for your boss on how this company should handle the privacy issue.

Endnotes

[1] "PC Penetration Increases in US," *NUA.net*, February 29, 2000 <www.nua.net/surveys/?f=VS&art_id=905355625&rel=true>.

[2] "Business and the Internet," *The Economist*, June 26, 1999, p. 17.

[3] David W. Moore, "Americans Say Internet Makes Their Lives Better," Gallup News Service, February 23, 2000 <www.gallup.com/poll/releases/pr000223.asp>.

[4] "US Adults Prefer E-mail to Post and Telephone," *NUA.net*, January 18, 2000 <www.nua.net/surveys/?f=VS&art_id=905355531&rel=true>.

[5] "Online Shopping Promises Consumers More Than It Delivers."

[6] Sun Microsystems press release, October 7, 2000.

[7] "U.S. Intranets Go Full Tilt as Spending Reaches a Staggering $10.9 Billion." International Data Corporation press release, July 15, 1999 <www.idc.com/Data/Internet/content/NET071599PR.htm>.

[8] Anne Fischer Lent, "Livin' la Vida Internet," *PC World*, January 11, 2000 <www.pcworld.com/pcwtoday/article/0,1510,14746,00.html>.

[9] Steve Fioretti and Bob D'Acquisto, "Advertising Takes a Ride on the Wireless Wave," *iMarketing News*, August 21, 2000, p. 19.

[10] The Direct Marketing Association, *Statistical Fact Book 1999*, p. 9.

[11] Ibid., p. 37.

[12] *Bob Coen's Insider's Report,* McCann-Erickson Worldgroup website June 2000 <www.mccann.com>.

[13] Quoted in Laura Hansen, "Dialing for Dollars," *Marketing Tools*, January–February 1997, p. 47.

[14] Kruti Trivedi, "Telemarketers Don't Want You, Just Your Answering Machine," *The Wall Street Journal*, August 16, 1999, p. B1.

[15] Charles Fishman, "This Is a Marketing Revolution," *Fast Company*, May 1999, p. 207.

[16] Joana Cmar, "One Step Ahead of the Competition: Implementing a Customer-Centric IVR System," *IMC Research Journal,* Spring 2001, p.4

[17] Jim Sterne, "In Praise of E-Mail," *Inc. Tech 2000*, September 15, 2000, p. 149.

[18] Bill McCloskey, "Rich Email: Part 1," *ClickZ Network*, February 24, 2000 <http://gt.clickz.com/cgi-bin/gt/sb/rm/rm.html?article=1357>.

[19] Sterne, "In Praise of E-Mail."

[20] McCloskey, "Rich Email: Part 1."

[21] "Email—Most Effective Online Marketing Tool," *Los Angeles Times*, January 27, 2000 <www.nua.net/surveys/?f=VS&art_id=905355553&rel=true>; and Sterne, "In Praise of E-mail."

[22] Sterne, "In Praise of E-Mail," p. 152.

[23] Anne D'Innocenzio, "Stores Catch Up with Net-Only Firms," *Boulder Daily Camera*, December 7, 2000, p. D1.

[24] "eMarketer Reports: Internet Economy Sound," *BrandEra Times*, June 12, 2000; John Zarocostas, "Internet Firms Neglect Logistics, Study says," *Business Plus*, February 28, 2000.

[25] Sarah Gilbert, "Web Page Offers More Connections," *Business Plus*, October 25, 1999, p. 4.

[26] Martin Lindstrom, "Morphing Offline into Online," *ClickZ Network*, August 26, 1999 <http://gt.clickz.com/cgi-bin/gt/wi/bm/bm.html?article=679>.

[27] Rachel Silverman, "Raiding Talent Via the Web," *The Wall Street Journal*, October 3, 2000, p. B1.

[28] Pamela Parker, "Dot-Com Companies Hit Public Radio Airwaves," *InternetNews.com*, March 20, 2000 <www.internetnews.com:80/bus-news/print/0,1089,3_323461,00.html>.

[29] NPD press release, February 7, 2000 <www.npd.com/corp/press/press_000207.htm>.

[30] Martin Lindstrom, "Rat Race Scurry" *ClickZ Network*, December 2, 1999 <http://gt.clickz.com/cgi-bin/gt/wi/bm/bm.html?article=1014>.

[31] Martin Lindstrom, "Dot-Com Branding Dilemma," *ClickZ Network*, February 24, 2000 <http://gt.clickz.com/cgi-bin/gt/wi/bm/bm.html?article=1356>; and Suein L. Hwang, "The Dot-Com Blur: Venture Capitalists Discover Marketing," *The Wall Street Journal*, February 16, 2000, p. A16.

[32] "Broadbase 'Sticky Factor' Study Finds 89% of Online Offers Not Targeted to Individual Customer Needs or Buying Behavior," Broadbase press release, February 25, 2000 <www.broadbase.com/news/press_sticky2.asp>.

[33] Hwang, "The Dot-Com Blur," p. A1.

[34] Mukul Pandya, "A Good Brand Is Hard to Buy," *The Wall Street Journal*, June 9, 2000, p. A18.

[35] "DoubleClick Cuts More Than 120 Employees," *Boulder Daily Camera,* December 6, 2000, p. 5D.

[36] Louis Whitman, "Dotcoms Shaping Up," *BrandEra Times*, April 25, 2000.

[37] Suein Hwang and Mylene Mangalindan, "Yahoo's Grand Vision for Web Advertising Takes Some Hard Hits," *The Wall Street Journal*, September 1, 2000, p. A1.

[38] Chan-Hoan Cho and John Leckenby, "The Effectiveness of Banner Advertising: Involvement and Click-Through," Association for Education in Journalism and Mass Communication conference presentation, August 2000.

[39] Jeffrey Graham, "Internet Advertising Best Practices: Five Rules to Brand By," *ClickZ Network*, October 25, 2000.

[40] Barb Palser, "Attack of the Killer Ads," *American Journalism Review*, March 2000, p. 64.

[41] Terry Lefton, "Blocking Those Internet Ads," from *Industry Standard*, reprinted in *Boulder Daily Camera's Business Plus*, April 23, 2001, p. 12.

[42] Marc Langheinrich, Atsuyoshi Nakamura, Naoki Abe, Tomonari Kamba, Yoshiyuki Koseki, *Unintrusive Customization Techniques for Web Advertising* <www8.org/w8-papers/2bcustomizing/unintrusive/unintrusive.html>.

[43] "Banners on the Decline," *CyberAtlas*, April 22, 1999 <http://cyberatlas.internet.com/big_picture/demographics/article/0,1323,5941_154461,00.html>.

[44] "Business and the Internet," p. 6.

[45] Paul Tulenko, "Design Web Page Basically," *Boulder Daily Camera*, February 26, 2000, p. 6D.

[46] Bob Tedeschi, "Web Merchants Go Multimedia," *New York Times*, March 13, 2000 <www.nytimes.com/library/tech/00/03/cyber/commerce/13commerce.html>.

[47] Stephen H. Wildstrom, "Untangle These Web Sites, Please," *Business Week*, August 30, 1999, p. 18.

[48] Clint Swett, "E-Mail Response May Come Now, Later or Not at All," *Business Plus*, February 6, 2000, p. 15.

[49] James Daly, "Editor's Note: Service First," *Business 2.0*, June 27, 2000, p. 5.

[50] John Zarocostas, "Internet Firms Neglect Logistics, Study Says," *Business Plus*, February 28, 2000.

[51] Tony Graham and Dee Martinez, "The Customer Service Side of Technolgy-Based Communication," *IMC Research Journal* 6 (Spring 2000), pp. 12-16; Jennifer Freedman and Ruby Sudoyo, "Technology's Effect on Customer Service: Building Meaningful Relationships through Dialogue," *IMC Research Journal* 5 (Spring 1999), pp. 3-8; Leigh Ann Steere and Timothy Weiss, "Is Technology Damaging Your Brand Images?" *IMC Research Journal* 4 (Spring 1998), pp. 17-25.

[52] Tom McNichol, "The New Privacy Wars," *USA Weekend*, May 16, 1996, pp. 16-17; Ellyn E. Spragins and Mary Hager, "Naked Before the World," *Newsweek*, June 30, 1997, p. 84.

[53] Susannah Fox, "Trust and Privacy Online; Why Americans Want to Rewrite the Rules," The Pew Internet and American Life Project, online posting, <www.pewinternet.org>, 2000.

[54] Michael Pastore, "Per Capita Online Spending Drops," *InternetNews.com*, January 3, 2000 <www.internetnews.com/ec-news/print/0,1089,4_272011,00.html>.

[55] Laurel Fortin, "Online Privacy Targeted in U.S.," *BrandEra Times*, May 31, 2000.

[56] D. Ian Hopper, "Privacy Group Breaks Ties with Amazon.com," *Boulder Daily Camera*, September 14, 2000, p. 3A.

[57] Jeri Clausing, "Self-Regulation of Internet Companies Is Poor," *The New York Times*, June 5, 1998.

[58] Jeri Clausing, "On Eve of Privacy Conference, Trade Groups Jockey for Position," *The New York Times*, June 23, 1998.

[59] Jeri Clausing, "Self-Regulation."

[60] David W. Moore, "Americans Say Internet Makes Their Lives Better," Gallup News Service, February 23, 2000 <www.gallup.com/poll/releases/pr000223.asp>.

[61] Sim D'Hertefelt, "Trust and the Perception of Security," *Interactionarchitect*, January 3, 2000 <www.interactionarchitect.com/research/report20000103shd.htm>.

[62] "Forrester Technographics® Finds Online Consumers Fearful of Privacy Violations," Forrester Research press release, October 27, 1999 <www.forrester.com/ER/Press/Release/0,1769,177,FF.html>.

13

Media Planning

Key Points in This Chapter

1. How do you explain the basic concepts used in comparing media?

2. What are the key media planning objectives and strategies?

3. How do you make decisions on combining media in a media mix?

Chapter Perspective
Planning Media Connections

As explained in Chapter 8, IMC makes use of data-driven communication. Databases enable magazines to insert a subscriber's name in an ad, telemarketers to use random dialing, and customer-service departments to use automated voice answering systems. They also let cable TV stations send certain brand messages to selected households, and let various marketers send selected brand messages to selected cellular phones. Media have become technologically complex. Media planners need to know how to leverage this technology.

As noted in Chapter 11, the goal of such leverage is not just message delivery but company–customer connection. The Minneapolis-based MC agency Fallon Worldwide recognizes that all types of message delivery systems create brand contact points that are important brand experiences. The overarching IMC objective, therefore, is to maximize all media-created brand contacts. According to Mark Goldstein, Fallon's chief marketing officer, connection is determined by the "five Ms" of media: the *moment* in which brand messages are delivered, the *mood* of customers or prospects at the time they receive or send brand messages, the *mindset* of customers and prospects, the *media* that carry the messages, and the *milieu* in which messages are exchanged.[1]

This way of thinking about media recognizes that its planning can be just as creative as designing a brand message. After a connection planning overview, this chapter describes some basic media planning concepts: audiences, reach, frequency, environment, and costs. It then explains how to create a media plan and, finally, looks at the whole media mix.

USING A MEDIA CONTEXT TO HELP REVIVE AN OLD BRAND
Lee Jeans Campaign by Fallon, Minneapolis, MN

Background: Why Buddy Lee Was Revived

Lee Jeans faced a critical brand problem. According to the heart of the jeans market, males and females ages 17–22, Lee Jeans were "not for me." They said Lee was "outdated," "boring," and "my mother's jeans." Fallon and Lee decided to reverse perceptions of the 105-year-old brand among these consumers by introducing a new sub-brand, Lee Dungarees, and reviving a diamond-in-the-rough icon uncovered in Lee's archives, Buddy Lee. (Buddy is Lee's vintage "spokes doll" from the 1920s (see Exhibit 13–1).

Lee's goal was to snap younger consumers' heads back and affect significant increases in key attribute measures including "brand for me" and "brand becoming more popular." In addition, Lee wanted to increase sales among young men and juniors.

The strategies: (1) guide fickle consumers down a path of discovery, allowing them to participate in discerning the meaning of the icon and the brand values; (2) fully integrate the positioning "jeans that won't hold you back" in all communications; (3) don't try too hard or risk rejection; and (4) use Buddy Lee to create a new definition of cool.

Stage I: Who is that cool guy?

Fallon designed a Discovery Phase to create intrigue in Buddy Lee and imbue him with coolness. The agency started by creating buzz locally and somewhat "underground." Using guerrilla tactics, brand communication was slightly ahead of the primary target, reaching leaders and influencers first. In these messages jeans were never mentioned . . . or the brand.

EXHIBIT 13-1

Reproduction of the original Buddy Lee "Spokes doll."

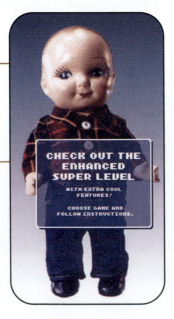

Consumers saw a phantom campaign of otherwise unidentified images of Buddy Lee wild posted, such as on walls bordering construction sites and other unusual places on the streets of trend areas in 15 major cities. Influential hipsters found random, small-space tune-in invitations to watch The Buddy Lee Story in music zines, alternative weeklies, and a CD-ROM (where Buddy became a fixture in the new music area). An underground network of web zines linked to the unbranded Buddy Lee website which told his story, but did not link to leejeans.com. The Buddy Lee site was interactive in that consumers could submit questions about Buddy and these were answered directly.

After bar-hopping and clubbing, the target came home and watched The Buddy Lee Story in between "South Park" episodes. The story ran as a two-part series of three-minute short films on late-late night cable. Next, the target saw nonbranded "Coming Soon" trailers on ESPN's Summer X Game's TV coverage. On-site X Games participants and spectators were the first to see the connection between Buddy Lee and Lee Dungarees jeans.

Stage II: Hey, those jeans are cool.

The brand maintained legitimacy among the "in" circle while moving from the narrowly targeted Discovery stage to a broader Launch stage. Ongoing proprietary trend-model and "cool meter" data, which Fallon derived by using account planning techniques with the target, helped predict favorite programming among the trend-leader target better than traditional demographic rating estimates. These measures separated hot from neutral program environments so that the brand connection would be truer—e.g., "Buffy the Vampire Slayer," "Dawson's Creek," and "Felicity" versus well-targeted but neutral programs such as "Melrose Place" and "90210." Fallon customized media schedules on FOX, The WB, ESPN 2, MTV, VH1, E!, and Comedy Central using consumer-endorsed programming. TV advertising revealed the Buddy Lee–Dungarees connection on messages carried on these channels for the first time. More recent TV commercials continued to use Buddy Lee as this cult hero (see Exhibit 13–2).

Results

Buddy Lee has become a bona fide pop-culture icon. Visuals of him continue to be modeled on a long list of celebrities (thanks to Fallon's aggressive T-shirt distribution to the young Hollywood elite). The wild postings appear as back drops on TV (e.g., "NYPD Blue") and in magazines (*Swing, Detour*). And the cost of a real Buddy Lee doll has risen from $250 up to $1,000, if you can find one.

This campaign created the most significant movement of any Lee Brand campaign in the last 12 years. Brand tracking also indicated significant changes in perceptions. Lee as a "brand becoming more popular" moved from 23 to 31 points and "cool to wear" moved from 26 to 35 points.

EXHIBIT 13-2

In TV commercials Buddy Lee meets a variety of strange characters.

More importantly, Lee saw a 3 percent brand market share growth in a flat to down category. Sell-in of Lee Dungarees' original straight leg was 300 percent higher than estimated. Sales grew 281 percent over the previous year among young men and 70 percent (off a larger base) among juniors.

Achieving these goals required an intimate consumer understanding as well as the courage and creativity to use new tools to create a media context which required media selection based on more than demographics and psychographics. Having customer insight as to why and how they consumed media, what they cared about, and how they choose brands provided a base for every message and delivery strategy employed. The media strategy was anything but vintage.

This case prepared with the generous help of Mark Goldstein, Fallon's chief marketing officer worldwide; Michelle Fitzgerald, media connection planner; and Bruce Tait, senior account planner.

MEDIA PLANNING OVERVIEW

Learning the strengths, weaknesses, and characteristics of the various media, which was the focus of Chapters 11 and 12, is the easy part of media planning. The more challenging part is being able to develop a media plan that cost-effectively achieves a given set of marketing objectives by serving each of the marketing communication functions.

Simply put, media planning is about determining the best mix of one-way and two-way media for a particular brand situation. The key is to balance message impact and cost. Media are often the largest single cost item in a marketing communication budget. General Motors, for example, spends worldwide over $3 billion a year on media. If media dollars are not wisely spent, and if the selected media do not allow brand messages to have maximum impact, money will be wasted and brand value will be lost.

Unfortunately, many academics as well as professionals still think of media only in terms of "advertising." Nothing could be further from the truth, as evidenced by the extensive use of media by all the MC functions.

Brand Contacts and Media

The media picture is getting bigger and broader and deeper because media planners recognize that there are many ways to interact with prospects and customers. This recognition has been slow in coming, however. It was not until the late 1980s, for example, that the Advertising Research Association recommended that its 30-year-old model for evaluating media effects be revised so it would be applicable to all marketing communication areas, not just advertising. Fallon Worldwide, which created the award-winning media plan for the Buddy Lee campaign described in the chapter opening case, knows that people can come in contact with a brand in a variety of ways, and that those contacts can be useful points of interaction. For some time Fallon has used account planners to design creative work that effectively touches the audience. Now the agency is doing the same thing in media by using "connection planners" to maximize the impact of all types of media that connect with the customer (see Exhibit 13–3).

Recall from Chapter 4 that there are three kinds of brand contacts points: (1) *intrinsic*, which automatically occur during the course of buying or using a brand;

(2) *customer-created*, which are those initiated by customers and prospects; and (3) *company-created*, which are the marketing communication planned messages that media deliver. A first step in media planning should be reviewing what messages are being delivered and received at the intrinsic and customer-created contact points. If these messages are negative, they will negate most company-created messages, which can result in a waste of media dollars (and, very possibly, a poor reflection on the marketing communication department and its agencies).

Another reason to identify intrinsic contact points is that they can provide additional "media" opportunities at virtually no cost. Intrinsic contacts, such as service delivery, packaging, and repair requests, represent opportunities for providing brand information and reinforcing brand relationships. Because they automatically demand the attention of customers, especially current customers, they provide a captive audience that should be receptive because these people are already interacting with the brand in some way.

Finally, intrinsic contacts are an excellent opportunity for encouraging customer feedback. To that end, when interactive media are part of a media plan, employees interacting with customers should be trained to listen during these interactions and record customer comments, perhaps even to ask specific questions designed to generate feedback on particular programs or planning decisions. Although media planners are not responsible for customer service and order taking, they should consider recommending that those who are responsible be prepared to capture all types of customer responses. All companies need to have a system in place that can readily receive messages from customers. Microsoft, for example, was overwhelmed with 40,000 phone calls a day when it announced a customer call-center number as part of its Windows 95 introduction.

As media continue to become more interactive, the dividing line between those used to send and those used to receive brand messages grows thinner. This is why cross-functional media planning is essential to integration.

EXHIBIT 13-3

The connection planners for the Buddy Lee campaign included (clockwise from rear right): Bruce Tait, Shawn O'Meara, Michelle Fitzgerald, Keith Faust, Harvey Mano, and Dodie Subler.

Media Planning and Buying Functions

Media planners perform four basic functions—conduct media research, determine media objectives and strategies, determine the media mix, and do the actual media buy. Media research involves analyzing both the target audience and media options. The information includes size and characteristics of the various media audiences, as well as effectiveness data on how well the various media deliver the audiences they promise. Most of the information comes from research companies that compile media statistics and profiles. Mediamark Research, Inc. (MRI), for example, provides data on demographic, lifestyle, product usage, and media usage from a sample of 25,000 consumers who are interviewed each year. Information Resources, Inc. (IRI), synthesizes the movement of billions of product purchases based on data from retail store scanners.

Media plans build on an analysis of brand contact points. Since there are an unlimited number of media options for creating brand contacts with customers and prospects, a media plan is a complex document that presents the decisions made about the most effective use of media time and space. The plan details which target segments, which media vehicles, to what extent, in which markets, at what times, and at what costs. Figure 13–1 identifies the key questions a media planner must answer.

FIGURE 13-1

The answers to these questions are the foundation of a media plan.

Media Plan Questions That Must Be Answered

Which targets?	Which media vehicles?	Use to what extent?	Which markets?	At what times?	At what costs?

Unless their media budget is extremely small, most brands use more than one medium, for several reasons. First, different media have different message delivery features, as explained in the previous two chapters. Second, media strategies, such as the one described in the chapter opening case about Lee Jeans, often call for a variety of media. Finally, no single communication vehicle generally can reach most of the target audience. Figure 13–2 summarizes the variety of media that were used for the Lee Dungarees launch. The chart not only gives the types of media used but also the amount budgeted to each area.

Media buying is *the execution of a media plan.* Media buyers negotiate with publishers, broadcasters, and other media representatives to arrange the most cost-effective contracts possible that will satisfy the media objectives. In buying media, it is not the lowest price that is most important but the return on the media investment in terms of effect on the target audience. Media buyers usually do post-buy analyses, which monitor the message placements that have run for a brand, to make sure the messages were delivered as promised.

FIGURE 13-2

Lee Dungarees Media Launch Plan

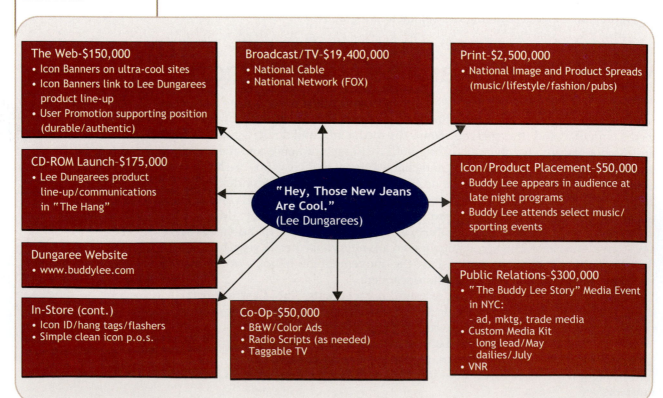

The Web-$150,000
- Icon Banners on ultra-cool sites
- Icon Banners link to Lee Dungarees product line-up
- User Promotion supporting position (durable/authentic)

CD-ROM Launch-$175,000
- Lee Dungarees product line-up/communications in "The Hang"

Dungaree Website
- www.buddylee.com

In-Store (cont.)
- Icon ID/hang tags/flashers
- Simple clean icon p.o.s.

Broadcast/TV-$19,400,000
- National Cable
- National Network (FOX)

"Hey, Those New Jeans Are Cool."
(Lee Dungarees)

Co-Op-$50,000
- B&W/Color Ads
- Radio Scripts (as needed)
- Taggable TV

Print-$2,500,000
- National Image and Product Spreads (music/lifestyle/fashion/pubs)

Icon/Product Placement-$50,000
- Buddy Lee appears in audience at late night programs
- Buddy Lee attends select music/sporting events

Public Relations-$300,000
- "The Buddy Lee Story" Media Event in NYC:
  - ad, mktg, trade media
- Custom Media Kit
  - long lead/May
  - dailies/July
- VNR

One trend that has affected media buying in recent years is the consolidation of media companies into major conglomerates, as mentioned in Chapter 3. Each of these companies is bundling its various vehicles to offer planners "cross-media buys." Hachette Filipacchi Magazines, for example, offers buyers the chance to send "integrated messages" using a variety of its vehicles (see Exhibit 13–4). A study commissioned by *Advertising Age* found that half of the companies and agencies surveyed said they had bought cross-media packages. The number one reason given for making these buys was not saving money, but rather "delivering an integrated marketing message across all [media] platforms."[2]

Media Integration

There are many different areas of a company's operations in which media plans need to be integrated. The most obvious is the overall marketing plan. When a new promotion or product is being introduced, media support is needed. But unless the planning is integrated, it is possible that the media will deliver brand messages at the wrong time. A common mistake is using media to announce a new product before that product has been produced or distributed.

Media and creative planning must be integrated so that a company does not miss opportunities for reaching the right audiences in a dynamic way. Media also must be integrated with each of the MC functional programs. For example, a publicity release for a new or improved product should be distributed before the advertising runs. Otherwise, the news value is negated and editors have no reason to use the publicity release.

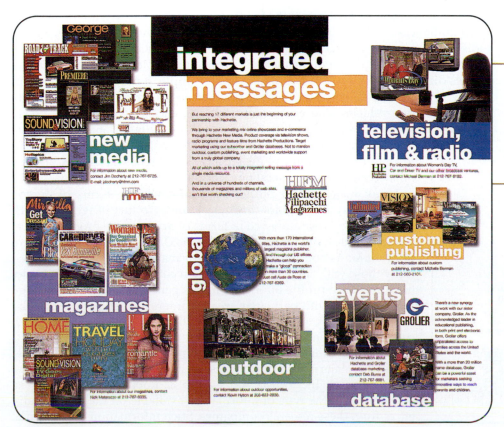

EXHIBIT 13-4

This promotional piece for Hachette Filipacchi Magazines promises marketers integrated messages in 17 different media.

Media planning may also be integrated into a company's business model—how it goes about conducting its business. A good example is how brick-and-mortar retailers have set up websites, enabling customers to buy online. By integrating the Internet medium into their business model, these retailers have been able to expand their overall business. Amazon.com has reversed the process, integrating a direct-mail catalog into its predominantly online business. The catalog shown in Exhibit 13–5 is for Amazon.com products other than books.

The decisions made in a media plan are as much art as science. The science dimension involves using numbers to derive solid quantitative justifications for the media selection decisions. The art is based on an understanding of the qualitative dimensions of how people use the various media. This chapter will present both the quantitative and qualitative tools used in media planning and buying. Regardless of position, researchers, media planners, and buyers have to understand a basic set of media planning concepts.

BASIC MEDIA PLANNING CONCEPTS

There is no way to know exactly how, and to what extent, brand messages delivered by various media will impact attitudes and behavior. In addition to experience, media planners rely on five basic concepts: media audiences, reach, frequency, media environment, and media costs.

Media Audiences

From the marketing and MC plan, the media planner will know who the brand's target audiences are. The planner's job is to select communication vehicles whose audience profiles most closely match those of the target audiences. The greater the match, the better. The extent of the match is determined by looking at how the audiences differ from the average population. For example, if the target audience is twice as likely as the average population to own a boat, communication vehicles whose audiences also are twice as likely to own a boat should be considered. In other words, every target market has certain **skews**, or *variations from the general population*. A skew is similar to an index. For example, physicians skew higher (i.e., index higher) on income than the general population.

Many major media profile their audiences in terms of demographics, psychographics (lifestyles), and product usage. That lets them analyze their audience in terms of appropriate products to be advertised (see the Ethics and Issues box). However, such detailed information is not always available for many media vehicles, especially those with small audiences. When communication vehicles do have audience-profile information, it is generally demographic. Vehicles dealing with particular areas of interest, such as sports, hobbies, or finance, are the ones most likely to have lifestyle and product-usage data in addition to demographic profiles.

Although some media do their own research to profile their audiences, the majority buy it from research companies such as Mediamark Research Inc. (MRI) and Gallup & Robinson. Table 13–1 is an example of the type of information available on magazine audiences from these research companies. Such information helps media

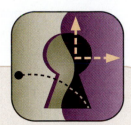

ETHICS AND ISSUES

Lighting Fire under Tobacco Media

In response to increasing government and social pressure for tobacco companies not to promote smoking to those under 18 years of age, cigarette maker Philip Morris announced in 2000 that it would no longer run advertising for Marlboro and its other brands in over 40 magazines that the company had been using. The dropped magazines were those that had 15 percent or more of their readers under 18. Some of these publications were *Glamour, Newsweek, Rolling Stone, People*, and *TV Guide*. The levels of youth readership were determined through surveys by Simmons Market Research Bureau and Mediamark Research, Inc. (MRI).

This isn't the first time cigarette media plans have been affected by social and legal pressures. In 1997, the Supreme Court upheld a Baltimore, Maryland, law that bans cigarette advertising on billboards and other outdoor locations near schools and other places that attract children.

Even in-store point-of-sale racks have come under scrutiny (see Exhibit 13–6). A Camel cigarette display that depicted a yellow-and-purple sports car with a trunk filled with packs of Camel cigarettes was criticized for its appeal to children. Such self-service displays, particularly those attractive to kids, have also been attacked because they make it possible for children to take a pack of cigarettes without asking for them from salesclerks. The U.S. Food and Drug Administration (FDA) has raised the question of whether these systems are in fact advertisements or merely ways to distribute a product. If they are ads, then they come under the jurisdiction of the FDA, with its authority to regulate advertising to children.

EXHIBIT 13-6

Is this Camel display strictly a way of distributing a product and/or a promotional device aimed specifically at children?

Think About It

What is the heart of the issue that affects the advertising and promotion of cigarettes? Does the list of magazines that were deleted from Philip Morris's media plan make sense to you? If 15 percent of the audience profile contains kids, do you feel that is justification for eliminating the magazine from the media buy?

Source: Matthew Rose, "Magazines Brace for Cigarette Ad Pullout," *The Wall Street Journal*, June 7, 2000, p. B5.

planners understand the audience of a particular vehicle and how it compares to the profile of their brands' targeted audiences. A later section of this chapter will explain how vehicle-audience data, along with cost data, are used to help planners in the media-buying process.

Trade publications and trade shows make it somewhat easier to select media for BtB targets. Each industry has its own publications and trade shows that attract well-defined product-category audiences. Because most BtB brands have smaller customer and prospect universes (compared to consumer brands), and

T A B L E 1 3 - 1 Magazine Audience Estimates

MRI Spring 2000 Cyber Stats
Survey Dates: March 1999–April 2000

	Total Adults	*Any online/ Internet Usage	Have Internet Access			Used the Internet in Past 30 Days			Used Online Service in Past 30 Days				
			Home/ Work/ Other	Home	Work	Home/ Work/ Other	Home	Work	Any Service	AOL	Compu-Serve	MSN	Prodigy
Total Adults	199438	90458	112949	77621	50476	86289	65471	40449	75409	38888	2370	13288	2639
	100.0	100.0	100.0	100.0	100.0	100.0	100.0	100.0	100.0	100.0	100.0	100.0	100.0
Men	48.0	49.8	48.5	49.3	52.3	49.8	50.1	52.7	49.3	48.7	49.9	48.6	49.5
Women	52.0	50.2	51.5	50.7	47.7	50.2	49.9	47.3	50.7	51.3	50.1	51.4	50.5
Graduated College Plus	22.5	38.0	33.6	38.6	49.2	38.8	41.6	53.1	37.8	35.5	47.4	37.7	32.6
Attended College	26.5	34.8	33.7	34.0	30.6	35.0	34.4	30.2	35.0	36.1	32.8	36.5	32.3
Did not Attend College	51.0	27.2	32.8	27.3	20.3	26.2	24.1	16.7	27.2	28.4	19.8	25.8	35.1
Age 18–34	32.5	39.7	37.9	35.1	34.9	39.8	36.6	34.6	40.3	41.6	34.9	43.0	42.7
Age 35–54	39.9	47.7	46.0	49.4	55.4	47.7	49.6	56.3	47.4	46.6	52.5	46.8	44.8
Age 55+	27.6	12.7	16.2	15.5	9.7	12.5	13.8	9.1	12.3	11.8	12.6	10.3	12.5
Employed Full Time	56.8	71.1	67.8	68.5	92.2	71.3	70.0	93.2	71.3	69.9	70.6	73.5	73.8
Employed Part-Time	8.6	10.5	10.4	10.4	7.5	10.6	10.8	6.5	10.5	11.6	11.9	11.8	9.6
Occupation													
Professional	10.4	18.7	16.5	18.9	26.8	19.2	20.5	28.2	18.2	16.3	18.9	18.8	15.2
Exec./Manager/Administrator	9.9	16.8	14.7	16.3	24.9	17.2	17.5	27.8	17.1	17.5	21.1	18.0	22.2
Clerical/Sales/Technical	18.9	26.4	24.8	23.7	32.3	26.4	24.2	32.2	27.1	27.2	23.8	29.5	18.4
Precision/Crafts/Repair	7.2	6.2	6.7	6.4	6.2	6.1	6.2	5.0	6.0	6.0	6.5	6.1	8.2
Census Region													
Northeast	19.7	19.9	20.1	20.3	19.2	19.8	20.1	19.2	20.9	23.5	16.2	17.2	19.7
North Central	23.1	23.0	23.6	21.9	23.6	23.3	22.1	23.5	21.9	20.4	24.0	23.9	21.1
South	35.4	32.6	32.7	33.0	33.5	32.4	32.4	33.2	32.2	32.2	34.8	38.9	34.9
West	21.8	24.6	23.6	24.9	23.7	24.5	25.3	24.0	25.0	23.8	25.0	20.0	24.3
Household Income													

T A B L E   13 - 1   Magazine Audience Estimates *(continued)*

$150,000 or More	4.1	7.6	6.7	8.5	9.7	7.8	8.7	10.7	8.0	9.1	9.3	6.8	6.5
$75,000—149,999	20.1	32.6	29.4	34.7	39.6	33.1	36.4	41.8	33.1	33.8	38.2	33.3	32.0
$50,000—74,999	20.7	26.2	25.7	26.9	27.4	26.2	26.5	26.8	26.0	25.2	24.9	26.0	26.0
Less Than $50,000	55.1	33.6	38.3	29.9	23.3	32.9	28.4	20.8	32.9	32.0	27.5	33.9	35.5
Job Function/Area of Responsibility													
Accounting	8.5	13.5	12.2	13.0	18.0	13.6	13.6	19.1	13.6	14.6	16.3	15.5	18.6
Banking	6.8	9.7	9.1	9.6	11.9	9.7	9.9	12.3	9.6	10.1	12.7	9.4	15.2
Engineering/Design/Research	6.2	11.3	9.8	10.7	17.2	11.6	11.7	19.1	10.9	10.3	14.8	15.4	15.5
Finance	6.5	10.6	9.3	9.7	14.5	10.7	10.2	16.0	10.6	10.6	13.4	11.8	14.4
General Management	12.7	19.9	18.2	19.3	27.7	20.1	20.0	29.1	19.8	20.2	26.3	22.9	24.2
International	0.9	1.8	1.5	1.7	2.9	1.8	1.8	3.4	1.8	1.9	2.2	2.7	4.5
MIS/EDP	1.5	2.9	2.5	2.8	4.9	3.1	3.2	5.7	2.7	2.1	3.9	4.1	4.6
Manufacturing	4.2	5.2	5.1	4.4	6.3	5.2	4.7	6.3	4.9	5.0	6.8	8.0	10.9
Marketing	6.6	11.3	10.0	11.0	15.0	11.4	11.6	16.3	11.2	12.0	16.6	12.8	13.4
Medical	4.8	6.9	6.7	7.1	8.2	7.1	7.1	7.7	6.8	7.3	7.6	7.5	7.6
Sales	12.6	18.0	16.6	17.4	20.8	18.0	18.0	22.0	18.0	18.6	23.6	19.4	17.5
County Size A	41.2	44.0	42.4	45.8	47.0	44.7	46.4	48.1	44.8	50.3	45.3	39.1	45.6
County Size B	29.9	30.4	30.5	30.2	30.3	30.4	30.0	30.3	31.0	31.1	32.1	30.0	29.0
County Size C	14.3	14.6	15.0	14.0	12.6	14.4	13.9	12.4	14.1	12.5	17.0	15.4	17.4
County Size D	14.6	10.9	12.1	10.0	10.2	10.5	9.6	9.2	10.0	6.2	5.6	15.5	7.9
Marital Status													
Single	23.7	27.5	26.0	23.4	22.6	27.7	24.5	23.3	28.4	30.5	25.3	30.9	28.1
Married	57.2	61.6	61.1	66.2	65.3	61.4	65.7	65.1	60.6	57.9	65.8	57.8	57.4
Other	19.1	10.9	12.9	10.3	12.0	10.9	9.7	11.6	10.9	11.5	8.9	11.3	14.5
Household Size													
1—2 Persons	47.9	40.2	41.0	37.9	41.8	40.4	39.0	42.6	39.5	37.7	43.1	42.6	46.6
3—4 Persons	36.9	44.4	43.3	45.9	44.6	44.3	45.6	44.4	44.5	45.4	45.6	42.6	41.7
5+ Persons	15.2	15.4	15.7	16.2	13.6	15.3	15.4	13.0	16.1	17.0	11.3	14.8	11.7
Any Child in Household	42.1	47.7	47.0	48.7	48.0	47.3	48.3	46.7	47.9	49.3	44.3	45.6	44.8
Type of Firm													
Business Firm	37.7	45.0	43.6	42.7	55.2	45.0	43.5	55.4	45.2	45.5	46.7	48.4	47.4
Government	9.7	15.0	13.8	13.8	21.8	15.3	14.5	21.7	14.5	12.9	12.7	18.1	12.5
Other	18.0	21.5	20.7	22.3	22.7	21.5	22.7	22.7	22.0	23.1	23.2	18.9	23.4

*Any online/Internet usage is a net of those who looked at or used the Internet or any online service at home, work, or any other place in the last 30 days.

more databases of these targets, as well as significantly higher average sales transactions, they can afford to make more use of expensive interactive media. Exhibit 13–7 is an example of how a trade publication describes and promotes its audience.

How to Determine CDIs, BDIs

A major decision in media planning is determining the best geographic areas in which to find the target audience. To help make these decisions, marketers use a **category development index (CDI),** which is *a numerical indicator of the relative consumption rate in a particular market for a particular product category.* For example, if the average household consumption of hot dogs in the United States is indexed at 100, then a city with a CDI of 200 means the average household in that city consumes twice the national average of hot dogs, while the average household in a city with a CDI of 50 consumes half the average.

To determine a category development index (CDI), you first must determine the average household (HH) consumption rate for a marketing universe, such as "total U.S." This number becomes the base against which the average household consumption rate of the product category is compared. For illustration, let's look at the processed meat category. We'll assume 1 billion pounds of processed meat are sold each year in the United States, which has 100 million households. This would mean the average annual household consumption is 10 pounds:

$$\frac{\text{Total pounds sold in the U.S. in a year}}{\text{Total number of households in U.S.}} = \text{Avg. lbs. per HH}$$

$$\frac{1,000,000,000 \text{ pounds of processed meat}}{100,000,000 \text{ million households}} = 10 \text{ lbs. per HH}$$

(The calculation can be made in whatever unit a category is sold—pounds, cases, jars. It should not be made in currency, however, because different brands charge different prices.)

Once the average household consumption is determined for the total marketplace, then average HH consumption can be determined for individual markets.

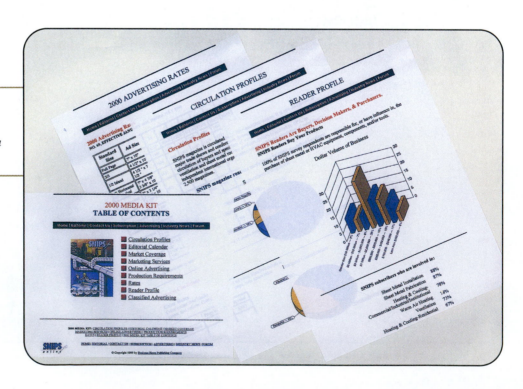

To do this, the total number of pounds sold in a market is divided by the total number of HHs in that market. The following shows the average pounds per household in Milwaukee, Wisconsin:

$$\frac{\text{Total pounds sold in Milwaukee}}{\text{Total households in Milwaukee}} = \text{Average lbs. per HH}$$

$$\frac{12,500,000 \text{ pounds sold in Milwaukee}}{500,000 \text{ households in Milwaukee}} = 25 \text{ lbs. per HH}$$

Once the average HH consumption is known for a particular market, such as 25 pounds for Milwaukee, the CDI is determined by dividing this number by the average national HH consumption rate, which in this illustration is 10 pounds per household. The result is multiplied by 100. Note: This means that an average CDI would be indexed at 100; anything above 100 is higher than the average, and anything below 100 is lower than the average.

$$\text{CDI} = \frac{25 \text{ lbs. in Milwaukee}}{10 \text{ lbs. nationally}} = 2.50 \times 100 = 250$$

This CDI of 250 says that the average Milwaukee HH consumes two and a half times as much processed meat as does the average U.S. HH. For this reason, processed meat companies' media plans will generally have more media weight in Milwaukee than in a market with a much lower CDI such as Los Angeles (whose processed meat CDI is about 65). CDIs tell marketers where they are mostly likely to get the best return on their media dollars.

While the CDI indicates relative development of a product category by geographic market, the **brand development index (BDI)** is *a numerical indicator of the relative development of a particular brand within a market*. The higher a BDI, the better that brand is doing in a market compared to all the other markets in which that brand is distributed. A BDI is used to compare a brand's individual market average household consumption to that brand's national average household consumption. As with CDI, a BDI of 100 is average, so when a market's BDI is below 100, it says the brand is underperforming compared to the average for all other markets in which the brand is distributed. One reason could be more competition, in which case the brand could plan for more media weight and promotions. Another explanation could be a weak sales force in that market.

Continuing the processed-meat illustration, the Oscar Mayer (OM) brand will be used as an example of a single brand to show how to figure a brand development index (BDI).

$$\frac{\text{Total pounds of brand's product sold in U.S.}}{\text{Total number of households in U.S.}} = \text{Avg. lbs. of OM per HH nationally}$$

$$\frac{500 \text{ million pounds of OM}}{100 \text{ million households}} = 5 \text{ lbs. OM per HH nationally}$$

$$\frac{3.5 \text{ million pounds sold in Milwaukee}}{500,000 \text{ households in Milwaukee}} = 7 \text{ lbs. OM per HH in Milwaukee}$$

$$\text{BDI} = \frac{7 \text{ lbs. in Milwaukee}}{5 \text{ lbs. nationally}} = 1.40 \times 100 = 140 \text{ Milwaukee BDI}$$

Reach

No matter how good an offer is or how creatively a brand message has been designed, it is useless until it reaches the target audience. **Reach** (also called **penetration**) is *the percentage of a specified audience exposed one or more times to a particular* *communication vehicle within a specified period*. Although exposure to a vehicle carrying a brand message does not guarantee that the brand's message itself will be received, that is the way reach is determined. In other words, reach is calculated for exposure to a magazine or TV program, not for any specific ad within the magazine or program. Reach is expressed as a percentage, although the percent sign is not used. For example, the equation R = 58 translates to a reach of 58 percent— that is, 58 out of 100 people (or HHs) in the target audience were exposed to the communication vehicle. Although reach can be based on any defined universe (e.g., all households in the United States, males over 18, all adults living in Illinois), reach is assumed to be stated in terms of households unless specified otherwise (see Exhibit 13–8).

The first step in determining the most effective reach for a message is to select communication vehicles whose audiences most closely match a brand's target audience. A maker of tennis equipment would likely consider tennis magazines, rather than automotive magazines, for example. Media planners must also know the reach of each vehicle being considered. For example, a chain of dry cleaners in Cleveland, Ohio, thinking of advertising in the *Cleveland Plain-Dealer*, would want to know what percentage of households in the paper's *coverage area* (or *universe*) regularly read this publication. Note the difference between the terms *coverage area* (the geographical area) and *reach* (the percentage of those within the coverage area who are regularly exposed to a vehicle). The *Plain-Dealer*'s coverage area is metropolitan Cleveland; its reach is 60 percent (60 percent of households in metro Cleveland regularly read this daily paper).

The coverage area for local TV stations is generally a 50- to 60-mile radius from a city center—the distance most broadcast signals travel. As mentioned in Chapter 11, this *TV broadcast coverage area* is called a **designated marketing area (DMA)**. Every county within the United States has been assigned to a DMA city. A county is assigned to the city from which 50 percent or more of the county's households receive their TV signals. As shown in Figure 13–3, the DMA for Seattle-Tacoma, Washington, includes several counties. Because TV has become such a dominant medium, most marketers now do local-market planning based on DMAs.

As with print, a broadcast station may have a wide coverage area but a low reach. Consider, for example, WKMG-TV, whose coverage area is the Orlando, Florida, DMA. Even though all households with TV sets in this DMA *can* receive the station, only a small portion actually have their sets on and tuned to WKMG-TV at one time. In fact, most WKMG-TV programs are seen by fewer than 10 percent of the households. Unlike print media, whose reach is fairly constant (because it is based mostly on subscriptions), the reach of broadcast and cable stations varies program by program.

Reach can also be based on such things as occupations, hobbies, sports, or in the case of BtB marketing, size of businesses. For example, say Sprint's small business division is interested in reaching owners and managers of small businesses nationwide. If it were considering advertising in *Business Week*, it would want to know what percentage of small businesses regularly receive *Business Week*.

Very seldom is a brand lucky enough to find a media vehicle whose reach is 100 percent of the brand's targeted audience, which is one reason it is necessary to use more than one vehicle in a given campaign. Yet planners must do their math homework carefully, because adding reach is not always simple. Suppose that, in a given coverage area, TV has a reach of 60 percent and newspapers 50 percent. This does not mean that placing brand messages in both media will result in a reach of 110 percent. In fact, when the two are combined, the reach may be well under 100 percent because of duplication. **Duplication** is *the*

EXHIBIT 13-8

Impact Media, a company that hangs product samples on doorknobs, uses this ad to compare its HH reach to that of local newspapers.

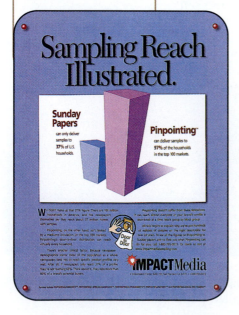

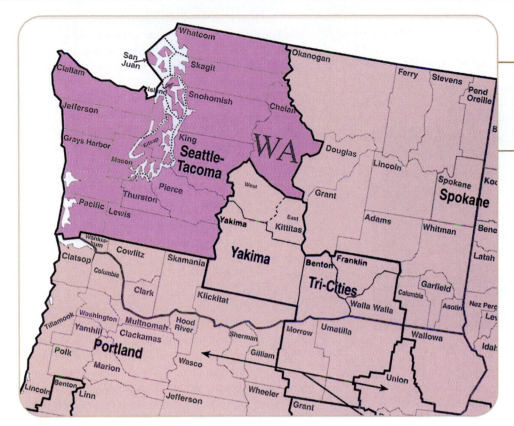

FIGURE 13-3

*Purple shaded area shows all
the counties making up the
Seattle-Tacoma DMA.*

overlapping coverage of two or more vehicles. If Sprint, again, decided to supplement its *Business Week* advertising by also running ads in *The Wall Street Journal*, in *Inc.* magazine, and on the MSNBC cable channel, there would be a lot of duplication. Some small businesses are exposed to two of these vehicles, some to three and a few to all four (see Figure 13–4). Generally speaking, while adding vehicles increases reach, it also increases duplication.

The extent of duplication is determined by research—asking people what media they regularly use. Most major media companies either conduct such surveys themselves or buy the information from independent research companies. Advertising agencies have software programs that compare different mixes of communication vehicles to determine duplication levels and the unduplicated reach of each mix. Remember, reach is the percentage of a target audience that has the opportunity to be exposed to one *or more* brand messages over a specified period of time.

Measuring Reach

In the case of radio and television, reach is determined by the rating of a particular program. As discussed in Chapter 11, these program ratings, which are provided by Nielsen Media Research and Arbitron, are estimates of average program viewership based on quarter-hour viewing/listening research. In essence, programs are the communication vehicles, rather than the stations themselves.

A program's rating is basically the same as its reach. Recall that one rating point equals 1 percent of a vehicle's coverage area. A broadcast rating of 5 means that 5 percent of the households in a station's coverage area were exposed to that particular program. The more households watching or listening to a particular program in a particular DMA, the higher that program's rating.

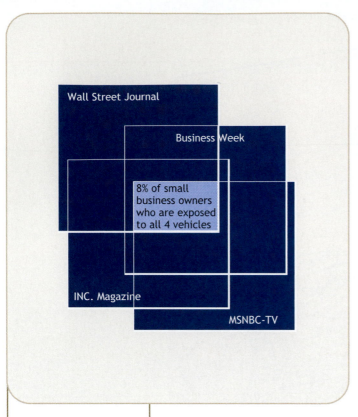

8% of small business owners who are exposed to all 4 vehicles

Wall Street Journal

Business Week

INC. Magazine

MSNBC-TV

FIGURE 13-4

Universe of small business owners; each box represents each vehicle's coverage of small businesses

The reach of specialized magazines is based on a universe defined by category interest or use. For example, the universe for the trade publication *Golf Course Management* would be all managers of golf courses.

The reach of outdoor advertising is determined by the percentage of cars in a metropolitan area that drive by billboards carrying a particular brand message within a 24-hour period. When using outdoor advertising, most companies display the brand message on multiple boards at the same time. If a brand message is posted on 10 outdoor boards spread throughout Nashville, Tennessee, for example, the reach is determined by the percentage of cars driving by these boards. If there are 200,000 cars registered in metro Nashville, and traffic counts show that 200,000 cars have driven by one or more of these boards within a 24-hour period, the reach is said to be 100 (i.e., 100 percent). In outdoor terms, this is known as a "100 showing." Unfortunately, traffic counts don't recognize duplication.

Another way to determine reach is by the number of message impressions. An **impression** is *one exposure to a brand message*. Media planners sometimes use impressions as a measure of reach when it is difficult to identify a universe (i.e., the basis on which a reach percentage can be figured). Internet brand messages are often figured in terms of impressions because it is still difficult to tell who in a target audience has access to the Internet. The number of visits to websites carrying a particular brand message determines the number of impressions for that brand message.

In the case of direct mail and telemarketing, the universe base for figuring reach is defined according to the company's identification of its market. For example, the Boston chapter of the Red Cross uses telemarketing in its annual fund drive and can define its universe as all households in the Boston metro area. If there are 400,000 households and 40,000 were called, the reach would be 10 (40,000 ÷ 400,000 = .10). A similar method is used to figure the reach of a direct-mail effort: Simply divide the number of mailings made by the total number of households or companies that make up the targeted universe.

Targeted Reach

Most marketers, regardless of what they are selling, are not interested in reaching all of the households or businesses in a particular communication vehicle's audience because some audience members are neither customers nor prospects. This is why it is best to do media planning based on **targeted reach,** which is *that portion of a communication vehicle's audience who are in a brand's target market.* For example, suppose a large lawn-and-garden shop in St. Louis, Missouri, that sells power mowers throughout the city has defined its target audience as metro area homeowners with lawns. It places an ad in the *St. Louis Post-Dispatch,* which has a 60 percent reach in the St. Louis market. If only half of the households receiving the newspaper have yards, however, then the *targeted reach* is 30 percent of the total metro area—half of the *Post-Dispatch*'s reach.

Targeted reach can be determined for any communication vehicle as long as the brand's target audience can be identified within a vehicle's audience. For example, let's say that Accenture (formerly Andersen Consulting) placed an ad in *Progressive Grocer* in order to create interest in a new inventory control program. Accenture's target is managers of stores with annual sales of $3 million or more. Of *Progressive Grocer*'s 60,000 readers, only 20,000 are managers of these large-volume stores. Therefore, the targeted reach for Andersen is only one-third (60,000 ÷ 20,000) of the trade magazine's total reach.

How Much Reach Is Enough?

In most cases it is cost-prohibitive for a brand to have 100 percent reach of a target market. So the question that must be answered is: How much reach is enough? The answer is: The percentage that is most cost-effective to achieve. That percentage is determined by calculating the point at which the cost to reach additional members of a target is more than these customers are worth in revenue. As Figure 13–5 shows, as the number of media exposures increases, the rate of increase in reach diminishes. A certain portion of a target audience is always less expensive to reach than other members because of their different levels of media usage. Those who consume the most media are the easiest to reach. There is an old saying in marketing: "Pick the low-hanging fruit first." In other words, don't waste time and money climbing to the top of a tree (to get at those who are hard to reach) until all the fruit that is easily reached from the ground has been picked.

Another factor that helps determine the reach objective, especially for consumer brands sold at retail, is where the brand is sold. Quite simply, if a brand has distribution only in the southwestern part of the United States, then that is the only geographical region that should receive brand messages. When a brand wants to expand into a new geographical area, most retail chains demand to see a media plan before agreeing to begin selling that brand. At the same time, most companies do not want to buy media in areas before it has distribution of its brand in stores doing 60 percent or more of the business in that area. This often becomes a catch-22 for marketers. On the one hand, if they promote a brand that has little or no distribution in a market, they are wasting money. On the other hand, if a retailer takes on a new brand and there are no brand messages to make people aware of the brand, it will sit on the store shelf and not move. Most major chains charge brands a **slotting fee** for taking on a new brand—an up-front payment made in exchange for guaranteed shelf space. In the case of many large chains, if the brand does not sell at an expected level within 90 days, the chains will quit carrying the

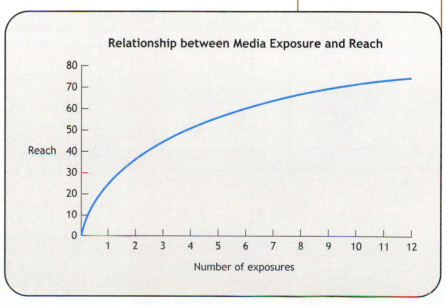

Relationship between Media Exposure and Reach

brand, but keep the slotting fee. Therefore, the pressure is on marketers to make sure that when they go into a new area and get distribution, there are enough media messages to create a demand for the brand.

Media Waste

A major concern of many marketers is **media waste,** defined as *brand messages sent to people who are neither customers nor prospects.* In the above example of Accenture's effort to target managers of large-volume stores, two-thirds of *Progressive Grocer's* circulation would be media waste for Accenture. Since marketers must pay for reaching a vehicle's total audience, media waste can translate into monetary waste. Exhibit 13–9 illustrates the pinpointed reach promised by a company that hangs product samples on doorknobs.

Having said this, it must also be pointed out that something more important than the percentage of media waste is cost per response. A communication vehicle that has a high percentage of media waste may still have a lower cost per response than other vehicles. This is discussed more thoroughly in Chapter 17, on direct response.

Frequency

In media planning, the word **frequency** refers to *the average number of times those who are reached have an opportunity to be exposed to a brand message within a specified time period.* (Note that this is a different use of the word than in Chapter 7, where frequency was described as part of a targeting strategy that measured recency, frequency, and monetary [RFM] values of a customer's catalog purchases.) To understand the difference between reach and frequency, think about this example: If an Atlanta, Georgia, Ford dealer ran an ad in the *Atlanta Journal* the same day a news release about the dealership appeared in the newspaper, whose coverage is 65 percent, the combined reach of both brand messages would still be 65, since the same households were exposed to both the ad and the news story. The frequency, however, would be 2. This is because each household receiving the *Journal* had the opportunity to see two brand messages about the Ford dealer. Frequency, then, is the result of message duplication.

Most media plans call for a frequency greater than 1. This is for several reasons, the first of which is to help ensure that the message itself gets exposed. Research done by companies such as Roper-Starch, Nielsen Media Research, Gallup & Robinson, and Readex, have documented what we intuitively know—exposure to any particular brand message will be far less than the exposure to the vehicle carrying that message. This means *message* exposure should be given more attention than *vehicle* exposure.

One study of television viewing behavior found that viewer disinterest plagues commercials twice as frequently as programs; the primary avoidance technique is doing something else and ignoring the screen

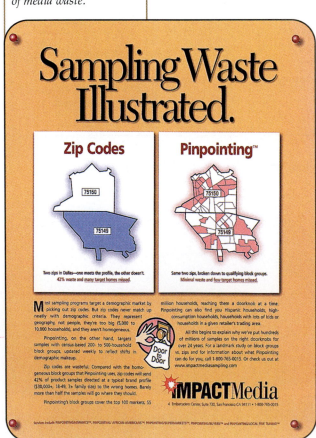

(reading, folding laundry, talking on the phone). Another ethnographic study found that when viewers who were actually watching TV encountered a commercial, they changed the channel 52 percent of the time.[3] Based on Nielsen People Meter reports (described in Chapter 11), only 25–35 percent of the average TV audience actually sees and pays attention to an average commercial. In the case of radio, only about 20 percent of listeners pay attention to the average commercial. For the average newspaper ad, the percentage is even smaller than this.[4] What this means is that, in practice, multiple *vehicle* exposures are needed to generate at least one *message* exposure among the target audience.

The second reason for multiple exposures is to increase the chance a message will be understood. The more complex the message, the more exposures will be needed in order for the target to fully understand what is being communicated. Finally, and perhaps most obviously, frequency increases the chance that a message will be remembered. You will recall from the discussion of communication in Chapter 4 that repetition is a major key to memory.

Effective Frequency

As with reach, a media planner must answer a similar question with frequency: How much is enough? An often-quoted guideline is that **effective frequency**, *the number of times a message needs to be seen to make an impression or achieve a specific level of awareness*, is somewhere between 3 and 10. In reality, this is not much of a guideline because the range is so wide. A 10 frequency, for example, requires a media budget over three times as large as that required for a frequency of 3. Most brands do not have this kind of budget flexibility. The "right" level of frequency is that which cost-effectively affects attitudes and/or behavior. One of the best ways for a company to determine this is to track customer responses, testing various levels of frequency.

Another reason the level of effective frequency will vary with every brand is that there are so many variables that determine the impact of a brand message. Some of these variables are:

1. *The offer—its value and complexity.* Making prospects understand that a local bank now offers "free checking" does not require nearly as much frequency as does getting them to understand that the bank offers four different savings-plan options (let alone getting them to remember what those options are and how they differ).

2. *The attention value of the medium itself.* Some media vehicles demand more attention than others, or attention of a different kind (an outdoor board may be startling, for example, but a TV commercial may command more sustained attention).

3. *The attention-getting power of the message itself.* The more creative and attention-getting a message is, the more likely it will have the desired effect.

4. *The target audience's level of need or desire to learn about a brand.* Some product categories are simply more interesting than others and automatically get attention more easily. Most people, for example, find cars more interesting than laundry detergents. When audience interest is high, less frequency may be needed.

5. *The MC objectives.* If the communication objective is to increase brand awareness rather than to change behavior, probably less frequency will be needed.

6. *Personal influences.* Word of mouth can greatly affect the impact of a message. If the word of mouth is negative, more frequency will be needed to help counter the negative messages.

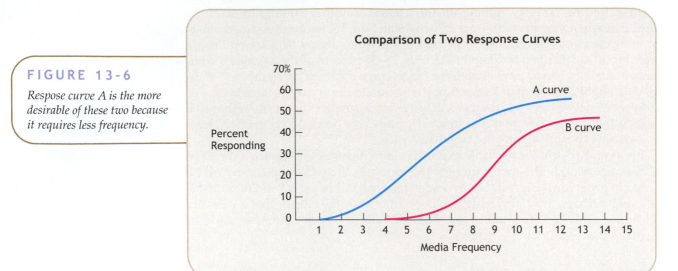

FIGURE 13-6

Respose curve A is the more desirable of these two because it requires less frequency.

7. *The amount of competitive brand messages.* Generally, the more frequency competitive brand messages have, the more frequency is needed for your brand. **Share of voice** is *the percentage of media spending in a particular category that comes from one brand.* Having a 25 share of voice means that, of all the media dollars spent in the category within a given time period, 25 percent came from this brand. Most marketers and media planners agree that a brand must maintain a competitive share of voice. In political campaigns, especially for national elections, candidates try to raise as much money as possible so they can have greater message frequency than their opponents.

The S curve in Figure 13–6 helps explain the concept of effective frequency by showing how different levels of frequency create difference levels of response. Most media planners agree that there must be a minimum level of frequency before any impact will occur. As the frequency continues to increase, however, there comes a point where additional increases have little or no effect. At this point, a marketer's return on the media investment becomes zero or negative. One of two things are generally happening at this point. Either most of the target audience who are going to respond have done so or *the brand messages that once attracted attention and motivated the target are no longer doing so*—a situation called **message wearout.**

Another important aspect of the frequency response curve is that it can shift to being more responsive or less responsive. Again in Figure 13–6, note that there are two S response curves. The A curve is the more desirable because it generates more response from a lower level of frequency, meaning the average cost per response is less than that of the B curve.

There are several variables that can influence whether the S curve is more or less efficient. One is the media being used and whether they are reaching those most likely to buy. Assume that response curves A and B were both for an ad offering a McDonald's Big Mac hamburger for 89 cents. The A response curve might represent a media mix that reached teenagers, while the B curve might represent a media mix that reached more middle-aged and older customers—those not nearly as interested in the offer. Another variable can be the offer itself. Suppose now that McDonald's sent two Big Mac offers to the same teen audience. Offer A advertised Big Macs for 89 cents, and offer B set the price at $1.19. Because the 89 cent offer is more attractive to the target audience, it would generate a higher response represented by A response curve.

Frequency Distribution Analysis

When planning frequency, it is important to keep in mind that frequency is an average, which means that some of those reached will have more exposures and others fewer than the frequency figure itself. For example, when a media plan has a frequency of 7, about half of the target audience will be exposed more than seven times and half less than seven times. For this reason, media planners often do a **frequency distribution analysis** (sometimes referred to as a **quintile analysis**). This is *an analysis that divides a target audience into equal segments and establishes an average frequency for each of these segments.* A quintile analysis, specifically, is when the audience is divided into five equal segments. (*Quintus* is the Latin word for "fifth.") For a media plan with a frequency of 7, a quintile analysis would indicate that the top 20 percent would receive six times as many exposure opportunities as the bottom 20 percent of the target audience, as the following shows:

Quintiles	Frequency
Top 20% of audience	12
Next 20%	9
Next 20%	6
Next 20%	4
Bottom 20%	2

In this example, 60 percent of the target was exposed less than seven times. Therefore, if it had been decided that seven exposures were important in order for the target to understand and remember a particular brand message, it would be necessary to have an overall frequency of 10 or more to guarantee that the *majority* of the target did, in fact, have at least seven opportunities to be exposed to the brand message.

Media Environment

Cable channels with specialized content, such as Home & Garden, the Weather Channel, the History Channel, and Arts and Entertainment (A & E) have developed strong brand environments for themselves and their audiences. They provide a prestigious media environment, and they have strong relationships with their audiences, who come to the channels with specific expectations. This means these audiences will be most receptive to product offerings related to program content. A manufacturer of plant fertilizer, for example, would likely do well by buying time on the Home & Garden channel.

Another consideration in media planning is the compatibility between a media vehicle's image and the brand's image. For some brands, having their messages in the *National Enquirer* and on the "Jerry Springer" show is no problem. However, these sensational vehicles would not provide a compatible media environment for such status brands as Tiffany's and Lexus, nor for even traditional family brands such as Hershey's chocolate, Kraft mayonnaise, or Johnson & Johnson baby shampoo.

A vehicle's image is determined not only by its content but also by the brands and products whose advertising it carries. The next time you are going through checkout at your local supermarket, look at copies of the various tabloids to see which brands and products have bought display and classified advertising space in these publications. You'll probably find ads for psychic readers, diet pills, sex aids, and dating services.

Although the practice was more prevalent in the early days of television, you still see on some packages and in some print ads the line "As seen on TV." For little-known brands, advertising on TV and in other media environments that are well respected can be an added value for a brand. In the United States, marketers pay two to three times beyond normal rates to advertise during the Super Bowl just to be associated with this spectacular global TV event.

As explained in Chapters 11 and 12, each medium has its own strengths and weaknesses. Table 13–2 is a summary of how major media compare with regard to other attributes that are often considered in media planning.

Media Cost

No brand has an unlimited amount of money to spend on media. Cost must always, therefore, be a consideration when making any kind of media decision. Although the costs of time and space are important to know, what is even more important to keep in mind is the cost for creating a lead or a purchase. An easy way to think about most media costs is to think how the post office charges for delivering mail. The more people you send something to, the more it costs. Also the bigger the pieces you send to each, the more it costs. The same for media—the larger the audience, the greater the cost, and the bigger the message (in length of time or size), the greater the cost. Because media costs are so important, they are discussed at several places in this book (see, e.g., Chapters 11 and 12).

"Free" Media

Marketers often talk about free media with regard to brand publicity and sending messages over the Internet. While it is true that these are exceptions to media costs based on size of audience and size of the message being delivered, there are indirect costs. For example, the way many brand publicity stories get placed is through personal contacts that the public relations people have with media editors. It often takes years of phone calls, press parties, and lunches to create a good relationship with these editors—all of which requires staff time and expenses. As for the Internet, creating and maintaining a website is not free, and responding to website traffic can be extremely expensive.

Cost per Thousand

To determine which are the best values among all the many vehicle alternatives, media planners use several tools. The most common are cost per thousand, cost per point, and cost per response.

Because the number of audience members (e.g., customers, households, businesses) is different for every communication vehicle, comparing the cost of a unit of time or space can often be misleading. It is much smarter to compare **cost per thousand (CPM),** *what a communication vehicle charges to deliver a message to 1,000 members of its audience.* A CPM is determined by using the following simple formula:

$$\frac{\text{Cost of ad unit} \times 1,000}{\text{Circulation or audience}} = \text{CPM}$$

Several examples will help explain. Radio station A charges $500 for a 60-second commercial, and station B charges $1,500. Both stations are in the same DMA. On the surface, it would seem that station A would be a much better buy because it charges $1,000 less for the same amount of time. But this can be extremely misleading. To

T A B L E   1 3 - 2   Relative Attributes of Major Media

	Magazine (local)	Newspaper	Outdoor	Television	Radio (local)	Direct mail	Tele-marketing	Internet	Phone	Pack-aging
Target Selectivity	good	poor	poor*	bdct. average/ cable good	good	best	best	good/ best**	best	best
Reach	average	best	high	high	low	low	low	low	low	best
Message impact	average	average	low	average	low	high	high	low	high	high
Geographic flexibility	poor	poor	good	national poor/ local good	good	good	good	low	best	good
Lead time to use	long	short	long	national long/ local short	short	medium	short	short	short	long
Ability to control time of exposure	poor	good	poor	best	best	good	best	best	best	poor
Where vehicles used most	home/ some away	home	out of home	home	home/ car	home/ office	home/ office	home/ office	home/ office/ car	home

*but good geographically
**e-mail is best

Based on "General Characteristics of Major Media Forms," in *Media Planning: A Practical Guide*, Jim Surmanek, NTC, 1995.

determine which is the better value, a planner must also know the size of the audience for each station's program in which the commercial would run. As shown in the following calculation, station A's audience is 30,000 and station B's is 120,000:

	Station A	Station B
Cost of a :60 time slot	$500	$1,500
Audience	30,000	120,000
CPM	$\dfrac{\$500 \times 1,000}{30,000} = \$16.66$	$\dfrac{\$1,500 \times 1,000}{120,000} = \$12.50$

As you can see, station B offers greater value, since its CPM is only $12.50, more than $4.00 less than station A's ($16.66).

The same CPM formula is used for comparing cost efficiencies of different print vehicles. As the following shows, magazine B offers a better CPM than magazine A, even though A's cost per page is less:

	Magazine A	Magazine B
Cost of a full page ad	$20,000	$30,000
Circulation	800,000	1,500,000
CPM	$\dfrac{\$20,000 \times 1,000}{800,000} = \$25$	$\dfrac{\$30,000 \times 1,000}{1,500,000} = \$20$

As discussed earlier, the best way to compare the reach of similar communication vehicles, however, is to compare targeted reach. This tells the cost after taking into account wasted circulation. The CPM formula applies, except that the targeted reach (in actual numbers) is substituted for the vehicle's total audience.

To show how this can change a media decision based on simple CPM, we'll use the two magazines in the calculation above and assume a target of "females with a college education who participate in outdoor sports." Magazine A reaches 200,000 households where our target lives and magazine B reaches 250,000. As you can see, the targeted cost per thousand (TCPM) is $20 lower for magazine A than for magazine B, even though the opposite was true when the two were compared on the basis of total audience CPM:

	Magazine A	Magazine B
Cost of a full page ad	$20,000	$30,000
Targeted circulation	200,000	250,000
TCPM	$\dfrac{\$20,000 \times 1,000}{200,000} = \$100$	$\dfrac{\$30,000 \times 1,000}{250,000} = \$120$

Cost per Point and Cost per Response

Similar to CPM is **cost per point (CPP)**, a measure *used to compare same-medium broadcast vehicles.* In this use, the word *point* is shorthand for *rating point,* which you will recall is 1 percent of a station's coverage area. Since the broadcast coverage areas for most TV and radio stations in a market is the DMA, a rating point represents the same number of households for all the market's stations.

You cannot, however, compare the CPP for a broadcast program in one DMA with that in another DMA. This is because every DMA has a different number of households, and thus a different basis for determining what 1 percent (i.e., one rating point) is. Take Chicago and Indianapolis, for example. One rating point in Indianapolis represents 9,633 households, while one rating point in Chicago represents 32,047 households. When you change the basis on which a percentage is figured, then the value of that percentage changes. Which would you rather have, 1 percent of $1,000 or 1 percent of $1 million? Obviously, there is a significant difference ($10 versus $10,000).

A word of caution: CPPs should be used to compare vehicles only within the same type of medium (e.g., one radio station versus another). They should not be used to compare two different types of vehicles, such as radio and TV or newspapers and radio. This is because each medium has its own strengths (which were discussed in Chapter 11).

Because the ultimate objective of any marketing communication program is to motivate the target audience to respond in some way, the ideal way to compare the cost effectiveness of different vehicles, regardless of their media type, is on the basis of the **cost per response (CPR)** generated by each of the vehicles, *a measure figured by dividing the media cost of using one vehicle by the number of responses generated by the message in that vehicle.* (This type of comparison assumes that the message, creative, and offer are held constant.) The desired response needs to be defined in any behavioral way, such as "bought the product," "made a store visit," or "requested more information about the brand or offer."

Here's one example how CPR is used. The Golden Moon, a neighborhood family Chinese restaurant, runs an ad in the local paper, which costs $810. Every one of the 30,000 households that subscribe or buy the paper is exposed to the ad. This means that it not only reaches people who live near the restaurant and like to eat in Chinese restaurants but also a lot of people who are not even prospects. Because the circulation is 30,000, and only 5,000 of the homes exposed to the ad are prospects, you could say that there is a lot of wasted circulation.

Before concluding that the local newspaper shouldn't be used again because of the high percentage of wasted reach, there are several questions that must be answered: (1) How many responses did the ad generate? (2) What was the cost of each response? and (3) Are there other media that are more cost-effective to use? The answer to the first question is that 90 couples responded by coming in for dinner. The owner was able to know this because the ad offered a free dessert to everyone who mentioned the ad. To answer the second question and determine the cost per response (CPR), we simply divide the number responding by the cost of the ad and then add the cost of each free dessert to the answer:

	Newspaper
Media cost	$810 for the ad
Number of responses	90

Cost per response $\dfrac{\$810}{90} = \$9 + \$2$ dessert $= \$11$ per response

To answer the third question—are there more cost-effective media?—the restaurant made the same offer using two other communication vehicles, radio and direct mail (each at a different time and each with a different free offer so the owner could determine to which media message customers were responding). The calculations below show the CPR results, including the cost of the free offer, when the offer was made by radio and by direct mail. As can be seen, the newspaper's cost per response was the lowest, even though the cost of the ad—$810—was more than the radio ad and nearly the same as the cost of direct mail.

	Radio	Direct Mail
Media cost	$540	$980
Number of responses	30	70

Cost per response $\dfrac{\$540}{30} = \$18 + \$2$ drink $= \$20$ $\dfrac{\$980}{70} = \$14 + \$2$ appetizer $= \$16$

When more than one vehicle is being used at a time in the same market, one way to determine which vehicle was responsible for which set of responses is to use coded coupons. Each ad is given a different code number that refers to a particular vehicle.

The above example has been kept simple for the sake of explanation. Most brands use a variety of communication vehicles (i.e., a media mix), which makes these analyses more complex but, with computers and good planning, still possible to do.

CREATING THE MEDIA PLAN

A media plan is designed to help accomplish marketing objectives. As with all types of marketing plans, media plans contain targets, objectives, strategies, and tactics. In most cases, setting media objectives is not too difficult because they are driven by the overall marketing strategies. The more difficult part is determining the best media strategies for achieving the objectives.

In many agencies and companies, message-design decisions are still made before media objectives and strategies are determined. When this is done, media planners must select media to fit the creative message. If only magazine ads and TV commercials have been prepared, for example, then magazine space and TV time are the only media that should be purchased. But, as stated before, media plans are increasingly being made alongside creative plans. This is because: a) there are now more media alternatives than ever before, b) because media are a major portion of most MC budgets, and c) because some audiences are so difficult to reach that media must first be selected and then messages designed accordingly, as was the situation in the Buddy Lee case (see Exhibit 13–10).

With cross-functional planning, creative and media departments work together, exploring the best message-design options for a brand while simultaneously exploring the best media options. When done in this way, media planning uses the advantages of each approach (e.g., certain key media are chosen and then messages are designed for them; certain key messages are designed and media are selected that can best deliver them). Exploring media opportunities in this way, and determining their cost efficiencies and impact, is an ongoing exercise in building a media plan. The planning guidelines that follow should be interpreted as directional, not absolute. In other words, to say that one-way media are more appropriate for creating brand awareness doesn't mean there is never a situation where interactive media could not be used cost-effectively to do this.

The type of product is another factor in media decisions. By their very nature, low-involvement products don't attract as much attention as high-involvement products. Therefore, when advertising detergent, paper towels, or industrial cleaning services, planners should consider more intrusive media. Another strategy, however, is selecting media whose editorial content creates a more receptive environment. For detergent and paper-towel brands, a "shelter" magazine such as *Better Homes & Gardens* or the Home & Garden Television channel would provide such an environment. On the other hand, high-involvement products such as luxury goods and entertainment offers can make use of print media where readers select what stories and ads they want to see.

EXHIBIT 13-10

Because of the increasing power of the Internet to reach targeted audiences, websites like this one for the Lee Jeans' "Buddy Lee" campaign was included by the Fallon agency as part of the brand's media plan.

Target Audiences

The size of a target audience, plus its degree of commonality, affects media decisions. For example, addressable media would be more appropriate for reaching 5,000 households in a city of 100,000 households than would mass media; on the other hand, if the target size in this same metro area is 50,000, mass media would probably be more cost-effective. Similarly, if the people in the target audience have a high degree of commonality, the more likely it is that niche media can be found that will reach a high percentage of that target. Furthermore, the more tightly targeted the audience, the more likely it is that interactive and addressable media will be cost-effective. In contrast, when there are few commonalities within a target audience, then mass media are often more cost-effective.

Media Objectives

Although the target audience is provided by the marketing plan, media planners must decide how best to reach the audience segments, such as heavy users, light users, prospects, and (for BtB marketing) members of the distribution channel. The following are the types of questions that media people must answer in order to create an integrated media plan:

- *What types of sales promotion offers should be made, at what times, and to whom?* Coupons, for example, are delivered by print media (broadcast media can't deliver coupons). Some companies are experimenting with offering coupons online that customers can print out. A concern with this delivery system, however, is that a customer may print out more than one coupon. Certain software programs can limit each computer to one coupon download, but this requires an additional cost for marketers.

- *What direct-response efforts (direct mail and telemarketing) are planned that will need other media support?* As will be explained in Chapter 17, supporting direct mail and telemarketing offers with other media can increase the response rate ("watch for introductory coupon arriving in the mail soon").

- *What are the major publicity programs, and to whom should news releases be sent?* A company that advertises in a BtB trade publication may find that publication more willing to accept a news release than one in which it does not advertise. Local media are also more receptive of press releases from major advertisers. In short, the idea is that you support us and we'll support you.

- *Are there new/improved product introductions planned?* When new products are introduced in the United States, they are often done so in a regional "rollout" rather than all at one time nationwide. This allows production to gradually increase its efficiencies and enables the MC plan to be tested. Media planners need to be aware of the rollout schedule. In Europe, rollouts are often done country by country because each country has its own sales and marketing teams.

- *What levels of distribution exist in targeted geographical areas?* As noted earlier, consumer products marketers should buy media in a given area only after a minimal level of distribution (generally 60 percent) has been achieved. If media dollars are invested with only 40 percent distribution, say, then 6 out of 10 people who are persuaded to look for the brand will probably not find it.

- *What is the relative importance of the brand's various targets?* In most cases, media planners must consider different segments among the target audience (e.g., heavy and light users, married and single people). Different reach and frequency objectives should be set for each, according to the overall objectives of the campaign.

- *To what extent do category sales fluctuate?* Seasonal, day-of-week, and geographical fluctuations are some of the purchasing variables media planners must consider.

Media objectives explain what needs to be accomplished in order to connect with customers and prospects. The two most general media objectives are reach and frequency. As with all marketing objectives, media objectives should be measurable. The following are examples of media objectives:

- *Reach:* Have a minimum reach of 65 during each of the first three quarters of the year, and 80 in last quarter.

- *Frequency:* Have a minimum frequency of 7 in markets where share is over 20 percent; have a minimum frequency of 10 in all other markets where there is brand distribution.

- *Target allocation:* Put 75 percent of media weight against prospective customers and 25 percent against current customers.

- *Timing:* Begin advertising one month before seasonal buying begins.

- *Cross-function reach:* Use media that will deliver coupons to 60 percent of the target audience.

- *Intermedia action:* Use media that will drive prospective customers to brand website, generating at least 20,000 site visits a month.

- *Interactivity:* Respond to 95 percent of customer/prospect-initiated e-mails within 24 hours.

- *Interactivity:* Operate customer-service center 24/7.

Media Strategy Considerations

Media strategies are ideas about *how* media objectives will be accomplished. To develop creative cost-effective media-use ideas requires an in-depth understanding of each medium's characteristics (described in Chapters 11 and 12), as well as a thorough understanding of the target audience, including its media and buying habits.

An idea about how to use media effectively is more than just identifying which media should be used ("spend half the money in TV, a fourth in newspapers, and a fourth in outdoor"). Media strategy is about how media can help create a brand experience and engage customers and prospects—a connection. Good media strategy requires creative aggregation of media and their applications, as Mark Goldstein, the worldwide brand director at the MC agency Fallon has said.[5]

> "Media are no longer planned and bought; instead they're created, aggregated, and partnered."
>
> Mark Goldstein, Worldwide Brand Director, Fallon

Recall from the chapter opening case how the Fallon agency used a strategic media idea to reposition Lee jeans. The planners selected media that reached the target audience at unexpected times (late, late night) in communication vehicles whose image said nontraditional, off-the-wall, wacky. Part of the media strategy of using a **teaser campaign**—*a series of messages that don't carry any brand identification but that are designed to create curiosity*—was to build interest in later brand messages. It also allowed the target audience, which resents being sold to, an opportunity to "discover" the Buddy Lee story with a more open mind-set.

A big media idea can also be based on customer retention and cost savings. For example, an entertainment ticketing agency that uses its database to find customers who have purchased tickets to see country-western entertainers can send those customers an automated e-mail and/or place an automated phone call to alert them to a just-scheduled Garth Brooks concert. Either message could give this target audience a chance to purchase tickets before the concert is widely advertised and thus allows them to get the best choice of seats—an added value for loyal customers. Automated e-mail and phone calls (1) have an extremely low cost, (2) demand attention, and (3) allow for a type of personalization that significantly increases the level of response.

Customers' Buying Decision Process

Media strategy should be driven by customers' buying decision processes, which were discussed in Chapter 5. For considered purchases, for example, the buying decision process often follows the AIDA model—attention, interest, desire, action. IBM uses the AIDA model to drive much of its media decisions. Each step in the process requires different media. As you will recall, AIDA is a cognitive model that is best applied to high-involvement products such as cars and computers. However, since targeted prospects are in various stages of the buying processes, most major high-involvement brands will use a mix of media so that customers and prospects will be engaged at each step. The more that is known about where customers and prospects are in their buying decision process, the more targeted the media and messages can be to their respective stages.

Strategy also has to be adjusted for audience size, complexity of the message, and the product's price points. For example, if you were selling high-end landscaping, you would probably get a list of the most expensive real estate neighborhoods in the metro area and use addressable media to reach owners in this segment. Because of the relatively small size of the audience and the high cost of the service, mass media would deliver too much waste.

For high-competition product categories such as computers and cars, mass media are useful to create attention and maintain brand awareness and interest. However, once a customer enters the desire and action stages for these products, interactive media (mail, e-mail, phone) may be more appropriate and effective. The closer to the action step, the more personal the message delivery needs to be. The more personal the message and the medium, generally the more impact the two will have (see Figure 13–7). Although interactive and addressable media are expensive, the cost often can be justified because of their ability to motivate behavior.

The importance of interactivity during the action stage cannot be overstated. In their early phases e-business companies such as CDnow and Amazon.com found that people often went to their company websites, filled shopping carts, got ready to check out, found themselves with a question and no way to get it answered, so abandoned their shopping carts. That's why many e-commerce companies now make their sites interactive and provide e-mail addresses and phone numbers, as well as hyperlinks to customer service. Making sure that an interested customer can talk to someone in person is vital in all considered-purchase situations, not just in e-commerce.

Response Media

With increasing use of interactive media, companies must be prepared not only to hear from customers but to also respond. Unfortunately, most companies have the media available but not enough personnel to prepare and send replies, especially in a timely fashion (within 24 hours for phone and mail contacts). One of the benefits of websites is that they can contain an unlimited amount of data that can answer customer and prospect questions. The challenge is to provide navigational guides that make it easy for website visitors to find the information they need. This can reduce the demand for a human response. Also automated answering systems (as described in Chapter 12), if properly designed, can take the place of live telephone. In banking, for example, customers who want to know how much they have in their checking accounts can get the answer without talking to a person. Many people call airlines to find out if planes are departing or arriving on time; making it easy for them to get this information (e.g., requiring them to simply punch in flight number) adds value to the service.

Many companies have found a useful response tool in proprietary software that allows customers to link to the company from their home computers. Print media have effectively been used to carry the CDs. An example is the Kinko's File Prep Tool shown in Exhibit 13–11, which was distributed with the November 2000 issue of the business magazine *Fast Company*. This CD can be used to send documents directly to Kinko's for printing. The various uses of response media are discussed in more detail in Chapter 17.

FIGURE 13-7

The more interactive the medium, the more impact it will generally have.

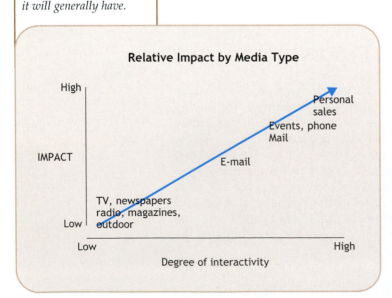

Relative Impact by Media Type

Personal sales
Events, phone
Mail
E-mail
TV, newspapers radio, magazines, outdoor

High
IMPACT
Low

Low — High
Degree of interactivity

Apertures

A media strategy used by the advertising agency DDB Worldwide combines an understanding of contact points and buyer decision processes. This agency uses the word **apertures** (which means "opening") to describe *any situation in which the target audience is most receptive to a brand message.* In photography, an aperture is the opening in a camera's lens. The further the lens is open (the wider its aperture), the more light that passes through. A narrow aperture allows relatively little light into a camera. The idea is that the more open a person is to receiving a message, the more impact that message can have. In a sports stadium for example, the spectators' aperture is much more open to brand messages related to food, drink, and sporting goods than it is to political messages, dietary aids, and life insurance offers. Thus, media strategy that is built by following customers through their daily lives can identify opportunities that take advantage of these apertures.

Self-Selection

Another media strategy that integrates creative and media planning is to use mass media to maximize the reach of a brand message that invites those interested to contact the company for more information. As described in Chapter 7, this kind of self-selection strategy is used to prompt prospects to "raise their hand." Once a prospect responds, then one-to-one, interactive media can be used to deliver personalized messages and further engage these prospects.

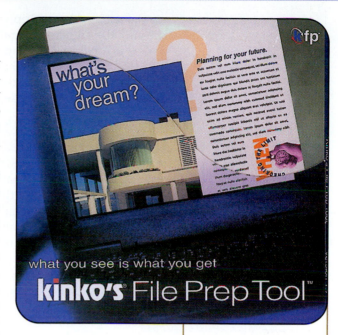

EXHIBIT 13-11

Magazines, mail, and even newspapers (that are delivered in plastic bags) are now carriers of CD-ROMs that can be used to connect online to a company.

Media Weight: Gross Rating Points

To allocate different levels of support for different target segments and different geographical areas, media planners use a concept called **media weight,** which is *an indication of the relative impact of a media mix.* For example, for products bought by one segment but used by another, such as hot dogs (parents buy them but children eat them), a weighting strategy could be 65 percent placed to reach parents and 35 percent placed to reach children.

Media weights can be figured in a variety of ways such as in terms of media dollars or in terms of reach and frequency. Some brands, for example, allocate media weight based on a percentage of sales. If Chicago has four times the sales of Indianapolis, for example, then Chicago would be allocated four times as many media dollars. The problem with comparing on the basis of dollars is that media costs vary from market to market. In this case, the CPM for a prime-time TV ad is approximately $30 in Chicago but only $22 in Indianapolis. So even though Chicago would be given four times as many media dollars, the brand would not be able to deliver four times as many messages in Chicago.

This is why *a combination of reach and frequency measures,* called **gross rating points (GRP),** is used when doing media planning for a variety of markets. GRPs are determined by multiplying reach (the number of people exposed to vehicles carrying the brand message) by frequency (the number of insertions or units purchased in a particular communication vehicle within a specified time period). For example, if 3M company had five ads in *Modern Office Supplies* magazine, which reaches 50 percent of the office-supply market (3M's target), then the total GRPs generated by these five insertions would be 250:

$$50\% \text{ reach} \times 5 \text{ insertions} = 250 \text{ GRPs}$$

GRPs ideally should be compared only for mixes of vehicles within the same medium. GRPs for TV, newspapers, and direct mail cannot be reliably compared because different media have different levels of impact. Does a 30-second TV ad have more or less impact than a half-page newspaper ad, an outdoor board, or a 60-second radio commercial? Each medium has its own characteristics that affect the impact of a brand message exposure.

Companies also figure media weights for competing brands in order to determine how much weight of their own to use in certain areas. For example, if Harley-Davidson found that Honda was significantly increasing its media weight to reach 16- to 24-year-olds, it may counter by increasing its media weight to reach this segment as well.

Targeted Rating Points

Remember the discussion about reach versus targeted reach? The same idea applies to GRPs. Marketers can and should look at media schedules in terms of targeted rating points (TRPs). This gives them a better idea of what percentage of a communication vehicle's audience is in the brand's target by accounting for the wasted reach. The following sections show how to calculate GRPs and TRPs.

Calculating GRPs

Using a national broadcast media mix of four TV programs, Table 13–3 demonstrates how gross rating points (GRPs) are figured. In this example, the universe is all TV households (HHs) in the United States. The reach of each program is determined by its rating. The frequency is the number of times a brand message ran in each program within a four-week period. The ads that ran in the *CBS Evening News* each had a reach of 6 because the program had a rating of 6. And because the ads ran five times they had a frequency of 5, making the GRPs generated by using this program 30:

$$6 \text{ (reach)} \times 5 \text{ (frequency)} = 30 \text{ GRPs}$$

TABLE 13-3   GRPs Based on Total U.S. HH Coverage

Programs	Program Rating		Frequency		GRPs
CBS Evening News	6	×	5	=	30
Friends	10	×	4	=	40
Law & Order	15	×	6	=	90
Monday Night Football	12	×	3	=	36
Total					196

Doing the same calculations for the other three programs and then adding the totals equals 196 GRPs, as the table shows.

What this literally means is that 196 percent of U.S. HHs were reached, which, of course, is mathematically impossible. Just as you can't eat more than 100 percent of a pie, you cannot reach more than 100 percent of an audience. The reason GRPs are often over 100 is duplication—the fact that many of those reached were reached more than once. In this example, some households who watched the "CBS Evening News" may not only have watched it more than once but may also have watched one or more "Law & Order" shows in which the ads ran. Other HHs that were reached may have seen more than one "Friends" show, as well as "Monday Night Football" at least once.

To determine the amount of duplication, agencies use computer programs based on audience research done by companies such as Simmons Market Research Bureau (SMRB). For the sake of discussion, let's assume that in Table 13–4 the computer models showed reach to be 49. Once this has been determined, the frequency can easily be found by simply dividing the total number of GRPs by the reach: 196 ÷ 49 = 4. Thus, in this example, 49 percent of U.S. households were, on average, exposed four times to the brand message. In reality, however, some of the 49 percent were only exposed one or two times, while very heavy TV viewers may have been exposed as many as 18 times (the total number of times the brand message was run).

Note again that R × F = GRPs. This is important because it illustrates the relationship between reach and frequency. When you have a set number of GRPs, increase one and the other must decrease. In the above example, the reach of 49 multiplied by the frequency of 4 equals 196. If the reach were 63, then the frequency would be approximately 3; if the frequency were increased to 5, then the reach would be reduced to around 39.

Calculating Targeted Rating Points

If AT&T is interested in reaching just HHs with incomes of over $75,000 a year and the company used the national media schedule shown in Table 13–4, the targeted rating points (TRPs) would be significantly less than 196 GRPs because many HHs reached by these programs have annual incomes below $75,000. As shown in Table 13–4 when figured on the basis of TRPs, the reach numbers are significantly less for each show although the frequency numbers don't change. "CBS Evening News'" targeted reach, for example, is only 3, indicating that half of the households tuned to the program were outside the target. The TRPs are only 92, much smaller than

TABLE 13-4   TRPs Based on HHs With Incomes of $75,000+

Programs	Targeted HH Rating		Frequency		TRPs
CBS Evening News	3	×	5	=	15
Friends	5	×	4	=	20
Law & Order	7	×	6	=	42
Monday Night Football	5	×	3	=	15
Total					92

196, suggesting a targeted reach of only 24; the frequency, however, would continue to be nearly the same: $92 \div 24 = 3.8$.

Media Scheduling

Three commonly used scheduling strategies are called flighting, continuous scheduling, and pulsing. Figure 13–8 demonstrates how these strategies differ.

Flighting is *a scheduling strategy in which planned messages run in intermittent periods*. Flighting is used for products whose sales fluctuate seasonally. It is also used when budgets are limited; the idea is that when media are running in flights, they will provide sufficient message impact to have a presence. With the huge amount of commercial message clutter that exists today, most media planners believe there must be a certain level of frequency or messages that will have little or no impact on the target audience; flighting can help them achieve this frequency without draining the budget.

The opposite of flighting is **continuous scheduling,** which means *placing media throughout the year with equal weight in each month*. This scheduling strategy is used more often by brands with large budgets and whose sales are fairly constant throughout the year. It is also a strategy used by retailers that desire to maintain a certain level of awareness. Another rationale for a continuous scheduling strategy is that when a product is frequently purchased or, in the case of BtB products, when the brand decision-making process is relatively long, prospects need constant brand reminders. **Pulsing** is *a combination of flighting and continuous strategies that provides a "floor" of media support throughout the year with periodic increases*. Fast-food and beverage companies with large media budgets often use a pulsing schedule.

Once a media schedule is worked out, it is presented as a flow chart such as the one in Figure 13–9 for Lee Jeans' Buddy Lee campaign.

Seasonality and Timing

If a product has seasonal fluctuations, media buys are generally scheduled with similar fluctuations. These do not occur simultaneously because marketing communication, with the exception of sales promotion, generally has a lag effect. For

FIGURE 13-8

Most companies use one of these three media scheduling strategies.

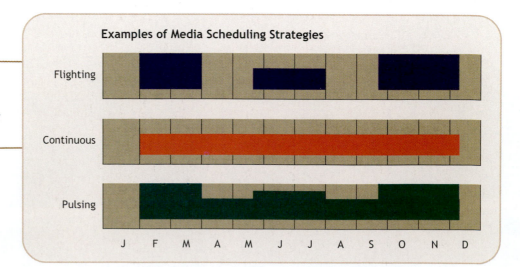

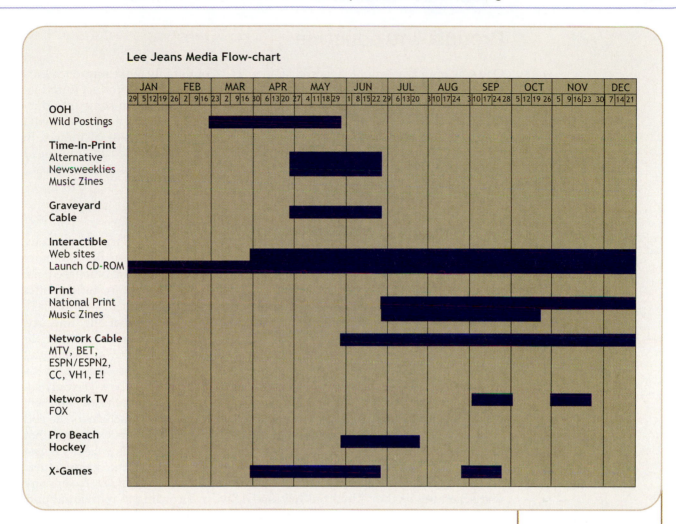

FIGURE 13-9

Bars and their thickness show when the various media are used and to what extent.

example, if tennis racket sales begin increasing in April in the northern part of the United States, then marketing communication should begin increasing in March.

In some categories, such as restaurants and movie theaters, sales vary by day of week, with the majority of sales coming on weekends. Media buys supporting these businesses are often scheduled Thursday–Saturday to reach people when they are making plans for the weekend. Finally, some brands schedule media by time of day. Breakfast foods, for example, may schedule brand messages to reach customers in the morning when they are thinking "breakfast."

In BtB media planning, often major trade shows require media support both prior to and during the shows in the markets where the shows are held. BtB media planning is also heavily influenced by introductions of new and improved products.

Promotional lead time differs category by category. Companies can plan their seasonal spending according to when competitors begin theirs, or experiment each year with different starting dates in a few markets. Timing is also determined by the brand message. An awareness/image message requires a longer lead time to have an effect than does a promotional offer message. A seasonal promotional offer, however, should be made only when the target audience is in a buying mood. Swimsuit manufacturer Jantzen, for example, might start its brand advertising in February but not run any promotional offers until April and May when the weather has turned nice and people are ready to buy.

Product Introduction

One way brands attempt to retain customers is to continually make improvements and expand product offers. Each major improvement and new-product introduction needs media support. The timing for this support varies. In some introductions, companies wait until the product is in distribution; in others, media placement begins ahead of time to build the interest and desire of customers. In the case of products sold through retail, media buys are scheduled slightly ahead of the product launch to motivate retailers to stock the new/improved products.

Purchase Cycle

Some marketers feel that a product's purchase cycle (i.e., how often customers buy the product) should influence media scheduling. The argument is that the more frequently products in a particular category, such as soft drinks, are purchased, the more frequency is needed for brand messages—and vice versa for infrequently purchased products such as refrigerators and cars. This argument would make sense if all the buyers of refrigerators and cars bought them all at one time, say, every three years. In reality, however, there is no major seasonal variation for durable products such as refrigerators and cars; they are constantly being bought.

For this reason, you see advertising for major-purchase items year-round because companies cannot know when each prospect will want to buy. The only solution to this problem is to track customers who make major purchases and then, on a customer-by-customer basis, send out brand messages as each nears the end of a purchase cycle. For example, let's say a manufacturer of fire trucks knows that the average fire district replaces its trucks every five years. This would suggest that four years after a district has purchased its fleet of trucks, the manufacturer should begin sending information on its newest models to this district. A company that schedules its individualized message delivery according to individual purchase cycles must have a good customer database and do customer tracking.

Media Mix

Determining a media mix involves two basic decisions—which media to use and how much of each. Most media plans include both one-way and interactive media, although the majority of plans are heavy on one-way media. The simple approach to a media mix focuses on selecting individual media; more sophisticated media planning aims to pick the combination of media that can create synergy.[6] There are hundreds of communication vehicles from which to choose but thousands of ways to combine them, hence the challenge of media planning.

There is no one best mix—every brand situation is different, and the mix should be driven by the media and marketing objectives. When the objective is to maximize reach, the more media used, the faster reach will increase. Table 13–5 shows the unduplicated reach when two different media are used. (This table is an approximation; every combination of two media varies.) For example, say one medium had a reach of 45 and the other a reach of 55. As shown, the combined reach (underlined) is 75.

Lead Time

Another factor in determining a media mix is the lead time available, which is based on a calculation of the number of days needed to produce the message. Any

T A B L E   1 3 - 5   Combined Reach of Two Media

Reach of Second Medium	Reach of One Medium					
	25	35	45	55	65	75
25	46	51	59	66	74	81
35		58	64	71	77	84
45			70	<u>75</u>	81	86
55				80	84	89
65					88	91
75						94

Source: Karsh & Hagan Communication Agency, 2000.

sudden changes in the marketing plan, which are more the rule than the exception, generally require changes in the media mix. When media budgets need to be kept flexible, it is best not to depend heavily on national TV and magazines because they demand relatively long lead times; and, once contracts are signed for space and time, it is difficult (although not always impossible) to get out of the commitment.

Media Concentration

Media mix strategy is influenced by the degree of concentration that is needed in a plan, and this is basically a qualitative decision. A more concentrated media mix uses fewer media and communication vehicles compared to a broad media mix, which uses more media types and vehicles.

A *concentrated media mix* strategy delivers greater frequency (at the expense of reach). Newspapers and magazines provide vehicle concentration because most are sent repeatedly (via subscriptions) to the same audience members. Audiences for broadcast programs are not as consistent and usually broader in their characteristics. Another rationale for a concentrated mix is that it may help build strong relationships with a smaller portion of a target audience, those who represent the heavy users. This may be more productive in the long term than building weaker relationships with a large audience. This is because those customers with a strong brand relationship are more likely to respond and more likely to talk positively about the brand to others.

Production costs are another factor in the decision to concentrate media. Using fewer media means that fewer messages need to be produced. If radio, TV, outdoor, and magazines are in a mix, four completely different message formats must be produced. For a small budget, such production can be a major expense. Finally, concentrating media dollars in fewer media can often result in getting more promotional support from these media—and better space and time—compared to spreading out the media buy and not being a significant customer for any of the vehicles used.

The primary benefit of a *broad media mix* is greater reach (though at the expense of frequency). For example, because heavy TV viewers are light readers of magazines, having both TV and magazines in a mix will provide greater reach than if

TECHNOLOGY IN ACTION

Optimizing the Media Buy

Which makes more sense—paying $400,000 for a spot on *Friends* or scattering spots across a dozen or more cable networks and syndicated shows? Savvy media planners know that, using the latter strategy, they can sometimes reach the same number of viewers and save as much as $100,000 on the buy.

Obviously, in this age of accountability, clients are pressuring agencies to prove they are making the most efficient media buys. One way agencies have found to better justify such decisions is to use *optimizer programs*, which are computer programs that move beyond analyzing program ratings to factor in various customer data in order to make the decision more precise.

Originally devised for European markets, these optimizer programs came to the United States when Nielsen Media Research made available data for real-time metered viewing patterns (from People Meters in some 5,000 homes). Optimizers are complex media planning models that combine the Nielsen data with other data from in-store scanners and customer profile databases.

Some agencies have developed their own proprietary optimizer models that factor in different types of data. The Bozell agency's optimizer program, for example, factors in a TV program's holding power, loyalty, and attentiveness. The media-buying company Media That Works factors in ad clutter. McCann's "Media in Mind" program takes into consideration consumers' state of mind (among other things) during media usage. The "Volume Rating Points" program by the Spectra research company adds an equation for sales volume per household using Nielsen's home-scanning program, in which 55,000 people scan their purchases in their home as they unload their shopping bags. These volume rating points move beyond ratings to indicate, for example, whether *ER* viewers purchase more cosmetics, soft drinks, or pain remedies than the viewers of *Frasier*. This is the latest application of single-source data—that is, purchasing data from in-store scanners.

Newer optimizer programs include ratings for other media besides television. J. Walter Thompson's "Thompson Total Marketing" program for its client Ford Motor Company, for example, links Nielsen data with Ford's customer-service database and evaluates print and broadcast for reach. It also includes reach estimates for other marketing communication functions such as events, public relations, product placement, and the Web.

Think About It

If you were asked to develop an optimizer program for a campaign designed to promote the Suzuki method of teaching music to children, what target audience features and media characteristics would you include in the optimizer program and why?

David Kiley, "Optimum Target," *Adweek*, May 18, 1998, pp. 39–42; Marc Gunther, "New Software Programs: TV Advertising," *Fortune*, May 11, 1998, pp. 26–27; Verne Gay, "Pumping Up the Volume," *Brandweek*, May 29, 2000, pp. U40–U44.

just one medium were used. See again Table 13–5, which shows how reach can be increased by combining two media.

Likewise, a broad media mix enables a brand to use media for different purposes at the same time, such as building awareness (TV), delivering coupons to increase action (magazines or newspapers), and getting immediate feedback (Internet and telephone).

Finally, some MC executives believe that a broader mix of media provides greater synergy (i.e., greater message synergy), although empirical evidence is weak for this belief. The argument is that if three different people tell you something it will have more impact than if one person tells it to you three times. This is particularly important for brands with small budgets that want to maximize the impact of their messages. It can maximize repetition in low-frequency media plans.

Creative Strategy Considerations

Creative strategy is a qualitative factor. When a brand message is relatively complex, it may require a concentrated mix, because greater frequency gives the target more opportunities to understand a message. Message complexity also suggests considering print rather than broadcast media because, as explained in Chapter 11, print can be read slowly, re-read, and even clipped and saved, unlike a broadcast brand message. Another way to say it is this: Sell the car on TV and sell the deal in newspapers. Also, when a message is fairly simple (e.g., "2 for 1 through Sunday"), a broad mix with a high level of reach (rather than frequency) may be appropriate.

One of the most important considerations in creating a media mix is to choose media that best deliver the message. As a DDB Worldwide media executive explained, "It is no longer enough to calculate a cost per thousand or other body-count figures. We also need to think about the qualitative benefits that different media vehicles can provide, such as conveying a message with authority or having the ability to be influential."[7]

The selection decisions at this level are based not only on an objective analysis of various media's ability to deliver on the plan's objectives, but also on how they can be used effectively to complement one another. Media-mix decision factors can be summarized as follows:

1. *Media cost/value.* Evaluate media costs and compare them with reach and frequency objectives, as well as impact on the target audience; generally speaking, the greater the impact, the more expensive and the less reach and frequency.

2. *Lead time.* Compare the length of the necessary lead time against the need for flexibility in production scheduling.

3. *Concentration.* Compare the reach and frequency objectives to determine whether to use a broad mix (focus on reach) or a concentrated mix (focus on frequency).

4. *Relationship building.* Use a more concentrated media mix to build strong relationships with current customers and a broader mix to reach more prospects.

5. *Number of targets.* Allow for different numbers of targets: The more target audiences identified in the plan, the more the need for a broader media mix.

6. *Number of objectives.* Consider all objectives: The more objectives specified, generally the greater the need for a variety of media to serve the different purposes.

7. *Synergy.* Create impact by having a variety of different messages saying the same thing or the same message in a variety of media.

8. *Brand differentiation.* For commodity products, use high levels of frequency (and a concentrated mix) to build familiarity.

9. *Production costs.* Analyze the budget and determine the level of production costs available—more communication vehicles means higher production costs.

10. *Message complexity.* For a complex message, focus on frequency and concentration; for a simple message, try more reach in a broader mix.

A FINAL NOTE: CLOSED-LOOP MEDIA MARKETING

Media brands, like other brands, can increase their visibility through brand extensions such as stores, related products, and merchandising materials. This notion is known as "closed-loop marketing." A media brand like *Martha Stewart Living* is both medium and product—in other words, it can deliver what it produces. An example of a TV channel that has developed a strong brand and a closed marketing loop is the Discovery Channel. Its chain of retail stores, the Discovery Stores, provides advertisers with media to create awareness as well as a channel of distribution for their products. These types of media offerings add value to brands because the media themselves have become respected brands.

Next to Martha Stewart, Disney is probably the best example of closed-loop marketing. It owns media properties, such as Walt Disney Studios and Touchstone. It also owns the ABC television network; ESPN; the Mighty Ducks hockey team and the Anaheim Angels baseball team; theme parks in California, Florida, Paris, and Tokyo; the Web portals Infoseek and Go Network; and Disney retail outlets.

Advertisers on ESPN, for example, can take advantage of ESPN's radio network, its magazine, its center next to Disneyworld in Florida, and its website. And ESPN special programming can be sold as videos in Disney's retail outlets. ESPN has become a branded medium that has its own unique identity and high level of prestige, especially when it comes to sports, but the strength of the brand is enhanced by its connection with Disney's image of quality entertainment.

Key Terms

media buying 460
skews 462
category development index (CDI) 466
brand development index (BDI) 467
reach (penetration) 467
designated marketing area (DMA) 468
duplication 468
impression 470
targeted reach 470
slotting fee 471
media waste 472
frequency 472
effective frequency 473

share of voice 474
message wearout 474
frequency distribution analysis (quintile analysis) 475
cost per thousand (CPM) 476
cost per point (CPP) 478
cost per response (CPR) 479
teaser campaign 483
aperture 485
media weight 485
gross rating point (GRP) 485
flighting 488
continuous scheduling 488
pulsing 488

Key Points Summary

Key Point 1: Basic Media Concepts

- *Media audience.* Media planners select media whose audiences most closely match the brand's target audience.

- *Reach and coverage*. Reach is the percentage of an audience that has the opportunity to be exposed to a brand message one or more times within a specified period; coverage is the percentage of a geographical area or category of customers that receive a particular communication vehicle.
- *Frequency*. Frequency is the average number of times those that are reached have an opportunity to be exposed to a brand message within a specified time period.
- *Media environment*. Media planners consider the compatibility between a communication vehicle's image and the brand's image.
- *Media costs*. Media planners compare media on their cost per thousand—what each vehicle charges to deliver a message to 1,000 members of its audience.

Key Point 2: Key Media Planning Activities

- *Media objectives*. Media objectives state who is to be reached, with what frequency, where, and at what time.
- *Media strategies*. How the media are used to accomplish the objectives includes analyzing, weighting, and scheduling the media as part of determining the media mix.

Key Point 3: Media Mix Decisions

Media are selected by comparing their characteristics with an eye as to which will be most cost-effective. More important, a media mix also considers the effects achieved by different combinations of media.

Lessons Learned

Key Point 1: Basic Media Concepts

a. What kind of information is available to match a medium's audience to the targeted audience? Where is such information obtained?
b. Explain in your own words, what the difference is between reach, coverage, and exposure.
c. Explain why duplication and waste are problems for media planners.
d. Find a news article that reports the rating of some recent television program. Is the figure cited in the story a high or a low rating level?
e. How do you determine how much reach is enough?
f. What is targeted reach, and why is it important to marketers?
g. What is effective frequency? What is message wearout? What are three factors that affect the evaluation of effective frequency and wearout?
h. What is frequency distribution analysis, and how is it used in media planning?
i. How do you compute a cost per thousand, and what does it tell you about a medium's audience?
j. What is the difference between CPM, TCPM, CPP, and CPR?

Key Point 2: Key Media Planning Activities

a. What information is included in a set of media objectives?
b. What is media weighting, and why is it used in media planning?
c. What is a GRP, and how is it computed?
d. What is the difference between a GRP and a TRP?
e. Find a print ad in a magazine or a newspaper that has an obvious seasonality factor and explain how seasonality drives the media buy.
f. What is the difference between flighting, continuous scheduling, and pulsing strategies? How is each used?

Key Point 3: Media Mix Decisions

a. Why is a media mix used in media planning?
b. What are three common media characteristics used in selecting media to use in a media plan?

c.   What are three decisions involved in determining the best media mix?

d.   What is the difference between a concentrated media mix and a broad media mix? Give an instance where each approach would be appropriate.

e.   How does the media mix reflect the creative strategy?

f.   Explain how media weighting decisions affect the way the media budget is allocated.

g.   The next time you are in a grocery or discount store, study the displays for cigarettes. Do you feel they are trying to reach kids? How are these displays signaling their target audience?

Chapter Challenge

Writing Assignment

In the discussion of reach, it was mentioned that reach is figured on the percentage of the target exposed to the vehicle or program, not on the percentage exposed to the brand message. How might that problem be remedied? Write a memo to your instructor that explains this problem and outlines some suggestions on what might be done to make the evaluation of a brand message's reach more reliable.

Presentation Assignment

Interview the advertising manager at a large company or retail store in your community. Summarize that company's media plan and media mix. Explain why the various media were chosen. Present this report to your classmates.

Internet Assignment

Analyze Lee Jeans' Buddy Lee website (www.buddylee.com). Develop a report for your instructor on how the website contributes to the image of the dungarees and speaks to the interests of the brand's target audience. For next year's campaign, what would you recommend doing with this website to make it even more relevant and interesting?

Additional Readings

Jugenheimer, Donald W.; Arnold M. Barban; and Peter B. Turk. *Advertising Media: Strategy and Tactics.* Dubuque, IA: Brown & Benchmark, 1992.

Surmanek, Jim. *Media Planning: A Practical Guide.* 3rd ed., Lincolnwood, IL: NTC Business Books, 1996.

Research Assignment

Read everything you can on the Nielsen ratings for television programs. What are the most common criticisms aimed at this research service? What are some of the suggestions being made to improve the quality of these ratings? What do you feel should be done to solve the problems that concern the critics of the Nielsen ratings?

Endnotes

[1] Mark Goldstein, speech at University of Colorado IMC Program, November 8, 2000.

[2] Jon Fine, "Cross-Media Catches Fire," *Advertising Age,* October 23, 2000, p. S2.

[3] Sandra E. Moriarty, "Explorations into the Commercial Encounter," *Proceedings of the 1991 Conference of the American Academy of Advertising,* Rebecca Holman, ed.; and Sandra E. Moriarty and Shu-Ling

Everett, "Commercial Breaks: A Viewing Behavior Study," *Journalism Quarterly* 71, no. 2, (Summer 1994), pp. 346-55.

[4]*TV Dimensions '98* (Media Dynamics, Inc., 1998), p. 480.

[5]Mark Goldstein, presentation at the University of Colorado-Boulder, November 8, 2000.

[6]Erwin Ephron, "A New Media-Mix Strategy," *Advertising Age,* February 28, 2000, p. S10.

[7]Michael White, personal correspondence with the author, March 17, 1993.

Part Four

Marketing Communication Functions

A few years ago, the Leo Burnett agency did a study that found that consumers identified all brand messages as "advertising." Although this agency did the study to prove that advertising was the soul of all brand messages, what it really pointed out is that consumers don't discriminate among MC functions.

Although it may be true that consumers confuse the various marketing communication functions, it is important for marketing communicators to understand that there are differences among the various functions, just as there are differences among the various types of media. There are four categories of marketing communication functions discussed in this part: those that primarily use mass media (advertising and public relations); those that use situations and places (sales promotion, packaging, point-of-purchase); those that use personal communication (direct-response and personal sales); and those that use experiences (events, sponsorships, trade shows, and customer service). By knowing the differences—the strengths and limitations—between each of the major MC functions, marketers are better able to select and integrate the MC functions most appropriate for each brand-building situation.

14

Advertising: The Awareness Builder

Key Points in This Chapter

1. What are advertising's strengths and limitations, and what role does it play in IMC?

2. What is merchandising, and how does it relate to IMC?

3. Why is packaging both an intrinsic and created brand contact point?

Chapter Perspective:
The Mass in Brand Building

The first category of functional areas includes those that rely heavily (although not exclusively) on mass media. Traditionally, advertising has been characterized as impersonal and one-way. It is impersonal in that ads are not directly addressed to the individual audience members. It is one-way because it cannot carry messages back to the company from the customer. When you see an ad on TV or in the newspaper, the only way you can respond to the company is through another communication channel.

Most important, mass media advertising has been used in marketing communication because its reach is broader than other forms of marketing communication. Historically, it was extremely important in the development of mass marketing, which means selling the same product to everyone using the same marketing mix.

As you will recall, in the brand decision process, the first step is problem or opportunity recognition. The next, especially in the cognitive model, is information searching. Mass media advertising can play a significant role in influencing these steps by creating awareness and helping position brands. Other mass media functions include merchandising and packaging. These two operate in the critical zone where brand decisions are being made or evaluated (e.g., in a store, particularly in an aisle of shelves, or at home as the product is being used).

This chapter first discusses mass media advertising in general—its functions, types, strengths, and limitations. The chapter then discusses merchandising as a driver of reminders, and packaging as the "last ad" consumers see before they make a purchase decision.

THE NATAL SHARKS WIN MORE THAN MATCHES
TBWA Hunt Lascaris, Durban, South Africa

In the mid-1990s the Natal Rugby Union, one of South Africa's provincial rugby organizations, adopted the shark as its official mascot and namesake. This was a daring move for a traditional rugby organization with its old-boy-club English heritage. A marketing communication campaign was needed, however, to create a powerful new brand identity for the team that would have international, as well as local, appeal. That was the assignment give to the TBWA Hunt Lascaris agency in Durban, South Africa. Despite limited funds to establish the new brand, the Natal Sharks (see Exhibit 14–1) became one of the highest profile rugby teams in the world in only three years. This case will explain the planning behind this award-winning brand-building effort.

Market Situation

In the mid-1990s there were a number of changes taking place in sports and entertainment industries both around the world and specifically in South Africa. The reacceptance of South Africa among the global community following the nation's democratic elections of 1994 (which ended a long period of racial apartheid) led to a flood of requests for music concert tours and sporting competition with this country. Sports brands had achieved an unprecedented level of status in South Africa. Reebok, Nike, and Adidas, among other labels, had become street-fashion brand names.

EXHIBIT 14-1

The Natal Shark mascot helps create and extend the team's brand identity.

The Natal Rugby Union was perceived as little different from other traditional, conservative sporting groups in South Africa. Its official emblem—a colonial-style crest featuring two leaping wildebeests—and its colloquial name "The Banana Boys" did little to challenge this perception. High-profile British soccer clubs with strong brand identities—such as the Manchester United, Chelsea, and Liverpool teams—had already demonstrated that sports merchandising could be highly lucrative. Successfully marketed sports teams were generating revenues from tickets, catering and food sales, and, surprisingly, merchandise. There was obviously a significant opportunity to introduce the latest sports marketing and advertising thinking into South African rugby.

To summarize the marketing situation with a SWOT analysis: the Natal Rugby Union's *strength* lay in its vision and professionalism, and its *weakness* lay in its lack of a brand identity. The *opportunity* to leverage the increasing popularity of international rugby, and the *threat* lay with the wide range of entertainment competition that was entering the South African market.

The Brand Strategy

In the light of the SWOT analysis described above, the overall brand strategy, then, was to create a powerful new identity for the team that would position it globally as an innovator in rugby and sports marketing, and engage a much broader audience than it had in the past. The strategy was designed to promote the whole brand experience, including the game, the facilities, and the pre- and postmatch activities and related entertainment, as well as the team. True to the IMC philosophy, everything related to the Natal Sharks became an essential part of the brand identity. The Sharks product can be divided into three broad categories: the team, the experience, and the merchandise.

The Team

The team could create a powerful, almost fanatical, emotional bond between consumers and the brand, due to the fact that it represented the sporting aspirations of partisan consumers. The possibility existed for a kind of blood loyalty, so to speak, which competitors would find difficult, if not impossible, to destroy.

The Experience

The experience at a Sharks game was, and still is, unequaled for two reasons: the generally good weather and the acres of space. First, the team's home city of Durban and province of KwaZula-Natal has a subtropical climate that, even in winter, creates balmy, generally dry evenings lending themselves to after-match outdoor activities. Second, Durban's King Park Stadium is surrounded by acres of rugby fields that are used for parking and corporate entertaining on match days, with up to 30 marquees (stages) forming a sprawling tent village surrounded by thousands of spectators' parked cars. So a visit to King's Park involves more than watching a game of rugby; it becomes a full afternoon and evening event that is as much about socializing as it is about sports. At the end of a game, there is no rush to go home. Instead, thousands of fans open their car boots (trunks) to extract folding picnic tables, hampers, braals (barbeques), and cooler boxes filled with iced refreshments.

The bond between team and supporters is strengthened as the players wander around the fields during the after-match party chatting with individual fans, playing rugby with youngsters, and signing autographs. The party sometimes lasts until the next morning.

The Merchandise

In the world of rugby, merchandise is the badge of the supporter—a combination of fashion statement and loyalty. The range of Natal Sharks merchandise includes more than 150 lines sold locally as well as internationally through mail order. Merchandise orders have come from as far away as New Zealand, Australia, and the United States.

A major element in promoting the merchandise was the creation of a stadium souvenir store, the Shark Cage, as well as other Shark Cage merchandise stores away from the stadium. Following the success of the original Shark Cage at the stadium, a new retail complex was built—the Ultimate Shopping Mall—which consisted of a bigger Shark Cage, ticket offices, and a Jawlers beer garden and coffee shop. (The word *jawler* is South African slang for a fun-loving party animal.) A multimedia experience and a museum are also part of the entertainment package.

Campaign Objectives

The overall long-term objectives for the Natal Sharks brand identity campaign were to:

- Establish a worldwide awareness of the Sharks brand.
- Create an understanding of the brand's values.
- Build the belief in the minds of the target audience that the Sharks brand is the most desirable sports brand.
- Activate trial of the match experience and purchase of the merchandise.
- Encourage advocacy by the target market of the Sharks experience and merchandise.
- Motivate loyal and continued support for the Sharks team and the Natal Rugby Union.

The short-term objectives for the campaign, which were designed to address specific issues, included the following:

- Attract spectators to low-key games.
- Announce the opening of the new Shark Cage souvenir shop.
- Promote the sale of merchandise.
- Promote the renewal and sales of season tickets.
- Invite spectators to attend the free 4:00 A.M. showing of the regional Super 12 semifinal.

In general, the Sharks brand identity campaign was aimed at the younger part of the market. A rugby game was a popular meeting place for fashion-conscious teenagers who were always dressed in the trendiest casual gear. But there were subcategories in the target audience. The local target included current and potential rugby fans who lived within an hour of the stadium. These were the target for ticketing, catering, and merchandise. At least 50 percent of ticket revenue was generated from sales to these private individuals.

The second important local market was the corporate sector. The majority of suites (private boxes) and many of the season tickets were held by this sector for use as corporate entertainment or staff incentives. This was also the primary source of patronage for the Marquee Village or Tent Town where the pre- and postmatch festivities take place.

The international target market included current and potential rugby fans around the world who were exposed to the game via the electronic media. In particular, there were thousands of KwaZula-Natalians who had moved to other parts of South Africa and the world yet still fanatically supported their hometown team.

Campaign Strategy

TBWA decided that, in the early stages, the focus was to be on the shark imagery to quickly establish the Natal Rubgy Union's new identity. The new brand's position was defined as "proud, professional, and predatory." Other communication objectives included the following:

- Establish the brand's values and personality as confident but not arrogant, mischievous but not evil, and strong yet friendly.

- Reinforce the team colors of black and white.
- Avoid parochialism in the message and choice of media.

There were a number of guidelines and mandates to follow in implementing the communication strategy:

- The team must adopt the name the Sharks.
- The icon should not be politically sensitive.
- The team identity should lend itself to unlimited theme, marketing, and merchandising opportunities.
- The newly named team must use advertising to gain a high level of awareness.
- Brand messages must be aimed at the younger spectator.
- The brand must adopt an attitude that sets it apart from other rugby teams but is not arrogant.

Message Delivery

A variety of media and marketing communication tools were used to launch this new brand identity. The media and tools used to deliver the messages included radio advertising, publicity, direct marketing, CD-ROM press kits, outdoor advertising, event posters, leaflets, merchandising signs, and programs.

Other, more limited reach tools included Shark-branded Christmas wrapping paper sold at the Shark Cage, nonpermanent tattoos that were given away or sold at various games, and a Shark car decal that was given away with most items of merchandise. One of the most visible embodiments of the Shark symbol was the seven-foot mascot whose costume was worn at all Shark events by a very tall man.

The licensing of Shark-related merchandise also added to the visibility and memorability of the new brand identity. A Natal Sharks music compact disc called *Shark Attack* was distributed nationally. Undertaken primarily as a brand-building exercise, the response was overwhelming, with the CD selling out by Christmas. Also, with the highly successful liquor sales in the stadium, one of the team's first licensed products was the "Shark Shooter," a vodka-based shooter in four flavors. Demand for Sharks merchandise soared. Within a year, many items were being sold at selected major retailers and Reebok outlets around the country. (Reebok is the apparel sponsor of the team.)

Events other than matches also were used to generate Shark enthusiasm. An innovative screening of the 1997 Super 12 semifinal between the Natal Sharks and an Auckland team that broadcast at 4:00 A.M. from New Zealand on a cold May winter morning attracted an unprecedented 5,000 spectators.

The strong image also spoke to the younger fans, which extended the brand's appeal and attracted more families and young people. It also led to a Junior Sharks Club, catering to young supporters up to 14 years old (see Exhibit 14–2).

Evaluation of the Sharks Campaign

While attendance at other rugby games stayed static or declined, support for the Natal Sharks grew until the number of spectators attending the Sharks home games had doubled. After three years of monitoring, the Natal Rugby Union became one of the leading global marketers in rugby. The support for the new brand built revenue in most areas of the Natal Rugby Union's business, including an increase in merchandise sales of 600 percent in the first three years. Revenue from

EXHIBIT 14-2

Example of brochure used to create and maintain interest in the Natal Sharks among young people through membership in a "Junior Shark's" club.

the sales of private suites, liquor sales, and other functions and beverages increased similarly.

Even though the Sharks failed to make the Currie Cup final in the first year of the team's identity program, the Natal Rugby Union was recognized by the Institute of Marketing Management (IMM) as the Marketing Organization of the Year. The IMM credited the Sharks' branding effort with raising the profile of both provincial rugby and the entertainment experience of home games.

As another endorsement of the campaign's success, other advertisers have also adopted the shark theme in their own advertising. For example, Reebok brags that it is "the official supplier of shark's teeth" in an ad for its boots. The Nike posters at the Currie Cup final piggybacked on the Sharks theme.

And, finally, media representatives, many of whom had condemned the radical change at the outset, lauded the building of the brand in their stories on the brand's success. Media coverage is certainly a major factor in the success of the campaign.

This case was adapted with permission from the Advertising and Marketing Effectiveness (AME) award-winning brief for the Natal Rugby Union Natal Sharks prepared by the TBWA Hunt Lascaris agency in Durban, South Africa.

MASS MEDIA ADVERTISING: THE AWARENESS BUILDER

Advertising is carried by a wide variety of media and often, especially for consumer brands, is a major portion of the MC budget. **Mass media advertising** consists of *nonpersonal, one-way, planned messages paid for by an identified sponsor and disseminated to a broad audience in order to influence their attitudes and behavior.*

Let's look at the six characteristics identified in the definition:

1. The fact that advertising is *nonpersonal* communication means that it is aimed at groups of people, not individuals. These targeted groups might be either consumers (such as people who attend the Natal Sharks rugby games) or trade

customers (such as owners and managers of stores that sell team merchandise).

2. Mass media advertising is *one-way* because the media it uses cannot carry messages back to the company from the customer; that is, it is not interactive. You see an ad on TV or in the newspaper, and the only way you can respond to the company is through another communication channel (e.g., telephone, mail, e–mail).

3. The planned message dimension refers to one of the great benefits of advertising: the message can be created and controlled by the advertiser to communicate a very precise idea and image. That was an important objective for the Natal Rugby Union, which needed to define its image and establish the Shark association (see Exhibit 14–3).

4. Naturally, the *sponsor* of the advertising message usually wants to be *identified*.

5. Media companies are *paid* for the space or time used to carry the advertiser's messages.

6. When effective, advertising *influences attitudes and behaviors*. For current customers, mass media advertising reinforces positive brand attitudes and behaviors. For new customers (and new products), it creates demand for a brand.

EXHIBIT 14-3

The Natal Sharks used intense imagery from the movie Jaws *to capture the predatory spirit of the team's new mascot.*

A good example of creating demand by changing a behavior comes from the pharmaceutical industry. In recent years, the U.S. government has allowed pharmaceutical companies to advertise prescription drugs directly to consumers. As a result, patients who never before asked for drugs by name are now inquiring about the cholesterol-reducing drug Zocor, the allergy drug Claritin, or the antidepressant Prozac.

Overview of the Advertising Industry

Advertising is a major factor in the economies of industrialized nations. In the United States, mass media ad spending per household is $1,600 a year—more than twice the total of almost every other country in the world. Only Japan, whose advertisers spend approximately $1,000 per household each year, comes anywhere near.

Mass media advertising was in a slump in the early 1990s but turned around at the end of the decade. According to McCann-Erickson's Robert Coen, who tracks the industry, U.S. firms spent more than $233 billion on advertising in the year 2000. That represented an 8.3 percent increase over 1999's $215 billion and a 70 percent increase over 1995's $137 billion.[1]

Spending on mass media advertising typically mirrors changes in a country's economy. In healthy economies, companies can justify spending more on advertising because customers are economically able to respond and buy. As an economy cools down and sales levels fall, many companies cut back on advertising (even though that is sometimes the opposite strategy from what most advertising agencies would recommend). During the last several years, the world economy overall has been fairly good. Many of the largest global advertisers increased their spending from 1998 to 1999, as shown in Table 14–1.[2] This economic situation also was a positive factor in the creation of the Natal Sharks brand, described in the chapter opening case.

The Function of Mass Media Advertising

Of all the tools marketing communicators use, mass media advertising is no doubt the most commonplace and the most visible. In fact, as the opening page of Part IV pointed out, advertising is so pervasive that consumers do not differentiate between mass media advertising and sales promotion or publicity and event sponsorship. The Natal rugby club built on this tendency by including events and merchandise as part of its "advertising" for the new Sharks brand.

Advertising's primary function is building brand awareness, as the trade ad in Exhibit 14–4 demonstrates. For new products and new companies, especially, building brand credibility and momentum, is also critical. Brand momentum is gained when brand awareness and positioning spread within the target audience at an increasing rate. For that reason, advertising planners in an IMC program may find themselves involved in planning and managing a brand's total communication program, and that may involve more than just traditional advertising. The IMC in Action box illustrates the work of a relatively small advertising agency that integrates clients' total brand communication as the basis for its "advertising" strategy.

TABLE 14-1	Changes in Media Advertising Spending for Top 10 Global Advertisers		
Advertiser	**Headquarters**	**1998 Media Spend ($ Billions)**	**% Increase from 1998**
Procter & Gamble	Cincinnati, OH, USA	$4,748	4%
Unilever	Rotterdam/London	3,429	9
Nestlé	Vevey, Switzerland	1,833	15
Ford Motor Company	Dearborn, MI, USA	2,230	10
General Motors	Detroit, MI, USA	3,194	1
Philip Morris	New York, NY, USA	1,980	1
DaimlerChrysler	Stuttgart, Germany	1,922	3
Toyota Motors	Toyota City, Japan	1,692	−2
Sony Corporation	Tokyo, Japan	1,337	10
Coca-Cola	Atlanta, GA, USA	1,327	2

Source: www.adage.com/dataplace/archives

IMC IN ACTION

The Ad Works When the Company Works

Adworks, a Washington, D.C., ad agency, is known for its cutting-edge work in reshaping its clients' entire marketing program as well as marketing communication. For its client the Nature Company, a chain of 107 retail stores selling nature-themed products, Adworks offered advice on what the retailer should and should not stock on its shelves. In its advertising strategy for the chain, Adworks argued that the ads should position the stores as a pathway to the "simple joys" of nature. So instead of featuring a $3,000 refractor telescope (one of the Nature Company's high-ticket products), Adworks' first television ad for the Nature Company focused on a $4.95 wooden birdcaller. The store's director of retail marketing observed that Adworks just doesn't "come up with a few clever words and images. They realize that even a great ad is just the first step in the whole process that leads to a sale."

For Ratner's Hair Cuttery, a small chain of salons run by Dennis Ratner, Adworks totally redesigned the look of the current ads and the image of the store presented in them. But more than that, the Adworks staff told Ratner that his salon should have only one price, that all cuts should include a shampoo, and that the staffers and premises needed a remake as well. Six years later, Ratner's Hair Cuttery had outlets in 16 East Coast states and ranked as the nation's largest privately owned chain of hair salons.

The question agencies like Adworks—and this can be any type of MC agency, not just ad agencies—have to ask themselves is whether or not they want to take a leadership position in integrating a client's total communication and brand-relationship-building program. If they do, then they need to consider all brand contact points, which means looking at the messages being delivered by sources other than advertising, such as product, service, and unplanned messages. Adworks aims to be a communication partner rather than just a supplier of advertising, however great the advertising might be. To do so, it has to look at the big picture of its clients' communication.

Think About It

Does it make sense for an advertising agency to offer a client advice on other types of messages, such as product and service messages? What is the difference between being a supplier of advertising and a communication partner?

Source: Adapted from Erik Ipsen, "The Big Show or Bust," *Fortune*, December 8, 1997, pp. 232A–232C.

Types of Advertising

Advertising is a very broad tool. To create a more specific understanding, people often put an adjective before the word *advertising* to indicate the kind or classification of advertising being discussed: sports advertising, retail advertising, print advertising, and so on.

Target Audiences

As discussed in Chapter 7, sophisticated marketers always direct their ads toward some segment of the population known as the target audience. The target audience is made up of customers and prospects who are in the market for a particular type of product, which can be categorized in terms of the product category or industry.

KEEP TECHNOLOGY FROM DIVIDING US ALL.

Religions split us. Politics polarize us. But incompatible technologies can truly come between us. Which is why, from the beginning, opened doors to new ideas like our "Java" technologies. If you set out to keep computing open, not closed, filled with more choices. we've spoken out for a more universal approach to computing: Network computing. And that's not less, the world pulls closer together, not further apart. Peace. THE NETWORK IS THE COMPUTER." ◆Sun Microsystems

EXHIBIT 14-5

Sun Microsystems is a global technology company that sells computer and Internet systems and services to other businesses.

There are two main types of target audiences: consumers and businesses. People who buy products for their own or someone else's personal use are called consumers; the advertising directed at them is called *consumer advertising*. Most of the advertising we see or hear daily in newspapers, in magazines, and on radio or TV is advertising created and placed for manufacturers or retailers of consumer products.

In contrast, *business advertising* is directed to people who buy or specify goods and services for business use (see Exhibit 14–5). This target audience may use these products in their own business, incorporate them in some other product they sell, or they may simply buy them wholesale and resell them at retail.

Media

Advertising may also be categorized according to the medium in which it appears: direct-mail advertising, print and broadcast advertising, and so on. Business or trade advertising (also called BtB advertising) tends to rely heavily on print media and appears in specialized business publications and trade magazines, as well as in direct-mail pieces sent to businesses.

Geography

There are four classifications of advertising based on geography: local, regional, national, and international. Advertising aimed at customers throughout a country is called *national advertising*. *Regional advertising* is used for products that are sold in only one or two regions of a country, which might cover several states or provinces. Many advertisers, such as department stores, auto dealers, restaurants, and banks, have customers in only one city or local trading area, so they use *local advertising*. Most local advertising is done by retailers, but not all retail advertising is local; large retailers like Sears, J. C. Penney, and Kmart have national image campaigns supplemented by local-market promotional advertising that focuses more on price. In recent years, many of the traditional barriers to trade have disappeared around the world. As a result, the field of *international advertising*—advertising aimed at foreign markets—has grown rapidly and become very important.

Strengths and Objectives of Mass Media Advertising

Different marketing communication tools are used for different reasons. In other words, when you identify the strengths of a marketing communication function like advertising, you identify what it can do more cost-effectively than other MC functions. Another way of depicting strengths is in terms of objectives—in other words, what you want to accomplish when you use that MC tool. For certain objectives, advertising may be more appropriate than public relations, direct marketing, or sales promotion.

As noted throughout this chapter, advertising's primary strength is in the area of building awareness. Advertising also (1) adds value to a brand, (2) is cost-effective in terms of impressions, and (3) offers control over the content and timing of the message.

The Added Value of Advertising

Advertising adds value to a brand by creating awareness and helping build, position, and reposition brands. The Evian ad in Exhibit 14–6 is an example of advertising being used to position a brand: The idea of making a martini with Evian (rather than the normal vodka or gin) is a way to say that Evian is a fancy, upscale bottled water.

Awareness

As you will recall from Chapter 5, awareness of a problem or opportunity is the first step in the brand decision process. Awareness is also important in the information-seeking stage. The easier it is for a customer or prospect to learn that a certain brand can solve a certain problem, the more likely it is that they will purchase that brand or at least give it further consideration. Advertising thus helps keep a brand top-of-mind, which means customers are more likely to buy the brand when they have a need in the product category because it will be the first brand they think of.

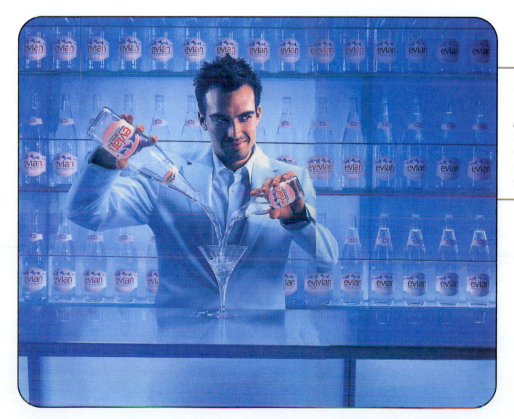

EXHIBIT 14-6

This ad makes a statement about the Evian brand of bottled water with its visual metaphor of a bartender mixing an Evian drink in a martini glass.

When it comes to luxury goods, advertising creates awareness that goes beyond potential buyers. Companies that make precision watches, expensive liquors, and high-end automobiles use mass media advertising not only to reach customers and prospects but also to reach the general public. The reason is that buyers of these status brands want others to know how special the brands are. A Rolex watch would not be as valuable as its price tag suggests if no one but the buyer had ever heard of a Rolex. In other words, people don't buy a Rolex just so they know what time it is.

Taco Bell's 1998 "Chihuahua" campaign, which featured a talking Mexican dog whose only desire was to consume Taco Bell food, has been praised as one of advertising's best brand-recognition success stories. Not only did the restaurant chain's sales increase after the campaign began, but sales of licensed products featuring the dog's image increased the company's revenue.[3] Yet, after featuring the Chihuahua "spokesdog" for two years, the company decided that its advertising needed to place more emphasis on the product and less on the Chihuahua.[4] This is a typical evolution of a successful character. The next time you see a commercial for Green Giant products, notice how little emphasis is given to the Jolly Green Giant. Once a character is established, it can do its job with less "face" time.

Source of Creative Ideas

Mass media advertising is able to build awareness because of the power of its creative ideas. To see a collection of highly creative television ads, check out AdCritic.com (www.adcritic.com), a website that archives good commercials. Although the big idea can come from any functional area, it comes from the advertising agency, because a major portion of consumer products companies' MC budgets is for mass media advertising. The Natal Rugby Union had used the shark reference before, but the idea of making it into a strong brand identity came from its agency, TBWA Hunt Lascaris, which then had to sell the idea to the rugby union. Thus, another of advertising's strengths is often to develop the big idea that serves as a central focus for all marketing communication messages.

Information

Another way advertising adds value is by communicating information about the brand, its features and benefits, and its location of sale. Advertising is particularly a good choice when the message is simple, such as "Coke six-packs, 99 cents this week at Wal-Mart." There is no need for personalizing this message or making it interactive in order for it to have an effect. And advertising in BtB marketing tends to emphasize its informational role because of the bottom-line and performance orientation of most BtB buyers.

Brand Positioning

Advertising has the power to create a psychological relationship between a brand and its users. As the Natal Sharks campaign demonstrates, advertising can create a brand personality, deliver a brand promise, and anchor a brand position in a creative and compelling manner. Such positioning creates the added value that customers acquire by using the brand.

In case after case, the best-selling brands in a product category are also typically the leading advertisers: Tide, Crest, and Marlboro, to name just a few. Although information is important, advertising forges the psychological link through emotional involvement. Whenever it can bring drama and emotion to a brand message, mass media advertising typically becomes the lead MC function.

The more complex a brand or an offer is, the less role there is for mass media advertising. However, once a mix of MC functions has successfully explained a brand, advertising can cost-effectively maintain awareness of the brand and differentiate it from competitors. Good examples of this come from the mass media advertising used by high-technology companies such as Lucent and Intel, which have each spent millions on advertising to help keep their complex systems and products top-of-mind with customers, prospects, and other stakeholders. Some call this *reminder advertising*; it, too, helps in maintaining a brand position (see Exhibit 14–7).

Cost-Effectiveness

As noted in Chapter 13, marketing communication costs can be considered in either of two ways: in absolute terms (i.e., how much the total bill is for the MC effort) and in terms of how many people are reached. A television commercial is probably the most expensive form an MC message can take in absolute terms. Yet, when you consider the reach of most television programs, then the cost per person reached becomes relatively low. Television is relatively *cost-effective* compared to other forms of marketing communication. Please note that throughout this chapter and the following ones, the discussion will refer either to cost (the actual size of the bill) or cost-effectiveness (the cost relative to the reach).

Control

Because advertising time and space are paid for by the marketer, the brand has complete control over what the ad says, and when and where it appears. In some cases (e.g., with tasteless or deceptive ads), a communication vehicle may refuse to run an ad as produced; however, most advertising content is accepted by the media and runs unchanged, which is one of advertising's greatest strengths.

IMC-Related Strengths

Two other strengths related to advertising's role in an IMC program come in the areas of self-selection and stakeholder communication. Regarding the first strength, when a brand is not sure who might be interested in its product, or when it is not able to select niche media that reach its target audience only, it can use mass media advertising to inexpensively motivate those who are interested in the brand to "hold up their hand." In other words, advertising enables prospective customers to self-select themselves for further brand communication. In such cases it is important to design in a response mechanism—e-mail address, toll-free number, website address—as part of the ad's message. And, in addition to the contact information in the ad, there also has to be a back-end system in place to handle the contact, a problem addressed in the Technology in Action box.

The second strength is that mass media advertising messages are seen by other stakeholders besides just customers—employees, investors, and the local community. It is difficult to measure the impact of advertising on these groups; however,

Proud Sponsor Of Major League Baseball.

EXHIBIT 14-7

This ad for Twizzlers uses the candy as stitching on a baseball to remind consumers, as well as employees and other business partners, that Twizzlers is a sponsor of major league baseball.

TECHNOLOGY IN ACTION

Dialing for Dealers

An example of how communication technology is helping build closer relationships between advertisers, the retailers providing their goods or services, and customers is a system called DealerQuik (see Exhibit 14-8). This service allows a company to run national advertising that includes a single toll-free number through which potential customers can be connected directly to the retailer closest to them. In the past, a national ad either had to list all the retailers in a given region and their telephone numbers or had to provide its own toll-free number and hire staff to answer phones and provide callers with information on retailers—a very time-consuming, expensive activity.

DealerQuik works this way. Let's say a customer in Dallas, Texas, sees an ad in *Time* magazine for a new lawn mower made by Toro, whose corporate office is in Minnesota. When the customer calls the 800 number in the ad, the DealerQuik system automatically connects the call to the retailer closest to the person making the call. This is done by using geographic recognition software that instantly identifies the location of the caller and then goes into a database of Toro retailers (which Toro has supplied and updates as necessary). Once the closest retailer is identified, the phone call is automatically redirected to that store; the customer does not need to do anything, and in fact is probably unaware of the call's redirection because it happens so quickly. Before the customer comes on the line, the service representative who answers the phone will hear a brief message saying the caller is interested in a Toro lawn mower, which is known by the computer because of the number that was called.

An added value to the DealerQuik system is that software handling the phone transaction records all calls. This enables the advertiser to measure exactly what response is being creating by its advertising. If the company wants to test several different media or message, it can use a different 800 number for each, thereby allowing responses to each to be kept separate. This integration of advertising and 800 numbers is a cost-efficient use of marketing communication.

EXHIBIT 14-8

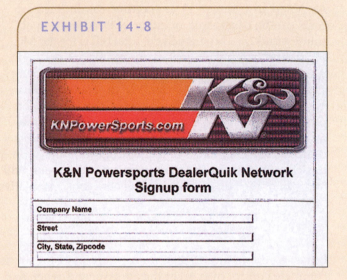

K&N Powersports DealerQuik Network Signup form

Company Name

Street

City, State, Zipcode

Think About It

How does the DealerQuik software help overcome mass media advertising's limitation as a one-way communication process? What are the benefits to the company, to the customer, and to the retailer of such a software program?

such impact is an important side benefit of advertising. Research has shown that employees feel encouraged to work harder and deliver higher levels of quality when they see advertising for their company.

Objectives

Most advertising we see is designed to elicit action at a later date. This is generally referred to as *brand image advertising* because it seeks to position and create

EXHIBIT 14-9

These four ads represent the evolution of the Sharks imagery from a traditional club to a blood-and-guts sports. Note the hat in the first one has the old logo, which is shown as a direct contrast to the sharp, pointed teeth of the new Sharks fan.

familiarity with the brand. Some awareness advertising is intended to reinforce a previous buying decision. In this case, it is typically called *reinforcement advertising*. Yet, image advertising goes well beyond simple awareness building or reinforcement. It is designed to position a brand firmly in the customer's mind, to build a particular association for the brand, and to give the brand personality and power. The Natal Sharks ads in Exhibit 14–9 are typical of the image-building visuals used in repositioning the rugby club. Advertising can also be used to help the sales department by generating leads of prospects who are known to be interested in the product category. Another type of behavioral objective is to open up opportunities for customers to initiate a conversation with the company.

Limitations of Mass-Media Advertising

For all its advantages, advertising also suffers from certain distinct disadvantages. These have all been mentioned in preceding chapters but are examined more closely in the following subsections.

Waste

Advertising often has a high level of waste. As noted in Chapter 13, mass media messages typically reach a large number of people who aren't in the market for the product. It's also harder to do pinpoint targeting with mass media advertising than with other marketing communication tools. To call mass media advertising wasteful, however, may be misleading because the economies of scale may offset the wasted reach. Also, waste in mass media buys has decreased in recent years as cable channels and magazines have become more specialized.

One-Way Communication

By now, mass media advertising's limitation as a form of one-way communication should be clear—in sum, sending messages from marketers to customers does not allow for a two-way dialogue. Most advertisers need to not only do a better job of targeting but also find ways to open up dialogue opportunities with customers and other stakeholders.

Low Credibility

Credibility is not seen as a strength of advertising because customers recognize ads as paid messages delivered on behalf of a brand. Many customers, in fact, jaded by decades of puffery, automatically discount the claims they hear in mass media ads—simply because it's advertising. And some, knowing that advertising claims are self-serving, profess to believe no advertising claims. This problem is further exacerbated by those advertisers and agencies that continue to exaggerate and overpromise.

The puffery image of advertising has become pervasive. During an IMC workshop conducted by the author in Europe, one account supervisor of a major international ad agency stated that she was working on a brand whose slogan was "The taste that lasts forever." To their credit, several of the other workshop participants immediately challenged the slogan, saying that the "taste" does not in fact last "forever." The account supervisor defended her client's slogan by saying to the group: "It doesn't matter if it's not true, because people know it's advertising and don't believe it anyway." Such a statement can become a self-fulfilling prophecy. To say the least, it is very damaging to the efforts of ethical marketers who want to use advertising as a tool to help develop lasting, purposeful relationships with customers and other stakeholders. Consumer resistance to advertising is discussed in the Ethics and Issues box here, and in more detail in Chapter 19, on ethics.

Clutter

Another major limitation of advertising is that there is just so much of it—across all media. Some estimate that consumers are now exposed to hundreds of commercial messages every day. Syndicated newspaper columnist John Leo has detailed the various ways advertising is creeping into unexpected places, such as cash machines and electronic ticker-tape ads in taxi cabs. In one column, he lamented a new program by Rio Network of Raleigh, North Carolina, that installs screens and speakers at gas pumps so that when a customer lifts the nozzle, the device delivers a sales message.[5]

The more advertising is everywhere, the more people criticize it and build up resistance to it. Customers for both consumer and BtB products have developed

E T H I C S   A N D   I S S U E S

Ad Jamming

One of advertising's biggest problems is criticism and outright resistance by articulate, well-educated people. In New Jersey, a coalition of artists known as Cicada Corps, has altered billboards, particularly for "sin" products such as liquor and cigarettes, that they believe are disproportionately placed in minority neighborhoods. One Newport cigarette billboard received a banner that read, "Healthy profits don't always require living customers."

Negativland, a San Francisco area band, got into the cultural criticism game with its recording called *Dispepsi*, a CD pieced together from bits of music, ads, and interviews that creates a scathing, although entertaining, commentary on the soft-drink company. As one band member commented, "It isn't that advertising per se is evil, it's the amount of it that's going on." The band coined the term *culture jamming* as a way to break through the might of giant marketers so that opposing viewpoints can be heard.

Likewise, a Cicada Corps member believes that, although defacing billboards is illegal, their actions are justified: "Alternatives have been taken away because they [big businesses] have all the money. We had to go underground."

The corporate response to these tactics is usually "no comment." But while marketers may look upon culture-jamming actions as too puny to worry about, some mainstream advertisers are imitating the hip, ironic attitude of ad resisters.

The Suissa Miller advertising agency, for example, produced a series of parody ads for Boston Chicken (now named Boston Market) mocking the severely underweight models who appear in ads for designer clothing maker Calvin Klein. And a campaign for Candie's colorful sneakers featured actress Jenny McCarthy at a miniature golf course, throwing her club in the air, accompanied by the line, "Just screw it." Viewers may have laughed, but athletic-shoe maker Nike, whose well-known "Just do it" campaign was clearly being mocked, saw nothing funny.

In a particularly hard-hitting ad during a St. Louis labor dispute with a Miller Brewing Company distributor, the Teamsters Union put up a billboard mocking a Miller ad. Instead of two bottles of beer in a snowbank with the line "Two Cold," the parody ad showed two frozen workers in a snowbank labeled "Too Cold." The Teamsters report that it has used similar parody ads to good effect in other labor disputes.

Think About It

What is it about parody ads that make them effective, if they are? As activists become more sophisticated in presenting their anti-advertising messages, do you think they will begin to have a widespread impact on the public?

Sources: Mary Kuntz, "Is Nothing Sacred?" *Business Week*, May 18, 1998, pp. 130–34; and John Leo, "Captives of the Advertising Culture," *Indianapolis Star*, December 31, 1997, p. A10.

---

mechanisms for blocking out most commercial messages. Technology has given us the video recorder and remote control, which enable us to physically screen out many TV commercial messages by either zipping through them on the VCR or zapping them altogether by changing channels.

A hidden cost of clutter is reduced advertising effectiveness. Because it takes more messages to have an effect in a cluttered MC environment, companies must increase their spending on communication. The result is a vicious circle: As advertisers rely more and more on media weight to overcome the clutter, the clutter grows ever thicker. The increasing ineffectiveness of advertising has given impetus to the concept of IMC as companies look for alternative ways to leverage their MC dollars, derive synergy from their communication efforts, and cultivate deeper relationships with their customers.

MERCHANDISING AND POP: THE REMINDER DRIVERS

Merchandising means *extending a brand image through promotional activities at the retail level.* One of the key elements in the Natal Sharks success story was its use of branded merchandise—and branded stores—to carry the brand imagery into a shopping experience. Exhibit 14–10 illustrates the way the merchandise and the shopping experience also became communication vehicles to reinforce the brand imagery.

The majority of the materials used for merchandising are **point-of-purchase (POP) materials,** *which are in-store display materials designed to call attention to a brand.* POP materials provide an ad at the point when customers and prospects are in their final brand decision-making stage. An off-shelf display is an in-store display of a brand in a location besides the one in which it regularly appears. The benefit of having off-shelf display is that a brand has a second opportunity to be noticed and considered by customers. Without question, the more in-store exposure a brand has, the better.

Knowing that most retail stores are always trying to reduce labor costs, some brands periodically use **shipper-displays** in order to get off-shelf display. These are *specially designed shipping cartons that when opened become display units complete with signage and a quantity of products ready for sale.* Shipper-displays demand little extra labor on the part of retailers. Flaps from the carton stand up to help call attention to the display and carry a brand message. Once the product is sold, the display carton is thrown away.

Merchandising is concerned with *how* a brand is displayed. Some food stores, for example, use different shelving and flooring in different sections (e.g., the bakery section or the all-natural products section) in an effort to make each one stand out. How different product categories are arranged in a store in relation to the traffic flow is another form of merchandising. For example, in the men's sections of department stores, ties are generally displayed next to dress shirts.

It's difficult to get a complete picture of merchandising, since it includes so many varied activities. It is estimated that marketers spent over $15 billion on POP materials in 2000—as much as they spent on specialties and consumer magazine advertising. The largest users of POP materials are restaurants ($1.1 billion) and apparel and footwear retailers ($1 billion). The fastest-growing categories using POP materials are foods and professional services.

Merchandising and POP materials provided by manufacturers (or for franchised stores by corporate headquarters) give the retailer ready-made, professionally designed brand messages. These materials include banners, signs, window posters, counter stands, floor stands, TV monitors, audiotapes for playing over the store's public-address system, shelf signs, end-cap (end-of-aisle) displays, and special display racks. Retail chains typically create many of their own merchandising materials. The ACTMEDIA ad in Exhibit 14–11 illustrates how in-store merchandising can become confusing if not properly integrated.

One of the most common POP materials is a **shelf talker,** *a printed card or sign stuck into the shelf's price rail.* Shelf talkers place information (such as recipes) and incentives (such as coupons and premium offers) for the brand on display in the critical "buying zone"

EXHIBIT 14-10

The Shark Cage souvenir shops were promoted with ads that tied the shark theme to merchandise and the shopping experience.

where customers make their product choices. Motion-activated coupon dispensers are small units attached to the price rail that eject a coupon when a person walks by. The unit has a brand identification on the side to provide even further brand communication.

In addition to signs and banners, manufacturers provide restaurants and bars with **table tents,** which are *small tent-shaped signs placed on tables to promote a certain dish or drink.* A variation is the Pizza Hut table talker in Exhibit 14-12, which Pizza Hut sends to local motels to put in their guest rooms to encourage pizza delivery orders.

There are agencies that specialize in designing promotional as well as permanent store interiors. If, for example, a store wanted to use a wine-and-cheese theme for a promotion, or even a store design, then Propaganda, a retail environment design agency based in San Francisco, would suggest such props as picnic baskets, deck chairs, picnic blankets, and photo posters of the countryside. Propaganda's CEO Keith Walton calls that "romancing the customer" with visual merchandising.[6]

The more investment and creativity a chain or independently owned retail store puts into its own store design and ambiance, the less receptive it is to POP from manufacturers. The argument is that most POP materials are strategically inconsistent with the in-store message retailers are trying to communicate—an argument that is difficult to refute. Increasingly, companies are recognizing that if in-store merchandising is to have a significant effect on sales, the materials have to be designed extremely well.

The more consumer pull a brand has, the more pressure manufacturers can place on retailers. For example, Rathers, an independent menswear store in Red Butte, Illinois, opened in 1887 selling Levi-Strauss merchandise. However, Levis recently notified the store that Rathers was losing its franchise for its mainstay Levis and Dockers lines because it did not conform to Levi's display and merchandising criteria. After considerable outcry from customers and the news media, Levi's reversed its decision and allowed the 110-year relationship to continue. For its part, Rathers has promised to do a better job of merchandising the Levis products.[7]

> " If it weren't for visual merchandising, you would walk into a store and everything would just be lying on the floor."
>
> Keith Walton, CEO, Propaganda

Strengths and Limitations of Merchandising

The greatest strength of merchandising and POP is that they direct attention to a brand or particular product offering at the point of sale. In doing so, they increase the level of customer consideration, which positively affects sales, especially for impulse items. Most important, they can nudge customers from a state of interest or desire to action—making a purchase. An American Dairy Association in-store promotion supported by POP increased sales by approximately one third.[8] When POP was used to support a candy and gum promotion, it increased sales nearly 400 percent compared to stores in which the POP was not used.[9] This indicates that POP can affect

EXHIBIT 14-11

This ad for ACTMEDIA, which designs in-store merchandising materials, dramatizes the decisions consumers make as they walk the aisles of a store.

TODAY, THE AVERAGE SUPERMARKET HAS 18,000 BRAND CHOICES. WHAT ARE YOUR CHANCES OF BEING NOTICED?

Today's shoppers are busy people. They're trying to balance multiple demands. They'll only spend 12 seconds selecting a product in your category. So don't leave their purchase decision to chance.

For 25 years ACTMEDIA has been leading the way with impactful programs that offer effective marketing solutions in-store. No one knows the store and the shopping experience more than we do. And no one delivers your message or incentive to your target audience better. In the right place and at the right time; 24 hours a day, seven days a week.

To find out more about ACTMEDIA's in-store solutions, call Patrick B. Harris, Sr. V. P. of Sales, at (203) 847-7610. Together we'll beat the odds.

ACTMEDIA
© ACTMEDIA, INC.

sales in all product categories and is especially powerful when used for impulse items.

The second most important strength of these MC functions is that they provide links between all of the out-of-store brand communication that customers have been exposed to and the in-store shopping experience. When properly done, the design and theme of POP reinforces the creative idea being used to support a brand campaign in other media and MC functional areas. In terms of the trade, merchandising and POP get the attention of the store's personnel and sales force and can inspire them to support a special promotion.

The biggest limitations of POP materials are (1) the retailer's resistance to using them and (2) the failure of salespeople to promote their use where POP is acceptable. Because display materials can significantly affect sales and are relatively inexpensive to use, most brands prepare them. Consequently, retailers are inundated with materials and forced to be selective in what items they allow in their stores.

In high-end stores, retailers may look upon the manufacturer's merchandising materials as cluttering the environment and detracting from the store's image. In supermarkets, for example, shelf space and floor space are precious. This means that retailers often can't use the special racks, sales aids, and promotional literature supplied by manufacturers. Many retailers are so pressed for time and personnel that roughly half of the promotional materials remain in the stock room unused and unassembled.

Because POP is place-based, meaning it is generally in only one location, a customer must come to or walk past that location in order to be exposed to the brand message. It is estimated that in drugstores and discount stores, only about 20 percent of store visitors browse most of the aisles.[10]

Because there are so many end-aisle displays, rail strips, and banners hanging from the ceilings in many stores, all designed to get attention, the retail environment can become visually numbing (see Exhibit 14–13). Studies that ask customers to recall what POP materials they saw when visiting indicate that only a small portion are remembered.

PACKAGING: THE LAST AD SEEN BEFORE BUYING

As the self-service concept in retailing has expanded, the package has become a particularly important brand message for consumer brands. In self-service stores, which nearly all retail stores are today, the package takes the place of the salesperson. As customers move through heavily stocked stores, shoppers scan shelves at the rate of 300 items a minute. Amid all this clutter, a package's job is to attract attention and communicate brand information (see Exhibit 14–14).

Packaging is an important part of a brand's identity, particularly for consumer packaged goods. Outside the United States, these are often referred to as fast-moving consumer goods (FMCGs). By whatever name you choose to call them, the important thing is that they are frequently purchased and their brand identity is conveyed by the package or label. In fact, the package is often the only brand message that distinguishes a branded product from a generic one.

A great example of proprietary packaging (a package design that is patented in order to prevent any other brand from using it) is the hourglass shape of the Coca-Cola bottle. It took Coke years to figure out how to replicate this hourglass shape in plastic bottles and, as a result of that success, introduced a 20-ounce contour plastic bottle. Now it is working on a design for a 20-ounce plastic cup in clear or green plastic in the famous contour shape that will compete with Pepsi's popular "Twist 'n Go" cup.[11]

A package is first of all a container. But more than that, a package also delivers a complex message about the product category and the brand's selling points, as well as the brand identity and image. Just as a store's design sends a strong message about a store, the design and labels on a package communicate important messages about the product it contains. A package is also an intrinsic brand message. A person cannot buy (in the store) or use (in the home or workplace) a packaged product without coming into contact with the brand message.

A package, in other words, is a medium for carrying a planned brand message. As with merchandising and POP materials, a package plays a critical role in brand decision making at the point of sale. There are close links between merchandising and packaging, since both add to, or subtract from, the experience that surrounds a purchase decision.

EXHIBIT 14-14

In the highly competitive cereal market, marketers rely on the design of their packages to make their brands visible and easy to find.

" You don't have to be a rocket scientist to realize the leverageable power in proprietary packaging. "

Coca-Cola spokesperson

Objectives of Packaging

One of the primary responsibilities of a package design is to link the product to the other brand messages to which the customer has been exposed. One way to do this is through the use of flags on the front of the package that can be used to call attention to product features as well as to present reminder messages that tie in with other MC efforts, such as advertising campaigns and special promotional offers.

The brand message transfer is strongest when package designers make sure the package is depicted in all package-goods advertising so that customers know what to look for. But the message transfer is also conveyed through the stylistics of the package's artwork. Celestial Seasonings' packaging, for example, uses delicate illustrations, soft colors, and quotes about life to reinforce its positioning as a New Age, natural, herbal tea.

In addition to brand-identity links, the package design has some very specific attention-getting objectives. To determine which colors, typography, and layout styles will attract the attention of busy shoppers, package designers study which items consumers notice and which ones they actually place in their shopping cart. One of the biggest success stories in packaging has been Pepsi's 32-ounce Twist 'n Go container introduced in 1999. It is spill-resistant, resealable, and designed to fit most car cup holders.

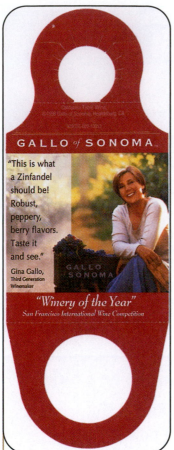

EXHIBIT 14–15

Tags like this can be used to add information to the product's packaging. In this case, the tag explains a type of wine and uses a representative of the wine-making family as an authority figure.

Although packages are most often thought of in conjunction with consumer packaged goods, the packaging concept applies to services just as well. The service "package" is the environment in which a service is delivered. How many times have you based the selection or rejection of a restaurant on its exterior or interior appearance? Likewise, for service personnel operating away from their place of business, their uniforms and the vehicles they drive become elements in the service "package."

The Package Is a Free Medium

Although seldom discussed as such, packaging is a major communication vehicle that companies can use to deliver whatever brand message they wish. Unfortunately, many manufacturers of packaged goods still consider a package primarily as a container. If you think of a package as a communication opportunity, however, then the media cost is zero because the package is "already there."

The number of people who walk down food, drug, and mass merchandiser aisles everyday is in the millions—far more than the number who watch an average prime-time TV show. What this means is that a brand's package is like a miniature outdoor board with millions of potential exposures each day. Companies that fail to make their packages attention-getting and appealing are missing a communication opportunity. The design cost to improve and modernize a package label, when spread over millions of exposures, not to mention purchases, is one of the best bargains in marketing communication.

The fact that the package is the last brand message that a prospective customer sees before making a brand choice is another strong rationale for making package design an important part of an IMC program. This is particularly true for brands and product lines that have little or no other marketing communication support. Techniques like the hang tag in Exhibit 14–15 are used to provide an additional on-product advertisement.

For example, one meat company produced a line of thin-sliced lunch meat that was sold in four-ounce plastic pouches. Because this line of six different meats had sales of only $25 million a year, the company could not cost-justify producing and running print or broadcast advertising for the line. The fact that it carried the corporate brand name, as did all the other 150 different products, was the only MC support the line had, which is why its sales increases were minimal year after year. Then, working with a packaging design firm and spending less than $100,000, the company redesigned the packaging, giving the products much more attention-getting power and appetite appeal. The result was a nearly $7 million increase in sales (a 27 percent increase) the first year after the new package was introduced. The return on the investment (ROI) paid for the cost of the redesign many, many times over.

Strengths and Limitations of Packaging

Packages both protect a product as it is distributed and facilitate transportation. But beyond those functional objectives, packages can also be used to make a strong visual statement that brings the brand personality to life, ties in with other marketing communication efforts, and delivers low-cost brand information and reminders in the critical "buy zone" in a store. Furthermore, a package continues to communicate after the buyer leaves the store. The package can provide important decision information, such as nutrition information and product claims like "caffeine free." It can also showcase promotions with flags like "official sponsor of the Olympics," or "free toy inside."

Sometimes the package itself can be an added value, particularly when it is designed to add convenience to a product. Aseptic juice packages (i.e., juice boxes), for example, created an entirely new category in the beverage market because they are not only portable and lightweight but also don't have to be refrigerated. Bottles that have a special nondrip spout provide added value for products like syrup and laundry detergent. Packages can even function as a premium when they become collector's items, such as Avon bottles, special holiday liquor bottles, and designer cans used to package teas, cookies, or crackers.

The biggest limitation for packaging is its potential for clogging up landfills. The long box often used to package CDs is one example of unnecessary overpackaging. The asceptic beverage box used for milk and juices turned out to be a nightmare for environmentalists because the thin layers of paper and plastic and the aluminum-foil lining are hard to separate. A number of companies are redesigning their packages in order to make them more disposable. Carnation has converted its pet food cans to recyclable aluminum. Heinz has replaced its perennial dump filler, the squeezable ketchup bottle, with one that can be more easily recycled.

A FINAL NOTE: EVERYTHING SAYS SHARKS

The Natal Rugby Union used a big idea—Sharks—as an identity link for its new brand image. This new position was communicated through advertising, merchandising, and packaging, among other MC tools, to create a new attitude for its team, the Natal Sharks. The power of advertising to reach a broad audience and build a high level of awareness was what led that team to its position as one of the leading global marketers in the rugged sport of rugby.

Although advertising is generally thought to be nonpersonal and one-way, the excitement generated by the new brand identity campaign was able to lock in the new team attitude of "proud, professional, and predatory" in the public mind. The message was continually reinforced, not only in traditional advertising but also in merchandising and the packaging of the team and its mascot, which carried the new team brand image to stores and the street. The Natal Sharks experience, which came alive in events and shopping, was reinforced by this reminder advertising, which demonstrates the IMC philosophy that everything carries a message and contributes to a brand image when it is focused and single-minded.

Key Terms

mass media advertising 506
merchandising 518
point-of-purchase (POP) materials 518

shipper displays 518
shelf talker 518
table tents 509

Key Point Summary

This chapter is focused on the marketing communication functions that use mass media to make contact with customers and other stakeholders. It describes mass media advertising and its primary strength, which is awareness building, it describes merchandising whose primary strength is in-store promotions, and it describes packaging which delivers the last message a consumer sees before making a purchase.

Key Point 1: Advertising's Strengths and Limitations

Advertising consists of nonpersonal one-way planned messages paid for by an identified sponsor and disseminated to a broad audience in order to influence their attitudes and behavior. Advertising can be classified in terms of media used, audience targeted, geographical reach, and the focus of its objectives. Advertising's strengths include the ability to reach large markets cost-effectively and the ability to build strong brands by creating a brand personality that adds value to a product. Advertising's limitations relate primarily to media waste, low credibility, and clutter.

Key Point 2: Merchandising

Merchandising refers to in-store promotional activities of manufacturers and retailers, which includes posters, signage, and product displays that are used to increase store traffic. Point-of-purchase materials are a type of merchandising.

Key Point 3: Package Design

More than a container, a package is a communication vehicle that delivers a complex brand message (identification cues, image, and selling points), ties in with other marketing communication, and delivers low-cost brand reminder information.

Lessons Learned

Key Point 1: Advertising's Strengths and Limitations

a. Why is advertising called "the awareness builder"?
b. List the six characteristics of advertising discussed in this chapter's definition of advertising.
c. What does it mean to say that advertising builds demand?
d. Build a scrapbook of ads (copies of print ads and written summaries of broadcast commercials) that illustrate the five types of advertising objectives discussed in this chapter.
e. Explain what it means to say that advertising creates a psychological relationship between a brand and its customers. How was that true for the Natal Sharks?
f. Why is reaching a mass market considered to be a strength of advertising? Why is it also considered a weakness?
g. Find an example of an advertising campaign that takes advantage of advertising's ability to both reach mass markets and add value through branding. Explain how these strengths are evident in the campaign.
h. Why is low credibility a limitation of advertising?
i. What is a hidden cost of clutter in terms of advertising effectiveness?
j. Create your own lampoon or parody ad. If you are not comfortable doing anti-advertising for a brand, then use the parody technique on the behalf of a good cause.

Key Point 2: Merchandising

a. Define merchandising.
b. In what ways is visual merchandising "theatrical"?
c. What is a point-of-purchase display? Give an example.

d.   What is the difference between a shelf talker and a table talker? Find examples of each.

e.   What are the key strengths and limitations of sales promotions?

f.   List at least three objectives that you might use in designing a sales promotion program.

g.   Visit your favorite store and analyze the visual messages that cue its personality and make it distinctive in its market. In addition to store design, what other merchandising materials did you observe in use in the store?

Key Point 3: Package Design

a.   What are the communication functions that a package performs?

b.   What does it mean to say that packages have a billboard function?

c.   Visit your local grocery store and identify the brand that has the most "shelf facings" (packages that face you as you stand in the aisle). Explain how this brand benefits from the billboard effect.

d.   What are the key strengths and limitations of packaging design?

e.   List at least three objectives that you might have in designing packaging.

Chapter Challenge

Writing Assignment

Visit the website of the Advertising Educational Foundation (www.aef.com). Find some piece of information about advertising that builds on the discussion in this chapter. Write a report on what you have found and how it extends your knowledge of how advertising works. Then visit the website of Adbusters (www.adbusters.org) and do the same type of analysis. Compare what you have learned from both sites.

Presentation Assignment

Analyze your university or college as a brand. Analyze how advertising contributes to the development of this brand. What is its identity, image, and reputation? Develop recommendations on what needs to be done to strengthen your school's branding, and present them to your class.

Internet Assignment

Consult AdCritic.com (www.adcritic.com) and find an ad that you think represents the strength of a creative idea. Explain how the ad works to create its impact.

Additional Readings

Aaker, David A., and Alexander L. Biel. *Brand Equity & Advertising*. Hillsdale, NJ: Lawrence Erlbaum, 1993.

Braunstein, Marc; Ned Levine; and Edward Levine. *Deep Branding on the Internet: Applying Heat and Pressure Online to Ensure a Lasting Brand*. Rocklin, CA: Prima Publishing, 2000.

Gladwell, Malcolm. *The Tipping Point: How Little Things Can Make a Big Difference*. Boston: Little Brown & Co., 2000.

Jones, John Philip, ed. *The Advertising Business*. Thousand Oaks, CA: Sage, 1999.

Ries, Laura, and Al Ries. *The 22 Immutable Laws of Branding: How to Build a Product or Service into a World-Class Brand*. New York: HarperCollins, 1998.

Roman, Kenneth, and Jane Maas. *The New How to Advertise*. New York: St. Martin's Press, 1992.

Sullivan, Luke. *"Hey, Whipple, Squeeze This," A Guide to Creating Great Ads*. New York: John Wiley & Sons, 1998.

Travis, Daryl, and Richard Branson. *Emotional Branding: How Successful Brands Gain the Irrational Edge*. Rocklin, CA: Prima Publishing, 2000.

Wells, William; John Burnett; and Sandra Moriarty. *Advertising Principles & Practice*. Upper Saddle River NJ: Prentice Hall, 1998.

Zeff, Robbin Lee, and Brad Aronson. *Advertising on the Internet,* 2nd ed. New York: John Wiley & Sons, 1999.

Research Assignment

From these books and other books and articles you can find, develop an argument either supporting or opposing the notion that advertising makes an important contribution to society.

Endnotes

[1] John Galvin, "Dirty Little Secret," *SmartBusinessMag.Com*, June 2000, p. 54.

[2] Jim Oates, of Leo Burnett, personal interview with author, Chicago, July 1995.

[3] Lowell Conn, "Old Dogs Learn Faster Tricks," *BrandEra.com*, March 1, 2000.

[4] Kathryn Kranhold, "Taco Bell Ads to Focus on Food, Not Dog," *The Wall Street Journal*, October 11, 1999, p. B10.

[5] John Leo, "Captives of the Advertising Culture," *Indianapolis Star*, December 31, 1997, p. A10.

[6] Jane Applegate, " 'Visual Merchandising' Sets Mood," *The Denver Post*, April 26, 1998, p. 7-I.

[7] "Divorce Retail Style," *Retrospectives in Marketing* 11, no. 2, April 1998, p. 2.

[8] "A. C. Nielsen Research Reveals Cheese Sales Skyrocket with In-Store Promotions," *POPAI News*, Marketplace 1990, p. 19.

[9] *The Point of Purchase Advertising Industry Fact Book*, 2000, p. 51.

[10] Website of POPAI, "Competitive Media Facts," July 2000.

[11] Kate MacArthur, "Fracas Hits the Fountain," *Advertising Age*, May 29, 2000, p. 46.

15

Public Relations: The Credibility Builder

Key Points in This Chapter

1. What is public relations, and how does it relate to IMC?

2. Why is corporate communication important to IMC programs?

3. What are the strengths and limitations of marketing public relations (MPR)?

Chapter Perspective:
The Relationship Angle

Public relations professionals have always understood the concept of relationships—after all, the word *relations* is part of their job title. In the brand decision process, public relations messages are particularly useful in announcing new products, helping prospects and customers find information, and establishing credibility for the brand.

Unfortunately, many marketing people in the past did not always recognize or appreciate the value of public relations departments. And, because of the turf battles between the two functions, public relations people typically focused on government, community, and media groups and were not much involved in the management of customer relationships.

Some major steps toward bringing marketing and public relations departments closer came in the early 1990s with the development of a concept called relationship marketing, pioneered by Regis McKenna, chairman of the consulting firm the McKenna Group. At the same time, courses devoted to relationship marketing began to develop in business schools around the world through the efforts of such scholars as Jag Sheth at Emory University in Atlanta, Christian Grönroos in Finland, and Rod Brodie in New Zealand. Although McKenna's background is public relations, he calls himself a marketing consultant. He challenged the marketing industry to become more "customer-centric" and better understand customer relationships. "Advertising, promotion, and market-share thinking are dead," writes McKenna, "and what counts are the relationships a company develops with its customers, suppliers, partners, distributors—even its competitors."[1]

IMC, with its relationship focus, is helping to introduce concepts to marketing professionals that public relations professionals have known about for years, such as the importance of stakeholder relationships. Marketing people are discovering the power and value of brand publicity to deliver highly effective, cost-efficient messages. At the same time, public relations people are learning more about marketing and using marketing concepts like branding and positioning to build corporate communication strategies.

This chapter begins with an overview of the public relations industry and the types of public relations. It then explores the concept of corporate communication, which is specifically concerned with building a company's image and reputation. The third main section is devoted to "marketing public relations," whose primary strength from an IMC perspective is building a brand's overall credibility.

SWIMMING TO INDUSTRY LEADERSHIP
Freshwater Software, Denver, Colorado

Freshwater Software is a company that helps other companies set up and manage their Internet sites for e-business. A leading provider of e-business solutions, Freshwater has produced a suite of software products that monitor the reliability of its clients' websites. In addition to dot-coms, Freshwater's customers include banks and online trading firms that depend on customers being able to access their portfolios and make transactions accurately and quickly.

Established in 1996 with 5 employees, the firm had grown to 48 employees by midyear 2000, when it was ranked as the second fastest-growing private company in the Denver, Colorado, metropolitan area. In addition to its explosive growth, the innovative software company is known for two things: a customer-centric business philosophy and a unique corporate culture. Both of these are given wide publicity by the company's public relations agency, Citigate Cunningham, that emphasizes branding in its communication planning.

Donna Auguste, Freshwater's president and co-founder, claims the growth is a product of the company's philosophy of listening to its clients. The company uses customer feedback to determine what products the fast-changing world of e-business will need next. To maximize the power and immediacy of feedback, Freshwater's software engineers also participate in customer-service duties.

The company's culture is based on sensitive teamwork, as well as a close working relationship with customers. Auguste is known for her ability to implement nontraditional team-building activities that inspire new ways of thinking and working in the high-tech environment. She was described by the *New York Times* as having "a flair for managing the teams that come together, with an extraordinary commitment, to build the software that breathes life into the machines."

Brand imagery is also an important part of the company's culture. The biggest visible statement of that can be found in Freshwater's corporate offices, where a maze of fish tanks line the desks and serve as cubicle dividers (see Exhibit 15–1). The meeting room resembles a submarine with gray walls and portholes. The company strives to be a fun place to work, and that attitude is carried out in the cartoon-style fish that serves as the corporate logo (see Exhibit 15–2).

Freshwater's primary product is its Global SiteReliance, an annual subscription service that is a unique blend of software, services, and a network operations center, which provides around-the-clock site monitoring. SiteScope™ monitors the entire transaction process of its clients' customers from order placement to delivery. It also provides reports on a nightly or weekly basis. Another product, SiteSeer™, provides Web administrators with a visitor's eye-view of their website.

Auguste explains that these products allow Web administrators to monitor the critical back-end processes that provide brand integrity for companies engaging in Web commerce, "where the rules of the competitive game don't allow for downtime or incomplete transactions." In experiencing the site as users do, managers monitor response times and can identify bottlenecks. Auguste explains that "the integrity of their brands is contingent upon users' website experiences." The online advertising service DoubleClick, for example, delivers advertising to 11,000 sites worldwide. It uses Freshwater's SiteScope to help ensure that its 1,500 servers are up and running 24 hours a day, seven days a week.

Citigate Cunningham has surrounded the growth of Freshwater Software with extensive publicity. Frequent news releases focus on the following types of information:

EXHIBIT 15-1

EXHIBIT 15-1

Freshwater's office interior manifests the company's name by using freshwater aquariums as office dividers.

- Product improvements: "Freshwater Software Launches Global SiteReliance to Remotely Manage e-business Growth"; "Freshwater Software Launches SiteScope 5.0 to Help e-businesses Grow."

- Recognition by industry sources: "Freshwater Software Ranked Second Fastest Growing Private Company in Denver Area"; "*Computerworld* Names Freshwater Software One of '100 Emerging Companies to Watch in 2000'"; "Freshwater's SiteScope Wins *PC Computing* 1999 MVP Award."

- Stories about its clients' use of Freshwater's products: "Freshwater to Enable eBusiness Growth for DoubleClick's Global Internet Advertising Solutions"; "Microsoft Selects Freshwater Software's SiteScope as Monitoring Solution for MSN.COM."

- Personal successes of its staff and management team: "Freshwater Receives U.S. Patent for eBusiness Transaction Monitoring"; "*Denver Business Journal*

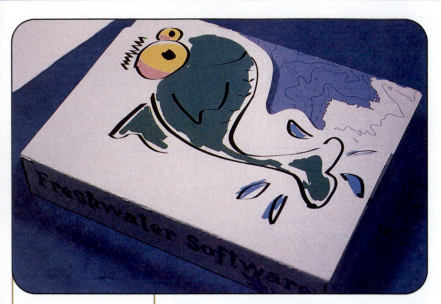

Names Freshwater CEO, Donna Auguste, Outstanding Woman in Business"; "Freshwater CTO John Meier Wins *Denver Business Journal's* Prestigious Forty Under 40 Award."

All of these news releases—along with numerous product and company fact sheets, customer lists and testimonials, and corporate executive bios—appear in the Freshwater press kit (see Exhibit 15–3).

Such publicity efforts have led to even more recognition for the company, such as being named one of the "100 Emerging Companies to Watch in 2000" by *Computerworld* magazine and as a Rising Star 2000 in the Deloitte & Touche Colorado Technology Fast 50, which recognizes the region's fastest-growing young technology companies. (Freshwater's revenues grew by 1,495 percent from 1996 to 1999.) These stories result from Citigate Cunningham's good media relations with the high-tech industry press. The visibility that results is good, but even more important is how this coverage is leveraged by the agency. The stories, for example, are available as reprints, which go in the press kit, but also are used by sales representatives and given to potential customers and business partners.

Other stories that testify to the quality of Freshwater's products are leveraged in the same way. One is a column called "The Motley Fool" in *Network World* newsletter, in which the author, Dwight Gibbs, says, "There are many tools in the market that let you monitor servers. We have found one that we think stands out. SiteScope from Freshwater Software is the best thing since sliced bread." *Performance Computing* devoted all of one issue's "Web Advisor" column to a positive review of SiteScope.

Citigate Cunningham presents the press kit to its media contacts in an imaginative box that contains brand promotion items carrying the company's cartoon-fish logo, such as mini-notebook/diary, a T-shirt, a pen made in the shape of the Freshwater fish, decals, and branded Post-it notes. Printed with depth navigation charts on the outside and printed blue both outside and in, the box itself is designed to reinforce Freshwater's brand image. The box is also used for other special events and client presentations, which is another way Citigate Cunningham leverages its ideas for greater promotional effect.

This case was provided by Freshwater Software and its agency, Citigate Cunningham, and used with their permission. Special thanks to Eric Beteille for his cooperation.

EXHIBIT 15-2

This mailing carton shows Freshwater's logo, a cartoon fish.

EXHIBIT 15-3

Freshwater's corporate backgrounding press kit contains much information about the company and its accomplishments.

THE PRACTICE OF PUBLIC RELATIONS

Public relations covers a very broad area and a wide variety of activities that seek to affect both public opinion and the opinion of specific stakeholders whose interests intersect with an organization. It can be a concept, a profession, and a management function, as well as a practice. Its objective is to create goodwill and understanding between an organization and its stakeholders—that is, positive stakeholder relationships.

In terms of its practice, authors James Grunig and Todd Hunt define **public relations** as "management of communication between an organization and its publics."[2] In elaborating on the notion of a variety of "publics," *Inside PR* magazine describes it as "a management discipline that encompasses a wide range of activities, from marketing and advertising to investor relations and government affairs." Denny Griswold, founder of *Public Relations News,* defines the practice even more broadly, as "the management function that evaluates public attitudes, identifies the policies and procedures of an individual or an organization with the public interest, and plans and executes a program of action to earn public understanding and acceptance."[3]

Although the interests of public relations and marketing overlap, in many organizations public relations, at least at the management level, operates separately from marketing with different goals. Fraser Seitel, in his public relations textbook, explains that "whereas marketing and sales have as their primary objective selling an organization's products, public relations attempts to sell the organization itself."[4]

This chapter will first discuss the general field of public relations, then look at corporate communication—what Seitel calls "selling the organization itself." Then it will move to a discussion of marketing public relations (MPR), which is the form of public relations most closely aligned with IMC.

Overview of the Public Relations Industry

Public relations is one of the fastest growing of all the communication functions used in IMC. As shown in Table 15–1, the top 100 firms worldwide increased billings by 25 percent between 1998 and 1999. In 1999, the average growth of the top 50 public relations firms was reported at 32 percent by the Council of Public Relations Firms.[5] Admittedly, some of this growth was the result of mergers and acquisitions, but the trend indicates how healthy this industry is. It is growing because of its ability to reach people with messages that contain a great deal of credibility. Philip Kotler, of Northwestern University's Kellogg School of Management, has noted the power of public relations to cut through message clutter.[6]

Compared to dollars spent on mass media advertising, public relations spending, at first glance, looks relatively

> "Public relations can account for its growth by its great versatility, its aptitude for drama, and its capacity to break through the information clutter and capture attention and interest."
>
> Philip Kotler, Kellogg School of Management, Northwestern University

TABLE 15-1	Changes in Revenue of Top 100 Public Relations Firms ($ Millions)		
	1998	1999	% Increase
U.S. revenue	$1,747	$2,242	28.4%
Worldwide revenue	2,528	3,153	24.7

Source: Council of Public Relations Firms, 1999 Public Relations Industry Rankings <www.prfirms.org/infocenter/1999factsheet.html>.

minor. This is misleading, however, because public relations has little or no media cost, which is the major portion of an advertising budget. The major cost in doing public relations includes staff time and personnel and department management, as well as the production of brochures, newsletters, annual reports, and corporate advertising.

Types of Public Relations

In an effort to maintain good relationships with all its important stakeholders, corporate public relations undertakes a variety of "relational" programs, or areas of practice, as Table 15–2 shows. The table indicates the range of "publics," or stakeholder audiences, that are targeted by traditional public relations programs, from government officials to employees, the financial community, and the media. These areas of expertise may be developed internally within a company, but they are also available from agencies, some of which provide a full range of programs (see Exhibit 15–4). These agencies may also focus on specific industries such as pharmaceuticals, agriculture, or high technology.

An example of how these various types of programs and stakeholders merge in a successful public relations effort comes from the launch of Maytag's Neptune,

T A B L E   1 5 - 2   Types of Public Relations Programs

Type	Description
Corporate relations	Managed by senior-level counselors, such programs focus on corporate identity, reputation management, and strategic counseling for top management. Responsibilities that are sometimes found in corporate relations include: • *Issues management:* functions that monitor public opinion and advise senior management, particularly in those companies in sensitive or controversial industries such as pharmaceuticals, liquor, and cigarettes. • *Community relations:* programs that involve the local community and address their concerns. • *Government relations (public affairs):* information programs for legislators, governmental bodies, and regulatory agencies. • *Industry relations:* activities that address the concerns of the industry in which the company competes.
Crisis management	A general plan designed to manage how a company responds when disaster strikes.
Marketing public relations (Brand publicity)	Programs that support product and brand communication and promotion, and that are directed primarily at consumers.
Media relations	Activities that distribute information to the media creating publicity for an organization; activities that cultivate relationships of trust with key reporters and editors.
Employee relations	Internal communication programs that keep employees informed and build their morale (can also be a part of internal marketing programs); employee relations can also include labor relations programs.
Financial or investor relations	Information programs for the financial community—investors, analysts, and the financial press.

which is featured in the IMC Strategy box (next page). The Neptune story illustrates how public relations can be used to announce news and create awareness among customers and other important stakeholders. The Neptune launch involved media relations, community relations, government relations, and financial relations. It is likely that such a successful new product launch involved Maytag's employees as well.

Public Relations Strategy and Planning

Public relations strategy can be focused on the corporate brand or a product brand. Whatever its focus, different public relations agencies have their own approaches to strategy development. For example, as noted in the chapter opening case, Citigate Cunningham is a public relations agency that specializes in brand building. In Citigate's approach, brand differentiation comes from managing a unique combination of perceptions and substance, a combination that delivers momentum to a brand.[7] Its work for Freshwater Software demonstrates the company's proprietary method, called Momentum Management. Ron Ricci, one of the creators of the Momentum Management philosophy, explains that, in physics, momentum is derived from the mass of a body or system and how fast it is moving in a particular direction. Those three concepts—mass, speed, and direction—are at the heart of Citigate's Momentum Management philosophy (see Figure 15–1). For Freshwater Software, the *mass* is the company's Internet monitoring software products and services, the *speed* can be expressed as constant change and innovation, and the *direction* is leadership in the industry.

Positioning is also a critical factor in Citigate Cunningham's approach to brand strategy. Its structured approach to building a positioning platform was introduced briefly in Chapter 9, in a discussion of how various agencies approach message strategy. First is the Positioning Statement, which summarizes the key elements of the brand's position. For Freshwater Software, the positioning statement was "Freshwater Software is the leading provider of comprehensive Internet growth solutions for e–business."

Next come the key Value Propositions, which are the selling premises behind the brand's differentiation. For Freshwater Software, the agency identified three benefits the firm offers its clients: growth in e-business, rapid implementation on a global scale, and brand integrity. Each of those three propositions was further developed with Key Messages, Proof Points, and Sound Bites. For example, under eBusiness Growth, the key message was that Freshwater Software's "managed services, technologies, and expertise are critical enablers of e-business growth." The four reasons why that statement is true focus on (1) the Internet model used by Freshwater to leverage growth, (2) corporate and company leadership, (3) the focus on growing customers' business, and (4) the critical role of business partners. The Sound Bites were quotes from customers that serve as testimonies to the effectiveness of Freshwater in delivering that particular Value Proposition.

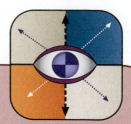

IMC STRATEGY

Maytag Takes a Spin with Public Relations

When appliance manufacturer Maytag launched its new Neptune, a revolutionary, high-efficiency front-loading washer, that entered a market dominated by top-loaders, it depended on public relations to get the story out. To get attention and visibility, Maytag and the public relations arm of its advertising agency, Leo Burnett, unveiled the product to the trade and media at a New York launch party hosted by Ol' Lonely, the Maytag Repairman. The event featured famous television moms Barbara Billingsley "Leave It to Beaver," June Lockhart "Lassie," "Lost in Space," Florence Henderson "The Brady Bunch," and Isabel Sanford "The Jeffersons."

But Maytag needed more than just visibility to support its high-efficiency claim. In order to drive home that message, Maytag worked with the U.S. Department of Energy (DOE) to conduct a live water-conservation test in Bern, Kansas (population 204). After replacing half of the small town's washers with a Neptune for six weeks, the DOE computed a 38 percent savings in overall water use. The successful demonstration was widely covered by the media, which added even more visibility to the new washer.

The Neptune launch was driven by public relations with very limited advertising. Maytag claims it was the most successful product launch in the company's history because it convinced consumers to trade for a new washer instead of waiting for theirs to wear out.

The raves of other stakeholders, such as financial analysts who were impressed by the company's innovative new product, also drove the Maytag stock price up 100 percent in a relatively short period.

Think About It

What was Maytag's primary selling message? Why did it elect to deliver that message with public relations rather than advertising?

Six Dimensions that Drive Brand Momentum

Category Leadership

Relevance of Value Proposition

Ecosystem Potential

Market Agility

Building Mass — Gaining Speed — Setting a Direction

Management Vision

Brand Integrity

Even though Citigate Cunningham is a public relations agency, it should be clear from an analysis of this document that its focus is on brand building. The tools that it uses—press releases, fact sheets, reprints, quotes from satisfied customers, and other promotional ideas—are all designed to communicate the brand position detailed in this Positioning Platform.

CORPORATE COMMUNICATION

Although most of the discussion so far has been on product line branding, there is another level of brand building: the corporate brand. The Freshwater case at the beginning of this chapter demonstrates how public relations activities can be used in support of corporate brand building and brand positioning.

Both advertising and public relations are involved in managing corporate and brand images and identities. Public relations programs generally have responsibility for managing corporate image; marketing is generally responsible for managing the image of product brands. The distinction between the two is sometimes fuzzy because they affect the other. For example, sometimes the corporate name is the same as the brand name (Nike, Disney); sometimes it is different (General Motors and Saturn; Procter & Gamble and Tide, Freshwater Software and SiteScope); and sometimes it is connected (Sony and the Sony Walkman). Regardless of the branding strategy used, there should be concern about how the product brand and the corporate brand reflect on and reinforce one another.

Public relations executives who work at a senior level in a company and advise top management on how the organization presents itself, are called **corporate communication executives.** These executives, and the public relations agencies that advise them, are very much focused on maintaining the corporate brand and corporate reputation.

Another focus of corporate communication executives is on opinion and issues management. Because of the powerful effect of public opinion, organizations of all kinds must consider the public impact of their actions and decisions, as well as the effect of changing public opinion on the organization's business opportunities. This is especially true in times of crisis, emergency, or disaster, but it also holds true for major policy decisions—changes in management or pricing, labor negotiations, new product offerings, closing or opening plants, or changes in distribution methods. Each decision affects different groups in different ways. Through effective public relations, managers hope to channel stakeholder opinions toward better understanding of issues and create more positive attitudes toward the company's actions.

Cargill, the largest privately held corporation in the United States, processes and distributes a wide array of food and agricultural products; the company has always been active in giving voice to farm-oriented public opinion. An example is the *Cargill Bulletin,* which is distributed free to farmers, policymakers, academics, and other opinion leaders. It's also available on the company's website. What makes the bulletin different is that it offers a spectrum of opinion—including Cargill's own—on agriculture issues. Another opinion program is the company's "community network," which consists of about 1,000 managers organized as a speakers' bureau and a platform for leadership in farm communities.

Most important, corporate communication executives are involved in the management of communication both internally and externally with key stakeholder groups. In a newsletter from the global public relations agency GCI Group (see Exhibit 15–5), an essay focuses on the importance of planning these communication efforts:

> As the nerve system of an organization, communication can be the conduit through which information is carried, disseminated, discussed, debated and ultimately incorporated into constructive action and long-term knowledge. Calls to action, goal setting, unifying behind a common mission—none of these things can be carried out without an effective communication plan.[8]

Corporate Advertising

It was mentioned in Chapter 14 that mass media advertising is itself used by most of the other MC functions. Public relations uses two different kinds of advertising: **public service announcements,** which are *ads for nonprofit organizations that run on time and space donated by the media,* and **corporate advertising,** which are *ads designed to build awareness of a company and explain what it does or believes.* Although public service announcements are for good causes (such as the Partnership for a Drug Free America—discussed later in this chapter), the most visible expression of the corporate communication focus is corporate advertising. Such advertising can have any number of purposes, such as:

- *Corporate identity.* Corporate identity advertising tries to establish a higher level of awareness of a company, its brands, and what it does. This is often the problem after a merger when several companies are trying to build awareness of a new corporate name. This advertising is often targeted to the financial community.

- *Advocacy.* Advocacy advertising is designed to state a corporate position on a controversial issue, such as a lumber company or chemical company speaking out on environmental concerns and proposed legislation.

- *Social issue.* Social issue advertising seeks to establish an image of a company as being socially responsible. In this category are ads for good causes that a company chooses to support.

Exhibit 15–6 illustrates an ad sponsored by Anheuser-Busch (makers of Budweiser, Michelob, and a wide assortment of other beers) intended to position the company as an advocate of responsible drinking. Even though public service and corporate advertising uses advertising techniques, they are often planned and executed by the public relations department. Corporate advertising is most frequently used by large, multiproduct companies or new companies that are the product of mergers or acquisitions. It is somewhat controversial because it is one of the most difficult types of marketing communication programs to evaluate in terms of its return on investment.

An example of a corporate advertising campaign used to reposition a corporate image comes from Cargill, mentioned above as the largest privately held company in the United States. In 1999, the company began a corporate campaign that sought to change its "invisible giant" image. One commercial features a rancher saddling his horse while his partner, who is sitting on a fence reading a newspaper, points to the headline "Cargill Develops Technology to Process Beef More Safely." The first man replies, "Yup. And look what they did with it," as the second man turns the page and finds another headline, which proclaims that Cargill will share its innovation with the entire

industry. The ad is remarkable, according to *Reputation Management* magazine, not only because it calls attention to Cargill but also because of its offer to share technologies that are good for the consumer, putting customers ahead of private gain. The campaign's theme—"It's not just what we do. It's how we do it"—is designed to emphasize that the company's values are what set it apart from the competition.[9]

Corporate advertising is generally created to reach a variety of target audiences. Firms that specialize in developing corporate identity programs and marketing communication campaigns claim that these efforts not only have a positive impact on employees, investors, and other members of the financial community but also help attract high-quality employees and increase sales.

Because it is less focused on bottom-line results than product advertising, corporate advertising increases when companies and the economy are doing well. For example, the percentage of U.S. companies that ran corporate ad campaigns went from 50 percent in 1992 to 63 percent in 1997, and the average annual amount spent increased over 30 percent during this period.[10]

One of the criticisms of corporate advertising is that it is placed in mass media and thus aimed at broad audiences. Very few viewers or readers of such advertising are stakeholders or potential stakeholders of the company being advertised.

Corporate Mission and Vision

A corporate communication program must be built on the bedrock of a solid corporate mission and vision. A central mission anchors the marketing communication and becomes the central focus of integrated communication.[11] A mission statement, which is often the responsibility of corporate communication, is an expression of a company's history, business philosophy, and distinctive competencies. This is its corporate purpose above and beyond making money—that is, the company's raison d'être.

The word *vision* is sometimes used interchangeably with *mission*. However, *vision* adds the ideas of direction and focus for the future growth of a company to the idea of mission. Cargill's vision is to raise living standards around the world by delivering increased value to producers and consumers. Its mission statement also identifies its key stakeholders:

> We will accomplish this vision by being the best at merchandising, processing, and distributing agricultural and other commodities. We will reinvest substantially all of our cash flow to provide needed products and services for our customers, rewarding career opportunities for our employees, and attractive long-term value for our shareholders. We will be a valued customer for our suppliers and responsible neighbors in our communities.[12]

In another example, when Carly Fiorina took over as CEO of Hewlett-Packard (HP), she determined that her first priority was to create a compelling vision for the high-tech company, one that would reposition it in the marketplace. A $200 million global branding campaign was created to launch Fiorina's vision of the HP story: "We are a company founded by inventors, fueled by invention, and adept at reinventing ourselves to track with new market opportunities." The campaign uses a visual of a garage to symbolize the company's founding in the 1940s by Bill Hewlett and Dave Packard in a one-car garage in Palo Alto, California. The campaign both celebrates HP's history and its sense of itself as an inventive organization and gives direction to the future operation of the company. The vision and the campaign also are an attempt to

EXHIBIT 15-6

In a campaign to position itself as supporting responsible drinking behavior, Anheuser-Busch runs ads helping parents deal with underage drinking.

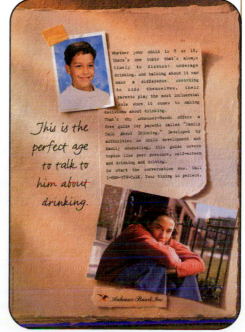

reposition HP's corporate brand, which, with its 130 different product groups and stifling bureaucracy, had become unfocused. Fiorina describes the campaign as "a 360-degree message," in that it starts with employees and "extends to everyone we work with and work for"—customers, business partners, shareholders.[13]

Similarly, when Steve Jobs came back to Apple Computer, he had to reinvent the company's vision: He had to make Apple cool again. Apple's first new corporate campaign under Jobs featured great creative thinkers of history and the slogan "Think Different" as a way to reinforce the company's association with creativity and its leadership in new computer ideas. The campaign was supported with the launch of new products, including the iMac, which, with its bubble-gum colors and distinctive design, became the most popular computer launch in history, according to Harry Pforzheimer, who heads the technology practices group in the Silicon Valley office of Edelman Public Relations.[14]

Corporate Culture

A corporation's culture is also built on the bedrock of mission and vision. As noted in Chapter 1, a **corporate culture** is the *pattern of shared values and beliefs that structure the way an organization's employees work and interact with each other and with stakeholders*. It determines whether a company encourages new ideas (such as IMC and cross-functional management) and rewards discussion and criticism, or whether it is closed to new ideas and encourages people to just follow the rules. Corporate culture is a concern of the highest level of senior management, and it takes its direction from the leadership style of the chief executive. Often programs that are designed to adjust corporate culture are managed by senior executives from corporate communication. Corporate culture just exists in some companies, but other companies care about how it is created and managed. Because of its dependence on employees, such an assignment may fall to the employee relations people, whether in public relations or human resources.

As noted at various points in this book, a company can't be integrated externally in its communication with stakeholders unless it is integrated internally. And that means the corporate culture must support the notions of information sharing and customer focus. It is difficult to implement an IMC program in a company that doesn't support cross-functional planning and reward efforts to increase the lifetime value of customers.

Change Agent

The process of realigning a corporate culture, repositioning a corporate brand, or reengineering an organization's structure—or implementing an IMC program—inevitably involves change throughout an organization. That's why managers who undertake such restructuring and refocusing must also be **change agents,** *people who understand the process of transformation and develop plans to guide an organization in the new direction*. The Hill and Knowlton ad in Exhibit 15–7 focuses on this important role and explains how the public relations agency can help with this transformation.

Corporate Image and Reputation

The difference between an *image* and a *reputation* is sometimes confusing, both for brands and organizations. An image can be created—but a reputation is earned. An image is more of a facade based on planned communication, such as advertising

EXHIBIT 15-7

Hill and Knowlton focuses attention in this ad on its ability to help companies that are undergoing change, reorganization, and transformation.

and brand publicity; reputation reflects how a company behaves, and it is based on what other stakeholders say about the company. **Reputation,** then, is *the esteem that a company or brand has in the eyes of its stakeholders; it represents the organization's core values and behaviors,* and is reflected in word-of-mouth, confirmatory statements by others, as well as personal experiences with a company or brand.

As Paul Holmes, editor of *Reputation Management,* argues in an editorial, a brand image is what a company believes about its products, but reputation is the brand plus behavior.[15] Both brand image and brand reputation are important and, ideally, they merge to create brand integrity. In Chapter 2, a brand was defined as the net sum of its relationships. Another way of describing a corporate brand, then, is that it is the sum of its image and reputation. These two elements together drive brand relationships.

An example of a company that understands brand integrity is Sara Lee, which recently offered its controversial cut-tobacco unit for sale. The division was a

> **" It is not only what the company says about its product, but also what it does."**
>
> Paul Holmes, *Reputation Management*

highly profitable business, but one that seemed to undercut the meaning of the company's slogan "Nobody doesn't like Sara Lee."

A recent Harris poll identified the organization most admired by Americans as the 100-year-old company best known for its baby powder and shampoo—Johnson & Johnson (J&J).[16] One reason J&J has maintained its high level of public esteem is that it puts its customers first. Its business credo, written in 1943, begins, "We believe our first responsibility is to the doctors, nurses and patients, to mothers and fathers, and all others who use our products and services." It puts that philosophy into action in its support of programs like Head Start. The ad in Exhibit 15–8, promotes Head Start as a program supported by J&J's Management Fellows Program, which provides business leadership and training for such organizations.

Corporate branding and reputation go hand in hand. A recent article in *Public Relations Quarterly* merges the marketing-based customer relationship management (CRM) philosophy with another CRM: corporate reputation management.[17] Thomas L. Harris, author of several books on marketing public relations, explains that a corporate brand "is a shorthand way of evoking in your mind all of the qualities you associate with a company."[18] These are primarily emotional connections based on experiences with the company, its behavior, and its products' performance. Similar to product brands, the corporate brand has trust—for example, J&J's high level of esteem—as its foundation. This point was noted by former J&J CEO James Burke, who defined a corporate brand as "the capitalized value of the trust between a company and its customer." The current CEO, Ralph S. Larsen, says, "Johnson & Johnson is more than a trademark. It's a 'trustmark.'"[19]

An indication of the need for marketing and public relations to work closely together in managing corporate reputation comes from a reputation question in Thomas L. Harris's study of Fortune 500 companies.[20] Harris found that when corporate public relations managers were asked how involved other executives were in managing the reputation of the firm, marketing and advertising managers were third on the list, behind public relations/public affairs managers and CEOs (see Table 15–3).

EXHIBIT 15-8

Johnson & Johnson's corporate slogan, "Caring for Generations," is brought to life in this ad, which reports on J&J's Management Fellows Program and its involvement with the Head Start program.

TABLE 15-3	Importance of Reputation Management
Type of Manager	Percentage of Respondents Who Cited Reputation Management as Important
Public relations/public affairs	60%
The CEO of the firm	51
Marketing/advertising	39
CFO/investor relations	27
Other top management	24
Middle management	11

Source: Thomas L. Harris/Impulse Research, "Corporate Communications Spending and Reputations of Fortune 500 Companies," Los Angeles, CA: Impulse Research Corp. Report, June 4, 1999, p. 16.

MARKETING PUBLIC RELATIONS

Marketers often talk, erroneously, about using "public relations" to help promote a brand. What they are really talking about is using **marketing public relations (MPR),** which is just one function of public relations and is defined as *the use of non-paid media to deliver positive brand information designed to positively influence customers and prospects.* The related but slightly more specific term **brand publicity** means *using news releases and other media tools to broaden awareness and knowledge of a brand or company.* While traditional corporate public relations focuses on a full range of stakeholder relationship programs (as Table 15–2 illustrated), MPR focuses more on customers and prospects, complementing other marketing efforts. The IMC in Action box illustrates how powerful public relations can be in a marketing communication program.

I M C   I N   A C T I O N

Fanning the *Goblet of Fire* PR Blaze

One of the hottest stories in marketing relations was the launch in 2000 of *Harry Potter and the Goblet of Fire*, the fourth book in the popular children's series. A blaze of publicity about the boy wizard was created, which included Sam Donaldson reading from the book on ABC's "This Week," an interview with author J. K. Rowling on "Sunday Morning on CBS," a *New York Times* article about a publicity stunt involving a train dubbed the Hogwarts Express, a Rowling interview with *Newsweek* editor Malcom Jones, and two consecutive appearances on the cover of *Newsweek*. On this day Harry beat out Arafat, Barak, Clinton, and the Mideast summit as the lead news story on the "Today" show.

The key to the publicity was the temporary embargo by the publisher, Scholastic Press. The idea was that booksellers were prohibited from selling any copies of the book until 12:00 midnight ushered in the launch date of July 8. The public relations ploy—which added drama to the coverage of little kids lining up at midnight to get their copies—was covered by almost every local and national print and broadcast medium in the United States and the United Kingdom. Pre-stories for the July 8 event began running in May. The CEO of the British brand consultancy company Interbrand compared the Harry Potter campaign, with its warehouse security, to the launch of a new car: "There is quite obsessive secrecy. All the news is kept under strict control. And you create a sense of expectation and anticipation."

Another publicity vehicle was the Hogwarts Express, an old-fashioned steam-powered train that moved from book signing to book signing at railway stations large and small around the United States and the United Kingdom. In London, more than 500 children took part in a sleepover party at bookseller Waterstone's flagship store in Piccadilly Circus.

Barnes & Noble, which wasn't even allowed to unpack its boxes until the magic midnight hour, sold more than 850,000 books in its stores and on its website. And independent booksellers everywhere sponsored midnight parties for their customers both young and old. The first weekend after the launch, Amazon.com shipped 375,000 copies, an event that also received national television news coverage and was celebrated in an ad by FedEx, which delivered the books.

But the launch was only the beginning. Late in 2001, Harry Potter's first motion picture was scheduled to be released with the same kind of publicity campaign. Estimates are that the revenues from the movie, books, toys, and other merchandise and licensing could be $5 to $10 billion. Quite a take for what is essentially a classic MPR case study.

Think About It

Why is this a good example of MPR? Why did Scholastic use public relations rather than advertising? What public relations tactics were in this product launch?

Sources: *Thomas L. Harris ViewsLetter* (Highland Park, IL: Thomas L. Harris & Co., July 2000), pp. 1–2; Paul Gray, "Harry's Magic Is Back Again," *Time*, July 17, 2000, pp. 70–71; "Marketers Count on Potter Film for Golden Touch," *USA Today*, July 18, 2000, p. 1; and Charles Batchelor and Charles Pretzlik, "Waterstones Potters but HMV Outcome Sings," *Financial Times*, July 12, 2000, p. 10.

As a result of the increasing emphasis on marketing, a major part of many public relations firms' income is coming from brand public relations activities. Harris has estimated that brand-related public relations is the fastest-growing segment in the public relations industry. More specifically, he estimates that up to 70 percent of public relations firms' revenue comes from marketing-related business.[21] Another indication of the importance of brand public relation is that 13 of the 15 largest public relations firms in the United States have been acquired by advertising agency conglomerates.[22]

MPR is used to build brand credibility, make product news announcements, and reach hard-to-reach target audiences with articles in special interest and trade publications. It is particularly useful in launching new products. In an IMC program, monitoring and influencing unplanned messages is an important responsibility of public relations. MPR can be just as creative as advertising in its effort to build brand relationships and positive brand images. Consider, for example, Harley-Davidson's unusual annual report (Exhibit 15–9).

EXHIBIT 15-9

This annual report was designed with a book jacket that unfolds to become a large poster showing the history of Harley-Davidson motorcycles.

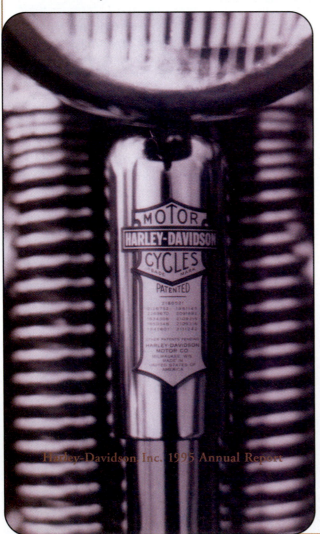

MPR complements the brand message strategy by (1) increasing brand message credibility; (2) delivering specifically targeted messages to niche demographic, psychographic, ethnic, or regional audiences; (3) influencing the influentials, opinion leaders, or trendsetters; and (4) increasing the involvement of customers and other stakeholders through special events.

With the growing interest in relationship marketing, two-way interactivity, and IMC, companies are beginning to learn more about relationship management from a public relations viewpoint. Authors James Grunig and Jon White explain that this public relations worldview is "symmetrical" (i.e., uses two-way communication), is idealistic about relationships, and is managerial focused.[23] This is in contrast to traditional product-and-sales focused worldview that relies primarily on one-way communication sent from a marketing department to customers. To create, in Grunig's words, more symmetrical relationships, public relations communication must also become more data-driven, a point Sandra Moriarty made in a *Public Relations Quarterly* article:

> As PR people become more proficient with databases and interactive technologies, two-way communication with stakeholders will continue to increase. As it does, there will need to be some serious creative thinking about what it means to participate in communication initiated by a wide range of stakeholders.[24]

Marketing and Public Relations

There is an organizational factor affecting the cooperation of marketing and public relations. In many companies, it is still the practice to separate the two departments. Public relations managers, particularly those who track issues and public opinions, typically report to the president of the organization. Meanwhile, marketing communication managers usually report to a vice president of marketing. In such situations, where there is no cross-functional organization, marketing communication and advertising planners may have little or no contact with the public relations department and its programs.

An example of the problems that this can cause comes from a 1998 issue of *The Wall Street Journal,* in which a full-page ad for the high-tech firm Bay Networks extolled the virtues of the company's electronic communication routing and switching capabilities. On the next page, the lead news story highlighted Bay Networks' disappointing sales.[25] If the company's advertising and public relations departments had talked, perhaps they could have avoided having these two conflicting messages appear back to back. Most marketers would agree that a negative news story will do more than cancel out the effects of a typical "brag and boast" ad.

In some companies, turf battles and philosophical differences between marketing and public relations have been referred to by some in public relations as "marketing imperialism." This term reflects the views of some public relations managers who fear that, in an IMC program, public relations might be made subordinate to marketing. This gulf seems to be decreasing, although it can still be found in some companies. Others have asked, jokingly, if perhaps marketing should report to public relations, given the latter's traditional role in managing a full range of stakeholder relationships, its function as a counsel on public opinion to senior management, and its emphasis on listening as well as talking to stakeholders.

Marketing managers, of course, have a bottom-line responsibility and have to produce market share and sales, which is a different type of bottom-line responsibility than managing a company's stakeholder communications. The tension between these marketing and public relations objectives is one of the reasons why IMC has become so important. Its emphasis on cross-functional management provides a structure for coordinating these activities without the threat of imperialism from either functional area.

In truth, advertising and public relations often work hand in hand. The reason small companies like Gardenburger (a maker of frozen veggie-burger patties) spend most or all their MC dollars on high-profile advertising, such as the Super Bowl, is because of the publicity it will generate. By the same token, for years, clothing retailer Benetton developed controversial ads not only to position its brand, but gain publicity without a big media budget.

Although advertising gets a lot of credit for creativity, original ideas are just as prized by the public relations industry, which has its own creativity award, the Silver Anvil, sponsored by the Public Relations Society of America (www.prsa.org).[26] An example comes from the Baltimore-based McCormick Company, which makes spices. Since 1977, the company has been printing its annual report with a scent that smells like one of its spices. Each year, the spice is kept a secret and the business section of the *Baltimore Sun* runs a pool whose participants guess the scent being used. The annual report not only gets attention for its novel aroma but also generates media coverage.[27] Another example of MPR creativity is Water Pik's "Two Hands Full" press kit, shown in Exhibit 15–10).

MPR Media

As noted in Chapter 10, public relations departments provide media representatives with publicity ideas in the form of news releases or feature stories (see Exhibit 15–11). **Gatekeepers**—*editors and reporters who select (or reject) stories for their publications or stations based on what they think will interest their audiences*—are an important target for brand publicity programs. The objective is to get these media professionals to print or run a given story.

But there are other important targets embedded in this news environment that reflect public relations' ability to leverage its relationship focus. Through word of mouth, such people can advocate a company or brand's position, and their advocacy is more credible than any other form of marketing communication. The process begins, however, by getting information to these people, and that usually

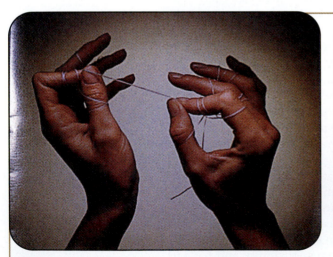
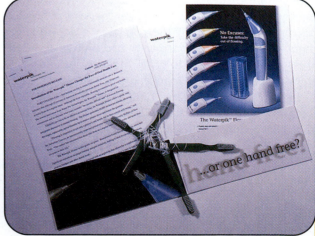

EXHIBIT 15-10

This award-winning press kit was developed to announce the Water Pik Flosser. In order to get the attention of gatekeepers—the editors and writers who decide what news is worth covering—the packet was designed with a toothbrush doll figure held together with dental floss.

happens through the use of tightly targeted mass media. Public relations is often able to manage this two-step process of influence—inform opinion leaders who then inform others—better than other MC functions.

In addition to targeted news releases, there are a variety of other media and programs used by public relations to gain publicity; these are listed in Table 15–4. Even if these programs don't directly involve mass media, such as special events and speeches, they may be designed to get media coverage. Unilever's Sunlight dishwashing detergent, for example, partnered with Whirlpool on an innovative way to build brand awareness and make news at the same time. The idea was to find America's messiest kitchen. The contest was promoted through a broad media relations campaign aimed at women's home, lifestyle, and feature editors. A "spring cleaning" press kit mailing, which targeted these editors, as well as daily newspapers in the top 100 markets and 10,000 local suburban weekly newspapers, generated nearly 125 stories and thousands of entries. Nearly 50 million impressions were delivered, with 100 percent of the stories communicating the fact that the contest was created by Unilever and the Sunlight brand.[28]

Note in Table 15–4 that public relations media include "new" media. Writer Steve Jarvis has described how the Internet has changed publicity fundamentals.[29]

Websites and e-mail have changed the way public relations departments operate, because they decrease the importance of the traditional gatekeeper. Corporate websites, in particular, have become very important sources of public information providing a profile of the company, its products, its employees, and its business philosophy. E-mail allows the public relations professional to instantaneously communicate with the media and reach critical stakeholder groups (employees, consumer groups, investment community). It also allows for more collaborative work in teams whose members may not be located in the same city, state, or country.

Table 15–4 also shows that a big part of public relations is fostering media relations. The following section looks more closely at public relations' use of news releases in particular.

ACCESSLINE
communications

WWW.ACCESSLINE.COM

Media Contacts:
Lambert Jemley
AccessLine Communications
(206) 686-1096
ljemley@accessline.com

Laura Engle
Citigate Cunningham
(512) 652-2712
lengle@cunningham.com

For Immediate Release

AccessLine Enhances Peoplesoft's Flexible Working Environment Through Hosted Communication Services

Two-Thousand Consultants Are Added to AccessLine Services

BELLEVUE, Wash. — April 5, 2000 — AccessLine Communications, the leader in hosted communications and voice services, has significantly expanded its relationship with PeopleSoft, a world leader in enterprise application software for eBusinesses, by providing more effective communications for an additional 2,000 of PeopleSoft's highly mobile staff and consultants. PeopleSoft initially selected AccessLine for its sales staff, who are constantly on the road and need voice services that convert remote locations — customer sites, hotels, homes — into connected and productive office environments.

PeopleSoft has completed rollout of AccessLine services to 2,000 employees of its world-class consulting division, thereby allowing them easy and efficient communications — no matter where they are. Through wireless technology and AccessLine's hosted services, PeopleSoft has provided its consulting employees the mobility and communications flexibility they need for their jobs.

"Previously, our communications systems couldn't provide a flexible working environment for our mobile employees, " said Neil Hennessy, vice president of Engineering at PeopleSoft. "Now through AccessLine, we are able to offer our employees cutting-edge communication tools for a truly mobile environment. They are finding themselves more productive and more empowered in their relationships with our customers, their fellow employees and their families."

AccessLine's regard for high-quality customer service is also key to the success of PeopleSoft's rapid implementation. AccessLine provided PeopleSoft employees with a "high touch environment." Employees were given one-on-one, virtual training and support during every aspect of installation — set up of service, a walk-through of options, step-by-step instructions — all in an extremely short period of time.

(more)

11201 SE 8th St. Suite 200 Bellevue WA 98004   Phone/Fax: 206 621 3500   Toll Free: 1 877 500 LINE

EXHIBIT 15-11

This press release was written to show how AccessLine, a leader in hosted communications and voice services, has been adopted by Peoplesoft. Each time a well-known new client signs up, it provides a news opportunity for AccessLine to promote its telecommunication services.

News Releases

Media relations are guided by journalism standards, principally a need for a news angle in a news release in order to have a story used. Journalists need material that is timely, relevant, topical, accurate, comprehensive, substantiated, concise, unbiased, and, ideally, exclusive, or at least with a special angle that an editor can use to make it a one-of-a-kind story.[30] These are the factors that editors and other media gatekeepers use in deciding whether or not to use a story or cover an event. Central to the editor's decision to use a publicity release or news tip is the extent to

> " The direct-to-consumer aspect of the corporate website has given public relations representatives used to schmoozing reporters a whole new audience and greater control over their messages."
>
> Steve Jarvis, *Marketing News*

TABLE 15-4 Marketing Public Relations Activities

Medium or Program	Description
News releases	Any form of print, visual, or broadcast announcement an organization makes available to the media about its activities; includes video news releases
Publications	Newsletters, magazines, or brochures used in all areas and all types of stakeholder relations programs
Annual reports	A financial report required of all publicly held companies
Corporate, issue, or advocacy advertising	Advertising used in support of an identity program or that promotes a company's viewpoint
Films and videos	Productions designed to promote a company's products and services; used in a variety of settings
Displays	Booths or other setups used in lobbies and other public gathering places to visually describe a company and initiate two-way communication
Public tours	Guided tours of a plant, office, or campus; often done for customers and the general public
Press kit	A packet of information that includes photographs and drawings, maps, histories, background facts, different stories on different aspects of the product or event, speeches, test results, along with person to be contacted for more information
Press conference	A press event in which corporate officials meet with media representatives to inform them about some major company-related story
Media tour	A spokesperson for a firm travels to selected cities and meets with as many local media representatives as possible; ideally includes live appearances on broadcast media
Media event	A special event, like a groundbreaking or grand opening, designed to gain media coverage, as well as create an involvement opportunity for stakeholders
Speeches	Public statements, often ghostwritten by public relations staff
Meetings and video conferences	Corporate meetings used for a variety of purposes (annual meetings with investors, sales meetings) and often planned by the public relations staff
Websites	A profile or overview of the company; may be the responsibility of the public relations department
E-mail	Often used for disseminating news releases, as well as employee and other stakeholder communication

which it has a "news peg" or a human interest angle. The Freshwater Software story, for example, appeared in the business section of the *Boulder Daily Camera* (see Exhibit 15–12) and resulted directly from a press release sent by Citigate Cunningham ("Boulder-Based Freshwater Software Expands Local Business with 24×7 Network Operations Center").

How do you define news? Table 15–5 lists some common reasons stories are selected to be used, or not used, by media editors. It is perfectly legitimate to create news—that is, to do something or find something that is the first, biggest, shortest, most expensive, oldest, longest, highest, or most unusual. Special events such as the Pillsbury Bake-Off, Tide's Dirtiest Kid contest, Saturn's "homecoming," and the M&M new colors contest were all specifically designed to be news events. Such events are often more important for the publicity they generate than for the extent of their contacts. This is true because the event usually involves a relatively small number of customers (and other stakeholders) but the publicity can reach millions more. Heinz made its package a news story when it used three different

TABLE 15-5   What Gets Covered?

How Gatekeepers Select News Stories
- *Impact:* What is the magnitude (past or potential) of the action or event?
- *Timeliness:* Is it a breaking news story or the latest development?
- *Proximity:* How local is the story angle?
- *Prominence:* To whom does it happen, or who is involved, and how important are they?
- *Conflict:* Is there tension or drama created by warring viewpoints?
- *Human interest:* How fun, entertaining, or emotionally engaging is the story idea; does it touch a chord?
- *Novelty:* Is it unusual or unpredictable?

Reasons Stories Are Rejected
- *Not timely:* If it's old news, it won't get used.
- *Not localized:* If there's not a local angle, the audience may not be interested.
- *No human interest:* If the audience cannot connect in some personal way, it will be judged dull.
- *Sloppy:* If it's poorly written, filmed, or recorded, it's not usable.

Source: Adapted from Matthew P. Gonring, "Global and Local Media Relations," in *The Handbook of Strategic Public Relations & Integrated Communications,* ed. Clarke L. Caywood (New York: McGraw-Hill, 1997), p. 67.

labels designed by kids on 10 million bottles of ketchup. This resulted in numerous print and broadcast stories that reached millions of ketchup users.

Because of the timeliness element, publicity, with its emphasis on a news announcement, should precede advertising and other marketing communication functions. This is particularly true for new product introductions, for example, where the news value is good for only a short time. Once the advertising begins, the gatekeeper will reject the product introduction release as old news. The challenge, however, is to continue to find story angles in order to keep the brand visible and top-of-mind even after its introduction.

The news release is the primary tool of publicity, and it can appear in both print and video forms. A service that distributes news releases is PR Newswire (see Exhibit 15–13), a company that delivers video, print, and audio news releases through a variety of media including satellite and the Internet.

Once a story has been identified, then it must be written up in a form that editors can use easily with a minimum of editing. The following list gives some ideas on how to prepare effective print news releases.[31]

News Release Tips

- Ask who, what, why, where, and when, and be sure that these questions are answered in every news story.
- Get the main news point into the first paragraph and preferably the first sentence. Organize paragraphs so that the most newsworthy points are at the top.
- Use short paragraphs with only one point per paragraph.
- Write stories to match the publication and its audience's interest.
- Write the story as if a journalist were writing it, not from the viewpoint or in the style of your company or senior executive.
- Keep the copy tight and concise. Draft, redraft, edit, polish, and cut everything superfluous out of the copy.

- Use journalistic style: short sentences, active verbs. Avoid long and inverted clauses, superlatives, pompous phrases, and jargon.
- Be accurate and factual. Never fudge an issue, exaggerate, or create a misleading impression.
- Substantiate any claims; document the facts; quote from reliable sources.

As described in Chapter 10, Video news releases (VNRs) are television news stories, or packages, produced by a company to feature a product or service and designed to run from 30 to 90 seconds on a news program. They are used when a story has a strong visual impact. A VNR, for example, produced by Golin/Harris Communications to announce the introduction of McDonald's Arch Deluxe sandwich depicted the unveiling of a foam version of the sandwich built over the famed Cinerama Dome on Hollywood's Sunset Boulevard. The videotape of the event reached some 233 million people.

VNRs are usually distributed to television stations along with a script. The VNR is also accompanied by a **B-roll,** which consists of *unedited footage from the VNR along with an introduction to the topic, more visuals, and sound bites from appropriate spokespersons.* Local stations can use the B-roll to assemble the story themselves with their own reporters on camera. VNRs can be distributed by videotape, satellite, or the Internet.

Because VNRs are expensive to produce (budgets can range from $5,000 to $100,000), the following factors should be considered when deciding on the use of a VNR:[32]

- Does the story have a strong visual impact?
- Does the video clarify or provide a new perspective on a news story or issue?
- Will it help a news department create a better story?
- Can the video be used as background footage while a station's reporter discusses the pertinent news copy?
- Can the organization provide unusual visual footage, or an interview, that stations can't get?

It was mentioned earlier that news releases can be disseminated by e-mail. Although e-mail is easy, some companies and PR firms use a wire service, such as Business Wire, that electronically transmits press releases to selected media, including newspapers, radio, television, and trade journals. Business Wire charges about $400 for each press release distributed through its services. Similar sources include Feature Photo (www.featurephoto.com), which distributes photos; MediaMap (www.mediamap.com), which has a database of media addresses; and West Glen communications (www.west-glen.com), which produces and distributes VNRs.

EXHIBIT 15-12

This is an example of a press release by the Citigate Cunningham agency for its client, Freshwater Software, and the newspaper story that resulted from it.

Boulder-Based Freshwater Software Expands ...siness With 24X7 Network Operations Center   http://www.freshwater.com/press/ExpandNOCRelease

Boulder-Based Freshwater Software Expands Local Business With 24X7 Network Operations Center

BOULDER, Colo.--(BUSINESS WIRE)--Oct. 5, 2000--Freshwater Software, the leading provider of comprehensive Internet growth solutions for eBusiness, is expanding the operation of its 24x7 network operations center (NOC) in Boulder, Colo.

Freshwater's expansion means a 20 percent increase in staff, with ten immediate openings for experienced NOC service professionals. The expansion will help Freshwater reach its year-end goal of 80 to 100 employees.

Freshwater's Boulder NOC services eBusinesses who use the company's remote managed service, Global SiteReliance, to manage their Web environments and ensure the quality of the end-user experience. Freshwater's Global SiteReliance customers include Intel Online Services and ePresence. The NOC is also available to other customers, including those who use Freshwater's internal and external monitoring services, SiteScope and SiteSeer, and want 24x7 technical support.

Freshwater Software has more than 2,500 leading eBusiness customers, including AltaVista, barnesandnoble.com, CNET, Merrill Lynch and GO.com.

"Freshwater is growing in anticipation of our eBusiness customers' own growth needs," said Heidi Dudek, NOC manager, responsible for Freshwater's day-to-day Boulder NOC operations. "We understand the complexities of growing an eBusiness. We meet industry needs by offering in-depth monitoring and management services that are essential to maintaining a consistent, high-quality Web experience for end users."

The NOC services Freshwater's personnel work with Freshwater's suite of Web environment monitoring and management tools and services -- Global SiteReliance, SiteScope and SiteSeer -- to pinpoint problems for quick resolution, or to design and implement a comprehensive monitoring solution from the ground up.

Today's NOC expansion marks the latest enhancement to the 22,000-sq. ft. space on Arapahoe Avenue occupied by Freshwater since March 2000.

About Freshwater Software

Freshwater Software Inc. provides comprehensive, global eBusiness environment monitoring and management solutions to enable eBusiness growth. Freshwater's solutions ensure that eBusinesses are available 24x7 and that they deliver a superior online experience for end users. Freshwater's product line includes Global SiteReliance for complete managed services, SiteScope for internal monitoring, and Global SiteSeer for external monitoring. Customers include AltaVista (a CMGI company), barnesandnoble.com (Nasdaq:BNBN), CNET (Nasdaq:CNET), Intel Online Services (an Intel Corp. company), Merrill Lynch (NYSE:MER) and GO.com (a Walt Disney Internet Group service). Founded in 1996 and headquartered in Boulder, Colo., Freshwater Software is a privately held company with venture capital support from Mayfield Fund and Mohr, Davidow Ventures. Visit www.freshwater.com or call 303/443-2266 for more information.

CONTACT: For Freshwater Software Inc., Boulder
Cunningham Public Relations
Heather Mechtly, 303/376-7276
hmechtly@citigatecunningham.com

Advertising versus Editorial

One issue related to publicity is the relationship between the editorial or news side and advertising. Although many readers of newspapers and magazines, and viewers of television, have little sense of the difference between ads and publicity stories, editors and advertisers are very conscious of the difference.

Most media in the United States are primarily supported by advertising. That means an important role is to deliver a certain type of audience. That point was made by Cyrus Curtis, founder of *Ladies' Home Journal*, in a speech to business executives in the late 1800s:

> The editor of the *Ladies' Home Journal* thinks we publish it for the benefit of American women. This is an illusion, but a very proper one for him to have. The real reason, the publisher's reason, is to give you who manufacture things American women want, a chance to tell them about your products.

Even so, most editors see their mission as bringing news to the public as fairly and objectively as possible. The *Los Angeles Times* created problems for itself when it lost sight of that mission. In an attempt to increase short-term profits, it devoted a Sunday magazine section to the city's new multisport arena, the Staples Center, with which it was sharing advertising revenue. The special section looked like a regular editorial section of the paper, but it was really an advertiser-supported supplement. The paper's own reporters were incensed when they found out that they were writing stories for a promotional piece, and their protests brought a great deal of negative publicity to the paper.

Because of the central role advertising plays, it is not unusual for companies to threaten to pull ads out of media that write negative stories about them. According to *Editor & Publisher* magazine, 97 percent of newspaper publishers say an advertiser has pulled ads because of a story it opposed.[33] Yet such a practice is unprofessional, if not naive, because the news media jealously guard the objectivity and independence of their news coverage and are not likely to respond to pressure from advertisers. As *Inside PR* magazines has noted, if a media company loses its objectivity, it may also likely lose its audience.[34]

An example of a more enlightened response comes from Shell. The giant oil company has been criticized fiercely by the magazine *Mother Jones*, most notably for its support of the Nigerian government, which some feel is one of the most abusive in the world. In spite of that, Shell runs banner ads on the MoJo Wire, the website of *Mother Jones*. An editor's note on the site makes it clear that the ads have not bought more favorable coverage and even provides links to almost every unfavorable story the magazine has written about Shell. Both were cited in *Reputation Management*: MoJo Wire for accepting the ads, despite reader criticism, and Shell for reaching out to its critics to provide both sides to a complicated issue.[35]

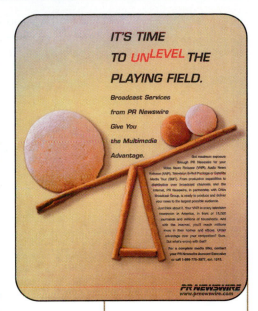

EXHIBIT 15-13

This ad for PR Newswire, a service that distributes news releases, promotes its multimedia capabilities.

> " The media's equity is tied closely to its objectivity."
>
> *Inside PR*

Strengths and Objectives of MPR

As the increased spending on MPR demonstrates, it is playing an increasingly important role in helping companies meet their IMC objectives. The types of IMC objectives that MPR is especially good at helping meet include the following: (1) to build a climate of acceptance for a company and its brands, (2) to increase brand awareness, (3) to increase the credibility and believability of brand claims, (4) to use news and human interest to break through commercial message clutter, (5) to reach hard-to-reach audiences through articles in special interest and trade publications, (6) to reach other stakeholder groups, and (7) to do all these things in a very cost-effective way. Each of these objectives is also an area of strength for the MPR function.

Brand Awareness

Effective media relations departments use publicity and the cultivation of media contacts to announce product news, create visibility for a brand, and position the brand as a category leader. In some MPR programs, publicity means getting the brand name mentioned in the mass media in as many different ways, times, and places as possible. The idea being that the more mentions in the press, the more top-of-mind awareness the brand will gain. This type of shot-gun strategy, however, may not be cost-effective. Like advertising, publicity should be targeted as much as possible. This is because placing stories takes time and effort (although the "media cost" is zero).

Awareness efforts also include appearances by corporate executives and brand mentions on news programs and talk shows. However, MPR is also concerned with moving beyond simple awareness and creating positive attitudes, as Exhibit 15–14 illustrates.

Some new products have even been successfully introduced using only brand publicity. Breathe Right nasal strips and Gatorade both relied on the on-camera use of the brand by athletes. Publicity can do it alone, however, only when the marketplace isn't too crowded and the product is unique. In a more competitive new product launch, media coverage in consumer and business publications is used to build customer awareness and provide information (see the IMC in Action box).

Acceptance and Credibility

Although brand awareness can be strengthened with MPR, publicity also is used to build credibility for the brand's claims. Media stories resulting from publicity efforts are more believable because of what is called **third-party endorsement**, *an objective perspective presented by a reputable source who has no personal interest in the success or failure of the product being endorsed.* This credibility strategy is the basis for passing out reprints of articles about the brand or a company's executives (see Exhibit 15–16). An example of the use of third-party endorsements comes from Steve Jobs's reshaping of Apple. Rather than relying on product claims in advertisements, the MPR team relied almost exclusively on comments from industry analysts. Apple, in turn, provided them with a steady flow of quotes and research data, and created chat rooms and user sites on the Internet to generate buzz, which the analysts noted.[36]

In a marketing communication program, credibility is also gained by establishing a position of good corporate citizenship and supporting a good cause, a practice that will be discussed in Chapter 19, on ethics.

Cost-Effectiveness

Recall that, although it costs money to have someone write a press release and distribute it, there is no charge for the time and space messages occupy in the mass media. That makes publicity considerably less expensive than mass media advertising and most other

EXHIBIT 15-14

Well-crafted public relations efforts are designed not only to get awareness but also to change the way people think.

There's a big difference between attracting their attention and changing the way they think.

Beaupre
&Co.

public relations counsel for high technology corporations

IMC IN ACTION

The Beetle's Back

In 1993, Volkswagen (VW) had so many problems with production in the North American market that it actually stopped making cars for eight months. During that time, in order to keep the dealers in business, the company used its ad budget to pay dealers $1,000 for each car they would have sold based on prior years' figures.

After a lot of corporate soul-searching and restructuring, VW emerged in 1998 with a model dubbed the New Beetle, hoping to rekindle some of the magic that had made the company and the car so popular in the 1960s (see Exhibit 15-15). *Advertising Age* columnist Bob Garfield predicted that the "Beetle would cruise even without fine ads." Ads by the Boston-based Arnold Agency used the popular VW "Drivers wanted" campaign theme, but the car was really launched by an impressive public relations effort long before the advertising hit. The effort was described as a public relations coup—almost everyone of driving age was aware of the new Beetle months before it was available in showrooms.

The Ruder-Finn public relations firm made it virtually impossible for people to miss reading, seeing, or hearing about the New Beetle. Tying in to 60s nostalgia, VW staged a love-in to introduce the Love Bug to 300 journalists from around the world. Young women in tie-dyed T-shirts handed out daisies and peace symbols. And in the ultimate nod to the days of flower power, the new bug came equipped with a bud vase. So did the press kit. The agency reported that there were 900 national and local television news segments featuring the new car the week of the launch. Matt Lauer, a long-time Beetle owner since the 60s, introduced the new model on the "Today Show." Harry Smith took a new red Beetle for a spin around Times Square. The New Beetle was such a success that it made the cover of *Business Week* even before it made the showrooms.

With a limited production run of 50,000 vehicles and rave reviews from the automotive and popular press, the New Beetle was the automotive success story of the 1990s. Dealers were allotted only a limited number of the little bugs, and, after they finally started rolling into showrooms, most dealers found themselves with a four- to five-month backlog of orders.

The question is: Will the New Beetle be the rejuvenation tonic that VW of America needed, or will it just be an example of a cultural "retro" icon that was revisited in a short period of marketplace hype?

EXHIBIT 15-15

The "new" VW Beetle was one of the biggest new-product success stories of the last decade. Brand publicity played a major role in this achievement.

Think About It

Plot the launch of the New Beetle in terms of its use of public relations and advertising. What other type of activity was used in support of the launch? What other activities might you have recommended?

Sources: Adapted from material in Thomas L. Harris, "The Bug Is Back," *MPR Update*, May 1998, pp. 1–2; and Greg Farrell, "Getting the Bugs Out," *Brandweek*, April 6, 1998, pp. 30–36, 40.

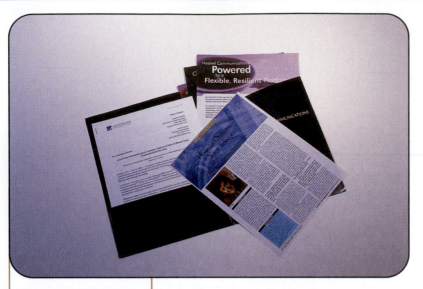

forms of mass communication. Given the impact of a news story, brand publicity then becomes a very cost-effective MC tactic. The Internet has made publicity efforts even more cost-effective, a fact reflected in a 1999 survey of brand managers, 42 percent of whom said public relations is the best discipline for brand building on the Internet, as opposed to 32 percent who preferred advertising.[37]

Clutter Busting

A problem for all brand messages is that they compete for attention in a very cluttered commercial message environment. Publicity breaks through the clutter of other commercial messages, particularly if the news is delivered in a creative way, such as an event that features a personal appearance.

Although there is a lot of information in the media, a brand message is intrinsically more attention-getting, interesting, and believable when it is news or human interest. Its power to capture attention can be considerably higher than an advertising message. For example, Heinz once made the "world's largest salad" by filling a portable swimming pool with salad makings and then covering it with gallons of a new Heinz dressing. Both TV and print editors ran human interest stories on the event, gaining brand exposure and awareness among millions of potential customers, despite the millions of dollars being spent on advertising by other salad dressing brands.

Reaching the Hard to Reach

Another role of MPR is to reach audiences that are difficult to reach with advertising and other brand messages—for example, upscale and well-educated audiences, such as business executives, who spend less time with television, radio, and popular magazines than other groups and therefore have limited exposure to traditional advertising. However, they do tend to read newspapers and special interest and industry publications. MPR also helps get around the communication roadblocks (e.g., secretaries and answering machines) that hinder sales calls and direct marketing.

Just as advertising reaches stakeholders other than customers, so does brand publicity. A professional public relations program is an ongoing process that molds and nourishes mutually beneficial, long-term relationships with all stakeholders.

Limitations of MPR

Although marketers control most brand MC messages to ensure their content, reach, and impact against a targeted audience, they have much less control over brand publicity because the messages are filtered through media gatekeepers—those editors and reporters who make the decision to run the story or not.

Also, as with image advertising, the impact of brand publicity is not easily measured because the majority of it is focused on affecting attitudes and opinions, changes that are difficult to attribute to messages from just one kind of MC function. In public relations, most measurement consists of counting the number of mentions, inches, or the amount of time a brand or company story receives in the media. It is difficult, however, to link these measures to behaviors and to the bottom line.

Another limitation is that public relations can only go so far. Editors will not run stories about the same company or brand too frequently (otherwise the communication vehicle loses its own credibility). Consequently, it is more difficult for public relations programs to create a frequency of mention in the same media vehicle. So, while public relations may offer greater credibility, advertising offers greater control and the awareness that comes from repetition. Another problem, and one that drives to the heart of its greatest strength, is public relations' own image, a credibility problem that is discussed in the Ethics and Issues box.

Other Public Relations Functions That Affect Brands

MPR is the most important area of public relations for marketing communication programs. However, there are other PR activities and programs that are also relevant to a company's or brand's success. They include crisis management, word of mouth, and social marketing.

ETHICS AND ISSUES

The Incredible Credibility Crisis

One of the biggest strengths of public relations is the credibility it brings to a brand through the use of third-party endorsements. This aura of credibility, however, is at odds with the image of professionals in the field, who are sometimes referred to disparagingly as flacks and spinmasters. This demeaning image is further reinforced by certain stories, like one that appeared in 2000 in the *New York Times* reporting a study finding that 25 percent of public relations professionals say they lie on their clients' behalf.

Equally damaging is another study, underwritten by the Public Relations Society of America and reported in the industry trade journal *Public Relations Quarterly*, that found public relations specialists to be third from the bottom in terms of a National Credibility Index of 44 different types of public figures. (The public figure at the top of the list was Supreme Court justice, followed by teacher; the bottom of the list was TV or radio talk-show host.)

It's incredible that an industry so concerned with the reputation of its clients would itself have such a bad reputation. Furthermore, with so much effort invested by public relations professionals in building positive corporate reputations, how come the public view of big business is generally so negative?

Think About It

What is the credibility problem faced by public relations, as well as by big business? What can be done to turn around this generally negative public opinion?

Sources: Alex Kuczynski, "In Public Relations, 25% Admit Lying," *New York Times*, May 8, 2000, p. 20; John F. Budd, Jr., "The Incredible Credibility Dilemma," *Public Relations Quarterly* 45, no. 3 (Fall 2000), pp. 22–28; Paul A. Holmes, "Big Business, Bad Reputation," *Reputation Management* 6, no. 7 (July–August 2000), pp. 2-4.

Crisis Management

Recall from Chapter 4 that a program designed to plan and manage a company's response when disaster strikes is called a crisis management plan. Such plans are focused on designating who will provide what information to media and employees during a crisis. Although designing and managing a crisis management plan is the responsibility of the director of public relations, the marketing department should be involved. This is because a crisis, by definition, means that a company's reputation and brand relationships will be negatively affected.

Proactive companies are realistic; they know that bad things happen. A manufacturing accident or product failure that causes serious injury or death may occur when a company least expects it. The larger a company is and the longer it is in business, the more likely it will have such a crisis.

An example of a product failure crisis was what Bridgestone/Firestone and Ford faced in 2000 when it was widely publicized that certain Firestone tires on Ford Explorers were breaking down and causing deadly accidents. This crisis resulted in the recall and replacement of millions of Firestone tires, as the ads in Exhibit 15–17 show.

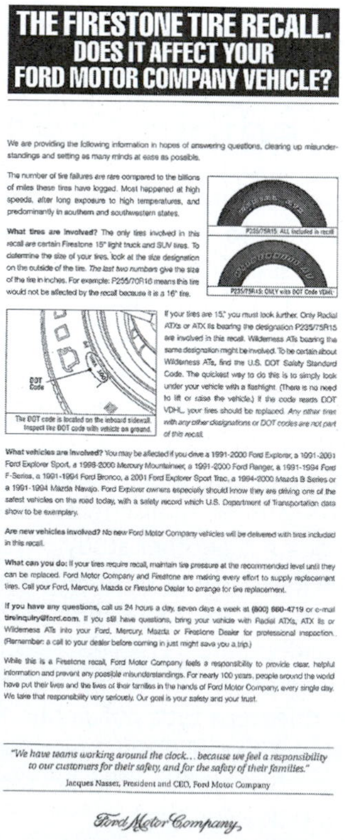

EXHIBIT 15-17

These were full-page ads that ran in The Wall Street Journal *after the tire recall was announced by Firestone and Ford. The objective in running such ads was to inform customers and attempt to restore public trust in the companies and their business practices.*

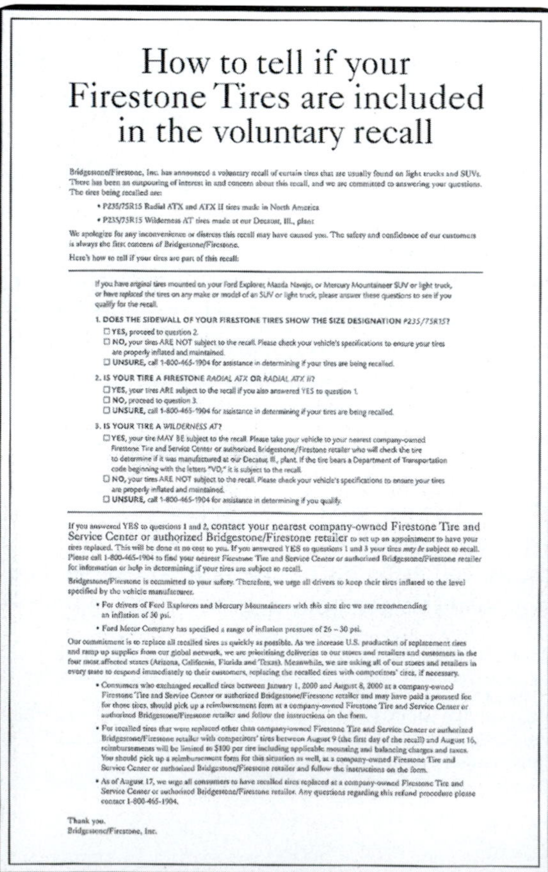

How to tell if your Firestone Tires are included in the voluntary recall

Bridgestone/Firestone, Inc. has announced a voluntary recall of certain tires that are usually found on light trucks and SUVs. There has been an outpouring of interest in and concern about this recall, and we are committed to answering your questions. The tires being recalled are:

- P235/75R15 Radial ATX and ATX II tires made in North America
- P235/75R15 Wilderness AT tires made at our Decatur, Ill., plant

We apologize for any inconvenience or distress this recall may have caused you. The safety and confidence of our customers is always the first concern of Bridgestone/Firestone.

Here's how to tell if your tires are part of this recall:

If you have original tires mounted on your Ford Explorer, Mazda Navajo, or Mercury Mountaineer SUV or light truck, or have replaced the tires on any make or model of an SUV or light truck, please answer these questions to see if you qualify for the recall.

1. DOES THE SIDEWALL OF YOUR FIRESTONE TIRES SHOW THE SIZE DESIGNATION *P235/75R15*?
   - ☐ YES, proceed to question 2.
   - ☐ NO, your tires ARE NOT subject to the recall. Please check your vehicle's specifications to ensure your tires are properly inflated and maintained.
   - ☐ UNSURE, call 1-800-465-1904 for assistance in determining if your tires are being recalled.
2. IS YOUR TIRE A FIRESTONE *RADIAL ATX* OR *RADIAL ATX II*?
   - ☐ YES, your tires ARE subject to the recall if you also answered YES to question 1.
   - ☐ NO, proceed to question 3.
   - ☐ UNSURE, call 1-800-465-1904 for assistance in determining if your tires are being recalled.
3. IS YOUR TIRE A *WILDERNESS AT*?
   - ☐ YES, your tire MAY BE subject to the recall. Please take your vehicle to your nearest company-owned Firestone Tire and Service Center or authorized Bridgestone/Firestone retailer who will check the tire to determine if it was manufactured at our Decatur, Ill., plant. If the tire bears a Department of Transportation code beginning with the letters "VD," it is subject to the recall.
   - ☐ NO, your tires ARE NOT subject to the recall. Please check your vehicle's specifications to ensure your tires are properly inflated and maintained.
   - ☐ UNSURE, call 1-800-465-1904 for assistance in determining if you qualify.

If you answered YES to questions 1 and 2, contact your nearest company-owned Firestone Tire and Service Center or authorized Bridgestone/Firestone retailer to set up an appointment to have your tires replaced. This will be done at no cost to you. If you answered YES to questions 1 and 3 your tires *may be* subject to recall. Please call 1-800-465-1904 to find your nearest Firestone Tire and Service Center or authorized Bridgestone/Firestone retailer for information or help in determining if your tires are subject to recall.

Bridgestone/Firestone is committed to your safety. Therefore, we urge all drivers to keep their tires inflated to the level specified by the vehicle manufacturer.

- For drivers of Ford Explorers and Mercury Mountaineers with this size tire we are recommending an inflation of 30 psi.
- Ford Motor Company has specified a range of inflation pressure of 26 – 30 psi.

Our commitment is to replace all recalled tires as quickly as possible. As we increase U.S. production of replacement tires and ramp up supplies from our global network, we are prioritizing deliveries to our stores and retailers and customers in the four most affected states (Arizona, California, Florida and Texas). Meanwhile, we are asking all of our stores and retailers in every state to respond immediately to their customers, replacing the recalled tires with competitors' tires, if necessary.

- Consumers who exchanged recalled tires between January 1, 2000 and August 8, 2000 at a company-owned Firestone Tire and Service Center or authorized Bridgestone/Firestone retailer and may have paid a prorated fee for those tires, should pick up a reimbursement form at a company-owned Firestone Tire and Service Center or authorized Bridgestone/Firestone retailer and follow the instructions on the form.
- For recalled tires that were replaced other than company-owned Firestone Tire and Service Center or authorized Bridgestone/Firestone retailer with competitors' tires between August 9 (the first day of the recall) and August 16, reimbursements will be limited to $100 per tire including applicable mounting and balancing charges and taxes. You should pick up a reimbursement form for this situation as well, at a company-owned Firestone Tire and Service Center or authorized Bridgestone/Firestone retailer and follow the instructions on the form.
- As of August 17, we urge all consumers to have recalled tires replaced at a company-owned Firestone Tire and Service Center or authorized Bridgestone/Firestone retailer. Any questions regarding this refund procedure please contact 1-800-465-1904.

Thank you.
Bridgestone/Firestone, Inc.

THE FIRESTONE TIRE RECALL.
DOES IT AFFECT YOUR
FORD MOTOR COMPANY VEHICLE?

We are providing the following information in hopes of answering questions, clearing up misunderstandings and setting as many minds at ease as possible.

The number of tire failures are rare compared to the billions of miles these tires have logged. Most happened at high speeds, after long exposure to high temperatures, and predominantly in southern and southwestern states.

P235/75R15: ALL included in recall

P235/75R15: ONLY with DOT Code VDHL

What tires are involved? The only tires involved in this recall are certain Firestone 15" light truck and SUV tires. To determine the size of your tires, look at the size designation on the outside of the tire. *The last two numbers* give the size of the tire in inches. For example: P255/70R16 means this tire would not be affected by the recall because it is a 16" tire.

DOT Code

The DOT code is located on the inboard sidewall. Inspect the DOT code with vehicle on ground.

If your tires are 15," you must look further. Only Radial ATXs or ATX IIs bearing the designation P235/75R15 are involved in this recall. Wilderness ATs bearing the same designation might be involved. To be certain about Wilderness ATs, find the U.S. DOT Safety Standard Code. The quickest way to do this is to simply look under your vehicle with a flashlight. (There is no need to lift or raise the vehicle.) If the code reads DOT VDHL, your tires should be replaced. *Any other tires with any other designations or DOT codes are not part of this recall.*

What vehicles are involved? You may be affected if you drive a 1991-2000 Ford Explorer, a 1991-2001 Ford Explorer Sport, a 1998-2000 Mercury Mountaineer, a 1991-2000 Ford Ranger, a 1991-1994 Ford F-Series, a 1991-1994 Ford Bronco, a 2001 Ford Explorer Sport Trac, a 1994-2000 Mazda B Series or a 1991-1994 Mazda Navajo. Ford Explorer owners especially should know they are driving one of the safest vehicles on the road today, with a safety record which U.S. Department of Transportation data show to be exemplary.

Are new vehicles involved? No new Ford Motor Company vehicles will be delivered with tires included in this recall.

What can you do: If your tires require recall, maintain tire pressure at the recommended level until they can be replaced. Ford Motor Company and Firestone are making every effort to supply replacement tires. Call your Ford, Mercury, Mazda or Firestone Dealer to arrange for tire replacement.

If you have any questions, call us 24 hours a day, seven days a week at **(800) 660-4719** or e-mail **tireinquiry@ford.com**. If you still have questions, bring your vehicle with Radial ATXs, ATX IIs or Wilderness ATs into your Ford, Mercury, Mazda or Firestone Dealer for professional inspection. (Remember: a call to your dealer before coming in just might save you a trip.)

While this is a Firestone recall, Ford Motor Company feels a responsibility to provide clear, helpful information and prevent any possible misunderstandings. For nearly 100 years, people around the world have put their lives and the lives of their families in the hands of Ford Motor Company, every single day. We take that responsibility very seriously. Our goal is your safety and your trust.

"We have teams working around the clock… because we feel a responsibility to our customers for their safety, and for the safety of their families."

Jacques Nasser, President and CEO, Ford Motor Company

Ford Motor Company

The crisis ignited when Bridgestone/Firestone's U.S. subsidiary called a press conference to announce that it was voluntarily recalling 6.5 million of its tires, which had been linked to 46 deaths in the United States, as well as to 300 other incidents. Clearly the announcement had major public relations implications for both Firestone and Ford, and both suffered damage to their reputations. According to an article in *Reputation Management*, Ford handled the crisis responsibly, with CEO Jacques Nasser prominent in the company's communication of concern for customers. Firestone's response, however, failed to inspire confidence. The Japanese-based company was clearly handicapped by its culture, which prompted a closed-mouth posture with the media and which was more focused on supplier and partner relationships, than on keeping consumers happy.[38] The result can be seen in Table 15–6, which reports the results of an opinion poll on the public's view of how the two companies handled the crisis.

The reason for having a crisis plan worked out *before* there is a crisis is so that the company is not forced to instantly forge a response when emotions are high and the media are knocking on the door with cameras and live video, anxious to tell the world how bad things are. In a sense, having a crisis management plan is like having a two-minute drill (a preselected set of plays) in football. When your team is behind and the clock is running out, there is no time to decide what plays to call. In the same way, during a crisis there is no time to plan—a company has to respond immediately or the media, customers, and others think the company is trying to hide something.

When a crisis does occur, public relations professionals advise (1) that only designated company executives talk to the media, (2) that they explain what happened as they understand it, (3) that they tell what the company is doing to minimize the damage (such as product recall), and (4) that they express sympathy and concern for injured parties and their families. What spokespeople should not say or suggest in any way, however, is that the company is responsible for what happened. Such an admission of *liability*—without knowing all the related facts, which can take weeks or months to gather and analyze—can result in the company's having to pay millions of dollars in compensation. This is not to say a company should not be responsible for its actions, but only that it should take time to accurately determine what its responsibilities really are in certain situations.

Brand Image Crises

After Burger King ran a promotion giving away Pokémon toys packaged inside a plastic ball, the company was shocked when it was reported that a baby suffocated

---

T A B L E   1 5 - 6   Survey Results Regarding the Ford/Firestone Tire Crisis

The numbers represent the percentage of respondents who rated each company's handling of the crisis as good or excellent.

	Ford	Firestone/Bridgestone
Level of honesty	53%	34%
Helpfulness	60	46
Speed of response	51	34

Source: Paul A. Holmes, "With Friends Like These...," *Reputation Management* 6, no. 7 (July–August 2000), p. 12.

and another child nearly died (half of the ball package had been placed over the mouth and nose of each victim). The company responded by recalling the ball packages (not the toys themselves). To encourage people to act, Burger King gave a free order of fries to each person who returned a ball package. At the time of the recall, the company had distributed over 20 million of the Pokémon toys. The recall, which was announced in a full-page *USA Today* ad, was not only a responsible thing to do, but a smart marketing move because it generated considerable publicity and motivated families to visit their local Burger King once again.

A common source of a marketing crisis is a sales promotion event or advertisement that goes awry. For example, both Kraft Foods in the United States and Hoover vacuum cleaners in England used contests that had flaws, allowing many more winners than planned. In the case of Kraft, because of a misprint, there were thousands claiming the first prize of a Dodge Caravan. As for Hoover, an aggressive sales promotion offer of two free plane tickets to the United States or continental Europe for the purchase of a vacuum cleaner or Maytag washing machine backfired when responses overwhelmed the company. It is important that marketing and public relations work together when a disaster occurs in product production, distribution, or promotional activities.

The bottom line of crisis communication is damage control. When a major disaster occurs, especially one resulting in death or serious injury, the damage has been done. And in this day of instant news, the world will soon be told about it. Look at what happened to Intel when a problem with its Pentium chip was discovered. Even before the mass media made it a big business story, it was being discussed on the Internet, whose audience is very important to Intel's reputation. When the crisis occurred, Intel's initial denial tarnished its previously stellar image. But Intel did learn and act. It has since hired people to monitor all major high-tech chat rooms and immediately report any negative comments about the brand.

Word of Mouth

When a brand competes in a crowded and cluttered category, some companies are finding that it might be better—and cheaper—to let customers discover cool new products themselves. The idea is to harness the power of positive word of mouth. It currently goes by several different names: *guerrilla marketing* usually applies to edgy, unconventional campaigns that generate word of mouth; *viral marketing* is a buzzword in Internet marketing to refer to the way communication spreads on the Internet. Whatever it's called, word of mouth is cheap because it doesn't rely on expensive media buys. It can, however, be reinforced by media stories, which is where public relations comes in.[39]

Word of mouth is a powerful tool because of its high level of credibility. And, if the topic is hot, it can spread like wildfire. George Silverman, president of a company that specializes in word-of-mouth campaigns, says they are up to 1,000 times more powerful than other forms of advertising. If a friend recommends a movie to you, he contends, you're 1,000 times more likely to see it than if you learned about it through an advertisement. It's not a new tactic; martinis, cigars, grunge fashions, Pokémon, Beanie Babies, Cabbage Patch dolls, mood rings, and Rubik's Cubes all benefited from buzz.

Another example comes from Levi Strauss's Red Line brand, which was launched without any advertising, only its own website. The product was delivered to a special group of trendy boutiques, and some posters were placed in underground clubs. The website featured interesting images that had nothing to do with jeans. The idea was to let the target market (fashion leaders) enjoy the thrill of discovering something new that they could introduce to their friends.

Social Marketing

Social marketing is *a type of public relations campaign that uses a variety of other MC functions to promote a social program or cause.* Information campaigns are mounted on behalf of everything from voter registration to disease prevention. One of the earliest efforts at social marketing was the "Smokey the Bear" campaign, which sought to reduce the number of forest fires. Managed by the Ad Council, a nonprofit arm of the advertising industry that undertakes social marketing campaigns as a public relations effort, the campaign has developed high visibility over the years. Other Ad Council campaigns include work for the National Negro College Fund ("A Mind Is a Terrible Thing to Waste,") and for the National Parks ("Take Pride in America"). The American Indian College Fund ad in Exhibit 15–18 is another example of social marketing.

One of the largest social marketing efforts is the Partnership for a Drug-Free America (PDFA), whose antidrug messages are aimed at teens and preteens as well as parents, teachers, and counselors. Media donations of time and space for public service announcements (PSAs) by the media have equaled almost $3 billion since 1986. Annual support moved from $115 million to $365 million in 1989 and 1990. The ads are created pro bono (which means they are done for free) by advertising agencies.[40]

The campaign has seen results; there are 10 million fewer adult drug users in the United States than there were in 1985, 50 percent fewer regular users of drugs, and 75 percent fewer cocaine users. At the end of the 1990s, drug-related crime was at a 20-year low. However, drug use among young people of high school age has been climbing since 1991. To combat that problem, the federal government is teaming with the PDFA to begin placing antidrug advertising in specific communication vehicles. The paid ads will be able to reach the at-risk markets more effectively than PSAs whose value has dwindled due to media splintering and market forces that are squeezing them off the air.

Mike Marshall / Sinte Gleska Univ. / SPQ 39
Major: Fine Arts / Ival: Financial Aid

American Indian College Fund
Educating the mind and spirit

Please call 1-800-776-FUND or visit www.collegefund.org.
Special thanks to the U.S. West foundation for underwriting production costs for this advertisement.

EXHIBIT 15-18

This campaign for the American Indian College Fund spotlights individual Native American students with a brief profile as part of a fund-raising effort.

A FINAL NOTE: REPUTATION AND RELATIONSHIPS

IMC programs that contribute to positive relationships move beyond image advertising and seek to affect reputation through credible brand messages. According to public relations professional Terrie Williams, putting relationships into public relations is critical because "people are starved for recognition."[41] She referred to psychologist Abraham Maslow's hierarchy of needs (see again Chapter 6) in explaining that acknowledgment and recognition are important dimensions of self-actualization. That's why customer recognition is an important factor in an IMC program as well.

Good citizenship, or social responsibility, is also an important part of a reputation program. Research has shown that consumers will change their buying habits to support companies they perceive as being socially responsible—which means they are environmentally responsible, treat their employees fairly, and/or work to make their communities better places to live.

Key Terms

corporate communication executives 537
public service announcements 538
corporate advertising 538
change agents 540
reputation 541
marketing public relations (MPR) 543

brand publicity 543
gatekeepers 546
B-roll 550
third-party endorsement 552
social marketing 559

Key Point Summary

This chapter is focused on public relations, whose primary strengths are building credibility and extending awareness and brand knowledge in an extremely cost-effective manner.

Key Point 1: Public Relations

Public relations is an MC function used to manage communication between an organization and its publics and create favorable relationships with a variety of different stakeholders who are targeted by the following types of programs: corporate relations (issues management, community relations, government relations, industry relations), marketing public relations, media relations, employee relations, and financial relations.

Key Point 2: Corporate Communication

Corporate communication manages a full range of stakeholder relationships. Its focus on the corporate brand is most evident in corporate advertising. Corporate communication is built on a solid mission, which is embedded in the corporate culture and reflected in the corporate image and reputation.

Key Point 3: Marketing Public Relations (MPR)

MPR encourages purchase and consumer satisfaction through credible communication of information that associates companies and their products with the needs, wants, concerns, and interests of consumers. It is used to build brand credibility, make product news announcements, and launch new products. The strengths of MPR include building a climate of acceptance for a company and its brands, increasing brand visibility, increasing the brand's level of credibility and believability, using news to break through MC clutter, and reaching hard-to-reach audiences through articles in special interest and trade publications. Limitations include the lack of control over publicity, the difficulty quantifying impact, and the inability of PR to guarantee frequency of exposure to the message over time.

Lessons Learned

Key Point 1: Public Relations

a.   Why is public relations a growth area in marketing communication?
b.   What are the key elements of public relations as given in the definitions quoted in this chapter?
c.   Which stakeholders are addressed by public relations programs?
d.   Which types of public relations programs listed in Table 15-2 can also be used in IMC programs?
e.   Do a search for a story about a new product launch, like the Maytag Neptune. In addition to the story placement itself, what other public relations tactics were used to introduce this product? What other MC functions were used?

Key Point 2: Corporate Communication

a. What is corporate communication?
b. What are the three types of corporate advertising? Find an example of each and explain the strategy behind the communication.
c. Why is corporate culture important to corporate communication managers, and how does it affect IMC programs?
d. What is the role of a change agent? How do change agents contribute to public relations and IMC programs?
e. What's the difference between corporate image and corporate reputation?
f. In what way is reputation important to an IMC program?

Key Point 3: Marketing Public Relations (MPR)

a. Define marketing public relations (MPR), and explain how it differs from public relations in general.
b. Explain how MRP can supplement an MC strategy.
c. List the four strengths of MPR.
d. In the marketing trade press, find an example of a marketing program that had to involve both acceptance programs and issues management in order to be successful.
e. What is a media gatekeeper, and why does that person create limitations for MPR's effectiveness?
f. What is the third-party endorsement factor in publicity, and what does it mean for MPR? Find an example of how a medium lends credibility to a story about a brand. Explain *how* this credibility is enhanced by the medium.

Chapter Challenge

Writing Assignment

Update the New Beetle story (see p. 553). Read everything you can find in the business and automotive trade press as well as consumer publications. Take a position on the question in the last paragraph of the box: Is the New Beetle a success story for the long term or just a flash of nostalgia?

Presentation Assignment

Analyze your university or college as a brand. How does public relations contribute to the development of the school's brand? What is the school's identity, image, and reputation? Develop recommendations on what needs to be done to strengthen your school's branding, and present them to your class.

Internet Assignment

The premier job site for the global public relations industry is Workinpr.com (www.workinpr.com). It is a partnership between the two leading U.S. public relations associations—the Public Relations Society of America (www.prsa.org) and the council of Public Relations Firms (www.prfirms.org). The workinpr.com site offers job-search capabilities as well as up-to-date industry research and career information. Explore all three of these sites and do an analysis of the field of public relations and how it relates to your personal interests and skills. Prepare a sheet with one column on the left that lists job requirements (what employers are looking for) and in the column on the right analyze yourself on these requirements. Write a conclusion that states whether public relations would be a good career option for you.

Additional Readings

Caywood, Clarke L., ed. *The Handbook of Strategic Public Relations & Integrated Communications*. New York: McGraw-Hill, 1997.

Harris, Thomas L. *Value-Added Public Relations: The Secret Weapon of Integrated Marketing*. Lincolnwood IL: NTC Business Books, 1998.

Rosen, Emanuel. *The Anatomy of Buzz: How to Create Word-of-Mouth Marketing*. New York: Doubleday, 2000.

Research Assignment

Consult the books above and other books and articles you can find on public relations. From these readings, develop an outline for a crisis management program for your school or college. In other words, if some disaster happens (e.g., a student is killed, a building burns down), what should your school or college do to minimize the damage to its reputation?

Endnotes

[1] Regis McKenna, *Relationship Marketing*, Reading, Mass: Addison-Wesley, 1991.

[2] James E. Grunig and Todd Hunt, *Managing Public Relations* (New York: Holt, Rinehart & Winston, 1984), p. 6.

[3] Quoted in Fraser P. Seitel, *The Practice of Public Relations*, 7th ed. (Upper Saddle River, NJ: Prentice Hall, 1998), p. 7.

[4] Seitel, ibid., p. 5.

[5] "Rep Briefs: By the Numbers," *Reputation Management* 6, no. 5 (May 2000), p. 18.

[6] Quoted in Thomas L. Harris, *Value-Added Public Relations: The Secret Weapon of Integrated Marketing* (Lincolnwood, IL: NTC Business Books, 1998), p. x.

[7] Ron Ricci, "Momentum Management: Why Momentum Eclipses Branding in the Information Age," *Journal of Integrated Communications*, 1999-2000, pp. 10-15.

[8] "Strategic Messaging: A Solution," *GCI Intelligence Quarterly* 1, no. 133.

[9] "An 'Invisible Giant' Awakens," *Reputation Management* 5, no. 2 (March-April 1999), pp. 68-70.

[10] Gordon Fairclough, "Crabs Sing to Give ITT Industries a 'Name'," *The Wall Street Journal*, September 17, 1998, p. B22.

[11] Tom Duncan and Sandra Moriarty, "A Process for Managing Brand Relationships," *Academy Monograph* (New York: PRSA Counselors Academy, 2000), pp. 11-12.

[12] "An 'Invisible Giant' Awakens," p. 70.

[13] "20/20 Vision," *Reputation Management* 6, no. 2 (February 2000), pp. 32-40.

[14] Ibid., pp. 38, 40.

[15] Paul A. Holmes, "Promise Keepers," *Reputation Management* 6, no. 3 (March 2000), p. 4.

[16] Thomas L. Harris, "Brand Maintenance," *Reputation Management* 6, no. 2 (February 2000), pp. 28-29.

[17] Prema Nakra, "Corporate Reputation Management: 'CRM' with a Strategic Twist?" *Public Relations Quarterly* 45, no. 2 (Summer 2000), pp. 35-42.

[18] Harris, "Brand Maintenance," p. 29.

[19] Quoted in ibid., p. 29.

[20] Harris, "Corporate Communications Spending & Reputations of Fortune 500 Companies," Los Angeles, CA: An Impulse Research Report, June 4, 1000. p. 16.

[21] Thomas L. Harris, *The Marketer's Guide to Public Relations: How Today's Top Companies Are Using the New PR to Gain a Competitive Edge* (New York: John Wiley & Sons, 1991), p. 9.

[22] Richard Rotman, "Why Can't They Get Along?" *Brandera.com*, May 30, 2000.

[23] James E. Grunig and Jon White, "The Effect of Worldviews on Public Relations Theory and Practice," in *Excellence in Public Relations and Communication Management*, ed. James E. Grunig (Hillsdale, NJ: Lawrence Erlbaum, 1992), p. 31.

[24]Sandra E. Moriarty, "PR and IMC: The Benefits of Integration," *Public Relations Quarterly* 39, no. 3 (Fall 1994), p. 41.

[25]David Bank, "Bay Networks' Results to Trail Forecasts," *The Wall Street Journal*, March 18, 1998, p. B4.

[26]Sandra E. Moriarty, "The Big Idea: Creativity in Public Relations," in *The Handbook of Strategic Public Relations and Integrated Communications*, ed. Clarke L. Caywood (New York: McGraw-Hill, 1997), pp. 554-63.

[27]John W. Felton, "A Generation of Attitudes," Vernon C. Schranz Distinguished Lectureship in Public Relations (Muncie, IN: Ball State University, 1994).

[28]"Next to Godliness," *Reputation Management* 6, no. 3 (March 2000), p. 17.

[29]Steve Jarvis, "How the Internet Is Changing Fundamentals of Publicity," *Marketing News*, July 17, 2000, p. 6.

[30]Roger Haywood, "Media Relations," in *Strategic Public Relations*, ed. Norman A. Hart (London: Macmillan Business Press, 1995), pp. 176-77.

[31]Ibid., pp. 178-79.

[32]Seitel, *The Practice of Public Relations*, p. 283.

[33]"RepBriefs: By the Numbers," *Reputation Management* 6, no. 2 (February 2000), p. 18.

[34]"From Gay-Bashing Ministers to Striking Umps, Agency Names Top PR Blunders of 1999," *Inside PR*, January 3, 2000, p. 10.

[35]"Reputation Watch: Shell," *Reputation Management* 6, no. 3 (March 2000), p. 11.

[36]"20/20 Vision," p. 40.

[37]"RepBriefs: By the Numbers," *Reputation Management* 5, no. 3 (May–June 1999), p. 12.

[38]Paul A. Holmes, "With Friends Like These...," *Reputation Management* 6, no. 8 (September 2000), pp. 12-15.

[39]Paul A. Holmes, "Guerilla Marketing: The Word on the Street," *Reputation Management* 6, no. 3 (March 2000), pp. 30-37.

[40]Richard D. Bonnette, "UnSelling Drugs with Paid Media," *Agency*, Spring 1998, pp. 67-69.

[41]Terrie Williams, "Putting Relationships Back into Public Relations," Vernon C. Schranz Distinguished Lectureship in Public Relations (Muncie, IN: Ball State University, 1996).

16

Sales Promotion: Intensifying Consideration

Key Points in This Chapter

1. How do sales promotions add value to a brand offering?

2. What are consumer sales promotions designed to accomplish and what are their strengths and limitations?

3. How do trade promotions work?

Chapter Perspective:
Intensifying the Brand Message

This chapter focuses on sales promotion, which is a marketing communication function that adds value to brand messages. A sales promotion intensifies a brand contact when a customer or prospect is in a buying or using situation. It operates where brand decisions are being evaluated and decisions are being made.

Although sales promotion's primary job is to affect behavior, it can (and should) also help create awareness and reinforce the brand image. The more complex and drawn-out the buying decision is for a product category, the more sales promotion can be used to help more prospects and customers through the decision process. These types of brand messages are highly persuasive because they provide tangible added value and are available for only a limited period, which creates a sense of immediacy.

Sales promotions are mostly one-way, nonpersonal messages. Sales promotions targeted at trade partners are designed to motivate the trade not only to buy more product but also to take other actions that will encourage end users to buy more of a brand. Consumer loyalty programs are a form of sales promotion that are key in helping retain and increase share of current customers' category spending. Because of the power of intensified brand contacts, sales promotions are often a major portion of a marketing communication budget for consumer packaged goods.

This chapter looks at sales promotion as a value-added function. The two main divisions are consumer sales promotions (which include various tools, from coupons to loyalty programs, and are carried by a variety of media) and trade promotions.

NESCAFÉ SERVES CONTINUOUS HAPPINESS
McCann-Erickson, Osaka, Japan

EFFECTIVENESS CASE

When the Japanese economy went into a deep recession in the 1990s, and coffee category sales leveled off, the Swiss-based food-and-beverage giant Nestlé found it necessary to increase the prices of its instant-coffee brand Nescafé. Under such circumstances, how would you intensify the relationship Nescafé has with its Japanese customers, reach new customers, involve more retailers, and increase sales of instant coffee in Japan?

The Osaka office of international advertising agency McCann-Erickson decided that sales promotion was the marketing communication tool that could best lead this campaign for Nescafé. A strategic promotional idea under the theme "Continuous Happiness Present" was created by the McCann team and executed over a period of several years. This award-winning promotional campaign was designed to promote Nestlé's "friendly and caring" brand values while simultaneously increasing sales of Nescafé instant coffees at higher prices (see Exhibit 16–1).

To Western students of marketing communications, the "Continuous Happiness Present" campaign may seem overly polite, too much of a soft sell. It must be kept in mind, however, that the Japanese, like other Asian people, often find American and European advertising and sales promotion offers to be too pushy and intrusive.

The Marketing Challenge

The marketplace environment was the source of most of the problems faced by McCann's management team. Nescafé was the best-selling brand in the Japanese instant-coffee market, with a 72 percent share. However, its sales had been falling in recent years due to severe competition with growing liquid-coffee sales, a harder environment in which to get in-store display opportunities, and heavy-discount sale pricing of other competitive brands.

EXHIBIT 16-1

A scene from one of the Nescafé TV commercials showing one of the winners of the flower promotion.

Campaign Strategy

In 1998, the Nestlé Japan Coffee Beverage Group launched the "Continuous Happiness Present" campaign, which was designed to promote Nescafé's friendly nature to consumers rather than winning them with a discount price strategy. The promotion was a closed lottery in the sense that entrants had to provide a proof of purchase (a legal requirement in Japan), in this case the Nescafé proof-of-purchase mark, which appears on all Nescafé products. Winners whose entries were drawn received a present—a beautiful pot of flowers every month for a whole year (thus "continuous happiness"). It was a large-scale continuity campaign that ran for two years with a total of 10,000 winners.

The flowers brought the "continuous happiness" theme to life as it delivered Nescafé brand reminders to the winners every month when their new present arrived. The Nescafé brand, then, came to mean friendly, caring, and happiness—values that are very important to Japanese consumers.

Message Delivery

The focus of the "Continuous Happiness" campaign was on the flower promotion sweepstakes, which was announced through TV and newspaper advertising, as well as on posters on trains (see Exhibit 16-2). (A large number of Japanese commute by train.) In addition, the campaign was supported by various other types of communication, such as entry cards, minigame brochures, and merchandising materials (display skirts, tray bands, wigglers, shelf posters, on-cap and neck-ring leaflets, and bookmarks).

EXHIBIT 16-2

The "Flower Train" promotion not only had banner ads announcing the promotion, it also had fresh flowers in an overhead container.

Since this campaign was also designed to get the support and assistance of retailers, McCann developed a trade promotion plan. A trade brochure explained the "flowerpot" promotion to retailers, and the company sent dealers display kits and a taste demonstration stand for doing in-store sampling.

The campaign used an integrated cross-media approach that integrated the supporting advertisements. For example, the TV commercial asked the viewers to "look at today's morning paper." TV was used to attract attention, and newspapers were used to help consumers understand the details of the promotion and how to enter the drawing. Further, a "Flower Train" commercial, which ran in the second phase of the promotional campaign, directed consumers to in-train promotional offers. For two weeks, many commuter train compartments were decorated with the "flowerpot" promotion announcement and several transit advertisements featured real flowers (which also required major maintenance efforts).

In addition to advertising, other promotional elements included coffee-mug giveaways at the point of purchase, an on-pack flower vase premium, and a telephone-card promotion. These were premiums that motivated some type of activity with the idea that the brand name, Nescafé, would be seen and made top-of-mind each time these premiums were used.

Evaluation of the Nescafé Campaign

The McCann team designed a campaign evaluation with two key criteria to gauge the campaign's effectiveness: (1) number of consumer applications, and (2) number of chain-store participants. Entries to the promotion could be directly translated into sales volume because a consumer had to buy a product to enter the drawing. The participation of chain supermarkets is crucial for the success of a retail promotional campaign because the greater the distribution and the bigger the in-store displays, the more sales are likely to increase.

This campaign was repeated for two years with consumer involvement escalating from year to year. The first year generated 2.7 million entries, and, the second year generated 3.8 million—an increase of 40 percent. Obviously, there was no erosion in this promotion as it continued from one year to the next. Instead, the continuity was evidence of the cumulative effects in consumers' minds of the happiness theme.

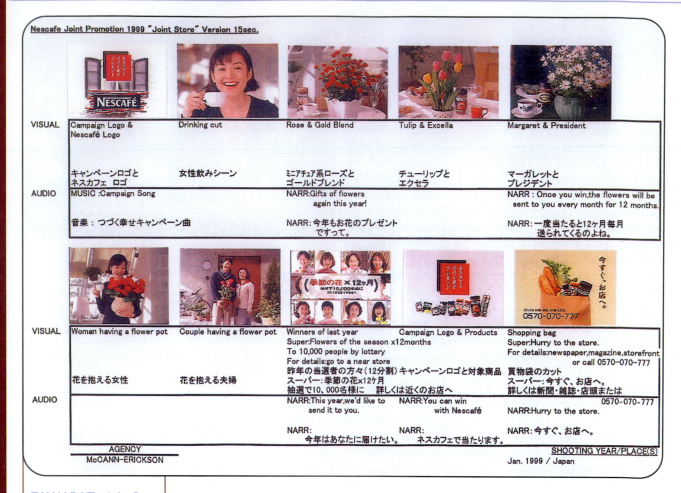

AGENCY
McCANN–ERICKSON

SHOOTING YEAR/PLACE(S)
Jan. 1999 / Japan

EXHIBIT 16-3

One of the TV photoboards, written in both Japanese and English, that made the flower offer.

In terms of chain-store participation, the promotional campaign generated a 41 percent increase in the participation of retailers. The "Continuous Happiness Present" promotional campaign also won international awards for its effectiveness and was the most successful promotion in Nestlé Japan's history.

What were the reasons for the campaign's success? First, the primary premium in this promotion was flowers, something that is appreciated by Japanese people of all ages. Also, the campaign had longevity, with its continuity concept of "delivering continuous happiness to consumers" for a year. Finally, the promotion was unique, something that had not been seen before in the Japanese market.

But the Nescafé flower promotion would have been incomplete without the integration of mass media advertising, special packaging, and in-store merchandising materials to support the flower sweepstakes. The photoboard (like a TV storyboard, except with still photos) in Exhibit 16–3 illustrates the development of the "Flowerpot" campaign idea, and also ties in the lottery promotion, before it ends with a product-line shot and a photo of a shopping bag with the brand prominently shown at the top.

This case was adapted with permission from the Advertising and Marketing Effectiveness (AME) award-winning brief for Nescafé prepared by the McCann-Erickson agency in Osaka, Japan.

SALES PROMOTION: THE VALUE-ADDED FUNCTION

The term *sales promotion* is sometimes misunderstood or confused with advertising. This is because sales promotion activities frequently use advertising to make the promotional offer known. **Sales promotion,** however, is a marketing communication function that encourages action by adding tangible value to a brand offering. More specifically, it is *a short-term, added-value offer designed to encourage and accelerate a response.* A *consumer* sales promotion offer is designed for end users or buyers; a *trade* sales promotion offer is designed for customers in the distribution channel, such as distributors, wholesalers, and retailers.

Let's consider some key concepts in the sales promotion definition. Sales promotion focuses on *adding value,* as Exhibit 16–4 illustrates. An added value includes such things as a chance to win a prize; a reduction in price (e.g., 20 percent off, two for the price of one, no finance charges for a year); prizes; extra product (e.g., 30 percent more coffee for the same price); free samples; and premiums (e.g., buy $30 worth of cosmetics and receive a cosmetic travel case free).

Trade sales promotions (which are generally referred to simply as trade promotions) include discounts; extra product (e.g., buy three cases, get one free); advertising support; and premiums. After price reductions, trips and cash rewards and are the most popular trade promotions. In BtB marketing, executive gifts (e.g., high-value premiums) are used to reward good customers.

As companies place more emphasis on retaining customers, sales promotions are often used as rewards for customer loyalty. United Airlines, for example, sends out free upgrades periodically to its "premier executives"—those who fly more than 25,000 miles a year on United. Retail stores often have exclusive showings and sales for their credit-card customers. Relationship marketing talks about moving beyond customer satisfaction and "delighting" customers, which can be achieved with the strategic use of sales promotions.

Two important things to note are, first, that these incentives are used to motivate customers to respond in some way that will lead to a sale and, second, that sales promotions are used to motivate customers at different points in the brand decision process. While advertising is often used to create awareness and interest, sales promotions are often used to create the next steps in buying behavior, such as desire and action. Automobile dealers, for example, offer free drinks and hot dogs just for visiting their showrooms, while those companies selling time-share properties offer free dinners and an overnight stay to those willing to listen to a sales pitch for the property. In other words, a prospect may be aware and even have some interest in a brand but not enough desire to actively seek the brand out or risk buying it, but an extra incentive can sometimes move a prospect into the desire and action stage. A sales promotion tied to a particular customer situation can have a large impact because of the prospect's personal involvement.

A critical element of sales promotion is that it works in the short term. If a reduction in price is offered too often, for example, customers begin to think of that reduced price as the regular price. Consequently, the reduction no longer has a sense of immediacy. By offering an extra incentive for only a short period of time, companies create a sense of immediacy: Customers know that if they don't respond they won't receive the "something extra" that is being offered. The bottom

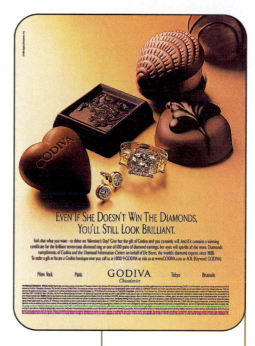

EXHIBIT 16-4

Even prestige brands use sales promotions. In this case, Godiva chocolate is sponsoring a sweepstakes in which the prize is diamonds. Notice how the image of the product is enhanced by the quality of the promotion.

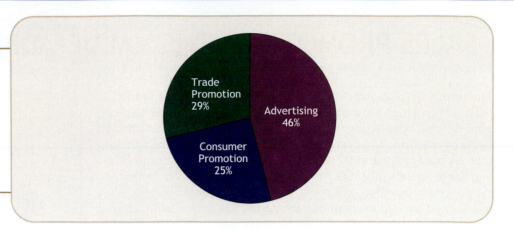

EXHIBIT 16-5

This ad seeks to engage the customer in a taste test; to motivate people to participate by trying Diet Dr Pepper, it includes a coupon for a free two-liter bottle. Note, however, the emphasis on the brand, which is another important objective of this sales promotion ad.

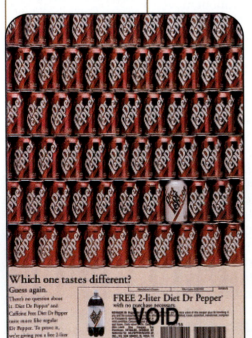

line is that the short-term aspect, the momentum created by the incentive, speeds up the brand decision-making process.

Some consider sales promotion complementary to advertising and personal selling because it can make both more effective. In reality, however, sales promotion is far more than supplementary. A study of marketing communication spending in the year 2000 across a wide range of consumer goods and services by *Promo* magazine once again confirmed that more money is spent on promotions (trade plus consumer) than on advertising as shown in Figure 16–1. What is surprising in this figure is that the trade promotion portion is smaller than that for advertising, because for years trade promotion spending (for consumer brands) was the largest piece of this pie. According to *Promo*'s study, consumer products companies spent $93.4 billion in 2000 on consumer promotions and $108.3 billion on trade promotions.

The increasing use of sales promotion reflects that the growing number of brand offerings has made the fight for shelf space in grocery, drug, and discount stores brutal. Just as in real estate, the more people who want to own, say, beachfront property, the higher the cost of that property. With more brands asking for distribution and shelf space, retail chains have realized that they can play one brand against another as a way to maximize sales promotion support from manufacturers.

Some say that a decline in brand loyalty has also been responsible for the increased sales promotion spending. Others argue, however, that it is the other way around—that the increase in sales promotion spending has conditioned customers to focus more on prices than on brands, and thus become less loyal. It is possible, however, to use sales promotion effectively to build a brand, as Exhibit 16–5 demonstrates.

How Sales Promotion Works

Keep in mind that the usual grocery-shopping trip takes about 27 minutes.[1] During that time, a shopper in the average store will select only 35 to 40 of the 7,000 available grocery items (30,000 if you include different sizes and flavors). Those selections depend on the customer's previous experience with brands and the marketing communications used to support the brand. Studies have shown that when sales promotion tools are used they can increase sales of a brand as much as 400 percent.

As an example of how a sales promotion effort works, consider the Maybelline HydraTime lipcolor offer in Exhibit 16–6. In addition to picturing the product and its shades of color, the card also states selling points (extended-wear, moisturizing), a price deal ("Save $1.00"), and a sample ("Try it now!"). On the back, it gives more information about the shades (their names), information about how the extended-wear feature works ("exclusive ColorBond™"), and a coupon that makes good on the "Save $1.00" offer on the front side.

In order to move their products through the distribution channel from the point of manufacture to the point of consumption, consumer-product marketers use two basic sales promotion strategies—push and pull.

Push strategies are *marketing communication efforts targeted at members of the distribution channels*. Manufacturers know that once a retailer, for example, has purchased several truckloads of a product, that retailer will work hard to make sure the product sells in order to recoup the cost of the product and make a profit on it. There is an old, rather crude saying in the produce and meat business that summarizes such a situation: "Sell it or smell it."

Pull strategies are *marketing communication efforts targeted at end users*. Brands use consumer promotions to motivate customers to come to stores to look for a specific brand, which "pulls" product off the shelf and creates a need for retailers to buy more to meet the consumer demand.

Most trade buyers can estimate how much pull will be created by certain kinds of promotions. Before the Contadina ad in Exhibit 16–7 ran, the buyers for the chains carrying Contadina were shown copies of the ad by Contadina's sales representatives. Buyers were told which communication vehicles would be carrying the ad and when, and given the specific number of coupons that would be distributed in their trading area. Using this information, a buyer would estimate, for example, that the Contadina coupon and advertising during the promotion period would increase (i.e., pull) Contadina sales by 25 percent. That buyer would then order 25 percent more cases than usual.

Most sales promotion programs include both push and pull strategies, using both consumer and trade promotions. In IMC the challenge is to integrate trade and consumer promotions both in timing and theme. In this way both efforts will create a positive synergy. Although push and pull are most frequently discussed in relation to consumer packaged goods, these strategies are also used in BtB, service, and considered-purchase products (i.e., durable goods). In the case of BtB, often the end users of products are not the same as those who make the buying decisions. Thus, the users become the consumers and the buyers become the "retailers." Having an integrated promotion program designed for both can be strategically sound. Buyers (or their companies) can be given certain incentives for buying, and users can be given incentives to try new or improved brands or to attend training sessions so that their use of the brand will be more satisfying and productive.

In the case of service products, such as insurance, banking, and transportation, the "trade" becomes the retail outlets and branches. Corporate and division offices often use "push" incentives to motivate their frontline employees to focus on certain products.

EXHIBIT 16-6

This Maybelline Hydra-Time lipcolor promotion contains a number of features including a price deal and a coupon, as well as product samples and product information.

Banks, for example, will often have competitions among their branches using premiums to reward those generating the most sales for new product offerings.

CONSUMER SALES PROMOTION TOOLS

Consumer sales promotion is designed to motivate prospects and customers to make a decision and buy the brand. There are a number of different sales promotion tools used in consumer promotion.

Although most of the popular sales promotion tools described below are used for consumer promotions, some are also adapted for BtB marketing. The following is a review of the most common consumer promotions used to trigger a brand-buying decision in the critical buy zone.

Coupons

A **coupon** is *a certificate with a stated value for a price reduction on a specified item.* Today, over 300 billion coupons are distributed every year in the United States, but only about 2 percent of these are ever redeemed. Coupons have to be distributed through some medium—newspapers or magazines, on packages, in store displays, or direct mail. Many reach consumers through colorful freestanding inserts (FSIs) in newspapers. FSIs have a slightly higher redemption rate than regular newspaper and magazine coupons, while coupons on packages ("on-packs") have the highest redemption levels.

Electronic coupons are high-tech coupons that are distributed in-store and on-line. Online coupons are issued by both individual companies and coupon distribution sites such as Cool Savings (www.coolsavings.com). This site requires that you register and provide a profile of yourself. It then shows you a checklist of lifestyle categories; the company will send coupon offers to you according to the categories you check off. Because customers opt-in and provide their profiles and interests, they redeem the coupons they receive at a higher rate than those distributed in newspapers and magazines.

In-store coupon distribution is handled in several ways: interactive touch-screen video kiosks at the point of purchase, coupons that are dispensed as a customer walks up to a certain product category, and instant-print coupons issued at the cash register while checking out. The latter are targeted based on what the customer has bought—a person who bought ice cream may be given a coupon for chocolate syrup. Some marketers use electronic coupons to target buyers of competitive brands. Someone who buys Kellogg cereal, for example, may be issued a coupon for a General Mills cereal. The strategy is that if the Kellogg buyers are at all dissatisfied, they will be motivated by the coupon to buy a General Mills cereal the next time, changing their brand choice.

Price Reductions

Short-term price reductions come in various forms: a featured price that is lower than the regular price, on-pack coupons, free goods ("buy one, get one free"), and enlarged packages ("30 more for same price"). Most price reductions are in the form of "featured products," which grocery stores use each week to attract shoppers. These items are generally emphasized in a store's local ad or in direct-mail flyers. When retailers receive a trade promotion, they pass the savings on to the customer in the form of price reductions. Sometimes, the retailer will even sacrifice some of its own profit margin in order to offer a motivating low price on a few featured items.

Another form of price reduction is reduced or extended credit. This incentive is often used with high-priced items such as appliances, furniture, and cars. Typical offers are "No payment till next year" and "Only 0.9% interest." When customers have a strong desire and their only barrier is money, extended-credit offers can be powerful incentives. "Buy now, pay later" promotions can, however, cause some customers to spend more than they can afford. When such easy credit is made available to teenagers, some say it creates an ethical dilemma, as discussed in the Ethics and Issues box.

Rebates

Some companies offer customers cash refunds known as rebates. Rebates are commonly offered for such items as clothing or household appliances (see Exhibit 16–8). Large rebates, like those given on cars, are handled by the seller. For small rebates, like those given for coffeemakers, the consumer must send the manufacturer proof of purchase (a receipt and a barcode label) and a completed rebate form. Many people purchase a product because of an advertised rebate but then never collect the rebate because they either forget about it or lose the rebate application or receipt. Failure to take advantage of rebates is called *slippage* and is the reason why marketers can offer such high-value rebates (those who do not take advantage of the offer essentially cover the costs of those who do). Yet slippage has also led to a decrease in the motivating power of rebates (customers aren't interested in an offer when they feel that getting the rebate is too much trouble) and thus to a decline in the practice in general.

EXHIBIT 16-8

Following the benefit-oriented copy, this Champion ad contains a rebate offer as the incentive to action.

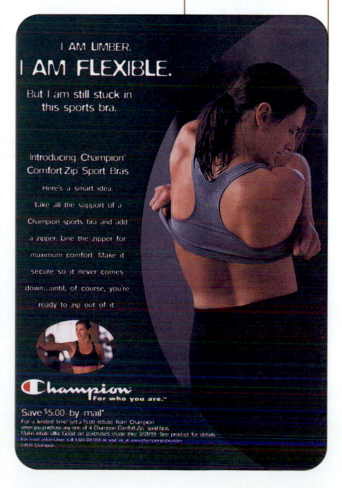

I AM LIMBER.
I AM FLEXIBLE.
But I am still stuck in this sports bra.

Introducing Champion Comfort Zip Sport Bras

Here's a smart idea. Take all the support of a Champion sports bra and add a zipper. Use the zipper for maximum comfort. Make it secure so it never comes down...until, of course, you're ready to zip out of it.

Champion
For who you are.™

Save $5.00 by mail*

ETHICS AND ISSUES

Can Teens Responsibly Handle Credit?

American Express has added a new product to its line, the Cobaltcard. (The creator of the card, Zowi Corp., has licensed the card to American Express.) What makes this a different kind of credit card is that it is aimed at 13- to 22-year-olds. Because this wide age range includes junior high schoolers as well as college seniors, some would argue that those in the low end of the age range may not have the maturity to handle a credit card (a parent must co-sign for anyone under 18).

To help introduce the new card, the company had a promotional tie-in with the MTV show *Road Rules*. The characters in the show were shown using the Cobaltcard to purchase supplies for one of their missions. Advertising both off- and online was also used to increase awareness and encourage teens to apply for the new card. According to Zowi's marketing director, the card is a "financial tool" for this age group, which spends $140 billion a year.

If the Cobaltcard and others like it become widely used, merchants will probably target teenagers even more aggressively than they already do, telling them they can satisfy their wants and desires even if they don't have the money now—all they need is that piece of plastic. When the president of Florida Consolidated Credit Counseling Services was asked about the impact of promoting teen credit cards, he said, simply, "It is going to be a boon to our business."

Think About It

Will easy credit lead teenagers into financial difficulty? Or is having a teen credit card a good way of learning to become financially responsible? If you were the owner of a retail bike store, would you encourage teens to come in and use their credit cards to buy bikes costing $500 or more?

Sources: "Getting Carded," *Promo*, December 2000, p. 13; and Lisa Marshall, "Charge!" *Boulder Daily Camera*, December 12, 2000, p. 1D.

Premiums

In the context of sales promotion, a **premium** is *an item offered free or at a bargain price to encourage some type of response.* Premiums that are most effective are those that are instantly available. Premiums can improve a brand's image, gain goodwill, broaden the customer base (by attracting new customers), produce an immediate increase in sales, and reward customers. A premium may be included in the product's package (in-pack premium), placed visibly on the package (on-pack premium), handed out in a store or at an event, or sent by mail.

The major challenge with premiums is finding an item that a high percentage of a target audience would be interested in having. Consumables such as movie tickets, gasoline, food, and beverages have proved to be popular as premiums. Another important criterion is that the net cost of a premium must be relatively low, especially compared to the price of the product for which it is being used. Items that customers enjoy having many variations of, such as caps, T-shirts, and cups, are widely used premiums.

Free is the most powerful sales promotion word a company can use (because we are all a bit greedy and like getting something for nothing). This is the reason that when a premium is being offered, the word *free* is strongly emphasized; it not only attracts attention to the brand message but is also a powerful motivator.

Premiums that can be made unique to a brand can also be attractive to customers. One example is a toy replica of a NASCAR racecar that is sponsored by

M&Ms. Although miniature toy cars are widely available in stores, the M&M-sponsored car is not (because M&M and NASCAR control the use of that particular car's reproduction). Selecting the right premium is a challenge. When choosing a premium, companies should ask the following questions:[2]

1. Does the premium have appeal for the majority of the target audience?
2. Does it have a perceived value?
3. Is it relevant to the product, brand image, and/or campaign idea?
4. Will customers and the trade easily recognize its nature and ready application?
5. Will it create an immediate behavioral response?
6. Is it a consumable or collectable (so customers will be attracted even though they already have one or more)?
7. Does it fit into the seasonal/promotional period?
8. Is it made domestically?
9. Does it have any safety/health concerns?
10. Can it be ordered and quickly reordered in limited quantities (to avoid unused inventories) that are still cost-effective?

Specialties

Like premiums, **specialties** are *incentives given free to customers and other stakeholders to help keep a brand's name top-of-mind*. Specialties are generally low-cost items such as calendars, rulers, coffee mugs, T-shirts, and pens. BtB marketers may give more costly items, such as desk sets, cellular telephones, briefcases, CD players, and watches, to executives or other representatives with whom the company has a relationship.

Spending in the promotional products category of specialties and premiums is now over $15 billion a year, more than is spent on consumer magazine advertising. All types of businesses, including nonprofit organizations, use specialties for occasions ranging from launching new products and opening new facilities (where creating a new customer base is an important objective), to rewarding current customers and reminding prospects of the brand.

The rationale for using specialty items is that people will think more positively about a brand that gives them something of value—the more added value, the greater the impact. Also, because most specialty items are tangible, those who receive them are exposed to the brand name multiple times (i.e., every time they look at the calendar or drink from the coffee mug), helping to keep the brand top-of-mind.

Sampling

An especially powerful pull strategy, **sampling** consists of *offering prospects the opportunity to try a product before making a buying decision*. Sampling is usually targeted through the purchase of select mailing lists or carried out in stores or at events. Research has found that the strategy seems to work better with women (73 percent positive response) than with men (57 percent).[3]

Sampling is one of the most costly of all sales promotions; however, it is also one of the most effective. The proposition is that a brand is so good that once people try it, they will want to buy it. Sampling offers the greatest credibility of all MC

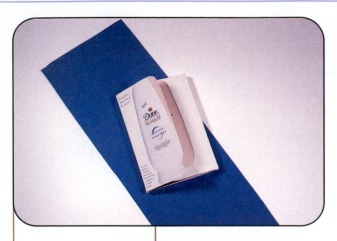

EXHIBIT 16-9

Dove introduced its new body wash, Nutrium, with this package containing a sample of the product and free shower pouf.

functions because it is based on the product's performance and can move a nonuser to become a loyal customer instantaneously—if the product lives up to the expectation that has been created for it. Sampling is most successful when a product is perceivably different from the competition.

Most in-store sampling programs are tied to a coupon campaign. Sometimes samples are distributed with related items (e.g., an on-pack sample of hair conditioner given free with the purchase of a shampoo), but this limits their distribution to those who buy the other product. A recent innovation in distribution is polybagging, in which samples are hung on doorknobs or delivered in plastic bags along with the daily newspaper or a monthly magazine. The Dove sampling promotion in Exhibit 16–9 can be delivered by mail or in a doorknob hanger.

In a practice similar to sampling, food and drug marketers use *combination offers*, such as a razor and a package of blades or a toothbrush with a tube of toothpaste, at a reduced price for the two. For best results, the items should be related. Sometimes, a combination offer may be used to introduce a new brand by tying its purchase to an established brand at a special price.

Sweepstakes and Contests

A **contest** is *a brand-sponsored competition that involves some form of skill and effort*. A **sweepstakes** is *a form of sales promotion that offers prizes based on a chance drawing of entrants' names*. Contests and sweepstakes are used to increase store traffic by requiring those who wish to enter to pick up an entry blank at a store or dealership. To encourage a large number of entries, these types of sales promotion should be kept as simple as possible. By law, the prize structure must be clearly stated and rules clearly defined. Because contests, especially, require some effort, the response rate is extremely low. Furthermore, a portion of those who do respond may be "professional" contest entrants who care nothing about the brand sponsoring the contest. "Professional" contest entrants simply do it for the fun of participating and the chance to win. Although sweepstakes and contests don't generate a high rate of response, they are helpful in setting up customer databases (because entrants have to submit their names and addresses and often are asked to answer other questions) and calling attention to a brand.

A **game** is *a sales promotion tool that has the chance element of a sweepstakes but is conducted over a longer time*. Grocery stores may design bingo-type games to build store traffic. The marketing advantage of a game is that customers must make repeat visits to the dealer to continue playing. Brand games have become popular ways to promote brands on the Internet.

Sweepstakes, contests, and games all require careful planning and monitoring. Companies must abide by state and federal regulations. For example, although it can *encourage* entrants to send in a proof of purchase, a company cannot *require* a purchase as a condition for entry, or else the sweepstakes becomes a lottery, which is illegal in most states. The law also requires that the odds of winning the sweepstakes be published on promotional materials.

Contests and sweepstakes must be advertised to be successful—and often they need dealer or retail support. Retailers must be encouraged to build special in-store displays to hold product, announce a sweepstakes, and provide entry forms. In this way, sweepstakes are used to get off-shelf display. Some contests and sweepstakes ask the entrant to name the product's local dealer so that the company may award prizes to the dealer that made the sale. This gives retailers extra incentive to promote the sweepstakes and the brand.

Tie-in Promotions

In a *tie-in promotion,* two or more products are advertised together, such as cheese and crackers. (The difference between a tie-in promotion and the combination offer mentioned earlier, under sampling, is that the two brands are not packaged together.) But, to obtain the offered savings, the customer must purchase both brands at the same time. This not only allows two brands to share the promotional costs but also lets each brand build from the other's image.

Loyalty Promotions

In a loyalty promotion, a company offers premiums or other incentives when a customer makes multiple purchases over time. The most simple of these is the coffee or gasoline punch card that allows a person a free coffee or a fill-up after a set number of purchases (e.g., "buy 10 and get the 11th one free"). This is a powerful sales promotion tool for helping retain and grow customers' share of spending. Because loyalty programs are so important, the following section explains them in more detail.

Loyalty Programs: The Retention Driver

As noted at various points throughout this book, sales promotion is one of the most powerful MC functions for helping retain customers. *Using promotions specifically de-signed for customer retention* is called **loyalty (or frequency) marketing**. Regardless of what name a company or agency gives it, a loyalty program represents a strategy for minimizing customer defections and increasing a brand's share of wallet.

Most loyalty programs have been built on discounts and impersonal gifts (toasters, fishing rods, golf clubs, dinnerware, jewelry). However, as Richard Barlow, chairman and CEO of Frequency Marketing, Inc., notes, after a decade of a hot economy, what people value now is not more stuff, but more satisfying personal experiences.[4] Frequent-flyer programs are so successful because they translate into trips and memories, a phenomenon being described as "the experience economy."

> "More compelling than stuff, are experiences—events, trips, places, sights, sounds, tastes that are out of the ordinary, memorable in their own right, precious in their uniqueness and fulfilling in a way that seems to make us more than we were."
>
> Richard Barlow, "The Net Upends Tenets of Loyalty Marketing"

How Loyalty Programs Work

Loyalty programs work best when brands have high fixed costs and low variable costs. Probably one of the best examples, again, is airlines.[5] When a plane goes from New York to London, the fixed costs associated with the trip are relatively high: gasoline, crew wages, amortized cost of the airplane, airport fees, and marketing

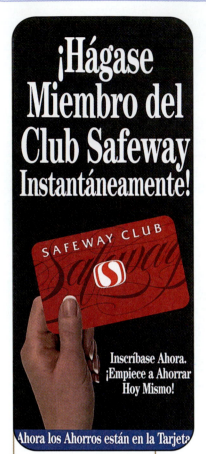

¡Hágase Miembro del Club Safeway Instantáneamente!

SAFEWAY CLUB

Inscríbase Ahora.
¡Empiece a Ahorrar
Hoy Mismo!

Ahora los Ahorros están en la Tarjeta

EXHIBIT 16-10

Targeted to a Hispanic audience, this Safeway Club brochure, which can be picked up at the checkout counter, explains in Spanish how the Safeway Club card program works.

costs. The additional costs associated with having each passenger on board, however, are quite low: basically the cost of beverages and food consumed by that passenger. Entertainment venues, credit-card companies, and cable and telephone companies are other types of businesses with high fixed and low variable costs. When such businesses have empty seats and extra capacity, providing their own product (e.g., trips, admissions) as a reward for being a loyal customer costs the brand relatively little. At the same time, the customer perceives the reward as being of high value and very motivational. In other words, unused services and goods become "promotional currency," which is paid to customers for being loyal. This can be a tie-breaker for customers in their choice between competing brands. The average hotel, for example, sells only about 70 percent of its rooms each night. This means 30 percent of the rooms sit vacant. If these vacant rooms are used to reward customers, a company can greatly increase the impact of its sales promotion programs with a minimal increase in actual budget.

Opportunities to join loyalty programs are delivered through mass media advertising, direct mail, and program literature at brand contact points, such as airline counters. The Safeway brochure in Exhibit 16–10 announces the Safeway Club program for a Spanish-speaking audience. E-commerce companies, like RagingBull.com, a company that serves individual investors, wanted a way to retain and reward its loyal Internet customer base. It turned to Perks.com, an Internet business that provides online customer loyalty programs, including an incentive-based website, catalog of rewards, research, data tracking, customer profiling, and customer service.

The best loyalty programs are strategic, meaning they are designed to achieve a certain objective and contain an idea for doing so. Because a loyalty program is, by its very nature, designed to retain customers and increase a customers' share of category spending, the first step is to determine why customers are leaving the brand or not giving the brand more of their business. If a bank, for example, finds that the major reason customers are leaving is poor service, it should set up a loyalty program for employees rather than customers. Employees or branches of the bank can then be rewarded for reducing the percentage of closed accounts.

When the airlines found that most frequent flyers belonged to three or more frequent-flyer programs, they began providing larger rewards to those who flew the most. United Airlines gives its Premier Executives (those who fly more than 25,000 miles a year on United) double rewards for all flights.

A good loyalty objective is: "Increase average customer lifetime from 8 to 10 years" or "Decrease the defection rate to 5 percent or less." A rather useless objective would be: "Begin a loyalty program." Clearly, a company must set standards for measurement and, more important, provide specific guidelines for what the loyalty program should be designed to do.

Loyalty Program Strengths and Limitations

The primary benefit, or strength, of a loyalty program is an increased level of customer retention, which means lower selling cost. A related benefit is that, because loyalty programs require customers to fill out forms, they can be an excellent vehicle for collecting database information. Another benefit is that these type of programs can differentiate a brand, which is especially important in a commodity category. Because so many brands in a product category are so similar in performance and price, customers must look hard to find a difference. A reward for loyalty may be the only thing that sets one brand apart from another. Besides the obvious cost savings of selling to a current customer (versus a new one) loyalty programs provide what is, in most cases, a pleasant brand experience that further engages customers. Rewards make customers feel good, and this feeling can motivate them to become brand ambassadors and to make brand referrals.

A limitation of loyalty programs is that they can overshadow the brand and take more resources to manage and administer than other forms of marketing communication used by the brand. It's also difficult to determine whether such programs are truly cost-effective especially when competitors offer similar programs. Do they cost more to administer than they are worth in increased revenue? Many companies do not have a clear answer to this question.

Managing a Loyalty Program

When beginning a loyalty program, a company must determine how customers become members. Will all those who make a purchase automatically become members, or do they need to sign up? Generally having customers opt in through their own effort ensures better results. Most programs require prospective members to fill out an application form that asks for customer profile information. This information is valuable not only to those managing the loyalty program but also to those in sales, those managing direct response, and those in customer service.

Once a program is up and running, a company must be sensitive to how many brand messages it sends to members. Loyalty programs that become intrusive and too aggressive in cross-selling can be counterproductive because customers will come to resent the misuse of the company database. The primary way to determine when this line is crossed is by listening to customers and asking for their feedback about the amount of brand messages they are receiving. Asking customers up front what product lines and types of brand information they are interested in receiving can also minimize negative effects.

Minimizing the cost of running a loyalty program is critical. While an airline may be using empty seats for rewards, it must ensure that it does not give away seats during heavy demand periods. Movie theaters often restrict the use of free passes to weeknights and weekend matinees. Similarly, when possible, rewards should be designed to increase sales. A free movie pass may be good only when used along with a purchased ticket.

An important part of the loyalty program strategy is to set the program up so that even after a person redeems a reward he or she is still in the program. When sending out free tickets, an airline should make sure the recipients still have unused miles in their accounts. Another aspect is to have an expiration date on rewards once they have been given out, since outstanding rewards are a financial liability.

Finally, when a loyalty program is designed, a company should discuss its "exit strategy"—how it can end the program should it not be profitable or no longer fit into the brand's overall marketing strategy. A loyalty program, more than almost anything else a marketing communication program does, sets specific expectations for its customers. A company should consider how these expectations can be changed when it's time for the program to end.

Media of Consumer Sales Promotion

It should be clear from the review of the different types of sales promotion that the industry uses every possible type of medium to deliver its brand messages to both consumer and trade audiences. Coupons, for example, appear in mass media advertising, in direct-mail pieces, on packages, and on the back of grocery sales

EXHIBIT 16-11

This is a plastic wrapper for delivering newspapers. The bottom contains a pouch in which a free Hallmark card is enclosed. The wrapper itself announces a line of 99-cent Hallmark cards.

receipts. Contests are announced in ads and at events. Samples are handed out in stores, but they are also mailed to homes and businesses (see Exhibit 16–11). The point is that every sales promotion needs a vehicle to carry it.

Many sales promotions, such as displays, are specially constructed and delivered by sales reps or distributors. Sales literature and manuals contain the information sales reps need about the various types of allowances and discounts they are able to offer customers.

The Internet is just beginning to become a sales promotion tool. However, Forrester Research has predicted that Internet sales promotion spending will account for 50 to 70 percent of Internet marketing budgets by 2003.[6] Saturn has used the Internet effectively in its prelaunch efforts to target young buyers for its new S-series cars. The automaker ran an online sweepstakes offering the target audience a chance to win a car and, in the process, gathered the names of more than 200,000 potential Saturn buyers.

Publishers Clearing House (PCH), famous for its multimillion-dollar direct-mail sweepstakes, has launched a Web company that represents an entirely new e-commerce business model. The company will leverage the promotion, marketing, and database resources of PCH to create a new customer experience. Site visitors will find a game-playing experience that, at the same time, exposes them to "winning deals" on a variety of merchandise and magazine offers. As site visitors play a game, and become interested in brand offerings, they can simply click on the brand mentioned and find out more information and how to order. Because of the game involvement, visitors are motivated to stay at the site longer than they would at sites simply offering a catalog of products.

Likewise, packaged-goods marketers are developing free-sample sites that provide them with customer feedback, in addition to an opportunity for customers to try a new product. Two sites offering this service are FreeSamples.com and StartSampling.com. Promotions.com is a BtB company that provides clients with tools for running online promotions, as well as permission-based direct marketing and targeted e-mail campaigns (see Exhibit 16–12).

Promotional efforts are sneaking onto electronic shopping carts as well. A software program from iChoose, Inc., searches its database of coupons and deals to find savings on the exact items a customer puts in his or her shopping cart. Fickle shoppers can be teased away at the promise of a 10 percent saving or a cheaper shipping fee.[7]

> **"We're permission-based marketing on steroids."**
>
> Kevin Dahlstrom, president of iChoose

Strengths of Consumer Sales Promotion

The strengths of the sales promotion functions can be found by looking at the types of marketing and MC objectives that sales promotion can help accomplish. In terms of the marketing program, sales promotion programs are designed to (1) increase distribution, (2) balance demand, (3) control inventory levels, and (4) respond to competitive programs. Before consumers can buy a retail product, it must be available on the store's shelf. Thus, marketers use trade promotions to gain new distributors and secure shelf space. Promotions *increase distribution* by lowering the risk for members of the distribution channel.

Knowing how important it is to have products available when customers want them, most companies—goods and services, consumer and BtB companies—work hard to keep adequate inventories. Service companies, similarly, staff up for traditionally busy times of the day, week, or year. When companies find they have too many goods on hand or service personnel who are not being kept busy, they use promotions to *balance demand* and *control inventory levels*. Rental car companies sometimes offer "three days for the price of two" on Friday-through-Monday rentals because this period spans both business and weekend rentals. For products that have irregular purchase cycles, promotions are used to level out the peaks and valleys in the sales curve.

Another common use of promotions is to *respond to competitive offerings*. To counter the introduction of a new competing brand, a company may use "loading" promotions in which customers are encouraged to buy in larger quantities than usual (i.e., to load up on a product). The idea is that if the demand for the new product is reduced, it will have a tougher time getting and keeping distribution. In the high-tech industry, companies are always coming out with improved hardware and software. A company that is behind may offer special pricing or extra product in order to prevent current customers from switching to the competing improved brand.

MC Objectives

Companies also use sales promotion to achieve certain MC objectives. Consumer programs are designed to (1) encourage trial, (2) increase frequency and/or quantity of purchases, (3) build customer databases and relationships, (4) reward and retain customers, (5) cross-sell, (6) extend the use of a brand, and (7) reinforce the brand image. To obtain and maintain shelf space, consumer products companies use sales promotions to *encourage trial*, as well as repurchase. America Online is well known for offering samples—limited periods of free Internet access—to increase trial and sign-ups. Coupons on and inside packages are designed to encourage repurchase.

The majority of those who take advantage of coupons and price reductions are current customers. Thus, companies aim to *increase frequency and/or quantity of purchases*. This is the reason for "buy one, get one free" offers. If you examine the pricing of these offers, you will note that the price of the one you buy is often the maximum retail price and that, when this price is divided in half, it is often close to the normal "on sale" price. In other words, the "buy one, get one free" offer is another way of packaging a regular promotion with one twist—it motivates the customer to buy two instead of one item at a time.

Because loyalty programs are specifically designed to increase repeat visits by regular customers, McDonald's appealed to its littlest customers with a promotion

EXHIBIT 16-12

Internet promotion company Promotions.com explains in this ad how to create effective online promotions.

EXHIBIT 16-13

By offering a new Teenie Beanie every few weeks, this was one of McDonald's best loyalty programs.

offering Teenie Beanies (small versions of the popular plush toys). This resulted in some store owners finding customers lined up as early as 5:30 A.M. waiting for the store to open (see Exhibit 16–13). Many McDonald's restaurants had to set up voice-mail systems to handle inquiries from customers wanting to know which of the toys were available in a particular week. One store even went so far to have its automated answering system say, "Teenie Beanie Central. We're selling Doby the Doberman." Another McDonald's store owner lamented the fact that he could get only a 21-day supply when the promotion first began because he knew his sales would double in that period. It was that kind of response that made the Teenie Beanie promotion one of the most successful efforts in the chain's history.

To increase the frequency of purchase, a company first identifies what the regular purchase frequency is. Say, for example, the average purchase frequency of shampoo is every three months. Knowing this, a brand may schedule its promotions two months apart. Once a product category reaches maturity, competition increases and promotions are often used to protect share of market and try to nudge it higher. At this point, companies may use promotional techniques to get consumers to buy larger quantities or to increase their frequency of use.

When companies know who their current customers are, they can use promotions to *build databases* with customer contact information and then plan programs to *reward and retain* these customers, particularly those that are most profitable. One brokerage firm, for example, sends out gifts of exotic candy and prime-cut steaks to customers at year-end; the more trading customers have done during the year, the more expensive the "thank you" premiums they receive. The IMC in Action box describes how supermarkets are targeting promotions to individual customers, or segments of one, based on their database information.

Promotions are also used to cross-sell, which, as you recall from Chapter 7, means encouraging current customers to try additional goods or services provided by a company. Because customers already are familiar with the brand and trust it enough to make repeat purchases, selling them on other products under the same brand or made by the same company can be more cost-effective than selling to those unfamiliar with the brand.

Promotions also can be used to *extend the use* of a brand. An example of a campaign designed to extend a product's uses comes from Nabisco's Grey Poupon mustard. The brand moved from its high-profile "pardon me" advertising campaign, with its Rolls-Royces and hoity-toity passengers, to a promotional campaign that positions the spicy mustard not just for sandwiches but as a cooking ingredient for other meals. Through a coupon redemption program, Nabisco offered promotional products such as measuring spoons and recipe books.[8]

Although sales promotions by design add something extra to a brand offering, what is added should not only be compatible with the brand's image but also reinforce that image. In frequent-flyer programs, not only are members rewarded on the basis of miles traveled, but the more they travel the more special they are made to feel. Heavy travelers on United Airlines, for example, are given a special toll-free number to call for reservations and flight information. Callers to this number are very seldom placed on hold.

IMC IN ACTION

Promotions for Segments of One

Technological advances have created a new type of sales promotion targeting: promotions sent to "segments of one"—that is, to individual customers. Grocery stores with special computer programs connected to their checkout scanners can print coupons on the back of the sales slips that are generated by each customer's purchases. Catalina, a promotion company that supplies this service, generates instant coupons at checkouts according to whether or not the customer is brand loyal. Tracking customer purchases over time allows the store to determine, on a given shopping trip, whether the customer is buying a particular brand for the first time or has been buying it regularly.

When a customer buys a jar of Jif peanut butter, for example, the store's computer goes instantly into that customer's history of purchases and shows whether that customer buys Jif regularly. If he does, then this triggers the computer to produce a coupon good for, say, $1 off on a purchase of three jars of Jif. For a different customer, one who only occasionally buys Jif, the computer will generate a coupon for 50 cents off one jar of Jif in order to increase the customer's

frequency and volume of purchases. A third customer comes along and buys Peter Pan peanut butter; if the computer shows that this person never buys Jif, she will receive a coupon for $1 off one jar of Jif in order to motivate her to try Jif.

As you can see, the promotional incentive differs depending on each person's brand choice history. The fewer times the customer has bought Jif in the past, the greater the incentive given for him or her to buy Jif the next time. Here's a summary of that strategy:

"Loyal customer" receives $1 off three.
"Switcher" receives 50 cents off one.
"Never buyer" receives $1 off one.

Catalina's computer keeps a history of everyone who uses a store card or charge card. This system can also be used for cross-promoting, such as giving a buyer of peanut butter a coupon for a particular brand of jelly.

Think About It

What is a segment of one? Why would a company want to target such a tiny market?

Limitations of Consumer Sales Promotion

Despite the fact that most sales promotions can show a more direct impact on sales than advertising, this MC function still has a questionable image. The reason for this image is that some marketers feel sales promotion is simply a way to "buy sales" as opposed to convincing people that a brand is a good value. Peter Breen, editor of *Promo* magazine, however, recently stated that marketers need to "forget all that nonsense about consumer promotion being the ugly stepchild of advertising."[9] To that end, the promotion industry is making efforts to become more strategic and less tactical—using promotions to move customers and prospects through the decision-making process rather than just reducing the price to move more items (see Exhibit 16–14). As one marketer stated in responding to a survey on sales promotion activities: "Increasingly, the gimmicks are gone. We must all step up to the challenge of adding real, brand-building value with promotions—the kind that sparks genuine consumer, retailer, and client interest."[10]

EXHIBIT 16-14

Using a scratch-off device, this promotion for Sprint is designed to move people through the trial stage in the decision process.

Although sales promotions can increase sales, they are not necessarily cost-effective. One analysis showed that only 16 percent of customer promotions were profitable. In other words, in 84 percent of the promotions, companies spent more than $1 to generate an extra $1 of profits.

Sales promotions are sometimes criticized for primarily attracting those who are searching for only the best deal, not a long-term brand relationship. These are customers who always try to buy what is on sale and are not loyal to any brand. In automotive marketing, for example, companies have had mixed experiences with online promotions that have brought masses of unqualified consumers into dealerships to enter sweepstakes and win prizes. Once again, targeting is the critical element.

Another limitation of sales promotion is that as soon as one brand in a category has a successful program, competitors soon follow. This usually negates added-value advantage and simply represents another cost of doing business. Two challenges for loyalty programs are keeping an accurate accounting of customer rewards and managing their disbursement. These programs can become so much a part of a brand's offering that if there is a problem with the reward program, the brand relationship can be weakened by the very program that was designed to strengthen it.

Another concern is that an overuse of promotional offers will negatively reposition the brand. A brand that is always on sale or always offering premiums will soon be known as the "price brand" or "deal brand," an image that most brands don't want to have. Most companies limit discounts. This is not only to protect the profitability of the brand but also to protect the retail price. In the soft-drink category, because Coke and Pepsi frequently run sales of 99 cents or less for a two-liter bottle, many customers refuse to buy until the price is reduced to this level (and then they stock up). For these people, 99 cents has become the regular price. Furthermore, brands that use trade discounts extensively find that when they cut back on these promotions, they may lose shelf space and then market share.

What is the appropriate balance between sales promotion and brand-building functions such as media advertising and publicity? Extensive research by the Coalition for Brand Equity shows that an overbalance of sales promotions has a negative impact on a brand. The coalition has therefore compiled the following guidelines:[11]

1. Excessive promotion at the expense of advertising may hurt profits. In the consumer packaged goods field, experts caution that trade and consumer promotion should not exceed 60 percent of the marketing communication budget. (This can vary from category to category.)

2. A higher ratio of advertising (relative to sales promotion) typically increases profits.

3. A high level of trade and consumer promotion, relative to advertising, has a positive effect on short-term market share but a negative effect on brand attitudes and long-term market share.

4. Without an effective advertising effort to emphasize brand image and quality, customers become deal-prone rather than brand-loyal.

5. Overemphasis on low prices eventually destroys brand equity.

> "Market leadership can be bought through bribes, but enduring profitable market leadership must be earned through building both brand value as well as volume."
>
> Larry Light, Coalition for Brand Equity

One of the major challenges of integrated marketing communication is to get the MC mix right. If too much of the communication mix is allocated to advertising, the brand may gain a high-quality, differentiated image but not enough volume to be a market leader. On the other hand, as Larry Light, the chairman of the Coalition for Brand Equity says, "Too much promotion, and the brand will have high volume but low profitability."[12]

TRADE AND BTB PROMOTIONS

As you will recall, businesses sell to other business either ingredients and parts, goods and services to help them run their business, or goods to be resold. When selling goods to be resold, businesses use trade promotions, which will be explained first, followed by an explanation of other types of BtB promotions.

Marketers doing trade promotions must always keep in mind that, according to the Robinson-Patman Act, passed by the U.S. Congress in 1936, trade promotions must be offered on an equal basis to all dealers and resellers who compete against each other. This means that, just because a manufacturer has a better relationship with chain A versus all its competitors, it cannot offer chain A a more valuable trade promotion than it offers chain B, chain C, and so on. It is legal, however, to offer varying discount levels based on quantities purchased. The more a store or chain buys, the larger the discount can be.

In the last decade there has been an increase in trade promotions, often at the expense of consumer promotions and advertising. There are several reasons for this. Accountability is number one; a company can more easily predict and measure what return it will receive for promotional spending, especially trade promotions, than it can for mass media advertising. Tied closely to this is management's demand to see short-term or immediate results. Top management is no longer willing to wait till the end of the year to see if there have been increases in brand share, sales, and profits. In one company, when sales fell below average for just one day, the CEO would write a memo to the head of marketing and sales asking what changes were going to be made to ensure the sales loss would be made up. Although such short-term thinking and micromanagement is the extreme, more top executives think short term than long term in today's competitive environment.

Another reason for the increase in trade promotion spending is that retail chains have gotten bigger, more powerful, and more demanding than ever before. Today, most branded goods need major chains more than the chains need the brands. Major chains have also become sophisticated marketers, doing a good job of analyzing their own sales, category by category and store by store. Scanner checkout systems enable chains to know which stores are selling what brands at what rate. When buyers for a major chain are presented promotions by marketers, they evaluate the promotions based on the following criteria:

1. How much per case is the promotion actually worth?
2. How will the chain be compensated—by a separate check, a reduction when paying the marketer's next invoice, or a credit against future purchases once proof of performance has been sent to marketer? (The easier and quicker the compensation, the more attractive the promotion.)
3. How much effort must the retailer put forth to receive the promotion? The more work involved (such as setting up off-shelf displays, reallocating shelf displays, featuring the brand in the retailer's ad), the less attractive the offer.

4. Does the offer violate any store policies? For example, some chains do not permit contests in which individual employees receive premiums or rewards from a manufacturer.

5. How much consumer advertising and promotion support will the brand have to complement the trade offer? The more, the better.

6. Will the promotion require handling items not already being carried? Will it require accepting different package configurations? Any changes in items or packaging configuration means more work for the retailer and therefore makes the promotion less attractive.

7. Can the retail chain buy extra product (more than can be sold in a particular region) and ship to another region where the brand is not being offered at a discount?

8. What is the promotional period—how long will the store or chain be able to buy at the promotional price?

9. How flexible is the required performance. Can a store put up window banners or have an in-store display rather than running a newspaper ad that mentions the brand?

10. Are the terms and timing of the promotional offer compatible with promotional offers from other brands within the product category?

Scanner data has also resulted in retail chains focusing on product category management. Instead of just looking at the sales of each brand (e.g., Fritos corn chips) within a product category, chains are closely analyzing sales of the category as a whole (e.g., salty snacks). They then experiment to determine the best mix of brands and the best use of that category's shelf space. When a brand fails to sell at the expected volume, the store puts pressure on the brand for more promotional support under threat of discontinuing ("de-authorizing") the brand. At this point, a brand's sales force often comes to the company's marketing department and asks for more advertising and sales promotion programs in order to increase sales and maintain distribution.

Trade Promotion Objectives

Like all promotions, trade promotions are used to motivate certain types of actions by channel members: (1) obtain or increase distribution of a brand, (2) have the brand featured in the store's advertising, and (3) expand amount of shelf display and/or get temporary off-shelf display. In essence, trade promotions offer retailers something of value in exchange for making an extra effort to increase a brand's sales.

Types of Trade Promotions

The essence of a trade promotion, in most cases, is a reduction in price. Yet price reductions come in many forms. The idea is that the manufacturer will financially make it worth a retailer's effort to "push" a brand. Trade promotion tactics include the following:

1. *Slotting allowances.* In response to the glut of new products, most retail chains demand one-time, up-front fees known as slotting allowances, which can range up to $40,000 per brand. To get distribution of a new brand, therefore, manufacturers have to pay the slotting allowance, which is considered a trade promotion expense. Retailers justify this because taking on a new brand requires them to allocate one or more "slots" (i.e., spaces) in their warehouses,

enter the new brand items into their computer and scanning programs, and rearrange shelf space within their stores where the new brand will be displayed. Because most store shelves are already filled, this generally means removing another brand.

Slotting allowances are controversial because manufacturers think they're being forced to subsidize the retailer's cost of doing business. Also, these high fees often prevent new brands, especially those not belonging to large companies, from getting distribution in the major chains. The U.S. Federal Trade Commission and the Bureau of Alcohol, Tobacco and Firearms periodically reconsider the legality of such allowances, but to date the practice continues. To a certain extent, slotting allowances encourage companies to sell their brands direct. With the advent of the Internet, direct sales have become easier, as will be discussed in Chapter 17.

2. *Off-invoice allowances.* An off-invoice allowance is a basic price reduction and is thus the simplest of all trade promotions, and the one channel members desire most. Retailers are encouraged to pass such price reductions on to customers in order to generate increased sales. During a designated promotion period, often 30 days, everything a retailer buys is discounted a certain percentage, generally between 5 and 20 percent. A problem with these type of allowances, though, is that some retailers will do "forward buying," meaning near the end of the promotion period they will buy another month's worth of the product and not discount it to the customer.

3. *Advertising/Performance allowances.* Manufacturers of consumer packaged goods offer performance allowances such as $1 or $2 a case to encourage retailers to advertise their brands. Similar allowances are used for department stores. Exhibit 16–15 highlights a promotion in which clothing maker Savane provided a special allowance to Dillard's department stores for featuring

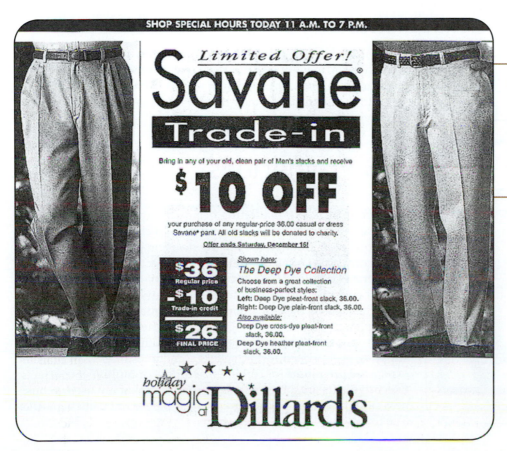

EXHIBIT 16-15

In this promotion the clothing manufacturer Savane offered Dillard's a special allowance in exchange for Dillard's running the special trade-in ad.

Savane products and agreeing to help collect used Savane-labeled clothing for charity.

In order for a retailer to receive such allowances, it must submit proof of performance—copies of a newspaper ad or affidavits of performance from radio or TV stations, along with invoices from these media. Most major brands provide retailers with prepared advertising materials—ads, glossy photos, sample radio and TV commercials—insisting that one or more of these materials be used in order to qualify for the allowances. Other ways retailers can perform is by having special displays at the end of an aisle (end caps), where the brand gets more exposure than it would on the shelf.

4. *Cooperative advertising allowances.* Many manufacturers have cooperative (co-op) advertising programs in which a certain percentage of everything the retailer buys is put into a special "co-op" fund. Then, when the retailer advertises the brand in newspapers, on radio, on TV, or in some other way, anywhere from 50 to 100 percent of the cost is paid for out of that dealer's co-op fund. Such funds allow retailers to promote a brand on their own schedule rather than in just the promotional periods designated by the brand itself.

5. *Buy-back allowances.* When introducing a new product, manufacturers sometimes offer to buy back the current stock of the brands they are replacing. To further convince retailers to take on products, some manufacturers guarantee that their brand will move by offering to buy back any of their own brand not sold within a specified period.

6. *Dealer contests.* To get retail dealers and their salespeople to reach specific sales goals or to stock a certain product, companies may offer special prizes and gifts. Travel-related contests in particular are popular. Many chains require that these types of rewards be made to the chain's headquarters and not to individual buyers. The chain then uses them to stage their own competitions. This is done to prevent buyers from making buying decisions that are not in the best interest of the chain.

7. *Dealer loaders.* A manufacturer may offer a premium to the dealer for purchase of a special product assortment or a specified dollar volume. An example would be a cooler used to stock soft drinks. After the promotion period, the premium belongs to the retailer, who may raffle it off or award it to an employee.

BtB Promotions

In other areas of BtB marketing beside the retail channel, companies use sales promotions not only to help close a sale but also to move prospects through the buying decision process. For example, some companies offer premiums if prospects agree to listen to a sales presentation or try a product on a trial basis. To encourage current customers to reorder more frequently, or to order in larger quantities when they do reorder, companies may offer volume or frequency discounts, free goods, or some other incentive (see Exhibit 16–16). On business items such as office supplies, cleaning supplies, and printed forms, sellers sometimes offer trips or other expensive premiums for certain-size orders or multiyear contracts. Executive gifts are a type of sales promotion that are used in business as an incentive or a reward to an employee or business partner (see Exhibit 16–17).

EXHIBIT 16-16

This ad promotes the products and services offered by the online arm of Staples. In order to stimulate action, it offers a price deal to businesses that respond.

Another use of sales promotion is to provide incentives for a company's own sales force or an outside sales force (such as a food broker or distributor). Although most salespeople are paid based on how much they sell, adding additional incentives can motivate them to increase their efforts.

A FINAL NOTE: PROMOTION AND STRATEGIC CREATIVITY

All areas of the sales promotion function use creativity to deliver their messages. The chapter opening case showed how Nescafé used a unique way to reach coffee drinkers and make them feel good about their morning coffee. People working in sales promotion (who admittedly are biased) say it is the most inventive area in all of marketing communication. One company, for example, mailed pieces of a short-wave radio to engineers with instructions on how to assemble the gadget. Once the engineers received their last piece, they were told where to tune in to receive the promotional message. The promotion was highly effective because the engineers were so intrigued by the inventiveness of the idea.

These areas also have to be integrated into the overall marketing program. When Oldsmobile launched its new Aurora model, it used an IMC program that included a direct-mail effort to invite luxury car owners in 10 cities to events where they could drive and compare the Aurora with Lexus, Infiniti, and Mercedes models. The promotion brought dealers together on one day and consumers together on the next. The auto manufacturer's lead agency, Leo Burnett, worked closely with Frankel & Company, a sales promotion agency, to manage all of the Oldsmobile promotional activities involved with this launch as well as the anniversary festivities.

Sometimes success of a promotion comes from the excitement that a creative idea can generate in the trade. For example, for a long time, Eckrich (a brand of processed meat) didn't use any type of consumer promotions. When it finally did use one—offering customers a Louisville Slugger bat for several proofs of purchase plus cash—sales went up 40 percent. The strange thing was that fewer than 50 bats were redeemed. It turned out that what made the promotion so successful was the excitement the offer created in the sales force and the trade. The salespeople worked harder, and the trade was willing to give the brand additional space in the store and in grocery ads. In other words, it may be hard to predict the payout of a creative idea by itself, but a creative idea can very definitely add to a promotion's success.

EXHIBIT 16-17

Tiffany's distinctive blue box signals a high-quality reward for employees or business partners.

SOME THINGS YOU REMEMBER FOR A LIFETIME

TIFFANY & CO.

Key Terms

sales promotion 569
push strategies 571
pull strategies 571
coupon 572
premium 574
specialties 575

sampling 575
contest 576
sweepstakes 576
game 576
loyalty (or frequency) marketing 577

Key Point Summary

Key Point 1: Consumer and Trade Promotions

Sales promotions include consumer and trade programs that add incentives to buy or participate, accelerating a product's movement from producer to consumer. Sales promotion drives an immediate response by adding something of tangible value to the offer.

Key Point 2: Consumer Sales Promotion

Consumer sales promotion, which is often used as part of a pull strategy, adds value to a transaction by motivating a response in the buy zone—that critical point when consumers are considering a purchase. Loyalty programs are used to help retain customers and increase the brand's share of wallet. Criticisms include attracting the wrong customers who are only interested in a deal and negatively repositioning the brand on a price image.

Key Point 3: Trade and BtB Promotions

Trade promotions are an important tool in a push strategy. They are used to gain the support of a brand by members of the distribution channel, especially retailers. In BtB marketing, sales promotions are used not only to help close a sale but also to move prospects through the brand decision process.

Lessons Learned

Key Point 1: Sales Promotion

a.   Define sales promotion, and explain its incentive function.
b.   Why is sales promotion referred to as a sales accelerator?
c.   What is the difference between a push strategy and a pull strategy?

Key Point 2: Consumer Sales Promotion

a.   What is the difference between a coupon and a rebate?
b.   What is the difference between a sweepstake and a contest? Find an example of one or the other and explain how it works. Which category do you believe it illustrates?
c.   Explain how specialties are used to deliver brand reminder messages.
d.   Check your medicine cabinet and pick one of your favorite products. How many different sales promotions can you identify as being used in support of this product? Consider not only the product's package but any other marketing communication you can find that promotes this brand.
e.   What are the key strengths and limitations of consumer sales promotions?
f.   List at least three objectives that you might have in designing a consumer sales promotion program.

g. Do an aisle check in your favorite drugstore. What products could profit most by identifying segments of one?
h. How do loyalty programs work? What objectives do they accomplish?
i. What are the strengths and limitations of loyalty programs?
j. This chapter said that loyalty programs work best when a brand has high fixed costs and low variable costs. Explain what that means.

Key Point 3: Trade Promotion

a. What is the most common form of trade promotion?
b. What do you need to know about the Robinson-Patman Act when you plan a trade promotion?
c. This chapter says there has been an increase in trade promotions versus consumer promotions. Why is that so?
d. How do slotting allowances, off-invoice allowances, and advertising performance allowances differ?

Chapter Challenge

Writing Assignment

Adopt a local store. Analyze its use of sales promotion, merchandising, specialty items, and corporate design. Is there a distinctive image and personality being presented in these materials and activities? What would you recommend to help the store tighten up its promotional program and create even greater impact?

Presentation Assignment

Read everything you can find about a special promotion used by one of the major fast-food chains such as McDonald's, Burger King, or Taco Bell. Explain how it worked and describe all the materials, events, and other MC supporting efforts. Prepare a presentation for your class that summarizes your analysis.

Internet Assignment

Check the music section of Amazon.com and the CDnow website. Identify the sales promotions efforts at both sites. Which one is more effective in its use of consumer sales promotions? Explain why you evaluate them so.

Additional Readings

Buzzell, Robert D.; John A. Quelch; and Walter J. Salmon. "The Costly Bargain of Sales Promotion." *Harvard Business Review* (March–April 1990), pp. 141–49.
Carmody, Bill. "Top 10 Online Promotion Pointers." *Promo*, December 2000, p. 47.
Levin, Gary. "Sponsors Put Pressure on for Accountability." *Advertising Age*, June 21, 1993, p. S-4.
Robinson, Brian. "Promotion Is a New Way to Make Brand Contact with Buyers," *Marketing News*, April 12, 1994, pp. 2, 16.
Schultz, Don E.; William A. Robinson; and Lisa A. Petrison. *Sales Promotion Essentials*, 2nd ed. Lincolnwood IL: NTC Business Books, 1993.
Totten, John C., and Martin P. Block. *Analyzing Sales Promotion*, 2nd. ed. Chicago: Dartnell Corp., 1994.

Research Assignment

Consult the books and articles listed above and other materials you find in the library that discuss the topic of promotional activities and brand relationships. Do you think they support or argue against the idea that using sales promotion deemphasizes brand equity and brand loyalty?

Endnotes

[1]*The Art of Sales Promotion* (New York: Sibel/Mohr, a sales promotion agency, 1981).

[2]Adapted from *The Art of Sales Promotion*.

[3]"The Test Bait," *Brandweek*, March 30, 1998, p. 27.

[4]Richard Barlow, "The Net Upends Tenets of Loyalty Marketing," *Advertising Age*, April 17, 2000, p. 46.

[5]Dennis L. Duffy, "Effective Design and Use of Loyalty Marketing and Frequency Marketing Programs," American Marketing Association Fall Workshop, Oak Brook, IL, 1999.

[6]Amanda Beeler, "Promotions.com Aims at Business Solutions," *Advertising Age*, January 31, 2000, p. 54.

[7]Ann Mack, "Choose Me," *Brandweek*, April 10, 2000, p. 106.

[8]"Different Tools for Different Strategies," *Promotional Sense* 3 no. 1 (Spring 1998), p. 2.

[9]Peter Breen, "Promotion Trends 2000" <www.promomagazine.com/content/report/2000>.

[10]Quoted in ibid.

[11]Larry Light, "At the Center of It All Is the Brand," *Advertising Age*, March 29, 1993, p. 22.

[12]Ibid.

17

The Personal Connection: Direct Response and Personal Sales

Key Points in This Chapter

1. What are the four major components of a direct-response piece?

2. What are the strengths and weaknesses of direct-response marketing?

3. What role does personal selling play in marketing communication?

4. What are the strengths and limitations of personal sales?

Chapter Perspective:
Making It Personal

As stressed throughout this book, one of the main things that differentiates IMC from the traditional practices of advertising and sales promotion is the increasing use of interactivity. The more personal this interactivity can be, the more persuasive it is. Direct marketing and personal sales have been around for decades; however, their use has drastically changed with the new communication and information technology. It's easier and less costly now than ever before to have more personal dialogue with customers, especially those who are most profitable. And customers are increasingly expecting and demanding personal contact with companies.

Direct response and personal selling affect all the steps of the brand decision process to some degree. Both functions are capable of handling the complete selling process from creating awareness of a problem or opportunity to helping customers review their buying decision. Where these functions have their greatest impact, however, is on closing the sale—the *decision* step. This is especially true in the marketing of BtB and higher-priced consumer products.

Direct marketing and personal sales also allow companies to measure their effectiveness quantitatively, and thus calculate their profitability for each customer. As companies continue to demand more accountability, direct-response marketing continues to grow.

If there is any place where speed, connectivity, and intangibles—the currency of the new high-tech marketplace—are having an impact, it's with direct marketing and personal sales. This chapter explains not only the basic principles of direct marketing and personal selling but also how these functions can be used to integrate customers and prospects into a company's operations.

CHARLOTTE PIPE AND FOUNDRY
Price McNabb

Founded in 1901 and still family-owned, Charlotte Pipe and Foundry in Charlotte, North Carolina, is the nation's leading manufacturer of cast-iron and plastic pipe and fittings for the plumbing industry (see Exhibit 17–1). The company's products are used in residential, commercial, and industrial applications. In 1998, the MC agency Price/McNabb began working with Charlotte Pipe and Foundry to help the company make the transition from a manufacturing focus to a marketing focus.

Pipe and fittings manufacturers sell their products through plumbing wholesalers, who often carry several competing brands. Pipe and fittings represent about 10 percent of the entire plumbing package in jobs. For large jobs, wholesalers often treat pipe and fittings as a "loss leader" (a product sold at a loss in order to entice customers to buy other, higher priced goods). Wholesalers hope to win the project by bidding low on the pipe and fittings—which enables them to make their profit on higher-margin categories like fixtures. As a result, a "pipe is pipe" commodity mentality has emerged in the marketplace.

Brand Relationships

Charlotte Pipe and Foundry recognized that the best way to counter a commodity mentality was to strengthen its brand. Therefore, the first activity undertaken by Price/McNabb was a qualitative brand audit, conducted (1) to gain an understanding of the brand and how it was perceived by customers and prospects, (2) to reach management consensus on brand intent, and (3) to begin a campaign to

EXHIBIT 17-1

This is an example of a BtB home page design for easy navigation (see menu bar at bottom of screen).

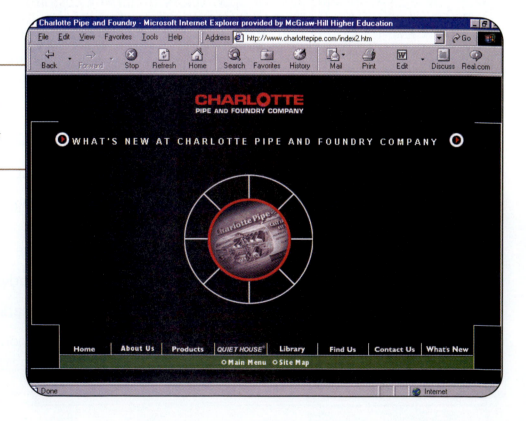

reinforce the most motivating brand attributes. This could be done only after determining key strengths, weaknesses, opportunities, and threats. Three key insights emerged from the audit:

1. Customers think of the Charlotte Pipe and Foundry brand in terms of organizational strengths over products. Customers who know Charlotte Pipe and Foundry had highly favorable perceptions of the company's integrity, service orientation, and commitment to the industry.

2. While Charlotte Pipe and Foundry had a reputation for honesty and integrity, companies in the pipe and fittings category lack any true branding or differentiation.

3. While brand loyalty in pipe and fittings is not strong, the fact that many contractors buy Charlotte Pipe and Foundry's products exclusively means that brand loyalty *can* exist.

Before branding work could begin, a baseline needed to be set. Price/McNabb conducted a quantitative benchmark survey as part of its SWOT analysis. Telephone interviews were completed with 200 plumbing contractors and 200 wholesalers. The key customer insight from the survey was that plumbing contractors can influence their wholesalers' decision on which brands of pipe and fittings the wholesaler carries. This suggested that, as a group, contractors were influential and that wholesalers were receptive to brand recommendations. The agency also conducted several focus groups among contractors, wholesalers, agency sales reps, and builder to provide additional insights and depth to the understanding of customer attitudes.

Although price was found to be a strong motivator, it was also found that quality matters. Many plumbers are willing to spend a little more for quality products than for ordinary products. The tolerances within certain pipes and fittings can cause installation problems that cost the contractors more than the money they saved buying cheaper pipe. They can achieve an overall lower installation cost with high-quality products because of a more consistent fit and fewer callbacks. It was also found that purchase decisions hinge on contractors' experiences with a supplier and the wholesaler's track record of having materials in stock, delivering orders on time, and providing the necessary service and support.

The IMC Campaign

From previous focus groups, it was evident that many contractors believed some brands (including Charlotte Pipe and Foundry) fit together better than others and that they tended to avoid brands they had had problems with in the past. There was consistent agreement that product "fit" and "a single source of accountability" were motivating factors, along with "getting materials when promised" and "orders are filled accurately."

The new strategy was to link these motivating factors to the brand's key communication messages. Charlotte Pipe and Foundry is the only U.S. company that makes pipes and fittings in both cast iron and plastic, and the only one that manufacturers to the middle of specifications, which reduces size variances and thus ensures a more consistent, snug fit than offered by competitors. With this background, the agency developed concept statements that revolved around a product "system." The notion of "system" was expanded to include operational and customer service "system" enhancements, all designed to help improve the business performance of contractor customers.

Focus groups with plumbing contractors were held to test concept statements and message points intended to drive the creative development process. The concepts tested well in terms of enhancing performance (easier to install, fewer callbacks) and accountability. Charlotte Pipe and Foundry's heritage of quality products and integrity made the message a strong, believable claim for the company. Viewed through a laddering approach, the strategy was as follows:

Company Features

- Only company that makes both cast-iron and plastic pipe and fittings.
- Only company that manufactures to the middle of the spec for a consistent fit.
- Operational, customer-service enhancements and improvements.

Contractor Benefits

- One-company accountability.
- Easier to install, fewer callbacks.
- Complete, on-time delivery.

Contractor Rewards

- No hassles.
- Increased productivity.
- Better margins.

The IMC campaign incorporated these messages, with a promise that the benefits and rewards of doing business with Charlotte Pipe and Foundry would result in contractors' improving their performance and enhancing their business reputation. The tag line "You Can't Beat the System" was created and incorporated into all creative pieces to drive home the message (see Exhibit 17–2).

The visual identity, tag line, and message strategy from the campaign have since been extended to the company's collateral, website (www.charlottepipe.com), packaging, and point-of-purchase materials. A "system" of capabilities, product, and technical literature was then developed to deliver on the message strategy in practice. The website delivers on the enhanced performance promise, with e-business activities designed to save contractors time and hassle. Fittings packaging was redesigned to reinforce the brand identity and tag line. Point-of-sale posters visually demonstrate the product "system" and provide installation tips to help contractors improve productivity.

In an effort to create a dialogue and help the company improve management of customer relationships, the company decided to set up a comprehensive sales and marketing database of customers and prospects. To help build the database, Price/McNabb recommended a pilot direct-marketing program designed not only to gather customer profile data but also to test promotional offers. The pilot program was designed to help determine customers'

- Demographic data (company size, commercial versus residential, repair versus new construction).
- Material preference (cast iron, plastic, or both).
- Current brand preference, if any.
- Purchasing habits, such as how many different brands they used and, where they made purchases.
- Experiences with other manufacturers regarding product performance and service.
- Level of brand loyalty (to current manufacturer brands).
- Level of Internet usage.

EXHIBIT 17-2

One of the print ads used by Charlotte Pipe.

The direct-marketing program involved sending personalized letters to contractors in key markets that explained the "systems" approach and asked for the contractors' assistance in gathering information. A survey was enclosed, along with a business reply envelope (see Exhibit 17–3). Two premiums were tested as an incentive to return the survey—a $1 bill and a hat emblazoned with the "You Can't Beat the System" tag line. The program drew a response rate of 15 percent and provided a wealth of customer data that can be used to further refine strategy and messages.

To extend the one-to-one dialogue and collect customer data from additional sources (inquiries from ads and publicity releases, telephone calls, website hits, trace-show booth visits, etc.) the agency revamped the company's inquiry management and fulfillment system. Initial inquiries are fulfilled with a capabilities brochure, along with a cover letter and a bingo card that asks customers to indicate what additional information they need. Fulfillment of requests for product literature seek additional customer feedback in an attempt to sustain the dialogue and move customers through the buying decision-making process.

Campaign Evaluation

The initial benchmark survey was replicated to measure effectiveness of the first year of the brand campaign. The results were very positive:

- Awareness of Charlotte Pipe and Foundry among contractors had increased substantially over the past year, particularly among residential contractors.
- Top-of-mind awareness of Charlotte Pipe and Foundry as a maker of plastic pipe and fittings increased by 17 percent.
- Top-of-mind awareness of Charlotte Pipe and Foundry as a maker of cast-iron pipe and fittings rose by 8 percent.
- Recall of Charlotte Pipe and Foundry advertising jumped by 18 percent.
- Significantly, awareness numbers for Charlotte Pipe and Foundry's key competitors remained flat over the same period.

Case Discussion Questions

1. Price/McNabb agency was asked to move Charlotte Pipe and Foundry from a manufacturing focus to a marketing focus. Explain how this campaign accomplished that objective.

2. Explain how customers were segmented, how their motivations were determined, and then how these motivating factors were addressed in the brand communication plan for the key audience segments.

3. From the information given in this case, develop a SWOT analysis for the Charlotte Pipe and Foundry campaign.

4. If you were asked to develop a proposal for the next year of this campaign, what else would you recommend?

Case drafted by Brad Muller, Account Supervisor, Price/McNabb.

EXHIBIT 17-3

Example of direct-marketing effort to collect data and begin a dialogue.

DIRECT RESPONSE: THE DIALOGUE BUILDER

When a company wants to be in direct contact with customers and potential customers without the intermediate step of going through a retailer, it uses **direct-response marketing,** which is *a closed-loop, interactive, database-driven messaging system that uses a broad range of media to create a behavioral response.* It combines a sales message with demand creation (using a message to intensify demand for a product) and fulfillment (delivery of the product or requested information). Over two-thirds of U.S. adults order products by mail, phone, and/or the Internet each year.[1]

The definition above has several key elements. *Closed-loop* means there is no distributor, wholesaler or retailer between the company making the offer and the customer. Only the two parties are involved, and all communication is between them. Direct marketing is called *interactive* because there is two-way communication between the company and customer; either can initiate the dialogue. Direct-response offers are designed to generate an immediate, *behavioral response,* as opposed to many advertising messages whose primary objective is to create awareness, offer information, or reinforce or change customer attitudes.

As a complete buying, selling, and distribution process, direct marketing is a microcosm of the entire marketing process. Whereas some businesses are 100 percent direct (i.e., they have no retail presence), companies such as Eddie Bauer and Victoria's Secret use direct-mail catalogs and websites and also have retail stores.

Figure 17–1 shows the flow chart used by the Direct Marketing Association (DMA) to describe the industry of direct marketing, as well as the process. It begins with a marketing focus that is guided by research and database building, as well as marketing objectives and strategy. Various media can deliver a direct-response offer, as the figure shows. The last section of the model identifies the response process: transaction, distribution, fulfillment, and follow-up. From this process information is extracted to update the customer database. Other marketing mix functions are also integrated into the response step.

Size and Scale of Direct-Response Marketing

According to the Direct Marketing Association (DMA), 1 out of every $17 (i.e., 5.8 percent) in U.S. sales today is related to direct marketing.[2] As Table 17–1 shows, slightly over half of direct-marketing-generated sales were for consumer goods in 1999. Moreover, the study found that more than half of all ad expenditures include an offer designed to prompt a potential customer to make a direct purchase, inquire for more information, or visit a store or dealership to make a specific purchase.

Direct marketing is one of the fastest-growing MC functions. Major social and technological changes over the last several decades have been fueling this growth. In the United States, for example, 58 percent of women now work outside the home; in Canada, the figure is 60 percent. So while families have more income, they have less time to spend shopping.

The proliferation of cell phones (along with traditional telephones), credit and debit cards, catalogs, and access to the Internet have increased opportunities for two-way communication between direct marketers and customers, and made shopping more convenient. Companies worldwide now provide toll-free numbers so customers can call to place orders or request information regardless of national boundaries. Toll-free numbers give companies immediate, direct responses and help them collect information to create and refine their databases.

Finally, the computer, now affordable for even the smallest businesses, enables users to both compile and analyze information, which helps them maximize their direct-marketing budgets. When the Fashion Bug chain of clothing stores, for example, installed a new database system, it suddenly discovered that 18 percent of its customers made purchases six or more times per year. This information enabled the company to contact its best customers to make sure they were completely satisfied and to keep them coming back. The database also enabled the company to study purchasing patterns, reduce costs, and reach new customers for new store openings.

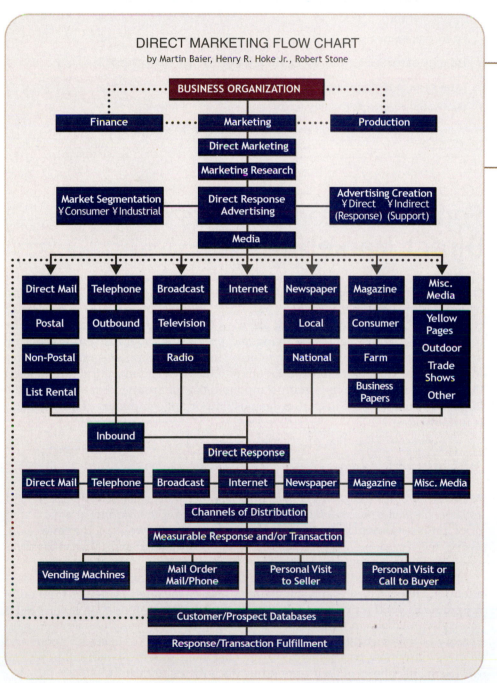

FIGURE 17-1

Note how direct marketing uses a variety of media.

Source: *Direct Marketing,* Oct. 2000, p. 3.

TABLE 17-1 Estimated Direct Marketing Impact on Total U.S. Sales ($Billions)

	1999	2003
Consumer DM sales	$ 819	$ 1,098
Direct orders	265	350
Lead generation	400	542
Traffic generation*	154	206
BtB DM sales	674	975
Direct orders	191	269
Lead generation	435	639
Traffic generation*	48	67
Total DM sales	$ 1,493	$ 2,073
Total sales in United States	$19,280	$23,866

*Motivated customers to a buying location, such as a retail store

Source: Direct Marketing Association's Statistical Fact Book '99, NYC. p. 287.

Four Basic Components of Direct Marketing

Direct-response has what is called *front-end* and *back-end operations*. The front-end operations include the marketing communication, the inbound and outbound call centers, and all other activities that are used to generate sales and inquires. The back-end operations include receiving and processing orders, inventory control, order shipping, invoicing, handling returns, and other customer-service functions. In essence, the front end sets expectations and the back end meets (or fails to meet) these expectations. The important components of the front end are the offer, the target audience, and the response; the most important component of the back end is fulfillment.

The Offer

An **offer** involves *everything, both tangible and intangible, promised by a company in exchange for money or some other desired behavior*. Besides the product at a particular price, an offer also includes the terms of payment, the guarantee, the time of delivery, and any promised premiums, as well as the image and other intangibles associated with a brand (see Exhibit 17–4).

Offers are designed to take a prospect through all the brand decision steps—attention, interest, desire, and action. In most cases the offer, as in sales promotion programs, is good for only a limited time period. This is done to give the offer a sense of immediacy and also to limit how long a company needs to maintain an inventory of that particular product. Also, direct marketers of consumer goods and services know from past responses that if customers don't respond within several weeks, the likelihood of their responding decreases significantly.

EXHIBIT 17-4

The Valdoro Mountain Lodge mailing offers recipients a chance to buy in to a new Hilton Grand Vacations Club Resort being built in Breckenridge, Colorado. The mailing includes a return card (and toll-free number and a website address) to encourage prospects to inquire about buying in to the timeshare.

Since the objective of a direct-response piece is to promote some kind of action, sales promotion devices—such as premiums, discounts on the product, and extended credit terms—are common incentives used to motivate action. Duplex Products, for instance, sells a prepaid long-distance calling-card package to research firms to help them increase response rates for their surveys. Survey prospects receive a mailing containing the phone card and instructions for responding to a telephone survey. Upon completion, they receive a personal identification number to activate the free long-distance minutes. This offer of an immediate reward provides an average response rate of 18 percent, two to three times higher than comparable research methods.

In business-to-business marketing, companies combine direct-response offers with sales promotions to stimulate an immediate response in the buying process. For example, an offer might say "Send for more information and receive a free subscription to *Business Week*"; "Visit our booth at the trade show and enter to win a trip to Europe"; or "Try our product for 30 days and receive a discount on your next order."

The Database

Although it is theoretically possible to do direct marketing without a database, it is not practical. Direct-marketing companies live and die according to the quality of their customer lists. Because of the costs involved, direct marketers seldom make a profit on their first sale to customers; they must therefore capture customers' names, addresses, and other relevant information so they can be sent additional offers (and become profitable customers). Also, without a database it is almost impossible to tell which offers performed better than others, another critical factor in building a successful direct-marketing business. The mailing in Exhibit 17–5 demonstrates how one veterinarian combines a reminder that shots are due with a magazine called *Healthy Pet*.

No matter how good and how creatively presented a direct offer is, however, it will not be successful if it is sent to the wrong people. The more carefully a database of customers and prospects is constructed, the higher the response rate will be. A brand's database can be compiled from lists of its customers and prospects, and from lists purchased from specialized companies called *list brokers*.

Good databases are essential in developing brand relationships because they allow marketers to identify the company's best customers, their value to the organization, and their needs and buying behavior. From this, marketers can create lifetime-value models based on historical and potential sales.

The marketer must have someone responsible for *list acquisition*—which means renting lists from list brokers—as well as managing the company's own house list. List management also includes finding **response lists,** which are made up of *people who have responded to related direct-marketing offers,* or **compiled lists,** which are *names and addresses collected from public sources,* such as car registrations.

Response lists are more costly to rent because the rate of response is generally higher than that from compiled lists. A response list should be evaluated on three critical factors, as described in Chapter 7: how recently those on the list have made a direct response purchase, how many direct response purchases they have made in the last 12 months, and how much they spent. This is called, as you may recall, recency, frequency, and monetary. The more recent the purchase, the greater the frequency, and the more the monetary amount, the better the prospects.

List brokers gather names and addresses from a variety of sources—direct-marketing companies, magazines, and collectors of warranty cards such as Polk Company. Companies that sell things such as appliances, cameras, luggage, and hair dryers often encourage customers to send in warranty cards; customers may or may not realize that the information they write down on these cards is bought and sold (or rented) by direct marketers. A growing source of lists are of e-mail addresses. The most costly e-mail lists are those where customers have given their permission to be contacted. Average list rental costs are $250 for 1,000 permission-based BtB names and about $200 for 1,000 permission-based consumer names.[3]

EXHIBIT 17-5

The Companion Animal Hospital mails a free magazine to its customers. The cover is localized with the names of the owner and the pet, as well as reminder information about shots that are due.

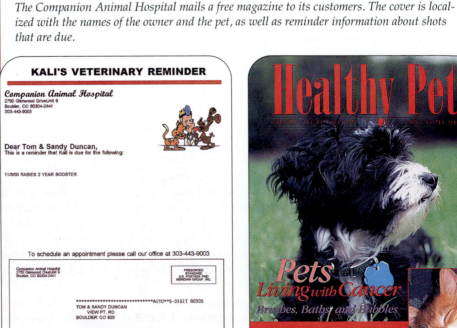

Managing direct-marketing lists is a daunting task, especially when the databases contain millions of names. Most large companies outsource list management to companies that specialize in this area. For those companies that do manage their lists in-house, a number of software programs are available to help them. To see examples of what these software programs provide, go to the websites of My-Points (www.mypoints.com) and Experian (www.experian.com).

One of the interesting aspects of direct-response marketing is that it breeds on its own success. When a direct-marketing program motivates customers to make their first purchase from a company, their names, addresses, and other relevant data go into the customer database. Information related to additional purchases and other interactions with the company are then added to each customer's personal file. This enables a company to target other products and messages accordingly.

The Response

In direct marketing, a **response** is defined as *something said or done in answer to a marketing communication message*. Like two hands clapping, the response and the offer work together. For example, the value of the offer—including any premiums, awards, or emotional appeals that are promised—is critically important to motivating the customer to respond in the desired way (see Exhibit 17–6). The customer may call a toll-free telephone number, visit a showroom, go to a website, respond to an invitation, send in a contribution to a charity or favorite cause, or become a member.

Although the customer must initiate the response, it is up to the company to facilitate and handle the response properly to ensure that the response results in the action desired. Customers who respond using a free phone call shouldn't be put on hold, waiting for a company representative. The longer the hold time, or the more layers of an automated voice menu the customer must go through, the more likely it is that the customer will hang up and a sale will be lost. When a customer does reach a representative, if that person is not able to answer questions or is rude, this also increases the possibilities that the customer will not complete an order. Also, if the product is not available for immediate shipping, the customer may decide not to wait. According to the DMA, approximately 10 percent of all catalog response orders cannot be immediately filled because the company is out of stock.

Fulfillment

The distribution side of direct marketing is called **fulfillment**—*getting the product or the information requested to the customer in a convenient, cost-effective, and timely fashion*. As noted earlier, this part of direct marketing is often referred to as the *back end;* the term came into use because in many companies the warehouse where products are stored and shipped is in the back end of the building. The fulfillment department is responsible not only for seeing that a product is shipped but also for managing the inventory, handling the billing, following up on back orders, restocking and issuing credit for returns, and handling exchanges. Another aspect of fulfillment is up-selling or cross-selling.

EXHIBIT 17-6

The Sunset *magazine promotion illustrates the use of a subscription offer that includes a motivation device—a free packet of seeds—and a return card that makes it easy for prospects to subscribe.*

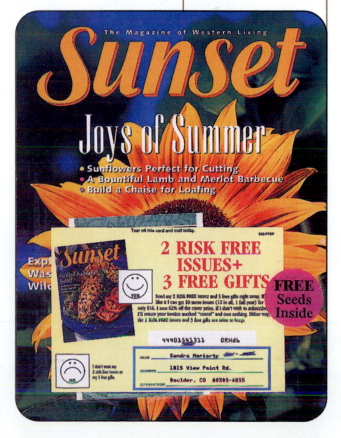

Time is an important element in fulfillment. U.S. law requires that orders received through direct-marketing solicitation must be filled promptly or the customer must be notified and given the opportunity to cancel the order and receive a full refund. But more important, a customer's desire or need for a product can diminish between the time an order is placed and the time it is received. If the interval is very long, a customer may cancel the order or return the shipped product.

Fulfillment can be either handled in-house or outsourced. Some companies use a combination, fulfilling some items themselves and outsourcing others, or they may receive and process orders themselves but outsource the mailing and invoicing. Magazines with a small circulation, for example, find that receiving and processing orders, generating labels and invoices, preparing statements to certify level of circulation, and managing the subscriber mailing list requires more overhead than can often be cost-justified. Therefore, they may outsource the handling of fulfillment to such companies as EDS, which is one of the country's largest fulfillment houses.

As for any company function, there are advantages and disadvantages for outsourcing fulfillment. Because of the volume of work, a fulfillment company knows what works and doesn't work, and it can better afford the latest hardware and software for handling all the logistical details. The downsides are that a company has less control and possibly higher cost (although if a company includes all the equipment and overhead needed to handle fulfillment, outsourcing can actually be cost-effective).

The Media of Direct Marketing

Direct marketers send their offers through a variety of media—direct mail, TV, radio, print, catalogs, telephone, and the Internet. Marketers often use mass media advertising to encourage people to contact the company—that is, to self-select themselves into the prospect database—and then use direct marketing to respond to these prospects. Exhibit 17–7 illustrates how interested prospects can be identified through a mass media advertising effort for a company-constructed list.

Catalog direct marketers such as L. L. Bean and Lands' End, home shopping channels such as QVC, and online marketers such as Amazon.com, are all engaged in direct marketing. The IMC in Action box explains how one such company works.

Types of Direct Response

Direct marketers face a basic communication question: What should be the balance of personal and nonpersonal messages in the marketing communication mix? There are degrees of message personalization, as shown in Table 17–2. You will also note in this table that there are various degrees of interactivity. At

EXHIBIT 17-7

The Catfish Institute in Mississippi used this attractive ad, which offered a recipe book, to change the image of catfish and encourage consumption. Interested consumers who responded became part of the institute's database.

THE REAL BEAUTY IS IN HOW IT TASTES.

IMC IN ACTION

Dialing for Flowers

One very successful direct marketer is 1-800-FLOW-ERS, a pioneer in using direct-response television advertising, telemarketing, and e-commerce to generate sales for local florists. The parent company, Teleway, an innovative relationship marketer, set up a network of 2,500 U.S. retail florists called BloomNet. Teleway creates, schedules, and runs direct-response advertising that generates business for this group.

To send a gift of flowers, you call the 800 number (or contact 1-800-FLOWERS.COM) and a local retailer within the recipient's zip code area delivers the flowers. Teleway receives orders from around the world in one of three telemarketing centers. Each order is transmitted within three minutes to a computer at the florist nearest the recipient's address. The florist makes up the bouquet from specifications and color photos in Teleway's manual and delivers the flowers.

In addition to television, the e-commerce company uses direct mail and radio to market its products. Direct mail catalogs are sent to consumer segments in a file of 1.5 million customers, and radio is used to generate orders from people at work or in their cars. Those who place flower orders may receive a follow-up postcard offering other Teleway products such as gift baskets, candy, or Florida oranges.

A Web pioneer since 1992, the company was named the "Top Gift Site on the Web" by ClicksGuide.com. It also has enlarged its Web presence by buying Great-food.com and consolidating the gourmet and specialty foods line with the FLOWERS line in an attempt to become the number one source for thoughtful gifts for all occasions.

Think About It

Why is 1-800-FLOWERS described as a direct marketer? How does such a company differ from other florist companies? How many different marketing communication tools does 1-800-FLOWERS use in its direct-marketing program?

Source: Adapted from William J. McDonald, *Direct Marketing: An Integrated Approach* (Burr Ridge, IL: Irwin/McGraw-Hill, 1998), p. 3.

---

one extreme is real-time interactivity, as in personal selling and telemarketing. Next is delayed-response interactivity, by which customers must wait, to some degree, to get the information they want. The least interactive media of all are the mass media, which require that customers go to another medium such as the Internet, telephone, or fax to respond.

A brand message in any of the mass media that asks the receiver (reader, viewer, or listener) to respond directly to the sender is called **direct-response advertising.** Some people confuse direct-response advertising with direct-mail advertising, incorrectly using the terms interchangeably. Direct-mail advertising is simply one type of direct-response message delivery. As noted in Chapter 12, the two mostly widely used direct-response media, by far, are the telephone and mail.

Telemarketing

Using the telephone to deliver an offer and take an order can be called either personal selling or direct marketing. For the sake of discussion, this book places it within the direct-marketing function. Where it actually resides in a company varies. The important things to understand are how it works, and when and where it is best used.

TABLE 17-2   The Personalization Continuum

Degree of Personalization	Initiation	Interactivity	Response	Message
High	Face-to-face personal selling	Interactive in real time	Personalized communication	Company-initiated
	Telemarketing, phone	Interactive in real time	Can be personalized (but often are scripted)	Company- or customer-initiated
	E-mail, fax	Delayed response	Can be personalized (but often are scripted)	Company- or customer-initiated
	Electronic kiosks, Internet	Instant information retrieval	Mass message	Customer-initiated
	Direct mail	Delayed customer response	Can be personalized but usually treated as a mass-media message (telephone response can be personal and interactive)	Company-initiated
	Catalogs, videos, CDs	Delayed response	Mass messages (telephone response can be personal and interactive)	Company-initiated
	Audiotext (900 numbers)	Delayed interaction	Impersonal mass messages; may or may not have a personal company response	Company-initiated
Low	Mass-media ads	Delayed response	Impersonal, mass message (telephone response can be personal and interactive)	Company-initiated

Although the practice has been used for decades, the term *telemarketing* is relatively new in popular use. Recall from Chapter 12 that telemarketing is defined as lead generation and qualification, selling, and receiving orders by phone. In 1999, marketers spent an estimated $66 billion on consumer and BtB telemarketing (about the same amount as spent in radio, magazines, and newspaper media combined) which generated an estimated $1.3 trillion worth of direct orders and leads. By year 2003, it is estimated that $84 billion will be spent on telemarketing in the United States.[4] There are several reasons why telemarketing receives such a large portion of many companies' MC budgets:

1. A company can accurately estimate its return on investment in a telemarketing program because the results are easy to measure.
2. Telemarketing cost significantly less per customer contact than face-to-face personal selling.
3. Telemarketing is extremely economical for maintaining frequent, personal contact with customers.
4. Assuming a company has a customer database, telemarketing is highly targeted.
5. Telephone messages can be personally tailored just as in face-to-face selling.

6. Customers can be reached faster through telemarketing than through most other forms of media.

Call Centers

Inbound and outbound calls take place in a **call center**—*a bank of telephones staffed by sales representatives whose dialogue is guided by computer-generated scripts* (see Exhibits 17–8). These scripts ensure that callers present an offer in the right order and record all the necessary response information. Without such scripts, the brand messages being delivered by the callers would probably be inconsistent.

Although most telemarketing is used for soliciting sales and receiving orders, it can also be used for doing surveys, setting appointments for salespeople, and handling customer service. Companies usually separate customer-service and survey work from solicitations and taking orders, however, because each of these requires special training.

Direct Mail

The Direct Marketing Association estimates that U.S. companies spent $42 billion on direct mail in 1999. Today's leading mail-order product categories are insurance, financial services, and department stores.

Surprisingly, although direct mail is an addressable medium, the majority of direct-mail offers are impersonal. The labor required to personalize each message is cost-prohibitive for most companies, but there are software programs that can automatically personalize messages to a certain extent. Even so, this software requires a detailed database of customer transactions plus some profile information for each customer—which many companies don't have.

Direct-mail advertising comes in a variety of formats from handwritten postcards to three-dimensional packages with moving parts. The traditional mailing, though, contains five pieces: an outer envelope, a letter, a brochure or similar selling piece, a business reply card (BRC), and an envelope for the BRC. Marketers have found that including several items in a mailing demands the recipient's attention and is more involving than using only one piece. The more time a person spends with any brand message, the more likely it is that the message will have an impact and generate a response.

Because one of the main expenses of using direct mail is postage, companies often "piggyback" their direct-mail offers; that is, they send their offer along with another company's mailing. Piggyback offers, also called statement stuffers, can appear with utility

EXHIBIT 17-8

a. This telemarketing script invites companies to be listed on a website through which they can promote their products.

Hi! I'm _____ calling from the CLIENT MEMBERSHIP PROGRAM. The CLIENT MEMBERSHIP PROGRAM has developed an industry specific website to promote products like yours in the worldwide market. The web site will list company information and product descriptions that support this specific industry.

- [If the company is *not a current member* of the CLIENT MEMBERSHIP PROGRAM, invite them to join the program by]: To best provide you with the tools to develop and support your product, THE CLIENT would like to invite you to review the benefits of joining the CLIENT MEMBERSHIP PROGRAM, a free program, by going to CLIENT MEMBERSHIP PROGRAM WEB SITE. You can then apply at CLIENT MEMBERSHIP PROGRAM WEB SITE.

We show your product [**Product Name Here**] is a potential candidate for the industry specific website. Do you have any other products that might apply to the specific industry Market? Open box needed to print product name/description/cats/subcats.

I have some questions for you in regard to that/those product/s. Do you have a few minutes that I can ask you some questions?
[Need to be able to record responses for each product listed]:

1) What operating system is this product running on? List versions in check box format.
   - [If their product is *active on Operating System "A"*]: I want to invite you to be featured as part of the CLIENT's Industry Specific Web site.

2) Is there a reference site for any of your Client-based installations? Create box for fill in info on company name, address, phone, web.

3) Do you support an international business opportunity with this product? Y or N

4) Who should be the point of contact for this program? Title? Phone #'? Email ID? Create fill in boxes for these fields.

The Industry Specific website information is available on the Web at <u>WEB</u> SITE. I want to thank you [**their name here**] for your time. If you have any questions or need assistance please call us at 800.945.6111, option 1-2. We would be happy to help! Have a great day!

Save info in database and record call in Activity Tracker.

EXHIBIT 17-8

b. This telemarketing script is for doing a sales follow-up to make sure the buyer received the software and has been able to install and use it.

Hi! I am _____ calling from CLIENT. Our records indicate your company recently purchased PRODUCT X for software development purposes. I wanted to follow up and talk to you about this purchase.

1. Are you developing software on the hardware system that was recently purchased?
* If yes, continue with the questions.
* If No, ask who is using the equipment (and ask to be transferred to them or get their phone number)
* If transferred, thank this person and repeat from the top with the new contact.

These questions will take approximately 10 minutes of your time. As an incentive, CLIENT would like to send you a complimentary gift [Gift is a size large (only) t-shirt to be sent].

2. Did you receive the box of software included with the hardware system?
_____ Yes   _____ NO
* If Yes, go down to question 3
* If No, ask 2a:
2a. Can you please give me your fax #?

3. Did you remember a brochure included with your subscription?
_____ Yes   _____ NO

4. Have you activated your software subscription?
_____ Yes   _____ NO
* If Yes, go to question 5
* If No, go to question 4A;

4a. Why haven't you activated your software subscription?/Comments: Can you please give me your fax #? _____ Also, I need to know how many machines did you order for which the software subscription has not been activated? [You will need to issue a serial number for *each* machine they ordered from the sheet titled 'serial #s' in the database. Be sure to record next to the serial number in the database what company that number was issued to.] I can fax you a software activation form that you can use to order your software over the Internet OR if you have time, I can walk you through the process right now. Your software will take approximately 1-2 weeks to arrive.

5. Do you find it valuable to include software with your hardware system?
_____ Yes   _____ NO

6. Do you find it valuable to receive automatic software updates (as opposed to single copy)?
_____ Yes   _____ NO

Now, I'm going to ask you a couple of general questions regarding the Hardware offering you received.

OVERALL PROGRAM SATISFACTION

7. How long did it take for your hardware system to arrive after your order was placed?
_____ 1 week or less   _____ 2-4 weeks   _____ 5-8 weeks   _____ More than 8 weeks

8. Overall, are you happy with your purchase?
_____ Yes   _____ NO
Comments:

9. Do you have any comments on what we can do to enhance this offering?
(Possible Answers, <u>DO NOT READ</u>)
_____ Lower the price
_____ Offer more selection
_____ Remove software
_____ Make it easier to purchase
_____ Other

10. Do you have any additional comments I can pass on?
Comments:

Thank you for your time. In order to send you your gift, please give me your name and address.
* Name =
* Company Name =
* Address =

[The size Large (only-no exceptions) T-shirt will be sent out in 1-2 weeks.]. I appreciate your input; have a great day!

bills, monthly reports from brokerage firms, periodic frequent-flyer reports to an airline's members, or monthly credit-card statements.

The cost of an average direct-mail piece (including postage) is $1.68, which is less than the cost of a BtB or consumer telemarketing call but more than the cost of an e-mail message.[5] The average response rate for direct mail is higher than for any of the mass media but below that of telemarketing and personal selling.

Catalogs

The largest direct marketers are the catalog companies. Catalogs describe and usually picture the products offered by a manufacturer, wholesaler, jobber, or retailer. Catalogs are used for both BtB and consumer marketing. Most mail-order companies specialize in certain areas, such as outdoor clothing and equipment (Sierra Trading Post), electronic gadgets (Sharper Image), and gourmet foods (Balducci's).

The most popular consumer-product category making use of catalogs is clothing, followed by home furnishings. This fact reflects the interests of the primary target for consumer catalogs: women.[6] According to the DMA, about 62 percent of adult women buy one or more items a year from catalogs (compared to 48 percent of adult men). Although a catalog itself is impersonal, customers can contact the company through a toll-free number or online, which opens up an opportunity for one-to-one conversation with a sales representative (see the L. L. Bean spread in Exhibit 17–9).

New media are changing the way catalogs look and perform. Some marketers now have a video brochure or catalog to augment the efforts of its sales staff or to use for prospecting. CD-ROMs are increasingly being used to "print" and distribute catalogs, because they are able to store millions of bits of information in a durable yet space-efficient format. CDs can cost less to produce than catalogs, and can feature full-motion sight, sound, color and music.

Most catalog marketers have also placed their catalogs on their websites. Because copy, graphics, and layouts for most brand messages are computer-generated,

EXHIBIT 17-9

This is an inside spread (two pages) from an L. L. Bean catalog. It includes an historical feature on the founder, the company's guarantee, and a customer-service commitment statement, along with a toll-free number. The intention of such copy is to reduce the element of risk people face when they order products from a catalog.

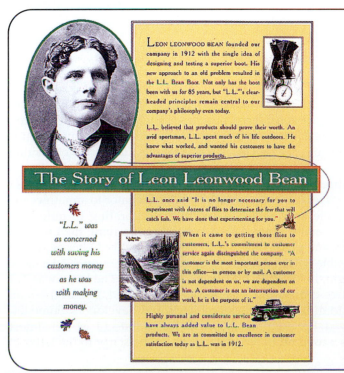

regardless of the medium that will be used, moving these bundles of digital data onto a website is increasingly easy to do. More important it allows catalogs to be kept up-to-date. A company can easily add and subtract items, and change prices in response to competitive and other marketplace changes.

Infomercials

Direct marketers' use of TV has increased in the last five years, particularly in the area of infomercials, which, as you recall from Chapter 11, are program-length advertisements that may run as long as 30 minutes. They are used to educate viewers about a product or service and then provide information on how to order. In 1997, more than 9 million adults purchased one or more items direct from a TV offer. Interestingly, the average cost of producing a 30-minute infomercial is about the same as producing a 30-second national TV spot—about $350,000.[7] The reason the average production cost is the same, despite the large difference in length, is that most infomercials use "talking heads" and only one studio set while many commercials use complex production techniques.

Measuring the Results

Measuring the basic cost-effectiveness of direct marketing programs does not require a Ph.D. in mathematics. For example, a percentage response in direct mail is calculated by dividing the number of responses by the number of mailed offers. If there were 50,000 responses from a mailing of 500,000, that would be a 10 percent response rate:

$$\frac{\text{Number of responses}}{\text{Number of offers mailed}} \quad = \quad \frac{50,000}{500,000} \quad = \quad .10 \quad = \quad 10\%$$

Conversion rates are computed based on the number of inquiries or direct responses generated by a mailing or advertisement. An inquiry is of little value until it is *converted* to an order. For example, if 1,000 responses produced 250 orders, then the conversion rate is 25 percent:

$$\frac{\text{Orders}}{\text{Total responses}} \quad = \quad \frac{250}{1,000} \quad = \quad .25 \quad = \quad 25\%$$

Although direct marketing can be a stand-alone MC function, it is also used along with other MC tools, and this is especially true in marketing business-to-business products or consumer-considered purchases such as financial services, cars, major appliances, and real estate. In these cases, the direct "response" that is desired may be a step in the buying process, such as taking a test drive or visiting a showroom.

An example of how direct response and personal selling can work together comes from a direct-mail teaser campaign created by Otis Elevator to announce the company's new Odyssey elevator, which is capable of operating in mile-high buildings. Based on a story about Frank Lloyd Wright's conceiving the idea of a mile-high building in 1956, and predicting that an elevator like the Odyssey would make such buildings possible within the next 20 years, the promotion used a letter allegedly written by Wright, in his style, and on his letterhead. The letter was put in an envelope with a three-cent stamp, inserted in a re-created, lost-in-the-mail envelope, and delivered to difficult-to-reach architects and developers. Some letters were even personalized. For example, distinguished architect I. M. Pei almost met Wright once but was scared off by Wright's dogs. A postscript in the letter to

Pei expressed regret that the dogs had prevented the meeting. This teaser campaign by Otis drew a 60 percent response rate from the architects and generated $2.5 billion in qualified leads for the sales force.[8]

As noted at various points throughout this book, professionals often make the mistake of thinking that if they simply use a variety of MC functions and media they are practicing IMC. The challenge to doing IMC, however, is to determine the best mix: the right amount of the right functions. In his book *Integrated Direct Marketing*, Ernan Roman provides an excellent example of how different media mixes and proportions can significantly change the level of response and cost per sale in direct marketing. For a manufacturer of telecommunications equipment, two campaigns (A and B) were tested. The immediate objective of the media messages in both campaigns was not to create sales, but to generate qualified leads. Personal selling was used to convert leads into sales. Note that both campaigns contained mass media advertising and direct mail but that campaign B also included telemarketing. In the more traditional campaign A, the majority of media dollars (70 percent) was spent on television and print advertising. In campaign B, the majority (65 percent) was spent on telemarketing, followed by direct mail (25 percent) and mass media advertising (10 percent). As the following table shows, both campaigns spent the same amount of money: $250,000: The difference in the number of leads generated by each campaign was dramatic: campaign B generated three times as many leads (3,750) as campaign A (2,250), as the following table shows:

Budget Allocations ($ Thousands)

	Campaign A		Campaign B	
TV and print advertising	70%	$175	10%	$25
Direct mail	30	75	25	63
Telemarketing	—	—	65	162
Total budget	100%	$250	100%	$250

Results by Medium

	Leads from A		Leads from B	
TV and print advertising	438	35%	375	10%
Direct mail	812	65	750	20
Telemarketing	—	—	2,625	70
Total leads	1,250	100%	3,750	100%

In campaign B, telemarketing calls were made to all those who received the direct-mail offer. Calls were made within a period of 24–72 hours after the direct mail was received. (TV and print began running two weeks before the mailing.) The result was that the cost per lead produced by campaign B ($67) was only one-third of that produced by A ($200):

$$\$250,000 \div 1,250 = \$200$$
$$\$250,000 \div 3,750 = \$67$$

More important than the cost per lead, however, is the cost per sale. As the following table shows, campaign B was far more cost-effective: $444 versus $6,250 per sale. Since the average transaction was $10,000, the MC selling cost (not including the personal selling cost) for campaign A was over half the price of the transaction—not a good situation to have in most cases.

	Cost-Per-Sale	
	Campaign A	**Campaign B**
Lead follow-ups	400	2,250
Conversion to sale	40	563
Cost per sale	$6,250	$444

As you can see, only a third (400 of 1,250) of the leads produced by campaign A were followed up, and of those, only 40 (10 percent) were converted into sales. For campaign B these figures were much better: 2,250 of the 3,750 leads (60 percent) were followed up and, of those, 563 (25 percent) were converted into sales. Campaign A generated lower figures because the leads it produced were of much lower quality, which is why fewer leads were followed up.

According to Roman, mass media brand messages often produce lower-quality leads because of the limited amount of information they can carry. Direct mail can carry more information, but even these messages are one-way until someone responds. In terms of the example, those who responded to campaign A versus campaign B didn't have as much information on which to decide whether or not they were truly interested in the offer. Furthermore, campaign B's use of telemarketing to follow up and add to the information supplied by the mass media advertising and direct mail allowed prospects to learn more about the offer. The better-informed prospects were able to say if they were really interested. So campaign B generated not only more leads but also higher-quality leads, meaning a higher percentage converted into sales.[9]

Testing

Before executing a direct-response effort, especially a large-scale one, a company should test one or more aspects of the proposed campaign. The following are some of the more common types of testing used:

- *List testing.* When addressable media are being used (e.g., mail, e-mail, telephone, fax), the list is one of the biggest variables affecting the rate of response. When a company has a list of 1 million people and mails to all of them at the same time, it is not testing but gambling.[10] Before committing to the costs of contacting a large list, the company should send the planned offer to a small sample of the list (5,000 to 10,000 people). If the response rate to this mailing meets or exceeds the planned objective, then the offer can be sent to the entire list with much less risk.

- *Offer testing.* As explained above, the offer includes many elements—product, price, credit terms, incentive for responding, guarantee, and so on. Each of these can be tested. The rationale for offer testing is especially strong if a part of the offer differs greatly from what the company usually does. For example, if the product has always had a one-year guarantee but the company decides to change it to three years, this warrants testing. Also, there are various combinations of an offer. For example, one combination could have a price of $59.95 along with a free Cross ballpoint pen (each of which costs the company $5): another offer could have a price of $54.95 and no incentive. Both offers cost the company the same; so the company should use the one that produces a significantly higher response than the other.

- *Creative/copy testing.* There are many different ways an offer can be explained and presented. Is a demonstration better than a testimonial? Does a cartoon character work better than a serious, straightforward presentation? Obviously, the creative treatment should be consistent with the overall brand creative strategy, but even within this parameter, there are many alternatives, each of which can affect the response rate.

- *Media mix testing.* Since different media reach different audiences with different effects (as the campaigns A and B example showed above), various combinations warrant testing. A company selling a new sun-protection product may test magazines going to three different "outdoor" audiences: hunting and fishing, gardening, and vacationing. Another type of media test is impact. Does a half-page ad generate at least twice the response rate of a quarter-page ad? Unless it does, the company should stick to the quarter-page ad, since a half-page ad costs twice as much.

- *Frequency testing.* Because current customers are a company's best customers, most companies that use direct marketing send current customers offers throughout the year. Testing the frequency of these offers— how many can profitably be sent within one year—is important. Contacting customers too much not only can be a waste of money (because people stop responding) but can also weaken brand relationships if customers become annoyed.

As direct marketing has become more widely used, with offers sometimes being delivered to 10 million or more households, testing has become very sophisticated and complicated. One basic rule of thumb, however, is quite simple: When testing one variable against another, it is critical that the samples for each test be representative of the total target audience. When testing a list, for example, every *n*th name should be chosen, rather than just taking the first 5,000 names from two different lists. When testing print media, split runs should be used, meaning that offers A and B each go into only half of the issues printed—that is, each goes into every other issue (see Chapter 11). Making these tests as scientifically pure as possible is a must, because even a quarter-percent difference in responses can be important (e.g., in a mailing of 10 million, a quarter percent represents 25,000 responses).

Strengths of Direct-Response Marketing

Direct response is the marketing communication function best suited to retaining and growing current customers. With the growth of database technologies, direct-response marketing has grown faster than any of the other marketing communication functions. Direct-response marketing is persuasive because most types of it are addressable. It can also open the door to personalized interactive customer communication and lead directly to a behavioral response. Furthermore, it can be both tightly targeted, and flexible, and it can generate immediate responses. But one of its greatest strengths is its accountability.

Because the primary objective of direct response is an observable response (e.g., buying a product, requesting information, visiting a store), it is the most accountable form of marketing communication. A marketer can know within days the attractiveness of an offer and the impact of the direct-marketing effort because the response is its own measurement tool. The variables of a direct-response program can be tested, which can significantly increase the cost-effectiveness of the final effort.

When direct-response messages are delivered using addressable media (mail, e-mail, phone), they can be sent to those most likely to respond. This reduces media waste. Flexibility is another strength. Most addressable media can be designed and used much quicker than can mass media. In the case of e-mail, a brand message can be written and distributed within minutes. Telemarketing scripts can be changed easily and quickly. Even direct mail (when a postcard or letter will do) can be designed, printed, and distributed within a few days. Message lengths can be whatever is needed and is restricted by only what the target audience can bear.

Another dimension of direct marketing's impact is that it generates immediate results. The response can happen—and usually does—within minutes (in the case of e-mail and phone) or at most within days of receiving the offer.

Limitations of Direct-Response Marketing

The primary disadvantage of direct-response marketing is its relatively high cost per customer or prospect reached. Direct-mail efforts, for example, may have costs per thousand (CPMs) up to $400. By comparison, the economies of scale of regular mass media advertising are CPMs of $15 to $50. This is why it is critical that direct-response messages be successful in creating more than an attitudinal response (which can be done with mass media messages). It is also critical that messages are correctly targeted for there always needs to be a certain level of response to more than pay for the campaign.

Direct marketing also suffers from clutter. People are deluged with mail and, increasingly, e-mail; and they are annoyed by poorly targeted "junk mail." Cable channels carry an increasing number of infomercials, and telemarketing pitches intrude on people at home and at work. Many consumers are also concerned with privacy (see Chapter 19). They don't like having their names sold by list vendors. In fact, numerous services have sprung up to help consumers reduce the amount of direct-response marketing to which they are subjected (see Exhibit 17–10).

There is also the risk that comes from not being able to see, touch, or try on a product before ordering it. Also, the high cost per contact has to be balanced against the higher price point and margin of the products being sold. Certain types of products—such as fresh produce, impulse products (candy bars), and small-ticket, mass-distributed convenience items (toothpicks, ballpoint pens)—are not likely to be sold through direct marketing—although that situation may change with the Internet.

In the past, direct marketers have been (and some still are) more sales oriented than relationship oriented. This high-pressure approach gives direct marketing a bad image. In the online environment, as described in Chapter 12, the practice of spamming—mass sending of e-mail—has generated a lot of protests. Most major portals now will not allow mass e-mailing. Web users like to feel they are in control, so they are particularly offended by unsolicited commercial messages directed at them. In Seattle, for example, a group of online users called the Forum for Responsible and Ethical E-mail (FREE) picketed a car dealer that tried to attract customers by bombarding them with unsolicited e-mails.[11]

PERSONAL SALES: THE FACE-TO-FACE FUNCTION

Everyone sells something at one time or another. Children sell lemonade, magazine subscriptions, and Girl Scout cookies. Students sell prom tickets and yearbook ads. Doctors sell exercise and diet programs to overweight patients. Lawyers sell briefs to skeptical judges. The fact is, many things, including ideas, are constantly being sold—by someone to somebody.

Personal sales involve one-to-one marketing using face-to-face communication. A more formal definition of **personal selling** is *two-way communication in which a seller interprets brand features in terms of buyer benefits.* Brand benefits come from not only product performance but also in the uncovering of needs and opportunities for the buyer, and, in the case of BtB customers, adding value to their operations and products.

As a business process and a profession, personal selling is more than "making a sale." As Table 17–3 shows, personal selling has evolved over the years. While once focused primarily on sales—a transaction-based approach—personal selling today must focus on solving customer problems and creating value for customers. This means working in a *partnership* with clients to come up with ideas that will reduce their costs and/or make their products more competitive and attractive (a practice also known as *enterprise* or *solution selling*). The partnering dimension of selling means that salespeople must learn as much about their customers' businesses as they know about their own. Salespeople then become the liaison between their company and customers, often selling as hard inside their own company as they do outside, in order to convince their company to make the necessary product and process changes that best serve their customers. Evidence of such customer focus often results in company executives asking the sales force: "Who are you working for, us or the customer?" The correct answer is "Both."

Today's professional salesperson is supported by information technology and the understanding that creating a good relationship will result in more sales than will the hard-sell, manipulative techniques of the past. Professional salespeople also realize that they are part of a total marketing communication organization and must conduct themselves in a way that is strategically consistent with all the other brand messages.

The role of personal selling varies by type of business and industry, the nature of the product or service, and the business strategy. Although most personal selling is for BtB brands, it is also a major MC function in selling consumer products such as insurance, real estate, cars, professional services, financial services, and other high-priced considered purchases. Where personal selling is used extensively, the salesperson is the company in the eyes of customers and prospects.

T A B L E   1 7 - 3   Evolution of Personal Selling

	Sales Era	Marketing Era	Partnering Era
Time period	Before 1960	1960-1990	After 1990
Objective	Making transactions	Satisfying needs	Building relationships
Role of salesperson	Persuader and order taker	Problem solver	Value creator

Source: Adapted from Barton Weitz, Stephen Castleberry, and John Tanner, *Selling* (Burr Ridge, IL: Irwin/McGraw-Hill, 1995), p. 12.

The Functions of Personal Sales

Personal selling's primary role is retaining and growing customers. Yet there is still a need for some attention to customer acquisition.

Retaining Current Customers

As stressed throughout this book, a company's current customers must not be taken for granted. Just because they have been buying from a company for years, there is no guarantee they will buy from the company next week.

Unfortunately, many businesses overemphasize acquiring customers at the expense of servicing current ones. An example of this can be found with marketing communication agencies themselves. Top managers—those most responsible for building their agencies and the executives considered by clients to be the most knowledgeable—often spend the majority of their time making new business pitches rather than working on accounts. They get back to work on the account only when the client is dissatisfied and threatening to switch agencies.

Because customer retention is the bottom line of a brand relationship, salespeople must do those things that create and maintain relationships. This means that a salesperson's number one objective is to create trust. This is accomplished by demonstrating dependability, competence, a customer orientation, honesty, and likability.[12] Some sales managers say that current customers should always be treated as new customers—with the same level of attention and care.

As in all areas of IMC, salespeople must create and manage customer expectations, not only of product performance but of all the other services that are expected in support of a brand. Once a product is sold, it is up to the salesperson to make sure the product arrives on time, that invoicing is properly handled, and that the customer knows how to use the product in the proper way. At the same time, the salesperson should be analyzing the customer's business to see in what ways the brand can further improve the customer's processes, sales, and profit. Salespeople are an information resource to their clients because they know how their products have been used by other companies and thus have a much broader perspective on the product's applications than any single customer can have. They can add value by not letting customers repeat mistakes made by other customers, as well as by sharing the ideas that work (as long as those ideas don't come from a customer's competitor).

Acquiring New Customers

With average annual customer turnover rates of approximately 15 to 20 percent, salespeople also need to acquire new customers to replace those that are lost. Customer acquisition is also a way to increase overall sales. The process of acquiring customers starts with sales leads. A **sales lead** is *a person or organization identified as being a prospect—someone able to benefit from the brand being sold.*

As mentioned earlier in this chapter, leads may come from a company's direct-response advertising or from publicity about the company or its brands. They include those who call in for information or respond by returning a business reply card (BRC) from a direct-mail piece or a "bingo card" from a trade or special interest magazine (see Exhibit 17–11). Leads may also come from referrals—satisfied customers, employees, even from competitors who feel a prospect is either too big or too small for them to handle.

Companies may generate leads by profiling current profitable customers. Profiling is done by mining the current customer database, as described in Chapter 8.

If a person has the same characteristics of current profitable customers, then he or she is likely to be a genuine prospect. If lists can't be found that include those characteristics, it may be necessary to create a set of criteria by merging several relevant lists based on management's knowledge of its market. For instance, by combining a database of technical information systems (IS) professionals with subscribers of a financial-services trade publication, a company could come up with a list of IS managers employed at companies with sales between, say, $200 and $500 million who have an interest in financial planning.

When Hewlett-Packard (HP) wanted to motivate its corporate customers to upgrade their equipment, the company segmented them by the volume of their previous purchases and then by the job description of the buyers for each of the companies. Specialized mailings were sent to people in each segment, who were then contacted by phone. The calls determined who was most likely to upgrade; those leads were sent to regional sales offices for personal follow-up. Said the HP marketing specialist who organized the effort, "Our conversion-to-lead ratio was extraordinarily high because we were talking to the right people with the right message."[13]

Another way to generate leads is by getting prospects to self-select, as described in Chapter 7. This is done by sending brand message via mass media and niche media to motivate those interested to identify themselves. Premiums are sometimes used to encourage prospects to provide profile information so that a salesperson can decide whether they are true prospects. When a customer takes the initiative in expressing interest in a product and providing profile information, that behavior can be highly predictive of future buying, as shown in Table 17–4.

SEND FOR
FREE INFORMATION
▼ FROM ADVERTISERS IN THIS SECTION ▼

Circle the numbers on the reply card that correspond to this list of companies:

OUTSOURCING

1. ADP
2. Arthur Andersen
3. AchieveGlobal
4. AT&T Solutions
5. Centrobe, An EDS Company
6. Compass America, Inc.
7. Consolidated Market Response
8. Corporate Project Resources, Inc.
9. Exelon
10. Express Personnel Services
11. Fusion Software Engineering Pvt. Ltd.
12. GE Information Services
13. Haas Corporation
14. Keane, Inc.
15. Lockheed Martin
16. Mastek Limited
17. Penske
18. PW Financial Solutions
19. Ryder Transportation Services
20. Sodexho Marriott Services
21. SOFTBANK Services Group
22. Wang Global

VARIABLE ANNUITIES

23. Aetna Retirement Services
24. Conseco
25. Golden American Life Insurance Company
26. Keyport Life Insurance Company
27. Lincoln Financial Group
28. Massachusetts Mutual Life Insurance Company
29. Nationwide/The BEST of AMERICA
30. Northwestern Mutual Life
31. Pacific Life
32. TIAA - CREF
33. Travelers Life & Annuity
34. VALIC

To receive information, circle the numbers below corresponding to numbers and companies listed above. Please type or print all information below.

Name

Title

Company

Address

City State Zip

Phone

Electronic Mail Address

1	2	3	4	5	6	7
8	9	10	11	12	13	14
15	16	17	18	19	20	21
22	23	24	25	26	27	28
29	30	31	32	33	34	

1. Title:
A. ❑ Chairman, President, CEO
B. ❑ Vice President
C. ❑ Financial Officer
D. ❑ CIO, MIS Executive
E. ❑ Other Company Officer
F. ❑ Owner/Partner
G. ❑ Middle Management
H. ❑ Professional (Doctor/Lawyer)
I. ❑ Non-Management
J. ❑ Other

2. Type of Firm
A. ❑ Manufacturing
B. ❑ Transportation, Communications, Public Utilities
C. ❑ Construction, Engineering, Mining, Oil/Gas
D. ❑ Information Technology
E. ❑ Other Industry
F. ❑ Banking/Finance
G. ❑ Wholesale/Retail Trade
H. ❑ Service
I. ❑ Government
J. ❑ Other

3. Number of employees in your company worldwide:
A. ❑ Small Office/Home Office
B. ❑ 5-49 D. ❑ 100-999
C. ❑ 50-99 E. ❑ 1,000 or more

S/T Offer expires September 22, 1998 July 20, 1998 NA

EXHIBIT 17-11

This is a bingo card. Readers of the magazine in which the card appears can mark the products and brands they would like to know more about and then send the card back to the magazine. The magazine then forwards the information to the brands. The idea is to allow the various brands listed on the card to generate leads.

TABLE 17-4 Making Strategic Use of Customer Contacts:

According to research done for Inquiry Systems and Analysis

- 60 percent of all inquirers purchase something within a year.
- 20 percent of inquirers have an immediate need.
- 10 percent are hot leads.
- 60 percent of inquirers also contact your competitors.
- 50 percent of all new business starts as an inquiry.

But most companies do not take advantage of these inquiries:

- 20 percent of inquirers never receive information.
- 40 percent of inquirers receive information too late to use it.
- 70 percent of inquirers are never contacted by a sales representative.

Source: Arthur M. Hughes, *The Complete Database Marketer* (Burr Ridge, IL: Irwin, 1996), p. 390.

IBM has embarked on several integrated, database-driven pilot campaigns that have generated three times as many qualified leads as did previous campaigns. A key component of these programs is asking customers what they are looking for in products and services and how they like to be contacted by the company—by mail, e-mail, phone, fax, brochures, salesperson's visit, or not at all.

One problem with managing lead generation is the interaction between salespeople and marketing departments, because these two groups often disagree about leads.[14] Marketing often sees a lead as anyone who inquires about the product, while sales defines a lead as someone ready to buy now. Marketing people complain that salespeople don't follow up on their leads, and salespeople argue that it's because many marketing-generated leads aren't worth following up. The heart of the problem is that each department wants the other to qualify the leads (a process explained below).

The Personal-Selling Process

The process of personal selling, particularly for acquiring new customers, involves generating leads, qualifying leads, making sales calls, closing the sale, and following up to build and maintain the customer relationship.

Qualifying Leads

Once leads are generated, they need to be qualified to determine whether they are genuine prospects. **Qualified leads** are *prospects who (1) have a real need or opportunity that the brand can address, (2) have the ability to pay for the good or service, (3) have the authority to buy, and (4) are approachable.* A company or person who buys infrequently or demands an unreasonably high level of service may not be a good lead.

When GM introduced its first electric car, it required all potential customers to fill out a customer profile application before a sales representative would meet with them. GM wanted to target those who were environmentally conscious, already owned at least two gasoline-powered cars, and had a household income over $120,000 a year. Because not all products are for all people, potential customers should be assisted in deciding whether a particular product or brand is for them. Exhibit 17–12 is an ad with a return-mail card whose purpose is to generate leads that can be contacted and further qualified.

The reason qualifying sales leads is so important is that the cost of a personal sales call outweighs that of most other MC functions. An average BtB sales call cost between $300 and $600, and some sales calls can run into the thousands. A person working for a highly specialized international company, such as one selling airport radar installations, may travel halfway around the world just to make one sales call, costing the company $10,000 or more. It is seldom cost-effective for salespeople to make "cold calls"—selling situations where they have no knowledge of how interested those being called on might be.

Another factor that makes qualifying leads important in BtB marketing is that it takes between three and seven personal sales contacts before a major sale is made.[15] This means a salesperson may make several expensive sales calls before realizing a prospect is not going to become a customer. The higher the quality of a lead, the more likely a prospect is to respond. And the higher the response rate, the lower the cost per sale.

Measurement of Personal-Selling Efforts

In personal selling, as in direct-response marketing, there are a number of measurements that can be used to evaluate the sales effort. A cost-per-call, for example, is calculated by comparing a salesperson's total costs to the number of calls made. A prospect call/close ratio can be determined by comparing the total number of prospect calls made to the number of who actually bought.

The best way to use these measurements is to track them to make sure they are going in the right direction. For example, if the overall company call-to-sale ratio is 5 to 1 this year (meaning one sale was made for every five sales calls), steps should be taken to make it 4.5 to 1 for the following year. Such ratios can be used to evaluate individual sale representatives. If the company call-to-sale ratio for the best salesperson is 3 to 1 and the ratio for the worst salesperson is 10 to 1, someone who comes in with an 11 to 1 ratio may well be advised to go work for the competition! Following are examples of how to figure some of these measurements.

Cost per Call $\quad \dfrac{\text{total sales costs}}{\text{number of calls made}} \quad = \quad \dfrac{\$2,500,000}{8,500} \quad = \quad \$294$

Call /Sales Ratio $\quad \dfrac{\text{number of calls made}}{\text{number of sales made}} \quad = \quad \dfrac{8,500}{1,700} \quad = \quad 5$

Sales Cost per Sale $\quad \dfrac{\text{total sales costs}}{\text{number of sales made}} \quad = \quad \dfrac{\$2,500,000}{1,700} \quad = \quad \$1,470$

The bottom line of any cost analysis, of course, is profitability. Determining individual customer profitability is now possible in those businesses where customers

---

EXHIBIT 17-12

This magazine ad for Ryder Transportation Services explains how the company's services are being used by Ace hardware. A reply card is tipped in (glued) to the ad to make response easy. When the cards come in, they are used to qualify the sales leads for Ryder's sales force.

It's time you got to know us on a first-name basis.

Find out how the people at Ryder can help your company save time and money – in practically no time. Return this card today.

❏ Please send me my free information kit.
❏ Please have a Ryder representative call me for a free consultation.

Name _____ Title _____

Company Name _____

Street Address _____ City _____ State _____ Zip _____

Business Phone _____ Best time to call _____

Call **1 800 RYDER OK**, ext. 612
www.ryder.com

Ryder®

Logistics and Transportation Solutions Worldwide

are known. (It is still not possible, however, for impulse purchases and other consumer packaged goods.) How to figure customer profitability is beyond the scope of this text; most marketing people leave the calculations to accounting departments. But, once the numbers are processed, they provide information that marketing people need to have when doing direct-response marketing and supporting personal sales.

For IMC, several other important measures of how well a salesperson is performing are (1) the average length of time an individual's accounts have been buying from the company, (2) the average annual sales and profitability of these accounts, and (3) the number of referrals made by these accounts. Because a primary IMC objective is to retain customers, the average customer lifetime should continue to increase if a salesperson is doing a good job. Also, current customers should be motivated to increase the quantity of their purchases from year to year. Finally, customers who have a good relationship with a salesperson and a brand will be more likely to recommend that person and brand to other companies.

SFA and CRM

Applying information technology to personal selling was originally called sales force automation (SFA). A vast majority of companies that first used SFA reported being disappointed with the return on their investment. Some of the reasons for this disappointment were that (1) time was not taken to properly train salespeople on how to use SFA; (2) the proper databases were not available, so information access was limited; and (3) SFA systems were not well integrated into the other information technology (IT) systems. Also, with interactive communication and the Internet, power began to shift from the sales side to the customer. As a result of these early shortcomings, companies selling SFA redesigned their systems to do more things, be more user friendly, and be easier to integrate into "legacy systems" (the software and hardware that companies were already using).

Because SFA acquired such a negative image, new and improved systems were introduced, such as customer relationship management (CRM) programs (described in Chapter 8), which bring more individualized attention and responsiveness to the sales process as a way to better nurture long-term customer relationships. Among marketers and IT people there is an ongoing debate as to whether CRM is much broader than SFA or is simply a more user-friendly, data-driven SFA system. According to one recent study, CRM can be divided into five categories of primary use:[16]

1. Sales force automation (accounts for 44 percent of all CRM use).
2. Customer service and technical support (27 percent).
3. Help desk for supporting channel members and others who have access to a company's extranet (20 percent).
4. Tracking of field service technicians (6 percent).
5. Support for planning, executing, and tracking marketing campaigns (3 percent but the fastest growing of all uses).

CRM is primarily a BtB tool (see Exhibit 17–13) and one that 70 percent of companies expect to have by 2005.[17] Because the major use of CRM is in automating the personal selling process, it is important to understand how it works and why it is of value to a company (when it does work). Because speed is so important in business today, a sale can easily be lost if a company spends too much time putting together an offer. Providing salespeople with laptops and modems to access relevant databases can significantly improve the efficiency and effectiveness of the typical sales call.

In essence, CRM makes salespeople better, more productive communicators. A salesperson using CRM can sit in a customer's office with a laptop computer; input that customer's needs; and, with a modem, access company databases to determine product design alternatives, product availability, prices, discounts available based on this customer's past volume, the customer's line of credit, and delivery schedules, among other things. Before leaving the customer's office, the salesperson is able to configure a customized product offering. Being able to do this type of communication quickly and accurately is an added value to customers and therefore a way to be more competitive.

From a company's perspective, CRM is also a way to manage customer leads and make sure salespeople are doing their job. By tracking leads and sales calls, and keeping customer and prospect profiles complete and up-to-date, CRM will enable a company to:[18]

- Know which leads were followed up and when, and what the results were.
- Give the leads that were not followed up to other salespeople.
- Determine why sales were not made (e.g., better competitive offer, dissatisfied with brand's current products or services, delivery not soon enough).
- Determine who within the prospect company has influence on the brand decision.
- Keep track of buyers who leave one company and go to another.

EXHIBIT 17-13

This ad for CRM company SalesLogix touts its CRM solutions designed for midsize B1B marketers.

Compensation and Rewards

Compensation systems are changing in personal selling. Traditionally, compensation was based totally or primarily on sales volume. Some companies still have salespeople work solely on **commission** (*a percentage of the sales price retained by the salesperson*). Often, top salespeople who work on 100 percent commission are some of the highest-paid people in a company. The problem with having commission be the major compensation driver is that it rewards transactions rather than long-term relationships.

In order to have a customer-relationship focus, companies have realized they must balance how they reward salespeople, because people respond to what is measured and rewarded. This is why salespeople are increasingly being evaluated and rewarded not only for sales but also for how long customers have bought from the company (retention), how much customers have increased their purchase quantities (customer growth), and how much they have been helped by the salesperson in solving problems and increasing productivity (customer satisfaction).

Special prizes, such as trips and other high-value premiums, are frequently used to increase sales in the short term. For a new product introduction, for example, salespeople may receive an extra incentive if 65 percent or more of their customers buy the new product within the first 90 days of its availability.

In addition to evaluating salespeople according to set objectives, companies are also asking customers to rate the salespeople that call on them. Because the success of personal selling can be so dependent on working with other people in an organization, some companies even ask people in their distribution, accounting, and customer-service departments to rate salespeople. It is critical that the salesperson's performance be consistent with the firm's positioning and reinforce its other marketing communications. What the salesperson says and does will either confirm or contradict the company's other brand messages.

Personal Selling Strengths and Limitations

The primary objective, and strength, of personal selling is building a trusting relationship. Any brochure or ad can lay out the benefits of a brand, but a personal sales experience can humanize a brand and a company, particularly when that interaction is supported by CRM (see Exhibit 17–14).

The greatest strength of personal selling, therefore, is two-way communication. It is the ultimate way to integrate a product and its features with customer wants, needs, and opportunities. Two-way communication is the most powerful form of persuasion—not only to encourage someone to buy but, more important, to encourage that person to remain a customer. By using face-to-face communication with the prospect, a skilled salesperson can observe a prospect's body language and encourage him or her to express objections. The one-to-one situation facilitates instant feedback to objections (which a good salesperson should anticipate and be prepared to address). Once a relationship is established, motivating sales becomes much easier.

Another strength of personal selling is its accountability and measurability. For this reason, personal selling is definitely numbers-driven. In most cases, a company can easily measure the sales generated by each salesperson in a specified period. Since most companies use commission-based compensation plans for the sales force, both companies and salespeople are concerned about how salespeople spend their time and what their sales records are.

Over time, it is very easy to determine how many of a salesperson's customers are still with the company and how many no longer are. It is also easy to determine how many sales each salesperson has generated. Sophisticated accounting software can now tell the overall profitability of each salesperson's customers. Using discounts, premiums, and other considerations can make a sale fairly easy, but the best salespeople are those who generate sales without making so many concessions that the company makes little or no profit on the transactions.

Personal selling is also flexible and allows sales messages to be tailored to each customer and prospect. It also allows instant changes in a sales presentation as the situation requires. Negotiation is another aspect of flexibility—with personal communication it is much

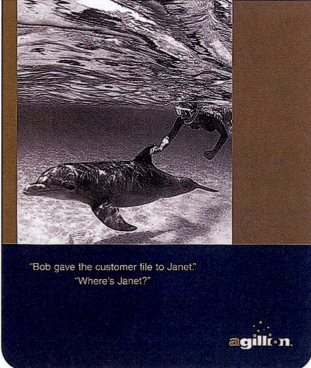

easier to find those terms that best suit the buyer's needs and to adjust the offer accordingly. If a buyer is primarily concerned with an earlier delivery date, for example, a salesperson may absorb the cost required to meet this date by getting the customer to either buy an additional amount or pay for the merchandise sooner.

Because good salespeople are in constant contact with their customers and know their customers' business, they can collect information and build valuable customer databases. A rich customer database offers vital information to marketing people, allowing them to prepare personalized, targeted messages. Such databases also become very valuable when a customer is assigned to a different salesperson.

Like all other MC functions, personal selling has it limitations. The most important limitation is its high cost. Maintaining a sales force is costly because it requires not only salaries (or commissions) but also sales call expenses, recruitment, training, and other internal support functions. Since it is basically a one-to-one medium, there are few economies of scale. In fact, two or three salespeople will sometimes go to an important customer's office to make a presentation or make multiple presentations if they represent different product lines. In personal selling, companies don't even think about cost per thousand (it would give most executives a heart attack). As mentioned above, just one personal sales call can run into the hundreds of dollars.

Another limitation is that some salespeople overemphasize making a quick sale and lack the patience to build relationships based on promising long-term leads. A study of 40,000 buyers found that only 11 percent of those who made purchases did so within three months of their first contact with the company. The study concluded: "It's important to put a relationship marketing program in place to nurture long-term leads."[19] This limitation, however, is not always the fault of salespeople. As noted above, compensation based on commissions nurtures the emphasis on transactions at the expense of relationships. Salespeople should be rewarded for generating sales, but when volume is the major portion of their focus, there is a tendency to overpromise in order to make a sale.

That human connection that was described as a strength can also create a dilemma—customers may develop loyalty to salespeople rather than to the company or the brand. Because a salesperson represents a company and is the primary person customers see and deal with, it is only natural that the salesperson "becomes" the company. If this is allowed to happen, it means that when salespeople change jobs, their customers may move with them. A partial solution to the problem is for the company to maintain a comprehensive database of customer contact information.

As you will recall, one of the strengths of personal selling is flexibility, but the flip side of that is often strategic inconsistency. When they begin to craft customer-specific sales deals, salespeople can create and deliver brand messages that are inconsistent with the overall brand strategy. An upscale, status brand positioning will not be reinforced if a salesperson continually encourages the company's customers to run sales.

Just as direct-response advertising is seen as intrusive and often in poor taste, personal selling has developed an *image problem* over the decades because of so much high-pressure selling and less-than-ethical practices. Thus, a common jibe is "Would you buy a used car from that person?" Many companies today give salespeople euphemistic titles like marketing associate, marketing representative, admissions coordinator, clinical liaison, professional services representative, or program manager. The idea is to counteract the rejection associated with the word *salesperson*.

As an indication of the reputation problem of personal selling, a study of college students conducted in 1997 in the United States, Britain, and Thailand found that students from these diverse areas all have a very low impression of sales as a career opportunity. Although 72 percent agreed with the statement "The financial rewards from selling are excellent," 40 percent believe that a salesperson's job security is poor. An example of the problem comes from a Mesa, Arizona, electrical wiring firm that got virtually no response to ads in college papers that said, "Looking for entry-level salespeople." When the same company instead ran an ad for marketing people, the résumés poured in.[20]

A FINAL NOTE: CONTACT WITH INTEGRITY

At a recent national forum of direct marketers, marketing with integrity was among the issues discussed. Marketers were told they must self-regulate, give consumers more control, and treat privacy like a customer-service issue, or they would risk legislation restricting access to the information they desperately need. They were also warned that the result of neglecting restraint would be lower response rates.

Similar issues plague personal selling. Both consumers and BtB customers still find some forms of sales calls to be intrusive and irritating. Marketers need to heed these warnings and develop methods, guidelines, and policies for responsible personal contact in marketing. These contacts, more than any other form of marketing communication, lend integrity (or a lack thereof) to a brand's reputation. However, if the contact provides information of value, it can dramatically lessen the irritation factor. In fact, it may set up a win–win situation for both the marketer and the customer.

Key Terms

direct-response marketing 600
offer 602
response lists 604
compiled lists 604
response 605
fulfillment 605

direct-response advertising 607
personal selling 617
sales lead 618
qualified leads 620
commission 623

Key Point Summary

Key Point 1: Direct-Response Components

Direct-response marketing seeks an immediate action and allows the customer to respond directly to the marketer, bypassing retail stores. The elements of a direct-response message include the offer, the response, and fulfillment. Direct-response tools offer varying degrees of personalization, from face-to-face direct sales and telemarketing, which are highly personalized; to e-mail, fax, and electronic kiosks, which are less personal although still interactive; to direct mail, catalogs, videos, CDs, and mass-media ads, which are usually not personalized.

Key Point 2: Direct-Response Strengths and Limitations

Direct response is valued because it is highly targeted, highly accountable, and cost-effective if the database is good. Limitations include a higher cost per contact, the image problems of "junk mail," spamming, telemarketing, and clutter.

Key Point 3: Personal Selling's Role

Personal sales is face-to-face selling using two-way communication in which a seller interprets brand features in terms of buyer benefits. It is effective in retaining current customers and managing relationships with them, as well as acquiring new customers, because face-to-face is the most persuasive of all forms of communication. The acquisition process for new customers involves generating and qualifying leads, making sales calls, closing the sale, and follow-up relationship management activities after the sale is made.

Key Point 4: Strengths and Limitations of Personal Sales

The strengths of personal sales include the power of personalized, two-way communication, relationship building, accountability, flexibility, and the ability to collect useful information in the process of making a sale. The limitations include its high cost, the overemphasis on sales transactions, customer loyalty to the sales rep rather than the company, strategic inconsistency, and the negative image of sales representatives in general.

Lessons Learned

Key Point 1: Direct-Response Components

a.   Define direct-response marketing.
b.   Why do we say that direct marketing is a "microcosm" of the entire marketing process?
c.   What role do databases play in a direct-marketing program?
d.   If you were a list manager for a national retail chain, what would be your duties?
e.   What are the three primary elements of direct-response marketing? Give an example of each from your own experience.
f.   Which type of direct marketing offers the greatest opportunity for personalization of the message? Which type offers the least opportunity?
g.   What is the difference between a highly interactive message and a highly personalized one?
h.   If you want an MC campaign to be heavy on opportunities for customer-initiated messages, what direct-marketing tools might you use?

Key Point 2: Strengths and Weaknesses of Direct Response

a.   What are the three primary strengths of direct-response marketing?
b.   Explain the three types of waste that can be avoided through the use of a database-driven, direct-marketing program.
c.   What are the three primary limitations of direct-response marketing?

Key Point 3: Personal Selling's Role

a.   This chapter makes the point that personal selling is more than "making a sale." Define personal selling and explain what is meant by that statement.
b.   Explain the evolution of personal selling and how the focus of the effort has changed over time.
c.   Explain how personal selling occurs at various points in the marketing process and what roles sales representatives typically play.
d.   How is personal selling used to acquire or retain a customer?
e.   What is lead generation?
f.   How are leads qualified?

g. This chapter says that sales calls should be considered as planned communication. What does that mean to a sales rep getting ready to make a call?

h. What is the most important thing to remember in giving a sales presentation?

i. What is aftermarketing, and why is it important?

Key Point 4: Strengths and Limitations of Personal Sales

a. Why is the personal nature of personal selling its greatest strength?

b. Why is personal selling more accountable than advertising or public relations?

c. Why do we say that personal selling is the best tool for relationship building?

d. What are the image problems that tarnish the reputation of personal selling, and what could a salesperson do to turn around these problems?

e. How does personal selling compare to advertising in cost per thousand?

Chapter Challenge

Writing Assignment

Visit a local store that has salesclerks on the floor. Analyze how they (1) greet a customer, (2) try to identify the customer's needs and match the needs to merchandise, (3) up-sell, (4) close the sale, and (5) make an effort to build a relationship with the customer. Are their efforts effective? Write a memo to the store's manager explaining what he or she could do to improve the performance of the sales clerks.

Presentation Assignment

Collect a week's worth of direct mail that comes to your mailbox. Analyze how personalized it is. Prepare a presentation to your class that sets up a continuum of personalization for your set of direct-mail pieces. In other words, which one is the most personalized, which one is the least personalized, and where would you put the other pieces in between?

Internet Assignment

Find the websites of three companies (addresses on packages and in brand messages). Contact these companies with an inquiry or complaint using the response instructions on each of their websites and keep track of: 1) how long it takes each company to respond, 2) rate each response on how personal it is (Was response personalized or a stock message?), 3) record to what extent your question was answered or your complaint addressed, and 4) record to what extent company made an effort find out more about you.

Additional Readings

McDonald, William J. *Direct Marketing: An Integrated Approach*. Burr Ridge, IL: Irwin/McGraw-Hill, 1998.

Nash, Edward. "The Roots of Direct Marketing." *Direct Marketing*, February 1995, pp. 38–40.

Peppers, Don, and Martha Rogers. *Enterprise One to One*. New York: Currency Doubleday, 1997.

Rapp, Stan, and Thomas I. Collins. *Maximarketing*. New York: McGraw-Hill, 1987.

Roman, Ernan. *Integrated Direct Marketing*. Lincolnwood, IL: NTC, 1995.

Stone, Bob. *Successful Direct Marketing Methods*. Lincolnwood, IL: NTC Business Books, 1994.

Vavra, Terry G. "The Database Marketing Imperative." *Marketing Management* 2 no. 1 (1993), pp. 47–57.

Weitz, Barton A.; Stephen B. Castleberry; and John F. Tanner. *Selling: Building Partnerships*, 2nd ed. Burr Ridge, IL: Irwin, 1995.

Wotruba, Thomas R. "The Evolution of Personal Selling." *Journal of Personal Selling & Sales Management* 11, no. 3 (Summer 1991), pp. 1–12.

Research Assignment

Review books and articles on the management of both personal selling and direct-response marketing. Prepare a report on how to communicate with customers in ways that are respectful—that is,—not irritating or needlessly intrusive—and that contribute to, rather than destroy, brand relationships.

Endnotes

[1] *DMA Statistical Fact Book 1999*, p. 3.

[2] Ibid. p. 287.

[3] Richard Levely, "On the Record: List Leaders of the Pack," *Directmag.com*, October 2000.

[4] *DMA Statistical Fact Book 1999*, pp. 285, 287.

[5] Ibid., p. 193.

[6] Ibid., p. 72.

[7] Ibid., pp. 285, 138.

[8] "As a Promotional Tactic, Re-creation Continues to Impress—and Produce Results," *Promotional Sense* 2, no. 4 (Winter 1997), p. 2.

[9] Ernan Roman, *Integrated Direct Marketing* (Lincolnwood, IL: NTC, 1995), p. 46.

[10] Edward Nash, "The Roots of Direct Marketing," *Direct Marketing*, February 1995, pp. 38-40.

[11] Peter Lewis, "Pickets Halt Car Dealer's 'Spam,'" *Boulder Daily Camera*, May 9, 1998, p. 5B.

[12] Barton Weitz, Stephen Castleberry, and John Tanner, *Selling* (Burr Ridge, IL: Irwin/McGraw-Hill, 1995), p. 386.

[13] Martin Evertt, "It's No Fluke," *Sales & Marketing Management*, April 1994.

[14] Bill Herr, "Bridging the Gap Between Marketing & Sales," *A&M Review*, April 1996, p. 24.

[15] Jim Obermayer, "Power Plays: Sales Leads Are Why You Exhibit," *Exhibit Show*, Baltimore, MD, October 4-8, 1999.

[16] Susan Breidenbach, "A Great Relationship—CRM Can Bomb Big," *Network World*, September 11, 2000.

[17] Jay and Adam Curry, *The Customer Marketing Method* (New York: Free Press, 2000), p. ix.

[18] Bernard Liautaud with Mark Hammond, *e-Business Intelligence* (New York: McGraw-Hill, 2001), p. 150.

[19] "Promising Long-Term Leads Are Too Often Lost through Impatience," *Promotional Sense* 3, no. 1 (Spring 1998), p. 2.

[20] Andy Cohen, "Sales Strikes Out on Campus," *Sales & Marketing Management*, November 1997, p. 13.

18

Experiential Contact: Events, Sponsorships, and Customer Service

Key Points in This Chapter

1. How do event marketing and sponsorships contribute to IMC?

2. What are the major types of events and sponsorships used in IMC?

3. Why is customer service so important in IMC?

4. What are the strengths and weaknesses of events, sponsorships, and customer service?

Chapter Perspective
Getting Involved with the Brand

With increased commercial message clutter and more brands from which to choose, brands must work harder not only to get the attention of customers and prospects but, more important, to have an impact on their attitudes and behavior. One way to do this is to involve target audiences in a brand experience. We know that people remember little of what they hear, slightly more of what they see, but nearly all of an experience in which they are involved. Therefore, customer involvement in a brand experience can be a valuable part of marketing communication.

The key word here is involvement. One of the principles of teamwork is getting people involved so they feel a part of what's happening, and feel ownership in the results.

This is the basic concept of using events and sponsorships, and maximizing the positive aspects of customer service. All of these activities, if properly designed and managed, can involve customers in a positive and memorable way, sending powerful brand messages. Events and sponsorships can work at any point in the brand decision process. Customer service, however, is primarily focused on that key evaluation step after the decision has been made.

This chapter is divided into two main sections. The first discusses events and sponsorships as "experience builders." The second discusses customer service as a "responsiveness driver."

JEANS FOR GENES
The Children's Medical Research Institute and John Bevins, Sydney, Australia

Recognized internationally for its work in unlocking the mysteries of genetic disorders, the Children's Medical Research Institute (CMRI) is one of Australia's leading research facilities. Based in Sydney, the institute studies the causes of genetic disorders such as spina bifida, Down's syndrome, muscular dystrophy, and childhood cancers. Primarily dependent on donations and grants, the CMRI receives little ongoing government funding.

The John Bevins agency in Sydney agreed to help the CMRI raise public awareness of children's medical research, along with desperately needed funding. The goal was to find an idea that would not only raise funds but also unite the community, engage the media, and generate corporate support and sponsorship. The resulting "Jeans for Genes" campaign not only raised more money than expected, with no media budget, but also won a Gold Medallion from the AME International Award Show. Even more, it touched the lives of all those who became involved.

The Marketing Challenge

Since its inception, the CMRI has relied almost solely on corporate and private donations. There are thousands of registered charities in Australia, all vying for the same charity dollars and equally deserving of funds. Their methods are as varied as their causes. Many charities have established a particular calendar day, or even week, on which to focus their energies. And, unlike the CMRI, some do have an advertising budget.

The CMRI had been engaged in a campaign built around the "Jeans for Genes" theme for several years. Each year had seen successive increases in the level of giving; however, the integrated campaign that began in 1998 and was recognized in the AME award brought the effort a new level of success.

Campaign Strategy

The campaign strategy was to create an event that would raise money and lots of it. Specific elements of the strategy were to:

- Invite all Australians to get involved in the Jeans for Genes Day and feel good about helping children achieve a healthier future.
- Increase the level of emotional attachment to the campaign.

Tracking studies from previous years had measured the level of awareness and recall of CMRI advertising and that of competitors. Using that information as a baseline, the goal of the "Jeans for Genes" campaign was to increase fund-raising by 27 percent over the previous years by broadening the collection base and increasing public awareness of the institute and its work. In addition, the behavioral objectives included:

- Increasing the number of coordinators by 30 percent.
- Increasing the number of schools participating by 23 percent.

- Increasing badge sales through retail outlets.
- Increasing the overall level of media support.

The broad target audience was all Australians, and the intention was to get as many people as possible involved at some level in supporting the "Jeans for Genes" campaign. More specifically, the campaign targeted several specific audiences:

- *The workplace:* Women 18 years and older were targeted to become coordinators. It was felt they would be the group most empathetic to the campaign and willing to assist with organizing and collecting money. Corporations and retail outlets were also contacted to broaden the base for collections and sponsorships.

- *Educational institutions*: Students, teachers, and mothers were targeted because of the nature of the research, which centered on children's health. Schools had been a traditional target of the campaign to organize various fund-raising and informational activities.

- *The media*: As a charity with no media budget, the CMRI had to gain the media gatekeepers' support for both public relations and advertising exposure to reach the general community.

Creative Strategy

Jeans for Genes Day was an event designed to unite Australians and science in the quest for better health for all children. The idea was that on the designated day, all Australians would wear jeans and make a donation. Jeans for Genes thus invited involvement on a wide scale—almost everyone in Australia owns a pair of jeans. The name Jeans for Genes could easily be related to the work of CMRI (genetic research) as well as to every person's daily life.

The Bevins team also saw this as both a brand-building campaign that had to build the idea of a brand (Jeans for Genes) and a direct-response campaign that had to generate giving of time and money. Without widespread support, the appeal would not work, so the campaign had to recruit for the cause as well as recruit participation.

Every piece in the campaign, every brand contact point, had to be true to the idea—the idea of linking the nature of the scientific research with wearing jeans. Bevins wanted people to donate money but also to have fun doing so. It therefore developed a new logo for the "Jeans for Genes" campaign that showed a pair of jeans with its legs intertwined, symbolically linking the jeans with a strand of DNA. The print part of the campaign was built around a simple visual idea that worked without explanation—a visual of a baby wrapped in a pair of jeans like a shawl. The image, aimed at existing and potential mothers but also relevant to the whole community, was carried in all campaign materials, from mailers to posters, kits, letterheads, advertising, and point-of-sale displays (see Exhibit 18–1).

EXHIBIT 18-1

This is one of the posters designed for the CMRI's awareness and fund-raising campaign.

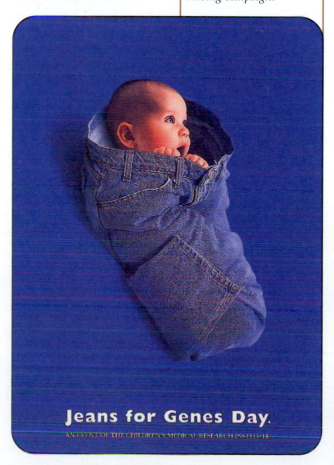

Jeans for Genes Day.

AN EVENT OF THE CHILDREN'S MEDICAL RESEARCH INSTITUTE.

Bevins decided to run the television commercial from the previous year, even though it did not feature the baby visual, because research had indicated strong recall, positive feelings, and support for the campaign. Reusing this commercial also allowed the CMRI to deploy its limited resources elsewhere more effectively.

Bevins's integrated campaign used direct marketing, an Internet site, advertising, and public relations. Following is how each of these MC functions were used to support the main MC function—the event of having everyone wear their jeans on Genes Day.

- *Direct marketing.* The agency sought involvement by corporations (number of workplaces and coordinators), schools, and the jeans industry through mail and phone contacts. Key jeans industry executives were invited to help since the Jeans for Genes Day was heavily promoting their product. There was unanimous support from these stakeholders, who participated with posters and point-of-sale displays. The industry also donated funds from every pair of jeans sold on the Genes Day.

- *Public relations.* In a related event, an auction of jean art contributed by celebrities such as John Travolta, Billy Joel, and Diane Keaton helped intensify public interest. News releases and transparencies of selected celebrity jeans art were distributed to the media, and photo opportunities were arranged with these personalities, football stars, and even the Queensland Premier, in their jeans. Celebrity interviews were also conducted on television talk shows and current-affairs programs.

- *Internet site.* All the auction items were exhibited on an Internet site with information about the CMRI. Site visitors could make bids on the artworks.

- *Advertising.* Public service advertising time and space, donated by the media, are key to the success of such a campaign. The Bevins team approached media representatives to seek their support and advice on how best to present the campaign in public service ads. The agency implemented a multimedia strategy after a successful launch to the media—television, radio, newspapers, and magazines—both metropolitan and regional. Each communication vehicle was invited to participate in the success of the campaign, and all contributed generously.

Evaluation of the Jeans for Genes Campaign

The idea of Jeans for Genes Day, which linked the nature of the cause with the act of wearing jeans and making a donation, was successful in differentiating the campaign and subsequently raising funds for the CMRI beyond the campaign's objectives. The objective was to increase fund-raising by 27 percent; however, the campaign actually generated an increase of 36 percent in funds raised over the previous year.

This case was adapted with permission from the Advertising and Marketing Effectiveness (AME) award-winning campaign created by the John Bevins agency, Australia, for the Children's Medical Research Institute.

EVENTS AND SPONSORSHIPS: THE EXPERIENCE BUILDERS

Tupperware is a direct-to-home marketing company that pioneered the use of an event as a selling tool—the Tupperware in-home party, which is the cornerstone of the company's marketing and distribution. The company has found that Tupperware's sales are driven by lively product demonstrations and a little bit of peer pressure. A Morgan Stanley analyst explained, "People at parties do feel a little bit of an obligation to buy."[1] As successful as that approach has been, it is now threatened by online marketing. Some Tupperware sales representatives have set up their own websites, much to the consternation of the Tupperware managers and other sales representatives, who feel the online sales technique will undercut their famous parties.

Tupperware parties are unique marketing experiences that represent what has become known as experiential marketing. Recall from Chapter 5 a discussion of Joseph Pine and James Gilmore's book *The Experience Economy*. The basic idea is that a brand can differentiate itself by creating an experience around its product. In other words, instead of selling product performance, companies should sell the brand experience.[2]

Chrysler uses this strategy in selling its Jeep Cherokee line of sport utility vehicles. It holds a camp each year in the Rocky Mountains to which Jeep Cherokee owners are invited (at each owner's expense). The purpose of the camp is to teach these owners how to drive off-road, in a safe and exciting way. It also provides owners with an opportunity to meet each other and build a brand community. The camp is an experience, and the experience helps define the brand. As you can imagine, when the campers return home, they are anxious to share their experience with friends and associates, creating "unplanned" brand advocacy messages through word of mouth.

According to Gilmore and Pine, for a brand experience to be successful it must offer enjoyment, knowledge, diversion, and/or beauty. The experience can be passive or active. Passive experiences are those that entertain or provide aesthetic enjoyment, such as visits to museums or demonstrations of a product. Active experiences are ones in which customers participate, such as learning or escaping—the key is a "sensory interaction," such as a "tasting" during a tour of a food or beverage plant.

Event Marketing

Events and sponsorships are designed to create involvement and intensify the experiential dimension of marketing communication. As companies have come to recognize how successful experiences are in bonding customers to a brand, there has been an explosion of **event marketing.** Although events are different from sponsorships, the two overlap because many events are sponsored. Not surprisingly, many of the guidelines are the same for each of these marketing communication functions. Event marketing will be explained first, and then sponsorships.

Event marketing, like the CMRI Jeans for Genes Day described in the chapter opening case, is *a significant situation or promotional happening that has a central focus and captures the attention and involvement of the target audience.* Companies and nonprofit organizations use events for several reasons: to involve target audiences; to associate a brand with a certain activity, lifestyle, or person; to reach hard-to-reach target audiences; to increase brand awareness; and to provide a platform for brand publicity. Embedded within the Jeans for Genes day was another event, a celebrity art auction (see Exhibit 18–2), that extended the reach and memorability of the fund-raising campaign.

Events can have a greater impact than any other MC function (with the exception of personal selling). This is because events are *involving.* An event is more memorable and motivating than passive brand messages, such as advertising, because those attending are participating in and part of the event. Events can also be used to help position or reposition a brand by associating it with a certain activity, such as the Olympics.

Because events have a single focus, they attract special audiences. In most cases, events are selected that reach a brand's current target. In order to reach women jeans wearers, for example, Levi Strauss & Co. sponsored the Sarah McLachlan-conceived Lilith Fair concert with a lineup of women-fronted acts. A second concert series—the Aware Tour—was also designed to build awareness of the brand as well as emerging artists. In addition to the summer concerts, the apparel company took the tours online to its Levi.com website. The focus on women, youth culture, and music is evident in various sections of the site, such as the event-focused "Backstage" and the "Webumentaries," which are cyber documentaries of new artists.[3]

Because events are special by definition, they can and should produce brand publicity and thus help create brand awareness and help keep a brand top-of-mind with its target audiences. Volvo, for example, estimates that its $4 million investment in helping set up and providing prize money for tennis events results in over 1.7 billion consumer impressions, an exposure equivalent to an estimated $24 million in advertising.

Types of Events

There are three primary ways in which companies use events: by creating them, participating in them, and sponsoring them. (Co-sponsored events, like the Olympics, will be explained later in this chapter.)

Created Events

Brand-created events include celebrations or other types of happenings. The SilverStream Software flyer in Exhibit 18–3 announces a seminar for the company's clients and prospective clients; such seminars are another type of created event. Created events are used to leverage the promotional aspects of such things as grand openings, brand or company anniversaries, new-product introductions, and annual meetings. When McDonald's sells a hamburger, it is not an event;

EXHIBIT 18-2

As part of the Jeans for Genes fund-raising event, celebrities donated jeans, which were then used by artists to create a piece of art related to that celebrity. These were then auctioned off.

when it sells its trillionth hamburger, however, an event can be created—which is what brand publicity people get paid for doing.

Each year, Kentucky Fried Chicken, like most franchise companies, has a convention to which all franchisees are invited, which is an example of a BtB event. The objective of the convention is to communicate information to the franchisees— that is, to introduce new products, procedures, cooking and store management processes; to provide a forum for franchisees to network and share ideas; and to enable corporate managers to interact with franchisees in a relaxed, pleasant environment. Most corporate meetings, especially those that involve franchisees (who don't have to attend), are held in "vacation" locations in order to maximize attendance.

While events attract and involve customers and other stakeholders, those who participate often represent only a small percentage of a brand's target audience. To make an event pay out, the company needs to include elements that will be of interest to the media, thus creating brand publicity as well. Grand openings and the introduction of new products are publicity events (see Chapter 14) designed to not only involve customers, prospects, and other stakeholders (e.g, employees, financial community) but also to make the six o'clock news or food pages. The more creative, fun, and exciting an event is, and the more people involved, the more likely it is that the event will generate brand publicity. Baskin-Robbins created an event when it built the world's largest ice-cream cake (5.5 tons) as a tie-in to International Ice Cream Month. Because the cake event was recognized by the *Guinness Book of World Records* and because it attracted hundreds of people, the event generated thousands of dollars worth of brand awareness for Baskin-Robbins (see Exhibit 18–4).

Specialized companies, known as event managers, develop everything from publicity stunts to internal company morale boosters. The Jack Morton Company, for example, which stages all kinds of events for corporations, uses the term *experiential communication* to sum up the many ways companies use live events to involve employees and other stakeholders and deliver corporate messages. When General Motors launched the new Corvette, Morton planned a cross-country "road rally," sending a convoy of 20 brand-new Corvettes along America's historical Route 66, which attracted the attention of Corvette enthusiasts from Chicago to Los Angeles as well as the media.

Event management includes organizing the event and its logistics, staffing it, and marketing it to participants, sponsors, and attendees. And then the event managers have to actually set up and run the event efficiently and safely. In other words, managing an event involves the use of almost every other form of marketing communication—advertising, sales promotion, public relations, and direct response.

Participating Events

Rather than creating an event, companies may choose to participate in an event created by someone else. Examples are trade shows, fairs, and exhibits. State and county fairs provide local businesses an opportunity to demonstrate their products for both consumers and local BtB customers. Most major metro areas also have annual auto, boat, and home and garden shows that attract consumers who are especially interested in these product categories. Companies choose to participate in an event

EXHIBIT 18-3

The SilverStream software company offered a free half-day seminar, which this brochure advertises, to demonstrate how to unify e-business applications that serve up databases, documents, photos, and video.

It was a silver and blue disk that hovered in the sky.

SilverStream

EXHIBIT 18-4

Baskin-Robbins created the world's largest ice-cream cake as a tie-in event for International Ice Cream Month.

according to the type of people it attracts. The more a show's attendees are similar to a brand's target audience, the more sense it makes to participate. Companies rent exhibit space at those types of shows. The larger the space and the larger the anticipated attendance, the more exhibit space costs. The most important participation events for BtB companies are trade shows.

Trade Shows

Trade shows are second only to personal selling as the most-used tool in BtB marketing communication. Pro-Team, a manufacturer of industrial vacuum cleaners, employs a full-time trade-show coordinator because trade shows are the company's number one marketing communication function. A **trade show** is *an event at which customers in a particular industry gather to attend training sessions and visit with suppliers and vendors to review their product offerings and innovations.* Suppliers set up booths at which they demonstrate their products, provide information, answer questions, and take orders. The average industry trade show has 10,000 attendees and includes 400 exhibits. Consumer trade shows, which are used to feature new models and products in such categories as cars, boats, and gardening, will average 45,000–50,000 attendees and 200 exhibits.[4]

Because of the tremendous importance of trade shows in industries like electronics and computers, some companies spend hundreds of thousands of dollars each year planning and staging exhibits. One of the largest trade shows, COMDEX, serves the computer industry (see Exhibit 18–5). More than 200,000 computer professionals, corporate buyers, and influencers from 130 countries attend COMDEX. Another 4,000 media and financial analysts attend, making it the most well-covered information technology event in the world.[5]

A new type of trade show is the private exhibit arranged by one or several suppliers for a client. Five companies in Indiana, for example, grouped together for a private exhibit held at the Indianapolis Chamber of Commerce. Using an Indy 500 theme, the invitations to exhibit were sound cards that, when opened, produced the high-speed roar of Indy cars. At the show, prospects had to visit all five booths to qualify for a grand prize drawing: two Indy 500 tickets. Of those invited, 27 percent responded, and those who attended produced about 100 new and qualified leads for each of the five sponsors.[6]

An extension of a trade-show exhibit is an online display and demonstration that is highlighted by live chat sessions, a "talk-to-the-company-president session," or some other attraction that would be of interest to customers and prospects. Some companies, for example, have offered online corporate seminars that have been successful in creating sales leads.

In planning for a trade-show exhibit, a company must decide what products to feature (there is seldom space or time enough to include all products), who will staff the booth, how to screen and qualify visitors

EXHIBIT 18-5

Booths at trade shows such as COMDEX, below, have become extremely elaborate and interactive.

to the booth, and how to capture names of qualified prospects. Some of the strategies used to maximize booth attendance are (1) sending out personal invitations a couple of weeks before the show, (2) designing a booth that is aesthetically inviting and pleasant to visit, and (3) using "borrowed interest," such as an entertainer, give-aways, or a drawing for a significant prize, to attract visitors. Table 18–1 contains a checklist for companies planning to have an exhibit at a trade show.

Because trade-show participation is a type of brand communication, the booth should be designed in a way that reinforces the brand/company image and positioning. Some high-tech companies, for example, use laser lights and modern electronic music to help reinforce their position as being on the cutting edge of technology.

Trade Show Strengths and Objectives

Companies participate in trade shows primarily to reinforce relationships with current customers and to create qualified leads for new customers. Trade shows provide opportunities to engage customers in personal communication and relationship-building activities, such as seminars and receptions. According to Jim Obermayer, co-author of *Managing Sales Leads*, trade shows are so important as a BtB marketing communication tool because:[7]

- On average, 83 percent of trade-show attendees have not seen a salesperson from their suppliers within the last 12 months.
- Over 80 percent of those who attend trade shows have buying authority or heavily influence brand choices.

T A B L E 1 8 - 1   Checklist for Exhibiting at a Trade Show

Several Months before Trade Show

- Determine measurable objectives for each major show with cross-functional team of sales, marketing, customer service, and trade-show coordinator.
- Design (or update) exhibit booth, making sure it is interactive and that it reinforces brand image.
- Select products and brands that will be displayed in booth, and determine which will be featured (generally the new and/or improved items).
- Select incentive to motivate customers and prospects to visit booth.

Several Weeks before Trade Show

- Determine who will staff booth (normally members of sales and marketing).
- Send out personal invitations to both current customers and prospects.
- Train people who will be staffing booth, showing them how to screen, qualify, and capture contact information of prospects.

After Trade Show

- Have people who staffed the booth fill out an exhibit evaluation form that helps determine what changes need to be made to improve booth productivity.
- Follow up with sales to see which leads have been contacted and how many sales were made.
- Determine the return on investment for the trade show appearance.

- Two-thirds of trade-show attendees plan to make brand buying decisions at the show.
- Trade-show-created leads cost 70 percent less to close than other leads.

Objectives for trade shows, therefore, should state how many customers and prospects the company wants to see and how many leads it wants to turn into sales. Because of the expense of exhibiting at trade shows, companies need to maximize the number of current customers and prospects that visit their booths in order to cost-justify the participation. The value of participating in a trade show can be determined by several measures: the number of customers and prospects who visit the booth, the amount of orders written at the show, the number of qualified leads obtained, and, most important, the number of sales resulting from these contacts.

Sponsorships

Sponsorship is *the financial support of an organization, person, or activity in exchange for brand publicity and association.* Sponsorships are big business, with over $8.7 billion being spent annually by corporate sponsors. Anheuser-Busch, the leader in sponsorships, spent $170 million in 1999.[8]

Sponsorships both differentiate and add value to brands. Nike, for example, sponsors champion golfer Tiger Woods because Woods is well-liked and respected by members of the brand's target audience. The association with Woods helps differentiate Nike from other marketers of sporting goods and also helps increase the status of the Nike brand. If a brand's customers and prospects, for example, enjoy National Association of Stock Car Auto Racing (NASCAR) events, presumably they will like the brands associated with a favorite NASCAR driver.

As you will recall from Chapter 2, one of the elements of a brand is its associations. Sponsorship is one of the primary ways a brand develops associations. The challenge is to find associations that reinforce the desired image of a brand. If the association is inconsistent with the brand's image and other messages, a sponsorship can do more harm than good—customers will be confused about what and who the brand actually is. Determining the consistency of image association is increasingly a two-way street. Groups and events are becoming increasingly selective about accepting sponsors. An example of a sponsorship in which the image is consistent and both parties can benefit is shown in Exhibit 18–6, which announces that clothing manufacturer Tommy Hilfiger will be sponsoring a tour by the rock band Rolling Stones.

Companies can sponsor a variety of things: media programs, events, individuals, teams, sport categories, cultural organizations, good causes, and so on. It's almost impossible to attend any kind of large function today, such as a rock concert or spring-break beach party, without being inundated by brand banners, posters, and samples. A good example is the annual College Fest event in Philadelphia, which attracts up to 10,000 students to its campus convention of music, fashion, games, and social events. During the College Fest, a variety of companies give out free coupons and samples at their exhibits. The following guidelines are used by companies in choosing sponsorships:

1. *Target audience.* The audience for what is being sponsored should have the same profile as the brand's target audience(s) within the geographical areas served by the brand.

EXHIBIT 18-6

Tommy Hilfiger's sponsorship of the Rolling Stones helps position the Hilfiger brand among the desired target audience (those who like the Rolling Stones–type music).

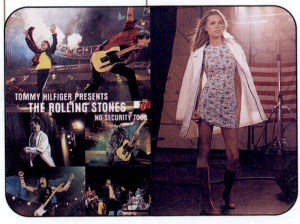

2. *Brand image reinforcement.* Sponsorships should be used in an environment that is consistent with a brand's positioning and image.

3. *Extendability.* The more brand exposure a sponsorship can provide, the more beneficial it can be. If the sponsorship is a multiyear relationship, for example, a company may consider promoting the sponsorship on its packaging, as many of the Olympic sponsors do. One of the main opportunities to look for is brand publicity that extends beyond that directly provided by the event itself.

4. *Brand involvement.* The more privileges a sponsorship provides, the better. Sponsorship of a museum, for example, could include the right to use the museum for a corporate social function, exclusive tours for customers and employees, and invitations to openings of new exhibits.

5. *Cost-effectiveness.* Some sponsorships produce enough brand message exposure that if the cost of the sponsorship were converted to a cost per thousand (CPM), it would be competitive with other media buys.

6. *Other sponsors.* When a company associates with an event or cause, it does so to enhance its own image and positioning. Because some organizations have many sponsors, a company would be wise to know who the other sponsors are. Most companies expect category exclusivity, which means none of its competitors will be a sponsor.

Sports Sponsorships

Although sponsorships cover a wide range of activities, two-thirds of event sponsorship spending is sports related. Sports event marketing accounts for a $7.6 billion investment by U.S. companies. As athletes, sports teams, and leagues at all levels have increasingly recognized the financial benefit of having sponsors—and, in turn, have realized that they can offer added value to brands—companies have found themselves with an increased range of sponsorship opportunities.

The single largest sporting event that attracts sponsors is the Olympic Games. Not only are the Olympics a huge advertising venue, but they also represent a huge sponsorship opportunity. Advertising brings in half of the event's revenue—more than $1.3 billion for the 2000 Games in Sydney—and global sponsorships bring in 21 percent. The lure of the event is its reach; some 3.7 billion people—more than half the world's population—tune in to one or more of the televised games.[9]

There are many ways to affiliate with the Olympics as a sponsor. There are sponsors for teams and sports, as well as countries. For example, one United States Olympic Committee (USOC) sponsor, General Motors, signed an eight-year contract to support the U.S. team and the winter Games in Salt Lake City. This gave General Motors exclusive category advertising rights in the United States through 2008, meaning no other automotive brand could have a similar sponsorship association. On a higher level there are worldwide Olympic sponsors, such as Xerox (see Exhibit 18–7) which pays close to $50 million for sponsorship rights, as described in the Global Focus box.

EXHIBIT 18-7

Xerox is one of The Olympic Partners, a select group of 11 companies whose worldwide advertising is allowed to carry the Olympic rings.

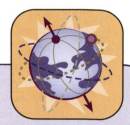

The Olympics Tops the List

On a worldwide level, The Olympic Partners (TOPs) is a group of 11 international corporations that join with the International Olympic Committee (IOC) for periods of four years. They pay an average of $50 million in cash, equipment, and services in order to be a member of the exclusive TOP club. They support the Olympic Movement in exchange for exclusive marketing rights within their categories in every country that is part of the movement, currently 198. The companies that signed on as Worldwide Partner through 2000 are listed below. The URLs are given here so you can check out their use of the Olympic rings on their websites.

Coca-Cola (www.cocacola.com)

John Hancock (www.jhancock.com)

IBM (www.ibm.com)

Kodak (www.kodak.com)

McDonald's (www.mcdonalds.com)

Panasonic (www.mei.co.jp)

Samsung (www.sosimple.com)

Sports Illustrated/Time Inc. (www.pathfinder.com/si)

UPS (www.ups.com)

Visa (www.visa.com)

Xerox (www.xerox.com)

Why bother with an Olympic sponsorship? Companies traditionally capitalize on the natural connection between themselves and the organization—ski manufacturers frequently support World Cup ski events, for example. For the sponsors in the TOP club, most tie into the inherent drama of the Olympic spirit, as well as the worldwide popularity of the event. McDonald's, for example, connects to the good family reputation of the Games, and Coca-Cola celebrates their festive nature (see Exhibit 18-8).

As a marketing vice president for McDonald's USA explains, sponsorship support is linking yourself with identifiable partnerships in a way that makes you more visible to your consumers. He said, "We pick and choose our sponsorships very carefully to fit who we are as a brand. It's come down to a couple of key relationships on a global basis, and the Olympics heads the list."

Does it work? Although some companies have found that they have gotten lost amid the clutter, companies that have the financial wherewithal to properly leverage their Olympic connection believe the investment is worthwhile. The Olympics overall remains a positive, powerful, worldwide movement despite its bits of negative publicity from the Salt Lake City scandal and occasional drug violations. Its sponsors hope some of the gold will rub off, and in most cases it does. One nine-nation study in 1996 found that 93 percent of the 4,500 respondents correctly identified the Olympic rings and that 74 percent associated them with success and high standards. And research has found that these positive feelings are transferable. Another multinational study found that 62 percent of the respondents view Olympic sponsors as modern and innovative and that 59 percent saw them as leaders in their industries. In the United States, these figures were 75 percent and 80 percent, respectively.

When UPS signed on to become one of the 10 worldwide sponsors of the Olympics, it saw that sponsorship as an unusual opportunity to gain global exposure, unify its diverse workforce, establish itself in the Atlanta community, and build long-term business relationships with other Olympic sponsors. In just two years, its research found positive effects in terms of

EXHIBIT 18-8

As this picture of the Olympic Park in Sydney, Australia, during the Olympic Games shows, Coke did an excellent job leveraging its presence at the Games in 2000.

these objectives. Some evidence was particularly compelling, such as a direct-mail promotion that brought in results that were three to four times higher than previous efforts. Another benefit was the impact the sponsorship had on uniting UPS's 38,000 worldwide employees.

Think About It

What are the reasons companies give for becoming an Olympic sponsor? How do such sponsorships work? What is required in order to make an Olympic sponsorship effective?

Source: Skip Rozin, "Why Corporate Support Is Good Business: The Olympic Partnership," *Fortune*, February 2, 1998, special advertising section, p. S2.

But even minor co-sponsorships can be leveraged if a company is willing to spend the extra money. Husqvarna North America (distributor of outdoor power tools), for example, has been a minor sponsor of NASCAR driver Bobby Labonte who is on the Joe Gibbs racing team (see Exhibit 18–9). Although Husqvarna's logo on Labonte's car is one of the smaller ones and is seldom seen by TV audiences or even the fans attending races, the company has benefited in other ways from the sponsorship. One reason Husqvarna chose to sponsor a Joe Gibbs car is that both Husqvarna's North American corporate offices and Joe Gibb's racing headquarters, where the race cars are built and maintained, are in Charlotte, North Carolina. The sponsorship allows Husqvarna to bring its dealers—that is, its current customers—to Gibbs's headquarters to see the cars being made and meet Gibbs and hear him talk about NASCAR racing. At the same time, dealers and prospective dealers are frequently invited to Husqvarna's corporate offices for training on how to better sell and repair Husqvarna products.

Husqvarna's sponsorship also includes using Joe Gibbs as a spokesperson for the company. He makes TV and radio commercials, as well as being used in print collateral materials. One of the popular POP pieces is a life-sized cardboard cutout of Joe Gibbs that dealers can place in their showrooms. To further leverage its NASCAR sponsorship, Husqvarna has an executive suite at Lowe's Motor Speedway, which is also in Charlotte. This provides Husqvarna another way to enrich the visits by dealers and prospective dealers when they are in town on race day.

As the Husqvarna example demonstrates, companies need to spend additional money beyond the sponsorship fee in order to fully leverage a sponsorship. Research has shown that, on average, a sponsor invests approximately two and a half times their sponsorship fee on advertising and promotion designed to make customers aware of the sponsorship and to involve them in some way.

EXHIBIT 18-9

Outdoor power tool manufacturer Husqvarna North America is a minor sponsor of NASCAR car driven by Bobby Labonte. Can you find the Husqvarna brand on Labonte's car?

Cause Marketing

A particular type of sponsorship is **cause marketing,** *a program in which a brand promises to donate money or other types of support to a nonprofit organization or social activity when a customer buys or uses the brand.* Recall from the chapter opening case that cause marketing is what made the CMRI Jeans for Genes campaign work.

An example is the American Express program to feed the homeless, which has donated two cents to homeless food kitchens for each credit card transaction made by its cardholders. The effort was supported by an advertising campaign stating, "Every time you use the American Express Card, you'll help

provide a meal for someone who is hungry." The campaign was estimated to have helped increase AmEx charge-card transactions by 8.4 percent, so in the short term, at least, this was a highly successful promotion. In order to control their financial liability when promising a contribution for each sales transaction, most brands (in small print) state that donations will be made up to a stated amount of money.

When the Internet search engine and navigational portal Lycos found itself struggling to build a brand identity and share-of-mind among many competitors, it used cause marketing. Following an important principle of cause marketing, it selected to help a nonprofit in a way that leveraged and demonstrated its expertise—searching. Lycos agreed to help the National Center for Missing and Exploited Children. The company learned that the most critical period in finding these children is within the first 72 hours of their disappearance. Because of the short lead time required for using the Internet, Lycos developed a system for distributing information and pictures of missing children as soon as their disappearance was reported. Lycos receive positive media coverage for its efforts, and saw an increase in the number of visits to its portal.[10]

Cause marketing has been described as "sales promotion with a PR spin."[11] It is generally short-term and can reflect a "cause du jour" mentality that makes it difficult to build any long-term association between the cause and the company. There is no question, however, that it can have a significant impact on sales. An example of an ad designed to get visibility for discount clothing retailer T. J. Maxx's support of the Save the Children organization is Exhibit 18–10.

Nonprofit organizations are increasingly offering themselves as a "cause" in order to tap into this type of corporate support. A *Promo* magazine special issue on cause marketing contained six pages of causes looking for corporate sponsors.[12] For a cause to be strategically integrated into a marketing communication program, it not only must be consistent with a brand's image but also needs to have a bottom-line payout (just as any promotion should do).

EXHIBIT 18-10

This ad identifies T. J. Maxx as a sponsor of the Save the Children organization.

Mission Marketing

In an IMC program, a more strategic approach than cause marketing is **mission marketing,** *a program that ties an organization's sponsorship efforts to the company's mission.* Recall from Chapter 9 that a mission is a sense of who a company is and what it is striving to accomplish, and it reflects the core values of a company or brand. Examples of mission statements are the following:[13]

- Merck pharmaceutical company: "Preserving and improving human life."
- Johnson & Johnson: "To alleviate pain and disease."
- General Electric: "Improving the quality of life through technology and innovation."

In order for a company to market its mission, it selects sponsorship opportunities that tie the company's mission with a larger public interest and build on the connection for the long term. An example would be furniture company Homestead House's support of Habitat for Humanity. Another example would be the forest products company Weyerhaeuser, which conducted a study of its contributions to find out if the company's philanthropic efforts coincided with its objectives. The result was a decision to make most of the company's contributions focused on the preservation of forests, countering the negative attitude many have about companies that cut down trees for commercial purposes. By focusing in this way, Weyerhaeuser has been able to get more impact from its contributions while, at the same time, becoming fundamentally more environmentally sensitive. It's a classic win–win situation.

While a profit-driven mission speaks to a small group of stakeholders (managers, investors), a socially responsible mission speaks to a much broader set of stakeholders (employees, the community, government, and customers) and gives them reason to support the company. The large retailer Target captures the community connection with its local donations, in particular its support of local community schools. It says that, every week, it gives $1 million back to the communities it serves (see Exhibit 18–11).

Avon's long-time support of breast-cancer research ties that company directly to an issue of concern to its target market—women. It also complements Avon's products—cosmetics. Cosmetics are designed to make women feel better about their physical appearance; reducing the risk of breast cancer helps them feel better about their physical health. This link makes it easier for Avon to gain visibility and credibility from its sponsorship. Likewise, McDonald's sponsorship of the Ronald McDonald House for families of children in hospitals reflects McDonald's tradition of being a family-focused restaurant.

Apple Computer's original mission to be "the computer for the rest of us," for example, unlocked computer literacy for children, as well as millions of people who had no interest in learning programming language. Although Apple had many management problems in the 1990s, it still has a devoted, almost cultlike following of people who believe passionately in the company because of its mission and the products that support that mission.

Companies that have built their business primarily on socially responsible missions include Ben & Jerry's, The Body Shop, and Tom's of Maine. In most cases, these companies do little advertising, instead relying on word-of-mouth reputation cues, brand publicity, and the Internet to advance their businesses. This is true mission marketing because the company's mission, which is to be socially responsible, is an integrative platform, one that drives all of its business practices. Although products from these companies may have high prices or be hard to find, consumers buy them because they believe in the company and its mission.

As The Body Shop found out, however, when a *Business Ethics* article was published questioning the company's environmental sourcing of product ingredients and its relationship with its franchisees, marketing a mission requires adhering to that mission because expectations have been set very high.[14] The Body Shop's website (www.usa.the-body-shop.com) now explains what organizations the company supports and provides links to those and the company's community partners. It combines information about The Body Shop's commitment to the various causes with how this cause relates to its products. By providing links to groups active in these areas, the site also urges visitors to take action. These elements of the company's site have both increased visitors' involvement with the site and provided further exposure and benefit to the company's nonprofit partners.[15]

The Internet has become a great tool to explain in more depth how mission marketing works. Swiss-based pharmaceuticals and agribusiness producer Novartis (owner of CIBA Vision) uses the Internet to give substance to the company's environmental claims. More than just a list of causes that its foundation supports, its website (www.info.novartis.com) features health, safety, and environmental reports, including specific company statistics. The site also features an online roundtable discussion with impartial experts and Novartis personnel that covers social and environmental issues related to the company's business. Novartis uses the Web to provide detailed information and balanced viewpoints, resulting in increased brand credibility.

EXHIBIT 18-11

Target stores use the company's shopping bags to announce the company's support of local communities.

Because of the increasing number of product choices and the similarity of many products, companies are looking for ways to give their brands an edge. Mission marketing is one way of doing that. Craig Smith explained this concept well in a *Harvard Business Review* article: "For the first time, businesses are backing philanthropic initiatives with real corporate muscle. . . They are funding those initiatives not only with philanthropic budgets but also from business units, such as marketing and human resources."[16]

Strengths and Limitations of Events and Sponsorships

Events and sponsorships enhance a company or brand's visibility by associating it with something positive, such as a cause or athletic event. Because of the involvement factor, events and sponsorships are also good relationship-building activities that emotionally bind customers to a company or brand, and they can be used to involve a variety of important stakeholders. Sponsors of major events and organizations, such as auto racing, college bowl games, symphonies, and museums, often receive season tickets or passes and other special privileges for their customers and employees.

As sponsorships have grown (currently at about 5 percent per year), so has the need for some way of measuring their impact. Most sponsorships should offer a 150–200 percent return on the cost of the sponsorship in terms of advertising and promotional opportunities, not to mention the goodwill and relationships that will arise from the affiliation. The Yankelovich agency's Express Lifestyle Tracking is a new service designed to help companies measure and evaluate the impact of sports and entertainment sponsorships. The system works by distributing survey cards to event attendees to capture data about their behavior and attitude following the event.

The biggest limitation of event sponsorships is that, depending on the scope of the event, they tend to directly involve only a small percentage of a brand's target audience. This is why the return on investment of most event sponsorship is determined not by the event itself, but by how well other MC functions leverage the sponsorship. Another problem is the control, or lack thereof, that a company has over the design and management of a sponsored event. This is explained in the Ethics and Issues box.

CUSTOMER SERVICE: THE RESPONSIVENESS DRIVER

Customer service is the seat belt of brand relationships. When a customer has a product question or problem, he or she usually contacts the customer-service department. How well the complaint or question is handled affects to what extent that relationship is injured, lost, or saved. Chapter 4 explained the three types of brand contacts—intrinsic, company-created, and customer-initiated. Customer service is the primary recipient of customer-initiated brand contacts.

Customers don't expect companies to be perfect, but they do expect problems to be corrected quickly. When they are, customers generally stay loyal. Automaker Chrysler had four recalls in the spring of 1994, yet its market share went up, which some observers attributed to the way Chrysler handled the recalls—quickly and honestly.

E T H I C S   A N D   I S S U E S

The Strategic Debates Behind a Sponsorship

When a company is a major sponsor of an event or cause, how much control should the sponsor have over the event or cause? Most organizations make it clear to sponsors that content and programming are off-limits to sponsors. The more financially secure an organization is, the more it can protect its integrity. The problem is subtle, however, with indirect pressures that can influence content or programming.

One community chorale organization makes an interesting example. Like many arts groups, the chorale's financial support came from season-ticket sales and sponsorships. Consequently, when each year's programs were planned, there was always a discussion as to how popular the musical selections for each program would be. On the one hand, the true artists argued for more performances of new works and some of the more complicated (and less popular) classical works. On the other hand, those responsible for paying the chorale's bills argued that if the group failed to play to its audience, there soon wouldn't be an audience. The result was always a compromise in which each group felt it had given in too much.

Another ethical issue concerns which events and causes get supported and which do not. Again, because one of the ways sponsors measure the effectiveness of a given effort is by how many people it reaches, this influences where the money goes. Thus, most sponsors want to be associated with popular events. As one observer found in a study of sponsorship in Great Britain, "Sponsors favor the performing over the visual arts; the known and the familiar over the novel; prestigious, well-established 'big names' amongst theaters, orchestras and galleries; and London over everywhere else."

Think About It

If a company is truly a good corporate citizen, should it want to influence programming and content? Should it only sponsor the most popular events? Since the company is spending its money, and controls all the other brand messages for which it pays, should it have a say in programming and content?

Source: Anthony Beck, "'But Where Can We Find Heineken?' Commercial Sponsorship of the Arts," *Political Quarterly* 61, no. 4 (1990), p. 393.

Certain industries—such as airlines, cable television providers, and utility companies—have a particular problem providing good customer service. As an article in *The Wall Street Journal* lamented, "Customer-service woes are now so pervasive in the telecom business that a cottage industry has sprung up to help customers weed through their bills and services. The [customers simply] do not know who to call for services."[17]

A specific example comes from a column in *Fortune* magazine, in which columnist Stewart Alsop lamented his treatment at the hands of the telecommunications company Sprint PCS. Not only did Alsop's column generate huge negative publicity for the company, but the troubles for Sprint continued in the following issue when letters from other unhappy customers seconded Alsop's concerns.[18]

Customer service is not just a stand-alone department but rather *an ongoing, companywide process that begins with the design of a product and continues through all operations of a company that directly or indirectly affect a customer.* In other words, customer service has both a conceptual and functional

> "I hate Sprint and spend way too much time fantasizing about its demise. I have friends who hate Sprint too, and we talk to one another like members of a support group. Whenever I'm in line at Sprint stores, I feel it is my duty to reach out to and dissuade as many prospective customers as I can."
>
> Letter to the Editor, *Fortune*

meaning. From a conceptual perspective, customer service conveys a helpful attitude that every employee should practice. However, like marketing, customer service is also a function with specific responsibilities. The functional meaning describes the responsibilities of a customer-service department, which means answering customers' questions and dealing with complaints.

The more customer-focused a company is throughout its operation, the fewer demands there will be on a customer-service department. For example, on the functional level, USAA, the giant insurance and financial services company, answers 80 percent of all phone calls within 20 seconds. On the conceptual level, all 16,500 USAA employees are provided the training and technology to do more than one task. A USAA associate selling a customer car insurance, for example, can also help that customer open a bank account.[19]

According to a study of 2,465 consumers by the DDB Worldwide advertising agency, the top five factors that had a "major influence" on customer retention were product quality/performance (96 percent rated this important), a company's method of handling complains (85 percent), the way a company handles a crisis in which it is at fault (73 percent), a challenge by a government agency about the safety of a company's products (60 percent), and an accusation of illegal or unethical trading practices (58 percent).[20] Note that dealing with customer complaints—an important customer-service task—was the second most important factor affecting retention. Companies are paying more attention to customer service these days for a number of reasons:[21]

1. *Competitive advantage:* Customer service offers a way to differentiate brands, although as more competitors improve their customer-service operations, the competitive advantage becomes an even greater challenge to maintain.

2. *Customers demands:* With more brands competing for customers' business, customers can demand more, especially in BtB dealings.

3. *Customer-service expectations:* The promise of good customer service is increasingly promised in brand messages. The more companies raise the expectation of good service, the more customers will demand it from all brands.

4. *Relationship maintenance:* When companies use customer service in a proactive way to maintain contact with customers, it gives customers fewer reasons to go elsewhere.

5. *Increased technological sophistication of product:* As new technology becomes a part of more and more products, customers increasingly need help and advice about using these products.

Customer Service Functions

The customer-service function is not performed the same way in all companies. It varies by size of company, industry, and orientation of business. In packaged-goods companies, such as Kraft and Procter & Gamble, hot lines are created primarily to handle consumer questions. High-tech companies have hot lines to provide instruction on the use of their products, as well as provide information. In small BtB companies, customer service may be the responsibility of sales or even product managers. In large BtB companies, sales representatives interact with customers before a purchase and customer-service representatives interact with them after the purchase—which creates a need for a cross-functional structure to keep communication consistent.

Complaints and Compliments

The Research Institute of America did a study for the White House Office of Consumer Affairs and found that 96.7 percent of those dissatisfied with a product or company don't complain to the company. However, 90 percent of these people do not buy again from that company. The study also found that dissatisfied customers talked, on the average, to nine other people about their negative brand experience. Thus, companies must find ways to encourage unhappy customers to contact the company rather than walk away.

British Airways (BA) found that half of its customers who had a problem with the airline, and did not let BA know they were dissatisfied, changed to another airline. However, of those who had a problem and discussed it with BA, 87 percent continued as customers.[22] The point is that a good customer-service department can generally keep customers from defecting if it has the opportunity to talk to them. The Target "Guest Comment Card" in Exhibit 18–12 is an example of how one company elicits this response.

Regaining the loyalty of an unhappy customer can sometimes actually result in a stronger brand relationship than existed before a customer had a problem. When the recovery process is properly handled, it is similar to a person getting a cut and ending up with scar tissue, which is tougher than regular skin. According to J. W. Marriott, chief executive officer of the Marriott hotel chain, "Sometimes those customers who you make that extra effort to gain back become the most loyal customers that you have."[23]

Another role of customer service is to provide a way for people to contact a company with suggestions and compliments. A major high-tech manufacturer has found that nearly one-fourth of the calls coming in to its customer-service department contain compliments on the company's products or service. Such information is useful in planning marketing communication strategy since it identifies points of strength and brand advantages that can be leveraged.

Customer Contact

A customer-service department can be proactive as well as reactive. Proactive policies—such as notifying BtB customers about anticipated shortages, product recalls, or other problems—are important in keeping current customers and minimizing their calls to the company. When a company knows it will be late shipping orders, then customers should be contacted and told about the delay.

Customer Feedback

The compliments and complaints described above are one form of customer feedback. A company may also take active steps to gather real-time feedback that can be extremely useful in strategic planning. Starbucks, the coffeeshop chain, uses a survey form with structured

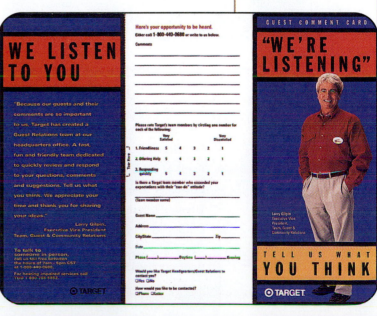

EXHIBIT 18-12

Target is known for its customer-service program that, among other things, takes merchandise back without asking questions. Its sensitive approach to customers can be seen in this comment card, which is prominently displayed at checkout stands in Target stores.

questions (see Exhibit 18–13). As Table 18–2 shows, customer service is the number one source of customer data, other than formal market research.

How Customer Service Works

From an organizational and structural perspective, the customer-service department is often similar to a telemarketing call center. In large companies, customer-service representatives work in a central area, each with a computer and phone headset. Representatives use computers to help answer customer questions, to record complaints, and in some cases to elicit structured feedback for the brand.

Inbound calls are routed to different representatives to maintain a balanced workload. When a call center has extremely sophisticated equipment and can identify incoming calls, however, key customers (e.g., most profitable customers) can be placed at the front of the queue so their wait is minimal and can be routed to the more senior representatives or a personally assigned representative to ensure better handling.

A variation is the Internet customer-service center. A survey of customer-support executives at Fortune 1,000 companies in 1998 found that more than half had Internet customer-service operations, using both the Web and e-mail. Another 25 percent were pilot-testing such operations.[24]

For years, call centers were notorious for using low-paid, untrained employees. Unfortunately, many top managers saw customer service merely as something the company had to have rather than as an opportunity to better manage

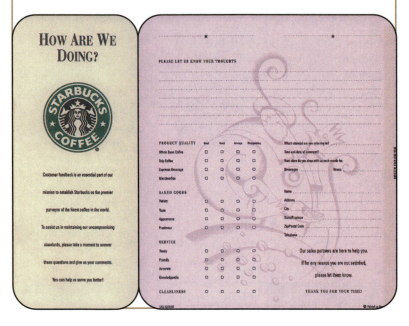

EXHIBIT 18-13

Starbucks makes an effort to elicit customer feedback using a survey form with a postage-paid business reply mailer.

TABLE 18-2 Sources of Customer Information	
Customer-service departments	90%
Salesforce interactions	87
Point of sale	75
Customer user group	64
Inbound telemarketing	53
Outbound telemarketing	52
Other	30
Warranty cards	27

Source: From Ernst & Young's *Marketing Planning Systems* as presented by Robert Wayland and Paul Cole in *Customer Connections* (Harvard Business School Press, 1997), p. 47.

customer relationships. With more emphasis on IMC and relationship marketing, this perspective is changing fast. Not only are companies providing higher salaries and more training to their customer-service representatives, but there is also more interaction between customer service and marketing.

As mentioned above, some companies are expanding customer service to their websites. MessageMedia, an e-mail marketing company, for example, offers a service product called SerivceSuite. This is designed to handle in-bound e-mails, either sorting them by keywords and providing automatic responses or routing those that don't fit into a response category to the proper department. It also provides real-time live chat with customer-service representatives. As Message Media's CEO Larry Jones states, customer service, whether online or handled in the traditional manner, is, from the customers' perspective, part of marketing.[25]

> "In the online world, customers don't see it [marketing and customer service] as two separate entities; they see it as one brand."
>
> Larry Jones, MessageMedia

Characteristics of Good Customer Service

Factors affecting the quality of customer service communication include representatives' accessibility, their product knowledge, attitude and personality, and responsiveness. To ensure that customer-service programs send positive brand messages, companies need to pay attention to these areas.

Accessibility

The challenge for marketing communicators is to encourage and facilitate those who have problems to let the company know. There are several ways companies can make themselves more accessible for their customers:

- Provide free phone numbers in all planned messages (e.g., ads, invoices, on packages, and in service manuals).
- Provide multiple ways for the company to be reached. In addition to a toll-free number, also provide a mailing address, fax number, and e-mail address.
- Train customer-contact employees how to handle and process complaints.

A major challenge for most customer-service departments is having enough staff during peak demand. The company sends a negative message whenever a customer cannot get through to customer service. The more difficult it is to reach the company, the more negative the message. If a company cannot afford to maintain an adequate staff, it can either give customers incentives to call during off-peak hours or provide answering machines that ask customers to leave a message, phone number, and best time to be reached.

Product Knowledge

Knowing how to answer people's questions is an absolutely essential characteristic of good customer service. Representatives need to have a thorough knowledge of the company's product line and how its products work. They must be able to trouble-shoot the product use and identify the points where customers will have questions, which is a particular problem with complex and high-tech products.

This level of knowledgability is acquired through a solid training program. Help-desk staffers should be completely familiar with the products before they hit the marketplace. At Roadrunner Sports, a running and sports-shoe catalog company, customer-service representatives are able to help customers buy shoes by phone because they have been trained in how to size and fit shoes and in how to match the right shoe for the right application, all over the phone.

Attitude and Behavior

People skills are just as important as technical knowledge, which is why those selected for handling customer-service calls need to be upbeat and positive. Because so much of customer service involves complaints from angry customers, representatives can become demoralized or defensive, which is obviously counterproductive. The Walt Disney Company, for example, is known for its courteous, enthusiastic staff (even though it does not pay significantly more than other companies). The company excels at profiling, recruiting, and hiring the types of people who can maintain a consistently positive attitude.

Those who are considered good at customer service have the following personality characteristics: professionalism, positive attitude, flexibility, reliability, ability to listen, and empathy.[26]

Responsiveness

In order for customer-service personnel to be responsive, they must have the authority to handle problems. Such authority is commonly called empowerment. Because there cannot be a rule or policy for every imaginable situation, employees must be trained and trusted to respond based on general, rather than specific, guidelines. Employees must be trusted to decide, for example, when taking a short-term loss will result in increasing and extending the lifetime value of a customer—and to differentiate these situations from customers attempting to take advantage of the company.

Customer-Service Support

Customer-service representatives should have access to customer databases. As explained in Chapter 12, such information enables them to individualize their communication. By bringing up a profile of a customer who has called or e-mailed with a complaint, representatives can quickly see what other interactions the customer has had with the company. Knowing this background allows representatives to "recognize" customers and have a more personal dialogue with them—something that can help defuse an angry customer. Federal Express uses such a system to handle over 250,000 customer phone calls a day.

The right technical support can improve customer service in several ways. It can route a call to the representative or department who has talked to the customer before—simply by scanning a caller's or e-mailer's profile, the computer can automatically identify the last representative who was in touch with the customer. A utility company, for example, can route incoming calls from a business customer to the same company representative who has handled calls from that business number in the past. Such systems eliminate name, address, and phone number recording errors; since customer information has already been recorded in a master file, it doesn't have to be recorded again.

Strengths and Limitations

If a company truly operates with a customer-focused philosophy that is apparent in the corporate culture and the commitment of top management, then all of the advantages of two-way communication can be reinforced on this critical front line. The personal encounters are more persuasive than mass-media marketing communication and can be used to overcome the negative feelings associated with product problems. In other words, the primary strength of customer service is its contribution to the maintenance of a customer relationship after the purchase has been made.

A limitation of customer service is that it is rarely managed as part of a marketing program, so the communication dimensions of the service may not be integrated into the overall marketing communication approach. Furthermore, training people to work in customer service represents a significant expense to the company, especially when turnover in this area is high.

The more complex a product offering, generally the more critical the role of customer service. For example, a company providing airplane parts and repairs for private aircraft will require a more extensive customer-service department and more technical training for the reps than a company making candy bars. Candy bars do not generate a lot of postpurchase questions. Aircraft parts, in contrast involve unique, project-specific, and sometimes unpredictable situations.

A FINAL NOTE: ADDING EXPERIENCE TO A BRAND RELATIONSHIP

Events, sponsorships, and customer service are critical dimensions of relationship marketing—they provide interactivity and the intensity of involvement that comes from having a personal experience. Experiential communication is persuasive because it increases the customer's level of attention, interest, and recall of a brand and company. These positive benefits of participation were at the heart of the highly successful Jeans for Genes program described in the chapter opening case.

As an MC function, experiential contact makes it possible for a company to develop a positive and highly involving brand experience. Furthermore, it offers an opportunity to tightly target an audience. By combining the persuasiveness of personal contact with the involvement of experience-focused communication, the tools described in this chapter can be used to maintain and, more important, grow effective relationships.

Key Terms

event marketing 635
trade show 638
sponsorship 640

cause marketing 643
mission marketing 644
customer service 647

Key Points Summary

Key Point 1: Event Marketing and Sponsorships

Event marketing refers to the strategic use of an event as part of a marketing program to reach a certain audience; sponsorships create a positive association in customers' minds between the event and a sponsoring company that underwrites the expenses of the event.

Key Point 2: Types of Events and Sponsorships

Event marketing includes events that are created by a company or organization and participation events, such as a trade show, in which a company is only one of many participants. Co-sponsored events, such as the Olympics, are promotional opportunities that allow a company to associate its brand with the event. The primary type of sponsorship is sports events. Others types of sponsorships include cause marketing and mission marketing.

Key Point 3: How Customer Service Works

Customer service is both a philosophy of business and a marketing communication function that assumes responsibility for customer satisfaction after the purchase. Customer-service programs are designed to handle complaints, initiate customer contact after the purchase, and elicit customer feedback.

Key Point 4: Strengths and Weaknesses of Events, Sponsorships, and Customer Service

Events and sponsorships are designed to associate the brand with something positive and create brand likability, as well as intensify customer relationships by increasing their customers' level of involvement with the brand. Their primary limitation is that they involve only a small percentage of a brand's target audience. Customer service's strength is its use of personal, two-way communication to maintain customer satisfaction after the purchase; its limitations come from the difficulty of training people to effectively manage the problems encountered in these situations and of coordinating marketing and customer-service programs.

Lessons Learned

Key Point 1: Events and Sponsorships

a.   What is the relationship between event marketing and sponsorships?
b.   Why is event marketing referred to as experiential communication, and how does it differ from marketing communication methods discussed in earlier chapters?
c.   What are the duties most commonly involved in event management?
d.   Check out the websites of three of the companies listed in the Global Focus box on p. 642. Do they use their Olympic sponsorship on their website? Is the sponsorship being effectively used? How would you recommend that these companies better leverage their association with the Olympics on their website?

Key Point 2: Types of Events and Sponsorships

a.   What is the difference between a created event and a participation event? Give an example of each.
b.   What departments or MC functions use events, and what do they hope to accomplish?
c.   What do events contribute to relationship programs?
d.   What is a trade show, who is its target, and what objectives might a company specify for its participation in such an event?
e.   How do sports event sponsorships work, and what are their objectives?
f.   Define cause marketing and mission marketing, and explain the differences between the two.

g.   Find an example of both cause marketing and mission marketing. How effective is each one at building brand relationships?

Key Point 3: Types of Customer Service

a.   Why do we say customer service drives responsiveness?
b.   What are the two meanings of customer service?
c.   Why is training such an important part of an effective customer-service program?
d.   What are the primary characteristics of a good customer-service program?
e.   Have you ever returned a product to a retailer or manufacturer? How was your return handled? What other services did the company's customer-service department offer?
f.   Have you ever called a company's toll-free number with a question about a product or service? How well did the help desk or hot line handle your question?

Key Point 4: Strengths and Limitations

a.   What are the primary strengths and limitations of event marketing and sponsorships?
b.   What are the primary strengths and limitations of customer service?
c.   Develop a set of typical objectives (at least three each) for event marketing, sponsorship, and customer service programs.

Chapter Challenge

Writing Assignment

Choose a local store or manufacturer in your market. Analyze the effectiveness of its experiential-communication programs. In other words, look at how it handles events and sponsorships, customer service, and cybermarketing. In what ways could the company improve its efforts in this area? Write a report to the marketing manager summarizing and explaining your findings.

Presentation Assignment

Based on your findings in the writing assignment given above, develop a relationship marketing plan for the company you chose. Identify the key stakeholders, their contact points with the company, and the messages being delivered at those contact points. What might the company do to better manage these relationships? In particular, how can experiential communication be used to grow the company's business with its customers? Prepare a presentation of the marketing plan for your class.

Internet Assignment

Consult one of the corporate websites listed below and analyze how the company handles customer interactivity. Look specifically for a toll-free phone number or e-mail address. Ask the customer-service representative a common question to find out how long it takes to get an answer and how satisfactory the answer is. Write a memo to your instructor on this company's customer service quality.

www.harley-davidson.com

www.cheerios.com

www.pizzahut.com

www.goodyear.com

www.ual.com (United Airlines)

www.sears.com

www.usmc.mil (Marine Corps)

www.target.com

www.starbucks.com

Additional Readings

Band, William A. *Creating Value for Customers: Designing and Implementing a Total Corporate Strategy*. New York: John Wiley & Sons, 1991.

Brady, Regina; Edward Forrest; and Richard Mizerski. *Cybermarketing: Your Interactive Marketing Consultant*, Lincolnwood IL: NTC, 1997.

Cespedes, Frank V. *Concurrent Marketing: Integrating Product, Sales, and Service.* Boston: Harvard Business School Press, 1995.

Christopher, Martin; Adrian Payne; and David Ballantyne. *Relationship Marketing: Bringing Quality, Customer Service, and Marketing Together*. Oxford, UK: Butterworth-Heinemann, 1991.

Cram, Tony. *The Power of Relationship Marketing; How to Keep Customers for Life*. London: Pitman Publishing, 1994.

Lowenstein, Michael. *Customer Retention: An Integrated Process for Keeping Your Best Customers.* Milwaukee, WI: ASQC Quality Press, 1995.

Newell, Frederick. *The New Rules of Marketing: How to Use One-to-One Relationship Marketing to Be the Leader in Your Industry*. New York: McGraw-Hill, 1997.

Research Assignment

From these books and other books and articles you find in the library, develop a paper on the strategic role of involvement in marketing communication persuasion. Conclude with a list of all of the different ways a company can create and strategically manage participatory experiences for customers and other key stakeholders.

Endnotes

[1] Quoted in Melanie Warner, "Can Tupperware Keep a Lid on the Web?" *Fortune*, January 12, 1998, p. 144.

[2] Joseph Pine II and James Gilmore, *The Experience Economy: Work Is Theatre and Every Business a Stage* (Boston: Harvard Business School Press, 1999).

[3] Bernhard Warner, "Levi.com Buttons Up Lilith Fair Tour Sponsorships," *Brandweek*, April 20, 1988, p. 40.

[4] Melinda Fulmer, "Tricks of the Trade Shows," *Los Angeles Times*, February 19, 1997, D1.

[5] COMDEX press release, January 26, 1998.

[6] "Private Trade Shows," *Promotional Sense* 3, no. 1. (Spring 1998), p. 2.

[7] Jim Obermayer, "Power Play: Sales Leads Are Why You Exhibit," presentation at Exhibitor Show, Baltimore, MD, Fall 1999.

[8] "RepBriefs by the Numbers," *Reputation Management* 6, no. 2. (February 2000), p. 18.

[9] David Sweet, "Bowing to TV, IOC Bars Web Use of Audio, Video from Olympics," *The Wall Street Journal*, August 2, 2000, p. B1.

[10] Stephanie Zschunke, "Cause Marketing: Lost and Found," *Reputation Management*, February 2000, p. 22.

[11] Tom Duncan and Sandra Moriarty, *Driving Brand Value* (New York: McGraw-Hill, 1997), p. 137.

[12] Daniel Shannon, "Doing Well by Doing Good: Special Report on Cause Marketing," *Promo*, February 1996, pp. 29-38.

[13] James Collins and Jerry Porras, *Built to Last* (New York: Harper Business, 1994), p. 69.

[14] Jon Entine, "Shattered Image," *Business Ethics*, September-October 1994, pp. 23-25.

[15] Laima Gaiglalas, "How Mission Marketing Can Help Build Brands," *The Advertiser*, Fall 2000.

[16] Craig Smith, "The New Corporate Philosophy," *Harvard Business Review*, May-June 1994, p. 48.

[17] *The Wall Street Journal*, January 19, 2000, p. B1.

[18] "Alsop to Sprint: Drop Dead," *Fortune*, July 24, 2000, p. 31.

[19] Ronald Henkoff, "Growing Your Company: Five Ways to Do It Right!" *Fortune*, November 25, 1996.

[20] "Consumers Eager to Know Values That Guide Business Decision," *Marketing News*, November 6, 1995, p. 5.

[21]Thomas Knect, Ralf Keszinski, and Felix A. Weber, "Making Profits After the Sale," *McKinsey Quarterly* 4 (1993), pp. 79-86.

[22]Charles Weiser, "Championing the Customer," *Harvard Business Review*, November–December 1995, p. 113.

[23]Christopher Lovelock, *Product Plus: How Product + Service = Competitive Advantage* (New York: McGraw-Hill, 1994), p. 214.

[24]"Serving Customers Online," *Sales & Marketing Management*, June 1998, p. 74.

[25]Quoted in Erika Stutzman, "Online Customer Service," *Boulder Daily Camera*, October 3, 2000, p. B1

[26]Christian Gronroos, *Service Management and Marketing* (Lanham, MD: Lexington Books, 1990), p. 47; and A. Parasuraman, V. A. Zeithaml, and L. L. Berry, "A Conceptual Model of Service Quality and Its Implications for Future Research," *Journal of Marketing*, Fall 1985, p. 47.

Part Five

The Big Picture

This part of the book looks at some of the overriding issues and practices that surround the practice of IMC. Chapter 19 focuses on the social, legal, and ethic issues that affect marketing communication. Chapter 20 looks at international and global marketing, and explores how marketing communication is affected by various cross-cultural practices and issues. Chapter 21 wraps up the book with a discussion of how marketing communication is evaluated in order to determine its effectiveness.

19

Social, Ethical, and Legal Issues

Key Points in This Chapter

1. What ethical issues relate to marketing communication?

2. What legal issues relate to marketing communication?

3. How is regulation managed in marketing communication?

Chapter Perspective
Managing MC with Sensitivity

In a marketplace economy, such as most developed nations have today, it is impossible to separate the social from the economic. In other words, many of the functions of the business world greatly affect society and social well-being and vice versa—what society feels and thinks about business can greatly affect business results.

Marketing communication exists in a socioeconomic environment. Every society and group establishes, to a greater or lesser extent, what is appropriate behavior for its organizations and members. These expectations are communicated in a variety of ways: traditions, public opinion, social and religious standards, professional codes, and government rules and regulations.

Marketing communication, because it is so public by its very nature, is constantly being scrutinized to see if it reinforces or undermines societal values. What makes the social evaluation of MC difficult is that there is no uniform set of values. Different audiences have different standards against which they evaluate MC. Nevertheless, marketing communicators must have a basic understanding of what is and is not acceptable, what is legal and illegal, and what is open to interpretation. This chapter focuses on explaining the issues, standards, guidelines, and regulations that have been put in place by various organizations and government bodies. The chapter's overriding objective is to make you sensitive to the social, ethical, and legal issues that relate to marketing communication and managing brand relationships. The first section looks at marketing communication within a social and economic context; the next section is a discussion of ethics, then an overview of regulatory and legal issues, concerns, and guidelines; the last section is a discussion of responsible professional behavior.

WINNING THE BIG BROTHER MATCH
Glennie Stamnes, Vancouver, British Columbia, Canada

It is difficult to convince people to give their hard-earned money to a charity, but it is even more difficult to inspire them to give some of their precious personal time. And, if your target is young to middle-aged men, it is even tougher still. The volunteer organization Big Brothers of British Columbia depends on these busy men to donate their time to be a father figure and mentor for fatherless boys aged 7 to 12 (see Exhibit 19–1). But the Vancouver-based Big Brothers program had a problem. There was a two-year waiting list of 200 young boys waiting to be matched with a suitable Big Brother.

How would you go about reaching concerned adult males to volunteer their time to this good cause—and do it with a small budget? That was the assignment given to the Glennie Stamnes Strategy agency in Vancouver. This case demonstrates how companies can use marketing communication in support of good causes. It also shows how social marketing can heighten the public's perception of a company. Social responsibility is becoming more and more important as consumers expect more good citizenship from the companies they support.

The Marketing Challenge

Vancouver is a dynamic, affluent city with high rent and housing costs. It is on the leading edge of technology and boasts a vibrant downtown core. It is one of the few cities in the world where you can ski at noon and sail in the evening. Vancouver residents consider themselves lucky in their lifestyles and would be shocked to know that the Big Brothers program was having a tough time finding volunteers.

Big Brothers of British Columbia is a nonprofit organization that operates on a minimal annual budget derived from donations, private fund-raising events, and limited support from the Canadian government and the United Way. Furthermore, in 1997, volunteerism in Canada was declining and all Canadian Big Brothers chapters were experiencing a decline in recruitment. Negative press relating to a local hockey-coach scandal and other molestation-by-mentor stories contributed to the decline as well.

Throughout that time the 40-year-old program consistently advertised—primarily with radio, small print ads, posters, and social events, as well as sporadic, generic television ads developed for the national organization. The advertising won awards but, unfortunately, did not produce incremental results. Traditional advertising, in other words, wasn't delivering the needed volunteers. The Glennie Stamnes team decided to use a strategy that told the story in a new way that appealed to emotions.

Campaign Strategy

The overall marketing objective of the Big Brothers campaign was to expand the market of local volunteers and compel the target audience to pick up the phone and call now. To achieve that end, the campaign was designed to "create a heightened awareness of the 'crisis' situation and get as many quality new Big Brother matches as soon as possible in a short window of time."

The campaign targeted male adults ages 25–54. It also was looking for a particular type of person—men who had inquired before and were aware of what it

EXHIBIT 19-1

Example of one of the new Big Brother brand messages.

BROTHER, CAN YOU SPARE SOME TIME?

876-2447

takes to become a Big Brother. The agency team called them "fence-sitters," believing that if it could effectively communicate the "crisis" situation, then these predisposed men would be surprised at the critical situation and rush to sign up.

Communication Strategy

Historically, Big Brothers marketing communication has taken a "feel-good" approach with scenes of Big and Little Brothers participating in activities together—throwing footballs, walking together in a park, or lying on the grass talking about "guy stuff." Another approach was based on a theme of "It only takes a little time." The Glennie Stamnes team took a 180-degree turn from these warm and fuzzy approaches.

The agency decided to take more of a crisis approach to the situation, much the same way the Red Cross would announce a severe blood shortage. Perhaps children weren't in danger, but the quality of many young lives was at stake. The campaign's big idea explained the problem simply: "Two years is too long." The call to action that signed off each ad was emphatic, earnest, and unique in its reference to Big Brothers: "Be a Brother now."

A television commercial was designed to make viewers feel a little uncomfortable without upsetting them. It showed a young boy in his room killing time and looking restless, listless, and hopeless. The outdoor posters and print ads used dramatic black-and-white portraits of boys with bold headlines across the images, such as: "We want to make two years of his life disappear." (See Exhibit 19–2.)

These executions were tough to sell to a nervous client who worried that the kids might look like easy prey to pedophiles. The agency team argued that the messages had to show hurt and frustration in order to create the expected emotional response from the fence-sitter target audience. The agency felt it couldn't be cautious since the initial two-month launch had to have enough impact to create the momentum to carry it through the rest of the year.

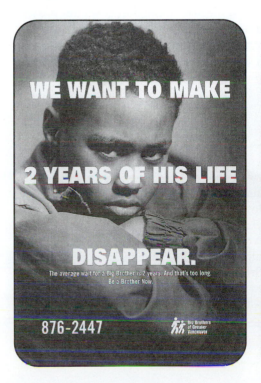

EXHIBIT 19-2

The print ads developed for the Big Brothers campaign were designed to position the Big Brother matchup problem as a crisis.

Media Strategy

Because of the crisis situation and small budget, this campaign was basically a public service effort using donated media space and time. Glennie Stamnes developed the strategy and creative for free, a practice known as *pro bono* work, but there was no point if no one saw the messages. The agency therefore had to also arrange for donations of time, space, and expertise in order to get the campaign seen.

Because of the emotional power required to move people to act, the agency knew television would be a key medium, but it was also the most expensive medium to produce and buy. To get around the problem of budget for buying television time, Glennie Stamnes came up with an innovative approach to public service advertising. A small amount of funding available from Big Brothers was used as seed money, an "honorarium" to motivate the stations to give the Big Brothers special consideration. Five stations were offered $3,333 (total budget of $16,665) and asked to air the television spot immediately in the best and most frequent times they could. The stations rallied around the idea and even continued to air the spot well after the requested two-month push.

Getting the commercial time lined up was important, but another task was getting a production team to donate time and expertise to produce the commercial. Fortunately, it had been a good year for television and movie crews in Vancouver, and many were looking for tax write-offs. The agency found a skilled crew that was happy to work in exchange for a tax slip from Big Brothers, as well as a local film supplier willing to donate film, and a young director who was looking to build up his experience and reputation.

Outdoor advertising was also used to increase the reach of the campaign. A local outdoor advertising firm donated 48 transit shelters—approximately 50 gross rating points daily—during the push. In addition, the company used the poster to fill any unsold periods as well. The transit advertising extended the reach into all areas of the Greater Vancouver region, and the additional frequency from the posters provided reminders throughout the campaign push.

After the initial success, the agency added local newspapers to the media mix to sustain the effort and target outlying suburban areas. Once again, production dollars were tight, but the agency simply reduced the size of the transit shelter posters for use in newspapers instead of creating new print ads—a cost-efficient choice.

Finally, the agency received an offer from Cineplex to film the transit poster and use it as a movie trailer, a short commercial before a featured film. This provided additional frequency and reached an audience that matched the Big Brothers' target profile.

Campaign Effectiveness

The objective was to get the fence-sitters to respond—and respond they did. With the very first ads, the responses from potential volunteers started pouring in. The campaign quickly reversed a four-year downward trend for the local Big Brothers chapter and resulted in an increase of 145 percent in the number of volunteers recruited over the previous year, from 279 volunteers to 683.

Not only did the campaign break all records, but the quality of the men enrolling was significantly higher. Big Brothers caseworkers observed that they had never before seen "such a dedicated and personable group of volunteers." And many of them were in fact the fence-sitters who had previously been in touch with the agency. This is probably the response factor that impressed the client the most.

Within three months, all 200 boys on the list had been matched. Moreover, there was now a waiting list of Big Brothers! The results caught the attention of other Big Brothers chapters across Canada, and the creative has been adapted for use in other markets.

As another indication of success, the tiny local campaign won an AME Gold Medallion for the most effective public service campaign worldwide. The campaign also was a winner of the Canadian "Cassies" national advertising award show.

This case was adapted with permission from the Advertising and Marketing Effectiveness (AME) award-winning brief for Big Brother prepared by the Glennie Stamnes agency in Vancover, B.C., Canada

THE ROLE OF MARKETING COMMUNICATION IN SOCIETY

The Big Brothers effort described in the chapter opening case was a public service campaign that illustrates the power marketing communication can have when used on behalf of a good cause. The Salvation Army ad in Exhibit 19–3 is another example of using the power of advertising to sell a socially responsible behavior. Critics, however, ask whether marketing communication has the same kind of power in creating a materialistic consumer culture.

The goals of an IMC program are to inform, persuade, and listen to all stakeholders. The listening component makes IMC a more socially responsible form of marketing communication than just using advertising or direct marketing. Unfortunately, most companies have been relatively ineffective when it comes to listening. For this reason, there is often a clash between social concerns and business practices on many issues such as the environment, social values, and designed obsolescence. Here is how one marketing communication function—advertising—has been portrayed by one observer:

> Regarded as a form of communication, it [advertising] has been criticized for playing on emotions, simplifying real human situations into stereotypes, exploiting anxieties, and employing techniques of intensive persuasion that amount to manipulation. Many social critics have stated that advertising is essentially concerned with exalting the materialistic virtues of consumption by exploiting achievement drives and emulative anxieties, employing tactics of hidden manipulation, playing on emotions, maximizing appeal and minimizing information, trivializing, eliminating objective considerations, contriving illogical situations, and generally reducing men, women, and children to the role of irrational consumer. Criticism expressed in such a way may be overstated, but it cannot be entirely brushed aside.[1]

For the most part, the criticisms made against advertising can be viewed as criticisms made against all forms of marketing communication because the ultimate goals—to influence buying decisions—is the same for each. Most consumers and social critics do not make a distinction between marketing communication functions when it comes to charges of overcommercialization and encouraging conspicuous

EXHIBIT 19-3

Marketing communication can be used on behalf of socially responsible causes, such as donations to the poor. However, the issue is whether it also spurs people to become too focused on materialism.

SHOP 'TIL YOU DROP.

NEED KNOWS NO SEASON

consumption—to them, *any* brand message that directly or indirectly encourages people to consume is suspect.

For an introduction to this world of criticism, go to www.adbusters.org or consult *Adbusters*, a magazine that comments on the social responsibility of advertising and marketing communication—or the perceived lack thereof. The three parody ads in Exhibit 19–4 are from a collection of *Adbusters* postcards.

EXHIBIT 19-4

Adbusters is a magazine that is critical of advertising and its role in creating a materialistic culture. These parody ads are typical of the critical approach used by the publication to make its points.

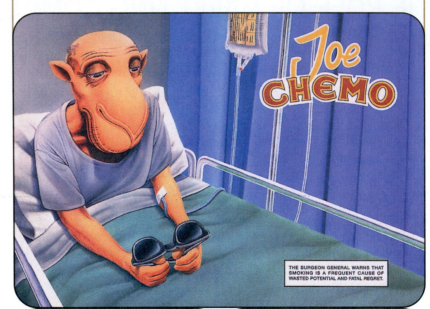

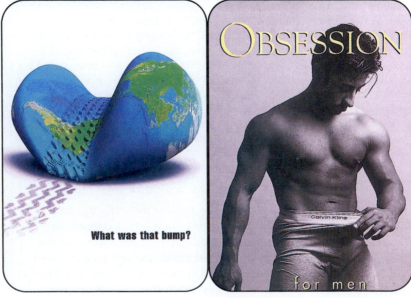

Does MC Mirror or Shape Society?

A decades-old debate concerns the degree of influence that MC has on customers and society as a whole. Critics say that advertising in particular, because of its creative skills and pervasiveness, has created a materialistic culture of conspicuous consumption. Not only are people persuaded to buy specific goods and services they don't want or need, but brand messages also present an idealistic profile of glamorous people, opulent lifestyles, and happiness, which can be had by buying the right brands. In this way, the critics argue, marketers shape how we live. Some brands, however, have recognized the social concern about advertising and have created ads that speak directly to the issue such as the Nike ad in Exhibit 19–5.

Defenders of MC say that marketers are given way too much credit for persuasive power. They note, for example, that of the hundreds of brand messages customers see and hear each day, few are remembered. They point out that 9 out of 10 new product ideas fail, which wouldn't be the case if marketers were as controlling as critics say they are. They also point out that companies spend billions of dollars on research to find out what customers want. If companies could sell anything they wanted to, then why waste money on customer research?

Finally, defenders argue that MC and society are intertwined and that MC is as much a mirror of public opinion as it is a shaper of consumer choices. Environmental issues, for example, became a major social concern in the late 1900s not because environmental responsibility was the subject of a strong MC effort, but rather because of an emerging social consciousness. The ad in Exhibit 19–6 illustrates Shell Oil's attempt to tie in with environmental concerns.

The purpose of MC, its defenders say, is to provide information and to help customers in the brand decision process. They admit that brand messages are designed to be persuasive, but the fact that much effort is made to send these messages only to those interested in the product category demonstrates that marketers know they can convince only a very small portion of the total population to buy. University of Colorado professor Richard Goode-Allen has developed what he calls "adilemmas." The overriding MC adilemmas, he says, are based on the following issues:

- If marketing communication doesn't work, does it mean businesses are wasting the billions of dollars they spend on it each year?
- If it does work, does it mean consumers have no conscious will?

In his forthcoming book, *Marketing Dilemmas*, Goode-Allen says the truth is somewhere in between these extremes and can be found only when people begin thinking differently about MC. On the one hand, critics need to take into consideration that most developed nations are based on a marketplace economy, which requires the production and distribution of goods and services for its existence. On the other hand, marketers must understand that the environment and customers' financial and emotional resources are finite and perishable.

Concerns about Marketing Communication

A survey of 1,000 adults conducted by the University of Illinois Cummings Center for Advertising Studies found that 51 percent of consumers are offended by marketing communication "sometimes or often," that 47 percent believe that most

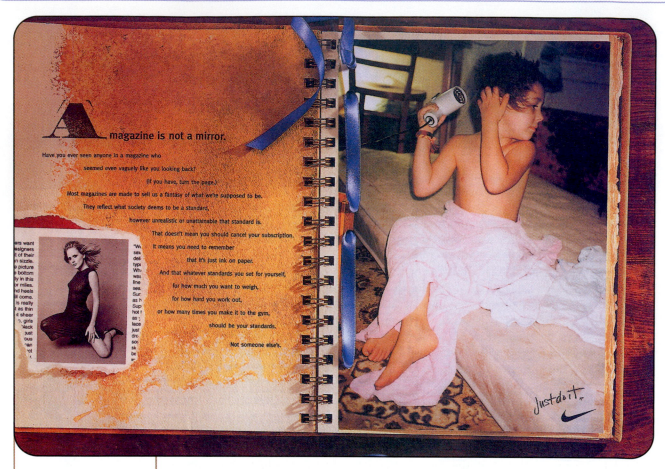

EXHIBIT 19-5

This Nike ad takes on the shape/mirror debate, directly informing the magazine's audience that they should remember it's just ink on paper.

brand messages insult their intelligence, and that 69 percent feel they are occasionally misled by brand messages.[2] The fact that many people have serious misgivings about marketing communication is a result of various perceptions, such as the following:

- It drives up the cost of products.
- It is used to sell inferior products and products that are not good for us.
- It sets unrealistic expectations.
- It is done in bad taste.
- It causes censorship.
- It causes visual pollution.
- It pushes one country's culture onto another.

Each of these is briefly discussed below.

- *Drives up the cost of products.* Some people feel that MC drives up the cost of goods and services because the cost of marketing is included in the cost of products. In other words, customers pay for being sold to. While it's true that as much as 25 percent of the price customers pay for some cosmetics goes to marketing, for most other products marketing costs are a relatively small percentage of the purchase price. In the case of cars, marketing costs generally account for 2 to 4 percent of the purchase price. Marketers also point out that often the cost of MC is more than offset by price reductions that result from MC encouraging competition in the marketplace. Howard

EXHIBIT 19-6

This ad for Shell expresses the company's ideas on profits versus principles in the destruction of rain forests.

Morgens, former president of Procter & Gamble, says, "We believe that advertising [i.e., marketing communication] is the most effective and efficient way to sell to the consumer. If we should ever find better methods of selling our type of products to the consumer, we'll leave advertising and turn to these other methods."[3]

- *Sells inferior products.* Another criticism is that MC encourages people to buy inferior products, which can be especially true of new products. As has been pointed out in this book, however, few companies make a profit by selling to a customer just once. And there is no faster way to kill an inferior brand than to convince many people to buy it, only to have them find out they have wasted their money. Customers don't continue to buy products that don't meet their expectations, which have been set by brand messages.

- *Sells unhealthy, dangerous products.* One issue that continues to be discussed is the appropriateness of promoting products that, though legal, may not be good for us, such as tobacco and alcohol. Antismoking advocates continue to push for bans on tobacco advertising. The compromise has been to reduce the exposure of tobacco brand messages to children, who cannot legally buy the product. Because of pressures from critics, manufacturers of such products often try to adopt a socially responsible spin in their advertising, as the Nike ad (Exhibit 19–5) illustrates.

- *Sets unrealistic expectations.* A relatively new concern over MC is the promotion of products to people who may not be allowed to buy them. Regulations concerning pharmaceutical advertising, for example, have been relaxed in recent years so that drug companies can now advertise prescription drugs directly to consumers. In 1997, *Reader's Digest* received $30 million a year from prescription-drug advertising, approximately one-fifth of its annual ad revenue.[4] Yet health insurance companies are trying to rein in spending on drugs and are not always willing to pay for every prescription that a member requests. So while brand messages encourage consumers to ask their doctors for new medicines, doctors are being encouraged (and sometimes forced) by health insurance companies to limit the number of people who use them. This conflict between what consumers are told will help them and what they have access to can generate anxiety and frustration.

- *Is done in bad taste.* There is an ongoing battle in many countries, including the United States, between those who want to establish standards of taste and morality in society and those who feel that open expression must be allowed and defended, even if this means people are sometimes exposed to things they find offensive. Many are concerned about marketers' use of sex and violence to gain attention and sell brands. Even when brand message content is not offensive to the target audience, it can be offensive to others. The First Amendment to the U.S. Constitution maintains that "Congress shall make no law . . . abridging the freedom of speech, or of the press." Some magazines and newspapers cite the First Amendment when they say they have the right to accept all advertising.[5] These publications often end up with ads for X-rated movies, cheap handguns, and inflammatory political causes.

- *Causes censorship.* Most media, however, strongly protect their right to pick and choose the ads they run. Besides having their own convictions about what messages are proper and not proper, they are also sensitive to all their advertisers as well as their audiences. An offense to either side could result in reduced revenue. When the media reject an ad, however, they are practicing a form of censorship. A few years ago, CNN was criticized for pulling off the air two ads that warned viewers about global warming. Richard Pollock, spokesperson for the Global Climate Information Project, the lobbying organization that paid for the ads, said, "I think this is totally a censorship issue. This is Ted Turner [CNN founder and now vice president of CNN's parent company Time Warner] pulling views that he personally doesn't like. He has decided to act as an information czar." Steve Haworth, a CNN spokesperson, said the decision had been made not by Turner but by the network's standards and practices committee. Haworth said that it was CNN's policy not to run advocacy ads when an issue is receiving intense news coverage. At the time the ads were first allowed on CNN, the topic was not a major issue. They were pulled, he said, when it "became increasingly apparent that our coverage was intensifying."[6]

- *Visual pollution.* Recall from Chapter 11's discussion of out-of-home advertising that some people consider the proliferation of outdoor advertising to be "visual pollution." Zoning laws in many states prohibit billboards in certain areas for aesthetic reasons. In newer commercial shopping strips, retail store signage is often restricted in size.

- *Pushes one country's culture onto another.* One of things every country exports to a certain extent is its culture. The increased attention given in recent years to global focus among businesses has led to an increase in the "export of culture." Some countries perceive the persuasiveness of American culture and American values as a threat. A writer in the *South China Post* recently noted: "Whether it is a case of the French going crazy over Jerry Lewis, the Germans channel surfing for "Baywatch," or Chinese teenagers idolizing Michael Jordan, there is no denying America's role as the supreme exporter of entertainment."[7] (Entertainment is one aspect of culture.)

There have been many examples where countries have sought to keep American culture out. Conservative Islamic countries have barred American television shows and movies. The Chinese have banned direct selling, forcing Avon, Amway, and other American companies to alter the way they do business there. The European Community requires all TV channels to carry at least 50 percent European programming. French officials try to limit the number of American films shown in France; some even called the movie *Jurassic Park* a "threat to [French] national identity."[8] In July 1998, there was a two-day meeting of 22 government ministers from around the world to find ways to counter the spread of American culture. What must be sorted out, however, is whether a country is "protecting" its citizens from "corrupting" outside influences or whether it is limiting choices and dictating tastes.

ETHICS AND MARKETING COMMUNICATION

Every society has certain moral and value standards, called *ethics*, that act as behavioral guidelines for its citizens. The ethics of organizations and individuals within that society are the benchmarks for determining what is right and wrong in different situations. Unlike government laws and regulations, which are specifically stated, ethics are generally not written down but rather held in the social consciousness of an organization or a population. Likewise, ethical behavior is governed only by public attitudes and feelings. Ethics are important in IMC because they provide the basis for the moral choices that individuals and organizations must make in their relationships with each other.

Marketing practices should be guided by an organization's ethics. Marketers should also ask whether brand messages and programs are aligned with the ethics of the brand's stakeholders. If not, stakeholder relationships will be weakened. In addition, unethical brand messages can reflect negatively on the agencies that create them and the media that distribute them.

It is not always easy, however, to establish just what is or is not ethical. For example, various conservative and liberal groups differ on whether corporate policies that provide insurance coverage for same-sex partners are ethical. As you will recall from Chapter 1, everything a company does, and sometimes what it doesn't do, can send a brand message. The types of policies a company sets down for its employees communicate that company's beliefs to its stakeholders and the public at large.

Because ethics are so subjective, some companies simply say that employees must not do anything illegal. In other words, they let the law define their ethics. As you will see in the following discussion, however, ethical issues exist even when a company is law-abiding. Therefore, companies need to discuss ethical issues and set guidelines for individual and corporate behavior. Just as brand messages should be strategically consistent, it is even more critical that corporate behavior be ethically consistent. The cross-functional group responsible for managing brand relationships will have to deal with ethics and should allow for open discussion.

Because ethics are so subjective, the best way to explain them is through example. The following sections present some of the major ethical issues frequently encountered in using marketing communications.

Stereotyping

As our society has become more aware of its diversity, people have become sensitized to cultural, ethnic, gender, and other differences. The challenge for brands is to develop messages that strike a chord with targeted audiences without reinforcing negative stereotypes. Even when using careful planning (e.g., testing copy with focus groups comprised of members from the targeted audience), companies may still alienate some people. For example, Taco Bell's use of a Spanish-speaking Chihuahua in a series of ads was well received by some Latinos but not by others, who were offended that the Mexican in the ad was a dog.

Sometimes advertisers are able to use messages that can be interpreted favorably by different audiences. Volkswagen created a highly popular television commercial in which two young men drove around town in a VW Golf, stopped to pick up an abandoned chair, then stopped again to dump it off because it smelled. While most viewers saw them as Generation X friends or roommates, gay audiences assumed they were a couple.

Advertising to women can be particularly difficult because appealing to one subset may alienate another. Childless women may not identify with messages directed to mothers; women who see themselves as overweight may resent messages directed to fitness buffs. Women are not a monolithic audience and can't be treated as such.

Companies can avoid making some groups uncomfortable or even angry by selecting highly targeted media for their brand message. One-to-one media are often best for sensitive products.

Targeting Vulnerable Groups

As the population as a whole has become more educated about marketing strategies and tactics, there has been increasing concern about messages specifically directed to less educated or sophisticated consumer groups. Some feel companies take "persuasive advantage" of the disadvantaged. Different groups have mounted efforts to ban the promotion of certain types of products from certain media targeted to certain audiences, such as children, minorities, the elderly, and people in developing countries.

Children

Marketing to children has come under question because even the most vigilant parents find it hard to screen all, or even a fraction, of the commercial messages their children see. In general, parents prefer to be the ones to shape their children's buying decisions. But when companies are free to advertise in and around schools, during children's programming on television, at sporting events, on product packaging and point-of-purchase displays, on the Internet, and in movies and at movie theaters, parents cannot possibly be on hand to help their children interpret all of these brand messages. Critics argue that children have neither the intellectual development nor the experience necessary to separate advertising puffery from facts, and that, therefore, they are overly vulnerable to persuasive brand messages.

The more children's tastes appear to be shaped by commercial messages rather than parental influences, the more support there is for regulation. However, groups that want to shield children from commercial messages have found it difficult to collect valid evidence to support their negative views (see the Ethics and Issues box).

Joe Camel and Kids

One of the most visible targets of anti-advertising groups in the last decade was tobacco company R. J. Reynolds' cartoon symbol, Joe Camel. While the company maintained it was not targeting children and teenagers, many antismoking advocates charged otherwise. Critics argued that using a cartoon character was a blatant attempt to influence children and teens favorably toward smoking. In apparent support of their concerns, a 1990 study found that, in the three years following Joe Camel's 1987 introduction in the United States, children's recognition of Camel cigarettes jumped from 0.5 percent to 32.8 percent. Furthermore, the study found that 30 percent of three year olds and 91.3 percent of six year olds recognized the cartoon smoker. The researchers concluded that recognition of Joe Camel was linked to an increase in smoking among teens: "Our data demonstrate that in just three years Camel's Old Joe cartoon character had an astounding influence on children's smoking behavior." Another study showed less dramatic, but still significant, results. According to the U.S. Centers for Disease Control and Prevention's Teenage Attitudes and Practices Survey, only 8.1 percent of U.S. teenagers bought Camels in 1989 but 13.3 percent did so in 1993. By 1991 Camels were the brand of choice among 12- to 17-year-old males and the most named brand among 12 to 13 year olds.

Even so, in 1994, U.S. Federal Trade Commission (FTC) ruled in a 3-2 vote that there was no evidence to link Joe Camel and increased smoking among children. It based its decision, in part, on a poll that indicated that while 95 percent of 10 to 17 year olds could identify Joe Camel as a cigarette logo, 97 percent among them had a negative view of smoking. The committee issued this statement: "If intuition and concern for children's health were a sufficient basis under the law for bringing a case, we have no doubt that a unanimous commission would have taken that action long ago. The issue here, however, was whether the record showed a link between the Joe Camel advertising campaign and increased smoking among children, not whether smoking has an effect on children or whether the health of children is important."

The investigation was reopened in 1996 after the FTC was petitioned by a bipartisan group of 67 members of Congress. The FTC was made aware of internal tobacco industry documents outlining plans to target youth and of more recent studies suggesting that cigarette advertising had more influence on children than peer pressure or parental smoking. One company document said that Camel "must increase its share penetration among the 14-24 age group, which have a new set of more liberal values and which represent tomorrow's cigarette business."

In 1997, the FTC charged R. J. Reynolds with unfair advertising practices. Still, two commissioners disagreed with that decision. Said one of them, Roscoe Starek III, "The issue in this case is whether the Joe Camel advertising campaign causes or is likely to cause children to begin or to continue smoking. As was true three years ago, intuition and concern for children's health are not the equivalent of—and should not be substituted for—evidence sufficient to find reason to believe that there is a causal connection between the Joe Camel advertising campaign and smoking by children."

In defense of using cartoon characters it has been pointed out that Met Life's use of Peanuts characters does not mean the company is attempting to sell life insurance to children. Yet even ad executives have questioned the motives of R. J. Reynolds and other tobacco companies. According to a survey of 300 advertising and marketing executives, 68 percent said that marketing cigarettes to teens who smoke is a goal of tobacco companies, and 59 percent said that marketing cigarettes to teens who do not smoke also is a goal.

In July 1997, R. J. Reynolds announced that it would retire Joe Camel and switch to advertising with more adult themes. Critics charged that the company did this only to avoid giving the FTC the internal documents (including market-share figures regarding underage smokers) the commission had requested.

Think About It

What did R. J. Reynolds do that opened the company up to criticism? Why couldn't the government prohibit the Joe Camel symbol either before or soon after R. J. Reynolds started to use it?

Sources: Joseph R. DiFranza and Joseph B. Type, "Who Profits from Tobacco Sales to Minors?" *Journal of the American Medical Association* 263 (May 23–30, 1990) pp. 3145, 3148, 3149–51; Jacob Sullum, "Cowboys, Camels, and Kids: Does Advertising Turn People into Smokers?" *Reason* 29, no. 11 (April 1998), p. 32; Sheryl Stolberg, "FTC Reveals It Has New Evidence in Joe Camel Case," *Los Angeles Times*, March 27, 1997, p. D1; Dissenting FTC Members: No Evidence against Old Joe," *Advertising Age*, June 2, 1997, p. 44; and Alan Kline, "When Ads Come On, Few Touch That Dial," *Washington Time*, January 6, 1997, p. D17.

The fact that schools are accepting and displaying brand messages in exchange for money, free equipment, and curriculum materials has received strong opposition by some parent groups. A company called rStar (formerly ZapMe) (www.rstar.com) for example, offers not only equipment and Internet access but also teacher aids such as electronic grade books, calendars, and shopping opportunities. This is an Internet application of the original in-school program offered by the Channel One Network, which was described in Chapter 4.

Companies have developed lesson plans and classroom videos that some believe are little more than corporate public relations messages aimed at young audiences. Dow Chemical has prepared an instructional video about the benefits of chemicals and Exxon has one using its 1989 Alaskan oil-spill cleanup as an example of environmental success. Chevron's video on global warming stresses that not all scientists agree that there is a problem.

According to a study by the nonprofit organization the Consumers Union, nearly 80 percent of corporate-sponsored school materials contained "biased or incomplete information [that] favors the company or its economic agenda." The study claimed that these materials are full of "self-interested, incomplete or discriminatory points of view [that] basically teach opinion as if it were fact."[9]

Marketers have learned, however, that if their material is obviously biased, little or none of it will be used. Ron Schmieder, president of the Plastic Bag Association, describes his organization's booklet titled "Don't Let a Good Thing Go to Waste," which is given free to grade school teachers, by saying: "'It's good public relations, plus it takes care of a need. We've tried to give a very balanced view of the solid waste issue."[10]

Minorities

Commercial messages are often targeted to different ethnic groups. Many consumer-products companies have developed Cinco de Mayo–themed promotions for Mexican Americans, for example. But when the products being promoted are perceived to be socially unacceptable, there are concerns about exploitation.

Several years ago, when R. J. Reynolds announced that it would introduce Uptown, a cigarette designed to appeal to black smokers, U.S. Secretary of Health and Human Services Louis Sullivan charged that the company was "cynically" targeting a group already suffering from smoking-related illness.[11]

There was similar criticism when G. Heileman Brewing Company planned to introduce a malt liquor called PowerMaster. Because per capita consumption of malt liquor has traditionally been relatively high in African-American communities, this campaign (and product) drew criticism from anti-alcohol groups and black leaders. They said that the last thing inner-city communities needed was an inexpensive drink with more alcohol. The Beer Institute countered by saying that it was patronizing for community leaders to suggest that blacks and Hispanics need more protection than the population at large.[12]

The Elderly

Consumer affairs offices and reporters are often alerted to questionable sales and marketing tactics specifically directed to the elderly. Some marketers use hard-sell pitches with puzzling details for this target audience (see Exhibit 19–7).

According to Robert Pitofsky, chair of the U.S. Federal Trade Commission (FTC), the elderly are often the targets of telemarketing fraud involving prize promotions, lottery clubs, charity solicitations, and investment offers. Concerned about the problem, the FTC developed the Partnership for Consumer Education to place messages about fraud in catalogs, billing statements, classified advertising, and public transportation to help the elderly be more cautious about responding to these offers.[13]

Developing Countries

Companies looking to expand business beyond current markets sometimes see opportunities in countries where there are fewer trade and product restrictions. Tobacco companies have come under criticism for using advertising in Asia, Eastern Europe, and South America that was long ago banned in the United States and Europe. Free Cigarettes, a Brazilian subsidiary of the international conglomerate British American Tobacco, has used ads that suggest smoking is an appropriate symbol of teenage rebellion. In one, a teen says, "First we go crazy, then we see what happens."[14]

Pharmaceutical companies have been accused of promoting unsafe drugs in developing countries. Studies have shown that advertisements, labels and package inserts often overstate benefits and understate risks in countries where government regulations are lacking or are not consistently enforced.[15]

EXHIBIT 19-7

This is an elderly woman who mistook a direct-mail solicitation from Publishers Clearing House for a notice that she had actually won a $1.1 million prize.

Offensive Brand Messages

To get a feel for different types of commercial messages, imagine a continuum. On one end are the very straightforward, objective, safe messages. If a company goes too far in this direction, it can end up with brand messages that are boring or easily forgotten. On the other end are the attention-grabbing messages. A company that goes too far in this direction can end up with messages that are too controversial and even offensive. Even marketing communication that is within legal bounds may not be ethical or socially acceptable.

As a promotional stunt, for example, a British insurance company sent 77 homing pigeons, each in a cage, to reporters in London to announce a new investment product. The reporters were instructed to release the pigeons and were told the one whose pigeon returned home first would receive a free case of whiskey. Animal rights groups were outraged, and even the Royal Pigeon Racing Association could not understand "why a responsible organization would send live birds to people without asking them first if they wanted them." The public relations firm that thought up the idea responded: "It just goes to show how sensitive some people are. We think that it was an innovative and clever idea."[16]

When talking about offensive advertising, people often point to sex and social taboos as two areas where brand messages often cross over the line.

EXHIBIT 19-8

Sex has been used to sell all kinds of products, including flowers.

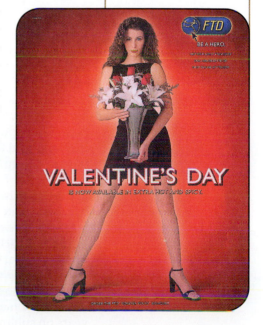

Sex

Sexual images are an attention-grabbing device (see Exhibit 19-8). That is why bikini-clad women have for years appeared in ads for auto parts (and about every other male-targeted product you can think of). But using sexual images that are unrelated to product claims may be a poor creative decision because these images can overpower the primary brand message. Also, with the attention comes scrutiny and possible protests from audiences. The sexual ads that have drawn the most protest are those that exploit women in general as sex objects and those that use underage models in sexually suggestive ways.

However, sexual mores (i.e., moral attitudes) are not the same in all cultures, so it is difficult to develop definitive sexual guidelines. Some ads that are acceptable in European cultures are considered in poor taste in America; likewise, some images that work in New York City would draw protests in Muncie, Indiana.

Taboo Topics

Different segments of the population consider certain products and topics to be inappropriate as the focus of public discussion and, especially, commercial messages. Feminine hygiene products and condoms are two such products. These were not advertised on American television for many years because stations feared the criticism they would get from their other advertisers and audiences.

In recent years, clothing manufacturer Benetton has generated a great deal of attention and publicity by using images widely considered by some people to be shocking and inappropriate: pictures of human hearts, a man dying of AIDS, and a priest kissing a nun. Just as people who buy sexy underwear aren't generally offended by ads for lingerie, people who are very liberal and often anti-establishment aren't offended by Benetton ads. Companies like Benetton are targeting their current customers and likely prospects; they expect these audiences will accept their ads and are thus inclined to ignore objections of other groups (i.e., those who would never buy the product anyway). This can be simplistic reasoning, however, because it overlooks other stakeholders who, as explained earlier in this book, can affect the profits of a company and brand just as much, if not more, than customers. The point is that brands don't have to offend others in order to appeal to their target audience. One of the basic creative challenges for marketing communication is to find a way to talk to and persuade customers and prospects that *doesn't* offend others.

Manipulation Issues

Marketers are expected to influence consumers to purchase goods and services. This influence can take many acceptable forms—product information, pricing, image, and so on. Some individuals and consumer groups suspect that this influence can also take on more insidious forms, akin to mind control and manipulation.

Subliminal advertising is said to contain *messages that are received subconsciously, below a person's perceptual threshold, causing a desired response.* Subliminal advertising became a popular topic in 1957 when a market researcher, James Vicary, claimed he had increased the sales of Coke and popcorn in a movie theater by inserting into the theater's feature film the phrases "Drink Coke" and "Eat popcorn" every five seconds but just for a fraction of a second. Although Vicary's claim caused a major stir in the advertising world, the fact that he refused to disclose the details of his study began to create doubt about the validity of his findings. The marketing community was soon convinced the technique was of no value, and the issue faded.[17]

In the 1970s, interest in subliminal advertising was revisited with the publication of several books by Wilson Bryan Key, including *Subliminal Seduction: Ad Media's Manipulation of a Not So Innocent America.* The books are long on anecdotes but extremely short on empirical evidence. The topic still receives attention occasionally from some researchers and academics; however, a review of research over the years on subliminal messages shows they are not a viable MC tool because there is

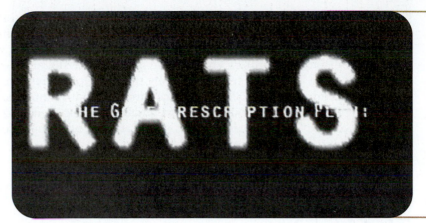

no proof that they work.[18] During the 2000 U.S. presidential campaigns, a TV commercial for Republican George W. Bush reignited the discussion of subliminal advertising. During the commercial, the word *RATS* briefly flashed on the screen when the Democratic Party was being discussed. (The ad's producer said that it was mistakenly left in when a frame containing the word Bureaucrats was cut from the ad.) Although some media stories called it subliminal advertising, the fact that the word was so obvious took it out of the "subliminal" category (see Exhibit 19–9). Nevertheless, the ad was quickly taken off the air.

Even if subliminal advertising worked, any company or MC agency that used it would be running the risk of creating negative publicity for itself. Who would want to buy from a company accused of secretly manipulating, even brainwashing, its customers?

LEGAL ASPECTS OF MARKETING COMMUNICATION

Unfortunately, it isn't enough to use public opinion to determine what is and is not appropriate in marketing communication. Most societies feel that the threat of inappropriate commercial messages is serious enough to warrant establishing laws regulating messages and penalties for those who deviate from the laws.

Several organizations have been set up to monitor commercial messages. They have been called upon to distinguish between acceptable persuasion, questionable sales pitches, and outright fraud. Responses range from tolerating the messages, to recommending changes, to taking legal action. The following sections discuss the types of legal questions marketers face along with examples of how watchdog organizations and government agencies respond to illegal activities.

Puffery

Puffery is *the use of hyperbole or exaggeration to promote a brand.* Calling a product the "best" or the "finest" may be an exaggeration that cannot be proved, but the use of such words is rarely challenged. The Uniform Commercial Code of 1996 maintains that puffery is acceptable unless a buyer can show that such language was intended to be interpreted as a fact or a promise.

Wal-Mart, however, used a tag line that didn't pass the puffery test. Competitors claimed that Wal-Mart's slogan "Always the low price. Always" implied that Wal-Mart had the *lowest* prices of all retailers. The National Advertising Division of the

Council of Better Business Bureau (both involved with industry self-regulation, which will be discussed later) reviewed the ad and deemed it misleading. Wal-Mart lost an appeal and changed its slogan to "Always low prices. Always Wal-Mart."[19]

Another example of puffery crossing the line was the slogan "Better Ingredients, Better Pizza," used for several years by the Papa John's restaurant chain. In 1999, Papa John's used the slogan in a commercial that mentioned competitor Pizza Hut. The issue was brought to court; judges said the mention of Pizza Hut created a "context" and thus the slogan became an indirect comparison that could not be substantiated and therefore was deceptive.

Questionable Business-to-Business Practices

Consumers aren't the only victims of unfair or unethical marketing practices. Sometimes vendors engage in certain practices that penalize either competitors or low-volume customers (e.g., retailers). Recall from Chapter 16 that the Robinson-Patman Act stipulates that any trade allowances granted to a company's wholesalers and retailers must be made available to all of them on an equal and proportional basis. In other words, a manufacturer is not allowed to show preferential treatment among competing groups of retailers. However, some retailers, usually independents and small chains, claim they have been victims of discriminatory practices that favor the largest chains, since the law does allow those who buy more to receive larger allowances.

Recall again from Chapter 16 that retailers often charge slotting allowances—fees a manufacture must pay to get its product on the shelf. Some also charge display fees for certain shelf locations (items sitting at eye level are more likely to sell than those displayed higher or lower). Over the years these allowances and fees have escalated so high that small companies cannot afford them. According to an article in the *Journal of Marketing*, "Currently, two schools of thought dominate the debate on these fees. One considers them a tool for improving distribution efficiency, whereas the other proposes that the fees operate as a mechanism for enhancing market power and damaging competition. Managers and public policymakers are uncertain as to the effects of slotting fees and the appropriate strategy to adopt [regarding their use]."[20]

Fraud

More serious in the universe of bad marketing communication practices than any of the questionable tactics listed above is outright fraud at either the consumer or BtB level. Generally, government agencies aggressively pursue companies that willingly mislead the public while offering no method of consumer recourse. They also are targeted when they have no track record of providing legitimate goods and services. Companies and individuals engaging in fraud face criminal penalties.

REGULATORY METHODS AND AGENCIES

A number of different systems deal with questionable marketing communication messages and practices, including industry self-regulation and government regulation. Table 19–1 lists key consumer-protection websites.

TABLE 19-1   Consumer-Protection Websites

Federal Trade Commission	*www.ftc.gov*
FTC report on Privacy	*www.ftc.gov/reports/privacy3/toc.htm*
OnlinePrivacy Alliance	*www.privacyalliance.org*
Commerce Department	*www.doc.gov*
Center for Media Education	*www.cme.org*
Direct Marketing Association	*www.the-dma.org*
Better Business Bureau	*www.bbb.org*
Center for Democracy and Technology	*www.cdt.org*
Electronic Privacy Information Center	*www.epic.org*
Privacy & American Business	*idt.net/~pab*
TRUSTe	*www.truste.org*
Consumer Affairs	*www.ConsumerAffairs.com*

The consumer affairs site at the end of the list is an independent source of consumer news, advocacy, and assistance. It provides a page for filing a complaint—a consumer incident report. If you fill out this report, Consumer Affairs will then pass your name to legal firms that may contact you about legal actions you might take. Although this is a useful site for consumers, managers should be aware that such sites exist and that there are people monitoring corporate behavior—people who can make life difficult for the company.

Self-Regulation

Most of the oversight within the marketing communication industry is handled through self-regulation rather than by government order. It is in the best interest of responsible businesses and trade organizations to maintain high standards, for several reasons. First, the more they do so, the less government interference there should be. Second, industries have learned from past experience that a few disreputable companies can create suspicion of an entire industry. Finally, the few companies that do not play by the rules have an unfair competitive advantage, at least in the short term. As the following discussion shows, self-regulation occurs at many levels.

Internal Policies

Most companies and the marketing communication agencies they work with have their own professional standards. Every business should have internal guidelines so that employees understand what kinds of messages and behaviors are and are not acceptable.

Although marketers and their MC agency staffs are not expected to be lawyers, they should know enough about the law to call for legal opinion when programs and practices may be close to the legal line. Most medium and large companies have a legal staff. It's always wise to make these people aware of major marketing communication programs, especially anything new and different. More than one person has lost a marketing job for failure to get legal counsel before initiating a program that turned out be illegal, resulting in costly reputation repairs and negative publicity.

MC agencies sometimes refuse to accept work from certain companies, such as tobacco companies. For the work they do accept, the agencies are responsible for verifying any claims made by their clients before using those claims in brand messages. Before being distributed publicly, the messages are usually reviewed by agency lawyers. Also, media companies may demand proof of claims before running brand messages. As mentioned earlier, when a claim is found to be misleading, everyone involved—the company making the claim, the agency that produced the ad, and the media running the ad—can face penalties.

Industry Standards

National trade organizations establish guidelines for their members. For example, the Distilled Spirits Council agreed to keep liquor advertising off radio beginning in 1936 and off TV beginning in 1948. (Recently, though, some liquor companies have started to deviate from that policy.) Doctors and lawyers did not advertise until some members challenged the bans enforced by the American Medical Association and the American Bar Associations.

Several advertising trade organizations (the American Association of Advertising Agencies, the American Advertising Federation, and the Association of National Advertisers) each have their own practice guidelines for their members. More important, they have united to create monitoring groups to deal with questionable advertising practices.

Although many members of trade groups welcome restrictions on marketing tactics as a way to maintain professional standards, some argue that such restrictions are simply a way to preserve the status quo and prevent newcomers from gaining a foothold in the marketplace. And some critics say that the only reason trade organizations develop codes is to head off government regulations. The Better Business Bureau's Children's Advertising Review Unit (CARU), for example, was set up in reaction to public criticisms and government hearings about potential restrictions on advertising to this vulnerable target audience.[21] As it turned out, however, Congress was not satisfied with industry self-regulation and in 1991 passed limits on televised child-oriented advertising. Table 19–2 summarizes the organizations that are involved in industry self-regulation.

Media Review

The magazine and newspaper trade associations have not set forth advertising guidelines for their members; however, individual media chains and local media outlets often set standards for advertising. Newspapers are more likely than other media to keep out ads that they believe their readers and advertisers might find objectionable.[22] A survey of 321 newspapers found that more than 71 percent asked for verification or substantiation of ad claims.[23] This same survey also indicated that, while 40 percent had a written policy outlining the types of ads they would accept or reject, many chose not to give any such explanations for fear of lawsuits. Rather, they inform advertisers that they reserve the right to reject any advertising. A survey of 184 magazines indicated they were most concerned about "good taste," which generally meant rejecting ads with sexual explicitness.[24]

For the most part, radio and television broadcasters have been highly active in self-regulation. As a matter of fact, in one area, the government said that broadcasters went too far. The National Association of Broadcasters (NAB) several decades ago developed a code for television and radio advertising. One of the codes, for example, prevented lingerie commercials from using live models. In

T A B L E   1 9 - 2   Industry Self-Regulation

Organization	Description
The Better Business Bureau (BBB)	This well-known national business organization with local chapters keeps files on violators of good business practices and makes these available to the public. Its BBB Code provides guidelines for ethical and responsible advertising, and its monthly publication, *Do's and Don'ts in Advertising Copy*, alerts subscribers to developments in advertising regulations and recent court rulings.
BBB's Children's Advertising Review Unit (CARU)	This unit of the BBB sets forth voluntary television advertising guidelines for makers of children's products.
National Advertising Review Council (NARC)	This organization was established by the Council of Better Business Bureaus and three different ad groups to promote and enforce standards of trust, accuracy, taste, morality, and social responsibility in advertising.
National Advertising Division (NAD)	This is the division of the NARC that monitors advertising and reviews complaints from consumers, consumer groups, competitors, local BBBs, trade associations, and others. Once presented with a complaint, it investigates the issue and asks for claim substantiation, if warranted. Where necessary, it will recommend that the advertiser change the questionable advertising. If the advertiser disagrees with the recommendation, the case can be appealed to the National Advertising Review Board. Since 1973, the NAD has looked at approximately 34,000 cases. As of 1997, only 25 of the advertisers had not agreed to abide by its decisions.
National Advertising Review Board (NARB)	This is the appeals board for NAD decisions. It becomes involved if the advertiser does not want to comply with the NAD recommendations. The NARB panel's decision is final. If the advertiser still does not want to comply, the case is referred to the appropriate government agency.

Source: Jim Barlow, "Watchdog Keeps Ad Claims in Line," *The Houston Chronicle*, March 6, 1997, p. 1.

1982, the U.S. Justice Department sued the NAB under antitrust laws. Today the major networks use the NAB codes as a guideline only.

Government Oversight

There are many federal agencies that have jurisdiction over one or more aspects of marketing communication. There are so many potential pitfalls in this area that marketers must know the limits of their own expertise and be prepared to consult with people who specialize in keeping up with government rules and regulations. Table 19–3 lists the major federal regulatory agencies in the United States that are involved with marketing communication.

T A B L E   1 9 - 3   Federal Regulatory Agencies Involved with MC

Agency	Description
Federal Trade Commission (FTC)	Charged with monitoring "unfair trade practices," the FCC regulates marketing communication for products sold through interstate commerce.
Federal Communications Commission (FCC)	The FCC oversees the radio, television, telephone, Internet, and telegraph industries.
Food and Drug Administration (FDA)	The FDA oversees labeling, packaging, branding, and advertising of packaged foods, medicine (including package inserts and product advertising), and medical devices. The Nutritional Labeling and Education Act established rules for food labels and the use of such terms as *fat free, low fat, light, reduced calories,* and *natural.*
United States Postal Service (USPS)	The USPS has jurisdiction over advertising and promotional messages sent through the U.S. mail. A staff is maintained to review magazines and other publications for deceptive or misleading advertising. The focus has been on health-related products, sweepstakes and game promotions, and pornography.
Bureau of Alcohol, Tobacco, and Firearms (BATF)	The BATF is a branch of the Treasury Department that oversees alcohol, tobacco, and firearm advertising and beer and wine labeling.
Patent and Trademark Office	This office becomes involved in cases involving unauthorized use of trademarks and logos.
U.S. Department of Agriculture	This cabinet-level department's responsibilities include overseeing meat and poultry labeling, and seed and insecticide advertising.
U.S. Department of Transportation (DOT)	The DOT is a cabinet-level department with responsibilities that include overseeing airline advertising and promotions (e.g., frequent-flyer programs).
U.S. Treasury Department	This cabinet-level department oversees advertising related to currency, coins, and bonds.
U.S. Labor Department	This cabinet-level department oversees advertising related to employers and unions.
Securities and Exchange Commission (SEC)	The SEC regulates marketing communication dealing with securities (e.g., stocks, bonds, mutual funds) and communication to the financial community.
Consumer Products Safety Commission	This government agency can call for corrective advertising for defective products.
Environmental Protection Agency (EPA)	The EPA's responsibilities include defining terms used in "green" advertising and regulating advertising and labeling of lawn care chemicals.

Federal Trade Commission (FTC)

The Federal Trade Commission (FTC), created by and directly responsible to Congress, has five members, who are appointed by the president and confirmed by the

Senate. Since 1914, it has been in charge of dealing with "unfair trade practices," although just what those are has never been fully spelled out.

One area the FTC regulates is marketing communication for products sold through interstate commerce. The FTC considers marketing communication deceptive if the messages mislead "reasonable consumers" to such an extent that their buying decisions are influenced—that is, the customers make a decision as a result of deception or confusion.

When there is a problem, the FTC can take one of several actions:

- *Affirmative disclosure.* The FTC can require a company to provide in its advertising certain information to outline product limitations or conditions.
- *Advertising substantiation.* The FTC can ask a company to show documentation if there are any challenges to the company's use of safety, performance, efficacy, quality, or competitive price claims.
- *Consent and cease-and-desist orders.* The FTC can caution a company about questionable advertising. If the company agrees to stop using the ads, it signs a consent order. If it does not agree, the FTC can issue a cease-and-desist order, which is a demand to stop running the ads in question. Companies not obeying this order are subject to civil suits.
- *Corrective advertising.* The FTC can also require a company to spend a certain percentage of its advertising budget to correct previous false advertising by running brand messages that explain that earlier messages were misleading or false.

In addition to advertising, the FTC has issued guidelines concerning coupons, warranties, and sweepstakes. Companies may not run lotteries, which are considered a form of gambling. One of the tests of a lottery is whether the program requires "consideration," meaning a consumer must buy something to enter. To get around this rule, companies allow customers to enter a sweepstakes by sending in a card on which the brand's name has been written.

State and Local Regulations

Many state and local governments have agencies that oversee marketing communication within their respective geographical jurisdictions. The National Association of Attorneys General has been particularly proactive in recent years, going after large corporations that individuals and even the federal government cannot afford to fight. Attorneys general from 40 states sued the department store chain Sears, for example, for using misleading tactics to secure payments from bankrupt customers. Fifty attorneys general sued Zeneca, a British chemicals manufacturer, because the company was using cash rebates connected to price fixing on farm chemicals.

Foreign Regulations

Each country has its own laws concerning commercial messages and government bodies that enforce such laws. In Puerto Rico, for example, rules for promotions have to be in Spanish as well as English; they have to be printed in at least one general-circulation newspaper once a week during the promotion; and a notary must be present during the drawing for a prize. In France, alcohol and tobacco advertising is prohibited, which is why Budweiser, a sponsor of the 1998 World Cup, was not allowed to advertise at the stadiums where the soccer matches were being held. In Quebec, Canada, labels have to be in both French and English because a major portion of the Quebec population is French speaking.

Issues involving unfair trade practices and advertising, pricing, or trade disputes involving international trading partners are sometimes resolved by the World Trade Organization, based in Geneva, Switzerland.

Another international regulatory organization that governs trade practices among European countries is the European Union. Standards are being set and trade barriers lowered by this government body so that Europe can act as a single continental trading entity, much like the United States. A major area of ongoing debate in the EU, however, regards restrictions on marketing communication.

Companies advertising internationally and on the Internet are also subject to foreign regulations. When Virgin Airlines, a British company, advertised its prices for its fare between Newark, New Jersey, and London, England, it did not disclose that a $38.91 tax would be added. While this may have been legal in Britain, the U.S. Department of Transportation fined Virgin $14,000 for the violation. The point is that each country has its own set of laws and regulations regarding commercial messages, and often they are not the same. (This is discussed in more detail in Chapter 20.)

Consumer Groups

A myriad of special-interest advocacy groups monitor commercial messages related to their causes. They often take their complaints public and organize boycotts when they deem it necessary. Although they have no legal powers, they can cause companies to change their marketing communication practices.

The Center for Science in the Public Interest is a nonprofit group that monitors the food industry. In 1995, it urged the U.S. Food and Drug Administration to revise its food labeling rules. Two examples were cited: General Mills' Berry Berry Kix was deemed mislabeled since the cereal didn't contain any berries and only a minimal amount of fruit products of any kind. The same company's Crispy Wheats 'n Raisins was billed on the package as "lightly sweetened, honey-touched whole wheat flakes and raisins," but the list of ingredients indicated that the cereal was 20 percent sugar by weight.[25]

OBLIGATIONS OF MARKETING COMMUNICATION PROFESSIONALS

Managing the social, ethical, and legal aspects of marketing communication is a complex task. MC managers need a general understanding of what can and cannot be done from a legal perspective, as well as what should and should not be done from an ethical perspective. They also need to know with whom to check for expert advice. In addition, they should have some sense as to what to do when conflicts arise.

Approval Processes

To minimize legal and other challenges to brand messages, every company should have an approval process that involves several message checkpoints. The approval steps vary by company, but in larger organizations, the process often includes the following steps:

1. Review by the marketing staff.
2. Review by the public relations department for perspectives of stakeholders other than customers. Are the messages inconsistent with these audiences' social, moral, and cultural standards?
3. Copy testing, not only for communication and persuasion, but for unintended messages.
4. Review by internal and (in the case of major campaigns) by external legal counsel.
5. Review by MC agency account team and agency lawyers.
6. Review by the media.

Dealing with Corporate Ethics

In order for MC professionals to practice ethical behavior, they must work in an environment where that behavior is encouraged and supported. Unfortunately, not all companies give such encouragement or support—and, too often, companies do the opposite. A company trying to meet certain financial goals may be tempted to cut corners when it comes to testing or labeling ingredients, honoring warranties, and providing the promised after-market service. These companies might also allow (or force) marketing communicators to overpromise in order to increase short-term sales.

All companies should have an ethics statement and new employees should expect to see it. Lack of an ethics policy may be a red flag alerting a new hire of potential problems in the MC program. Like a crisis plan, an ethics statement should be clearly spelled out and discussed. Problems within the company and incidents outside the company should be used as examples to clarify what is expected of employees. Some companies conduct periodic ethics audits to encourage awareness of various issues that the company is either currently facing or might face in the future.

An ethics statement can offer some protection to employees who are being pressured to engage in behavior that they believe is wrong. If such behavior has already been identified as unacceptable, then the employee can point to it as a reason to refuse to cooperate. If an employee is still being pressured to do something that is unethical or illegal, then his or her wisest choice would be to leave the company; to stay with the company would be to risk serious damage to the employee's whole career.

A FINAL NOTE: SOCIAL MARKETING

While there are some social groups that continually criticize marketing communication practices, there are others—such as the Big Brothers of British Columbia—that embrace MC and use it to promote social causes. The same persuasive practices designed to sell products and build brand relationships can be used to help solve social problems. Public relations expert Bill Novelli, who is president of the Campaign for Tobacco-Free Kids, has said, "[Problem-solving] is what marketing does, because it is a process that forges a close relationship among strategies, audience, and behaviors."[26] Recall from Chapter 15 that using marketing to address societal problems is called social marketing.

Social marketing has proved successful in many cases. Thailand dramatically reduced the number of men becoming infected by HIV (the virus that causes

AIDS) by encouraging them to use condoms and reduce their visits to prostitutes. Two years after the government-funded campaign began, the frequency of HIV infection in military recruits had dropped fivefold and the frequency of other sexually transmitted diseases had decreased tenfold.[27]

Social marketing is not without controversy, however. Antidrug campaigns, for example, have been criticized for targeting the wrong problems (e.g., focusing on illegal drugs rather than alcohol abuse); for glamorizing drug use (by combining attractive actors and actresses with violent images); and wasting taxpayer money (by having no effect or, worse, being counterproductive). In 1998, the Congress approved an initial budget of $195 million to be spent on antidrug television, radio, print, billboard, and interactive media. Said Thomas A. Hedrick, vice chairman of the Partnership for a Drug-Free America, "For the first time we will be able to buy the time slots in the best media vehicles, just like Nike or McDonald's or Pepsi does on a regular basis." But, countered Ethan Nadelmann, director of the Lindesmith Center, a drug policy research organization, "For the past 10 years, our nation's kids have been bombarded with anti-drug messages, and it is these same kids who are experimenting with more drugs. While these ads are well intended, this money could be better spent on programs that are proven effective in reducing drug use, such as after-school programs and treatment on demand."[28]

At the very least, social marketing shows that MC is a set of tools that can be used for promoting social issues as well as for selling soap and soft drinks. What is often overlooked is that MC itself is not inherently good or bad; it is only the messenger. When it is used to sell such things as tobacco and alcohol, should the anger and resentment be directed at MC or at the products themselves and the marketers behind them?

Key Terms

subliminal advertising 676   puffery 677

Key Point Summary

Key Point 1: Ethical Issues

Certain standards of right and wrong are applied to commercial messages. Ethical issues include stereotypes, vulnerable groups, offensive messages, and manipulation.

Key Point 2: Legal Issues

Marketing communication's primary legal challenges are in the areas of false, incomplete, misleading, and unfair messages. Questionable tactics include practicing bait-and-switch and burying important details in small print. Competitive challenges come from brand and package infringement and pricing promotions. Fraud is the most serious legal issue.

Key Point 3: Regulation

Most MC industries, companies, and media willingly police themselves for potential ethical lapses so that they can maintain high standards and avoid the involvement of government agencies. There are an exhaustive number of government rules and regulations (at the local, state, national, and international levels) with which marketers must comply. While no one can know all the rules, each MC planner should know which government body's oversight responsibility is important to the brand and when to seek expert advice.

Lessons Learned

Key Point 1: Ethical Behavior

a. How would you define ethics?
b. What are sensitive areas in marketing communication? Do you think MC shapes society or mirrors it? Explain your answer.
c. Find an example of a marketing message that offends you or someone you know. Explain why.
d. Find five examples of cigarette marketing communication and list the messages they appear to be sending and to whom. What ethical concerns do they raise, if any?
e. Find an example of a social marketing campaign and analyze how it relates to various stakeholder groups.

Key Point 2: Legal Issues

a. What is the NAD?
b. How are puffery and fraud different from each other?
c. Find an example of a false or misleading piece of marketing communication and explain why you believe it has problems.
d. How and in what areas do competitors get involved in challenging a brand's communication?

Key Point 3: Regulation

a. What is the primary federal government agency overseeing advertising in the United States?
b. What is the difference between the FTC and the FCC in terms of their oversight responsibilities for marketing communication in the United States?
c. What is the role of your state's attorney general in overseeing marketing communication?
d. You are planning to launch a new soft drink, first in the United States and then in Europe. List as many regulatory agencies as you can that might factor into the launch, and explain their involvement with this launch.

Chapter Challenge

Writing Assignment

You are applying for a job with a large multiproduct, multinational company. Are there any products or services you personally could not promote? What are they and why? You have been asked by this company to state your personal ethics on unacceptable products; write a 500-word essay that explains your position.

Presentation Assignment

You are in charge of developing a direct mail piece to be used locally by the Chevrolet dealer in your town. What information should be in the dealer's database that would be useful to identify the target market? How could you use this information to personalize the message without irritating the prospective customer? Prepare a mock-up of the mailing and present it to your class.

Internet Assignment

Visit Junkbusters.com, Epic.org, Privacycouncil.com, and Webwasher.com to determine what they advise you to do about the social, ethical, and legal issues associated with e-commerce.

Additional Readings

Barone, Michael, and Paul Miniard. "How and When Factural Ad Claims Mislead Consumers." *Journal of Marketing Research*, February 1999, pp. 58–74

Frith, Katherine Toland. *Undressing the Ad: Reading Culture in Advertising*. New York: Peter Lang, 1997.

Liebig, James E. *Merchants of Vision*. San Francisco: Berrett-Koehler, 1994.

Scott, Mary, and Howard Rothman. *Companies with a Conscience*. New York: Citadel Press (Carol Publishing), 1994.

Thomas, Rosamund. "Developing an Ethical Image: Managing Your Reputation via Corporate Branding." *Journal of Brand Management,* January 1999, pp. 198–210

Research Assignment

Consult these and other related books and magazines to identify the key social responsibility issues that affect IMC. (Every issue of *Adbusters* contains stories related to misleading ads and marketing manipulation.) Develop your own personal statement of ethical behavior for yourself as a marketing communication professional.

Endnotes

[1] Sean MacBride, *Many Voices, One World: Communication and Society* (New York: Unipub [UNESCO], 1980).

[2] "Avoid Insulting Women's Intelligence: Give Then Ads that Inform as Well as Entertain," *About Women & Marketing* 10, no. 12 (December 1997), p. 7.

[3] Quoted in David Ogilvy, *Ogilvy on Advertising* (New York: Crown, 1983).

[4] Yuminko Ono, "Magazines Spar with Television over Drug Ads," *The Wall Street Journal,* October 10, 1997, p. B8.

[5] Herbert J. Rotfeld, "Power and Limitations of Media Clearance Practices and Advertising Self-Regulation," *Journal of Public Policy & Marketing* 11, no. 1 (Spring 1992), p. 93.

[6] David Bauder, "CNN Pulls Two Ads on Global Warming," *Boulder Daily Camera,* October 5, 1997, p. 14A.

[7] Simon Beck, "World Gangs Up on US 'culture,'" *South China Morning Post,* July 5, 1998, p. 12.

[8] Tyler Cowen, "French Kiss-Off: How Protectionism Has Hurt French Films," *Reason* 30, no. 3 (July 1998), p. 40.

[9] Jim Drinkard, "Lobbyists Trying to Sway Younger Minds," *USA Today,* June 23, 1998, p. 7A.

[10] Lisa Sarkis Neaville, "Molding Young Minds: Firms Spend Big to Get Views into Public Schools," *Plastics News,* October 30, 1995, p. 1.

[11] James R. Schiffman, "After Uptown, Are Some Niches Out?" *The Wall Street Journal,* January 22, 1990, pp. B1, B8.

[12] Alan Farnham, "Biggest Business Goofs of 1991," *Fortune,* Jnauary 13, 1992, pp. 80–83.

[13] "U.S. FTC: Consumers Lose Billions Annually to Fraud, FTC Chairman Tells Senate Subcommittee," *M2 Presswire,* February 6, 1998.

[14] "Love Is Playing with Fire," *Forbes,* November 3, 1997, p. 39.

[15] David B. Menkes, "Hazardous Drugs in Developing Countries: The Market May Be Healthier Than the People," *British Medical Journal* 315, 7122, (December 13, 1997), p. 1557.

[16] "First Mad Cows, Now Mad about Pigeons," *Inside PR* 2, no. 39 (July 22, 1996).

[17] Cecil Adams, "The Straight Dope," *Chicago Reader,* 1999 <www.chicagoreader.com>.

[18] Joel Saegert, "Why Marketing Should Quit Giving Subliminal Advertising the Benefit of the Doubt," *Psychology and Marketing,* 1987, pp. 107–20; Myron Gable, Henry T. Wilkins, Lynn Harris, and Richard Feinberg, "An Evaluation of Subliminally Embedded Sexual Stimuli in Graphics," *Journal of Advertising* 16, no. 1 (1987), pp. 26–31.

[19] Diane Richard, "Local Advertisers Turn to Arbitration to Resolve Disputes over Ads," *Minneapolis-St. Paul City Business* 15, no. 9 (August 1, 1997), p. 1.

[20]Paul Bloom, Gregory Gundlach, and Joseph Cannon, "Slotting Allowances and Fees: Schools of Thought and the Views of Practicing Managers," *Journal of Marketing*, April 2000, p. 92.

[21]Herbert J. Rotfeld, "Power and Limitations of Media Clearance Practices and Advertising Self-Regulation," *Journal of Public Policy & Marketing* 11, no. 1 (Spring 1992), p. 90.

[22]Steve Pasternack and Sandra H. Utz, "Newspapers' Policies on Rejection of Ads for Products and Services," *Journalism Quarterly* 65 (Fall 1988), pp. 695–701.

[23]Herbert J. Rotfeld, Kathleen T. Lacher, and Michael S. LaTour, "Newspapers' Standards for Acceptable Advertising," *Journal of Advertising Research*, September–October 1996, pp. 37–48.

[24]Herbert J. Rotfeld and Patrick R. Parsons, "Self-Regulation and Magazine Advertising," *Journal of Advertising* 18, no. 4, (Winter 1989) pp. 33–40.

[25]Sheila Calamba, Group Targets 36 Products It Says Have 'Misleading' Labels; Several "General Mills Cereals, Snacks on the List," Minneapolis *Star Tribune*, August 3, 1995, p. 1D.

[26]" Smoking Guns: PR/Marketing's Role in a Healthier America," *PR News* 53, no. 21 (April 21, 1997).

[27]Susan Okie, "Thai Condom Campaign Cuts HIV Infections," *Washington Post*, March 3, 1998, p. Z5.

[28]Courtney Kane, "A Federal Agency Starts a Paid Campaign Today to Influence Young People to Stay Away from Drugs," *New York Times*, July 9, 1998, p. D3.

20

International Marketing Communication

Key Points in This Chapter

1. How is international marketing different from global marketing?

2. How does culture affect marketing communication strategies?

3. How are international markets segmented and targeted?

4. How do marketers plan international message strategies and media plans?

Chapter Perspective
Marketing to the World

Businesses are experiencing phenomenal opportunities to expand internationally. The ease of doing so, however, depends on which countries they choose to enter, what products they are selling, and what methods they choose to build brand relationships.

International marketers face many challenges related to different cultures, languages, and levels of economic development. Adapting brand messages while at the same time maintaining strategic brand consistency requires a delicate balance. Cross-functional planning becomes all the more important when brand messages are being sent across national borders.

Most companies today are "international" even if they don't sell outside their national borders. This is because some or most of their raw materials or equipment comes from other countries. And even if all of their customers and materials are domestic, their competitors may very easily come from other countries. All companies today must therefore consider international issues in analyzing their competitive position.

This chapter distinguishes between international marketing and global marketing. It goes on to discuss cultural factors in international MC, including cultural sensitivity and social responsibility. Segmenting and targeting are special challenges for international marketers, as are message design and delivery.

WHISKAS CREATES A TINY TIGER
BBDO, Düsseldorf, Germany

In the highly competitive cat-food market in the late 1990s, growth rates were nearly zero in most European markets, and all products were seen to perform essentially the same. The Whiskas brand management team at the European office of parent company Mars, Incorporated, decided that the brand needed to differentiate itself, and that the way to do so was to emphasize the emotional core of the brand on which its relationship with consumers was built. It did this by introducing a brand character, a gray tabby called the Tiny Tiger (see Exhibit 20–1).

The Marketing Challenge

Revamping this venerable brand was the challenge given to the Düsseldorf, Germany, office of the international MC agency BBDO. A truly international brand sold worldwide, Whiskas had a 14-country European market. It also had many competitors. In addition to Mars's four other European brands, there were also strong entries from Nestlé and Purina. All these brands were fighting for a share of the market, creating a negative trend in 1997 for Whiskas.

Historically, the differentiating factors in the cat-food segment were health, taste, and nutrition. In the late 1990s, all the brands performed essentially the same on these factors. Whiskas had long been successful with the proposition " Whiskas is the preferred food for cats." However, as the competition improved, the Whiskas brand lost its competitive edge.

Campaign Strategy

The objectives of the Whiskas "Tiny Tiger" campaign were to differentiate the Whiskas brand from the competition, to make cat owners feel they had a role in the feeding choice, and to make owners feel good about spending more money for Whiskas. Regardless of country, the target audience for Whiskas is universal: female cat owners between 19 and 65 years of age who are responsible for buying the cat food.

EXHIBIT 20-1

The small gray tabby cat became the main character of Whiskas new campaign.

Creative Strategy

In terms of the brand strategy, the "Tiny Tiger" campaign was designed to give the Whiskas brand a heart by focusing on the brand's core essence, which is "care" (see Exhibit 20–2). The Whiskas brand needed to reflect the core benefit of well-being—"the best way to care for your cat"— a benefit that is universally appreciated across the diverse European market. This strategy allowed the BBDO team to focus on those attributes that are most motivating in each market and determine the balance between the nutrition and enjoyment appeals. Caring is an emotional strategy, but this approach also allowed a degree of rationality.

The creative concept was stated as follows: "With Whiskas you can take the best care of your cat. You can see it and you can hear it. Every day." The creative tactics brought that idea to life with a satisfied cat on the lap framed in the Whiskas mask and the sound effect of a cat's purring. In addition, the silver tabby cat character, Tiny Tiger, was created as the hero of the campaign. These three integrated elements—the cat visual, the purring, and the silver tabby— became the Whiskas key brand signals. The simple graphics of the print ads were designed to showcase these brand identity elements (see Exhibit 20–3).

Message Delivery

The "Tiny Tiger" campaign used a full range of marketing communication functions:

- Television, radio, print, and outdoor advertising.
- In-store promotions.
- Point-of-purchase activities.
- Direct marketing.
- A sales video and sales folder for the sales team to use with the trade audience.
- Internet activities, including a website in Germany (www.Whiskas.de).
- Licensed materials (a silver tabby stuffed toy).

Message Delivery Strategy

For the advertising, the emphasis was placed on television and, to a lesser extent, print and outdoor. Research determined that cat owners want to see cats in motion, so television provided important visual impact. Print was used in more specialized and targeted publications to reach true cat enthusiasts and communicate detailed information about the product. Outdoor offered a unique way to portray the silver tabby cat in a bigger-than-life medium.

Executing an international campaign is always difficult. In this case, the strategy was to use a standardized format with only a change in language for different markets. Because the creative idea was universal, the

EXHIBIT 20-2

This cover and inside spread from the German Whiskas brochure on kitten care introduces the silver tabby brand character, Tiny Tiger, as a kitten.

BBDO team felt that using standardized messages would provide more useful synergy for the brand than attempting to adapt the creative idea to different cultural groups. However, different executions were found to work better in different markets, so the strategy was localized by matching the best-performing executions to each country.

The agency created 11 television spots to launch the "Tiny Tiger" campaign. The campaign also introduced a new single-serve pouch, a line of kitten food, and a cat treat (pocket kibble). The spot "Purr," for example, which used all three of the key brand signals—the satisfied cat on the lap, the sound effect of the cat purring, and the silver tabby—showed high involvement of the owner and performed well in all markets. To see how the executions were targeted locally, consider two of the spots, "Cat Shuffle" and "Mmmeat," which were found from tests to do particularly well in France. "Cat Shuffle" succeeded in communicating functional benefits (taste and freshness) as well as emotional benefits (well-being), and "Mmmeat," which created the highest level of brand awareness in that market, and focused more on the functional benefits of the best way to care for your cat.

Other Marketing Communication Strategies

In order to reach the loyal Whiskas user effectively, BBDO designed a promotion to generate new addresses in the Whiskas database. In Germany, the agency elicited huge responses with two promotion strategies: a 15-second tag to the "It's in Your Hands" commercial and a "kitten starter pack," which included various products essential in the care of a new kitten. Of those customers who called the company as a result of the promotions, 70 percent were new additions to the database.

Direct marketing was another important part of the MC mix. Whiskas sponsored a quarterly magazine, kitten brochures in stores, and a shop on the Internet site. Other sales promotions included sampling of dry products and kitten products, and in-store promotions for both the can and the new pouch. Packaging was also a part of the mix; a new brand label was created featuring the silver tabby cat, which tied the campaign directly to the product on the store shelf.

Evaluation of the Whiskas Campaign

Total European sales results from January to August 1998 showed a significant turnaround from a negative growth rate and drop in share to a positive growth rate. An even larger increase in growth rate and share was noted in 1999.

The effort was so successful that the campaign was deemed an award winner at the Advertising and Marketing Effectiveness (AME) international award show. More important, it has launched a brand repositioning that has extended beyond Western Europe to other regions such as Poland, Hungary, the Czech Republic, the Baltics, Russia, and the United Kingdom, as well as Brazil and Argentina in South America. Billboards with the silver tabby have also been used in Mexico. And the Tiny Tiger shows up on the new pouch packages in all markets, including the United States. The increasingly widespread use of the brand character shows how a good idea developed in one country (Germany) for a regional market (Europe) can, if successful, evolve into a global theme.

This case was adapted with permission from the Advertising and Marketing Effectiveness (AME) award-winning brief for Whiskas was prepared by the BBDO agency in Düsseldorf, Germany.

EXHIBIT 20-3

This outdoor board with the headline "Makes Your Tiny Tiger Purr" in German and the tag line "Every Day" summarizes the elements of the brand strategy.

DEFINING GLOBAL MARKETING

Most companies market their products in the countries where their headquarters are located. *Companies that focus their marketing* efforts on their home countries are called **national** (or **domestic**) **marketers.** A national market, then, is an individual country—such as Germany, Australia, or Mexico—and a national brand is one that is sold in only one country.

Companies that market products in several different countries are said to be **international marketers.** Most companies engaged in international marketing treat each country as a separate market, and one that is "foreign" from the home country.[1]

Then there are the **global marketers,** *companies that consider their market to be just one—the world.* Generally speaking, brands sold around the world are called global brands. A company involved in global marketing focuses on world market opportunities, not limiting itself to individual countries or regions. This does not mean that global companies have to enter every country in the world; it does mean "widening the company's business horizons to encompass the world when identifying business opportunities."[2] Most companies start locally, expand nationally, move into international marketing, and then, when their brands have proved themselves, become global brands.

Multinationals are a special type of international marketer. They are *companies that have built a corporate network of subsidiaries and affiliates with whom they trade and that engage in international sales in various countries.* They develop market power through the strength of these alliances. Multinationals create their own international markets internally from within the group of affiliates. A more formal definition of a multinational is "a corporation that owns (in whole or in part), controls, and manages income-generating assets in more than one country . . . engaging in international production, sales, and distribution of goods and services across national boundaries."[3] For the multinational, "foreignness" is relatively meaningless since the company is not strongly tied to a home country. The market power of these multinationals generated the protests from consumer activists that arose in 2000 at the World Trade Organization meetings in Seattle and in Prague. The activists were worried about the economic power and social responsibility of these relatively stateless companies, which seemingly answer to no government.

Successful Global Companies

One of the best examples of a global marketer is Coca-Cola, whose products are distributed in more than 195 countries (see Exhibit 20–4). Coke is generally recognized as one of the best-known, strongest brands in the world. Its enviable global position results in part from the company's willingness to work with local distributors and to support local marketing efforts.[4]

McDonald's, a fast-food marketer known for its predictable quality and service, has brought the Golden Arches to more than 110 different countries (see Exhibit 20–5). The secret to its success is its ability to set up a standardized restaurant system anyplace in the world. Moving to a global stage was a

EXHIBIT 20-5

This is an example of a German ad for McDonald's tie-in with the Olympics.

strategic decision for McDonald's after it saw a slowing of growth in the U.S. fast-food industry. By 1997, the number of restaurants outside the United States had reached 23,000 and accounted for 49 percent of McDonald's sales.[5]

Other major international marketers include Germany's Mercedes-Benz (whose corporate parent is Daimler-Chrysler), which is a brand name recognized around the world; Japan's Toyota and Honda, both of which started out exporting cars from Japan, but now have invested in manufacturing in numerous countries. Other important global marketers and their home countries are:

Canada: Campeau.

Finland: Nokia, Marimekko.

France: Cartier, Chanel, Louis Vuitton, Hermes, Christian Dior, Renault, Yves Saint Laurent, Yoplait, Thompson (RCA).

Germany: Mercedes-Benz, BMW, Henkel, Hoechst, Lufthansa, Siemens, Volkswagen, Porsche.

Italy: Benetton, Armani, Ferrari, Gucci, Valentino, Alfa Romeo.

Japan: Bridgestone, Hitachi, Honda, Komatsu, Mitsubishi, Sanyo, Sony, Toshiba, Toyota.

Korea: Daewoo, Hyundai, Kia, Samsung.

Netherlands/United Kingdom: Shell/Royal Dutch, Unilever.

Netherlands: KLM, Philips.

Sweden: Electrolux, Ikea, SAS.

Switzerland: Ciba-Geigy, Nestlé, Novartis, Roche Holding.

United Kingdom: British Airlines, Jaguar, Rolls-Royce, Burberry's, Wedgwood.

THE CULTURAL FACTOR

Culture is a major consideration in targeting customers internationally. The word **culture** refers to *the learned behaviors of a people that come from traditions passed on from generation to generation.* It is manifested in how people dress and what they eat, as well as in their music, religion, and entertainment. Culture also includes values and ways of looking at the world—how people act, think, and respond emotionally. It is the glue that binds a group of people together.[6] The question for MC professionals is: How does culture influence customer behavior in response to brand messages?

When doing international marketing communication planning, companies must assess a country or target group's culture as part of the SWOT analysis. This involves analyzing customers' attitudes and beliefs, motivations, and perceptions as they relate to a product category, the brand, and its usage. A basic principle is that these culturally embedded traits should affect brand message strategies differently in each country.[7]

Since culture and communication are closely related, the cultural factor is important in planning cross-cultural marketing communication strategies and evaluating their effectiveness. The idea is to see whether there are different response patterns for different cultural groups.

Cultural Differences and Similarities

There are debates in marketing about how important cultural differences and similarities are in planning international brand messages. On the one hand are managers who believe that all cultures are different and that, therefore, brand messages should always be customized for the local culture. On the other hand are managers who believe that there are universals, such as love and happiness, that can be the basis for cross-cultural campaigns. And the more specific the target (business travelers, computer users), the more likely that their needs are similar, regardless of country or culture. A Procter & Gamble executive explained the company's approach to the global marketing of its Pampers disposable diapers as follows: "Babies' bottoms are the same everywhere."

In these situations, managers believe that the brand messages can be standardized around the world. Exhibit 20–6 illustrates the commonalities in international banking. The point of the ad is that listening to customers is even more important in international than in domestic marketing communication.

If customer segments are homogeneous between countries and across borders, as in the Whiskas example in the chapter opening case, then, clearly, standardized strategies make sense. If they are not, then there is a need for adaptive strategies. This can create an incredibly complex international marketing program, however, with many opportunities for brand inconsistency—obviously a problem for an IMC manager.

Many marketers believe that the demographic and psychographic segments that cross borders—such as business travelers—respond to brand messages in similar ways. Researchers Sak Onkvisit and John Shaw, however, have found more differences than similarities in consumer responses to marketing efforts. In many product categories, consumer demographics and behavioral responses vary by country. In a review of research studies into cultural differences and similarities, Onkvisit and Shaw concluded: "The evidence is quite overwhelming that consumer/market homogeneity on a global basis does not exist."[8] Some products are definitely "culture bound"—see, for example, Exhibit 20–7, which shows a video game that is especially popular in Asian countries.

When money talks, we know better what's saying.

EXHIBIT 20-6

Even a cliché like "Money talks" transcends cultural boundaries in this international ad, written in English by a Brazilian bank in a Mexican magazine for companies doing business in Mexico.

EXHIBIT 20-7

Each culture has its own special types of entertainment.

An IMC principle is *that the degree of cultural difference is often related to the product category.* Some products, such as medicine, computers, and telecommunication, do not differ much by country, although other products, such as food and fashion, may have significant differences. In the Whiskas case, the brand's managers used research to determine that owning and caring for a cat were fairly universal factors related to this product category.

Researchers John Quelch and Edward Hoff found that consumer products, established products, and products with simple technologies are the most culturally bound, while industrial products and services, new products, and complex new technologies are the least culturally bound. Not surprisingly, business-to-business brand messages from a variety of countries have been found to be relatively unrelated to cultural differences.[9]

Food products are considered difficult to sell globally because of entrenched national eating habits and tastes. Olive oil sells well in the Mediterranean countries, but less well in Scandinavia. Cold cereal with milk is a distinctively North American breakfast, one that has been slow to catch on in Europe and Asia. Even so, many national foods, such as tacos, pita bread, croissants, curry dishes, sushi, gyros, and yogurt have moved around the world to varying degrees.

So what's a manager to believe? Obviously the cultural question complicates the practice of one-voice, one-look strategies. Whiskas campaign managers found that cat owners all want to be seen as caring. Yet they also found differences in how that caring is expressed. Therefore, different brand message executions were used accordingly.

Because of the need to plot cultural differences and similarities, international IMC calls for an even more complex plan for strategic consistency than does national IMC. (This will be discussed in more detail later in this chapter.) As Figure 20–1 illustrates, the question of cultural differences is complex because of different levels of culture. Even within a country, where one might presume there is a great deal of national identity, there still may be different cultures, traditions, and languages, as the breakups in the former Soviet Union and Yugoslavia demonstrated. There are similarities and differences at both the national and regional levels, and these have to be factored in to any message strategy. On a global scale, there are differences in the level of industrialization that may also affect message strategies.

FIGURE 20-1

Cultural differences exist at different levels around the world.

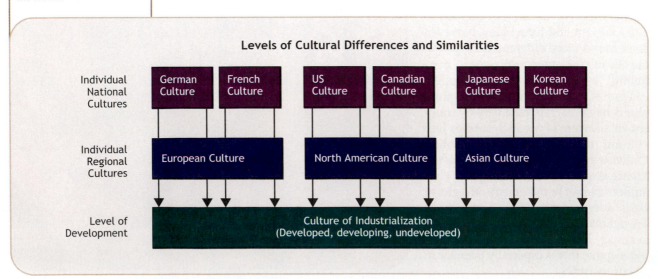

Culture and Values

Culture functions as a lens that determines how the world is seen, and that lens reflects the values of the people within the culture.[10] **Values** are *enduring points of view that a certain way of thinking and behaving is preferable to a different way of thinking and behaving.*[11] Values involve judgments of good or bad, right or wrong. In IMC, it may be an important strategy to link values with a company's mission and understand how culture interacts with brand relationships and a customer-focus philosophy.

Values can affect the way people respond to marketing communication. For example, a study of the differences between Chinese and Hong Kong television commercials found that brand messages in the two markets were characterized by different sets of cultural values. The five cultural values that dominated Chinese ads were "modernity," "family," "tradition," "technology," and "collectivism." The five dominant values in Hong Kong ads were "quality," effectiveness," "economy," "enjoyment," and "modernity." The Chinese commercials used more symbolic values, while the Hong Kong commercials were more utilitarian.[12]

Dimensions of Culture

A number of studies have found similarities and differences in mass media advertising used in different cultures—and that can include cultures within a country, such as the Hispanic or Asian cultures in the United States. Generally, these studies have found that ads in Eastern cultures are more emotional or symbolic, whereas those in Western cultures are more practical, utilitarian, hard-sell, or informative.[13]

High and Low Context

Another way of explaining the differences found in cross-cultural studies is in terms of the cultural context surrounding a message. Edward Hall has classified countries as either high-context or low-context cultures, depending on whether the context—the nonverbal elements surrounding the message—carries meaning and is a significant part of the message.[14] For example, an informational strategy or hard-sell approach in a brand message will probably be more successful in low-context cultures, such as the United States, where people don't rely as much on context to interpret the message as they do in Asian cultures. Dramas and imagery may be more appropriate for high-context cultures, such as Japan and France, where there is more dependence on the context to signal the appropriate message. This distinction can be summarized as follows:

High-context: Cultures that pay close attention to the physical environment in which the message takes place. Relatively little information is found in the explicit message; people in these cultures are more sensitive to nonverbal cues.

Low context: Cultures that rely on the explicit message to carry most of the information. There is relatively less reliance on nonverbal cues.

Hofstede's Dimensions

Another approach used in evaluating international brand messages is to analyze the components of culture as Geert Hofstede has done and use them to develop message strategies. In a study of 50 countries, he identified four basic components of culture as follows:[15]

- Power distance: hierarchical versus egalitarian.
- Uncertainty avoidance: tolerance of risk.
- Collectivism versus individualism.
- Feminine versus masculine.

A study of Korean and U.S. agency executives, based on an analysis of Hofstede's dimensions, found that there were differences in how the two groups viewed ethical questions relating to the practice of advertising. For example, a greater orientation to collectivism, hierarchy, and structure contributes to strong company loyalty in Korea, more so than in U.S. agencies.[16]

But even in Asia, there are differences in cultural responses to marketing communication. For example, researchers have found that advertising appeals in Taiwan and Hong Kong tend to be dominated more by "Westernized" cultural values than by traditional Chinese values.[17] One explanation for this is that Western goods have a certain cachet, especially for people in newly developed countries.

How can an understanding of Hofstede and Hall help in planning IMC? Researchers have found that Hofstede's individualism–collectivism corresponds to Hall's high- and low-context cultures—that is, low-context cultures are individualistic; high-context are collectivist.[18] Further, they have identified high-context, collective societies to be mostly Asian and South American—cultures that value social harmony and selflessness. Low-context, individualistic cultures are mostly European and North American; people in these cultures tend to value self-realization and see themselves as independent, self-contained, autonomous. Such an analysis helps to explain the different brand message strategies used in communicating with people in these countries.

Figure 20–2 adapts Hall's context category and Hofstede's four factors—each one presented as a continuum—to set up a chart for evaluating the cultural dimensions of a target market. This chart assigns countries to opposite ends of the spectrum in order to demonstrate they differ on these dimensions. In planning a campaign, however, MC managers would need to conduct research to plot the actual positions and develop cultural profiles for target groups in different countries.

Cultural dimensions also can be used to analyze organizations and how people work and communicate within them. In China, for example, business interaction is complex. Gareth Chang, head of Star TV, explained that communication in China "takes a formal and an informal interaction, a balance of the two."[19] A basic principle in most Asian countries is that before a business relationship is cemented, such as a client/agency relationship, the people who will be working together must get along socially, as well as professionally. So in these countries, part of the brand relationship building, especially for BtB products, often takes place on golf courses and in restaurants.

Cultural Sensitivity and Social Responsibility

A critical competency for people managing cross-cultural communication is to develop cultural sensitivity. One way to develop good relations with people who are culturally diverse is to develop sensitivity to communication styles and the problems and misunderstandings they can create.[20] Having cultural awareness—a sense of the cultural differences and similarities— is the first step in becoming culturally sensitive. Flexibility is a second important factor in a manager's relationship proficiency. These traits are particularly important when international cross-functional teams are assembled.

Media Sensitivity

Global media are magnifying the sensitivity issue. With the development of huge media conglomerates—such as Sony's entertainment division, Columbia TriStar, Time Warner's TV production units, and News Corp.'s Star TV—American and European popular culture spread all over the world. And then something happened: these conglomerates not only discovered local programming, they discovered that in many cases their audiences preferred local shows. So now Columbia TriStar is producing *Chinese Restaurant*, a series in Mandarin Chinese about a young Chinese woman in Los Angeles. The show is carried by 100 Chinese television stations. Columbia TriStar also has become the owner of Super TV, a Mandarin-language channel that reaches 77 percent of the 5.1 million homes in Taiwan. Other Columbia TriStar production houses are located in India, Latin America, and several Asian cities. Columbia has also set up shop in Germany to go into foreign-language film production in Europe.

Rupert Murdoch's News Corp. bought Hong Kong–based Star TV with the intention of blanketing Asia with English-language channels, a move that backfired. The satellite gave News Corp. a huge footprint in Asia; however, the company soon found that its unwillingness to localize programming was a misstep.[21] Since

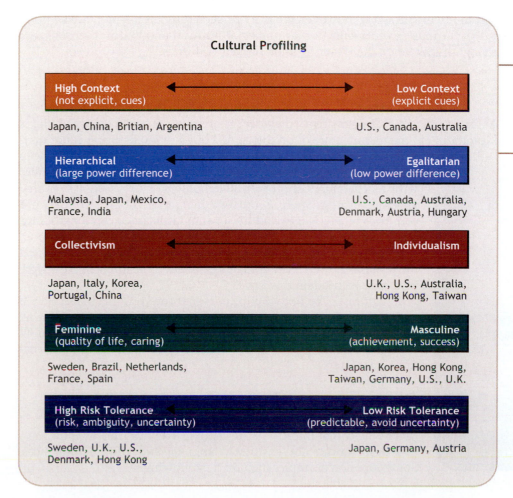

FIGURE 20-2

This chart shows how countries differ on several cultural dimensions.

then, Star's real success story is its Mandarin-language Phoenix channel. In partnership with two Hong Kong companies, Phoenix reaches some 170 million educated upscale viewers in China, including those in Beijing and the prosperous southern city of Guangzhou.

The model for both television and film is the music industry, where the dominant global companies have discovered two revenue streams by delivering international hits as well as local music. What is emerging is a two-tier production system. English is the language of international blockbuster films, TV series, CDs, and advertising, but local language hits are equally as important.

Cultural Imperialism

Another debate that hinges on cultural sensitivity is the issue of **cultural imperialism,** a phrase that refers to *the impact that a more dominant culture has on another less dominant culture.*

The cultural imperialism criticism is based on the notion that American movies, television programs, and especially advertising, all promote materialism and a heightened consumption culture. Brand messages and program content from the United States also violate local taboos, such as those of Muslim countries against showing women in bathing suits and other revealing clothing. Opposition to cultural imperialism has led to bans and restrictions on certain brand messages in come countries. In Malaysia, for example, all television programs and commercials have to be produced in the country using local producers and models. In 1998, China allowed only 10 foreign-made films to be shown in the country; in 1999, it announced that it would ban all unauthorized reception of foreign TV. Because of satellite broadcasting, however, the ban has been difficult to enforce. The point is that various governments, for a number of political and cultural reasons, are trying to slow down the Westernization of their countries.

Exploitation

A dimension of cultural sensitivity that focuses on issues of social responsibility is exploitation in the manufacture of products. Although manufacturing is not marketing communication, it is important to note that business practices that are seen as exploitive send a message that can harm a brand's relationship with its customers and other stakeholders. That's why issues that generate protest, such as outsourcing production to third-world countries where wages and living standards are exceptionally low, may lead to a perception of a company as not being socially responsible. Nike, among others, has been attacked for such practices, and the protests at the World Trade Organization meetings in 2000 were primarily focused on this issue.

In contrast, The Body Shop (personal care products) and Ben & Jerry's (ice cream) are companies built on a philosophy of protecting the environment and supporting indigenous people. The ad in Exhibit 20–8 attempts to separate The Body Shop from other international marketers.

Cultural Mistakes

Marketing communication is susceptible to cultural errors if the message designers are not sensitive to language and cultural differences. Some common examples include the following:[22]

EXHIBIT 20-8

The Body Shop calls attention to the practices of other international marketers, those that outsource manufacturing and use "sweatshop labor," in contrast to its own philosophy of buying ingredients and products from indigenous people and supporting their economic development in a positive way.

- In Thailand, a U.S.-designed ad for Listerine was ineffective because it showed a boy and girl being affectionate to each other in public, a relationship that violated the cultural norms of the country.
- In France, Colgate introduced its Cue toothpaste only to find out later that cue sounds like a certain obscene word in French.
- In Germany, Pepsi's slogan "Come alive, you're in the Pepsi generation" was translated as "Come out of the grave."
- Pepsodent's promise of white teeth backfired in Southeast Asia, where betelnut chewing makes yellow teeth common.
- The brewer Carlsberg had to add a third elephant to its beer label in Africa, where two elephants are a symbol of bad luck.

The use of color can be a sensitive cultural concern, a fact that can create serious problems for global brands that desire consistency in their brand messages. In Japan, China, and many other Asian countries, the color white is for mourning, as is purple in many Latin American countries. Gold is a strong positive color for Chinese, but not when it is combined with black, as in the Benson & Hedges cigarette branding. Ikea, an international furniture retailer based in Sweden, uses the colors blue and yellow, the colors of the Swedish flag—but not in Denmark, a country that was in the past occupied by the Swedes and where that color combination has a negative connotation.[23]

SEGMENTING INTERNATIONAL TARGET MARKETS

There are three ways to classify global or international markets: by geography, by level of development, and by cohort group. Understanding these distinctions is a first step in the SWOT analysis and in identifying target audiences.

By Geography

The distinctions made earlier in defining different types of international and global marketing also describe geographic markets. The most common geographical classifications are local markets (national or domestic) and international markets, which can be regional or global.

Regional marketing in international markets is done in countries that are geographically close, usually within the same continent. In such markets, products are distributed easily between countries. With the development of alliances such as the EU and NAFTA, regional marketing has gained importance. In Europe, nearly all trade barriers have been eliminated among EU member nations selling within the EU. Similarly, NAFTA was designed to reduce trade barriers between Canada, the United States, and Mexico. In Asia there are several groups of countries with varying degrees of unification.

By Level of Development

Another way to segment markets is in terms of the level of development of the country. The **developed markets** in Europe, Scandinavia, North America, Australia, and Japan can be described as *markets in which consumption patterns are focused more on wants and desires than on basic needs.* Consumers in developed countries can easily meet their physical needs (food, clothing, shelter) and thus have money to spend on nonessential goods and services, which include interesting and novel experiences. The characteristics of developed markets include:

- High levels of literacy.
- A high standard of living.
- An infrastructure that supports health care and education.
- A wide variety of media and high rates of media penetration.

North America, with its accelerating economy in the past decade, has been the fastest-growing of the developed markets. The United States accounted for 43 percent of world ad expenditures in 1999, and experts predict it will have 44 percent by 2002, which is more than the 13 next largest markets combined. For decades, Europe has been the focus of many media and marketing efforts. Switzerland, for example, is home to some of the world's truly multinational corporations, many of which have been dominant in their categories since the beginning of the 20th century.

Japan is slowly recovering from its 1990's economic slowdown; however, Japan remains a relatively closed market that is difficult for foreign marketers to enter. Australia is also a difficult market to enter due to fairly tight regulation and its geographic isolation.

Many of the Far East or Pacific Rim countries, such as Thailand, Vietnam, the Phillippines, Indonesia, and China, are considered **developing markets.** These are *markets in which the consumption patterns are clearly expanding from necessities to wants and desires.* Mainland China, with a population of 1.2 billion, is the largest market in this category, while Malaysia has the fastest-growing economy. Some of the other countries in the Far East region, such as South Korea, Taiwan, Singapore, and Hong Kong, have well-developed economies.

> "They're placing their biggest bets in Asia, where startup costs are enormous, the regulatory environment is unpredictable, the advertising market is as yet undeveloped and audiences are measured by the billion."
>
> Frank Rose, "Think Globally, Script Locally"

In spite of the Asian economic slowdown and all the other problems faced in Asia in the 1990s, the region is seen as having great potential, according to Frank Rose, writing in *Fortune* magazine.[24] International companies have again been investing heavily in Asia. With its 3 billion people, Asia comprises about two-fifths of the world's population, as well as some of the most promising markets in the world. China, for example, has some 305 million television households that now can be reached via satellite as well as land-based stations. The country was closed to marketing until 1978, when economic reforms led to sustained growth and a more open market.

India, too, is a developing market, and the Middle East is slowly opening its doors to Western thought and trade. Dubai, capital of the United Arab Emirates, is a key city in the southern part of the Mideast region and Riyadh, capital of Saudia Arabia, is also a major center of industrialization. Israel is an exception in this region, of course, because it already has a highly developed economy.

In Africa, Egypt is an expanding economy. The industrialized South Africa offers a stabilized economy and a huge potential for marketers as its African consumer culture emerges. Diverse cultures and closed borders remain in some areas of South America, but strong market opportunities exist in many of the countries, particularly Argentina and Brazil, which means product choice is becoming much more important to consumers.

Undeveloped markets are *markets in which consumption patterns remain focused on basic needs.* Challenges to marketers in these regions include lack of media, a relatively high level of illiteracy, low disposable income, and lack of marketing infrastructure such as distribution systems. As undeveloped countries modernize, market opportunities will be created, although the consumer orientation will be more focused on meeting basic needs than on wants for some years to come. Much of Africa, outside the big cities, falls into this category. The IMC in Action box explains how one marketing entrepreneur is developing methods to reach people in these markets and begin to develop their awareness of brands.

By Cultural Cohort Group

A **cultural cohort,** which is based on anthropologists' analysis of cross-cultural groups, is *a demographic or psychographic group that slices across multiple cultures.* In other words, it is a global community with a unifying interest.[25] The cohort approach to international segmentation uses a stratification method in which customers with similar characteristics, and therefore common wants and needs can be grouped together, despite national boundaries. Examples include mothers of infants, business travelers, and cat owners. Recall from the chapter opening case that the target audience for Whiskas was considered universal: female cat owners who

IMC IN ACTION

Building Brands in the Bush

Busi Skenjana is a South African woman who is pioneering techniques to build brands in the townships of South Africa, using nonconventional media. Skenjana is president of Soweto-based IXesha Marketing Focus, which is a promotions agency that offers packaged-goods brands an entry into township retailing. Her unusual route to building brand awareness takes her not to traditional media, but to dirt roads leading to village social and cultural events, such as weddings and funerals.

She has found that entertainment, celebrations, and events like funerals provide opportunities for visibility for the brands she represents. She does it by bringing in all the equipment, furnishings, food, and other accouterments needed to stage the event, such as pans and bowls for the food, tents, banners, limos, portable stages, even toilets—all of them branded. For example, a branded bridal limousine carries the message "Here comes the [brand X] bride." After all, the same brand does sponsor the Bride of the Year award

in local newspapers. And Skenjana makes sure that all the little shops in the township are stocked with the brands sponsoring the event.

It's a win-win approach to brand promotion. The celebrants get a larger and more extravagant event at no cost, and the brands get an introduction—and one with positive associations—to a newly developing market. It's an innovative way to reach customers who have access to very little media, and to do so in a way that is relevant to their lives.

Think About It

What is the key problem faced in reaching customers in undeveloped markets? How does IXesha Marketing Focus reach its target markets?

Source: Busi Skenjana, "Building Brands in a Fragmented Media Society," IMM-MASA Conference, Johannesburg, South Africa, March 10, 1998.

are responsible for buying the cat food. Cultural cohorts are particularly noticeable in the high-tech, fashion, and entertainment industries.

The Global Youth Market

The youth market is one of the most distinct global cohort groups and a particularly important global community for many marketers. But even within this group, there are still segments based upon values, personalities, and lifestyles. In a study of more than 27,000 teenagers in 44 countries, the 500-million member group was divided into six distinct value segments. In other words, the study found that teens are not necessarily alike worldwide, even within countries; however, there are still lifestyle characteristics that cross national borders.[26] These six segments are defined in Figure 20–3.

The music video channel MTV is an example of a powerful worldwide media vehicle that reaches the global youth market. It is also a premier platform for marketers trying to reach a cultural-cohort segment. Although most teens listen to the same kinds of music, MTV has found that there are regional and national differences, particularly in language. For that reason, MTV now airs 22 different feeds around the world, all tailored for their respective markets. All the channels, however, reflect the familiar, frenetic look and feel of the original MTV. The channel's managers learned in MTV's early foray into the European market that, while the world's youth might all say "I want my MTV!" they didn't want a copycat version of the U.S. channel.

Viacom, the channel's owner, estimates that every second of every day almost 2 million people are watching MTV, and 1.2 million of them are tuning in from outside the United States.[27] In the early 2000s, MTV reached 116 million homes in Asia and China—46 million more than in the United States. Since nearly two-thirds of Asia's 3 billion people are under the age of 35, MTV's growth in the region has been explosive, as it attracts those valuable trendsetting early adopters.

As a way to develop relationships with its viewers, MTV sponsors parties in the United Kingdom, Russia, and the Philippines, which are showcases for MTV's sponsoring brands, such as Nike, Gap, and Levi's. Compaq's European manager attributes a 12 percent increase in profit in Europe to the company's presence on MTV. He explains, "Young people trust MTV, and they trust what is shown on MTV."[28]

FIGURE 20-3

This is one way to view the global youth market. Note the special interests of each segment.

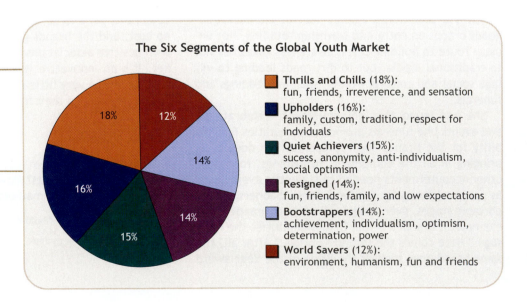

The Six Segments of the Global Youth Market

Thrills and Chills (18%):
fun, friends, irreverence, and sensation

Upholders (16%):
family, custom, tradition, respect for indviduals

Quiet Achievers (15%):
sucess, anonymity, anti-individualism, social optimism

Resigned (14%):
fun, friends, family, and low expectations

Bootstrappers (14%):
achievement, individualism, optimism, determination, power

World Savers (12%):
environment, humanism, fun and friends

MESSAGE DESIGN: THINK GLOBALLY, ACT LOCALLY

Although the world is becoming more of a single, homogeneous marketplace, there will always be economic, geographical, cultural, political, demographic, and technological differences that stand in the way of a truly level playing field. Even if people buy the same products, that doesn't mean they buy them for the same reasons. International marketers are faced with the challenge of taking advantage of new communication technology to reach millions of customers quickly and cost-effectively while ensuring that they are not sacrificing their desired brand image.

Standardize or Localize?

Globalization, standardization, and localization are three different MC strategies for global or international brands. **Standardization** refers to *a brand message strategy designed for one specific market and then extended to many additional markets.* **Globalization,** in contrast, refers to *a brand message strategy that is designed at the outset for multiple countries and that takes into consideration market and customer similarities and differences.*[29] Whiskas ran ads for its kitten food in different countries with only a change in language, because the company's MC agency determined through testing that the ad had a universal appeal (see Exhibit 20–9). **Localization** is *a strategy that adapts and modifies a brand message to make it more compatible with local market culture.*

The debate about the best international strategy has been going on since the early 1960s. It became a central issue in the early 1980s when a controversial article in the *Harvard Business Review* by Harvard professor Theodore Levitt called for companies to move to standardized global marketing strategies.[30] Research findings consistently show that standardization is problematic at best because of differences in cultural values. However, corporate managers continue to argue for standardization in the hope of better controlling the presentation of a brand's image, as well as benefiting from the cost-efficiencies of a single campaign.

Combination Strategies

The answer may lie somewhere in between. A recent report on global best practices found that most multinationals are operating with a two-tier strategy: global headquarters determine the broad strategic direction for the brand and the regional or local groups execute it locally.[31] Such an approach is sometimes referred to as a combination strategy.[32] As Jiafei Yin explains, this approach combines the advantages of both strategies—consistent brand image development and successful communication accommodating cultural differences.[33] Figure 20–4 illustrates the continuum of strategic options from totally standardized to totally localized.

In other words, planning an IMC strategy for an international or global brand may not be as simple as deciding whether to standardize or not. The brand imagery and logo, for example, are easier to standardize than are models, settings, and language. Think of all the various strategic decisions involved in a campaign. Figure 20–5 breaks out 12 dimensions of strategy and gives examples of the elements that need to be considered in the standardization/localization decision.

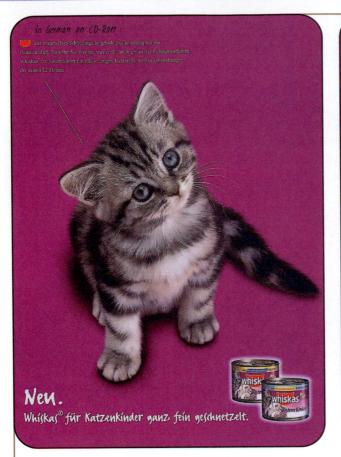

EXHIBIT 20-9

This ad for Whiskas Kitten Food runs in both English-speaking and German-speaking countries with only the language changed accordingly.

FIGURE 20-4

As this continuum illustrates, the balance of localization and standardization can greatly vary.

Source: Adapted from Sandra Moriarty and Tom Duncan, "Global Advertising: Issues and Practices," *Current Issues & Research in Advertising* 13, nos. 1 and 2 (1991), p. 317

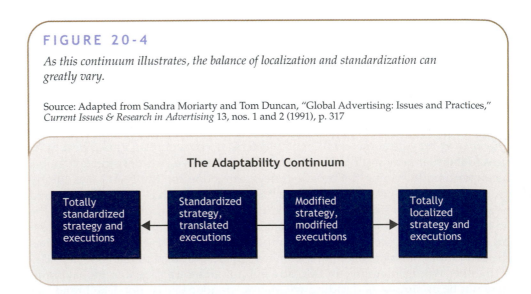

Local offices sometimes resent being forced to use global campaigns and inevitably will make the argument that the standardized campaign doesn't adequately address the local market. That's another reason for the increasing use of

The Standardization Model

Area	Easier to Standardize - More Difficult to Standardize
Product Category	Hi Tech Hi Touch, High Fashion / Industrial, Computers / Fun Services Foods, Cigarettes / Homecare Decorating / Food, Beer / Contraceptives Bikinis
Product Life Cycle	New product .... Older product with local strategies
Objectives	Advertising .... Media / Sales promotion
Targeting	Intntl. youth market, bus. travelers / Indust. buyers / New mothers / Home-makers / Blue collar workers / Subsistence farmers
Positioning	Universal need and target .... Culturally determined tastes
Branding	Common name and image / Modified name or image / Local name or image / Local name and image
Creative Strategy	Image / Benefit / Informative
Advertising Message	Creative concept, theme .... Execution details
Production	Central production / Central production & local modifications / Produced locally
Media	Planning .... Buying
Media Availability	Media conglomerates, satellite TV / Intnl. mags, nwsprs, / Natl. mags, nwsprs, TV / Outdoor / PoP, direct response / Local TV, radio nwsprs
Research	Secondary .... Primary

FIGURE 20-5

Examples of various levels of standardization and localization applications.

Source: Sandra E. Moriarty and Tom Duncan, "Global Advertising: Issues and Practices," *Current Issues and Research in Advertising* 13, no. 1 and 2 (1991), pp. 313–341.

combination strategies that standardize some elements of the brand strategy and localize other elements of the execution.

One survey of 87 multinational companies that market in China, Taiwan, Hong Kong, and Singapore found that 31 percent of the advertising decisions were made using the same strategy as the home market, while 68 percent used a different strategy.[34] Robert Hite and Cynthia Fraser found in 1988 that 66 percent of the international companies they surveyed used a combination strategy; only 9 percent used a standardized strategy, and 37 percent used a localized strategy.[35] Ten years later, a major study of advertising in China by Jiafei Yin found that little had changed: The majority of the international companies surveyed about their practices in China used a combination strategy.[36]

Yin concluded that the majority of the companies surveyed have abandoned standardization. The only exception was the electronics industry, in which no company used a localized strategy, suggesting that high-tech markets are less affected by cultural differences than other types of markets. Furthermore, she observed that even in the emerging markets of developing countries, some degree of localization is a preferred strategy for most companies, rather than the less costly and more efficient standardization approach. Some researchers have found, however, that, although global integration can be done using either a standardization or localization approach, coordination is probably more difficult with the latter.[37]

The general principle seems to be that it isn't a question of "Think globally" or "Think locally," but rather, "Think globally and act locally." Companies wishing to launch global marketing campaigns must still play in the local arena of local media, varying government regulations, wide cultural differences, and ever-changing stages of economic and demographic development. Although many of the world's economic and cultural barriers have fallen in recent years, international companies cannot ignore the remaining barriers if they hope to reach their customers on a global scale.

MESSAGE DELIVERY: MEDIA AND TECHNOLOGY

There are three basic media strategies being used to reach multinational and global markets. The first is to localize media mixes based on what mix of media are available in each country. The second is to use international publications and satellite TV, whose footprint covers various regions of the world. A **broadcast footprint** is *the geographical area in which there is reception from a satellite transmission.* The third way to deliver media across borders is to participate in programs that have transnational audiences, such as sporting events like Soccer's World Cup and the Olympics (see the Global Focus box).

Level of Media Development

As with economic development, countries differ in the area of media development. In South Africa, for example, there are only a few TV channels, compared to dozens in the North American and European countries. In developing countries where communication vehicles are limited, as is literacy, radio and posters or billboards dominate the media schedule. In such places, the search is on for nontraditional vehicles and sales promotions that can reach customers in rural villages.

Media growth in China has been phenomenal as the market economy has opened up. China has about 2,200 general publications and trade magazines and newspapers, up from 186 in 1978, and more than 3,000 TV and radio stations. Ninety-six percent of Chinese urban homes now have color television sets, and the number of Internet users reached 4 million at the end of 1999.[38]

The Growth in International Media

John Perriss, CEO of Zenith Media Worldwide, a media buying company, predicts exceptional growth in the early years of the 21st century because of the vibrant ad

GLOBAL FOCUS

Capturing the World Cup Audience

The Olympics reaches a worldwide audience, but few other sporting events have that much global attention. Soccer probably comes the closest; however, it misses out in the United States, which is a major target for sports marketing.

Coca-Cola, Gillette, and McDonald's each spent $20 to $40 million to be an official sponsor of the 1998 World Cup, soccer's month-long global championship series (see Exhibit 20-10). Unless they saw those brand names on the billboards surrounding the fields, English-speaking Americans had little awareness of these promotional efforts by these brands. None of the three bought commercial time on the English-language networks carrying the matches live to the United States. However, Coke and McDonald's did advertise on the Spanish-language Univision network, which broadcasts in the United States.

So why this huge investment by American companies to reach international audiences? All three companies signed on as sponsors mainly to market themselves outside the United States to audiences that are fervent about soccer. With all its supporting marketing communication around the world, Coca-Cola reportedly spent more than $200 million on MC to leverage its World Cup sponsorship.

So when will the U.S. market become part of the soccer game? Marketers estimate that it will take years for Americans to be as passionate about soccer as they are about baseball or football. The TV ratings seem to confirm that. ABC's broadcast of the opening U.S. match with Germany had a rating of 4.4 in major markets, compared to a 5.8 rating four years earlier for the U.S. opener against Switzerland. As an approach to building the American audience during the 1998 World Cup, Coke conducted soccer clinics in 31 U.S. cities and sent a group of youngsters to France to serve as World Cup flag bearers and ball kids.

Soccer also presents unusual challenges for marketers because the matches have no natural time-outs and the networks are reluctant to break away from the action for commercials. Sponsors' names do appear in the on-screen box showing the score and game clock, and of course the in-stadium banner ads receive a lot of TV exposure. But ads run only before and after the matches and at halftime.

Think About It

Why are soccer sponsors reluctant to advertise on U.S. television broadcasts? What needs to happen to make this as attractive as other international sporting events, such as the Olympics?

Source: Adapted from Skip Wollenberg, "Advertisers Low-Key in Marketing World Cup in U.S.," *Boulder Daily Camera,* June 20, 1998, p. 6B.

EXHIBIT 20-10

market and thriving global market.[39] Worldwide ad revenues are expected to grow to $360 billion in 2002. A breakdown of expenditures for major advertising media in 1998 and predictions for 2002 are given in Table 20–1. (Keep in mind these "advertising" figures also include sales promotion and direct-response offers.) Much of the ad growth is expected from new media companies, with expenditures predicted to triple in the early 2000s. The year 2000, in particular, with its U.S. election and the Sydney Olympics, drove much of the recent growth.

TABLE 20-1	World Advertising Expenditures for Major Media (TV, Press, Radio, Cinema, Outdoor; $ Billions)*		
Region	1998	2002 (Est.)	% Increase
North America	$121	$156	22%
Europe	79	101	22
Asia/Pacific	54	66	18
Latin America	23	26	12
Africa/Middle East	7	10	31

*Figures do not include direct mail and telemarketing.

Source: Adapted from "Global Ad Expenditures Still Accelerating," *Direct Marketing*, March 2000, p. 17.

Print advertising, specifically outdoor, magazines and newspapers, has historically offered international advertisers the best way to reach cross-cultural markets. Many U.S. publications such as *Time, Newsweek, USA Today, Cosmopolitan,* and *The Wall Street Journal* publish their issues in multiple languages and distribute throughout the world.

You might not think of outdoor media as being global, but one of the largest outdoor advertising companies in the world, the France-based JCDecaux company, has nearly half a million display locations spread throughout 1,300 cities in 33 countries. JCDecaux is also the inventor of, and world's largest provider of, "street furniture" (bus benches and shelters) and the world leader in airport and subway posters. In the United States, it is the largest provider of shopping-mall poster displays.

While print is still the most-used advertising vehicle for international marketers, satellite technology is quickly making television the medium for the masses. Yet the fastest-growing development, of course, is occurring with the Internet.

Internet: A True Global Medium

> "We want to build Europe's largest Internet provider [T-Online], step-by-step, in to the leading pan-European Internet brand."
>
> Ron Sommer, CEO, Deutsche Telekom

As Internet usage continues to grow throughout the world, companies are trying to identify who the users are and how they can get their brand message out to as many of them as possible. The largest Internet service provider in Europe is T-Online, owned by Germany's telecommunication leader, Deutsche Telekom. As of 2000, T-Online served 6.5 million customers and was accessible to over half of all European households and businesses. As a quote from Deutsche Telekom's CEO, Ron Sommer, in a recent *Wall Street Journal* article suggests, media companies are as concerned about branding as providers of other types of products are.[40] Exhibit 20–11 shows the home page for bCentral (http://store.bcentral.com/intl/), an international promotion portal that helps companies engaged in e-commerce promote their sites in a variety of languages.

E-commerce companies, such as Amazon.com, the online auction company eBay, and Bol.com AG (the online unit of the German media giant Bertelsmann AG) are pushing into international business. They are developing local-language sites across Europe and Asia. Amazon.com operates language-specific sites in Germany and France. It has also exported products to customers in 160 other countries where customers access the site in English. Online auctioneer eBay has a dedicated site for the United Kingdom, but its European rival, QXL, is pioneering a different approach. QXL has moved from nation to nation, launching local sites in some and buying established companies in others, and it now operates in 12 different languages with 12 different currencies.

Online communities are often classified by the languages used as opposed to the geographic region. E-commerce marketers who try to rely on English as an international business language often find that their customers want to do business in their own languages. The Adero ad in Exhibit 20–12 illustrates this problem. A study completed in June 2000 identified the percentages of online users by language. These findings are listed in Table 20–2.

E-commerce expanded faster in South Korea than any other nation between 1998 and 2000. E-commerce is a big business in Korea, where such companies as E*Trade benefit from the fact that 50 percent of Korean stock trading is now on the Net.[41] One particular use of the Internet that is distinctively Korean is the "PC Room," a combination Internet café (without the coffee) and game arcade. There are some 15,000 PC Rooms in South Korea, complete with Web video cameras and rows of computers jammed in as tightly as they will fit. Although many South Koreans have Internet access on home PCs, they come to the PC Rooms for souped-up terminals with high-speed links and super graphics, for the camaraderie, and for the help of resident computer geeks who stand by to fix problems instantly. Men tend to spend their time there playing games, while women chat online. Computer games also have become a major "sport" marketing arena in South Korea, where at least a thousand professional gamers are sponsored and paid generous salaries by online game manufacturers. The best Korean game players have fan clubs, participate in big game tournaments, and make TV news shows.

The emerging Web market looks different in Japan than in other countries because of the Japanese fascination with handheld electronic appliances, such as the mobile phone, rather than the computer. For example, a cell-phone company offered a handset that hooks up to the Internet; a year later, it had signed up 5 million users. Wireless communication, in other words, is driving the shape and development of Internet marketing in Japan.

And e-commerce works differently, as well. In Japan, online orders can be placed one day and the goods picked up the next at one of the ubiquitous local convenience stores or even a gas station. That means 7-Eleven, with its 8,000 outlets in Japan, is positioned to be the biggest distributor of e-commerce merchandise.

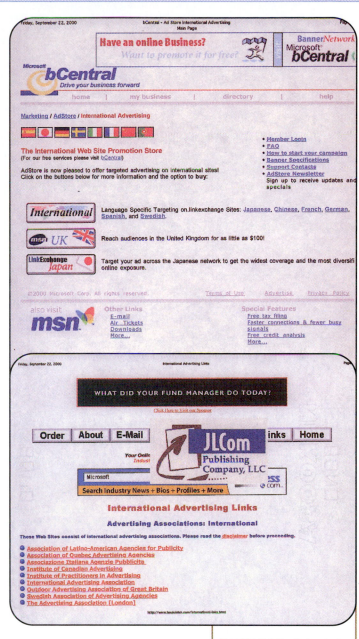

EXHIBIT 20-11

Developing international advertising for Internet sites is difficult because of the different languages. The portal bCentral is a service that helps with language-specific targeting.

Global Tracking Systems for the Internet

While multinational corporations are trying to reach the world's proliferation of Internet users, they must do so in a targeted, constructive manner, just as they would use any other advertising medium. One of the tools now available to international companies is a new global tracking service for advertisers, launched by ACNielsen. Prior to ACNielsen's research service, marketers relied on market measurements that varied by types of information collected, methods used, and level of accuracy. The research company promises consistently gathered information about the number of people and households per country with access to the Internet, their online browsing and purchasing habits, and the rates of access at home, work, or other locations.[42]

As Internet technology becomes more common throughout the world and more tracking and research services are developed, international advertisers will look to the Internet as an integrated brand message vehicle to carry sales promotion offers, publicity releases, and ad messages. Most important, companies will use the Internet to develop an online dialogue with customers.

Media Convergence

Media convergence is a term used to describe *the bringing together of phone, television, and the computer, along with a variety of other new technologies, such as smart cards, pagers, personal digital assistants, and satellite navigational systems.* Brand messages may take on an entirely different shape as wireless communication makes use of all these technologies. This is particularly true in those early-adopter countries that have pioneered the development of wireless communication, such as the Scandinavian countries and Japan.

Picture a butcher shop in Stockholm, Sweden, where customers are offered a discount for waving their wireless cell phones through an infrared sensor that records the telephone's number. Near closing time on one particular day, the butcher is anxious to move some prime cuts of Argentine beef. Using the store's customer database, he sends out a special offer by an automated phone message to customers who have ordered Argentine beef before—and who happen to be within, say, three blocks. The mobile phone network finds these customers, pages them, and delivers a message about the special deal, complete with a mouthwatering picture of a sizzling steak. The butcher's wireless company charges a few cents for each message delivered; however, he may recover that cost with the revenue from the Bordeaux ad message delivered at the same time as the beef offer. Customers who buy online get a discount, and the charges are automatically credited against their phone's debit card.[43]

In Japan, Honda is building cybercars that can connect to the Internet. Its Internavi system uses a computer satellite mapping system, a modem and mobile phone, Internet browser capability, and a dashboard-mounted paperback-sized screen. It's possible to provide drivers with guides to restaurants, a list of leisure activities, and event schedules.

Media Regulation

Developing an international media plan, however, is not simple—not only because of the varied pattern of local media, but also because of the different regulations. Although some media are being privatized in countries as diverse as Israel and Russia, governments around the world still own and control most broadcast media, and many still do not permit advertising. In Norway, there is only one commercial Norwegian TV channel. Others limit advertising to a certain number of minutes per hour or per day. European Union guidelines allow only 12 minutes of commercial messages per hour and mandate at least 20 minutes of programming between commercial breaks. However, there are few restrictions on newspapers and magazines.

Despite individual country regulations barring or limiting TV advertising, households in these countries are increasingly being reached with TV commercials that are carried by satellite broadcasting companies, such as Columbia TriStar and Sky TV.

Many countries also limit or fully prevent the use of certain media such as direct mail and telemarketing. Good information about media use and audience profiles isn't available in every country, especially developing countries. Circulation figures aren't always reliable, audience demographics may be sketchy, ad rates may vary greatly, and mailing lists and phone numbers may not exist in a directory or in a database. And because of costs, the methods used in media research may be considerably different from one market to another, making comparisons virtually impossible. Because of the media variations in each country, most international marketers assign national media planning and buying responsibilities to in-country media specialists rather than running the risk of faulty, centralized media planning.

TABLE 20-2   Online Language Populations

Language	Percentage of Internet Users
Dutch	1.8%
Italian	3.0
Korean	3.5
French	3.9
Chinese	5.4
Spanish	5.8
German	5.9
Japanese	8.1
English	51.3

Source: "Global Internet Statistics (by Language)," June 2000 <www.glreach.com/globstats/index.php3>.

FINAL NOTE: INTEGRATION AT THE INTERNATIONAL LEVEL

When companies sell their products outside their home country, IMC practices and principles are even more important than when they sell them domestically. Building stakeholder relationships with global customers, agencies, media, and channels of distribution can be highly complex and certainly requires cross-functional planning and monitoring.

The goal of most businesses is to market their products or services to the largest group of potential customers at the lowest possible cost. This strategy would suggest that a company should use a standardized or global message to reach large numbers of customers through international markets, as the Whiskas case demonstrated. Although this standardized international marketing strategy may work for some brands and may offer various efficiency benefits for a company, in most cases international businesses need to take local economic, cultural, political, legal, demographic, and media factors into consideration, market by market.

Reaching customers in various countries with a positive and lasting brand image calls for a complex yet integrated strategy. The challenge remains how to maintain strategic consistency with an international or worldwide group of stakeholders, media, and agency/client partnerships. Building brand relationships is complicated at this level, but the same basic integration issues are still driving the strategies.

Key Terms

national (or domestic) marketers 695
international marketers 695
global marketers 695
multinationals 695
culture 696
values 699
cultural imperialism 702
developed markets 703

developing markets 704
undeveloped markets 704
cultural cohort 705
standardization 707
globalization 707
localization 707
broadcast footprint 710
media convergence 714

Key Point Summary

Key Point 1: Different Types of International Marketing

National (or domestic) marketing programs are designed for marketing within a country; international marketing programs are for companies that market in a number of different countries; and global marketers sell their products in many countries around the world. Multinational companies are powerful corporate structures built on a network of subsidiaries and affiliates that market to each other, as well as to external companies.

Key Point 2: The Impact of Culture

Cultural differences and similarities reflect people's values. MC planners must be sensitive to these differences. Media sensitivity, cultural imperialism, exploitation, and cultural mistakes are all problem areas that marketers must understand.

Key Point 3: Segmenting International Markets

International markets are segmented by geography, by level of market economy development, and by cultural cohort groups. Understanding these differences is an important part of conducting a SWOT analysis for a product marketed internationally.

Key Point 4: Planning International Message and Media Strategies

The big issue in planning international message strategies is deciding on the extent of standardization or localization appropriate for a particular type of product marketed in various countries. Many companies use a combination strategy. Likewise, in creating a media plan for international markets, a decision has to be made about using local media or media that reach across borders. Such decisions are becoming increasingly complex—yet also hold great potential—due to the growth of the Internet and to media convergence.

Lessons Learned

Key Point 1: Different Types of International Marketing

a. What are the differences between national, international, and global, marketing? What is a multinational company?
b. List three of the major trends that are driving the move to international marketing, and explain their impact on marketing.

Key Point 2: The Impact of Culture

a. Define culture and explain where in the planning of a marketing communication program it becomes a factor.
b. What is the nature of the debate about cultural differences and similarities?
c. If you were to summarize the difference in values between Western and Asian cultures, what values would you identify?
d. Explain the difference between a high-context and a low-context culture. How does context affect marketing communication?
e. Explain the concern that some countries have with cultural or Western imperialism. Find an ad that you think might incite the imperialism issue and explain why you think the ad's strategy might create a problem in an international marketing plan.

Key Point 3: Segmenting International Markets

a. What are the three ways international markets can be segmented and targeted? Explain how these factors make a difference in an MC strategy.
b. What are the characteristics of developed markets, developing markets, and undeveloped markets? How do each of these affect a marketing communication strategy?
c. What is a cultural cohort group, and why is this concept important in international marketing communication? Give an example of such a group.

Key Point 4: Planning International Message and Media Plans

a. What is meant by standardization? By localization?

b. What is a combination strategy? How does the "adaptability continuum" in Figure 20–4 (p. 708) explain the differences in this approach?

c. Explain the phrase "Think globally, act locally."

d. What are the three basic media strategies used to reach multinational audiences?

e. What does media convergence mean? Give an example.

Chapter Challenge

Writing Assignment

Identify a product that is sold in your country and another country. (A good place to start looking is in your school's library in a magazine like *Elle* or *Figaro*.) Collect an ad for that brand in both languages. In a paper, analyze the brand's use of standardization or localization.

Presentation Assignment

Set up a debate between two teams of students; one team supports the idea that standardization is a useful strategy, and the other team supports the idea that localization is the only way to develop an effective marketing communication plan. Both teams should also consider the issue of cultural imperialism in making their statements.

Internet Assignment

Consult Amazon.com's website. Print off the first page of each offering from a different country or in a different language. Analyze the appearance of these pages in terms of their strategic consistency.

Additional Readings

de Mooij, Marieke. *Advertising Worldwide*, 2nd ed. Hertfordshire, UK: Prentice Hall Europe, 1994.
—— *Global Marketing and Advertising: Understanding Cultural Paradoxes*. Thousand Oaks, CA: Sage, 1998.
Keegan, Warren J. *Global Marketing Management*, 6th ed. Upper Saddle River, NJ: Prentice Hall, 1999.
Levitt, Theodore. "The Globalization of Markets," *Harvard Business Review*, May–June 1983, pp. 92–102.
Mueller, Barbara. *International Advertising: Communicating Across Cultures*. Belmont, CA: Wadsworth, 1995.
Ohmae, Kenneth. "Managing in a Borderless World," *Harvard Business Review*, May–June 1989, pp. 152-61.

Research Assignment

Consult these books and articles and others you might find on international marketing communication, and develop a review of factors that lead to more effective integrated marketing communication on the international level.

Endnotes

[1] Philip Cateora, *International Marketing* (Homewood, IL: Irwin, 1993), p. vii.

[2] Warren Keegan, *Global Marketing Management*, 6th ed. (Upper Saddle River, NJ: Prentice Hall, 1999), pp. 8-9.

[3] Stanley Paliwoda, *International Marketing* (London: Heinemann, 1986), p. 2.

[4] Keegan, *Global Marketing Management*, p. 9.

[5] Ibid., p. 6.

[6] Marieke de Mooij, *Global Marketing and Advertising: Understanding Cultural Paradoxes* (Thousand Oaks, CA: Sage, 1998), p. 43.

[7] Subhash Jain, *International Marketing Management*, 3rd ed. (Boston: PWS-Kent, 1990), p. 229.

[8] Sak Onkvisit and John Shaw, "Standardized International Advertising: Some Research Issues and Implications," *Journal of Marketing Research* 39, no. 6 (1999), pp. 19-24; and Frenkel Ter Hofstede, Jan-Benedict Steenkamp, and Michel Wedel, "International Market Segmentation Based on Consumer-Product Relations," *Journal of Marketing Research* 36, no. 1 (1999), pp. 1-17.

[9] John Quelch and Edward Hoff, "Customizing Global Marketing," *Harvard Business Review*, May-June 1986, pp. 59-68.

[10] Grant McCracken, 1986, "Culture and Consumption: A Theoretical Account of the Structure and Movement of the Cultural Meaning of Consumer Goods," *Journal of Consumer Research* 13 (1986), pp. 71-84.

[11] M. Rokeach, *The Nature of Human Values* (New York: Free Press, 1973), p. 5.

[12] Hong Cheng and Kara Chan, "One Country, Two Systems: Cultural Values Reflected in Chinese and Hong Kong Television Commercials," *Proceedings of the 2000 Conference of the American Academy of Advertising*, ed. Mary Alice Shaver (East Lansing: Michigan State University, 2000), p. 110.

[13] Jee Young Lee and Trina Sego, "Culture in Advertising on the World Wide Web: Executional Elements of South Korean and U.S. Banner Advertisements," *Proceedings of the 2000 Conference of the American Academy of Advertising*, ed. Mary Alice Shaver (East Lansing: Michigan State University, 2000), p. 198; Gordon Miracle, Beate Bluhm, Juergen Bluhm, Yung Kyun Choi, and Hairong Li, "The Relationship between Cultural Variables and the Amount and Type of Information in Korean and German Television Commercials," in *Proceedings of the 1998 Conference of the American Academy of Advertising*, ed. Darrel D. Muehling (Pullman, WA: Washington State University, 1998), pp. 9-15; and Jyotika Ramaprasad and Kazumi Hasegawa, "An Analysis of Japanese Television Commercials," *Journalism Quarterly*, 67 (Fall 1990), pp. 1025-33.

[14] Edward Hall, *Beyond Culture* (New York: Anchor Press-Doubleday, 1976).

[15] Geert H. Hofstede, *Culture's Consequences: International Differences in Work-Related Values* (Beverly Hills, CA: Sage, 1980); *Cultures and Organizations: Software of the Mind* (New York: McGraw-Hill, 1991); "The Cultural Relativity of Organization Practices and Theories," *Journal of International Business Studies* 14, no.2 (1983), pp. 75-89.

[16] Young Sook Moon and George R. Franke, "Cultural Influences on Agency Practitioners' Ethical Perceptions: A Comparison of Korea and the U.S.," *Journal of Advertising* 29, no. 1 (Spring 2000), pp. 51-65.

[17] Alan Shao, Mary Anne Raymond, and Charles Taylor, "Shifting Advertising Appeals in Taiwan," *Journal of Advertising Research*, November-December 1999, pp. 61-69.

[18] W. C. Gudykunst and S. Ting-Toomey, *Culture and Interpersonal Communication* (Newbury Park, CA: Sage, 1988); and B. C. Deng, "The Influence of Individualism-Collectivism on Conflict Management Style: A Cross-Culture Comparison between Taiwanese and U.S. Business Employees," master's thesis (Sacramento: California State University, 1992).

[19] Rose, p. 160.

[20] T. J. Knutson, R. Komolsevin, P. Chatiketu, and V. Smith, "Rhetorical Sensitivity and Willingness to Communicate: A Comparison of Thai and U.S. American Samples with Implications for Intercultural Communication Effectiveness," International Communication Association Annual conference, Acapulco, Mexico, June 2000.

[21] Rose, "Think Globally, Script Locally," p. 158.

[22] These are compiled from Jain, *International Marketing Management*, pp. 227-28.

[23] Marieke de Mooij, *Global Marketing and Advertising: Understanding Cultural Paradoxes* (Thousand Oaks, CA: Sage, 1998), p. 56.

[24] Frank Rose, "Think Globally, Script Locally," *Fortune*, November 8, 1999, p. 160.

[25] Tom Duncan, "A Mother's a Mother," *Marketing and Media Decisions*, May 1990, p. 120.

[26] Elissa Moses, *The $100 Billion Allowance: Accessing the Global Teen Market* (New York: Wiley, 2000).

[27] Brett Pulley and Andrew Tanzer, "Summer's Gemstone," *Forbes*, February 21, 2000, pp. 107-11.

[28] Quoted in ibid., p. 107.

[29] Onkvisit and Show, "Standardized International Advertising."

[30] Theodore Levitt, "The Globalization of Markets," *Harvard Business Review,* May–June 1983, pp. 92–102.

[31] Marilyn Roberts, "2000 International Advertising Pre-Conference: The Global Best Practices Roundtable," *Proceedings of the 2000 Conference of the American Academy of Advertising,* ed. Mary Alice Shaver (East Lansing: Michigan State University, 2000), pp. 239–41.

[32] Onkvisit and Shaw, "Standardized International Advertising."

[33] Yin, "International Advertising Strategies in China," p. 30.

[34] Susan H. C. Tai, "Advertising in Asia: Localize or Regionalize?" *International Journal of Advertising* 16, no. 1 (1997), pp. 48–61.

[35] Robert Hite and Cynthia Fraser, "International Advertising Strategies of Multinational Corporations," *Journal of Advertising Research* 28, no. 4 (1988), pp. 9–17.

[36] Yin, "International Advertising Strategies in China," pp. 25–35.

[37] Stephen Gould, Dawn Lerman, and Andreas Green, "Agency Perceptions and Practices on Global IMC," *Journal of Advertising Research* 39, no. 1 (1999), pp. 7–20.

[38] Alfred Che, "The Challenge of China," Reputation Management, March 2000, p. 62.

[39] Quoted in "Global Ad Expenditures Still Accelerating," *Direct Marketing,* March 2000, pp. 16–17.

[40] William Boston, "Investors Cheer T-Online Plan to Take Over Spanish Portal," *The Wall Street Journal,* September 5, 2000, p. A25.

[41] Benjamin Fulford, "All Wired Up in Korea," *Forbes,* March 20, 2000, pp. 102–5.

[42] William Pulver, "Nielsen NetRatings Global Internet Trends," ACNielsen.com, September 7, 2000.

[43] Stephen Baker, "Reach Out and Sell Someone," *Business Week E.Biz,* February 7, 2000, pp. EB50–52.

21

Measurement, Evaluation, and Effectiveness

Key Points in This Chapter

1. How does the IMC audit evaluate IMC processes?

2. How should the evaluation of brand messages be conducted?

3. What are the common methods used in IMC evaluation?

4. What are relationship metrics?

Chapter Perspective
The Mandate for Accountability

Accountability is a must in business today. Starting all the way at the top—with the board of directors, who answer to shareholders—down to the smallest department, there is always someone wanting to know how and why money was spent, how the spending helped generate more sales and profits, and whether the money was spent in the most effective way. Because many of the elements that drive brand equity are intangible, such as brand awareness, brand knowledge, and customer satisfaction, measurement is more complicated that simply looking at sales and profits

The demand to be accountable is increasing because of the availability of technology that tracks sales and profitability. Such things as scanner data, customer databases, and automated customer service operations are generating enormous amounts of marketing data that can be used to evaluate MC programs. As a matter of fact, in many companies, the primary challenge is not collecting more information but analyzing and making use of the information that already exists.

One of the most important ways to meet this challenge is to measure and evaluate brand messages and customer interactions. This includes generating feedback on brand strategies and the different brand messages and campaigns that are used. This chapter discusses two types of IMC audits—the mini-audit and the in-depth audit. It then considers evaluation and measurement of brand messages in general before looking at specific methods. It ends with a discussion of the benefits and limitations of evaluation.

EFFECTIVENESS CASE

BUITONI REPOSITIONS ITS BRAND IMAGE
McCann-Erickson Italiana, Milan, Italy

Buitoni was a historic trademark in the Italian food industry, yet it represented a fairly unexciting traditional line of Italian food products—crispbread and small pasta. It's a common problem: How do you appear innovative without walking away from your traditional expertise? This case describes McCann-Erickson Italiana's "*Star Bene a Tavola*" campaign, which marked the successful repositioning of the Buitoni brand, an effort that began in the 1980s and extended 15 years. The objective was to change the perception of the pasta brand from dull and dietetic to innovative and fresh (see Exhibit 21–1). To track the effectiveness of the effort, McCann needed a comprehensive research effort.

The Marketing Challenge

The repositioning began after brand image research found that Buitoni's image profile and personality traits were suffering, despite a high level of consumer awareness. Buitoni was primarily identified with dietetic foods that were healthy but flavorless. This created a disadvantage relative to the other strong competitors in the food industry. In terms of products and advertising values, the competitors' images were richer, more dynamic, and more contemporary.

Buitoni was bought by Swiss-based Nestlé in 1988. The new parent company began the process of brand rejuvenation by developing new products meeting consumers' demands for both more taste and more convenience. Fresh pasta and sauces were the first steps toward innovation. They were soon followed by frozen foods, such as pizza and ready-made frozen meals.

EXHIBIT 21-1

As this scene from a Buitoni TV commercial shows, the brand has been given a more modern, emotional image.

The objective of the long-term repositioning effort was to create an image of Buitoni as the modern interpreter of Italian cuisine and to do this by being close and relevant to the new needs of Italian consumers. Italian consumer research found that there was a positive attitude toward new ideas in the food sector but, at the same time, resistance to giving up the taste and the pleasure of traditional foods simply for the sake of convenience. For Italians, eating is a social and family experience. The research found that the table is the place where Italians experience and express relaxed, warm, welcoming, and genuine social relations. At the table, not only do you enjoy the flavor of good food, but you also enjoy the pleasure of good company.

Message Strategy

In addition to repositioning the Buitoni brand, the campaign hoped to create market expansion, either by category or geography. The communication objectives were to:

- Provide support for the Buitoni brand's new positioning.
- Give individual products personality and credibility.
- Create a world of positive values for the brand.

Based on an understanding of the Italian perception of eating and the importance of the table as the place where warm social events are experienced, the McCann team created the concept of *star bene a tavola,* which roughly translates to "have a good life at the table." This slogan became the tag line for the campaign

Buitoni's competitors placed their emphasis on formal situations and food as a duty (daily meals), and they paid attention to food preparation rather than food enjoyment. In contrast, Buitoni chose to identify with a more genuine pleasure: the conviviality of the informal table.

To convey the brand's emotional and strategic values and to make individual products recognizable, personable, and distinctive within the competitive field, McCann chose a celebrity testimonial format. The chosen actor, Diego Abatantuono, was an up-and-coming movie star in Italian cinema. His personality brought alive the values of friendliness and affinity, and linked those values to the brand. He represented the most positive side of "Italianness": He was lively, cheerful, extroverted, and ironic. He expressed pleasure in good food, conviviality, and friendship, and he had the unaffected nature of the bon vivant.

In one advertisement, Diego, a recognized gourmet, surprises his friends by offering them a genuine, traditional recipe that has been rediscovered and adapted by Buitoni with care and respect for tradition (reflecting the company's gastronomic expertise), but with modern simplicity and convenience (reflecting the company's technological ability/innovation).

In every execution the story played on the product's functional benefit, which became the centerpoint of the representation of friendly conviviality. The good-humored irony conveyed by the tone of voice of the advertisements gave authenticity and amusement to the situation.

Message Delivery Strategies

The Buitoni repositioning campaign used television, radio, and print advertising for awareness and image building. Sales promotion activities also were used to get closer to the consumer. Buitoni advertisements were targeted to households; therefore, McCann's advertising relied on television, especially in the launch phase when the communication objective was to build awareness.

Media planning can be just as creative as the work of the writers and designers creating the message, particularly when it comes to stretching a budget. An example comes from the way the McCann team stretched its TV budget. Given the competitive environment on television, the Milan McCann team sought to maintain a high level of awareness after the launch phase by short TV commercials (15 seconds). This strategy made it possible to be on air for more weeks than would have been possible with longer commercials, thus keeping the brand image more top-of-mind. Even without a budget that would allow Buitoni to advertise each product continuously, the brand could feature one product per week on the air. Tracking studies were the key to the media strategy. The McCann team chose the best weeks to be on air by comparing sell data with cost/gross rating points to find advertising cost-effectiveness per week and per product. The overall plan was the result of combining Buitoni's budget and its weekly effectiveness estimates.

Evaluation

Brand image research carried out in the late 1990s found excellent results for the brand repositioning. Buitoni's image changed from that of a traditional (i.e., old), authoritative, average-quality brand to that of a company offering intelligent solutions to contemporary food needs and desires. Buitoni is now seen as a megabrand with a tradition of expertise serving multiple specialist categories. It brings together Italian good taste and the most modern technology in support of genuine, traditional recipes.

Conclusion

The Buitoni repositioning campaign was able to synthesize brand values for the consumer. The messages underscored the company's friendliness and closeness, its warm and welcoming modernity, and its credibility and authority in a way that was relaxed and self-assured. "Star bene a tavola" is now Buitoni's communication territory, a broad but well-defined image territory where the variety of products have a distinctive and appealing personality for the consumer.

As the campaign's strategy evolved, it saw excellent sales results, good brand image and advertising tracking results, and advertising staying power. After many years, the "Star bene a tavola" campaign is still delivering positive results in popularity and increasing renown. The effectiveness of this long-term repositioning effort was recognized at the Advertising and Marketing Effectiveness award show.

This case was adapted with permission from the Advertising and Marketing Effectiveness (AME) award-winning brief for the repositioning of the Buitoni prepared by the McCann-Erickson Italiana office in Milan, Italy.

EVALUATING THE IMC PROCESSES

Completing his term as chairman of the American Association of Advertising Agencies, David Bell remarked, "Nothing remains more critical to the health and rigor of our business than proving what we all know: that advertising [MC] really works; that it works in the ways that are relevant to our clients; and that it helps drive American business."[1] The trade publication *Advertising Age* echoed Bell's words when it wrote that increasingly cost-conscious marketers "are demanding that agencies be held more accountable for their work by demonstrating value for what they charge."[2]

These two quotes point to the need for *evaluation* in the IMC process. Evaluation must include such critical areas as cross-functional planning and monitoring; brand messages creation; media planning and buying; and listening to customers and capturing their complaints, suggestions, and compliments. It's these IMC processes that strengthen the brand relationships that drive profitable brands. As stated near the beginning of this book, a company cannot fully develop relationships externally until relationships have been developed internally. For that reason, this chapter will begin with a discussion of an internal IMC audit and how it is conducted.

The IMC Mini-Audit

Processes are more important in IMC than in the practice of traditional marketing because more processes are used, and they must be integrated to be effective. IMC requires more interaction with customers and other key stakeholders, more internal sharing of information, and more cross-functional planning for, and monitoring of, brand relationships. Because these are critical processes, they need to be controlled, which can be done only if they are periodically evaluated and monitored. One way to do this is with a process audit. Figure 21–1 is an IMC mini-audit that organizations can use to get a quick read on just how integrated they are.

The IMC In-Depth Audit

The **IMC audit,** on which the IMC mini-audit in Figure 21–1 is based, was developed in the University of Colorado's IMC graduate program. It is *an in-depth research method for evaluating IMC relationship-building efforts.* It examines the organizational structure, as well as the extent of understanding of MC objectives and strategies within the organization and the extent to which people agree with them. It also measures to what extent planned brand messages are strategically consistent. An important element of the audit is a *gap analysis,* which compares what is actually being done to what managers and executives say is being done. Exhibit 21–2 is a creative depiction of the gap between promise and performance.

Before a company can be integrated in the eyes of customers and other stakeholders, it must have an integrated process for developing its marketing communications and brand relationships—in other words, a corporate culture and organization that encourage and facilitate cross-functional management. Just as important, it must have managers who have a basic understanding of, and respect for, the strengths of each of the major marketing communication functions.

Internal communication systems are particularly important in cross-functional management. If the MC process is not managed and executed by people who are in constant touch with each other, the result will be confusion rather than communication. MC planners must keep in mind that, unlike the car industry, which can announce a recall when it discovers it has

FIGURE 21-1

This 20-question mini-audit is a good and easy way for an organization to quickly test its level of integration.

IMC Mini-Audit

Circle the number that best describes how your organization operates regarding each of the following statements. If you *don't know* how well your organization is doing for a given item, circle DK (Don't Know). If a question does not apply to your organization, leave it blank.

		Never			Always		

Organizational Infrastructure

1. In our company, the process of managing brand/company reputation and building stakeholder relationships is a cross-functional responsibility that includes departments such as production, operations, sales finance, and human resources, as well as marketing. — 1 2 3 4 5 DK

2. The people managing our communication programs demonstrate a good understanding of the strengths and weaknesses of ALL major marketing communication tools such as direct response, public relations sales promotion, advertising, and packaging when putting marketing communication plans together. — 1 2 3 4 5 DK

3. We do a good job of internal marketing, informing all areas of the organization about our objectives and marketing programs. — 1 2 3 4 5 DK

4. Our major communication agencies have at least monthly contact with each other regarding our communication programs and activities. — 1 2 3 4 5 DK

Interactivity

5. Our media plan is a strategic balance between mass media and one-to-one media. — 1 2 3 4 5 DK

6. Special programs are in place to facilitate customer inquiries and complaints. — 1 2 3 4 5 DK

7. We use customer databases that capture customer inquiries, complaints, compliments, as well as sales behavior (e.g., trial, repeat, frequency of purchase, type of purchases). — 1 2 3 4 5 DK

8. Our customer databases are easily accessible (internally) and user-friendly. — 1 2 3 4 5 DK

Mission Marketing

9. Our organization's mission is a key consideration and is evident in our marketing communication plans. — 1 2 3 4 5 DK

10. Our mission provides an additional reason for customers and other key stakeholders to believe our messages and support our company. — 1 2 3 4 5 DK

11. Our corporate philanthropic efforts are concentrated in one specific area or program. — 1 2 3 4 5 DK

Strategic Consistency

12. All of our planned brand messages (e.g., advertising, sales promotion, PR, packaging) are strategically consistent. — 1 2 3 4 5 DK

13. We periodically review all our brand messages to determine to what extent they are strategically consistent. — 1 2 3 4 5 DK

14. We consciously think about what brand messages are being sent by our pricing, distribution, product performance, customer-service operations, and by persons and organizations outside the control of the company. — 1 2 3 4 5 DK

Planning and Evaluating

15. When doing our marketing communication planning, a SWOT analysis is used to determine the strengths and opportunities we can leverage, and the weaknesses and threats we need to address.	1	2	3	4	5	DK
16. We use a zero-based approach in marketing communication planning.	1	2	3	4	5	DK
17. When doing annual marketing communication planning, we make sure intrinsic brand contact points are sending positive brand messages and that these contacts are being fully leveraged before investing in creating new brand contact points.	1	2	3	4	5	DK
18. Our company uses some type of tracking study to evaluate the strength of our relationships with customers and other key stakeholder groups.	1	2	3	4	5	DK
19. Our marketing strategies maximize the unique strengths of the various marketing communication functions (e.g., public relations, direct response, advertising, event sponsorships, trade promotions, packaging).	1	2	3	4	5	DK
20. The overall objective of our marketing communication program is to create and nourish profitable relationships with customers and other stakeholders by strategically controlling or influencing all messages sent to these groups, and encouraging purposeful dialogue with them.	1	2	3	4	5	DK

Add scores (minus blank items and DKs) and divide by 20.   Score _____

installed defective parts, it is virtually impossible to recall a million brand messages to replace a broken promise or to align inconsistent messages.

The in-depth IMC audit takes about two months to complete. Table 21–1 outlines the basic steps that are involved.

Examples of Audit Findings

An audit can identify problems a company doesn't even know it has. For example, in one high-tech manufacturing firm, the director of marketing believed the company was totally integrated and would learn little from the audit. The audit discovered, however, that the opposite was true. The marketing communication department, for example, spent most of its budget on trade magazine advertisements and very little on direct marketing even though the company, which sold a very specialized product, had only 200 customers. The MC department had little knowledge of, and made little use of, the company's customer databases.

The following are more examples of other actual audit findings:[3]

- *Confusion about objectives.* In one company, managers gave 9 different responses when asked what the corporate marketing communication objectives were and 10 different responses for the brand marketing communication objectives. Obviously, when people are working against different message objectives, it is impossible to have message consistency, which was confirmed by a content analyses undertaken as part of the audit.

- *Lack of agreement on message themes.* In a retail chain that had begun advertising "Low Prices Every Day," there was no agreement among managers on the definition of what this did or should mean regarding the chain's pricing strategy. Out of seven different explanations of what this new strategy meant, none was given by more than 15 percent of the managers.

TABLE 21-1   Steps in Conducting an IMC Audit

1. *Orientation meeting.*

   a. Prior to this meeting, the audit team reviews basic reports describing the organization and its business.

   b. At the meeting, company executives give the audit team an overview of the company.

   c. Executives also provide audit team a copy of the organization's marketing and MC objectives, and an overview of the processes used to generate brand relationship-building programs. These objectives become one of the standards against which the audit findings are evaluated.

   d. Executives and the audit team agree on a list of people to be interviewed and set a timetable for the interviews.

   e. The company appoints an internal audit coordinator.

   f. Within a week of this meeting, the company must approve the audit instruments.

2. *On-site interviews.* The audit team conducts interviews of 60 to 90 minutes with all key people involved in influencing and/or producing marketing programs and managing customer relationships. It is also recommended that outside communication agency account managers be interviewed.

   Interviews are designed to measure each manager's:

   a. Perceptions of the organization's brand objectives and his or her responsibilities in helping meet these objectives.

   b. Knowledge of the major marketing communication functions. For example, how well does an advertising person understand the strengths and weaknesses of PR?

   c. Understanding of, and attitude toward, integrating the organization's marketing communication efforts.

   d. Interaction and cooperation with all the other communication units in regard to planning and executing message and media programs.

   e. Use of customer and other stakeholder databases.

   f. Value perception of each primary stakeholder group.

3. *Content analysis.* At the time of the interviews, the audit team collects samples of all selling messages (advertising, press releases, packaging, product instructions, etc.) used within the last 12 months. The team then systematically analyzes these for consistency of message, image and portrayal of company/brand positioning, and consistency with stated marketing communication objectives.

4. *Tabulation and analysis.* The audit team analyzes the interview findings, along with the results of the content analysis, and determines the organization's level of integration. It then compares these findings to the organization's marketing and communication objectives.

5. *Final report.* The audit team presents both a written and an oral report that identifies strengths and weaknesses of the organization's brand relationship managing process and makes recommendations as to how the weaknesses can be addressed and the strengths leveraged.

In a national consumer goods company, one message theme was used in 100 percent of television advertising, but only 22 percent of other advertising; another theme was used in 80 percent of television advertising, but only 20 percent of the sales promotion materials.

- *Lack of agreement on primary stakeholders.* In a health care facility, patients and their families received the third highest rating of importance when all responses were averaged, but this same group ranked eighth when only senior management responses were averaged. Political leaders were ninth on the list when all responses were averaged, but third on the list for public affairs/public relations. The audit was not investigating specific stakeholders to whom specific types of messages are addressed by specific departments, but rather the overall importance to the organization of the various stakeholders.

- *Messages not targeted to primary stakeholder groups.* In one company it was found that 24 percent of all printed messages were not targeted to any of the high-priority stakeholder groups identified by management, and only 1 percent was specifically directed to the target audience rated most important.

- *Not enough information available.* Most marketing managers say that only about half the time do they receive enough information from other departments to do their jobs effectively. In some cases the desired information did not exist; however, many times it did, and these managers were unaware of it or how to access it. The types of information frequently mentioned as difficult to get were sales results, research results, and promotional and other special marketing plans for specific events and programs.

- *Limited use of research results.* In one packaged-goods company, which was spending approximately $150 million on marketing communication, 37 percent of the managers said they did not know of any market analysis being done by the company, 33 percent said some was being done but didn't know if it was being used, and 15 percent said very little was used.

- *Little knowledge of annual planning.* In one company, 60 percent of the managers did not know how the budget was allocated among departments, and half of the managers did not know to what extent each year's communication plan compared to the previous one.

- *Little understanding of evaluation.* In a high-tech company selling computer components to other manufactures, 35 percent did not know if or how the company evaluated its marketing communication programs. Of those who said the company did evaluate these programs, half did not know what was evaluated and over a third did not know how the results of those evaluations were used in marketing communication planning.

- *Limited use of computers for networking and consumer databases.* In one company, which had a relatively small number of industrial customers, customer buying behavior was not captured, although there were many opportunities for doing so.

Benefits of an IMC Audit

Companies that have had IMC audits done have realized benefits that far outweigh the time and cost it takes to conduct the audit. As stated earlier, the main purpose of the audit is to identify process gaps and barriers (i.e., those procedures and departments that are obstructing or slowing down the development of consistent messages), inadequacies in properly handling purposeful dialogue, and the unrealized potential of merchandising the corporate mission. Specifically, an IMC audit has many benefits:

- The audit objectively shows to what extent planned messages contain a consistent strategy.
- The audit identifies the degree of consensus and focus among managers. It reveals the extent to which managers are working toward the same MC objectives and have the same understandings about the brand's strengths and weaknesses, targets, brand position, and competitive advantages.

- The audit identifies the level of coordination (or lack thereof) between communication units, both internally and externally.

- The audit indicates which units or people need to increase their core competency in integration and in their basic understanding of, and appreciation for, the strengths and weakness of each MC tool.

- Conducting an audit not only sends a message to the marketing communications staff and outside communication agencies that their jobs are important, but also sends the message throughout the organization that management believes in and endorses integration.

- The audit provides a basis for refocusing and reallocating resources against the primary objectives.

- Audit findings give top management an objective basis on which to provide more effective leadership in marketing and relationship building, and they make top management aware that building and nourishing relationships is a cross-functional challenge and responsibility.

Communication Audits

Similar to an IMC audit is the *communication audit*, which is used in public relations. According to Fraser Seitel, a communication audit is "an increasingly important method of research in public relations work."[4] A communication audit evaluates an organization's reputation, determines how the organization is perceived by its own employees and members of the community, measures the readership of PR publications such as annual reports and news releases, and evaluates the organization's role as a corporate citizen.

One version of a communication audit is that created by the agency GCI Group. Called a Corporate Brand Study, this audit includes the following steps:[5]

1. Internal: Management survey
   - Optional: Employee survey

2. External: Key stakeholder survey

3. Assessment
   - Gap analysis
   - Structural equation modeling
   - Sensitivity analysis
   - Competitive analysis

4. Strategic communication planning

5. Communication program implementation

6. Evaluation: Follow-up study; measure results

Although the communication and IMC audits are basically evaluation tools, they also can help design a road map that an organization can use to become more integrated and customer focused. They provide an objective, well-documented list of what must be changed in order for a company to maximize the benefits of integration before beginning the next step, which is to develop integrated communication strategies.

EVALUATION AND MEASUREMENT OF BRAND MESSAGES

MC evaluation and measurement programs are types of research conducted both during the development of brand message strategies and after the completion of a campaign. In either case, the basic objective is to predict or determine *results*—that is, the changes in behavior and/or attitudes created by an offer, a promotion, a campaign, a company response, or some other type of brand message. Exhibit 21–3 draws attention to the importance of results in all areas of business.

Other objectives of evaluation and measurement include (1) reducing risk, (2) providing direction, (3) determining to what extent marketing communication programs met objectives, and (4) determining to what extent the communication effort proved to be a good investment of the company's money. The Buitoni campaign described in the chapter opening case resulted from research that determined there was a need for a change in the brand's position. The resulting campaign also involved tracking the effectiveness of the effort from product to product as well as from year to year.

Important as they are, however, MC measurement and evaluation need to be put into perspective. The vast majority of brand messages have never been, and never will be, formally measured or evaluated. Most decisions as to whether or not to use a particular brand message are based on the judgment of a marketing manager (or some other client or agency executive) because there is not enough at risk to justify spending money to evaluate every single message.

Generally speaking, MC evaluation is done only when companies (1) have sizable media budgets and (2) stand to suffer significant financial losses should the brand messages fail to achieve the MC objectives. While some marketing executives feel their personal judgment is sufficient to evaluate brand messages and campaigns, most *smart* executives in these situations prefer to base their "use/don't use" decisions on some type of objective evaluation.

Although the majority of individual brand messages are never formally evaluated, the selling concept or creative strategy on which a brand message is based may have been rigorously tested. Once an idea for an advertising campaign has been tested and has proved itself, that idea may be executed for a couple of years with no further testing other than tracking studies (which are explained later in this chapter).

Even when an evaluation is deemed necessary, there are several questions that need to be answered to justify the expense:

1. What should be evaluated?

2. What information already exists?

3. At what stage should the MC message or campaign be evaluated?

EXHIBIT 21-3

Accountability is a big issue in marketing communication, as in other areas of business. This ad points to the fact that the insurance and financial services company Cigna accepts responsibility for getting results for its clients.

How come no company has ever used this slogan?

Given the fact that results are what business is all about, isn't it just a little ironic that no company has ever associated itself with the statement below? It is, however, understandable.

After all, if there ever was a double-edged slogan, this is it.

We get paid for results.

For, once you promise results, you had better be prepared to deliver, be judged, and be held accountable for them.

At the CIGNA companies, we operate on a simple principle: Clients come to us for results.

And the reason they keep coming back is because we give them their money's worth.

By accepting that responsibility, we have become a leader in many fields. Business insurance. Employee benefits. Managed health care. Pension and investment management.

From now on, you'll see the words—we get paid for results—next to our logo. Not as a window dressing. But rather because they are the essence of who we are and what we do. To learn more, write us at One Liberty Place, Dept. RA, Phila., PA 19103.

Because, if you're not paying for results, what are you paying for?

What Should Be Evaluated?

Evaluation is generally undertaken for critical decisions that involve a lot of money, resources, and/or staff time, such as changing a logo or launching a year-long campaign. The idea is to determine the probability of success up front, before the money is spent. In particular, marketers want to know whether the level of success will be high enough to justify the program's cost, an analysis that shows the return on investment (ROI).

The Cost/Value Factor

A company should conduct brand message research when the risks are high and the cost/value of the research is reasonable. The more that is at risk, the more developmental evaluations and measurements should be used.

For example, if Pillsbury is considering replacing its familiar Doughboy with a more modern character, the company would probably spend hundreds of thousands of dollars testing and evaluating alternatives before making such a high-risk decision. This is because hundreds of *millions* of dollars have been invested in building awareness of the Doughboy as spokesperson for the brand. It's a big decision than can cost the company dearly if the wrong decision is made.

On the other hand, if the company is planning to introduce a new cornbread product, using the Doughboy in brand messages related to the launch, it would not be worth spending money to evaluate whether the Doughboy should or should not wear a cowboy bandana in the ads. The extent of the bandana's impact on the overall brand message would be so minor that spending time and money researching the question would not be cost-effective.

The important thing to remember is that there are always costs to evaluation. One cost is payment to participants, a practice commonly used with focus groups. The ad in Exhibit 21–4 focuses on this type of cost.

There are, however, some MC measurements that can be made with very little cost. Recall the explanation of *split-runs* in Chapter 11. For a few hundred dollars extra, two versions of a print ad can be run in a magazine or newspaper to measure the difference in response for two different offers, headlines, illustrations, or other message components. The same technique can be used in direct mail or with other types of promotional brochures and offers. Although the risk of using one offer versus another may not be great, the cost of measuring is relatively small and thus the cost-value of the measurement is very good.

Also, evaluations should measure only those things that can be changed. One manufacturing company asked its dealers how satisfied they were with a number of operational areas. Three areas of the business always received low scores, but no changes were made. When the president of the company was asked why not, he explained that making such changes would be too costly. Unfortunately, the company continued to ask these questions, which not only took time and money but also served as a reminder to the dealers of things they didn't like about the company.

What Information Already Exists?

As mentioned at various points in this book, many companies have enormous amounts of data that could be (but have not been) used for evaluative purposes. A good example is a situation that occurred at a public health organization several years ago. When the level of public discussion of acquired immune deficiency syndrome (AIDS) was very high, the organization hired a major advertising agency to conduct focus groups across the United States to see what major questions the average person had about this disease. At the same time, the organization hired a consultant to evaluate the organization's call center, which was set up to answer health questions from medical personnel and the general public. In the course of his audit, the consultant noticed that the representatives made notes on most of the calls they handled. When asked the purpose of the notes, he was told they were to help the representatives keep track of the number of calls handled and the subject of the calls so they could do their weekly performance report. Once the weekly reports were written, the notes were thrown away.

In further observations, the consultant found that the notes often included the questions being asked by those who called into the center. Not surprisingly, many of the calls were about AIDS. Those within the organization who had requested the AIDS focus groups did not realize this information was coming in to the organization's call center each day. The problem was that the people who asked for the focus groups were separate from the call center people. Because there was no cross-functional organization involving these two groups, the organization paid thousands of dollars to gather data that it was already collecting.

Similar situations exist in many companies. For example, marketing departments seldom work closely with customer-service departments and consequently have little knowledge of what customers are saying about the brand and company. Also many companies that issue product warranty cards never tabulate those that are returned—and thus never collect the valuable customer profile information the cards contain. The point is that before a research project is started, it is wise to make sure the information desired does not already exist.

When Should Evaluation Be Conducted?

Evaluation can be done at several stages during the development and execution of MC campaigns. The first stage is market research into customer perceptions to determine whether the brand's position needs reinforcing, changing, or repositioning. Recall that it was this kind of market research that determined that Buitoni had a brand image problem. Then, after message ideas have been generated, **concept testing,** which consists of *tests that measure the effectiveness of the rough ideas that become brand and campaign themes.* Next is copytesting, which was mentioned in Chapter 10 as a type of research that evaluates brand message executions in a rough form before they are finally produced. Then there is **concurrent testing,** which is *testing that tracks the performance of messages as they are run* (see Exhibit 21–5). Some companies only test at one stage, others at more than one—again depending on how much the company wants to invest in minimizing its risks. A specific kind of concurrent testing, the tracking study, will be described later in this chapter.

Finally, there is **evaluative testing,** which *measures the performance of the brand messages against their objectives at the conclusion of the program.* The closer a message is to its finished form and the more realistic the testing environment,

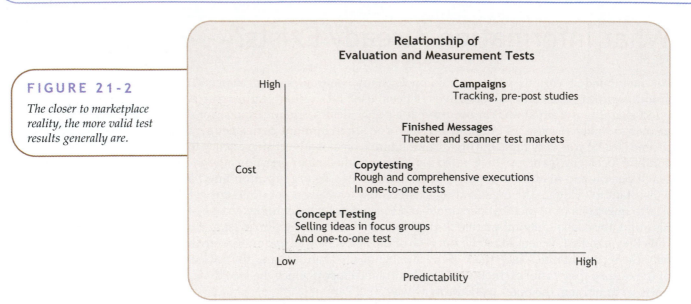

FIGURE 21-2

The closer to marketplace reality, the more valid test results generally are.

the more predictability a measurement generally has, as shown in Figure 21–2. (Some of the terms in this figure may be unfamiliar to you; they will be explained later in this chapter.)

The Critical Role of Objectives

As stated earlier, an effective marketing communication program is one that meets its objectives. This means that MC planners must set measurable objectives. All organizations measure sales and profits. In nonprofit organizations "sales" translate to such things as donations, volunteer hours, and function attendance. The problem with using sales results to evaluate the impact of marketing communication, however, is that MC represents only one set of variables that affect these measures. Product performance, pricing, distribution, and competition all help determine sales, share, and profits. Consequently, the effectiveness of MC activities must be measured by results that are directly related to their objectives. Only in the areas of direct marketing and some sales promotion is it possible to easily gauge message effectiveness by sales. Other MC results include brand awareness, brand knowledge, attitude change, and customer satisfaction. Although these measures are also influenced by other factors, they are generally the focus of marketing communications measuring efforts.

Measuring Objectives

Although every MC plan is different, most plans are designed to increase one or more of the following communication objectives: understanding and recall of brand information (knowledge); the creation of brand awareness and image (awareness); the creation of attitude change and preference (persuasion); trial and repeat buying (behavior); and the development of customer acquisition, retention, and growth (relationship building). If the objective calls for a 10 percent increase in brand awareness, for example, then brand awareness should be measured.

If the objectives are behavioral results, such things as requests for more information, trial, and showroom visits are the easiest to measure. As explained in Chapters 16 and 17, one of the primary strengths of both sales promotion and direct response is their measurability. The number of prospects and customers who respond to a promotion or offer (e.g., buying, sampling, requesting more information, visiting store or trade show booth) can be compared to the targeted population to determine a response rate or percentage.

Measuring changes in attitudes and opinions is more difficult because these changes exist only in people's heads. Also researchers do not agree about whether attitude changes lead to behavior changes—or, if they do, to what extent. Nevertheless, most marketers and academics agree that increases in such things as brand awareness, knowledge, and brand preference are critical indicators of communication effectiveness and are therefore worth measuring and evaluating.

Baselines and Benchmarks

An important factor in setting measurable objectives is knowing the **baseline**—that is, *the beginning point, or where things stood right before the MC effort began.* In other words, if you want to increase awareness by 10 percent, then you have to know what the current level of awareness is in order gauge the amount of change—10 percent of what? If 60 percent of the target audience is aware of a brand, and the objective is to increase awareness by 10 percent, then the desired outcome would be an awareness level of 66 percent (60 × .10 = 6, which is added to the base of 60). The objective would be stated like this:

> The objective is to increase the awareness level from 60 percent to 66 percent, an increase of 10 percent, within a one-year period.

A tracking study of the launch of Buitoni's Bella Napoli Pizza product, for example, found that the product had gained a critical level of penetration. The communication effectiveness was determined by the following:

- *Awareness:* The 43 percent level of awareness at the prelaunch stage (1995) rose to 98 percent two years later, surpassing the main competitor, Findus, which held an 84 percent awareness level during the same period.

- *Brand usership:* Buitoni's penetration went from 11 percent during the prelaunch phase to 59 percent after the launch.

The bottom line for marketing communication effectiveness is sales figures. Thanks to the communication support provided by the launch of Pizza Bella Napoli in 1996, Buitoni Pizzas registered a 61 percent growth in sales volume and a 76 percent increase in value in the following two years. Buitoni Pasta Fresca, which benefited from a successful new product in 1996, grew by 100 percent in volume and 95 percent in value from the proceeding year.

MEASUREMENT AND EVALUATION METHODS

The vast majority of developmental evaluations and measurements, as mentioned above, are done for advertising concepts and strategies that are supported by large media budgets. If a company makes three TV commercials, spends $15 million on media time and space, and then finds that the messages are not communicating or persuading, it has wasted both the production costs and the $15 million. Table 21–2 lists the elements and developmental stages of brand messages most frequently measured, the types of measuring methods used, and the format in which the evaluations and measurements take place. (Again, some of the terms may be unfamiliar to you; these are explained in the following sections.)

TABLE 21-2   Measurement and Evaluation Methods

Element to Be Tested	Measurement Methods	Message-Testing Format
Concept, creative strategy	Focus groups, intercept surveys, projective tests	Idea statements, visuals on display boards
Awareness, brand knowledge	Surveys	Phone, e-mail, customer service interactions
Communication and persuasion	Focus groups, one to one, laboratory, e-mail	Rough layouts, comps
Recognition, recall	Magazine portfolio, day-after phone survey, theater	Finished executions, anamatics
Physiological responses	Eye tracking, galvanic skin response	Laboratory one to one
Packaging impact	Tachistoscope, observation	Laboratory one to one, in store/aisle
Pilot test	Scanner test-markets	Finished executions
Customer knowledge, attitudes, behavior	Tracking studies	Phone, e-mail
Copytesting (post-test)	Split-run, scanner data, awareness, attitude change, sales	Finished executions

Concept, Creative Strategy Testing

The first step in developing a campaign is to determine the most compelling message concept, creative theme, or primary selling proposition. An example of a concept test is one that was done by a U.S.-based frozen-food company. Its food technicians developed a frozen pasta sauce that consumers could make from a package containing chunks of frozen vegetables and a packet of seasoning and thickener. All the consumer had to do was place the ingredients in a skillet along with some water and oil and cook for 20 minutes.

The challenge was to come up with a message concept that accurately described the product and its benefits in a believable and persuasive manner. The company didn't know whether to focus on the convenience of preparation, the great taste, or the ingredients. Working with its advertising agency, the company wrote the following three concept statements, which were shown to three focus groups of the target audience—women who had families and who liked to cook. Each statement was printed in large letters on poster board. In each focus group, the order in which the three concepts were presented was changed to avoid order bias.

Concept A: Now, in only 20 minutes you can conveniently prepare a delicious-tasting pasta sauce made from flash-frozen vegetables and a secret mix of Italian spices.

Concept B: A rich, thick pasta sauce that is so delicious, your family will not believe you made it yourself.

Concept C: Because it is a unique blend of flash-frozen Italian tomatoes, onions, celery, peppers, and hearty Italian spices, this is the finest-tasting pasta sauce you will ever make.

After all three concepts were displayed, participants were asked to write down and then discuss which one best described a product they would be most likely to buy and why. The "whys" are the most important aspect of concept testing. The key finding about the pasta sauce was that few believed that a great-tasting sauce could be made in only 20 minutes. This resulted in final copy that promised "a great tasting sauce that you don't have to cook all day."

There are several ways to test creative concepts. One is to use an **intercept survey**—*a survey in which people in a mall or at an event are stopped and asked to respond to a short questionnaire.* The questions ask them to compare various concepts and comment on them. These are not scientifically reliable studies, but rather methods of getting a quick response for diagnostic purposes. It tells whether people being interviewed understand a concept and, if so, if they like or dislike it.

A **focus group** is *an evaluation technique in which 8 to 12 members of a brand's target audience, led by a moderator, discuss some aspect of a brand, product category, or message strategy.* Discussions last one to two hours, and participants are paid anywhere from $25 to $200 for participating. The higher fees are for professionals such as doctors and lawyers.

The main benefits of focus group research is diagnostic; the idea is to learn more about a category, competing brands, and message strategies from the user's perspective. When a participant says that a brand is "not easy to use," a good discussion leader then probes to find out why this is so and what could be done to improve its ease of use. Some people call focus groups "red flag" research. This means focus groups are a good place to hear about problems. Sometimes when people are working closely on a project, such as a commercial or a set of print ads, they can overlook the obvious. Focus groups help catch these oversights.

Focus group findings should not be projected to a brand's total population because (1) the number of participants is too small, (2) the participants do not represent a randomly selected sample, and (3) quite often two or three "strong" people in a group dominate the discussion, often biasing the views of others. Despite these shortcomings, however, focus groups can provide customer insights that can be valuable help in developing brand messages.

Copytesting for Predicting Communication and Persuasion

Copytesting can be used either while the brand message is in development or after it appears. The ad in Exhibit 21–6 for Insight Express, which is a spinoff of NFO (a panel research company that evaluates campaigns and other brand messages online), illustrates how different people involved in the development of a creative idea may see its potential differently from the audience for whom it is intended.

All brand messages should, to some extent, do two things—communicate and persuade. To make sure these two message objectives are achieved, companies use several different measuring techniques. As explained in Chapter 4, communication happens when the receiver of a message arrives at the same meaning as was intended by the sender who encoded the message. Persuasion takes place when recipients of a message change their attitudes and/or behavior in the direction desired. Copytesting measures both of these.

Measuring Communication Effects

Copytesting can be used to measure and evaluate several aspects of communication: attention, brand/message awareness and knowledge, and emotional and physiological responses, which are briefly discussed below.

Attention

The ability of a brand message to get attention is an important aspect of communication. One way to test the attention-getting power of a package, ad, or other brand message is by using a **tachistoscope,** *a device that exposes a brand message briefly to test participants so that researchers can measure how long it takes for a certain message or elements to be communicated.* Test using a tachistoscope are called *t-tests.* Respondents are seated before a screen containing a small hole that they are asked to look through. Behind the screen, but in complete darkness, is the ad or other stimulus, such as a logo, to be tested. The researcher illuminates the object for a very short but specific amount of time, such as a second or two, and then asks respondents what they saw. To illustrate, say that a company wants to test the attention-getting power of a promotional offer printed on a package of frozen vegetables. The t-test would be set up to see how many times the package must be illuminated for one second before respondents saw the promotional announcement on the package. If there were three different executions, the one requiring the fewest exposures would be considered the most attention-getting.

A t-test may also be used to compare package designs. A selection of competitive packages, including the test package, are arranged behind the screen similarly to how they would be displayed in a store. Respondents are asked to look through the hole and find the brand being tested. Once the light comes on, it stays on until respondents say they see the test brand and can correctly say where it is displayed (upper left, lower right, etc.). This is called a find-time test. By testing several different package designs, the measure helps determine which one is most attention-getting. Because the average shopper spends only 20 to 30 seconds making a brand selection in most categories, the quicker a package can be spotted, the more likely it is to be purchased.

EXHIBIT 21-6

This ad for Insight Express promotes the company's high-speed market feedback and research.

Awareness and Knowledge

Companies commonly measure consumers' brand awareness and knowledge. There are two types of brand awareness that are measured—recognition and recall. *Recognition* is the act of identifying and remembering that you have seen something. Identifying a person you know within a crowd of people is recognition. *Recall* (or *unaided awareness*) is the more difficult process of bringing forth a brand message from memory. You may recognize a person in a crowd, but you may not be able to recall the person's name. Researchers measure recall by asking respondents to name all the brands they can think of in a particular product category. The researchers then give the respondents any brand names they did not mention and ask whether the respondents have heard of those brands (a process called *aided awareness*). As you might expect, aided awareness (recognition) scores are always higher than unaided awareness (recall) scores. (See the box titled "The Starch Challenge" for a discussion of one type of awareness testing.)

A measure of magazine ad recall is provided by Gallup & Robinson's Impact Test, which gives respondents (who have been screened for certain demographic characteristics) a magazine to take home and read. The following day the respondents are called and asked to recall as many ads as they can from the magazine. For the ads that are recalled, respondents are asked what brand claims they remember and how likely they are to buy the brand.

Recall measurements of TV commercials—called *post-tests* because the commercials have already been made and are on air—are done in a similar way. Respondents are called and asked if they have watched a certain show the day before. If they say yes, they are asked if they saw a commercial for a product in a particular category (e.g., hair sprays, cars, brokerage services, computers). If the answer is yes, they are asked what the brand was and what they recall about the commercial. Those who don't recall the particular commercial being studied are then asked if they remember a commercial for the brand being measured (a recognition question).

Some of the concerns with post-tests are that program content can influence a score, as can the number of competitive commercials that are running at the same time. And, as with the print tests, there is always a question as to what is actually being remembered—the message execution or the brand claims. It has also been found that well-known brands normally have higher scores than do new and less well-known brands just because of the familiarity factor.

Awareness and brand knowledge can be affected by both content and delivery. Harris Interactive has a service that tracks total media usage. An online panel of 3,000 people are sent a digital-diary survey that takes them through the previous day, prompting them to recall all media usage, including time spent online, at a movie theater, watching regular and prerecorded TV programs and videos, and reading newspapers or magazines. Panels such as this can be used to determine media habits of target audiences and to measure a media mix's impact on them versus a control group.

To determine media habit differences between Internet users and nonusers (or light users), the Harris Interactive survey is administered periodically offline (by phone). One of the findings is that Internet users spend less time reading newspapers but more time reading magazines than do nonusers or light users of the Internet.

Brand knowledge requires a more in-depth measurement than does brand recall. To measure how much respondents know about a brand and to what extent they see it as different it from its competitors, researchers use phone and e-mail surveys. Brand knowledge can also be measured with one-to-one personal interviews, but this expensive method is often not cost-justified. Brand awareness and knowledge measurements are frequently used to evaluate a new or revised campaign effort. Measurements are done as pre- and post-tests (i.e., before and after a campaign runs).

The Starch Challenge

It's very difficult to link message responses to behavioral responses. An example comes from the long-standing research service offered by the INRA/Starch company. Although this service was abandoned in the late 1990s, it's useful to see how the Starch test operated in order to understand the difficulty of using measures like this to predict message effectiveness.

For many years, the Starch Readership Report was one of the most widely used recognition measures in print evaluation programs. Starch measured the readership of ads in approximately 100 magazines and newspapers (both consumer and BtB). For each issue, 200 respondents were screened to make sure they had spent time reading the particular issue being studied. These respondents were then taken through the magazine by an interviewer, who pointed to each ad that was being measured. For each ad, respondents were asked if they remembered seeing it and, if so, how much of the ad they had read or looked at. From these answers, each ad was given three scores: Noted (those who noted the ad), Seen/Associated (those who read or looked at some of the ad), and Read Most (those who read or looked at the majority of the ad).

The assumption was that the higher the Read Most score, the more involving the ad, and thus the more likely it was effective in communicating the message and persuading the audience. Because some product categories are naturally more interesting to readers than others, a brand's ad score was compared to other ads in the same category to determine its meaning. The Starch program had category norms to use in this comparison.

A major limitation of this type of measurement is that communication and persuasion can only be inferred. Some brand messages attract a lot of attention but leave readers with little knowledge about the brand itself.

Industry criticism regarding Starch measures came primarily from the newspaper industry, where researchers argued that the ad noting scores devalued the newspaper audience attention patterns. There were also criticisms of the way the sample newspapers were chosen; whether they reflected local, as opposed to national, newspaper readership; and whether the scores can be used to reliably represent the readership of the publication.

Think About It

What did the Starch scores attempt to measure, and how did they do it? Why are measures like this subject to criticism? What were the criticisms aimed at this program? Do you believe a test like this would be useful to people who create and manage brand messages?

Source: Robert L. Oney, "The Case Against Ad-Noting Scores," *Research Federation Forum* 31, no. 1, January–February 1997, p. 1; and Mike Donatello, "New Starch Norms on the Horizon, But Will They Be Better?" *Research Federation Forum* 3, no. 1, January–February 1997, p. 2.

Emotional Responses

Recognizing the power of emotions in brand decision making, and also the fact that emotions are difficult for many people to express, MC agency BBDO Worldwide has developed a test that measures emotional responses to brand messages. The agency's proprietary Emotional Measurement System lets respondents communicate their emotions by selecting photographs of individuals with various emotional expressions. After respondents are shown a set of brand messages, they are asked to select from dozens of these individual-expression photos (which have been extensively studied and categorized) the ones that best illustrate how the brand messages made them feel. The selected photos are used to "emotionally profile" each set of brand messages shown. This allows the agency and client to select the brand message that comes closest to creating the emotional response that is desired.

An important emotional response that can be measured is likability. Traditionally many MC managers felt that it didn't matter whether customers liked an ad or not, as long as it built awareness. More recently, a study by the Advertising Research Foundation (ARF) of different pretesting methods found that likability was a powerful predictor of sales success.

The likability of a brand message can be measured by using a continuum with two extremes such as "I loved the message" and "I hated the message." Respondents choose a number on the scale (usually from 1 to 5 or from 1 to 7) that best indicates their feeling. Likability tests consider such factors as:

- Relevance (personally meaningful).
- Believability, credibility (convincing and true to life).
- Interest (intriguing, fascinating, engaging).
- Enjoyment (entertaining, warm).
- Familiarity (comfortable).
- Surprise (pleasantly surprising).

Physiological Responses

Sometimes how we feel emotionally about something affects how we respond to it physically—whether or not we are aware of those responses. According to neurologist Richard Restak, "We have reason to doubt that full awareness of our motives, drives, and other mental activities may be possible."[6] Recognizing that people sometimes are not willing or capable of expressing what they really think or feel about a brand message, measures of physiological responses have been developed. Because companies seldom use these tests, they will be described only briefly. The reason for limited use is that the tests are relatively expensive to conduct and the findings are often difficult to interpret.

Probably the most widely discussed physiological test is the *galvanic skin response test*, which uses an instrument called a galvanometer, to measure minute electrical currents. It is the same basic instrument used in lie detectors. For marketing communications, however, the purpose is to measure to what extent respondents are stimulated or aroused when exposed to a variety of brand messages. Researchers have found that there can be a correlation between level of stimulation and purchase behavior.[7]

Two other tests have to do with eyes—pupil dilation and eye tracking. The *pupil dilation measure* follows the same concept as the galvanic skin response measurement. The more the pupil dilates, the greater the indication of involvement in the brand message being shown. The *eye-tracking instrument* uses an infrared beam to follow the eye, converting its movement to traces on the ad being tested. Measurements show which ad elements attract the most attention. This can be helpful in measuring what is known in the MC industry as "vampire creative"—message elements that detract from the purpose of the brand message.

Measuring Persuasion Effects

Although focus groups are often used to test communication, they are not as reliable for testing persuasion. The reason for this is that there is a low correlation between what people say they will do and what they actually do, especially when it comes to brand selection. "Intend-to-buy" scores—another name for persuasion scores and preference measures—have fooled many companies. Therefore, several levels and methods of persuasion testing have been developed, each providing a little more validity than the one before: theater setting, theater/store, scanner market tests, and conventional test markets. The more a test simulates real life and includes behavioral responses, the more validity the persuasion score will have.

Theater Tests

After focus groups, companies use **theater tests,** such as Market Research Inc.'s ASI test (developed by Burke Marketing Research), to measure persuasion effects. These are *tests in which people are invited to a local location for the purpose, they are told, of critiquing a TV program, but actually for the purpose of evaluating their response to a brand message.* Before the showing, participants are asked to complete a questionnaire that asks what brands in certain categories they prefer (it also asks for some demographic data). Respondents are then shown the program, which contains six to eight commercials. Three or four of these are the commercials being tested. Following the showing, respondents are asked about the program; they are also asked what commercials they remember seeing (a measure of advertising recall). They are then shown a second program, also containing the test commercials. Following this, they are asked to indicate their preference for brands in a variety of categories similar to the first questionnaire they completed. The difference in the preference scores between the pre- and post-tests for the brands being tested indicates the level of persuasion.

These laboratory persuasion scores can be given meaning only after they are compared to **norms,** which are *average product category scores accumulated over the years by the research company.* Also, companies doing this type of research try to get as much follow-up sales data as they can from their clients to correlate lab findings with actual sales results.

Theater Test with Purchase

The next level of persuasion validity involves forced-purchases after the theater showing of a brand message. Instead of having participants complete the last questionnaire described above, respondents are given tokens and taken into another room that is set up as a small store. The shelves are stocked with all the major brands in each of the product categories of the test commercials. Respondents are told to use their tokens to buy whichever brands they want. By recording each person's brand choices and comparing these choices to those indicated on the initial brand-usage questionnaire, researchers can determine how many respondents switched brands. The more that switched, the higher the persuasion score for the respective test commercial.

One advantage of the theater tests is that **animatics** (*rough video footage*) can be used instead of finished commercials. Although finished ads are preferred so they don't look out of place or inferior, using animatics saves companies a great amount of production costs. A weakness of theater tests is that, because participants are aware they are being tested, they can still project intend-to-buy responses that do not necessarily correspond to their normal behavior. Forced-purchase decisions can provide only directional answers regarding persuasion (an ad is persuasive or not persuasive); they cannot be used to say that the test commercial would increase sales by x percent.

Test Marketing

Test marketing is probably the most valid persuasion test of all because it takes place over the long term in a competitive marketplace. Test marketing is *a research* *design, in which an MC campaign is run in two to four markets for anywhere from 3 to 12 months.* Brand sales are compared to those in similar control markets (those in which the brand has about the same share and is faced with the same major competitors). The problems with using test markets are (1) they take a long time, (2) testing exposes your new ideas to competitors, and (3) market tests are expensive. In test marketing, all MC materials must be in finished form, and at least 200 customers need to be interviewed in each of the test and control markets both before and after the test market runs. One type of test marketing is the scanner market test. Another is a tracking study.

Scanner Market Tests

The third level of validity is the **scanner market test** (also called a *single-source test*), which is *a tracking of a household's purchases.* Several of the major research companies (ACNielsen, Information Resources, and SAMI/Burke) provide this type of testing service. Each of these services has made special arrangements with chain stores and local cable operators and newspapers in selected small- to medium-sized markets throughout the United States. In each of these markets researchers have recruited a panel of household members that agree to have a buyer identification card (like a frequent-buyer card) scanned every time they go shopping so their purchases can be tracked (see Exhibit 21–7). Within each market's panel, participants are divided into two groups, the test group and the control group. The cable company sends the test commercial only to those in the test group. At the same time, newspaper test ads are substituted for regular ads in papers that are delivered to the test households.

Scanner market tests can be used in the short term to evaluate sales promotion offers, which, if successful, generally increase sales within days of running. These tests can also be used for more long-term evaluation, such as a brand's repositioning or a new campaign theme. One of the benefits of scanner tests is that, by tracking weekly (or even daily) sales, researchers can determine just how long it takes for marketing communication to have an effect. The more frequently a product category is purchased, the more telling such a test generally is and the less time it requires. Differences in purchases between the test and control households determine the extent of the promotional impact.

Although participating households know they are members of a research panel, they have no idea what brands are being tested. Because brand selections are made in real stores with respondents using their own money, there is nothing other than the test MC messages to influence the results. Also, results are based on actual sales data, not on scores that have to be translated into sales. Furthermore, this type of test is not obvious to competitors.

There are a couple of shortcomings, however. Scanner market tests have high costs—several times the cost of theater tests—because not only must researchers use finished brand messages, but households must be compensated for participating, stores must be paid for providing scanner data for the test and control groups, and the cable and newspaper media charge a premium for special handling of the test messages. Another limitation is that the percentage of the test panel that makes purchases in the test brand's product category can be relatively small, making projections to a national market difficult.

EXHIBIT 21-7

Check-out scanners can track the purchases of selected HHs that agree to participate in research studies.

Tracking Studies

Used most frequently by companies that have multi-million-dollar MC budgets, **tracking studies** are *periodic surveys that show the trend in brand awareness, trial, repeat, and customer satisfaction of a brand and its competitors.* Tracking studies can also be used to test a new campaign or other major changes in the marketing and marketing communication mix. This is done by making the change in a couple of the markets being tracked, then using the other markets that are being tracked as control markets.

Tracking studies are one of the best methods for evaluating long-term marketing communication and relationship-building results. Most tracking studies are done by phone (although for brands whose users are also heavy Internet users, they can be done online) in several different markets every three to six months. Brands that can afford to do so often track a sample of their strong, weak, and new markets. Unless a company has a database of category users, random dialing is used to find respondents. In the case of service brands, customer satisfaction tracking studies are often ongoing, with customer interviews being conducted each day or week.

To illustrate what is asked in a study that tracks awareness, trial, and repeat, Figure 21–3 lists typical questions that a car rental company might ask. To the right of each question is an explanation of the question. Following the screening question, the five questions dealing with awareness, trial, and repeat are standard on tracking studies. The remaining questions are customized for each brand and each survey wave (each study is called a wave). These diagnostic questions help explain why a brand is growing or declining in sales and share. One processed-meat company conducted a tracking study that always included questions on quality and taste. When it was found that the scores for "tastes great" were falling, the TV advertising (which was the primary MC function) was revised to include more shots of taste satisfaction—close-ups of delicious-looking sandwiches and of people smiling while eating. Within six months after the new advertising began running, taste satisfaction scores began to increase.

Although a tracking study is designed to show trends over time, the results of one wave of interviews can often provide valuable insights into the strengths and weaknesses of a brand's marketing program. Both absolute numbers and the relationship between the various numbers need to be analyzed. Obviously, there are many messages—planned, product, service, and unplanned—that affect tracking scores. Tracking study analyses, however, can often help companies spot MC problem areas. Table 21–3 is a hypothetical set of tracking scores that could be obtained from the questions in Figure 21–3, followed by how these scores could be interpreted and the changes the scores might suggest in each brand's marketing efforts.

TABLE 21-3   Tracking Study Scores*

	Brand A	Brand B	Brand C
Top-of-mind (TOM) awareness	40%	20%	15%
Unaided awareness	62	62	38
Aided awareness	90	85	70
Trial	65	65	20
Repeat purchase	38	10	15

*Numbers are hypothetical.

FIGURE 21-3
Tracking Study Questions

Sample Tracking Study Questions

Questions and Answers

Q: Have you rented a car within the last six months?
A: Yes.

Q: Please tell me all the brands of rental cars you can think of.
A: Brand A, Brand B

Q: Which of these brands are you familiar with: Brand C, Brand D, Brand E?
A: Brand C, Brand E.

Q: From which of these companies have you rented a car at least once during the last 12 months?
A: Brand A, Brand B.

Q: From which of these companies have you rented a car **more** than once during the last 12 months?
A: Brand A.

Q: On a scale of 1 to 5, with 5 being the highest rating, how would you rate Brand A's customer service? How would you rate Brand B's?
A: Four for Brand A; two for Brand B.

Q: On a scale of 1 to 5, with 5 being the highest rating, how would you rate the quality of car that you rented from Brand A? From Brand B?
A: Four for Brand A; two for Brand B.

Q: On a scale of 1 to 5, with 5 being the highest rating, how likely would you be to recommend Brand A to someone else? Brand B?
A: Four for Brand A; two for Brand B.

Explanation

Screening question. This question is asked first to make sure the respondent is a category user. If the answer is no, the interview is terminated.

Recall question. The first brand name mentioned is tabulated as the top-of-mind (TOM) brand. There is generally a high correlation between a brand's TOM score and the brand's market share. This is because customers are more likely to mention first the brand they use most. All others mentioned are classified as "unaided" mentions. These are brands that the respondents can recall.

Recognition question. Interviewer asks for each of the brands being measured that the respondent did not mention in the answer to the recall question. The brands with which the respondent is familiar are classified as "aided" mentions. These are the brands that were not recalled but were recognized.

Trial question. The answer to this question indicates which brands the respondent has tried/sampled.

Brand menu question. This answer indicates those brands the respondent feels are OK to use, the ones to which the respondent is loyal.

Here begins the customized questions. This particular one is measuring the perceived level of customer service.

This might be asked to see if the perceived difference in car quality is enough to be used as a copy point in brand messages.

This type of question is generally considered as being the most predictive of brand loyalty. If a customer is very likely to recommend a brand to someone else, that customer is very likely to make a repeat purchase.

* Answers are hypothetical.

The column of numbers for Brand A are what brand managers dream of—they are very good. The 40 percent top-of-mind is the percentage of respondents who mentioned Hertz first when responding to the recall question ("Please tell me all the brands of rental car brands you can think of.") This score is close to the brand's market share and shows that Brand A is by far the number one car rental brand. The fact that nearly two-thirds of those aware of Brand A have rented at least once in the last 12 months is a good ratio and suggests that there are few, if any, marketing communication concerns. The fact that half have rented more than once in this period is also healthy, especially in a competitive category such as rental cars, where the actual product differences are minimal.

The numbers for Brand B have both good and bad news. The fact that Brand B's top-of-mind awareness is only half that of Brand A suggests that Brand B may need greater brand message frequency and/or more memorable brand messages. The conversion from awareness to trial numbers is very good, as nearly three out of four of those aware have tried Brand B. That only one out of six makes a repeat purchase, however, indicates a severe problem. One explanation is that expectations were set too high, causing renters to be disappointed. Another and more likely explanation is that the brand was inferior; long lines, unavailability, or dirty or underperforming cars may be part of the product inferiority.

Because the top three Brand C scores are considerably lower than those for Brand A and Brand B, it could suggest that Brand C is not spending enough on marketing communications. If competitive spending reports show that Brand C is, in fact, spending nearly the same as the other two brands, this would then indicate that the brand messages are not communicating or not persuading (fewer than one out of three respondents familiar with the brand have even tried it in the last 12 months). The low top-of-mind scores and unaided scores could also suggest poor media selection—not reaching the target audience. The good news in these scores is that three-fourths of those who tried Brand C repeated, a much higher percentage of conversion than either Brand A or Brand B. This suggests that Brand C should also invest much more in promotion in order to motivate trial because the findings show that once customers try Brand C, the majority make repeat rentals.

Real-Time Tracking

The biggest problem with most customer satisfaction tracking studies is that the research takes so long to implement that the findings are not timely. Who cares what customers were saying three or six months ago? The Internet is solving that problem because it allows almost instantaneous data reporting. Immediate feedback from a website provides information on a real-time basis that can be used in monitoring and changing strategies. Karl Weiss, president of Market Perceptions, Inc., explains that an "intelligent" online reporting system also can alert managers about customer satisfaction problems as they develop and point to the sources of these problems.[8]

Weiss uses the following example: Let's say the director of customer satisfaction at a large, regional hospital network of three hospitals surveys patients daily. A Real-time Notification System™ can be set up that allows the director to monitor critical parameters (e.g., courtesy of attending nurses, patient's involvement in determining care/treatment, courtesy shown to visitors) and compare them to the hospital's norms—both as a group (the aggregate scores) and for the individual hospitals. Every time the data reporting system finds that the results fall below the thresholds that have been set for each parameter, an e-mail alert is sent to the director responsible. Figure 21–4 illustrates how one parameter—courtesy to visitors—might be monitored. When the percent of respondents scoring "courtesy of staff to visitors" falls below the organization's norm of 75 percent, a "red flag" e-mail message is automatically generated.

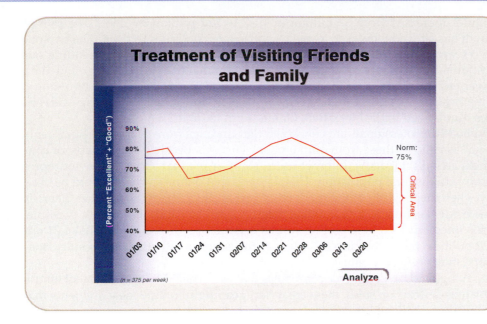

FIGURE 21-4

Example of real-time reporting and tracking of customer satisfaction.

Source: Market Perceptions, Inc.

BtB Measurement

Because most BtB marketing communication budgets are not as large as those for consumer brands, BtB companies generally don't do as much copy and media evaluation. Tracking studies, for example, are most typically used for consumer products, but there is nothing that prevents BtB brands from using them other than cost.

Because a much larger portion of most BtB budgets goes into personal selling, BtB companies often use other forms of measurement such as advisory boards, customer evaluation forms, and surveys of industry consultants and members of the trade press. Advisory boards are generally made up of customers (both channel members and end users) but can also include suppliers, consultants, and academics who specialize in relevant areas. The purpose of these groups is to tell companies what they are doing right and what they could be doing better.

IBM ThinkPad, for example, has a marketing advisory board made up of marketing directors from noncompeting companies, suppliers of marketing services, and academics who specialize in marketing and IMC. Each year, for two days, the group is presented with everything from marketing plans, special promotions, packaging ideas, and new product ideas to creative work and asks for reactions and suggestions.

Customer and other types of advisory groups can provide helpful feedback to companies, but there are limitations to this type of MC evaluation. Normally, the customer advisory groups are quite small and are not representative of the company's customer base. Some members of these groups can also have their own agendas and therefore bias their comments according to what best suits their own company needs and desires.

Online Measurement and Evaluation

Conducting online evaluations makes sense not only for measuring online marketing efforts but also for replacing or complementing mail and phone surveys. Although online research still accounts for only a small portion of the $6 billion market research industry in the United States, it has been growing. Online research revenues increased from \$7 million in 1997 to \$72 million in 1999.[9] The rate of growth has slowed, however, as the response rate continues to drop. The two online research areas that hold the most promise are panel surveying (sending out questionnaires to those who have agreed beforehand to participate) and data delivery (distributing measurement findings online). Three major benefits of doing online measurements are high speeds, low costs, and narrow targeting—advantages dramatized in the Greenfield Online ad in Exhibit 21–8.

Some MC professionals are concerned that findings from online measurements are not as valid as those from offline phone surveys. Because the majority of consumers are still not active Internet users, some argue that samples are not representative of the total population. This suggests that online surveys should be used only when the majority of the product's target audience uses the Internet. There is some evidence, however, that online measures can be valid. In 1998, for example, Harris Interactive's online polling system correctly predicted the results of 21 out of 22 political races; this success rate was the same as or better than results from several major telephone surveys.[10]

Although most e-commerce companies that undertake MC measurement efforts focus those efforts on sales, there are other meaningful online measurements that can be taken. Online tests can measure:

- The number who requested brand information.
- The number who completed a customer profile.
- The number who made complaints.
- The types of people who visit the site.
- The frequency of visits.
- The number who participate in chat sessions.
- The number and quality of website mentions in the media and by other third parties.
- The type and popularity of other sites that request to be linked to the company's site.

Having this type of evaluative information can help companies improve their websites, online offers, and other online relationship-building efforts.

Online Panels versus Spam Surveys

Although spam mailings of research questions can quickly generate a large number of responses, it is difficult to know who responded. It is known that, even if respondents are required to provide personal profile data, approximately 25 percent of those respondents provide false data. Another problem of spam research is that, just as telemarketing has made phone survey work difficult to do (the participation refusal rate is now close to 50 percent), it will make online research more difficult and costly to do. People ignore the unsolicited surveys because they either confuse them with sales offers or are annoyed by receiving too much unsolicited e-mail in general.

At various points in this book, "permission marketing" is mentioned. The same concept applies to doing surveys. The most successful surveys invite people to participate. Not only do people need to give their permission to be sent surveys, but they also must provide personal profiles in order to be in a research panel. This not only ensures a much higher response rate but also provides a database of customer profiles that can be used to match the survey respondents to the target audience of a brand for which the research is being done.

America OnLine (AOL) owns an online research company called DMS. This company recruits respondents from AOL's 20-million-plus members. To motivate members to participate, AOL offers various incentives, including credits that reduce AOL membership fees. Other major online research companies (e.g., Harris and Greenfield) as well as offline research companies (e.g., NFO and NPD Group) also have sizable prerecruited panels from which they can select representative brand-audience samples. Recruiting panel members is an ongoing job and requires advertising and tie-in promotions with a variety of websites.

Holding focus group discussions online offers several advantages, such as saving the cost of renting a research facility and paying high fees for participation. Advertain.com (www.advertain.com) is one of the companies that sets up and runs online focus groups. Operationally, an **online focus group** is *a chat room to which selected people have been invited to meet at a specified time with a moderator.* These groups are most successful when participants are either customers or prospects selected from a highly controlled panel. This helps ensure that participants (1) are who they say they are and (2) are motivated to participate. Because online participants aren't sitting across from each other as in a traditional focus group setting, the timid are more likely to respond and people are more likely to challenge and disagree with the more outspoken and aggressive participants. At the same time, there are disadvantages. Face-to-face groups provide a certain amount of body language that is lost online. Online discussions also lack the display of dynamics and emotions that can be a measure of how relevant a certain brand aspect is.

Media Metrix is a company that tracks online media usage of members of a recruited panel. Participants sign up to participate and give permission for their online activities to be recorded. The software for doing the tracking is downloaded by the participants, and their activities are uploaded and sent to Media Metrix for analysis. Such panels provide online marketers a way to measure who is participating and what other online sites attract their customers. Also, changes of website content and presentation or changes in the mix of links with other sites, for example, can be evaluated with Media Metrix findings.

In sum, MC planners who intend to use online evaluation should consider the following:

Guidelines for Online Evaluation

- *Use respondents from a prerecruited panel.* This provides several advantages: Respondents are known (online users are notorious for disguising their identity), respondents can be chosen who best match the brand's target profile, the questionnaire is not perceived as intrusive, and respondents feel an obligation to respond.

- *Ensure quick download.* Since respondents are doing the company a favor, the questionnaire should download quickly and the instructions should be very clear.

- *Limit questionnaire length.* As with the above point, companies must respect respondents' time. Experts suggest that questionnaires take no more than 15 minutes to complete.[11]

- *Make navigation effortless.* The more work it takes for respondents to complete a survey, the lower the response rate will be.

- *Limit contact frequency.* Because most online surveys are done with panels, if members of the panels are asked to participate too often, they may drop out of the panel. The right frequency depends on the incentives offered, the product category, and the length of the questionnaires. The effect of frequency on response rate is something that can be easily tracked and evaluated. When the response rate begins to decrease and all other conditions are the same, frequency should be reduced.

Advantages and Disadvantages of Online Surveying

Online surveys have both advantages and disadvantages when compared to mail and telephone surveys. Online surveys are faster to prepare and distribute, and responses are received faster—days compared to weeks for the return of mail questionnaires. Compared to using the telephone, the number of questionnaires completed in a day is not limited by the number of phone interviewers—theoretically thousands of online questionnaires can be completed at the same time since they are self-administered and automatically reported. Online surveys provide more flexibility. They can show not only print messages but also audio and video, which offline studies can do only in certain expensive locations. Unlike mail questionnaires, online surveys can be quickly changed when questions are found to be unclear or misleading; also, data are cleaned as they are collected. For example, if respondents are asked to do a ranking and assign the same number to two factors, they will instantly be made aware of the error and asked to do it correctly. Finally, as finished questionnaires are returned, unlike mail questionnaires, they are instantly coded and tabulated without need for entering data manually.[12]

Although most research professionals agree that online research will become more widely used, it does have its limitations. Random sampling produces very low returns. As mentioned earlier, online respondents can hide their identity. Although phone respondents can also do this, area codes and some phone-number prefixes indicate a geographical location for which there are demographic profiles against which respondent profiles can be compared. Also because respondents can hide their identity, competitors can opt in to a brand's research panel, hide their identity, and learn what products and ideas the brand is studying. Other concerns are that online samples are not representative and that the research frame (i.e., the population from which the respondents are drawn) is not well defined.[13]

Relationship Metrics

For the most part, measurements of brand awareness, recall, recognition, trial, and repeat purchases are diagnostics that help explain why brand relationships are strong or weak. To give these findings more meaning, researchers must combine them with direct measures of brand relationships, called **relationship metrics.** These are *a type of output control developed specifically for IMC programs to track the development of brand relationships.*[14] They help explain sales and share trends and provide diagnostic information as a basis for more accurate forecasting.

Some companies feel that brand relationships can be evaluated by simply asking customers if they are satisfied. Yet more than 70 percent of customers who defect may have been "satisfied." Research by Thomas O. Jones and W. Earl Sasser has found that there is a large gulf between satisfied customers and *completely* satisfied customers. The key to generating superior long-term financial performance is to turn the former into the latter.[15]

Although companies should continually ask customers if their wants, needs, and concerns are being addressed, in order not to overlook the obvious, as the Delta ad in Exhibit 21–9 illustrates, there are several reasons why this should not be the extent of measuring "satisfaction." First, the idea of asking what customers want and need will seldom open the door to any creative ideas or competitive advantages. Most customers are not trained to be creative in their responses to satisfaction surveys. As one pundit puts it: "The biggest lie in the restaurant business is the answer to the question: 'How was your dinner?'" A company must look for

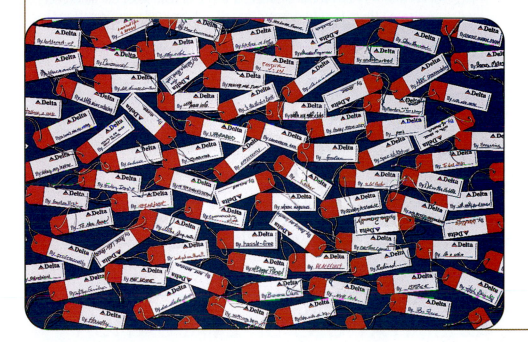

the underlying problems, as well as future wants and needs. As a former senior vice president of Hewlett-Packard put it, you need to have an "imaginative understanding of the user's needs." [16]

The various metrics that companies use most successfully include lifetime customer value (LTCV) quintile analysis; recency frequency, and monetary indexes (collectively referred to as RFM analysis); referral index; and share of wallet. They have been discussed earlier in this book and are summarized as follows:

- *LTCV quintile analysis.* The LTCV concept was introduced in Chapter 2, and quintile analysis was discussed in Chapter 13. Here, the concepts are combined. Somewhat similar to a customer profitability measure, but with a more long-term perspective, LTCV means dividing customers into five equal groups based on their lifetime customer value (LTCV). In the top group would be those 20 percent with the highest LTCV, and in the bottom group the 20 percent with the lowest LTCV. Tracking the average LTCV of each of these five groups will profile a company's source of revenue. Ideally, the averages in all five groups will continue to increase. A red flag could be the increase in the top group and a decrease in all the others, indicating that the basis of support is shrinking even though total revenue may be unchanged or even slightly increasing.

- *Recency, frequency, monetary (RFM) analysis.* As mentioned in Chapter 7, the direct-response industry has discovered that the more recently people have bought, that the more often they buy, and the more they spend, the better customers they are. In particular, the average purchase frequency—the percentage of customers who purchased within the last 30 days (period will vary depending on product category)—indicates to what extent acquired customers are becoming loyal. Sales could be increasing, but if the average customer is buying less frequently, this could mean the support base is weakening. Similarly, the more a customer spends, the more likely it is that the customer will continue the relationship.

- *Referral index.* This tracks the percentage of new business resulting from a customer or other stakeholder recommending the brand. It applies best to large-ticket and service products where it is possible to ask new customers what motivated them to choose your brand. Referrals are confirmation that you are doing what you are saying you will do for customers. Because referrals are one of the key behaviors of brand advocates (the highest level of brand relationships), a higher referral index score generally indicates an increase in the number of brand advocates—a good indication that your relationship-building practices are working.

- *Share of wallet.* Because the most profitable customers, especially in packaged-goods categories, buy multiple brands, one brand objective is to get an increasing percentage of these customers' category purchases. Scanner data is helpful in determining this share trend.

When any of the metrics shows a negative trend, a company needs to find out, first, which areas of the company are sending the messages that are causing the negative trend and, second, what needs to be done to correct these messages. The same diagnostic approach should be used when a trend makes a significant jump. Determining why it jumped may enable a company to leverage certain brand messages still further.

BENEFITS AND LIMITATIONS OF EVALUATION[17]

Evaluating the processes and results of marketing communication has many obvious benefits, but it also has several limitations. In most cases, the point of evaluation is to increase productivity of brand messages, as Exhibit 21–10 illustrates.

Benefits

Some of the most important benefits of evaluation are that it reduces risk, enriches planning, provides controls, and helps document the contributions of the MC programs and activities:

- *Reduces risks.* One of the ongoing expectations of marketing communication is to be creative. By definition, being creative means doing things differently, in new ways. The only problem with this is that predicting results is much more difficult when things are done in new ways. But if new creative strategies, media mixes, and brand messages can be evaluated before they are produced or used throughout a brand's marketing area, the risk of failure can be reduced.

- *Enriches planning and managing.* Without knowing how a brand is performing, it is impossible to make intelligent decisions about managing relationships and the communication that drives these relationships. Think about the important role measurements play in the simple task of driving a car. Imagine trying to drive safely without a speedometer to show how fast you are driving; without a gauge to show how much gasoline is left; or without a temperature gauge that tells whether the engine has overheated. The more measurements you have about the status of your car and its performance, the better you can manage the car's performance and upkeep. The same is true with any aspect of business, including marketing communication and brand relationships.

- *Provides controls.* The larger a brand, generally the more people, departments, and outside agencies involved in its marketing communication activities. The more people involved, the more controls are needed to make sure plans are being properly executed and procedures are being followed. One of the characteristics that helps build trust is consistency. Through constant evaluation of brand messages and interactions with customers and other key stakeholders, a brand can work to maintain consistency. Tracking studies and audits are important ways to control processes. Scores for awareness, communication, and persuasion are often the basis for agency compensation.

- *Documents MC contributions.* Because much of what MC does can't be directly linked to sales and profit, it is necessary to have surrogate measures that can be correlated to sales and profits. For example, by tracking increases in awareness and trial and showing a correlation with increases in sales, an MC department can justify the budget it has been allocated. Often, it can use these findings as rationale for requesting budget increases.

Limitations

The limitations or weaknesses of doing evaluative measurements are several: cost, time, validity and projectability, reduced creativity, and an overdependence on research and numbers.

- *Cost.* Costs for staff time, along with payments to outside measurement services that operate facilities and equipment and often actually do

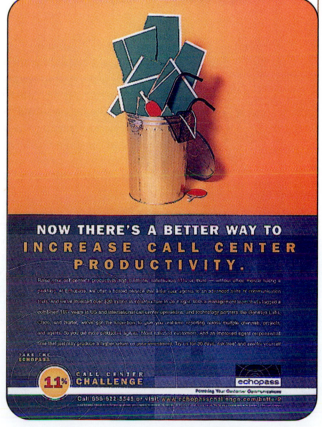

the measurements, can run into thousands of dollars for the simplest of tests. For companies with multimillion-dollar budgets, these costs are normally not a concern, but for a medium- or small-size business, the costs can be prohibitive. This is why most copytesting is only done for national and international advertising TV and print campaigns.

- *Time.* Evaluation takes time. Conducting focus groups in three or four cities can take a couple of months from the time they are first thought of to the analysis of findings. The shortcoming of all evaluation efforts, and especially measurements of marketing communication efforts, is that customers, competitors, and other elements in the marketplace are always changing. So even if an advertising, a publicity, or a promotional program tests well, conditions can change by the time these messages and programs are rolled out to the brand's entire marketing area. When this happens, the results may not turn out as predicted.

- *Validity and projectability.* All measurements are done on samples of respondents. It is sometimes difficult to get a sample that is representative of a brand's customers and prospects. Talking to a different mix of customers than those in the target audience means that the two groups will probably respond differently. If companies try to save money by reducing sample sizes, this can lower validity. Another danger is looking at subsample responses when the total sample size is only big enough to project answers to questions asked of the total sample. For example, findings from a representative sample of 200 teenagers can be projected with a fairly high degree of confidence. However, if a company wants to look at responses of only those teenagers who are heavy Internet users, this number may be only 70, which is not large enough to project to all teenagers who are heavy Internet users.

- *Reduced creativity.* Some marketers strongly believe that if brand massages are measured on the basis of advertising recall, creatives will work to make the advertising memorable with little concern about increasing brand knowledge and awareness of brand benefits. Some creatives feel that copytests, especially those done under laboratory conditions, do not reflect how the brand messages would perform in the marketplace. They argue that creative work cannot be reduced to numbers. Consequently, when told their work needs to have more brand mentions, more pictures of the package, and so on, they can become discouraged and put in less creative effort.

- *Overdependence on research.* Too much of a good thing can be bad. If an MC department insists on researching everything, and doing so until the results are exactly what it wants, it may lose many opportunities. Just as there are some managers that prefer to make decisions without research (what is sometimes called "shooting from the hip"), there are others that are so risk-averse they are afraid to make any major decision without a lot of measurement support. Calling for more and more measurements to be done is also a way to avoid having to make a decision.

A FINAL NOTE: CONTINUOUS FEEDBACK

Measurement and evaluation involve more than just the accumulation of data and the monitoring of sales. If used strategically, evaluation becomes an important source of feedback information in both MC message development and future planning.

One objective of good program evaluation is that feedback be as current and continuous as possible. Federal Express, for example, compiles its effectiveness indicators on a daily basis. Its evaluation program includes both output and process control information. FedEx also compiles monthly indicators for all marketing communication areas, including advertising and publicity, and it conducts an online employee survey every three months. Managers get the results and use them for discussions with employees. They act on the survey information immediately wherever changes in procedures are needed. Senior managers have a sales district where they are required to spend a few days every year to get close to customers and the front line of the sales and marketing efforts.

It is often said that, for managers making important decisions, it is lonely at the top. But as Anders Gronstedt, who studied the Federal Express communication system points out, with continuous information about communication effectiveness, it never gets lonely for communication managers when they have the information they need to make their strategic decisions.[18]

Key Terms

IMC audit 727	focus group 739	scanner market test 745
concept testing 735	tachitoscope 740	tracking studies 746
concurrent testing 735	theater tests 744	online focus group 751
evaluative testing 735	norms 744	relationship metrics 752
baseline 737	animatics 744	
intercept survey 739	test marketing 744	

Key Point Summary

Key Point 1: The IMC Audit and Process Evaluation

Process evaluation in an IMC program is conducted using an IMC audit that investigates relationship-building efforts by examining the organization, processes, and strategic consistency of messages being delivered at all contact points.

Key Point 2: Conducting Brand Message Evaluation

In planning the evaluation of brand messages, the critical questions are: What should be evaluated? What information already exists? and When should the evaluation be conducted? Evaluation is conducted to determine whether the MC efforts met their objectives.

Key Point 3: Methods

The primary categories of measurement are concept testing, copytesting for both communication measures, persuasion measures, BtB evaluation methods, and online research. MC planners must keep in mind that communication effects (attention, awareness, emotional reactions) do not always translate into persuasion effects (actual changes in buying behavior). Tracking studies are important for predicting the latter.

Key Point 4: IMC Metrics

In the those IMC areas where sales impact can justifiably be used to evaluate the program, various kinds of ratios are computed to calculate and compare the cost efficiency of the programs. These calculations determine whether the effort was worth the cost.

Lessons Learned

Key Point 1: The IMC Audit and Process Evaluation

a. Why would you want to bother conducting an IMC audit? What would you learn?
b. Who is involved in an IMC audit?
c. What tools are used in an IMC audit, and what information do they uncover?
d. What is the difference between an IMC audit and a communication audit?

Key Point 2: Brand Message Research

a. What is the primary reason for evaluating brand messages before they run?
b. In what way does evaluation reduce risk?
c. How and why is the cost/value factor important in conducting evaluation research?
d. What role do objectives play in evaluation?

Key Point 3: Methods

a. What is concept testing, and why is it used?
b. When copytesting is conducted to evaluate the communication impact of a brand message, what kind of effects are investigated?
c. Describe three types of tests that evaluate the persuasive effectiveness of a brand message.
d. Explain how online interactions can be used for research purposes.
e. How are awareness and perception studies used in the evaluation of marketing communication?
f. What's the difference between pre- and post-testing?
g. You work as a creative person in an agency; the person next to you works as the marketing manager for a company. Explain how the two of you might differ in your views about copytesting.
h. Explain the debate in the industry about the use of marketplace measures to evaluate the effectiveness of advertising and public relations.
i. Build a chart that has two columns and a row for each of the following MC functions: advertising, public relations, sales promotion, direct response, events and sponsorships, and personal sales. In the first column, list a major brand message objective for each of these areas. In the second column, identify a method that might be used to evaluate the area's effectiveness at achieving that objective.

Key Point 4: IMC Metrics

a. You are designing an evaluation program for a direct-marketing effort that will sell computers to college students. List and explain three types of cost-efficiency measurements that you might use to determine whether the effort is successful.
b. In your own words, explain the underlying logic behind lifetime customer value quintile analysis.
c. What does RFM stand for, and what is included in this type of evaluation?

Chapter Challenge

Writing Assignment

Pick a local company and develop an evaluation program for its marketing communication program. In a 2-page memo, outline and explain all the various types of research and evaluation methods that you would recommend be used.

Presentation Assignment

Develop a program to evaluate relationships for your favorite restaurant. Present to your class a set of relationship metrics, and explain what information they uncover and how that information can be used in developing MC strategies.

Internet Assignment

Visit InsightExpress's website (www.insightexpress.com) for an example of the types of services online research companies provide. Prepare a report for your instructor on how and when to use the services of this company.

Additional Readings

Duncan, Tom, and Sandra E. Moriarty. "The IMC Audit: Testing the Fabric of Integration." *Integrated Marketing Communication Research Journal* 3, no.1 (Spring 1997), pp. 3–10.

Henderson, Wayne. "The IMC Scale: A tool for Evaluating IMC Usage." *Integrated Marketing Communication Research Journal* 3, no. 1 (Spring 1997), pp. 11–17.

Jones, John Philip. *When Ads Work: New Proof That Advertising Triggers Sales.* New York: Lexington Books, 1995.

Lutz, Richard J. "Some General Observations about Research on Integrated Marketing Communications," *Integrated Communication: Synergy of Persuasive Voices,* eds. Esther Thorson and Jeri Moore. Mahwah, NJ: Lawrence Erlbaum, 1996.

Pavlik, John. *Public Relations: What Research Tells Us.* Newbury Park CA: Sage, 1987.

Research Assignment

From the books on this list and any other relevant articles and books that you can find, outline how an IMC program that aims to achieve the goal of effectiveness should be evaluated.

Endnotes

1. David Bell, "Bozell's Bell Paints Active Future for 4A's," *Advertising Age,* April 7, 1997, p. 26.
2. Laura Petrecca, "Agencies Urged to Show the Worth of Their Work," *Advertising Age,* April 14, 1997, pp. 3, 54.
3. For several years the author developed and directed the IMC audits performed by the IMC graduate students at the University of Colorado. These are some of the findings of the audits done under his supervision.
4. Frazer Seitel, *The Practice of Public Relations* (Upper Saddle River, NJ: Prentice Hall, 1998), p. 110.
5. "Building a Powerhouse Corporate Brand," *GCI Intelligence Quarterly* 1, no. 11 (no date), p. 2.
6. Quoted from Restak's 1996 book, *Brainscapes,* by David Wolfe in "What Your Customers Can't Say," *American Demographics,* February 1998, p. 24.

[7]Priscilla LaBarbare and Joel Tucciarone, "GSR Reconsidered: A Behavior-Based Approach to Evaluating and Improving the Sales Potency of Advertising," *Journal of Advertising Research,* September–October 1995, p. 35.

[8]Karl Weiss, "Internet Research: Harnessing the Power of the Internet with Online Data Reporting," *Alert* 38, no. 6 (June 2000), pp. 1–3.

[9]Maryann Jones Thompson, "When Market Research Turns into Marketing," *Online Newsletter*, August 23, 1999, quoting Jack Honomichl, publisher of *Inside Research*.

[10]Ibid.

[11]Geneva J. King, "Today's Marketing Data Research Companies: The News You Need, When You Need It," *Online Newsletter*, July 7, 2000.

[12]Adapted from Phil Levine and Bill Ahlhauser, "Internet Interviewing—Pro," *Marketing Research,* Summer 1999, p. 35.

[13]Dale Kulp and Rick Hunter, "Internet Interviewing—Con," *Marketing Research*, Summer 1999, p. 36.

[14]Tom Duncan and Sandra Moriarty, *Driving Brand Value* (New York: McGraw-Hill, 1997), pp. 262–63.

[15]Thomas O. Jones and W. Earl Sasser, Jr., "Why Satisfied Customers Defect," *Harvard Business Review*, November–December 1995, pp. 88–99.

[16]Gregory H. Watson, *Strategic Benchmarking* (New York: John Wiley, 1993), p. 10.

[17]Audrey Ward and Jeremy Hebert, "Content Analysis: A Tool for Evaluating Perception Against Reality," *IMC Research Journal* 2, no. 1 (Spring 1996), pp. 28–31.

[18]Anders Gronstedt and Anders Hogstrom, "Benchmarking Public Relations: The Volvo Story," *The Strategist*, Fall 1998, p. 10.

Glossary

A

account manager   a supervisor who serves as a liaison between the client and the agency.

account planner   a type of strategic planner who specializes in gathering consumer insights and using them to develop message strategies and who can speak on the consumer's behalf in the development of message strategies.

account planning   using research and brand insights to bring a strong consumer focus to the planning of marketing communication.

activity-based costing   a process for capturing and allocating the cost of handling each customer on a customer-by-customer basis.

addressable media   media that carry messages to identifiable customers or prospects.

affective response   a response that involves emotional processing and results in preferring (or not preferring) a brand and developing a conviction about it.

affiliates   local market stations that agree to carry programming and commercials provided by the network.

analytical database applications   those that allow companies to examine customer transactions and interactions.

aperture   situations in which the target audience is most receptive to a brand message.

appeals   powers that motivate the audience or excite their interest.

art director   the person responsible for the nonverbal aspect of the brand message—the design—which determines the visual look and feel of a planned message.

attention   the conscious narrowing of mental and emotional focus.

attitudes   dispositions regarding objects, people, and ideas associated with a brand.

audiotext   a recorded message that provides information (e.g., the weather, sports scores) via a toll-free or toll number.

awareness   getting a message past the senses—the point of initial exposure—and into the consciousness.

B

B-roll   unedited footage from the video news release (VNR) along with introduction to the topic, more visuals, and sound bites from appropriate spokepersons.

banner ads   small ads placed on websites, generally running at the top, bottom, or side of a screen page.

baseline   the beginning point, or where things stood right before the MC effort began.

behavioral segmenting   segmenting a market according to product usage.

belief   a conclusion based on information and/or experiences with a brand.

benefit segmenting   segmenting a market according to the benefits customers seek as the result of using a brand.

benefits   selling premises that describe the product in terms of what it can do for the user.

big idea   a creative concept that translates the strategy into an umbrella theme that unites all the various brand messages and contributes consistency to the brand image.

bleed ads   ads with graphics that go to the edge of the page.

body copy   the text of the brand message.

borrowed interest   interest created in a brand message through associating it with something else, related or not, that customers find relevant.

brainstorming   a formal process in which a group of 6 to 10 people gather together for the purpose of generating a multitude of new ideas.

brand   a perception of an integrated bundle of information and experiences that distinguishes a company and/or its product offerings from the competition.

brand contact point   every brand-related, information-bearing interaction that a customer or potential customer has with a brand.

brand development index (BDI)   a numerical indicator of the relative development of a particular brand within a market.

brand equity   the intangible value of a company beyond its physical net assets.

brand extension   the application of an established brand name to new product offerings.

brand identity   identification cues, such as brand symbols, colors, and distinctive typography, that together create recognition of the brand.

brand image   an impression created by brand messages and experiences and assimilated into a perception through information processing.

brand knowledge   acquiring an understanding of the brand and its benefits.

brand loyalty   a measure of the attachment that a customer has to a brand as expressed by repeat purchases.

brand managers or product managers   those who manage a brand or product line.

brand messages   all the messages customers and other stakeholders receive from and about a brand that affect what they think about the brand.

brand position   how a brand compares to its competitors in the minds of customers, prospects, and stakeholders.

briefs   statements that summarize the research and the insights for the creative team, and help the team identify the direction and focus for their creative and media ideas.

broadcast footprint   the geographical area in which there is reception from a satellite transmission.

budget   a fixed amount of money for a fixed period of time to be used for a specific purpose.

business philosophy   an approach to doing business that is usually either internally focused on products and processes, or externally focused on customers and their needs.

business plan   a detailed explanation of how a company will generate revenue, profit, and brand equity.

buy zone   the space, either on the shelf or off the shelf, where a product is displayed.

C

campaign   selection and execution of a mix of media and MC functions to achieve certain MC objectives.

category development index (CDI)   a numerical indicator of the relative consumption rate in a particular market for a particular product category.

cause marketing   a program in which a brand promises to donate money or other types of support to a nonprofit organization or social activity when a customer buys or uses the brand.

change agents   people who understand the process of transformation and develop plans to guide an organization in a new direction.

chat rooms   websites in which people can engage in real-time interaction with other people.

claims   product-centered selling premises that describe the product in terms of its features and benefits.

classified ads   small-space, words-only ads presented in a category labeled section with no editorial content surrounding it.

classified display ads   ads in the classified section that include graphics and larger sizes of type.

click-through   the act of responding by clicking on a link to go directly to a particular website.

cognitive dissonance   the psychological contradiction between belief and desired action.

cognitive learning theory   a view of learning as a mental process involving thinking, reasoning, and understanding.

cognitive response   a response to a brand message driven by reasoning, judgment, or knowledge.

column inch   a space that is one column wide and one inch tall.

commercial pod   the commercial break in a TV program.

commission   a percentage of the sales price retained by an agency or salesperson.

commodity products   goods and services offered by different companies that have few or no distinguishing characteristics.

communication   the sending and receiving of messages.

communication vehicles   specific publications, networks, channels, stations, and programs that make up a medium.

competitive advantages   brand superiority created by offering customers something more or different than what is offered by other companies.

compiled lists   names and addresses collected from public sources.

concept testing   tests that measure the effectiveness of the rough ideas that become brand and campaign themes.

concurrent testing   testing that tracks the performance of messages as they are run.

conditioned learning theory   a view of learning as a trial-and-error process.

contest   a brand-sponsored competition that involves some form of skill and effort.

continuous scheduling   placing media throughout the year with equal weight in each month.

controlled-circulation publications   trade, industrial, and organizational magazines that are distributed free to those working in a given product area or affiliated with a given organization.

cookie   an online tracking tool.

cooperative advertising program   a system in which a manufacturer pays a portion (normally half) of the cost when a local retailer advertises the manufacturer's brand.

copytesting   testing the effectiveness of a brand message, a creative concept, or elements such as a headline, slogan, or visual for creative impact and understandability.

copywriter   a person who has the task of developing the verbal brand message—the copy (words).

corporate advertising   ads designed to build awareness of a company and explain what it does or believes.

corporate culture   the pattern of shared values and beliefs that structure the way an organization's employees work and interact with each other and with stakeholders.

corporate image   the overall perception of an organization.

cost per point (CPP)   the cost to reach 1 percent of a defined audience.

cost per response (CPR)   a measure figured by dividing the media cost by the number of responses generated.

cost per thousand (CPM)   what a communication vehicle charges to deliver a message to 1,000 members of its audience.

coupon   a certificate with a stated value for a price reduction on a specified item.

creative boutique   an agency of creative specialists, usually writers and designers, who work for clients and other agencies in the development of the brand messages.

creative brief a document used to "brief" those who actually plan and create the brand messages, and provide them with key strategic directions.

creative director one who supervises the development of the creative idea and its execution.

creative platform a fully developed creative strategy document (similar to a creative brief).

creative process a formal procedure for increasing productivity and innovative output by an individual or a group.

crisis management plan a communication plan for handling the types of disasters that can be anticipated.

cross-functional planning planning that involves multiple departments and functions.

cross-selling using the sale of one product to promote the sale of related products.

cultural cohort a demographic or psychographic group that exists in multiple cultures.

cultural imperialism the impact that Western, especially American, media and products have on other cultures.

culture the attitudes and behaviors of a people that come from the tradition that is passed on from generation to generation.

customer relationship management (CRM) a database-driven approach to managing customer relationships.

customer relationships a series of interactions between individuals and a company over time.

customer service a process for responding to customers.

customers those who have purchased the brand at least once within a designated period.

D

data mining the sifting and sorting of the information warehoused in a database.

data overlay combining two or more databases in order to expand the amount of information about each customer.

database a collection of related information that is stored and organized in a way that allows easy access and analysis.

database management system (DBMS) software that records customer information, tracks customer interactions, and links customer databases that are already in existence.

daypart a block of time identified by a station for the purpose of setting ad rates.

decoding the process the receiver goes through to understand a message by interpreting what the words, pictures, and/or sounds in the message mean.

demand the amount of a good or service customers are willing and able to buy.

demographics definable statistical measures, such as age and life stage, gender, ethnicity, religion, income,

education, occupation, marital status, household size, age of children, and home ownership.

designated marketing area (DMA) TV broadcast coverage area.

developed markets economically developed areas in which consumption patterns are focused more on wants and desires than on basic needs.

developing markets markets in which the consumption patterns are expanding from necessities to wants and desires.

direct-response advertising a brand message in any of the mass media that asks the receiver (reader, viewer, or listener) to respond directly to the sender.

direct-response marketing a closed-loop, interactive, database-driven messaging system that uses a broad range of media to create a behavioral response.

display ads ads that generally contain more graphics and white space than copy and appear next to editorial content.

display copy copy in a type size that is larger than the body copy.

domain name the general term for the name of a node on the Internet.

duplication the overlapping coverage of two or more media vehicles.

E

effective frequency the number of times a message needs to be seen to make an impression or achieve a specific level of awareness.

employee empowerment giving front-line employees who are in contact with customers the power to make decisions about problems that affect customer relationships.

encoding the process of putting a message into words, pictures, and/or sounds that convey the sender's intended meaning.

event a planned promotional happening that has a central focus and captures the attention and involvement of the target audience.

event marketing the use of special events as a promotional tool in a brand's marketing program.

evoked set all those brands that customers have judged to be acceptable.

exchange the process by which money (or something else of value) is traded for goods or services, that is, the physical activity of a transaction.

extranet a limited-access website that links suppliers, distributors, and other partners to the company.

F

feature articles colorful stories with high human interest.

fee a fixed, periodic payment for performing certain work.

feedback a response to a message that is conveyed back to the source.

flighting   a media scheduling strategy in which planned messages run in intermittent periods.

focus group   an evaluation technique in which 8 to 12 members of a brand's target audience, led by a moderator, discuss some aspect of a brand, product category, or message strategy.

forums   public websites where people can post notes on a given topic.

free lancers   independent creative people who are self-employed and take on assignments for an agency or a marketer on a project-by-project basis.

freestanding inserts (FSIs)   supplements that contain ads, most with coupons, for a variety of national brands.

frequency   the average number of times those who are reached have an opportunity to be exposed to a brand message within a specified time period.

frequency distribution analysis (sometimes referred to as a quintile analysis)   an analysis that divides a target audience into equal segments and establishes an average frequency for each of these segments.

fulfillment   getting the product or the information requested to the customer in a convenient, cost-effective, and timely fashion.

full-service agency   a marketing communication agency that provides all or most of the services needed in its area of specialization.

G

game   a sales promotion tool that has the chance element of a sweepstakes but is conducted over a longer time.

gatekeepers   editors and reporters who select (or reject) stores for their publications or stations based on what they think will interest their audiences.

generic products   goods that are not labeled with a traditional brand name.

geodemographic segmenting   a process that combines geographic and demographic data to identify and segment customers and prospects.

geographical information system (GIS)   a software program that combines geographical databases with customer databases and analyzes sales and other transactions based on geography.

global marketers   companies that market their products worldwide.

gross rating point (GRP)   a combination of reach and frequency measures that indicates the "weight" of a media schedule.

H

heavy users   those customers who buy an above-average amount of a given product.

high-involvement products   those for which customers perceive differences among brands and are willing to invest prepurchase decision-making energy.

hits   individual Internet site visits.

home page   the opening page of a website.

hyperlinks (also called links)   buttons or other sensitive areas on the page that, when clicked on, move the viewer to another page or site.

I

image messages   messages that either present an attractive personality for the product or indirectly suggest to customers that they can acquire a certain style by using a particular brand.

image transfer   a process by which members of a target audience who have been exposed to the sights and sounds of a brand's TV message, recall the visual elements of the message when they are exposed to a similar sound track on radio.

IMC (integrated marketing communication)   a cross-functional process for creating and nourishing profitable relationships with customers and other stakeholders by strategically controlling or influencing all messages sent to these groups and encouraging data-driven, purposeful dialogue with them.

IMC audit   an in-depth research method for evaluating brand relationship-building efforts.

impression   one exposure to a brand message.

infomercial   a 30-minute commercial program that demonstrates a product, presents testimonials from satisfied users, and offers viewers one or more ways to buy the product direct.

ingredient branding   using a brand name of a product component in the promotion of another branded product.

in-house ad agency   a department within a company that is responsible for producing some or all of that company's marketing communications.

interactive media   two-way media, which allow both companies and customers to send and receive messages.

interactive TV   the convergence of computers, television, and the Internet.

intercept survey   a survey in which people in a mall or at an event are stopped and asked to respond to a questionnaire.

internal marketing   an ongoing program that promotes the customer-focus philosophy and keeps employees informed of important marketing activities that affect both them and the company's customers.

international marketers   companies that market products in several different countries.

internet   a worldwide system of linked computer networks.

interstitials   ads that pop up in a separate frame on a screen page.

intranets   websites that are accessible only to employees and contain proprietary information.

L

layout   an arrangement of the elements making up a print message.

learning   a change in the knowledge base that comes from exposure to new information or experiences.

life stages the different periods in life of an individual or family.

lifestyle the way people live their lives as well as how they choose to spend their money, time, and energy.

lifetime customer value (LTCV) an estimate of how much a given customer contributes to a company's profit over the average number of years the average customer buys from a company.

listservs (also sometimes spelled listserves) electronic mailing lists.

localization a strategy that adapts a brand message to make it more compatible with a local market culture.

logo a brand symbol, or a distinctive graphic design used to indicate a product's source or ownership.

low-involvement products products bought on impulse or without much consideration.

loyalty (or frequency) marketing using promotions to motivate repeat purchases and for customer retention.

M

marginal analysis examining the ratio of spending to sales and profit.

market the group of actual or potential buyers for a product; can also be a geographical area (e.g., the Chicago "market").

marketing the process of creating and providing what customers want in return for something they are willing to give (money, time, or membership).

marketing communication (MC) the collective term for all the communication functions used in marketing a product.

marketing communication (MC) mix the selection of MC functions used at a given time as part of a marketing program.

marketing concept a philosophy of business that focuses on meeting customer wants and needs.

marketing mix the selection of product (design, production), price, place (distribution), and promotion.

marketing plan a set of objectives, strategies, and tactics orchestrating all of the organization's marketing activities designed to help the company achieve its financial objectives.

marketing process the planning, executing, and evaluating of activities that produce exchanges between an organization and customers.

marketing public relations (MPR) the use of nonpaid media messages to deliver positive brand information designed to positively influence customers and prospects.

marketing services the department that specializes in managing the marketing communication functional areas.

mass customization the process of personalizing customer interaction with a company on a large scale.

mass marketing selling the same product in the same way to everyone.

mass media all broad-based communication media that reach a large and diverse population.

mass media advertising nonpersonal, one-way, planned messages paid for by an identified sponsor and disseminated to a broad audience in order to influence their attitudes and behavior.

MC suppliers the specialists who help MC agencies actually produce their work.

media collective term for the methods used to carry messages.

media buying the execution of a media plan, the purchasing of time and space to carry brand messages.

media buying services agencies that specialize in buying time and space, that is, placing brand messages in the media.

media convergence the bringing together of phone, Internet, television, and the computer, along with a variety of other new technologies, such as smart cards, pagers, personal digital assistants, and satellite navigational systems.

media kit a package of publicity information that includes a variety of materials related to a brand and/or to an event, including background information.

media menu all the communication vehicles available to the consumer, as well as to the marketer.

media mix a plan that identifies the most effective media vehicles to use to create positive brand contacts.

media partners the vehicles through which marketing communication messages are carried to (and from) the target audiences.

media share the percentage of those using a radio/TV at a particular time in a designated area who are tuned to a particular station.

media waste brand messages sent to people who are neither customers nor prospects.

media weight an indication of the relative impact of a media mix.

medium (plural media) a vehicle or means by which a message can be transmitted.

merchandising in-store promotional activities and materials of manufacturers and retailers.

merge/purge a process that eliminates duplications in a database.

message the information being transmitted from source to receiver.

message wearout the brand messages that once attracted attention and motivated the target are no longer doing so.

mission what a company stands for, represents, or does well.

mission marketing a program that ties an organization's sponsorship efforts to the company's mission.

monetary a measure of the amount a customer has spent with a company over a given period.

multinationals companies that have built a corporate network of subsidiaries and affiliates with whom they trade and that engage in international sales in various countries.

multi-tier branding when two or more brands (all owned by the same company) are used in the identification of a product.

N

national (or domestic) marketers companies that focus their marketing efforts on their home countries.

navigation the process by which people access a website, find the information they want, and move around within the site and to other related sites.

needs the biological and psychological motivations that drive attitudes and actions.

news release a news story written by an organization to get publicity for itself or one of its brands.

niche markets markets that are relatively small or highly focused on one particular interest area.

noise all the internal and external distractions that fight for attention when a receiver is processing a message.

norms average product category test scores accumulated over the years by a research company.

O

objectives what is to be accomplished.

offer everything, both tangible and intangible, promised by a company in exchange for money or some other desired behavior.

one-to-one marketing customizing products and marketing communication for an individual person or company according to individual needs.

one-voice, one-look consistency the type of consistency that occurs when all the marketing communication activities—the planned messages—have the same look and tone.

online focus group a chat room to which selected people have been invited to meet at a specified time with a moderator.

operational database applications where the data are used to help the company to improve its interactions with customers.

opinion leaders people who are highly visible in the community, in the media, or in industry and who are consulted about their opinions.

opt-in e-mail e-mail that is sent only to those who have indicated they want to receive it.

opt-out e-mail messages that a company sends automatically until notified not to.

out-of-home media communication vehicles that the target audience is only exposed to away from home.

P

Pareto rule states that 80 percent of a brand's sales come from 20 percent of its customers.

pass-along number of people who read a publication in addition to subscribers or buyers.

personal selling two-way communication one-to-one, with the ultimate objective of creating sales.

persuasion the act of creating changes in beliefs, attitudes, and behaviors.

place-based media customer destinations where brand messages can be displayed.

point-of-purchase (POP) materials on- and off-shelf display materials designed to call attention to a brand.

portal a search engine for a select number of sites.

preemptable rate a relatively low rate that doesn't guarantee a given commercial will run at a given time.

premium an item offered free or at a bargain price to encourage some type of response.

pro forma a breakdown of forecasted sales on a per unit basis.

producers agents hired to handle such major tasks as the filming of television commercials and special events films.

product any good, service, or idea produced and/or provided by an organization.

product placement a marketing communication practice in which branded products or brand names are featured visibly in a movie or television program.

promotional flags brand messages that call attention to current sales-promotion offers.

prospecting using data on hand to identify prospective customer types.

prospects creating brand contacts to identify high potential customers.

psychographics measures that classify customers in terms of their attitudes, interests, and opinions.

public relations management of communication between an organization and its stakeholders.

public service announcements ads for nonprofit organizations that run on time and space donated by the media.

publicity news releases and other brand messages that are media delivered without charge.

puffery the use of hyperbole or exaggeration to promote a brand.

pull strategies marketing communication efforts targeted at end users.

pulsing a combination of flighting and continuous media strategies.

purposeful dialogue communication that is mutually beneficial for the customer and the company.

push strategies marketing communication efforts targeted at members of the distribution channels.

Q

qualified leads prospects who (1) have a need or opportunity that the brand can address, (2) have the ability to pay for the good or service, (3) have the authority to buy, and (4) are approachable.

R

rate card a list of advertising space costs and discounts.

reach (also called penetration) the percentage of a specified audience exposed one or more times to a particular communication vehicle within a specified period.

recency a measure of how recently a customer has purchased from a company.

relationship metrics a type of output controls developed specifically for IMC programs to test the profitability of brand relationships.

reputation the esteem that a company or brand has in the eyes of its stakeholders.

response something said or done in answer to a marketing communication message.

response lists people who have responded to related direct-marketing offers.

retainer an arrangement in which a client contracts to work with an agency for a year or more and pay that agency a certain amount.

S

sales lead a person or organization identified as being a prospect—someone able to benefit from the brand being sold.

sampling offering prospects the opportunity to try a product before making a buying decision.

scanner market test (also called a single-source test) tracking of a household's purchase via retail electronic check-out scanners.

search engine Internet tool that finds websites based on keywords.

segmenting grouping customers or prospects according to common characteristics, needs, wants, and/or desires.

selective perception the process used to decide what is worthy of attention.

self-selection (or aggregation segmentation) a method of segmenting prospects that motivates potential customers to "raise their hands"—i.e. identify themselves as being interested in what the brand has to offer.

selling premise the logic behind the offer or what in the offer should motivate someone to buy or respond.

share of voice the percentage of media spending in a particular category that comes from one brand.

share of wallet the percentage of a customer's spending in a product category for one particular brand.

shelf talker printed card or sign on a retail shelf's price rail.

shipper displays specially designed shipping cartons that when opened become display units complete with signage and a quantity of products ready for sale.

showings the basic units of sale for outdoor advertising.

signature a distinctive way of printing the brand name.

situation analysis an analysis of everything that could affect a company's marketing effort, brand equity, and profitability.

skews variations from an average or standard.

slotting fee an up-front payment made by a manufacturer to a retailer for guaranteed shelf space for a new product.

social marketing a campaign that uses a variety of MC functions to promote a social program or cause.

source credibility the extent to which the message sender is believable.

spam unsolicited e-mail whose purpose is to sell a product or service.

special interest groups groups of people who organize themselves around a specific political or social issue.

specialties incentives given free to customers and other prospects to keep a brand's name top-of-mind.

split-run a process in which a marketer places one ad in half of a magazine's circulation and a different ad in the other half to determine which ad pulled best.

sponsorship the financial support of an organization, person, or activity in exchange for brand publicity and association.

spot buys when regional or national companies buy broadcast time only in certain markets.

stakeholders individuals or groups who can affect, or be affected by, an organization.

standard advertising unit (SAU) a set of predetermined advertising spaces that are constant in size in every newspaper that has adopted the SAU standards.

standardization a strategy of using the same brand message in different countries.

storyboard a selection of scenes from a TV commercial that tells the visual "story."

strategic business unit (SBU) a product-, brand-, or market-based division that operates as a profit center within the company.

strategic consistency the coordination of all types of messages that create or cue brand images, positions, and reputations in the minds of customers and other stakeholders.

strategic planning a process of developing and maintaining a fit between the organization's goals and capabilities and changing marketing opportunities.

style a manner of expression.

subliminal advertising messages that are received subconsciously, below a person's perceptual threshold.

supplement inserts inserts that are preprinted by an advertiser and enclosed with a newspaper.

sweepstakes a form of sales promotion that offers prizes based on a chance drawing of entrants' names.

SWOT analysis a structured evaluation of internal situations (strengths and weaknesses) and external situations (opportunities and threats) that can help and hurt a brand.

synergy an interaction of individual parts that results in the whole being greater than the sum of those parts.

T

table tents small tent-shaped signs placed on tables to promote a certain dish or drink.

tachistoscope   a device that exposes a brand message briefly to test participants so that researchers can measure how long it takes for certain messages or elements to be communicated.

target audience   a group that has significant potential to respond positively to a brand message.

targeted reach   that portion of a media vehicle's audience who are in a brand's target market.

targeting   analyzing, evaluating, and prioritizing those market segments deemed most profitable to pursue.

teaser campaign   a series of messages that don't carry any brand identification but that are designed to create curiosity.

telemarketing   the practice of using the telephone to deliver a brand message designed to create a sale or sales lead.

telephony   the technical name for the transmission of sound between two points.

test marketing   a research design in which a MC campaign is run in two to four small- to medium-sized geographical markets for anywhere from 3 to 12 months; brand sales are compared to those in similar control markets.

theater tests   tests in which people are invited to a location for the purpose, they are told, of critiquing a TV program, but actually for the purpose of evaluating their response to brand messages.

third-party endorsement   an objective perspective presented by a reputable source who has no personal interest in the success or failure of the brand being endorsed.

tone   a general atmosphere or a manner of expression.

tracking studies   periodic surveys that show the trend in brand awareness, trial, repeat, and customer satisfaction of a brand and its competitors.

trade show   an event at which customers in a particular industry gather to attend training sessions and visit with suppliers and vendors to review their product offerings and innovations.

trademark   a sign of someone's business designed to differentiate that person's work from others.

traffic manager   an agency person who controls the flow of work through the approval and production process.

typeface   a set of letters and numbers with a particular or distinguishing design.

U

undeveloped markets   markets in which consumption patterns remain focused on basic needs.

unique selling proposition (USP)   a selling premise based on a feature that differentiates a product from its competition.

up-selling   encouraging customers to buy a more expensive product than they had in mind.

V

values   enduring points of view that a certain way of thinking and behaving is preferable to an opposite or different way of thinking and behaving.

virtual communities   groups of people who focus on certain online activities, establish relationships with one another, and begin to form an identity among themselves.

visualization   the first step in the process of developing an execution; the process of turning the creative concept into a visual.

W

webmaster   someone who manages a website.

Z

zero-based planning   determining objectives and strategies based on current brand and marketplace conditions; the current conditions are considered the zero point.

Brand Index

Name Index

Subject Index

McGraw-Hill/Irwin Series in Marketing